POKÉMON™

HEARTGOLD VERSION · SOULSILVER VERSION

Pokédex
Official Pocket Version

STAFF

PUBLISHED BY
The Pokémon Company International
333 108th Ave NE, Suite 1900
Bellevue, WA 98004

TM, ® & © The Pokémon Company
International 2010
All rights reserved.

EDITOR-IN-CHIEF
Michael G. Ryan

EDITORS
Kellyn Ballard
Blaise Selby

ACKNOWLEDGEMENTS
Colin Palmer
Yasuhiro Usui
Katherine Fang
Cris Silvestri
Kazuya Kitamura
Ian Levenstein
Eve Eschenbacher
Hollie Beg
Eoin Sanders

TRANSLATION SERVICES
Claire Samuels

DESIGN & PRODUCTION
Prima Games
Mario De Govia
Shaida Boroumand
Melissa Smith
Jamie Knight
Stephanie Sanchez

ISBN: 978-0-307-46948-9
Library of Congress Catalog Card Number:
2010906231
10 11 12 13 GG 10 9 8 7 6 5 4 3 2 1

Published in the United States using
materials from the *Pokémon HeartGold* and
*SoulSilver Official Complete Clear Guide
Johto Adventure* and *Johto Pokédex* and
the *Pokémon HeartGold and SoulSilver
Official Complete Clear Guide Kanto
Adventure* and *National Pokédex*. Published
in Japan 2009 by Media Factory, Inc.

SPECIAL THANKS TO
Editor: Shusuke Motomiya and ONEUP, Inc.
Design & Layout: RAGTIME CO., LTD., and
SUZUKIKOUBOU, Inc.

Pokémon Alphabetical Index

How to Use the National Pokédex

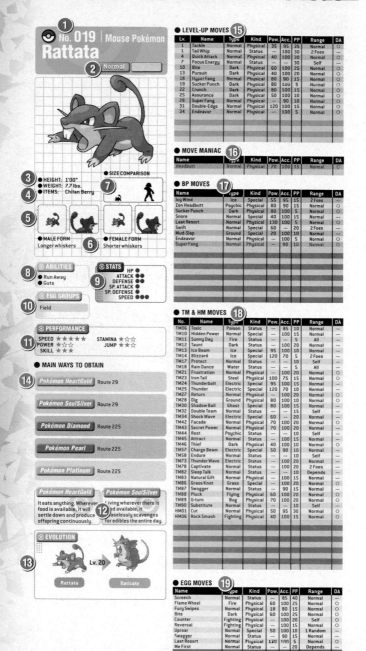

(1) ● No. 019 | Mouse Pokémon
Rattata

(2) Normal

(3) ● HEIGHT: 1'00"
(4) ● WEIGHT: 7.7 lbs.
● ITEMS: Chilan Berry

(7) ● SIZE COMPARISON

(5)
● MALE FORM
Longer whiskers

(6) ● FEMALE FORM
Shorter whiskers

(8) ⊙ ABILITIES
● Run Away
● Guts

(9) ⊙ STATS
HP ●
ATTACK ●●
DEFENSE ●●
SP. ATTACK ●
SP. DEFENSE ●
SPEED ●●●

(10) ⊙ EGG GROUPS
Field

(11) ⊙ PERFORMANCE
SPEED ★★★★★   STAMINA ★☆☆
POWER ★☆☆   JUMP ★★☆
SKILL ★★★

● MAIN WAYS TO OBTAIN

(14)
Pokémon HeartGold	Route 29
Pokémon SoulSilver	Route 29
Pokémon Diamond	Route 225
Pokémon Pearl	Route 225
Pokémon Platinum	Route 225

(12)
| Pokémon HeartGold | Pokémon SoulSilver |
| It eats anything. Wherever food is available, it will settle down and produce offspring continuously. | Living wherever there is food available, it ceaselessly scavenges for edibles the entire day. |

(13) ⊙ EVOLUTION

Rattata → Lv. 20 → Raticate

● LEVEL-UP MOVES **(15)**

Lv.	Name	Type	Kind	Pow.	Acc.	PP	Range	DA
1	Tackle	Normal	Physical	35	95	35	Normal	○
1	Tail Whip	Normal	Status	—	100	30	Normal	
4	Quick Attack	Normal	Physical	40	100	30	Normal	○
7	Focus Energy	Normal	Status	—	—	30	Self	—
10	Bite	Dark	Physical	60	100	25	Normal	○
13	Pursuit	Dark	Physical	40	100	20	Normal	○
16	Hyper Fang	Normal	Physical	80	90	15	Normal	○
19	Sucker Punch	Dark	Physical	80	100	5	Normal	○
22	Crunch	Dark	Physical	80	100	15	Normal	○
25	Assurance	Dark	Physical	50	100	10	Normal	○
28	Super Fang	Normal	Physical	—	90	10	Normal	○
31	Double-Edge	Normal	Physical	120	100	15	Normal	○
34	Endeavor	Normal	Physical	—	100	5	Normal	○

● MOVE MANIAC **(16)**

Name	Type	Kind	Pow.	Acc.	PP	Range	DA
Headbutt	Normal	Physical	70	100	15	Normal	○

● BP MOVES **(17)**

Name	Type	Kind	Pow.	Acc.	PP	Range	DA
Icy Wind	Ice	Special	55	95	15	2 Foes	—
Zen Headbutt	Psychic	Physical	80	90	15	Normal	○
Sucker Punch	Dark	Physical	80	100	5	Normal	○
Snore	Normal	Special	40	100	15	Normal	—
Last Resort	Normal	Physical	130	100	5	Normal	○
Swift	Normal	Special	60	—	20	2 Foes	—
Mud-Slap	Ground	Special	20	100	10	Normal	—
Endeavor	Normal	Physical	—	100	5	Normal	○
Super Fang	Normal	Physical	—	90	10	Normal	○

● TM & HM MOVES **(18)**

No.	Name	Type	Kind	Pow.	Acc.	PP	Range	DA
TM06	Toxic	Poison	Status	—	85	10	Normal	—
TM10	Hidden Power	Normal	Special	—	100	15	Normal	—
TM11	Sunny Day	Fire	Status	—	—	5	All	—
TM12	Taunt	Dark	Status	—	100	20	Normal	—
TM13	Ice Beam	Ice	Special	95	100	10	Normal	—
TM14	Blizzard	Ice	Special	120	70	5	2 Foes	—
TM17	Protect	Normal	Status	—	—	10	Self	—
TM18	Rain Dance	Water	Status	—	—	5	All	—
TM21	Frustration	Normal	Physical	—	100	20	Normal	○
TM23	Iron Tail	Steel	Physical	100	75	15	Normal	○
TM24	Thunderbolt	Electric	Special	95	100	15	Normal	—
TM25	Thunder	Electric	Special	120	70	10	Normal	—
TM27	Return	Normal	Physical	—	100	20	Normal	○
TM28	Dig	Ground	Physical	80	100	10	Normal	○
TM30	Shadow Ball	Ghost	Special	80	100	15	Normal	—
TM32	Double Team	Normal	Status	—	—	15	Self	—
TM34	Shock Wave	Electric	Special	60	—	20	Normal	—
TM42	Facade	Normal	Physical	70	100	20	Normal	○
TM43	Secret Power	Normal	Physical	70	100	20	Normal	—
TM44	Rest	Psychic	Status	—	—	10	Self	—
TM45	Attract	Normal	Status	—	100	15	Normal	—
TM46	Thief	Dark	Physical	40	100	10	Normal	○
TM57	Charge Beam	Electric	Special	50	90	10	Normal	—
TM58	Endure	Normal	Status	—	—	10	Self	—
TM73	Thunder Wave	Electric	Status	—	100	20	Normal	—
TM78	Captivate	Normal	Status	—	100	20	2 Foes	—
TM82	Sleep Talk	Normal	Status	—	—	10	Depends	—
TM83	Natural Gift	Normal	Physical	—	100	15	Normal	○
TM86	Grass Knot	Grass	Special	—	100	20	Normal	○
TM87	Swagger	Normal	Status	—	90	15	Normal	—
TM88	Pluck	Flying	Physical	60	100	20	Normal	○
TM89	U-turn	Bug	Physical	70	100	20	Normal	○
TM90	Substitute	Normal	Status	—	—	10	Self	—
HM01	Cut	Normal	Physical	50	95	30	Normal	○
HM06	Rock Smash	Fighting	Physical	40	100	15	Normal	○

● EGG MOVES **(19)**

Name	Type	Kind	Pow.	Acc.	PP	Range	DA
Screech	Normal	Status	—	85	40	Normal	—
Flame Wheel	Fire	Physical	60	100	25	Normal	○
Fury Swipes	Normal	Physical	18	80	15	Normal	○
Bite	Dark	Physical	60	100	25	Normal	○
Counter	Fighting	Physical	—	100	20	Self	○
Reversal	Fighting	Physical	—	100	15	Normal	○
Uproar	Normal	Special	50	100	10	1 Random	—
Swagger	Normal	Status	—	90	15	Normal	—
Last Resort	Normal	Physical	120	100	5	Normal	○
Me First	Normal	Status	—	—	20	Depends	—

Basic Data

1) National Pokédex Number

The National Pokédex number of the Pokémon.

2) Type

The Pokémon's type. Some Pokémon have two types.

3) Height and Weight

The height and weight of the Pokémon.

4) Held Item

The item that is sometimes held by the Pokémon when you encounter it in the wild in places such as tall grass, caves, and the ocean.

5) Gender

It shows whether the Pokémon has two genders. Some Pokémon's gender is unknown.

6) Male and Female Forms

Some Pokémon look a little bit different between male and female. Comments describe the differences between the two forms. If they share the same form, the common form is shown.

7) Size Comparison

The size of the Pokémon is compared to that of the hero/heroine.

8) Ability

The Pokémon's Ability. If two Abilities are listed, each individual Pokémon will have one of the two.

9) Stats

For each of the six key Pokémon stats, the number of dots (maximum of 6) indicates how readily that stat increases in comparison to other Pokémon.

10) Egg Group

The Egg group the Pokémon belongs to. Some Pokémon belong to two groups.

11) Performance

These are stats that affect how well a Pokémon performs in the Pokéathlon sports competition. The number of orange stars indicates the base Performance level, and white stars indicate how much further each Performance stat can be raised (maximum is five stars). For example, ★★☆ means that the Pokémon's standard Performance is 2, but can go up to 3. Performance level varies depending on the day of the week, the Pokémon's Nature, and what kinds of Aprijuice you use.

12) Pokédex Entry

It's the Pokémon summaries given in the Pokédex. Both the *Pokémon HeartGold* and *SoulSilver Version* entries are included.

13) Evolution

The course of Evolution for the Pokémon, as well as any conditions governing its Evolution.

How to Obtain

14) Main Ways to Obtain

One main method to obtain the Pokémon is shown. The ways to obtain in *Pokémon Diamond, Pearl,* and *Platinum* Versions are also shown.

Moves It Can Learn

15) Level-Up Moves

A list of the moves the Pokémon can learn by leveling up.

16) Move Maniac

A list of the moves that the Move Maniac can teach the Pokémon.

17) BP Moves

A list of the moves that can be learned in exchange for BP (Battle Points) obtained in the Battle Frontier.

18) TM & HM Moves

A list of the moves the Pokémon can learn by using a TM or an HM.

19) Egg Moves

These moves are occasionally learned by the Pokémon upon hatching from an Egg, as long as they are known by the male Pokémon you leave at the Pokémon Day Care.

Chart Key

Lv. ....The level at which the move can be learned

No. ....The TM's number

Type ......The move's type

Kind ......Whether the move is a physical, special, or status move

Pow. ......The move's attack power

Acc. ....The move's accuracy

PP ....How many times the move can be used

Range ...The number and type of targets that the move affects

DA ....Whether the move is a direct attack that makes physical contact with the target

Type Matchup Chart

Types are assigned both to moves and to the Pokémon receiving them. These types can greatly affect the amount of damage dealt or received in battle, so learn how they stand up against one another and give yourself an advantage in battle.

Attacking Pokémon's Move Type \ Defending Pokémon's Type	Normal	Fire	Water	Grass	Electric	Ice	Fighting	Poison	Ground	Flying	Psychic	Bug	Rock	Ghost	Dragon	Dark	Steel
Normal													△	×			△
Fire		△	△	◎		◎						◎	△		△		◎
Water		◎	△	△					◎				◎		△		
Grass		△	◎	△					◎	△		△	◎		△		△
Electric			◉	△	△				×	◉					△		
Ice		△	△	◎		△			◎	◎					◎		△
Fighting	◎					◎		△		△	△	△	◎	×		◎	◎
Poison				◎				△	△				△	△			×
Ground		◎		△	◎			◎		×		△	◎				◎
Flying				◎	△		◎					◎	△				△
Psychic							◎	◎			△					×	△
Bug		△		◎			△	△		△	◎			△		◎	△
Rock		◎				◎	△		△	◎		◎					△
Ghost	×										◎			◎		△	△
Dragon															◎		△
Dark							△				◎			◉		△	△
Steel		△	△		△	◎							◎				△

Legend

◎	Very effective — "It's super effective!"	x2
△	Not too effective — "It's not very effective…"	x0.5
×	No effect — "It doesn't affect…"	x0
(No Icon)	Normal damage	x1

- Fire-type Pokémon cannot be afflicted with the Burned condition.
- Grass-type Pokémon are immune to Leech Seed.
- Ice-type Pokémon cannot be afflicted with the Frozen condition, and take no damage from the Hail weather condition.
- Poison-type Pokémon cannot be afflicted with a Poison or a Badly Poisoned condition, even when switching in with Toxic Spikes in play. Poison-type Pokémon nullify Toxic Spikes (unless these Pokémon are also Flying type or have the Levitate Ability).
- Ground-type Pokémon are immune to Thunder Wave and to damage from the Sandstorm weather condition.
- Flying-type Pokémon cannot be damaged by Spikes when switching in, or become afflicted with a Poison or Badly Poisoned condition due to switching in with Toxic Spikes in play.
- Rock-type Pokémon are immune to damage from the Sandstorm weather condition.
- Steel-type Pokémon are immune to damage from the Sandstorm weather condition.

How to obtain Pokémon

In order to succeed on your adventure, you'll have to partner up with Pokémon and use their powers to help you. For that reason, you'd better get acquainted with the various methods of obtaining Pokémon.

● How to obtain Pokémon

⊙ Catch wild Pokémon

Most Pokémon inhabit places like fields, caves, and bodies of water. Go discover and catch them.

⊙ Evolve them through battle

As Pokémon build up their strength by battling, some of them will evolve. After Evolution, the Pokémon's name and appearance will change.

⊙ Get them through story events

You can get Pokémon or Pokémon Eggs as the story unfolds, so be sure to talk to townspeople.

⊙ Link trade with friends

Some Pokémon are especially hard to obtain. The easiest way to get them is by trading with a friend.

Pokémon Distributed in Events

Not all Pokémon can be obtained through regular gameplay. To get certain rare Pokémon, you'll have to attend a Pokémon event or connect to Nintendo Wi-Fi Connection. The Legendary Pokémon below are only available through special events and not through regular gameplay—check the official Pokémon website at Pokemon.com for updates on how to obtain these Pokémon.

● Pokémon Distributed in Events So Far

Celebi

⊙ Notes

Celebi can be transferred from Pal Park once acquired in *Pokémon FireRed, LeafGreen, Ruby, Sapphire,* or *Emerald* version.

Mew

⊙ Notes

If you fulfill certain conditions in the WiiWare game *My Pokémon Ranch,* Hayley will trade you a Mew. Note that *My Pokémon Ranch* is only compatible with *Pokémon Diamond* or *Pearl Version,* and can't be used with *Pokémon HeartGold* or *SoulSilver Version.*

Jirachi

⊙ Notes

Jirachi can be transferred from Pal Park once acquired in *Pokémon FireRed, LeafGreen, Ruby, Sapphire,* or *Emerald* version.

Deoxys

Deoxys can be transferred from Pal Park once acquired in *Pokémon Ruby*, *Sapphire*, or *Emerald version*.

Manaphy

Notes

Manaphy is only available through distribution at special events.*

Darkrai

Notes

Darkrai is only available through distribution at special events.

Shaymin

Notes

Shaymin is only available through distribution at special events.

Arceus

Notes

Arceus is only available through distribution at special events.

*Since Phione can be obtained by hatching Eggs, it is not classified as a Legendary Pokémon.

Battling makes Pokémon stronger

A Pokémon grows and becomes stronger by battling. If it wins a battle, it gains Exp. Points (Experience Points). Once it accumulates enough Experience Points, it levels up and gets a stat increase. Take care in training your Pokémon to make it powerful.

Earn Exp. Points to level up.

WEEDLE ♀Lv3

SENTRET ♀Lv3

What will SENTRET do?

Pokémon evolve by leveling up

Some Pokémon can evolve into new Pokémon with different names, appearances, or moves. There are several ways to evolve Pokémon, but the most basic method is through battling and earning Experience Points to level up.

Don't blink, or you'll miss the magical moment when Evolution occurs.

SKIPLOOM is evolving!

● Evolution example: Hoppip

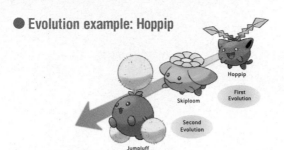

Hoppip

First Evolution

Skiploom

Second Evolution

Jumpluff

● Key Evolution methods

◉ Use special stones

Special stones, such as the Moon Stone or Dusk Stone, have the power to instantly trigger a Pokémon Evolution.

◉ Strengthen your friendship

Take good care of a Pokémon and it'll return the favor. Some Pokémon evolve if they level up while they're on friendly terms with you.

It looks really happy!
It must love you a lot.

◉ Fulfill certain conditions

Some Pokémon can only evolve once you fulfill certain conditions. You may need to have them learn a particular move or set up your party in the right configuration, for example.

TANGELA learned AncientPower!

◉ Link trade

Some Pokémon evolve when they're traded. Many of these Pokémon also need to be holding a certain item during the trade.

Learn how to catch wild Pokémon

You can't catch wild Pokémon without a Poké Ball. Even so, Pokémon won't just hop into a Poké Ball—they can be hard to catch unless you tire them out first. Increase your odds of success by knocking down their HP to the lowest possible amount.

You want HP to be as low as possible.

What will POLIWHIRL do?

● How to make catching Pokémon easier

1 Inflict status conditions

Some Pokémon moves inflict status conditions on their targets. A Pokémon saddled with a status condition is easier to catch. Out of the six status conditions, Sleep and Frozen are the most effective. Lower the target's HP and use status conditions to maximize your chances of success.

Sleep and Frozen are effective.

The wild ZUBAT is fast asleep.

There are many different kinds of Poké Balls, each specialized for a certain use. For instance, the Net Ball excels at catching Water- and Bug-type Pokémon. Always use a Poké Ball that's effective for the type of Pokémon you want to catch—it's a basic Pokémon-catching principle.

Teach your party useful Pokémon-catching moves

As explained above, lowering a wild Pokémon's HP and using status conditions makes it easier to catch Pokémon. To do this, use moves like False Swipe and Spore—these moves are more convenient for catching wild Pokémon than other moves. You'll want your team to include Pokémon capable of using these moves.

● Examples of moves good for catching Pokémon

False Swipe   Always leaves the target with at least 1 HP, even if the move would have KO'd it

Spore   100% chance of inflicting Sleep status

● Example: a useful Pokémon that can learn both False Swipe and Spore

Parasect

Catch a Paras in Ilex Forest or the Safari Zone, and raise it to Lv. 17 to teach it Spore. Then raise it to Lv. 24 to evolve it into Parasect, and use TM54 to teach it False Swipe.

Tricks to increase your Pokémon encounter rate

In fields, inside caves, or wherever Pokémon are found, there are tricks you can use to increase your chance of encountering wild Pokémon. If you're hoping to run into a particular Pokémon, try techniques from the list below. On the other hand, there are ways to lower your wild Pokémon encounter rate, too. Use those tricks if you'd rather avoid meeting any wild Pokémon, such as when your team is injured.

● How to increase your wild Pokémon encounter rate

1. Ride your Bicycle
2. Turn the radio dial to Pokémon Music and play the Pokémon march
3. Walk through the tall grass
4. Use the White Flute
5. Put a Pokémon with the Arena Trap, Suction Cups, Sticky Hold, No Guard, or Illuminate Ability at the head of your party

● How to lower your wild Pokémon encounter rate

1. Walk, don't run (avoid using the Running Shoes)

2. Turn the radio dial to Pokémon Music and play the Pokémon lullaby

3. Have your lead Pokémon hold the Cleanse Tag

4. Use the Black Flute

5. Put a Pokémon with the Stench, White Smoke, Sand Veil, Quick Feet, or Snow Cloak Ability at the head of your party

Pokémon can learn various moves

Pokémon can learn all kinds of moves, which are useful both in battle and on your adventure in general. There are many different moves, each with its own unique effects. If you put some thought into developing move sets, your Pokémon will stand out as an individual.

A Pokémon can learn up to four moves.

● Three fundamental kinds of moves

Attack Moves	Defense Moves	Status Moves
These moves do damage by attacking the enemy. There are many variations on the basic attack move. Some moves also inflict status conditions, while others let your Pokémon take the first attack.	When your opponent has you in a tight spot, defense moves are a good idea. These moves can restore HP or cure status conditions. There are also defense moves that do everything from leeching an opponent's HP to regenerating HP each turn.	These moves strengthen the user or weaken an opponent. They can do anything from raising a Pokémon's stats to inflicting status conditions that gradually drain an opponent's HP. There's even a move that forces the other Trainer to swap out Pokémon.

● How to teach moves to Pokémon

◉ Level them up

Pokémon can learn various moves at predetermined levels. Once they reach a certain level, they can learn the appropriate move.

◉ Use a TM

A TM (Technical Machine) is an item that teaches a move to a single Pokémon. There are 92 different TMs, and each TM is only good for one use.

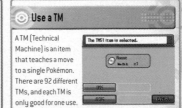

◉ Use an HM

Each HM (Hidden Machine) is programmed with a special move. An HM can teach that move to an unlimited number of Pokémon.

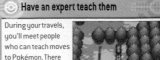

◉ Have an expert teach them

During your travels, you'll meet people who can teach moves to Pokémon. There are several different moves that can be learned this way.

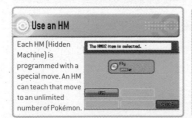

● No. 001 | Seed Pokémon
Bulbasaur

Grass   Poison

- **HEIGHT:** 2'04"
- **WEIGHT:** 15.2 lbs.
- **ITEMS:** None

● SIZE COMPARISON

● MALE/FEMALE HAVE SAME FORM

⊙ ABILITIES
- Overgrow

⊙ STATS
HP	●●
ATTACK	●●
DEFENSE	●●
SP. ATTACK	●●●
SP. DEFENSE	●●●
SPEED	●●

⊙ EGG GROUPS
Monster

Grass

⊙ PERFORMANCE
SPEED ★★☆	STAMINA ★★★☆
POWER ★★☆	JUMP ★★★
SKILL ★★★☆	

● MAIN WAYS TO OBTAIN

Pokémon HeartGold	Receive from Professor Oak in Pallet Town (after defeating Red)
Pokémon SoulSilver	Receive from Professor Oak in Pallet Town (after defeating Red)
Pokémon Diamond	—
Pokémon Pearl	—
Pokémon Platinum	—

Pokémon HeartGold	Pokémon SoulSilver
The seed on its back is filled with nutrients. The seed grows steadily larger as its body grows.	It carries a seed on its back right from birth. As it grows older, the seed also grows larger.

⊙ EVOLUTION

Lv. 16   Lv. 32

Bulbasaur   Ivysaur   Venusaur

● LEVEL-UP MOVES
Lv.	Name	Type	Kind	Pow.	Acc.	PP	Range	DA
1	Tackle	Normal	Physical	35	95	35	Normal	○
3	Growl	Normal	Status	—	100	40	2 Foes	—
7	Leech Seed	Grass	Status	—	90	10	Normal	—
9	Vine Whip	Grass	Physical	35	100	15	Normal	○
13	PoisonPowder	Poison	Status	—	75	35	Normal	—
13	Sleep Powder	Grass	Status	—	75	15	Normal	—
15	Take Down	Normal	Physical	90	85	20	Normal	○
19	Razor Leaf	Grass	Physical	55	95	25	Normal	—
21	Sweet Scent	Normal	Status	—	100	20	2 Foes	—
25	Growth	Normal	Status	—	—	40	Self	—
27	Double-Edge	Normal	Physical	120	100	15	Normal	○
31	Worry Seed	Grass	Status	—	100	10	Normal	—
33	Synthesis	Grass	Status	—	—	5	Self	—
37	Seed Bomb	Grass	Physical	80	100	15	Normal	—

● MOVE MANIAC
Name	Type	Kind	Pow.	Acc.	PP	Range	DA
Headbutt	Normal	Physical	70	100	15	Normal	○

● BP MOVES
Name	Type	Kind	Pow.	Acc.	PP	Range	DA
Fury Cutter	Bug	Physical	10	95	20	Normal	○
Knock Off	Dark	Physical	20	100	20	Normal	○
Snore	Normal	Special	40	100	15	Normal	—
Synthesis	Grass	Status	—	—	5	Self	—
String Shot	Bug	Status	—	95	40	2 Foes	—
Worry Seed	Grass	Status	—	100	10	Normal	—
Mud-Slap	Ground	Special	20	100	10	Normal	—
Seed Bomb	Grass	Physical	80	100	15	Normal	—

● TM & HM MOVES
No.	Name	Type	Kind	Pow.	Acc.	PP	Range	DA
TM06	Toxic	Poison	Status	—	85	10	Normal	—
TM09	Bullet Seed	Grass	Physical	10	100	30	Normal	—
TM10	Hidden Power	Normal	Special	—	100	15	Normal	—
TM11	Sunny Day	Fire	Status	—	—	5	All	—
TM17	Protect	Normal	Status	—	—	10	Self	—
TM19	Giga Drain	Grass	Special	60	100	10	Normal	—
TM21	Frustration	Normal	Physical	—	100	20	Normal	○
TM22	SolarBeam	Grass	Special	120	100	10	Normal	—
TM27	Return	Normal	Physical	—	100	20	Normal	○
TM32	Double Team	Normal	Status	—	—	15	Self	—
TM36	Sludge Bomb	Poison	Special	90	100	10	Normal	—
TM42	Facade	Normal	Physical	70	100	20	Normal	○
TM43	Secret Power	Normal	Physical	70	100	20	Normal	—
TM44	Rest	Psychic	Status	—	—	10	Self	—
TM45	Attract	Normal	Status	—	100	15	Normal	—
TM53	Energy Ball	Grass	Special	80	100	10	Normal	—
TM58	Endure	Normal	Status	—	—	10	Self	—
TM70	Flash	Normal	Status	—	100	20	Normal	—
TM75	Swords Dance	Normal	Status	—	—	30	Self	—
TM78	Captivate	Normal	Status	—	100	20	2 Foes	—
TM82	Sleep Talk	Normal	Status	—	—	10	Depends	—
TM83	Natural Gift	Normal	Physical	—	100	15	Normal	—
TM86	Grass Knot	Grass	Special	—	100	20	Normal	○
TM87	Swagger	Normal	Status	—	90	15	Normal	—
TM90	Substitute	Normal	Status	—	—	10	Self	—
HM01	Cut	Normal	Physical	50	95	30	Normal	○
HM04	Strength	Normal	Physical	80	100	15	Normal	○
HM06	Rock Smash	Fighting	Physical	40	100	15	Normal	○

● EGG MOVES
Name	Type	Kind	Pow.	Acc.	PP	Range	DA
Light Screen	Psychic	Status	—	—	30	2 Allies	—
Skull Bash	Normal	Physical	100	100	15	Normal	○
Safeguard	Normal	Status	—	—	25	2 Allies	—
Charm	Normal	Status	—	100	20	Normal	—
Petal Dance	Grass	Special	90	100	20	1 Random	○
Magical Leaf	Grass	Special	60	—	20	Normal	—
GrassWhistle	Grass	Status	—	55	15	Normal	—
Curse	???	Status	—	—	10	Normal/Self	—
Ingrain	Grass	Status	—	—	20	Self	—
Nature Power	Normal	Status	—	—	20	Depends	—
Amnesia	Psychic	Status	—	—	20	Self	—
Leaf Storm	Grass	Special	140	90	5	Normal	—
Power Whip	Grass	Physical	120	85	10	Normal	○
Sludge	Poison	Special	65	100	20	Normal	—

LEVEL-UP MOVES

Lv.	Name	Type	Kind	Pow.	Acc.	PP	Range	DA
1	Tackle	Normal	Physical	35	95	35	Normal	○
1	Growl	Normal	Status	—	100	40	2 Foes	—
1	Leech Seed	Grass	Status	—	90	10	Normal	—
3	Growl	Normal	Status	—	100	40	2 Foes	—
7	Leech Seed	Grass	Status	—	90	10	Normal	—
9	Vine Whip	Grass	Physical	35	100	15	Normal	○
13	PoisonPowder	Poison	Status	—	75	35	Normal	—
13	Sleep Powder	Grass	Status	—	75	15	Normal	—
15	Take Down	Normal	Physical	90	85	20	Normal	○
20	Razor Leaf	Grass	Physical	55	95	25	2 Foes	—
23	Sweet Scent	Normal	Status	—	100	20	2 Foes	—
28	Growth	Normal	Status	—	—	40	Self	—
31	Double-Edge	Normal	Physical	120	100	15	Normal	○
36	Worry Seed	Grass	Status	—	100	10	Normal	—
39	Synthesis	Grass	Status	—	—	5	Self	—
44	SolarBeam	Grass	Special	120	100	10	Normal	—

MOVE MANIAC

Name	Type	Kind	Pow.	Acc.	PP	Range	DA
Headbutt	Normal	Physical	20	100	15	Normal	○

BP MOVES

Name	Type	Kind	Pow.	Acc.	PP	Range	DA
Fury Cutter	Bug	Physical	10	95	20	Normal	○
Knock Off	Dark	Physical	20	100	20	Normal	○
Snore	Normal	Special	40	100	15	Normal	—
Synthesis	Grass	Status	—	—	5	Self	—
String Shot	Bug	Status	—	95	40	2 Foes	—
Worry Seed	Grass	Status	—	100	10	Normal	—
Mud-Slap	Ground	Special	20	100	10	Normal	—
Seed Bomb	Grass	Physical	80	100	15	Normal	—

TM & HM MOVES

No.	Name	Type	Kind	Pow.	Acc.	PP	Range	DA
TM06	Toxic	Poison	Status	—	85	10	Normal	—
TM09	Bullet Seed	Grass	Physical	10	100	30	Normal	—
TM10	Hidden Power	Normal	Special	—	100	15	Normal	—
TM11	Sunny Day	Fire	Status	—	—	5	All	—
TM17	Protect	Normal	Status	—	—	10	Self	—
TM19	Giga Drain	Grass	Special	60	100	10	Normal	—
TM21	Frustration	Normal	Physical	—	100	20	Normal	○
TM22	SolarBeam	Grass	Special	120	100	10	Normal	—
TM27	Return	Normal	Physical	—	100	20	Normal	○
TM32	Double Team	Normal	Status	—	—	15	Self	—
TM36	Sludge Bomb	Poison	Special	90	100	10	Normal	—
TM42	Facade	Normal	Physical	70	100	20	Normal	○
TM43	Secret Power	Normal	Physical	70	100	20	Normal	—
TM44	Rest	Psychic	Status	—	—	10	Self	—
TM45	Attract	Normal	Status	—	100	15	Normal	—
TM53	Energy Ball	Grass	Special	80	100	10	Normal	—
TM58	Endure	Normal	Status	—	—	10	Self	—
TM70	Flash	Normal	Status	—	100	20	Normal	—
TM75	Swords Dance	Normal	Status	—	—	30	Self	—
TM78	Captivate	Normal	Status	—	100	20	2 Foes	—
TM82	Sleep Talk	Normal	Status	—	—	10	Depends	—
TM83	Natural Gift	Normal	Physical	—	100	15	Normal	—
TM86	Grass Knot	Grass	Special	—	100	20	Normal	○
TM87	Swagger	Normal	Status	—	90	15	Normal	—
TM90	Substitute	Normal	Status	—	—	10	Self	—
HM01	Cut	Normal	Physical	50	95	30	Normal	○
HM04	Strength	Normal	Physical	80	100	15	Normal	○
HM06	Rock Smash	Fighting	Physical	40	100	15	Normal	○

No. 002 | Seed Pokémon
Ivysaur

Grass Poison

- **HEIGHT:** 3'03"
- **WEIGHT:** 28.7 lbs.
- **ITEMS:** None

● SIZE COMPARISON

● MALE/FEMALE HAVE SAME FORM

ABILITIES
● Overgrow

STATS
HP ●●
ATTACK ●●●
DEFENSE ●●●
SP. ATTACK ●●●●
SP. DEFENSE ●●●
SPEED ●●●

EGG GROUPS
Monster

Grass

PERFORMANCE

SPEED ★★	STAMINA ★★★★☆
POWER ★★☆	JUMP ★★★
SKILL ★★★★☆	

MAIN WAYS TO OBTAIN

Pokémon HeartGold — Level up Bulbasaur to Lv. 16

Pokémon SoulSilver — Level up Bulbasaur to Lv. 16

Pokémon Diamond — —

Pokémon Pearl — —

Pokémon Platinum — —

Pokémon HeartGold
Exposure to sunlight adds to its strength. Sunlight also makes the bud on its back grow larger.

Pokémon SoulSilver
If the bud on its back starts to smell sweet, it is evidence that the large flower will soon bloom.

EVOLUTION

Lv. 16   Lv. 32

Bulbasaur   Ivysaur   Venusaur

● No. 003 | Seed Pokémon
Venusaur

Grass | Poison

- ● HEIGHT: 6'07"
- ● WEIGHT: 220.5 lbs.
- ● ITEMS: None

● SIZE COMPARISON

● MALE FORM
No pistil

● FEMALE FORM
Pistil protruded

● ABILITIES
- ● Overgrow

● STATS
HP ●●●
ATTACK ●●●
DEFENSE ●●●
SP. ATTACK ●●●●
SP. DEFENSE ●●●●
SPEED ●●●●

● EGG GROUPS
Monster
Grass

● PERFORMANCE
SPEED ★☆
POWER ★★★★☆
SKILL ★★★

STAMINA ★★★★★
JUMP ★★

● MAIN WAYS TO OBTAIN

Pokémon HeartGold	Level up Ivysaur to Lv. 32
Pokémon SoulSilver	Level up Ivysaur to Lv. 32
Pokémon Diamond	—
Pokémon Pearl	—
Pokémon Platinum	—

| Pokémon HeartGold | Pokémon SoulSilver |
| By spreading the broad petals of its flower and catching the sun's rays, it fills its body with power. | It is able to convert sunlight into energy. As a result, it is more powerful in the summertime. |

● EVOLUTION

Lv. 16   Lv. 32

Bulbasaur   Ivysaur   Venusaur

● LEVEL-UP MOVES

Lv.	Name	Type	Kind	Pow.	Acc.	PP	Range	DA
1	Tackle	Normal	Physical	35	95	35	Normal	○
1	Growl	Normal	Status	—	100	40	2 Foes	—
1	Leech Seed	Grass	Status	—	90	10	Normal	—
1	Vine Whip	Grass	Physical	35	100	15	Normal	○
3	Growl	Normal	Status	—	100	40	2 Foes	—
7	Leech Seed	Grass	Status	—	90	10	Normal	—
9	Vine Whip	Grass	Physical	35	100	15	Normal	○
13	PoisonPowder	Poison	Status	—	75	35	Normal	—
13	Sleep Powder	Grass	Status	—	75	15	Normal	—
15	Take Down	Normal	Physical	90	85	20	Normal	○
20	Razor Leaf	Grass	Physical	55	95	25	2 Foes	—
23	Sweet Scent	Normal	Status	—	100	20	2 Foes	—
28	Growth	Normal	Status	—	—	40	Self	—
31	Double-Edge	Normal	Physical	120	100	15	Normal	○
32	Petal Dance	Grass	Special	90	100	20	1 Random	—
39	Worry Seed	Grass	Status	—	100	10	Normal	—
45	Synthesis	Grass	Status	—	—	5	Self	—
53	SolarBeam	Grass	Special	120	100	10	Normal	—

● MOVE MANIAC

Name	Type	Kind	Pow.	Acc.	PP	Range	DA
Headbutt	Normal	Physical	70	100	15	Normal	—
Frenzy Plant	Grass	Special	150	90	5	Normal	—

● BP MOVES

Name	Type	Kind	Pow.	Acc.	PP	Range	DA
Fury Cutter	Bug	Physical	10	95	20	Normal	○
Knock Off	Dark	Physical	20	100	20	Normal	○
Snore	Normal	Special	40	100	15	Normal	—
Synthesis	Grass	Status	—	—	5	Self	—
String Shot	Bug	Status	—	95	40	2 Foes	—
Worry Seed	Grass	Status	—	100	10	Normal	—
Block	Normal	Status	—	—	5	Normal	—
Mud-Slap	Ground	Special	20	100	10	Normal	—
Outrage	Dragon	Physical	120	100	15	1 Random	○
Seed Bomb	Grass	Physical	80	100	15	Normal	—

● TM & HM MOVES

No.	Name	Type	Kind	Pow.	Acc.	PP	Range	DA
TM05	Roar	Normal	Status	—	100	20	Normal	—
TM06	Toxic	Poison	Status	—	85	10	Normal	—
TM09	Bullet Seed	Grass	Physical	10	100	30	Normal	—
TM10	Hidden Power	Normal	Special	—	100	15	Normal	—
TM11	Sunny Day	Fire	Status	—	—	5	All	—
TM15	Hyper Beam	Normal	Special	150	90	5	Normal	—
TM17	Protect	Normal	Status	—	—	10	Self	—
TM19	Giga Drain	Grass	Special	60	100	10	Normal	—
TM21	Frustration	Normal	Physical	—	100	20	Normal	○
TM22	SolarBeam	Grass	Special	120	100	10	Normal	—
TM26	Earthquake	Ground	Physical	100	100	10	2 Foes/1 Ally	—
TM27	Return	Normal	Physical	—	100	20	Normal	○
TM32	Double Team	Normal	Status	—	—	15	Self	—
TM36	Sludge Bomb	Poison	Special	90	100	10	Normal	—
TM42	Facade	Normal	Physical	70	100	20	Normal	○
TM43	Secret Power	Normal	Physical	70	100	20	Normal	—
TM44	Rest	Psychic	Status	—	—	10	Self	—
TM45	Attract	Normal	Status	—	100	15	Normal	—
TM53	Energy Ball	Grass	Special	80	100	10	Normal	—
TM58	Endure	Normal	Status	—	—	10	Self	—
TM68	Giga Impact	Normal	Physical	150	90	5	Normal	○
TM70	Flash	Normal	Status	—	100	20	Normal	—
TM75	Swords Dance	Normal	Status	—	—	30	Self	—
TM78	Captivate	Normal	Status	—	100	20	2 Foes	—
TM82	Sleep Talk	Normal	Status	—	—	10	Depends	—
TM83	Natural Gift	Normal	Physical	—	100	15	Normal	—
TM86	Grass Knot	Grass	Special	—	100	20	Normal	○
TM87	Swagger	Normal	Status	—	90	15	Normal	—
TM90	Substitute	Normal	Status	—	—	10	Self	—
HM01	Cut	Normal	Physical	50	95	30	Normal	○
HM04	Strength	Normal	Physical	80	100	15	Normal	○
HM06	Rock Smash	Fighting	Physical	40	100	15	Normal	○
HM08	Rock Climb	Normal	Physical	90	85	20	Normal	○

● LEVEL-UP MOVES

Lv.	Name	Type	Kind	Pow.	Acc.	PP	Range	DA
1	Scratch	Normal	Physical	40	100	35	Normal	○
1	Growl	Normal	Status	—	100	40	2 Foes	—
7	Ember	Fire	Special	40	100	25	Normal	—
10	SmokeScreen	Normal	Status	—	100	20	Normal	—
16	Dragon Rage	Dragon	Special	—	100	10	Normal	—
19	Scary Face	Normal	Status	—	90	10	Normal	—
25	Fire Fang	Fire	Physical	65	95	15	Normal	○
28	Slash	Normal	Physical	70	100	20	Normal	○
34	Flamethrower	Fire	Special	95	100	15	Normal	—
37	Fire Spin	Fire	Special	15	70	15	Normal	—

● MOVE MANIAC

Name	Type	Kind	Pow.	Acc.	PP	Range	DA
Headbutt	Normal	Physical	70	100	15	Normal	○

● BP MOVES

Name	Type	Kind	Pow.	Acc.	PP	Range	DA
Fury Cutter	Bug	Physical	10	95	20	Normal	○
ThunderPunch	Electric	Physical	75	100	15	Normal	○
Fire Punch	Fire	Physical	75	100	15	Normal	○
Snore	Normal	Special	40	100	15	Normal	—
Swift	Normal	Special	60	—	20	2 Foes	—
Mud-Slap	Ground	Special	20	100	10	Normal	—
Heat Wave	Fire	Special	100	90	10	2 Foes	—

● TM & HM MOVES

No.	Name	Type	Kind	Pow.	Acc.	PP	Range	DA
TM01	Focus Punch	Fighting	Physical	150	100	20	Normal	○
TM02	Dragon Claw	Dragon	Physical	80	100	15	Normal	○
TM06	Toxic	Poison	Status	—	85	10	Normal	—
TM10	Hidden Power	Normal	Special	—	100	15	Normal	—
TM11	Sunny Day	Fire	Status	—	—	5	All	—
TM17	Protect	Normal	Status	—	—	10	Self	—
TM21	Frustration	Normal	Physical	—	100	20	Normal	○
TM23	Iron Tail	Steel	Physical	100	75	15	Normal	○
TM27	Return	Normal	Physical	—	100	20	Normal	○
TM28	Dig	Ground	Physical	80	100	10	Normal	○
TM31	Brick Break	Fighting	Physical	75	100	15	Normal	○
TM32	Double Team	Normal	Status	—	—	15	Self	—
TM35	Flamethrower	Fire	Special	95	100	15	Normal	—
TM38	Fire Blast	Fire	Special	120	85	5	Normal	—
TM39	Rock Tomb	Rock	Physical	50	80	10	Normal	○
TM40	Aerial Ace	Flying	Physical	60	—	20	Normal	○
TM42	Facade	Normal	Physical	70	100	20	Normal	○
TM43	Secret Power	Normal	Physical	70	100	20	Normal	○
TM44	Rest	Psychic	Status	—	—	10	Self	—
TM45	Attract	Normal	Status	—	100	15	Normal	—
TM50	Overheat	Fire	Special	140	90	5	Normal	—
TM56	Fling	Dark	Physical	—	100	10	Normal	—
TM58	Endure	Normal	Status	—	—	10	Self	—
TM61	Will-O-Wisp	Fire	Status	—	75	15	Normal	—
TM65	Shadow Claw	Ghost	Physical	70	100	15	Normal	○
TM75	Swords Dance	Normal	Status	—	—	30	Self	—
TM78	Captivate	Normal	Status	—	100	20	2 Foes	—
TM80	Rock Slide	Rock	Physical	75	90	10	2 Foes	—
TM82	Sleep Talk	Normal	Status	—	—	10	Depends	—
TM83	Natural Gift	Normal	Physical	—	100	15	Normal	—
TM87	Swagger	Normal	Status	—	90	15	Normal	—
TM90	Substitute	Normal	Status	—	—	10	Self	—
HM01	Cut	Normal	Physical	50	95	30	Normal	○
HM04	Strength	Normal	Physical	80	100	15	Normal	○
HM06	Rock Smash	Fighting	Physical	40	100	15	Normal	○

● EGG MOVES

Name	Type	Kind	Pow.	Acc.	PP	Range	DA
Belly Drum	Normal	Status	—	—	10	Self	—
AncientPower	Rock	Special	60	100	5	Normal	—
Rock Slide	Rock	Physical	75	90	10	2 Foes	—
Bite	Dark	Physical	60	100	25	Normal	○
Outrage	Dragon	Physical	120	100	15	1 Random	○
Beat Up	Dark	Physical	10	100	10	Normal	—
Swords Dance	Normal	Status	—	—	30	Self	—
Dragon Dance	Dragon	Status	—	—	20	Self	—
Crunch	Dark	Physical	80	100	15	Normal	○
Dragon Rush	Dragon	Physical	100	75	10	Normal	○
Metal Claw	Steel	Physical	50	95	35	Normal	○
Flare Blitz	Fire	Physical	120	100	15	Normal	○
Counter	Fighting	Physical	—	100	20	Self	○

● **No. 004** | Lizard Pokémon
Charmander

`Fire`

- ● **HEIGHT:** 2'00"
- ● **WEIGHT:** 18.7 lbs.
- ● **ITEMS:** None

● SIZE COMPARISON

● MALE/FEMALE HAVE SAME FORM

⊕ ABILITIES
- ● Blaze

⊕ STATS
HP	●
ATTACK	●●
DEFENSE	●●
SP. ATTACK	●●●
SP. DEFENSE	●●●
SPEED	●●●

⊕ EGG GROUPS
Monster

Dragon

⊕ PERFORMANCE
SPEED ★★★	STAMINA ★☆☆
POWER ★☆☆☆☆	JUMP ★★★
SKILL ★★★☆	

● MAIN WAYS TO OBTAIN

Pokémon HeartGold — Receive from Professor Oak in Pallet Town (after defeating Red)

Pokémon SoulSilver — Receive from Professor Oak in Pallet Town (after defeating Red)

Pokémon Diamond — —

Pokémon Pearl — —

Pokémon Platinum — —

Pokémon HeartGold — The flame on its tail shows the strength of its life force. If it is weak, the flame also burns weakly.

Pokémon SoulSilver — The flame on its tail indicates CHARMANDER's life force. If it is healthy, the flame burns brightly.

⊕ EVOLUTION

Charmander — Lv. 16 — Charmeleon — Lv.32 — Charizard

● No. 005 | Flame Pokémon
Charmeleon

Fire

● HEIGHT: 3'07"
● WEIGHT: 41.9 lbs.
● ITEMS: None

● MALE/FEMALE HAVE SAME FORM

● SIZE COMPARISON

● ABILITIES
● Blaze

● STATS
HP ●●
ATTACK ●●●
DEFENSE ●●
SP. ATTACK ●●●
SP. DEFENSE ●●●
SPEED ●●●●

● EGG GROUPS
Monster
Dragon

● PERFORMANCE
SPEED ★★★
POWER ★★☆☆
SKILL ★★★☆
STAMINA ★★
JUMP ★★★

● MAIN WAYS TO OBTAIN

Pokémon HeartGold	Level up Charmander to Lv. 16
Pokémon SoulSilver	Level up Charmander to Lv. 16
Pokémon Diamond	—
Pokémon Pearl	—
Pokémon Platinum	—

| Pokémon HeartGold | Pokémon SoulSilver |
| It is very hotheaded by nature, so it constantly seeks opponents. It calms down only when it wins. | It has a barbaric nature. In battle, it whips its fiery tail around and slashes away with sharp claws. |

● EVOLUTION

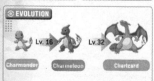

Charmander — Lv. 16 — Charmeleon — Lv. 32 — Charizard

● LEVEL-UP MOVES

Lv.	Name	Type	Kind	Pow.	Acc.	PP	Range	DA
1	Scratch	Normal	Physical	40	100	35	Normal	○
1	Growl	Normal	Status	—	100	40	2 Foes	—
1	Ember	Fire	Special	40	100	25	Normal	—
7	Ember	Fire	Special	40	100	25	Normal	—
10	SmokeScreen	Normal	Status	—	100	20	Normal	—
17	Dragon Rage	Dragon	Special	—	100	10	Normal	—
21	Scary Face	Normal	Status	—	90	10	Normal	—
28	Fire Fang	Fire	Physical	65	95	15	Normal	○
32	Slash	Normal	Physical	70	100	20	Normal	○
39	Flamethrower	Fire	Special	95	100	15	Normal	—
43	Fire Spin	Fire	Special	15	70	15	Normal	—

● MOVE MANIAC

Name	Type	Kind	Pow.	Acc.	PP	Range	DA
Headbutt	Normal	Physical	70	100	15	Normal	—

● BP MOVES

Name	Type	Kind	Pow.	Acc.	PP	Range	DA
Fury Cutter	Bug	Physical	10	95	20	Normal	○
ThunderPunch	Electric	Physical	75	100	15	Normal	○
Fire Punch	Fire	Physical	75	100	15	Normal	○
Snore	Normal	Special	40	100	15	Normal	—
Swift	Normal	Special	60	—	20	2 Foes	—
Mud-Slap	Ground	Special	20	100	10	Normal	—
Heat Wave	Fire	Special	100	90	10	2 Foes	—

● TM & HM MOVES

No.	Name	Type	Kind	Pow.	Acc.	PP	Range	DA
TM01	Focus Punch	Fighting	Physical	150	100	20	Normal	○
TM02	Dragon Claw	Dragon	Physical	80	100	15	Normal	○
TM06	Toxic	Poison	Status	—	85	10	Normal	—
TM10	Hidden Power	Normal	Special	—	100	15	Normal	—
TM11	Sunny Day	Fire	Status	—	—	5	All	—
TM17	Protect	Normal	Status	—	—	10	Self	—
TM21	Frustration	Normal	Physical	—	100	20	Normal	○
TM27	Return	Normal	Physical	—	100	20	Normal	○
TM28	Dig	Ground	Physical	80	100	10	Normal	○
TM31	Brick Break	Fighting	Physical	75	100	15	Normal	○
TM32	Double Team	Normal	Status	—	—	15	Self	—
TM35	Flamethrower	Fire	Special	95	100	15	Normal	—
TM38	Fire Blast	Fire	Special	120	85	5	Normal	—
TM39	Rock Tomb	Rock	Physical	50	80	10	Normal	○
TM40	Aerial Ace	Flying	Physical	60	—	20	Normal	○
TM42	Facade	Normal	Physical	70	100	20	Normal	○
TM43	Secret Power	Normal	Physical	70	100	20	Normal	○
TM44	Rest	Psychic	Status	—	—	10	Self	—
TM45	Attract	Normal	Status	—	100	15	Normal	—
TM50	Overheat	Fire	Special	140	90	5	Normal	—
TM56	Fling	Dark	Physical	—	100	10	Normal	○
TM58	Endure	Normal	Status	—	—	10	Self	—
TM61	Will-O-Wisp	Fire	Status	—	75	15	Normal	—
TM65	Shadow Claw	Ghost	Physical	70	100	15	Normal	○
TM75	Swords Dance	Normal	Status	—	—	30	Self	—
TM78	Captivate	Normal	Status	—	100	20	2 Foes	—
TM80	Rock Slide	Rock	Physical	75	90	10	2 Foes	—
TM82	Sleep Talk	Normal	Status	—	—	10	Depends	—
TM83	Natural Gift	Normal	Physical	—	100	15	Normal	—
TM87	Swagger	Normal	Status	—	90	15	Normal	—
TM90	Substitute	Normal	Status	—	—	10	Self	—
HM01	Cut	Normal	Physical	50	95	30	Normal	○
HM04	Strength	Normal	Physical	80	100	15	Normal	○
HM06	Rock Smash	Fighting	Physical	40	100	15	Normal	○

● LEVEL-UP MOVES

Lv.	Name	Type	Kind	Pow.	Acc.	PP	Range	DA
1	Dragon Claw	Dragon	Physical	80	100	15	Normal	○
1	Shadow Claw	Ghost	Physical	70	100	15	Normal	○
1	Air Slash	Flying	Special	75	95	20	Normal	○
1	Scratch	Normal	Physical	40	100	35	Normal	○
1	Growl	Normal	Status	—	100	40	2 Foes	—
1	Ember	Fire	Special	40	100	25	Normal	—
1	SmokeScreen	Normal	Status	—	100	20	Normal	—
7	Ember	Fire	Special	40	100	25	Normal	—
10	SmokeScreen	Normal	Status	—	100	20	Normal	—
17	Dragon Rage	Dragon	Special	—	100	10	Normal	—
21	Scary Face	Normal	Status	—	90	10	Normal	—
28	Fire Fang	Fire	Physical	65	95	15	Normal	○
32	Slash	Normal	Physical	70	100	20	Normal	○
36	Wing Attack	Flying	Physical	60	100	35	Normal	○
42	Flamethrower	Fire	Special	95	100	15	Normal	—
49	Fire Spin	Fire	Special	15	70	15	Normal	—
59	Heat Wave	Fire	Special	100	90	10	2 Foes	—
66	Flare Blitz	Fire	Physical	120	100	15	Normal	○

● MOVE MANIAC

Name	Type	Kind	Pow.	Acc.	PP	Range	DA
Headbutt	Normal	Physical	70	100	15	Normal	○
Blast Burn	Fire	Special	150	90	5	Normal	—

● BP MOVES

Name	Type	Kind	Pow.	Acc.	PP	Range	DA
Fury Cutter	Bug	Physical	10	95	20	Normal	○
ThunderPunch	Electric	Physical	75	100	15	Normal	○
Fire Punch	Fire	Physical	75	100	15	Normal	○
Ominous Wind	Ghost	Special	60	100	5	Normal	—
Air Cutter	Flying	Special	55	95	25	2 Foes	—
Snore	Normal	Special	40	100	15	Normal	—
Swift	Normal	Special	60	—	20	2 Foes	—
Tailwind	Flying	Status	—	—	30	2 Allies	—
Mud-Slap	Ground	Special	20	100	10	Normal	—
Outrage	Dragon	Physical	120	100	15	1 Random	○
Twister	Dragon	Special	40	100	20	2 Foes	—
Heat Wave	Fire	Special	100	90	10	2 Foes	—

● TM & HM MOVES

No.	Name	Type	Kind	Pow.	Acc.	PP	Range	DA
TM01	Focus Punch	Fighting	Physical	150	100	20	Normal	○
TM02	Dragon Claw	Dragon	Physical	80	100	15	Normal	○
TM05	Roar	Normal	Status	—	100	20	Normal	—
TM06	Toxic	Poison	Status	—	85	10	Normal	—
TM10	Hidden Power	Normal	Special	—	100	15	Normal	—
TM11	Sunny Day	Fire	Status	—	—	5	All	—
TM15	Hyper Beam	Normal	Special	150	90	5	Normal	—
TM17	Protect	Normal	Status	—	—	10	Self	—
TM21	Frustration	Normal	Physical	—	100	20	Normal	○
TM22	SolarBeam	Grass	Special	120	100	10	Normal	—
TM23	Iron Tail	Steel	Physical	100	75	15	Normal	○
TM26	Earthquake	Ground	Physical	100	100	10	2 Foes/1 Ally	—
TM27	Return	Normal	Physical	—	100	20	Normal	○
TM28	Dig	Ground	Physical	80	100	10	Normal	○
TM31	Brick Break	Fighting	Physical	75	100	15	Normal	○
TM32	Double Team	Normal	Status	—	—	15	Self	—
TM35	Flamethrower	Fire	Special	95	100	15	Normal	—
TM38	Fire Blast	Fire	Special	120	85	5	Normal	—
TM39	Rock Tomb	Rock	Physical	50	80	10	Normal	—
TM40	Aerial Ace	Flying	Physical	60	—	20	Normal	○
TM42	Facade	Normal	Physical	70	100	20	Normal	○
TM43	Secret Power	Normal	Physical	70	100	20	Normal	—
TM44	Rest	Psychic	Status	—	—	10	Self	—
TM45	Attract	Normal	Status	—	100	15	Normal	—
TM47	Steel Wing	Steel	Physical	70	90	25	Normal	○
TM50	Overheat	Fire	Special	140	90	5	Normal	—
TM51	Roost	Flying	Status	—	—	10	Self	—
TM52	Focus Blast	Fighting	Special	120	70	5	Normal	—
TM56	Fling	Dark	Physical	—	100	10	Normal	—
TM58	Endure	Normal	Status	—	—	10	Self	—
TM59	Dragon Pulse	Dragon	Special	90	100	10	Normal	—
TM61	Will-O-Wisp	Fire	Status	—	75	15	Normal	—
TM65	Shadow Claw	Ghost	Physical	70	100	15	Normal	○
TM68	Giga Impact	Normal	Physical	150	90	5	Normal	○
TM75	Swords Dance	Normal	Status	—	—	30	Self	—
TM78	Captivate	Normal	Status	—	100	20	2 Foes	—
TM80	Rock Slide	Rock	Physical	75	90	10	2 Foes	—
TM82	Sleep Talk	Normal	Status	—	—	10	Depends	—
TM83	Natural Gift	Normal	Physical	—	100	15	Normal	—
TM87	Swagger	Normal	Status	—	90	15	Normal	—
TM90	Substitute	Normal	Status	—	—	10	Self	—
HM01	Cut	Normal	Physical	50	95	30	Normal	○
HM02	Fly	Flying	Physical	90	95	15	Normal	○
HM04	Strength	Normal	Physical	80	100	15	Normal	○
HM06	Rock Smash	Fighting	Physical	40	100	15	Normal	○

Charizard

Fire | Flying

● HEIGHT: 5'02"
● WEIGHT: 199.5 lbs.
● ITEMS: None

● SIZE COMPARISON

● MALE/FEMALE HAVE SAME FORM

● ABILITIES
● Blaze

● STATS
HP ●●●
ATTACK ●●●●
DEFENSE ●●●
SP. ATTACK ●●●●
SP. DEFENSE ●●●
SPEED ●●●●

● EGG GROUPS
Monster
Dragon

● PERFORMANCE
SPEED ★★★
POWER ★★★
SKILL ★★
STAMINA ★★★★☆
JUMP ★★★★★

● MAIN WAYS TO OBTAIN

Pokémon HeartGold	Level up Charmeleon to Lv. 36
Pokémon SoulSilver	Level up Charmeleon to Lv. 36
Pokémon Diamond	—
Pokémon Pearl	—
Pokémon Platinum	—

Pokémon HeartGold
If CHARIZARD becomes furious, the flame at the tip of its tail flares up in a light blue shade.

Pokémon SoulSilver
Breathing intense, hot flames, it can melt almost anything. Its breath inflicts terrible pain on enemies.

● EVOLUTION

Lv. 16 | Lv. 32

Charmander | Charmeleon | Charizard

No. 007 | Tiny Turtle Pokémon
Squirtle

Water

- **HEIGHT:** 1'08"
- **WEIGHT:** 19.8 lbs.
- **ITEMS:** None

SIZE COMPARISON

● MALE/FEMALE HAVE SAME FORM

⊚ ABILITIES
● Torrent

⊚ STATS
HP ●●
ATTACK ●●
DEFENSE ●●●
SP. ATTACK ●●
SP. DEFENSE ●●
SPEED ●●

⊚ EGG GROUPS
Monster

Water 1

⊚ PERFORMANCE
SPEED ★★★   STAMINA ★★★★
POWER ★☆☆   JUMP ★★
SKILL ★★★☆

● MAIN WAYS TO OBTAIN

Pokémon HeartGold	Receive from Professor Oak in Pallet Town [after defeating Red]
Pokémon SoulSilver	Receive from Professor Oak in Pallet Town [after defeating Red]
Pokémon Diamond	—
Pokémon Pearl	—
Pokémon Platinum	—

| Pokémon HeartGold | Pokémon SoulSilver |
| The shell is soft when it is born. It soon becomes so resilient, prodding fingers will bounce off it. | The shell, which hardens soon after it is born, is resilient. If you poke it, it will bounce back out. |

⊚ EVOLUTION

Squirtle — Lv. 16 — Wartortle — Lv. 36 — Blastoise

● LEVEL-UP MOVES

Lv.	Name	Type	Kind	Pow.	Acc.	PP	Range	DA
1	Tackle	Normal	Physical	35	95	35	Normal	○
4	Tail Whip	Normal	Status	—	100	30	2 Foes	—
7	Bubble	Water	Special	20	100	30	2 Foes	—
10	Withdraw	Water	Status	—	—	40	Self	—
13	Water Gun	Water	Special	40	100	25	Normal	—
16	Bite	Dark	Physical	60	100	25	Normal	○
19	Rapid Spin	Normal	Physical	20	100	40	Normal	○
22	Protect	Normal	Status	—	—	10	Self	—
25	Water Pulse	Water	Special	60	100	20	Normal	—
28	Aqua Tail	Water	Physical	90	90	10	Normal	○
31	Skull Bash	Normal	Physical	100	100	15	Normal	○
34	Iron Defense	Steel	Status	—	—	15	Self	—
37	Rain Dance	Water	Status	—	—	5	All	—
40	Hydro Pump	Water	Special	120	80	5	Normal	—

● MOVE MANIAC

Name	Type	Kind	Pow.	Acc.	PP	Range	DA
Headbutt	Normal	Physical	70	100	15	Normal	○

● BP MOVES

Name	Type	Kind	Pow.	Acc.	PP	Range	DA
Dive	Water	Physical	80	100	10	Normal	○
Icy Wind	Ice	Special	55	95	15	2 Foes	—
Ice Punch	Ice	Physical	75	100	15	Normal	○
Zen Headbutt	Psychic	Physical	80	90	15	Normal	○
Snore	Normal	Special	40	100	15	Normal	—
Mud-Slap	Ground	Special	20	100	10	Normal	—
Rollout	Rock	Physical	30	90	20	Normal	○
Aqua Tail	Water	Physical	90	90	10	Normal	○
Iron Defense	Steel	Status	—	—	15	Self	—

● TM & HM MOVES

No.	Name	Type	Kind	Pow.	Acc.	PP	Range	DA
TM01	Focus Punch	Fighting	Physical	150	100	20	Normal	○
TM03	Water Pulse	Water	Special	60	100	20	Normal	—
TM06	Toxic	Poison	Status	—	85	10	Normal	—
TM07	Hail	Ice	Status	—	—	10	All	—
TM10	Hidden Power	Normal	Special	—	100	15	Normal	—
TM13	Ice Beam	Ice	Special	95	100	10	Normal	—
TM14	Blizzard	Ice	Special	120	70	5	2 Foes	—
TM17	Protect	Normal	Status	—	—	10	Self	—
TM18	Rain Dance	Water	Status	—	—	5	All	—
TM21	Frustration	Normal	Physical	—	100	20	Normal	○
TM23	Iron Tail	Steel	Physical	100	75	15	Normal	○
TM27	Return	Normal	Physical	—	100	20	Normal	○
TM28	Dig	Ground	Physical	80	100	10	Normal	○
TM31	Brick Break	Fighting	Physical	75	100	15	Normal	○
TM32	Double Team	Normal	Status	—	—	15	Self	—
TM39	Rock Tomb	Rock	Physical	50	80	10	Normal	○
TM42	Facade	Normal	Physical	70	100	20	Normal	○
TM43	Secret Power	Normal	Physical	70	100	20	Normal	—
TM44	Rest	Psychic	Status	—	—	10	Self	—
TM45	Attract	Normal	Status	—	100	15	Normal	—
TM55	Brine	Water	Special	65	100	10	Normal	—
TM56	Fling	Dark	Physical	—	100	10	Normal	—
TM58	Endure	Normal	Status	—	—	10	Self	—
TM74	Gyro Ball	Steel	Physical	—	100	5	Normal	○
TM78	Captivate	Normal	Status	—	100	20	2 Foes	—
TM82	Sleep Talk	Normal	Status	—	—	10	Depends	—
TM83	Natural Gift	Normal	Physical	—	100	15	Normal	—
TM87	Swagger	Normal	Status	—	90	15	Normal	—
TM90	Substitute	Normal	Status	—	—	10	Self	—
HM03	Surf	Water	Special	95	100	15	2 Foes/1 Ally	—
HM04	Strength	Normal	Physical	80	100	15	Normal	○
HM05	Whirlpool	Water	Special	15	70	15	Normal	—
HM06	Rock Smash	Fighting	Physical	40	100	15	Normal	○
HM07	Waterfall	Water	Physical	80	100	15	Normal	○

● EGG MOVES

Name	Type	Kind	Pow.	Acc.	PP	Range	DA
Mirror Coat	Psychic	Special	—	100	20	Self	—
Haze	Ice	Status	—	—	30	All	—
Mist	Ice	Status	—	—	30	2 Allies	—
Foresight	Normal	Status	—	—	40	Normal	—
Flail	Normal	Physical	—	100	15	Normal	○
Refresh	Normal	Status	—	—	20	Self	—
Mud Sport	Ground	Status	—	—	15	All	—
Yawn	Normal	Status	—	—	10	Normal	—
Muddy Water	Water	Special	95	85	10	2 Foes	—
Fake Out	Normal	Physical	40	100	10	Normal	○
Aqua Ring	Water	Status	—	—	20	Self	—
Aqua Jet	Water	Physical	40	100	20	Normal	○
Water Spout	Water	Special	150	100	5	2 Foes	—

● LEVEL-UP MOVES

Lv.	Name	Type	Kind	Pow.	Acc.	PP	Range	DA
1	Tackle	Normal	Physical	35	95	35	Normal	○
1	Tail Whip	Normal	Status	—	100	30	2 Foes	—
1	Bubble	Water	Special	20	100	30	2 Foes	—
4	Tail Whip	Normal	Status	—	100	30	2 Foes	—
7	Bubble	Water	Special	20	100	30	2 Foes	—
10	Withdraw	Water	Status	—	—	40	Self	—
13	Water Gun	Water	Special	40	100	25	Normal	—
16	Bite	Dark	Physical	60	100	25	Normal	○
20	Rapid Spin	Normal	Physical	20	100	40	Normal	○
24	Protect	Normal	Status	—	—	10	Self	—
28	Water Pulse	Water	Special	60	100	20	Normal	—
32	Aqua Tail	Water	Physical	90	90	10	Normal	○
36	Skull Bash	Normal	Physical	100	100	15	Normal	○
40	Iron Defense	Steel	Status	—	—	15	Self	—
44	Rain Dance	Water	Status	—	—	5	All	—
48	Hydro Pump	Water	Special	120	80	5	Normal	—

● MOVE MANIAC

Name	Type	Kind	Pow.	Acc.	PP	Range	DA
Headbutt	Normal	Physical	70	100	15	Normal	○

● BP MOVES

Name	Type	Kind	Pow.	Acc.	PP	Range	DA
Dive	Water	Physical	80	100	10	Normal	○
Icy Wind	Ice	Special	55	95	15	2 Foes	—
Ice Punch	Ice	Physical	75	100	15	Normal	○
Zen Headbutt	Psychic	Physical	80	90	15	Normal	○
Snore	Normal	Special	40	100	15	Normal	—
Mud-Slap	Ground	Special	20	100	10	Normal	—
Rollout	Rock	Physical	30	90	20	Normal	○
Aqua Tail	Water	Physical	90	90	10	Normal	○
Iron Defense	Steel	Status	—	—	15	Self	—

● TM & HM MOVES

No.	Name	Type	Kind	Pow.	Acc.	PP	Range	DA
TM01	Focus Punch	Fighting	Physical	150	100	20	Normal	○
TM03	Water Pulse	Water	Special	60	100	20	Normal	—
TM06	Toxic	Poison	Status	—	85	10	Normal	—
TM07	Hail	Ice	Status	—	—	10	All	—
TM10	Hidden Power	Normal	Special	—	100	15	Normal	—
TM13	Ice Beam	Ice	Special	95	100	10	Normal	—
TM14	Blizzard	Ice	Special	120	70	5	2 Foes	—
TM17	Protect	Normal	Status	—	—	10	Self	—
TM18	Rain Dance	Water	Status	—	—	5	All	—
TM21	Frustration	Normal	Physical	—	100	20	Normal	○
TM23	Iron Tail	Steel	Physical	100	75	15	Normal	○
TM27	Return	Normal	Physical	—	100	20	Normal	○
TM28	Dig	Ground	Physical	80	100	10	Normal	○
TM31	Brick Break	Fighting	Physical	75	100	15	Normal	○
TM32	Double Team	Normal	Status	—	—	15	Self	—
TM39	Rock Tomb	Rock	Physical	50	80	10	Normal	○
TM42	Facade	Normal	Physical	70	100	20	Normal	○
TM43	Secret Power	Normal	Physical	70	100	20	Normal	○
TM44	Rest	Psychic	Status	—	—	10	Self	—
TM45	Attract	Normal	Status	—	100	15	Normal	—
TM55	Brine	Water	Special	65	100	10	Normal	—
TM56	Fling	Dark	Physical	—	100	10	Normal	○
TM58	Endure	Normal	Status	—	—	10	Self	—
TM74	Gyro Ball	Steel	Physical	—	100	5	Normal	○
TM78	Captivate	Normal	Status	—	100	20	2 Foes	—
TM82	Sleep Talk	Normal	Status	—	—	10	Depends	—
TM83	Natural Gift	Normal	Physical	—	100	15	Normal	—
TM87	Swagger	Normal	Status	—	90	15	Normal	—
TM90	Substitute	Normal	Status	—	—	10	Self	—
HM03	Surf	Water	Special	95	100	15	2 Foes/1 Ally	—
HM04	Strength	Normal	Physical	80	100	15	Normal	○
HM05	Whirlpool	Water	Special	15	70	15	Normal	—
HM06	Rock Smash	Fighting	Physical	40	100	15	Normal	○
HM07	Waterfall	Water	Physical	80	100	15	Normal	○

● No. 008 | Turtle Pokémon

Wartortle

Water

● **HEIGHT:** 3'03"
● **WEIGHT:** 49.6 lbs.
● **ITEMS:** None

● SIZE COMPARISON

● MALE/FEMALE HAVE SAME FORM

● ABILITIES
● Torrent

● STATS
HP ●●
ATTACK ●●●
DEFENSE ●●●
SP. ATTACK ●●●
SP. DEFENSE ●●●
SPEED ●●●

● EGG GROUPS
Monster
Water 1

● PERFORMANCE
SPEED ★★☆☆☆ STAMINA ★★★☆☆
POWER ★★☆☆☆ JUMP ★★★☆☆
SKILL ★★★★☆

● MAIN WAYS TO OBTAIN

Pokémon HeartGold — Level up Squirtle to Lv. 16

Pokémon SoulSilver — Level up Squirtle to Lv. 16

Pokémon Diamond — —

Pokémon Pearl — —

Pokémon Platinum — —

Pokémon HeartGold
It is a well-established symbol of longevity. If its shell has algae on it, that WARTORTLE is very old.

Pokémon SoulSilver
It cleverly controls its furry ears and tail to maintain its balance while swimming.

● EVOLUTION
Lv. 16   Lv. 36
Squirtle   Wartortle   Blastoise

No. 009 | Shellfish Pokémon
Blastoise

Water

- **HEIGHT:** 5'03"
- **WEIGHT:** 188.5 lbs.
- **ITEMS:** None

● SIZE COMPARISON

● MALE/FEMALE HAVE SAME FORM

⊕ ABILITIES
- Torrent

⊕ STATS
HP ●●●
ATTACK ●●●●
DEFENSE ●●●●
SP. ATTACK ●●●●
SP. DEFENSE ●●●●
SPEED ●●●

⊕ EGG GROUPS
Monster
Water 1

⊕ PERFORMANCE
SPEED ★★★
POWER ★★★★☆
SKILL ★★☆
STAMINA ★★★★☆
JUMP ★★☆

● MAIN WAYS TO OBTAIN

Pokémon HeartGold — Level up Wartortle to Lv. 36

Pokémon SoulSilver — Level up Wartortle to Lv. 36

Pokémon Diamond — —

Pokémon Pearl — —

Pokémon Platinum — —

Pokémon HeartGold	Pokémon SoulSilver
It deliberately makes itself heavy so it can withstand the recoil of the water jets it fires.	The rocket cannons on its shell fire jets of water capable of punching holes through thick steel.

⊕ EVOLUTION

Squirtle → Lv. 16 → Wartortle → Lv. 36 → Blastoise

● LEVEL-UP MOVES

Lv.	Name	Type	Kind	Pow.	Acc.	PP	Range	DA
1	Flash Cannon	Steel	Special	80	100	15	Normal	—
1	Tackle	Normal	Physical	35	95	35	Normal	○
1	Tail Whip	Normal	Status	—	100	30	2 Foes	—
1	Bubble	Water	Special	20	100	30	2 Foes	—
1	Withdraw	Water	Status	—	—	40	Self	—
4	Tail Whip	Normal	Status	—	100	30	2 Foes	—
7	Bubble	Water	Special	20	100	30	2 Foes	—
10	Withdraw	Water	Status	—	—	40	Self	—
13	Water Gun	Water	Special	40	100	25	Normal	—
16	Bite	Dark	Physical	60	100	25	Normal	○
20	Rapid Spin	Normal	Physical	20	100	40	Normal	○
24	Protect	Normal	Status	—	—	10	Self	—
28	Water Pulse	Water	Special	60	100	20	Normal	—
32	Aqua Tail	Water	Physical	90	90	10	Normal	○
39	Skull Bash	Normal	Physical	100	100	15	Normal	○
46	Iron Defense	Steel	Status	—	—	15	Self	—
53	Rain Dance	Water	Status	—	—	5	All	—
60	Hydro Pump	Water	Special	120	80	5	Normal	—

● MOVE MANIAC

Name	Type	Kind	Pow.	Acc.	PP	Range	DA
Headbutt	Normal	Physical	70	100	15	Normal	○
Hydro Cannon	Water	Special	150	90	5	Normal	—

● BP MOVES

Name	Type	Kind	Pow.	Acc.	PP	Range	DA
Dive	Water	Physical	80	100	10	Normal	○
Icy Wind	Ice	Special	55	95	15	2 Foes	—
Ice Punch	Ice	Physical	75	100	15	Normal	○
Zen Headbutt	Psychic	Physical	80	90	15	Normal	○
Snore	Normal	Special	40	100	15	Normal	—
Mud-Slap	Ground	Special	20	100	10	Normal	—
Rollout	Rock	Physical	30	90	20	Normal	○
Aqua Tail	Water	Physical	90	90	10	Normal	○
Outrage	Dragon	Physical	120	100	15	1 Random	○
Signal Beam	Bug	Special	75	100	15	Normal	—
Iron Defense	Steel	Status	—	—	15	Self	—

● TM & HM MOVES

No.	Name	Type	Kind	Pow.	Acc.	PP	Range	DA
TM01	Focus Punch	Fighting	Physical	150	100	20	Normal	○
TM03	Water Pulse	Water	Special	60	100	20	Normal	—
TM05	Roar	Normal	Status	—	100	20	Normal	—
TM06	Toxic	Poison	Status	—	85	10	Normal	—
TM07	Hail	Ice	Status	—	—	10	All	—
TM10	Hidden Power	Normal	Special	—	100	15	Normal	—
TM13	Ice Beam	Ice	Special	95	100	10	Normal	—
TM14	Blizzard	Ice	Special	120	70	5	2 Foes	—
TM15	Hyper Beam	Normal	Special	150	90	5	Normal	—
TM17	Protect	Normal	Status	—	—	10	Self	—
TM18	Rain Dance	Water	Status	—	—	5	All	—
TM21	Frustration	Normal	Physical	—	100	20	Normal	○
TM23	Iron Tail	Steel	Physical	100	75	15	Normal	○
TM26	Earthquake	Ground	Physical	100	100	10	2 Foes/1 Ally	—
TM27	Return	Normal	Physical	—	100	20	Normal	○
TM28	Dig	Ground	Physical	80	100	10	Normal	○
TM31	Brick Break	Fighting	Physical	75	100	15	Normal	○
TM32	Double Team	Normal	Status	—	—	15	Self	—
TM39	Rock Tomb	Rock	Physical	50	80	10	Normal	○
TM42	Facade	Normal	Physical	70	100	20	Normal	○
TM43	Secret Power	Normal	Physical	70	100	20	Normal	○
TM44	Rest	Psychic	Status	—	—	10	Self	—
TM45	Attract	Normal	Status	—	100	15	Normal	—
TM52	Focus Blast	Fighting	Special	120	70	5	Normal	—
TM55	Brine	Water	Special	65	100	10	Normal	—
TM56	Fling	Dark	Physical	—	100	10	Normal	—
TM58	Endure	Normal	Status	—	—	10	Self	—
TM68	Giga Impact	Normal	Physical	150	90	5	Normal	○
TM72	Avalanche	Ice	Physical	60	100	10	Normal	○
TM74	Gyro Ball	Steel	Physical	—	100	5	Normal	○
TM78	Captivate	Normal	Status	—	100	20	2 Foes	—
TM80	Rock Slide	Rock	Physical	75	90	10	2 Foes	—
TM82	Sleep Talk	Normal	Status	—	—	10	Depends	—
TM83	Natural Gift	Normal	Physical	—	100	15	Normal	—
TM87	Swagger	Normal	Status	—	90	15	Normal	—
TM90	Substitute	Normal	Status	—	—	10	Self	—
TM91	Flash Cannon	Steel	Special	80	100	10	Normal	—
HM03	Surf	Water	Special	95	100	15	2 Foes/1 Ally	—
HM04	Strength	Normal	Physical	80	100	15	Normal	○
HM05	Whirlpool	Water	Special	15	70	15	Normal	—
HM06	Rock Smash	Fighting	Physical	40	100	15	Normal	○
HM07	Waterfall	Water	Physical	80	100	15	Normal	○
HM08	Rock Climb	Normal	Physical	90	85	20	Normal	○

● LEVEL-UP MOVES

Lv.	Name	Type	Kind	Pow.	Acc.	PP	Range	DA
1	Tackle	Normal	Physical	35	95	35	Normal	○
1	String Shot	Bug	Status	—	95	40	2 Foes	—
15	Bug Bite	Bug	Physical	60	100	20	Normal	○

● MOVE MANIAC

Name	Type	Kind	Pow.	Acc.	PP	Range	DA

● BP MOVES

Name	Type	Kind	Pow.	Acc.	PP	Range	DA
Bug Bite	Bug	Physical	60	100	20	Normal	○
Snore	Normal	Special	40	100	15	Normal	—
String Shot	Bug	Status	—	95	40	2 Foes	—

● TM & HM MOVES

No.	Name	Type	Kind	Pow.	Acc.	PP	Range	DA

No. 010 | Worm Pokémon
Caterpie

Bug

● HEIGHT: 1'00"
● WEIGHT: 6.4 lbs.
● ITEMS: None

● SIZE COMPARISON

● MALE/FEMALE HAVE SAME FORM

⊙ ABILITIES
● Shield Dust

⊙ STATS
HP ●●
ATTACK ●
DEFENSE ●●
SP. ATTACK ●
SP. DEFENSE ●
SPEED ●●

⊙ EGG GROUPS
Bug

⊙ PERFORMANCE
SPEED ★★☆
POWER ★☆☆
SKILL ★★★★
STAMINA ★★☆
JUMP ★★

● MAIN WAYS TO OBTAIN

Pokémon HeartGold	Bug-Catching Contest at the National Park (after obtaining the National Pokédex/Tuesday)
Pokémon SoulSilver	Bug-Catching Contest at the National Park (after obtaining the National Pokédex/Tuesday)
Pokémon Diamond	Route 204 (after obtaining the National Pokédex, insert *Pokémon FireRed* into your Nintendo DS's Game Pak slot)
Pokémon Pearl	Route 204 (after obtaining the National Pokédex, insert *Pokémon FireRed* into your Nintendo DS's Game Pak slot)
Pokémon Platinum	Route 204 (after obtaining the National Pokédex, insert *Pokémon FireRed* into your Nintendo DS's Game Pak slot)

Pokémon HeartGold	*Pokémon SoulSilver*
For protection, it releases a horrible stench from the antennae on its head to drive away enemies.	Its feet have suction cups designed to stick to any surface. It tenaciously climbs trees to forage.

⊙ EVOLUTION

Lv. 7   Lv. 10

Caterpie   Metapod   Butterfree

● No. 011 | Cocoon Pokémon
Metapod

Bug

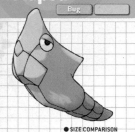

- **HEIGHT:** 2'04"
- **WEIGHT:** 21.8 lbs.
- **ITEMS:** None

● SIZE COMPARISON

● MALE/FEMALE HAVE SAME FORM

⬡ ABILITIES
● Shed Skin

⬡ STATS
HP ●●
ATTACK ●
DEFENSE ●●
SP. ATTACK ●
SP. DEFENSE ●
SPEED ●

⬡ EGG GROUPS
Bug

⬡ PERFORMANCE
SPEED ★☆☆   STAMINA ★★★★☆
POWER ★☆☆   JUMP ★★☆
SKILL ★

● MAIN WAYS TO OBTAIN

Pokémon HeartGold	Bug-Catching Contest at the National Park (after obtaining the National Pokédex/Tuesday)
Pokémon SoulSilver	Bug-Catching Contest at the National Park (after obtaining the National Pokédex/Tuesday)
Pokémon Diamond	Eterna Forest (after obtaining the National Pokédex, insert *Pokémon FireRed* into your Nintendo DS's Game Pak slot)
Pokémon Pearl	Eterna Forest (after obtaining the National Pokédex, insert *Pokémon FireRed* into your Nintendo DS's Game Pak slot)
Pokémon Platinum	Eterna Forest (after obtaining the National Pokédex, insert *Pokémon FireRed* into your Nintendo DS's Game Pak slot)

Pokémon HeartGold	**Pokémon SoulSilver**
Inside the shell, it is soft and weak as it prepares to evolve. It stays motionless in the shell.	It prepares for evolution by hardening its shell as much as possible to protect its soft body.

⬡ EVOLUTION

Caterpie — Lv. 7 → Metapod — Lv. 10 → Butterfree

● LEVEL-UP MOVES

Lv.	Name	Type	Kind	Pow.	Acc.	PP	Range	DA
1	Harden	Normal	Status	—	—	30	Self	—
7	Harden	Normal	Status	—	—	30	Self	—

● MOVE MANIAC

Name	Type	Kind	Pow.	Acc.	PP	Range	DA

● BP MOVES

Name	Type	Kind	Pow.	Acc.	PP	Range	DA
Bug Bite	Bug	Physical	60	100	20	Normal	○
String Shot	Bug	Status	—	95	40	2 Foes	—
Iron Defense	Steel	Status	—	—	15	Self	—

● TM & HM MOVES

No.	Name	Type	Kind	Pow.	Acc.	PP	Range	DA

● LEVEL-UP MOVES

Lv.	Name	Type	Kind	Pow.	Acc.	PP	Range	DA
1	Confusion	Psychic	Special	50	100	25	Normal	—
10	Confusion	Psychic	Special	50	100	25	Normal	—
12	PoisonPowder	Poison	Status	—	75	35	Normal	—
12	Stun Spore	Grass	Status	—	75	30	Normal	—
12	Sleep Powder	Grass	Status	—	75	15	Normal	—
16	Gust	Flying	Special	40	100	35	Normal	—
18	Supersonic	Normal	Status	—	55	20	Normal	—
22	Whirlwind	Normal	Status	—	100	20	Normal	—
24	Psybeam	Psychic	Special	65	100	20	Normal	—
28	Silver Wind	Bug	Special	60	100	5	Normal	—
30	Tailwind	Flying	Status	—	—	30	2 Allies	—
34	Safeguard	Normal	Status	—	—	25	2 Allies	—
36	Captivate	Normal	Status	—	100	20	2 Foes	—
40	Bug Buzz	Bug	Special	90	100	10	Normal	—

● MOVE MANIAC

Name	Type	Kind	Pow.	Acc.	PP	Range	DA

● BP MOVES

Name	Type	Kind	Pow.	Acc.	PP	Range	DA
Ominous Wind	Ghost	Special	60	100	5	Normal	—
Air Cutter	Flying	Special	55	95	25	2 Foes	—
Bug Bite	Bug	Physical	60	100	20	Normal	O
Snore	Normal	Special	40	100	15	Normal	—
Swift	Normal	Special	60	—	20	2 Foes	—
String Shot	Bug	Status	—	95	40	2 Foes	—
Tailwind	Flying	Status	—	—	30	2 Allies	—
Signal Beam	Bug	Special	75	100	15	Normal	—
Twister	Dragon	Special	40	100	20	2 Foes	—

● TM & HM MOVES

No.	Name	Type	Kind	Pow.	Acc.	PP	Range	DA

● No. 012 | Butterfly Pokémon
Butterfree

`Bug` `Flying`

- ● HEIGHT: 3'07"
- ● WEIGHT: 70.5 lbs.
- ● ITEMS: SilverPowder

● SIZE COMPARISON

● MALE FORM
Lower parts of wings are white

● FEMALE FORM
Lower parts of wings have a black spot

◉ ABILITIES
- ● Compoundeyes

◉ STATS
HP	●●
ATTACK	●●
DEFENSE	●●●
SP. ATTACK	●●●
SP. DEFENSE	●●●●
SPEED	●●●

◉ EGG GROUPS
Bug

◉ PERFORMANCE

SPEED ★★☆☆		STAMINA ★★☆	
POWER ★★☆		JUMP ★★★★★	
SKILL ★★☆			

● MAIN WAYS TO OBTAIN

Pokémon HeartGold	Bug-Catching Contest at the National Park (after obtaining the National Pokédex/Tuesday)
Pokémon SoulSilver	Bug-Catching Contest at the National Park (after obtaining the National Pokédex/Tuesday)
Pokémon Diamond	Level up Metapod to Lv. 10
Pokémon Pearl	Level up Metapod to Lv. 10
Pokémon Platinum	Level up Metapod to Lv. 10

Pokémon HeartGold	Pokémon SoulSilver
It collects honey every day. It rubs honey onto the hairs on its legs to carry it back to its nest.	Water-repellent powder on its wings enables it to collect honey, even in the heaviest of rains.

◉ EVOLUTION

Caterpie — Lv. 7 → Metapod — Lv. 10 → Butterfree

No. 013 | Hairy Bug Pokémon
Weedle

Bug | **Poison**

- **HEIGHT:** 1'00"
- **WEIGHT:** 7.1 lbs.
- **ITEMS:** None

● SIZE COMPARISON

● MALE/FEMALE HAVE SAME FORM

⊙ ABILITIES
● Shield Dust

⊙ STATS
HP ●
ATTACK ●●
DEFENSE ●
SP. ATTACK ●
SP. DEFENSE ●
SPEED ●●

⊙ EGG GROUPS
Bug

⊙ PERFORMANCE
SPEED ★☆☆   STAMINA ★☆☆
POWER ★★☆☆   JUMP ★★
SKILL ★★★☆

● MAIN WAYS TO OBTAIN

Pokémon HeartGold	Bug-Catching Contest at the National Park (after obtaining the National Pokédex/Tuesday)
Pokémon SoulSilver	Bug-Catching Contest at the National Park (after obtaining the National Pokédex/Tuesday)
Pokémon Diamond	Route 204 (after obtaining the National Pokédex, insert *Pokémon LeafGreen* into your Nintendo DS's Game Pak slot)
Pokémon Pearl	Route 204 (after obtaining the National Pokédex, insert *Pokémon LeafGreen* into your Nintendo DS's Game Pak slot)
Pokémon Platinum	Route 204 (after obtaining the National Pokédex, insert *Pokémon LeafGreen* into your Nintendo DS's Game Pak slot)

Pokémon HeartGold	*Pokémon SoulSilver*
Its poison stinger is very powerful. Its bright-colored body is intended to warn off its enemies.	It attacks using a two-inch poison barb on its head. It can usually be found under the leaves it eats.

⊙ EVOLUTION

Weedle — Lv. 7 → Kakuna — Lv. 10 → Beedrill

● LEVEL-UP MOVES

Lv.	Name	Type	Kind	Pow.	Acc.	PP	Range	DA
1	Poison Sting	Poison	Physical	15	100	35	Normal	—
1	String Shot	Bug	Status	—	95	40	2 Foes	—
15	Bug Bite	Bug	Physical	60	100	20	Normal	○

● MOVE MANIAC

Name	Type	Kind	Pow.	Acc.	PP	Range	DA

● BP MOVES

Name	Type	Kind	Pow.	Acc.	PP	Range	DA
Bug Bite	Bug	Physical	60	100	20	Normal	○
String Shot	Bug	Status	—	95	40	2 Foes	—

● TM & HM MOVES

No.	Name	Type	Kind	Pow.	Acc.	PP	Range	DA

● LEVEL-UP MOVES

Lv.	Name	Type	Kind	Pow.	Acc.	PP	Range	DA
1	Harden	Normal	Status	—	—	30	Self	—
7	Harden	Normal	Status	—	—	30	Self	—

● MOVE MANIAC

Name	Type	Kind	Pow.	Acc.	PP	Range	DA

● BP MOVES

Name	Type	Kind	Pow.	Acc.	PP	Range	DA
Bug Bite	Bug	Physical	60	100	20	Normal	○
String Shot	Bug	Status	—	95	40	2 Foes	—
Iron Defense	Steel	Status	—	—	15	Self	—

● TM & HM MOVES

No.	Name	Type	Kind	Pow.	Acc.	PP	Range	DA

⦿ No. 014 | Cocoon Pokémon
Kakuna

Bug Poison

● **HEIGHT:** 2'00"
● **WEIGHT:** 22.0 lbs.
● **ITEMS:** None

● SIZE COMPARISON

● MALE/FEMALE HAVE SAME FORM

⊙ ABILITIES
● Shed Skin

⊙ STATS
HP ●●
ATTACK ●●
DEFENSE ●●
SP. ATTACK ●
SP. DEFENSE ●
SPEED ●●

⊙ EGG GROUPS
Bug

⊙ PERFORMANCE
SPEED ★☆☆　　STAMINA ★★★★☆
POWER ★☆☆　　JUMP ★★☆
SKILL ★

● MAIN WAYS TO OBTAIN

Pokémon HeartGold	Bug-Catching Contest at the National Park (after obtaining the National Pokédex/Tuesday)
Pokémon SoulSilver	Bug-Catching Contest at the National Park (after obtaining the National Pokédex/Tuesday)
Pokémon Diamond	Eterna Forest (after obtaining the National Pokédex, insert *Pokémon LeafGreen* into your Nintendo DS's Game Pak slot)
Pokémon Pearl	Eterna Forest (after obtaining the National Pokédex, insert *Pokémon LeafGreen* into your Nintendo DS's Game Pak slot)
Pokémon Platinum	Eterna Forest (after obtaining the National Pokédex, insert *Pokémon LeafGreen* into your Nintendo DS's Game Pak slot)

Pokémon HeartGold
Although it is a cocoon, it can move a little. It can extend its poison barb if it is attacked.

Pokémon SoulSilver
From this form, it will grow into an adult. As its body becomes softer, the external shell hardens.

⊙ EVOLUTION

Weedle　Lv. 7　Kakuna　Lv. 10　Beedrill

No. 015 | Poison Bee Pokémon
Beedrill

Bug **Poison**

- **HEIGHT:** 3'03"
- **WEIGHT:** 65.0 lbs.
- **ITEMS:** Poison Barb

● SIZE COMPARISON

● MALE/FEMALE HAVE SAME FORM

⊕ ABILITIES
- Swarm

⊕ STATS
HP	●●
ATTACK	●●●
DEFENSE	●●●
SP. ATTACK	●●
SP. DEFENSE	●●●
SPEED	●●●

⊕ EGG GROUPS
Bug

⊕ PERFORMANCE
SPEED ★★★☆	STAMINA ★★
POWER ★☆☆☆	JUMP ★★★★★
SKILL ★★★☆	

● MAIN WAYS TO OBTAIN

Pokémon HeartGold	Bug-Catching Contest at the National Park (after obtaining the National Pokédex/Tuesday)
Pokémon SoulSilver	Bug-Catching Contest at the National Park (after obtaining the National Pokédex/Tuesday)
Pokémon Diamond	Level up Kakuna to Lv. 10
Pokémon Pearl	Level up Kakuna to Lv. 10
Pokémon Platinum	Level up Kakuna to Lv. 10

Pokémon HeartGold	Pokémon SoulSilver
It can take down any opponent with its powerful poison stingers. It sometimes attacks in swarms.	It has three poison barbs. The barb on its tail secretes the most powerful poison.

⊕ EVOLUTION

Weedle — Lv. 7 → Kakuna — Lv. 10 → Beedrill

● LEVEL-UP MOVES
Lv.	Name	Type	Kind	Pow.	Acc.	PP	Range	DA
1	Fury Attack	Normal	Physical	15	85	20	Normal	○
10	Fury Attack	Normal	Physical	15	85	20	Normal	○
13	Focus Energy	Normal	Status	—	—	30	Self	—
16	Twineedle	Bug	Physical	25	100	20	Normal	—
19	Rage	Normal	Physical	20	100	20	Normal	○
22	Pursuit	Dark	Physical	40	100	20	Normal	○
25	Toxic Spikes	Poison	Status	—	—	20	2 Foes	—
28	Pin Missile	Bug	Physical	14	85	20	Normal	—
31	Agility	Psychic	Status	—	—	30	Self	—
34	Assurance	Dark	Physical	50	100	10	Normal	○
37	Poison Jab	Poison	Physical	80	100	20	Normal	○
40	Endeavor	Normal	Physical	—	100	5	Normal	○

● MOVE MANIAC
Name	Type	Kind	Pow.	Acc.	PP	Range	DA

● BP MOVES
Name	Type	Kind	Pow.	Acc.	PP	Range	DA
Fury Cutter	Bug	Physical	10	95	20	Normal	○
Ominous Wind	Ghost	Special	60	100	5	Normal	—
Air Cutter	Flying	Special	55	95	25	2 Foes	—
Knock Off	Dark	Physical	20	100	20	Normal	○
Bug Bite	Bug	Physical	60	100	20	Normal	○
Snore	Normal	Special	40	100	15	Normal	—
Swift	Normal	Special	60	—	20	2 Foes	—
String Shot	Bug	Status	—	95	40	2 Foes	—
Tailwind	Flying	Status	—	—	30	2 Allies	—
Endeavor	Normal	Physical	—	100	5	Normal	○

● TM & HM MOVES
No.	Name	Type	Kind	Pow.	Acc.	PP	Range	DA
TM06	Toxic	Poison	Status	—	85	10	Normal	—
TM10	Hidden Power	Normal	Special	—	100	15	Normal	—
TM11	Sunny Day	Fire	Status	—	—	5	All	—
TM15	Hyper Beam	Normal	Special	150	90	5	Normal	—
TM17	Protect	Normal	Status	—	—	10	Self	—
TM19	Giga Drain	Grass	Special	60	100	10	Normal	—
TM21	Frustration	Normal	Physical	—	100	20	Normal	○
TM22	SolarBeam	Grass	Special	120	100	10	Normal	—
TM27	Return	Normal	Physical	—	100	20	Normal	○
TM31	Brick Break	Fighting	Physical	75	100	15	Normal	○
TM32	Double Team	Normal	Status	—	—	15	Self	—
TM36	Sludge Bomb	Poison	Special	90	100	10	Normal	—
TM40	Aerial Ace	Flying	Physical	60	—	20	Normal	○
TM42	Facade	Normal	Physical	70	100	20	Normal	○
TM43	Secret Power	Normal	Physical	70	100	20	Normal	○
TM44	Rest	Psychic	Status	—	—	10	Self	—
TM45	Attract	Normal	Status	—	100	15	Normal	—
TM46	Thief	Dark	Physical	40	100	10	Normal	○
TM51	Roost	Flying	Status	—	—	10	Self	—
TM54	False Swipe	Normal	Physical	40	100	40	Normal	○
TM58	Endure	Normal	Status	—	—	10	Self	—
TM62	Silver Wind	Bug	Special	60	100	5	Normal	—
TM66	Payback	Dark	Physical	50	100	10	Normal	○
TM68	Giga Impact	Normal	Physical	150	90	5	Normal	○
TM70	Flash	Normal	Status	—	100	20	Normal	—
TM75	Swords Dance	Normal	Status	—	—	30	Self	—
TM78	Captivate	Normal	Status	—	100	20	2 Foes	—
TM81	X-Scissor	Bug	Physical	80	100	15	Normal	○
TM82	Sleep Talk	Normal	Status	—	—	10	Depends	—
TM83	Natural Gift	Normal	Physical	—	100	15	Normal	○
TM84	Poison Jab	Poison	Physical	80	100	20	Normal	○
TM87	Swagger	Normal	Status	—	90	15	Normal	—
TM89	U-turn	Bug	Physical	70	100	20	Normal	○
TM90	Substitute	Normal	Status	—	—	10	Self	—
HM01	Cut	Normal	Physical	50	95	30	Normal	○
HM06	Rock Smash	Fighting	Physical	40	100	15	Normal	○

● LEVEL-UP MOVES

Lv.	Name	Type	Kind	Pow.	Acc.	PP	Range	DA
1	Tackle	Normal	Physical	35	95	35	Normal	○
5	Sand-Attack	Ground	Status	—	100	15	Normal	—
9	Gust	Flying	Special	40	100	35	Normal	—
13	Quick Attack	Normal	Physical	40	100	30	Normal	○
17	Whirlwind	Normal	Status	—	100	20	Normal	—
21	Twister	Dragon	Special	40	100	20	2 Foes	—
25	FeatherDance	Flying	Status	—	100	15	Normal	—
29	Agility	Psychic	Status	—	—	30	Self	—
33	Wing Attack	Flying	Physical	60	100	35	Normal	○
37	Roost	Flying	Status	—	—	10	Self	—
41	Tailwind	Flying	Status	—	—	30	2 Allies	—
45	Mirror Move	Flying	Status	—	—	20	Depends	—
49	Air Slash	Flying	Special	75	95	20	Normal	—

● MOVE MANIAC

Name	Type	Kind	Pow.	Acc.	PP	Range	DA

● BP MOVES

Name	Type	Kind	Pow.	Acc.	PP	Range	DA
Ominous Wind	Ghost	Special	60	100	5	Normal	—
Air Cutter	Flying	Special	55	95	25	2 Foes	—
Snore	Normal	Special	40	100	15	Normal	—
Swift	Normal	Special	60	—	20	2 Foes	—
Uproar	Normal	Special	50	100	10	1 Random	—
Tailwind	Flying	Status	—	—	30	2 Allies	—
Mud-Slap	Ground	Special	20	100	10	Normal	—
Twister	Dragon	Special	40	100	20	2 Foes	—
Heat Wave	Fire	Special	100	90	10	2 Foes	—

● TM & HM MOVES

No.	Name	Type	Kind	Pow.	Acc.	PP	Range	DA
TM06	Toxic	Poison	Status	—	85	10	Normal	—
TM10	Hidden Power	Normal	Special	—	100	15	Normal	—
TM11	Sunny Day	Fire	Status	—	—	5	All	—
TM17	Protect	Normal	Status	—	—	10	Self	—
TM18	Rain Dance	Water	Status	—	—	5	All	—
TM21	Frustration	Normal	Physical	—	100	20	Normal	○
TM27	Return	Normal	Physical	—	100	20	Normal	○
TM32	Double Team	Normal	Status	—	—	15	Self	—
TM40	Aerial Ace	Flying	Physical	60	—	20	Normal	○
TM42	Facade	Normal	Physical	70	100	20	Normal	○
TM43	Secret Power	Normal	Physical	70	100	20	Normal	○
TM44	Rest	Psychic	Status	—	—	10	Self	—
TM45	Attract	Normal	Status	—	100	15	Normal	—
TM46	Thief	Dark	Physical	40	100	10	Normal	○
TM47	Steel Wing	Steel	Physical	70	90	25	Normal	○
TM51	Roost	Flying	Status	—	—	10	Self	—
TM58	Endure	Normal	Status	—	—	10	Self	—
TM78	Captivate	Normal	Status	—	100	20	2 Foes	—
TM82	Sleep Talk	Normal	Status	—	—	10	Depends	—
TM83	Natural Gift	Normal	Physical	—	100	15	Normal	—
TM87	Swagger	Normal	Status	—	90	15	Normal	—
TM88	Pluck	Flying	Physical	60	100	20	Normal	○
TM89	U-turn	Bug	Physical	70	100	20	Normal	○
TM90	Substitute	Normal	Status	—	—	10	Self	—
HM02	Fly	Flying	Physical	90	95	15	Normal	○

● EGG MOVES

Name	Type	Kind	Pow.	Acc.	PP	Range	DA
Pursuit	Dark	Physical	40	100	20	Normal	○
Faint Attack	Dark	Physical	60	—	20	Normal	○
Foresight	Normal	Status	—	—	40	Normal	—
Steel Wing	Steel	Physical	70	90	25	Normal	○
Air Cutter	Flying	Special	55	95	25	2 Foes	—
Air Slash	Flying	Special	75	95	20	Normal	—
Brave Bird	Flying	Physical	120	100	15	Normal	○
Uproar	Normal	Special	50	100	10	1 Random	—

⬤ No. 016 | Tiny Bird Pokémon
Pidgey

`Normal` `Flying`

- **HEIGHT:** 1'00"
- **WEIGHT:** 4.0 lbs.
- **ITEMS:** None

● SIZE COMPARISON

● MALE/FEMALE HAVE SAME FORM

⊚ ABILITIES
- Keen Eye
- Tangled Feet

⊚ STATS
- HP ●
- ATTACK ● ●
- DEFENSE ● ●
- SP. ATTACK ●
- SP. DEFENSE ●
- SPEED ● ● ●

⊚ EGG GROUPS
Flying

⊚ PERFORMANCE
SPEED ★★★☆☆   STAMINA ★★☆
POWER ★★☆   JUMP ★★★☆☆
SKILL ★★★☆

● MAIN WAYS TO OBTAIN

Pokémon HeartGold	Route 29 (morning and afternoon only)
Pokémon SoulSilver	Route 29 (morning and afternoon only)
Pokémon Diamond	Route 229 (mass outbreak)
Pokémon Pearl	Route 229 (mass outbreak)
Pokémon Platinum	Route 229

Pokémon HeartGold
It usually hides in tall grass. Because it dislikes fighting, it protects itself by kicking up sand.

Pokémon SoulSilver
Common in grassy areas and forests, it is very docile and will chase off enemies by flapping up sand.

⊚ EVOLUTION

Lv. 18 — Lv. 36

Pidgey   Pidgeotto   Pidgeot

Pidgeotto

Normal | Flying

- **HEIGHT:** 3'07"
- **WEIGHT:** 41.9 lbs.
- **ITEMS:** None

● SIZE COMPARISON

● MALE/FEMALE HAVE SAME FORM

⊛ ABILITIES
- Keen Eye
- Tangled Feet

⊛ STATS
HP ●●
ATTACK ●●●
DEFENSE ●●
SP. ATTACK ●●
SP. DEFENSE ●●
SPEED ●●●

⊛ EGG GROUPS
Flying

⊛ PERFORMANCE
SPEED ★★★☆
POWER ★★☆
SKILL ★★☆

STAMINA ★★☆☆
JUMP ★★★★★

● MAIN WAYS TO OBTAIN

Pokémon HeartGold	Route 43 (morning and afternoon only)
Pokémon SoulSilver	Route 43 (morning and afternoon only)
Pokémon Diamond	Level up Pidgey to Lv. 18
Pokémon Pearl	Level up Pidgey to Lv. 18
Pokémon Platinum	Level up Pidgey to Lv. 18

Pokémon HeartGold	Pokémon SoulSilver
It has outstanding vision. However high it flies, it is able to distinguish the movements of its prey.	It renders its prey immobile using well-developed claws, then carries the prey more than 60 miles to its nest.

⊛ EVOLUTION

Pidgey — Lv. 18 → Pidgeotto — Lv. 36 → Pidgeot

● LEVEL-UP MOVES

Lv.	Name	Type	Kind	Pow.	Acc.	PP	Range	DA
1	Tackle	Normal	Physical	35	95	35	Normal	○
1	Sand-Attack	Ground	Status	—	100	15	Normal	—
1	Gust	Flying	Special	40	100	35	Normal	—
5	Sand-Attack	Ground	Status	—	100	15	Normal	—
9	Gust	Flying	Special	40	100	35	Normal	—
13	Quick Attack	Normal	Physical	40	100	30	Normal	○
17	Whirlwind	Normal	Status	—	100	20	Normal	—
22	Twister	Dragon	Special	40	100	20	2 Foes	—
27	FeatherDance	Flying	Status	—	100	15	Normal	—
32	Agility	Psychic	Status	—	—	30	Self	—
37	Wing Attack	Flying	Physical	60	100	35	Normal	○
42	Roost	Flying	Status	—	—	10	Self	—
47	Tailwind	Flying	Status	—	—	30	2 Allies	—
52	Mirror Move	Flying	Status	—	—	20	Depends	—
57	Air Slash	Flying	Special	75	95	20	Normal	—

● MOVE MANIAC

Name	Type	Kind	Pow.	Acc.	PP	Range	DA

● BP MOVES

Name	Type	Kind	Pow.	Acc.	PP	Range	DA
Ominous Wind	Ghost	Special	60	100	5	Normal	—
Air Cutter	Flying	Special	55	95	25	2 Foes	—
Snore	Normal	Special	40	100	15	Normal	—
Swift	Normal	Special	60	—	20	2 Foes	—
Uproar	Normal	Special	50	100	10	1 Random	—
Tailwind	Flying	Status	—	—	30	2 Allies	—
Mud-Slap	Ground	Special	20	100	10	Normal	—
Twister	Dragon	Special	40	100	20	2 Foes	—
Heat Wave	Fire	Special	100	90	10	2 Foes	—

● TM & HM MOVES

No.	Name	Type	Kind	Pow.	Acc.	PP	Range	DA
TM06	Toxic	Poison	Status	—	85	10	Normal	—
TM10	Hidden Power	Normal	Special	—	100	15	Normal	—
TM11	Sunny Day	Fire	Status	—	—	5	All	—
TM17	Protect	Normal	Status	—	—	10	Self	—
TM18	Rain Dance	Water	Status	—	—	5	All	—
TM21	Frustration	Normal	Physical	—	100	20	Normal	○
TM27	Return	Normal	Physical	—	100	20	Normal	○
TM32	Double Team	Normal	Status	—	—	15	Self	—
TM40	Aerial Ace	Flying	Physical	60	—	20	Normal	○
TM42	Facade	Normal	Physical	70	100	20	Normal	○
TM43	Secret Power	Normal	Physical	70	100	20	Normal	○
TM44	Rest	Psychic	Status	—	—	10	Self	—
TM45	Attract	Normal	Status	—	100	15	Normal	—
TM46	Thief	Dark	Physical	40	100	10	Normal	○
TM47	Steel Wing	Steel	Physical	70	90	25	Normal	○
TM51	Roost	Flying	Status	—	—	10	Self	—
TM58	Endure	Normal	Status	—	—	10	Self	—
TM78	Captivate	Normal	Status	—	100	20	2 Foes	—
TM82	Sleep Talk	Normal	Status	—	—	10	Depends	—
TM83	Natural Gift	Normal	Physical	—	100	15	Normal	○
TM87	Swagger	Normal	Status	—	90	15	Normal	—
TM88	Pluck	Flying	Physical	60	100	20	Normal	○
TM89	U-turn	Bug	Physical	70	100	20	Normal	○
TM90	Substitute	Normal	Status	—	—	10	Self	—
HM02	Fly	Flying	Physical	90	95	15	Normal	○

● LEVEL-UP MOVES

Lv.	Name	Type	Kind	Pow.	Acc.	PP	Range	DA
1	Tackle	Normal	Physical	35	95	35	Normal	○
1	Sand-Attack	Ground	Status	—	100	15	Normal	—
1	Gust	Flying	Special	40	100	35	Normal	—
1	Quick Attack	Normal	Physical	40	100	30	Normal	○
5	Sand-Attack	Ground	Status	—	100	15	Normal	—
9	Gust	Flying	Special	40	100	35	Normal	—
13	Quick Attack	Normal	Physical	40	100	30	Normal	○
17	Whirlwind	Normal	Status	—	100	20	Normal	—
22	Twister	Dragon	Special	40	100	20	2 Foes	—
27	FeatherDance	Flying	Status	—	100	15	Normal	—
32	Agility	Psychic	Status	—	—	30	Self	—
38	Wing Attack	Flying	Physical	60	100	35	Normal	○
44	Roost	Flying	Status	—	—	10	Self	—
50	Tailwind	Flying	Status	—	—	30	2 Allies	—
56	Mirror Move	Flying	Status	—	—	20	Depends	—
62	Air Slash	Flying	Special	75	95	20	Normal	—

● MOVE MANIAC

Name	Type	Kind	Pow.	Acc.	PP	Range	DA

● BP MOVES

Name	Type	Kind	Pow.	Acc.	PP	Range	DA
Ominous Wind	Ghost	Special	60	100	5	Normal	—
Air Cutter	Flying	Special	55	95	25	2 Foes	—
Snore	Normal	Special	40	100	15	Normal	—
Swift	Normal	Special	60	—	20	2 Foes	—
Uproar	Normal	Special	50	100	10	1 Random	—
Tailwind	Flying	Status	—	—	30	2 Allies	—
Mud-Slap	Ground	Special	20	100	10	Normal	—
Twister	Dragon	Special	40	100	20	2 Foes	—
Heat Wave	Fire	Special	100	90	10	2 Foes	—
Sky Attack	Flying	Physical	140	90	5	Normal	—

● TM & HM MOVES

No.	Name	Type	Kind	Pow.	Acc.	PP	Range	DA
TM06	Toxic	Poison	Status	—	85	10	Normal	—
TM10	Hidden Power	Normal	Special	—	100	15	Normal	—
TM11	Sunny Day	Fire	Status	—	—	5	All	—
TM15	Hyper Beam	Normal	Special	150	90	5	Normal	—
TM17	Protect	Normal	Status	—	—	10	Self	—
TM18	Rain Dance	Water	Status	—	—	5	All	—
TM21	Frustration	Normal	Physical	—	100	20	Normal	○
TM27	Return	Normal	Physical	—	100	20	Normal	○
TM32	Double Team	Normal	Status	—	—	15	Self	—
TM40	Aerial Ace	Flying	Physical	60	—	20	Normal	○
TM42	Facade	Normal	Physical	70	100	20	Normal	○
TM43	Secret Power	Normal	Physical	70	100	20	Normal	○
TM44	Rest	Psychic	Status	—	—	10	Self	—
TM45	Attract	Normal	Status	—	100	15	Normal	—
TM46	Thief	Dark	Physical	40	100	10	Normal	○
TM47	Steel Wing	Steel	Physical	70	90	25	Normal	○
TM51	Roost	Flying	Status	—	—	10	Self	—
TM58	Endure	Normal	Status	—	—	10	Self	—
TM68	Giga Impact	Normal	Physical	150	90	5	Normal	○
TM78	Captivate	Normal	Status	—	100	20	2 Foes	—
TM82	Sleep Talk	Normal	Status	—	—	10	Depends	—
TM83	Natural Gift	Normal	Physical	—	100	15	Normal	—
TM87	Swagger	Normal	Status	—	90	15	Normal	—
TM88	Pluck	Flying	Physical	60	100	20	Normal	○
TM89	U-turn	Bug	Physical	70	100	20	Normal	○
TM90	Substitute	Normal	Status	—	—	10	Self	—
HM02	Fly	Flying	Physical	90	95	15	Normal	○

 ● No. **018** | Bird Pokémon
Pidgeot

`Normal` `Flying`

- ● **HEIGHT:** 4'11"
- ● **WEIGHT:** 87.1 lbs.
- ● **ITEMS:** None

● SIZE COMPARISON

● MALE/FEMALE HAVE SAME FORM

⊘ ABILITIES
- ● Keen Eye
- ● Tangled Feet

⊘ EGG GROUPS
Flying

⊘ STATS
- HP ●●●○
- ATTACK ●●●○
- DEFENSE ●●●○
- SP. ATTACK ●●○○
- SP. DEFENSE ●●●○
- SPEED ●●●●

⊘ PERFORMANCE
- SPEED ★★★☆ STAMINA ★★★☆
- POWER ★★★☆ JUMP ★★★★★
- SKILL ★★☆

● MAIN WAYS TO OBTAIN

Pokémon HeartGold Level up Pidgeotto to Lv. 36

Pokémon SoulSilver Level up Pidgeotto to Lv. 36

Pokémon Diamond Level up Pidgeotto to Lv. 36

Pokémon Pearl Level up Pidgeotto to Lv. 36

Pokémon Platinum Level up Pidgeotto to Lv. 36

Pokémon HeartGold
Its well-developed chest muscles make it strong enough to whip up a gusty windstorm with just a few flaps.

Pokémon SoulSilver
It spreads its beautiful wings wide to frighten its enemies. It can fly at Mach 2 speed.

⊘ EVOLUTION

Lv. 18   Lv. 36

Pidgey   Pidgeotto   Pidgeot

No. 019 | Mouse Pokémon
Rattata

Normal

● LEVEL-UP MOVES

Lv.	Name	Type	Kind	Pow.	Acc.	PP	Range	DA
1	Tackle	Normal	Physical	35	95	35	Normal	○
1	Tail Whip	Normal	Status	—	100	30	2 Foes	—
4	Quick Attack	Normal	Physical	40	100	30	Normal	○
7	Focus Energy	Normal	Status	—	—	30	Self	—
10	Bite	Dark	Physical	60	100	25	Normal	○
13	Pursuit	Dark	Physical	40	100	20	Normal	○
16	Hyper Fang	Normal	Physical	80	90	15	Normal	○
19	Sucker Punch	Dark	Physical	80	100	5	Normal	○
22	Crunch	Dark	Physical	80	100	15	Normal	○
25	Assurance	Dark	Physical	50	100	10	Normal	○
28	Super Fang	Normal	Physical	—	90	10	Normal	○
31	Double-Edge	Normal	Physical	120	100	15	Normal	○
34	Endeavor	Normal	Physical	—	100	5	Normal	○

● MOVE MANIAC

Name	Type	Kind	Pow.	Acc.	PP	Range	DA
Headbutt	Normal	Physical	70	100	15	Normal	○

● BP MOVES

Name	Type	Kind	Pow.	Acc.	PP	Range	DA
Icy Wind	Ice	Special	55	95	15	2 Foes	—
Zen Headbutt	Psychic	Physical	80	90	15	Normal	○
Sucker Punch	Dark	Physical	80	100	5	Normal	○
Snore	Normal	Special	40	100	15	Normal	—
Last Resort	Normal	Physical	130	100	5	Normal	○
Swift	Normal	Special	60	—	20	2 Foes	—
Mud-Slap	Ground	Special	20	100	10	Normal	—
Endeavor	Normal	Physical	—	100	5	Normal	○
Super Fang	Normal	Physical	—	90	10	Normal	○

● HEIGHT: 1'00"
● WEIGHT: 7.7 lbs.
● ITEMS: Chilan Berry

● SIZE COMPARISON

● MALE FORM
Longer whiskers

● FEMALE FORM
Shorter whiskers

● ABILITIES
● Run Away
● Guts

● STATS
HP ●
ATTACK ●●
DEFENSE ●●
SP. ATTACK ●
SP. DEFENSE ●
SPEED ●●●

● EGG GROUPS
Field

● PERFORMANCE
SPEED ★★★★★   STAMINA ★☆☆
POWER ★☆☆   JUMP ★★☆
SKILL ★★★

● MAIN WAYS TO OBTAIN

Pokémon HeartGold — Route 29

Pokémon SoulSilver — Route 29

Pokémon Diamond — Route 225

Pokémon Pearl — Route 225

Pokémon Platinum — Route 225

Pokémon HeartGold
It eats anything. Wherever food is available, it will settle down and produce offspring continuously.

Pokémon SoulSilver
Living wherever there is food available, it ceaselessly scavenges for edibles the entire day.

● EVOLUTION

Rattata → Lv. 20 → Raticate

● TM & HM MOVES

No.	Name	Type	Kind	Pow.	Acc.	PP	Range	DA
TM06	Toxic	Poison	Status	—	85	10	Normal	—
TM10	Hidden Power	Normal	Special	—	100	15	Normal	—
TM11	Sunny Day	Fire	Status	—	—	5	All	—
TM12	Taunt	Dark	Status	—	100	20	Normal	—
TM13	Ice Beam	Ice	Special	95	100	10	Normal	—
TM14	Blizzard	Ice	Special	120	70	5	2 Foes	—
TM17	Protect	Normal	Status	—	—	10	Self	—
TM18	Rain Dance	Water	Status	—	—	5	All	—
TM21	Frustration	Normal	Physical	—	100	20	Normal	○
TM23	Iron Tail	Steel	Physical	100	75	15	Normal	○
TM24	Thunderbolt	Electric	Special	95	100	15	Normal	—
TM25	Thunder	Electric	Special	120	70	10	Normal	—
TM27	Return	Normal	Physical	—	100	20	Normal	○
TM28	Dig	Ground	Physical	80	100	10	Normal	○
TM30	Shadow Ball	Ghost	Special	80	100	15	Normal	—
TM32	Double Team	Normal	Status	—	—	15	Self	—
TM34	Shock Wave	Electric	Special	60	—	20	Normal	—
TM42	Facade	Normal	Physical	70	100	20	Normal	○
TM43	Secret Power	Normal	Physical	70	100	20	Normal	○
TM44	Rest	Psychic	Status	—	—	10	Self	—
TM45	Attract	Normal	Status	—	100	15	Normal	—
TM46	Thief	Dark	Physical	40	100	10	Normal	○
TM57	Charge Beam	Electric	Special	50	90	10	Normal	—
TM58	Endure	Normal	Status	—	—	10	Self	—
TM73	Thunder Wave	Electric	Status	—	100	20	Normal	—
TM78	Captivate	Normal	Status	—	100	20	2 Foes	—
TM82	Sleep Talk	Normal	Status	—	—	10	Depends	—
TM83	Natural Gift	Normal	Physical	—	100	15	Normal	○
TM86	Grass Knot	Grass	Special	—	100	20	Normal	○
TM87	Swagger	Normal	Status	—	90	15	Normal	—
TM88	Pluck	Flying	Physical	60	100	20	Normal	○
TM89	U-turn	Bug	Physical	70	100	20	Normal	○
TM90	Substitute	Normal	Status	—	—	10	Self	—
HM01	Cut	Normal	Physical	50	95	30	Normal	○
HM06	Rock Smash	Fighting	Physical	40	100	15	Normal	○

● EGG MOVES

Name	Type	Kind	Pow.	Acc.	PP	Range	DA
Screech	Normal	Status	—	85	40	Normal	—
Flame Wheel	Fire	Physical	60	100	25	Normal	○
Fury Swipes	Normal	Physical	18	80	15	Normal	○
Bite	Dark	Physical	60	100	25	Normal	○
Counter	Fighting	Physical	—	100	20	Self	○
Reversal	Fighting	Physical	—	100	15	Normal	○
Uproar	Normal	Special	50	100	10	1 Random	—
Swagger	Normal	Status	—	90	15	Normal	—
Last Resort	Normal	Physical	130	100	5	Normal	○
Me First	Normal	Status	—	—	20	Depends	—

● LEVEL-UP MOVES

Lv.	Name	Type	Kind	Pow.	Acc.	PP	Range	DA
1	Swords Dance	Normal	Status	—	—	30	Self	—
1	Tackle	Normal	Physical	35	95	35	Normal	○
1	Tail Whip	Normal	Status	—	100	30	2 Foes	—
1	Quick Attack	Normal	Physical	40	100	30	Normal	○
1	Focus Energy	Normal	Status	—	—	30	Self	—
4	Quick Attack	Normal	Physical	40	100	30	Normal	○
7	Focus Energy	Normal	Status	—	—	30	Self	—
10	Bite	Dark	Physical	60	100	25	Normal	○
13	Pursuit	Dark	Physical	40	100	20	Normal	○
16	Hyper Fang	Normal	Physical	80	90	15	Normal	○
19	Sucker Punch	Dark	Physical	80	100	5	Normal	○
20	Scary Face	Normal	Status	—	90	10	Normal	—
24	Crunch	Dark	Physical	80	100	15	Normal	○
29	Assurance	Dark	Physical	50	100	10	Normal	○
34	Super Fang	Normal	Physical	—	90	10	Normal	○
39	Double-Edge	Normal	Physical	120	100	15	Normal	○
44	Endeavor	Normal	Physical	—	100	5	Normal	○

● MOVE MANIAC

Name	Type	Kind	Pow.	Acc.	PP	Range	DA
Headbutt	Normal	Physical	70	100	15	Normal	○

● BP MOVES

Name	Type	Kind	Pow.	Acc.	PP	Range	DA
Icy Wind	Ice	Special	55	95	15	2 Foes	—
Zen Headbutt	Psychic	Physical	80	90	15	Normal	○
Sucker Punch	Dark	Physical	80	100	5	Normal	○
Snore	Normal	Special	40	100	15	Normal	—
Last Resort	Normal	Physical	130	100	5	Normal	○
Swift	Normal	Special	60	—	20	2 Foes	—
Mud-Slap	Ground	Special	20	100	10	Normal	—
Endeavor	Normal	Physical	—	100	5	Normal	○
Super Fang	Normal	Physical	—	90	10	Normal	○

● TM & HM MOVES

No.	Name	Type	Kind	Pow.	Acc.	PP	Range	DA
TM05	Roar	Normal	Status	—	100	20	Normal	—
TM06	Toxic	Poison	Status	—	85	10	Normal	—
TM10	Hidden Power	Normal	Special	—	100	15	Normal	—
TM11	Sunny Day	Fire	Status	—	—	5	All	—
TM12	Taunt	Dark	Status	—	100	20	Normal	—
TM13	Ice Beam	Ice	Special	95	100	10	Normal	—
TM14	Blizzard	Ice	Special	120	70	5	2 Foes	—
TM15	Hyper Beam	Normal	Special	150	90	5	Normal	—
TM17	Protect	Normal	Status	—	—	10	Self	—
TM18	Rain Dance	Water	Status	—	—	5	All	—
TM21	Frustration	Normal	Physical	—	100	20	Normal	○
TM23	Iron Tail	Steel	Physical	100	75	15	Normal	○
TM24	Thunderbolt	Electric	Special	95	100	15	Normal	—
TM25	Thunder	Electric	Special	120	70	10	Normal	—
TM27	Return	Normal	Physical	—	100	20	Normal	○
TM28	Dig	Ground	Physical	80	100	10	Normal	○
TM30	Shadow Ball	Ghost	Special	80	100	15	Normal	—
TM32	Double Team	Normal	Status	—	—	15	Self	—
TM34	Shock Wave	Electric	Special	60	—	20	Normal	—
TM42	Facade	Normal	Physical	70	100	20	Normal	○
TM43	Secret Power	Normal	Physical	70	100	20	Normal	○
TM44	Rest	Psychic	Status	—	—	10	Self	—
TM45	Attract	Normal	Status	—	100	15	Normal	—
TM46	Thief	Dark	Physical	40	100	10	Normal	○
TM57	Charge Beam	Electric	Special	50	90	10	Normal	—
TM58	Endure	Normal	Status	—	—	10	Self	—
TM68	Giga Impact	Normal	Physical	150	90	5	Normal	○
TM73	Thunder Wave	Electric	Status	—	100	20	Normal	—
TM75	Swords Dance	Normal	Status	—	—	30	Self	—
TM78	Captivate	Normal	Status	—	100	20	2 Foes	—
TM82	Sleep Talk	Normal	Status	—	—	10	Depends	—
TM83	Natural Gift	Normal	Physical	—	100	15	Normal	○
TM86	Grass Knot	Grass	Special	—	100	20	Normal	—
TM87	Swagger	Normal	Status	—	90	15	Normal	—
TM88	Pluck	Flying	Physical	60	100	20	Normal	○
TM89	U-turn	Bug	Physical	70	100	20	Normal	○
TM90	Substitute	Normal	Status	—	—	10	Self	—
HM01	Cut	Normal	Physical	50	95	30	Normal	○
HM04	Strength	Normal	Physical	80	100	15	Normal	○
HM06	Rock Smash	Fighting	Physical	40	100	15	Normal	○

● No. 020 | Mouse Pokémon
Raticate

Normal

- ● **HEIGHT:** 2'04"
- ● **WEIGHT:** 40.8 lbs.
- ● **ITEMS:** Chilan Berry

● SIZE COMPARISON

- ● **MALE FORM**
  Longer whiskers
- ● **FEMALE FORM**
  Shorter whiskers

⊙ ABILITIES
- ● Run Away
- ● Guts

⊙ STATS
HP	●●
ATTACK	●●●
DEFENSE	●●●
SP.ATTACK	●●
SP.DEFENSE	●●●
SPEED	●●●●

⊙ EGG GROUPS
Field

⊙ PERFORMANCE
SPEED ★★★★☆	STAMINA ★★☆
POWER ★★★☆	JUMP ★★★
SKILL ★★★	

● MAIN WAYS TO OBTAIN

Pokémon HeartGold	Route 38
Pokémon SoulSilver	Route 38
Pokémon Diamond	Route 225
Pokémon Pearl	Route 225
Pokémon Platinum	Route 225

Pokémon HeartGold	**Pokémon SoulSilver**
Gnaws on anything with its tough fangs. It can even topple concrete buildings by gnawing on them.	Its whiskers help it to maintain balance. Its fangs never stop growing, so it gnaws to pare them down.

⊙ EVOLUTION

Rattata → Lv. 20 → Raticate

Spearow

Normal | Flying

- **HEIGHT:** 1'00"
- **WEIGHT:** 4.4 lbs.
- **ITEMS:** None

- **SIZE COMPARISON**

- **MALE/FEMALE HAVE SAME FORM**

ABILITIES
- Keen Eye

STATS
- HP ●
- ATTACK ●●●
- DEFENSE ●●
- SP. ATTACK ●
- SP. DEFENSE ●
- SPEED ●●●

EGG GROUPS
Flying

PERFORMANCE
SPEED ★★★☆☆   STAMINA ★☆☆
POWER ★★☆☆   JUMP ★★★☆☆
SKILL ★☆☆

MAIN WAYS TO OBTAIN

Pokémon HeartGold	Route 33 (morning and afternoon only)
Pokémon SoulSilver	Route 33 (morning and afternoon only)
Pokémon Diamond	Route 225
Pokémon Pearl	Route 225
Pokémon Platinum	Route 225

Pokémon HeartGold	Pokémon SoulSilver
It flaps its short wings to flush out insects from tall grass. It then plucks them with its stubby beak.	Very protective of its territory, it flaps its short wings busily to dart around at high speed.

EVOLUTION

Spearow   Lv. 20 →   Fearow

● LEVEL-UP MOVES

Lv.	Name	Type	Kind	Pow.	Acc.	PP	Range	DA
1	Peck	Flying	Physical	35	100	35	Normal	○
1	Growl	Normal	Status	—	100	40	2 Foes	—
5	Leer	Normal	Status	—	100	30	2 Foes	—
9	Fury Attack	Normal	Physical	15	85	20	Normal	○
13	Pursuit	Dark	Physical	40	100	20	Normal	○
17	Aerial Ace	Flying	Physical	60	—	20	Normal	○
21	Mirror Move	Flying	Status	—	—	20	Depends	—
25	Agility	Psychic	Status	—	—	30	Self	—
29	Assurance	Dark	Physical	50	100	10	Normal	○
33	Roost	Flying	Status	—	—	10	Self	—
37	Drill Peck	Flying	Physical	80	100	20	Normal	○

● MOVE MANIAC

Name	Type	Kind	Pow.	Acc.	PP	Range	DA

● BP MOVES

Name	Type	Kind	Pow.	Acc.	PP	Range	DA
Ominous Wind	Ghost	Special	60	100	5	Normal	—
Air Cutter	Flying	Special	55	95	25	2 Foes	—
Snore	Normal	Special	40	100	15	Normal	—
Swift	Normal	Special	60	—	20	2 Foes	—
Tailwind	Flying	Status	—	—	30	2 Allies	—
Mud-Slap	Ground	Special	20	100	10	Normal	—
Twister	Dragon	Special	40	100	20	2 Foes	—
Heat Wave	Fire	Special	100	90	10	2 Foes	—

● TM & HM MOVES

No.	Name	Type	Kind	Pow.	Acc.	PP	Range	DA
TM06	Toxic	Poison	Status	—	85	10	Normal	—
TM10	Hidden Power	Normal	Special	—	100	15	Normal	—
TM11	Sunny Day	Fire	Status	—	—	5	All	—
TM17	Protect	Normal	Status	—	—	10	Self	—
TM18	Rain Dance	Water	Status	—	—	5	All	—
TM21	Frustration	Normal	Physical	—	100	20	Normal	○
TM27	Return	Normal	Physical	—	100	20	Normal	○
TM32	Double Team	Normal	Status	—	—	15	Self	—
TM40	Aerial Ace	Flying	Physical	60	—	20	Normal	○
TM42	Facade	Normal	Physical	70	100	20	Normal	○
TM43	Secret Power	Normal	Physical	70	100	20	Normal	○
TM44	Rest	Psychic	Status	—	—	10	Self	—
TM45	Attract	Normal	Status	—	100	15	Normal	—
TM46	Thief	Dark	Physical	40	100	10	Normal	○
TM47	Steel Wing	Steel	Physical	70	90	25	Normal	○
TM51	Roost	Flying	Status	—	—	10	Self	—
TM58	Endure	Normal	Status	—	—	10	Self	—
TM78	Captivate	Normal	Status	—	100	20	2 Foes	—
TM82	Sleep Talk	Normal	Status	—	—	10	Depends	—
TM83	Natural Gift	Normal	Physical	—	100	15	Normal	—
TM87	Swagger	Normal	Status	—	90	15	Normal	—
TM88	Pluck	Flying	Physical	60	100	20	Normal	○
TM89	U-turn	Bug	Physical	70	100	20	Normal	○
TM90	Substitute	Normal	Status	—	—	10	Self	—
HM02	Fly	Flying	Physical	90	95	15	Normal	○

● EGG MOVES

Name	Type	Kind	Pow.	Acc.	PP	Range	DA
Faint Attack	Dark	Physical	60	—	20	Normal	○
False Swipe	Normal	Physical	40	100	40	Normal	○
Scary Face	Normal	Status	—	90	10	Normal	—
Quick Attack	Normal	Physical	40	100	30	Normal	○
Tri Attack	Normal	Special	80	100	10	Normal	—
Astonish	Ghost	Physical	30	100	15	Normal	○
Sky Attack	Flying	Physical	140	90	5	Normal	○
Whirlwind	Normal	Status	—	100	20	Normal	—
Uproar	Normal	Special	50	100	10	1 Random	—
FeatherDance	Flying	Status	—	100	15	Normal	—

● LEVEL-UP MOVES

Lv.	Name	Type	Kind	Pow.	Acc.	PP	Range	DA
1	Pluck	Flying	Physical	60	100	20	Normal	○
1	Peck	Flying	Physical	35	100	35	Normal	○
1	Growl	Normal	Status	—	100	40	2 Foes	—
1	Leer	Normal	Status	—	100	30	2 Foes	—
1	Fury Attack	Normal	Physical	15	85	20	Normal	○
5	Leer	Normal	Status	—	100	30	2 Foes	—
9	Fury Attack	Normal	Physical	15	85	20	Normal	○
13	Pursuit	Dark	Physical	40	100	20	Normal	○
17	Aerial Ace	Flying	Physical	60	—	20	Normal	○
23	Mirror Move	Flying	Status	—	—	20	Depends	—
29	Agility	Psychic	Status	—	—	30	Self	—
35	Assurance	Dark	Physical	50	100	10	Normal	○
41	Roost	Flying	Status	—	—	10	Self	—
47	Drill Peck	Flying	Physical	80	100	20	Normal	○

● MOVE MANIAC

Name	Type	Kind	Pow.	Acc.	PP	Range	DA

● BP MOVES

Name	Type	Kind	Pow.	Acc.	PP	Range	DA
Ominous Wind	Ghost	Special	60	100	5	Normal	—
Air Cutter	Flying	Special	55	95	25	2 Foes	—
Snore	Normal	Special	40	100	15	Normal	—
Swift	Normal	Special	60	—	20	2 Foes	—
Tailwind	Flying	Status	—	—	30	2 Allies	—
Mud-Slap	Ground	Special	20	100	10	Normal	—
Twister	Dragon	Special	40	100	20	2 Foes	—
Heat Wave	Fire	Special	100	90	10	2 Foes	—
Sky Attack	Flying	Physical	140	90	5	Normal	—

● TM & HM MOVES

No.	Name	Type	Kind	Pow.	Acc.	PP	Range	DA
TM06	Toxic	Poison	Status	—	85	10	Normal	—
TM10	Hidden Power	Normal	Special	—	100	15	Normal	—
TM11	Sunny Day	Fire	Status	—	—	5	All	—
TM15	Hyper Beam	Normal	Special	150	90	5	Normal	—
TM17	Protect	Normal	Status	—	—	10	Self	—
TM18	Rain Dance	Water	Status	—	—	5	All	—
TM21	Frustration	Normal	Physical	—	100	20	Normal	○
TM27	Return	Normal	Physical	—	100	20	Normal	○
TM32	Double Team	Normal	Status	—	—	15	Self	—
TM40	Aerial Ace	Flying	Physical	60	—	20	Normal	○
TM42	Facade	Normal	Physical	70	100	20	Normal	○
TM43	Secret Power	Normal	Physical	70	100	20	Normal	○
TM44	Rest	Psychic	Status	—	—	10	Self	—
TM45	Attract	Normal	Status	—	100	15	Normal	—
TM46	Thief	Dark	Physical	40	100	10	Normal	○
TM47	Steel Wing	Steel	Physical	70	90	25	Normal	○
TM51	Roost	Flying	Status	—	—	10	Self	—
TM58	Endure	Normal	Status	—	—	10	Self	—
TM68	Giga Impact	Normal	Physical	150	90	5	Normal	○
TM78	Captivate	Normal	Status	—	100	20	2 Foes	—
TM82	Sleep Talk	Normal	Status	—	—	10	Depends	—
TM83	Natural Gift	Normal	Physical	—	100	15	Normal	○
TM87	Swagger	Normal	Status	—	90	15	Normal	—
TM88	Pluck	Flying	Physical	60	100	20	Normal	○
TM89	U-turn	Bug	Physical	70	100	20	Normal	○
TM90	Substitute	Normal	Status	—	—	10	Self	—
HM02	Fly	Flying	Physical	90	95	15	Normal	○

● No. 022 | Beak Pokémon
Fearow

Normal　Flying

- **HEIGHT:** 3'11"
- **WEIGHT:** 83.8 lbs.
- **ITEMS:** Sharp Beak

● SIZE COMPARISON

● MALE/FEMALE HAVE SAME FORM

◎ ABILITIES
● Keen Eye

◎ EGG GROUPS
Flying

◎ STATS
- HP ●●
- ATTACK ●●●●
- DEFENSE ●●●
- SP. ATTACK ●●●
- SP. DEFENSE ●●●
- SPEED ●●●●

◎ PERFORMANCE
SPEED ★★★★　STAMINA ★★☆
POWER ★★★★☆　JUMP ★★★★★
SKILL ★☆☆

● MAIN WAYS TO OBTAIN

Pokémon HeartGold　Route 47

Pokémon SoulSilver　Route 47

Pokémon Diamond　Route 225

Pokémon Pearl　Route 225

Pokémon Platinum　Route 225

Pokémon HeartGold
It shoots itself suddenly high into the sky, then plummets down in one fell swoop to strike its prey.

Pokémon SoulSilver
It cleverly uses its thin, long beak to pluck and eat small insects that hide under the ground.

◎ EVOLUTION

Lv. 20

Spearow　Fearow

⬤ No. 023 | Snake Pokémon
Ekans

Poison

● HEIGHT: 6'07"
● WEIGHT: 15.2 lbs.
● ITEMS: None

● SIZE COMPARISON

● MALE/FEMALE HAVE SAME FORM

⚙ ABILITIES
● Intimidate
● Shed Skin

⚙ STATS
HP ●●
ATTACK ●●●
DEFENSE ●●●
SP. ATTACK ●●
SP. DEFENSE ●●●
SPEED ●●●

⚙ EGG GROUPS
Field

Dragon

⚙ PERFORMANCE

SPEED ★★★☆	STAMINA ★★☆
POWER ★★★☆	JUMP ★★☆
SKILL ★★★	

● MAIN WAYS TO OBTAIN

Pokémon HeartGold	Goldenrod Game Corner prize (700 Coins)
Pokémon SoulSilver	Route 32
Pokémon Diamond	Route 212, Pastoria City side (after obtaining the National Pokédex, insert Pokémon FireRed into your Nintendo DS's Game Pak slot)
Pokémon Pearl	Route 212, Pastoria City side (after obtaining the National Pokédex, insert Pokémon FireRed into your Nintendo DS's Game Pak slot)
Pokémon Platinum	Route 212, Pastoria City side (after obtaining the National Pokédex, insert Pokémon FireRed into your Nintendo DS's Game Pak slot)

Pokémon HeartGold	Pokémon SoulSilver
It can freely detach its jaw to swallow large prey whole. It can become too heavy to move, however.	It always hides in grass. When first born, it has no poison, so its bite is painful, but harmless.

⚙ EVOLUTION

Ekans — Lv. 22 → Arbok

● LEVEL-UP MOVES

Lv.	Name	Type	Kind	Pow.	Acc.	PP	Range	DA
1	Wrap	Normal	Physical	15	85	20	Normal	○
1	Leer	Normal	Status	—	100	30	2 Foes	—
4	Poison Sting	Poison	Physical	15	100	35	Normal	—
9	Bite	Dark	Physical	60	100	25	Normal	○
12	Glare	Normal	Status	—	75	30	Normal	—
17	Screech	Normal	Status	—	85	40	Normal	—
20	Acid	Poison	Special	40	100	30	2 Foes	—
25	Stockpile	Normal	Status	—	—	20	Self	—
25	Swallow	Normal	Status	—	—	10	Self	—
25	Spit Up	Normal	Special	—	100	10	Normal	—
28	Mud Bomb	Ground	Special	65	85	10	Normal	—
33	Gastro Acid	Poison	Status	—	100	10	Normal	—
36	Haze	Ice	Status	—	—	30	All	—
41	Gunk Shot	Poison	Physical	120	70	5	Normal	—

● MOVE MANIAC

Name	Type	Kind	Pow.	Acc.	PP	Range	DA
Headbutt	Normal	Physical	70	100	15	Normal	○

● BP MOVES

Name	Type	Kind	Pow.	Acc.	PP	Range	DA
Snore	Normal	Special	40	100	15	Normal	—
Spite	Ghost	Status	—	100	10	Normal	—
Aqua Tail	Water	Physical	90	90	10	Normal	○
Gastro Acid	Poison	Status	—	100	10	Normal	—
Gunk Shot	Poison	Physical	120	70	5	Normal	—
Seed Bomb	Grass	Physical	80	100	15	Normal	—

● TM & HM MOVES

No.	Name	Type	Kind	Pow.	Acc.	PP	Range	DA
TM06	Toxic	Poison	Status	—	85	10	Normal	—
TM10	Hidden Power	Normal	Special	—	100	15	Normal	—
TM11	Sunny Day	Fire	Status	—	—	5	All	—
TM17	Protect	Normal	Status	—	—	10	Self	—
TM18	Rain Dance	Water	Status	—	—	5	All	—
TM19	Giga Drain	Grass	Special	60	100	10	Normal	—
TM21	Frustration	Normal	Physical	—	100	20	Normal	○
TM23	Iron Tail	Steel	Physical	100	75	15	Normal	○
TM26	Earthquake	Ground	Physical	100	100	10	2 Foes/1 Ally	—
TM27	Return	Normal	Physical	—	100	20	Normal	○
TM28	Dig	Ground	Physical	80	100	10	Normal	○
TM32	Double Team	Normal	Status	—	—	15	Self	—
TM36	Sludge Bomb	Poison	Special	90	100	10	Normal	—
TM39	Rock Tomb	Rock	Physical	50	80	10	Normal	—
TM41	Torment	Dark	Status	—	100	15	Normal	—
TM42	Facade	Normal	Physical	70	100	20	Normal	○
TM43	Secret Power	Normal	Physical	70	100	20	Normal	—
TM44	Rest	Psychic	Status	—	—	10	Self	—
TM45	Attract	Normal	Status	—	100	15	Normal	—
TM46	Thief	Dark	Physical	40	100	10	Normal	○
TM49	Snatch	Dark	Status	—	—	10	Depends	—
TM58	Endure	Normal	Status	—	—	10	Self	—
TM66	Payback	Dark	Physical	50	100	10	Normal	○
TM78	Captivate	Normal	Status	—	100	20	2 Foes	—
TM79	Dark Pulse	Dark	Special	80	100	15	Normal	—
TM80	Rock Slide	Rock	Physical	75	90	10	2 Foes	—
TM82	Sleep Talk	Normal	Status	—	—	10	Depends	—
TM83	Natural Gift	Normal	Physical	—	100	15	Normal	—
TM84	Poison Jab	Poison	Physical	80	100	20	Normal	○
TM87	Swagger	Normal	Status	—	90	15	Normal	—
TM90	Substitute	Normal	Status	—	—	10	Self	—
HM04	Strength	Normal	Physical	80	100	15	Normal	○

● EGG MOVES

Name	Type	Kind	Pow.	Acc.	PP	Range	DA
Pursuit	Dark	Physical	40	100	20	Normal	○
Slam	Normal	Physical	80	75	20	Normal	○
Spite	Ghost	Status	—	100	10	Normal	—
Beat Up	Dark	Physical	10	100	10	Normal	○
Poison Fang	Poison	Physical	50	100	15	Normal	○
Scary Face	Normal	Status	—	90	10	Normal	—
Poison Tail	Poison	Physical	50	100	25	Normal	○
Disable	Normal	Status	—	80	20	Normal	—
Switcheroo	Dark	Status	—	100	10	Normal	—

● LEVEL-UP MOVES

Lv.	Name	Type	Kind	Pow.	Acc.	PP	Range	DA
1	Ice Fang	Ice	Physical	65	95	15	Normal	○
1	Thunder Fang	Electric	Physical	65	95	15	Normal	○
1	Fire Fang	Fire	Physical	65	95	15	Normal	○
1	Wrap	Normal	Physical	15	85	20	Normal	—
1	Leer	Normal	Status	—	100	30	2 Foes	—
1	Poison Sting	Poison	Physical	15	100	35	Normal	—
1	Bite	Dark	Physical	60	100	25	Normal	—
4	Poison Sting	Poison	Physical	15	100	35	Normal	—
9	Bite	Dark	Physical	60	100	25	Normal	○
12	Glare	Normal	Status	—	75	30	Normal	—
17	Screech	Normal	Status	—	85	40	Normal	—
20	Acid	Poison	Special	40	100	30	2 Foes	—
22	Crunch	Dark	Physical	80	100	15	Normal	○
28	Stockpile	Normal	Status	—	—	20	Self	—
28	Swallow	Normal	Status	—	—	10	Self	—
28	Spit Up	Normal	Special	—	100	10	Normal	—
34	Mud Bomb	Ground	Special	65	85	10	Normal	—
42	Gastro Acid	Poison	Status	—	100	10	Normal	—
48	Haze	Ice	Status	—	—	30	All	—
56	Gunk Shot	Poison	Physical	120	70	5	Normal	—

● MOVE MANIAC

Name	Type	Kind	Pow.	Acc.	PP	Range	DA
Headbutt	Normal	Physical	70	100	15	Normal	—

● BP MOVES

Name	Type	Kind	Pow.	Acc.	PP	Range	DA
Snore	Normal	Special	40	100	15	Normal	—
Spite	Ghost	Status	—	100	10	Normal	—
Aqua Tail	Water	Physical	90	90	10	Normal	○
Gastro Acid	Poison	Status	—	100	10	Normal	—
Gunk Shot	Poison	Physical	120	70	5	Normal	—
Seed Bomb	Grass	Physical	80	100	15	Normal	—

● TM & HM MOVES

No.	Name	Type	Kind	Pow.	Acc.	PP	Range	DA
TM06	Toxic	Poison	Status	—	85	10	Normal	—
TM10	Hidden Power	Normal	Special	—	100	15	Normal	—
TM11	Sunny Day	Fire	Status	—	—	5	All	—
TM15	Hyper Beam	Normal	Special	150	90	5	Normal	—
TM17	Protect	Normal	Status	—	—	10	Self	—
TM18	Rain Dance	Water	Status	—	—	5	All	—
TM19	Giga Drain	Grass	Special	60	100	10	Normal	—
TM21	Frustration	Normal	Physical	—	100	20	Normal	○
TM23	Iron Tail	Steel	Physical	100	75	15	Normal	○
TM26	Earthquake	Ground	Physical	100	100	10	2 Foes/1 Ally	—
TM27	Return	Normal	Physical	—	100	20	Normal	○
TM28	Dig	Ground	Physical	80	100	10	Normal	○
TM32	Double Team	Normal	Status	—	—	15	Self	—
TM36	Sludge Bomb	Poison	Special	90	100	10	Normal	—
TM39	Rock Tomb	Rock	Physical	50	80	10	Normal	—
TM41	Torment	Dark	Status	—	100	15	Normal	—
TM42	Facade	Normal	Physical	70	100	20	Normal	○
TM43	Secret Power	Normal	Physical	70	100	20	Normal	—
TM44	Rest	Psychic	Status	—	—	10	Self	—
TM45	Attract	Normal	Status	—	100	15	Normal	—
TM46	Thief	Dark	Physical	40	100	10	Normal	—
TM49	Snatch	Dark	Status	—	—	10	Depends	—
TM58	Endure	Normal	Status	—	—	10	Self	—
TM66	Payback	Dark	Physical	50	100	10	Normal	○
TM68	Giga Impact	Normal	Physical	150	90	5	Normal	○
TM78	Captivate	Normal	Status	—	100	20	2 Foes	—
TM79	Dark Pulse	Dark	Special	80	100	15	Normal	—
TM80	Rock Slide	Rock	Physical	75	90	10	2 Foes	—
TM82	Sleep Talk	Normal	Status	—	—	10	Depends	—
TM83	Natural Gift	Normal	Physical	—	100	15	Normal	—
TM84	Poison Jab	Poison	Physical	80	100	20	Normal	○
TM87	Swagger	Normal	Status	—	90	15	Normal	—
TM90	Substitute	Normal	Status	—	—	10	Self	—
HM04	Strength	Normal	Physical	80	100	15	Normal	○

No. 024 | Cobra Pokémon
Arbok

Poison

● HEIGHT: 11'06"
● WEIGHT: 143.3 lbs.
● ITEMS: None

● SIZE COMPARISON

● MALE/FEMALE HAVE SAME FORM

● ABILITIES
● Intimidate
● Shed Skin

● STATS
HP ●●
ATTACK ●●●●
DEFENSE ●●●
SP. ATTACK ●●●
SP. DEFENSE ●●●
SPEED ●●●●

● EGG GROUPS
Field

Dragon

● PERFORMANCE
SPEED ★★★☆   STAMINA ★★☆☆
POWER ★★★★☆   JUMP ★★☆
SKILL ★★★

● MAIN WAYS TO OBTAIN

Pokémon HeartGold — Level up Ekans to Lv. 22

Pokémon SoulSilver — Route 27

Pokémon Diamond — Pastoria Great Marsh (after obtaining the National Pokédex, insert *Pokémon FireRed* into your Nintendo DS's Game Pak slot)

Pokémon Pearl — Pastoria Great Marsh (after obtaining the National Pokédex, insert *Pokémon FireRed* into your Nintendo DS's Game Pak slot)

Pokémon Platinum — Pastoria Great Marsh (after obtaining the National Pokédex, insert *Pokémon FireRed* into your Nintendo DS's Game Pak slot)

Pokémon HeartGold — Transfixing prey with the face-like pattern on its belly, it binds and poisons the frightened victim.

Pokémon SoulSilver — With a very vengeful nature, it won't give up the chase, no matter how far, once it targets its prey.

● EVOLUTION

Ekans   Lv. 22   Arbok

No. 025 | Mouse Pokémon
Pikachu

Electric

- **HEIGHT:** 1'04"
- **WEIGHT:** 13.2 lbs.
- **ITEMS:** Oran Berry
  Light Ball

● SIZE COMPARISON

● MALE FORM
Flat tail

● FEMALE FORM
Notched tail

⊙ ABILITIES
● Static

⊙ STATS
- HP ●
- ATTACK ●●
- DEFENSE ●●
- SP. ATTACK ●●
- SP. DEFENSE ●●
- SPEED ●●●●

⊙ EGG GROUPS
Field

Fairy

⊙ PERFORMANCE
SPEED ★★★☆	STAMINA ★★★☆
POWER ★★★☆	JUMP ★★★☆
SKILL ★★★☆	

● MAIN WAYS TO OBTAIN

Pokémon HeartGold	Viridian Forest
Pokémon SoulSilver	Viridian Forest
Pokémon Diamond	Trophy Garden at the Pokémon Mansion on Route 212
Pokémon Pearl	Trophy Garden at the Pokémon Mansion on Route 212
Pokémon Platinum	Trophy Garden at the Pokémon Mansion on Route 212

Pokémon HeartGold	Pokémon SoulSilver
This intelligent Pokémon roasts hard berries with electricity to make them tender enough to eat.	It raises its tail to check its surroundings. The tail is sometimes struck by lightning in this pose.

⊙ EVOLUTION

Pichu — Level up with high friendship → Pikachu — Use Thunderstone → Raichu

● LEVEL-UP MOVES

Lv.	Name	Type	Kind	Pow.	Acc.	PP	Range	DA
1	ThunderShock	Electric	Special	40	100	30	Normal	—
1	Growl	Normal	Status	—	100	40	2 Foes	—
5	Tail Whip	Normal	Status	—	100	30	2 Foes	—
10	Thunder Wave	Electric	Status	—	100	20	Normal	—
13	Quick Attack	Normal	Physical	40	100	30	Normal	○
18	Double Team	Normal	Status	—	—	15	Self	—
21	Slam	Normal	Physical	80	75	20	Normal	○
26	Thunderbolt	Electric	Special	95	100	15	Normal	—
29	Feint	Normal	Physical	50	100	10	Normal	—
34	Agility	Psychic	Status	—	—	30	Self	—
37	Discharge	Electric	Special	80	100	15	2 Foes/1 Ally	—
42	Light Screen	Psychic	Status	—	—	30	2 Allies	—
45	Thunder	Electric	Special	120	70	10	Normal	—

● MOVE MANIAC

Name	Type	Kind	Pow.	Acc.	PP	Range	DA
Headbutt	Normal	Physical	70	100	15	Normal	○

● BP MOVES

Name	Type	Kind	Pow.	Acc.	PP	Range	DA
ThunderPunch	Electric	Physical	75	100	15	Normal	○
Knock Off	Dark	Physical	20	100	20	Normal	○
Snore	Normal	Special	40	100	15	Normal	—
Helping Hand	Normal	Status	—	—	20	1 Ally	—
Magnet Rise	Electric	Status	—	—	10	Self	—
Swift	Normal	Special	60	—	20	2 Foes	—
Mud-Slap	Ground	Special	20	100	10	Normal	—
Rollout	Rock	Physical	30	90	20	Normal	○
Signal Beam	Bug	Special	75	100	15	Normal	—

● TM & HM MOVES

No.	Name	Type	Kind	Pow.	Acc.	PP	Range	DA
TM01	Focus Punch	Fighting	Physical	150	100	20	Normal	○
TM06	Toxic	Poison	Status	—	85	10	Normal	—
TM10	Hidden Power	Normal	Special	—	100	15	Normal	—
TM16	Light Screen	Psychic	Status	—	—	30	2 Allies	—
TM17	Protect	Normal	Status	—	—	10	Self	—
TM18	Rain Dance	Water	Status	—	—	5	All	—
TM21	Frustration	Normal	Physical	—	100	20	Normal	○
TM23	Iron Tail	Steel	Physical	100	75	15	Normal	○
TM24	Thunderbolt	Electric	Special	95	100	15	Normal	—
TM25	Thunder	Electric	Special	120	70	10	Normal	—
TM27	Return	Normal	Physical	—	100	20	Normal	○
TM28	Dig	Ground	Physical	80	100	10	Normal	○
TM31	Brick Break	Fighting	Physical	75	100	15	Normal	○
TM32	Double Team	Normal	Status	—	—	15	Self	—
TM34	Shock Wave	Electric	Special	60	—	20	Normal	—
TM42	Facade	Normal	Physical	70	100	20	Normal	○
TM43	Secret Power	Normal	Physical	70	100	20	Normal	—
TM44	Rest	Psychic	Status	—	—	10	Self	—
TM45	Attract	Normal	Status	—	100	15	Normal	—
TM56	Fling	Dark	Physical	—	100	10	Normal	—
TM57	Charge Beam	Electric	Special	50	90	10	Normal	—
TM58	Endure	Normal	Status	—	—	10	Self	—
TM70	Flash	Normal	Status	—	100	20	Normal	—
TM73	Thunder Wave	Electric	Status	—	100	20	Normal	—
TM78	Captivate	Normal	Status	—	100	20	2 Foes	—
TM82	Sleep Talk	Normal	Status	—	—	10	Depends	—
TM83	Natural Gift	Normal	Physical	—	100	15	Normal	—
TM86	Grass Knot	Grass	Special	—	100	20	Normal	○
TM87	Swagger	Normal	Status	—	90	15	Normal	—
TM90	Substitute	Normal	Status	—	—	10	Self	—
HM04	Strength	Normal	Physical	80	100	15	Normal	○
HM06	Rock Smash	Fighting	Physical	40	100	15	Normal	○

● LEVEL-UP MOVES

Lv.	Name	Type	Kind	Pow.	Acc.	PP	Range	DA
1	ThunderShock	Electric	Special	40	100	30	Normal	—
1	Tail Whip	Normal	Status	—	100	30	2 Foes	—
1	Quick Attack	Normal	Physical	40	100	30	Normal	○
1	Thunderbolt	Electric	Special	95	100	15	Normal	—

● MOVE MANIAC

Name	Type	Kind	Pow.	Acc.	PP	Range	DA
Headbutt	Normal	Physical	70	100	15	Normal	○

● BP MOVES

Name	Type	Kind	Pow.	Acc.	PP	Range	DA
ThunderPunch	Electric	Physical	75	100	15	Normal	○
Knock Off	Dark	Physical	20	100	20	Normal	○
Snore	Normal	Special	40	100	15	Normal	—
Helping Hand	Normal	Status	—	—	20	1 Ally	—
Magnet Rise	Electric	Status	—	—	10	Self	—
Swift	Normal	Special	60	—	20	2 Foes	—
Mud-Slap	Ground	Special	20	100	10	Normal	—
Rollout	Rock	Physical	30	90	20	Normal	○
Signal Beam	Bug	Special	75	100	15	Normal	—

● TM & HM MOVES

No.	Name	Type	Kind	Pow.	Acc.	PP	Range	DA
TM01	Focus Punch	Fighting	Physical	150	100	20	Normal	○
TM06	Toxic	Poison	Status	—	85	10	Normal	—
TM10	Hidden Power	Normal	Special	—	100	15	Normal	—
TM15	Hyper Beam	Normal	Special	150	90	5	Normal	—
TM16	Light Screen	Psychic	Status	—	—	30	2 Allies	—
TM17	Protect	Normal	Status	—	—	10	Self	—
TM18	Rain Dance	Water	Status	—	—	5	All	—
TM21	Frustration	Normal	Physical	—	100	20	Normal	○
TM23	Iron Tail	Steel	Physical	100	75	15	Normal	○
TM24	Thunderbolt	Electric	Special	95	100	15	Normal	—
TM25	Thunder	Electric	Special	120	70	10	Normal	—
TM27	Return	Normal	Physical	—	100	20	Normal	○
TM28	Dig	Ground	Physical	80	100	10	Normal	○
TM31	Brick Break	Fighting	Physical	75	100	15	Normal	○
TM32	Double Team	Normal	Status	—	—	15	Self	—
TM34	Shock Wave	Electric	Special	60	—	20	Normal	—
TM42	Facade	Normal	Physical	70	100	20	Normal	○
TM43	Secret Power	Normal	Physical	70	100	20	Normal	○
TM44	Rest	Psychic	Status	—	—	10	Self	—
TM45	Attract	Normal	Status	—	100	15	Normal	—
TM46	Thief	Dark	Physical	40	100	10	Normal	○
TM52	Focus Blast	Fighting	Special	120	70	5	Normal	—
TM56	Fling	Dark	Physical	—	100	10	Normal	○
TM57	Charge Beam	Electric	Special	50	90	10	Normal	—
TM58	Endure	Normal	Status	—	—	10	Self	—
TM68	Giga Impact	Normal	Physical	150	90	5	Normal	○
TM70	Flash	Normal	Status	—	100	20	Normal	—
TM73	Thunder Wave	Electric	Status	—	100	20	Normal	—
TM78	Captivate	Normal	Status	—	100	20	2 Foes	—
TM82	Sleep Talk	Normal	Status	—	—	10	Depends	—
TM83	Natural Gift	Normal	Physical	—	100	15	Normal	○
TM86	Grass Knot	Grass	Special	—	100	20	Normal	—
TM87	Swagger	Normal	Status	—	90	15	Normal	—
TM90	Substitute	Normal	Status	—	—	10	Self	—
HM04	Strength	Normal	Physical	80	100	15	Normal	○
HM06	Rock Smash	Fighting	Physical	40	100	15	Normal	○

○ No. 026 | Mouse Pokémon
Raichu

Electric

- ● HEIGHT: 2'07"
- ● WEIGHT: 66.1 lbs.
- ● ITEMS: None

● SIZE COMPARISON

● MALE FORM
Pointy tail end

● FEMALE FORM
Flat tail end

⊛ ABILITIES
● Static

⊛ STATS
HP	●●
ATTACK	●●●
DEFENSE	●●
SP. ATTACK	●●●
SP. DEFENSE	●●
SPEED	●●●●

⊛ EGG GROUPS
Field
Fairy

⊛ PERFORMANCE
SPEED ★★☆		STAMINA ★★★★☆	
POWER ★★★★☆		JUMP ★★☆	
SKILL ★★★★☆			

● MAIN WAYS TO OBTAIN

Pokémon HeartGold	Use Thunderstone on Pikachu
Pokémon SoulSilver	Use Thunderstone on Pikachu
Pokémon Diamond	Use Thunderstone on Pikachu
Pokémon Pearl	Use Thunderstone on Pikachu
Pokémon Platinum	Use Thunderstone on Pikachu

Pokémon HeartGold	Pokémon SoulSilver
When its electricity builds, its muscles are stimulated, and it becomes more aggressive than usual.	If the electric pouches in its cheeks become fully charged, both ears will stand straight up.

⊛ EVOLUTION

| Pichu | Level up with high friendship | Pikachu | Use Thunderstone | Raichu |

● No. 027 | Mouse Pokémon
Sandshrew

Ground

- ● HEIGHT: 2'00"
- ● WEIGHT: 26.5 lbs.
- ● ITEMS: Quick Claw

● SIZE COMPARISON

● MALE/FEMALE HAVE SAME FORM

● ABILITIES
● Sand Veil

● STATS
- HP ●●
- ATTACK ●●●
- DEFENSE ●●●
- SP. ATTACK ●
- SP. DEFENSE ●
- SPEED ●●

● EGG GROUPS
Field

● PERFORMANCE
SPEED ★★★☆	STAMINA ★★☆
POWER ★★★	JUMP ★★☆
SKILL ★★★☆☆	

● MAIN WAYS TO OBTAIN

Pokémon HeartGold	Union Cave 1F
Pokémon SoulSilver	Safari Zone (Desert Area)
Pokémon Diamond	Wayward Cave (after obtaining the National Pokédex, insert Pokémon LeafGreen into your Nintendo DS's Game Pak slot)
Pokémon Pearl	Wayward Cave (after obtaining the National Pokédex, insert Pokémon LeafGreen into your Nintendo DS's Game Pak slot)
Pokémon Platinum	Wayward Cave (after obtaining the National Pokédex, insert Pokémon LeafGreen into your Nintendo DS's Game Pak slot)

Pokémon HeartGold	Pokémon SoulSilver
If it fell from a great height, this Pokémon could save itself by rolling into a ball and bouncing.	Disliking water, it lives in deep burrows in arid areas. It can roll itself instantly into a ball.

● EVOLUTION
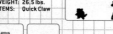
Sandshrew — Lv. 22 — Sandslash

● LEVEL-UP MOVES
Lv.	Name	Type	Kind	Pow.	Acc.	PP	Range	DA
1	Scratch	Normal	Physical	40	100	35	Normal	○
3	Defense Curl	Normal	Status	—	—	40	Self	—
7	Sand-Attack	Ground	Status	—	100	15	Normal	—
9	Poison Sting	Poison	Physical	15	100	35	Normal	○
13	Rapid Spin	Normal	Physical	20	100	40	Normal	○
15	Swift	Normal	Special	60	—	20	2 Foes	—
19	Fury Swipes	Normal	Physical	18	80	15	Normal	○
21	Rollout	Rock	Physical	30	90	20	Normal	○
25	Fury Cutter	Bug	Physical	10	95	20	Normal	○
27	Sand Tomb	Ground	Physical	15	70	15	Normal	—
31	Slash	Normal	Physical	70	100	20	Normal	○
33	Gyro Ball	Steel	Physical	—	100	5	Normal	○
37	Sandstorm	Rock	Status	—	—	10	All	—

● MOVE MANIAC
Name	Type	Kind	Pow.	Acc.	PP	Range	DA
Headbutt	Normal	Physical	70	100	15	Normal	○

● BP MOVES
Name	Type	Kind	Pow.	Acc.	PP	Range	DA
Fury Cutter	Bug	Physical	10	95	20	Normal	○
Knock Off	Dark	Physical	20	100	20	Normal	○
Snore	Normal	Special	40	100	15	Normal	—
Swift	Normal	Special	60	—	20	2 Foes	—
Mud-Slap	Ground	Special	20	100	10	Normal	—
Rollout	Rock	Physical	30	90	20	Normal	○
Earth Power	Ground	Special	90	100	10	Normal	—
Super Fang	Normal	Physical	—	90	10	Normal	○

● TM & HM MOVES
No.	Name	Type	Kind	Pow.	Acc.	PP	Range	DA
TM01	Focus Punch	Fighting	Physical	150	100	20	Normal	○
TM06	Toxic	Poison	Status	—	85	10	Normal	—
TM10	Hidden Power	Normal	Special	—	100	15	Normal	—
TM11	Sunny Day	Fire	Status	—	—	5	All	—
TM17	Protect	Normal	Status	—	—	10	Self	—
TM21	Frustration	Normal	Physical	—	100	20	Normal	○
TM23	Iron Tail	Steel	Physical	100	75	15	Normal	○
TM26	Earthquake	Ground	Physical	100	100	10	2 Foes/1 Ally	○
TM27	Return	Normal	Physical	—	100	20	Normal	○
TM28	Dig	Ground	Physical	80	100	10	Normal	○
TM31	Brick Break	Fighting	Physical	75	100	15	Normal	○
TM32	Double Team	Normal	Status	—	—	15	Self	—
TM37	Sandstorm	Rock	Status	—	—	10	All	—
TM39	Rock Tomb	Rock	Physical	50	80	10	Normal	○
TM40	Aerial Ace	Flying	Physical	60	—	20	Normal	○
TM42	Facade	Normal	Physical	70	100	20	Normal	○
TM43	Secret Power	Normal	Physical	70	100	20	Normal	○
TM44	Rest	Psychic	Status	—	—	10	Self	—
TM45	Attract	Normal	Status	—	100	15	Normal	—
TM46	Thief	Dark	Physical	40	100	10	Normal	○
TM56	Fling	Dark	Physical	—	100	10	Normal	○
TM58	Endure	Normal	Status	—	—	10	Self	—
TM65	Shadow Claw	Ghost	Physical	70	100	15	Normal	○
TM74	Gyro Ball	Steel	Physical	—	100	5	Normal	○
TM75	Swords Dance	Normal	Status	—	—	30	Self	—
TM76	Stealth Rock	Rock	Status	—	—	20	2 Foes	—
TM78	Captivate	Normal	Status	—	100	20	2 Foes	—
TM80	Rock Slide	Rock	Physical	75	90	10	2 Foes	—
TM81	X-Scissor	Bug	Physical	80	100	15	Normal	○
TM82	Sleep Talk	Normal	Status	—	—	10	Depends	—
TM83	Natural Gift	Normal	Physical	—	100	15	Normal	—
TM84	Poison Jab	Poison	Physical	80	100	20	Normal	○
TM87	Swagger	Normal	Status	—	90	15	Normal	—
TM90	Substitute	Normal	Status	—	—	10	Self	—
HM01	Cut	Normal	Physical	50	95	30	Normal	○
HM04	Strength	Normal	Physical	80	100	15	Normal	○
HM06	Rock Smash	Fighting	Physical	40	100	15	Normal	○
HM08	Rock Climb	Normal	Physical	90	85	20	Normal	○

● EGG MOVES
Name	Type	Kind	Pow.	Acc.	PP	Range	DA
Flail	Normal	Physical	—	100	15	Normal	○
Safeguard	Normal	Status	—	—	25	2 Allies	—
Counter	Fighting	Physical	—	100	20	Self	—
Rapid Spin	Normal	Physical	20	100	40	Normal	○
Rock Slide	Rock	Physical	75	90	10	2 Foes	—
Metal Claw	Steel	Physical	50	95	35	Normal	○
Swords Dance	Normal	Status	—	—	30	Self	—
Crush Claw	Normal	Physical	75	95	10	Normal	○
Night Slash	Dark	Physical	70	100	15	Normal	○
Mud Shot	Ground	Special	55	95	15	Normal	—

● LEVEL-UP MOVES

Lv.	Name	Type	Kind	Pow.	Acc.	PP	Range	DA
1	Scratch	Normal	Physical	40	100	35	Normal	○
1	Defense Curl	Normal	Status	—	—	40	Self	—
1	Sand-Attack	Ground	Status	—	100	15	Normal	—
3	Defense Curl	Normal	Status	—	—	40	Self	—
7	Sand-Attack	Ground	Status	—	100	15	Normal	—
9	Poison Sting	Poison	Physical	15	100	35	Normal	—
13	Rapid Spin	Normal	Physical	20	100	40	Normal	○
15	Swift	Normal	Special	60	—	20	2 Foes	—
19	Fury Swipes	Normal	Physical	18	80	15	Normal	○
21	Rollout	Rock	Physical	30	90	20	Normal	○
22	Crush Claw	Normal	Physical	75	95	10	Normal	○
28	Fury Cutter	Bug	Physical	10	95	20	Normal	○
33	Sand Tomb	Ground	Physical	15	70	15	Normal	—
40	Slash	Normal	Physical	70	100	20	Normal	○
45	Gyro Ball	Steel	Physical	—	100	5	Normal	○
52	Sandstorm	Rock	Status	—	—	10	All	—

● MOVE MANIAC

Name	Type	Kind	Pow.	Acc.	PP	Range	DA
Headbutt	Normal	Physical	70	100	15	Normal	○

● BP MOVES

Name	Type	Kind	Pow.	Acc.	PP	Range	DA
Fury Cutter	Bug	Physical	10	95	20	Normal	○
Knock Off	Dark	Physical	20	100	20	Normal	○
Snore	Normal	Special	40	100	15	Normal	—
Swift	Normal	Special	60	—	20	2 Foes	—
Mud-Slap	Ground	Special	20	100	10	Normal	—
Rollout	Rock	Physical	30	90	20	Normal	○
Earth Power	Ground	Special	90	100	10	Normal	—
Super Fang	Normal	Physical	—	90	10	Normal	○

● TM & HM MOVES

No.	Name	Type	Kind	Pow.	Acc.	PP	Range	DA
TM01	Focus Punch	Fighting	Physical	150	100	20	Normal	○
TM06	Toxic	Poison	Status	—	85	10	Normal	—
TM10	Hidden Power	Normal	Special	—	100	15	Normal	—
TM11	Sunny Day	Fire	Status	—	—	5	All	—
TM15	Hyper Beam	Normal	Special	150	90	5	Normal	—
TM17	Protect	Normal	Status	—	—	10	Self	—
TM21	Frustration	Normal	Physical	—	100	20	Normal	○
TM23	Iron Tail	Steel	Physical	100	75	15	Normal	○
TM26	Earthquake	Ground	Physical	100	100	10	2 Foes/1 Ally	○
TM27	Return	Normal	Physical	—	100	20	Normal	○
TM28	Dig	Ground	Physical	80	100	10	Normal	○
TM31	Brick Break	Fighting	Physical	75	100	15	Normal	○
TM32	Double Team	Normal	Status	—	—	15	Self	—
TM37	Sandstorm	Rock	Status	—	—	10	All	—
TM39	Rock Tomb	Rock	Physical	50	80	10	Normal	—
TM40	Aerial Ace	Flying	Physical	60	—	20	Normal	○
TM42	Facade	Normal	Physical	70	100	20	Normal	○
TM43	Secret Power	Normal	Physical	70	100	20	Normal	○
TM44	Rest	Psychic	Status	—	—	10	Self	—
TM45	Attract	Normal	Status	—	100	15	Normal	—
TM46	Thief	Dark	Physical	40	100	10	Normal	○
TM52	Focus Blast	Fighting	Special	120	70	5	Normal	—
TM56	Fling	Dark	Physical	—	100	10	Normal	○
TM58	Endure	Normal	Status	—	—	10	Self	—
TM65	Shadow Claw	Ghost	Physical	70	100	15	Normal	○
TM68	Giga Impact	Normal	Physical	150	90	5	Normal	○
TM71	Stone Edge	Rock	Physical	100	80	5	Normal	—
TM74	Gyro Ball	Steel	Physical	—	100	5	Normal	○
TM75	Swords Dance	Normal	Status	—	—	30	Self	—
TM76	Stealth Rock	Rock	Status	—	—	20	2 Foes	—
TM78	Captivate	Normal	Status	—	100	20	2 Foes	—
TM80	Rock Slide	Rock	Physical	75	90	10	2 Foes	—
TM81	X-Scissor	Bug	Physical	80	100	15	Normal	○
TM82	Sleep Talk	Normal	Status	—	—	10	Depends	—
TM83	Natural Gift	Normal	Physical	—	100	15	Normal	—
TM84	Poison Jab	Poison	Physical	80	100	20	Normal	○
TM87	Swagger	Normal	Status	—	90	15	Normal	—
TM90	Substitute	Normal	Status	—	—	10	Self	—
HM01	Cut	Normal	Physical	50	95	30	Normal	○
HM04	Strength	Normal	Physical	80	100	15	Normal	○
HM06	Rock Smash	Fighting	Physical	40	100	15	Normal	○
HM08	Rock Climb	Normal	Physical	90	85	20	Normal	○

○ No. 028 | Mouse Pokémon
Sandslash

Ground

● HEIGHT: 3'03"
● WEIGHT: 65.0 lbs.
● ITEMS: Quick Claw

● SIZE COMPARISON

● MALE/FEMALE HAVE SAME FORM

⊙ ABILITIES
● Sand Veil

⊙ STATS
HP ●●●
ATTACK ●●●●
DEFENSE ●●●●
SP. ATTACK ●●●
SP. DEFENSE ●●
SPEED ●●●

⊙ EGG GROUPS
Field

⊙ PERFORMANCE

SPEED ★★☆ STAMINA ★★★
POWER ★★★☆ JUMP ★★
SKILL ★★★★☆

● MAIN WAYS TO OBTAIN

Pokémon HeartGold	Safari Zone (Desert Area)
Pokémon SoulSilver	Safari Zone (Desert Area)
Pokémon Diamond	Route 228 (after obtaining the National Pokédex, insert *Pokémon LeafGreen* into your Nintendo DS's Game Pak slot)
Pokémon Pearl	Route 228 (after obtaining the National Pokédex, insert *Pokémon LeafGreen* into your Nintendo DS's Game Pak slot)
Pokémon Platinum	Route 228 (after obtaining the National Pokédex, insert *Pokémon LeafGreen* into your Nintendo DS's Game Pak slot)

Pokémon HeartGold	*Pokémon SoulSilver*
In an attempt to hide itself, it will run around at top speed to kick up a blinding dust storm.	If it digs at an incredible pace, it may snap off its spikes and claws. They grow back in a day.

⊙ EVOLUTION

Sandshrew → Lv. 22 → Sandslash

● No. 029 | Poison Pin Pokémon
Nidoran♀

Poison

● HEIGHT: 1'04"
● WEIGHT: 15.4 lbs.
● ITEMS: None

● SIZE COMPARISON

● FEMALE FORM

● ABILITIES
● Poison Point
● Rivalry

● STATS
HP ●●
ATTACK ●●
DEFENSE ●●
SP. ATTACK ●●
SP. DEFENSE ●●
SPEED ●●

● EGG GROUPS
Monster
Field

● PERFORMANCE
SPEED ★★★★☆   STAMINA ★★★
POWER ★★☆
SKILL ★★☆   JUMP ★★☆

● MAIN WAYS TO OBTAIN

Pokémon HeartGold	Route 35
Pokémon SoulSilver	Route 35
Pokémon Diamond	Route 201 (use Poké Radar)
Pokémon Pearl	Route 201 (occasionally appears when you use Poké Radar)
Pokémon Platinum	Route 201 (use Poké Radar)

Pokémon HeartGold	Pokémon SoulSilver
The poison hidden in its small horn is extremely potent. Even a tiny scratch can have fatal results.	Although not very combative, it will torment its foes with poison spikes if it is threatened in any way.

● EVOLUTION

Lv. 16 → Use Moon Stone →

Nidoran♀ → Nidorina → Nidoqueen

● LEVEL-UP MOVES

Lv.	Name	Type	Kind	Pow.	Acc.	PP	Range	DA
1	Growl	Normal	Status	—	100	40	2 Foes	—
1	Scratch	Normal	Physical	40	100	35	Normal	○
7	Tail Whip	Normal	Status	—	100	30	2 Foes	—
9	Double Kick	Fighting	Physical	30	100	30	Normal	—
13	Poison Sting	Poison	Physical	15	100	35	Normal	—
19	Fury Swipes	Normal	Physical	18	80	15	Normal	○
21	Bite	Dark	Physical	60	100	25	Normal	○
25	Helping Hand	Normal	Status	—	—	20	1 Ally	—
31	Toxic Spikes	Poison	Status	—	—	20	2 Foes	—
33	Flatter	Dark	Status	—	100	15	Normal	—
37	Crunch	Dark	Physical	80	100	15	Normal	○
43	Captivate	Normal	Status	—	100	20	2 Foes	—
45	Poison Fang	Poison	Physical	50	100	15	Normal	○

● MOVE MANIAC

Name	Type	Kind	Pow.	Acc.	PP	Range	DA
Headbutt	Normal	Physical	70	100	15	Normal	○

● BP MOVES

Name	Type	Kind	Pow.	Acc.	PP	Range	DA
Snore	Normal	Special	40	100	15	Normal	—
Helping Hand	Normal	Status	—	—	20	1 Ally	—
Mud-Slap	Ground	Special	20	100	10	Normal	—
Super Fang	Normal	Physical	—	90	10	Normal	○

● TM & HM MOVES

No.	Name	Type	Kind	Pow.	Acc.	PP	Range	DA
TM03	Water Pulse	Water	Special	60	100	20	Normal	—
TM06	Toxic	Poison	Status	—	85	10	Normal	—
TM10	Hidden Power	Normal	Special	—	100	15	Normal	—
TM11	Sunny Day	Fire	Status	—	—	5	All	—
TM13	Ice Beam	Ice	Special	95	100	10	Normal	—
TM14	Blizzard	Ice	Special	120	70	5	2 Foes	—
TM17	Protect	Normal	Status	—	—	10	Self	—
TM18	Rain Dance	Water	Status	—	—	5	All	—
TM21	Frustration	Normal	Physical	—	100	20	Normal	○
TM23	Iron Tail	Steel	Physical	100	75	15	Normal	○
TM24	Thunderbolt	Electric	Special	95	100	15	Normal	—
TM25	Thunder	Electric	Special	120	70	10	Normal	—
TM27	Return	Normal	Physical	—	100	20	Normal	○
TM28	Dig	Ground	Physical	80	100	10	Normal	○
TM32	Double Team	Normal	Status	—	—	15	Self	—
TM34	Shock Wave	Electric	Special	60	—	20	Normal	—
TM36	Sludge Bomb	Poison	Special	90	100	10	Normal	—
TM40	Aerial Ace	Flying	Physical	60	—	20	Normal	○
TM42	Facade	Normal	Physical	70	100	20	Normal	○
TM43	Secret Power	Normal	Physical	70	100	20	Normal	○
TM44	Rest	Psychic	Status	—	—	10	Self	—
TM45	Attract	Normal	Status	—	100	15	Normal	—
TM46	Thief	Dark	Physical	40	100	10	Normal	○
TM58	Endure	Normal	Status	—	—	10	Self	—
TM65	Shadow Claw	Ghost	Physical	70	100	15	Normal	○
TM78	Captivate	Normal	Status	—	100	20	2 Foes	—
TM82	Sleep Talk	Normal	Status	—	—	10	Depends	—
TM83	Natural Gift	Normal	Physical	—	100	15	Normal	—
TM84	Poison Jab	Poison	Physical	80	100	20	Normal	○
TM87	Swagger	Normal	Status	—	90	15	Normal	—
TM90	Substitute	Normal	Status	—	—	10	Self	—
HM01	Cut	Normal	Physical	50	95	30	Normal	○
HM04	Strength	Normal	Physical	80	100	15	Normal	○
HM06	Rock Smash	Fighting	Physical	40	100	15	Normal	○

● EGG MOVES

Name	Type	Kind	Pow.	Acc.	PP	Range	DA
Supersonic	Normal	Status	—	55	20	Normal	—
Disable	Normal	Status	—	80	20	Normal	—
Take Down	Normal	Physical	90	85	20	Normal	○
Focus Energy	Normal	Status	—	—	30	Self	—
Charm	Normal	Status	—	100	20	Normal	—
Counter	Fighting	Physical	—	100	20	Normal	○
Beat Up	Dark	Physical	10	100	10	Normal	—
Pursuit	Dark	Physical	40	100	20	Normal	○
Skull Bash	Normal	Physical	100	100	15	Normal	○

● LEVEL-UP MOVES

Lv.	Name	Type	Kind	Pow.	Acc.	PP	Range	DA
1	Growl	Normal	Status	—	100	40	2 Foes	—
1	Scratch	Normal	Physical	40	100	35	Normal	O
7	Tail Whip	Normal	Status	—	100	30	2 Foes	—
9	Double Kick	Fighting	Physical	30	100	30	Normal	O
13	Poison Sting	Poison	Physical	15	100	35	Normal	O
20	Fury Swipes	Normal	Physical	18	80	15	Normal	O
23	Bite	Dark	Physical	60	100	25	Normal	O
28	Helping Hand	Normal	Status	—	—	20	1 Ally	—
35	Toxic Spikes	Poison	Status	—	—	20	2 Foes	—
38	Flatter	Dark	Status	—	100	15	Normal	—
43	Crunch	Dark	Physical	80	100	15	Normal	O
50	Captivate	Normal	Status	—	100	20	2 Foes	—
58	Poison Fang	Poison	Physical	50	100	15	Normal	O

● MOVE MANIAC

Name	Type	Kind	Pow.	Acc.	PP	Range	DA
Headbutt	Normal	Physical	70	100	15	Normal	O

● BP MOVES

Name	Type	Kind	Pow.	Acc.	PP	Range	DA
Snore	Normal	Special	40	100	15	Normal	—
Helping Hand	Normal	Status	—	—	20	1 Ally	—
Mud-Slap	Ground	Special	20	100	10	Normal	—
Super Fang	Normal	Physical	—	90	10	Normal	O

● TM & HM MOVES

No.	Name	Type	Kind	Pow.	Acc.	PP	Range	DA
TM03	Water Pulse	Water	Special	60	100	20	Normal	—
TM06	Toxic	Poison	Status	—	85	10	Normal	—
TM10	Hidden Power	Normal	Special	—	100	15	Normal	—
TM11	Sunny Day	Fire	Status	—	—	5	All	—
TM13	Ice Beam	Ice	Special	95	100	10	Normal	—
TM14	Blizzard	Ice	Special	120	70	5	2 Foes	—
TM17	Protect	Normal	Status	—	—	10	Self	—
TM18	Rain Dance	Water	Status	—	—	5	All	—
TM21	Frustration	Normal	Physical	—	100	20	Normal	O
TM23	Iron Tail	Steel	Physical	100	75	15	Normal	O
TM24	Thunderbolt	Electric	Special	95	100	15	Normal	—
TM25	Thunder	Electric	Special	120	70	10	Normal	—
TM27	Return	Normal	Physical	—	100	20	Normal	O
TM28	Dig	Ground	Physical	80	100	10	Normal	O
TM32	Double Team	Normal	Status	—	—	15	Self	—
TM34	Shock Wave	Electric	Special	60	—	20	Normal	—
TM36	Sludge Bomb	Poison	Special	90	100	10	Normal	—
TM40	Aerial Ace	Flying	Physical	60	—	20	Normal	O
TM42	Facade	Normal	Physical	70	100	20	Normal	O
TM43	Secret Power	Normal	Physical	70	100	20	Normal	O
TM44	Rest	Psychic	Status	—	—	10	Self	—
TM45	Attract	Normal	Status	—	100	15	Normal	—
TM46	Thief	Dark	Physical	40	100	10	Normal	O
TM58	Endure	Normal	Status	—	—	10	Self	—
TM65	Shadow Claw	Ghost	Physical	70	100	15	Normal	O
TM78	Captivate	Normal	Status	—	100	20	2 Foes	—
TM82	Sleep Talk	Normal	Status	—	—	10	Depends	—
TM83	Natural Gift	Normal	Physical	—	100	15	Normal	—
TM84	Poison Jab	Poison	Physical	80	100	20	Normal	O
TM87	Swagger	Normal	Status	—	90	15	Normal	—
TM90	Substitute	Normal	Status	—	—	10	Self	—
HM01	Cut	Normal	Physical	50	95	30	Normal	O
HM04	Strength	Normal	Physical	80	100	15	Normal	O
HM06	Rock Smash	Fighting	Physical	40	100	15	Normal	O

● No. 030 | Poison Pin Pokémon
Nidorina

Poison

- **SIZE COMPARISON**
- **HEIGHT:** 1'00"
- **WEIGHT:** 4.0 lbs.
- **ITEMS:** None

● **FEMALE FORM**

⊙ ABILITIES
- Poison Point
- Rivalry

⊙ STATS
- HP ●●●
- ATTACK ●●●
- DEFENSE ●●●
- SP. ATTACK ●●
- SP. DEFENSE ●●
- SPEED ●●●

⊙ EGG GROUPS
No Egg has ever been discovered

⊙ PERFORMANCE
SPEED ★★★☆	STAMINA ★★★☆
POWER ★★★☆	JUMP ★★★☆
SKILL ★★☆	

● MAIN WAYS TO OBTAIN

Pokémon HeartGold	Route 13
Pokémon SoulSilver	Route 13
Pokémon Diamond	Route 221 (use Poké Radar)
Pokémon Pearl	Route 221 (occasionally appears when you use Poké Radar)
Pokémon Platinum	Valor Lakefront (use Poké Radar)

Pokémon HeartGold	Pokémon SoulSilver
When feeding its young, it first chews the food into a paste, then spits it out for the offspring.	It has a calm and caring nature. Because its horn grows slowly, it prefers not to fight.

⊙ EVOLUTION

Nidoran♀ → (Lv. 16) → Nidorina → (Use Moon Stone) → Nidoqueen

No. 031 | Drill Pokémon
Nidoqueen

Poison | Ground

- **HEIGHT:** 4'03"
- **WEIGHT:** 132.3 lbs.
- **ITEMS:** None

● SIZE COMPARISON

● FEMALE FORM

⚙ ABILITIES
- Poison Point
- Rivalry

⚙ STATS
HP	●●●
ATTACK	●●●●
DEFENSE	●●●●
SP. ATTACK	●●●
SP. DEFENSE	●●●
SPEED	●●●

⚙ EGG GROUPS
No Egg has ever been discovered

⚙ PERFORMANCE
SPEED ★★☆	STAMINA ★★★★★
POWER ★★★★☆	JUMP ★★
SKILL ★★★	

● MAIN WAYS TO OBTAIN

Pokémon HeartGold	Use Moon Stone on Nidorina
Pokémon SoulSilver	Use Moon Stone on Nidorina
Pokémon Diamond	Use Moon Stone on Nidorina
Pokémon Pearl	Use Moon Stone on Nidorina
Pokémon Platinum	Use Moon Stone on Nidorina

Pokémon HeartGold	Pokémon SoulSilver
Its body is covered with needle-like scales. It never shows signs of shrinking from any attack.	It uses its scaly, rugged body to seal the entrance of its nest and protect its young from predators.

⚙ EVOLUTION

Nidoran♀ → Nidorina → (Use Moon Stone) → Nidoqueen
Lv. 16

● LEVEL-UP MOVES
Lv.	Name	Type	Kind	Pow.	Acc.	PP	Range	DA
1	Scratch	Normal	Physical	40	100	35	Normal	○
1	Tail Whip	Normal	Status	—	100	30	2 Foes	—
1	Double Kick	Fighting	Physical	30	100	30	Normal	○
1	Poison Sting	Poison	Physical	15	100	35	Normal	○
23	Body Slam	Normal	Physical	85	100	15	Normal	○
43	Earth Power	Ground	Special	90	100	10	Normal	—
58	Superpower	Fighting	Physical	120	100	5	Normal	○

● MOVE MANIAC
Name	Type	Kind	Pow.	Acc.	PP	Range	DA
Headbutt	Normal	Physical	70	100	15	Normal	○

● BP MOVES
Name	Type	Kind	Pow.	Acc.	PP	Range	DA
Fury Cutter	Bug	Physical	10	95	20	Normal	○
Icy Wind	Ice	Special	55	95	15	2 Foes	—
ThunderPunch	Electric	Physical	75	100	15	Normal	○
Fire Punch	Fire	Physical	75	100	15	Normal	○
Ice Punch	Ice	Physical	75	100	15	Normal	○
Snore	Normal	Special	40	100	15	Normal	—
Helping Hand	Normal	Status	—	—	20	1 Ally	—
Uproar	Normal	Special	50	100	10	1 Random	—
Mud-Slap	Ground	Special	20	100	10	Normal	—
Superpower	Fighting	Physical	120	100	5	Normal	○
Aqua Tail	Water	Physical	90	90	10	Normal	○
Outrage	Dragon	Physical	120	100	15	1 Random	○
Earth Power	Ground	Special	90	100	10	Normal	—
Super Fang	Normal	Physical	—	90	10	Normal	○

● TM & HM MOVES
No.	Name	Type	Kind	Pow.	Acc.	PP	Range	DA
TM01	Focus Punch	Fighting	Physical	150	100	20	Normal	○
TM03	Water Pulse	Water	Special	60	100	20	Normal	—
TM05	Roar	Normal	Status	—	100	20	Normal	—
TM06	Toxic	Poison	Status	—	85	10	Normal	—
TM10	Hidden Power	Normal	Special	—	100	15	Normal	—
TM11	Sunny Day	Fire	Status	—	—	5	All	—
TM12	Taunt	Dark	Status	—	100	20	Normal	—
TM13	Ice Beam	Ice	Special	95	100	10	Normal	—
TM14	Blizzard	Ice	Special	120	100	5	2 Foes	—
TM15	Hyper Beam	Normal	Special	150	90	5	Normal	—
TM17	Protect	Normal	Status	—	—	10	Self	—
TM18	Rain Dance	Water	Status	—	—	5	All	—
TM21	Frustration	Normal	Physical	—	100	20	Normal	○
TM23	Iron Tail	Steel	Physical	100	75	15	Normal	○
TM24	Thunderbolt	Electric	Special	95	100	15	Normal	—
TM25	Thunder	Electric	Special	120	70	10	Normal	—
TM26	Earthquake	Ground	Physical	100	100	10	2 Foes/1 Ally	—
TM27	Return	Normal	Physical	—	100	20	Normal	○
TM28	Dig	Ground	Physical	80	100	10	Normal	○
TM30	Shadow Ball	Ghost	Special	80	100	15	Normal	—
TM31	Brick Break	Fighting	Physical	75	100	15	Normal	○
TM32	Double Team	Normal	Status	—	—	15	Self	—
TM34	Shock Wave	Electric	Special	60	—	20	Normal	—
TM35	Flamethrower	Fire	Special	95	100	15	Normal	—
TM36	Sludge Bomb	Poison	Special	90	100	10	Normal	—
TM37	Sandstorm	Rock	Status	—	—	10	All	—
TM38	Fire Blast	Fire	Special	120	85	5	Normal	—
TM39	Rock Tomb	Rock	Physical	50	80	10	Normal	○
TM40	Aerial Ace	Flying	Physical	60	—	20	Normal	○
TM41	Torment	Dark	Status	—	100	15	Normal	—
TM42	Facade	Normal	Physical	70	100	20	Normal	○
TM43	Secret Power	Normal	Physical	70	100	20	Normal	—
TM44	Rest	Psychic	Status	—	—	10	Self	—
TM45	Attract	Normal	Status	—	100	15	Normal	—
TM46	Thief	Dark	Physical	40	100	10	Normal	○
TM52	Focus Blast	Fighting	Special	120	70	5	Normal	—
TM56	Fling	Dark	Physical	—	100	10	Normal	○
TM58	Endure	Normal	Status	—	—	10	Self	—
TM59	Dragon Pulse	Dragon	Special	90	100	10	Normal	—
TM65	Shadow Claw	Ghost	Physical	70	100	15	Normal	○
TM68	Giga Impact	Normal	Physical	150	90	5	Normal	○
TM71	Stone Edge	Rock	Physical	100	80	5	Normal	○
TM72	Avalanche	Ice	Physical	60	100	10	Normal	○
TM76	Stealth Rock	Rock	Status	—	—	20	2 Foes	—
TM78	Captivate	Normal	Status	—	100	20	2 Foes	—
TM80	Rock Slide	Rock	Physical	75	90	10	2 Foes	—
TM82	Sleep Talk	Normal	Status	—	—	10	Depends	—
TM83	Natural Gift	Normal	Physical	—	100	15	Normal	○
TM84	Poison Jab	Poison	Physical	80	100	20	Normal	○
TM87	Swagger	Normal	Status	—	90	15	Normal	—
TM90	Substitute	Normal	Status	—	—	10	Self	—
HM01	Cut	Normal	Physical	50	95	30	Normal	○
HM03	Surf	Water	Special	95	100	15	2 Foes/1 Ally	—
HM04	Strength	Normal	Physical	80	100	15	Normal	○
HM05	Whirlpool	Water	Special	15	70	15	Normal	—
HM06	Rock Smash	Fighting	Physical	40	100	15	Normal	○
HM08	Rock Climb	Normal	Physical	90	85	20	Normal	○

● LEVEL-UP MOVES

Lv.	Name	Type	Kind	Pow.	Acc.	PP	Range	DA
1	Leer	Normal	Status	—	100	30	2 Foes	—
1	Peck	Flying	Physical	35	100	35	Normal	○
7	Focus Energy	Normal	Status	—	—	30	Self	—
9	Double Kick	Fighting	Physical	30	100	30	Normal	○
13	Poison Sting	Poison	Physical	15	100	35	Normal	—
19	Fury Attack	Normal	Physical	15	85	20	Normal	—
21	Horn Attack	Normal	Physical	65	100	25	Normal	○
25	Helping Hand	Normal	Status	—	—	20	1 Ally	—
31	Toxic Spikes	Poison	Status	—	—	20	2 Foes	—
33	Flatter	Dark	Status	—	100	15	Normal	—
37	Poison Jab	Poison	Physical	80	100	20	Normal	○
43	Captivate	Normal	Status	—	100	20	2 Foes	—
45	Horn Drill	Normal	Physical	—	30	5	Normal	○

● MOVE MANIAC

Name	Type	Kind	Pow.	Acc.	PP	Range	DA
Headbutt	Normal	Physical	70	100	15	Normal	○

● BP MOVES

Name	Type	Kind	Pow.	Acc.	PP	Range	DA
Sucker Punch	Dark	Physical	80	100	5	Normal	○
Snore	Normal	Special	40	100	15	Normal	—
Helping Hand	Normal	Status	—	—	20	1 Ally	—
Mud-Slap	Ground	Special	20	100	10	Normal	—
Super Fang	Normal	Physical	—	90	10	Normal	○

● TM & HM MOVES

No.	Name	Type	Kind	Pow.	Acc.	PP	Range	DA
TM03	Water Pulse	Water	Special	60	100	20	Normal	—
TM06	Toxic	Poison	Status	—	85	10	Normal	—
TM10	Hidden Power	Normal	Special	—	100	15	Normal	—
TM11	Sunny Day	Fire	Status	—	—	5	All	—
TM13	Ice Beam	Ice	Special	95	100	10	Normal	—
TM14	Blizzard	Ice	Special	120	70	5	2 Foes	—
TM17	Protect	Normal	Status	—	—	10	Self	—
TM18	Rain Dance	Water	Status	—	—	5	All	—
TM21	Frustration	Normal	Physical	—	100	20	Normal	○
TM23	Iron Tail	Steel	Physical	100	75	15	Normal	○
TM24	Thunderbolt	Electric	Special	95	100	15	Normal	—
TM25	Thunder	Electric	Special	120	70	10	Normal	—
TM27	Return	Normal	Physical	—	100	20	Normal	○
TM28	Dig	Ground	Physical	80	100	10	Normal	○
TM32	Double Team	Normal	Status	—	—	15	Self	—
TM34	Shock Wave	Electric	Special	60	—	20	Normal	—
TM36	Sludge Bomb	Poison	Special	90	100	10	Normal	—
TM42	Facade	Normal	Physical	70	100	20	Normal	○
TM43	Secret Power	Normal	Physical	70	100	20	Normal	○
TM44	Rest	Psychic	Status	—	—	10	Self	—
TM45	Attract	Normal	Status	—	100	15	Normal	—
TM46	Thief	Dark	Physical	40	100	10	Normal	○
TM58	Endure	Normal	Status	—	—	10	Self	—
TM65	Shadow Claw	Ghost	Physical	70	100	15	Normal	○
TM78	Captivate	Normal	Status	—	100	20	2 Foes	—
TM82	Sleep Talk	Normal	Status	—	—	10	Depends	—
TM83	Natural Gift	Normal	Physical	—	100	15	Normal	—
TM84	Poison Jab	Poison	Physical	80	100	20	Normal	○
TM87	Swagger	Normal	Status	—	90	15	Normal	—
TM90	Substitute	Normal	Status	—	—	10	Self	—
HM01	Cut	Normal	Physical	50	95	30	Normal	○
HM04	Strength	Normal	Physical	80	100	15	Normal	○
HM06	Rock Smash	Fighting	Physical	40	100	15	Normal	○

● EGG MOVES

Name	Type	Kind	Pow.	Acc.	PP	Range	DA
Counter	Fighting	Physical	—	100	20	Self	○
Disable	Normal	Status	—	80	20	Normal	—
Supersonic	Normal	Status	—	55	20	Normal	—
Take Down	Normal	Physical	90	85	20	Normal	○
Amnesia	Psychic	Status	—	—	20	Self	—
Confusion	Psychic	Special	50	100	25	Normal	—
Beat Up	Dark	Physical	10	100	10	Normal	—
Sucker Punch	Dark	Physical	80	100	5	Normal	○
Head Smash	Rock	Physical	150	80	5	Normal	○

● No. 032 | Poison Point Pokémon
Nidoran♂

`Poison`

- ● HEIGHT: 1'08"
- ● WEIGHT: 19.8 lbs.
- ● ITEMS: None

● SIZE COMPARISON

● MALE FORM

● ABILITIES
- ● Poison Point
- ● Rivalry

● STATS
- HP ●●
- ATTACK ●●
- DEFENSE ●●
- SP. ATTACK ●●
- SP. DEFENSE ●●
- SPEED ●●

● EGG GROUPS
Monster

Field

● PERFORMANCE
- SPEED ★★★★☆
- POWER ★★☆☆
- SKILL ★★☆
- STAMINA ★★☆
- JUMP ★★☆

● MAIN WAYS TO OBTAIN

Pokémon HeartGold	Route 35
Pokémon SoulSilver	Route 35
Pokémon Diamond	Route 201 (occasionally appears when you use Poké Radar)
Pokémon Pearl	Route 201 (use Poké Radar)
Pokémon Platinum	Route 201 (use Poké Radar)

Pokémon HeartGold

It is small, but its horn is filled with poison. It charges then stabs with the horn to inject poison.

Pokémon SoulSilver

It raises its big ears to check its surroundings. It will strike first if it senses any danger.

● EVOLUTION

Lv. 16 → Use Moon Stone →

Nidoran♂ → Nidorino → Nidoking

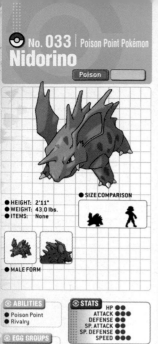

● No. 033 | Poison Point Pokémon
Nidorino

`Poison`

- ● HEIGHT: 2'11"
- ● WEIGHT: 43.0 lbs.
- ● ITEMS: None

● SIZE COMPARISON

● MALE FORM

● ABILITIES
- ● Poison Point
- ● Rivalry

● STATS
HP	●●
ATTACK	●●●
DEFENSE	●●●
SP. ATTACK	●●
SP. DEFENSE	●●
SPEED	●●●

● EGG GROUPS
Monster

Field

● PERFORMANCE
SPEED ★★★☆☆
POWER ★★★☆
SKILL ★★☆

STAMINA ★★★☆
JUMP ★★☆

● MAIN WAYS TO OBTAIN

Pokémon HeartGold — Route 13

Pokémon SoulSilver — Route 13

Pokémon Diamond — Route 221 (occasionally appears when you use Poké Radar)

Pokémon Pearl — Route 221 (use Poké Radar)

Pokémon Platinum — Valor Lakefront (use Poké Radar)

Pokémon HeartGold
It raises its big ears to check its surroundings. If it senses anything, it attacks immediately.

Pokémon SoulSilver
Quick to anger, it stabs enemies with its horn to inject a powerful poison when it becomes agitated.

● EVOLUTION

Nidoran♂ — Lv. 16 — Nidorino — Use Moon Stone — Nidoking

● LEVEL-UP MOVES
Lv.	Name	Type	Kind	Pow.	Acc.	PP	Range	DA
1	Leer	Normal	Status	—	100	30	2 Foes	—
1	Peck	Flying	Physical	35	100	35	Normal	○
7	Focus Energy	Normal	Status	—	—	30	Self	—
9	Double Kick	Fighting	Physical	30	100	30	Normal	○
13	Poison Sting	Poison	Physical	15	100	35	Normal	—
20	Fury Attack	Normal	Physical	15	85	20	Normal	○
23	Horn Attack	Normal	Physical	65	100	25	Normal	○
28	Helping Hand	Normal	Status	—	—	20	1 Ally	—
35	Toxic Spikes	Poison	Status	—	—	20	2 Foes	—
38	Flatter	Dark	Status	—	100	15	Normal	—
43	Poison Jab	Poison	Physical	80	100	20	Normal	○
50	Captivate	Normal	Status	—	100	20	2 Foes	—
58	Horn Drill	Normal	Physical	—	30	5	Normal	○

● MOVE MANIAC
Name	Type	Kind	Pow.	Acc.	PP	Range	DA
Headbutt	Normal	Physical	70	100	15	Normal	○

● BP MOVES
Name	Type	Kind	Pow.	Acc.	PP	Range	DA
Sucker Punch	Dark	Physical	80	100	5	Normal	○
Snore	Normal	Special	40	100	15	Normal	—
Helping Hand	Normal	Status	—	—	20	1 Ally	—
Mud-Slap	Ground	Special	20	100	10	Normal	—
Super Fang	Normal	Physical	—	90	10	Normal	○

● TM & HM MOVES
No.	Name	Type	Kind	Pow.	Acc.	PP	Range	DA
TM03	Water Pulse	Water	Special	60	100	20	Normal	—
TM06	Toxic	Poison	Status	—	85	10	Normal	—
TM10	Hidden Power	Normal	Special	—	100	15	Normal	—
TM11	Sunny Day	Fire	Status	—	—	5	All	—
TM13	Ice Beam	Ice	Special	95	100	10	Normal	—
TM14	Blizzard	Ice	Special	120	70	5	2 Foes	—
TM17	Protect	Normal	Status	—	—	10	Self	—
TM18	Rain Dance	Water	Status	—	—	5	All	—
TM21	Frustration	Normal	Physical	—	100	20	Normal	○
TM23	Iron Tail	Steel	Physical	100	75	15	Normal	○
TM24	Thunderbolt	Electric	Special	95	100	15	Normal	—
TM25	Thunder	Electric	Special	120	70	10	Normal	—
TM27	Return	Normal	Physical	—	100	20	Normal	○
TM28	Dig	Ground	Physical	80	100	10	Normal	○
TM32	Double Team	Normal	Status	—	—	15	Self	—
TM34	Shock Wave	Electric	Special	60	—	20	Normal	—
TM36	Sludge Bomb	Poison	Special	90	100	10	Normal	—
TM42	Facade	Normal	Physical	70	100	20	Normal	○
TM43	Secret Power	Normal	Physical	70	100	20	Normal	○
TM44	Rest	Psychic	Status	—	—	10	Self	—
TM45	Attract	Normal	Status	—	100	15	Normal	—
TM46	Thief	Dark	Physical	40	100	10	Normal	○
TM58	Endure	Normal	Status	—	—	10	Self	—
TM65	Shadow Claw	Ghost	Physical	70	100	15	Normal	○
TM78	Captivate	Normal	Status	—	100	20	2 Foes	—
TM82	Sleep Talk	Normal	Status	—	—	10	Depends	—
TM83	Natural Gift	Normal	Physical	—	100	15	Normal	—
TM84	Poison Jab	Poison	Physical	80	100	20	Normal	○
TM87	Swagger	Normal	Status	—	90	15	Normal	—
TM90	Substitute	Normal	Status	—	—	10	Self	—
HM01	Cut	Normal	Physical	50	95	30	Normal	○
HM04	Strength	Normal	Physical	80	100	15	Normal	○
HM06	Rock Smash	Fighting	Physical	40	100	15	Normal	○

LEVEL-UP MOVES

Lv.	Name	Type	Kind	Pow.	Acc.	PP	Range	DA
1	Peck	Flying	Physical	35	100	35	Normal	○
1	Focus Energy	Normal	Status	—	—	30	Self	—
1	Double Kick	Fighting	Physical	30	100	30	Normal	○
1	Poison Sting	Poison	Physical	15	100	35	Normal	○
23	Thrash	Normal	Physical	90	100	20	1 Random	○
43	Earth Power	Ground	Special	90	100	10	Normal	—
58	Megahorn	Bug	Physical	120	85	10	Normal	○

MOVE MANIAC

Name	Type	Kind	Pow.	Acc.	PP	Range	DA
Headbutt	Normal	Physical	70	100	15	Normal	○

BP MOVES

Name	Type	Kind	Pow.	Acc.	PP	Range	DA
Fury Cutter	Bug	Physical	10	95	20	Normal	○
Icy Wind	Ice	Special	55	95	15	2 Foes	○
ThunderPunch	Electric	Physical	75	100	15	Normal	○
Fire Punch	Fire	Physical	75	100	15	Normal	○
Ice Punch	Ice	Physical	75	100	15	Normal	○
Sucker Punch	Dark	Physical	80	100	5	Normal	○
Snore	Normal	Special	40	100	15	Normal	—
Helping Hand	Normal	Status	—	—	20	1 Ally	—
Uproar	Normal	Special	50	100	10	1 Random	—
Mud-Slap	Ground	Special	20	100	10	Normal	—
Superpower	Fighting	Physical	120	100	5	Normal	○
Aqua Tail	Water	Physical	90	90	10	Normal	○
Outrage	Dragon	Physical	120	100	15	1 Random	○
Earth Power	Ground	Special	90	100	10	Normal	—
Super Fang	Normal	Physical	—	90	10	Normal	—

TM & HM MOVES

No.	Name	Type	Kind	Pow.	Acc.	PP	Range	DA
TM01	Focus Punch	Fighting	Physical	150	100	20	Normal	○
TM03	Water Pulse	Water	Special	60	100	20	Normal	—
TM05	Roar	Normal	Status	—	100	20	Normal	—
TM06	Toxic	Poison	Status	—	85	10	Normal	—
TM10	Hidden Power	Normal	Special	—	100	15	Normal	—
TM11	Sunny Day	Fire	Status	—	—	5	All	—
TM12	Taunt	Dark	Status	—	100	20	Normal	—
TM13	Ice Beam	Ice	Special	95	100	10	Normal	—
TM14	Blizzard	Ice	Special	120	70	5	2 Foes	—
TM15	Hyper Beam	Normal	Special	150	90	5	Normal	—
TM17	Protect	Normal	Status	—	—	10	Self	—
TM18	Rain Dance	Water	Status	—	—	5	All	—
TM21	Frustration	Normal	Physical	—	100	20	Normal	○
TM23	Iron Tail	Steel	Physical	100	75	15	Normal	○
TM24	Thunderbolt	Electric	Special	95	100	15	Normal	—
TM25	Thunder	Electric	Special	120	70	10	Normal	—
TM26	Earthquake	Ground	Physical	100	100	10	2 Foes/1 Ally	○
TM27	Return	Normal	Physical	—	100	20	Normal	○
TM28	Dig	Ground	Physical	80	100	10	Normal	○
TM30	Shadow Ball	Ghost	Special	80	100	15	Normal	—
TM31	Brick Break	Fighting	Physical	75	100	15	Normal	○
TM32	Double Team	Normal	Status	—	—	15	Self	—
TM34	Shock Wave	Electric	Special	60	—	20	Normal	—
TM35	Flamethrower	Fire	Special	95	100	15	Normal	—
TM36	Sludge Bomb	Poison	Special	90	100	10	Normal	—
TM37	Sandstorm	Rock	Status	—	—	10	All	—
TM38	Fire Blast	Fire	Special	120	85	5	Normal	—
TM39	Rock Tomb	Rock	Physical	50	80	10	Normal	○
TM41	Torment	Dark	Status	—	100	15	Normal	—
TM42	Facade	Normal	Physical	70	100	20	Normal	○
TM43	Secret Power	Normal	Physical	70	100	20	Normal	—
TM44	Rest	Psychic	Status	—	—	10	Self	—
TM45	Attract	Normal	Status	—	100	15	Normal	—
TM46	Thief	Dark	Physical	40	100	10	Normal	○
TM52	Focus Blast	Fighting	Special	120	70	5	Normal	—
TM56	Fling	Dark	Physical	—	100	10	Normal	—
TM58	Endure	Normal	Status	—	—	10	Self	—
TM59	Dragon Pulse	Dragon	Special	90	100	10	Normal	—
TM65	Shadow Claw	Ghost	Physical	70	100	15	Normal	○
TM68	Giga Impact	Normal	Physical	150	90	5	Normal	○
TM71	Stone Edge	Rock	Physical	100	80	5	Normal	—
TM72	Avalanche	Ice	Physical	60	100	10	Normal	○
TM76	Stealth Rock	Rock	Status	—	—	20	2 Foes	—
TM78	Captivate	Normal	Status	—	100	20	2 Foes	—
TM80	Rock Slide	Rock	Physical	75	90	10	2 Foes	—
TM82	Sleep Talk	Normal	Status	—	—	10	Depends	—
TM83	Natural Gift	Normal	Physical	—	100	15	Normal	—
TM84	Poison Jab	Poison	Physical	80	100	20	Normal	○
TM87	Swagger	Normal	Status	—	90	15	Normal	—
TM90	Substitute	Normal	Status	—	—	10	Self	—
HM01	Cut	Normal	Physical	50	95	30	Normal	○
HM03	Surf	Water	Special	95	100	15	2 Foes/1 Ally	—
HM04	Strength	Normal	Physical	80	100	15	Normal	○
HM05	Whirlpool	Water	Special	15	70	15	Normal	—
HM06	Rock Smash	Fighting	Physical	40	100	15	Normal	○
HM08	Rock Climb	Normal	Physical	90	85	20	Normal	○

◉ No. 034 | Drill Pokémon
Nidoking

Poison **Ground**

● SIZE COMPARISON

● HEIGHT: 4'07"
● WEIGHT: 136.7 lbs.
● ITEMS: None

● MALE FORM

⊘ ABILITIES
● Poison Point
● Rivalry

⊘ STATS
HP	●●●
ATTACK	●●●●
DEFENSE	●●●●
SP. ATTACK	●●●●
SP. DEFENSE	●●●●
SPEED	●●●●

⊘ EGG GROUPS
Monster
Field

⊘ PERFORMANCE
SPEED ★★☆   STAMINA ★★★☆
POWER ★★★★★   JUMP ★★
SKILL ★★★

● MAIN WAYS TO OBTAIN

Pokémon HeartGold	Use Moon Stone on Nidorino
Pokémon SoulSilver	Use Moon Stone on Nidorino
Pokémon Diamond	Use Moon Stone on Nidorino
Pokémon Pearl	Use Moon Stone on Nidorino
Pokémon Platinum	Use Moon Stone on Nidorino

Pokémon HeartGold	**Pokémon SoulSilver**
It swings its big tail around during battle. If its foe flinches, it will charge with its sturdy body.	Its tail is thick and powerful. If it binds an enemy, it can render the victim helpless quite easily.

⊘ EVOLUTION

Nidoran♂ → Nidorino → (Use Moon Stone) → Nidoking

Lv. 16

No. 035 | Fairy Pokémon
Clefairy

`Normal`

- **HEIGHT:** 2'00"
- **WEIGHT:** 16.5 lbs.
- **ITEMS:** Leppa Berry
  Moon Stone

● SIZE COMPARISON

● MALE/FEMALE HAVE SAME FORM

⊕ ABILITIES
- Cute Charm
- Magic Guard

⊕ STATS
HP	●●●
ATTACK	●●
DEFENSE	●●
SP. ATTACK	●●●
SP. DEFENSE	●●●
SPEED	●●

⊕ EGG GROUPS
Fairy

⊕ PERFORMANCE
SPEED ★★★★☆   STAMINA ★★☆☆
POWER ★☆☆☆   JUMP ★★☆
SKILL ★★★☆☆

● MAIN WAYS TO OBTAIN

Pokémon HeartGold	Mt. Moon
Pokémon SoulSilver	Mt. Moon
Pokémon Diamond	Mt. Coronet 2F, 3F
Pokémon Pearl	Mt. Coronet 2F, 3F
Pokémon Platinum	Mt. Coronet (morning and night only)

Pokémon HeartGold
The moonlight that it stores in the wings on its back apparently gives it the ability to float in midair.

Pokémon SoulSilver
Its adorable behavior and cry make it highly popular. However, this cute Pokémon is rarely found.

⊕ EVOLUTION

Cleffa — Level up with high friendship → Clefairy — Use Moon Stone → Clefable

● LEVEL-UP MOVES

Lv.	Name	Type	Kind	Pow.	Acc.	PP	Range	DA
1	Pound	Normal	Physical	40	100	35	Normal	O
1	Growl	Normal	Status	—	100	40	2 Foes	—
4	Encore	Normal	Status	—	100	5	Normal	—
7	Sing	Normal	Status	—	55	15	Normal	—
10	DoubleSlap	Normal	Physical	15	85	10	Normal	O
13	Defense Curl	Normal	Status	—	—	40	Self	—
16	Follow Me	Normal	Status	—	—	20	Self	—
19	Minimize	Normal	Status	—	—	20	Self	—
22	Wake-Up Slap	Fighting	Physical	60	100	10	Normal	O
25	Cosmic Power	Psychic	Status	—	—	20	Self	—
28	Lucky Chant	Normal	Status	—	—	30	2 Allies	—
31	Metronome	Normal	Status	—	—	10	Depends	—
34	Gravity	Psychic	Status	—	—	5	All	—
37	Moonlight	Normal	Status	—	—	5	Self	—
40	Light Screen	Psychic	Status	—	—	30	2 Allies	—
43	Meteor Mash	Steel	Physical	100	85	10	Normal	O
46	Healing Wish	Psychic	Status	—	—	10	Self	—

● MOVE MANIAC

Name	Type	Kind	Pow.	Acc.	PP	Range	DA
Headbutt	Normal	Physical	70	100	15	Normal	O

● BP MOVES

Name	Type	Kind	Pow.	Acc.	PP	Range	DA
Icy Wind	Ice	Special	55	95	15	2 Foes	—
ThunderPunch	Electric	Physical	75	100	15	Normal	O
Fire Punch	Fire	Physical	75	100	15	Normal	O
Ice Punch	Ice	Physical	75	100	15	Normal	O
Zen Headbutt	Psychic	Physical	80	90	15	Normal	O
Trick	Psychic	Status	—	100	10	Normal	—
Knock Off	Dark	Physical	20	100	20	Normal	O
Snore	Normal	Special	40	100	15	Normal	—
Helping Hand	Normal	Status	—	—	20	1 Ally	—
Last Resort	Normal	Physical	130	100	5	Normal	O
Gravity	Psychic	Status	—	—	5	All	—
Magic Coat	Psychic	Status	—	—	15	Self	—
Role Play	Psychic	Status	—	—	10	Normal	—
Heal Bell	Normal	Status	—	—	5	All Allies	—
Mud-Slap	Ground	Special	20	100	10	Normal	O
Rollout	Rock	Physical	30	90	20	Normal	O
Endeavor	Normal	Physical	—	100	5	Normal	O
Signal Beam	Bug	Special	75	100	15	Normal	O
Bounce	Flying	Physical	85	85	5	Normal	O

● TM & HM MOVES

No.	Name	Type	Kind	Pow.	Acc.	PP	Range	DA
TM01	Focus Punch	Fighting	Physical	150	100	20	Normal	O
TM03	Water Pulse	Water	Special	60	100	20	Normal	—
TM04	Calm Mind	Psychic	Status	—	—	20	Self	—
TM06	Toxic	Poison	Status	—	85	10	Normal	—
TM10	Hidden Power	Normal	Special	—	100	15	Normal	—
TM11	Sunny Day	Fire	Status	—	—	5	All	—
TM13	Ice Beam	Ice	Special	95	100	10	Normal	—
TM14	Blizzard	Ice	Special	120	70	5	2 Foes	—
TM16	Light Screen	Psychic	Status	—	—	30	2 Allies	—
TM17	Protect	Normal	Status	—	—	10	Self	—
TM18	Rain Dance	Water	Status	—	—	5	All	—
TM20	Safeguard	Normal	Status	—	—	25	2 Allies	—
TM21	Frustration	Normal	Physical	—	100	20	Normal	O
TM22	SolarBeam	Grass	Special	120	100	10	Normal	—
TM23	Iron Tail	Steel	Physical	100	75	15	Normal	O
TM24	Thunderbolt	Electric	Special	95	100	15	Normal	—
TM25	Thunder	Electric	Special	120	70	10	Normal	—
TM27	Return	Normal	Physical	—	100	20	Normal	O
TM28	Dig	Ground	Physical	80	100	10	Normal	O
TM29	Psychic	Psychic	Special	90	100	10	Normal	—
TM30	Shadow Ball	Ghost	Special	80	100	15	Normal	—
TM31	Brick Break	Fighting	Physical	75	100	15	Normal	O
TM32	Double Team	Normal	Status	—	—	15	Self	—
TM33	Reflect	Psychic	Status	—	—	20	2 Allies	—
TM34	Shock Wave	Electric	Special	60	—	20	Normal	—
TM35	Flamethrower	Fire	Special	95	100	15	Normal	—
TM38	Fire Blast	Fire	Special	120	85	5	Normal	—
TM42	Facade	Normal	Physical	70	100	20	Normal	O
TM43	Secret Power	Normal	Physical	70	100	20	Normal	O
TM44	Rest	Psychic	Status	—	—	10	Self	—
TM45	Attract	Normal	Status	—	100	15	Normal	—
TM56	Fling	Dark	Physical	—	100	10	Normal	O
TM57	Charge Beam	Electric	Special	50	90	10	Normal	—
TM58	Endure	Normal	Status	—	—	10	Self	—
TM60	Drain Punch	Fighting	Physical	60	100	5	Normal	O
TM67	Recycle	Normal	Status	—	—	10	Self	—
TM70	Flash	Normal	Status	—	100	20	Normal	—
TM73	Thunder Wave	Electric	Status	—	100	20	Normal	—
TM76	Stealth Rock	Rock	Status	—	—	20	2 Foes	—
TM77	Psych Up	Normal	Status	—	—	10	Normal	—
TM78	Captivate	Normal	Status	—	100	20	2 Foes	—
TM82	Sleep Talk	Normal	Status	—	—	10	Depends	—
TM83	Natural Gift	Normal	Physical	—	100	15	Normal	O
TM85	Dream Eater	Psychic	Special	100	100	15	Normal	—
TM86	Grass Knot	Grass	Special	—	100	20	Normal	O
TM87	Swagger	Normal	Status	—	90	15	Normal	—
TM90	Substitute	Normal	Status	—	—	10	Self	—
HM04	Strength	Normal	Physical	80	100	15	Normal	O
HM06	Rock Smash	Fighting	Physical	40	100	15	Normal	O

● LEVEL-UP MOVES

Lv.	Name	Type	Kind	Pow.	Acc.	PP	Range	DA
1	Sing	Normal	Status	—	55	15	Normal	—
1	DoubleSlap	Normal	Physical	15	85	10	Normal	○
1	Minimize	Normal	Status	—	—	20	Self	—
1	Metronome	Normal	Status	—	—	10	Depends	—

● MOVE MANIAC

Name	Type	Kind	Pow.	Acc.	PP	Range	DA
Headbutt	Normal	Physical	70	100	15	Normal	○

● BP MOVES

Name	Type	Kind	Pow.	Acc.	PP	Range	DA
Icy Wind	Ice	Special	55	95	15	2 Foes	—
ThunderPunch	Electric	Physical	75	100	15	Normal	○
Fire Punch	Fire	Physical	75	100	15	Normal	○
Ice Punch	Ice	Physical	75	100	15	Normal	○
Zen Headbutt	Psychic	Physical	80	90	15	Normal	○
Trick	Psychic	Status	—	100	10	Normal	—
Knock Off	Dark	Physical	20	100	20	Normal	○
Snore	Normal	Special	40	100	15	Normal	—
Helping Hand	Normal	Status	—	—	20	1 Ally	—
Last Resort	Normal	Physical	130	100	5	Normal	○
Gravity	Psychic	Status	—	—	5	All	—
Magic Coat	Psychic	Status	—	—	15	Self	—
Role Play	Psychic	Status	—	—	10	Normal	—
Heal Bell	Normal	Status	—	—	5	All Allies	—
Mud-Slap	Ground	Special	20	100	10	Normal	○
Rollout	Rock	Physical	30	90	20	Normal	○
Endeavor	Normal	Physical	—	100	5	Normal	—
Signal Beam	Bug	Special	75	100	15	Normal	—
Bounce	Flying	Physical	85	85	5	Normal	○

● TM & HM MOVES

No.	Name	Type	Kind	Pow.	Acc.	PP	Range	DA
TM01	Focus Punch	Fighting	Physical	150	100	20	Normal	○
TM03	Water Pulse	Water	Special	60	100	20	Normal	—
TM04	Calm Mind	Psychic	Status	—	—	20	Self	—
TM06	Toxic	Poison	Status	—	85	10	Normal	—
TM10	Hidden Power	Normal	Special	—	100	15	Normal	—
TM11	Sunny Day	Fire	Status	—	—	5	All	—
TM13	Ice Beam	Ice	Special	95	100	10	Normal	—
TM14	Blizzard	Ice	Special	120	70	5	2 Foes	—
TM15	Hyper Beam	Normal	Special	150	90	5	Normal	—
TM16	Light Screen	Psychic	Status	—	—	30	2 Allies	—
TM17	Protect	Normal	Status	—	—	10	Self	—
TM18	Rain Dance	Water	Status	—	—	5	All	—
TM20	Safeguard	Normal	Status	—	—	25	2 Allies	—
TM21	Frustration	Normal	Physical	—	100	20	Normal	○
TM22	SolarBeam	Grass	Special	120	100	10	Normal	—
TM23	Iron Tail	Steel	Physical	100	75	15	Normal	○
TM24	Thunderbolt	Electric	Special	95	100	15	Normal	—
TM25	Thunder	Electric	Special	120	70	10	Normal	—
TM27	Return	Normal	Physical	—	100	20	Normal	○
TM28	Dig	Ground	Physical	80	100	10	Normal	○
TM29	Psychic	Psychic	Special	90	100	10	Normal	—
TM30	Shadow Ball	Ghost	Special	80	100	15	Normal	—
TM31	Brick Break	Fighting	Physical	75	100	15	Normal	○
TM32	Double Team	Normal	Status	—	—	15	Self	—
TM33	Reflect	Psychic	Status	—	—	20	2 Allies	—
TM34	Shock Wave	Electric	Special	60	—	20	Normal	—
TM35	Flamethrower	Fire	Special	95	100	15	Normal	—
TM38	Fire Blast	Fire	Special	120	85	5	Normal	—
TM42	Facade	Normal	Physical	70	100	20	Normal	○
TM43	Secret Power	Normal	Physical	70	100	20	Normal	—
TM44	Rest	Psychic	Status	—	—	10	Self	—
TM45	Attract	Normal	Status	—	100	15	Normal	—
TM49	Snatch	Dark	Status	—	—	10	Depends	—
TM52	Focus Blast	Fighting	Special	120	70	5	Normal	—
TM56	Fling	Dark	Physical	—	100	10	Normal	○
TM57	Charge Beam	Electric	Special	50	90	10	Normal	—
TM58	Endure	Normal	Status	—	—	10	Self	—
TM60	Drain Punch	Fighting	Physical	60	100	5	Normal	○
TM67	Recycle	Normal	Status	—	—	10	Self	—
TM68	Giga Impact	Normal	Physical	150	90	5	Normal	○
TM70	Flash	Normal	Status	—	100	20	Normal	—
TM73	Thunder Wave	Electric	Status	—	100	20	Normal	—
TM76	Stealth Rock	Rock	Status	—	—	20	2 Foes	—
TM77	Psych Up	Normal	Status	—	—	10	Normal	—
TM78	Captivate	Normal	Status	—	100	20	2 Foes	—
TM82	Sleep Talk	Normal	Status	—	—	10	Depends	—
TM83	Natural Gift	Normal	Physical	—	100	15	Normal	—
TM85	Dream Eater	Psychic	Special	100	100	15	Normal	—
TM86	Grass Knot	Grass	Special	—	100	20	Normal	○
TM87	Swagger	Normal	Status	—	90	15	Normal	—
TM90	Substitute	Normal	Status	—	—	10	Self	—
HM04	Strength	Normal	Physical	80	100	15	Normal	○
HM06	Rock Smash	Fighting	Physical	40	100	15	Normal	○

 No. **036** | Fairy Pokémon

Clefable

Normal

● HEIGHT: 4'03"
● WEIGHT: 88.2 lbs.
● ITEMS: None

● SIZE COMPARISON

● MALE/FEMALE HAVE SAME FORM

◈ ABILITIES
● Cute Charm
● Magic Guard

◈ STATS
HP ●●●●
ATTACK ●●●
DEFENSE ●●●
SP. ATTACK ●●●●
SP. DEFENSE ●●●●
SPEED ●●●

◈ EGG GROUPS
Fairy

◈ PERFORMANCE

SPEED ★★★ STAMINA ★★★☆☆
POWER ★★★ JUMP ★★☆
SKILL ★★★★☆

● MAIN WAYS TO OBTAIN

Pokémon HeartGold	Use Moon Stone on Clefairy
Pokémon SoulSilver	Use Moon Stone on Clefairy
Pokémon Diamond	Use Moon Stone on Clefairy
Pokémon Pearl	Use Moon Stone on Clefairy
Pokémon Platinum	Use Moon Stone on Clefairy

Pokémon HeartGold
With its acute hearing, it can pick up sounds from far away. It usually hides in quiet places.

Pokémon SoulSilver
Its very sensitive ears let it distinguish distant sounds. As a result, it prefers quiet places.

◈ EVOLUTION

Cleffa → Level up with high friendship → Clefairy → Use Moon Stone → Clefable

No. 037 | Fox Pokémon
Vulpix

Fire

- **HEIGHT:** 2'00"
- **WEIGHT:** 21.8 lbs.
- **ITEMS:** Rawst Berry

SIZE COMPARISON

● **MALE/FEMALE HAVE SAME FORM**

ABILITIES
- Flash Fire

EGG GROUPS
Field

STATS
HP	●
ATTACK	●●
DEFENSE	●●
SP. ATTACK	●●
SP. DEFENSE	●●
SPEED	●●●

PERFORMANCE
SPEED ★★★★☆ STAMINA ★★☆
POWER ★★☆ JUMP ★★★
SKILL ★★★☆

MAIN WAYS TO OBTAIN

Pokémon HeartGold	—
Pokémon SoulSilver	Route 36
Pokémon Diamond	Route 209 (after obtaining the National Pokédex, insert *Pokémon LeafGreen* into your Nintendo DS's Game Pak slot)
Pokémon Pearl	Route 209 (after obtaining the National Pokédex, insert *Pokémon LeafGreen* into your Nintendo DS's Game Pak slot)
Pokémon Platinum	Route 209 (after obtaining the National Pokédex, insert *Pokémon LeafGreen* into your Nintendo DS's Game Pak slot)

Pokémon HeartGold
As it develops, its single white tail gains color and splits into six. It is quite warm and cuddly.

Pokémon SoulSilver
If it is attacked by an enemy that is stronger than itself, it feigns injury to fool the enemy and escapes.

EVOLUTION

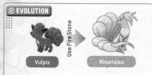

Use Fire Stone

Vulpix → Ninetales

LEVEL-UP MOVES
Lv.	Name	Type	Kind	Pow.	Acc.	PP	Range	DA
1	Ember	Fire	Special	40	100	25	Normal	—
4	Tail Whip	Normal	Status	—	100	30	2 Foes	—
7	Roar	Normal	Status	—	100	20	Normal	—
11	Quick Attack	Normal	Physical	40	100	30	Normal	○
14	Will-O-Wisp	Fire	Status	—	75	15	Normal	—
17	Confuse Ray	Ghost	Status	—	100	10	Normal	—
21	Imprison	Psychic	Status	—	—	10	Self	—
24	Flamethrower	Fire	Special	95	100	15	Normal	—
27	Safeguard	Normal	Status	—	—	25	2 Allies	—
31	Payback	Dark	Physical	50	100	10	Normal	○
34	Fire Spin	Fire	Special	15	70	15	Normal	—
37	Captivate	Normal	Status	—	100	20	2 Foes	—
41	Grudge	Ghost	Status	—	—	5	Self	—
44	Extrasensory	Psychic	Special	80	100	30	Normal	—
47	Fire Blast	Fire	Special	120	85	5	Normal	—

MOVE MANIAC
Name	Type	Kind	Pow.	Acc.	PP	Range	DA
Headbutt	Normal	Physical	70	100	15	Normal	○

BP MOVES
Name	Type	Kind	Pow.	Acc.	PP	Range	DA
Ominous Wind	Ghost	Special	60	100	5	Normal	—
Zen Headbutt	Psychic	Physical	80	90	15	Normal	○
Snore	Normal	Special	40	100	15	Normal	—
Spite	Ghost	Status	—	100	10	Normal	—
Swift	Normal	Special	60	—	20	2 Foes	—
Role Play	Psychic	Status	—	—	10	Normal	—
Heat Wave	Fire	Special	100	90	10	2 Foes	—
Pain Split	Normal	Status	—	—	20	Normal	—

TM & HM MOVES
No.	Name	Type	Kind	Pow.	Acc.	PP	Range	DA
TM05	Roar	Normal	Status	—	100	20	Normal	—
TM06	Toxic	Poison	Status	—	85	10	Normal	—
TM10	Hidden Power	Normal	Special	—	100	15	Normal	—
TM11	Sunny Day	Fire	Status	—	—	5	All	—
TM17	Protect	Normal	Status	—	—	10	Self	—
TM20	Safeguard	Normal	Status	—	—	25	2 Allies	—
TM21	Frustration	Normal	Physical	—	100	20	Normal	○
TM23	Iron Tail	Steel	Physical	100	75	15	Normal	○
TM27	Return	Normal	Physical	—	100	20	Normal	○
TM28	Dig	Ground	Physical	80	100	10	Normal	○
TM32	Double Team	Normal	Status	—	—	15	Self	—
TM35	Flamethrower	Fire	Special	95	100	15	Normal	—
TM38	Fire Blast	Fire	Special	120	85	5	Normal	—
TM42	Facade	Normal	Physical	70	100	20	Normal	○
TM43	Secret Power	Normal	Physical	70	100	20	Normal	—
TM44	Rest	Psychic	Status	—	—	10	Self	—
TM45	Attract	Normal	Status	—	100	15	Normal	—
TM50	Overheat	Fire	Special	140	90	5	Normal	—
TM58	Endure	Normal	Status	—	—	10	Self	—
TM61	Will-O-Wisp	Fire	Status	—	75	15	Normal	—
TM66	Payback	Dark	Physical	50	100	10	Normal	○
TM77	Psych Up	Normal	Status	—	—	10	Normal	—
TM78	Captivate	Normal	Status	—	100	20	2 Foes	—
TM79	Dark Pulse	Dark	Special	80	100	15	Normal	—
TM82	Sleep Talk	Normal	Status	—	—	10	Depends	—
TM83	Natural Gift	Normal	Physical	—	100	15	Normal	—
TM87	Swagger	Normal	Status	—	90	15	Normal	—
TM90	Substitute	Normal	Status	—	—	10	Self	—

EGG MOVES
Name	Type	Kind	Pow.	Acc.	PP	Range	DA
Faint Attack	Dark	Physical	60	—	20	Normal	○
Hypnosis	Psychic	Status	—	60	20	Normal	—
Flail	Normal	Physical	—	100	15	Normal	○
Spite	Ghost	Status	—	100	10	Normal	—
Disable	Normal	Status	—	80	20	Normal	—
Howl	Normal	Status	—	—	40	Self	—
Psych Up	Normal	Status	—	—	10	Normal	—
Heat Wave	Fire	Special	100	90	10	2 Foes	—
Flare Blitz	Fire	Physical	120	100	15	Normal	○
Extrasensory	Psychic	Special	80	100	30	Normal	—
Energy Ball	Grass	Special	80	100	10	Normal	—
Power Swap	Psychic	Status	—	—	10	Normal	—

● LEVEL-UP MOVES

Lv.	Name	Type	Kind	Pow.	Acc.	PP	Range	DA
1	Nasty Plot	Dark	Status	—	—	20	Self	—
1	Ember	Fire	Special	40	100	25	Normal	—
1	Quick Attack	Normal	Physical	40	100	30	Normal	○
1	Confuse Ray	Ghost	Status	—	100	10	Normal	—
1	Safeguard	Normal	Status	—	—	25	2 Allies	—

● MOVE MANIAC

Name	Type	Kind	Pow.	Acc.	PP	Range	DA
Headbutt	Normal	Physical	70	100	15	Normal	○

● BP MOVES

Name	Type	Kind	Pow.	Acc.	PP	Range	DA
Ominous Wind	Ghost	Special	60	100	5	Normal	—
Zen Headbutt	Psychic	Physical	80	90	15	Normal	○
Snore	Normal	Special	40	100	15	Normal	—
Spite	Ghost	Status	—	100	10	Normal	—
Swift	Normal	Special	60	—	20	2 Foes	—
Role Play	Psychic	Status	—	—	10	Normal	—
Heat Wave	Fire	Special	100	90	10	2 Foes	—
Pain Split	Normal	Status	—	—	20	Normal	—

● TM & HM MOVES

No.	Name	Type	Kind	Pow.	Acc.	PP	Range	DA
TM04	Calm Mind	Psychic	Status	—	—	20	Self	—
TM05	Roar	Normal	Status	—	100	20	Normal	—
TM06	Toxic	Poison	Status	—	85	10	Normal	—
TM10	Hidden Power	Normal	Special	—	100	15	Normal	—
TM11	Sunny Day	Fire	Status	—	—	5	All	—
TM15	Hyper Beam	Normal	Special	150	90	5	Normal	—
TM17	Protect	Normal	Status	—	—	10	Self	—
TM20	Safeguard	Normal	Status	—	—	25	2 Allies	—
TM21	Frustration	Normal	Physical	—	100	20	Normal	○
TM22	SolarBeam	Grass	Special	120	100	10	Normal	—
TM23	Iron Tail	Steel	Physical	100	75	15	Normal	○
TM27	Return	Normal	Physical	—	100	20	Normal	○
TM28	Dig	Ground	Physical	80	100	10	Normal	○
TM32	Double Team	Normal	Status	—	—	15	Self	—
TM35	Flamethrower	Fire	Special	95	100	15	Normal	—
TM38	Fire Blast	Fire	Special	120	85	5	Normal	—
TM42	Facade	Normal	Physical	70	100	20	Normal	○
TM43	Secret Power	Normal	Physical	70	100	20	Normal	○
TM44	Rest	Psychic	Status	—	—	10	Self	—
TM45	Attract	Normal	Status	—	100	15	Normal	—
TM50	Overheat	Fire	Special	140	90	5	Normal	—
TM58	Endure	Normal	Status	—	—	10	Self	—
TM61	Will-O-Wisp	Fire	Status	—	75	15	Normal	—
TM66	Payback	Dark	Physical	50	100	10	Normal	○
TM68	Giga Impact	Normal	Physical	150	90	5	Normal	○
TM77	Psych Up	Normal	Status	—	—	10	Self	—
TM78	Captivate	Normal	Status	—	100	20	2 Foes	—
TM79	Dark Pulse	Dark	Special	80	100	15	Normal	—
TM82	Sleep Talk	Normal	Status	—	—	10	Depends	—
TM83	Natural Gift	Normal	Physical	—	100	15	Normal	—
TM85	Dream Eater	Psychic	Special	100	100	15	Normal	—
TM87	Swagger	Normal	Status	—	90	15	Normal	—
TM90	Substitute	Normal	Status	—	—	10	Self	—

● HEIGHT: 3'07"
● WEIGHT: 43.9 lbs.
● ITEMS: None

● SIZE COMPARISON

● MALE/FEMALE HAVE SAME FORM

⊙ ABILITIES
● Flash Fire

⊙ STATS
HP ●●●
ATTACK ●●●
DEFENSE ●●●
SP. ATTACK ●●●
SP. DEFENSE ●●●●
SPEED ●●●●

⊙ EGG GROUPS
Field

⊙ PERFORMANCE
SPEED ★★★☆
POWER ★★☆
SKILL ★★★★☆
STAMINA ★★☆
JUMP ★★★

● MAIN WAYS TO OBTAIN

Pokémon HeartGold	—
Pokémon SoulSilver	Use Fire Stone on Vulpix
Pokémon Diamond	Use Fire Stone on Vulpix
Pokémon Pearl	Use Fire Stone on Vulpix
Pokémon Platinum	Use Fire Stone on Vulpix

Pokémon HeartGold
Some legends claim that each of its nine tails has its own unique type of special mystical power.

Pokémon SoulSilver
Its nine beautiful tails are filled with a wondrous energy that could keep it alive for 1,000 years.

⊙ EVOLUTION

Use Fire Stone

Vulpix → Ninetales

● No. 039 | Balloon Pokémon
Jigglypuff

Normal

- ● HEIGHT: 1'08"
- ● WEIGHT: 12.1 lbs.
- ● ITEMS: None

● SIZE COMPARISON

● MALE/FEMALE HAVE SAME FORM

● ABILITIES
- Cute Charm

● STATS
- HP ●●●●
- ATTACK ●●
- DEFENSE ●●
- SP. ATTACK ●●
- SP. DEFENSE ●●
- SPEED ●

● EGG GROUPS
Fairy

● PERFORMANCE
- SPEED ★★★☆☆
- POWER ★★☆☆
- SKILL ★★☆☆
- STAMINA ★★★☆☆
- JUMP ★★★

● MAIN WAYS TO OBTAIN

Pokémon HeartGold	Route 3 (morning and night only)
Pokémon SoulSilver	Route 3 (morning and night only)
Pokémon Diamond	Trophy Garden at the Pokémon Mansion on Route 212 (after obtaining the National Pokédex, talk to Mr. Backlot)
Pokémon Pearl	Trophy Garden at the Pokémon Mansion on Route 212 (after obtaining the National Pokédex, talk to Mr. Backlot)
Pokémon Platinum	Trophy Garden at the Pokémon Mansion on Route 212 (after obtaining the National Pokédex, talk to Mr. Backlot)

Pokémon HeartGold
If it inflates to sing a lullaby, it can perform longer and cause sure drowsiness in its audience.

Pokémon SoulSilver
Looking into its cute, round eyes causes it to sing a relaxing melody, inducing its enemies to sleep.

● EVOLUTION

Igglybuff → (Level up with high friendship) → Jigglypuff → (Use Moon Stone) → Wigglytuff

● LEVEL-UP MOVES

Lv.	Name	Type	Kind	Pow.	Acc.	PP	Range	DA
1	Sing	Normal	Status	—	55	15	Normal	—
5	Defense Curl	Normal	Status	—	—	40	Self	—
9	Pound	Normal	Physical	40	100	35	Normal	○
13	Disable	Normal	Status	—	80	20	Normal	—
17	Rollout	Rock	Physical	30	90	20	Normal	○
21	DoubleSlap	Normal	Physical	15	85	10	Normal	○
25	Rest	Psychic	Status	—	—	10	Self	—
29	Body Slam	Normal	Physical	85	100	15	Normal	○
33	Gyro Ball	Steel	Physical	—	100	5	Normal	○
37	Wake-Up Slap	Fighting	Physical	60	100	10	Normal	○
41	Mimic	Normal	Status	—	—	10	Normal	—
45	Hyper Voice	Normal	Special	90	100	10	2 Foes	—
49	Double-Edge	Normal	Physical	120	100	15	Normal	○

● MOVE MANIAC

Name	Type	Kind	Pow.	Acc.	PP	Range	DA
Headbutt	Normal	Physical	70	100	15	Normal	○

● BP MOVES

Name	Type	Kind	Pow.	Acc.	PP	Range	DA
Icy Wind	Ice	Special	55	95	15	2 Foes	—
ThunderPunch	Electric	Physical	75	100	15	Normal	○
Fire Punch	Fire	Physical	75	100	15	Normal	○
Ice Punch	Ice	Physical	75	100	15	Normal	○
Knock Off	Dark	Physical	20	100	20	Normal	○
Snore	Normal	Special	40	100	15	Normal	—
Helping Hand	Normal	Status	—	—	20	1 Ally	—
Last Resort	Normal	Physical	130	100	5	Normal	○
Gravity	Psychic	Status	—	—	5	All	—
Magic Coat	Psychic	Status	—	—	15	Self	—
Role Play	Psychic	Status	—	—	10	Normal	—
Heal Bell	Normal	Status	—	—	5	All Allies	—
Mud-Slap	Ground	Special	20	100	10	Normal	—
Rollout	Rock	Physical	30	90	20	Normal	○
Endeavor	Normal	Physical	—	100	5	Normal	○
Bounce	Flying	Physical	85	85	5	Normal	○
Pain Split	Normal	Status	—	—	20	Normal	—

● TM & HM MOVES

No.	Name	Type	Kind	Pow.	Acc.	PP	Range	DA
TM01	Focus Punch	Fighting	Physical	150	100	20	Normal	○
TM03	Water Pulse	Water	Special	60	100	20	Normal	—
TM06	Toxic	Poison	Status	—	85	10	Normal	—
TM10	Hidden Power	Normal	Special	—	100	15	Normal	—
TM11	Sunny Day	Fire	Status	—	—	5	All	—
TM13	Ice Beam	Ice	Special	95	100	10	Normal	—
TM14	Blizzard	Ice	Special	120	70	5	2 Foes	—
TM16	Light Screen	Psychic	Status	—	—	30	2 Allies	—
TM17	Protect	Normal	Status	—	—	10	Self	—
TM18	Rain Dance	Water	Status	—	—	5	All	—
TM20	Safeguard	Normal	Status	—	—	25	2 Allies	—
TM21	Frustration	Normal	Physical	—	100	20	Normal	○
TM22	SolarBeam	Grass	Special	120	100	10	Normal	—
TM24	Thunderbolt	Electric	Special	95	100	15	Normal	—
TM25	Thunder	Electric	Special	120	70	10	Normal	—
TM27	Return	Normal	Physical	—	100	20	Normal	○
TM28	Dig	Ground	Physical	80	100	10	Normal	○
TM29	Psychic	Psychic	Special	90	100	10	Normal	—
TM30	Shadow Ball	Ghost	Special	80	100	15	Normal	—
TM31	Brick Break	Fighting	Physical	75	100	15	Normal	○
TM32	Double Team	Normal	Status	—	—	15	Self	—
TM33	Reflect	Psychic	Status	—	—	20	2 Allies	—
TM34	Shock Wave	Electric	Special	60	—	20	Normal	—
TM35	Flamethrower	Fire	Special	95	100	15	Normal	—
TM38	Fire Blast	Fire	Special	120	85	5	Normal	—
TM42	Facade	Normal	Physical	70	100	20	Normal	○
TM43	Secret Power	Normal	Physical	70	100	20	Normal	○
TM44	Rest	Psychic	Status	—	—	10	Self	—
TM45	Attract	Normal	Status	—	100	15	Normal	—
TM49	Snatch	Dark	Status	—	—	10	Depends	—
TM56	Fling	Dark	Physical	—	100	10	Normal	○
TM57	Charge Beam	Electric	Special	50	90	10	Normal	—
TM58	Endure	Normal	Status	—	—	10	Self	—
TM60	Drain Punch	Fighting	Physical	60	100	5	Normal	○
TM67	Recycle	Normal	Status	—	—	10	Self	—
TM70	Flash	Normal	Status	—	100	20	Normal	—
TM73	Thunder Wave	Electric	Status	—	100	20	Normal	—
TM74	Gyro Ball	Steel	Physical	—	100	5	Normal	○
TM76	Stealth Rock	Rock	Status	—	—	20	2 Foes	—
TM77	Psych Up	Normal	Status	—	—	10	Normal	—
TM78	Captivate	Normal	Status	—	100	20	2 Foes	—
TM82	Sleep Talk	Normal	Status	—	—	10	Self	—
TM83	Natural Gift	Normal	Physical	—	100	15	Normal	○
TM85	Dream Eater	Psychic	Special	100	100	15	Normal	—
TM86	Grass Knot	Grass	Special	—	100	20	Normal	—
TM87	Swagger	Normal	Status	—	90	15	Normal	—
TM90	Substitute	Normal	Status	—	—	10	Self	—
HM04	Strength	Normal	Physical	80	100	15	Normal	○

● LEVEL-UP MOVES

Lv.	Name	Type	Kind	Pow.	Acc.	PP	Range	DA
1	Sing	Normal	Status	—	55	15	Normal	—
1	Disable	Normal	Status	—	80	20	Normal	—
1	Defense Curl	Normal	Status	—	—	40	Self	—
1	DoubleSlap	Normal	Physical	15	85	10	Normal	○

● MOVE MANIAC

Name	Type	Kind	Pow.	Acc.	PP	Range	DA
Headbutt	Normal	Physical	70	100	15	Normal	○

● BP MOVES

Name	Type	Kind	Pow.	Acc.	PP	Range	DA
Icy Wind	Ice	Special	55	95	15	2 Foes	—
ThunderPunch	Electric	Physical	75	100	15	Normal	○
Fire Punch	Fire	Physical	75	100	15	Normal	○
Ice Punch	Ice	Physical	75	100	15	Normal	○
Knock Off	Dark	Physical	20	100	20	Normal	○
Snore	Normal	Special	40	100	15	Normal	—
Helping Hand	Normal	Status	—	—	20	1 Ally	—
Last Resort	Normal	Physical	130	100	5	Normal	○
Gravity	Psychic	Status	—	—	5	All	—
Magic Coat	Psychic	Status	—	—	15	Self	—
Role Play	Psychic	Status	—	—	10	Normal	—
Heal Bell	Normal	Status	—	—	5	All Allies	—
Mud-Slap	Ground	Special	20	100	10	Normal	—
Rollout	Rock	Physical	30	90	20	Normal	○
Endeavor	Normal	Physical	—	100	5	Normal	○
Bounce	Flying	Physical	85	85	5	Normal	○
Pain Split	Normal	Status	—	—	20	Normal	—

● TM & HM MOVES

No.	Name	Type	Kind	Pow.	Acc.	PP	Range	DA
TM01	Focus Punch	Fighting	Physical	150	100	20	Normal	○
TM03	Water Pulse	Water	Special	60	100	20	Normal	—
TM06	Toxic	Poison	Status	—	85	10	Normal	—
TM10	Hidden Power	Normal	Special	—	100	15	Normal	—
TM11	Sunny Day	Fire	Status	—	—	5	All	—
TM13	Ice Beam	Ice	Special	95	100	10	Normal	—
TM14	Blizzard	Ice	Special	120	70	5	2 Foes	—
TM15	Hyper Beam	Normal	Special	150	90	5	Normal	—
TM16	Light Screen	Psychic	Status	—	—	30	2 Allies	—
TM17	Protect	Normal	Status	—	—	10	Self	—
TM18	Rain Dance	Water	Status	—	—	5	All	—
TM20	Safeguard	Normal	Status	—	—	25	2 Allies	—
TM21	Frustration	Normal	Physical	—	100	20	Normal	○
TM22	SolarBeam	Grass	Special	120	100	10	Normal	—
TM24	Thunderbolt	Electric	Special	95	100	15	Normal	—
TM25	Thunder	Electric	Special	120	70	10	Normal	—
TM27	Return	Normal	Physical	—	100	20	Normal	○
TM28	Dig	Ground	Physical	80	100	10	Normal	○
TM29	Psychic	Psychic	Special	90	100	10	Normal	—
TM30	Shadow Ball	Ghost	Special	80	100	15	Normal	—
TM31	Brick Break	Fighting	Physical	75	100	15	Normal	○
TM32	Double Team	Normal	Status	—	—	15	Self	—
TM33	Reflect	Psychic	Status	—	—	20	2 Allies	—
TM34	Shock Wave	Electric	Special	60	—	20	Normal	—
TM35	Flamethrower	Fire	Special	95	100	15	Normal	—
TM38	Fire Blast	Fire	Special	120	85	5	Normal	—
TM42	Facade	Normal	Physical	70	100	20	Normal	○
TM43	Secret Power	Normal	Physical	70	100	20	Normal	—
TM44	Rest	Psychic	Status	—	—	10	Self	—
TM45	Attract	Normal	Status	—	100	15	Normal	—
TM49	Snatch	Dark	Status	—	—	10	Depends	—
TM52	Focus Blast	Fighting	Special	120	70	5	Normal	—
TM56	Fling	Dark	Physical	—	100	10	Normal	—
TM57	Charge Beam	Electric	Special	50	90	10	Normal	—
TM58	Endure	Normal	Status	—	—	10	Self	—
TM60	Drain Punch	Fighting	Physical	60	100	5	Normal	—
TM67	Recycle	Normal	Status	—	—	10	Self	—
TM68	Giga Impact	Normal	Physical	150	90	5	Normal	○
TM70	Flash	Normal	Status	—	100	20	Normal	—
TM73	Thunder Wave	Electric	Status	—	100	20	Normal	—
TM74	Gyro Ball	Steel	Physical	—	100	5	Normal	○
TM76	Stealth Rock	Rock	Status	—	—	20	2 Foes	—
TM77	Psych Up	Normal	Status	—	—	10	Normal	—
TM78	Captivate	Normal	Status	—	100	20	2 Foes	—
TM82	Sleep Talk	Normal	Status	—	—	10	Depends	—
TM83	Natural Gift	Normal	Physical	—	100	15	Normal	—
TM85	Dream Eater	Psychic	Special	100	100	15	Normal	—
TM86	Grass Knot	Grass	Special	—	100	20	Normal	—
TM87	Swagger	Normal	Status	—	90	15	Normal	—
TM90	Substitute	Normal	Status	—	—	10	Self	—
HM04	Strength	Normal	Physical	80	100	15	Normal	○

● No. 040 | Balloon Pokémon
Wigglytuff

Normal

- **HEIGHT:** 3'03"
- **WEIGHT:** 26.5 lbs.
- **ITEMS:** None

● SIZE COMPARISON

● MALE/FEMALE HAVE SAME FORM

◈ ABILITIES
● Cute Charm

◈ STATS
HP	●●●●●
ATTACK	●●●●
DEFENSE	●●●
SP. ATTACK	●●●
SP. DEFENSE	●●
SPEED	●●

◈ EGG GROUPS
Fairy

◈ PERFORMANCE
SPEED ★★★☆	STAMINA ★★★★☆
POWER ★★★☆	JUMP ★★☆
SKILL ★★★☆	

● MAIN WAYS TO OBTAIN

Pokémon HeartGold	Use Moon Stone on Jigglypuff

Pokémon SoulSilver	Use Moon Stone on Jigglypuff

Pokémon Diamond	Use Moon Stone on Jigglypuff

Pokémon Pearl	Use Moon Stone on Jigglypuff

Pokémon Platinum	Use Moon Stone on Jigglypuff

Pokémon HeartGold
Their fur feels so good that if two of them snuggle together, they won't want to be separated.

Pokémon SoulSilver
It has a very fine fur. Take care not to make it angry, or it may inflate steadily and hit with a body slam.

◈ EVOLUTION

Igglybuff → (Level up with high friendship) → Jigglypuff → (Use Moon Stone) → Wigglytuff

● No. 041 | Bat Pokémon
Zubat

Poison | Flying

● HEIGHT: 2'07"
● WEIGHT: 16.5 lbs.
● ITEMS: None

● SIZE COMPARISON

● MALE FORM
Bigger fangs

● FEMALE FORM
Smaller fangs

⊙ ABILITIES
● Inner Focus

⊙ STATS
HP	●
ATTACK	●●
DEFENSE	●●
SP. ATTACK	●
SP. DEFENSE	●●
SPEED	●●●

⊙ EGG GROUPS
Flying

⊙ PERFORMANCE
SPEED ★★★★☆   STAMINA ★☆☆
POWER ★☆☆   JUMP ★★★★★
SKILL ★☆☆☆☆

● MAIN WAYS TO OBTAIN

Pokémon HeartGold	Route 32 (morning and night only)
Pokémon SoulSilver	Route 32 (morning and night only)
Pokémon Diamond	Oreburgh Gate 1F
Pokémon Pearl	Oreburgh Gate 1F
Pokémon Platinum	Oreburgh Gate 1F

Pokémon HeartGold	Pokémon SoulSilver
While flying, it constantly emits ultrasonic waves from its mouth to check its surroundings.	Capable of flying safely in dark places, it emits ultrasonic cries to check for any obstacles.

⊙ EVOLUTION

Zubat — Lv. 22 — Golbat — Level up with high friendship — Crobat

● LEVEL-UP MOVES

Lv.	Name	Type	Kind	Pow.	Acc.	PP	Range	DA
1	Leech Life	Bug	Physical	20	100	15	Normal	○
5	Supersonic	Normal	Status	—	55	20	Normal	—
9	Astonish	Ghost	Physical	30	100	15	Normal	○
13	Bite	Dark	Physical	60	100	25	Normal	○
17	Wing Attack	Flying	Physical	60	100	35	Normal	○
21	Confuse Ray	Ghost	Status	—	100	10	Normal	—
25	Air Cutter	Flying	Special	55	95	25	2 Foes	—
29	Mean Look	Normal	Status	—	—	5	Normal	—
33	Poison Fang	Poison	Physical	50	100	15	Normal	○
37	Haze	Ice	Status	—	—	30	All	—
41	Air Slash	Flying	Special	75	95	20	Normal	—

● MOVE MANIAC

Name	Type	Kind	Pow.	Acc.	PP	Range	DA

● BP MOVES

Name	Type	Kind	Pow.	Acc.	PP	Range	DA
Ominous Wind	Ghost	Special	60	100	5	Normal	—
Air Cutter	Flying	Special	55	95	25	2 Foes	—
Zen Headbutt	Psychic	Physical	80	90	15	Normal	○
Snore	Normal	Special	40	100	15	Normal	—
Swift	Normal	Special	60	—	20	2 Foes	—
Uproar	Normal	Special	50	100	10	1 Random	—
Tailwind	Flying	Status	—	—	30	2 Allies	—
Twister	Dragon	Special	40	100	20	2 Foes	—
Heat Wave	Fire	Special	100	90	10	2 Foes	—
Super Fang	Normal	Physical	—	90	10	Normal	○

● TM & HM MOVES

No.	Name	Type	Kind	Pow.	Acc.	PP	Range	DA
TM06	Toxic	Poison	Status	—	85	10	Normal	—
TM10	Hidden Power	Normal	Special	—	100	15	Normal	—
TM11	Sunny Day	Fire	Status	—	—	5	All	—
TM12	Taunt	Dark	Status	—	100	20	Normal	—
TM17	Protect	Normal	Status	—	—	10	Self	—
TM18	Rain Dance	Water	Status	—	—	5	All	—
TM19	Giga Drain	Grass	Special	60	100	10	Normal	—
TM21	Frustration	Normal	Physical	—	100	20	Normal	○
TM27	Return	Normal	Physical	—	100	20	Normal	○
TM30	Shadow Ball	Ghost	Special	80	100	15	Normal	—
TM32	Double Team	Normal	Status	—	—	15	Self	—
TM36	Sludge Bomb	Poison	Special	90	100	10	Normal	—
TM40	Aerial Ace	Flying	Physical	60	—	20	Normal	○
TM41	Torment	Dark	Status	—	100	15	Normal	—
TM42	Facade	Normal	Physical	70	100	20	Normal	○
TM43	Secret Power	Normal	Physical	70	100	20	Normal	○
TM44	Rest	Psychic	Status	—	—	10	Self	—
TM45	Attract	Normal	Status	—	100	15	Normal	—
TM46	Thief	Dark	Physical	40	100	10	Normal	○
TM47	Steel Wing	Steel	Physical	70	90	25	Normal	○
TM49	Snatch	Dark	Status	—	—	10	Depends	—
TM51	Roost	Flying	Status	—	—	10	Self	—
TM58	Endure	Normal	Status	—	—	10	Self	—
TM66	Payback	Dark	Physical	50	100	10	Normal	○
TM78	Captivate	Normal	Status	—	100	20	2 Foes	—
TM82	Sleep Talk	Normal	Status	—	—	10	Depends	—
TM83	Natural Gift	Normal	Physical	—	100	15	Normal	—
TM87	Swagger	Normal	Status	—	90	15	Normal	—
TM88	Pluck	Flying	Physical	60	100	20	Normal	○
TM89	U-turn	Bug	Physical	70	100	20	Normal	○
TM90	Substitute	Normal	Status	—	—	10	Self	—
HM02	Fly	Flying	Physical	90	95	15	Normal	○

● EGG MOVES

Name	Type	Kind	Pow.	Acc.	PP	Range	DA
Quick Attack	Normal	Physical	40	100	30	Normal	○
Pursuit	Dark	Physical	40	100	20	Normal	○
Faint Attack	Dark	Physical	60	—	20	Normal	○
Gust	Flying	Special	40	100	35	Normal	○
Whirlwind	Normal	Status	—	100	20	Normal	—
Curse	???	Status	—	—	10	Normal/Self	—
Nasty Plot	Dark	Status	—	—	20	Self	—
Hypnosis	Psychic	Status	—	60	20	Normal	—
Zen Headbutt	Psychic	Physical	80	90	15	Normal	○
Brave Bird	Flying	Physical	120	100	15	Normal	○

● LEVEL-UP MOVES

Lv.	Name	Type	Kind	Pow.	Acc.	PP	Range	DA
1	Screech	Normal	Status	—	85	40	Normal	—
1	Leech Life	Bug	Physical	20	100	15	Normal	○
1	Supersonic	Normal	Status	—	55	20	Normal	—
1	Astonish	Ghost	Physical	30	100	15	Normal	○
5	Supersonic	Normal	Status	—	55	20	Normal	—
9	Astonish	Ghost	Physical	30	100	15	Normal	○
13	Bite	Dark	Physical	60	100	25	Normal	○
17	Wing Attack	Flying	Physical	60	100	35	Normal	○
21	Confuse Ray	Ghost	Status	—	100	10	Normal	—
27	Air Cutter	Flying	Special	55	95	25	2 Foes	—
33	Mean Look	Normal	Status	—	—	5	Normal	—
39	Poison Fang	Poison	Physical	50	100	15	Normal	○
45	Haze	Ice	Status	—	—	30	All	—
51	Air Slash	Flying	Special	75	95	20	Normal	—

● MOVE MANIAC

Name	Type	Kind	Pow.	Acc.	PP	Range	DA

● BP MOVES

Name	Type	Kind	Pow.	Acc.	PP	Range	DA
Ominous Wind	Ghost	Special	60	100	5	Normal	—
Air Cutter	Flying	Special	55	95	25	2 Foes	—
Zen Headbutt	Psychic	Physical	80	90	15	Normal	○
Snore	Normal	Special	40	100	15	Normal	—
Swift	Normal	Special	60	—	20	2 Foes	—
Uproar	Normal	Special	50	100	10	1 Random	—
Tailwind	Flying	Status	—	—	30	2 Allies	—
Twister	Dragon	Special	40	100	20	2 Foes	—
Heat Wave	Fire	Special	100	90	10	2 Foes	—
Super Fang	Normal	Physical	—	90	10	Normal	○

● TM & HM MOVES

No.	Name	Type	Kind	Pow.	Acc.	PP	Range	DA
TM06	Toxic	Poison	Status	—	85	10	Normal	—
TM10	Hidden Power	Normal	Special	—	100	15	Normal	—
TM11	Sunny Day	Fire	Status	—	—	5	All	—
TM12	Taunt	Dark	Status	—	100	20	Normal	—
TM15	Hyper Beam	Normal	Special	150	90	5	Normal	—
TM17	Protect	Normal	Status	—	—	10	Self	—
TM18	Rain Dance	Water	Status	—	—	5	All	—
TM19	Giga Drain	Grass	Special	60	100	10	Normal	—
TM21	Frustration	Normal	Physical	—	100	20	Normal	○
TM27	Return	Normal	Physical	—	100	20	Normal	○
TM30	Shadow Ball	Ghost	Special	80	100	15	Normal	—
TM32	Double Team	Normal	Status	—	—	15	Self	—
TM36	Sludge Bomb	Poison	Special	90	100	10	Normal	—
TM40	Aerial Ace	Flying	Physical	60	—	20	Normal	○
TM41	Torment	Dark	Status	—	100	15	Normal	—
TM42	Facade	Normal	Physical	70	100	20	Normal	○
TM43	Secret Power	Normal	Physical	70	100	20	Normal	○
TM44	Rest	Psychic	Status	—	—	10	Self	—
TM45	Attract	Normal	Status	—	100	15	Normal	—
TM46	Thief	Dark	Physical	40	100	10	Normal	○
TM47	Steel Wing	Steel	Physical	70	90	25	Normal	○
TM49	Snatch	Dark	Status	—	—	10	Depends	—
TM51	Roost	Flying	Status	—	—	10	Self	—
TM58	Endure	Normal	Status	—	—	10	Self	—
TM66	Payback	Dark	Physical	50	100	10	Normal	○
TM68	Giga Impact	Normal	Physical	150	90	5	Normal	○
TM78	Captivate	Normal	Status	—	100	20	2 Foes	—
TM82	Sleep Talk	Normal	Status	—	—	10	Depends	—
TM83	Natural Gift	Normal	Physical	—	100	15	Normal	—
TM87	Swagger	Normal	Status	—	90	15	Normal	—
TM88	Pluck	Flying	Physical	60	100	20	Normal	○
TM89	U-turn	Bug	Physical	70	100	20	Normal	○
TM90	Substitute	Normal	Status	—	—	10	Self	—
HM02	Fly	Flying	Physical	90	95	15	Normal	○

⬤ No. 042 | Bat Pokémon
Golbat

`Poison` `Flying`

- ● HEIGHT: 5'03"
- ● WEIGHT: 121.3 lbs.
- ● ITEMS: None

● SIZE COMPARISON

● MALE FORM
Bigger fangs

● FEMALE FORM
Smaller fangs

⚙ ABILITIES
● Inner Focus

⚙ STATS
HP ●●●
ATTACK ●●●
DEFENSE ●●●
SP. ATTACK ●●●
SP. DEFENSE ●●●
SPEED ●●●●

⚙ EGG GROUPS
Flying

⚙ PERFORMANCE

SPEED ★★★★☆ STAMINA ★★★☆
POWER ★★☆ JUMP ★★★★★
SKILL ★☆☆

● MAIN WAYS TO OBTAIN

Pokémon HeartGold	Union Cave B2F
Pokémon SoulSilver	Union Cave B2F
Pokémon Diamond	Lost Tower 5F
Pokémon Pearl	Lost Tower 5F
Pokémon Platinum	Lost Tower 5F

Pokémon HeartGold
However hard its victim's hide may be, it punctures with sharp fangs and gorges itself with blood.

Pokémon SoulSilver
It can drink more than 10 ounces of blood at once. If it has too much, it gets heavy and flies clumsily.

⚙ EVOLUTION

Zubat → Lv. 22 → Golbat → Level up with high friendship → Crobat

No. 043 | Weed Pokémon
Oddish

Grass | Poison

● HEIGHT: 1'08"
● WEIGHT: 11.9 lbs.
● ITEMS: None

● SIZE COMPARISON

● MALE/FEMALE HAVE SAME FORM

● ABILITIES
● Chlorophyll

● STATS
HP ●●
ATTACK ●●
DEFENSE ●●
SP. ATTACK ●●●
SP. DEFENSE ●●●
SPEED ●

● EGG GROUPS
Grass

● PERFORMANCE
SPEED ★★★☆☆   STAMINA ★★★★
POWER ★☆☆☆   JUMP ★★★
SKILL ★★☆

● MAIN WAYS TO OBTAIN

Pokémon HeartGold	Ilex Forest (night only)
Pokémon SoulSilver	Ilex Forest (night only)
Pokémon Diamond	Route 229
Pokémon Pearl	Route 229
Pokémon Platinum	Route 224 (night only)

Pokémon HeartGold
Awakened by moonlight, it roams actively at night. In the day, it stays quietly underground.

Pokémon SoulSilver
If exposed to moonlight, it starts to move. It roams far and wide at night to scatter its seeds.

● EVOLUTION

Oddish — Lv. 21 → Gloom — Use Leaf Stone → Vileplume
Use Sun Stone → Bellossom

● LEVEL-UP MOVES

Lv.	Name	Type	Kind	Pow.	Acc.	PP	Range	DA
1	Absorb	Grass	Special	20	100	25	Normal	—
5	Sweet Scent	Normal	Status	—	100	20	2 Foes	—
9	Acid	Poison	Special	40	100	30	2 Foes	—
13	PoisonPowder	Poison	Status	—	75	35	Normal	—
15	Stun Spore	Grass	Status	—	75	30	Normal	—
17	Sleep Powder	Grass	Status	—	75	15	Normal	—
21	Mega Drain	Grass	Special	40	100	15	Normal	—
25	Lucky Chant	Normal	Status	—	—	30	2 Allies	—
29	Natural Gift	Normal	Physical	—	100	15	Normal	—
33	Moonlight	Normal	Status	—	—	5	Self	—
37	Giga Drain	Grass	Special	60	100	10	Normal	—
41	Petal Dance	Grass	Special	90	100	20	1 Random	○

● MOVE MANIAC

Name	Type	Kind	Pow.	Acc.	PP	Range	DA

● BP MOVES

Name	Type	Kind	Pow.	Acc.	PP	Range	DA
Snore	Normal	Special	40	100	15	Normal	—
Synthesis	Grass	Status	—	—	5	Self	—
Worry Seed	Grass	Status	—	100	10	Normal	—
Gastro Acid	Poison	Status	—	100	10	Normal	—
Seed Bomb	Grass	Physical	80	100	15	Normal	—

● TM & HM MOVES

No.	Name	Type	Kind	Pow.	Acc.	PP	Range	DA
TM06	Toxic	Poison	Status	—	85	10	Normal	—
TM09	Bullet Seed	Grass	Physical	10	100	30	Normal	—
TM10	Hidden Power	Normal	Special	—	100	15	Normal	—
TM11	Sunny Day	Fire	Status	—	—	5	All	—
TM17	Protect	Normal	Status	—	—	10	Self	—
TM19	Giga Drain	Grass	Special	60	100	10	Normal	—
TM21	Frustration	Normal	Physical	—	100	20	Normal	○
TM22	SolarBeam	Grass	Special	120	100	10	Normal	—
TM27	Return	Normal	Physical	—	100	20	Normal	○
TM32	Double Team	Normal	Status	—	—	15	Self	—
TM36	Sludge Bomb	Poison	Special	90	100	10	Normal	—
TM42	Facade	Normal	Physical	70	100	20	Normal	○
TM43	Secret Power	Normal	Physical	70	100	20	Normal	○
TM44	Rest	Psychic	Status	—	—	10	Self	—
TM45	Attract	Normal	Status	—	100	15	Normal	—
TM53	Energy Ball	Grass	Special	80	100	10	Normal	—
TM58	Endure	Normal	Status	—	—	10	Self	—
TM70	Flash	Normal	Status	—	100	20	Normal	—
TM75	Swords Dance	Normal	Status	—	—	30	Self	—
TM78	Captivate	Normal	Status	—	100	20	2 Foes	—
TM82	Sleep Talk	Normal	Status	—	—	10	Depends	—
TM83	Natural Gift	Normal	Physical	—	100	15	Normal	—
TM86	Grass Knot	Grass	Special	—	100	20	Normal	○
TM87	Swagger	Normal	Status	—	90	15	Normal	—
TM90	Substitute	Normal	Status	—	—	10	Self	—
HM01	Cut	Normal	Physical	50	95	30	Normal	○

● EGG MOVES

Name	Type	Kind	Pow.	Acc.	PP	Range	DA
Swords Dance	Normal	Status	—	—	30	Self	—
Razor Leaf	Grass	Physical	55	95	25	2 Foes	—
Flail	Normal	Physical	—	100	15	Normal	○
Synthesis	Grass	Status	—	—	5	Self	—
Charm	Normal	Status	—	100	20	Normal	—
Ingrain	Grass	Status	—	—	20	Self	—
Tickle	Normal	Status	—	100	20	Normal	—
Teeter Dance	Normal	Status	—	100	20	2 Foes/1 Ally	—

● LEVEL-UP MOVES

Lv.	Name	Type	Kind	Pow.	Acc.	PP	Range	DA
1	Absorb	Grass	Special	20	100	25	Normal	—
1	Sweet Scent	Normal	Status	—	100	20	2 Foes	—
1	Acid	Poison	Special	40	100	30	2 Foes	—
5	Sweet Scent	Normal	Status	—	100	20	2 Foes	—
9	Acid	Poison	Special	40	100	30	2 Foes	—
13	PoisonPowder	Poison	Status	—	75	35	Normal	—
15	Stun Spore	Grass	Status	—	75	15	Normal	—
17	Sleep Powder	Grass	Status	—	75	15	Normal	—
23	Mega Drain	Grass	Special	40	100	15	Normal	—
29	Lucky Chant	Normal	Status	—	—	30	2 Allies	—
35	Natural Gift	Normal	Physical	—	100	15	Normal	—
41	Moonlight	Normal	Status	—	—	5	Self	—
47	Giga Drain	Grass	Special	60	100	10	Normal	—
53	Petal Dance	Grass	Special	90	100	20	1 Random	○

● MOVE MANIAC

Name	Type	Kind	Pow.	Acc.	PP	Range	DA

● BP MOVES

Name	Type	Kind	Pow.	Acc.	PP	Range	DA
Snore	Normal	Special	40	100	15	Normal	—
Synthesis	Grass	Status	—	—	5	Self	—
Worry Seed	Grass	Status	—	100	10	Normal	—
Gastro Acid	Poison	Status	—	100	10	Normal	—
Seed Bomb	Grass	Physical	80	100	15	Normal	—

● TM & HM MOVES

No.	Name	Type	Kind	Pow.	Acc.	PP	Range	DA
TM06	Toxic	Poison	Status	—	85	10	Normal	—
TM09	Bullet Seed	Grass	Physical	10	100	30	Normal	—
TM10	Hidden Power	Normal	Special	—	100	15	Normal	—
TM11	Sunny Day	Fire	Status	—	—	5	All	—
TM17	Protect	Normal	Status	—	—	10	Self	—
TM19	Giga Drain	Grass	Special	60	100	10	Normal	—
TM21	Frustration	Normal	Physical	—	100	20	Normal	○
TM22	SolarBeam	Grass	Special	120	100	10	Normal	—
TM27	Return	Normal	Physical	—	100	20	Normal	○
TM32	Double Team	Normal	Status	—	—	15	Self	—
TM36	Sludge Bomb	Poison	Special	90	100	10	Normal	—
TM42	Facade	Normal	Physical	70	100	20	Normal	○
TM43	Secret Power	Normal	Physical	70	100	20	Normal	—
TM44	Rest	Psychic	Status	—	—	10	Self	—
TM45	Attract	Normal	Status	—	100	15	Normal	—
TM53	Energy Ball	Grass	Special	80	100	10	Normal	—
TM56	Fling	Dark	Physical	—	100	10	Normal	—
TM58	Endure	Normal	Status	—	—	10	Self	—
TM60	Drain Punch	Fighting	Physical	60	100	5	Normal	○
TM70	Flash	Normal	Status	—	100	20	Normal	—
TM75	Swords Dance	Normal	Status	—	—	30	Self	—
TM78	Captivate	Normal	Status	—	100	20	2 Foes	—
TM82	Sleep Talk	Normal	Status	—	—	10	Depends	—
TM83	Natural Gift	Normal	Physical	—	100	15	Normal	—
TM86	Grass Knot	Grass	Special	—	100	20	Normal	○
TM87	Swagger	Normal	Status	—	90	15	Normal	—
TM90	Substitute	Normal	Status	—	—	10	Self	—
HM01	Cut	Normal	Physical	50	95	30	Normal	○

● SIZE COMPARISON

- ● HEIGHT: 2'07"
- ● WEIGHT: 19.0 lbs.
- ● ITEMS: None

● MALE FORM
Smaller spots on petals

● FEMALE FORM
Larger spots on petals

◉ ABILITIES

● Chlorophyll

◉ STATS

HP	●●
ATTACK	●●●
DEFENSE	●●●
SP. ATTACK	●●●●
SP. DEFENSE	●●●●
SPEED	●●

◉ EGG GROUPS

Grass

◉ PERFORMANCE

SPEED ★★☆☆	STAMINA ★★★★☆
POWER ★☆☆☆	JUMP ★★★
SKILL ★★☆☆	

● MAIN WAYS TO OBTAIN

Pokémon HeartGold	Route 48
Pokémon SoulSilver	Route 48
Pokémon Diamond	Route 229
Pokémon Pearl	Route 229
Pokémon Platinum	Route 229

Pokémon HeartGold

What appears to be drool is actually sweet honey. It is very sticky and clings stubbornly if touched.

Pokémon SoulSilver

It secretes a sticky, drool-like honey. Although sweet, it smells too repulsive to get very close.

◉ EVOLUTION

Use Leaf Stone

Vileplume

Lv. 21　Use Sun Stone

Oddish　Gloom

Bellossom

No. 045 | Flower Pokémon
Vileplume

`Grass` `Poison`

● HEIGHT: 3'11"
● WEIGHT: 41.0 lbs.
● ITEMS: None

● SIZE COMPARISON

● MALE FORM
Smaller spots on petals

● FEMALE FORM
Larger spots on petals

ABILITIES
● Chlorophyll

STATS
HP ●●●
ATTACK ●●●
DEFENSE ●●●
SP. ATTACK ●●●●
SP. DEFENSE ●●●●
SPEED ●●

EGG GROUPS
Grass

PERFORMANCE
SPEED ★★
POWER ★★★
SKILL ★★★
STAMINA ★★★★★
JUMP ★★☆

MAIN WAYS TO OBTAIN

Pokémon HeartGold	Use Leaf Stone on Gloom
Pokémon SoulSilver	Use Leaf Stone on Gloom
Pokémon Diamond	Use Leaf Stone on Gloom
Pokémon Pearl	Use Leaf Stone on Gloom
Pokémon Platinum	Use Leaf Stone on Gloom

Pokémon HeartGold
It has the world's largest petals. With every step, the petals shake out heavy clouds of toxic pollen.

Pokémon SoulSilver
The bud bursts into bloom with a bang. It then starts scattering allergenic, poisonous pollen.

EVOLUTION

Oddish → (Lv. 21) → Gloom → (Use Leaf Stone) → Vileplume
Gloom → (Use Sun Stone) → Bellossom

● LEVEL-UP MOVES

Lv.	Name	Type	Kind	Pow.	Acc.	PP	Range	DA
1	Mega Drain	Grass	Special	40	100	15	Normal	—
1	Aromatherapy	Grass	Status	—	—	5	All Allies	—
1	Stun Spore	Grass	Status	—	75	30	Normal	—
1	Poison Powder	Poison	Status	—	75	35	Normal	—
53	Petal Dance	Grass	Special	90	100	20	1 Random	○
65	SolarBeam	Grass	Special	120	100	10	Normal	—

● MOVE MANIAC

Name	Type	Kind	Pow.	Acc.	PP	Range	DA

● BP MOVES

Name	Type	Kind	Pow.	Acc.	PP	Range	DA
Snore	Normal	Special	40	100	15	Normal	—
Synthesis	Grass	Status	—	—	5	Self	—
Worry Seed	Grass	Status	—	100	10	Normal	—
Gastro Acid	Poison	Status	—	100	10	Normal	—
Seed Bomb	Grass	Physical	80	100	15	Normal	—

● TM & HM MOVES

No.	Name	Type	Kind	Pow.	Acc.	PP	Range	DA
TM06	Toxic	Poison	Status	—	85	10	Normal	—
TM09	Bullet Seed	Grass	Physical	10	100	30	Normal	—
TM10	Hidden Power	Normal	Special	—	100	15	Normal	—
TM11	Sunny Day	Fire	Status	—	—	5	All	—
TM15	Hyper Beam	Normal	Special	150	90	5	Normal	—
TM17	Protect	Normal	Status	—	—	10	Self	—
TM19	Giga Drain	Grass	Special	60	100	10	Normal	—
TM21	Frustration	Normal	Physical	—	100	20	Normal	○
TM22	SolarBeam	Grass	Special	120	100	10	Normal	—
TM27	Return	Normal	Physical	—	100	20	Normal	○
TM32	Double Team	Normal	Status	—	—	15	Self	—
TM36	Sludge Bomb	Poison	Special	90	100	10	Normal	—
TM42	Facade	Normal	Physical	70	100	20	Normal	○
TM43	Secret Power	Normal	Physical	70	100	20	Normal	—
TM44	Rest	Psychic	Status	—	—	10	Self	—
TM45	Attract	Normal	Status	—	100	15	Normal	—
TM53	Energy Ball	Grass	Special	80	100	10	Normal	—
TM56	Fling	Dark	Physical	—	100	10	Normal	—
TM58	Endure	Normal	Status	—	—	10	Self	—
TM60	Drain Punch	Fighting	Physical	60	100	5	Normal	○
TM68	Giga Impact	Normal	Physical	150	90	5	Normal	○
TM70	Flash	Normal	Status	—	100	20	Normal	—
TM75	Swords Dance	Normal	Status	—	—	30	Self	—
TM78	Captivate	Normal	Status	—	100	20	2 Foes	—
TM82	Sleep Talk	Normal	Status	—	—	10	Depends	—
TM83	Natural Gift	Normal	Physical	—	100	15	Normal	—
TM86	Grass Knot	Grass	Special	—	100	20	Normal	○
TM87	Swagger	Normal	Status	—	90	15	Normal	—
TM90	Substitute	Normal	Status	—	—	10	Self	—
HM01	Cut	Normal	Physical	50	95	30	Normal	○

● LEVEL-UP MOVES

Lv.	Name	Type	Kind	Pow.	Acc.	PP	Range	DA
1	Scratch	Normal	Physical	40	100	35	Normal	○
6	Stun Spore	Grass	Status	—	75	30	Normal	—
6	PoisonPowder	Poison	Status	—	75	35	Normal	—
11	Leech Life	Bug	Physical	20	100	15	Normal	○
17	Spore	Grass	Status	—	100	15	Normal	—
22	Slash	Normal	Physical	70	100	20	Normal	○
27	Growth	Normal	Status	—	—	40	Self	—
33	Giga Drain	Grass	Special	60	100	10	Normal	—
38	Aromatherapy	Grass	Status	—	—	5	All Allies	—
43	X-Scissor	Bug	Physical	80	100	15	Normal	○

● MOVE MANIAC

Name	Type	Kind	Pow.	Acc.	PP	Range	DA

● BP MOVES

Name	Type	Kind	Pow.	Acc.	PP	Range	DA
Fury Cutter	Bug	Physical	10	95	20	Normal	○
Knock Off	Dark	Physical	20	100	20	Normal	—
Bug Bite	Bug	Physical	60	100	20	Normal	○
Snore	Normal	Special	40	100	15	Normal	—
Synthesis	Grass	Status	—	—	5	Self	—
String Shot	Bug	Status	—	95	40	2 Foes	—
Worry Seed	Grass	Status	—	100	10	Normal	—
Seed Bomb	Grass	Physical	80	100	15	Normal	○

● TM & HM MOVES

No.	Name	Type	Kind	Pow.	Acc.	PP	Range	DA
TM06	Toxic	Poison	Status	—	85	10	Normal	—
TM09	Bullet Seed	Grass	Physical	10	100	30	Normal	—
TM10	Hidden Power	Normal	Special	—	100	15	Normal	—
TM11	Sunny Day	Fire	Status	—	—	5	All	—
TM17	Protect	Normal	Status	—	—	10	Self	—
TM19	Giga Drain	Grass	Special	60	100	10	Normal	—
TM21	Frustration	Normal	Physical	—	100	20	Normal	○
TM22	SolarBeam	Grass	Special	120	100	10	Normal	—
TM27	Return	Normal	Physical	—	100	20	Normal	○
TM28	Dig	Ground	Physical	80	100	10	Normal	○
TM31	Brick Break	Fighting	Physical	75	100	15	Normal	○
TM32	Double Team	Normal	Status	—	—	15	Self	—
TM36	Sludge Bomb	Poison	Special	90	100	10	Normal	—
TM40	Aerial Ace	Flying	Physical	60	—	20	Normal	○
TM42	Facade	Normal	Physical	70	100	20	Normal	○
TM43	Secret Power	Normal	Physical	70	100	20	Normal	—
TM44	Rest	Psychic	Status	—	—	10	Self	—
TM45	Attract	Normal	Status	—	100	15	Normal	—
TM46	Thief	Dark	Physical	40	100	10	Normal	○
TM53	Energy Ball	Grass	Special	80	100	10	Normal	—
TM54	False Swipe	Normal	Physical	40	100	40	Normal	○
TM58	Endure	Normal	Status	—	—	10	Self	—
TM70	Flash	Normal	Status	—	100	20	Normal	—
TM75	Swords Dance	Normal	Status	—	—	30	Self	—
TM78	Captivate	Normal	Status	—	100	20	2 Foes	—
TM81	X-Scissor	Bug	Physical	80	100	15	Normal	○
TM82	Sleep Talk	Normal	Status	—	—	10	Depends	—
TM83	Natural Gift	Normal	Physical	—	100	15	Normal	—
TM86	Grass Knot	Grass	Special	—	100	20	Normal	—
TM87	Swagger	Normal	Status	—	90	15	Normal	—
TM90	Substitute	Normal	Status	—	—	10	Self	—
HM01	Cut	Normal	Physical	50	95	30	Normal	○
HM06	Rock Smash	Fighting	Physical	40	100	15	Normal	○

● EGG MOVES

Name	Type	Kind	Pow.	Acc.	PP	Range	DA
False Swipe	Normal	Physical	40	100	40	Normal	○
Screech	Normal	Status	—	85	40	Normal	—
Counter	Fighting	Physical	—	100	20	Self	○
Psybeam	Psychic	Special	65	100	20	Normal	—
Flail	Normal	Physical	—	100	15	Normal	○
Sweet Scent	Normal	Status	—	100	20	2 Foes	—
Light Screen	Psychic	Status	—	—	30	2 Allies	—
Pursuit	Dark	Physical	40	100	20	Normal	○
Metal Claw	Steel	Physical	50	95	35	Normal	○
Bug Bite	Bug	Physical	60	100	20	Normal	○
Cross Poison	Poison	Physical	70	100	20	Normal	○
Agility	Psychic	Status	—	—	30	Self	—

○ No. **046** | Mushroom Pokémon

Paras

`Bug` `Grass`

● SIZE COMPARISON

- ● HEIGHT: 1'00"
- ● WEIGHT: 11.9 lbs.
- ● ITEMS: TinyMushroom
  Big Mushroom

● MALE/FEMALE HAVE SAME FORM

⊛ ABILITIES
- ● Effect Spore
- ● Dry Skin

⊛ STATS
HP	●
ATTACK	●●●
DEFENSE	●●●
SP. ATTACK	●●
SP. DEFENSE	●●
SPEED	●

⊛ EGG GROUPS
Bug

Grass

⊛ PERFORMANCE
SPEED ★★☆☆☆   STAMINA ★★★
POWER ★☆☆☆   JUMP ★★☆
SKILL ★★★☆

● MAIN WAYS TO OBTAIN

Pokémon HeartGold	Ilex Forest
Pokémon SoulSilver	Ilex Forest
Pokémon Diamond	Pastoria Great Marsh (after obtaining the National Pokédex/changes daily)
Pokémon Pearl	Pastoria Great Marsh (after obtaining the National Pokédex/changes daily)
Pokémon Platinum	Pastoria Great Marsh (after obtaining the National Pokédex/changes daily)

Pokémon HeartGold

It is doused with mushroom spores when it is born. As its body grows, mushrooms sprout from its back.

Pokémon SoulSilver

As its body grows, large mushrooms named tochukaso start sprouting out of its back.

⊛ EVOLUTION

Paras — Lv. 24 → Parasect

Parasect

Bug | Grass

- **HEIGHT:** 3'03"
- **WEIGHT:** 65.0 lbs.
- **ITEMS:** TinyMushroom / Big Mushroom

● SIZE COMPARISON

● MALE/FEMALE HAVE SAME FORM

● ABILITIES
- Effect Spore
- Dry Skin

● STATS
HP	●●
ATTACK	●●●●
DEFENSE	●●●●
SP. ATTACK	●●●
SP. DEFENSE	●●●
SPEED	●

● EGG GROUPS
Bug

Grass

● PERFORMANCE
SPEED ★☆☆ STAMINA ★★★★★
POWER ★★☆☆ JUMP ★★☆
SKILL ★★★☆

● MAIN WAYS TO OBTAIN

Pokémon HeartGold	Cerulean Cave
Pokémon SoulSilver	Cerulean Cave
Pokémon Diamond	Level up Paras to Lv. 24
Pokémon Pearl	Level up Paras to Lv. 24
Pokémon Platinum	Level up Paras to Lv. 24

Pokémon HeartGold	Pokémon SoulSilver
It stays mostly in dark, damp places, the preference not of the bug, but of the big mushroom on its back.	The larger the mushroom on its back grows, the stronger the mushroom spores it scatters.

● EVOLUTION

Paras — Lv. 24 → Parasect

● LEVEL-UP MOVES

Lv.	Name	Type	Kind	Pow.	Acc.	PP	Range	DA
1	Cross Poison	Poison	Physical	70	100	20	Normal	○
1	Scratch	Normal	Physical	40	100	35	Normal	○
1	Stun Spore	Grass	Status	—	75	30	Normal	—
1	PoisonPowder	Poison	Status	—	75	35	Normal	—
1	Leech Life	Bug	Physical	20	100	15	Normal	○
6	Stun Spore	Grass	Status	—	75	30	Normal	—
6	PoisonPowder	Poison	Status	—	75	35	Normal	—
11	Leech Life	Bug	Physical	20	100	15	Normal	○
17	Spore	Grass	Status	—	100	15	Normal	—
22	Slash	Normal	Physical	70	100	20	Normal	○
30	Growth	Normal	Status	—	—	40	Self	—
39	Giga Drain	Grass	Special	60	100	10	Normal	—
47	Aromatherapy	Grass	Status	—	—	5	All Allies	—
55	X-Scissor	Bug	Physical	80	100	15	Normal	○

● MOVE MANIAC

Name	Type	Kind	Pow.	Acc.	PP	Range	DA

● BP MOVES

Name	Type	Kind	Pow.	Acc.	PP	Range	DA
Fury Cutter	Bug	Physical	10	95	20	Normal	○
Knock Off	Dark	Physical	20	100	20	Normal	○
Bug Bite	Bug	Physical	60	100	20	Normal	○
Snore	Normal	Special	40	100	15	Normal	—
Synthesis	Grass	Status	—	—	5	Self	—
String Shot	Bug	Status	—	95	40	2 Foes	—
Worry Seed	Grass	Status	—	100	10	Normal	—
Seed Bomb	Grass	Physical	80	100	15	Normal	—

● TM & HM MOVES

No.	Name	Type	Kind	Pow.	Acc.	PP	Range	DA
TM06	Toxic	Poison	Status	—	85	10	Normal	—
TM09	Bullet Seed	Grass	Physical	10	100	30	Normal	—
TM10	Hidden Power	Normal	Special	—	100	15	Normal	—
TM11	Sunny Day	Fire	Status	—	—	5	All	—
TM15	Hyper Beam	Normal	Special	150	90	5	Normal	—
TM17	Protect	Normal	Status	—	—	10	Self	—
TM19	Giga Drain	Grass	Special	60	100	10	Normal	—
TM21	Frustration	Normal	Physical	—	100	20	Normal	○
TM22	SolarBeam	Grass	Special	120	100	10	Normal	—
TM27	Return	Normal	Physical	—	100	20	Normal	○
TM28	Dig	Ground	Physical	80	100	10	Normal	○
TM31	Brick Break	Fighting	Physical	75	100	15	Normal	○
TM32	Double Team	Normal	Status	—	—	15	Self	—
TM36	Sludge Bomb	Poison	Special	90	100	10	Normal	—
TM40	Aerial Ace	Flying	Physical	60	—	20	Normal	○
TM42	Facade	Normal	Physical	70	100	20	Normal	○
TM43	Secret Power	Normal	Physical	70	100	20	Normal	—
TM44	Rest	Psychic	Status	—	—	10	Self	—
TM45	Attract	Normal	Status	—	100	15	Normal	—
TM46	Thief	Dark	Physical	40	100	10	Normal	○
TM53	Energy Ball	Grass	Special	80	100	10	Normal	—
TM54	False Swipe	Normal	Physical	40	100	40	Normal	○
TM58	Endure	Normal	Status	—	—	10	Self	—
TM68	Giga Impact	Normal	Physical	150	90	5	Normal	○
TM70	Flash	Normal	Status	—	100	20	Normal	—
TM75	Swords Dance	Normal	Status	—	—	30	Self	—
TM78	Captivate	Normal	Status	—	100	20	2 Foes	—
TM81	X-Scissor	Bug	Physical	80	100	15	Normal	○
TM82	Sleep Talk	Normal	Status	—	—	10	Depends	—
TM83	Natural Gift	Normal	Physical	—	100	15	Normal	—
TM86	Grass Knot	Grass	Special	—	100	20	Normal	○
TM87	Swagger	Normal	Status	—	90	15	Normal	—
TM90	Substitute	Normal	Status	—	—	10	Self	—
HM01	Cut	Normal	Physical	50	95	30	Normal	○
HM06	Rock Smash	Fighting	Physical	40	100	15	Normal	○

● LEVEL-UP MOVES

Lv.	Name	Type	Kind	Pow.	Acc.	PP	Range	DA
1	Tackle	Normal	Physical	35	95	35	Normal	○
1	Disable	Normal	Status	—	80	20	Normal	—
1	Foresight	Normal	Status	—	—	40	Normal	—
5	Supersonic	Normal	Status	—	55	20	Normal	—
11	Confusion	Psychic	Special	50	100	25	Normal	—
13	PoisonPowder	Poison	Status	—	75	35	Normal	—
17	Leech Life	Bug	Physical	20	100	15	Normal	○
23	Stun Spore	Grass	Status	—	75	30	Normal	—
25	Psybeam	Psychic	Special	65	100	20	Normal	—
29	Sleep Powder	Grass	Status	—	75	15	Normal	—
35	Signal Beam	Bug	Special	75	100	15	Normal	—
37	Zen Headbutt	Psychic	Physical	80	90	15	Normal	○
41	Poison Fang	Poison	Physical	50	100	15	Normal	○
47	Psychic	Psychic	Special	90	100	10	Normal	—

● MOVE MANIAC

Name	Type	Kind	Pow.	Acc.	PP	Range	DA

● BP MOVES

Name	Type	Kind	Pow.	Acc.	PP	Range	DA
Zen Headbutt	Psychic	Physical	80	90	15	Normal	○
Bug Bite	Bug	Physical	60	100	20	Normal	—
Snore	Normal	Special	40	100	15	Normal	—
Swift	Normal	Special	60	—	20	2 Foes	—
String Shot	Bug	Status	—	95	40	2 Foes	—
Signal Beam	Bug	Special	75	100	15	Normal	—

● TM & HM MOVES

No.	Name	Type	Kind	Pow.	Acc.	PP	Range	DA
TM06	Toxic	Poison	Status	—	85	10	Normal	—
TM10	Hidden Power	Normal	Special	—	100	15	Normal	—
TM11	Sunny Day	Fire	Status	—	—	5	All	—
TM17	Protect	Normal	Status	—	—	10	Self	—
TM19	Giga Drain	Grass	Special	60	100	10	Normal	—
TM21	Frustration	Normal	Physical	—	100	20	Normal	○
TM22	SolarBeam	Grass	Special	120	100	10	Normal	—
TM27	Return	Normal	Physical	—	100	20	Normal	○
TM29	Psychic	Psychic	Special	90	100	10	Normal	—
TM32	Double Team	Normal	Status	—	—	15	Self	—
TM36	Sludge Bomb	Poison	Special	90	100	10	Normal	—
TM42	Facade	Normal	Physical	70	100	20	Normal	○
TM43	Secret Power	Normal	Physical	70	100	20	Normal	—
TM44	Rest	Psychic	Status	—	—	10	Self	—
TM45	Attract	Normal	Status	—	100	15	Normal	—
TM46	Thief	Dark	Physical	40	100	10	Normal	○
TM48	Skill Swap	Psychic	Status	—	—	10	Normal	—
TM58	Endure	Normal	Status	—	—	10	Self	—
TM70	Flash	Normal	Status	—	100	20	Normal	—
TM78	Captivate	Normal	Status	—	100	20	2 Foes	—
TM82	Sleep Talk	Normal	Status	—	—	10	Depends	—
TM83	Natural Gift	Normal	Physical	—	100	15	Normal	—
TM87	Swagger	Normal	Status	—	90	15	Normal	—
TM90	Substitute	Normal	Status	—	—	10	Self	—

● EGG MOVES

Name	Type	Kind	Pow.	Acc.	PP	Range	DA
Baton Pass	Normal	Status	—	—	40	Self	—
Screech	Normal	Status	—	85	40	Normal	—
Giga Drain	Grass	Special	60	100	10	Normal	—
Signal Beam	Bug	Special	75	100	15	Normal	—
Agility	Psychic	Status	—	—	30	Self	—
Morning Sun	Normal	Status	—	—	5	Self	—
Toxic Spikes	Poison	Status	—	—	20	2 Foes	—
Bug Bite	Bug	Physical	60	100	20	Normal	○

◎ No. 048 | Insect Pokémon
Venonat

`Bug` `Poison`

● **HEIGHT:** 3'03"
● **WEIGHT:** 66.1 lbs.
● **ITEMS:** None

● SIZE COMPARISON

● MALE/FEMALE HAVE SAME FORM

◎ ABILITIES
● Compoundeyes
● Tinted Lens

◎ STATS
HP ●●
ATTACK ●●
DEFENSE ●●
SP. ATTACK ●●
SP. DEFENSE ●●
SPEED ●●

◎ EGG GROUPS
Bug

◎ PERFORMANCE
SPEED ★★★★☆   STAMINA ★★★☆
POWER ★★☆   JUMP ★★☆
SKILL ★★☆

● MAIN WAYS TO OBTAIN

Pokémon HeartGold	Route 43 (morning and night only)
Pokémon SoulSilver	Route 43 (morning and night only)
Pokémon Diamond	Route 229 (occasionally appears when you use Poké Radar)
Pokémon Pearl	Route 229 (occasionally appears when you use Poké Radar)
Pokémon Platinum	Route 229 (occasionally appears when you use Poké Radar)

Pokémon HeartGold

Its eyes also function as radar units. It catches and eats small bugs that hide in darkness.

Pokémon SoulSilver

Poison oozes from all over its body. It catches and eats small bugs at night that are attracted by light.

◎ EVOLUTION

Venonat → Lv. 31 → Venomoth

Venomoth

Bug | Poison

- **HEIGHT:** 4'11"
- **WEIGHT:** 27.6 lbs.
- **ITEMS:** Shed Shell

● SIZE COMPARISON

● MALE/FEMALE HAVE SAME FORM

⊕ ABILITIES
- Shield Dust
- Tinted Lens

⊕ STATS
HP	●●●
ATTACK	●●●
DEFENSE	●●●
SP. ATTACK	●●●
SP. DEFENSE	●●●●
SPEED	●●●●

⊕ EGG GROUPS
Bug

⊕ PERFORMANCE
SPEED ★★★	STAMINA ★☆☆
POWER ★☆☆	JUMP ★★★★★
SKILL ★★★	

● MAIN WAYS TO OBTAIN

Pokémon HeartGold — Route 25 (night only)

Pokémon SoulSilver — Route 25 (night only)

Pokémon Diamond — Route 229 (use Poké Radar)

Pokémon Pearl — Route 229 (use Poké Radar)

Pokémon Platinum — Route 229 (use Poké Radar)

Pokémon HeartGold
When it attacks, it flaps its large wings violently to scatter its poisonous powder all around.

Pokémon SoulSilver
The powder on its wings is poisonous if it is dark in hue. If it is light in hue, it causes paralysis.

⊕ EVOLUTION

Venonat → Lv. 31 → Venomoth

● LEVEL-UP MOVES

Lv.	Name	Type	Kind	Pow.	Acc.	PP	Range	DA
1	Silver Wind	Bug	Special	60	100	5	Normal	—
1	Tackle	Normal	Physical	35	95	35	Normal	○
1	Disable	Normal	Status	—	80	20	Normal	—
1	Foresight	Normal	Status	—	—	40	Normal	—
1	Supersonic	Normal	Status	—	55	20	Normal	—
5	Supersonic	Normal	Status	—	55	20	Normal	—
11	Confusion	Psychic	Special	50	100	25	Normal	—
13	PoisonPowder	Poison	Status	—	75	35	Normal	—
17	Leech Life	Bug	Physical	20	100	15	Normal	—
23	Stun Spore	Grass	Status	—	75	30	Normal	∪
25	Psybeam	Psychic	Special	65	100	20	Normal	—
29	Sleep Powder	Grass	Status	—	75	15	Normal	—
31	Gust	Flying	Special	40	100	35	Normal	—
37	Signal Beam	Bug	Special	75	100	15	Normal	—
41	Zen Headbutt	Psychic	Physical	80	90	15	Normal	○
47	Poison Fang	Poison	Physical	50	100	15	Normal	○
55	Psychic	Psychic	Special	90	100	10	Normal	—
59	Bug Buzz	Bug	Special	90	100	10	Normal	—

● MOVE MANIAC

Name	Type	Kind	Pow.	Acc.	PP	Range	DA

● BP MOVES

Name	Type	Kind	Pow.	Acc.	PP	Range	DA
Ominous Wind	Ghost	Special	60	100	5	Normal	—
Air Cutter	Flying	Special	55	95	25	2 Foes	—
Zen Headbutt	Psychic	Physical	80	90	15	Normal	○
Bug Bite	Bug	Physical	60	100	20	Normal	○
Snore	Normal	Special	40	100	15	Normal	—
Swift	Normal	Special	60	—	20	2 Foes	—
String Shot	Bug	Status	—	95	40	2 Foes	—
Tailwind	Flying	Status	—	—	30	2 Allies	—
Signal Beam	Bug	Special	75	100	15	Normal	—
Twister	Dragon	Special	40	100	20	2 Foes	—

● TM & HM MOVES

No.	Name	Type	Kind	Pow.	Acc.	PP	Range	DA
TM06	Toxic	Poison	Status	—	85	10	Normal	—
TM10	Hidden Power	Normal	Special	—	100	15	Normal	—
TM11	Sunny Day	Fire	Status	—	—	5	All	—
TM15	Hyper Beam	Normal	Special	150	90	5	Normal	—
TM17	Protect	Normal	Status	—	—	10	Self	—
TM19	Giga Drain	Grass	Special	60	100	10	Normal	—
TM21	Frustration	Normal	Physical	—	100	20	Normal	○
TM22	SolarBeam	Grass	Special	120	100	10	Normal	—
TM27	Return	Normal	Physical	—	100	20	Normal	○
TM29	Psychic	Psychic	Special	90	100	10	Normal	—
TM32	Double Team	Normal	Status	—	—	15	Self	—
TM36	Sludge Bomb	Poison	Special	90	100	10	Normal	—
TM40	Aerial Ace	Flying	Physical	60	—	20	Normal	○
TM42	Facade	Normal	Physical	70	100	20	Normal	○
TM43	Secret Power	Normal	Physical	70	100	20	Normal	—
TM44	Rest	Psychic	Status	—	—	10	Self	—
TM45	Attract	Normal	Status	—	100	15	Normal	—
TM46	Thief	Dark	Physical	40	100	10	Normal	○
TM48	Skill Swap	Psychic	Status	—	—	10	Normal	—
TM51	Roost	Flying	Status	—	—	10	Self	—
TM53	Energy Ball	Grass	Special	80	100	10	Normal	—
TM58	Endure	Normal	Status	—	—	10	Self	—
TM62	Silver Wind	Bug	Special	60	100	5	Normal	—
TM68	Giga Impact	Normal	Physical	150	90	5	Normal	○
TM70	Flash	Normal	Status	—	100	20	Normal	—
TM78	Captivate	Normal	Status	—	100	20	2 Foes	—
TM82	Sleep Talk	Normal	Status	—	—	10	Depends	—
TM83	Natural Gift	Normal	Physical	—	100	15	Normal	—
TM87	Swagger	Normal	Status	—	90	15	Normal	—
TM89	U-turn	Bug	Physical	70	100	20	Normal	○
TM90	Substitute	Normal	Status	—	—	10	Self	—

● LEVEL-UP MOVES

Lv.	Name	Type	Kind	Pow.	Acc.	PP	Range	DA
1	Scratch	Normal	Physical	40	100	35	Normal	○
1	Sand-Attack	Ground	Status	—	100	15	Normal	—
4	Growl	Normal	Status	—	100	40	2 Foes	—
7	Astonish	Ghost	Physical	30	100	15	Normal	○
12	Magnitude	Ground	Physical	—	100	30	2 Foes/1 Ally	○
15	Mud-Slap	Ground	Special	20	100	10	Normal	—
18	Dig	Ground	Physical	80	100	10	Normal	○
23	Sucker Punch	Dark	Physical	80	100	5	Normal	○
26	Earth Power	Ground	Special	90	100	10	Normal	—
29	Mud Bomb	Ground	Special	65	85	10	Normal	—
34	Slash	Normal	Physical	70	100	20	Normal	○
37	Earthquake	Ground	Physical	100	100	10	2 Foes/1 Ally	○
40	Fissure	Ground	Physical	—	30	5	Normal	—

● MOVE MANIAC

Name	Type	Kind	Pow.	Acc.	PP	Range	DA

● BP MOVES

Name	Type	Kind	Pow.	Acc.	PP	Range	DA
Sucker Punch	Dark	Physical	80	100	5	Normal	○
Snore	Normal	Special	40	100	15	Normal	—
Mud-Slap	Ground	Special	20	100	10	Normal	—
Earth Power	Ground	Special	90	100	10	Normal	—

● TM & HM MOVES

No.	Name	Type	Kind	Pow.	Acc.	PP	Range	DA
TM06	Toxic	Poison	Status	—	85	10	Normal	—
TM10	Hidden Power	Normal	Special	—	100	15	Normal	—
TM11	Sunny Day	Fire	Status	—	—	5	All	—
TM17	Protect	Normal	Status	—	—	10	Self	—
TM21	Frustration	Normal	Physical	—	100	20	Normal	○
TM26	Earthquake	Ground	Physical	100	100	10	2 Foes/1 Ally	○
TM27	Return	Normal	Physical	—	100	20	Normal	○
TM28	Dig	Ground	Physical	80	100	10	Normal	○
TM32	Double Team	Normal	Status	—	—	15	Self	—
TM36	Sludge Bomb	Poison	Special	90	100	10	Normal	—
TM37	Sandstorm	Rock	Status	—	—	10	All	—
TM39	Rock Tomb	Rock	Physical	50	80	10	Normal	—
TM40	Aerial Ace	Flying	Physical	60	—	20	Normal	○
TM42	Facade	Normal	Physical	70	100	20	Normal	—
TM43	Secret Power	Normal	Physical	70	100	20	Normal	—
TM44	Rest	Psychic	Status	—	—	10	Self	—
TM45	Attract	Normal	Status	—	100	15	Normal	—
TM46	Thief	Dark	Physical	40	100	10	Normal	○
TM58	Endure	Normal	Status	—	—	10	Self	—
TM65	Shadow Claw	Ghost	Physical	70	100	15	Normal	○
TM76	Stealth Rock	Rock	Status	—	—	20	2 Foes	—
TM78	Captivate	Normal	Status	—	100	20	2 Foes	—
TM80	Rock Slide	Rock	Physical	75	90	10	2 Foes	—
TM82	Sleep Talk	Normal	Status	—	—	10	Depends	—
TM83	Natural Gift	Normal	Physical	—	100	15	Normal	—
TM87	Swagger	Normal	Status	—	90	15	Normal	—
TM90	Substitute	Normal	Status	—	—	10	Self	—
HM01	Cut	Normal	Physical	50	95	30	Normal	○
HM06	Rock Smash	Fighting	Physical	40	100	15	Normal	○

● EGG MOVES

Name	Type	Kind	Pow.	Acc.	PP	Range	DA
Faint Attack	Dark	Physical	60	—	20	Normal	○
Screech	Normal	Status	—	85	40	Normal	—
AncientPower	Rock	Special	60	100	5	Normal	—
Pursuit	Dark	Physical	40	100	20	Normal	○
Beat Up	Dark	Physical	10	100	10	Normal	—
Uproar	Normal	Special	50	100	10	1 Random	—
Rock Slide	Rock	Physical	75	90	10	2 Foes	—
Mud Bomb	Ground	Special	65	85	10	Normal	—
Astonish	Ghost	Physical	30	100	15	Normal	○
Reversal	Fighting	Physical	—	100	15	Normal	—

No. 050 | Mole Pokémon
Diglett

Ground

- ● HEIGHT: 0'08"
- ● WEIGHT: 1.8 lbs.
- ● ITEMS: Soft Sand

● SIZE COMPARISON

● MALE/FEMALE HAVE SAME FORM

◎ ABILITIES
- Sand Veil
- Arena Trap

◎ STATS
HP ●
ATTACK ●●
DEFENSE ●
SP. ATTACK ●
SP. DEFENSE ●
SPEED ●●●●

◎ EGG GROUPS
Field

◎ PERFORMANCE

SPEED ★★★★☆　　STAMINA ★★★☆
POWER ★☆　　　　JUMP ★
SKILL ★★★☆

● MAIN WAYS TO OBTAIN

Pokémon HeartGold Route 48

Pokémon SoulSilver Route 48

Pokémon Diamond Route 228

Pokémon Pearl Route 228

Pokémon Platinum Route 228

Pokémon HeartGold
Its skin is very thin. If it is exposed to light, its blood heats up, causing it to grow weak.

Pokémon SoulSilver
If a DIGLETT digs through a field, it leaves the soil perfectly tilled and ideal for planting crops.

◎ EVOLUTION

Lv. 26

Diglett　　　Dugtrio

● No. 051 | Mole Pokémon
Dugtrio

Ground

● HEIGHT: 2'04"
● WEIGHT: 73.4 lbs.
● ITEMS: Soft Sand

● SIZE COMPARISON

● MALE/FEMALE HAVE SAME FORM

● ABILITIES
● Sand Veil
● Arena Trap

● STATS
HP ●
ATTACK ●●●
DEFENSE ●●
SP. ATTACK ●●
SP. DEFENSE ●●
SPEED ●●●●●

● EGG GROUPS
Field

● PERFORMANCE
SPEED ★★★★☆   STAMINA ★★★★
POWER ★★★☆   JUMP ★
SKILL ★★☆

● MAIN WAYS TO OBTAIN

Pokémon HeartGold	DIGLETT's Cave
Pokémon SoulSilver	DIGLETT's Cave
Pokémon Diamond	Route 228
Pokémon Pearl	Route 228
Pokémon Platinum	Route 228

Pokémon HeartGold
Its three heads bob separately up and down to loosen the soil nearby, making it easier for it to burrow.

Pokémon SoulSilver
Extremely powerful, they can dig through even the hardest ground to a depth of over 60 miles.

● EVOLUTION
Diglett → Lv. 26 → Dugtrio

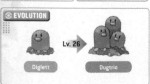

● LEVEL-UP MOVES

Lv.	Name	Type	Kind	Pow.	Acc.	PP	Range	DA
1	Night Slash	Dark	Physical	70	100	15	Normal	○
1	Tri Attack	Normal	Special	80	100	10	Normal	—
1	Scratch	Normal	Physical	40	100	35	Normal	○
1	Sand-Attack	Ground	Status	—	100	15	Normal	—
4	Growl	Normal	Status	—	100	40	2 Foes	—
7	Astonish	Ghost	Physical	30	100	15	Normal	○
12	Magnitude	Ground	Physical	—	100	30	2 Foes/1 Ally	—
15	Mud-Slap	Ground	Special	20	100	10	Normal	—
18	Dig	Ground	Physical	80	100	10	Normal	○
23	Sucker Punch	Dark	Physical	80	100	5	Normal	○
26	Sand Tomb	Ground	Physical	15	70	15	Normal	—
28	Earth Power	Ground	Special	90	100	10	Normal	—
33	Mud Bomb	Ground	Special	65	85	10	Normal	—
40	Slash	Normal	Physical	70	100	20	Normal	—
45	Earthquake	Ground	Physical	100	100	10	2 Foes/1 Ally	○
50	Fissure	Ground	Physical	—	30	5	Normal	—

● MOVE MANIAC

Name	Type	Kind	Pow.	Acc.	PP	Range	DA

● BP MOVES

Name	Type	Kind	Pow.	Acc.	PP	Range	DA
Sucker Punch	Dark	Physical	80	100	5	Normal	○
Snore	Normal	Special	40	100	15	Normal	—
Mud-Slap	Ground	Special	20	100	10	Normal	—
Earth Power	Ground	Special	90	100	10	Normal	—

● TM & HM MOVES

No.	Name	Type	Kind	Pow.	Acc.	PP	Range	DA
TM06	Toxic	Poison	Status	—	85	10	Normal	—
TM10	Hidden Power	Normal	Special	—	100	15	Normal	—
TM11	Sunny Day	Fire	Status	—	—	5	All	—
TM15	Hyper Beam	Normal	Special	150	90	5	Normal	—
TM17	Protect	Normal	Status	—	—	10	Self	—
TM21	Frustration	Normal	Physical	—	100	20	Normal	○
TM26	Earthquake	Ground	Physical	100	100	10	2 Foes/1 Ally	○
TM27	Return	Normal	Physical	—	100	20	Normal	○
TM28	Dig	Ground	Physical	80	100	10	Normal	○
TM32	Double Team	Normal	Status	—	—	15	Self	—
TM36	Sludge Bomb	Poison	Special	90	100	10	Normal	—
TM37	Sandstorm	Rock	Status	—	—	10	All	—
TM39	Rock Tomb	Rock	Physical	50	80	10	Normal	—
TM40	Aerial Ace	Flying	Physical	60	—	20	Normal	○
TM42	Facade	Normal	Physical	70	100	20	Normal	○
TM43	Secret Power	Normal	Physical	70	100	20	Normal	—
TM44	Rest	Psychic	Status	—	—	10	Self	—
TM45	Attract	Normal	Status	—	100	15	Normal	—
TM46	Thief	Dark	Physical	40	100	10	Normal	○
TM58	Endure	Normal	Status	—	—	10	Self	—
TM65	Shadow Claw	Ghost	Physical	70	100	15	Normal	○
TM68	Giga Impact	Normal	Physical	150	90	5	Normal	○
TM71	Stone Edge	Rock	Physical	100	80	5	Normal	—
TM76	Stealth Rock	Rock	Status	—	—	20	2 Foes	—
TM78	Captivate	Normal	Status	—	100	20	2 Foes	—
TM80	Rock Slide	Rock	Physical	75	90	10	2 Foes	—
TM82	Sleep Talk	Normal	Status	—	—	10	Depends	—
TM83	Natural Gift	Normal	Physical	—	100	15	Normal	—
TM87	Swagger	Normal	Status	—	90	15	Normal	—
TM90	Substitute	Normal	Status	—	—	10	Self	—
HM01	Cut	Normal	Physical	50	95	30	Normal	○
HM06	Rock Smash	Fighting	Physical	40	100	15	Normal	○

● LEVEL-UP MOVES

Lv.	Name	Type	Kind	Pow.	Acc.	PP	Range	DA
1	Scratch	Normal	Physical	40	100	35	Normal	○
1	Growl	Normal	Status	—	100	40	2 Foes	—
6	Bite	Dark	Physical	60	100	25	Normal	○
9	Fake Out	Normal	Physical	40	100	10	Normal	○
14	Fury Swipes	Normal	Physical	18	80	15	Normal	○
17	Screech	Normal	Status	—	85	40	Normal	—
22	Faint Attack	Dark	Physical	60	—	20	Normal	○
25	Taunt	Dark	Status	—	100	20	Normal	—
30	Pay Day	Normal	Physical	40	100	20	Normal	○
33	Slash	Normal	Physical	70	100	20	Normal	○
38	Nasty Plot	Dark	Status	—	—	20	Self	—
41	Assurance	Dark	Physical	50	100	10	Normal	○
46	Captivate	Normal	Status	—	100	20	2 Foes	—
49	Night Slash	Dark	Physical	70	100	15	Normal	○
54	Feint	Normal	Physical	50	100	10	Normal	—

● MOVE MANIAC

Name	Type	Kind	Pow.	Acc.	PP	Range	DA
Headbutt	Normal	Physical	70	100	15	Normal	○

● BP MOVES

Name	Type	Kind	Pow.	Acc.	PP	Range	DA
Icy Wind	Ice	Special	55	95	15	2 Foes	—
Knock Off	Dark	Special	20	100	20	Normal	○
Snore	Normal	Special	40	100	15	Normal	—
Spite	Ghost	Status	—	100	10	Normal	—
Last Resort	Normal	Physical	130	100	5	Normal	○
Swift	Normal	Special	60	—	20	2 Foes	—
Uproar	Normal	Special	50	100	10	1 Random	—
Mud-Slap	Ground	Special	20	100	10	Normal	—
Gunk Shot	Poison	Physical	120	70	5	Normal	—
Seed Bomb	Grass	Physical	80	100	15	Normal	—

● TM & HM MOVES

No.	Name	Type	Kind	Pow.	Acc.	PP	Range	DA
TM03	Water Pulse	Water	Special	60	100	20	Normal	—
TM06	Toxic	Poison	Status	—	85	10	Normal	—
TM10	Hidden Power	Normal	Special	—	100	15	Normal	—
TM11	Sunny Day	Fire	Status	—	—	5	All	—
TM12	Taunt	Dark	Status	—	100	20	Normal	—
TM17	Protect	Normal	Status	—	—	10	Self	—
TM18	Rain Dance	Water	Status	—	—	5	All	—
TM21	Frustration	Normal	Physical	—	100	20	Normal	○
TM23	Iron Tail	Steel	Physical	100	75	15	Normal	○
TM24	Thunderbolt	Electric	Special	95	100	15	Normal	—
TM25	Thunder	Electric	Special	120	70	10	Normal	—
TM27	Return	Normal	Physical	—	100	20	Normal	○
TM28	Dig	Ground	Physical	80	100	10	Normal	○
TM30	Shadow Ball	Ghost	Special	80	100	15	Normal	—
TM32	Double Team	Normal	Status	—	—	15	Self	—
TM34	Shock Wave	Electric	Special	60	—	20	Normal	—
TM40	Aerial Ace	Flying	Physical	60	—	20	Normal	○
TM41	Torment	Dark	Status	—	100	15	Normal	—
TM42	Facade	Normal	Physical	70	100	20	Normal	○
TM43	Secret Power	Normal	Physical	70	100	20	Normal	○
TM44	Rest	Psychic	Status	—	—	10	Self	—
TM45	Attract	Normal	Status	—	100	15	Normal	—
TM46	Thief	Dark	Physical	40	100	10	Normal	○
TM49	Snatch	Dark	Status	—	—	10	Normal	—
TM58	Endure	Normal	Status	—	—	10	Self	—
TM65	Shadow Claw	Ghost	Physical	70	100	15	Normal	○
TM66	Payback	Dark	Physical	50	100	10	Normal	○
TM70	Flash	Normal	Status	—	100	20	Normal	—
TM77	Psych Up	Normal	Status	—	—	10	Normal	—
TM78	Captivate	Normal	Status	—	100	20	2 Foes	—
TM79	Dark Pulse	Dark	Special	80	100	15	Normal	—
TM82	Sleep Talk	Normal	Status	—	—	10	Depends	—
TM83	Natural Gift	Normal	Physical	—	100	15	Normal	—
TM85	Dream Eater	Psychic	Special	100	100	15	Normal	—
TM87	Swagger	Normal	Status	—	90	15	Normal	—
TM89	U-turn	Bug	Physical	70	100	20	Normal	○
TM90	Substitute	Normal	Status	—	—	10	Self	—
HM01	Cut	Normal	Physical	50	95	30	Normal	○

● EGG MOVES

Name	Type	Kind	Pow.	Acc.	PP	Range	DA
Spite	Ghost	Status	—	100	10	Normal	—
Charm	Normal	Status	—	100	20	Normal	—
Hypnosis	Psychic	Status	—	60	20	Normal	—
Amnesia	Psychic	Status	—	—	20	Self	—
Psych Up	Normal	Status	—	—	10	Normal	—
Assist	Normal	Status	—	—	20	Depends	—
Odor Sleuth	Normal	Status	—	—	40	Normal	—
Flail	Normal	Physical	—	100	15	Normal	○
Last Resort	Normal	Physical	130	100	5	Normal	○
Punishment	Dark	Physical	—	100	5	Normal	○
Tail Whip	Normal	Status	—	100	30	2 Foes	—

No. 052 | Scratch Cat Pokémon
Meowth

Normal

- **HEIGHT:** 1'04"
- **WEIGHT:** 9.3 lbs.
- **ITEMS:** Quick Claw

● SIZE COMPARISON

● MALE/FEMALE HAVE SAME FORM

● ABILITIES
- Pickup
- Technician

● STATS
HP ●
ATTACK ●●
DEFENSE ●●
SP. ATTACK ●●
SP. DEFENSE ●●
SPEED ●●●●

● EGG GROUPS
Field

● PERFORMANCE
SPEED ★★★★   STAMINA ★
POWER ★☆   JUMP ★★★☆
SKILL ★★★★

● MAIN WAYS TO OBTAIN

Pokémon HeartGold	—
Pokémon SoulSilver	Route 38
Pokémon Diamond	Trophy Garden at the Pokémon Mansion on Route 212 (after obtaining the National Pokédex, talk to Mr. Backlot)
Pokémon Pearl	Trophy Garden at the Pokémon Mansion on Route 212 (after obtaining the National Pokédex, talk to Mr. Backlot)
Pokémon Platinum	Trophy Garden at the Pokémon Mansion on Route 212 (after obtaining the National Pokédex, talk to Mr. Backlot)

Pokémon HeartGold
It is fascinated by round objects. It can't stop playing with them until it tires and falls asleep.

Pokémon SoulSilver
It loves anything that shines. It especially adores coins that it picks up and secretly hoards.

● EVOLUTION

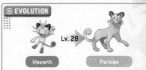

Meowth   Lv. 28   Persian

No. 053 | Classy Cat Pokémon
Persian

Normal

- **HEIGHT:** 3'03"
- **WEIGHT:** 70.5 lbs.
- **ITEMS:** Quick Claw

● SIZE COMPARISON

● MALE/FEMALE HAVE SAME FORM

ABILITIES
- Limber
- Technician

STATS
HP	●●
ATTACK	●●●
DEFENSE	●●●
SP. ATTACK	●●
SP. DEFENSE	●●
SPEED	●●●●●

EGG GROUPS
Field

PERFORMANCE
SPEED ★★★★☆   STAMINA ★
POWER ★★☆   JUMP ★★★
SKILL ★★★☆☆

MAIN WAYS TO OBTAIN

Pokémon HeartGold	—
Pokémon SoulSilver	Route 7
Pokémon Diamond	Level up Meowth to Lv. 28
Pokémon Pearl	Level up Meowth to Lv. 28
Pokémon Platinum	Level up Meowth to Lv. 28

Pokémon HeartGold	**Pokémon SoulSilver**
Many adore it for its sophisticated air. However, it will lash out and scratch for little reason.	Its lithe muscles allow it to walk without making a sound. It attacks in an instant.

EVOLUTION

Meowth → Lv. 28 → Persian

● LEVEL-UP MOVES

Lv.	Name	Type	Kind	Pow.	Acc.	PP	Range	DA
1	Switcheroo	Dark	Status	—	100	10	Normal	—
1	Scratch	Normal	Physical	40	100	35	Normal	○
1	Growl	Normal	Status	—	100	40	2 Foes	—
1	Bite	Dark	Physical	60	100	25	Normal	○
1	Fake Out	Normal	Physical	40	100	10	Normal	○
6	Bite	Dark	Physical	60	100	25	Normal	○
9	Fake Out	Normal	Physical	40	100	10	Normal	○
14	Fury Swipes	Normal	Physical	18	80	15	Normal	○
17	Screech	Normal	Status	—	85	40	Normal	—
22	Faint Attack	Dark	Physical	60	—	20	Normal	○
25	Taunt	Dark	Status	—	100	20	Normal	—
32	Power Gem	Rock	Special	70	100	20	Normal	—
37	Slash	Normal	Physical	70	100	20	Normal	○
44	Nasty Plot	Dark	Status	—	—	20	Self	—
49	Assurance	Dark	Physical	50	100	10	Normal	○
56	Captivate	Normal	Status	—	100	20	2 Foes	—
61	Night Slash	Dark	Physical	70	100	15	Normal	○
68	Feint	Normal	Physical	50	100	10	Normal	—

● MOVE MANIAC

Name	Type	Kind	Pow.	Acc.	PP	Range	DA
Headbutt	Normal	Physical	70	100	15	Normal	○

● BP MOVES

Name	Type	Kind	Pow.	Acc.	PP	Range	DA
Icy Wind	Ice	Special	55	95	15	2 Foes	—
Knock Off	Dark	Physical	20	100	20	Normal	○
Snore	Normal	Special	40	100	15	Normal	—
Spite	Ghost	Status	—	100	10	Normal	—
Last Resort	Normal	Physical	130	100	5	Normal	○
Swift	Normal	Special	60	—	20	2 Foes	—
Uproar	Normal	Special	50	100	10	1 Random	—
Mud-Slap	Ground	Special	20	100	10	Normal	—
Gunk Shot	Poison	Physical	120	70	5	Normal	—
Seed Bomb	Grass	Physical	80	100	15	Normal	—

● TM & HM MOVES

No.	Name	Type	Kind	Pow.	Acc.	PP	Range	DA
TM03	Water Pulse	Water	Special	60	100	20	Normal	—
TM05	Roar	Normal	Status	—	100	20	Normal	—
TM06	Toxic	Poison	Status	—	85	10	Normal	—
TM10	Hidden Power	Normal	Special	—	100	15	Normal	—
TM11	Sunny Day	Fire	Status	—	—	5	All	—
TM12	Taunt	Dark	Status	—	100	20	Normal	—
TM15	Hyper Beam	Normal	Special	150	90	5	Normal	—
TM17	Protect	Normal	Status	—	—	10	Self	—
TM18	Rain Dance	Water	Status	—	—	5	All	—
TM21	Frustration	Normal	Physical	—	100	20	Normal	○
TM23	Iron Tail	Steel	Physical	100	75	15	Normal	○
TM24	Thunderbolt	Electric	Special	95	100	15	Normal	—
TM25	Thunder	Electric	Special	120	70	10	Normal	—
TM27	Return	Normal	Physical	—	100	20	Normal	○
TM28	Dig	Ground	Physical	80	100	10	Normal	○
TM30	Shadow Ball	Ghost	Special	80	100	15	Normal	—
TM32	Double Team	Normal	Status	—	—	15	Self	—
TM34	Shock Wave	Electric	Special	60	—	20	Normal	—
TM40	Aerial Ace	Flying	Physical	60	—	20	Normal	○
TM41	Torment	Dark	Status	—	100	15	Normal	—
TM42	Facade	Normal	Physical	70	100	20	Normal	○
TM43	Secret Power	Normal	Physical	70	100	20	Normal	○
TM44	Rest	Psychic	Status	—	—	10	Self	—
TM45	Attract	Normal	Status	—	100	15	Normal	—
TM46	Thief	Dark	Physical	40	100	10	Normal	○
TM49	Snatch	Dark	Status	—	—	10	Depends	—
TM58	Endure	Normal	Status	—	—	10	Self	—
TM63	Embargo	Dark	Status	—	100	15	Normal	—
TM65	Shadow Claw	Ghost	Physical	70	100	15	Normal	○
TM66	Payback	Dark	Physical	50	100	10	Normal	○
TM68	Giga Impact	Normal	Physical	150	90	5	Normal	○
TM70	Flash	Normal	Status	—	100	20	Normal	—
TM77	Psych Up	Normal	Status	—	—	10	Normal	—
TM78	Captivate	Normal	Status	—	100	20	2 Foes	—
TM79	Dark Pulse	Dark	Special	80	100	15	Normal	—
TM82	Sleep Talk	Normal	Status	—	—	10	Depends	—
TM83	Natural Gift	Normal	Physical	—	100	15	Normal	—
TM85	Dream Eater	Psychic	Special	100	100	15	Normal	—
TM87	Swagger	Normal	Status	—	90	15	Normal	—
TM89	U-turn	Bug	Physical	70	100	20	Normal	○
TM90	Substitute	Normal	Status	—	—	10	Self	—
HM01	Cut	Normal	Physical	50	95	30	Normal	○

● LEVEL-UP MOVES

Lv.	Name	Type	Kind	Pow.	Acc.	PP	Range	DA
1	Water Sport	Water	Status	—	—	15	All	—
1	Scratch	Normal	Physical	40	100	35	Normal	○
5	Tail Whip	Normal	Status	—	100	30	2 Foes	—
9	Water Gun	Water	Special	40	100	25	Normal	—
14	Disable	Normal	Status	—	80	20	Normal	—
18	Confusion	Psychic	Special	50	100	25	Normal	—
22	Water Pulse	Water	Special	60	100	20	Normal	—
27	Fury Swipes	Normal	Physical	18	80	15	Normal	○
31	Screech	Normal	Status	—	85	40	Normal	—
35	Psych Up	Normal	Status	—	—	10	Normal	—
40	Zen Headbutt	Psychic	Physical	80	90	15	Normal	○
44	Amnesia	Psychic	Status	—	—	20	Self	—
48	Hydro Pump	Water	Special	120	80	5	Normal	—

● MOVE MANIAC

Name	Type	Kind	Pow.	Acc.	PP	Range	DA
Headbutt	Normal	Physical	70	100	15	Normal	○

● BP MOVES

Name	Type	Kind	Pow.	Acc.	PP	Range	DA
Dive	Water	Physical	80	100	10	Normal	○
Icy Wind	Ice	Special	55	95	15	2 Foes	—
Ice Punch	Ice	Physical	75	100	15	Normal	○
Zen Headbutt	Psychic	Physical	80	90	15	Normal	○
Snore	Normal	Special	40	100	15	Normal	—
Swift	Normal	Special	60	—	20	2 Foes	—
Worry Seed	Grass	Status	—	100	10	Normal	—
Role Play	Psychic	Status	—	—	10	Normal	—
Mud-Slap	Ground	Special	20	100	10	Normal	—
Aqua Tail	Water	Physical	90	90	10	Normal	○
Signal Beam	Bug	Special	75	100	15	Normal	—

● TM & HM MOVES

No.	Name	Type	Kind	Pow.	Acc.	PP	Range	DA
TM01	Focus Punch	Fighting	Physical	150	100	20	Normal	○
TM03	Water Pulse	Water	Special	60	100	20	Normal	—
TM04	Calm Mind	Psychic	Status	—	—	20	Self	—
TM06	Toxic	Poison	Status	—	85	10	Normal	—
TM07	Hail	Ice	Status	—	—	10	All	—
TM10	Hidden Power	Normal	Special	—	100	15	Normal	—
TM13	Ice Beam	Ice	Special	95	100	10	Normal	—
TM14	Blizzard	Ice	Special	120	70	5	2 Foes	—
TM17	Protect	Normal	Status	—	—	10	Self	—
TM18	Rain Dance	Water	Status	—	—	5	All	—
TM21	Frustration	Normal	Physical	—	100	20	Normal	○
TM23	Iron Tail	Steel	Physical	100	75	15	Normal	○
TM27	Return	Normal	Physical	—	100	20	Normal	○
TM28	Dig	Ground	Physical	80	100	10	Normal	○
TM29	Psychic	Psychic	Special	90	100	10	Normal	—
TM31	Brick Break	Fighting	Physical	75	100	15	Normal	○
TM32	Double Team	Normal	Status	—	—	15	Self	—
TM40	Aerial Ace	Flying	Physical	60	—	20	Normal	○
TM42	Facade	Normal	Physical	70	100	20	Normal	○
TM43	Secret Power	Normal	Physical	70	100	20	Normal	○
TM44	Rest	Psychic	Status	—	—	10	Self	—
TM45	Attract	Normal	Status	—	100	15	Normal	—
TM55	Brine	Water	Special	65	100	10	Normal	—
TM56	Fling	Dark	Physical	—	100	10	Normal	—
TM58	Endure	Normal	Status	—	—	10	Self	—
TM65	Shadow Claw	Ghost	Physical	70	100	15	Normal	○
TM70	Flash	Normal	Status	—	100	20	Normal	—
TM77	Psych Up	Normal	Status	—	—	10	Normal	—
TM78	Captivate	Normal	Status	—	100	20	2 Foes	—
TM82	Sleep Talk	Normal	Status	—	—	10	Depends	—
TM83	Natural Gift	Normal	Physical	—	100	15	Normal	—
TM87	Swagger	Normal	Status	—	90	15	Normal	—
TM90	Substitute	Normal	Status	—	—	10	Self	—
HM03	Surf	Water	Special	95	100	15	2 Foes/1 Ally	—
HM04	Strength	Normal	Physical	80	100	15	Normal	○
HM05	Whirlpool	Water	Special	15	70	15	Normal	—
HM06	Rock Smash	Fighting	Physical	40	100	15	Normal	○
HM07	Waterfall	Water	Physical	80	100	15	Normal	○

● EGG MOVES

Name	Type	Kind	Pow.	Acc.	PP	Range	DA
Hypnosis	Psychic	Status	—	60	20	Normal	—
Psybeam	Psychic	Special	65	100	20	Normal	—
Foresight	Normal	Status	—	—	40	Normal	—
Light Screen	Psychic	Status	—	—	30	2 Allies	—
Future Sight	Psychic	Special	80	90	15	Normal	—
Psychic	Psychic	Special	90	100	10	Normal	—
Cross Chop	Fighting	Physical	100	80	5	Normal	○
Refresh	Normal	Status	—	—	20	Self	—
Confuse Ray	Ghost	Status	—	100	10	Normal	—
Yawn	Normal	Status	—	—	10	Normal	—
Mud Bomb	Ground	Special	65	85	10	Normal	—
Encore	Normal	Status	—	100	5	Normal	—

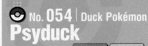

● No. 054 | Duck Pokémon
Psyduck

Water

- **HEIGHT:** 2'07"
- **WEIGHT:** 43.2 lbs.
- **ITEMS:** None

● SIZE COMPARISON

● MALE/FEMALE HAVE SAME FORM

● ABILITIES
- Damp
- Cloud Nine

● STATS
- HP ●●
- ATTACK ●●●
- DEFENSE ●●●
- SP. ATTACK ●●●
- SP. DEFENSE ●●●
- SPEED ●●●

● EGG GROUPS
- Water 1
- Field

● PERFORMANCE
- SPEED ★★☆☆☆
- POWER ★★☆☆☆
- SKILL ★★☆☆☆
- STAMINA ★★☆☆☆
- JUMP ★★★☆☆

● MAIN WAYS TO OBTAIN

Pokémon HeartGold	Ilex Forest (water surface)
Pokémon SoulSilver	Ilex Forest (water surface)
Pokémon Diamond	Oreburgh Gate B1F
Pokémon Pearl	Oreburgh Gate B1F
Pokémon Platinum	Oreburgh Gate 1F

Pokémon HeartGold

It has mystical powers but doesn't recall that it has used them. That is why it always looks puzzled.

Pokémon SoulSilver

If its chronic headache peaks, it may exhibit odd powers. It seems unable to recall such an episode.

● EVOLUTION

Psyduck → Lv. 33 → Golduck

● No. 055 | Duck Pokémon
Golduck

Water

● HEIGHT: 5'02"
● WEIGHT: 168.9 lbs.
● ITEMS: None

● SIZE COMPARISON

● MALE/FEMALE HAVE SAME FORM

● ABILITIES
● Damp
● Cloud Nine

● STATS
HP ●●●
ATTACK ●●●●
DEFENSE ●●●●
SP. ATTACK ●●●●
SP. DEFENSE ●●●●
SPEED ●●●●

● EGG GROUPS
Water 1
Field

● PERFORMANCE
SPEED ★★★
POWER ★★★☆
SKILL ★★☆
STAMINA ★★★★
JUMP ★★★☆

● MAIN WAYS TO OBTAIN

Pokémon HeartGold	Ilex Forest (water surface) or Safari Zone (Wetland Area: if Rock objects are placed, may appear in tall grass)
Pokémon SoulSilver	Ilex Forest (water surface) or Safari Zone (Wetland Area: if Rock objects are placed, may appear in tall grass)
Pokémon Diamond	Lake Verity (water surface)
Pokémon Pearl	Lake Verity (water surface)
Pokémon Platinum	Lake Verity (water surface)

| Pokémon HeartGold | Pokémon SoulSilver |
| When it swims at full speed using its long, webbed limbs, its forehead somehow begins to glow. | It appears by waterways at dusk. It may use telekinetic powers if its forehead glows mysteriously. |

● EVOLUTION

Psyduck → Lv. 33 → Golduck

● LEVEL-UP MOVES

Lv.	Name	Type	Kind	Pow.	Acc.	PP	Range	DA
1	Aqua Jet	Water	Physical	40	100	20	Normal	○
1	Water Sport	Water	Status	—	—	15	All	—
1	Scratch	Normal	Physical	40	100	35	Normal	○
1	Tail Whip	Normal	Status	—	100	30	2 Foes	—
1	Water Gun	Water	Special	40	100	25	Normal	—
5	Tail Whip	Normal	Status	—	100	30	2 Foes	—
9	Water Gun	Water	Special	40	100	25	Normal	—
14	Disable	Normal	Status	—	80	20	Normal	—
18	Confusion	Psychic	Special	50	100	25	Normal	—
22	Water Pulse	Water	Special	60	100	20	Normal	—
27	Fury Swipes	Normal	Physical	18	80	15	Normal	○
31	Screech	Normal	Status	—	85	40	Normal	—
37	Psych Up	Normal	Status	—	—	10	Normal	—
44	Zen Headbutt	Psychic	Physical	80	90	15	Normal	○
50	Amnesia	Psychic	Status	—	—	20	Self	—
56	Hydro Pump	Water	Special	120	80	5	Normal	—

● MOVE MANIAC

Name	Type	Kind	Pow.	Acc.	PP	Range	DA
Headbutt	Normal	Physical	70	100	15	Normal	○

● BP MOVES

Name	Type	Kind	Pow.	Acc.	PP	Range	DA
Dive	Water	Physical	80	100	10	Normal	○
Fury Cutter	Bug	Physical	10	95	20	Normal	○
Icy Wind	Ice	Special	55	95	15	2 Foes	—
Ice Punch	Ice	Physical	75	100	15	Normal	○
Zen Headbutt	Psychic	Physical	80	90	15	Normal	○
Snore	Normal	Special	40	100	15	Normal	—
Swift	Normal	Special	60	—	20	2 Foes	—
Worry Seed	Grass	Status	—	100	10	Normal	—
Role Play	Psychic	Status	—	—	10	Normal	—
Mud-Slap	Ground	Special	20	100	10	Normal	—
Aqua Tail	Water	Physical	90	90	10	Normal	—
Signal Beam	Bug	Special	75	100	15	Normal	—
Low Kick	Fighting	Physical	—	100	20	Normal	○

● TM & HM MOVES

No.	Name	Type	Kind	Pow.	Acc.	PP	Range	DA
TM01	Focus Punch	Fighting	Physical	150	100	20	Normal	○
TM03	Water Pulse	Water	Special	60	100	20	Normal	—
TM04	Calm Mind	Psychic	Status	—	—	20	Self	—
TM06	Toxic	Poison	Status	—	85	10	Normal	—
TM07	Hail	Ice	Status	—	—	10	All	—
TM10	Hidden Power	Normal	Special	—	100	15	Normal	—
TM13	Ice Beam	Ice	Special	95	100	10	Normal	—
TM14	Blizzard	Ice	Special	120	70	5	2 Foes	—
TM15	Hyper Beam	Normal	Special	150	90	5	Normal	—
TM17	Protect	Normal	Status	—	—	10	Self	—
TM18	Rain Dance	Water	Status	—	—	5	All	—
TM21	Frustration	Normal	Physical	—	100	20	Normal	○
TM23	Iron Tail	Steel	Physical	100	75	15	Normal	○
TM27	Return	Normal	Physical	—	100	20	Normal	○
TM28	Dig	Ground	Physical	80	100	10	Normal	○
TM29	Psychic	Psychic	Special	90	100	10	Normal	○
TM31	Brick Break	Fighting	Physical	75	100	15	Normal	—
TM32	Double Team	Normal	Status	—	—	15	Self	—
TM40	Aerial Ace	Flying	Physical	60	—	20	Normal	—
TM42	Facade	Normal	Physical	70	100	20	Normal	○
TM43	Secret Power	Normal	Physical	70	100	20	Normal	—
TM44	Rest	Psychic	Status	—	—	10	Self	—
TM45	Attract	Normal	Status	—	100	15	Normal	—
TM52	Focus Blast	Fighting	Special	120	70	5	Normal	—
TM55	Brine	Water	Special	65	100	10	Normal	—
TM56	Fling	Dark	Physical	—	100	10	Normal	—
TM58	Endure	Normal	Status	—	—	10	Self	—
TM65	Shadow Claw	Ghost	Physical	70	100	15	Normal	○
TM68	Giga Impact	Normal	Physical	150	90	5	Normal	○
TM70	Flash	Normal	Status	—	100	20	Normal	—
TM77	Psych Up	Normal	Status	—	—	10	Normal	—
TM78	Captivate	Normal	Status	—	100	20	2 Foes	—
TM82	Sleep Talk	Normal	Status	—	—	10	Depends	—
TM83	Natural Gift	Normal	Physical	—	100	15	Normal	—
TM87	Swagger	Normal	Status	—	90	15	Normal	—
TM90	Substitute	Normal	Status	—	—	10	Self	—
HM03	Surf	Water	Special	95	100	15	2 Foes / 1 Ally	—
HM04	Strength	Normal	Physical	80	100	15	Normal	○
HM05	Whirlpool	Water	Special	15	70	15	Normal	○
HM06	Rock Smash	Fighting	Physical	40	100	15	Normal	○
HM07	Waterfall	Water	Physical	80	100	15	Normal	○
HM08	Rock Climb	Normal	Physical	90	85	20	Normal	○

● LEVEL-UP MOVES

Lv.	Name	Type	Kind	Pow.	Acc.	PP	Range	DA
1	Covet	Normal	Physical	40	100	40	Normal	○
1	Scratch	Normal	Physical	40	100	35	Normal	○
1	Low Kick	Fighting	Physical	—	100	20	Normal	○
1	Leer	Normal	Status	—	100	30	2 Foes	—
1	Focus Energy	Normal	Status	—	—	30	Self	—
9	Fury Swipes	Normal	Physical	18	80	15	Normal	○
13	Karate Chop	Fighting	Physical	50	100	25	Normal	○
17	Seismic Toss	Fighting	Physical	—	100	20	Normal	○
21	Screech	Normal	Status	—	85	40	Normal	—
25	Assurance	Dark	Physical	50	100	10	Normal	○
33	Swagger	Normal	Status	—	90	15	Normal	—
37	Cross Chop	Fighting	Physical	100	80	5	Normal	○
41	Thrash	Normal	Physical	90	100	20	1 Random	○
45	Punishment	Dark	Physical	—	100	5	Normal	○
49	Close Combat	Fighting	Physical	120	100	5	Normal	○

● MOVE MANIAC

Name	Type	Kind	Pow.	Acc.	PP	Range	DA
Headbutt	Normal	Physical	70	100	15	Normal	○

● BP MOVES

Name	Type	Kind	Pow.	Acc.	PP	Range	DA
ThunderPunch	Electric	Physical	75	100	15	Normal	○
Fire Punch	Fire	Physical	75	100	15	Normal	○
Ice Punch	Ice	Physical	75	100	15	Normal	○
Vacuum Wave	Fighting	Special	40	100	30	Normal	—
Spite	Ghost	Status	—	100	10	Normal	—
Helping Hand	Normal	Status	—	—	20	1 Ally	—
Swift	Normal	Special	60	—	20	2 Foes	—
Uproar	Normal	Special	50	100	10	1 Random	—
Role Play	Psychic	Status	—	—	10	Normal	—
Mud-Slap	Ground	Special	20	100	10	Normal	—
Endeavor	Normal	Physical	—	100	5	Normal	—
Outrage	Dragon	Physical	120	100	15	1 Random	○
Gunk Shot	Poison	Physical	120	70	5	Normal	○
Seed Bomb	Grass	Physical	80	100	15	Normal	○
Low Kick	Fighting	Physical	—	100	20	Normal	○

● TM & HM MOVES

No.	Name	Type	Kind	Pow.	Acc.	PP	Range	DA
TM01	Focus Punch	Fighting	Physical	150	100	20	Normal	○
TM06	Toxic	Poison	Status	—	85	10	Normal	—
TM08	Bulk Up	Fighting	Status	—	—	20	Self	—
TM10	Hidden Power	Normal	Special	—	100	15	Normal	—
TM11	Sunny Day	Fire	Status	—	—	5	All	—
TM12	Taunt	Dark	Status	—	100	20	Normal	—
TM17	Protect	Normal	Status	—	—	10	Self	—
TM18	Rain Dance	Water	Status	—	—	5	All	—
TM21	Frustration	Normal	Physical	—	100	20	Normal	○
TM23	Iron Tail	Steel	Physical	100	75	15	Normal	○
TM24	Thunderbolt	Electric	Special	95	100	15	Normal	—
TM25	Thunder	Electric	Special	120	70	10	Normal	—
TM26	Earthquake	Ground	Physical	100	100	10	2 Foes/1 Ally	—
TM27	Return	Normal	Physical	—	100	20	Normal	○
TM28	Dig	Ground	Physical	80	100	10	Normal	○
TM31	Brick Break	Fighting	Physical	75	100	15	Normal	○
TM32	Double Team	Normal	Status	—	—	15	Self	—
TM39	Rock Tomb	Rock	Physical	50	80	10	Normal	—
TM40	Aerial Ace	Flying	Physical	60	—	20	Normal	○
TM42	Facade	Normal	Physical	70	100	20	Normal	○
TM43	Secret Power	Normal	Physical	70	100	20	Normal	—
TM44	Rest	Psychic	Status	—	—	10	Self	—
TM45	Attract	Normal	Status	—	100	15	Normal	—
TM46	Thief	Dark	Physical	40	100	10	Normal	○
TM50	Overheat	Fire	Special	140	90	5	Normal	—
TM52	Focus Blast	Fighting	Special	120	70	5	Normal	—
TM56	Fling	Dark	Physical	—	100	10	Normal	—
TM58	Endure	Normal	Status	—	—	10	Self	—
TM66	Payback	Dark	Physical	50	100	10	Normal	○
TM78	Captivate	Normal	Status	—	100	20	2 Foes	—
TM80	Rock Slide	Rock	Physical	75	90	10	2 Foes	—
TM82	Sleep Talk	Normal	Status	—	—	10	Depends	—
TM83	Natural Gift	Normal	Physical	—	100	15	Normal	—
TM84	Poison Jab	Poison	Physical	80	100	20	Normal	○
TM87	Swagger	Normal	Status	—	90	15	Normal	—
TM89	U-turn	Bug	Physical	70	100	20	Normal	○
TM90	Substitute	Normal	Status	—	—	10	Self	—
HM04	Strength	Normal	Physical	80	100	15	Normal	○
HM06	Rock Smash	Fighting	Physical	40	100	15	Normal	○
HM08	Rock Climb	Normal	Physical	90	85	20	Normal	○

● EGG MOVES

Name	Type	Kind	Pow.	Acc.	PP	Range	DA
Rock Slide	Rock	Physical	75	90	10	2 Foes	—
Foresight	Normal	Status	—	—	40	Normal	—
Meditate	Psychic	Status	—	—	40	Self	—
Counter	Fighting	Physical	—	100	20	Self	○
Reversal	Fighting	Physical	—	100	15	Normal	○
Beat Up	Dark	Physical	10	100	10	Normal	—
Revenge	Fighting	Physical	60	100	10	Normal	○
SmellingSalt	Normal	Physical	60	100	10	Normal	○
Close Combat	Fighting	Physical	120	100	5	Normal	○
Encore	Normal	Status	—	100	5	Normal	—

◉ No. 056 | Pig Monkey Pokémon
Mankey

Fighting

● HEIGHT: 1'08"
● WEIGHT: 61.7 lbs.
● ITEMS: Payapa Berry

● SIZE COMPARISON

● MALE/FEMALE HAVE SAME FORM

⬡ ABILITIES
- Vital Spirit
- Anger Point

⬡ STATS
HP ●
ATTACK ●●●
DEFENSE ●●
SP. ATTACK ●
SP. DEFENSE ●●
SPEED ●●●

⬡ EGG GROUPS
Field

⬡ PERFORMANCE
SPEED ★★★☆ STAMINA ★☆
POWER ★★☆ JUMP ★★☆
SKILL ★★★★☆

● MAIN WAYS TO OBTAIN

Pokémon HeartGold | Route 42

Pokémon SoulSilver | —

Pokémon Diamond | Route 225 (occasionally appears when you use Poké Radar)

Pokémon Pearl | Route 225 (occasionally appears when you use Poké Radar)

Pokémon Platinum | Route 225 (occasionally appears when you use Poké Radar)

Pokémon HeartGold
It is extremely ill-tempered. Groups of them will attack any handy target for no reason.

Pokémon SoulSilver
It's unsafe to approach if it gets violently enraged for no reason and can't distinguish friends from foes.

⬡ EVOLUTION

Mankey → Lv. 28 → Primeape

No. 057 | Pig Monkey Pokémon
Primeape

Fighting

● LEVEL-UP MOVES

Lv.	Name	Type	Kind	Pow.	Acc.	PP	Range	DA
1	Fling	Dark	Physical	—	100	10	Normal	—
1	Scratch	Normal	Physical	40	100	35	Normal	O
1	Low Kick	Fighting	Physical	—	100	20	Normal	O
1	Leer	Normal	Status	—	100	30	2 Foes	—
1	Focus Energy	Normal	Status	—	—	30	Self	—
9	Fury Swipes	Normal	Physical	18	80	15	Normal	O
13	Karate Chop	Fighting	Physical	50	100	25	Normal	O
17	Seismic Toss	Fighting	Physical	—	100	20	Normal	—
21	Screech	Normal	Status	—	85	40	Normal	—
25	Assurance	Dark	Physical	50	100	10	Normal	O
28	Rage	Normal	Physical	20	100	20	Normal	O
35	Swagger	Normal	Status	—	90	15	Normal	—
41	Cross Chop	Fighting	Physical	100	80	5	Normal	O
47	Thrash	Normal	Physical	90	100	20	1 Random	O
53	Punishment	Dark	Physical	—	100	5	Normal	O
59	Close Combat	Fighting	Physical	120	100	5	Normal	O

● MOVE MANIAC

Name	Type	Kind	Pow.	Acc.	PP	Range	DA
Headbutt	Normal	Physical	70	100	15	Normal	O

● BP MOVES

Name	Type	Kind	Pow.	Acc.	PP	Range	DA
ThunderPunch	Electric	Physical	75	100	15	Normal	O
Fire Punch	Fire	Physical	75	100	15	Normal	O
Ice Punch	Ice	Physical	75	100	15	Normal	O
Vacuum Wave	Fighting	Special	40	100	30	Normal	—
Spite	Ghost	Status	—	100	10	Normal	—
Helping Hand	Normal	Status	—	—	20	1 Ally	—
Swift	Normal	Special	60	—	20	2 Foes	—
Uproar	Normal	Special	50	100	10	1 Random	—
Role Play	Psychic	Status	—	—	10	Normal	—
Mud-Slap	Ground	Special	20	100	10	Normal	—
Endeavor	Normal	Physical	—	100	5	Normal	O
Outrage	Dragon	Physical	120	100	15	1 Random	O
Gunk Shot	Poison	Physical	120	70	5	Normal	O
Seed Bomb	Grass	Physical	80	100	15	Normal	O
Low Kick	Fighting	Physical	—	100	20	Normal	O

● HEIGHT: 3'03"
● WEIGHT: 70.5 lbs.
● ITEMS: Payapa Berry

● SIZE COMPARISON

● MALE/FEMALE HAVE SAME FORM

● ABILITIES
● Vital Spirit
● Anger Point

● STATS
HP ●●
ATTACK ●●●
DEFENSE ●●●
SP. ATTACK ●●●
SP. DEFENSE ●●●
SPEED ●●●●

● EGG GROUPS
Field

● PERFORMANCE
SPEED ★★★
POWER ★★★★☆
SKILL ★
STAMINA ★★☆
JUMP ★★☆

● MAIN WAYS TO OBTAIN

Pokémon HeartGold Cerulean Cave

Pokémon SoulSilver —

Pokémon Diamond Route 225 (use Poké Radar)

Pokémon Pearl Route 225 (use Poké Radar)

Pokémon Platinum Route 225 (use Poké Radar)

Pokémon HeartGold
If approached while asleep, it may awaken and angrily give chase in a groggy state of semi-sleep.

Pokémon SoulSilver
It becomes wildly furious if it even senses someone looking at it. It chases anyone that meets its glare.

● EVOLUTION

Lv. 28

Mankey — Primeape

● TM & HM MOVES

No.	Name	Type	Kind	Pow.	Acc.	PP	Range	DA
TM01	Focus Punch	Fighting	Physical	150	100	20	Normal	O
TM06	Toxic	Poison	Status	—	85	10	Normal	—
TM08	Bulk Up	Fighting	Status	—	—	20	Self	—
TM10	Hidden Power	Normal	Special	—	100	15	Normal	—
TM11	Sunny Day	Fire	Status	—	—	5	All	—
TM12	Taunt	Dark	Status	—	100	20	Normal	—
TM15	Hyper Beam	Normal	Special	150	90	5	Normal	—
TM17	Protect	Normal	Status	—	—	10	Self	—
TM18	Rain Dance	Water	Status	—	—	5	All	—
TM21	Frustration	Normal	Physical	—	100	20	Normal	O
TM23	Iron Tail	Steel	Physical	100	75	15	Normal	O
TM24	Thunderbolt	Electric	Special	95	100	15	Normal	—
TM25	Thunder	Electric	Special	120	70	10	Normal	—
TM26	Earthquake	Ground	Physical	100	100	10	2 Foes/1 Ally	—
TM27	Return	Normal	Physical	—	100	20	Normal	O
TM28	Dig	Ground	Physical	80	100	10	Normal	O
TM31	Brick Break	Fighting	Physical	75	100	15	Normal	O
TM32	Double Team	Normal	Status	—	—	15	Self	—
TM39	Rock Tomb	Rock	Physical	50	80	10	Normal	O
TM40	Aerial Ace	Flying	Physical	60	—	20	Normal	O
TM42	Facade	Normal	Physical	70	100	20	Normal	—
TM43	Secret Power	Normal	Physical	70	100	20	Normal	—
TM44	Rest	Psychic	Status	—	—	10	Self	—
TM45	Attract	Normal	Status	—	100	15	Normal	—
TM46	Thief	Dark	Physical	40	100	10	Normal	O
TM50	Overheat	Fire	Special	140	90	5	Normal	—
TM52	Focus Blast	Fighting	Special	120	70	5	Normal	—
TM56	Fling	Dark	Physical	—	100	10	Normal	—
TM58	Endure	Normal	Status	—	—	10	Self	—
TM66	Payback	Dark	Physical	50	100	10	Normal	O
TM68	Giga Impact	Normal	Physical	150	90	5	Normal	O
TM71	Stone Edge	Rock	Physical	100	80	5	Normal	—
TM78	Captivate	Normal	Status	—	100	20	2 Foes	—
TM80	Rock Slide	Rock	Physical	75	90	10	2 Foes	—
TM82	Sleep Talk	Normal	Status	—	—	10	Depends	—
TM83	Natural Gift	Normal	Physical	—	100	15	Normal	—
TM84	Poison Jab	Poison	Physical	80	100	20	Normal	O
TM87	Swagger	Normal	Status	—	90	15	Normal	—
TM89	U-turn	Bug	Physical	70	100	20	Normal	O
TM90	Substitute	Normal	Status	—	—	10	Self	—
HM04	Strength	Normal	Physical	80	100	15	Normal	O
HM06	Rock Smash	Fighting	Physical	40	100	15	Normal	O
HM08	Rock Climb	Normal	Physical	90	85	20	Normal	O

● LEVEL-UP MOVES

Lv.	Name	Type	Kind	Pow.	Acc.	PP	Range	DA
1	Bite	Dark	Physical	60	100	25	Normal	○
1	Roar	Normal	Status	—	100	20	Normal	—
6	Ember	Fire	Special	40	100	25	Normal	—
9	Leer	Normal	Status	—	100	30	2 Foes	—
14	Odor Sleuth	Normal	Status	—	—	40	Normal	—
17	Helping Hand	Normal	Status	—	—	20	1 Ally	—
20	Flame Wheel	Fire	Physical	60	100	25	Normal	○
25	Reversal	Fighting	Physical	—	100	15	Normal	○
28	Fire Fang	Fire	Physical	65	95	15	Normal	○
31	Take Down	Normal	Physical	90	85	20	Normal	○
34	Flamethrower	Fire	Special	95	100	15	Normal	—
39	Agility	Psychic	Status	—	—	30	Self	—
42	Crunch	Dark	Physical	80	100	15	Normal	○
45	Heat Wave	Fire	Special	100	90	10	2 Foes	—
48	Flare Blitz	Fire	Physical	120	100	15	Normal	○

● MOVE MANIAC

Name	Type	Kind	Pow.	Acc.	PP	Range	DA
Headbutt	Normal	Physical	70	100	15	Normal	○

● BP MOVES

Name	Type	Kind	Pow.	Acc.	PP	Range	DA
Snore	Normal	Special	40	100	15	Normal	—
Helping Hand	Normal	Status	—	—	20	1 Ally	—
Swift	Normal	Special	60	—	20	2 Foes	—
Mud-Slap	Ground	Special	20	100	10	Normal	—
Heat Wave	Fire	Special	100	90	10	2 Foes	—

● TM & HM MOVES

No.	Name	Type	Kind	Pow.	Acc.	PP	Range	DA
TM05	Roar	Normal	Status	—	100	20	Normal	—
TM06	Toxic	Poison	Status	—	85	10	Normal	—
TM10	Hidden Power	Normal	Special	—	100	15	Normal	—
TM11	Sunny Day	Fire	Status	—	—	5	All	—
TM17	Protect	Normal	Status	—	—	10	Self	—
TM21	Frustration	Normal	Physical	—	100	20	Normal	○
TM23	Iron Tail	Steel	Physical	100	75	15	Normal	○
TM27	Return	Normal	Physical	—	100	20	Normal	○
TM28	Dig	Ground	Physical	80	100	10	Normal	○
TM32	Double Team	Normal	Status	—	—	15	Self	—
TM35	Flamethrower	Fire	Special	95	100	15	Normal	—
TM38	Fire Blast	Fire	Special	120	85	5	Normal	—
TM40	Aerial Ace	Flying	Physical	60	—	20	Normal	○
TM42	Facade	Normal	Physical	70	100	20	Normal	○
TM43	Secret Power	Normal	Physical	70	100	20	Normal	○
TM44	Rest	Psychic	Status	—	—	10	Self	—
TM45	Attract	Normal	Status	—	100	15	Normal	—
TM46	Thief	Dark	Physical	40	100	10	Normal	○
TM50	Overheat	Fire	Special	140	90	5	Normal	—
TM58	Endure	Normal	Status	—	—	10	Self	—
TM61	Will-O-Wisp	Fire	Status	—	75	15	Normal	—
TM78	Captivate	Normal	Status	—	100	20	2 Foes	—
TM82	Sleep Talk	Normal	Status	—	—	10	Depends	—
TM83	Natural Gift	Normal	Physical	—	100	15	Normal	—
TM87	Swagger	Normal	Status	—	90	15	Normal	—
TM90	Substitute	Normal	Status	—	—	10	Self	—
HM04	Strength	Normal	Physical	80	100	15	Normal	○
HM06	Rock Smash	Fighting	Physical	40	100	15	Normal	○

● EGG MOVES

Name	Type	Kind	Pow.	Acc.	PP	Range	DA
Body Slam	Normal	Physical	85	100	15	Normal	○
Safeguard	Normal	Status	—	—	25	2 Allies	—
Crunch	Dark	Physical	80	100	15	Normal	○
Thrash	Normal	Physical	90	100	20	1 Random	○
Fire Spin	Fire	Special	15	70	15	Normal	—
Howl	Normal	Status	—	—	40	Self	—
Heat Wave	Fire	Special	100	90	10	2 Foes	—
Double-Edge	Normal	Physical	120	100	15	Normal	○
Flare Blitz	Fire	Physical	120	100	15	Normal	○
Morning Sun	Normal	Status	—	—	5	Self	—

No. 058 | Puppy Pokémon
Growlithe

Fire

- **HEIGHT:** 2'04"
- **WEIGHT:** 41.9 lbs.
- **ITEMS:** Rawst Berry

● SIZE COMPARISON

● MALE/FEMALE HAVE SAME FORM

● ABILITIES
- Intimidate
- Flash Fire

● STATS
- HP ●●
- ATTACK ●●●
- DEFENSE ●●
- SP. ATTACK ●●●
- SP. DEFENSE ●●
- SPEED ●●●

● EGG GROUPS
Field

● PERFORMANCE
- SPEED ★★★☆
- POWER ★★★☆
- SKILL ★★★☆
- STAMINA ★★☆
- JUMP ★★★☆

● MAIN WAYS TO OBTAIN

Pokémon HeartGold — Route 36

Pokémon SoulSilver — —

Pokémon Diamond — Route 201 (after obtaining the National Pokédex, insert *Pokémon FireRed* into your Nintendo DS's Game Pak slot)

Pokémon Pearl — Route 201 (after obtaining the National Pokédex, insert *Pokémon FireRed* into your Nintendo DS's Game Pak slot)

Pokémon Platinum — Route 201 (after obtaining the National Pokédex, insert *Pokémon FireRed* into your Nintendo DS's Game Pak slot)

Pokémon HeartGold — It has a brave and trustworthy nature. It fearlessly stands up to bigger and stronger foes.

Pokémon SoulSilver — Extremely loyal, it will fearlessly bark at any opponent to protect its own Trainer from harm.

● EVOLUTION

Growlithe → Use Fire Stone → Arcanine

No. 059 | Legendary Pokémon
Arcanine

Fire

LEVEL-UP MOVES

Lv.	Name	Type	Kind	Pow.	Acc.	PP	Range	DA
1	Thunder Fang	Electric	Physical	65	95	15	Normal	○
1	Bite	Dark	Physical	60	100	25	Normal	○
1	Roar	Normal	Status	—	100	20	Normal	—
1	Fire Fang	Fire	Physical	65	95	15	Normal	○
1	Odor Sleuth	Normal	Status	—	—	40	Normal	—
39	ExtremeSpeed	Normal	Physical	80	100	5	Normal	○

MOVE MANIAC

Name	Type	Kind	Pow.	Acc.	PP	Range	DA
Headbutt	Normal	Physical	70	100	15	Normal	○

BP MOVES

Name	Type	Kind	Pow.	Acc.	PP	Range	DA
Snore	Normal	Special	40	100	15	Normal	—
Helping Hand	Normal	Status	—	—	20	1 Ally	—
Swift	Normal	Special	60	—	20	2 Foes	—
Mud-Slap	Ground	Special	20	100	10	Normal	—
Iron Head	Steel	Physical	80	100	15	Normal	○
Heat Wave	Fire	Special	100	90	10	2 Foes	—

- **HEIGHT:** 6'03"
- **WEIGHT:** 341.7 lbs.
- **ITEMS:** None

SIZE COMPARISON

MALE/FEMALE HAVE SAME FORM

ABILITIES
- Intimidate
- Flash Fire

STATS
HP	●●●
ATTACK	●●●●
DEFENSE	●●●●
SP. ATTACK	●●●●
SP. DEFENSE	●●●
SPEED	●●●●

EGG GROUPS
Field

PERFORMANCE

SPEED ★★★★☆   STAMINA ★★☆
POWER ★★★★☆   JUMP ★★☆
SKILL ★☆

MAIN WAYS TO OBTAIN

Pokémon HeartGold	Use Fire Stone on Growlithe
Pokémon SoulSilver	—
Pokémon Diamond	Use Fire Stone on Growlithe
Pokémon Pearl	Use Fire Stone on Growlithe
Pokémon Platinum	Use Fire Stone on Growlithe

Pokémon HeartGold	Pokémon SoulSilver
This legendary Chinese Pokémon is considered magnificent. Many people are enchanted by its grand mane.	Its magnificent bark conveys a sense of majesty. Anyone hearing it can't help but grovel before it.

EVOLUTION

Use Fire Stone

Growlithe → Arcanine

TM & HM MOVES

No.	Name	Type	Kind	Pow.	Acc.	PP	Range	DA
TM05	Roar	Normal	Status	—	100	20	Normal	—
TM06	Toxic	Poison	Status	—	85	10	Normal	—
TM10	Hidden Power	Normal	Special	—	100	15	Normal	—
TM11	Sunny Day	Fire	Status	—	—	5	All	—
TM15	Hyper Beam	Normal	Special	150	90	5	Normal	—
TM17	Protect	Normal	Status	—	—	10	Self	—
TM21	Frustration	Normal	Physical	—	100	20	Normal	○
TM22	SolarBeam	Grass	Special	120	100	10	Normal	—
TM23	Iron Tail	Steel	Physical	100	75	15	Normal	○
TM27	Return	Normal	Physical	—	100	20	Normal	○
TM28	Dig	Ground	Physical	80	100	10	Normal	○
TM32	Double Team	Normal	Status	—	—	15	Self	—
TM35	Flamethrower	Fire	Special	95	100	15	Normal	—
TM38	Fire Blast	Fire	Special	120	85	5	Normal	—
TM40	Aerial Ace	Flying	Physical	60	—	20	Normal	○
TM42	Facade	Normal	Physical	70	100	20	Normal	○
TM43	Secret Power	Normal	Physical	70	100	20	Normal	○
TM44	Rest	Psychic	Status	—	—	10	Self	—
TM45	Attract	Normal	Status	—	100	15	Normal	—
TM46	Thief	Dark	Physical	40	100	10	Normal	○
TM50	Overheat	Fire	Special	140	90	5	Normal	—
TM58	Endure	Normal	Status	—	—	10	Self	—
TM59	Dragon Pulse	Dragon	Special	90	100	10	Normal	—
TM61	Will-O-Wisp	Fire	Status	—	75	15	Normal	—
TM68	Giga Impact	Normal	Physical	150	90	5	Normal	○
TM78	Captivate	Normal	Status	—	100	20	2 Foes	—
TM82	Sleep Talk	Normal	Status	—	—	10	Depends	—
TM83	Natural Gift	Normal	Physical	—	100	15	Normal	—
TM87	Swagger	Normal	Status	—	90	15	Normal	—
TM90	Substitute	Normal	Status	—	—	10	Self	—
HM04	Strength	Normal	Physical	80	100	15	Normal	○
HM06	Rock Smash	Fighting	Physical	40	100	15	Normal	○
HM08	Rock Climb	Normal	Physical	90	85	20	Normal	○

● LEVEL-UP MOVES

Lv.	Name	Type	Kind	Pow.	Acc.	PP	Range	DA
1	Water Sport	Water	Status	—	—	15	All	—
5	Bubble	Water	Special	20	100	30	2 Foes	—
8	Hypnosis	Psychic	Status	—	60	20	Normal	—
11	Water Gun	Water	Special	40	100	25	Normal	—
15	DoubleSlap	Normal	Physical	15	85	10	Normal	O
18	Rain Dance	Water	Status	—	—	5	All	—
21	Body Slam	Normal	Physical	85	100	15	Normal	O
25	BubbleBeam	Water	Special	65	100	20	Normal	—
28	Mud Shot	Ground	Special	55	95	15	Normal	—
31	Belly Drum	Normal	Status	—	—	10	Self	—
35	Wake-Up Slap	Fighting	Physical	60	100	10	Normal	O
38	Hydro Pump	Water	Special	120	80	5	Normal	—
41	Mud Bomb	Ground	Special	65	85	10	Normal	—

● MOVE MANIAC

Name	Type	Kind	Pow.	Acc.	PP	Range	DA
Headbutt	Normal	Physical	70	100	15	Normal	O

● BP MOVES

Name	Type	Kind	Pow.	Acc.	PP	Range	DA
Dive	Water	Physical	80	100	10	Normal	O
Icy Wind	Ice	Special	55	95	15	2 Foes	—
Snore	Normal	Special	40	100	15	Normal	—
Helping Hand	Normal	Status	—	—	20	1 Ally	—

● TM & HM MOVES

No.	Name	Type	Kind	Pow.	Acc.	PP	Range	DA
TM03	Water Pulse	Water	Special	60	100	20	Normal	—
TM06	Toxic	Poison	Status	—	85	10	Normal	—
TM07	Hail	Ice	Status	—	—	10	All	—
TM10	Hidden Power	Normal	Special	—	100	15	Normal	—
TM13	Ice Beam	Ice	Special	95	100	10	Normal	—
TM14	Blizzard	Ice	Special	120	70	5	2 Foes	—
TM17	Protect	Normal	Status	—	—	10	Self	—
TM18	Rain Dance	Water	Status	—	—	5	All	—
TM21	Frustration	Normal	Physical	—	100	20	Normal	O
TM27	Return	Normal	Physical	—	100	20	Normal	O
TM28	Dig	Ground	Physical	80	100	10	Normal	O
TM29	Psychic	Psychic	Special	90	100	10	Normal	—
TM32	Double Team	Normal	Status	—	—	15	Self	—
TM42	Facade	Normal	Physical	70	100	20	Normal	O
TM43	Secret Power	Normal	Physical	70	100	20	Normal	O
TM44	Rest	Psychic	Status	—	—	10	Self	—
TM45	Attract	Normal	Status	—	100	15	Normal	—
TM46	Thief	Dark	Physical	40	100	10	Normal	O
TM58	Endure	Normal	Status	—	—	10	Self	—
TM78	Captivate	Normal	Status	—	100	20	2 Foes	—
TM82	Sleep Talk	Normal	Status	—	—	10	Depends	—
TM83	Natural Gift	Normal	Physical	—	100	15	Normal	—
TM87	Swagger	Normal	Status	—	90	15	Normal	—
TM90	Substitute	Normal	Status	—	—	10	Self	—
HM03	Surf	Water	Special	95	100	15	2 Foes/1 Ally	—
HM05	Whirlpool	Water	Special	15	70	15	Normal	—
HM07	Waterfall	Water	Physical	80	100	15	Normal	O

● EGG MOVES

Name	Type	Kind	Pow.	Acc.	PP	Range	DA
Mist	Ice	Status	—	—	30	2 Allies	—
Splash	Normal	Status	—	—	40	Self	—
BubbleBeam	Water	Special	65	100	20	Normal	—
Haze	Ice	Status	—	—	30	All	—
Mind Reader	Normal	Status	—	—	5	Normal	—
Water Sport	Water	Status	—	—	15	All	—
Ice Ball	Ice	Physical	30	90	20	Normal	O
Mud Shot	Ground	Special	55	95	15	Normal	—
Refresh	Normal	Status	—	—	20	Self	—
Endeavor	Normal	Physical	—	100	5	Normal	O
Encore	Normal	Status	—	100	5	Normal	—

● HEIGHT: 2'00"
● WEIGHT: 27.3 lbs.
● ITEMS: None

● SIZE COMPARISON

● MALE/FEMALE HAVE SAME FORM

⊘ ABILITIES
● Water Absorb
● Damp

⊘ STATS
HP ●
ATTACK ●●
DEFENSE ●●
SP. ATTACK ●●
SP. DEFENSE ●●●
SPEED ●●●●

⊘ EGG GROUPS
Water 1

⊘ PERFORMANCE

SPEED ★★★☆ STAMINA ★★★☆☆
POWER ★☆ JUMP ★★☆☆☆
SKILL ★★☆

● MAIN WAYS TO OBTAIN

Pokémon HeartGold Route 30 (water surface)

Pokémon SoulSilver Route 30 (water surface)

Pokémon Diamond Route 227 (water surface)

Pokémon Pearl Route 227 (water surface)

Pokémon Platinum Route 227 (water surface)

Pokémon HeartGold
Because it is inept at walking on its newly grown legs, it always swims around in water.

Pokémon SoulSilver
The direction of its belly spiral differs by area. The equator is thought to have an effect on this.

⊘ EVOLUTION

Poliwag — Lv. 25 → Poliwhirl
Use Water Stone → Poliwrath
Have it hold King's Rock and trade it → Politoed

No. 061 | Tadpole Pokémon
Poliwhirl

Water

● LEVEL-UP MOVES

Lv.	Name	Type	Kind	Pow.	Acc.	PP	Range	DA
1	Water Sport	Water	Status	—	—	15	All	—
1	Bubble	Water	Special	20	100	30	2 Foes	—
1	Hypnosis	Psychic	Status	—	60	20	Normal	—
5	Bubble	Water	Special	20	100	30	2 Foes	—
8	Hypnosis	Psychic	Status	—	60	20	Normal	—
11	Water Gun	Water	Special	40	100	25	Normal	—
15	DoubleSlap	Normal	Physical	15	85	10	Normal	○
18	Rain Dance	Water	Status	—	—	5	All	—
21	Body Slam	Normal	Physical	85	100	15	Normal	—
27	BubbleBeam	Water	Special	65	100	20	Normal	—
32	Mud Shot	Ground	Special	55	95	15	Normal	—
37	Belly Drum	Normal	Status	—	—	10	Self	—
43	Wake-Up Slap	Fighting	Physical	60	100	10	Normal	○
48	Hydro Pump	Water	Special	120	80	5	Normal	—
53	Mud Bomb	Ground	Special	65	85	10	Normal	—

● MOVE MANIAC

Name	Type	Kind	Pow.	Acc.	PP	Range	DA
Headbutt	Normal	Physical	70	100	15	Normal	○

● BP MOVES

Name	Type	Kind	Pow.	Acc.	PP	Range	DA
Dive	Water	Physical	80	100	10	Normal	○
Icy Wind	Ice	Special	55	95	15	2 Foes	—
Ice Punch	Ice	Physical	75	100	15	Normal	○
Snore	Normal	Special	40	100	15	Normal	—
Helping Hand	Normal	Status	—	—	20	1 Ally	—
Mud-Slap	Ground	Special	20	100	10	Normal	—

● HEIGHT: 3'03"
● WEIGHT: 44.1 lbs.
● ITEMS: King's Rock

● SIZE COMPARISON

● MALE/FEMALE HAVE SAME FORM

◎ ABILITIES
● Water Absorb
● Damp

◎ STATS
HP ●●○
ATTACK ●●●○
DEFENSE ●●●○
SP. ATTACK ●●○
SP. DEFENSE ●●○
SPEED ●●●●

◎ EGG GROUPS
Water 1

◎ PERFORMANCE
SPEED ★★☆
POWER ★★★
SKILL ★★★
STAMINA ★★★☆
JUMP ★★★☆

● MAIN WAYS TO OBTAIN

Pokémon HeartGold	Route 30 (water surface)
Pokémon SoulSilver	Route 30 (water surface)
Pokémon Diamond	Route 225 (water surface)
Pokémon Pearl	Route 225 (water surface)
Pokémon Platinum	Route 225 (water surface)

Pokémon HeartGold
The swirl on its belly subtly undulates. Staring at it may gradually cause drowsiness.

Pokémon SoulSilver
The skin on most of its body is moist. However, the skin on its belly spiral feels smooth.

◎ EVOLUTION

Poliwag → Lv. 25 → Poliwhirl

Use Water Stone → Poliwrath

Have it hold King's Rock and trade it → Politoed

● TM & HM MOVES

No.	Name	Type	Kind	Pow.	Acc.	PP	Range	DA
TM01	Focus Punch	Fighting	Physical	150	100	20	Normal	○
TM03	Water Pulse	Water	Special	60	100	20	Normal	—
TM06	Toxic	Poison	Status	—	85	10	Normal	—
TM07	Hail	Ice	Status	—	—	10	All	—
TM10	Hidden Power	Normal	Special	—	100	15	Normal	—
TM13	Ice Beam	Ice	Special	95	100	10	Normal	—
TM14	Blizzard	Ice	Special	120	70	5	2 Foes	—
TM17	Protect	Normal	Status	—	—	10	Self	—
TM18	Rain Dance	Water	Status	—	—	5	All	—
TM21	Frustration	Normal	Physical	—	100	20	Normal	○
TM26	Earthquake	Ground	Physical	100	100	10	2 Foes/1 Ally	—
TM27	Return	Normal	Physical	—	100	20	Normal	○
TM28	Dig	Ground	Physical	80	100	10	Normal	○
TM29	Psychic	Psychic	Special	90	100	10	Normal	—
TM31	Brick Break	Fighting	Physical	75	100	15	Normal	○
TM32	Double Team	Normal	Status	—	—	15	Self	—
TM42	Facade	Normal	Physical	70	100	20	Normal	○
TM43	Secret Power	Normal	Physical	70	100	20	Normal	—
TM44	Rest	Psychic	Status	—	—	10	Self	—
TM45	Attract	Normal	Status	—	100	15	Normal	—
TM46	Thief	Dark	Physical	40	100	10	Normal	○
TM56	Fling	Dark	Physical	—	100	10	Normal	—
TM58	Endure	Normal	Status	—	—	10	Self	—
TM78	Captivate	Normal	Status	—	100	20	2 Foes	—
TM82	Sleep Talk	Normal	Status	—	—	10	Depends	—
TM83	Natural Gift	Normal	Physical	—	100	15	Normal	—
TM87	Swagger	Normal	Status	—	90	15	Normal	—
TM90	Substitute	Normal	Status	—	—	10	Self	—
HM03	Surf	Water	Special	95	100	15	2 Foes/1 Ally	—
HM04	Strength	Normal	Physical	80	100	15	Normal	○
HM05	Whirlpool	Water	Special	15	70	15	Normal	—
HM06	Rock Smash	Fighting	Physical	40	100	15	Normal	○
HM07	Waterfall	Water	Physical	80	100	15	Normal	○

● LEVEL-UP MOVES

Lv.	Name	Type	Kind	Pow.	Acc.	PP	Range	DA
1	BubbleBeam	Water	Special	65	100	20	Normal	—
1	Hypnosis	Psychic	Status	—	60	20	Normal	—
1	DoubleSlap	Normal	Physical	15	85	10	Normal	—
1	Submission	Fighting	Physical	80	80	25	Normal	○
43	DynamicPunch	Fighting	Physical	100	50	5	Normal	○
53	Mind Reader	Normal	Status	—	—	5	Normal	—

● MOVE MANIAC

Name	Type	Kind	Pow.	Acc.	PP	Range	DA
Headbutt	Normal	Physical	70	100	15	Normal	○

● BP MOVES

Name	Type	Kind	Pow.	Acc.	PP	Range	DA
Dive	Water	Physical	80	100	10	Normal	○
Icy Wind	Ice	Special	55	95	15	2 Foes	—
Ice Punch	Ice	Physical	75	100	15	Normal	○
Vacuum Wave	Fighting	Special	40	100	30	Normal	—
Snore	Normal	Special	40	100	15	Normal	—
Helping Hand	Normal	Status	—	—	20	1 Ally	—
Mud-Slap	Ground	Special	20	100	10	Normal	—

● TM & HM MOVES

No.	Name	Type	Kind	Pow.	Acc.	PP	Range	DA
TM01	Focus Punch	Fighting	Physical	150	100	20	Normal	○
TM03	Water Pulse	Water	Special	60	100	20	Normal	—
TM06	Toxic	Poison	Status	—	85	10	Normal	—
TM07	Hail	Ice	Status	—	—	10	All	—
TM08	Bulk Up	Fighting	Status	—	—	20	Self	—
TM10	Hidden Power	Normal	Special	—	100	15	Normal	—
TM13	Ice Beam	Ice	Special	95	100	10	Normal	—
TM14	Blizzard	Ice	Special	120	70	5	2 Foes	—
TM15	Hyper Beam	Normal	Special	150	90	5	Normal	—
TM17	Protect	Normal	Status	—	—	10	Self	—
TM18	Rain Dance	Water	Status	—	—	5	All	—
TM21	Frustration	Normal	Physical	—	100	20	Normal	○
TM26	Earthquake	Ground	Physical	100	100	10	2 Foes/1 Ally	—
TM27	Return	Normal	Physical	—	100	20	Normal	○
TM28	Dig	Ground	Physical	80	100	10	Normal	○
TM29	Psychic	Psychic	Special	90	100	10	Normal	—
TM31	Brick Break	Fighting	Physical	75	100	15	Normal	○
TM32	Double Team	Normal	Status	—	—	15	Self	—
TM39	Rock Tomb	Rock	Physical	50	80	10	Normal	—
TM42	Facade	Normal	Physical	70	100	20	Normal	○
TM43	Secret Power	Normal	Physical	70	100	20	Normal	—
TM44	Rest	Psychic	Status	—	—	10	Self	—
TM45	Attract	Normal	Status	—	100	15	Normal	—
TM46	Thief	Dark	Physical	40	100	10	Normal	○
TM52	Focus Blast	Fighting	Special	120	70	5	Normal	—
TM56	Fling	Dark	Physical	—	100	10	Normal	○
TM58	Endure	Normal	Status	—	—	10	Self	—
TM66	Payback	Dark	Physical	50	100	10	Normal	○
TM68	Giga Impact	Normal	Physical	150	90	5	Normal	○
TM78	Captivate	Normal	Status	—	100	20	2 Foes	—
TM80	Rock Slide	Rock	Physical	75	90	10	2 Foes	—
TM82	Sleep Talk	Normal	Status	—	—	10	Depends	—
TM83	Natural Gift	Normal	Physical	—	100	15	Normal	—
TM84	Poison Jab	Poison	Physical	80	100	20	Normal	○
TM87	Swagger	Normal	Status	—	90	15	Normal	—
TM90	Substitute	Normal	Status	—	—	10	Self	—
HM03	Surf	Water	Special	95	100	15	2 Foes/1 Ally	—
HM04	Strength	Normal	Physical	80	100	15	Normal	○
HM05	Whirlpool	Water	Special	15	70	15	Normal	—
HM06	Rock Smash	Fighting	Physical	40	100	15	Normal	○
HM07	Waterfall	Water	Physical	80	100	15	Normal	○
HM08	Rock Climb	Normal	Physical	90	85	20	Normal	○

● No. 062 | Tadpole Pokémon
Poliwrath
`Water` `Fighting`

- ● HEIGHT: 4'03"
- ● WEIGHT: 119.0 lbs.
- ● ITEMS: None
- ● SIZE COMPARISON

● MALE/FEMALE HAVE SAME FORM

⊜ ABILITIES
- ● Water Absorb
- ● Damp

⊜ EGG GROUPS
Water 1

⊜ STATS
- HP ●●●
- ATTACK ●●●●
- DEFENSE ●●●●
- SP. ATTACK ●●●●
- SP. DEFENSE ●●●●
- SPEED ●●●

● PERFORMANCE
SPEED ★ ☆ STAMINA ★★★★ ☆
POWER ★★★★★ JUMP ★★
SKILL ★★★ ☆

● MAIN WAYS TO OBTAIN

Pokémon HeartGold	Use Water Stone on Poliwhirl
Pokémon SoulSilver	Use Water Stone on Poliwhirl
Pokémon Diamond	Use Water Stone on Poliwhirl
Pokémon Pearl	Use Water Stone on Poliwhirl
Pokémon Platinum	Use Water Stone on Poliwhirl

Pokémon HeartGold
This strong and skilled swimmer is even capable of crossing the Pacific Ocean just by kicking.

Pokémon SoulSilver
Although an energetic, skilled swimmer that uses all of its muscles, it lives on dry land.

⊜ EVOLUTION

Use Water Stone → Poliwrath

Have it hold King's Rock and trade it → Politoed

Poliwag → Lv. 25 → Poliwhirl

● No. 063 | Psi Pokémon
Abra

Psychic

- **HEIGHT:** 2'11"
- **WEIGHT:** 43.0 lbs.
- **ITEMS:** TwistedSpoon

● SIZE COMPARISON

● MALE/FEMALE HAVE SAME FORM

◎ ABILITIES
- Synchronize
- Inner Focus

◎ STATS
HP	●
ATTACK	●
DEFENSE	●
SP. ATTACK	●●●●●
SP. DEFENSE	●●
SPEED	●●●●

◎ EGG GROUPS
Human-Like

◎ PERFORMANCE
SPEED ★☆☆☆☆	STAMINA ★☆☆☆
POWER ★	JUMP ★★★☆
SKILL ★★★★☆	

● MAIN WAYS TO OBTAIN

Pokémon HeartGold	Route 34
Pokémon SoulSilver	Route 34
Pokémon Diamond	Route 203
Pokémon Pearl	Route 203
Pokémon Platinum	Route 203

Pokémon HeartGold
It senses impending attacks and teleports away to safety before the actual attacks can strike.

Pokémon SoulSilver
If it decides to teleport randomly, it evokes the illusion that it has created copies of itself.

◎ EVOLUTION

Lv. 16 → Trade it →

Abra → Kadabra → Alakazam

● LEVEL-UP MOVES
Lv.	Name	Type	Kind	Pow.	Acc.	PP	Range	DA
1	Teleport	Psychic	Status	—	—	20	Self	—

● MOVE MANIAC
Name	Type	Kind	Pow.	Acc.	PP	Range	DA
Headbutt	Normal	Physical	70	100	15	Normal	○

● BP MOVES
Name	Type	Kind	Pow.	Acc.	PP	Range	DA
ThunderPunch	Electric	Physical	75	100	15	Normal	○
Fire Punch	Fire	Physical	75	100	15	Normal	○
Ice Punch	Ice	Physical	75	100	15	Normal	○
Zen Headbutt	Psychic	Physical	80	90	15	Normal	○
Trick	Psychic	Status	—	100	10	Normal	—
Knock Off	Dark	Physical	20	100	20	Normal	○
Snore	Normal	Special	40	100	15	Normal	—
Gravity	Psychic	Status	—	—	5	All	—
Magic Coat	Psychic	Status	—	—	15	Self	—
Role Play	Psychic	Status	—	—	10	Normal	—
Signal Beam	Bug	Special	75	100	15	Normal	—

● TM & HM MOVES
No.	Name	Type	Kind	Pow.	Acc.	PP	Range	DA
TM01	Focus Punch	Fighting	Physical	150	100	20	Normal	○
TM04	Calm Mind	Psychic	Status	—	—	20	Self	—
TM06	Toxic	Poison	Status	—	85	10	Normal	—
TM10	Hidden Power	Normal	Special	—	100	15	Normal	—
TM11	Sunny Day	Fire	Status	—	—	5	All	—
TM12	Taunt	Dark	Status	—	100	20	Normal	—
TM16	Light Screen	Psychic	Status	—	—	30	2 Allies	—
TM17	Protect	Normal	Status	—	—	10	Self	—
TM18	Rain Dance	Water	Status	—	—	5	All	—
TM20	Safeguard	Normal	Status	—	—	25	2 Allies	—
TM21	Frustration	Normal	Physical	—	100	20	Normal	○
TM23	Iron Tail	Steel	Physical	100	75	15	Normal	○
TM27	Return	Normal	Physical	—	100	20	Normal	○
TM29	Psychic	Psychic	Special	90	100	10	Normal	—
TM30	Shadow Ball	Ghost	Special	80	100	15	Normal	—
TM32	Double Team	Normal	Status	—	—	15	Self	—
TM33	Reflect	Psychic	Status	—	—	20	2 Allies	—
TM34	Shock Wave	Electric	Special	60	—	20	Normal	—
TM41	Torment	Dark	Status	—	100	15	Normal	—
TM42	Facade	Normal	Physical	70	100	20	Normal	○
TM43	Secret Power	Normal	Physical	70	100	20	Normal	○
TM44	Rest	Psychic	Status	—	—	10	Self	—
TM45	Attract	Normal	Status	—	100	15	Normal	—
TM46	Thief	Dark	Physical	40	100	10	Normal	○
TM48	Skill Swap	Psychic	Status	—	—	10	Normal	—
TM49	Snatch	Dark	Status	—	—	10	Depends	—
TM53	Energy Ball	Grass	Special	80	100	10	Normal	—
TM56	Fling	Dark	Physical	—	100	10	Normal	—
TM57	Charge Beam	Electric	Special	50	90	10	Normal	—
TM58	Endure	Normal	Status	—	—	10	Self	—
TM60	Drain Punch	Fighting	Physical	60	100	5	Normal	○
TM63	Embargo	Dark	Status	—	100	15	Normal	—
TM67	Recycle	Normal	Status	—	—	10	Self	—
TM70	Flash	Normal	Status	—	100	20	Normal	—
TM73	Thunder Wave	Electric	Status	—	100	20	Normal	—
TM77	Psych Up	Normal	Status	—	—	10	Normal	—
TM78	Captivate	Normal	Status	—	100	20	2 Foes	—
TM82	Sleep Talk	Normal	Status	—	—	10	Depends	—
TM83	Natural Gift	Normal	Physical	—	100	15	Normal	—
TM85	Dream Eater	Psychic	Special	100	100	15	Normal	—
TM86	Grass Knot	Grass	Special	—	100	20	Normal	○
TM87	Swagger	Normal	Status	—	90	15	Normal	—
TM90	Substitute	Normal	Status	—	—	10	Self	—
TM92	Trick Room	Psychic	Status	—	—	5	All	—

● EGG MOVES
Name	Type	Kind	Pow.	Acc.	PP	Range	DA
Encore	Normal	Status	—	100	5	Normal	—
Barrier	Psychic	Status	—	—	30	Self	—
Knock Off	Dark	Physical	20	100	20	Normal	○
Fire Punch	Fire	Physical	75	100	15	Normal	○
ThunderPunch	Electric	Physical	75	100	15	Normal	○
Ice Punch	Ice	Physical	75	100	15	Normal	○
Power Trick	Psychic	Status	—	—	10	Self	—
Guard Swap	Psychic	Status	—	—	10	Normal	—

● LEVEL-UP MOVES

Lv.	Name	Type	Kind	Pow.	Acc.	PP	Range	DA
1	Teleport	Psychic	Status	—	—	20	Self	—
1	Kinesis	Psychic	Status	—	80	15	Normal	—
1	Confusion	Psychic	Special	50	100	25	Normal	—
16	Confusion	Psychic	Special	50	100	25	Normal	—
18	Disable	Normal	Status	—	80	20	Normal	—
22	Miracle Eye	Psychic	Status	—	—	40	Normal	—
24	Psybeam	Psychic	Special	65	100	20	Normal	—
28	Reflect	Psychic	Status	—	—	20	2 Allies	—
30	Recover	Normal	Status	—	—	10	Self	—
34	Psycho Cut	Psychic	Physical	70	100	20	Normal	—
36	Role Play	Psychic	Status	—	—	10	Normal	—
40	Psychic	Psychic	Special	90	100	10	Normal	—
42	Future Sight	Psychic	Special	80	90	15	Normal	—
46	Trick	Psychic	Status	—	100	10	Normal	—

● MOVE MANIAC

Name	Type	Kind	Pow.	Acc.	PP	Range	DA
Headbutt	Normal	Physical	70	100	15	Normal	○

● BP MOVES

Name	Type	Kind	Pow.	Acc.	PP	Range	DA
ThunderPunch	Electric	Physical	75	100	15	Normal	○
Fire Punch	Fire	Physical	75	100	15	Normal	○
Ice Punch	Ice	Physical	75	100	15	Normal	○
Zen Headbutt	Psychic	Physical	80	90	15	Normal	○
Trick	Psychic	Status	—	100	10	Normal	—
Knock Off	Dark	Physical	20	100	20	Normal	○
Snore	Normal	Special	40	100	15	Normal	—
Gravity	Psychic	Status	—	—	5	All	—
Magic Coat	Psychic	Status	—	—	15	Self	—
Role Play	Psychic	Status	—	—	10	Normal	—
Signal Beam	Bug	Special	75	100	15	Normal	—

● TM & HM MOVES

No.	Name	Type	Kind	Pow.	Acc.	PP	Range	DA
TM01	Focus Punch	Fighting	Physical	150	100	20	Normal	○
TM04	Calm Mind	Psychic	Status	—	—	20	Self	—
TM06	Toxic	Poison	Status	—	85	10	Normal	—
TM10	Hidden Power	Normal	Special	—	100	15	Normal	—
TM11	Sunny Day	Fire	Status	—	—	5	All	—
TM12	Taunt	Dark	Status	—	100	20	Normal	—
TM16	Light Screen	Psychic	Status	—	—	30	2 Allies	—
TM17	Protect	Normal	Status	—	—	10	Self	—
TM18	Rain Dance	Water	Status	—	—	5	All	—
TM20	Safeguard	Normal	Status	—	—	25	2 Allies	—
TM21	Frustration	Normal	Physical	—	100	20	Normal	○
TM23	Iron Tail	Steel	Physical	100	75	15	Normal	○
TM27	Return	Normal	Physical	—	100	20	Normal	○
TM29	Psychic	Psychic	Special	90	100	10	Normal	—
TM30	Shadow Ball	Ghost	Special	80	100	15	Normal	—
TM32	Double Team	Normal	Status	—	—	15	Self	—
TM33	Reflect	Psychic	Status	—	—	20	2 Allies	—
TM34	Shock Wave	Electric	Special	60	—	20	Normal	—
TM41	Torment	Dark	Status	—	100	15	Normal	—
TM42	Facade	Normal	Physical	70	100	20	Normal	○
TM43	Secret Power	Normal	Physical	70	100	20	Normal	—
TM44	Rest	Psychic	Status	—	—	10	Self	—
TM45	Attract	Normal	Status	—	100	15	Normal	—
TM46	Thief	Dark	Physical	40	100	10	Normal	—
TM48	Skill Swap	Psychic	Status	—	—	10	Normal	—
TM49	Snatch	Dark	Status	—	—	10	Depends	—
TM53	Energy Ball	Grass	Special	80	100	10	Normal	—
TM56	Fling	Dark	Physical	—	100	10	Normal	—
TM57	Charge Beam	Electric	Special	50	90	10	Normal	—
TM58	Endure	Normal	Status	—	—	10	Self	—
TM60	Drain Punch	Fighting	Physical	60	100	5	Normal	○
TM63	Embargo	Dark	Status	—	100	15	Normal	—
TM67	Recycle	Normal	Status	—	—	10	Self	—
TM70	Flash	Normal	Status	—	100	20	Normal	—
TM73	Thunder Wave	Electric	Status	—	100	20	Normal	—
TM77	Psych Up	Normal	Status	—	—	10	Normal	—
TM78	Captivate	Normal	Status	—	100	20	2 Foes	—
TM82	Sleep Talk	Normal	Status	—	—	10	Depends	—
TM83	Natural Gift	Normal	Physical	—	100	15	Normal	—
TM85	Dream Eater	Psychic	Special	100	100	15	Normal	○
TM86	Grass Knot	Grass	Special	—	100	20	Normal	—
TM87	Swagger	Normal	Status	—	90	15	Normal	—
TM90	Substitute	Normal	Status	—	—	10	Self	—
TM92	Trick Room	Psychic	Status	—	—	5	All	—

Kadabra

Psychic

- ● HEIGHT: 4'03"
- ● WEIGHT: 124.6 lbs.
- ● ITEMS: TwistedSpoon

● SIZE COMPARISON

- ● MALE FORM
  Longer whiskers
- ● FEMALE FORM
  Shorter whiskers

● ABILITIES
- ● Synchronize
- ● Inner Focus

● STATS
- HP ●
- ATTACK ●●
- DEFENSE ●●
- SP. ATTACK ●●●●●
- SP. DEFENSE ●●●
- SPEED ●●●●●

● EGG GROUPS
Human-Like

● PERFORMANCE

SPEED ★★★☆   STAMINA ★★☆
POWER ★☆☆   JUMP ★★☆
SKILL ★★★★☆

● MAIN WAYS TO OBTAIN

Pokémon HeartGold Cerulean Cave

Pokémon SoulSilver Cerulean Cave

Pokémon Diamond Route 215

Pokémon Pearl Route 215

Pokémon Platinum Route 215

Pokémon HeartGold
It possesses strong spiritual power. The more danger it faces, the stronger its psychic power.

Pokémon SoulSilver
If it uses its abilities, it emits special alpha waves that cause machines to malfunction.

● EVOLUTION

Abra → (Lv. 16) → Kadabra → (Trade it) → Alakazam

No. 065 | Psi Pokémon
Alakazam

Psychic

- **HEIGHT:** 4'11"
- **WEIGHT:** 105.8 lbs.
- **ITEMS:** None

● **MALE FORM**
Longer whiskers

● **FEMALE FORM**
Shorter whiskers

● **SIZE COMPARISON**

ABILITIES
- Synchronize
- Inner Focus

EGG GROUPS
Human-Like

STATS
HP	●●
ATTACK	●●
DEFENSE	●●
SP. ATTACK	●●●●●●
SP. DEFENSE	●●●●
SPEED	●●●●●

PERFORMANCE
SPEED ★★★☆ STAMINA ★
POWER ★ JUMP ★★
SKILL ★★★★★

MAIN WAYS TO OBTAIN

Pokémon HeartGold — Link trade Kadabra

Pokémon SoulSilver — Link trade Kadabra

Pokémon Diamond — Link trade Kadabra

Pokémon Pearl — Link trade Kadabra

Pokémon Platinum — Link trade Kadabra

Pokémon HeartGold
Closing both its eyes heightens all its other senses. This enables it to use its abilities to their extremes.

Pokémon SoulSilver
Its brain cells multiply continually until it dies. As a result, it remembers everything.

EVOLUTION
Abra — Lv. 16 — Kadabra — Trade it — Alakazam

● **LEVEL-UP MOVES**

Lv.	Name	Type	Kind	Pow.	Acc.	PP	Range	DA
1	Teleport	Psychic	Status	—	—	20	Self	—
1	Kinesis	Psychic	Status	—	80	15	Normal	—
1	Confusion	Psychic	Special	50	100	25	Normal	—
16	Confusion	Psychic	Special	50	100	25	Normal	—
18	Disable	Normal	Status	—	80	20	Normal	—
22	Miracle Eye	Psychic	Status	—	—	40	Normal	—
24	Psybeam	Psychic	Special	65	100	20	Normal	—
28	Reflect	Psychic	Status	—	—	20	2 Allies	—
30	Recover	Normal	Status	—	—	10	Self	—
34	Psycho Cut	Psychic	Physical	70	100	20	Normal	—
36	Calm Mind	Psychic	Status	—	—	20	Self	—
40	Psychic	Psychic	Special	90	100	10	Normal	—
42	Future Sight	Psychic	Special	80	90	15	Normal	—
46	Trick	Psychic	Status	—	100	10	Normal	—

● **MOVE MANIAC**

Name	Type	Kind	Pow.	Acc.	PP	Range	DA
Headbutt	Normal	Physical	70	100	15	Normal	○

● **BP MOVES**

Name	Type	Kind	Pow.	Acc.	PP	Range	DA
ThunderPunch	Electric	Physical	75	100	15	Normal	○
Fire Punch	Fire	Physical	75	100	15	Normal	○
Ice Punch	Ice	Physical	75	100	15	Normal	○
Zen Headbutt	Psychic	Physical	80	90	15	Normal	○
Trick	Psychic	Status	—	100	10	Normal	—
Knock Off	Dark	Physical	20	100	20	Normal	○
Snore	Normal	Special	40	100	15	Normal	—
Gravity	Psychic	Status	—	—	5	All	—
Magic Coat	Psychic	Status	—	—	15	Self	—
Role Play	Psychic	Status	—	—	10	Normal	—
Signal Beam	Bug	Special	75	100	15	Normal	—

● **TM & HM MOVES**

No.	Name	Type	Kind	Pow.	Acc.	PP	Range	DA
TM01	Focus Punch	Fighting	Physical	150	100	20	Normal	○
TM04	Calm Mind	Psychic	Status	—	—	20	Self	—
TM06	Toxic	Poison	Status	—	85	10	Normal	—
TM10	Hidden Power	Normal	Special	—	100	15	Normal	—
TM11	Sunny Day	Fire	Status	—	—	5	All	—
TM12	Taunt	Dark	Status	—	100	20	Normal	—
TM15	Hyper Beam	Normal	Special	150	90	5	Normal	—
TM16	Light Screen	Psychic	Status	—	—	30	2 Allies	—
TM17	Protect	Normal	Status	—	—	10	Self	—
TM18	Rain Dance	Water	Status	—	—	5	All	—
TM20	Safeguard	Normal	Status	—	—	25	2 Allies	—
TM21	Frustration	Normal	Physical	—	100	20	Normal	○
TM23	Iron Tail	Steel	Physical	100	75	15	Normal	○
TM27	Return	Normal	Physical	—	100	20	Normal	○
TM29	Psychic	Psychic	Special	90	100	10	Normal	—
TM30	Shadow Ball	Ghost	Special	80	100	15	Normal	—
TM33	Double Team	Normal	Status	—	—	15	Self	—
TM34	Shock Wave	Electric	Special	60	—	20	Normal	—
TM41	Torment	Dark	Status	—	100	15	Normal	—
TM42	Facade	Normal	Physical	70	100	20	Normal	○
TM43	Secret Power	Normal	Physical	70	100	20	Normal	○
TM44	Rest	Psychic	Status	—	—	10	Self	—
TM45	Attract	Normal	Status	—	100	15	Normal	—
TM46	Thief	Dark	Physical	40	100	10	Normal	○
TM48	Skill Swap	Psychic	Status	—	—	10	Normal	—
TM49	Snatch	Dark	Status	—	—	10	Depends	—
TM52	Focus Blast	Fighting	Special	120	70	5	Normal	—
TM53	Energy Ball	Grass	Special	80	100	10	Normal	—
TM56	Fling	Dark	Physical	—	100	10	Normal	—
TM57	Charge Beam	Electric	Special	50	90	10	Normal	—
TM58	Endure	Normal	Status	—	—	10	Self	—
TM60	Drain Punch	Fighting	Physical	60	100	5	Normal	○
TM63	Embargo	Dark	Status	—	100	15	Normal	—
TM67	Recycle	Normal	Status	—	—	10	Self	—
TM68	Giga Impact	Normal	Physical	150	90	5	Normal	○
TM70	Flash	Normal	Status	—	100	20	Normal	—
TM73	Thunder Wave	Electric	Status	—	100	20	Normal	—
TM77	Psych Up	Normal	Status	—	—	10	Normal	—
TM78	Captivate	Normal	Status	—	100	20	2 Foes	—
TM82	Sleep Talk	Normal	Status	—	—	10	Depends	—
TM83	Natural Gift	Normal	Physical	—	100	15	Normal	—
TM85	Dream Eater	Psychic	Special	100	100	15	Normal	—
TM86	Grass Knot	Grass	Special	—	100	20	Normal	○
TM87	Swagger	Normal	Status	—	90	15	Normal	—
TM90	Substitute	Normal	Status	—	—	10	Self	—
TM92	Trick Room	Psychic	Status	—	—	5	All	—

● LEVEL-UP MOVES

Lv.	Name	Type	Kind	Pow.	Acc.	PP	Range	DA
1	Low Kick	Fighting	Physical	—	100	20	Normal	○
1	Leer	Normal	Status	—	100	30	2 Foes	—
7	Focus Energy	Normal	Status	—	—	30	Self	—
10	Karate Chop	Fighting	Physical	50	100	25	Normal	○
13	Foresight	Normal	Status	—	—	40	Normal	—
19	Seismic Toss	Fighting	Physical	—	100	20	Normal	○
22	Revenge	Fighting	Physical	60	100	10	Normal	○
25	Vital Throw	Fighting	Physical	70	—	10	Normal	○
31	Submission	Fighting	Physical	80	80	25	Normal	○
34	Wake-Up Slap	Fighting	Physical	60	100	10	Normal	○
37	Cross Chop	Fighting	Physical	100	80	5	Normal	○
43	Scary Face	Normal	Status	—	90	10	Normal	—
46	DynamicPunch	Fighting	Physical	100	50	5	Normal	○

● MOVE MANIAC

Name	Type	Kind	Pow.	Acc.	PP	Range	DA
Headbutt	Normal	Physical	70	100	15	Normal	○

● BP MOVES

Name	Type	Kind	Pow.	Acc.	PP	Range	DA
ThunderPunch	Electric	Physical	75	100	15	Normal	○
Fire Punch	Fire	Physical	75	100	15	Normal	○
Ice Punch	Ice	Physical	75	100	15	Normal	○
Vacuum Wave	Fighting	Special	40	100	30	Normal	—
Snore	Normal	Special	40	100	15	Normal	—
Helping Hand	Normal	Status	—	—	20	1 Ally	—
Role Play	Psychic	Status	—	—	10	Normal	—
Mud-Slap	Ground	Special	20	100	10	Normal	○
Superpower	Fighting	Physical	120	100	5	Normal	○
Low Kick	Fighting	Physical	—	100	20	Normal	○

● TM & HM MOVES

No.	Name	Type	Kind	Pow.	Acc.	PP	Range	DA
TM01	Focus Punch	Fighting	Physical	150	100	20	Normal	○
TM06	Toxic	Poison	Status	—	85	10	Normal	—
TM08	Bulk Up	Fighting	Status	—	—	20	Self	—
TM10	Hidden Power	Normal	Special	—	100	15	Normal	—
TM11	Sunny Day	Fire	Status	—	—	5	All	—
TM17	Protect	Normal	Status	—	—	10	Self	—
TM18	Rain Dance	Water	Status	—	—	5	All	—
TM21	Frustration	Normal	Physical	—	100	20	Normal	○
TM26	Earthquake	Ground	Physical	100	100	10	2 Foes/1 Ally	○
TM27	Return	Normal	Physical	—	100	20	Normal	○
TM28	Dig	Ground	Physical	80	100	10	Normal	○
TM31	Brick Break	Fighting	Physical	75	100	15	Normal	○
TM32	Double Team	Normal	Status	—	—	15	Self	—
TM35	Flamethrower	Fire	Special	95	100	15	Normal	—
TM38	Fire Blast	Fire	Special	120	85	5	Normal	—
TM39	Rock Tomb	Rock	Physical	50	80	10	Normal	○
TM42	Facade	Normal	Physical	70	100	20	Normal	○
TM43	Secret Power	Normal	Physical	70	100	20	Normal	—
TM44	Rest	Psychic	Status	—	—	10	Self	—
TM45	Attract	Normal	Status	—	100	15	Normal	—
TM46	Thief	Dark	Physical	40	100	10	Normal	○
TM52	Focus Blast	Fighting	Special	120	70	5	Normal	—
TM56	Fling	Dark	Physical	—	100	10	Normal	○
TM58	Endure	Normal	Status	—	—	10	Self	—
TM66	Payback	Dark	Physical	50	100	10	Normal	○
TM78	Captivate	Normal	Status	—	100	20	2 Foes	—
TM80	Rock Slide	Rock	Physical	75	90	10	2 Foes	○
TM82	Sleep Talk	Normal	Status	—	—	10	Depends	—
TM83	Natural Gift	Normal	Physical	—	100	15	Normal	—
TM84	Poison Jab	Poison	Physical	80	100	20	Normal	○
TM87	Swagger	Normal	Status	—	90	15	Normal	—
TM90	Substitute	Normal	Status	—	—	10	Self	—
HM04	Strength	Normal	Physical	80	100	15	Normal	○
HM06	Rock Smash	Fighting	Physical	40	100	15	Normal	○
HM08	Rock Climb	Normal	Physical	90	85	20	Normal	○

● EGG MOVES

Name	Type	Kind	Pow.	Acc.	PP	Range	DA
Light Screen	Psychic	Status	—	—	30	2 Allies	—
Meditate	Psychic	Status	—	—	40	Self	—
Rolling Kick	Fighting	Physical	60	85	15	Normal	○
Encore	Normal	Status	—	100	5	Normal	—
SmellingSalt	Normal	Physical	60	100	10	Normal	○
Counter	Fighting	Physical	—	100	20	Self	○
Rock Slide	Rock	Physical	75	90	10	2 Foes	○
Close Combat	Fighting	Physical	120	100	5	Normal	○
Fire Punch	Fire	Physical	75	100	15	Normal	○
ThunderPunch	Electric	Physical	75	100	15	Normal	○
Ice Punch	Ice	Physical	75	100	15	Normal	○
Bullet Punch	Steel	Physical	40	100	30	Normal	○
Power Trick	Psychic	Status	—	—	10	Self	—

● No. 066 | Superpower Pokémon
Machop

Fighting

● SIZE COMPARISON

● HEIGHT: 2'07"
● WEIGHT: 43.0 lbs.
● ITEMS: None

● MALE/FEMALE HAVE SAME FORM

⊙ ABILITIES
● Guts
● No Guard

⊙ STATS
HP ●●●
ATTACK ●●●
DEFENSE ●●●
SP. ATTACK ●●
SP. DEFENSE ●●
SPEED ●●

⊙ EGG GROUPS
Human-Like

⊙ PERFORMANCE
SPEED ★★★☆		STAMINA ★★☆
POWER ★★★☆		JUMP ★★
SKILL ★☆☆		

● MAIN WAYS TO OBTAIN

Pokémon HeartGold Mt. Mortar

Pokémon SoulSilver Mt. Mortar

Pokémon Diamond Route 207

Pokémon Pearl Route 207

Pokémon Platinum Route 207

Pokémon HeartGold
Always brimming with power, it passes time by lifting boulders. Doing so makes it even stronger.

Pokémon SoulSilver
It loves to work out and build its muscles. It is never satisfied, even if it trains hard all day long.

⊙ EVOLUTION

Machop — Lv. 28 → Machoke — Trade it → Machamp

Machoke

Fighting

- **HEIGHT:** 4'11"
- **WEIGHT:** 155.4 lbs.
- **ITEMS:** None

● SIZE COMPARISON

● MALE/FEMALE HAVE SAME FORM

● ABILITIES
- Guts
- No Guard

● STATS
HP	●●●
ATTACK	●●●●
DEFENSE	●●●
SP. ATTACK	●●
SP. DEFENSE	●●
SPEED	●●

● EGG GROUPS
Human-Like

● PERFORMANCE
SPEED ★★
POWER ★★★★
SKILL ★★☆

STAMINA ★★★☆
JUMP ★★

● MAIN WAYS TO OBTAIN

Pokémon HeartGold	Cliff Cave
Pokémon SoulSilver	Cliff Cave
Pokémon Diamond	Route 210, Celestic Town side
Pokémon Pearl	Route 210, Celestic Town side
Pokémon Platinum	Route 210, Celestic Town side

Pokémon HeartGold
It always goes at its full power, but this very tough and durable Pokémon never gets tired.

Pokémon SoulSilver
The muscles covering its body team with power. Even when still, it exudes an amazing sense of strength.

● EVOLUTION

Machop —Lv. 28→ Machoke —Trade it→ Machamp

● LEVEL-UP MOVES
Lv.	Name	Type	Kind	Pow.	Acc.	PP	Range	DA
1	Low Kick	Fighting	Physical	—	100	20	Normal	○
1	Leer	Normal	Status	—	100	30	2 Foes	—
1	Focus Energy	Normal	Status	—	—	30	Self	—
7	Focus Energy	Normal	Status	—	—	30	Self	—
10	Karate Chop	Fighting	Physical	50	100	25	Normal	○
13	Foresight	Normal	Status	—	—	40	Normal	—
19	Seismic Toss	Fighting	Physical	—	100	20	Normal	○
22	Revenge	Fighting	Physical	60	100	10	Normal	○
25	Vital Throw	Fighting	Physical	70	—	10	Normal	○
32	Submission	Fighting	Physical	80	80	25	Normal	○
36	Wake-Up Slap	Fighting	Physical	60	100	10	Normal	○
40	Cross Chop	Fighting	Physical	100	80	5	Normal	○
44	Scary Face	Normal	Status	—	90	10	Normal	—
51	DynamicPunch	Fighting	Physical	100	50	5	Normal	○

● MOVE MANIAC
Name	Type	Kind	Pow.	Acc.	PP	Range	DA
Headbutt	Normal	Physical	70	100	15	Normal	○

● BP MOVES
Name	Type	Kind	Pow.	Acc.	PP	Range	DA
ThunderPunch	Electric	Physical	75	100	15	Normal	○
Fire Punch	Fire	Physical	75	100	15	Normal	○
Ice Punch	Ice	Physical	75	100	15	Normal	○
Vacuum Wave	Fighting	Special	40	100	30	Normal	—
Snore	Normal	Special	40	100	15	Normal	—
Helping Hand	Normal	Status	—	—	20	1 Ally	—
Role Play	Psychic	Status	—	—	10	Normal	—
Mud-Slap	Ground	Special	20	100	10	Normal	—
Superpower	Fighting	Physical	120	100	5	Normal	○
Low Kick	Fighting	Physical	—	100	20	Normal	○

● TM & HM MOVES
No.	Name	Type	Kind	Pow.	Acc.	PP	Range	DA
TM01	Focus Punch	Fighting	Physical	150	100	20	Normal	○
TM06	Toxic	Poison	Status	—	85	10	Normal	—
TM08	Bulk Up	Fighting	Status	—	—	20	Self	—
TM10	Hidden Power	Normal	Special	—	100	15	Normal	—
TM11	Sunny Day	Fire	Status	—	—	5	All	—
TM17	Protect	Normal	Status	—	—	10	Self	—
TM18	Rain Dance	Water	Status	—	—	5	All	—
TM21	Frustration	Normal	Physical	—	100	20	Normal	○
TM26	Earthquake	Ground	Physical	100	100	10	2 Foes/1 Ally	—
TM27	Return	Normal	Physical	—	100	20	Normal	○
TM28	Dig	Ground	Physical	80	100	10	Normal	○
TM31	Brick Break	Fighting	Physical	75	100	15	Normal	○
TM32	Double Team	Normal	Status	—	—	15	Self	—
TM35	Flamethrower	Fire	Special	95	100	15	Normal	—
TM38	Fire Blast	Fire	Special	120	85	5	Normal	—
TM39	Rock Tomb	Rock	Physical	50	80	10	Normal	—
TM42	Facade	Normal	Physical	70	100	20	Normal	○
TM43	Secret Power	Normal	Physical	70	100	20	Normal	—
TM44	Rest	Psychic	Status	—	—	10	Self	—
TM45	Attract	Normal	Status	—	100	15	Normal	—
TM46	Thief	Dark	Physical	40	100	10	Normal	○
TM52	Focus Blast	Fighting	Special	120	70	5	Normal	—
TM56	Fling	Dark	Physical	—	100	10	Normal	—
TM58	Endure	Normal	Status	—	—	10	Self	—
TM66	Payback	Dark	Physical	50	100	10	Normal	○
TM78	Captivate	Normal	Status	—	100	20	2 Foes	—
TM80	Rock Slide	Rock	Physical	75	90	10	2 Foes	—
TM82	Sleep Talk	Normal	Status	—	—	10	Depends	—
TM83	Natural Gift	Normal	Physical	—	100	15	Normal	—
TM84	Poison Jab	Poison	Physical	80	100	20	Normal	○
TM87	Swagger	Normal	Status	—	90	15	Normal	—
TM90	Substitute	Normal	Status	—	—	10	Self	—
HM04	Strength	Normal	Physical	80	100	15	Normal	○
HM06	Rock Smash	Fighting	Physical	40	100	15	Normal	○
HM08	Rock Climb	Normal	Physical	90	85	20	Normal	○

● LEVEL-UP MOVES

Lv.	Name	Type	Kind	Pow.	Acc.	PP	Range	DA
1	Low Kick	Fighting	Physical	—	100	20	Normal	○
1	Leer	Normal	Status	—	100	30	2 Foes	—
1	Focus Energy	Normal	Status	—	—	30	Self	—
7	Focus Energy	Normal	Status	—	—	30	Self	—
10	Karate Chop	Fighting	Physical	50	100	25	Normal	○
13	Foresight	Normal	Status	—	—	40	Normal	—
19	Seismic Toss	Fighting	Physical	—	100	20	Normal	○
22	Revenge	Fighting	Physical	60	100	10	Normal	○
25	Vital Throw	Fighting	Physical	70	—	10	Normal	○
32	Submission	Fighting	Physical	80	80	25	Normal	○
36	Wake-Up Slap	Fighting	Physical	60	100	10	Normal	○
40	Cross Chop	Fighting	Physical	100	80	5	Normal	○
44	Scary Face	Normal	Status	—	90	10	Normal	—
51	DynamicPunch	Fighting	Physical	100	50	5	Normal	○

● MOVE MANIAC

Name	Type	Kind	Pow.	Acc.	PP	Range	DA
Headbutt	Normal	Physical	70	100	15	Normal	○

● BP MOVES

Name	Type	Kind	Pow.	Acc.	PP	Range	DA
ThunderPunch	Electric	Physical	75	100	15	Normal	○
Fire Punch	Fire	Physical	75	100	15	Normal	○
Ice Punch	Ice	Physical	75	100	15	Normal	○
Vacuum Wave	Fighting	Special	40	100	30	Normal	—
Snore	Normal	Special	40	100	15	Normal	—
Helping Hand	Normal	Status	—	—	20	1 Ally	—
Role Play	Psychic	Status	—	—	10	Normal	—
Mud-Slap	Ground	Special	20	100	10	Normal	—
Superpower	Fighting	Physical	120	100	5	Normal	○
Low Kick	Fighting	Physical	—	100	20	Normal	○

● TM & HM MOVES

No.	Name	Type	Kind	Pow.	Acc.	PP	Range	DA
TM01	Focus Punch	Fighting	Physical	150	100	20	Normal	○
TM06	Toxic	Poison	Status	—	85	10	Normal	—
TM08	Bulk Up	Fighting	Status	—	—	20	Self	—
TM10	Hidden Power	Normal	Special	—	100	15	Normal	—
TM11	Sunny Day	Fire	Status	—	—	5	All	—
TM15	Hyper Beam	Normal	Special	150	90	5	Normal	—
TM17	Protect	Normal	Status	—	—	10	Self	—
TM18	Rain Dance	Water	Status	—	—	5	All	—
TM21	Frustration	Normal	Physical	—	100	20	Normal	○
TM26	Earthquake	Ground	Physical	100	100	10	2 Foes / 1 Ally	—
TM27	Return	Normal	Physical	—	100	20	Normal	○
TM28	Dig	Ground	Physical	80	100	10	Normal	○
TM31	Brick Break	Fighting	Physical	75	100	15	Normal	○
TM32	Double Team	Normal	Status	—	—	15	Self	—
TM35	Flamethrower	Fire	Special	95	100	15	Normal	—
TM38	Fire Blast	Fire	Special	120	85	5	Normal	—
TM39	Rock Tomb	Rock	Physical	50	80	10	Normal	○
TM42	Facade	Normal	Physical	70	100	20	Normal	○
TM43	Secret Power	Normal	Physical	70	100	20	Normal	○
TM44	Rest	Psychic	Status	—	—	10	Self	—
TM45	Attract	Normal	Status	—	100	15	Normal	—
TM46	Thief	Dark	Physical	40	100	10	Normal	○
TM52	Focus Blast	Fighting	Special	120	70	5	Normal	—
TM56	Fling	Dark	Physical	—	100	10	Normal	○
TM58	Endure	Normal	Status	—	—	10	Self	—
TM66	Payback	Dark	Physical	50	100	10	Normal	○
TM68	Giga Impact	Normal	Physical	150	90	5	Normal	○
TM71	Stone Edge	Rock	Physical	100	80	5	Normal	○
TM78	Captivate	Normal	Status	—	100	20	2 Foes	—
TM80	Rock Slide	Rock	Physical	75	90	10	2 Foes	—
TM82	Sleep Talk	Normal	Status	—	—	10	Depends	—
TM83	Natural Gift	Normal	Physical	—	100	15	Normal	—
TM84	Poison Jab	Poison	Physical	80	100	20	Normal	○
TM87	Swagger	Normal	Status	—	90	15	Normal	—
TM90	Substitute	Normal	Status	—	—	10	Self	—
HM04	Strength	Normal	Physical	80	100	15	Normal	○
HM06	Rock Smash	Fighting	Physical	40	100	15	Normal	○
HM08	Rock Climb	Normal	Physical	90	85	20	Normal	○

No. 068 | Superpower Pokémon
Machamp

Fighting

- ● HEIGHT: 5'03"
- ● WEIGHT: 286.6 lbs.
- ● ITEMS: None

● SIZE COMPARISON

● MALE/FEMALE HAVE SAME FORM

⊚ ABILITIES
- ● Guts
- ● No Guard

⊚ STATS
- HP ●●●
- ATTACK ●●●●●
- DEFENSE ●●●●
- SP. ATTACK ●●
- SP. DEFENSE ●●●
- SPEED ●●●

⊚ EGG GROUPS
Human-Like

⊚ PERFORMANCE
- SPEED ★☆
- POWER ★★★★★
- SKILL ★★★★
- STAMINA ★★★
- JUMP ★★

● MAIN WAYS TO OBTAIN

Pokémon HeartGold	Link trade Machoke
Pokémon SoulSilver	Link trade Machoke
Pokémon Diamond	Link trade Machoke
Pokémon Pearl	Link trade Machoke
Pokémon Platinum	Link trade Machoke

Pokémon HeartGold
It quickly swings its four arms to rock its opponents with ceaseless punches and chops from all angles.

Pokémon SoulSilver
It uses its four powerful arms to pin the limbs of its foe, then throws the victim over the horizon.

⊚ EVOLUTION

Machop → Lv. 28 → Machoke → Trade it → Machamp

No. 069 | Flower Pokémon
Bellsprout

`Grass` `Poison`

- **HEIGHT:** 2'04"
- **WEIGHT:** 8.8 lbs.
- **ITEMS:** None

● **SIZE COMPARISON**

● MALE/FEMALE HAVE SAME FORM

● ABILITIES
- Chlorophyll

● STATS
HP	●●
ATTACK	●●●
DEFENSE	●●●
SP. ATTACK	●●●
SP. DEFENSE	●●
SPEED	●●

● EGG GROUPS
Grass

● PERFORMANCE
SPEED ★★☆	STAMINA ★★★☆☆
POWER ★★☆	JUMP ★★☆
SKILL ★★	

● MAIN WAYS TO OBTAIN

Pokémon HeartGold	Route 31
Pokémon SoulSilver	Route 31
Pokémon Diamond	Route 229
Pokémon Pearl	Route 229
Pokémon Platinum	Route 224 (morning and afternoon only)

Pokémon HeartGold
Even though its body is extremely skinny, it is blindingly fast when catching its prey.

Pokémon SoulSilver
It plants its feet deep underground to replenish water. It can't escape its enemy while it's rooted.

● EVOLUTION

Bellsprout — Lv. 21 → Weepinbell — Use Leaf Stone → Victreebel

● LEVEL-UP MOVES
Lv.	Name	Type	Kind	Pow.	Acc.	PP	Range	DA
1	Vine Whip	Grass	Physical	35	100	15	Normal	○
7	Growth	Normal	Status	—	—	40	Self	—
11	Wrap	Normal	Physical	15	85	20	Normal	○
13	Sleep Powder	Grass	Status	—	75	15	Normal	—
15	PoisonPowder	Poison	Status	—	75	35	Normal	—
17	Stun Spore	Grass	Status	—	75	30	Normal	—
23	Acid	Poison	Special	40	100	30	2 Foes	—
27	Knock Off	Dark	Physical	20	100	20	Normal	○
29	Sweet Scent	Normal	Status	—	100	20	2 Foes	—
35	Gastro Acid	Poison	Status	—	100	10	Normal	—
39	Razor Leaf	Grass	Physical	55	95	25	2 Foes	—
41	Slam	Normal	Physical	80	75	20	Normal	○
47	Wring Out	Normal	Special	—	100	5	Normal	○

● MOVE MANIAC
Name	Type	Kind	Pow.	Acc.	PP	Range	DA

● BP MOVES
Name	Type	Kind	Pow.	Acc.	PP	Range	DA
Knock Off	Dark	Physical	20	100	20	Normal	○
Sucker Punch	Dark	Physical	80	100	5	Normal	○
Snore	Normal	Special	40	100	15	Normal	—
Synthesis	Grass	Status	—	—	5	Self	—
Worry Seed	Grass	Status	—	100	10	Normal	—
Gastro Acid	Poison	Status	—	100	10	Normal	—
Seed Bomb	Grass	Physical	80	100	15	Normal	—

● TM & HM MOVES
No.	Name	Type	Kind	Pow.	Acc.	PP	Range	DA
TM06	Toxic	Poison	Status	—	85	10	Normal	—
TM09	Bullet Seed	Grass	Physical	10	100	30	Normal	—
TM10	Hidden Power	Normal	Special	—	100	15	Normal	—
TM11	Sunny Day	Fire	Status	—	—	5	All	—
TM17	Protect	Normal	Status	—	—	10	Self	—
TM19	Giga Drain	Grass	Special	60	100	10	Normal	—
TM21	Frustration	Normal	Physical	—	100	20	Normal	○
TM22	SolarBeam	Grass	Special	120	100	10	Normal	—
TM27	Return	Normal	Physical	—	100	20	Normal	○
TM32	Double Team	Normal	Status	—	—	15	Self	—
TM36	Sludge Bomb	Poison	Special	90	100	10	Normal	—
TM42	Facade	Normal	Physical	70	100	20	Normal	○
TM43	Secret Power	Normal	Physical	70	100	20	Normal	—
TM44	Rest	Psychic	Status	—	—	10	Self	—
TM45	Attract	Normal	Status	—	100	15	Normal	—
TM46	Thief	Dark	Physical	40	100	10	Normal	○
TM53	Energy Ball	Grass	Special	80	100	10	Normal	—
TM58	Endure	Normal	Status	—	—	10	Self	—
TM70	Flash	Normal	Status	—	100	20	Normal	—
TM75	Swords Dance	Normal	Status	—	—	30	Self	—
TM78	Captivate	Normal	Status	—	100	20	2 Foes	—
TM82	Sleep Talk	Normal	Status	—	—	10	Depends	—
TM83	Natural Gift	Normal	Physical	—	100	15	Normal	—
TM86	Grass Knot	Grass	Special	—	100	20	Normal	—
TM87	Swagger	Normal	Status	—	90	15	Normal	—
TM90	Substitute	Normal	Status	—	—	10	Self	—
HM01	Cut	Normal	Physical	50	95	30	Normal	○

● EGG MOVES
Name	Type	Kind	Pow.	Acc.	PP	Range	DA
Swords Dance	Normal	Status	—	—	30	Self	—
Encore	Normal	Status	—	100	5	Normal	—
Reflect	Psychic	Status	—	—	20	2 Allies	—
Synthesis	Grass	Status	—	—	5	Self	—
Leech Life	Bug	Physical	20	100	15	Normal	○
Ingrain	Grass	Status	—	—	20	Self	—
Magical Leaf	Grass	Special	60	—	20	Normal	—
Worry Seed	Grass	Status	—	100	10	Normal	—
Tickle	Normal	Status	—	100	20	Normal	—
Weather Ball	Normal	Special	50	100	10	Normal	—

● LEVEL-UP MOVES

Lv.	Name	Type	Kind	Pow.	Acc.	PP	Range	DA
1	Vine Whip	Grass	Physical	35	100	15	Normal	○
1	Growth	Normal	Status	—	—	40	Self	—
1	Wrap	Normal	Physical	15	85	20	Normal	○
7	Growth	Normal	Status	—	—	40	Self	—
11	Wrap	Normal	Physical	15	85	20	Normal	○
13	Sleep Powder	Grass	Status	—	75	15	Normal	—
15	Poison Powder	Poison	Status	—	75	35	Normal	—
17	Stun Spore	Grass	Status	—	75	30	Normal	—
23	Acid	Poison	Special	40	100	30	2 Foes	—
27	Knock Off	Dark	Physical	20	100	20	Normal	○
29	Sweet Scent	Normal	Status	—	100	20	2 Foes	—
35	Gastro Acid	Poison	Status	—	100	10	Normal	—
39	Razor Leaf	Grass	Physical	55	95	25	2 Foes	—
41	Slam	Normal	Physical	80	75	20	Normal	○
47	Wring Out	Normal	Special	—	100	5	Normal	○

● MOVE MANIAC

Name	Type	Kind	Pow.	Acc.	PP	Range	DA

● BP MOVES

Name	Type	Kind	Pow.	Acc.	PP	Range	DA
Knock Off	Dark	Physical	20	100	20	Normal	○
Sucker Punch	Dark	Physical	80	100	5	Normal	○
Snore	Normal	Special	40	100	15	Normal	—
Synthesis	Grass	Status	—	—	5	Self	—
Worry Seed	Grass	Status	—	100	10	Normal	—
Gastro Acid	Poison	Status	—	100	10	Normal	—
Seed Bomb	Grass	Physical	80	100	15	Normal	—

● TM & HM MOVES

No.	Name	Type	Kind	Pow.	Acc.	PP	Range	DA
TM06	Toxic	Poison	Status	—	85	10	Normal	—
TM09	Bullet Seed	Grass	Physical	10	100	30	Normal	—
TM10	Hidden Power	Normal	Status	—	100	15	Normal	—
TM11	Sunny Day	Fire	Status	—	—	5	All	—
TM17	Protect	Normal	Status	—	—	10	Self	—
TM19	Giga Drain	Grass	Special	60	100	10	Normal	—
TM21	Frustration	Normal	Physical	—	100	20	Normal	○
TM22	SolarBeam	Grass	Special	120	100	10	Normal	—
TM27	Return	Normal	Physical	—	100	20	Normal	○
TM32	Double Team	Normal	Status	—	—	15	Self	—
TM36	Sludge Bomb	Poison	Special	90	100	10	Normal	—
TM42	Facade	Normal	Physical	70	100	20	Normal	○
TM43	Secret Power	Normal	Physical	70	100	20	Normal	○
TM44	Rest	Psychic	Status	—	—	10	Self	—
TM45	Attract	Normal	Status	—	100	15	Normal	—
TM46	Thief	Dark	Physical	40	100	10	Normal	○
TM53	Energy Ball	Grass	Special	80	100	10	Normal	—
TM58	Endure	Normal	Status	—	—	10	Self	—
TM70	Flash	Normal	Status	—	100	20	Normal	—
TM75	Swords Dance	Normal	Status	—	—	30	Self	—
TM78	Captivate	Normal	Status	—	100	20	2 Foes	—
TM82	Sleep Talk	Normal	Status	—	—	10	Depends	—
TM83	Natural Gift	Normal	Physical	—	100	15	Normal	—
TM86	Grass Knot	Grass	Special	—	100	20	Normal	○
TM87	Swagger	Normal	Status	—	90	15	Normal	—
TM90	Substitute	Normal	Status	—	—	10	Self	—
HM01	Cut	Normal	Physical	50	95	30	Normal	○

● No. 070 | Flycatcher Pokémon
Weepinbell

Grass **Poison**

- **HEIGHT:** 3'03"
- **WEIGHT:** 14.1 lbs.
- **ITEMS:** None

● SIZE COMPARISON

● MALE/FEMALE HAVE SAME FORM

● ABILITIES
● Chlorophyll

● STATS
HP ●●
ATTACK ●●●●
DEFENSE ●●●
SP. ATTACK ●●●●
SP. DEFENSE ●●●
SPEED ●●●

● EGG GROUPS
Grass

● PERFORMANCE
SPEED ★☆
POWER ★★★
SKILL ★★
STAMINA ★★★★
JUMP ★★★

● MAIN WAYS TO OBTAIN

Pokémon HeartGold	Route 44
Pokémon SoulSilver	Route 44
Pokémon Diamond	Route 224
Pokémon Pearl	Route 224
Pokémon Platinum	Route 224

Pokémon HeartGold
Even though it is filled with acid, it does not melt because it also oozes a protective fluid.

Pokémon SoulSilver
If its prey is bigger than its mouth, it slices up the victim with sharp leaves, then eats every morsel.

● EVOLUTION

Lv. 21

Use Leaf Stone

Bellsprout — Weepinbell — Victreebel

No. 071 | Flycatcher Pokémon

Victreebel

Grass **Poison**

- **HEIGHT:** 5'07"
- **WEIGHT:** 34.2 lbs.
- **ITEMS:** None

● SIZE COMPARISON

● MALE/FEMALE HAVE SAME FORM

ABILITIES
- Chlorophyll

STATS
HP	●●●
ATTACK	●●●●
DEFENSE	●●●
SP. ATTACK	●●●●
SP. DEFENSE	●●
SPEED	●●●

EGG GROUPS
Grass

PERFORMANCE
SPEED ★	STAMINA ★★★★
POWER ★★★★	JUMP ★★★
SKILL ★★★☆	

MAIN WAYS TO OBTAIN

Pokémon HeartGold	Use Leaf Stone on Weepinbell
Pokémon SoulSilver	Use Leaf Stone on Weepinbell
Pokémon Diamond	Use Leaf Stone on Weepinbell
Pokémon Pearl	Use Leaf Stone on Weepinbell
Pokémon Platinum	Use Leaf Stone on Weepinbell

Pokémon HeartGold	Pokémon SoulSilver
Acid that has dissolved many prey becomes sweeter, making it even more effective at attracting prey.	This horrifying plant Pokémon attracts prey with aromatic honey, then melts them in its mouth.

EVOLUTION

Bellsprout → Weepinbell → Victreebel
Lv. 21 → Use Leaf Stone

● LEVEL-UP MOVES

Lv.	Name	Type	Kind	Pow.	Acc.	PP	Range	DA
1	Stockpile	Normal	Status	—	—	20	Self	—
1	Swallow	Normal	Status	—	—	10	Self	—
1	Spit Up	Normal	Special	—	100	10	Normal	—
1	Vine Whip	Grass	Physical	35	100	15	Normal	○
1	Sleep Powder	Grass	Status	—	75	15	Normal	—
1	Sweet Scent	Normal	Status	—	100	20	2 Foes	—
1	Razor Leaf	Grass	Physical	55	95	25	2 Foes	—
47	Leaf Storm	Grass	Special	140	90	5	Normal	—
47	Leaf Blade	Grass	Physical	90	100	15	Normal	○

● MOVE MANIAC

Name	Type	Kind	Pow.	Acc.	PP	Range	DA

● BP MOVES

Name	Type	Kind	Pow.	Acc.	PP	Range	DA
Knock Off	Dark	Physical	20	100	20	Normal	○
Sucker Punch	Dark	Physical	80	100	5	Normal	○
Snore	Normal	Special	40	100	15	Normal	—
Synthesis	Grass	Status	—	—	5	Self	—
Worry Seed	Grass	Status	—	100	10	Normal	—
Gastro Acid	Poison	Status	—	100	10	Normal	—
Seed Bomb	Grass	Physical	80	100	15	Normal	—

● TM & HM MOVES

No.	Name	Type	Kind	Pow.	Acc.	PP	Range	DA
TM06	Toxic	Poison	Status	—	85	10	Normal	—
TM09	Bullet Seed	Grass	Physical	10	100	30	Normal	—
TM10	Hidden Power	Normal	Special	—	100	15	Normal	—
TM11	Sunny Day	Fire	Status	—	—	5	All	—
TM15	Hyper Beam	Normal	Special	150	90	5	Normal	—
TM17	Protect	Normal	Status	—	—	10	Self	—
TM19	Giga Drain	Grass	Special	60	100	10	Normal	—
TM21	Frustration	Normal	Physical	—	100	20	Normal	○
TM22	SolarBeam	Grass	Special	120	100	10	Normal	—
TM27	Return	Normal	Physical	—	100	20	Normal	○
TM32	Double Team	Normal	Status	—	—	15	Self	—
TM36	Sludge Bomb	Poison	Special	90	100	10	Normal	—
TM42	Facade	Normal	Physical	70	100	20	Normal	○
TM43	Secret Power	Normal	Physical	70	100	20	Normal	—
TM44	Rest	Psychic	Status	—	—	10	Self	—
TM45	Attract	Normal	Status	—	100	15	Normal	—
TM46	Thief	Dark	Physical	40	100	10	Normal	○
TM53	Energy Ball	Grass	Special	80	100	10	Normal	—
TM58	Endure	Normal	Status	—	—	10	Self	—
TM68	Giga Impact	Normal	Physical	150	90	5	Normal	○
TM70	Flash	Normal	Status	—	100	20	Normal	—
TM75	Swords Dance	Normal	Status	—	—	30	Self	—
TM78	Captivate	Normal	Status	—	100	20	2 Foes	—
TM82	Sleep Talk	Normal	Status	—	—	10	Depends	—
TM83	Natural Gift	Normal	Physical	—	100	15	Normal	—
TM86	Grass Knot	Grass	Special	—	100	20	Normal	○
TM87	Swagger	Normal	Status	—	90	15	Normal	—
TM90	Substitute	Normal	Status	—	—	10	Self	—
HM01	Cut	Normal	Physical	50	95	30	Normal	○

● LEVEL-UP MOVES

Lv.	Name	Type	Kind	Pow.	Acc.	PP	Range	DA
1	Poison Sting	Poison	Physical	15	100	35	Normal	—
5	Supersonic	Normal	Status	—	55	20	Normal	—
8	Constrict	Normal	Physical	10	100	35	Normal	○
12	Acid	Poison	Special	40	100	30	2 Foes	—
15	Toxic Spikes	Poison	Status	—	—	20	2 Foes	—
19	BubbleBeam	Water	Special	65	100	20	Normal	—
22	Wrap	Normal	Physical	15	85	20	Normal	○
26	Barrier	Psychic	Status	—	—	30	Self	—
29	Water Pulse	Water	Special	60	100	20	Normal	—
33	Poison Jab	Poison	Physical	80	100	20	Normal	○
36	Screech	Normal	Status	—	85	40	Normal	—
40	Hydro Pump	Water	Special	120	80	5	Normal	—
43	Wring Out	Normal	Special	—	100	5	Normal	○

● MOVE MANIAC

Name	Type	Kind	Pow.	Acc.	PP	Range	DA

● BP MOVES

Name	Type	Kind	Pow.	Acc.	PP	Range	DA
Dive	Water	Physical	80	100	10	Normal	—
Icy Wind	Ice	Special	55	95	15	2 Foes	—
Knock Off	Dark	Physical	20	100	20	Normal	○
Snore	Normal	Special	40	100	15	Normal	—
Magic Coat	Psychic	Status	—	—	15	Self	—

● TM & HM MOVES

No.	Name	Type	Kind	Pow.	Acc.	PP	Range	DA
TM03	Water Pulse	Water	Special	60	100	20	Normal	—
TM06	Toxic	Poison	Status	—	85	10	Normal	—
TM07	Hail	Ice	Status	—	—	10	All	—
TM10	Hidden Power	Normal	Special	—	100	15	Normal	—
TM13	Ice Beam	Ice	Special	95	100	10	Normal	—
TM14	Blizzard	Ice	Special	120	70	5	2 Foes	—
TM17	Protect	Normal	Status	—	—	10	Self	—
TM18	Rain Dance	Water	Status	—	—	5	All	—
TM19	Giga Drain	Grass	Special	60	100	10	Normal	—
TM21	Frustration	Normal	Physical	—	100	20	Normal	○
TM27	Return	Normal	Physical	—	100	20	Normal	○
TM32	Double Team	Normal	Status	—	—	15	Self	—
TM36	Sludge Bomb	Poison	Special	90	100	10	Normal	—
TM42	Facade	Normal	Physical	70	100	20	Normal	○
TM43	Secret Power	Normal	Physical	70	100	20	Normal	○
TM44	Rest	Psychic	Status	—	—	10	Self	—
TM45	Attract	Normal	Status	—	100	15	Normal	—
TM46	Thief	Dark	Physical	40	100	10	Normal	○
TM55	Brine	Water	Special	65	100	10	Normal	—
TM58	Endure	Normal	Status	—	—	10	Self	—
TM66	Payback	Dark	Physical	50	100	10	Normal	○
TM75	Swords Dance	Normal	Status	—	—	30	Self	—
TM78	Captivate	Normal	Status	—	100	20	2 Foes	—
TM82	Sleep Talk	Normal	Status	—	—	10	Depends	—
TM83	Natural Gift	Normal	Physical	—	100	15	Normal	—
TM84	Poison Jab	Poison	Physical	80	100	20	Normal	○
TM87	Swagger	Normal	Status	—	90	15	Normal	—
TM90	Substitute	Normal	Status	—	—	10	Self	—
HM01	Cut	Normal	Physical	50	95	30	Normal	○
HM03	Surf	Water	Special	95	100	15	2 Foes/1 Ally	—
HM05	Whirlpool	Water	Special	15	70	15	Normal	—
HM07	Waterfall	Water	Physical	80	100	15	Normal	—

● EGG MOVES

Name	Type	Kind	Pow.	Acc.	PP	Range	DA
Aurora Beam	Ice	Special	65	100	20	Normal	—
Mirror Coat	Psychic	Special	—	100	20	Self	—
Rapid Spin	Normal	Physical	20	100	40	Normal	○
Haze	Ice	Status	—	—	30	All	—
Safeguard	Normal	Status	—	—	25	2 Allies	—
Confuse Ray	Ghost	Status	—	100	10	Normal	—
Knock Off	Dark	Physical	20	100	20	Normal	○
Acupressure	Normal	Status	—	—	30	1 Ally	—
Muddy Water	Water	Special	95	85	10	2 Foes	—

No. 072 | Jellyfish Pokémon
Tentacool

Water **Poison**

- ● HEIGHT: 2'11"
- ● WEIGHT: 100.3 lbs.
- ● ITEMS: Poison Barb

● SIZE COMPARISON

● MALE/FEMALE HAVE SAME FORM

⊙ ABILITIES
- ● Clear Body
- ● Liquid Ooze

⊙ STATS
HP ●
ATTACK ●●
DEFENSE ●●
SP. ATTACK ●●
SP. DEFENSE ●●●●
SPEED ●●●

⊙ EGG GROUPS
Water 3

⊙ PERFORMANCE
SPEED ★★☆   STAMINA ★★★☆
POWER ★★☆   JUMP ★★☆
SKILL ★★★☆☆

● MAIN WAYS TO OBTAIN

Pokémon HeartGold	New Bark Town (water surface)
Pokémon SoulSilver	New Bark Town (water surface)
Pokémon Diamond	Route 205 (water surface)
Pokémon Pearl	Route 205 (water surface)
Pokémon Platinum	Route 205 (water surface)

Pokémon HeartGold
When the tide goes out, dehydrated TENTACOOL remains can be found washed up on the shore.

Pokémon SoulSilver
It drifts aimlessly in waves. Very difficult to see in water, it may not be noticed until it stings.

⊙ EVOLUTION

Lv. 30

Tentacool → Tentacruel

No. 073 | Jellyfish Pokémon
Tentacruel

Water | **Poison**

- **HEIGHT:** 6'03"
- **WEIGHT:** 341.7 lbs.
- **ITEMS:** None

● SIZE COMPARISON

● MALE/FEMALE HAVE SAME FORM

⊛ ABILITIES
- Clear Body
- Liquid Ooze

⊛ STATS
HP ●●●
ATTACK ●●●
DEFENSE ●●●
SP. ATTACK ●●●●
SP. DEFENSE ●●●●●
SPEED ●●●●

⊛ EGG GROUPS
Water 3

⊛ PERFORMANCE
SPEED ★★★☆
POWER ★★☆☆
SKILL ★★★☆
STAMINA ★★☆☆
JUMP ★★★☆

● MAIN WAYS TO OBTAIN

Pokémon HeartGold	Route 36
Pokémon SoulSilver	—
Pokémon Diamond	Route 224 (water surface)
Pokémon Pearl	Route 224 (water surface)
Pokémon Platinum	Route 224 (water surface)

Pokémon HeartGold
It has a brave and trustworthy nature. It fearlessly stands up to bigger and stronger foes.

Pokémon SoulSilver
In battle, it extends all 80 of its tentacles to entrap its opponent inside a poisonous net.

⊛ EVOLUTION

Tentacool — Lv. 30 → Tentacruel

● LEVEL-UP MOVES

Lv.	Name	Type	Kind	Pow.	Acc.	PP	Range	DA
1	Poison Sting	Poison	Physical	15	100	35	Normal	—
1	Supersonic	Normal	Status	—	55	20	Normal	—
1	Constrict	Normal	Physical	10	100	35	Normal	O
5	Supersonic	Normal	Status	—	55	20	Normal	—
8	Constrict	Normal	Physical	10	100	35	Normal	O
12	Acid	Poison	Special	40	100	30	2 Foes	—
15	Toxic Spikes	Poison	Status	—	—	20	2 Foes	—
19	BubbleBeam	Water	Special	65	100	10	Normal	—
22	Wrap	Normal	Physical	15	85	20	Normal	O
26	Barrier	Psychic	Status	—	—	30	Self	—
29	Water Pulse	Water	Special	60	100	20	Normal	—
36	Poison Jab	Poison	Physical	80	100	20	Normal	O
42	Screech	Normal	Status	—	85	40	Normal	—
49	Hydro Pump	Water	Special	120	80	5	Normal	—
55	Wring Out	Normal	Special	—	100	5	Normal	O

● MOVE MANIAC

Name	Type	Kind	Pow.	Acc.	PP	Range	DA

● BP MOVES

Name	Type	Kind	Pow.	Acc.	PP	Range	DA
Dive	Water	Physical	80	100	10	Normal	O
Icy Wind	Ice	Special	55	95	15	2 Foes	—
Knock Off	Dark	Physical	20	100	20	Normal	O
Snore	Normal	Special	40	100	15	Normal	—
Magic Coat	Psychic	Status	—	—	15	Self	—

● TM & HM MOVES

No.	Name	Type	Kind	Pow.	Acc.	PP	Range	DA
TM03	Water Pulse	Water	Special	60	100	20	Normal	—
TM06	Toxic	Poison	Status	—	85	10	Normal	—
TM07	Hail	Ice	Status	—	—	10	All	—
TM10	Hidden Power	Normal	Special	—	100	15	Normal	—
TM13	Ice Beam	Ice	Special	95	100	10	Normal	—
TM14	Blizzard	Ice	Special	120	70	5	2 Foes	—
TM15	Hyper Beam	Normal	Special	150	90	5	Normal	—
TM17	Protect	Normal	Status	—	—	10	Self	—
TM18	Rain Dance	Water	Status	—	—	5	All	—
TM19	Giga Drain	Grass	Special	60	100	10	Normal	—
TM21	Frustration	Normal	Physical	—	100	20	Normal	O
TM27	Return	Normal	Physical	—	100	20	Normal	O
TM32	Double Team	Normal	Status	—	—	15	Self	—
TM36	Sludge Bomb	Poison	Special	90	100	10	Normal	—
TM42	Facade	Normal	Physical	70	100	20	Normal	O
TM43	Secret Power	Normal	Physical	70	100	20	Normal	—
TM44	Rest	Psychic	Status	—	—	10	Self	—
TM45	Attract	Normal	Status	—	100	15	Normal	—
TM46	Thief	Dark	Physical	40	100	10	Normal	O
TM55	Brine	Water	Special	65	100	10	Normal	—
TM58	Endure	Normal	Status	—	—	10	Self	—
TM66	Payback	Dark	Physical	50	100	10	Normal	O
TM68	Giga Impact	Normal	Physical	150	90	5	Normal	O
TM75	Swords Dance	Normal	Status	—	—	30	Self	—
TM78	Captivate	Normal	Status	—	100	20	2 Foes	—
TM82	Sleep Talk	Normal	Status	—	—	10	Depends	—
TM83	Natural Gift	Normal	Physical	—	100	15	Normal	—
TM84	Poison Jab	Poison	Physical	80	100	20	Normal	O
TM87	Swagger	Normal	Status	—	90	15	Normal	—
TM90	Substitute	Normal	Status	—	—	10	Self	—
HM01	Cut	Normal	Physical	50	95	30	Normal	O
HM03	Surf	Water	Special	95	100	15	2 Foes/1 Ally	—
HM05	Whirlpool	Water	Special	15	70	15	Normal	—
HM07	Waterfall	Water	Physical	80	100	15	Normal	O

● LEVEL-UP MOVES

Lv.	Name	Type	Kind	Pow.	Acc.	PP	Range	DA
1	Tackle	Normal	Physical	35	95	35	Normal	○
1	Defense Curl	Normal	Status	—	—	40	Self	—
4	Mud Sport	Ground	Status	—	—	15	All	—
8	Rock Polish	Rock	Status	—	—	20	Self	—
11	Rock Throw	Rock	Physical	50	90	15	Normal	—
15	Magnitude	Ground	Physical	—	100	30	2 Foes/1 Ally	—
18	Selfdestruct	Normal	Physical	200	100	5	2 Foes/1 Ally	—
22	Rollout	Rock	Physical	30	90	20	Normal	○
25	Rock Blast	Rock	Physical	25	80	10	Normal	—
29	Earthquake	Ground	Physical	100	100	10	2 Foes/1 Ally	—
32	Explosion	Normal	Physical	250	100	5	2 Foes/1 Ally	—
36	Double-Edge	Normal	Physical	120	100	15	Normal	○
39	Stone Edge	Rock	Physical	100	80	5	Normal	—

● MOVE MANIAC

Name	Type	Kind	Pow.	Acc.	PP	Range	DA
Headbutt	Normal	Physical	70	100	15	Normal	○

● BP MOVES

Name	Type	Kind	Pow.	Acc.	PP	Range	DA
ThunderPunch	Electric	Physical	75	100	15	Normal	○
Fire Punch	Fire	Physical	75	100	15	Normal	○
Sucker Punch	Dark	Physical	80	100	5	Normal	○
Snore	Normal	Special	40	100	15	Normal	—
Block	Normal	Status	—	—	5	Normal	—
Mud-Slap	Ground	Special	20	100	10	Normal	—
Rollout	Rock	Physical	30	90	20	Normal	○
Superpower	Fighting	Physical	120	100	5	Normal	○
AncientPower	Rock	Special	60	100	5	Normal	—
Earth Power	Ground	Special	90	100	10	Normal	—

● TM & HM MOVES

No.	Name	Type	Kind	Pow.	Acc.	PP	Range	DA
TM01	Focus Punch	Fighting	Physical	150	100	20	Normal	○
TM06	Toxic	Poison	Status	—	85	10	Normal	—
TM10	Hidden Power	Normal	Special	—	100	15	Normal	—
TM11	Sunny Day	Fire	Status	—	—	5	All	—
TM17	Protect	Normal	Status	—	—	10	Self	—
TM21	Frustration	Normal	Physical	—	100	20	Normal	○
TM26	Earthquake	Ground	Physical	100	100	10	2 Foes/1 Ally	—
TM27	Return	Normal	Physical	—	100	20	Normal	○
TM28	Dig	Ground	Physical	80	100	10	Normal	○
TM31	Brick Break	Fighting	Physical	75	100	15	Normal	○
TM32	Double Team	Normal	Status	—	—	15	Self	—
TM35	Flamethrower	Fire	Special	95	100	15	Normal	—
TM37	Sandstorm	Rock	Status	—	—	10	All	—
TM38	Fire Blast	Fire	Special	120	85	5	Normal	—
TM39	Rock Tomb	Rock	Physical	50	80	10	Normal	—
TM42	Facade	Normal	Physical	70	100	20	Normal	○
TM43	Secret Power	Normal	Physical	70	100	20	Normal	○
TM44	Rest	Psychic	Status	—	—	10	Self	—
TM45	Attract	Normal	Status	—	100	15	Normal	—
TM56	Fling	Dark	Physical	—	100	10	Normal	—
TM58	Endure	Normal	Status	—	—	10	Self	—
TM64	Explosion	Normal	Physical	250	100	5	2 Foes/1 Ally	—
TM69	Rock Polish	Rock	Status	—	—	20	Self	—
TM71	Stone Edge	Rock	Physical	100	80	5	Normal	—
TM74	Gyro Ball	Steel	Physical	—	100	5	Normal	○
TM76	Stealth Rock	Rock	Status	—	—	20	2 Foes	—
TM78	Captivate	Normal	Status	—	100	20	2 Foes	—
TM80	Rock Slide	Rock	Physical	75	90	10	2 Foes	—
TM82	Sleep Talk	Normal	Status	—	—	10	Depends	—
TM83	Natural Gift	Normal	Physical	—	100	15	Normal	—
TM87	Swagger	Normal	Status	—	90	15	Normal	—
TM90	Substitute	Normal	Status	—	—	10	Self	—
HM04	Strength	Normal	Physical	80	100	15	Normal	○
HM06	Rock Smash	Fighting	Physical	40	100	15	Normal	○
HM08	Rock Climb	Normal	Physical	90	85	20	Normal	○

● EGG MOVES

Name	Type	Kind	Pow.	Acc.	PP	Range	DA
Mega Punch	Normal	Physical	80	85	20	Normal	○
Rock Slide	Rock	Physical	75	90	10	2 Foes	—
Block	Normal	Status	—	—	5	Normal	—
Hammer Arm	Fighting	Physical	100	90	10	Normal	○
Flail	Normal	Physical	—	100	15	Normal	—
Curse	???	Status	—	—	10	Normal/Self	—

Geodude

Rock   Ground

● HEIGHT: 1'04"
● WEIGHT: 44.1 lbs.
● ITEMS: Everstone

● SIZE COMPARISON

● MALE/FEMALE HAVE SAME FORM

◎ ABILITIES
● Rock Head
● Sturdy

◎ STATS
HP ●
ATTACK ●●●
DEFENSE ●●●●
SP. ATTACK ●
SP. DEFENSE ●
SPEED ●

◎ EGG GROUPS
Mineral

◎ PERFORMANCE

SPEED ★☆☆   STAMINA ★★★☆
POWER ★★★   JUMP ★★
SKILL ★☆

● MAIN WAYS TO OBTAIN

Pokémon HeartGold — Union Cave

Pokémon SoulSilver — Union Cave

Pokémon Diamond — Oreburgh Gate 1F

Pokémon Pearl — Oreburgh Gate 1F

Pokémon Platinum — Oreburgh Gate 1F

Pokémon HeartGold
Most people may not notice, but a closer look should reveal that there are many GEODUDE around.

Pokémon SoulSilver
It uses its arms to steadily climb steep mountain paths. It swings its fists around if angered.

◎ EVOLUTION

Lv. 25   Trade it

Geodude   Graveler   Golem

Graveler

`Rock` `Ground`

● **HEIGHT:** 3'03"
● **WEIGHT:** 44.1 lbs.
● **ITEMS:** King's Rock

● **SIZE COMPARISON**

● **MALE/FEMALE HAVE SAME FORM**

⊙ ABILITIES
● Rock Head
● Sturdy

⊙ STATS
HP ●●
ATTACK ●●●●
DEFENSE ●●●●●
SP. ATTACK ●●
SP. DEFENSE ●●
SPEED ●●

⊙ EGG GROUPS
Mineral

⊙ PERFORMANCE
SPEED ★☆☆
POWER ★★★★
SKILL ★★
STAMINA ★★★☆
JUMP ★★

● MAIN WAYS TO OBTAIN

Pokémon HeartGold Route 45

Pokémon SoulSilver Route 45

Pokémon Diamond Route 214

Pokémon Pearl Route 214

Pokémon Platinum Route 214

Pokémon HeartGold
With a free and uncaring nature, it doesn't mind if pieces break off while it rolls down mountains.

Pokémon SoulSilver
A slow walker, it rolls to move. It pays no attention to any object that happens to be in its path.

⊙ EVOLUTION

Geodude — Lv. 25 → Graveler — Trade it → Golem

● LEVEL-UP MOVES

Lv.	Name	Type	Kind	Pow.	Acc.	PP	Range	DA
1	Tackle	Normal	Physical	35	95	35	Normal	○
1	Defense Curl	Normal	Status	—	—	40	Self	—
1	Mud Sport	Ground	Status	—	—	15	All	—
1	Rock Polish	Rock	Status	—	—	20	Self	—
4	Mud Sport	Ground	Status	—	—	15	All	—
8	Rock Polish	Rock	Status	—	—	20	Self	—
11	Rock Throw	Rock	Physical	50	90	15	Normal	—
15	Magnitude	Ground	Physical	—	100	30	2 Foes/1 Ally	—
18	Selfdestruct	Normal	Physical	200	100	5	2 Foes/1 Ally	—
22	Rollout	Rock	Physical	30	90	20	Normal	○
27	Rock Blast	Rock	Physical	25	80	10	Normal	—
33	Earthquake	Ground	Physical	100	100	10	2 Foes/1 Ally	—
38	Explosion	Normal	Physical	250	100	5	2 Foes/1 Ally	—
44	Double-Edge	Normal	Physical	120	100	15	Normal	○
49	Stone Edge	Rock	Physical	100	80	5	Normal	—

● MOVE MANIAC

Name	Type	Kind	Pow.	Acc.	PP	Range	DA
Headbutt	Normal	Physical	70	100	15	Normal	○

● BP MOVES

Name	Type	Kind	Pow.	Acc.	PP	Range	DA
ThunderPunch	Electric	Physical	75	100	15	Normal	○
Fire Punch	Fire	Physical	75	100	15	Normal	○
Sucker Punch	Dark	Physical	80	100	5	Normal	○
Snore	Normal	Special	40	100	15	Normal	—
Block	Normal	Status	—	—	5	Normal	—
Mud-Slap	Ground	Special	20	100	10	Normal	—
Rollout	Rock	Physical	30	90	20	Normal	○
Superpower	Fighting	Physical	120	100	5	Normal	○
AncientPower	Rock	Special	60	100	5	Normal	—
Earth Power	Ground	Special	90	100	10	Normal	—

● TM & HM MOVES

No.	Name	Type	Kind	Pow.	Acc.	PP	Range	DA
TM01	Focus Punch	Fighting	Physical	150	100	20	Normal	○
TM06	Toxic	Poison	Status	—	85	10	Normal	—
TM10	Hidden Power	Normal	Special	—	100	10	Normal	—
TM11	Sunny Day	Fire	Status	—	—	5	All	—
TM17	Protect	Normal	Status	—	—	10	Self	—
TM21	Frustration	Normal	Physical	—	100	20	Normal	○
TM26	Earthquake	Ground	Physical	100	100	10	2 Foes/1 Ally	—
TM27	Return	Normal	Physical	—	100	20	Normal	○
TM28	Dig	Ground	Physical	80	100	10	Normal	○
TM31	Brick Break	Fighting	Physical	75	100	15	Normal	—
TM32	Double Team	Normal	Status	—	—	15	Self	—
TM35	Flamethrower	Fire	Special	95	100	15	Normal	—
TM37	Sandstorm	Rock	Status	—	—	10	All	—
TM38	Fire Blast	Fire	Special	120	85	5	Normal	—
TM39	Rock Tomb	Rock	Physical	50	80	10	Normal	—
TM42	Facade	Normal	Physical	70	100	20	Normal	○
TM43	Secret Power	Normal	Physical	70	100	20	Normal	—
TM44	Rest	Psychic	Status	—	—	10	Self	—
TM45	Attract	Normal	Status	—	100	15	Normal	—
TM56	Fling	Dark	Physical	—	100	10	Normal	—
TM58	Endure	Normal	Status	—	—	10	Self	—
TM64	Explosion	Normal	Physical	250	100	5	2 Foes/1 Ally	—
TM69	Rock Polish	Rock	Status	—	—	20	Self	—
TM71	Stone Edge	Rock	Physical	100	80	5	Normal	—
TM74	Gyro Ball	Steel	Physical	—	100	5	Normal	○
TM76	Stealth Rock	Rock	Status	—	—	20	2 Foes	—
TM78	Captivate	Normal	Status	—	100	20	2 Foes	—
TM80	Rock Slide	Rock	Physical	75	90	10	2 Foes	—
TM82	Sleep Talk	Normal	Status	—	—	10	Depends	—
TM83	Natural Gift	Normal	Physical	—	100	15	Normal	—
TM87	Swagger	Normal	Status	—	90	15	Normal	—
TM90	Substitute	Normal	Status	—	—	10	Self	—
HM04	Strength	Normal	Physical	80	100	15	Normal	○
HM06	Rock Smash	Fighting	Physical	40	100	15	Normal	○
HM08	Rock Climb	Normal	Physical	90	85	20	Normal	○

● LEVEL-UP MOVES

Lv.	Name	Type	Kind	Pow.	Acc.	PP	Range	DA
1	Tackle	Normal	Physical	35	95	35	Normal	○
1	Defense Curl	Normal	Status	—	—	40	Self	—
1	Mud Sport	Ground	Status	—	—	15	All	—
1	Rock Polish	Rock	Status	—	—	20	Self	—
4	Mud Sport	Ground	Status	—	—	15	All	—
8	Rock Polish	Rock	Status	—	—	20	Self	—
11	Rock Throw	Rock	Physical	50	90	15	Normal	—
15	Magnitude	Ground	Physical	—	100	30	2 Foes/1 Ally	—
18	Selfdestruct	Normal	Physical	200	100	5	2 Foes/1 Ally	—
22	Rollout	Rock	Physical	30	90	20	Normal	○
27	Rock Blast	Rock	Physical	25	80	10	Normal	—
33	Earthquake	Ground	Physical	100	100	10	2 Foes/1 Ally	—
38	Explosion	Normal	Physical	250	100	5	2 Foes/1 Ally	—
44	Double-Edge	Normal	Physical	120	100	15	Normal	○
49	Stone Edge	Rock	Physical	100	80	5	Normal	—

● MOVE MANIAC

Name	Type	Kind	Pow.	Acc.	PP	Range	DA
Headbutt	Normal	Physical	70	100	15	Normal	○

● BP MOVES

Name	Type	Kind	Pow.	Acc.	PP	Range	DA
Fury Cutter	Bug	Physical	10	95	20	Normal	○
ThunderPunch	Electric	Physical	75	100	15	Normal	○
Fire Punch	Fire	Physical	75	100	15	Normal	○
Sucker Punch	Dark	Physical	80	100	5	Normal	○
Snore	Normal	Special	40	100	15	Normal	—
Block	Normal	Status	—	—	5	Normal	—
Mud-Slap	Ground	Special	20	100	10	Normal	—
Rollout	Rock	Physical	30	90	20	Normal	○
Superpower	Fighting	Physical	120	100	5	Normal	○
Iron Head	Steel	Physical	80	100	15	Normal	○
AncientPower	Rock	Special	60	100	5	Normal	—
Earth Power	Ground	Special	90	100	10	Normal	—

● TM & HM MOVES

No.	Name	Type	Kind	Pow.	Acc.	PP	Range	DA
TM01	Focus Punch	Fighting	Physical	150	100	20	Normal	○
TM05	Roar	Normal	Status	—	100	20	Normal	—
TM06	Toxic	Poison	Status	—	85	10	Normal	—
TM10	Hidden Power	Normal	Special	—	100	15	Normal	—
TM11	Sunny Day	Fire	Status	—	—	5	All	—
TM15	Hyper Beam	Normal	Special	150	90	5	Normal	—
TM17	Protect	Normal	Status	—	—	10	Self	—
TM21	Frustration	Normal	Physical	—	100	20	Normal	○
TM26	Earthquake	Ground	Physical	100	100	10	2 Foes/1 Ally	—
TM27	Return	Normal	Physical	—	100	20	Normal	○
TM28	Dig	Ground	Physical	80	100	10	Normal	○
TM31	Brick Break	Fighting	Physical	75	100	15	Normal	○
TM32	Double Team	Normal	Status	—	—	15	Self	—
TM35	Flamethrower	Fire	Special	95	100	15	Normal	—
TM37	Sandstorm	Rock	Status	—	—	10	All	—
TM38	Fire Blast	Fire	Special	120	85	5	Normal	—
TM39	Rock Tomb	Rock	Physical	50	80	10	Normal	—
TM42	Facade	Normal	Physical	70	100	20	Normal	○
TM43	Secret Power	Normal	Physical	70	100	20	Normal	—
TM44	Rest	Psychic	Status	—	—	10	Self	—
TM45	Attract	Normal	Status	—	100	15	Normal	—
TM52	Focus Blast	Fighting	Special	120	70	5	Normal	—
TM56	Fling	Dark	Physical	—	100	10	Normal	○
TM58	Endure	Normal	Status	—	—	10	Self	—
TM64	Explosion	Normal	Physical	250	100	5	2 Foes/1 Ally	—
TM68	Giga Impact	Normal	Physical	150	90	5	Normal	○
TM69	Rock Polish	Rock	Status	—	—	20	Self	—
TM71	Stone Edge	Rock	Physical	100	80	5	Normal	—
TM74	Gyro Ball	Steel	Physical	—	100	5	Normal	○
TM76	Stealth Rock	Rock	Status	—	—	20	2 Foes	—
TM78	Captivate	Normal	Status	—	100	20	2 Foes	—
TM80	Rock Slide	Rock	Physical	75	90	10	2 Foes	—
TM82	Sleep Talk	Normal	Status	—	—	10	Depends	—
TM83	Natural Gift	Normal	Physical	—	100	15	Normal	—
TM87	Swagger	Normal	Status	—	90	15	Normal	—
TM90	Substitute	Normal	Status	—	—	10	Self	—
HM04	Strength	Normal	Physical	80	100	15	Normal	○
HM06	Rock Smash	Fighting	Physical	40	100	15	Normal	○
HM08	Rock Climb	Normal	Physical	90	85	20	Normal	○

● No. 076 | Megaton Pokémon
Golem

Rock | Ground

- ● HEIGHT: 4'07"
- ● WEIGHT: 661.4 lbs.
- ● ITEMS: None

● SIZE COMPARISON

● MALE/FEMALE HAVE SAME FORM

⊘ ABILITIES
- ● Rock Head
- ● Sturdy

⊘ EGG GROUPS
Mineral

⊘ STATS
HP	●●●
ATTACK	●●●●●
DEFENSE	●●●●●
SP. ATTACK	●●
SP. DEFENSE	●●
SPEED	●●

⊘ PERFORMANCE
SPEED ★★	STAMINA ★★★★
POWER ★★★★	JUMP ★★
SKILL ★☆	

● MAIN WAYS TO OBTAIN

Pokémon HeartGold Link trade Graveler

Pokémon SoulSilver Link trade Graveler

Pokémon Diamond Link trade Graveler

Pokémon Pearl Link trade Graveler

Pokémon Platinum Link trade Graveler

Pokémon HeartGold
It sheds its skin once a year. The discarded shell immediately hardens and crumbles away.

Pokémon SoulSilver
It is capable of blowing itself up. It uses this explosive force to jump from mountain to mountain.

⊘ EVOLUTION

Geodude — Lv. 25 → Graveler — Trade it → Golem

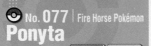

No. 077 | Fire Horse Pokémon
Ponyta

Fire

- **HEIGHT:** 3'03"
- **WEIGHT:** 66.1 lbs.
- **ITEMS:** Shuca Berry

● SIZE COMPARISON

● MALE/FEMALE HAVE SAME FORM

⚙ ABILITIES
- Run Away
- Flash Fire

⚙ STATS
HP ●●
ATTACK ●●●●
DEFENSE ●●●
SP. ATTACK ●●●
SP. DEFENSE ●●●
SPEED ●●●●

⚙ EGG GROUPS
Field

⚙ PERFORMANCE
SPEED ★★★☆☆ STAMINA ★★★
POWER ★★ JUMP ★★★★
SKILL ★★

● MAIN WAYS TO OBTAIN

Pokémon HeartGold	Route 26
Pokémon SoulSilver	Route 26
Pokémon Diamond	Route 206
Pokémon Pearl	Route 206
Pokémon Platinum	Route 206

Pokémon HeartGold	Pokémon SoulSilver
It is a weak runner immediately after birth. It gradually becomes faster by chasing after its parents.	Its hind legs, which have hooves that are harder than diamond, kick back at any presence it senses behind it.

⚙ EVOLUTION

Ponyta — Lv. 40 → Rapidash

● LEVEL-UP MOVES

Lv.	Name	Type	Kind	Pow.	Acc.	PP	Range	DA
1	Growl	Normal	Status	—	100	40	2 Foes	—
1	Tackle	Normal	Physical	35	95	35	Normal	○
6	Tail Whip	Normal	Status	—	100	30	2 Foes	—
10	Ember	Fire	Special	40	100	25	Normal	—
15	Flame Wheel	Fire	Physical	60	100	25	Normal	○
19	Stomp	Normal	Physical	65	100	20	Normal	○
24	Fire Spin	Fire	Special	15	70	15	Normal	—
28	Take Down	Normal	Physical	90	85	20	Normal	○
33	Agility	Psychic	Status	—	—	30	Self	—
37	Fire Blast	Fire	Special	120	85	5	Normal	—
42	Bounce	Flying	Physical	85	85	5	Normal	○
46	Flare Blitz	Fire	Physical	120	100	15	Normal	○

● MOVE MANIAC

Name	Type	Kind	Pow.	Acc.	PP	Range	DA
Headbutt	Normal	Physical	70	100	15	Normal	○

● BP MOVES

Name	Type	Kind	Pow.	Acc.	PP	Range	DA
Snore	Normal	Special	40	100	15	Normal	—
Swift	Normal	Special	60	—	20	2 Foes	—
Bounce	Flying	Physical	85	85	5	Normal	○
Heat Wave	Fire	Special	100	90	10	2 Foes	—

● TM & HM MOVES

No.	Name	Type	Kind	Pow.	Acc.	PP	Range	DA
TM06	Toxic	Poison	Status	—	85	10	Normal	—
TM10	Hidden Power	Normal	Special	—	100	15	Normal	—
TM11	Sunny Day	Fire	Status	—	—	5	All	—
TM17	Protect	Normal	Status	—	—	10	Self	—
TM21	Frustration	Normal	Physical	—	100	20	Normal	○
TM22	SolarBeam	Grass	Special	120	100	10	Normal	—
TM23	Iron Tail	Steel	Physical	100	75	15	Normal	○
TM27	Return	Normal	Physical	—	100	20	Normal	○
TM32	Double Team	Normal	Status	—	—	15	Self	—
TM35	Flamethrower	Fire	Special	95	100	15	Normal	—
TM38	Fire Blast	Fire	Special	120	85	5	Normal	—
TM42	Facade	Normal	Physical	70	100	20	Normal	○
TM43	Secret Power	Normal	Physical	70	100	20	Normal	○
TM44	Rest	Psychic	Status	—	—	10	Self	—
TM45	Attract	Normal	Status	—	100	15	Normal	—
TM50	Overheat	Fire	Special	140	90	5	Normal	—
TM58	Endure	Normal	Status	—	—	10	Self	—
TM61	Will-O-Wisp	Fire	Status	—	75	15	Normal	—
TM78	Captivate	Normal	Status	—	100	20	2 Foes	—
TM82	Sleep Talk	Normal	Status	—	—	10	Depends	—
TM83	Natural Gift	Normal	Physical	—	100	15	Normal	—
TM87	Swagger	Normal	Status	—	90	15	Normal	—
TM90	Substitute	Normal	Status	—	—	10	Self	—
HM04	Strength	Normal	Physical	80	100	15	Normal	○

● EGG MOVES

Name	Type	Kind	Pow.	Acc.	PP	Range	DA
Flame Wheel	Fire	Physical	60	100	25	Normal	○
Thrash	Normal	Physical	90	100	20	1 Random	○
Double Kick	Fighting	Physical	30	100	30	Normal	○
Hypnosis	Psychic	Status	—	60	20	Normal	—
Charm	Normal	Status	—	100	20	Normal	—
Double-Edge	Normal	Physical	120	100	15	Normal	○
Horn Drill	Normal	Physical	—	30	5	Normal	○
Morning Sun	Normal	Status	—	—	5	Self	—

● LEVEL-UP MOVES

Lv.	Name	Type	Kind	Pow.	Acc.	PP	Range	DA
1	Poison Jab	Poison	Physical	80	100	20	Normal	○
1	Megahorn	Bug	Physical	120	85	10	Normal	—
1	Growl	Normal	Status	—	100	40	2 Foes	—
1	Quick Attack	Normal	Physical	40	100	30	Normal	—
1	Tail Whip	Normal	Status	—	100	30	2 Foes	—
1	Ember	Fire	Special	40	100	25	Normal	—
6	Tail Whip	Normal	Status	—	100	30	2 Foes	—
10	Ember	Fire	Special	40	100	25	Normal	—
15	Flame Wheel	Fire	Physical	60	100	25	Normal	○
19	Stomp	Normal	Physical	65	100	20	Normal	○
24	Fire Spin	Fire	Special	15	70	15	Normal	—
28	Take Down	Normal	Physical	90	85	20	Normal	○
33	Agility	Psychic	Status	—	—	30	Self	—
37	Fire Blast	Fire	Special	120	85	5	Normal	—
40	Fury Attack	Normal	Physical	15	85	20	Normal	—
47	Bounce	Flying	Physical	85	85	5	Normal	○
56	Flare Blitz	Fire	Physical	120	100	15	Normal	○

● MOVE MANIAC

Name	Type	Kind	Pow.	Acc.	PP	Range	DA
Headbutt	Normal	Physical	70	100	15	Normal	○

● BP MOVES

Name	Type	Kind	Pow.	Acc.	PP	Range	DA
Snore	Normal	Special	40	100	15	Normal	—
Swift	Normal	Special	60	—	20	2 Foes	—
Bounce	Flying	Physical	85	85	5	Normal	○
Heat Wave	Fire	Special	100	90	10	2 Foes	—

● TM & HM MOVES

No.	Name	Type	Kind	Pow.	Acc.	PP	Range	DA
TM06	Toxic	Poison	Status	—	85	10	Normal	—
TM10	Hidden Power	Normal	Special	—	100	15	Normal	—
TM11	Sunny Day	Fire	Status	—	—	5	All	—
TM15	Hyper Beam	Normal	Special	150	90	5	Normal	—
TM17	Protect	Normal	Status	—	—	10	Self	—
TM21	Frustration	Normal	Physical	—	100	20	Normal	○
TM22	SolarBeam	Grass	Special	120	100	10	Normal	—
TM23	Iron Tail	Steel	Physical	100	75	15	Normal	○
TM27	Return	Normal	Physical	—	100	20	Normal	○
TM32	Double Team	Normal	Status	—	—	15	Self	—
TM35	Flamethrower	Fire	Special	95	100	15	Normal	—
TM38	Fire Blast	Fire	Special	120	85	5	Normal	—
TM42	Facade	Normal	Physical	70	100	20	Normal	○
TM43	Secret Power	Normal	Physical	70	100	20	Normal	—
TM44	Rest	Psychic	Status	—	—	10	Self	—
TM45	Attract	Normal	Status	—	100	15	Normal	—
TM50	Overheat	Fire	Special	140	90	5	Normal	—
TM58	Endure	Normal	Status	—	—	10	Self	—
TM61	Will-O-Wisp	Fire	Status	—	75	15	Normal	—
TM68	Giga Impact	Normal	Physical	150	90	5	Normal	○
TM78	Captivate	Normal	Status	—	100	20	2 Foes	—
TM82	Sleep Talk	Normal	Status	—	—	10	Depends	—
TM83	Natural Gift	Normal	Physical	—	100	15	Normal	—
TM84	Poison Jab	Poison	Physical	80	100	20	Normal	○
TM87	Swagger	Normal	Status	—	90	15	Normal	—
TM90	Substitute	Normal	Status	—	—	10	Self	—
HM04	Strength	Normal	Physical	80	100	15	Normal	○

Rapidash

Fire

- **HEIGHT:** 5'07"
- **WEIGHT:** 209.4 lbs.
- **ITEMS:** Shuca Berry

● SIZE COMPARISON

● MALE/FEMALE HAVE SAME FORM

⊘ ABILITIES
- Run Away
- Flash Fire

⊘ STATS
HP ●●
ATTACK ●●●●
DEFENSE ●●●
SP. ATTACK ●●●●
SP. DEFENSE ●●●
SPEED ●●●●●

⊘ EGG GROUPS
Field

⊘ PERFORMANCE
SPEED ★★★★★   STAMINA ★★★☆
POWER ★★★☆   JUMP ★★★☆
SKILL ★★

● MAIN WAYS TO OBTAIN

Pokémon HeartGold	Route 28
Pokémon SoulSilver	Route 28
Pokémon Diamond	Level up Ponyta to Lv. 40
Pokémon Pearl	Level up Ponyta to Lv. 40
Pokémon Platinum	Level up Ponyta to Lv. 40

Pokémon HeartGold
At full gallop, its four hooves barely touch the ground because it moves so incredibly fast.

Pokémon SoulSilver
With incredible acceleration, it reaches its top speed of 150 mph after running just 10 steps.

⊘ EVOLUTION

Ponyta → Lv. 40 → Rapidash

No. 079 | Dopey Pokémon
Slowpoke

Water | Psychic

● HEIGHT: 3'11"
● WEIGHT: 79.4 lbs.
● ITEMS: Lagging Tail

● SIZE COMPARISON

● MALE/FEMALE HAVE SAME FORM

● ABILITIES
● Oblivious
● Own Tempo

● STATS
HP ●●●
ATTACK ●●●
DEFENSE ●●●
SP. ATTACK ●●●
SP. DEFENSE ●
SPEED ●

● EGG GROUPS
Monster
Water 1

● PERFORMANCE
SPEED ★
POWER ★★
SKILL ★★☆☆☆
STAMINA ★★★★☆
JUMP ★★

● MAIN WAYS TO OBTAIN

Pokémon HeartGold	SLOWPOKE Well
Pokémon SoulSilver	SLOWPOKE Well
Pokémon Diamond	—
Pokémon Pearl	Route 205, Eterna City side [use Poké Radar]
Pokémon Platinum	Route 205, Eterna City side [use Poké Radar]

Pokémon HeartGold
It lazes vacantly near water. If something bites its tail, it won't even notice for a whole day.

Pokémon SoulSilver
A sweet sap leaks from its tail's tip. Although not nutritious, the tail is pleasant to chew on.

● EVOLUTION

Lv. 37

Slowpoke

Slowbro

Have it hold King's Rock and trade it

Slowking

● LEVEL-UP MOVES

Lv.	Name	Type	Kind	Pow.	Acc.	PP	Range	DA
1	Curse	???	Status	—	—	10	Normal/Self	—
1	Yawn	Normal	Status	—	—	10	Normal	—
1	Tackle	Normal	Physical	35	95	35	Normal	○
6	Growl	Normal	Status	—	100	40	2 Foes	—
11	Water Gun	Water	Special	40	100	25	Normal	—
15	Confusion	Psychic	Special	50	100	25	Normal	—
20	Disable	Normal	Status	—	80	20	Normal	—
25	Headbutt	Normal	Physical	70	100	15	Normal	○
29	Water Pulse	Water	Special	60	100	20	Normal	○
34	Zen Headbutt	Psychic	Physical	80	90	15	Normal	○
39	Slack Off	Normal	Status	—	—	10	Self	—
43	Amnesia	Psychic	Status	—	—	20	Self	—
48	Psychic	Psychic	Special	90	100	10	Normal	—
53	Rain Dance	Water	Status	—	—	5	All	—
57	Psych Up	Normal	Status	—	—	10	Normal	—

● MOVE MANIAC

Name	Type	Kind	Pow.	Acc.	PP	Range	DA
Headbutt	Normal	Physical	70	100	15	Normal	○

● BP MOVES

Name	Type	Kind	Pow.	Acc.	PP	Range	DA
Dive	Water	Physical	80	100	10	Normal	○
Icy Wind	Ice	Special	55	95	15	2 Foes	—
Zen Headbutt	Psychic	Physical	80	90	15	Normal	○
Trick	Psychic	Status	—	100	10	Normal	—
Snore	Normal	Special	40	100	15	Normal	—
Swift	Normal	Special	60	—	20	2 Foes	—
Magic Coat	Psychic	Status	—	—	15	Self	—
Block	Normal	Status	—	—	5	Normal	—
Mud-Slap	Ground	Special	20	100	10	Normal	—
Aqua Tail	Water	Physical	90	90	10	Normal	—
Signal Beam	Bug	Special	75	100	15	Normal	—

● TM & HM MOVES

No.	Name	Type	Kind	Pow.	Acc.	PP	Range	DA
TM03	Water Pulse	Water	Special	60	100	20	Normal	—
TM04	Calm Mind	Psychic	Status	—	—	20	Self	—
TM06	Toxic	Poison	Status	—	85	10	Normal	—
TM07	Hail	Ice	Status	—	—	10	All	—
TM10	Hidden Power	Normal	Special	—	100	15	Normal	—
TM11	Sunny Day	Fire	Status	—	—	5	All	—
TM13	Ice Beam	Ice	Special	95	100	10	Normal	—
TM14	Blizzard	Ice	Special	120	70	5	2 Foes	—
TM16	Light Screen	Psychic	Status	—	—	30	2 Allies	—
TM17	Protect	Normal	Status	—	—	10	Self	—
TM18	Rain Dance	Water	Status	—	—	5	All	—
TM20	Safeguard	Normal	Status	—	—	25	2 Allies	—
TM21	Frustration	Normal	Physical	—	100	20	Normal	—
TM23	Iron Tail	Steel	Physical	100	75	15	Normal	—
TM26	Earthquake	Ground	Physical	100	100	10	2 Foes/1 Ally	—
TM27	Return	Normal	Physical	—	100	20	Normal	—
TM28	Dig	Ground	Physical	80	100	10	Normal	—
TM29	Psychic	Psychic	Special	90	100	10	Normal	—
TM30	Shadow Ball	Ghost	Special	80	100	15	Normal	—
TM32	Double Team	Normal	Status	—	—	15	Self	—
TM35	Flamethrower	Fire	Special	95	100	15	Normal	—
TM38	Fire Blast	Fire	Special	120	85	5	Normal	—
TM42	Facade	Normal	Physical	70	100	20	Normal	—
TM43	Secret Power	Normal	Physical	70	100	20	Normal	—
TM44	Rest	Psychic	Status	—	—	10	Self	—
TM45	Attract	Normal	Status	—	100	15	Normal	—
TM48	Skill Swap	Psychic	Status	—	—	10	Normal	—
TM55	Brine	Water	Special	65	100	10	Normal	—
TM58	Endure	Normal	Status	—	—	10	Self	—
TM67	Recycle	Normal	Status	—	—	10	Self	—
TM70	Flash	Normal	Status	—	100	20	Normal	—
TM73	Thunder Wave	Electric	Status	—	100	20	Normal	—
TM77	Psych Up	Normal	Status	—	—	10	Normal	—
TM78	Captivate	Normal	Status	—	100	20	2 Foes	—
TM82	Sleep Talk	Normal	Status	—	—	10	Depends	—
TM83	Natural Gift	Normal	Physical	—	100	15	Normal	—
TM85	Dream Eater	Psychic	Special	100	100	15	Normal	—
TM86	Grass Knot	Grass	Special	—	100	20	Normal	—
TM87	Swagger	Normal	Status	—	90	15	Normal	—
TM90	Substitute	Normal	Status	—	—	10	Self	—
TM92	Trick Room	Psychic	Status	—	—	5	All	—
HM03	Surf	Water	Special	95	100	15	2 Foes/1 Ally	—
HM04	Strength	Normal	Physical	80	100	15	Normal	—
HM05	Whirlpool	Water	Special	15	70	15	Normal	—

● EGG MOVES

Name	Type	Kind	Pow.	Acc.	PP	Range	DA
Safeguard	Normal	Status	—	—	25	2 Allies	—
Belly Drum	Normal	Status	—	—	10	Self	—
Future Sight	Psychic	Special	80	90	15	Normal	—
Stomp	Normal	Physical	65	100	20	Normal	○
Mud Sport	Ground	Status	—	—	15	All	—
Sleep Talk	Normal	Status	—	—	10	Depends	—
Snore	Normal	Special	40	100	15	Normal	—
Me First	Normal	Status	—	—	20	Depends	—
Block	Normal	Status	—	—	5	Normal	—
Zen Headbutt	Psychic	Physical	80	90	15	Normal	○

● LEVEL-UP MOVES

Lv.	Name	Type	Kind	Pow.	Acc.	PP	Range	DA
1	Curse	???	Status	—	—	10	Normal/Self	—
1	Yawn	Normal	Status	—	—	10	Normal	—
1	Tackle	Normal	Physical	35	95	35	Normal	○
1	Growl	Normal	Status	—	100	40	2 Foes	—
6	Growl	Normal	Status	—	100	40	2 Foes	—
11	Water Gun	Water	Special	40	100	25	Normal	—
15	Confusion	Psychic	Special	50	100	25	Normal	—
20	Disable	Normal	Status	—	80	20	Normal	—
25	Headbutt	Normal	Physical	70	100	15	Normal	○
29	Water Pulse	Water	Special	60	100	20	Normal	—
34	Zen Headbutt	Psychic	Physical	80	90	15	Normal	○
37	Withdraw	Water	Status	—	—	40	Self	—
41	Slack Off	Normal	Status	—	—	10	Self	—
47	Amnesia	Psychic	Status	—	—	20	Self	—
54	Psychic	Psychic	Special	90	100	10	Normal	—
61	Rain Dance	Water	Status	—	—	5	All	—
67	Psych Up	Normal	Status	—	—	10	Normal	—

● MOVE MANIAC

Name	Type	Kind	Pow.	Acc.	PP	Range	DA
Headbutt	Normal	Physical	70	100	15	Normal	○

● BP MOVES

Name	Type	Kind	Pow.	Acc.	PP	Range	DA
Dive	Water	Physical	80	100	10	Normal	○
Fury Cutter	Bug	Physical	10	95	20	Normal	○
Icy Wind	Ice	Special	55	95	15	2 Foes	—
Ice Punch	Ice	Physical	75	100	15	Normal	○
Zen Headbutt	Psychic	Physical	80	90	15	Normal	○
Trick	Psychic	Status	—	100	10	Normal	—
Snore	Normal	Special	40	100	15	Normal	—
Swift	Normal	Special	60	—	20	2 Foes	—
Magic Coat	Psychic	Status	—	—	15	Self	—
Block	Normal	Status	—	—	5	Normal	—
Mud-Slap	Ground	Special	20	100	10	Normal	—
Aqua Tail	Water	Physical	90	90	10	Normal	○
Signal Beam	Bug	Special	75	100	15	Normal	—
Iron Defense	Steel	Status	—	—	15	Self	—

● TM & HM MOVES

No.	Name	Type	Kind	Pow.	Acc.	PP	Range	DA
TM01	Focus Punch	Fighting	Physical	150	100	20	Normal	○
TM03	Water Pulse	Water	Special	60	100	20	Normal	—
TM04	Calm Mind	Psychic	Status	—	—	20	Self	—
TM06	Toxic	Poison	Status	—	85	10	Normal	—
TM07	Hail	Ice	Status	—	—	10	All	—
TM10	Hidden Power	Normal	Special	—	100	15	Normal	—
TM11	Sunny Day	Fire	Status	—	—	5	All	—
TM13	Ice Beam	Ice	Special	95	100	10	Normal	—
TM14	Blizzard	Ice	Special	120	70	5	2 Foes	—
TM15	Hyper Beam	Normal	Special	150	90	5	Normal	—
TM16	Light Screen	Psychic	Status	—	—	30	2 Allies	—
TM17	Protect	Normal	Status	—	—	10	Self	—
TM18	Rain Dance	Water	Status	—	—	5	All	—
TM20	Safeguard	Normal	Status	—	—	25	2 Allies	—
TM21	Frustration	Normal	Physical	—	100	20	Normal	○
TM23	Iron Tail	Steel	Physical	100	75	15	Normal	○
TM26	Earthquake	Ground	Physical	100	100	10	2 Foes/1 Ally	—
TM27	Return	Normal	Physical	—	100	20	Normal	○
TM28	Dig	Ground	Physical	80	100	10	Normal	○
TM29	Psychic	Psychic	Special	90	100	10	Normal	—
TM30	Shadow Ball	Ghost	Special	80	100	15	Normal	—
TM31	Brick Break	Fighting	Physical	75	100	15	Normal	○
TM32	Double Team	Normal	Status	—	—	15	Self	—
TM35	Flamethrower	Fire	Special	95	100	15	Normal	—
TM38	Fire Blast	Fire	Special	120	85	5	Normal	—
TM42	Facade	Normal	Physical	70	100	20	Normal	—
TM43	Secret Power	Normal	Physical	70	100	20	Normal	—
TM44	Rest	Psychic	Status	—	—	10	Self	—
TM45	Attract	Normal	Status	—	100	15	Normal	—
TM48	Skill Swap	Psychic	Status	—	—	10	Normal	—
TM52	Focus Blast	Fighting	Special	120	70	5	Normal	—
TM55	Brine	Water	Special	65	100	10	Normal	—
TM56	Fling	Dark	Physical	—	100	10	Normal	—
TM58	Endure	Normal	Status	—	—	10	Self	—
TM60	Drain Punch	Fighting	Physical	60	100	5	Normal	○
TM67	Recycle	Normal	Status	—	—	10	Self	—
TM68	Giga Impact	Normal	Physical	150	90	5	Normal	○
TM70	Flash	Normal	Status	—	100	20	Normal	—
TM72	Avalanche	Ice	Special	60	100	10	Normal	—
TM73	Thunder Wave	Electric	Status	—	100	20	Normal	—
TM77	Psych Up	Normal	Status	—	—	10	Normal	—
TM78	Captivate	Normal	Status	—	100	20	2 Foes	—
TM82	Sleep Talk	Normal	Status	—	—	10	Depends	—
TM83	Natural Gift	Normal	Physical	—	100	15	Normal	—
TM85	Dream Eater	Psychic	Special	100	100	15	Normal	—
TM86	Grass Knot	Grass	Special	—	100	20	Normal	—
TM87	Swagger	Normal	Status	—	90	15	Normal	—
TM90	Substitute	Normal	Status	—	—	10	Self	—
TM92	Trick Room	Psychic	Status	—	—	5	All	—
HM03	Surf	Water	Special	95	100	15	2 Foes/1 Ally	—
HM04	Strength	Normal	Physical	80	100	15	Normal	○
HM05	Whirlpool	Water	Special	15	70	15	Normal	—
HM06	Rock Smash	Fighting	Physical	40	100	15	Normal	○

No. 080 | Hermit Crab Pokémon
Slowbro

Water Psychic

● **HEIGHT:** 5'03"
● **WEIGHT:** 173.1 lbs.
● **ITEMS:** King's Rock

● SIZE COMPARISON

● MALE/FEMALE HAVE SAME FORM

◎ ABILITIES
● Oblivious
● Own Tempo

◎ STATS
HP ●●●●
ATTACK ●●●●
DEFENSE ●●●●
SP. ATTACK ●●●●
SP. DEFENSE ●●●
SPEED ●

◎ EGG GROUPS
Monster

Water 1

◎ PERFORMANCE
SPEED ★   STAMINA ★★★★★
POWER ★★★   JUMP ★★☆
SKILL ★★☆☆☆

● MAIN WAYS TO OBTAIN

Pokémon HeartGold — SLOWPOKE Well B2F (water surface)

Pokémon SoulSilver — SLOWPOKE Well B2F (water surface)

Pokémon Diamond — —

Pokémon Pearl — Level up Slowpoke to Lv. 37

Pokémon Platinum — Level up Slowpoke to Lv. 37

Pokémon HeartGold — If the tail-biting SHELLDER is thrown off in a harsh battle, it reverts to being an ordinary SLOWPOKE.

Pokémon SoulSilver — Naturally dull to begin with, it lost its ability to feel pain due to SHELLDER's seeping poison.

◎ EVOLUTION

Slowpoke → (Lv. 37) → Slowbro

Slowpoke → Have it hold King's Rock and trade it → Slowking

No. 081 | Magnet Pokémon
Magnemite

`Electric` `Steel`

- **HEIGHT:** 1'00"
- **WEIGHT:** 13.2 lbs.
- **ITEMS:** Metal Coat

● **SIZE COMPARISON**

● **MALE/FEMALE HAVE SAME FORM**

⊛ ABILITIES
- Magnet Pull
- Sturdy

⊛ EGG GROUPS
Mineral

⊛ STATS
- HP ●
- ATTACK ●●
- DEFENSE ●●●
- SP. ATTACK ●●●●
- SP. DEFENSE ●●●●●
- SPEED ●●

⊛ PERFORMANCE
SPEED ★★★★ STAMINA ★☆
POWER ★☆ JUMP ★★★☆
SKILL ★★★☆

● MAIN WAYS TO OBTAIN

Pokémon HeartGold	Route 38
Pokémon SoulSilver	Route 38
Pokémon Diamond	Fuego Ironworks (mass outbreak)
Pokémon Pearl	Fuego Ironworks (mass outbreak)
Pokémon Platinum	Fuego Ironworks

Pokémon HeartGold	Pokémon SoulSilver
It is attracted by electromagnetic waves. It may approach Trainers if they are using their Pokégear.	The units at the sides of its body generate anti-gravity energy to keep it aloft in the air.

⊛ EVOLUTION

Magnemite — Lv. 30 → Magneton — Level up at Mt. Coronet* → Magnezone

● LEVEL-UP MOVES

Lv.	Name	Type	Kind	Pow.	Acc.	PP	Range	DA
1	Metal Sound	Steel	Status	--	85	40	Normal	--
1	Tackle	Normal	Physical	35	95	35	Normal	--
6	ThunderShock	Electric	Special	40	100	30	Normal	○
11	Supersonic	Normal	Status	--	55	20	Normal	--
14	SonicBoom	Normal	Special	--	90	20	Normal	--
17	Thunder Wave	Electric	Status	--	100	20	Normal	--
22	Spark	Electric	Physical	65	100	20	Normal	○
27	Lock-On	Normal	Status	--	--	5	Normal	--
30	Magnet Bomb	Steel	Physical	60	--	20	Normal	--
33	Screech	Normal	Status	--	85	40	Normal	--
38	Discharge	Electric	Special	80	100	15	2 Foes/1 Ally	--
43	Mirror Shot	Steel	Special	65	85	10	Normal	--
46	Magnet Rise	Electric	Status	--	--	10	Self	--
49	Gyro Ball	Steel	Physical	--	100	5	Normal	○
54	Zap Cannon	Electric	Special	120	50	5	Normal	--

● MOVE MANIAC

Name	Type	Kind	Pow.	Acc.	PP	Range	DA

● BP MOVES

Name	Type	Kind	Pow.	Acc.	PP	Range	DA
Snore	Normal	Special	40	100	15	Normal	--
Magnet Rise	Electric	Status	--	--	10	Self	--
Swift	Normal	Special	60	--	20	2 Foes	--
Gravity	Psychic	Status	--	--	5	All	--
Magic Coat	Psychic	Status	--	--	15	Self	--
Rollout	Rock	Physical	30	90	20	Normal	○
Signal Beam	Bug	Special	75	100	15	Normal	--
Iron Defense	Steel	Status	--	--	15	Self	--

● TM & HM MOVES

No.	Name	Type	Kind	Pow.	Acc.	PP	Range	DA
TM06	Toxic	Poison	Status	--	85	10	Normal	--
TM10	Hidden Power	Normal	Special	--	100	15	Normal	--
TM11	Sunny Day	Fire	Status	--	--	5	All	--
TM16	Light Screen	Psychic	Status	--	--	30	2 Allies	--
TM17	Protect	Normal	Status	--	--	10	Self	--
TM18	Rain Dance	Water	Status	--	--	5	All	--
TM21	Frustration	Normal	Physical	30	100	20	Normal	○
TM24	Thunderbolt	Electric	Special	95	100	15	Normal	--
TM25	Thunder	Electric	Special	120	70	10	Normal	--
TM27	Return	Normal	Physical	--	100	20	Normal	○
TM32	Double Team	Normal	Status	--	--	15	Self	--
TM33	Reflect	Psychic	Status	--	--	20	2 Allies	--
TM34	Shock Wave	Electric	Special	60	--	20	Normal	--
TM42	Facade	Normal	Physical	70	100	20	Normal	○
TM43	Secret Power	Normal	Physical	70	100	20	Normal	--
TM44	Rest	Psychic	Status	--	--	10	Self	--
TM57	Charge Beam	Electric	Special	50	90	10	Normal	--
TM58	Endure	Normal	Status	--	--	10	Self	--
TM64	Explosion	Normal	Physical	250	100	5	2 Foes/1 Ally	--
TM67	Recycle	Normal	Status	--	--	10	Self	--
TM70	Flash	Normal	Status	--	100	20	Normal	--
TM73	Thunder Wave	Electric	Status	--	100	20	Normal	--
TM74	Gyro Ball	Steel	Physical	--	100	5	Normal	○
TM77	Psych Up	Normal	Status	--	--	10	Normal	--
TM82	Sleep Talk	Normal	Status	--	--	10	Depends	--
TM83	Natural Gift	Normal	Physical	--	100	15	Normal	--
TM87	Swagger	Normal	Status	--	90	15	Normal	--
TM90	Substitute	Normal	Status	--	--	10	Self	--
TM91	Flash Cannon	Steel	Special	80	100	10	Normal	--

*Unable to evolve in Pokémon HeartGold or SoulSilver Version. Transfer from Diamond, Pearl, or Platinum Version.

● LEVEL-UP MOVES

Lv.	Name	Type	Kind	Pow.	Acc.	PP	Range	DA
1	Tri Attack	Normal	Special	80	100	10	Normal	—
1	Metal Sound	Steel	Status	—	85	40	Normal	—
1	Tackle	Normal	Physical	35	95	35	Normal	○
1	ThunderShock	Electric	Special	40	100	30	Normal	—
1	Supersonic	Normal	Status	—	55	20	Normal	—
6	ThunderShock	Electric	Special	40	100	30	Normal	—
11	Supersonic	Normal	Status	—	55	20	Normal	—
14	SonicBoom	Normal	Special	—	90	20	Normal	—
17	Thunder Wave	Electric	Status	—	100	20	Normal	—
22	Spark	Electric	Physical	65	100	20	Normal	○
27	Lock-On	Normal	Status	—	—	5	Normal	—
30	Magnet Bomb	Steel	Physical	60	—	20	Normal	—
34	Screech	Normal	Status	—	85	40	Normal	—
40	Discharge	Electric	Special	80	100	15	2 Foes/1 Ally	—
46	Mirror Shot	Steel	Special	65	85	10	Normal	—
50	Magnet Rise	Electric	Status	—	—	10	Self	—
54	Gyro Ball	Steel	Physical	—	100	5	Normal	○
60	Zap Cannon	Electric	Special	120	50	5	Normal	—

● MOVE MANIAC

Name	Type	Kind	Pow.	Acc.	PP	Range	DA

● BP MOVES

Name	Type	Kind	Pow.	Acc.	PP	Range	DA
Snore	Normal	Special	40	100	15	Normal	—
Magnet Rise	Electric	Status	—	—	10	Self	—
Swift	Normal	Special	60	—	20	2 Foes	—
Gravity	Psychic	Status	—	—	5	All	—
Magic Coat	Psychic	Status	—	—	15	Self	—
Rollout	Rock	Physical	30	90	20	Normal	○
Signal Beam	Bug	Special	75	100	15	Normal	—
Iron Defense	Steel	Status	—	—	15	Self	—

● TM & HM MOVES

No.	Name	Type	Kind	Pow.	Acc.	PP	Range	DA
TM06	Toxic	Poison	Status	—	85	10	Normal	—
TM10	Hidden Power	Normal	Special	—	100	15	Normal	—
TM11	Sunny Day	Fire	Status	—	—	5	All	—
TM15	Hyper Beam	Normal	Special	150	90	5	Normal	—
TM16	Light Screen	Psychic	Status	—	—	30	2 Allies	—
TM17	Protect	Normal	Status	—	—	10	Self	—
TM18	Rain Dance	Water	Status	—	—	5	All	—
TM21	Frustration	Normal	Physical	—	100	20	Normal	○
TM24	Thunderbolt	Electric	Special	95	100	15	Normal	—
TM25	Thunder	Electric	Special	120	70	10	Normal	—
TM27	Return	Normal	Physical	—	100	20	Normal	○
TM32	Double Team	Normal	Status	—	—	15	Self	—
TM33	Reflect	Psychic	Status	—	—	20	2 Allies	—
TM34	Shock Wave	Electric	Special	60	—	20	Normal	—
TM42	Facade	Normal	Physical	70	100	20	Normal	○
TM43	Secret Power	Normal	Physical	70	100	20	Normal	—
TM44	Rest	Psychic	Status	—	—	10	Self	—
TM57	Charge Beam	Electric	Special	50	90	10	Normal	—
TM58	Endure	Normal	Status	—	—	10	Self	—
TM64	Explosion	Normal	Physical	250	100	5	2 Foes/1 Ally	—
TM67	Recycle	Normal	Status	—	—	10	Self	—
TM68	Giga Impact	Normal	Physical	150	90	5	Normal	○
TM70	Flash	Normal	Status	—	100	20	Normal	—
TM73	Thunder Wave	Electric	Status	—	100	20	Normal	—
TM74	Gyro Ball	Steel	Physical	—	100	5	Normal	○
TM77	Psych Up	Normal	Status	—	—	10	Normal	—
TM82	Sleep Talk	Normal	Status	—	—	10	Depends	—
TM83	Natural Gift	Normal	Physical	—	100	15	Normal	—
TM87	Swagger	Normal	Status	—	90	15	Normal	—
TM90	Substitute	Normal	Status	—	—	10	Self	—
TM91	Flash Cannon	Steel	Special	80	100	10	Normal	—

No. 082 | Magnet Pokémon
Magneton

Electric | Steel

- **HEIGHT:** 3'03"
- **WEIGHT:** 132.3 lbs.
- **ITEMS:** Metal Coat

● SIZE COMPARISON

● MALE/FEMALE HAVE SAME FORM

● ABILITIES
- Magnet Pull
- Sturdy

● STATS
- HP ●●
- ATTACK ●●●
- DEFENSE ●●●●
- SP. ATTACK ●●●●●
- SP. DEFENSE ●●●●
- SPEED ●●●

● EGG GROUPS
Mineral

● PERFORMANCE
- SPEED ★★★
- POWER ★★☆
- SKILL ★★★★
- STAMINA ★★★☆
- JUMP ★★★☆

● MAIN WAYS TO OBTAIN

Pokémon HeartGold — Safari Zone (Peak Area)

Pokémon SoulSilver — Safari Zone (Peak Area)

Pokémon Diamond — Level up Magnemite to Lv. 30

Pokémon Pearl — Level up Magnemite to Lv. 30

Pokémon Platinum — Victory Road 2F

Pokémon HeartGold
Three MAGNEMITE are linked by a strong magnetic force. Earaches will occur if you get too close.

Pokémon SoulSilver
The MAGNEMITE are united by a magnetism so powerful, it dries all moisture in its vicinity.

● EVOLUTION

Magnemite → Lv. 30 → Magneton → Level up at Mt. Coronet* → Magnezone

* Unable to evolve in *Pokémon HeartGold* or *SoulSilver Version*. Transfer from *Diamond*, *Pearl*, or *Platinum Version*.

No. 083 | Wild Duck Pokémon
Farfetch'd

`Normal` `Flying`

● HEIGHT: 2'07"
● WEIGHT: 33,1 lbs.
● ITEMS: Stick

● SIZE COMPARISON

● MALE/FEMALE HAVE SAME FORM

ABILITIES
● Keen Eye
● Inner Focus

STATS
HP	●●
ATTACK	●●●
DEFENSE	●●●
SP. ATTACK	●●
SP. DEFENSE	●●
SPEED	●●●

EGG GROUPS
Flying
Field

PERFORMANCE
SPEED ★★☆	STAMINA ★★★
POWER ★★☆☆	JUMP ★★★☆
SKILL ★★☆	

MAIN WAYS TO OBTAIN

Pokémon HeartGold	Route 38 or Safari Zone [Wetland Area: if Forest objects are placed, may appear in tall grass]
Pokémon SoulSilver	Route 38 or Safari Zone [Wetland Area: if Forest objects are placed, may appear in tall grass]
Pokémon Diamond	Route 221 [mass outbreak]
Pokémon Pearl	Route 221 [mass outbreak]
Pokémon Platinum	Route 221 [mass outbreak]

Pokémon HeartGold	Pokémon SoulSilver
If anyone tries to disturb where the essential plant stalks grow, it uses its own stalk to thwart them.	If it eats the plant stalk it carries as emergency rations, it runs off in search of a new stalk.

EVOLUTION

Does not evolve

● LEVEL-UP MOVES
Lv.	Name	Type	Kind	Pow.	Acc.	PP	Range	DA
1	Poison Jab	Poison	Physical	80	100	20	Normal	○
1	Peck	Flying	Physical	35	100	35	Normal	○
1	Sand-Attack	Ground	Status	—	100	15	Normal	—
1	Leer	Normal	Status	—	100	30	2 Foes	—
1	Fury Cutter	Bug	Physical	10	95	20	Normal	○
7	Fury Attack	Normal	Physical	15	85	20	Normal	○
9	Knock Off	Dark	Physical	20	100	20	Normal	○
13	Aerial Ace	Flying	Physical	60	—	20	Normal	○
19	Slash	Normal	Physical	70	100	20	Normal	○
21	Air Cutter	Flying	Special	55	95	25	2 Foes	—
25	Swords Dance	Normal	Status	—	—	30	Self	—
31	Agility	Psychic	Status	—	—	30	Self	—
33	Night Slash	Dark	Physical	70	100	15	Normal	○
37	Air Slash	Flying	Special	75	95	20	Normal	—
43	Feint	Normal	Physical	50	100	10	Normal	○
45	False Swipe	Normal	Physical	40	100	40	Normal	○

● MOVE MANIAC
Name	Type	Kind	Pow.	Acc.	PP	Range	DA
Headbutt	Normal	Physical	70	100	15	Normal	○

● BP MOVES
Name	Type	Kind	Pow.	Acc.	PP	Range	DA
Fury Cutter	Bug	Physical	10	95	20	Normal	○
Ominous Wind	Ghost	Special	60	100	5	Normal	—
Air Cutter	Flying	Special	55	95	25	2 Foes	—
Knock Off	Dark	Physical	20	100	20	Normal	○
Snore	Normal	Special	40	100	15	Normal	—
Last Resort	Normal	Physical	130	100	5	Normal	○
Swift	Normal	Special	60	—	20	2 Foes	—
Uproar	Normal	Special	50	100	10	1 Random	—
Mud-Slap	Ground	Special	20	100	10	Normal	—
Twister	Dragon	Special	40	100	20	2 Foes	—
Heat Wave	Fire	Special	100	90	10	2 Foes	—

● TM & HM MOVES
No.	Name	Type	Kind	Pow.	Acc.	PP	Range	DA
TM06	Toxic	Poison	Status	—	85	10	Normal	—
TM10	Hidden Power	Normal	Special	—	100	15	Normal	—
TM11	Sunny Day	Fire	Status	—	—	5	All	—
TM17	Protect	Normal	Status	—	—	10	Self	—
TM21	Frustration	Normal	Physical	—	100	20	Normal	○
TM23	Iron Tail	Steel	Physical	100	75	15	Normal	○
TM27	Return	Normal	Physical	—	100	20	Normal	○
TM32	Double Team	Normal	Status	—	—	15	Self	—
TM40	Aerial Ace	Flying	Physical	60	—	20	Normal	○
TM42	Facade	Normal	Physical	70	100	20	Normal	○
TM43	Secret Power	Normal	Physical	70	100	20	Normal	○
TM44	Rest	Psychic	Status	—	—	10	Self	—
TM45	Attract	Normal	Status	—	100	15	Normal	—
TM46	Thief	Dark	Physical	40	100	10	Normal	○
TM47	Steel Wing	Steel	Physical	70	90	25	Normal	○
TM51	Roost	Flying	Status	—	—	10	Self	—
TM54	False Swipe	Normal	Physical	40	100	40	Normal	○
TM58	Endure	Normal	Status	—	—	10	Self	—
TM75	Swords Dance	Normal	Status	—	—	30	Self	—
TM77	Psych Up	Normal	Status	—	—	10	Normal	—
TM78	Captivate	Normal	Status	—	100	20	2 Foes	—
TM82	Sleep Talk	Normal	Status	—	—	10	Depends	—
TM83	Natural Gift	Normal	Physical	—	100	15	Normal	—
TM84	Poison Jab	Poison	Physical	80	100	20	Normal	○
TM87	Swagger	Normal	Status	—	90	15	Normal	—
TM88	Pluck	Flying	Physical	60	100	20	Normal	○
TM89	U-turn	Bug	Physical	70	100	20	Normal	○
TM90	Substitute	Normal	Status	—	—	10	Self	—
HM01	Cut	Normal	Physical	50	95	30	Normal	○
HM02	Fly	Flying	Physical	90	95	15	Normal	○

● EGG MOVES
Name	Type	Kind	Pow.	Acc.	PP	Range	DA
Steel Wing	Steel	Physical	70	90	25	Normal	○
Foresight	Normal	Status	—	—	40	Normal	—
Mirror Move	Flying	Status	—	—	20	Depends	—
Gust	Flying	Special	40	100	35	Normal	—
Quick Attack	Normal	Physical	40	100	30	Normal	○
Flail	Normal	Physical	—	100	15	Normal	○
FeatherDance	Flying	Status	—	100	15	Normal	—
Curse	???	Status	—	—	10	Normal/Self	—
Covet	Normal	Physical	40	100	40	Normal	○
Mud-Slap	Ground	Special	20	100	10	Normal	—
Night Slash	Dark	Physical	70	100	15	Normal	○
Leaf Blade	Grass	Physical	90	100	15	Normal	○

● LEVEL-UP MOVES

Lv.	Name	Type	Kind	Pow.	Acc.	PP	Range	DA
1	Peck	Flying	Physical	35	100	35	Normal	○
1	Growl	Normal	Status	—	100	40	2 Foes	—
5	Quick Attack	Normal	Physical	40	100	30	Normal	○
10	Rage	Normal	Physical	20	100	20	Normal	○
14	Fury Attack	Normal	Physical	15	85	20	Normal	○
19	Pursuit	Dark	Physical	40	100	20	Normal	○
23	Uproar	Normal	Special	50	100	10	1 Random	—
28	Acupressure	Normal	Status	—	—	30	1 Ally	—
32	Double Hit	Normal	Physical	35	90	10	Normal	○
37	Agility	Psychic	Status	—	—	30	Self	—
41	Drill Peck	Flying	Physical	80	100	20	Normal	○
46	Endeavor	Normal	Physical	—	100	5	Normal	○

● MOVE MANIAC

Name	Type	Kind	Pow.	Acc.	PP	Range	DA

● BP MOVES

Name	Type	Kind	Pow.	Acc.	PP	Range	DA
Air Cutter	Flying	Special	55	95	25	2 Foes	—
Knock Off	Dark	Physical	20	100	20	Normal	○
Snore	Normal	Special	40	100	15	Normal	—
Swift	Normal	Special	60	—	20	2 Foes	—
Uproar	Normal	Special	50	100	10	1 Random	—
Mud-Slap	Ground	Special	20	100	10	Normal	—
Endeavor	Normal	Physical	—	100	5	Normal	○

● TM & HM MOVES

No.	Name	Type	Kind	Pow.	Acc.	PP	Range	DA
TM06	Toxic	Poison	Status	—	85	10	Normal	—
TM10	Hidden Power	Normal	Special	—	100	15	Normal	—
TM11	Sunny Day	Fire	Status	—	—	5	All	—
TM17	Protect	Normal	Status	—	—	10	Self	—
TM21	Frustration	Normal	Physical	—	100	20	Normal	○
TM27	Return	Normal	Physical	—	100	20	Normal	○
TM32	Double Team	Normal	Status	—	—	15	Self	—
TM40	Aerial Ace	Flying	Physical	60	—	20	Normal	○
TM42	Facade	Normal	Physical	70	100	20	Normal	○
TM43	Secret Power	Normal	Physical	70	100	20	Normal	○
TM44	Rest	Psychic	Status	—	—	10	Self	—
TM45	Attract	Normal	Status	—	100	15	Normal	—
TM46	Thief	Dark	Physical	40	100	10	Normal	○
TM47	Steel Wing	Steel	Physical	70	90	25	Normal	○
TM51	Roost	Flying	Status	—	—	10	Self	—
TM58	Endure	Normal	Status	—	—	10	Self	—
TM78	Captivate	Normal	Status	—	100	20	2 Foes	—
TM82	Sleep Talk	Normal	Status	—	—	10	Depends	—
TM83	Natural Gift	Normal	Physical	—	100	15	Normal	○
TM87	Swagger	Normal	Status	—	90	15	Normal	—
TM88	Pluck	Flying	Physical	60	100	20	Normal	○
TM90	Substitute	Normal	Status	—	—	10	Self	—
HM02	Fly	Flying	Physical	90	95	15	Normal	○

● EGG MOVES

Name	Type	Kind	Pow.	Acc.	PP	Range	DA
Quick Attack	Normal	Physical	40	100	30	Normal	○
Supersonic	Normal	Status	—	55	20	Normal	—
Haze	Ice	Status	—	—	30	All	—
Faint Attack	Dark	Physical	60	—	20	Normal	○
Flail	Normal	Physical	—	100	15	Normal	○
Endeavor	Normal	Physical	—	100	5	Normal	○
Mirror Move	Flying	Status	—	—	20	Depends	—
Brave Bird	Flying	Physical	120	100	15	Normal	○

◎ No. 084 | Twin Bird Pokémon
Doduo

`Normal` `Flying`

- **HEIGHT:** 3'03"
- **WEIGHT:** 14.1 lbs.
- **ITEMS:** None

● SIZE COMPARISON

● MALE FORM
Black necks

● FEMALE FORM
Brown necks

⊛ ABILITIES
- Run Away
- Early Bird

⊛ STATS
- HP ●
- ATTACK ●●●●
- DEFENSE ●●●
- SP. ATTACK ●
- SP. DEFENSE ●
- SPEED ●●●

⊛ EGG GROUPS
Flying

⊛ PERFORMANCE

SPEED ★★★★☆	STAMINA ★★☆☆
POWER ★★★☆	JUMP ★★☆
SKILL ★★☆	

● MAIN WAYS TO OBTAIN

Pokémon HeartGold — Route 28 (morning and afternoon only)

Pokémon SoulSilver — Route 28 (morning and afternoon only)

Pokémon Diamond — Route 201 (mass outbreak)

Pokémon Pearl — Route 201 (mass outbreak)

Pokémon Platinum — Route 201 (mass outbreak)

Pokémon HeartGold
By alternately raising and lowering its two heads, it balances itself to be more stable while running.

Pokémon SoulSilver
It races through grassy plains with powerful strides, leaving footprints up to four inches deep.

⊛ EVOLUTION
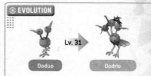

Doduo → Lv. 31 → Dodrio

No. 085 | Triple Bird Pokémon
Dodrio

Normal Flying

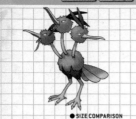

- **HEIGHT:** 5'11"
- **WEIGHT:** 187.8 lbs.
- **ITEMS:** Sharp Beak

● SIZE COMPARISON

● MALE FORM
Black necks

● FEMALE FORM
Brown necks

⊙ ABILITIES
- Run Away
- Early Bird

⊙ STATS
HP	●●
ATTACK	●●●●●
DEFENSE	●●●
SP. ATTACK	●●
SP. DEFENSE	●●
SPEED	●●●●

⊙ EGG GROUPS
Flying

⊙ PERFORMANCE
SPEED ★★★★☆   STAMINA ★★
POWER ★★★★   JUMP ★★★
SKILL ★★

● MAIN WAYS TO OBTAIN

Pokémon HeartGold — Route 28 (morning and afternoon only)

Pokémon SoulSilver — Route 28 (morning and afternoon only)

Pokémon Diamond — Level up Doduo to Lv. 31

Pokémon Pearl — Level up Doduo to Lv. 31

Pokémon Platinum — Level up Doduo to Lv. 31

Pokémon HeartGold
It collects data and plans three times as wisely, but it may think too much and fall into a state of immobility.

Pokémon SoulSilver
If one of the heads gets to eat, the others will be satisfied, too, and they will stop squabbling.

⊙ EVOLUTION

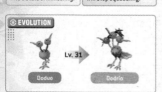

Doduo → Lv. 31 → Dodrio

● LEVEL-UP MOVES
Lv.	Name	Type	Kind	Pow.	Acc.	PP	Range	DA
1	Pluck	Flying	Physical	60	100	20	Normal	○
1	Peck	Flying	Physical	35	100	35	Normal	○
1	Growl	Normal	Status	—	100	40	2 Foes	—
1	Quick Attack	Normal	Physical	40	100	30	Normal	○
1	Rage	Normal	Physical	20	100	20	Normal	○
5	Quick Attack	Normal	Physical	40	100	30	Normal	○
10	Rage	Normal	Physical	20	100	20	Normal	○
14	Fury Attack	Normal	Physical	15	85	20	Normal	○
19	Pursuit	Dark	Physical	40	100	20	Normal	○
23	Uproar	Normal	Special	50	100	10	1 Random	—
28	Acupressure	Normal	Status	—	—	30	1 Ally	—
34	Tri Attack	Normal	Special	80	100	10	Normal	—
41	Agility	Psychic	Status	—	—	30	Self	—
47	Drill Peck	Flying	Physical	80	100	20	Normal	○
54	Endeavor	Normal	Physical	—	100	5	Normal	○

● MOVE MANIAC
Name	Type	Kind	Pow.	Acc.	PP	Range	DA

● BP MOVES
Name	Type	Kind	Pow.	Acc.	PP	Range	DA
Air Cutter	Flying	Special	55	95	25	2 Foes	—
Knock Off	Dark	Physical	20	100	20	Normal	○
Snore	Normal	Special	40	100	15	Normal	—
Swift	Normal	Special	60	—	20	2 Foes	—
Uproar	Normal	Special	50	100	10	1 Random	—
Mud-Slap	Ground	Special	20	100	10	Normal	—
Endeavor	Normal	Physical	—	100	5	Normal	○
Sky Attack	Flying	Physical	140	90	5	Normal	—

● TM & HM MOVES
No.	Name	Type	Kind	Pow.	Acc.	PP	Range	DA
TM06	Toxic	Poison	Status	—	85	10	Normal	—
TM10	Hidden Power	Normal	Special	—	100	15	Normal	—
TM11	Sunny Day	Fire	Status	—	—	5	All	—
TM12	Taunt	Dark	Status	—	100	20	Normal	—
TM15	Hyper Beam	Normal	Special	150	90	5	Normal	—
TM17	Protect	Normal	Status	—	—	10	Self	—
TM21	Frustration	Normal	Physical	—	100	20	Normal	○
TM27	Return	Normal	Physical	—	100	20	Normal	○
TM32	Double Team	Normal	Status	—	—	15	Self	—
TM40	Aerial Ace	Flying	Physical	60	—	20	Normal	○
TM41	Torment	Dark	Status	—	100	15	Normal	—
TM42	Facade	Normal	Physical	70	100	20	Normal	○
TM43	Secret Power	Normal	Physical	70	100	20	Normal	○
TM44	Rest	Psychic	Status	—	—	10	Self	—
TM45	Attract	Normal	Status	—	100	15	Normal	—
TM46	Thief	Dark	Physical	40	100	10	Normal	○
TM47	Steel Wing	Steel	Physical	70	90	25	Normal	○
TM51	Roost	Flying	Status	—	—	10	Self	—
TM58	Endure	Normal	Status	—	—	10	Self	—
TM66	Payback	Dark	Physical	50	100	10	Normal	○
TM68	Giga Impact	Normal	Physical	150	90	5	Normal	○
TM78	Captivate	Normal	Status	—	100	20	2 Foes	—
TM82	Sleep Talk	Normal	Status	—	—	10	Depends	—
TM83	Natural Gift	Normal	Physical	—	100	15	Normal	—
TM87	Swagger	Normal	Status	—	90	15	Normal	—
TM88	Pluck	Flying	Physical	60	100	20	Normal	○
TM90	Substitute	Normal	Status	—	—	10	Self	—
HM02	Fly	Flying	Physical	90	95	15	Normal	○

● LEVEL-UP MOVES

Lv.	Name	Type	Kind	Pow.	Acc.	PP	Range	DA
1	Headbutt	Normal	Physical	70	100	15	Normal	○
3	Growl	Normal	Status	—	100	40	2 Foes	—
7	Water Sport	Water	Status	—	—	15	All	—
11	Icy Wind	Ice	Special	55	95	15	2 Foes	—
13	Encore	Normal	Status	—	100	5	Normal	—
17	Ice Shard	Ice	Physical	40	100	30	Normal	—
21	Rest	Psychic	Status	—	—	10	Self	—
23	Aqua Ring	Water	Status	—	—	20	Self	—
27	Aurora Beam	Ice	Special	65	100	20	Normal	—
31	Aqua Jet	Water	Physical	40	100	20	Normal	○
33	Brine	Water	Special	65	100	10	Normal	—
37	Take Down	Normal	Physical	90	85	20	Normal	○
41	Dive	Water	Physical	80	100	10	Normal	○
43	Aqua Tail	Water	Physical	90	90	10	Normal	○
47	Ice Beam	Ice	Special	95	100	10	Normal	—
51	Safeguard	Normal	Status	—	—	25	2 Allies	—

● MOVE MANIAC

Name	Type	Kind	Pow.	Acc.	PP	Range	DA
Headbutt	Normal	Physical	70	100	15	Normal	○

● BP MOVES

Name	Type	Kind	Pow.	Acc.	PP	Range	DA
Dive	Water	Physical	80	100	10	Normal	○
Icy Wind	Ice	Special	55	95	15	2 Foes	—
Snore	Normal	Special	40	100	15	Normal	—
Aqua Tail	Water	Physical	90	90	10	Normal	○
Signal Beam	Bug	Special	75	100	15	Normal	—

● TM & HM MOVES

No.	Name	Type	Kind	Pow.	Acc.	PP	Range	DA
TM03	Water Pulse	Water	Special	60	100	20	Normal	—
TM06	Toxic	Poison	Status	—	85	10	Normal	—
TM07	Hail	Ice	Status	—	—	10	All	—
TM10	Hidden Power	Normal	Special	—	100	15	Normal	—
TM13	Ice Beam	Ice	Special	95	100	10	Normal	—
TM14	Blizzard	Ice	Special	120	70	5	2 Foes	—
TM17	Protect	Normal	Status	—	—	10	Self	—
TM18	Rain Dance	Water	Status	—	—	5	All	—
TM20	Safeguard	Normal	Status	—	—	25	2 Allies	—
TM21	Frustration	Normal	Physical	—	100	20	Normal	○
TM27	Return	Normal	Physical	—	100	20	Normal	○
TM32	Double Team	Normal	Status	—	—	15	Self	—
TM42	Facade	Normal	Physical	70	100	20	Normal	○
TM43	Secret Power	Normal	Physical	70	100	20	Normal	—
TM44	Rest	Psychic	Status	—	—	10	Self	—
TM45	Attract	Normal	Status	—	100	15	Normal	—
TM46	Thief	Dark	Physical	40	100	10	Normal	○
TM55	Brine	Water	Special	65	100	10	Normal	—
TM56	Fling	Dark	Physical	—	100	10	Normal	○
TM58	Endure	Normal	Status	—	—	10	Self	—
TM78	Captivate	Normal	Status	—	100	20	2 Foes	—
TM82	Sleep Talk	Normal	Status	—	—	10	Depends	—
TM83	Natural Gift	Normal	Physical	—	100	15	Normal	—
TM87	Swagger	Normal	Status	—	90	15	Normal	—
TM90	Substitute	Normal	Status	—	—	10	Self	—
HM03	Surf	Water	Special	95	100	15	2 Foes/1 Ally	—
HM05	Whirlpool	Water	Special	15	70	15	Normal	—
HM07	Waterfall	Water	Physical	80	100	15	Normal	○

● EGG MOVES

Name	Type	Kind	Pow.	Acc.	PP	Range	DA
Lick	Ghost	Physical	20	100	30	Normal	○
Perish Song	Normal	Status	—	—	5	All	—
Disable	Normal	Status	—	80	20	Normal	—
Horn Drill	Normal	Physical	—	30	5	Normal	○
Slam	Normal	Physical	80	75	20	Normal	○
Encore	Normal	Status	—	100	5	Normal	—
Fake Out	Normal	Physical	40	100	10	Normal	○
Icicle Spear	Ice	Physical	10	100	30	Normal	○
Signal Beam	Bug	Special	75	100	15	Normal	—
Stockpile	Normal	Status	—	—	20	Self	—
Swallow	Normal	Status	—	—	10	Self	—
Spit Up	Normal	Special	—	100	10	Normal	—

◎ No. 086 | Sea Lion Pokémon
Seel

`Water`

- **● HEIGHT:** 2'11"
- **● WEIGHT:** 100.3 lbs.
- **● ITEMS:** Poison Barb

● SIZE COMPARISON

● MALE/FEMALE HAVE SAME FORM

◎ ABILITIES
- Thick Fat
- Hydration

◎ STATS
- HP ●●
- ATTACK ●●
- DEFENSE ●●
- SP. ATTACK ●●
- SP. DEFENSE ●●●
- SPEED ●●

◎ EGG GROUPS
- Water 1
- Field

◎ PERFORMANCE
- SPEED ★★☆
- POWER ★★☆
- SKILL ★★
- STAMINA ★★★☆
- JUMP ★★☆

● MAIN WAYS TO OBTAIN

Pokémon HeartGold — Whirl Islands

Pokémon SoulSilver — Whirl Islands

Pokémon Diamond — Route 226 (water surface)

Pokémon Pearl — —

Pokémon Platinum — Find its Egg at the Pokémon Day Care and hatch it

Pokémon HeartGold

Although it can't walk well on land, it is a graceful swimmer. It especially loves being in frigid seas.

Pokémon SoulSilver

In daytime, it is often found asleep on the seabed in shallow waters. Its nostrils close while it swims.

◎ EVOLUTION

Seel — Lv. 34 → Dewgong

Dewgong

`Water` `Ice`

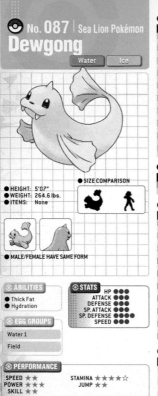

- **HEIGHT:** 5'02"
- **WEIGHT:** 264.6 lbs.
- **ITEMS:** None

● **SIZE COMPARISON**

● **MALE/FEMALE HAVE SAME FORM**

⊙ ABILITIES
- Thick Fat
- Hydration

⊙ STATS
- HP ●●●
- ATTACK ●●●●
- DEFENSE ●●●
- SP. ATTACK ●●●
- SP. DEFENSE ●●●●
- SPEED ●●●

⊙ EGG GROUPS
Water 1

Field

⊙ PERFORMANCE
- SPEED ★★
- POWER ★★★
- SKILL ★★
- STAMINA ★★★★☆
- JUMP ★★

● MAIN WAYS TO OBTAIN

Pokémon HeartGold	Seafoam Islands B3F
Pokémon SoulSilver	Seafoam Islands B3F
Pokémon Diamond	Route 226 (water surface)
Pokémon Pearl	—
Pokémon Platinum	Victory Road 1F (Route 224 side, water surface)

Pokémon HeartGold
Its streamlined body has little drag in water. The colder the temperature, the friskier it gets.

Pokémon SoulSilver
It loves frigid seas with ice floes. It uses its long tail to change swimming direction quickly.

⊙ EVOLUTION

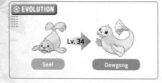

Seel → Lv. 34 → Dewgong

● LEVEL-UP MOVES

Lv.	Name	Type	Kind	Pow.	Acc.	PP	Range	DA
1	Headbutt	Normal	Physical	70	100	15	Normal	○
1	Growl	Normal	Status	—	100	40	2 Foes	—
1	Signal Beam	Bug	Special	75	100	15	Normal	—
1	Icy Wind	Ice	Special	55	95	15	2 Foes	—
3	Growl	Normal	Status	—	100	40	2 Foes	—
7	Signal Beam	Bug	Special	75	100	15	Normal	—
11	Icy Wind	Ice	Special	55	95	15	2 Foes	—
13	Encore	Normal	Status	—	100	5	Normal	—
17	Ice Shard	Ice	Physical	40	100	30	Normal	—
21	Rest	Psychic	Status	—	—	10	Self	—
23	Aqua Ring	Water	Status	—	—	20	Self	—
27	Aurora Beam	Ice	Special	65	100	20	Normal	—
31	Aqua Jet	Water	Physical	40	100	20	Normal	○
33	Brine	Water	Special	65	100	10	Normal	—
34	Sheer Cold	Ice	Special	—	30	5	Normal	—
37	Take Down	Normal	Physical	90	85	20	Normal	○
41	Dive	Water	Physical	80	100	10	Normal	○
43	Aqua Tail	Water	Physical	90	90	10	Normal	○
47	Ice Beam	Ice	Special	95	100	10	Normal	—
51	Safeguard	Normal	Status	—	—	25	2 Allies	—

● MOVE MANIAC

Name	Type	Kind	Pow.	Acc.	PP	Range	DA
Headbutt	Normal	Physical	70	100	15	Normal	○

● BP MOVES

Name	Type	Kind	Pow.	Acc.	PP	Range	DA
Dive	Water	Physical	80	100	10	Normal	○
Icy Wind	Ice	Special	55	95	15	2 Foes	—
Snore	Normal	Special	40	100	15	Normal	—
Aqua Tail	Water	Physical	90	90	10	Normal	○
Signal Beam	Bug	Special	75	100	15	Normal	—

● TM & HM MOVES

No.	Name	Type	Kind	Pow.	Acc.	PP	Range	DA
TM03	Water Pulse	Water	Special	60	100	20	Normal	—
TM06	Toxic	Poison	Status	—	85	10	Normal	—
TM07	Hail	Ice	Status	—	—	10	All	—
TM10	Hidden Power	Normal	Special	—	100	15	Normal	—
TM13	Ice Beam	Ice	Special	95	100	10	Normal	—
TM14	Blizzard	Ice	Special	120	70	5	2 Foes	—
TM15	Hyper Beam	Normal	Special	150	90	5	Normal	—
TM17	Protect	Normal	Status	—	—	10	Self	—
TM18	Rain Dance	Water	Status	—	—	5	All	—
TM20	Safeguard	Normal	Status	—	—	25	2 Allies	—
TM21	Frustration	Normal	Physical	—	100	20	Normal	○
TM27	Return	Normal	Physical	—	100	20	Normal	○
TM32	Double Team	Normal	Status	—	—	15	Self	—
TM42	Facade	Normal	Physical	70	100	20	Normal	○
TM43	Secret Power	Normal	Physical	70	100	20	Normal	○
TM44	Rest	Psychic	Status	—	—	10	Self	—
TM45	Attract	Normal	Status	—	100	15	Normal	—
TM46	Thief	Dark	Physical	40	100	10	Normal	○
TM55	Brine	Water	Special	65	100	10	Normal	—
TM56	Fling	Dark	Physical	—	100	10	Normal	○
TM58	Endure	Normal	Status	—	—	10	Self	—
TM68	Giga Impact	Normal	Physical	150	90	5	Normal	○
TM72	Avalanche	Ice	Physical	60	100	10	Normal	○
TM78	Captivate	Normal	Status	—	100	20	2 Foes	—
TM82	Sleep Talk	Normal	Status	—	—	10	Depends	—
TM83	Natural Gift	Normal	Physical	—	100	15	Normal	○
TM87	Swagger	Normal	Status	—	90	15	Normal	—
TM90	Substitute	Normal	Status	—	—	10	Self	—
HM03	Surf	Water	Special	95	100	15	2 Foes/1 Ally	—
HM05	Whirlpool	Water	Special	15	70	15	Normal	—
HM07	Waterfall	Water	Physical	80	100	15	Normal	○

● LEVEL-UP MOVES

Lv.	Name	Type	Kind	Pow.	Acc.	PP	Range	DA
1	Poison Gas	Poison	Status	—	55	40	Normal	—
1	Pound	Normal	Physical	40	100	35	Normal	○
4	Harden	Normal	Status	—	—	30	Self	—
7	Mud-Slap	Ground	Special	20	100	10	Normal	—
12	Disable	Normal	Status	—	80	20	Normal	—
17	Minimize	Normal	Status	—	—	20	Self	—
20	Sludge	Poison	Special	65	100	20	Normal	—
23	Mud Bomb	Ground	Special	65	85	10	Normal	—
28	Fling	Dark	Physical	—	100	10	Normal	—
33	Screech	Normal	Status	—	85	40	Normal	—
36	Sludge Bomb	Poison	Special	90	100	10	Normal	—
39	Acid Armor	Poison	Status	—	—	40	Self	—
44	Gunk Shot	Poison	Physical	120	70	5	Normal	—
49	Memento	Dark	Status	—	100	10	Normal	—

● MOVE MANIAC

Name	Type	Kind	Pow.	Acc.	PP	Range	DA

● BP MOVES

Name	Type	Kind	Pow.	Acc.	PP	Range	DA
ThunderPunch	Electric	Physical	75	100	15	Normal	○
Fire Punch	Fire	Physical	75	100	15	Normal	○
Ice Punch	Ice	Physical	75	100	15	Normal	○
Snore	Normal	Special	40	100	15	Normal	—
Mud-Slap	Ground	Special	20	100	10	Normal	—
Gunk Shot	Poison	Physical	120	70	5	Normal	—
Pain Split	Normal	Status	—	—	20	Normal	—

● TM & HM MOVES

No.	Name	Type	Kind	Pow.	Acc.	PP	Range	DA
TM06	Toxic	Poison	Status	—	85	10	Normal	—
TM10	Hidden Power	Normal	Special	—	100	15	Normal	—
TM11	Sunny Day	Fire	Status	—	—	5	All	—
TM12	Taunt	Dark	Status	—	100	20	Normal	—
TM17	Protect	Normal	Status	—	—	10	Self	—
TM18	Rain Dance	Water	Status	—	—	5	All	—
TM19	Giga Drain	Grass	Special	60	100	10	Normal	—
TM21	Frustration	Normal	Physical	—	100	20	Normal	○
TM24	Thunderbolt	Electric	Special	95	100	15	Normal	—
TM25	Thunder	Electric	Special	120	70	10	Normal	—
TM27	Return	Normal	Physical	—	100	20	Normal	○
TM28	Dig	Ground	Physical	80	100	10	Normal	—
TM30	Shadow Ball	Ghost	Special	80	100	15	Normal	—
TM32	Double Team	Normal	Status	—	—	15	Self	—
TM34	Shock Wave	Electric	Special	60	—	20	Normal	—
TM35	Flamethrower	Fire	Special	95	100	15	Normal	—
TM36	Sludge Bomb	Poison	Special	90	100	10	Normal	—
TM38	Fire Blast	Fire	Special	120	85	5	Normal	—
TM39	Rock Tomb	Rock	Physical	50	80	10	Normal	—
TM41	Torment	Dark	Status	—	100	15	Normal	—
TM42	Facade	Normal	Physical	70	100	20	Normal	○
TM43	Secret Power	Normal	Physical	70	100	20	Normal	○
TM44	Rest	Psychic	Status	—	—	10	Self	—
TM45	Attract	Normal	Status	—	100	15	Normal	—
TM46	Thief	Dark	Physical	40	100	10	Normal	○
TM56	Fling	Dark	Physical	—	100	10	Normal	—
TM58	Endure	Normal	Status	—	—	10	Self	—
TM64	Explosion	Normal	Physical	250	100	5	2 Foes/1 Ally	—
TM66	Payback	Dark	Physical	50	100	10	Normal	○
TM78	Captivate	Normal	Status	—	100	20	2 Foes	—
TM80	Rock Slide	Rock	Physical	75	90	10	2 Foes	—
TM82	Sleep Talk	Normal	Status	—	—	10	Depends	—
TM83	Natural Gift	Normal	Physical	—	100	15	Normal	—
TM84	Poison Jab	Poison	Physical	80	100	20	Normal	○
TM87	Swagger	Normal	Status	—	90	15	Normal	—
TM90	Substitute	Normal	Status	—	—	10	Self	—
HM04	Strength	Normal	Physical	80	100	15	Normal	○

● EGG MOVES

Name	Type	Kind	Pow.	Acc.	PP	Range	DA
Haze	Ice	Status	—	—	30	All	—
Mean Look	Normal	Status	—	—	5	Normal	—
Lick	Ghost	Physical	20	100	30	Normal	○
Imprison	Psychic	Status	—	—	10	Self	—
Curse	???	Status	—	—	10	Normal/Self	—
Shadow Punch	Ghost	Physical	60	—	20	Normal	—
Explosion	Normal	Physical	250	100	5	2 Foes/1 Ally	—
Shadow Sneak	Ghost	Physical	40	100	30	Normal	—
Stockpile	Normal	Status	—	—	20	Self	—
Swallow	Normal	Status	—	—	10	Self	—
Spit Up	Normal	Special	—	100	10	Normal	—

◎ No. 088 | Sludge Pokémon
Grimer

`Poison`

● HEIGHT: 2'11"
● WEIGHT: 66.1 lbs.
● ITEMS: Nugget

● SIZE COMPARISON

● MALE/FEMALE HAVE SAME FORM

◎ ABILITIES
● Stench
● Sticky Hold

◎ STATS
HP ●●●
ATTACK ●●●
DEFENSE ●●
SP. ATTACK ●●
SP. DEFENSE ●●
SPEED ●

◎ EGG GROUPS
Amorphous

◎ PERFORMANCE

SPEED ★
POWER ★★★☆
SKILL ★★
STAMINA ★★★★☆
JUMP ★★

● MAIN WAYS TO OBTAIN

Pokémon HeartGold — Safari Zone (Marshland Area)

Pokémon SoulSilver — Safari Zone (Marshland Area)

Pokémon Diamond — Route 212, Pastoria City side (use Poké Radar)

Pokémon Pearl — Route 212, Pastoria City side (use Poké Radar)

Pokémon Platinum — Route 212, Pastoria City side (use Poké Radar)

Pokémon HeartGold
As it moves, it loses bits of its body, from which new GRIMER emerge. This worsens the stench around it.

Pokémon SoulSilver
Wherever GRIMER has passed, so many germs are left behind that no plants will ever grow again.

◎ EVOLUTION

Grimer → Lv. 38 → Muk

No. 089 | Sludge Pokémon
Muk

Poison

● LEVEL-UP MOVES

Lv.	Name	Type	Kind	Pow.	Acc.	PP	Range	DA
1	Poison Gas	Poison	Status	—	55	40	Normal	—
1	Pound	Normal	Physical	40	100	35	Normal	○
1	Harden	Normal	Status	—	—	30	Self	—
1	Mud-Slap	Ground	Special	20	100	10	Normal	—
4	Harden	Normal	Status	—	—	30	Self	—
7	Mud-Slap	Ground	Special	20	100	10	Normal	—
12	Disable	Normal	Status	—	80	20	Normal	—
17	Minimize	Normal	Status	—	—	20	Self	—
20	Sludge	Poison	Special	65	100	20	Normal	—
23	Mud Bomb	Ground	Special	65	85	10	Normal	—
28	Fling	Dark	Physical	—	100	10	Normal	—
33	Screech	Normal	Status	—	85	40	Normal	—
36	Sludge Bomb	Poison	Special	90	100	10	Normal	—
44	Acid Armor	Poison	Status	—	—	40	Self	—
54	Gunk Shot	Poison	Physical	120	70	5	Normal	—
65	Memento	Dark	Status	—	100	10	Normal	—

● MOVE MANIAC

Name	Type	Kind	Pow.	Acc.	PP	Range	DA

● BP MOVES

Name	Type	Kind	Pow.	Acc.	PP	Range	DA
ThunderPunch	Electric	Physical	75	100	15	Normal	○
Fire Punch	Fire	Physical	75	100	15	Normal	○
Ice Punch	Ice	Physical	75	100	15	Normal	○
Snore	Normal	Special	40	100	15	Normal	—
Block	Normal	Special	—	—	5	Normal	—
Mud-Slap	Ground	Special	20	100	10	Normal	—
Gunk Shot	Poison	Physical	120	70	5	Normal	—
Pain Split	Normal	Status	—	—	20	Normal	—

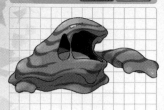

● HEIGHT: 3'11"
● WEIGHT: 66.1 lbs.
● ITEMS: Nugget

● SIZE COMPARISON

● MALE/FEMALE HAVE SAME FORM

⊙ ABILITIES
● Stench
● Sticky Hold

⊙ STATS
HP ●●●●
ATTACK ●●●●
DEFENSE ●●●
SP. ATTACK ●●●
SP. DEFENSE ●●●●
SPEED ●●

⊙ EGG GROUPS
Amorphous

⊙ PERFORMANCE
SPEED ★☆☆☆☆   STAMINA ★★★★★
POWER ★★★★   JUMP ★★☆☆☆
SKILL ★☆☆☆☆

● MAIN WAYS TO OBTAIN

Pokémon HeartGold	Route 17
Pokémon SoulSilver	Route 17
Pokémon Diamond	Level up Grimer to Lv. 38
Pokémon Pearl	Level up Grimer to Lv. 38
Pokémon Platinum	Level up Grimer to Lv. 38

Pokémon HeartGold
They love to gather in smelly areas where sludge accumulates, making the stench around them worse.

Pokémon SoulSilver
Its body is made of a powerful poison. Touching it accidentally will cause a fever that requires bed rest.

⊙ EVOLUTION

Grimer — Lv. 38 — Muk

● TM & HM MOVES

No.	Name	Type	Kind	Pow.	Acc.	PP	Range	DA
TM01	Focus Punch	Fighting	Physical	150	100	20	Normal	○
TM06	Toxic	Poison	Status	—	85	10	Normal	—
TM10	Hidden Power	Normal	Special	—	100	15	Normal	—
TM11	Sunny Day	Fire	Status	—	—	5	All	—
TM12	Taunt	Dark	Status	—	100	20	Normal	—
TM15	Hyper Beam	Normal	Special	150	90	5	Normal	—
TM17	Protect	Normal	Status	—	—	10	Self	—
TM18	Rain Dance	Water	Status	—	—	5	All	—
TM19	Giga Drain	Grass	Special	60	100	10	Normal	—
TM21	Frustration	Normal	Physical	—	100	20	Normal	○
TM24	Thunderbolt	Electric	Special	95	100	15	Normal	—
TM25	Thunder	Electric	Special	120	70	10	Normal	—
TM27	Return	Normal	Physical	—	100	20	Normal	○
TM28	Dig	Ground	Physical	80	100	10	Normal	—
TM30	Shadow Ball	Ghost	Special	80	100	15	Normal	—
TM31	Brick Break	Fighting	Physical	75	100	15	Normal	○
TM32	Double Team	Normal	Status	—	—	15	Self	—
TM34	Shock Wave	Electric	Special	60	—	20	Normal	—
TM35	Flamethrower	Fire	Special	95	100	15	Normal	—
TM36	Sludge Bomb	Poison	Special	90	100	10	Normal	—
TM38	Fire Blast	Fire	Special	120	85	5	Normal	—
TM39	Rock Tomb	Rock	Physical	50	80	10	Normal	—
TM41	Torment	Dark	Status	—	100	15	Normal	—
TM42	Facade	Normal	Physical	70	100	20	Normal	○
TM43	Secret Power	Normal	Physical	70	100	20	Normal	—
TM44	Rest	Psychic	Status	—	—	10	Self	—
TM45	Attract	Normal	Status	—	100	15	Normal	—
TM46	Thief	Dark	Physical	40	100	10	Normal	○
TM52	Focus Blast	Fighting	Special	120	70	5	Normal	—
TM56	Fling	Dark	Physical	—	100	10	Normal	—
TM58	Endure	Normal	Status	—	—	10	Self	—
TM64	Explosion	Normal	Physical	250	100	5	2 Foes/1 Ally	—
TM66	Payback	Dark	Physical	50	100	10	Normal	○
TM68	Giga Impact	Normal	Physical	150	90	5	Normal	—
TM78	Captivate	Normal	Status	—	100	20	2 Foes	—
TM79	Dark Pulse	Dark	Special	80	100	15	Normal	—
TM80	Rock Slide	Rock	Physical	75	90	10	2 Foes	—
TM82	Sleep Talk	Normal	Status	—	—	10	Depends	—
TM83	Natural Gift	Normal	Physical	—	100	15	Normal	—
TM84	Poison Jab	Poison	Physical	80	100	20	Normal	○
TM87	Swagger	Normal	Status	—	90	15	Normal	—
TM90	Substitute	Normal	Status	—	—	10	Self	—
HM04	Strength	Normal	Physical	80	100	15	Normal	○
HM06	Rock Smash	Fighting	Physical	40	100	15	Normal	○

● LEVEL-UP MOVES

Lv.	Name	Type	Kind	Pow.	Acc.	PP	Range	DA
1	Tackle	Normal	Physical	35	95	35	Normal	○
4	Withdraw	Water	Status	—	—	40	Self	—
8	Supersonic	Normal	Status	—	55	20	Normal	—
13	Icicle Spear	Ice	Physical	10	100	30	Normal	—
16	Protect	Normal	Status	—	—	10	Self	—
20	Leer	Normal	Status	—	100	30	2 Foes	—
25	Clamp	Water	Physical	35	75	10	Normal	○
28	Ice Shard	Ice	Physical	40	100	30	Normal	—
32	Aurora Beam	Ice	Special	65	100	20	Normal	—
37	Whirlpool	Water	Special	15	70	15	Normal	—
40	Iron Defense	Steel	Status	—	—	15	Self	—
44	Brine	Water	Special	65	100	10	Normal	—
49	Ice Beam	Ice	Special	95	100	10	Normal	—

● MOVE MANIAC

Name	Type	Kind	Pow.	Acc.	PP	Range	DA

● BP MOVES

Name	Type	Kind	Pow.	Acc.	PP	Range	DA
Dive	Water	Physical	80	100	10	Normal	○
Icy Wind	Ice	Special	55	95	15	2 Foes	—
Snore	Normal	Special	40	100	15	Normal	—
Swift	Normal	Special	60	—	20	2 Foes	—
Iron Defense	Steel	Status	—	—	15	Self	—

● TM & HM MOVES

No.	Name	Type	Kind	Pow.	Acc.	PP	Range	DA
TM03	Water Pulse	Water	Special	60	100	20	Normal	—
TM06	Toxic	Poison	Status	—	85	10	Normal	—
TM07	Hail	Ice	Status	—	—	10	All	—
TM10	Hidden Power	Normal	Special	—	100	15	Normal	—
TM13	Ice Beam	Ice	Special	95	100	10	Normal	—
TM14	Blizzard	Ice	Special	120	70	5	2 Foes	—
TM17	Protect	Normal	Status	—	—	10	Self	—
TM18	Rain Dance	Water	Status	—	—	5	All	—
TM21	Frustration	Normal	Physical	—	100	20	Normal	○
TM27	Return	Normal	Physical	—	100	20	Normal	○
TM32	Double Team	Normal	Status	—	—	15	Self	—
TM42	Facade	Normal	Physical	70	100	20	Normal	○
TM43	Secret Power	Normal	Physical	70	100	20	Normal	○
TM44	Rest	Psychic	Status	—	—	10	Self	—
TM45	Attract	Normal	Status	—	100	15	Normal	—
TM55	Brine	Water	Special	65	100	10	Normal	—
TM58	Endure	Normal	Status	—	—	10	Self	—
TM64	Explosion	Normal	Physical	250	100	5	2 Foes/1 Ally	—
TM66	Payback	Dark	Physical	50	100	10	Normal	—
TM78	Captivate	Normal	Status	—	100	20	2 Foes	—
TM82	Sleep Talk	Normal	Status	—	—	10	Self	—
TM83	Natural Gift	Normal	Physical	—	100	15	Normal	—
TM87	Swagger	Normal	Status	—	90	15	Normal	—
TM90	Substitute	Normal	Status	—	—	10	Self	—
HM03	Surf	Water	Special	95	100	15	2 Foes/1 Ally	—
HM05	Whirlpool	Water	Special	15	70	15	Normal	—

● EGG MOVES

Name	Type	Kind	Pow.	Acc.	PP	Range	DA
BubbleBeam	Water	Special	65	100	20	Normal	—
Take Down	Normal	Physical	90	85	20	Normal	○
Barrier	Psychic	Status	—	—	30	Self	—
Rapid Spin	Normal	Physical	20	100	40	Normal	○
Screech	Normal	Status	—	85	40	Normal	—
Icicle Spear	Ice	Physical	10	100	30	Normal	—
Mud Shot	Ground	Special	55	95	15	Normal	—
Rock Blast	Rock	Physical	25	80	10	Normal	—

◉ No. 090 | Bivalve Pokémon
Shellder

Water

● **HEIGHT:** 1'00"
● **WEIGHT:** 8.8 lbs.
● **ITEMS:** Pearl
　　　　　 Big Pearl

● SIZE COMPARISON

● MALE/FEMALE HAVE SAME FORM

◉ ABILITIES
● Shell Armor
● Skill Link

◉ STATS
- HP ●●●
- ATTACK ●●●●
- DEFENSE ●●●●●
- SP. ATTACK ●●●●
- SP. DEFENSE ●●
- SPEED ●●

◉ EGG GROUPS
Water 3

◉ PERFORMANCE
SPEED ★★★☆　　STAMINA ★★★☆
POWER ★★★　　　JUMP ★★
SKILL ★★

● MAIN WAYS TO OBTAIN

Pokémon HeartGold　New Bark Town (Good Rod)

Pokémon SoulSilver　New Bark Town (Good Rod)

Pokémon Diamond　Route 205 (Super Rod)

Pokémon Pearl　Route 205 (Super Rod)

Pokémon Platinum　Route 205 (Super Rod)

Pokémon HeartGold
It swims facing backward by opening and closing its two-piece shell. It is surprisingly fast.

Pokémon SoulSilver
Grains of sand trapped in its shells mix with its body fluids to form beautiful pearls.

◉ EVOLUTION

Shellder

Use Water Stone

Cloyster

No. 091 | Bivalve Pokémon
Cloyster

Water | Ice

- **HEIGHT:** 4'11"
- **WEIGHT:** 292.1 lbs.
- **ITEMS:** None

● SIZE COMPARISON

● MALE/FEMALE HAVE SAME FORM

● ABILITIES
- Shell Armor
- Skill Link

● STATS
HP	●●
ATTACK	●●●●
DEFENSE	●●●●●
SP. ATTACK	●●●●
SP. DEFENSE	●●
SPEED	●●●

● EGG GROUPS
Water 3

● PERFORMANCE
SPEED ★☆	STAMINA ★★★★
POWER ★★★★☆	JUMP ★★
SKILL ★	

● MAIN WAYS TO OBTAIN

Pokémon HeartGold — Use Water Stone on Shellder

Pokémon SoulSilver — Use Water Stone on Shellder

Pokémon Diamond — Use Water Stone on Shellder

Pokémon Pearl — Use Water Stone on Shellder

Pokémon Platinum — Use Water Stone on Shellder

Pokémon HeartGold
Once it slams its shell shut, it is impossible to open, even by those with superior strength.

Pokémon SoulSilver
CLOYSTER that live in seas with harsh tidal currents grow large, sharp spikes on their shells.

● EVOLUTION

Shellder
→ Use Water Stone →

Cloyster

● LEVEL-UP MOVES
Lv.	Name	Type	Kind	Pow.	Acc.	PP	Range	DA
1	Toxic Spikes	Poison	Status	—	—	20		—
1	Withdraw	Water	Status	—	—	40		—
1	Supersonic	Normal	Status	—	55	20		—
1	Aurora Beam	Ice	Special	65	100	20		—
1	Protect	Normal	Status	—	—	10		—
28	Spikes	Ground	Status	—	—	20		—
40	Spike Cannon	Normal	Physical	20	100	15		—

● MOVE MANIAC
Name	Type	Kind	Pow.	Acc.	PP	Range	DA
							—
							—

● BP MOVES
Name	Type	Kind	Pow.	Acc.	PP	Range	DA
Dive	Water	Physical	80	100	10	Normal	○
Icy Wind	Ice	Special	55	95	15	2 Foes	—
Snore	Normal	Special	40	100	15	Normal	—
Swift	Normal	Special	60	—	20	2 Foes	—
Signal Beam	Bug	Special	75	100	15	Normal	—
Iron Defense	Steel	Status	—	—	15	Self	—

● TM & HM MOVES
No.	Name	Type	Kind	Pow.	Acc.	PP	Range	DA
TM03	Water Pulse	Water	Special	60	100	20	Normal	—
TM06	Toxic	Poison	Status	—	85	10	Normal	—
TM07	Hail	Ice	Status	—	—	10	All	—
TM10	Hidden Power	Normal	Special	—	100	15	Normal	—
TM13	Ice Beam	Ice	Special	95	100	10	Normal	—
TM14	Blizzard	Ice	Special	120	70	5	2 Foes	—
TM15	Hyper Beam	Normal	Special	150	90	5	Normal	—
TM17	Protect	Normal	Status	—	—	10	Self	—
TM18	Rain Dance	Water	Status	—	—	5	All	—
TM21	Frustration	Normal	Physical	—	100	20	Normal	○
TM27	Return	Normal	Physical	—	100	20	Normal	○
TM32	Double Team	Normal	Status	—	—	15	Self	—
TM41	Torment	Dark	Status	—	100	15	Normal	—
TM42	Facade	Normal	Physical	70	100	20	Normal	○
TM43	Secret Power	Normal	Physical	70	100	20	Normal	—
TM44	Rest	Psychic	Status	—	—	10	Self	—
TM45	Attract	Normal	Status	—	100	15	Normal	—
TM55	Brine	Water	Special	65	100	10	Normal	—
TM58	Endure	Normal	Status	—	—	10	Self	—
TM64	Explosion	Normal	Physical	250	100	5	2 Foes/1 Ally	—
TM66	Payback	Dark	Physical	50	100	10	Normal	○
TM68	Giga Impact	Normal	Physical	150	90	5	Normal	○
TM72	Avalanche	Ice	Physical	60	100	10	Normal	○
TM78	Captivate	Normal	Status	—	100	20	2 Foes	—
TM82	Sleep Talk	Normal	Status	—	—	10	Depends	—
TM83	Natural Gift	Normal	Physical	—	100	15	Normal	—
TM84	Poison Jab	Poison	Physical	80	100	20	Normal	○
TM87	Swagger	Normal	Status	—	90	15	Normal	—
TM90	Substitute	Normal	Status	—	—	10	Self	—
HM03	Surf	Water	Special	95	100	15	2 Foes/1 Ally	—
HM05	Whirlpool	Water	Special	15	70	15	Normal	—

● LEVEL-UP MOVES

Lv.	Name	Type	Kind	Pow.	Acc.	PP	Range	DA
1	Hypnosis	Psychic	Status	—	60	20	Normal	—
1	Lick	Ghost	Physical	20	100	30	Normal	○
5	Spite	Ghost	Status	—	100	10	Normal	—
8	Mean Look	Normal	Status	—	—	5	Normal	—
12	Curse	???	Status	—	—	10	Normal/Self	—
15	Night Shade	Ghost	Special	—	100	15	Normal	—
19	Confuse Ray	Ghost	Status	—	100	10	Normal	—
22	Sucker Punch	Dark	Physical	80	100	5	Normal	○
26	Payback	Dark	Physical	50	100	10	Normal	○
29	Shadow Ball	Ghost	Special	80	100	15	Normal	—
33	Dream Eater	Psychic	Special	100	100	15	Normal	—
36	Dark Pulse	Dark	Special	80	100	15	Normal	○
40	Destiny Bond	Ghost	Status	—	—	5	Self	—
43	Nightmare	Ghost	Status	—	100	15	Normal	—

● MOVE MANIAC

Name	Type	Kind	Pow.	Acc.	PP	Range	DA

● BP MOVES

Name	Type	Kind	Pow.	Acc.	PP	Range	DA
Icy Wind	Ice	Special	55	95	15	2 Foes	—
ThunderPunch	Electric	Physical	75	100	15	Normal	○
Fire Punch	Fire	Physical	75	100	15	Normal	○
Ice Punch	Ice	Physical	75	100	15	Normal	○
Ominous Wind	Ghost	Special	60	100	5	Normal	—
Trick	Psychic	Status	—	100	10	Normal	—
Knock Off	Dark	Physical	20	100	20	Normal	○
Sucker Punch	Dark	Physical	80	100	5	Normal	○
Snore	Normal	Special	40	100	15	Normal	—
Spite	Ghost	Status	—	100	10	Normal	—
Uproar	Normal	Special	50	100	10	1 Random	—
Pain Split	Normal	Status	—	—	20	Normal	—

● TM & HM MOVES

No.	Name	Type	Kind	Pow.	Acc.	PP	Range	DA
TM06	Toxic	Poison	Status	—	85	10	Normal	—
TM10	Hidden Power	Normal	Special	—	100	15	Normal	—
TM11	Sunny Day	Fire	Status	—	—	5	All	—
TM12	Taunt	Dark	Status	—	100	20	Normal	—
TM17	Protect	Normal	Status	—	—	10	Self	—
TM18	Rain Dance	Water	Status	—	—	5	All	—
TM19	Giga Drain	Grass	Special	60	100	10	Normal	—
TM21	Frustration	Normal	Physical	—	100	20	Normal	○
TM24	Thunderbolt	Electric	Special	95	100	15	Normal	—
TM27	Return	Normal	Physical	—	100	20	Normal	○
TM29	Psychic	Psychic	Special	90	100	10	Normal	—
TM30	Shadow Ball	Ghost	Special	80	100	15	Normal	—
TM32	Double Team	Normal	Status	—	—	15	Self	—
TM36	Sludge Bomb	Poison	Special	90	100	10	Normal	—
TM41	Torment	Dark	Status	—	100	15	Normal	—
TM42	Facade	Normal	Physical	70	100	20	Normal	—
TM43	Secret Power	Normal	Physical	70	100	20	Normal	—
TM44	Rest	Psychic	Status	—	—	10	Self	—
TM45	Attract	Normal	Status	—	100	15	Normal	—
TM46	Thief	Dark	Physical	40	100	10	Normal	—
TM48	Skill Swap	Psychic	Status	—	—	10	Normal	—
TM49	Snatch	Dark	Status	—	—	10	Depends	—
TM53	Energy Ball	Grass	Special	80	100	10	Normal	—
TM58	Endure	Normal	Status	—	—	10	Self	—
TM61	Will-O-Wisp	Fire	Status	—	75	15	Normal	—
TM63	Embargo	Dark	Status	—	100	15	Normal	—
TM64	Explosion	Normal	Physical	250	100	5	2 Foes/1 Ally	—
TM66	Payback	Dark	Physical	50	100	10	Normal	—
TM77	Psych Up	Normal	Status	—	—	10	Self	—
TM78	Captivate	Normal	Status	—	100	20	2 Foes	—
TM79	Dark Pulse	Dark	Special	80	100	15	Normal	—
TM82	Sleep Talk	Normal	Status	—	—	10	Depends	—
TM83	Natural Gift	Normal	Physical	—	100	15	Normal	—
TM85	Dream Eater	Psychic	Special	100	100	15	Normal	—
TM87	Swagger	Normal	Status	—	90	15	Normal	—
TM90	Substitute	Normal	Status	—	—	10	Self	—
TM92	Trick Room	Psychic	Status	—	—	5	All	—

● EGG MOVES

Name	Type	Kind	Pow.	Acc.	PP	Range	DA
Psywave	Psychic	Special	—	80	15	Normal	—
Perish Song	Normal	Status	—	—	5	All	—
Haze	Ice	Status	—	—	30	All	—
Astonish	Ghost	Physical	30	100	15	Normal	○
Will-O-Wisp	Fire	Status	—	75	15	Normal	—
Grudge	Ghost	Status	—	—	5	Self	—
Explosion	Normal	Physical	250	100	5	2 Foes/1 Ally	—
Fire Punch	Fire	Physical	75	100	15	Normal	○
Ice Punch	Ice	Physical	75	100	15	Normal	○
ThunderPunch	Electric	Physical	75	100	15	Normal	○
Disable	Normal	Status	—	80	20	Normal	—

◉ No. 092 | Gas Pokémon
Gastly

Ghost | Poison

- ● HEIGHT: 4'03"
- ● WEIGHT: 0.2 lbs.
- ● ITEMS: None

● SIZE COMPARISON

● MALE/FEMALE HAVE SAME FORM

◉ ABILITIES
- Levitate

◉ STATS
HP ●
ATTACK ●●
DEFENSE ●
SP. ATTACK ●●●●
SP. DEFENSE ●
SPEED ●●●●

◉ EGG GROUPS
Amorphous

◉ PERFORMANCE
SPEED ★★★★   STAMINA ★☆
POWER ★   JUMP ★★★☆
SKILL ★★★★

● MAIN WAYS TO OBTAIN

Pokémon HeartGold	Sprout Tower (night only)
Pokémon SoulSilver	Sprout Tower (night only)
Pokémon Diamond	Old Chateau
Pokémon Pearl	Old Chateau
Pokémon Platinum	Old Chateau

Pokémon HeartGold
With its gas-like body, it can sneak into any place it desires. However, it can be blown away by wind.

Pokémon SoulSilver
Its body is made of gas. Despite lacking substance, it can envelop an opponent of any size and cause suffocation.

◉ EVOLUTION

Lv. 25 — Trade it

Gastly → Haunter → Gengar

No. 093 | Gas Pokémon
Haunter

Ghost Poison

- **HEIGHT:** 5'03"
- **WEIGHT:** 0.2 lbs.
- **ITEMS:** None

● SIZE COMPARISON

● MALE/FEMALE HAVE SAME FORM

⚙ ABILITIES
- Levitate

⚙ STATS
HP ●●
ATTACK ●●
DEFENSE ●●
SP. ATTACK ●●●●●
SP. DEFENSE ●●●●
SPEED ●●●●

⚙ EGG GROUPS
Amorphous

⚙ PERFORMANCE
SPEED ★★★☆
POWER ★
SKILL ★★★★☆
STAMINA ★★★☆
JUMP ★★★☆

● MAIN WAYS TO OBTAIN

Pokémon HeartGold	Safari Zone (Forest Area)
Pokémon SoulSilver	Safari Zone (Forest Area)
Pokémon Diamond	Turnback Cave
Pokémon Pearl	Turnback Cave
Pokémon Platinum	Turnback Cave

Pokémon HeartGold
In total darkness, where nothing is visible, HAUNTER lurks, silently stalking its next victim.

Pokémon SoulSilver
Its tongue is made of gas. If licked, its victim starts shaking constantly until death eventually comes.

⚙ EVOLUTION

Gastly — Lv. 25 → Haunter — Trade it → Gengar

● LEVEL-UP MOVES

Lv.	Name	Type	Kind	Pow.	Acc.	PP	Range	DA
1	Hypnosis	Psychic	Status	—	60	20	Normal	—
1	Lick	Ghost	Physical	20	100	30	Normal	○
1	Spite	Ghost	Status	—	100	10	Normal	—
5	Spite	Ghost	Status	—	100	10	Normal	—
8	Mean Look	Normal	Status	—	—	5	Normal	—
12	Curse	???	Status	—	—	10	Normal/Self	—
15	Night Shade	Ghost	Special	—	100	15	Normal	—
19	Confuse Ray	Ghost	Status	—	100	10	Normal	—
22	Sucker Punch	Dark	Physical	80	100	5	Normal	○
25	Shadow Punch	Ghost	Physical	60	—	20	Normal	○
28	Payback	Dark	Physical	50	100	10	Normal	○
33	Shadow Ball	Ghost	Special	80	100	15	Normal	—
39	Dream Eater	Psychic	Special	100	100	15	Normal	—
44	Dark Pulse	Dark	Special	80	100	15	Normal	—
50	Destiny Bond	Ghost	Status	—	—	5	Self	—
55	Nightmare	Ghost	Status	—	100	15	Normal	—

● MOVE MANIAC

Name	Type	Kind	Pow.	Acc.	PP	Range	DA

● BP MOVES

Name	Type	Kind	Pow.	Acc.	PP	Range	DA
Icy Wind	Ice	Special	55	95	15	2 Foes	—
ThunderPunch	Electric	Physical	75	100	15	Normal	○
Fire Punch	Fire	Physical	75	100	15	Normal	○
Ice Punch	Ice	Physical	75	100	15	Normal	○
Ominous Wind	Ghost	Special	60	100	5	Normal	—
Trick	Psychic	Status	—	100	10	Normal	—
Knock Off	Dark	Physical	20	100	20	Normal	○
Sucker Punch	Dark	Physical	80	100	5	Normal	○
Snore	Normal	Special	40	100	15	Normal	—
Spite	Ghost	Status	—	100	10	Normal	—
Uproar	Normal	Special	50	100	10	1 Random	—
Pain Split	Normal	Status	—	—	20	Normal	—

● TM & HM MOVES

No.	Name	Type	Kind	Pow.	Acc.	PP	Range	DA
TM06	Toxic	Poison	Status	—	85	10	Normal	—
TM10	Hidden Power	Normal	Special	—	100	15	Normal	—
TM11	Sunny Day	Fire	Status	—	—	5	All	—
TM12	Taunt	Dark	Status	—	100	20	Normal	—
TM17	Protect	Normal	Status	—	—	10	Self	—
TM18	Rain Dance	Water	Status	—	—	5	All	—
TM19	Giga Drain	Grass	Special	60	100	10	Normal	—
TM21	Frustration	Normal	Physical	—	100	20	Normal	○
TM24	Thunderbolt	Electric	Special	95	100	15	Normal	—
TM27	Return	Normal	Physical	—	100	20	Normal	○
TM29	Psychic	Psychic	Special	90	100	10	Normal	—
TM30	Shadow Ball	Ghost	Special	80	100	15	Normal	—
TM32	Double Team	Normal	Status	—	—	15	Self	—
TM36	Sludge Bomb	Poison	Special	90	100	10	Normal	—
TM41	Torment	Dark	Status	—	100	15	Normal	—
TM42	Facade	Normal	Physical	70	100	20	Normal	○
TM43	Secret Power	Normal	Physical	70	100	20	Normal	○
TM44	Rest	Psychic	Status	—	—	10	Self	—
TM45	Attract	Normal	Status	—	100	15	Normal	—
TM46	Thief	Dark	Physical	40	100	10	Normal	○
TM48	Skill Swap	Psychic	Status	—	—	10	Normal	—
TM49	Snatch	Dark	Status	—	—	10	Depends	—
TM53	Energy Ball	Grass	Special	80	100	10	Normal	—
TM56	Fling	Dark	Physical	—	100	10	Normal	—
TM58	Endure	Normal	Status	—	—	10	Self	—
TM61	Will-O-Wisp	Fire	Status	—	75	15	Normal	—
TM63	Embargo	Dark	Status	—	100	15	Normal	—
TM64	Explosion	Normal	Physical	250	100	5	2 Foes/1 Ally	—
TM65	Shadow Claw	Ghost	Physical	70	100	15	Normal	○
TM66	Payback	Dark	Physical	50	100	10	Normal	○
TM77	Psych Up	Normal	Status	—	—	10	Normal	—
TM78	Captivate	Normal	Status	—	100	20	2 Foes	—
TM79	Dark Pulse	Dark	Special	80	100	15	Normal	—
TM82	Sleep Talk	Normal	Status	—	—	10	Depends	—
TM83	Natural Gift	Normal	Physical	—	100	15	Normal	—
TM84	Poison Jab	Poison	Physical	80	100	20	Normal	○
TM85	Dream Eater	Psychic	Special	100	100	15	Normal	—
TM87	Swagger	Normal	Status	—	90	15	Normal	—
TM90	Substitute	Normal	Status	—	—	10	Self	—
TM92	Trick Room	Psychic	Status	—	—	5	All	—

● LEVEL-UP MOVES

Lv.	Name	Type	Kind	Pow.	Acc.	PP	Range	DA
1	Hypnosis	Psychic	Status	—	60	20	Normal	—
1	Lick	Ghost	Physical	20	100	30	Normal	○
1	Spite	Ghost	Status	—	100	10	Normal	—
5	Spite	Ghost	Status	—	100	10	Normal	—
8	Mean Look	Normal	Status	—	—	5	Normal	—
12	Curse	???	Status	—	—	10	Normal/Self	—
15	Night Shade	Ghost	Special	—	100	15	Normal	—
19	Confuse Ray	Ghost	Status	—	100	10	Normal	—
22	Sucker Punch	Dark	Physical	80	100	5	Normal	○
25	Shadow Punch	Ghost	Physical	60	—	20	Normal	○
28	Payback	Dark	Physical	50	100	10	Normal	○
33	Shadow Ball	Ghost	Special	80	100	15	Normal	—
39	Dream Eater	Psychic	Special	100	100	15	Normal	—
44	Dark Pulse	Dark	Special	80	100	15	Normal	—
50	Destiny Bond	Ghost	Status	—	—	5	Self	—
55	Nightmare	Ghost	Status	—	100	15	Normal	—

● MOVE MANIAC

Name	Type	Kind	Pow.	Acc.	PP	Range	DA
Headbutt	Normal	Physical	70	100	15	Normal	○

● BP MOVES

Name	Type	Kind	Pow.	Acc.	PP	Range	DA
Icy Wind	Ice	Special	55	95	15	2 Foes	—
ThunderPunch	Electric	Physical	75	100	15	Normal	○
Fire Punch	Fire	Physical	75	100	15	Normal	○
Ice Punch	Ice	Physical	75	100	15	Normal	○
Ominous Wind	Ghost	Special	60	100	5	Normal	—
Trick	Psychic	Status	—	100	10	Normal	—
Knock Off	Dark	Physical	20	100	20	Normal	○
Sucker Punch	Dark	Physical	80	100	5	Normal	○
Snore	Normal	Special	40	100	15	Normal	—
Spite	Ghost	Status	—	100	10	Normal	—
Uproar	Normal	Special	50	100	10	1 Random	—
Role Play	Psychic	Status	—	—	10	Normal	—
Pain Split	Normal	Status	—	—	20	Normal	—

● TM & HM MOVES

No.	Name	Type	Kind	Pow.	Acc.	PP	Range	DA
TM01	Focus Punch	Fighting	Physical	150	100	20	Normal	○
TM06	Toxic	Poison	Status	—	85	10	Normal	—
TM10	Hidden Power	Normal	Special	—	100	15	Normal	—
TM11	Sunny Day	Fire	Status	—	—	5	All	—
TM12	Taunt	Dark	Status	—	100	20	Normal	—
TM15	Hyper Beam	Normal	Special	150	90	5	Normal	—
TM17	Protect	Normal	Status	—	—	10	Self	—
TM18	Rain Dance	Water	Status	—	—	5	All	—
TM19	Giga Drain	Grass	Special	60	100	10	Normal	—
TM21	Frustration	Normal	Physical	—	100	20	Normal	○
TM24	Thunderbolt	Electric	Special	95	100	15	Normal	—
TM25	Thunder	Electric	Special	120	70	10	Normal	—
TM27	Return	Normal	Physical	—	100	20	Normal	○
TM29	Psychic	Psychic	Special	90	100	10	Normal	—
TM30	Shadow Ball	Ghost	Special	80	100	15	Normal	—
TM31	Brick Break	Fighting	Physical	75	100	15	Normal	○
TM32	Double Team	Normal	Status	—	—	15	Self	—
TM36	Sludge Bomb	Poison	Special	90	100	10	Normal	—
TM41	Torment	Dark	Status	—	100	15	Normal	—
TM42	Facade	Normal	Physical	70	100	20	Normal	○
TM43	Secret Power	Normal	Physical	70	100	20	Normal	○
TM44	Rest	Psychic	Status	—	—	10	Self	—
TM45	Attract	Normal	Status	—	100	15	Normal	—
TM46	Thief	Dark	Physical	40	100	10	Normal	○
TM48	Skill Swap	Psychic	Status	—	—	10	Normal	—
TM49	Snatch	Dark	Status	—	—	10	Depends	—
TM52	Focus Blast	Fighting	Special	120	100	5	Normal	—
TM53	Energy Ball	Grass	Special	80	100	10	Normal	—
TM56	Fling	Dark	Physical	—	100	10	Normal	○
TM58	Endure	Normal	Status	—	—	10	Self	—
TM60	Drain Punch	Fighting	Physical	60	100	5	Normal	○
TM61	Will-O-Wisp	Fire	Status	—	75	15	Normal	—
TM63	Embargo	Dark	Status	—	100	15	Normal	—
TM64	Explosion	Normal	Physical	250	100	5	2 Foes/1 Ally	—
TM65	Shadow Claw	Ghost	Physical	70	100	15	Normal	○
TM66	Payback	Dark	Physical	50	100	10	Normal	○
TM68	Giga Impact	Normal	Physical	150	90	5	Normal	○
TM77	Psych Up	Normal	Status	—	—	10	Normal	—
TM78	Captivate	Normal	Status	—	100	20	2 Foes	—
TM79	Dark Pulse	Dark	Special	80	100	15	Normal	—
TM82	Sleep Talk	Normal	Status	—	—	10	Depends	—
TM83	Natural Gift	Normal	Physical	—	100	15	Normal	—
TM84	Poison Jab	Poison	Physical	80	100	20	Normal	○
TM85	Dream Eater	Psychic	Special	100	100	15	Normal	—
TM87	Swagger	Normal	Status	—	90	15	Normal	—
TM90	Substitute	Normal	Status	—	—	10	Self	—
TM92	Trick Room	Psychic	Status	—	—	5	All	—
HM04	Strength	Normal	Physical	80	100	15	Normal	○
HM06	Rock Smash	Fighting	Physical	40	100	15	Normal	○

● HEIGHT: 4'11"
● WEIGHT: 89.3 lbs.
● ITEMS: None

● SIZE COMPARISON

● MALE/FEMALE HAVE SAME FORM

⊙ ABILITIES
● Levitate

⊙ STATS
HP ●●
ATTACK ●●●
DEFENSE ●●●
SP. ATTACK ●●●●●
SP. DEFENSE ●●●
SPEED ●●●●●

⊙ EGG GROUPS
Amorphous

⊙ PERFORMANCE
SPEED ★★☆   STAMINA ★★★★
POWER ★★☆   JUMP ★★☆
SKILL ★★★★★

● MAIN WAYS TO OBTAIN

Pokémon HeartGold — Link trade Haunter

Pokémon SoulSilver — Link trade Haunter

Pokémon Diamond — Old Chateau 2F, 2nd room from right (after obtaining the National Pokédex, insert Pokémon Ruby into your Nintendo DS's Game Pak slot)

Pokémon Pearl — Old Chateau 2F, 2nd room from right (after obtaining the National Pokédex, insert Pokémon Ruby into your Nintendo DS's Game Pak slot)

Pokémon Platinum — Old Chateau 2F, 2nd room from right (after obtaining the National Pokédex, insert Pokémon Ruby into your Nintendo DS's Game Pak slot)

Pokémon HeartGold
It steals heat from its surroundings. If you feel a sudden chill, it is certain that a GENGAR appeared.

Pokémon SoulSilver
To steal the life of its target, it slips into the prey's shadow and silently waits for an opportunity.

⊙ EVOLUTION

Lv. 25   Trade it

Gastly   Haunter   Gengar

⦿ No. 095 | Rock Snake Pokémon
Onix

Rock Ground

- **HEIGHT:** 28'10"
- **WEIGHT:** 463.0 lbs.
- **ITEMS:** None

⦿ SIZE COMPARISON

● MALE/FEMALE HAVE SAME FORM

⦿ ABILITIES
- Rock Head
- Sturdy

⦿ STATS
HP	●
ATTACK	●●
DEFENSE	●●●●●●
SP. ATTACK	●●
SP. DEFENSE	●●
SPEED	●●●

⦿ EGG GROUPS
Mineral

⦿ PERFORMANCE
SPEED ★★★☆   STAMINA ★★★★
POWER ★★   JUMP ★★☆
SKILL ★☆

● MAIN WAYS TO OBTAIN

Pokémon HeartGold	Union Cave (night only)
Pokémon SoulSilver	Union Cave (night only)
Pokémon Diamond	Oreburgh Mine B1F
Pokémon Pearl	Oreburgh Mine B1F
Pokémon Platinum	Oreburgh Mine B1F

Pokémon HeartGold	Pokémon SoulSilver
It twists and squirms through the ground. The thunderous roar of its tunneling echoes a long way.	It rapidly bores through the ground at 50 mph by squirming and twisting its massive, rugged body.

⦿ EVOLUTION

Onix → Steelix (Have it hold Metal Coat and trade it)

● LEVEL-UP MOVES
Lv.	Name	Type	Kind	Pow.	Acc.	PP	Range	DA
1	Mud Sport	Ground	Status	—	—	15	All	—
1	Tackle	Normal	Physical	35	95	35	Normal	○
1	Harden	Normal	Status	—	—	30	Self	—
1	Bind	Normal	Physical	15	75	20	Normal	○
6	Screech	Normal	Status	—	85	40	Normal	—
9	Rock Throw	Rock	Physical	50	90	15	Normal	—
14	Rage	Normal	Physical	20	100	20	Normal	○
17	Rock Tomb	Rock	Physical	50	80	10	Normal	—
22	Sandstorm	Rock	Status	—	—	10	All	—
25	Slam	Normal	Physical	80	75	20	Normal	○
30	Rock Polish	Rock	Status	—	—	20	Self	—
33	DragonBreath	Dragon	Special	60	100	20	Normal	—
38	Curse	???	Status	—	—	10	Normal/Self	—
41	Iron Tail	Steel	Physical	100	75	15	Normal	○
46	Sand Tomb	Ground	Physical	15	70	15	Normal	—
49	Double-Edge	Normal	Physical	120	100	15	Normal	○
54	Stone Edge	Rock	Physical	100	80	5	Normal	—

● MOVE MANIAC
Name	Type	Kind	Pow.	Acc.	PP	Range	DA
Headbutt	Normal	Physical	70	100	15	Normal	○

● BP MOVES
Name	Type	Kind	Pow.	Acc.	PP	Range	DA
Snore	Normal	Special	40	100	15	Normal	—
Block	Normal	Status	—	—	5	Normal	—
Mud-Slap	Ground	Special	20	100	10	Normal	—
Rollout	Rock	Physical	30	90	20	Normal	○
Iron Head	Steel	Physical	80	100	15	Normal	○
AncientPower	Rock	Special	60	100	5	Normal	—
Earth Power	Ground	Special	90	100	10	Normal	—
Twister	Dragon	Special	40	100	20	2 Foes	—

● TM & HM MOVES
No.	Name	Type	Kind	Pow.	Acc.	PP	Range	DA
TM05	Roar	Normal	Status	—	100	20	Normal	—
TM06	Toxic	Poison	Status	—	85	10	Normal	—
TM10	Hidden Power	Normal	Special	—	100	15	Normal	—
TM11	Sunny Day	Fire	Status	—	—	5	All	—
TM12	Taunt	Dark	Status	—	100	20	Normal	—
TM17	Protect	Normal	Status	—	—	10	Self	—
TM21	Frustration	Normal	Physical	—	100	20	Normal	○
TM23	Iron Tail	Steel	Physical	100	75	15	Normal	○
TM26	Earthquake	Ground	Physical	100	100	10	2 Foes/1 Ally	—
TM27	Return	Normal	Physical	—	100	20	Normal	○
TM28	Dig	Ground	Physical	80	100	10	Normal	○
TM32	Double Team	Normal	Status	—	—	15	Self	—
TM37	Sandstorm	Rock	Status	—	—	10	All	—
TM39	Rock Tomb	Rock	Physical	50	80	10	Normal	—
TM41	Torment	Dark	Status	—	100	15	Normal	—
TM42	Facade	Normal	Physical	70	100	20	Normal	○
TM43	Secret Power	Normal	Physical	70	100	20	Normal	○
TM44	Rest	Psychic	Status	—	—	10	Self	—
TM45	Attract	Normal	Status	—	100	15	Normal	—
TM58	Endure	Normal	Status	—	—	10	Self	—
TM59	Dragon Pulse	Dragon	Special	90	100	10	Normal	—
TM64	Explosion	Normal	Physical	250	100	5	2 Foes/1 Ally	—
TM66	Payback	Dark	Physical	50	100	10	Normal	○
TM69	Rock Polish	Rock	Status	—	—	20	Self	—
TM71	Stone Edge	Rock	Physical	100	80	5	Normal	—
TM74	Gyro Ball	Steel	Physical	—	100	5	Normal	○
TM76	Stealth Rock	Rock	Status	—	—	20	2 Foes	—
TM77	Psych Up	Normal	Status	—	—	10	Self	—
TM78	Captivate	Normal	Status	—	100	20	2 Foes	—
TM80	Rock Slide	Rock	Physical	75	90	10	2 Foes	—
TM82	Sleep Talk	Normal	Status	—	—	10	Depends	—
TM83	Natural Gift	Normal	Physical	—	100	15	Normal	—
TM87	Swagger	Normal	Status	—	90	15	Normal	—
TM90	Substitute	Normal	Status	—	—	10	Self	—
TM91	Flash Cannon	Steel	Special	80	100	10	Normal	—
HM04	Strength	Normal	Physical	80	100	15	Normal	○
HM06	Rock Smash	Fighting	Physical	40	100	15	Normal	○
HM08	Rock Climb	Normal	Physical	90	85	20	Normal	○

● EGG MOVES
Name	Type	Kind	Pow.	Acc.	PP	Range	DA
Rock Slide	Rock	Physical	75	90	10	2 Foes	—
Flail	Normal	Physical	—	100	15	Normal	—
Explosion	Normal	Physical	250	100	5	2 Foes/1 Ally	—
Block	Normal	Status	—	—	5	Normal	—
Defense Curl	Normal	Status	—	—	40	Self	—
Rollout	Rock	Physical	30	90	20	Normal	○
Rock Blast	Rock	Physical	25	80	10	Normal	—

● LEVEL-UP MOVES

Lv.	Name	Type	Kind	Pow.	Acc.	PP	Range	DA
1	Pound	Normal	Physical	40	100	35	Normal	○
1	Hypnosis	Psychic	Status	—	60	20	Normal	—
7	Disable	Normal	Status	—	80	20	Normal	—
9	Confusion	Psychic	Special	50	100	25	Normal	—
15	Headbutt	Normal	Physical	70	100	15	Normal	○
18	Poison Gas	Poison	Status	—	55	40	Normal	—
21	Meditate	Psychic	Status	—	—	40	Self	—
26	Psybeam	Psychic	Special	65	100	20	Normal	—
29	Psych Up	Normal	Status	—	—	10	Normal	—
32	Headbutt	Normal	Physical	70	100	15	Normal	○
37	Swagger	Normal	Status	—	90	15	Normal	—
40	Psychic	Psychic	Special	90	100	10	Normal	—
43	Nasty Plot	Dark	Status	—	—	20	Self	—
50	Zen Headbutt	Psychic	Physical	80	90	15	Normal	○
53	Future Sight	Psychic	Special	80	90	15	Normal	—

● MOVE MANIAC

Name	Type	Kind	Pow.	Acc.	PP	Range	DA
Headbutt	Normal	Physical	70	100	15	Normal	○

● BP MOVES

Name	Type	Kind	Pow.	Acc.	PP	Range	DA
ThunderPunch	Electric	Physical	75	100	15	Normal	○
Fire Punch	Fire	Physical	75	100	15	Normal	○
Ice Punch	Ice	Physical	75	100	15	Normal	○
Zen Headbutt	Psychic	Physical	80	90	15	Normal	○
Trick	Psychic	Status	—	100	10	Normal	—
Magic Coat	Psychic	Status	—	—	15	Self	—
Role Play	Psychic	Status	—	—	10	Normal	—
Signal Beam	Bug	Special	75	100	15	Normal	—
Low Kick	Fighting	Physical	—	100	20	Normal	—

● TM & HM MOVES

No.	Name	Type	Kind	Pow.	Acc.	PP	Range	DA
TM01	Focus Punch	Fighting	Physical	150	100	20	Normal	○
TM04	Calm Mind	Psychic	Status	—	—	20	Self	—
TM06	Toxic	Poison	Status	—	85	10	Normal	—
TM10	Hidden Power	Normal	Special	—	100	15	Normal	—
TM11	Sunny Day	Fire	Status	—	—	5	All	—
TM12	Taunt	Dark	Status	—	100	20	Normal	—
TM16	Light Screen	Psychic	Status	—	—	30	2 Allies	—
TM17	Protect	Normal	Status	—	—	10	Self	—
TM18	Rain Dance	Water	Status	—	—	5	All	—
TM20	Safeguard	Normal	Status	—	—	25	2 Allies	—
TM21	Frustration	Normal	Physical	—	100	20	Normal	○
TM27	Return	Normal	Physical	—	100	20	Normal	○
TM29	Psychic	Psychic	Special	90	100	10	Normal	—
TM30	Shadow Ball	Ghost	Special	80	100	15	Normal	—
TM31	Brick Break	Fighting	Physical	75	100	15	Normal	○
TM32	Double Team	Normal	Status	—	—	15	Self	—
TM33	Reflect	Psychic	Status	—	—	20	2 Allies	—
TM41	Torment	Dark	Status	—	100	15	Normal	—
TM42	Facade	Normal	Physical	70	100	20	Normal	○
TM43	Secret Power	Normal	Physical	70	100	20	Normal	○
TM44	Rest	Psychic	Status	—	—	10	Self	—
TM45	Attract	Normal	Status	—	100	15	Normal	—
TM46	Thief	Dark	Physical	40	100	10	Normal	○
TM48	Skill Swap	Psychic	Status	—	—	10	Normal	—
TM49	Snatch	Dark	Status	—	—	10	Depends	—
TM56	Fling	Dark	Physical	—	100	10	Normal	—
TM58	Endure	Normal	Status	—	—	10	Self	—
TM60	Drain Punch	Fighting	Physical	60	100	5	Normal	○
TM67	Recycle	Normal	Status	—	—	10	Self	—
TM70	Flash	Normal	Status	—	100	20	Normal	—
TM73	Thunder Wave	Electric	Status	—	100	20	Normal	—
TM77	Psych Up	Normal	Status	—	—	10	Normal	—
TM78	Captivate	Normal	Status	—	100	20	2 Foes	—
TM82	Sleep Talk	Normal	Status	—	—	10	Depends	—
TM83	Natural Gift	Normal	Physical	—	100	15	Normal	—
TM85	Dream Eater	Psychic	Special	100	100	15	Normal	—
TM86	Grass Knot	Grass	Special	—	100	20	Normal	○
TM87	Swagger	Normal	Status	—	90	15	Normal	—
TM90	Substitute	Normal	Status	—	—	10	Self	—
TM92	Trick Room	Psychic	Status	—	—	5	All	—

● EGG MOVES

Name	Type	Kind	Pow.	Acc.	PP	Range	DA
Barrier	Psychic	Status	—	—	30	Self	—
Assist	Normal	Status	—	—	20	Depends	—
Role Play	Psychic	Status	—	—	10	Normal	—
Fire Punch	Fire	Physical	75	100	15	Normal	○
ThunderPunch	Electric	Physical	75	100	15	Normal	○
Ice Punch	Ice	Physical	75	100	15	Normal	○
Nasty Plot	Dark	Status	—	—	20	Self	—
Flatter	Dark	Status	—	100	15	Normal	—
Psycho Cut	Psychic	Physical	70	100	20	Normal	—
Guard Swap	Psychic	Status	—	—	10	Normal	—

No. 096 | Hypnosis Pokémon

Drowzee

`Psychic`

- **HEIGHT:** 3'03"
- **WEIGHT:** 132.3 lbs.
- **ITEMS:** Metal Coat

● SIZE COMPARISON

● MALE/FEMALE HAVE SAME FORM

◉ ABILITIES
- Insomnia
- Forewarn

◉ STATS
HP	●●
ATTACK	●●
DEFENSE	●●
SP. ATTACK	●●
SP. DEFENSE	●●●●
SPEED	●●

◉ EGG GROUPS
Human-Like

◉ PERFORMANCE
SPEED ★☆☆   STAMINA ★★★★☆
POWER ★★★☆   JUMP ★★☆
SKILL ★★☆

● MAIN WAYS TO OBTAIN

Pokémon HeartGold — Route 34

Pokémon SoulSilver — Route 34

Pokémon Diamond — Route 215 (mass outbreak)

Pokémon Pearl — Route 215 (mass outbreak)

Pokémon Platinum — Route 215 (mass outbreak)

Pokémon HeartGold
If you think that you had a good dream but you can't remember it, a DROWZEE has probably eaten it.

Pokémon SoulSilver
It remembers every dream it eats. It rarely eats the dreams of adults because children's are much tastier.

◉ EVOLUTION

Drowzee → Lv. 26 → Hypno

No. 097 | Hypnosis Pokémon
Hypno

Psychic

- **HEIGHT:** 5'03"
- **WEIGHT:** 166.7 lbs.
- **ITEMS:** None

- **MALE FORM** Shorter mane
- **FEMALE FORM** Longer mane

ABILITIES
- Insomnia
- Forewarn

EGG GROUPS
Human-Like

STATS
HP	●●●
ATTACK	●●●
DEFENSE	●●●
SP. ATTACK	●●●●
SP. DEFENSE	●●●●●
SPEED	●●●

PERFORMANCE
SPEED ★★☆
POWER ★★☆
SKILL ★★★★☆
STAMINA ★★★
JUMP ★★★

MAIN WAYS TO OBTAIN

Pokémon HeartGold — Safari Zone (Swamp Area, night only)

Pokémon SoulSilver — Safari Zone (Swamp Area, night only)

Pokémon Diamond — Level up Drowzee to Lv. 26

Pokémon Pearl — Level up Drowzee to Lv. 26

Pokémon Platinum — Level up Drowzee to Lv. 26

Pokémon HeartGold — When it is very hungry, it puts humans it meets to sleep, then it feasts on their dreams.

Pokémon SoulSilver — Always holding a pendulum that it swings at a steady rhythm, it causes drowsiness in anyone nearby.

EVOLUTION

Drowzee — Lv. 26 — Hypno

LEVEL-UP MOVES
Lv.	Name	Type	Kind	Pow.	Acc.	PP	Range	DA
1	Nightmare	Ghost	Status	—	100	15	Normal	—
1	Switcheroo	Dark	Status	—	100	10	Normal	—
1	Pound	Normal	Physical	40	100	35	Normal	○
1	Hypnosis	Psychic	Status	—	60	20	Normal	—
1	Disable	Normal	Status	—	80	20	Normal	—
1	Confusion	Psychic	Special	50	100	25	Normal	—
7	Disable	Normal	Status	—	80	20	Normal	—
9	Confusion	Psychic	Special	50	100	25	Normal	—
15	Headbutt	Normal	Physical	70	100	15	Normal	○
18	Poison Gas	Poison	Status	—	55	40	Normal	—
21	Meditate	Psychic	Status	—	—	40	Self	—
28	Psybeam	Psychic	Special	65	100	20	Normal	—
33	Psych Up	Normal	Status	—	—	10	Normal	—
38	Headbutt	Normal	Physical	70	100	15	Normal	○
45	Swagger	Normal	Status	—	90	15	Normal	—
50	Psychic	Psychic	Special	90	100	10	Normal	—
55	Nasty Plot	Dark	Status	—	—	20	Self	—
64	Zen Headbutt	Psychic	Physical	80	90	15	Normal	○
69	Future Sight	Psychic	Special	80	90	15	Normal	—

MOVE MANIAC
Name	Type	Kind	Pow.	Acc.	PP	Range	DA
Headbutt	Normal	Physical	70	100	15	Normal	○

BP MOVES
Name	Type	Kind	Pow.	Acc.	PP	Range	DA
ThunderPunch	Electric	Physical	75	100	15	Normal	○
Fire Punch	Fire	Physical	75	100	15	Normal	○
Ice Punch	Ice	Physical	75	100	15	Normal	○
Zen Headbutt	Psychic	Physical	80	90	15	Normal	○
Trick	Psychic	Status	—	100	10	Normal	—
Magic Coat	Psychic	Status	—	—	15	Self	—
Role Play	Psychic	Status	—	—	10	Normal	—
Signal Beam	Bug	Special	75	100	15	Normal	—
Low Kick	Fighting	Physical	—	100	20	Normal	○

TM & HM MOVES
No.	Name	Type	Kind	Pow.	Acc.	PP	Range	DA
TM01	Focus Punch	Fighting	Physical	150	100	20	Normal	○
TM04	Calm Mind	Psychic	Status	—	—	20	Self	—
TM06	Toxic	Poison	Status	—	85	10	Normal	—
TM10	Hidden Power	Normal	Special	—	100	15	Normal	—
TM11	Sunny Day	Fire	Status	—	—	5	All	—
TM12	Taunt	Dark	Status	—	100	20	Normal	—
TM15	Hyper Beam	Normal	Special	150	90	5	Normal	—
TM16	Light Screen	Psychic	Status	—	—	30	2 Allies	—
TM17	Protect	Normal	Status	—	—	10	Self	—
TM18	Rain Dance	Water	Status	—	—	5	All	—
TM20	Safeguard	Normal	Status	—	—	25	2 Allies	—
TM21	Frustration	Normal	Physical	—	100	20	Normal	○
TM27	Return	Normal	Physical	—	100	20	Normal	○
TM29	Psychic	Psychic	Special	90	100	10	Normal	—
TM30	Shadow Ball	Ghost	Special	80	100	15	Normal	—
TM31	Brick Break	Fighting	Physical	75	100	15	Normal	○
TM32	Double Team	Normal	Status	—	—	15	Self	—
TM33	Reflect	Psychic	Status	—	—	20	2 Allies	—
TM41	Torment	Dark	Status	—	100	15	Normal	—
TM42	Facade	Normal	Physical	70	100	20	Normal	○
TM43	Secret Power	Normal	Physical	70	100	20	Normal	○
TM44	Rest	Psychic	Status	—	—	10	Self	—
TM45	Attract	Normal	Status	—	100	15	Normal	—
TM46	Thief	Dark	Physical	40	100	10	Normal	○
TM48	Skill Swap	Psychic	Status	—	—	10	Normal	—
TM49	Snatch	Dark	Status	—	—	10	Depends	—
TM52	Focus Blast	Fighting	Special	120	70	5	Normal	—
TM56	Fling	Dark	Physical	—	100	10	Normal	—
TM58	Endure	Normal	Status	—	—	10	Self	—
TM60	Drain Punch	Fighting	Physical	60	100	5	Normal	○
TM67	Recycle	Normal	Status	—	—	10	Self	—
TM68	Giga Impact	Normal	Physical	150	90	5	Normal	○
TM70	Flash	Normal	Status	—	100	20	Normal	—
TM73	Thunder Wave	Electric	Status	—	100	20	Normal	—
TM77	Psych Up	Normal	Status	—	—	10	Normal	—
TM78	Captivate	Normal	Status	—	100	20	2 Foes	—
TM82	Sleep Talk	Normal	Status	—	—	10	Depends	—
TM83	Natural Gift	Normal	Physical	—	100	15	Normal	—
TM85	Dream Eater	Psychic	Special	100	100	15	Normal	—
TM86	Grass Knot	Grass	Special	—	100	20	Normal	○
TM87	Swagger	Normal	Status	—	90	15	Normal	—
TM90	Substitute	Normal	Status	—	—	10	Self	—
TM92	Trick Room	Psychic	Status	—	—	5	All	—

● LEVEL-UP MOVES

Lv.	Name	Type	Kind	Pow.	Acc.	PP	Range	DA
1	Mud Sport	Ground	Status	—	—	15	All	—
1	Bubble	Water	Special	20	100	30	2 Foes	—
5	ViceGrip	Normal	Physical	55	100	30	Normal	○
9	Leer	Normal	Status	—	100	30	2 Foes	—
11	Harden	Normal	Status	—	—	30	Self	—
15	BubbleBeam	Water	Special	65	100	10	Normal	—
19	Mud Shot	Ground	Special	55	95	15	Normal	—
21	Metal Claw	Steel	Physical	50	95	35	Normal	○
25	Stomp	Normal	Physical	65	100	20	Normal	○
29	Protect	Normal	Status	—	—	10	Self	—
31	Guillotine	Normal	Physical	—	30	5	Normal	○
35	Slam	Normal	Physical	80	75	20	Normal	○
39	Brine	Water	Special	65	100	10	Normal	—
41	Crabhammer	Water	Physical	90	85	10	Normal	○
45	Flail	Normal	Physical	—	100	15	Normal	○

● MOVE MANIAC

Name	Type	Kind	Pow.	Acc.	PP	Range	DA

● BP MOVES

Name	Type	Kind	Pow.	Acc.	PP	Range	DA
Dive	Water	Physical	80	100	10	Normal	○
Fury Cutter	Bug	Physical	10	95	20	Normal	○
Icy Wind	Ice	Special	55	95	15	2 Foes	—
Knock Off	Dark	Physical	20	100	20	Normal	○
Snore	Normal	Special	40	100	15	Normal	—
Mud-Slap	Ground	Special	20	100	10	Normal	—
Superpower	Fighting	Physical	120	100	5	Normal	○
AncientPower	Rock	Special	60	100	5	Normal	—
Iron Defense	Steel	Status	—	—	15	Self	—

● TM & HM MOVES

No.	Name	Type	Kind	Pow.	Acc.	PP	Range	DA
TM03	Water Pulse	Water	Special	60	100	20	Normal	—
TM06	Toxic	Poison	Status	—	85	10	Normal	—
TM07	Hail	Ice	Status	—	—	10	All	—
TM10	Hidden Power	Normal	Special	—	100	15	Normal	—
TM13	Ice Beam	Ice	Special	95	100	10	Normal	—
TM14	Blizzard	Ice	Special	120	70	5	Normal	—
TM17	Protect	Normal	Status	—	—	10	Self	—
TM18	Rain Dance	Water	Status	—	—	5	All	—
TM21	Frustration	Normal	Physical	—	100	20	Normal	○
TM27	Return	Normal	Physical	—	100	20	Normal	○
TM28	Dig	Ground	Physical	80	100	10	Normal	○
TM31	Brick Break	Fighting	Physical	75	100	15	Normal	○
TM32	Double Team	Normal	Status	—	—	15	Self	—
TM39	Rock Tomb	Rock	Physical	50	80	10	Normal	○
TM42	Facade	Normal	Physical	70	100	20	Normal	○
TM43	Secret Power	Normal	Physical	70	100	20	Normal	○
TM44	Rest	Psychic	Status	—	—	10	Self	—
TM45	Attract	Normal	Status	—	100	15	Normal	—
TM46	Thief	Dark	Physical	40	100	10	Normal	○
TM54	False Swipe	Normal	Physical	40	100	40	Normal	○
TM55	Brine	Water	Special	65	100	10	Normal	—
TM56	Fling	Dark	Physical	—	100	10	Normal	○
TM58	Endure	Normal	Status	—	—	10	Self	—
TM75	Swords Dance	Normal	Status	—	—	30	Self	—
TM78	Captivate	Normal	Status	—	100	20	2 Foes	—
TM80	Rock Slide	Rock	Physical	75	90	10	2 Foes	○
TM81	X-Scissor	Bug	Physical	80	100	15	Normal	○
TM82	Sleep Talk	Normal	Status	—	—	10	Depends	—
TM83	Natural Gift	Normal	Physical	—	100	15	Normal	—
TM87	Swagger	Normal	Status	—	90	15	Normal	—
TM90	Substitute	Normal	Status	—	—	10	Self	—
HM01	Cut	Normal	Physical	50	95	30	Normal	○
HM03	Surf	Water	Special	95	100	15	2 Foes/1 Ally	—
HM04	Strength	Normal	Physical	80	100	15	Normal	○
HM05	Whirlpool	Water	Special	15	70	15	Normal	—
HM06	Rock Smash	Fighting	Physical	40	100	15	Normal	○

● EGG MOVES

Name	Type	Kind	Pow.	Acc.	PP	Range	DA
Dig	Ground	Physical	80	100	10	Normal	○
Haze	Ice	Status	—	—	30	All	—
Amnesia	Psychic	Status	—	—	20	Self	—
Flail	Normal	Physical	—	100	15	Normal	○
Slam	Normal	Physical	80	75	20	Normal	○
Knock Off	Dark	Physical	20	100	20	Normal	○
Swords Dance	Normal	Status	—	—	30	Self	—
Tickle	Normal	Status	—	100	20	Normal	—
AncientPower	Rock	Special	60	100	5	Normal	—
Agility	Psychic	Status	—	—	30	Self	—

◉ No. 098 | River Crab Pokémon
Krabby

Water

● SIZE COMPARISON

● HEIGHT: 1'04"
● WEIGHT: 14.3 lbs.
● ITEMS: None

● MALE/FEMALE HAVE SAME FORM

◉ ABILITIES
● Hyper Cutter
● Shell Armor

◉ STATS
HP ●
ATTACK ●●●●
DEFENSE ●●●●
SP. ATTACK ●●
SP. DEFENSE ●●
SPEED ●●

◉ EGG GROUPS
Water 3

◉ PERFORMANCE
SPEED ★★☆
POWER ★★★★
SKILL ★☆☆
STAMINA ★★★☆
JUMP ★★☆

● MAIN WAYS TO OBTAIN

Pokémon HeartGold — Whirl Islands

Pokémon SoulSilver — Whirl Islands

Pokémon Diamond — Route 226 (mass outbreak)

Pokémon Pearl — Route 226 (mass outbreak)

Pokémon Platinum — Route 226 (mass outbreak)

Pokémon HeartGold
If it senses danger approaching, it cloaks itself with bubbles from its mouth so it will look bigger.

Pokémon SoulSilver
The pincers break off easily. If it loses a pincer, it somehow becomes incapable of walking sideways.

◉ EVOLUTION

Lv. 28

Krabby → Kingler

No. 099 | Pincer Pokémon
Kingler

Water

● HEIGHT: 4'03"
● WEIGHT: 132.3 lbs.
● ITEMS: None

● SIZE COMPARISON

● MALE/FEMALE HAVE SAME FORM

◎ ABILITIES
● Hyper Cutter
● Shell Armor

◎ STATS
HP ●●
ATTACK ●●●●●
DEFENSE ●●●●●
SP. ATTACK ●●
SP. DEFENSE ●●
SPEED ●●●

◎ EGG GROUPS
Water 3

◎ PERFORMANCE
SPEED ★★☆
POWER ★★★★☆
SKILL ★★☆
STAMINA ★★★★☆
JUMP ★★

● MAIN WAYS TO OBTAIN

Pokémon HeartGold	Cliff Cave
Pokémon SoulSilver	Cliff Cave
Pokémon Diamond	Level up Krabby to Lv. 28
Pokémon Pearl	Level up Krabby to Lv. 28
Pokémon Platinum	Level up Krabby to Lv. 28

Pokémon HeartGold	Pokémon SoulSilver
It can hardly lift its massive, overgrown pincer. The pincer's size makes it difficult to aim properly.	Its pincers grow peculiarly large. If it lifts the pincers too fast, it loses its balance and staggers.

◎ EVOLUTION

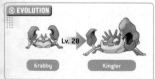

Krabby — Lv. 28 → Kingler

● LEVEL-UP MOVES

Lv.	Name	Type	Kind	Pow.	Acc.	PP	Range	DA
1	Mud Sport	Ground	Status	—	—	15	All	—
1	Bubble	Water	Special	20	100	30	2 Foes	—
1	ViceGrip	Normal	Physical	55	100	30	Normal	○
5	ViceGrip	Normal	Physical	55	100	30	Normal	○
9	Leer	Normal	Status	—	100	30	2 Foes	—
11	Harden	Normal	Status	—	—	30	Self	—
15	BubbleBeam	Water	Special	65	100	20	Normal	—
19	Mud Shot	Ground	Special	55	95	15	Normal	—
21	Metal Claw	Steel	Physical	50	95	35	Normal	○
25	Stomp	Normal	Physical	65	100	20	Normal	○
32	Protect	Normal	Status	—	—	10	Self	—
37	Guillotine	Normal	Physical	—	30	5	Normal	○
44	Slam	Normal	Physical	80	75	20	Normal	○
51	Brine	Water	Special	65	100	10	Normal	—
56	Crabhammer	Water	Physical	90	85	10	Normal	○
63	Flail	Normal	Physical	—	100	15	Normal	○

● MOVE MANIAC

Name	Type	Kind	Pow.	Acc.	PP	Range	DA

● BP MOVES

Name	Type	Kind	Pow.	Acc.	PP	Range	DA
Dive	Water	Physical	80	100	10	Normal	○
Fury Cutter	Bug	Physical	10	95	20	Normal	○
Icy Wind	Ice	Special	55	95	15	2 Foes	—
Knock Off	Dark	Physical	20	100	20	Normal	○
Snore	Normal	Special	40	100	15	Normal	—
Mud-Slap	Ground	Special	20	100	10	Normal	—
Superpower	Fighting	Physical	120	100	5	Normal	○
AncientPower	Rock	Special	60	100	5	Normal	—
Iron Defense	Steel	Status	—	—	15	Self	—

● TM & HM MOVES

No.	Name	Type	Kind	Pow.	Acc.	PP	Range	DA
TM03	Water Pulse	Water	Special	60	100	20	Normal	—
TM06	Toxic	Poison	Status	—	85	10	Normal	—
TM07	Hail	Ice	Status	—	—	10	All	—
TM10	Hidden Power	Normal	Special	—	100	15	Normal	—
TM13	Ice Beam	Ice	Special	95	100	10	Normal	—
TM14	Blizzard	Ice	Special	120	70	5	2 Foes	—
TM15	Hyper Beam	Normal	Special	150	90	5	Normal	—
TM17	Protect	Normal	Status	—	—	10	Self	—
TM18	Rain Dance	Water	Status	—	—	5	All	—
TM21	Frustration	Normal	Physical	—	100	20	Normal	○
TM27	Return	Normal	Physical	—	100	20	Normal	○
TM28	Dig	Ground	Physical	80	100	10	Normal	○
TM31	Brick Break	Fighting	Physical	75	100	15	Normal	○
TM32	Double Team	Normal	Status	—	—	15	Self	—
TM39	Rock Tomb	Rock	Physical	50	80	10	Normal	○
TM42	Facade	Normal	Physical	70	100	20	Normal	○
TM43	Secret Power	Normal	Physical	70	100	20	Normal	○
TM44	Rest	Psychic	Status	—	—	10	Self	—
TM45	Attract	Normal	Status	—	100	15	Normal	—
TM46	Thief	Dark	Physical	40	100	10	Normal	○
TM54	False Swipe	Normal	Physical	40	100	40	Normal	○
TM55	Brine	Water	Special	65	100	10	Normal	—
TM56	Fling	Dark	Physical	—	100	10	Normal	○
TM58	Endure	Normal	Status	—	—	10	Self	—
TM68	Giga Impact	Normal	Physical	150	90	5	Normal	○
TM75	Swords Dance	Normal	Status	—	—	30	Self	—
TM78	Captivate	Normal	Status	—	100	20	2 Foes	—
TM80	Rock Slide	Rock	Physical	75	90	10	2 Foes	—
TM81	X-Scissor	Bug	Physical	80	100	15	Normal	○
TM82	Sleep Talk	Normal	Status	—	—	10	Depends	—
TM83	Natural Gift	Normal	Physical	—	100	15	Normal	○
TM87	Swagger	Normal	Status	—	90	15	Normal	—
TM90	Substitute	Normal	Status	—	—	10	Self	—
HM01	Cut	Normal	Physical	50	95	30	Normal	○
HM03	Surf	Water	Special	95	100	15	2 Foes/1 Ally	—
HM04	Strength	Normal	Physical	80	100	15	Normal	○
HM05	Whirlpool	Water	Special	15	70	15	Normal	—
HM06	Rock Smash	Fighting	Physical	40	100	15	Normal	○

● LEVEL-UP MOVES

Lv.	Name	Type	Kind	Pow.	Acc.	PP	Range	DA
1	Charge	Electric	Status	—	—	20	Self	—
5	Tackle	Normal	Physical	35	95	35	Normal	○
8	SonicBoom	Normal	Special	—	90	20	Normal	—
12	Spark	Electric	Physical	65	100	20	Normal	○
15	Rollout	Rock	Physical	30	90	20	Normal	○
19	Screech	Normal	Status	—	85	40	Normal	—
22	Light Screen	Psychic	Status	—	—	30	2 Allies	—
26	Charge Beam	Electric	Special	50	90	10	Normal	—
29	Selfdestruct	Normal	Physical	200	100	5	2 Foes/1 Ally	—
33	Swift	Normal	Special	60	—	20	2 Foes	—
36	Magnet Rise	Electric	Status	—	—	10	Self	—
40	Gyro Ball	Steel	Physical	—	100	5	Normal	○
43	Explosion	Normal	Physical	250	100	5	2 Foes/1 Ally	—
47	Mirror Coat	Psychic	Special	—	100	20	Self	—

● MOVE MANIAC

Name	Type	Kind	Pow.	Acc.	PP	Range	DA
Headbutt	Normal	Physical	70	100	15	Normal	○

● BP MOVES

Name	Type	Kind	Pow.	Acc.	PP	Range	DA
Sucker Punch	Dark	Physical	80	100	5	Normal	○
Snore	Normal	Special	40	100	15	Normal	—
Magnet Rise	Electric	Status	—	—	10	Self	—
Swift	Normal	Special	60	—	20	2 Foes	—
Magic Coat	Psychic	Status	—	—	15	Self	—
Rollout	Rock	Physical	30	90	20	Normal	○
Signal Beam	Bug	Special	75	100	15	Normal	—

● TM & HM MOVES

No.	Name	Type	Kind	Pow.	Acc.	PP	Range	DA
TM06	Toxic	Poison	Status	—	85	10	Normal	—
TM10	Hidden Power	Normal	Special	—	100	15	Normal	—
TM12	Taunt	Dark	Status	—	100	20	Normal	—
TM16	Light Screen	Psychic	Status	—	—	30	2 Allies	—
TM17	Protect	Normal	Status	—	—	10	Self	—
TM18	Rain Dance	Water	Status	—	—	5	All	—
TM21	Frustration	Normal	Physical	—	100	20	Normal	○
TM24	Thunderbolt	Electric	Special	95	100	15	Normal	—
TM25	Thunder	Electric	Special	120	70	10	Normal	—
TM27	Return	Normal	Physical	—	100	20	Normal	○
TM32	Double Team	Normal	Status	—	—	15	Self	—
TM34	Shock Wave	Electric	Special	60	—	20	Normal	—
TM41	Torment	Dark	Status	—	100	15	Normal	—
TM42	Facade	Normal	Physical	70	100	20	Normal	○
TM43	Secret Power	Normal	Physical	70	100	20	Normal	○
TM44	Rest	Psychic	Status	—	—	10	Self	—
TM46	Thief	Dark	Physical	40	100	10	Normal	○
TM57	Charge Beam	Electric	Special	50	90	10	Normal	—
TM58	Endure	Normal	Status	—	—	10	Self	—
TM64	Explosion	Normal	Physical	250	100	5	2 Foes/1 Ally	—
TM70	Flash	Normal	Status	—	100	20	Normal	—
TM73	Thunder Wave	Electric	Status	—	100	20	Normal	—
TM74	Gyro Ball	Steel	Physical	—	100	5	Normal	○
TM82	Sleep Talk	Normal	Status	—	—	10	Depends	—
TM83	Natural Gift	Normal	Physical	—	100	15	Normal	—
TM87	Swagger	Normal	Status	—	90	15	Normal	—
TM90	Substitute	Normal	Status	—	—	10	Self	—

● **HEIGHT:** 1'08"
● **WEIGHT:** 22.9 lbs.
● **ITEMS:** None

● SIZE COMPARISON

● GENDER UNKNOWN

● ABILITIES
● Soundproof
● Static

● STATS
HP ●
ATTACK ●
DEFENSE ●●
SP. ATTACK ●●
SP. DEFENSE ●●
SPEED ●●●●

● EGG GROUPS
Mineral

● PERFORMANCE

SPEED ★★★★★ STAMINA ★☆
POWER ★☆ JUMP ★★★★☆
SKILL ★★★

● MAIN WAYS TO OBTAIN

Pokémon HeartGold Route 10

Pokémon SoulSilver Route 10

Pokémon Diamond Route 218 (mass outbreak)

Pokémon Pearl Route 218 (mass outbreak)

Pokémon Platinum Route 218 (mass outbreak)

Pokémon HeartGold
It rolls to move. If the ground is uneven, a sudden jolt from hitting a bump can cause it to explode.

Pokémon SoulSilver
It was discovered when Poké Balls were introduced. It is said that there is some connection.

● EVOLUTION

Voltorb — Lv. 30 — Electrode

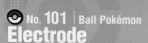

No. 101 | Ball Pokémon
Electrode

Electric

- **HEIGHT:** 3'11"
- **WEIGHT:** 146.8 lbs.
- **ITEMS:** None

● SIZE COMPARISON

● GENDER UNKNOWN

⊙ ABILITIES
- Soundproof
- Static

⊙ STATS
HP	●●
ATTACK	●●
DEFENSE	●●●
SP. ATTACK	●●●●
SP. DEFENSE	●●●
SPEED	●●●●●●

⊙ EGG GROUPS
Mineral

⊙ PERFORMANCE
SPEED ★★★★★	STAMINA ★★★☆
POWER ★★☆	JUMP ★★☆☆
SKILL ★★☆	

● MAIN WAYS TO OBTAIN

Pokémon HeartGold — Team Rocket's HQ (story event)

Pokémon SoulSilver — Team Rocket's HQ (story event)

Pokémon Diamond — Level up Voltorb to Lv. 30

Pokémon Pearl — Level up Voltorb to Lv. 30

Pokémon Platinum — Level up Voltorb to Lv. 30

Pokémon HeartGold
It is dangerous. If it has too much electricity and has nothing to do, it amuses itself by exploding.

Pokémon SoulSilver
It stores an overflowing amount of electric energy inside its body. Even a small shock makes it explode.

⊙ EVOLUTION

Voltorb → Lv. 30 → Electrode

● LEVEL-UP MOVES
Lv.	Name	Type	Kind	Pow.	Acc.	PP	Range	DA
1	Charge	Electric	Status	—	—	20	Self	—
1	Tackle	Normal	Physical	35	95	35	Normal	—
1	SonicBoom	Normal	Special	—	90	20	Normal	—
1	Spark	Electric	Physical	65	100	20	Normal	○
5	Tackle	Normal	Physical	35	95	35	Normal	—
8	SonicBoom	Normal	Special	—	90	20	Normal	—
12	Spark	Electric	Physical	65	100	20	Normal	○
15	Rollout	Rock	Physical	30	90	20	Normal	○
19	Screech	Normal	Status	—	85	40	Normal	—
22	Light Screen	Psychic	Status	—	—	30	2 Allies	—
26	Charge Beam	Electric	Special	50	90	10	Normal	—
29	Selfdestruct	Normal	Physical	200	100	5	2 Foes/1 Ally	—
35	Swift	Normal	Special	60	—	20	2 Foes	—
40	Magnet Rise	Electric	Status	—	—	10	Self	—
46	Gyro Ball	Steel	Physical	—	100	5	Normal	○
51	Explosion	Normal	Physical	250	100	5	2 Foes/1 Ally	—
57	Mirror Coat	Psychic	Special	—	100	10	Self	—

● MOVE MANIAC
Name	Type	Kind	Pow.	Acc.	PP	Range	DA
Headbutt	Normal	Physical	70	100	15	Normal	○

● BP MOVES
Name	Type	Kind	Pow.	Acc.	PP	Range	DA
Sucker Punch	Dark	Physical	80	100	5	Normal	○
Snore	Normal	Special	40	100	15	Normal	—
Magnet Rise	Electric	Status	—	—	10	Self	—
Swift	Normal	Special	60	—	20	2 Foes	—
Magic Coat	Psychic	Status	—	—	15	Self	—
Rollout	Rock	Physical	30	90	20	Normal	○
Signal Beam	Bug	Special	75	100	15	Normal	—

● TM & HM MOVES
No.	Name	Type	Kind	Pow.	Acc.	PP	Range	DA
TM06	Toxic	Poison	Status	—	85	10	Normal	—
TM10	Hidden Power	Normal	Special	—	100	15	Normal	—
TM12	Taunt	Dark	Status	—	100	20	Normal	—
TM15	Hyper Beam	Normal	Special	150	90	5	Normal	—
TM16	Light Screen	Psychic	Status	—	—	30	2 Allies	—
TM17	Protect	Normal	Status	—	—	10	Self	—
TM18	Rain Dance	Water	Status	—	—	5	All	—
TM21	Frustration	Normal	Physical	—	100	20	Normal	○
TM24	Thunderbolt	Electric	Special	95	100	15	Normal	—
TM25	Thunder	Electric	Special	120	70	10	Normal	—
TM27	Return	Normal	Physical	—	100	20	Normal	○
TM32	Double Team	Normal	Status	—	—	15	Self	—
TM34	Shock Wave	Electric	Special	60	—	20	Normal	—
TM41	Torment	Dark	Status	—	100	15	Normal	—
TM42	Facade	Normal	Physical	70	100	20	Normal	○
TM43	Secret Power	Normal	Physical	70	100	20	Normal	○
TM44	Rest	Psychic	Status	—	—	10	Self	—
TM46	Thief	Dark	Physical	40	100	10	Normal	○
TM57	Charge Beam	Electric	Special	50	90	10	Normal	—
TM58	Endure	Normal	Status	—	—	10	Self	—
TM64	Explosion	Normal	Physical	250	100	5	2 Foes/1 Ally	—
TM68	Giga Impact	Normal	Physical	150	90	5	Normal	○
TM70	Flash	Normal	Status	—	100	20	Normal	—
TM73	Thunder Wave	Electric	Status	—	100	20	Normal	—
TM74	Gyro Ball	Steel	Physical	—	100	5	Normal	○
TM82	Sleep Talk	Normal	Status	—	—	10	Depends	—
TM83	Natural Gift	Normal	Physical	—	100	15	Normal	—
TM87	Swagger	Normal	Status	—	90	15	Normal	—
TM90	Substitute	Normal	Status	—	—	10	Self	—

● LEVEL-UP MOVES

Lv.	Name	Type	Kind	Pow.	Acc.	PP	Range	DA
1	Barrage	Normal	Physical	15	85	20	Normal	—
1	Uproar	Normal	Special	50	100	10	1 Random	—
1	Hypnosis	Psychic	Status	—	60	20	Normal	—
1	Reflect	Psychic	Status	—	—	20	2 Allies	—
11	Leech Seed	Grass	Status	—	90	10	Normal	—
17	Bullet Seed	Grass	Physical	10	100	30	Normal	—
19	Stun Spore	Grass	Status	—	75	30	Normal	—
21	PoisonPowder	Poison	Status	—	75	35	Normal	—
23	Sleep Powder	Grass	Status	—	75	15	Normal	—
27	Confusion	Psychic	Special	50	100	25	Normal	—
33	Worry Seed	Grass	Status	—	100	10	Normal	—
37	Natural Gift	Normal	Physical	—	100	15	Normal	—
43	SolarBeam	Grass	Special	120	100	10	Normal	—
47	Psychic	Psychic	Special	90	100	10	Normal	—

● MOVE MANIAC

Name	Type	Kind	Pow.	Acc.	PP	Range	DA

● BP MOVES

Name	Type	Kind	Pow.	Acc.	PP	Range	DA
Snore	Normal	Special	40	100	15	Normal	—
Synthesis	Grass	Status	—	—	5	Self	—
Uproar	Normal	Special	50	100	10	1 Random	—
Gravity	Psychic	Status	—	—	5	All	—
Worry Seed	Grass	Status	—	100	10	Normal	—
Rollout	Rock	Physical	30	90	20	Normal	○
AncientPower	Rock	Special	60	100	5	Normal	—
Seed Bomb	Grass	Physical	80	100	15	Normal	—

● TM & HM MOVES

No.	Name	Type	Kind	Pow.	Acc.	PP	Range	DA
TM06	Toxic	Poison	Status	—	85	10	Normal	—
TM09	Bullet Seed	Grass	Physical	10	100	30	Normal	—
TM10	Hidden Power	Normal	Special	—	100	15	Normal	—
TM11	Sunny Day	Fire	Status	—	—	5	All	—
TM16	Light Screen	Psychic	Status	—	—	30	2 Allies	—
TM17	Protect	Normal	Status	—	—	10	Self	—
TM19	Giga Drain	Grass	Special	60	100	10	Normal	—
TM21	Frustration	Normal	Physical	—	100	20	Normal	○
TM22	SolarBeam	Grass	Special	120	100	10	Normal	—
TM27	Return	Normal	Physical	—	100	20	Normal	○
TM29	Psychic	Psychic	Special	90	100	10	Normal	—
TM32	Double Team	Normal	Status	—	—	15	Self	—
TM33	Reflect	Psychic	Status	—	—	20	2 Allies	—
TM36	Sludge Bomb	Poison	Special	90	100	10	Normal	—
TM42	Facade	Normal	Physical	70	100	20	Normal	○
TM43	Secret Power	Normal	Physical	70	100	20	Normal	—
TM44	Rest	Psychic	Status	—	—	10	Self	—
TM45	Attract	Normal	Status	—	100	15	Normal	—
TM46	Thief	Dark	Physical	40	100	10	Normal	○
TM48	Skill Swap	Psychic	Status	—	—	10	Normal	—
TM53	Energy Ball	Grass	Special	80	100	10	Normal	—
TM58	Endure	Normal	Status	—	—	10	Self	—
TM64	Explosion	Normal	Physical	250	100	5	2 Foes/1 Ally	—
TM70	Flash	Normal	Status	—	100	20	Normal	—
TM75	Swords Dance	Normal	Status	—	—	30	Self	—
TM77	Psych Up	Normal	Status	—	—	10	Normal	—
TM78	Captivate	Normal	Status	—	100	20	2 Foes	—
TM82	Sleep Talk	Normal	Status	—	—	10	Depends	—
TM83	Natural Gift	Normal	Physical	—	100	15	Normal	—
TM85	Dream Eater	Psychic	Special	100	100	15	Normal	—
TM86	Grass Knot	Grass	Special	—	100	20	Normal	○
TM87	Swagger	Normal	Status	—	90	15	Normal	—
TM90	Substitute	Normal	Status	—	—	10	Self	—
TM92	Trick Room	Psychic	Status	—	—	5	All	—
HM04	Strength	Normal	Physical	80	100	15	Normal	○

● EGG MOVES

Name	Type	Kind	Pow.	Acc.	PP	Range	DA
Synthesis	Grass	Status	—	—	5	Self	—
Moonlight	Normal	Status	—	—	5	Self	—
Reflect	Psychic	Status	—	—	20	2 Allies	—
AncientPower	Rock	Special	60	100	5	Normal	—
Psych Up	Normal	Status	—	—	10	Normal	—
Ingrain	Grass	Status	—	—	20	Self	—
Curse	???	Status	—	—	10	Normal/Self	—
Nature Power	Normal	Status	—	—	20	Depends	—
Lucky Chant	Normal	Status	—	—	30	2 Allies	—
Leaf Storm	Grass	Special	140	90	5	Normal	—
Power Swap	Psychic	Status	—	—	10	Normal	—

⊙ No. 102 | Egg Pokémon
Exeggcute

Grass | Psychic

● HEIGHT: 1'04"
● WEIGHT: 5.5 lbs.
● ITEMS: None

● SIZE COMPARISON

● MALE/FEMALE HAVE SAME FORM

⊙ ABILITIES
● Chlorophyll

⊙ STATS
HP ●●
ATTACK ●●
DEFENSE ●●●
SP. ATTACK ●●●
SP. DEFENSE ●●
SPEED ●●

⊙ EGG GROUPS
Grass

⊙ PERFORMANCE
SPEED ★★★   STAMINA ★★★★
POWER ★★☆   JUMP ★★☆
SKILL ★★☆

● MAIN WAYS TO OBTAIN

Pokémon HeartGold	New Bark Town (use Headbutt)
Pokémon SoulSilver	New Bark Town (use Headbutt)
Pokémon Diamond	Pastoria Great Marsh (after obtaining the National Pokédex (changes daily)
Pokémon Pearl	Pastoria Great Marsh (after obtaining the National Pokédex (changes daily)
Pokémon Platinum	Pastoria Great Marsh (after obtaining the National Pokédex (changes daily)

Pokémon HeartGold
Their shells are very durable. Even if they crack, they can survive without spilling their contents.

Pokémon SoulSilver
Using telepathy only, they can employ, they always form a cluster of six EXEGGCUTE.

⊙ EVOLUTION

Exeggcute

Use Leaf Stone

Exeggutor

No. 103 | Coconut Pokémon
Exeggutor

Grass | Psychic

- **HEIGHT:** 6'02"
- **WEIGHT:** 264.6 lbs.
- **ITEMS:** None

● SIZE COMPARISON

● MALE/FEMALE HAVE SAME FORM

⊛ ABILITIES
- Chlorophyll

⊛ EGG GROUPS
Grass

⊛ STATS
- HP ●●●●
- ATTACK ●●●●
- DEFENSE ●●●
- SP. ATTACK ●●●●●
- SP. DEFENSE ●●
- SPEED ●●●

⊛ PERFORMANCE
SPEED ★★☆　　STAMINA ★★★★
POWER ★★★☆　JUMP ★★☆
SKILL ★★★

● MAIN WAYS TO OBTAIN

Pokémon HeartGold	Use the Leaf Stone on Exeggcute
Pokémon SoulSilver	Use the Leaf Stone on Exeggcute
Pokémon Diamond	Use the Leaf Stone on Exeggcute
Pokémon Pearl	Use the Leaf Stone on Exeggcute
Pokémon Platinum	Use the Leaf Stone on Exeggcute

| Pokémon HeartGold | Pokémon SoulSilver |
| Its three heads think independently. However, they are friendly and never appear to squabble. | If a head drops off, it emits a telepathic call in search of others to form an EXEGGCUTE cluster. |

⊛ EVOLUTION

Exeggcute — Use Leaf Stone → Exeggutor

● LEVEL-UP MOVES

Lv.	Name	Type	Kind	Pow.	Acc.	PP	Range	DA
1	Seed Bomb	Grass	Physical	80	100	15	Normal	—
1	Barrage	Normal	Physical	15	85	20	Normal	—
1	Hypnosis	Psychic	Status	—	60	20	Normal	—
1	Confusion	Psychic	Special	50	100	25	Normal	—
1	Stomp	Normal	Physical	65	100	20	Normal	○
17	Stomp	Normal	Physical	65	100	20	Normal	○
27	Egg Bomb	Normal	Physical	100	75	10	Normal	—
37	Wood Hammer	Grass	Physical	120	100	15	Normal	○
47	Leaf Storm	Grass	Special	140	90	5	Normal	—

● MOVE MANIAC

Name	Type	Kind	Pow.	Acc.	PP	Range	DA
Headbutt	Normal	Physical	70	100	15	Normal	○

● BP MOVES

Name	Type	Kind	Pow.	Acc.	PP	Range	DA
Zen Headbutt	Psychic	Physical	80	90	15	Normal	○
Snore	Normal	Special	40	100	15	Normal	—
Synthesis	Grass	Status	—	—	5	Self	—
Gravity	Psychic	Status	—	—	5	All	—
Worry Seed	Grass	Status	—	100	10	Normal	—
Rollout	Rock	Physical	30	90	20	Normal	○
AncientPower	Rock	Special	60	100	5	Normal	—
Seed Bomb	Grass	Physical	80	100	15	Normal	—
Low Kick	Fighting	Physical	—	100	20	Normal	○

● TM & HM MOVES

No.	Name	Type	Kind	Pow.	Acc.	PP	Range	DA
TM06	Toxic	Poison	Status	—	85	10	Normal	—
TM09	Bullet Seed	Grass	Physical	10	100	30	Normal	—
TM10	Hidden Power	Normal	Special	—	100	15	Normal	—
TM11	Sunny Day	Fire	Status	—	—	5	All	—
TM15	Hyper Beam	Normal	Special	150	90	5	Normal	—
TM16	Light Screen	Psychic	Status	—	—	30	2 Allies	—
TM17	Protect	Normal	Status	—	—	10	Self	—
TM19	Giga Drain	Grass	Special	60	100	10	Normal	—
TM21	Frustration	Normal	Physical	—	100	20	Normal	○
TM22	SolarBeam	Grass	Special	120	100	10	Normal	—
TM27	Return	Normal	Physical	—	100	20	Normal	○
TM29	Psychic	Psychic	Special	90	100	10	Normal	—
TM32	Double Team	Normal	Status	—	—	15	Self	—
TM33	Reflect	Psychic	Status	—	—	20	2 Allies	—
TM36	Sludge Bomb	Poison	Special	90	100	10	Normal	—
TM42	Facade	Normal	Physical	70	100	20	Normal	○
TM43	Secret Power	Normal	Physical	70	100	20	Normal	○
TM44	Rest	Psychic	Status	—	—	10	Self	—
TM45	Attract	Normal	Status	—	100	15	Normal	—
TM46	Thief	Dark	Physical	40	100	10	Normal	○
TM48	Skill Swap	Psychic	Status	—	—	10	Normal	—
TM53	Energy Ball	Grass	Special	80	100	10	Normal	—
TM58	Endure	Normal	Status	—	—	10	Self	—
TM64	Explosion	Normal	Physical	250	100	5	2 Foes/1 Ally	—
TM68	Giga Impact	Normal	Physical	150	90	5	Normal	—
TM70	Flash	Normal	Status	—	100	20	Normal	—
TM75	Swords Dance	Normal	Status	—	—	30	Self	—
TM77	Psych Up	Normal	Status	—	—	10	Self	—
TM78	Captivate	Normal	Status	—	100	20	2 Foes	—
TM82	Sleep Talk	Normal	Status	—	—	10	Depends	—
TM83	Natural Gift	Normal	Physical	—	100	15	Normal	—
TM85	Dream Eater	Psychic	Special	100	100	15	Normal	—
TM86	Grass Knot	Grass	Special	—	100	20	Normal	○
TM87	Swagger	Normal	Status	—	90	15	Normal	—
TM90	Substitute	Normal	Status	—	—	10	Self	—
TM92	Trick Room	Psychic	Status	—	—	5	All	—
HM04	Strength	Normal	Physical	80	100	15	Normal	○

● LEVEL-UP MOVES

Lv.	Name	Type	Kind	Pow.	Acc.	PP	Range	DA
1	Growl	Normal	Status	—	100	40	2 Foes	—
3	Tail Whip	Normal	Status	—	100	30	2 Foes	—
7	Bone Club	Ground	Physical	65	85	20	Normal	—
11	Headbutt	Normal	Physical	70	100	15	Normal	○
13	Leer	Normal	Status	—	100	30	2 Foes	—
17	Focus Energy	Normal	Status	—	—	30	Self	—
21	Bonemerang	Ground	Physical	50	90	10	Normal	—
23	Rage	Normal	Physical	20	100	20	Normal	—
27	False Swipe	Normal	Physical	40	100	40	Normal	—
31	Thrash	Normal	Physical	90	100	20	1 Random	○
33	Fling	Dark	Physical	—	100	10	Normal	—
37	Bone Rush	Ground	Physical	25	80	10	Normal	—
41	Endeavor	Normal	Physical	—	100	5	Normal	○
43	Double-Edge	Normal	Physical	120	100	15	Normal	○

● MOVE MANIAC

Name	Type	Kind	Pow.	Acc.	PP	Range	DA
Headbutt	Normal	Physical	70	100	15	Normal	—

● BP MOVES

Name	Type	Kind	Pow.	Acc.	PP	Range	DA
Fury Cutter	Bug	Physical	10	95	20	Normal	○
Icy Wind	Ice	Special	55	95	15	2 Foes	—
ThunderPunch	Electric	Physical	75	100	15	Normal	○
Fire Punch	Fire	Physical	75	100	15	Normal	○
Knock Off	Dark	Physical	20	100	20	Normal	○
Snore	Normal	Special	40	100	15	Normal	—
Uproar	Normal	Special	50	100	10	1 Random	—
Mud-Slap	Ground	Special	20	100	10	Normal	—
Endeavor	Normal	Physical	—	100	5	Normal	○
Earth Power	Ground	Special	90	100	10	Normal	—
Iron Defense	Steel	Status	—	—	15	Self	—
Low Kick	Fighting	Physical	—	100	20	Normal	○

● TM & HM MOVES

No.	Name	Type	Kind	Pow.	Acc.	PP	Range	DA
TM01	Focus Punch	Fighting	Physical	150	100	20	Normal	○
TM06	Toxic	Poison	Status	—	85	10	Normal	—
TM10	Hidden Power	Normal	Special	—	100	15	Normal	—
TM11	Sunny Day	Fire	Status	—	—	5	All	—
TM13	Ice Beam	Ice	Special	95	100	10	Normal	—
TM14	Blizzard	Ice	Special	120	70	5	2 Foes	—
TM17	Protect	Normal	Status	—	—	10	Self	—
TM21	Frustration	Normal	Physical	—	100	20	Normal	○
TM23	Iron Tail	Steel	Physical	100	75	15	Normal	○
TM26	Earthquake	Ground	Physical	100	100	10	2 Foes/1 Ally	—
TM27	Return	Normal	Physical	—	100	20	Normal	○
TM28	Dig	Ground	Physical	80	100	10	Normal	○
TM31	Brick Break	Fighting	Physical	75	100	15	Normal	○
TM32	Double Team	Normal	Status	—	—	15	Self	—
TM35	Flamethrower	Fire	Special	95	100	15	Normal	—
TM37	Sandstorm	Rock	Status	—	—	10	All	—
TM38	Fire Blast	Fire	Special	120	85	5	Normal	—
TM39	Rock Tomb	Rock	Physical	50	80	10	Normal	—
TM40	Aerial Ace	Flying	Physical	60	—	20	Normal	○
TM42	Facade	Normal	Physical	70	100	20	Normal	○
TM43	Secret Power	Normal	Physical	70	100	20	Normal	—
TM44	Rest	Psychic	Status	—	—	10	Self	—
TM45	Attract	Normal	Status	—	100	15	Normal	—
TM46	Thief	Dark	Physical	40	100	10	Normal	—
TM54	False Swipe	Normal	Physical	40	100	40	Normal	○
TM56	Fling	Dark	Physical	—	100	10	Normal	—
TM58	Endure	Normal	Status	—	—	10	Self	—
TM75	Swords Dance	Normal	Status	—	—	30	Self	—
TM76	Stealth Rock	Rock	Status	—	—	20	2 Foes	—
TM78	Captivate	Normal	Status	—	100	20	2 Foes	—
TM80	Rock Slide	Rock	Physical	75	90	10	2 Foes	—
TM82	Sleep Talk	Normal	Status	—	—	10	Depends	—
TM83	Natural Gift	Normal	Physical	—	100	15	Normal	—
TM87	Swagger	Normal	Status	—	90	15	Normal	—
TM90	Substitute	Normal	Status	—	—	10	Self	—
HM04	Strength	Normal	Physical	80	100	15	Normal	○
HM06	Rock Smash	Fighting	Physical	40	100	15	Normal	○
HM08	Rock Climb	Normal	Physical	90	85	20	Normal	○

● EGG MOVES

Name	Type	Kind	Pow.	Acc.	PP	Range	DA
Rock Slide	Rock	Physical	75	90	10	2 Foes	—
AncientPower	Rock	Special	60	100	5	Normal	—
Belly Drum	Normal	Status	—	—	10	Self	—
Screech	Normal	Status	—	85	40	Normal	—
Skull Bash	Normal	Physical	100	100	15	Normal	○
Perish Song	Normal	Status	—	—	5	All	—
Swords Dance	Normal	Status	—	—	30	Self	—
Double Kick	Fighting	Physical	30	100	30	Normal	○
Iron Head	Steel	Physical	80	100	15	Normal	○
Detect	Fighting	Status	—	—	5	Self	—

No. 104 | Lonely Pokémon
Cubone

Ground

● **HEIGHT:** 1'04"
● **WEIGHT:** 14.3 lbs.
● **ITEMS:** Thick Club

● SIZE COMPARISON

● MALE/FEMALE HAVE SAME FORM

◎ ABILITIES
● Rock Head
● Lightningrod

◎ STATS
HP ●●
ATTACK ●●
DEFENSE ●●●●
SP. ATTACK ●●
SP. DEFENSE ●●
SPEED ●●

◎ EGG GROUPS
Monster

◎ PERFORMANCE

SPEED ★★★★	STAMINA ★★☆
POWER ★☆☆☆	JUMP ★★★
SKILL ★★★	

● MAIN WAYS TO OBTAIN

Pokémon HeartGold	Safari Zone (Desert Area, morning and afternoon only)
Pokémon SoulSilver	Safari Zone (Desert Area, morning and afternoon only)
Pokémon Diamond	Route 203 (mass outbreak)
Pokémon Pearl	Route 203 (mass outbreak)
Pokémon Platinum	Route 203 (mass outbreak)

Pokémon HeartGold	Pokémon SoulSilver
If it is sad or lonely, the skull it wears shakes and emits a plaintive and mournful sound.	It always wears the skull of its dead mother, so no one has any idea what its hidden face looks like.

◎ EVOLUTION

Lv. 28

Cubone → Marowak

No. 105 | Bone Keeper Pokémon
Marowak

Ground

- **HEIGHT:** 3'03"
- **WEIGHT:** 99.2 lbs.
- **ITEMS:** Thick Club

● SIZE COMPARISON

● MALE/FEMALE HAVE SAME FORM

⚙ ABILITIES
- Rock Head
- Lightningrod

⚙ STATS
HP	●●
ATTACK	●●●●
DEFENSE	●●●●
SP. ATTACK	●●
SP. DEFENSE	●●●
SPEED	●●

⚙ EGG GROUPS
Flying

Field

⚙ PERFORMANCE
SPEED ★★☆ STAMINA ★★★★
POWER ★★★★☆ JUMP ★★
SKILL ★★★

● MAIN WAYS TO OBTAIN

Pokémon HeartGold	Safari Zone (Desert Area, morning and afternoon only)
Pokémon SoulSilver	Safari Zone (Desert Area, morning and afternoon only)
Pokémon Diamond	Level up Cubone to Lv. 28
Pokémon Pearl	Level up Cubone to Lv. 28
Pokémon Platinum	Level up Cubone to Lv. 28

Pokémon HeartGold	Pokémon SoulSilver
It has been seen pounding boulders with the bone it carries in order to tap out messages to others.	It collects bones from an unknown place. Some whisper that a MAROWAK graveyard exists somewhere in the world.

⚙ EVOLUTION

Cubone — Lv. 28 → Marowak

● LEVEL-UP MOVES

Lv.	Name	Type	Kind	Pow.	Acc.	PP	Range	DA
1	Growl	Normal	Status	—	100	40	2 Foes	—
1	Tail Whip	Normal	Status	—	100	30	2 Foes	—
1	Bone Club	Ground	Physical	65	85	20	Normal	—
1	Headbutt	Normal	Physical	70	100	15	Normal	○
3	Tail Whip	Normal	Status	—	100	30	2 Foes	—
7	Bone Club	Ground	Physical	65	85	20	Normal	—
11	Headbutt	Normal	Physical	70	100	15	Normal	○
13	Leer	Normal	Status	—	100	30	2 Foes	—
17	Focus Energy	Normal	Status	—	—	30	Self	—
21	Bonemerang	Ground	Physical	50	90	10	Normal	—
23	Rage	Normal	Physical	20	100	20	Normal	○
27	False Swipe	Normal	Physical	40	100	40	Normal	○
33	Thrash	Normal	Physical	90	100	10	1 Random	○
37	Fling	Dark	Physical	—	100	10	Normal	—
43	Bone Rush	Ground	Physical	25	80	10	Normal	—
49	Endeavor	Normal	Physical	—	100	5	Normal	○
53	Double-Edge	Normal	Physical	120	100	15	Normal	○

● MOVE MANIAC

Name	Type	Kind	Pow.	Acc.	PP	Range	DA
Headbutt	Normal	Physical	70	100	15	Normal	○

● BP MOVES

Name	Type	Kind	Pow.	Acc.	PP	Range	DA
Fury Cutter	Bug	Physical	10	95	20	Normal	○
Icy Wind	Ice	Special	55	95	15	2 Foes	—
ThunderPunch	Electric	Physical	75	100	15	Normal	○
Fire Punch	Fire	Physical	75	100	15	Normal	○
Knock Off	Dark	Physical	20	100	20	Normal	○
Snore	Normal	Special	40	100	15	Normal	—
Uproar	Normal	Special	50	100	10	1 Random	—
Mud-Slap	Ground	Special	20	100	10	Normal	—
Endeavor	Normal	Physical	—	100	5	Normal	—
Outrage	Dragon	Physical	120	100	15	1 Random	○
Earth Power	Ground	Special	90	100	10	Normal	—
Iron Defense	Steel	Status	—	—	15	Self	—
Low Kick	Fighting	Physical	—	100	20	Normal	○

● TM & HM MOVES

No.	Name	Type	Kind	Pow.	Acc.	PP	Range	DA
TM01	Focus Punch	Fighting	Physical	150	100	20	Normal	○
TM06	Toxic	Poison	Status	—	85	10	Normal	—
TM10	Hidden Power	Normal	Special	—	100	15	Normal	—
TM11	Sunny Day	Fire	Status	—	—	5	All	—
TM13	Ice Beam	Ice	Special	95	100	10	Normal	—
TM14	Blizzard	Ice	Special	120	70	5	2 Foes	—
TM15	Hyper Beam	Normal	Special	150	90	5	Normal	—
TM17	Protect	Normal	Status	—	—	10	Self	—
TM21	Frustration	Normal	Physical	—	100	20	Normal	○
TM23	Iron Tail	Steel	Physical	100	75	15	Normal	○
TM26	Earthquake	Ground	Physical	100	100	10	2 Foes/1 Ally	—
TM27	Return	Normal	Physical	—	100	20	Normal	○
TM28	Dig	Ground	Physical	80	100	10	Normal	○
TM31	Brick Break	Fighting	Physical	75	100	15	Normal	○
TM32	Double Team	Normal	Status	—	—	15	Self	—
TM37	Sandstorm	Rock	Status	—	—	10	All	—
TM35	Flamethrower	Fire	Special	95	100	15	Normal	—
TM38	Fire Blast	Fire	Special	120	85	5	Normal	—
TM39	Rock Tomb	Rock	Physical	50	80	10	Normal	○
TM40	Aerial Ace	Flying	Physical	60	—	20	Normal	○
TM42	Facade	Normal	Physical	70	100	20	Normal	○
TM43	Secret Power	Normal	Physical	70	100	20	Normal	—
TM44	Rest	Psychic	Status	—	—	10	Self	—
TM45	Attract	Normal	Status	—	100	15	Normal	—
TM46	Thief	Dark	Physical	40	100	10	Normal	○
TM52	Focus Blast	Fighting	Special	120	70	5	Normal	—
TM54	False Swipe	Normal	Physical	40	100	40	Normal	○
TM56	Fling	Dark	Physical	—	100	10	Normal	○
TM58	Endure	Normal	Status	—	—	10	Self	—
TM68	Giga Impact	Normal	Physical	150	90	5	Normal	○
TM71	Stone Edge	Rock	Physical	100	80	5	Normal	○
TM75	Swords Dance	Normal	Status	—	—	30	Self	—
TM76	Stealth Rock	Rock	Status	—	—	20	2 Foes	—
TM78	Captivate	Normal	Status	—	100	20	2 Foes	—
TM80	Rock Slide	Rock	Physical	75	90	10	2 Foes	—
TM82	Sleep Talk	Normal	Status	—	—	10	Depends	—
TM83	Natural Gift	Normal	Physical	—	100	15	Normal	—
TM87	Swagger	Normal	Status	—	90	15	Normal	—
TM90	Substitute	Normal	Status	—	—	10	Self	—
HM04	Strength	Normal	Physical	80	100	15	Normal	○
HM06	Rock Smash	Fighting	Physical	40	100	15	Normal	○
HM08	Rock Climb	Normal	Physical	90	85	20	Normal	○

● LEVEL-UP MOVES

Lv.	Name	Type	Kind	Pow.	Acc.	PP	Range	DA
1	Revenge	Fighting	Physical	60	100	10	Normal	○
1	Double Kick	Fighting	Physical	30	100	30	Normal	○
5	Meditate	Psychic	Status	—	—	40	Self	—
9	Rolling Kick	Fighting	Physical	60	85	15	Normal	○
13	Jump Kick	Fighting	Physical	85	95	25	Normal	○
17	Brick Break	Fighting	Physical	75	100	15	Normal	○
21	Focus Energy	Normal	Status	—	—	30	Self	—
25	Feint	Normal	Physical	50	100	10	Normal	—
29	Hi Jump Kick	Fighting	Physical	100	90	20	Normal	○
33	Mind Reader	Normal	Status	—	—	5	Normal	—
37	Foresight	Normal	Status	—	—	40	Normal	—
41	Blaze Kick	Fire	Physical	85	90	10	Normal	○
45	Endure	Normal	Status	—	—	10	Self	—
49	Mega Kick	Normal	Physical	120	75	5	Normal	○
53	Close Combat	Fighting	Physical	120	100	5	Normal	○
57	Reversal	Fighting	Physical	—	100	15	Normal	○

● MOVE MANIAC

Name	Type	Kind	Pow.	Acc.	PP	Range	DA
Headbutt	Normal	Physical	70	100	15	Normal	○

● BP MOVES

Name	Type	Kind	Pow.	Acc.	PP	Range	DA
Vacuum Wave	Fighting	Special	40	100	30	Normal	—
Knock Off	Dark	Physical	20	100	20	Normal	○
Sucker Punch	Dark	Physical	80	100	5	Normal	○
Snore	Normal	Special	40	100	15	Normal	—
Helping Hand	Normal	Status	—	—	20	1 Ally	—
Swift	Normal	Special	60	—	20	2 Foes	—
Role Play	Psychic	Status	—	—	10	Normal	—
Mud-Slap	Ground	Special	20	100	10	Normal	—
Superpower	Fighting	Physical	120	100	5	Normal	○
Bounce	Flying	Physical	85	85	5	Normal	○
Low Kick	Fighting	Physical	—	100	20	Normal	○

● TM & HM MOVES

No.	Name	Type	Kind	Pow.	Acc.	PP	Range	DA
TM01	Focus Punch	Fighting	Physical	150	100	20	Normal	○
TM06	Toxic	Poison	Status	—	85	10	Normal	—
TM08	Bulk Up	Fighting	Status	—	—	20	Self	—
TM10	Hidden Power	Normal	Special	—	100	15	Normal	—
TM11	Sunny Day	Fire	Status	—	—	5	All	—
TM17	Protect	Normal	Status	—	—	10	Self	—
TM18	Rain Dance	Water	Status	—	—	5	All	—
TM21	Frustration	Normal	Physical	—	100	20	Normal	○
TM26	Earthquake	Ground	Physical	100	100	10	2 Foes/1 Ally	○
TM27	Return	Normal	Physical	—	100	20	Normal	○
TM31	Brick Break	Fighting	Physical	75	100	15	Normal	○
TM32	Double Team	Normal	Status	—	—	15	Self	—
TM39	Rock Tomb	Rock	Physical	50	80	10	Normal	○
TM42	Facade	Normal	Physical	70	100	20	Normal	○
TM43	Secret Power	Normal	Physical	70	100	20	Normal	○
TM44	Rest	Psychic	Status	—	—	10	Self	—
TM45	Attract	Normal	Status	—	100	15	Normal	—
TM46	Thief	Dark	Physical	40	100	10	Normal	○
TM52	Focus Blast	Fighting	Special	120	70	5	Normal	—
TM56	Fling	Dark	Physical	—	100	10	Normal	○
TM58	Endure	Normal	Status	—	—	10	Self	—
TM71	Stone Edge	Rock	Physical	100	80	5	Normal	○
TM78	Captivate	Normal	Status	—	100	20	2 Foes	—
TM80	Rock Slide	Rock	Physical	75	90	10	2 Foes	○
TM82	Sleep Talk	Normal	Status	—	—	10	Depends	—
TM83	Natural Gift	Normal	Physical	—	100	15	Normal	○
TM84	Poison Jab	Poison	Physical	80	100	20	Normal	○
TM87	Swagger	Normal	Status	—	90	15	Normal	—
TM90	Substitute	Normal	Status	—	—	10	Self	—
HM04	Strength	Normal	Physical	80	100	15	Normal	○
HM06	Rock Smash	Fighting	Physical	40	100	15	Normal	○
HM08	Rock Climb	Normal	Physical	90	85	20	Normal	○

◉ No. 106 | Kicking Pokémon
Hitmonlee

Fighting

- **HEIGHT:** 4'11"
- **WEIGHT:** 109.8 lbs.
- **ITEMS:** None

● SIZE COMPARISON

● MALE FORM

⊙ ABILITIES
- Limber
- Reckless

⊙ EGG GROUPS
Human-Like

⊙ STATS
- HP ●●
- ATTACK ●●●●●
- DEFENSE ●●
- SP. ATTACK ●
- SP. DEFENSE ●●●●
- SPEED ●●●●

⊙ PERFORMANCE
- SPEED ★★★
- POWER ★★★★
- SKILL ★★☆
- STAMINA ★★☆
- JUMP ★★★★

Pokémon HeartGold
Make Tyrogue's Attack higher than its Defense, then level it up to Lv. 20

Pokémon SoulSilver
Make Tyrogue's Attack higher than its Defense, then level it up to Lv. 20

Pokémon Diamond
Make Tyrogue's Attack higher than its Defense, then level it up to Lv. 20

Pokémon Pearl
Make Tyrogue's Attack higher than its Defense, then level it up to Lv. 20

Pokémon Platinum
Make Tyrogue's Attack higher than its Defense, then level it up to Lv. 20

Pokémon HeartGold
This amazing Pokémon has an awesome sense of balance. It can kick in succession from any position.

Pokémon SoulSilver
If it starts kicking repeatedly, both legs will stretch even longer to strike a fleeing foe.

⊙ EVOLUTION

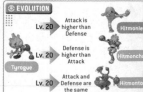

Tyrogue — Lv. 20 Attack is higher than Defense → Hitmonlee

Lv. 20 Defense is higher than Attack → Hitmonchan

Lv. 20 Attack and Defense are the same → Hitmontop

No. 107 | Punching Pokémon
Hitmonchan

Fighting

- **HEIGHT:** 4'07"
- **WEIGHT:** 110.7 lbs.
- **ITEMS:** None

● SIZE COMPARISON

● MALE FORM

ABILITIES
- Keen Eye
- Iron Fist

EGG GROUPS
Human-Like

STATS
- HP ●●
- ATTACK ●●●●
- DEFENSE ●●●
- SP. ATTACK ●●●
- SP. DEFENSE ●●●
- SPEED ●●●●

PERFORMANCE
- SPEED ★★★☆
- POWER ★★★☆
- SKILL ★★★☆☆
- STAMINA ★★★★
- JUMP ★★☆

Pokémon HeartGold	Make Tyrogue's Defense higher than its Attack, then level it up to Lv. 20
Pokémon SoulSilver	Make Tyrogue's Defense higher than its Attack, then level it up to Lv. 20
Pokémon Diamond	Make Tyrogue's Defense higher than its Attack, then level it up to Lv. 20
Pokémon Pearl	Make Tyrogue's Defense higher than its Attack, then level it up to Lv. 20
Pokémon Platinum	Make Tyrogue's Defense higher than its Attack, then level it up to Lv. 20

Pokémon HeartGold	**Pokémon SoulSilver**
Its punches slice the air. However, it seems to need a short break after fighting for three minutes.	Its punches are launched at such high speed, even a slight graze could cause a burn.

EVOLUTION

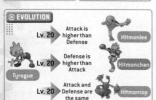

Tyrogue → Lv. 20 Attack is higher than Defense → Hitmonlee

Tyrogue → Lv. 20 Defense is higher than Attack → Hitmonchan

Tyrogue → Lv. 20 Attack and Defense are the same → Hitmontop

● LEVEL-UP MOVES

Lv.	Name	Type	Kind	Pow.	Acc.	PP	Range	DA
1	Revenge	Fighting	Physical	60	100	10	Normal	○
1	Comet Punch	Normal	Physical	18	85	15	Normal	○
6	Agility	Psychic	Status	—	—	30	Self	—
11	Pursuit	Dark	Physical	40	100	20	Normal	○
16	Mach Punch	Fighting	Physical	40	100	30	Normal	○
16	Bullet Punch	Steel	Physical	40	100	30	Normal	○
21	Feint	Normal	Physical	50	100	10	Normal	—
26	Vacuum Wave	Fighting	Special	40	100	30	Normal	—
31	ThunderPunch	Electric	Physical	75	100	15	Normal	○
31	Ice Punch	Ice	Physical	75	100	15	Normal	○
31	Fire Punch	Fire	Physical	75	100	15	Normal	○
36	Sky Uppercut	Fighting	Physical	85	90	15	Normal	○
41	Mega Punch	Normal	Physical	80	85	20	Normal	○
46	Detect	Fighting	Status	—	—	5	Self	—
51	Counter	Fighting	Physical	—	100	5	Self	○
56	Close Combat	Fighting	Physical	120	100	5	Normal	○

● MOVE MANIAC

Name	Type	Kind	Pow.	Acc.	PP	Range	DA
Headbutt	Normal	Physical	70	100	15	Normal	○

● BP MOVES

Name	Type	Kind	Pow.	Acc.	PP	Range	DA
ThunderPunch	Electric	Physical	75	100	15	Normal	○
Fire Punch	Fire	Physical	75	100	15	Normal	○
Ice Punch	Ice	Physical	75	100	15	Normal	○
Vacuum Wave	Fighting	Special	40	100	30	Normal	—
Snore	Normal	Special	40	100	15	Normal	—
Helping Hand	Normal	Status	—	—	20	1 Ally	—
Swift	Normal	Special	60	—	20	2 Foes	—
Role Play	Psychic	Status	—	—	10	Normal	—
Mud-Slap	Ground	Special	20	100	10	Normal	○
Low Kick	Fighting	Physical	—	100	20	Normal	○

● TM & HM MOVES

No.	Name	Type	Kind	Pow.	Acc.	PP	Range	DA
TM01	Focus Punch	Fighting	Physical	150	100	20	Normal	○
TM06	Toxic	Poison	Status	—	85	10	Normal	—
TM08	Bulk Up	Fighting	Status	—	—	20	Self	—
TM10	Hidden Power	Normal	Special	—	100	15	Normal	—
TM11	Sunny Day	Fire	Status	—	—	5	All	—
TM17	Protect	Normal	Status	—	—	10	Self	—
TM18	Rain Dance	Water	Status	—	—	5	All	—
TM21	Frustration	Normal	Physical	—	100	20	Normal	○
TM26	Earthquake	Ground	Physical	100	100	10	2 Foers/1 Ally	—
TM27	Return	Normal	Physical	—	100	20	Normal	○
TM31	Brick Break	Fighting	Physical	75	100	15	Normal	○
TM32	Double Team	Normal	Status	—	—	15	Self	—
TM39	Rock Tomb	Rock	Physical	50	80	10	Normal	○
TM42	Facade	Normal	Physical	70	100	20	Normal	○
TM43	Secret Power	Normal	Physical	70	100	20	Normal	○
TM44	Rest	Psychic	Status	—	—	10	Self	—
TM45	Attract	Normal	Status	—	100	15	Normal	—
TM46	Thief	Dark	Physical	40	100	10	Normal	○
TM52	Focus Blast	Fighting	Special	120	70	5	Normal	—
TM56	Fling	Dark	Physical	—	100	10	Normal	○
TM58	Endure	Normal	Status	—	—	10	Self	—
TM60	Drain Punch	Fighting	Physical	60	100	5	Normal	○
TM71	Stone Edge	Rock	Physical	100	80	5	Normal	○
TM78	Captivate	Normal	Status	—	100	20	2 Foes	—
TM80	Rock Slide	Rock	Physical	75	90	10	2 Foes	○
TM82	Sleep Talk	Normal	Status	—	—	10	Depends	—
TM83	Natural Gift	Normal	Physical	—	100	15	Normal	—
TM87	Swagger	Normal	Status	—	90	15	Normal	—
TM90	Substitute	Normal	Status	—	—	10	Self	—
HM04	Strength	Normal	Physical	80	100	15	Normal	○
HM06	Rock Smash	Fighting	Physical	40	100	15	Normal	○
HM08	Rock Climb	Normal	Physical	90	85	20	Normal	○

● LEVEL-UP MOVES

Lv.	Name	Type	Kind	Pow.	Acc.	PP	Range	DA
1	Lick	Ghost	Physical	20	100	30	Normal	○
5	Supersonic	Normal	Status	—	55	20	Normal	—
9	Defense Curl	Normal	Status	—	—	40	Self	—
13	Knock Off	Dark	Physical	20	100	20	Normal	○
17	Wrap	Normal	Physical	15	85	20	Normal	—
21	Stomp	Normal	Physical	65	100	20	Normal	○
25	Disable	Normal	Status	—	80	20	Normal	—
29	Slam	Normal	Physical	80	75	20	Normal	○
33	Rollout	Rock	Physical	30	90	20	Normal	○
37	Me First	Normal	Status	—	—	20	Depends	—
41	Refresh	Normal	Status	—	—	20	Self	—
45	Screech	Normal	Status	—	85	40	Normal	—
49	Power Whip	Grass	Physical	120	85	10	Normal	○
53	Wring Out	Normal	Special	—	100	5	Normal	○

● MOVE MANIAC

Name	Type	Kind	Pow.	Acc.	PP	Range	DA
Headbutt	Normal	Physical	70	100	15	Normal	○

● BP MOVES

Name	Type	Kind	Pow.	Acc.	PP	Range	DA
Icy Wind	Ice	Special	55	95	15	2 Foes	—
ThunderPunch	Electric	Physical	75	100	15	Normal	○
Fire Punch	Fire	Physical	75	100	15	Normal	○
Ice Punch	Ice	Physical	75	100	15	Normal	○
Zen Headbutt	Psychic	Physical	80	90	15	Normal	○
Knock Off	Dark	Physical	20	100	20	Normal	○
Snore	Normal	Special	40	100	15	Normal	—
Mud-Slap	Ground	Special	20	100	10	Normal	—
Rollout	Rock	Physical	30	90	20	Normal	○
Aqua Tail	Water	Physical	90	90	10	Normal	○

● TM & HM MOVES

No.	Name	Type	Kind	Pow.	Acc.	PP	Range	DA
TM01	Focus Punch	Fighting	Physical	150	100	20	Normal	○
TM03	Water Pulse	Water	Special	60	100	20	Normal	—
TM06	Toxic	Poison	Status	—	85	10	Normal	—
TM10	Hidden Power	Normal	Special	—	100	15	Normal	—
TM11	Sunny Day	Fire	Status	—	—	5	All	—
TM13	Ice Beam	Ice	Special	95	100	10	Normal	—
TM14	Blizzard	Ice	Special	120	70	5	2 Foes	—
TM15	Hyper Beam	Normal	Special	150	90	5	Normal	—
TM17	Protect	Normal	Status	—	—	10	Self	—
TM18	Rain Dance	Water	Status	—	—	5	All	—
TM21	Frustration	Normal	Physical	—	100	20	Normal	○
TM22	SolarBeam	Grass	Special	120	100	10	Normal	—
TM23	Iron Tail	Steel	Physical	100	75	15	Normal	○
TM24	Thunderbolt	Electric	Special	95	100	15	Normal	—
TM25	Thunder	Electric	Special	120	70	10	Normal	—
TM26	Earthquake	Ground	Physical	100	100	10	2 Foes/1 Ally	○
TM27	Return	Normal	Physical	—	100	20	Normal	○
TM28	Dig	Ground	Physical	80	100	10	Normal	○
TM30	Shadow Ball	Ghost	Special	80	100	15	Normal	—
TM31	Brick Break	Fighting	Physical	75	100	15	Normal	○
TM32	Double Team	Normal	Status	—	—	15	Self	—
TM34	Shock Wave	Electric	Special	60	—	20	Normal	—
TM35	Flamethrower	Fire	Special	95	100	15	Normal	—
TM37	Sandstorm	Rock	Status	—	—	10	All	—
TM38	Fire Blast	Fire	Special	120	85	5	Normal	—
TM39	Rock Tomb	Rock	Physical	50	80	10	Normal	○
TM42	Facade	Normal	Physical	70	100	20	Normal	○
TM43	Secret Power	Normal	Physical	70	100	20	Normal	○
TM44	Rest	Psychic	Status	—	—	10	Self	—
TM45	Attract	Normal	Status	—	100	15	Normal	—
TM46	Thief	Dark	Physical	40	100	10	Normal	○
TM56	Fling	Dark	Physical	—	100	10	Normal	○
TM58	Endure	Normal	Status	—	—	10	Self	—
TM68	Giga Impact	Normal	Physical	150	90	5	Normal	○
TM75	Swords Dance	Normal	Status	—	—	30	Self	—
TM77	Psych Up	Normal	Status	—	—	10	Normal	—
TM78	Captivate	Normal	Status	—	100	20	2 Foes	—
TM80	Rock Slide	Rock	Physical	75	90	10	2 Foes	—
TM82	Sleep Talk	Normal	Status	—	—	10	Depends	—
TM83	Natural Gift	Normal	Physical	—	100	15	Normal	—
TM85	Dream Eater	Psychic	Special	100	100	15	Normal	—
TM87	Swagger	Normal	Status	—	90	15	Normal	—
TM90	Substitute	Normal	Status	—	—	10	Self	—
HM01	Cut	Normal	Physical	50	95	30	Normal	○
HM03	Surf	Water	Special	95	100	15	2 Foes/1 Ally	—
HM04	Strength	Normal	Physical	80	100	15	Normal	○
HM05	Whirlpool	Water	Special	15	70	15	Normal	—
HM06	Rock Smash	Fighting	Physical	40	100	15	Normal	○
HM08	Rock Climb	Normal	Physical	90	85	20	Normal	○

● EGG MOVES

Name	Type	Kind	Pow.	Acc.	PP	Range	DA
Belly Drum	Normal	Status	—	—	10	Self	—
Magnitude	Ground	Physical	—	100	30	2 Foes/1 Ally	—
Body Slam	Normal	Physical	85	100	15	Normal	○
Curse	???	Status	—	—	10	Normal/Self	—
SmellingSalt	Normal	Physical	60	100	10	Normal	○
Sleep Talk	Normal	Status	—	—	10	Depends	—
Snore	Normal	Special	40	100	15	Normal	—
Substitute	Normal	Status	—	—	10	Self	—
Amnesia	Psychic	Status	—	—	20	Self	—
Hammer Arm	Fighting	Physical	100	90	10	Normal	○
Muddy Water	Water	Special	95	85	10	2 Foes	—

● No. 108 | Licking Pokémon
Lickitung

Normal

● SIZE COMPARISON

● HEIGHT: 3'11"
● WEIGHT: 144.4 lbs.
● ITEMS: Lagging Tail

● MALE/FEMALE HAVE SAME FORM

● ABILITIES
● Own Tempo
● Oblivious

● STATS
HP ●●●
ATTACK ●●●
DEFENSE ●●●
SP. ATTACK ●●●
SP. DEFENSE ●●●
SPEED ●

● EGG GROUPS
Monster

● PERFORMANCE
SPEED ★★☆　　STAMINA ★★★★☆
POWER ★★★☆　JUMP ★★☆
SKILL ★★☆

● MAIN WAYS TO OBTAIN

Pokémon HeartGold Route 44

Pokémon SoulSilver Route 44

Pokémon Diamond Lake Valor (mass outbreak)

Pokémon Pearl Lake Valor (mass outbreak)

Pokémon Platinum Route 215

Pokémon HeartGold
Its tongue has well-developed nerves that run to the very tip, so it can be deftly manipulated.

Pokémon SoulSilver
Its long tongue, slathered with a gooey saliva, sticks to anything, so it is very useful.

● EVOLUTION

Lickitung → Lickilicky

Level it up to Lv. 33 and teach it Rollout. Or, level it up once it knows Rollout.

No. 109 | Poison Gas Pokémon
Koffing

Poison

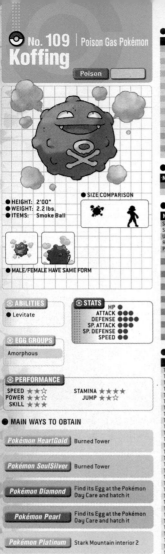

- **HEIGHT:** 2'00"
- **WEIGHT:** 2.2 lbs.
- **ITEMS:** Smoke Ball

● SIZE COMPARISON

● MALE/FEMALE HAVE SAME FORM

ABILITIES
- Levitate

STATS
HP ●
ATTACK ●●●
DEFENSE ●●●●
SP. ATTACK ●●●●
SP. DEFENSE ●●
SPEED ●●

EGG GROUPS
Amorphous

PERFORMANCE
SPEED ★★☆　　STAMINA ★★★★
POWER ★★☆　　JUMP ★★☆
SKILL ★★★

● MAIN WAYS TO OBTAIN

Pokémon HeartGold	Burned Tower
Pokémon SoulSilver	Burned Tower
Pokémon Diamond	Find its Egg at the Pokémon Day Care and hatch it
Pokémon Pearl	Find its Egg at the Pokémon Day Care and hatch it
Pokémon Platinum	Stark Mountain interior 2

Pokémon HeartGold
In total darkness, where nothing is visible, HAUNTER lurks, silently stalking its next victim.

Pokémon SoulSilver
The poisonous gases it contains are a little bit lighter than air, keeping it slightly airborne.

EVOLUTION

Koffing　→ Lv. 35 →　Weezing

● LEVEL-UP MOVES

Lv.	Name	Type	Kind	Pow.	Acc.	PP	Range	DA
1	Poison Gas	Poison	Status	—	55	40	Normal	—
1	Tackle	Normal	Physical	35	95	35	Normal	○
6	Smog	Poison	Special	20	70	20	Normal	—
10	SmokeScreen	Normal	Status	—	100	20	Normal	—
15	Assurance	Dark	Physical	50	100	10	Normal	○
19	Selfdestruct	Normal	Physical	200	100	5	2 Foes/1 Ally	—
24	Sludge	Poison	Special	65	100	20	Normal	—
28	Haze	Ice	Status	—	—	30	All	—
33	Gyro Ball	Steel	Physical	—	100	5	Normal	○
37	Explosion	Normal	Physical	250	100	5	2 Foes/1 Ally	—
42	Sludge Bomb	Poison	Special	90	100	10	Normal	—
46	Destiny Bond	Ghost	Status	—	—	5	Self	—
51	Memento	Dark	Status	—	100	10	Normal	—

● MOVE MANIAC

Name	Type	Kind	Pow.	Acc.	PP	Range	DA

● BP MOVES

Name	Type	Kind	Pow.	Acc.	PP	Range	DA
Snore	Normal	Special	40	100	15	Normal	—
Spite	Ghost	Status	—	100	10	Normal	—
Uproar	Normal	Special	50	100	10	1 Random	—
Rollout	Rock	Physical	30	90	20	Normal	○
Pain Split	Normal	Status	—	—	20	Normal	—

● TM & HM MOVES

No.	Name	Type	Kind	Pow.	Acc.	PP	Range	DA
TM06	Toxic	Poison	Status	—	85	10	Normal	—
TM10	Hidden Power	Normal	Special	—	100	15	Normal	—
TM11	Sunny Day	Fire	Status	—	—	5	All	—
TM12	Taunt	Dark	Status	—	100	20	Normal	—
TM17	Protect	Normal	Status	—	—	10	Self	—
TM18	Rain Dance	Water	Status	—	—	5	All	—
TM21	Frustration	Normal	Physical	70	100	20	Normal	○
TM24	Thunderbolt	Electric	Special	95	100	15	Normal	—
TM25	Thunder	Electric	Special	120	70	10	Normal	—
TM27	Return	Normal	Physical	—	100	20	Normal	○
TM30	Shadow Ball	Ghost	Special	80	100	15	Normal	—
TM32	Double Team	Normal	Status	—	—	15	Self	—
TM34	Shock Wave	Electric	Special	60	—	20	Normal	—
TM35	Flamethrower	Fire	Special	95	100	15	Normal	—
TM36	Sludge Bomb	Poison	Special	90	100	10	Normal	—
TM38	Fire Blast	Fire	Special	120	85	5	Normal	—
TM41	Torment	Dark	Status	—	100	15	Normal	—
TM42	Facade	Normal	Physical	70	100	20	Normal	○
TM43	Secret Power	Normal	Physical	70	100	20	Normal	○
TM44	Rest	Psychic	Status	—	—	10	Self	—
TM45	Attract	Normal	Status	—	100	15	Normal	—
TM46	Thief	Dark	Physical	40	100	10	Normal	○
TM58	Endure	Normal	Status	—	—	10	Self	—
TM61	Will-O-Wisp	Fire	Status	—	75	15	Normal	—
TM64	Explosion	Normal	Physical	250	100	5	2 Foes/1 Ally	—
TM66	Payback	Dark	Physical	50	100	10	Normal	○
TM70	Flash	Normal	Status	—	100	20	Normal	—
TM74	Gyro Ball	Steel	Physical	—	100	5	Normal	○
TM79	Dark Pulse	Dark	Special	80	100	15	Normal	—
TM82	Sleep Talk	Normal	Status	—	—	10	Depends	—
TM83	Natural Gift	Normal	Physical	—	100	15	Normal	—
TM87	Swagger	Normal	Status	—	90	15	Normal	—
TM90	Substitute	Normal	Status	—	—	10	Self	—

● EGG MOVES

Name	Type	Kind	Pow.	Acc.	PP	Range	DA
Screech	Normal	Status	—	85	40	Normal	—
Psywave	Psychic	Special	—	80	15	Normal	—
Psybeam	Psychic	Special	65	100	20	Normal	—
Destiny Bond	Ghost	Status	—	—	5	Self	—
Pain Split	Normal	Status	—	—	20	Normal	—
Will-O-Wisp	Fire	Status	—	75	15	Normal	—
Grudge	Ghost	Status	—	—	5	Self	—
Spite	Ghost	Status	—	100	10	Normal	—
Curse	???	Status	—	—	10	Normal/Self	—

● LEVEL-UP MOVES

Lv.	Name	Type	Kind	Pow.	Acc.	PP	Range	DA
1	Poison Gas	Poison	Status	—	55	40	Normal	—
1	Tackle	Normal	Physical	35	95	35	Normal	○
1	Smog	Poison	Special	20	70	20	Normal	—
1	SmokeScreen	Normal	Status	—	100	20	Normal	—
6	Smog	Poison	Special	20	70	20	Normal	—
10	SmokeScreen	Normal	Status	—	100	20	Normal	—
15	Assurance	Dark	Physical	50	100	10	Normal	○
19	Selfdestruct	Normal	Physical	200	100	5	2 Foes/1 Ally	—
24	Sludge	Poison	Special	65	100	20	Normal	—
28	Haze	Ice	Status	—	—	30	All	—
33	Double Hit	Normal	Physical	35	90	10	Normal	○
40	Explosion	Normal	Physical	250	100	5	2 Foes/1 Ally	—
48	Sludge Bomb	Poison	Special	90	100	10	Normal	—
55	Destiny Bond	Ghost	Status	—	—	5	Self	—
63	Memento	Dark	Status	—	100	10	Normal	—

● MOVE MANIAC

Name	Type	Kind	Pow.	Acc.	PP	Range	DA
—							—

● BP MOVES

Name	Type	Kind	Pow.	Acc.	PP	Range	DA
Snore	Normal	Special	40	100	15	Normal	—
Spite	Ghost	Status	—	100	10	Normal	—
Uproar	Normal	Special	50	100	10	1 Random	—
Rollout	Rock	Physical	30	90	20	Normal	○
Pain Split	Normal	Status	—	—	20	Normal	—

● TM & HM MOVES

No.	Name	Type	Kind	Pow.	Acc.	PP	Range	DA
TM06	Toxic	Poison	Status	—	85	10	Normal	—
TM10	Hidden Power	Normal	Special	—	100	15	Normal	—
TM11	Sunny Day	Fire	Status	—	—	5	All	—
TM12	Taunt	Dark	Status	—	100	20	Normal	—
TM15	Hyper Beam	Normal	Special	150	90	5	Normal	—
TM17	Protect	Normal	Status	—	—	10	Self	—
TM18	Rain Dance	Water	Status	—	—	5	All	—
TM21	Frustration	Normal	Physical	—	100	20	Normal	○
TM24	Thunderbolt	Electric	Special	95	100	15	Normal	—
TM25	Thunder	Electric	Special	120	70	10	Normal	—
TM27	Return	Normal	Physical	—	100	20	Normal	○
TM30	Shadow Ball	Ghost	Special	80	100	15	Normal	—
TM32	Double Team	Normal	Status	—	—	15	Self	—
TM34	Shock Wave	Electric	Special	60	—	20	Normal	—
TM35	Flamethrower	Fire	Special	95	100	15	Normal	—
TM36	Sludge Bomb	Poison	Special	90	100	10	Normal	—
TM38	Fire Blast	Fire	Special	120	85	5	Normal	—
TM41	Torment	Dark	Status	—	100	15	Normal	—
TM42	Facade	Normal	Physical	70	100	20	Normal	—
TM43	Secret Power	Normal	Physical	70	100	20	Normal	○
TM44	Rest	Psychic	Status	—	—	10	Self	—
TM45	Attract	Normal	Status	—	100	15	Normal	—
TM46	Thief	Dark	Physical	40	100	10	Normal	○
TM58	Endure	Normal	Status	—	—	10	Self	—
TM61	Will-O-Wisp	Fire	Status	—	75	15	Normal	—
TM64	Explosion	Normal	Physical	250	100	5	2 Foes/1 Ally	—
TM66	Payback	Dark	Physical	50	100	10	Normal	○
TM68	Giga Impact	Normal	Physical	150	90	5	Normal	—
TM70	Flash	Normal	Status	—	100	20	Normal	—
TM74	Gyro Ball	Steel	Physical	—	100	5	Normal	—
TM78	Captivate	Normal	Status	—	100	20	2 Foes	—
TM79	Dark Pulse	Dark	Special	80	100	15	Normal	—
TM82	Sleep Talk	Normal	Status	—	—	10	Depends	—
TM83	Natural Gift	Normal	Physical	—	100	15	Normal	—
TM87	Swagger	Normal	Status	—	90	15	Normal	—
TM90	Substitute	Normal	Status	—	—	10	Self	—

◉ No. 110 | Poison Gas Pokémon
Weezing

Poison

- ● HEIGHT: 3'11"
- ● WEIGHT: 20.9 lbs.
- ● ITEMS: Smoke Ball

● SIZE COMPARISON

● MALE/FEMALE HAVE SAME FORM

◎ ABILITIES
- ● Levitate

◎ STATS
HP ●●
ATTACK ●●●●
DEFENSE ●●●●●
SP. ATTACK ●●●●
SP. DEFENSE ●●●
SPEED ●●●

◎ EGG GROUPS
Amorphous

◎ PERFORMANCE
SPEED ★★	STAMINA ★★★★
POWER ★★★☆	JUMP ★★☆
SKILL ★★☆	

● MAIN WAYS TO OBTAIN

Pokémon HeartGold — Safari Zone (Marshland Area, morning and afternoon only)

Pokémon SoulSilver — Safari Zone (Marshland Area, morning and afternoon only)

Pokémon Diamond — Route 227

Pokémon Pearl — Route 227

Pokémon Platinum — Route 227

Pokémon HeartGold
If one of the twin KOFFING inflates, the other one deflates. It constantly mixes its poisonous gases.

Pokémon SoulSilver
Top-grade perfume is made using its internal poison gases by diluting them to the highest level.

◎ EVOLUTION

Lv. 35

Koffing → Weezing

No. 111 | Spikes Pokémon
Rhyhorn

`Ground` `Rock`

- **HEIGHT:** 3'03"
- **WEIGHT:** 253.5 lbs.
- **ITEMS:** None

● **SIZE COMPARISON**

● **MALE FORM**
Longer horn

● **FEMALE FORM**
Shorter horn

ABILITIES
- Lightningrod
- Rock Head

STATS
- HP ●●●○○
- ATTACK ●●●●○
- DEFENSE ●●●●○
- SP. ATTACK ●○○○○
- SP. DEFENSE ●●○○○
- SPEED ●○○○○

EGG GROUPS
Monster

Field

PERFORMANCE
- SPEED ★★☆☆☆
- POWER ★★★☆☆
- SKILL ★☆☆☆☆
- STAMINA ★★★☆
- JUMP ★★☆

MAIN WAYS TO OBTAIN

Pokémon HeartGold	Victory Road
Pokémon SoulSilver	Victory Road
Pokémon Diamond	Route 227
Pokémon Pearl	Route 227
Pokémon Platinum	Route 227

Pokémon HeartGold	Pokémon SoulSilver
It is inept at turning because of its four short legs. It can only charge and run in one direction.	It doesn't care if there is anything in its way. It just charges and destroys all obstacles.

EVOLUTION

Lv. 42

Have it hold Protector and trade it

Rhyhorn → Rhydon → Rhyperior

● LEVEL-UP MOVES

Lv.	Name	Type	Kind	Pow.	Acc.	PP	Range	DA
1	Horn Attack	Normal	Physical	65	100	25	Normal	○
1	Tail Whip	Normal	Status	—	100	30	2 Foes	—
9	Stomp	Normal	Physical	65	100	20	Normal	○
13	Fury Attack	Normal	Physical	15	85	20	Normal	○
21	Scary Face	Normal	Status	—	90	10	Normal	—
25	Rock Blast	Rock	Physical	25	80	10	Normal	—
33	Take Down	Normal	Physical	90	85	20	Normal	○
37	Horn Drill	Normal	Physical	—	30	5	Normal	—
45	Stone Edge	Rock	Physical	100	80	5	Normal	—
49	Earthquake	Ground	Physical	100	100	10	2 Foes/1 Ally	—
57	Megahorn	Bug	Physical	120	85	10	Normal	○

● MOVE MANIAC

Name	Type	Kind	Pow.	Acc.	PP	Range	DA
Headbutt	Normal	Physical	70	100	15	Normal	○

● BP MOVES

Name	Type	Kind	Pow.	Acc.	PP	Range	DA
Icy Wind	Ice	Special	55	95	15	2 Foes	—
Snore	Normal	Special	40	100	15	Normal	—
Spite	Ghost	Status	—	100	10	Normal	—
Uproar	Normal	Special	50	100	10	1 Random	—
Mud-Slap	Ground	Special	20	100	10	Normal	—
Rollout	Rock	Physical	30	90	20	Normal	○
Superpower	Fighting	Physical	120	100	5	Normal	○
Aqua Tail	Water	Physical	90	90	10	Normal	○
Endeavor	Normal	Physical	—	100	5	Normal	—
AncientPower	Rock	Special	60	100	5	Normal	—
Earth Power	Ground	Special	90	100	10	Normal	—

● TM & HM MOVES

No.	Name	Type	Kind	Pow.	Acc.	PP	Range	DA
TM05	Roar	Normal	Status	—	100	20	Normal	—
TM06	Toxic	Poison	Status	—	85	10	Normal	—
TM10	Hidden Power	Normal	Special	—	100	15	Normal	—
TM11	Sunny Day	Fire	Status	—	—	5	All	—
TM13	Ice Beam	Ice	Special	95	100	10	Normal	—
TM14	Blizzard	Ice	Special	120	70	5	2 Foes	—
TM17	Protect	Normal	Status	—	—	10	Self	—
TM18	Rain Dance	Water	Status	—	—	5	All	—
TM21	Frustration	Normal	Physical	—	100	20	Normal	○
TM23	Iron Tail	Steel	Physical	100	75	15	Normal	○
TM24	Thunderbolt	Electric	Special	95	100	15	Normal	—
TM25	Thunder	Electric	Special	120	70	10	Normal	—
TM26	Earthquake	Ground	Physical	100	100	10	2 Foes/1 Ally	—
TM27	Return	Normal	Physical	—	100	20	Normal	○
TM28	Dig	Ground	Physical	80	100	10	Normal	○
TM32	Double Team	Normal	Status	—	—	15	Self	—
TM34	Shock Wave	Electric	Special	60	—	20	Normal	—
TM35	Flamethrower	Fire	Special	95	100	15	Normal	—
TM37	Sandstorm	Rock	Status	—	—	10	All	—
TM38	Fire Blast	Fire	Special	120	85	5	Normal	—
TM39	Rock Tomb	Rock	Physical	50	80	10	Normal	○
TM42	Facade	Normal	Physical	70	100	20	Normal	○
TM43	Secret Power	Normal	Physical	70	100	20	Normal	○
TM44	Rest	Psychic	Status	—	—	10	Self	—
TM45	Attract	Normal	Status	—	100	15	Normal	—
TM46	Thief	Dark	Physical	40	100	10	Normal	○
TM58	Endure	Normal	Status	—	—	10	Self	—
TM59	Dragon Pulse	Dragon	Special	90	100	10	Normal	—
TM66	Payback	Dark	Physical	50	100	10	Normal	○
TM69	Rock Polish	Rock	Status	—	—	20	Self	—
TM71	Stone Edge	Rock	Physical	100	80	5	Normal	—
TM75	Swords Dance	Normal	Status	—	—	30	Self	—
TM76	Stealth Rock	Rock	Status	—	—	20	2 Foes	—
TM78	Captivate	Normal	Status	—	100	20	2 Foes	—
TM80	Rock Slide	Rock	Physical	75	90	10	2 Foes	—
TM82	Sleep Talk	Normal	Status	—	—	10	Depends	—
TM83	Natural Gift	Normal	Physical	—	100	15	Normal	—
TM84	Poison Jab	Poison	Physical	80	100	20	Normal	○
TM87	Swagger	Normal	Status	—	90	15	Normal	—
TM90	Substitute	Normal	Status	—	—	10	Self	—
HM04	Strength	Normal	Physical	80	100	15	Normal	○
HM06	Rock Smash	Fighting	Physical	40	100	15	Normal	○
HM08	Rock Climb	Normal	Physical	90	85	20	Normal	○

● EGG MOVES

Name	Type	Kind	Pow.	Acc.	PP	Range	DA
Crunch	Dark	Physical	80	100	15	Normal	○
Reversal	Fighting	Physical	—	100	15	Normal	○
Rock Slide	Rock	Physical	75	90	10	2 Foes	—
Counter	Fighting	Physical	—	100	20	Self	—
Magnitude	Ground	Physical	—	100	30	2 Foes/1 Ally	—
Swords Dance	Normal	Status	—	—	30	Self	—
Curse	???	Status	—	—	10	Normal/Self	—
Crush Claw	Normal	Physical	75	95	10	Normal	○
Dragon Rush	Dragon	Physical	100	75	10	Normal	○
Ice Fang	Ice	Physical	65	95	15	Normal	○
Fire Fang	Fire	Physical	65	95	15	Normal	○
Thunder Fang	Electric	Physical	65	95	15	Normal	○
Skull Bash	Normal	Physical	100	100	15	Normal	○

LEVEL-UP MOVES

Lv.	Name	Type	Kind	Pow.	Acc.	PP	Range	DA
1	Horn Attack	Normal	Physical	65	100	25	Normal	○
1	Tail Whip	Normal	Status	—	100	30	2 Foes	○
1	Stomp	Normal	Physical	65	100	20	Normal	○
1	Fury Attack	Normal	Physical	15	85	20	Normal	○
9	Stomp	Normal	Physical	65	100	20	Normal	○
13	Fury Attack	Normal	Physical	15	85	20	Normal	○
21	Scary Face	Normal	Status	—	90	10	Normal	—
25	Rock Blast	Rock	Physical	25	80	10	Normal	—
33	Take Down	Normal	Physical	90	85	20	Normal	○
37	Horn Drill	Normal	Physical	—	30	5	Normal	○
42	Hammer Arm	Fighting	Physical	100	90	10	Normal	○
45	Stone Edge	Rock	Physical	100	80	5	Normal	—
49	Earthquake	Ground	Physical	100	100	10	2 Foes/1 Ally	—
57	Megahorn	Bug	Physical	120	85	10	Normal	○

MOVE MANIAC

Name	Type	Kind	Pow.	Acc.	PP	Range	DA
Headbutt	Normal	Physical	70	100	15	Normal	○

BP MOVES

Name	Type	Kind	Pow.	Acc.	PP	Range	DA
Fury Cutter	Bug	Physical	10	95	20	Normal	—
Icy Wind	Ice	Special	55	95	15	2 Foes	—
ThunderPunch	Electric	Physical	75	100	15	Normal	○
Fire Punch	Fire	Physical	75	100	15	Normal	○
Ice Punch	Ice	Physical	75	100	15	Normal	○
Snore	Normal	Special	40	100	15	Normal	—
Spite	Ghost	Status	—	100	10	Normal	—
Uproar	Normal	Special	50	100	10	1 Random	—
Block	Normal	Status	—	—	5	Normal	—
Mud-Slap	Ground	Special	20	100	10	Normal	—
Rollout	Rock	Physical	30	90	20	Normal	○
Superpower	Fighting	Physical	120	100	5	Normal	○
Aqua Tail	Water	Physical	90	90	10	Normal	○
Endeavor	Normal	Physical	—	100	5	Normal	○
Outrage	Dragon	Physical	120	100	15	1 Random	○
AncientPower	Rock	Special	60	100	5	Normal	—
Earth Power	Ground	Special	90	100	10	Normal	—

TM & HM MOVES

No.	Name	Type	Kind	Pow.	Acc.	PP	Range	DA
TM01	Focus Punch	Fighting	Physical	150	100	20	Normal	○
TM05	Roar	Normal	Status	—	100	20	Normal	—
TM06	Toxic	Poison	Status	—	85	10	Normal	—
TM10	Hidden Power	Normal	Special	—	100	15	Normal	—
TM11	Sunny Day	Fire	Status	—	—	5	All	—
TM13	Ice Beam	Ice	Special	95	100	10	Normal	—
TM14	Blizzard	Ice	Special	120	70	5	2 Foes	—
TM15	Hyper Beam	Normal	Special	150	90	5	Normal	—
TM17	Protect	Normal	Status	—	—	10	Self	—
TM18	Rain Dance	Water	Status	—	—	5	All	—
TM21	Frustration	Normal	Physical	—	100	20	Normal	○
TM23	Iron Tail	Steel	Physical	100	75	15	Normal	○
TM24	Thunderbolt	Electric	Special	95	100	15	Normal	—
TM25	Thunder	Electric	Special	120	70	10	Normal	—
TM26	Earthquake	Ground	Physical	100	100	10	2 Foes/1 Ally	—
TM27	Return	Normal	Physical	—	100	20	Normal	○
TM28	Dig	Ground	Physical	80	100	10	Normal	○
TM31	Brick Break	Fighting	Physical	75	100	15	Normal	○
TM32	Double Team	Normal	Status	—	—	15	Self	—
TM34	Shock Wave	Electric	Special	60	—	20	Normal	—
TM35	Flamethrower	Fire	Special	95	100	15	Normal	—
TM37	Sandstorm	Rock	Status	—	—	10	All	—
TM38	Fire Blast	Fire	Special	120	85	5	Normal	—
TM39	Rock Tomb	Rock	Physical	50	80	10	Normal	○
TM42	Facade	Normal	Physical	70	100	20	Normal	○
TM43	Secret Power	Normal	Physical	70	100	20	Normal	○
TM44	Rest	Psychic	Status	—	—	10	Self	—
TM45	Attract	Normal	Status	—	100	15	Normal	—
TM46	Thief	Dark	Physical	40	100	10	Normal	○
TM52	Focus Blast	Fighting	Special	120	70	5	Normal	—
TM56	Fling	Dark	Physical	—	100	10	Normal	○
TM58	Endure	Normal	Status	—	—	10	Self	—
TM59	Dragon Pulse	Dragon	Special	90	100	10	Normal	—
TM65	Shadow Claw	Ghost	Physical	70	100	15	Normal	○
TM66	Payback	Dark	Physical	50	100	10	Normal	○
TM68	Giga Impact	Normal	Physical	150	90	5	Normal	○
TM69	Rock Polish	Rock	Status	—	—	20	Self	—
TM71	Stone Edge	Rock	Physical	100	80	5	Normal	—
TM72	Avalanche	Ice	Physical	60	100	10	Normal	○
TM75	Swords Dance	Normal	Status	—	—	30	Self	—
TM76	Stealth Rock	Rock	Status	—	—	20	2 Foes	—
TM78	Captivate	Normal	Status	—	100	20	2 Foes	—
TM80	Rock Slide	Rock	Physical	75	90	10	2 Foes	—
TM82	Sleep Talk	Normal	Status	—	—	10	Depends	—
TM83	Natural Gift	Normal	Physical	—	100	15	Normal	—
TM84	Poison Jab	Poison	Physical	80	100	20	Normal	○
TM87	Swagger	Normal	Status	—	90	15	Normal	—
TM90	Substitute	Normal	Status	—	—	10	Self	—
HM01	Cut	Normal	Physical	50	95	30	Normal	○
HM03	Surf	Water	Special	95	100	15	2 Foes/1 Ally	—
HM04	Strength	Normal	Physical	80	100	15	Normal	○
HM05	Whirlpool	Water	Special	15	70	15	Normal	—
HM06	Rock Smash	Fighting	Physical	40	100	15	Normal	○
HM08	Rock Climb	Normal	Physical	90	85	20	Normal	○

● No. 112 | Drill Pokémon
Rhydon

`Ground` `Rock`

● HEIGHT: 6'03"
● WEIGHT: 264.6 lbs.
● ITEMS: None

● SIZE COMPARISON

● MALE FORM
Longer horn

● FEMALE FORM
Shorter horn

⊙ ABILITIES
● Lightningrod
● Rock Head

⊙ STATS
HP ●●●●
ATTACK ●●●●●
DEFENSE ●●●●●
SP. ATTACK ●●
SP. DEFENSE ●●
SPEED ●●

⊙ EGG GROUPS
Monster
Field

⊙ PERFORMANCE

SPEED ★★
POWER ★★★★☆
SKILL ★★☆

STAMINA ★★★★☆
JUMP ★★☆

● MAIN WAYS TO OBTAIN

Pokémon HeartGold	Safari Zone (Savannah Area): if Rock objects are placed, may appear in tall grass)
Pokémon SoulSilver	Safari Zone (Savannah Area): if Rock objects are placed, may appear in tall grass)
Pokémon Diamond	Route 227
Pokémon Pearl	Route 227
Pokémon Platinum	Victory Road 1F

Pokémon HeartGold
Its rugged hide protects it from even the heat of lava. However, the hide also makes it insensitive.

Pokémon SoulSilver
Its brain developed when it began walking on hind legs. Its thick hide protects it even in magma.

⊙ EVOLUTION

Rhyhorn → (Lv. 42) → Rhydon → (Have it hold Protector and trade it) → Rhyperior

No. 113 | Egg Pokémon
Chansey

Normal

- **HEIGHT:** 3'07"
- **WEIGHT:** 76.3 lbs.
- **ITEMS:** Oval Stone
  Lucky Egg

● SIZE COMPARISON

● FEMALE FORM

● LEVEL-UP MOVES

Lv.	Name	Type	Kind	Pow.	Acc.	PP	Range	DA
1	Pound	Normal	Physical	40	100	35	Normal	○
1	Growl	Normal	Status	—	100	40	2 Foes	—
5	Tail Whip	Normal	Status	—	100	30	2 Foes	—
9	Refresh	Normal	Status	—	—	20	Self	—
12	Softboiled	Normal	Status	—	—	10	Self	—
16	DoubleSlap	Normal	Physical	15	85	10	Normal	○
20	Minimize	Normal	Status	—	—	20	Self	—
23	Sing	Normal	Status	—	55	15	Normal	—
27	Fling	Dark	Physical	—	100	10	Normal	—
31	Defense Curl	Normal	Status	—	—	40	Self	—
34	Light Screen	Psychic	Status	—	—	30	2 Allies	—
38	Egg Bomb	Normal	Physical	100	75	10	Normal	○
42	Healing Wish	Psychic	Status	—	—	10	Self	—
46	Double-Edge	Normal	Physical	120	100	15	Normal	○

● MOVE MANIAC

Name	Type	Kind	Pow.	Acc.	PP	Range	DA
Headbutt	Normal	Physical	70	100	15	Normal	○

● BP MOVES

Name	Type	Kind	Pow.	Acc.	PP	Range	DA
Icy Wind	Ice	Special	55	95	15	2 Foes	—
ThunderPunch	Electric	Physical	75	100	15	Normal	○
Fire Punch	Fire	Physical	75	100	15	Normal	○
Ice Punch	Ice	Physical	75	100	15	Normal	○
Zen Headbutt	Psychic	Physical	80	90	15	Normal	○
Snore	Normal	Special	40	100	15	Normal	—
Helping Hand	Normal	Status	—	—	20	1 Ally	—
Last Resort	Normal	Physical	130	100	5	Normal	○
Gravity	Psychic	Status	—	—	5	All	—
Heal Bell	Normal	Status	—	—	5	All Allies	—
Mud-Slap	Ground	Special	20	100	10	Normal	○
Rollout	Rock	Physical	30	90	20	Normal	○
Endeavor	Normal	Physical	—	100	5	Normal	—

⊘ ABILITIES

- Natural Cure
- Serene Grace

⊘ STATS

HP	●●●●●●
ATTACK	●
DEFENSE	●
SP. ATTACK	●
SP. DEFENSE	●●●●
SPEED	●●

⊘ EGG GROUPS

Fairy

⊘ PERFORMANCE

SPEED ★★☆	STAMINA ★★★★★
POWER ★☆☆☆	JUMP ★★★
SKILL ★☆☆☆	

Pokémon HeartGold
Route 13 or level up Happiny while it holds the Oval Stone between 4:00 A.M. and 8:00 P.M.

Pokémon SoulSilver
Route 13 or level up Happiny while it holds the Oval Stone between 4:00 A.M. and 8:00 P.M.

Pokémon Diamond
Route 13 or level up Happiny while it holds the Oval Stone between 4:00 A.M. and 8:00 P.M.

Pokémon Pearl
Route 13 or level up Happiny while it holds the Oval Stone between 4:00 A.M. and 8:00 P.M.

Pokémon Platinum
Route 13 or level up Happiny while it holds the Oval Stone between 4:00 A.M. and 8:00 P.M.

Pokémon HeartGold
It walks carefully to prevent its egg from breaking. However, it is extremely fast at running away.

Pokémon SoulSilver
Being few in number and difficult to capture, it is said to bring happiness to the Trainer who catches it.

⊘ EVOLUTION

Happiny → Have it hold Oval Stone and then level it up between 4:00 A.M. and 8:00 P.M. → Chansey → Level up with high friendship → Blissey

● TM & HM MOVES

No.	Name	Type	Kind	Pow.	Acc.	PP	Range	DA
TM01	Focus Punch	Fighting	Physical	150	100	20	Normal	○
TM03	Water Pulse	Water	Special	60	100	20	Normal	—
TM04	Calm Mind	Psychic	Status	—	—	20	Self	—
TM06	Toxic	Poison	Status	—	85	10	Normal	—
TM07	Hail	Ice	Status	—	—	10	All	—
TM10	Hidden Power	Normal	Special	—	100	15	Normal	—
TM11	Sunny Day	Fire	Status	—	—	5	All	—
TM13	Ice Beam	Ice	Special	95	100	10	Normal	—
TM14	Blizzard	Ice	Special	120	70	5	2 Foes	—
TM15	Hyper Beam	Normal	Special	150	90	5	Normal	—
TM16	Light Screen	Psychic	Status	—	—	30	2 Allies	—
TM17	Protect	Normal	Status	—	—	10	Self	—
TM18	Rain Dance	Water	Status	—	—	5	All	—
TM20	Safeguard	Normal	Status	—	—	25	2 Allies	—
TM21	Frustration	Normal	Physical	—	100	20	Normal	○
TM22	SolarBeam	Grass	Special	120	100	10	Normal	—
TM23	Iron Tail	Steel	Physical	100	75	15	Normal	○
TM24	Thunderbolt	Electric	Special	95	100	15	Normal	—
TM25	Thunder	Electric	Special	120	70	10	Normal	—
TM26	Earthquake	Ground	Physical	100	100	10	2 Foes & 1 Ally	—
TM27	Return	Normal	Physical	—	100	20	Normal	○
TM29	Psychic	Psychic	Special	90	100	10	Normal	—
TM30	Shadow Ball	Ghost	Special	80	100	15	Normal	—
TM31	Brick Break	Fighting	Physical	75	100	15	Normal	○
TM32	Double Team	Normal	Status	—	—	15	Self	—
TM34	Shock Wave	Electric	Special	60	—	20	Normal	—
TM35	Flamethrower	Fire	Special	95	100	15	Normal	—
TM37	Sandstorm	Normal	Status	—	—	10	All	—
TM38	Fire Blast	Fire	Special	120	85	5	Normal	—
TM39	Rock Tomb	Rock	Physical	50	80	10	Normal	○
TM42	Facade	Normal	Physical	70	100	20	Normal	○
TM43	Secret Power	Normal	Physical	70	100	20	Normal	○
TM44	Rest	Psychic	Status	—	—	10	Self	—
TM45	Attract	Normal	Status	—	100	15	Normal	—
TM48	Skill Swap	Psychic	Status	—	—	10	Normal	—
TM49	Snatch	Dark	Status	—	—	10	Depends	—
TM56	Fling	Dark	Physical	—	100	10	Normal	—
TM57	Charge Beam	Electric	Special	50	90	10	Normal	—
TM58	Endure	Normal	Status	—	—	10	Self	—
TM60	Drain Punch	Fighting	Physical	60	100	5	Normal	○
TM67	Recycle	Normal	Status	—	—	10	Self	—
TM68	Giga Impact	Normal	Physical	150	90	5	Normal	○
TM70	Flash	Normal	Status	—	100	20	Normal	—
TM73	Thunder Wave	Electric	Status	—	100	20	Normal	—
TM76	Stealth Rock	Rock	Status	—	—	20	2 Foes	—
TM77	Psych Up	Normal	Status	—	—	10	Normal	—
TM78	Captivate	Normal	Status	—	100	20	2 Foes	—
TM80	Rock Slide	Rock	Physical	75	90	10	2 Foes	○
TM82	Sleep Talk	Normal	Status	—	—	10	Depends	—
TM83	Natural Gift	Normal	Physical	—	100	15	Normal	—
TM85	Dream Eater	Psychic	Special	100	100	15	Normal	—
TM86	Grass Knot	Grass	Special	—	100	20	Normal	○
TM87	Swagger	Normal	Status	—	90	15	Normal	—
TM90	Substitute	Normal	Status	—	—	10	Self	—
HM04	Strength	Normal	Physical	80	100	15	Normal	○
HM06	Rock Smash	Fighting	Physical	40	100	15	Normal	○
HM08	Rock Climb	Normal	Physical	90	85	20	Normal	○

● EGG MOVES

Name	Type	Kind	Pow.	Acc.	PP	Range	DA
Present	Normal	Physical	—	90	15	Normal	—
Metronome	Normal	Status	—	—	10	Depends	—
Heal Bell	Normal	Status	—	—	5	All Allies	—
Aromatherapy	Grass	Status	—	—	5	All Allies	—
Substitute	Normal	Status	—	—	10	Self	—
Counter	Fighting	Physical	—	100	20	Normal	○
Helping Hand	Normal	Status	—	—	20	1 Ally	—
Gravity	Psychic	Status	—	—	5	All	—
Mud Bomb	Ground	Special	65	85	10	Normal	—

● LEVEL-UP MOVES

Lv.	Name	Type	Kind	Pow.	Acc.	PP	Range	DA
1	Ingrain	Grass	Status	—	—	20	Self	—
1	Constrict	Normal	Physical	10	100	35	Normal	○
5	Sleep Powder	Grass	Status	—	75	15	Normal	—
8	Absorb	Grass	Special	20	100	25	Normal	—
12	Growth	Normal	Status	—	—	40	Self	—
15	PoisonPowder	Poison	Status	—	75	35	Normal	—
19	Vine Whip	Grass	Physical	35	100	15	Normal	○
22	Bind	Normal	Physical	15	75	20	Normal	○
26	Mega Drain	Grass	Special	40	100	15	Normal	—
29	Stun Spore	Grass	Status	—	75	30	Normal	—
33	AncientPower	Rock	Special	60	100	5	Normal	—
36	Knock Off	Dark	Physical	20	100	20	Normal	○
40	Natural Gift	Normal	Physical	—	100	15	Normal	—
43	Slam	Normal	Physical	80	75	20	Normal	○
47	Tickle	Normal	Status	—	100	20	Normal	—
50	Wring Out	Normal	Special	—	100	5	Normal	○
54	Power Whip	Grass	Physical	120	85	10	Normal	○

● MOVE MANIAC

Name	Type	Kind	Pow.	Acc.	PP	Range	DA
Headbutt	Normal	Physical	70	100	15	Normal	—

● BP MOVES

Name	Type	Kind	Pow.	Acc.	PP	Range	DA
Knock Off	Dark	Physical	20	100	20	Normal	○
Snore	Normal	Special	40	100	15	Normal	—
Synthesis	Grass	Status	—	—	5	Self	—
Worry Seed	Grass	Status	—	100	10	Normal	—
AncientPower	Rock	Special	60	100	5	Normal	—
Seed Bomb	Grass	Physical	80	100	15	Normal	—
Pain Split	Normal	Status	—	—	20	Normal	—

● TM & HM MOVES

No.	Name	Type	Kind	Pow.	Acc.	PP	Range	DA
TM06	Toxic	Poison	Status	—	85	10	Normal	—
TM09	Bullet Seed	Grass	Physical	10	100	30	Normal	—
TM10	Hidden Power	Normal	Special	—	100	15	Normal	—
TM11	Sunny Day	Fire	Status	—	—	5	All	—
TM15	Hyper Beam	Normal	Special	150	90	5	Normal	—
TM17	Protect	Normal	Status	—	—	10	Self	—
TM19	Giga Drain	Grass	Special	60	100	10	Normal	—
TM21	Frustration	Normal	Physical	—	100	20	Normal	○
TM22	SolarBeam	Grass	Special	120	100	10	Normal	—
TM27	Return	Normal	Physical	—	100	20	Normal	○
TM32	Double Team	Normal	Status	—	—	15	Self	—
TM33	Reflect	Psychic	Status	—	—	20	2 Allies	—
TM34	Shock Wave	Electric	Special	60	—	20	Normal	—
TM36	Sludge Bomb	Poison	Special	90	100	10	Normal	—
TM42	Facade	Normal	Physical	70	100	20	Normal	○
TM43	Secret Power	Normal	Physical	70	100	20	Normal	—
TM44	Rest	Psychic	Status	—	—	10	Self	—
TM45	Attract	Normal	Status	—	100	15	Normal	—
TM46	Thief	Dark	Physical	40	100	10	Normal	○
TM53	Energy Ball	Grass	Special	80	100	10	Normal	—
TM58	Endure	Normal	Status	—	—	10	Self	—
TM68	Giga Impact	Normal	Physical	150	90	5	Normal	○
TM70	Flash	Normal	Status	—	100	20	Normal	—
TM75	Swords Dance	Normal	Status	—	—	30	Self	—
TM77	Psych Up	Normal	Status	—	—	10	Self	—
TM78	Captivate	Normal	Status	—	100	20	2 Foes	—
TM82	Sleep Talk	Normal	Status	—	—	10	Depends	—
TM83	Natural Gift	Normal	Physical	—	100	15	Normal	—
TM86	Grass Knot	Grass	Special	—	100	20	Normal	○
TM87	Swagger	Normal	Status	—	90	15	Normal	—
TM90	Substitute	Normal	Status	—	—	10	Self	—
HM01	Cut	Normal	Physical	50	95	30	Normal	○
HM06	Rock Smash	Fighting	Physical	40	100	15	Normal	—

● EGG MOVES

Name	Type	Kind	Pow.	Acc.	PP	Range	DA
Flail	Normal	Physical	—	100	15	Normal	○
Confusion	Psychic	Special	50	100	25	Normal	—
Mega Drain	Grass	Special	40	100	15	Normal	—
Reflect	Psychic	Status	—	—	20	2 Allies	—
Amnesia	Psychic	Status	—	—	20	Self	—
Leech Seed	Grass	Status	—	90	10	Normal	—
Nature Power	Normal	Status	—	—	20	Depends	—
Endeavor	Normal	Physical	—	100	5	Normal	○
Leaf Storm	Grass	Special	140	90	5	Normal	—
Power Swap	Psychic	Status	—	—	10	Normal	—

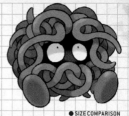

☉ No. 114 | Vine Pokémon
Tangela

Grass

- **HEIGHT:** 3'03"
- **WEIGHT:** 77.2 lbs.
- **ITEMS:** None

● SIZE COMPARISON

● MALE/FEMALE HAVE SAME FORM

⊘ ABILITIES
- Chlorophyll
- Leaf Guard

⊘ STATS
HP	●●
ATTACK	●●
DEFENSE	●●●●●
SP. ATTACK	●●●●
SP. DEFENSE	●
SPEED	●●●

⊘ EGG GROUPS
Grass

⊘ PERFORMANCE
SPEED ★★☆	STAMINA ★★★☆
POWER ★★☆	JUMP ★★☆
SKILL ★★★★	

● MAIN WAYS TO OBTAIN

Pokémon HeartGold — Route 44

Pokémon SoulSilver — Route 44

Pokémon Diamond — —

Pokémon Pearl — —

Pokémon Platinum — Pastoria Great Marsh

Pokémon HeartGold
The vines that cloak its entire body are always jiggling. They effectively unnerve its foes.

Pokémon SoulSilver
It tangles any moving thing with its vines. Their subtle shaking is ticklish if you get ensnared.

⊘ EVOLUTION

Tangela — Tangrowth

Level it up to Lv. 33 and teach it AncientPower. Or, level it up once it knows AncientPower.

No. 115 | Parent Pokémon
Kangaskhan

Normal

- **HEIGHT:** 7'03"
- **WEIGHT:** 176.4 lbs.
- **ITEMS:** None

● SIZE COMPARISON

● FEMALE FORM

ABILITIES
- Early Bird
- Scrappy

STATS
HP	●●●●
ATTACK	●●●●
DEFENSE	●●●●
SP. ATTACK	●●●
SP. DEFENSE	●●●
SPEED	●●●●

EGG GROUPS
Monster

PERFORMANCE
SPEED ★★★☆☆	STAMINA ★★★☆☆
POWER ★★★☆☆	JUMP ★★
SKILL ★★★☆☆	

● MAIN WAYS TO OBTAIN

Pokémon HeartGold	Safari Zone (Wasteland Area, morning and afternoon only)
Pokémon SoulSilver	Safari Zone (Wasteland Area, morning and afternoon only)
Pokémon Diamond	Pastoria Great Marsh (after obtaining the National Pokédex / changes daily)
Pokémon Pearl	Pastoria Great Marsh (after obtaining the National Pokédex / changes daily)
Pokémon Platinum	Pastoria Great Marsh (after obtaining the National Pokédex / changes daily)

Pokémon HeartGold	**Pokémon SoulSilver**
If it is safe, the young gets out of the belly pouch to play. The adult keeps a close eye on the youngster.	To protect its young, it will never give up during battle, no matter how badly wounded it is.

EVOLUTION
Does not evolve

● LEVEL-UP MOVES
Lv.	Name	Type	Kind	Pow.	Acc.	PP	Range	DA
1	Comet Punch	Normal	Physical	18	85	15	Normal	○
1	Leer	Normal	Status	—	100	30	2 Foes	—
7	Fake Out	Normal	Physical	40	100	10	Normal	○
10	Tail Whip	Normal	Status	—	100	30	2 Foes	—
13	Bite	Dark	Physical	60	100	25	Normal	○
19	Mega Punch	Normal	Physical	80	85	20	Normal	○
22	Rage	Normal	Physical	20	100	20	Normal	○
25	Dizzy Punch	Normal	Physical	70	100	10	Normal	○
31	Crunch	Dark	Physical	80	100	15	Normal	○
34	Endure	Normal	Status	—	—	10	Self	—
37	Outrage	Dragon	Physical	120	100	15	1 Random	○
43	Double Hit	Normal	Physical	35	90	10	Normal	○
46	Sucker Punch	Dark	Physical	80	100	5	Normal	○
49	Reversal	Fighting	Physical	—	100	15	Normal	○

● MOVE MANIAC
Name	Type	Kind	Pow.	Acc.	PP	Range	DA
Headbutt	Normal	Physical	70	100	15	Normal	○

● BP MOVES
Name	Type	Kind	Pow.	Acc.	PP	Range	DA
Fury Cutter	Bug	Physical	10	95	20	Normal	○
Icy Wind	Ice	Special	55	95	15	2 Foes	—
ThunderPunch	Electric	Physical	75	100	15	Normal	○
Fire Punch	Fire	Physical	75	100	15	Normal	○
Ice Punch	Ice	Physical	75	100	15	Normal	○
Sucker Punch	Dark	Physical	80	100	5	Normal	○
Snore	Normal	Special	40	100	15	Normal	—
Spite	Ghost	Status	—	100	10	Normal	—
Helping Hand	Normal	Status	—	—	20	1 Ally	—
Uproar	Normal	Special	50	100	10	1 Random	—
Mud-Slap	Ground	Special	20	100	10	Normal	—
Aqua Tail	Water	Physical	90	90	10	Normal	○
Endeavor	Normal	Physical	—	100	5	Normal	○
Outrage	Dragon	Physical	120	100	15	1 Random	○
Low Kick	Fighting	Physical	—	100	20	Normal	○

● TM & HM MOVES
No.	Name	Type	Kind	Pow.	Acc.	PP	Range	DA
TM01	Focus Punch	Fighting	Physical	150	100	20	Normal	○
TM03	Water Pulse	Water	Special	60	100	20	Normal	—
TM05	Roar	Normal	Status	—	100	20	Normal	—
TM06	Toxic	Poison	Status	—	85	10	Normal	—
TM07	Hail	Ice	Status	—	—	10	All	—
TM10	Hidden Power	Normal	Special	—	100	15	Normal	—
TM11	Sunny Day	Fire	Status	—	—	5	All	—
TM13	Ice Beam	Ice	Special	95	100	10	Normal	—
TM14	Blizzard	Ice	Special	120	70	5	2 Foes	—
TM15	Hyper Beam	Normal	Special	150	90	5	Normal	—
TM17	Protect	Normal	Status	—	—	10	Self	—
TM18	Rain Dance	Water	Status	—	—	5	All	—
TM21	Frustration	Normal	Physical	—	100	20	Normal	○
TM22	SolarBeam	Grass	Special	120	100	10	Normal	—
TM23	Iron Tail	Steel	Physical	100	75	15	Normal	○
TM24	Thunderbolt	Electric	Special	95	100	15	Normal	—
TM25	Thunder	Electric	Special	120	70	10	Normal	—
TM26	Earthquake	Ground	Physical	100	100	10	2 Foes/1 Ally	○
TM27	Return	Normal	Physical	—	100	20	Normal	○
TM28	Dig	Ground	Physical	80	100	10	Normal	○
TM30	Shadow Ball	Ghost	Special	80	100	15	Normal	—
TM31	Brick Break	Fighting	Physical	75	100	15	Normal	○
TM32	Double Team	Normal	Status	—	—	15	Self	—
TM34	Shock Wave	Electric	Special	60	—	20	Normal	—
TM35	Flamethrower	Fire	Special	95	100	15	Normal	—
TM37	Sandstorm	Rock	Status	—	—	10	All	—
TM38	Fire Blast	Fire	Special	120	85	5	Normal	—
TM39	Rock Tomb	Rock	Physical	50	80	10	Normal	○
TM40	Aerial Ace	Flying	Physical	60	—	20	Normal	○
TM42	Facade	Normal	Physical	70	100	20	Normal	○
TM43	Secret Power	Normal	Physical	70	100	20	Normal	○
TM44	Rest	Psychic	Status	—	—	10	Self	—
TM45	Attract	Normal	Status	—	100	15	Normal	—
TM46	Thief	Dark	Physical	40	100	10	Normal	○
TM52	Focus Blast	Fighting	Special	120	70	5	Normal	—
TM56	Fling	Dark	Physical	—	100	10	Normal	○
TM58	Endure	Normal	Status	—	—	10	Self	—
TM60	Drain Punch	Fighting	Physical	60	100	5	Normal	○
TM65	Shadow Claw	Ghost	Physical	70	100	15	Normal	○
TM68	Giga Impact	Normal	Physical	150	90	5	Normal	○
TM72	Avalanche	Ice	Physical	60	100	10	Normal	○
TM78	Captivate	Normal	Status	—	100	20	2 Foes	—
TM80	Rock Slide	Rock	Physical	75	90	10	2 Foes	○
TM82	Sleep Talk	Normal	Status	—	—	10	Depends	—
TM83	Natural Gift	Normal	Physical	—	100	15	Normal	○
TM87	Swagger	Normal	Status	—	90	15	Normal	—
TM90	Substitute	Normal	Status	—	—	10	Self	—
HM01	Cut	Normal	Physical	50	95	30	Normal	○
HM03	Surf	Water	Special	95	100	15	2 Foes/1 Ally	—
HM04	Strength	Normal	Physical	80	100	15	Normal	○
HM05	Whirlpool	Water	Special	15	70	15	Normal	—
HM06	Rock Smash	Fighting	Physical	40	100	15	Normal	○
HM08	Rock Climb	Normal	Physical	90	85	20	Normal	○

● EGG MOVES
Name	Type	Kind	Pow.	Acc.	PP	Range	DA
Stomp	Normal	Physical	65	100	20	Normal	○
Foresight	Normal	Status	—	—	40	Normal	—
Focus Energy	Normal	Status	—	—	30	Self	—
Safeguard	Normal	Status	—	—	25	2 Allies	—
Disable	Normal	Status	—	80	20	Normal	—
Counter	Fighting	Physical	—	100	20	Self	○
Crush Claw	Normal	Physical	75	95	10	Normal	○
Substitute	Normal	Status	—	—	10	Self	—
Double-Edge	Normal	Physical	120	100	15	Normal	○
Endeavor	Normal	Physical	—	100	5	Normal	○
Hammer Arm	Fighting	Physical	100	90	10	Normal	○

● LEVEL-UP MOVES

Lv.	Name	Type	Kind	Pow.	Acc.	PP	Range	DA
1	Bubble	Water	Special	20	100	30	2 Foes	—
4	SmokeScreen	Normal	Status	—	100	20	Normal	—
8	Leer	Normal	Status	—	100	30	2 Foes	—
11	Water Gun	Water	Special	40	100	25	Normal	—
14	Focus Energy	Normal	Status	—	—	30	Self	—
18	BubbleBeam	Water	Special	65	100	20	Normal	—
23	Agility	Psychic	Status	—	—	30	Self	—
26	Twister	Dragon	Special	40	100	20	2 Foes	—
30	Brine	Water	Special	65	100	10	Normal	—
35	Hydro Pump	Water	Special	120	80	5	Normal	—
38	Dragon Dance	Dragon	Status	—	—	20	Self	—
42	Dragon Pulse	Dragon	Special	90	100	10	Normal	—

● MOVE MANIAC

Name	Type	Kind	Pow.	Acc.	PP	Range	DA
Headbutt	Normal	Physical	70	100	15	Normal	—

● BP MOVES

Name	Type	Kind	Pow.	Acc.	PP	Range	DA
Dive	Water	Physical	80	100	10	Normal	○
Icy Wind	Ice	Special	55	95	15	2 Foes	—
Snore	Normal	Special	40	100	15	Normal	—
Swift	Normal	Special	60	—	20	2 Foes	—
Outrage	Dragon	Physical	120	100	15	1 Random	○
Signal Beam	Bug	Special	75	100	15	Normal	—
Twister	Dragon	Special	40	100	20	2 Foes	—
Bounce	Flying	Physical	85	85	5	Normal	○

● TM & HM MOVES

No.	Name	Type	Kind	Pow.	Acc.	PP	Range	DA
TM03	Water Pulse	Water	Special	60	100	20	Normal	—
TM06	Toxic	Poison	Status	—	85	10	Normal	—
TM07	Hail	Ice	Status	—	—	10	All	—
TM10	Hidden Power	Normal	Special	—	100	15	Normal	—
TM13	Ice Beam	Ice	Special	95	100	10	Normal	—
TM14	Blizzard	Ice	Special	120	70	5	2 Foes	—
TM17	Protect	Normal	Status	—	—	10	Self	—
TM18	Rain Dance	Water	Status	—	—	5	All	—
TM21	Frustration	Normal	Physical	—	100	20	Normal	○
TM27	Return	Normal	Physical	—	100	20	Normal	○
TM32	Double Team	Normal	Status	—	—	15	Self	—
TM42	Facade	Normal	Physical	70	100	20	Normal	○
TM43	Secret Power	Normal	Physical	70	100	20	Normal	○
TM44	Rest	Psychic	Status	—	—	10	Self	—
TM45	Attract	Normal	Status	—	100	15	Normal	—
TM55	Brine	Water	Special	65	100	10	Normal	—
TM58	Endure	Normal	Status	—	—	10	Self	—
TM59	Dragon Pulse	Dragon	Special	90	100	10	Normal	—
TM78	Captivate	Normal	Status	—	100	20	2 Foes	—
TM82	Sleep Talk	Normal	Status	—	—	10	Depends	—
TM83	Natural Gift	Normal	Physical	—	100	15	Normal	○
TM87	Swagger	Normal	Status	—	90	15	Normal	—
TM90	Substitute	Normal	Status	—	—	10	Self	—
TM91	Flash Cannon	Steel	Special	80	100	10	Normal	—
HM03	Surf	Water	Special	95	100	15	2 Foes / 1 Ally	—
HM05	Whirlpool	Water	Special	15	70	15	Normal	—
HM07	Waterfall	Water	Physical	80	100	15	Normal	○

● EGG MOVES

Name	Type	Kind	Pow.	Acc.	PP	Range	DA
Flail	Normal	Physical	—	100	15	Normal	○
Aurora Beam	Ice	Special	65	100	20	Normal	—
Octazooka	Water	Special	65	85	10	Normal	—
Disable	Normal	Status	—	80	20	Normal	—
Splash	Normal	Status	—	—	40	Self	—
Dragon Rage	Dragon	Special	—	100	10	Normal	—
DragonBreath	Dragon	Special	60	100	20	Normal	—
Signal Beam	Bug	Special	75	100	15	Normal	—
Razor Wind	Normal	Special	80	100	10	2 Foes	—
Muddy Water	Water	Special	95	85	10	2 Foes	—

⬤ No. 116 Dragon Pokémon
Horsea

Water

- ● **HEIGHT:** 1'04"
- ● **WEIGHT:** 17.6 lbs.
- ● **ITEMS:** Dragon Scale

● **SIZE COMPARISON**

● MALE/FEMALE HAVE SAME FORM

◎ ABILITIES
- ● Swift Swim
- ● Sniper

◎ STATS
- HP ●
- ATTACK ●●
- DEFENSE ●●●
- SP. ATTACK ●●●
- SP. DEFENSE ●
- SPEED ●●●

◎ EGG GROUPS
Water 1

Dragon

◎ PERFORMANCE
SPEED ★★☆☆☆ STAMINA ★★★☆
POWER ★★★☆☆ JUMP ★★
SKILL ★☆☆

● MAIN WAYS TO OBTAIN

Pokémon HeartGold Whirl Islands (water surface)

Pokémon SoulSilver Whirl Islands (water surface)

Pokémon Diamond Route 226 (Good Rod)

Pokémon Pearl Route 226 (Good Rod)

Pokémon Platinum Route 226 (Good Rod)

Pokémon HeartGold
If attacked by a larger enemy, it quickly swims to safety by adeptly controlling its well-developed dorsal fin.

Pokémon SoulSilver
Its big, developed fins move rapidly, allowing it to swim backward while still facing forward.

◎ EVOLUTION

Horsea → Seadra — Lv. 32 → Kingdra

Have it hold Dragon Scale and trade it

⬤ No. 117 | Dragon Pokémon
Seadra

Water

- ⬤ HEIGHT: 3'11"
- ⬤ WEIGHT: 55.1 lbs.
- ⬤ ITEMS: Dragon Scale

⬤ SIZE COMPARISON

⬤ MALE/FEMALE HAVE SAME FORM

⬤ ABILITIES
- ⬤ Poison Point
- ⬤ Sniper

⬤ STATS
HP	⬤⬤
ATTACK	⬤⬤⬤
DEFENSE	⬤⬤⬤⬤
SP. ATTACK	⬤⬤⬤⬤
SP. DEFENSE	⬤⬤
SPEED	⬤⬤⬤⬤

⬤ EGG GROUPS
Water 1

Dragon

⬤ PERFORMANCE
SPEED ★★☆
POWER ★★☆
SKILL ★★★★
STAMINA ★★★☆
JUMP ★★☆

⬤ MAIN WAYS TO OBTAIN

Pokémon HeartGold	Whirl Islands, entrance to the Waterfall Basin (water surface)
Pokémon SoulSilver	Whirl Islands, entrance to the Waterfall Basin (water surface)
Pokémon Diamond	Route 226 (Super Rod)
Pokémon Pearl	Route 226 (Super Rod)
Pokémon Platinum	Route 226 (Super Rod)

Pokémon HeartGold	Pokémon SoulSilver
An examination of its cells revealed the presence of a gene not found in HORSEA. It became a hot topic.	Its fin-tips leak poison. Its fins and bones are highly valued as ingredients in herbal medicine.

⬤ EVOLUTION

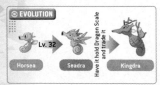

Horsea → (Lv. 32) → Seadra → (Have it hold Dragon Scale and trade it) → Kingdra

⬤ LEVEL-UP MOVES
Lv.	Name	Type	Kind	Pow.	Acc.	PP	Range	DA
1	Bubble	Water	Special	20	100	30	2 Foes	—
1	SmokeScreen	Normal	Status	—	100	20	Normal	—
1	Leer	Normal	Status	—	100	30	2 Foes	—
1	Water Gun	Water	Special	40	100	25	Normal	—
4	SmokeScreen	Normal	Status	—	100	20	Normal	—
8	Leer	Normal	Status	—	100	30	2 Foes	—
11	Water Gun	Water	Special	40	100	25	Normal	—
14	Focus Energy	Normal	Status	—	—	30	Self	—
18	BubbleBeam	Water	Special	65	100	20	Normal	—
23	Agility	Psychic	Status	—	—	30	Self	—
26	Twister	Dragon	Special	40	100	20	2 Foes	—
30	Brine	Water	Special	65	100	10	Normal	—
40	Hydro Pump	Water	Special	120	80	5	Normal	—
48	Dragon Dance	Dragon	Status	—	—	20	Self	—
57	Dragon Pulse	Dragon	Special	90	100	10	Normal	—

⬤ MOVE MANIAC
Name	Type	Kind	Pow.	Acc.	PP	Range	DA
Headbutt	Normal	Physical	70	100	15	Normal	⬤

⬤ BP MOVES
Name	Type	Kind	Pow.	Acc.	PP	Range	DA
Dive	Water	Physical	80	100	10	Normal	⬤
Icy Wind	Ice	Special	55	95	15	2 Foes	—
Snore	Normal	Special	40	100	15	Normal	—
Swift	Normal	Special	60	—	20	2 Foes	—
Outrage	Dragon	Physical	120	100	15	1 Random	⬤
Signal Beam	Bug	Special	75	100	15	Normal	—
Twister	Dragon	Special	40	100	20	2 Foes	—
Bounce	Flying	Physical	85	85	5	Normal	⬤

⬤ TM & HM MOVES
No.	Name	Type	Kind	Pow.	Acc.	PP	Range	DA
TM03	Water Pulse	Water	Special	60	100	20	Normal	—
TM06	Toxic	Poison	Status	—	85	10	Normal	—
TM07	Hail	Ice	Status	—	—	10	All	—
TM10	Hidden Power	Normal	Special	—	100	15	Normal	—
TM13	Ice Beam	Ice	Special	95	100	10	Normal	—
TM14	Blizzard	Ice	Special	120	70	5	2 Foes	—
TM15	Hyper Beam	Normal	Special	150	90	5	Normal	—
TM17	Protect	Normal	Status	—	—	10	Self	—
TM18	Rain Dance	Water	Status	—	—	5	All	—
TM21	Frustration	Normal	Physical	—	100	20	Normal	⬤
TM27	Return	Normal	Physical	—	100	20	Normal	⬤
TM32	Double Team	Normal	Status	—	—	15	Self	—
TM42	Facade	Normal	Physical	70	100	20	Normal	⬤
TM43	Secret Power	Normal	Physical	70	100	20	Normal	—
TM44	Rest	Psychic	Status	—	—	10	Self	—
TM45	Attract	Normal	Status	—	100	15	Normal	—
TM55	Brine	Water	Special	65	100	10	Normal	—
TM58	Endure	Normal	Status	—	—	10	Self	—
TM59	Dragon Pulse	Dragon	Special	90	100	10	Normal	—
TM68	Giga Impact	Normal	Physical	150	90	5	Normal	⬤
TM78	Captivate	Normal	Status	—	100	20	2 Foes	—
TM82	Sleep Talk	Normal	Status	—	—	10	Depends	—
TM83	Natural Gift	Normal	Physical	—	100	15	Normal	—
TM87	Swagger	Normal	Status	—	90	15	Normal	—
TM90	Substitute	Normal	Status	—	—	10	Self	—
TM91	Flash Cannon	Steel	Special	80	100	10	Normal	—
HM03	Surf	Water	Special	95	100	15	2 Foes/1 Ally	—
HM05	Whirlpool	Water	Special	15	70	15	Normal	—
HM07	Waterfall	Water	Physical	80	100	15	Normal	⬤

● LEVEL-UP MOVES

Lv.	Name	Type	Kind	Pow.	Acc.	PP	Range	DA
1	Peck	Flying	Physical	35	100	35	Normal	○
1	Tail Whip	Normal	Status	—	100	30	2 Foes	—
1	Water Sport	Water	Status	—	—	15	All	—
7	Supersonic	Normal	Status	—	55	20	Normal	—
11	Horn Attack	Normal	Physical	65	100	25	Normal	○
17	Water Pulse	Water	Special	60	100	20	Normal	—
21	Flail	Normal	Physical	—	100	15	Normal	○
27	Aqua Ring	Water	Status	—	—	20	Self	—
31	Fury Attack	Normal	Physical	15	85	20	Normal	○
37	Waterfall	Water	Physical	80	100	15	Normal	○
41	Horn Drill	Normal	Physical	—	30	5	Normal	○
47	Agility	Psychic	Status	—	—	30	Self	—
51	Megahorn	Bug	Physical	120	85	10	Normal	○

● MOVE MANIAC

Name	Type	Kind	Pow.	Acc.	PP	Range	DA

● BP MOVES

Name	Type	Kind	Pow.	Acc.	PP	Range	DA
Dive	Water	Physical	80	100	10	Normal	○
Fury Cutter	Bug	Physical	10	95	20	Normal	○
Icy Wind	Ice	Special	55	95	15	2 Foes	—
Knock Off	Dark	Physical	20	100	20	Normal	○
Snore	Normal	Special	40	100	15	Normal	—
Swift	Normal	Special	60	—	20	2 Foes	—
Mud-Slap	Ground	Special	20	100	10	Normal	—
Aqua Tail	Water	Physical	90	90	10	Normal	○
Bounce	Flying	Physical	85	85	5	Normal	○

● TM & HM MOVES

No.	Name	Type	Kind	Pow.	Acc.	PP	Range	DA
TM03	Water Pulse	Water	Special	60	100	20	Normal	—
TM06	Toxic	Poison	Status	—	85	10	Normal	—
TM07	Hail	Ice	Status	—	—	10	All	—
TM10	Hidden Power	Normal	Special	—	100	15	Normal	—
TM13	Ice Beam	Ice	Special	95	100	10	Normal	—
TM14	Blizzard	Ice	Special	120	70	5	2 Foes	—
TM17	Protect	Normal	Status	—	—	10	Self	—
TM18	Rain Dance	Water	Status	—	—	5	All	—
TM21	Frustration	Normal	Physical	—	100	20	Normal	○
TM27	Return	Normal	Physical	—	100	20	Normal	○
TM32	Double Team	Normal	Status	—	—	15	Self	—
TM42	Facade	Normal	Physical	70	100	20	Normal	○
TM43	Secret Power	Normal	Physical	70	100	20	Normal	—
TM44	Rest	Psychic	Status	—	—	10	Self	—
TM45	Attract	Normal	Status	—	100	15	Normal	—
TM58	Endure	Normal	Status	—	—	10	Self	—
TM78	Captivate	Normal	Status	—	100	20	2 Foes	—
TM82	Sleep Talk	Normal	Status	—	—	10	Depends	—
TM83	Natural Gift	Normal	Physical	—	100	15	Normal	—
TM84	Poison Jab	Poison	Physical	80	100	20	Normal	○
TM87	Swagger	Normal	Status	—	90	15	Normal	—
TM90	Substitute	Normal	Status	—	—	10	Self	—
HM03	Surf	Water	Special	95	100	15	2 Foes/1 Ally	—
HM05	Whirlpool	Water	Special	15	70	15	Normal	—
HM07	Waterfall	Water	Physical	80	100	15	Normal	○

● EGG MOVES

Name	Type	Kind	Pow.	Acc.	PP	Range	DA
Psybeam	Psychic	Special	65	100	20	Normal	—
Haze	Ice	Status	—	—	30	All	—
Hydro Pump	Water	Special	120	80	5	Normal	—
Sleep Talk	Normal	Status	—	—	10	Depends	—
Mud Sport	Ground	Status	—	—	15	All	—
Mud-Slap	Ground	Special	20	100	10	Normal	—
Aqua Tail	Water	Physical	90	90	10	Normal	○
Body Slam	Normal	Physical	85	100	15	Normal	○

● **No. 118** | Goldfish Pokémon
Goldeen

Water

● **HEIGHT:** 2'00"
● **WEIGHT:** 33.1 lbs.
● **ITEMS:** None

● SIZE COMPARISON

● **MALE FORM**
Longer horn

● **FEMALE FORM**
Shorter horn

⊕ ABILITIES
● Swift Swim
● Water Veil

⊕ STATS
HP ●●
ATTACK ●●●
DEFENSE ●●
SP. ATTACK ●●
SP. DEFENSE ●●
SPEED ●●●

⊕ EGG GROUPS
Water 2

⊕ PERFORMANCE

SPEED ★★★☆   STAMINA ★☆
POWER ★★☆☆   JUMP ★★★
SKILL ★★☆

● MAIN WAYS TO OBTAIN

Pokémon HeartGold   SLOWPOKE Well (Old Rod)

Pokémon SoulSilver   SLOWPOKE Well (Old Rod)

Pokémon Diamond   Route 203 (Good Rod)

Pokémon Pearl   Route 203 (Good Rod)

Pokémon Platinum   Route 203 (Good Rod)

Pokémon HeartGold
Its dorsal, pectoral and tail fins wave elegantly in water. That is why it is known as the water dancer.

Pokémon SoulSilver
A strong swimmer, it is capable of swimming nonstop up fast streams at a steady speed of five knots per hour.

⊕ EVOLUTION

Lv. 33

Goldeen → Seaking

⬤ No. 119 | Goldfish Pokémon
Seaking

Water

● **LEVEL-UP MOVES**

Lv.	Name	Type	Kind	Pow.	Acc.	PP	Range	DA
1	Poison Jab	Poison	Physical	80	100	20	Normal	○
1	Peck	Flying	Physical	35	100	35	Normal	○
1	Tail Whip	Normal	Status	—	100	30	2 Foes	—
1	Water Sport	Water	Status	—	—	15	All	—
1	Supersonic	Normal	Status	—	55	20	Normal	—
7	Supersonic	Normal	Status	—	55	20	Normal	—
11	Horn Attack	Normal	Physical	65	100	25	Normal	○
17	Water Pulse	Water	Special	60	100	20	Normal	—
21	Flail	Normal	Physical	—	100	15	Normal	○
27	Aqua Ring	Water	Status	—	—	20	Self	—
31	Fury Attack	Normal	Physical	15	85	20	Normal	○
40	Waterfall	Water	Physical	80	100	15	Normal	○
47	Horn Drill	Normal	Physical	—	30	5	Normal	○
56	Agility	Psychic	Status	—	—	30	Self	—
63	Megahorn	Bug	Physical	120	85	10	Normal	○

● **MOVE MANIAC**

Name	Type	Kind	Pow.	Acc.	PP	Range	DA
							—
							—

● **BP MOVES**

Name	Type	Kind	Pow.	Acc.	PP	Range	DA
Dive	Water	Physical	80	100	10	Normal	○
Fury Cutter	Bug	Physical	10	95	20	Normal	○
Icy Wind	Ice	Special	55	95	15	2 Foes	—
Knock Off	Dark	Physical	20	100	20	Normal	○
Snore	Normal	Special	40	100	15	Normal	—
Swift	Normal	Special	60	—	20	2 Foes	—
Mud-Slap	Ground	Special	20	100	10	Normal	—
Aqua Tail	Water	Physical	90	90	10	Normal	○
Bounce	Flying	Physical	85	85	5	Normal	○

● **HEIGHT:** 4'03"
● **WEIGHT:** 86.0 lbs.
● **ITEMS:** None

● **SIZE COMPARISON**

● **MALE FORM**
Longer horn

● **FEMALE FORM**
Shorter horn

⊛ **ABILITIES**
● Swift Swim
● Water Veil

⊛ **STATS**
HP ●●●
ATTACK ●●●●
DEFENSE ●●●
SP. ATTACK ●●●
SP. DEFENSE ●●●
SPEED ●●●

⊛ **EGG GROUPS**
Water 2

⊛ **PERFORMANCE**
SPEED ★★☆☆ STAMINA ★★★
POWER ★★★☆ JUMP ★★☆
SKILL ★★☆

● **MAIN WAYS TO OBTAIN**

Pokémon HeartGold Route 42 (water surface)

Pokémon SoulSilver Route 42 (water surface)

Pokémon Diamond Route 203 (Super Rod)

Pokémon Pearl Route 203 (Super Rod)

Pokémon Platinum Route 203 (Super Rod)

Pokémon HeartGold
During spawning season, SEAKING gather from all over, causing rivers to appear a brilliant red.

Pokémon SoulSilver
Using its horn, it bores holes in riverbed boulders, making nests to prevent its eggs from washing away.

⊛ **EVOLUTION**

Goldeen — Lv. 33 → Seaking

● **TM & HM MOVES**

No.	Name	Type	Kind	Pow.	Acc.	PP	Range	DA
TM03	Water Pulse	Water	Special	60	100	20	Normal	—
TM06	Toxic	Poison	Status	—	85	10	Normal	—
TM07	Hail	Ice	Status	—	—	10	All	—
TM10	Hidden Power	Normal	Special	—	100	15	Normal	—
TM13	Ice Beam	Ice	Special	95	100	10	Normal	—
TM14	Blizzard	Ice	Special	120	70	5	2 Foes	—
TM15	Hyper Beam	Normal	Special	150	90	5	Normal	—
TM17	Protect	Normal	Status	—	—	10	Self	—
TM18	Rain Dance	Water	Status	—	—	5	All	—
TM21	Frustration	Normal	Physical	—	100	20	Normal	○
TM27	Return	Normal	Physical	—	100	20	Normal	○
TM32	Double Team	Normal	Status	—	—	15	Self	—
TM42	Facade	Normal	Physical	70	100	20	Normal	○
TM43	Secret Power	Normal	Physical	70	100	20	Normal	○
TM44	Rest	Psychic	Status	—	—	10	Self	—
TM45	Attract	Normal	Status	—	100	15	Normal	—
TM58	Endure	Normal	Status	—	—	10	Self	—
TM68	Giga Impact	Normal	Physical	150	90	5	Normal	○
TM78	Captivate	Normal	Status	—	100	20	2 Foes	—
TM82	Sleep Talk	Normal	Status	—	—	10	Depends	—
TM83	Natural Gift	Normal	Physical	—	100	15	Normal	○
TM84	Poison Jab	Poison	Physical	80	100	20	Normal	○
TM87	Swagger	Normal	Status	—	90	15	Normal	—
TM90	Substitute	Normal	Status	—	—	10	Self	—
HM03	Surf	Water	Special	95	100	15	2 Foes/1 Ally	—
HM05	Whirlpool	Water	Special	15	70	15	Normal	—
HM07	Waterfall	Water	Physical	80	100	15	Normal	—

● LEVEL-UP MOVES

Lv.	Name	Type	Kind	Pow.	Acc.	PP	Range	DA
1	Tackle	Normal	Physical	35	95	35	Normal	○
1	Harden	Normal	Status	—	—	30	Self	—
6	Water Gun	Water	Special	40	100	25	Normal	—
10	Rapid Spin	Normal	Physical	20	100	40	Normal	—
15	Recover	Normal	Status	—	—	10	Self	—
19	Camouflage	Normal	Status	—	—	20	Self	—
24	Swift	Normal	Special	60	—	20	2 Foes	—
28	BubbleBeam	Water	Special	65	100	20	Normal	—
33	Minimize	Normal	Status	—	—	20	Self	—
37	Gyro Ball	Steel	Physical	—	100	5	Normal	○
42	Light Screen	Psychic	Status	—	—	30	2 Allies	—
46	Power Gem	Rock	Special	70	100	20	Normal	—
51	Cosmic Power	Psychic	Status	—	—	20	Self	—
55	Hydro Pump	Water	Special	120	80	5	Normal	—

● MOVE MANIAC

Name	Type	Kind	Pow.	Acc.	PP	Range	DA
							—
							—

● BP MOVES

Name	Type	Kind	Pow.	Acc.	PP	Range	DA
Dive	Water	Physical	80	100	10	Normal	○
Icy Wind	Ice	Special	55	95	15	2 Foes	—
Snore	Normal	Special	40	100	15	Normal	—
Swift	Normal	Special	60	—	20	2 Foes	—
Gravity	Psychic	Status	—	—	5	All	—
Magic Coat	Psychic	Status	—	—	15	Self	—
Rollout	Rock	Physical	30	90	20	Normal	○
Signal Beam	Bug	Special	75	100	15	Normal	—
Twister	Dragon	Special	40	100	20	2 Foes	—
Pain Split	Normal	Status	—	—	20	Normal	—

● TM & HM MOVES

No.	Name	Type	Kind	Pow.	Acc.	PP	Range	DA
TM03	Water Pulse	Water	Special	60	100	20	Normal	—
TM06	Toxic	Poison	Status	—	85	10	Normal	—
TM07	Hail	Ice	Status	—	—	10	All	—
TM10	Hidden Power	Normal	Special	—	100	15	Normal	—
TM13	Ice Beam	Ice	Special	95	100	10	Normal	—
TM14	Blizzard	Ice	Special	120	70	5	2 Foes	—
TM16	Light Screen	Psychic	Status	—	—	30	2 Allies	—
TM17	Protect	Normal	Status	—	—	10	Self	—
TM18	Rain Dance	Water	Status	—	—	5	All	—
TM21	Frustration	Normal	Physical	—	100	20	Normal	○
TM24	Thunderbolt	Electric	Special	95	100	15	Normal	—
TM25	Thunder	Electric	Special	120	70	10	Normal	—
TM27	Return	Normal	Physical	—	100	20	Normal	○
TM29	Psychic	Psychic	Special	90	100	10	Normal	—
TM32	Double Team	Normal	Status	—	—	15	Self	—
TM33	Reflect	Psychic	Status	—	—	20	2 Allies	—
TM42	Facade	Normal	Physical	70	100	20	Normal	—
TM43	Secret Power	Normal	Physical	70	100	20	Normal	—
TM44	Rest	Psychic	Status	—	—	10	Self	—
TM55	Brine	Water	Special	65	100	10	Normal	—
TM58	Endure	Normal	Status	—	—	10	Self	—
TM67	Recycle	Normal	Status	—	—	10	Self	—
TM70	Flash	Normal	Status	—	100	20	Normal	—
TM73	Thunder Wave	Electric	Status	—	100	20	Normal	—
TM74	Gyro Ball	Steel	Physical	—	100	5	Normal	○
TM77	Psych Up	Normal	Status	—	—	10	Normal	—
TM82	Sleep Talk	Normal	Status	—	—	10	Depends	—
TM83	Natural Gift	Normal	Physical	—	100	15	Normal	—
TM87	Swagger	Normal	Status	—	90	15	Normal	—
TM90	Substitute	Normal	Status	—	—	10	Self	—
TM91	Flash Cannon	Steel	Special	80	100	10	Normal	—
HM03	Surf	Water	Special	95	100	15	2 Foes/1 Ally	—
HM05	Whirlpool	Water	Special	15	70	15	Normal	—
HM07	Waterfall	Water	Physical	80	100	15	Normal	○

● No. 120 | Star Shape Pokémon
Staryu

Water

- ● HEIGHT: 2'07"
- ● WEIGHT: 76.1 lbs.
- ● ITEMS: Stardust
  Star Piece

● SIZE COMPARISON

● GENDER UNKNOWN

⊕ ABILITIES
- ● Illuminate
- ● Natural Cure

⊕ STATS
HP	●
ATTACK	●●
DEFENSE	●●
SP. ATTACK	●●●
SP. DEFENSE	●●●
SPEED	●●●●

⊕ EGG GROUPS
Water 3

⊕ PERFORMANCE
SPEED ★★★★☆　　STAMINA ★★☆
POWER ★☆☆　　　JUMP ★★★
SKILL ★★★

● MAIN WAYS TO OBTAIN

Pokémon HeartGold　Cherrygrove City (Good Rod, night only)

Pokémon SoulSilver　Cherrygrove City (Good Rod, night only)

Pokémon Diamond　Canalave City (Super Rod)

Pokémon Pearl　Canalave City (Super Rod)

Pokémon Platinum　Canalave City (Super Rod)

Pokémon HeartGold	**Pokémon SoulSilver**
At night, the middle of its body slowly flickers with the same rhythm as a human heartbeat.	Even if its body is torn, it can regenerate as long as the glowing central core remains intact.

⊕ EVOLUTION

 Use Water Stone

Staryu — Starmie

No. 121 | Mysterious Pokémon
Starmie

Water **Psychic**

- **HEIGHT:** 3'07"
- **WEIGHT:** 176.4 lbs.
- **ITEMS:** None

SIZE COMPARISON

GENDER UNKNOWN

ABILITIES
- Illuminate
- Natural Cure

STATS
HP	●●
ATTACK	●●●
DEFENSE	●●●
SP. ATTACK	●●●●
SP. DEFENSE	●●●●
SPEED	●●●●●

EGG GROUPS
Water 3

PERFORMANCE
SPEED ★★★★☆ STAMINA ★★☆
POWER ★★☆☆☆ JUMP ★★★★
SKILL ★★★

MAIN WAYS TO OBTAIN

Pokémon HeartGold Use Water Stone on Staryu

Pokémon SoulSilver Use Water Stone on Staryu

Pokémon Diamond Use Water Stone on Staryu

Pokémon Pearl Use Water Stone on Staryu

Pokémon Platinum Use Water Stone on Staryu

Pokémon HeartGold
The middle section of its body is called the core. It glows in a different color each time it is seen.

Pokémon SoulSilver
Regardless of the environment it lives in, its body grows to form a symmetrical geometric shape.

EVOLUTION
 Use Water Stone
Staryu → Starmie

● LEVEL-UP MOVES
Lv.	Name	Type	Kind	Pow.	Acc.	PP	Range	DA
1	Water Gun	Water	Special	40	100	25	Normal	—
1	Rapid Spin	Normal	Physical	20	100	40	Normal	○
1	Recover	Normal	Status	—	—	10	Self	—
1	Swift	Normal	Special	60	—	20	2 Foes	—
28	Confuse Ray	Ghost	Status	—	100	10	Normal	—

● MOVE MANIAC
Name	Type	Kind	Pow.	Acc.	PP	Range	DA

● BP MOVES
Name	Type	Kind	Pow.	Acc.	PP	Range	DA
Dive	Water	Physical	80	100	10	Normal	○
Icy Wind	Ice	Special	55	95	15	2 Foes	—
Trick	Psychic	Status	—	100	10	Normal	—
Snore	Normal	Special	40	100	15	Normal	—
Swift	Normal	Special	60	—	20	2 Foes	—
Gravity	Psychic	Status	—	—	5	All	—
Magic Coat	Psychic	Status	—	—	15	Self	—
Rollout	Rock	Physical	30	90	20	Normal	○
Signal Beam	Bug	Special	75	100	15	Normal	—
Twister	Dragon	Special	40	100	20	2 Foes	—
Pain Split	Normal	Status	—	—	20	Normal	—

● TM & HM MOVES
No.	Name	Type	Kind	Pow.	Acc.	PP	Range	DA
TM03	Water Pulse	Water	Special	60	100	20	Normal	—
TM06	Toxic	Poison	Status	—	85	10	Normal	—
TM07	Hail	Ice	Status	—	—	10	All	—
TM10	Hidden Power	Normal	Special	—	100	15	Normal	—
TM13	Ice Beam	Ice	Special	95	100	10	Normal	—
TM14	Blizzard	Ice	Special	120	70	5	2 Foes	—
TM15	Hyper Beam	Normal	Special	150	90	5	Normal	—
TM16	Light Screen	Psychic	Status	—	—	30	2 Allies	—
TM17	Protect	Normal	Status	—	—	10	Self	—
TM18	Rain Dance	Water	Status	—	—	5	All	—
TM21	Frustration	Normal	Physical	—	100	20	Normal	○
TM24	Thunderbolt	Electric	Special	95	100	15	Normal	—
TM25	Thunder	Electric	Special	120	70	10	Normal	—
TM27	Return	Normal	Physical	—	100	20	Normal	○
TM29	Psychic	Psychic	Special	90	100	10	Normal	—
TM32	Double Team	Normal	Status	—	—	15	Self	—
TM33	Reflect	Psychic	Status	—	—	20	2 Allies	—
TM42	Facade	Normal	Physical	70	100	20	Normal	○
TM43	Secret Power	Normal	Physical	70	100	20	Normal	—
TM44	Rest	Psychic	Status	—	—	10	Self	—
TM48	Skill Swap	Psychic	Status	—	—	10	Normal	—
TM55	Brine	Water	Special	65	100	10	Normal	—
TM58	Endure	Normal	Status	—	—	10	Self	—
TM67	Recycle	Normal	Status	—	—	10	Self	—
TM68	Giga Impact	Normal	Physical	150	90	5	Normal	○
TM70	Flash	Normal	Status	—	100	20	Normal	—
TM72	Avalanche	Ice	Physical	60	100	10	Normal	○
TM73	Thunder Wave	Electric	Status	—	100	20	Normal	—
TM74	Gyro Ball	Steel	Physical	—	100	5	Normal	○
TM77	Psych Up	Normal	Status	—	—	10	Normal	—
TM82	Sleep Talk	Normal	Status	—	—	10	Depends	—
TM83	Natural Gift	Normal	Physical	—	100	15	Normal	○
TM85	Dream Eater	Psychic	Special	100	100	15	Normal	—
TM86	Grass Knot	Grass	Special	—	100	20	Normal	○
TM87	Swagger	Normal	Status	—	90	15	Normal	—
TM90	Substitute	Normal	Status	—	—	10	Self	—
TM91	Flash Cannon	Steel	Special	80	100	10	Normal	—
TM92	Trick Room	Psychic	Status	—	—	5	All	—
HM03	Surf	Water	Special	95	100	15	2 Foes/1 Ally	—
HM05	Whirlpool	Water	Special	15	70	15	Normal	—
HM07	Waterfall	Water	Physical	80	100	15	Normal	○

● LEVEL-UP MOVES

Lv.	Name	Type	Kind	Pow.	Acc.	PP	Range	DA
1	Magical Leaf	Grass	Special	60	—	20	Normal	—
1	Power Swap	Psychic	Status	—	—	10	Normal	—
1	Guard Swap	Psychic	Status	—	—	10	Normal	—
1	Barrier	Psychic	Status	—	—	30	Self	—
1	Copycat	Normal	Status	—	—	20	Self	—
4	Confusion	Psychic	Special	50	100	25	Normal	—
8	Meditate	Psychic	Status	—	—	40	Self	—
11	Encore	Normal	Status	—	100	5	Normal	—
15	DoubleSlap	Normal	Physical	15	85	10	Normal	○
18	Mimic	Normal	Status	—	—	10	Normal	—
22	Light Screen	Psychic	Status	—	—	30	2 Allies	—
22	Reflect	Psychic	Status	—	—	20	2 Allies	—
25	Psybeam	Psychic	Special	65	100	20	Normal	—
29	Substitute	Normal	Status	—	—	10	Self	—
32	Recycle	Normal	Status	—	—	10	Self	—
36	Trick	Psychic	Status	—	100	10	Normal	—
39	Psychic	Psychic	Special	90	100	10	Normal	—
43	Role Play	Psychic	Status	—	—	10	Normal	—
46	Baton Pass	Normal	Status	—	—	40	Self	—
50	Safeguard	Normal	Status	—	—	25	2 Allies	—

● MOVE MANIAC

Name	Type	Kind	Pow.	Acc.	PP	Range	DA
Headbutt	Normal	Physical	70	100	15	Normal	—

● BP MOVES

Name	Type	Kind	Pow.	Acc.	PP	Range	DA
ThunderPunch	Electric	Physical	75	100	15	Normal	○
Fire Punch	Fire	Physical	75	100	15	Normal	○
Ice Punch	Ice	Physical	75	100	15	Normal	○
Zen Headbutt	Psychic	Physical	80	90	15	Normal	○
Trick	Psychic	Status	—	100	10	Normal	—
Snore	Normal	Special	40	100	15	Normal	—
Helping Hand	Normal	Status	—	—	20	1 Ally	—
Magic Coat	Psychic	Status	—	—	15	Self	—
Role Play	Psychic	Status	—	—	10	Normal	—
Mud-Slap	Ground	Special	20	100	10	Normal	—
Signal Beam	Bug	Special	75	100	15	Normal	—
Iron Defense	Steel	Status	—	—	15	Self	—

● TM & HM MOVES

No.	Name	Type	Kind	Pow.	Acc.	PP	Range	DA
TM01	Focus Punch	Fighting	Physical	150	100	20	Normal	○
TM04	Calm Mind	Psychic	Status	—	—	20	Self	—
TM06	Toxic	Poison	Status	—	85	10	Normal	—
TM10	Hidden Power	Normal	Special	—	100	15	Normal	—
TM11	Sunny Day	Fire	Status	—	—	5	All	—
TM12	Taunt	Dark	Status	—	100	20	Normal	—
TM15	Hyper Beam	Normal	Special	150	90	5	Normal	—
TM16	Light Screen	Psychic	Status	—	—	30	2 Allies	—
TM17	Protect	Normal	Status	—	—	10	Self	—
TM18	Rain Dance	Water	Status	—	—	5	All	—
TM20	Safeguard	Normal	Status	—	—	25	2 Allies	—
TM21	Frustration	Normal	Physical	—	100	20	Normal	○
TM22	SolarBeam	Grass	Special	120	100	10	Normal	—
TM24	Thunderbolt	Electric	Special	95	100	15	Normal	—
TM25	Thunder	Electric	Special	120	70	10	Normal	—
TM27	Return	Normal	Physical	—	100	20	Normal	○
TM29	Psychic	Psychic	Special	90	100	10	Normal	—
TM30	Shadow Ball	Ghost	Special	80	100	15	Normal	—
TM31	Brick Break	Fighting	Physical	75	100	15	Normal	○
TM32	Double Team	Normal	Status	—	—	15	Self	—
TM33	Reflect	Psychic	Status	—	—	20	2 Allies	—
TM34	Shock Wave	Electric	Special	60	—	20	Normal	—
TM40	Aerial Ace	Flying	Physical	60	—	20	Normal	○
TM41	Torment	Dark	Status	—	100	15	Normal	—
TM42	Facade	Normal	Physical	70	100	20	Normal	○
TM43	Secret Power	Normal	Physical	70	100	20	Normal	○
TM44	Rest	Psychic	Status	—	—	10	Self	—
TM45	Attract	Normal	Status	—	100	15	Normal	—
TM46	Thief	Dark	Physical	40	100	10	Normal	○
TM48	Skill Swap	Psychic	Status	—	—	10	Normal	—
TM49	Snatch	Dark	Status	—	—	10	Depends	—
TM52	Focus Blast	Fighting	Special	120	70	5	Normal	—
TM53	Energy Ball	Grass	Special	80	100	10	Normal	—
TM56	Fling	Dark	Physical	—	100	10	Normal	○
TM57	Charge Beam	Electric	Special	50	90	10	Normal	—
TM58	Endure	Normal	Status	—	—	10	Self	—
TM60	Drain Punch	Fighting	Physical	60	100	5	Normal	○
TM66	Payback	Dark	Physical	50	100	10	Normal	○
TM67	Recycle	Normal	Status	—	—	10	Self	—
TM68	Giga Impact	Normal	Physical	150	90	5	Normal	○
TM70	Flash	Normal	Status	—	100	20	Normal	—
TM73	Thunder Wave	Electric	Status	—	100	20	Normal	—
TM77	Psych Up	Normal	Status	—	—	10	Normal	—
TM78	Captivate	Normal	Status	—	100	20	2 Foes	—
TM82	Sleep Talk	Normal	Status	—	—	10	Depends	—
TM83	Natural Gift	Normal	Physical	—	100	15	Normal	—
TM85	Dream Eater	Psychic	Special	100	100	15	Normal	—
TM86	Grass Knot	Grass	Special	—	100	20	Normal	—
TM87	Swagger	Normal	Status	—	90	15	Normal	—
TM90	Substitute	Normal	Status	—	—	10	Self	—
TM92	Trick Room	Psychic	Status	—	—	5	All	—

● EGG MOVES

Name	Type	Kind	Pow.	Acc.	PP	Range	DA
Future Sight	Psychic	Special	80	90	15	Normal	—
Hypnosis	Psychic	Status	—	60	20	Normal	—
Mimic	Normal	Status	—	—	10	Normal	—
Psych Up	Normal	Status	—	—	10	Normal	—
Fake Out	Normal	Physical	40	100	10	Normal	○
Trick	Psychic	Status	—	100	10	Normal	—
Confuse Ray	Ghost	Status	—	100	10	Normal	—
Wake-Up Slap	Fighting	Physical	60	100	10	Normal	○
Teeter Dance	Normal	Status	—	100	20	2 Foes/1 Ally	—
Nasty Plot	Dark	Status	—	—	20	Self	—

◉ No. 122 | Barrier Pokémon
Mr. Mime

Psychic

● HEIGHT: 4'03"
● WEIGHT: 120.1 lbs.
● ITEMS: Leppa Berry

● SIZE COMPARISON

● MALE/FEMALE HAVE SAME FORM

◎ ABILITIES
● Soundproof
● Filter

◎ STATS
HP ●
ATTACK ●●
DEFENSE ●●●
SP. ATTACK ●●●●
SP. DEFENSE ●●●●●●●
SPEED ●●●●

◎ EGG GROUPS
Human-Like

◎ PERFORMANCE

SPEED ★★☆	STAMINA ★★★☆
POWER ★★☆	JUMP ★★★
SKILL ★★★★☆	

● MAIN WAYS TO OBTAIN

Pokémon HeartGold	Celadon Game Corner prize (3,333 Coins)
Pokémon SoulSilver	Celadon Game Corner prize (3,333 Coins)
Pokémon Diamond	Route 218
Pokémon Pearl	Level up Mime Jr. to Lv. 18 and have it learn Mimic, or level it up once it knows Mimic
Pokémon Platinum	Route 218

Pokémon HeartGold	Pokémon SoulSilver
A skilled mime from birth, it gains the ability to create invisible objects as it matures.	Its fingertips emit a peculiar force field that hardens air to create an actual wall.

◎ EVOLUTION

Level it up to Lv. 18 and teach it Mimic, or level it up once it knows Mimic.

Mime Jr.

Mr. Mime

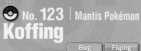

No. 123 | Mantis Pokémon
Koffing

Bug | Flying

● HEIGHT: 4'11"
● WEIGHT: 123.5 lbs.
● ITEMS: None

● SIZE COMPARISON

● MALE FORM
Shorter abdomen

● FEMALE FORM
Longer abdomen

● ABILITIES
● Swarm
● Technician

● STATS
HP ●●●
ATTACK ●●●●●
DEFENSE ●●●
SP. ATTACK ●●●
SP. DEFENSE ●●●
SPEED ●●●●●

● EGG GROUPS
Bug

● PERFORMANCE
SPEED ★★★☆
POWER ★★★☆
SKILL ★★★☆☆
STAMINA ★★
JUMP ★★★★☆

● MAIN WAYS TO OBTAIN

Pokémon HeartGold	Bug-Catching Contest at the National Park
Pokémon SoulSilver	Bug-Catching Contest at the National Park
Pokémon Diamond	Route 229
Pokémon Pearl	—
Pokémon Platinum	Route 210

| Pokémon HeartGold | Pokémon SoulSilver |
| It slashes through grass with its sharp scythes, moving too fast for the human eye to track. | When it moves, it leaves only a blur. If it hides in grass, its protective coloration makes it invisible. |

● EVOLUTION

Scyther

Have it hold Metal Coat and trade it

Scizor

● LEVEL-UP MOVES

Lv.	Name	Type	Kind	Pow.	Acc.	PP	Range	DA
1	Vacuum Wave	Fighting	Special	40	100	30	Normal	—
1	Quick Attack	Normal	Physical	40	100	30	Normal	○
1	Leer	Normal	Status	—	100	30	2 Foes	—
5	Focus Energy	Normal	Status	—	—	30	Self	—
9	Pursuit	Dark	Physical	40	100	20	Normal	○
13	False Swipe	Normal	Physical	40	100	40	Normal	○
17	Agility	Psychic	Status	—	—	30	Self	—
21	Wing Attack	Flying	Physical	60	100	35	Normal	○
25	Fury Cutter	Bug	Physical	10	95	20	Normal	○
29	Slash	Normal	Physical	70	100	20	Normal	○
33	Razor Wind	Normal	Special	80	100	10	2 Foes	—
37	Double Team	Normal	Status	—	—	15	Self	—
41	X-Scissor	Bug	Physical	80	100	15	Normal	○
45	Night Slash	Dark	Physical	70	100	15	Normal	○
49	Double Hit	Normal	Physical	35	90	10	Normal	○
53	Air Slash	Flying	Special	75	95	20	Normal	—
57	Swords Dance	Normal	Status	—	—	30	Self	—
61	Feint	Normal	Physical	50	100	10	Normal	—

● MOVE MANIAC

Name	Type	Kind	Pow.	Acc.	PP	Range	DA
Headbutt	Normal	Physical	70	100	15	Normal	○

● BP MOVES

Name	Type	Kind	Pow.	Acc.	PP	Range	DA
Fury Cutter	Bug	Physical	10	95	20	Normal	○
Ominous Wind	Ghost	Special	60	100	5	Normal	—
Knock Off	Dark	Physical	20	100	20	Normal	○
Bug Bite	Bug	Physical	60	100	20	Normal	○
Snore	Normal	Special	40	100	15	Normal	—
Swift	Normal	Special	60	—	20	2 Foes	—
Tailwind	Flying	Status	—	—	30	2 Allies	—

● TM & HM MOVES

No.	Name	Type	Kind	Pow.	Acc.	PP	Range	DA
TM06	Toxic	Poison	Status	—	85	10	Normal	—
TM10	Hidden Power	Normal	Special	—	100	15	Normal	—
TM11	Sunny Day	Fire	Status	—	—	5	All	—
TM15	Hyper Beam	Normal	Special	150	90	5	Normal	—
TM17	Protect	Normal	Status	—	—	10	Self	—
TM18	Rain Dance	Water	Status	—	—	5	All	—
TM21	Frustration	Normal	Physical	—	100	20	Normal	○
TM27	Return	Normal	Physical	—	100	20	Normal	○
TM31	Brick Break	Fighting	Physical	75	100	15	Normal	○
TM32	Double Team	Normal	Status	—	—	15	Self	—
TM40	Aerial Ace	Flying	Physical	60	—	20	Normal	○
TM42	Facade	Normal	Physical	70	100	20	Normal	○
TM43	Secret Power	Normal	Physical	70	100	20	Normal	○
TM44	Rest	Psychic	Status	—	—	10	Self	—
TM45	Attract	Normal	Status	—	100	15	Normal	—
TM46	Thief	Dark	Physical	40	100	10	Normal	○
TM47	Steel Wing	Steel	Physical	70	90	25	Normal	○
TM51	Roost	Flying	Status	—	—	10	Self	—
TM54	False Swipe	Normal	Physical	40	100	40	Normal	○
TM58	Endure	Normal	Status	—	—	10	Self	—
TM62	Silver Wind	Bug	Special	60	100	5	Normal	—
TM68	Giga Impact	Normal	Physical	150	90	5	Normal	○
TM75	Swords Dance	Normal	Status	—	—	30	Self	—
TM78	Captivate	Normal	Status	—	100	20	2 Foes	—
TM81	X-Scissor	Bug	Physical	80	100	15	Normal	○
TM82	Sleep Talk	Normal	Status	—	—	10	Depends	—
TM83	Natural Gift	Normal	Physical	—	100	15	Normal	○
TM87	Swagger	Normal	Status	—	90	15	Normal	—
TM89	U-turn	Bug	Physical	70	100	20	Normal	○
TM90	Substitute	Normal	Status	—	—	10	Self	—
HM01	Cut	Normal	Physical	50	95	30	Normal	○
HM06	Rock Smash	Fighting	Physical	40	100	15	Normal	○

● EGG MOVES

Name	Type	Kind	Pow.	Acc.	PP	Range	DA
Counter	Fighting	Physical	—	100	20	Normal	○
Safeguard	Normal	Status	—	—	25	2 Allies	—
Baton Pass	Normal	Status	—	—	40	Self	—
Razor Wind	Normal	Special	80	100	10	2 Foes	—
Reversal	Fighting	Physical	—	100	15	Normal	○
Light Screen	Psychic	Status	—	—	30	2 Allies	—
Endure	Normal	Status	—	—	10	Self	—
Silver Wind	Bug	Special	60	100	5	Normal	—
Bug Buzz	Bug	Special	90	100	10	Normal	—
Night Slash	Dark	Physical	70	100	15	Normal	○

● LEVEL-UP MOVES

Lv.	Name	Type	Kind	Pow.	Acc.	PP	Range	DA
1	Pound	Normal	Physical	40	100	35	Normal	○
1	Lick	Ghost	Physical	20	100	30	Normal	○
1	Lovely Kiss	Normal	Status	—	75	10	Normal	—
1	Powder Snow	Ice	Special	40	100	25	2 Foes	—
5	Lick	Ghost	Physical	20	100	30	Normal	○
8	Lovely Kiss	Normal	Status	—	75	10	Normal	—
11	Powder Snow	Ice	Special	40	100	25	2 Foes	—
15	DoubleSlap	Normal	Physical	15	85	10	Normal	○
18	Ice Punch	Ice	Physical	75	100	15	Normal	○
21	Mean Look	Normal	Status	—	—	5	Normal	—
25	Fake Tears	Dark	Status	—	100	20	Normal	—
28	Wake-Up Slap	Fighting	Physical	60	100	10	Normal	○
33	Avalanche	Ice	Physical	60	100	10	Normal	○
39	Body Slam	Normal	Physical	85	100	15	Normal	○
44	Wring Out	Normal	Special	—	100	5	Normal	—
49	Perish Song	Normal	Status	—	—	5	All	—
55	Blizzard	Ice	Special	120	70	5	2 Foes	—

● MOVE MANIAC

Name	Type	Kind	Pow.	Acc.	PP	Range	DA
Headbutt	Normal	Physical	70	100	15	Normal	○

● BP MOVES

Name	Type	Kind	Pow.	Acc.	PP	Range	DA
Icy Wind	Ice	Special	55	95	15	2 Foes	—
Ice Punch	Ice	Physical	75	100	15	Normal	○
Zen Headbutt	Psychic	Physical	80	90	15	Normal	○
Trick	Psychic	Status	—	100	10	Normal	—
Snore	Normal	Special	40	100	15	Normal	—
Helping Hand	Normal	Status	—	—	20	1 Ally	—
Magic Coat	Psychic	Status	—	—	15	Self	—
Role Play	Psychic	Status	—	—	10	Normal	—
Heal Bell	Normal	Status	—	—	5	All Allies	—
Mud-Slap	Ground	Special	20	100	10	Normal	—
Signal Beam	Bug	Special	75	100	15	Normal	—

● TM & HM MOVES

No.	Name	Type	Kind	Pow.	Acc.	PP	Range	DA
TM01	Focus Punch	Fighting	Physical	150	100	20	Normal	○
TM03	Water Pulse	Water	Special	60	100	20	Normal	—
TM04	Calm Mind	Psychic	Status	—	—	20	Self	—
TM06	Toxic	Poison	Status	—	85	10	Normal	—
TM07	Hail	Ice	Status	—	—	10	All	—
TM10	Hidden Power	Normal	Special	—	100	15	Normal	—
TM12	Taunt	Dark	Status	—	100	20	Normal	—
TM13	Ice Beam	Ice	Special	95	100	10	Normal	—
TM14	Blizzard	Ice	Special	120	70	5	2 Foes	—
TM15	Hyper Beam	Normal	Special	150	90	5	Normal	—
TM16	Light Screen	Psychic	Status	—	—	30	2 Allies	—
TM17	Protect	Normal	Status	—	—	10	Self	—
TM18	Rain Dance	Water	Status	—	—	5	All	—
TM21	Frustration	Normal	Physical	—	100	20	Normal	○
TM27	Return	Normal	Physical	—	100	20	Normal	○
TM29	Psychic	Psychic	Special	90	100	10	Normal	—
TM30	Shadow Ball	Ghost	Special	80	100	15	Normal	—
TM31	Brick Break	Fighting	Physical	75	100	15	Normal	○
TM32	Double Team	Normal	Status	—	—	15	Self	—
TM33	Reflect	Psychic	Status	—	—	20	2 Allies	—
TM41	Torment	Dark	Status	—	100	15	Normal	—
TM42	Facade	Normal	Physical	70	100	20	Normal	○
TM43	Secret Power	Normal	Physical	70	100	20	Normal	○
TM44	Rest	Psychic	Status	—	—	10	Self	—
TM45	Attract	Normal	Status	—	100	15	Normal	—
TM46	Thief	Dark	Physical	40	100	10	Normal	○
TM48	Skill Swap	Psychic	Status	—	—	10	Normal	—
TM52	Focus Blast	Fighting	Special	120	70	5	Normal	—
TM53	Energy Ball	Grass	Special	80	100	10	Normal	—
TM56	Fling	Dark	Physical	—	100	10	Normal	○
TM58	Endure	Normal	Status	—	—	10	Self	—
TM60	Drain Punch	Fighting	Physical	60	100	5	Normal	○
TM66	Payback	Dark	Physical	50	100	10	Normal	○
TM67	Recycle	Normal	Status	—	—	10	Self	—
TM68	Giga Impact	Normal	Physical	150	90	5	Normal	○
TM70	Flash	Normal	Status	—	100	20	Normal	—
TM72	Avalanche	Ice	Physical	60	100	10	Normal	○
TM77	Psych Up	Normal	Status	—	—	10	Self	—
TM78	Captivate	Normal	Status	—	100	20	2 Foes	—
TM82	Sleep Talk	Normal	Status	—	—	10	Depends	—
TM83	Natural Gift	Normal	Physical	—	100	15	Normal	—
TM85	Dream Eater	Psychic	Special	100	100	15	Normal	—
TM86	Grass Knot	Grass	Special	—	100	20	Normal	—
TM87	Swagger	Normal	Status	—	90	15	Normal	—
TM90	Substitute	Normal	Status	—	—	10	Self	—
TM92	Trick Room	Psychic	Status	—	—	5	All	—

● No. 124 | Human Shape Pokémon
Jynx

Ice　Psychic

● HEIGHT: 4'07"
● WEIGHT: 89.5 lbs.
● ITEMS: Aspear Berry

● SIZE COMPARISON

● FEMALE FORM

● ABILITIES
● Oblivious
● Forewarn

● STATS
HP ●●
ATTACK ●●●●
DEFENSE ●●●●
SP. ATTACK ●●●●●
SP. DEFENSE ●●●●
SPEED ●●●

● EGG GROUPS
Human-Like

● PERFORMANCE
SPEED ★★　　　　STAMINA ★★★★
POWER ★★★☆　　JUMP ★★☆
SKILL ★★☆

● MAIN WAYS TO OBTAIN

Pokémon HeartGold Ice Path

Pokémon SoulSilver Ice Path

Pokémon Diamond Level up Smoochum to Lv. 30

Pokémon Pearl Level up Smoochum to Lv. 30

Pokémon Platinum Snowpoint Temple B1F

Pokémon HeartGold
It rocks its body rhythmically. It appears to alter the rhythm depending on how it is feeling.

Pokémon SoulSilver
It speaks a language similar to that of humans. However, it seems to use dancing to communicate.

● EVOLUTION

Smoochum　Lv. 30　Jynx

Electabuzz

Electric

- **HEIGHT:** 3'07"
- **WEIGHT:** 66.1 lbs.
- **ITEMS:** None

● SIZE COMPARISON

● MALE/FEMALE HAVE SAME FORM

⊙ ABILITIES
- Static

⊙ STATS
HP	●●
ATTACK	●●●●
DEFENSE	●●●
SP. ATTACK	●●●●
SP. DEFENSE	●●●
SPEED	●●●●●

⊙ EGG GROUPS
Human-Like

⊙ PERFORMANCE
SPEED ★★★☆	STAMINA ★★★☆
POWER ★★★☆	JUMP ★★★
SKILL ★★★☆	

● MAIN WAYS TO OBTAIN

Pokémon HeartGold	Route 10
Pokémon SoulSilver	Route 10
Pokémon Diamond	Level up Elekid to Lv. 30
Pokémon Pearl	Level up Elekid to Lv. 30
Pokémon Platinum	Route 222

Pokémon HeartGold
Electricity runs across the surface of its body. In darkness, its entire body glows a whitish-blue.

Pokémon SoulSilver
Its body constantly discharges electricity. Getting close to it will make your hair stand on end.

⊙ EVOLUTION

Lv. 30 → Have it hold Electirizer and trade it →

Elekid — Electabuzz — Electivire

● LEVEL-UP MOVES
Lv.	Name	Type	Kind	Pow.	Acc.	PP	Range	DA
1	Quick Attack	Normal	Physical	40	100	30	Normal	—
1	Leer	Normal	Status	—	100	30	2 Foes	—
1	ThunderShock	Electric	Special	40	100	30	Normal	—
7	ThunderShock	Electric	Special	40	100	30	Normal	—
10	Low Kick	Fighting	Physical	—	100	20	Normal	○
16	Swift	Normal	Special	60	—	20	2 Foes	—
19	Shock Wave	Electric	Special	60	—	20	Normal	—
25	Light Screen	Psychic	Status	—	—	30	2 Allies	—
28	ThunderPunch	Electric	Physical	75	100	15	Normal	—
37	Discharge	Electric	Special	80	100	15	2 Foes/1 Ally	—
43	Thunderbolt	Electric	Special	95	100	15	Normal	—
52	Screech	Normal	Status	—	85	40	Normal	—
58	Thunder	Electric	Special	120	70	10	Normal	—

● MOVE MANIAC
Name	Type	Kind	Pow.	Acc.	PP	Range	DA
Headbutt	Normal	Physical	70	100	15	Normal	○

● BP MOVES
Name	Type	Kind	Pow.	Acc.	PP	Range	DA
ThunderPunch	Electric	Physical	75	100	15	Normal	○
Fire Punch	Fire	Physical	75	100	15	Normal	○
Ice Punch	Ice	Physical	75	100	15	Normal	○
Snore	Normal	Special	40	100	15	Normal	—
Helping Hand	Normal	Status	—	—	20	1 Ally	—
Magnet Rise	Electric	Status	—	—	10	Self	—
Swift	Normal	Special	60	—	20	2 Foes	—
Mud-Slap	Ground	Special	20	100	10	Normal	—
Signal Beam	Bug	Special	75	100	15	Normal	—
Low Kick	Fighting	Physical	—	100	20	Normal	○

● TM & HM MOVES
No.	Name	Type	Kind	Pow.	Acc.	PP	Range	DA
TM01	Focus Punch	Fighting	Physical	150	100	20	Normal	○
TM06	Toxic	Poison	Status	—	85	10	Normal	—
TM10	Hidden Power	Normal	Special	—	100	15	Normal	—
TM15	Hyper Beam	Normal	Special	150	90	5	Normal	—
TM16	Light Screen	Psychic	Status	—	—	30	2 Allies	—
TM17	Protect	Normal	Status	—	—	10	Self	—
TM18	Rain Dance	Water	Status	—	—	5	All	—
TM21	Frustration	Normal	Physical	—	100	20	Normal	○
TM23	Iron Tail	Steel	Physical	100	75	15	Normal	○
TM24	Thunderbolt	Electric	Special	95	100	15	Normal	—
TM25	Thunder	Electric	Special	120	70	10	Normal	—
TM27	Return	Normal	Physical	—	100	20	Normal	○
TM29	Psychic	Psychic	Special	90	100	10	Normal	—
TM31	Brick Break	Fighting	Physical	75	100	15	Normal	○
TM32	Double Team	Normal	Status	—	—	15	Self	—
TM34	Shock Wave	Electric	Special	60	—	20	Normal	—
TM42	Facade	Normal	Physical	70	100	20	Normal	○
TM43	Secret Power	Normal	Physical	70	100	20	Normal	○
TM44	Rest	Psychic	Status	—	—	10	Self	—
TM45	Attract	Normal	Status	—	100	15	Normal	—
TM46	Thief	Dark	Physical	40	100	10	Normal	○
TM52	Focus Blast	Fighting	Special	120	70	5	Normal	—
TM56	Fling	Dark	Physical	—	100	10	Normal	○
TM57	Charge Beam	Electric	Special	50	90	10	Normal	—
TM58	Endure	Normal	Status	—	—	10	Self	—
TM68	Giga Impact	Normal	Physical	150	90	5	Normal	○
TM70	Flash	Normal	Status	—	100	20	Normal	—
TM73	Thunder Wave	Electric	Status	—	100	20	Normal	—
TM78	Captivate	Normal	Status	—	100	20	2 Foes	—
TM82	Sleep Talk	Normal	Status	—	—	10	Depends	—
TM83	Natural Gift	Normal	Physical	—	100	15	Normal	○
TM87	Swagger	Normal	Status	—	90	15	Normal	—
TM90	Substitute	Normal	Status	—	—	10	Self	—
HM04	Strength	Normal	Physical	80	100	15	Normal	○
HM06	Rock Smash	Fighting	Physical	40	100	15	Normal	○
HM08	Rock Climb	Normal	Physical	90	85	20	Normal	○

● LEVEL-UP MOVES

Lv.	Name	Type	Kind	Pow.	Acc.	PP	Range	DA
1	Smog	Poison	Special	20	70	20	Normal	—
1	Leer	Normal	Status	—	100	30	2 Foes	—
1	Ember	Fire	Special	40	100	25	Normal	—
7	Ember	Fire	Special	40	100	25	Normal	—
10	SmokeScreen	Normal	Status	—	100	20	Normal	—
16	Faint Attack	Dark	Physical	60	—	20	Normal	○
19	Fire Spin	Fire	Special	15	70	15	Normal	—
25	Confuse Ray	Ghost	Status	—	100	10	Normal	—
28	Fire Punch	Fire	Physical	75	100	15	Normal	○
36	Lava Plume	Fire	Special	80	100	15	2 Foes/1 Ally	—
41	Flamethrower	Fire	Special	95	100	15	Normal	—
49	Sunny Day	Fire	Status	—	—	5	All	—
54	Fire Blast	Fire	Special	120	85	5	Normal	—

● MOVE MANIAC

Name	Type	Kind	Pow.	Acc.	PP	Range	DA
Headbutt	Normal	Physical	70	100	15	Normal	○

● BP MOVES

Name	Type	Kind	Pow.	Acc.	PP	Range	DA
ThunderPunch	Electric	Physical	75	100	15	Normal	○
Fire Punch	Fire	Physical	75	100	15	Normal	○
Snore	Normal	Special	40	100	15	Normal	—
Helping Hand	Normal	Status	—	—	20	1 Ally	—
Mud-Slap	Ground	Special	20	100	10	Normal	—
Heat Wave	Fire	Special	100	90	10	2 Foes	—
Low Kick	Fighting	Physical	—	100	20	Normal	○

● TM & HM MOVES

No.	Name	Type	Kind	Pow.	Acc.	PP	Range	DA
TM01	Focus Punch	Fighting	Physical	150	100	20	Normal	○
TM06	Toxic	Poison	Status	—	85	10	Normal	—
TM10	Hidden Power	Normal	Special	—	100	15	Normal	—
TM11	Sunny Day	Fire	Status	—	—	5	All	—
TM15	Hyper Beam	Normal	Special	150	90	5	Normal	—
TM17	Protect	Normal	Status	—	—	10	Self	—
TM21	Frustration	Normal	Physical	—	100	20	Normal	○
TM23	Iron Tail	Steel	Physical	100	75	15	Normal	○
TM27	Return	Normal	Physical	—	100	20	Normal	○
TM29	Psychic	Psychic	Special	90	100	10	Normal	—
TM31	Brick Break	Fighting	Physical	75	100	15	Normal	○
TM32	Double Team	Normal	Status	—	—	15	Self	—
TM35	Flamethrower	Fire	Special	95	100	15	Normal	—
TM38	Fire Blast	Fire	Special	120	85	5	Normal	—
TM42	Facade	Normal	Physical	70	100	20	Normal	○
TM43	Secret Power	Normal	Physical	70	100	20	Normal	—
TM44	Rest	Psychic	Status	—	—	10	Self	—
TM45	Attract	Normal	Status	—	100	15	Normal	—
TM46	Thief	Dark	Physical	40	100	10	Normal	○
TM50	Overheat	Fire	Special	140	90	5	Normal	—
TM52	Focus Blast	Fighting	Special	120	70	5	Normal	—
TM56	Fling	Dark	Physical	—	100	10	Normal	○
TM58	Endure	Normal	Status	—	—	10	Self	—
TM61	Will-O-Wisp	Fire	Status	—	75	15	Normal	—
TM68	Giga Impact	Normal	Physical	150	90	5	Normal	○
TM78	Captivate	Normal	Status	—	100	20	2 Foes	—
TM82	Sleep Talk	Normal	Status	—	—	10	Depends	—
TM83	Natural Gift	Normal	Physical	—	100	15	Normal	—
TM87	Swagger	Normal	Status	—	90	15	Normal	—
TM90	Substitute	Normal	Status	—	—	10	Self	—
HM04	Strength	Normal	Physical	80	100	15	Normal	○
HM06	Rock Smash	Fighting	Physical	40	100	15	Normal	○
HM08	Rock Climb	Normal	Physical	90	85	20	Normal	○

⦿ No. 126 | Spitfire Pokémon
Magmar

Fire

- ● HEIGHT: 4'03"
- ● WEIGHT: 98.1 lbs.
- ● ITEMS: None

● SIZE COMPARISON

● MALE/FEMALE HAVE SAME FORM

⦿ ABILITIES
- ● Flame Body

⦿ STATS
HP ●●
ATTACK ●●●●
DEFENSE ●●●
SP. ATTACK ●●●●
SP. DEFENSE ●●●
SPEED ●●●

⦿ EGG GROUPS
Human-Like

⦿ PERFORMANCE
SPEED ★★   STAMINA ★★★★☆
POWER ★★☆   JUMP ★★☆
SKILL ★★★★☆

● MAIN WAYS TO OBTAIN

Pokémon HeartGold	Burned Tower B1F
Pokémon SoulSilver	Burned Tower B1F
Pokémon Diamond	Level up Magby to Lv. 30
Pokémon Pearl	Level up Magby to Lv. 30
Pokémon Platinum	Fuego Ironworks

Pokémon HeartGold
It dislikes cold places, so it blows scorching flames to make the environment suitable for itself.

Pokémon SoulSilver
The fiery surface of its body gives off a wavering, rippling glare that is similar to the sun.

⦿ EVOLUTION

Lv. 30 — Have it hold Magmarizer and trade it

Magby → Magmar → Magmortar

⦿ No. 127 | Stag Beetle Pokémon
Pinsir

Bug

- **HEIGHT:** 4'11"
- **WEIGHT:** 121.3 lbs.
- **ITEMS:** None

● SIZE COMPARISON

● MALE/FEMALE HAVE SAME FORM

⦿ ABILITIES
- Hyper Cutter
- Mold Breaker

⦿ STATS
HP	●●
ATTACK	●●●●
DEFENSE	●●●●
SP. ATTACK	●●
SP. DEFENSE	●●●
SPEED	●●●●

⦿ EGG GROUPS
Bug

⦿ PERFORMANCE
SPEED ★★
POWER ★★★★☆
SKILL ★★★☆

STAMINA ★★★★☆
JUMP ★★☆

● MAIN WAYS TO OBTAIN

Pokémon HeartGold	Bug-Catching Contest at the National Park
Pokémon SoulSilver	Bug-Catching Contest at the National Park
Pokémon Diamond	—
Pokémon Pearl	Route 229
Pokémon Platinum	Route 229 (mass outbreak)

Pokémon HeartGold
With its pincer horns, it digs burrows to sleep in at night. In the morning, damp soil clings to its body.

Pokémon SoulSilver
It swings its long pincer horns wildly to attack. During cold periods, it hides deep in forests.

⦿ EVOLUTION

Does not evolve

● LEVEL-UP MOVES

Lv.	Name	Type	Kind	Pow.	Acc.	PP	Range	DA
1	ViceGrip	Normal	Physical	55	100	30	Normal	—
1	Focus Energy	Normal	Status	—	—	30	Self	—
4	Bind	Normal	Physical	15	75	20	Normal	○
8	Seismic Toss	Fighting	Physical	—	100	20	Normal	○
13	Harden	Normal	Status	—	—	30	Self	—
18	Revenge	Fighting	Physical	60	100	10	Normal	○
21	Brick Break	Fighting	Physical	75	100	15	Normal	○
25	Vital Throw	Fighting	Physical	70	—	10	Normal	○
30	X-Scissor	Bug	Physical	80	100	15	Normal	○
35	Thrash	Normal	Physical	90	100	10	1 Random	○
38	Swords Dance	Normal	Status	—	—	30	Self	—
42	Submission	Fighting	Physical	80	80	25	Normal	○
47	Guillotine	Normal	Physical	—	30	5	Normal	○
52	Superpower	Fighting	Physical	120	100	5	Normal	○

● MOVE MANIAC

Name	Type	Kind	Pow.	Acc.	PP	Range	DA
Headbutt	Normal	Physical	70	100	15	Normal	○

● BP MOVES

Name	Type	Kind	Pow.	Acc.	PP	Range	DA
Fury Cutter	Bug	Physical	10	95	20	Normal	○
Knock Off	Dark	Physical	20	100	20	Normal	○
Snore	Normal	Special	40	100	15	Normal	—
String Shot	Bug	Status	—	95	40	2 Foes	—
Superpower	Fighting	Physical	120	100	5	Normal	○
Iron Defense	Steel	Status	—	—	15	Self	—

● TM & HM MOVES

No.	Name	Type	Kind	Pow.	Acc.	PP	Range	DA
TM01	Focus Punch	Fighting	Physical	150	100	20	Normal	○
TM06	Toxic	Poison	Status	—	85	10	Normal	—
TM08	Bulk Up	Fighting	Status	—	—	20	Self	—
TM10	Hidden Power	Normal	Special	—	100	15	Normal	—
TM11	Sunny Day	Fire	Status	—	—	5	All	—
TM15	Hyper Beam	Normal	Special	150	90	5	Normal	—
TM17	Protect	Normal	Status	—	—	10	Self	—
TM18	Rain Dance	Water	Status	—	—	5	All	—
TM21	Frustration	Normal	Physical	—	100	20	Normal	○
TM26	Earthquake	Ground	Physical	100	100	10	2 Foes/1 Ally	—
TM27	Return	Normal	Physical	—	100	20	Normal	○
TM28	Dig	Ground	Physical	80	100	10	Normal	○
TM31	Brick Break	Fighting	Physical	75	100	15	Normal	○
TM32	Double Team	Normal	Status	—	—	15	Self	—
TM39	Rock Tomb	Rock	Physical	50	80	10	Normal	○
TM42	Facade	Normal	Physical	70	100	20	Normal	○
TM43	Secret Power	Normal	Physical	70	100	20	Normal	○
TM44	Rest	Psychic	Status	—	—	10	Self	—
TM45	Attract	Normal	Status	—	100	15	Normal	—
TM46	Thief	Dark	Physical	40	100	10	Normal	○
TM52	Focus Blast	Fighting	Special	120	70	5	Normal	—
TM54	False Swipe	Normal	Physical	40	100	40	Normal	○
TM56	Fling	Dark	Physical	—	100	10	Normal	—
TM58	Endure	Normal	Status	—	—	10	Self	—
TM68	Giga Impact	Normal	Physical	150	90	5	Normal	○
TM71	Stone Edge	Rock	Physical	100	80	5	Normal	—
TM75	Swords Dance	Normal	Status	—	—	30	Self	—
TM76	Stealth Rock	Rock	Status	—	—	20	2 Foes	—
TM78	Captivate	Normal	Status	—	100	20	2 Foes	—
TM80	Rock Slide	Rock	Physical	75	90	10	2 Foes	—
TM81	X-Scissor	Bug	Physical	80	100	15	Normal	○
TM82	Sleep Talk	Normal	Status	—	—	10	Depends	—
TM83	Natural Gift	Normal	Physical	—	100	15	Normal	—
TM87	Swagger	Normal	Status	—	90	15	Normal	—
TM90	Substitute	Normal	Status	—	—	10	Self	—
HM01	Cut	Normal	Physical	50	95	30	Normal	○
HM04	Strength	Normal	Physical	80	100	15	Normal	○
HM06	Rock Smash	Fighting	Physical	40	100	15	Normal	○
HM08	Rock Climb	Normal	Physical	90	85	20	Normal	○

● EGG MOVES

Name	Type	Kind	Pow.	Acc.	PP	Range	DA
Fury Attack	Normal	Physical	15	85	20	Normal	○
Flail	Normal	Physical	—	100	15	Normal	○
False Swipe	Normal	Physical	40	100	40	Normal	○
Faint Attack	Dark	Physical	60	—	20	Normal	—
Quick Attack	Normal	Physical	40	100	30	Normal	○
Close Combat	Fighting	Physical	120	100	5	Normal	—
Feint	Normal	Physical	50	100	10	Normal	—

● LEVEL-UP MOVES

Lv.	Name	Type	Kind	Pow.	Acc.	PP	Range	DA
1	Tackle	Normal	Physical	35	95	35	Normal	○
3	Tail Whip	Normal	Status	—	100	30	2 Foes	—
5	Rage	Normal	Physical	20	100	20	Normal	○
8	Horn Attack	Normal	Physical	65	100	25	Normal	○
11	Scary Face	Normal	Status	—	90	10	Normal	—
15	Pursuit	Dark	Physical	40	100	20	Normal	○
19	Rest	Psychic	Status	—	—	10	Self	—
24	Payback	Dark	Physical	50	100	10	Normal	○
29	Zen Headbutt	Psychic	Physical	80	90	15	Normal	○
35	Take Down	Normal	Physical	90	85	20	Normal	○
41	Swagger	Normal	Status	—	90	15	Normal	—
48	Thrash	Normal	Physical	90	100	20	1 Random	○
55	Giga Impact	Normal	Physical	150	90	5	Normal	○

● MOVE MANIAC

Name	Type	Kind	Pow.	Acc.	PP	Range	DA
Headbutt	Normal	Physical	70	100	15	Normal	○

● BP MOVES

Name	Type	Kind	Pow.	Acc.	PP	Range	DA
Icy Wind	Ice	Special	55	95	15	2 Foes	—
Zen Headbutt	Psychic	Physical	80	90	15	Normal	○
Snore	Normal	Special	40	100	15	Normal	—
Spite	Ghost	Status	—	100	10	Normal	—
Helping Hand	Normal	Status	—	—	20	1 Ally	—
Uproar	Normal	Special	50	100	10	1 Random	—
Role Play	Psychic	Status	—	—	10	Normal	—
Iron Head	Steel	Physical	80	100	15	Normal	○
Endeavor	Normal	Physical	—	100	5	Normal	○
Outrage	Dragon	Physical	120	100	15	1 Random	○

● TM & HM MOVES

No.	Name	Type	Kind	Pow.	Acc.	PP	Range	DA
TM03	Water Pulse	Water	Special	60	100	20	Normal	—
TM06	Toxic	Poison	Status	—	85	10	Normal	—
TM10	Hidden Power	Normal	Special	—	100	15	Normal	—
TM11	Sunny Day	Fire	Status	—	—	5	All	—
TM13	Ice Beam	Ice	Special	95	100	10	Normal	—
TM14	Blizzard	Ice	Special	120	70	5	2 Foes	—
TM15	Hyper Beam	Normal	Special	150	90	5	Normal	—
TM17	Protect	Normal	Status	—	—	10	Self	—
TM18	Rain Dance	Water	Status	—	—	5	All	—
TM21	Frustration	Normal	Physical	—	100	20	Normal	○
TM22	SolarBeam	Grass	Special	120	100	10	Normal	—
TM23	Iron Tail	Steel	Physical	100	75	15	Normal	○
TM24	Thunderbolt	Electric	Special	95	100	15	Normal	—
TM25	Thunder	Electric	Special	120	70	10	Normal	—
TM26	Earthquake	Ground	Physical	100	100	10	2 Foes/1 Ally	○
TM27	Return	Normal	Physical	—	100	20	Normal	○
TM32	Double Team	Normal	Status	—	—	15	Self	—
TM34	Shock Wave	Electric	Special	60	—	20	Normal	—
TM35	Flamethrower	Fire	Special	95	100	15	Normal	—
TM37	Sandstorm	Rock	Status	—	—	10	All	—
TM38	Fire Blast	Fire	Special	120	85	5	Normal	—
TM39	Rock Tomb	Rock	Physical	50	80	10	Normal	○
TM42	Facade	Normal	Physical	70	100	20	Normal	○
TM43	Secret Power	Normal	Physical	70	100	20	Normal	○
TM44	Rest	Psychic	Status	—	—	10	Self	—
TM45	Attract	Normal	Status	—	100	15	Normal	—
TM58	Endure	Normal	Status	—	—	10	Self	—
TM66	Payback	Dark	Physical	50	100	10	Normal	○
TM68	Giga Impact	Normal	Physical	150	90	5	Normal	○
TM71	Stone Edge	Rock	Physical	100	80	5	Normal	○
TM78	Captivate	Normal	Status	—	100	20	2 Foes	—
TM80	Rock Slide	Rock	Physical	75	90	10	2 Foes	—
TM82	Sleep Talk	Normal	Status	—	—	10	Depends	—
TM83	Natural Gift	Normal	Physical	—	100	15	Normal	—
TM87	Swagger	Normal	Status	—	90	15	Normal	—
TM90	Substitute	Normal	Status	—	—	10	Self	—
HM03	Surf	Water	Special	95	100	15	2 Foes/1 Ally	—
HM04	Strength	Normal	Physical	80	100	15	Normal	○
HM05	Whirlpool	Water	Special	15	70	15	Normal	—
HM06	Rock Smash	Fighting	Physical	40	100	15	Normal	○
HM08	Rock Climb	Normal	Physical	90	85	20	Normal	○

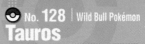

No. 128 | Wild Bull Pokémon
Tauros

Normal

- ● HEIGHT: 4'07"
- ● WEIGHT: 194.9 lbs.
- ● ITEMS: None
- ● SIZE COMPARISON

● MALE FORM

● ABILITIES
- ● Intimidate
- ● Anger Point

● STATS
- HP ●●●
- ATTACK ●●●●
- DEFENSE ●●●●
- SP. ATTACK ●●
- SP. DEFENSE ●●●
- SPEED ●●●●●

● EGG GROUPS
Field

● PERFORMANCE
SPEED ★★★☆   STAMINA ★★☆☆☆
POWER ★★★★☆   JUMP ★★
SKILL ★★

● MAIN WAYS TO OBTAIN

Pokémon HeartGold — Route 38

Pokémon SoulSilver — Route 38

Pokémon Diamond — Route 209 (use Poké Radar)

Pokémon Pearl — Route 209 (use Poké Radar)

Pokémon Platinum — Route 210 in Solaceon Town (use Poké Radar)

Pokémon HeartGold	Pokémon SoulSilver
They fight each other by locking horns. The herd's protector takes pride in its battle-scarred horns.	After heightening its will to fight by whipping itself with its three tails, it charges at full speed.

● EVOLUTION

Does not evolve

No. 129 | Fish Pokémon
Magikarp

`Water`

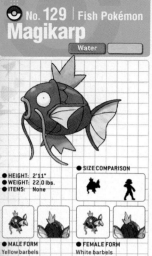

- **HEIGHT:** 2'11"
- **WEIGHT:** 22.0 lbs.
- **ITEMS:** None

● SIZE COMPARISON

● **MALE FORM**
Yellow barbels

● **FEMALE FORM**
White barbels

⊙ ABILITIES
- Swift Swim

⊙ STATS
- HP ●
- ATTACK ●
- DEFENSE ●●
- SP. ATTACK ●
- SP. DEFENSE ●
- SPEED ●●●●

⊙ EGG GROUPS
Water 2

Dragon

⊙ PERFORMANCE
SPEED ★☆☆☆☆   STAMINA ★☆☆☆☆
POWER ★☆☆☆☆   JUMP ★★☆☆☆
SKILL ★★☆☆☆

● MAIN WAYS TO OBTAIN

Pokémon HeartGold	Route 43 (water surface)
Pokémon SoulSilver	Route 43 (water surface)
Pokémon Diamond	Route 203 (Old Rod)
Pokémon Pearl	Route 203 (Old Rod)
Pokémon Platinum	Route 203 (Old Rod)

Pokémon HeartGold
An underpowered, pathetic Pokémon. It may jump high on rare occasions, but usually not more than seven feet.

Pokémon SoulSilver
For no reason, it jumps and splashes about, making it easy for predators like PIDGEOTTO to catch it mid-jump.

⊙ EVOLUTION

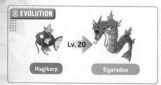

Magikarp — Lv. 20 → Gyarados

● LEVEL-UP MOVES

Lv.	Name	Type	Kind	Pow.	Acc.	PP	Range	DA
1	Splash	Normal	Status	—	—	40	Self	
15	Tackle	Normal	Physical	35	95	35	Normal	○
30	Flail	Normal	Physical	—	100	15	Normal	○

● MOVE MANIAC

Name	Type	Kind	Pow.	Acc.	PP	Range	DA

● BP MOVES

Name	Type	Kind	Pow.	Acc.	PP	Range	DA
Bounce	Flying	Physical	85	85	5	Normal	○

● TM & HM MOVES

No.	Name	Type	Kind	Pow.	Acc.	PP	Range	DA

● LEVEL-UP MOVES

Lv.	Name	Type	Kind	Pow.	Acc.	PP	Range	DA
1	Thrash	Normal	Physical	90	100	20	1 Random	—
20	Bite	Dark	Physical	60	100	25	Normal	—
23	Dragon Rage	Dragon	Special	—	100	10	Normal	—
26	Leer	Normal	Status	—	100	30	2 Foes	—
29	Twister	Dragon	Special	40	100	20	2 Foes	—
32	Ice Fang	Ice	Physical	65	95	15	Normal	○
35	Aqua Tail	Water	Physical	90	90	10	Normal	—
38	Rain Dance	Water	Status	—	—	5	All	—
41	Hydro Pump	Water	Special	120	80	5	Normal	—
44	Dragon Dance	Dragon	Status	—	—	20	Self	—
47	Hyper Beam	Normal	Special	150	90	5	Normal	—

● MOVE MANIAC

Name	Type	Kind	Pow.	Acc.	PP	Range	DA
Headbutt	Normal	Physical	70	100	15	Normal	○

● BP MOVES

Name	Type	Kind	Pow.	Acc.	PP	Range	DA
Dive	Water	Physical	80	100	10	Normal	○
Icy Wind	Ice	Special	55	95	15	2 Foes	—
Snore	Normal	Special	40	100	15	Normal	—
Spite	Ghost	Status	—	100	10	Normal	—
Uproar	Normal	Special	50	100	10	1 Random	—
Iron Head	Steel	Physical	80	100	15	Normal	○
Aqua Tail	Water	Physical	90	90	10	Normal	—
Outrage	Dragon	Physical	120	100	15	1 Random	—
Twister	Dragon	Special	40	100	20	2 Foes	—
Bounce	Flying	Physical	85	85	5	Normal	○

● TM & HM MOVES

No.	Name	Type	Kind	Pow.	Acc.	PP	Range	DA
TM03	Water Pulse	Water	Special	60	100	20	Normal	—
TM05	Roar	Normal	Status	—	100	20	Normal	—
TM06	Toxic	Poison	Status	—	85	10	Normal	—
TM07	Hail	Ice	Status	—	—	10	All	—
TM10	Hidden Power	Normal	Special	—	100	15	Normal	—
TM12	Taunt	Dark	Status	—	100	20	Normal	—
TM13	Ice Beam	Ice	Special	95	100	10	Normal	—
TM14	Blizzard	Ice	Special	120	70	5	2 Foes	—
TM15	Hyper Beam	Normal	Special	150	90	5	Normal	—
TM17	Protect	Normal	Status	—	—	10	Self	—
TM18	Rain Dance	Water	Status	—	—	5	All	—
TM21	Frustration	Normal	Physical	—	100	20	Normal	○
TM24	Thunderbolt	Electric	Special	95	100	15	Normal	—
TM25	Thunder	Electric	Special	120	70	10	Normal	—
TM26	Earthquake	Ground	Physical	100	100	10	2 Foes/1 Ally	○
TM27	Return	Normal	Physical	—	100	20	Normal	○
TM32	Double Team	Normal	Status	—	—	15	Self	—
TM35	Flamethrower	Fire	Special	95	100	15	Normal	—
TM37	Sandstorm	Rock	Status	—	—	10	All	—
TM38	Fire Blast	Fire	Special	120	85	5	Normal	—
TM41	Torment	Dark	Status	—	100	15	Normal	—
TM42	Facade	Normal	Physical	70	100	20	Normal	○
TM43	Secret Power	Normal	Physical	70	100	20	Normal	○
TM44	Rest	Psychic	Status	—	—	10	Self	—
TM45	Attract	Normal	Status	—	100	15	Normal	—
TM55	Brine	Water	Special	65	100	10	Normal	—
TM58	Endure	Normal	Status	—	—	10	Self	—
TM59	Dragon Pulse	Dragon	Special	90	100	10	Normal	—
TM66	Payback	Dark	Physical	50	100	10	Normal	○
TM68	Giga Impact	Normal	Physical	150	90	5	Normal	○
TM71	Stone Edge	Rock	Physical	100	80	5	Normal	○
TM72	Avalanche	Ice	Physical	60	100	10	Normal	○
TM73	Thunder Wave	Electric	Status	—	100	20	Normal	—
TM78	Captivate	Normal	Status	—	100	20	2 Foes	—
TM79	Dark Pulse	Dark	Special	80	100	15	Normal	—
TM82	Sleep Talk	Normal	Status	—	—	10	Depends	—
TM83	Natural Gift	Normal	Physical	—	100	15	Normal	—
TM87	Swagger	Normal	Status	—	90	15	Normal	—
TM90	Substitute	Normal	Status	—	—	10	Self	—
HM03	Surf	Water	Special	95	100	15	2 Foes/1 Ally	○
HM04	Strength	Normal	Physical	80	100	15	Normal	○
HM05	Whirlpool	Water	Special	15	70	15	Normal	—
HM06	Rock Smash	Fighting	Physical	40	100	15	Normal	○
HM07	Waterfall	Water	Physical	80	100	15	Normal	○

● No. 130 | Atrocious Pokémon
Gyarados

Water **Flying**

- ● HEIGHT: 21'04"
- ● WEIGHT: 518.1 lbs.
- ● ITEMS: None

● SIZE COMPARISON

● MALE FORM
Blue barbels

● FEMALE FORM
White barbels

● ABILITIES
- ● Intimidate

● STATS
HP ●●●●
ATTACK ●●●●●
DEFENSE ●●●●
SP. ATTACK ●●●
SP. DEFENSE ●●●
SPEED ●●●●

● EGG GROUPS
Water 2

Dragon

● PERFORMANCE

SPEED ★★☆   STAMINA ★★★☆
POWER ★★★★★   JUMP ★★★★☆
SKILL ★☆

● MAIN WAYS TO OBTAIN

Pokémon HeartGold — Lake of Rage (water surface)

Pokémon SoulSilver — Lake of Rage (water surface)

Pokémon Diamond — Route 203 (Super Rod)

Pokémon Pearl — Route 203 (Super Rod)

Pokémon Platinum — Route 203 (Super Rod)

Pokémon HeartGold

They say that during past strife, GYARADOS would appear and leave blazing ruins in its wake.

Pokémon SoulSilver

Once it appears, it goes on a rampage. It remains enraged until it demolishes everything around it.

● EVOLUTION

Magikarp   Lv. 20   Gyarados

No. 131 | Transport Pokémon
Lapras

Water **Ice**

● HEIGHT: 8'02"
● WEIGHT: 485.0 lbs.
● ITEMS: None

● SIZE COMPARISON

● MALE/FEMALE HAVE SAME FORM

⊛ ABILITIES
● Water Absorb
● Shell Armor

⊛ STATS
HP ●●●●●
ATTACK ●●●●
DEFENSE ●●●●
SP. ATTACK ●●●●
SP. DEFENSE ●●●●
SPEED ●●●

⊛ EGG GROUPS
Monster

Water 1

⊛ PERFORMANCE
SPEED ★★☆
POWER ★★★☆
SKILL ★★★☆
STAMINA ★★★★☆
JUMP ★★★

● MAIN WAYS TO OBTAIN

Pokémon HeartGold — Safari Zone (Rocky Beach Area, water surface)

Pokémon SoulSilver — Safari Zone (Rocky Beach Area, water surface)

Pokémon Diamond — Victory Road 1F Back 2 (water surface)

Pokémon Pearl — Victory Road 1F Back 2 (water surface)

Pokémon Platinum — Victory Road 1F Back 2 (water surface)

Pokémon HeartGold — They have gentle hearts. Because they rarely fight, many have been caught. Their number has dwindled.

Pokémon SoulSilver — It ferries people across the sea on its back. It may sing an enchanting cry if it is in a good mood.

⊛ EVOLUTION
Does not evolve

● LEVEL-UP MOVES

Lv.	Name	Type	Kind	Pow.	Acc.	PP	Range	DA
1	Sing	Normal	Status	—	55	15	Normal	—
1	Growl	Normal	Status	—	100	40	2 Foes	—
1	Water Gun	Water	Special	40	100	25	Normal	—
4	Mist	Ice	Status	—	—	30	2 Allies	—
7	Confuse Ray	Ghost	Status	—	100	10	Normal	—
10	Ice Shard	Ice	Physical	40	100	30	Normal	—
14	Water Pulse	Water	Special	60	100	20	Normal	—
18	Body Slam	Normal	Physical	85	100	15	Normal	○
22	Rain Dance	Water	Status	—	—	5	All	—
27	Perish Song	Normal	Status	—	—	5	All	—
32	Ice Beam	Ice	Special	95	100	10	Normal	—
37	Brine	Water	Special	65	100	10	Normal	—
43	Safeguard	Normal	Status	—	—	25	2 Allies	—
49	Hydro Pump	Water	Special	120	80	5	Normal	—
55	Sheer Cold	Ice	Special	—	30	5	Normal	—

● MOVE MANIAC

Name	Type	Kind	Pow.	Acc.	PP	Range	DA
Headbutt	Normal	Physical	70	100	15	Normal	○

● BP MOVES

Name	Type	Kind	Pow.	Acc.	PP	Range	DA
Dive	Water	Physical	80	100	10	Normal	○
Icy Wind	Ice	Special	55	95	15	2 Foes	—
Zen Headbutt	Psychic	Physical	80	90	15	Normal	○
Snore	Normal	Special	40	100	15	Normal	—
Heal Bell	Normal	Status	—	—	5	All Allies	—
Block	Normal	Status	—	—	5	Normal	—
Iron Head	Steel	Physical	80	100	15	Normal	○
Aqua Tail	Water	Physical	90	90	10	Normal	○
Outrage	Dragon	Physical	120	100	15	1 Random	○
AncientPower	Rock	Special	60	100	5	Normal	—
Signal Beam	Bug	Special	75	100	15	Normal	—

● TM & HM MOVES

No.	Name	Type	Kind	Pow.	Acc.	PP	Range	DA
TM03	Water Pulse	Water	Special	60	100	20	Normal	—
TM05	Roar	Normal	Status	—	100	20	Normal	—
TM06	Toxic	Poison	Status	—	85	10	Normal	—
TM07	Hail	Ice	Status	—	—	10	All	—
TM10	Hidden Power	Normal	Special	—	100	15	Normal	—
TM13	Ice Beam	Ice	Special	95	100	10	Normal	—
TM14	Blizzard	Ice	Special	120	70	5	2 Foes	—
TM15	Hyper Beam	Normal	Special	150	90	5	Normal	—
TM17	Protect	Normal	Status	—	—	10	Self	—
TM18	Rain Dance	Water	Status	—	—	5	All	—
TM20	Safeguard	Normal	Status	—	—	25	2 Allies	—
TM21	Frustration	Normal	Physical	—	100	20	Normal	○
TM23	Iron Tail	Steel	Physical	100	75	15	Normal	○
TM24	Thunderbolt	Electric	Special	95	100	15	Normal	—
TM25	Thunder	Electric	Special	120	70	10	Normal	—
TM27	Return	Normal	Physical	—	100	20	Normal	○
TM29	Psychic	Psychic	Special	90	100	10	Normal	—
TM32	Double Team	Normal	Status	—	—	15	Self	—
TM34	Shock Wave	Electric	Special	60	—	20	Normal	—
TM42	Facade	Normal	Physical	70	100	20	Normal	○
TM43	Secret Power	Normal	Physical	70	100	20	Normal	—
TM44	Rest	Psychic	Status	—	—	10	Self	—
TM45	Attract	Normal	Status	—	100	15	Normal	—
TM55	Brine	Water	Special	65	100	10	Normal	—
TM58	Endure	Normal	Status	—	—	10	Self	—
TM59	Dragon Pulse	Dragon	Special	90	100	10	Normal	—
TM68	Giga Impact	Normal	Physical	150	90	5	Normal	○
TM72	Avalanche	Ice	Physical	60	100	10	Normal	○
TM78	Captivate	Normal	Status	—	100	20	2 Foes	—
TM82	Sleep Talk	Normal	Status	—	—	10	Depends	—
TM83	Natural Gift	Normal	Physical	—	100	15	Normal	—
TM85	Dream Eater	Psychic	Special	100	100	15	Normal	—
TM87	Swagger	Normal	Status	—	90	15	Normal	—
TM90	Substitute	Normal	Status	—	—	10	Self	—
HM03	Surf	Water	Special	95	100	15	2 Foes/1 Ally	—
HM04	Strength	Normal	Physical	80	100	15	Normal	○
HM05	Whirlpool	Water	Special	15	70	15	Normal	—
HM06	Rock Smash	Fighting	Physical	40	100	15	Normal	○
HM07	Waterfall	Water	Physical	80	100	15	Normal	○

● EGG MOVES

Name	Type	Kind	Pow.	Acc.	PP	Range	DA
Foresight	Normal	Status	—	—	40	Normal	—
Substitute	Normal	Status	—	—	10	Self	—
Tickle	Normal	Status	—	100	20	Normal	—
Refresh	Normal	Status	—	—	20	Self	—
Dragon Dance	Dragon	Status	—	—	20	Self	—
Curse	???	Status	—	—	10	Normal/Self	—
Sleep Talk	Normal	Status	—	—	10	Depends	—
Horn Drill	Normal	Physical	—	30	5	Normal	○
AncientPower	Rock	Special	60	100	5	Normal	—
Whirlpool	Water	Special	15	70	15	Normal	—
Fissure	Ground	Physical	—	30	5	Normal	—

● LEVEL-UP MOVES

Lv.	Name	Type	Kind	Pow.	Acc.	PP	Range	DA
1	Transform	Normal	Status	—	—	10	Normal	—

● MOVE MANIAC

Name	Type	Kind	Pow.	Acc.	PP	Range	DA

● BP MOVES

Name	Type	Kind	Pow.	Acc.	PP	Range	DA

● TM & HM MOVES

No.	Name	Type	Kind	Pow.	Acc.	PP	Range	DA

No. 132 | Transform Pokémon
Ditto

Normal

- **HEIGHT:** 1'00"
- **WEIGHT:** 8.8 lbs.
- **ITEMS:** Quick Powder, Metal Powder

● SIZE COMPARISON

● GENDER UNKNOWN

⊘ ABILITIES
● Limber

⊘ STATS
HP ●●
ATTACK ●●
DEFENSE ●●
SP. ATTACK ●●
SP. DEFENSE ●●
SPEED ●●

⊘ EGG GROUPS
Ditto

⊘ PERFORMANCE
SPEED ★★☆☆☆   STAMINA ★★☆☆☆
POWER ★★☆☆☆   JUMP ★★☆☆☆
SKILL ★★☆☆☆

● MAIN WAYS TO OBTAIN

Pokémon HeartGold	Route 34 or Safari Zone (Wetland Area: If Water objects are placed, may appear in tall grass)
Pokémon SoulSilver	Route 34 or Safari Zone (Wetland Area: If Water objects are placed, may appear in tall grass)
Pokémon Diamond	Route 218 (use Poké Radar)
Pokémon Pearl	Route 218 (use Poké Radar)
Pokémon Platinum	Trophy Garden at the Pokémon Mansion on Route 212 (after obtaining the National Pokédex, talk to Mr. Backlot)

Pokémon HeartGold	**Pokémon SoulSilver**
It can transform into anything. When it sleeps, it changes into a stone to avoid being attacked.	Its transformation ability is perfect. However, if made to laugh, it can't maintain its disguise.

⊘ EVOLUTION

Does not evolve

No. 133 | Evolution Pokémon
Eevee

Normal

● LEVEL-UP MOVES

Lv.	Name	Type	Kind	Pow.	Acc.	PP	Range	DA
1	Tail Whip	Normal	Status	—	100	30	2 Foes	—
1	Tackle	Normal	Physical	35	95	35	Normal	—
1	Helping Hand	Normal	Status	—	—	20	1 Ally	—
8	Sand-Attack	Ground	Status	—	100	15	Normal	—
15	Growl	Normal	Status	—	100	40	2 Foes	—
22	Quick Attack	Normal	Physical	40	100	30	Normal	○
29	Bite	Dark	Physical	60	100	25	Normal	○
36	Baton Pass	Normal	Status	—	—	40	Self	—
43	Take Down	Normal	Physical	90	85	20	Normal	○
50	Last Resort	Normal	Physical	130	100	5	Normal	○
57	Trump Card	Normal	Special	—	—	5	Normal	○

● MOVE MANIAC

Name	Type	Kind	Pow.	Acc.	PP	Range	DA
Headbutt	Normal	Physical	70	100	15	Normal	○

● BP MOVES

Name	Type	Kind	Pow.	Acc.	PP	Range	DA
Snore	Normal	Special	40	100	15	Normal	—
Helping Hand	Normal	Status	—	—	20	1 Ally	—
Last Resort	Normal	Physical	130	100	5	Normal	○
Swift	Normal	Special	60	—	20	2 Foes	—
Heal Bell	Normal	Status	—	—	5	All Allies	—
Mud-Slap	Ground	Special	20	100	10	Normal	—

● SIZE COMPARISON

● HEIGHT: 1'00"
● WEIGHT: 14.3 lbs.
● ITEMS: None

● MALE/FEMALE HAVE SAME FORM

⊛ ABILITIES
● Run Away
● Adaptability

⊛ STATS
HP ●●
ATTACK ●●
DEFENSE ●●
SP. ATTACK ●●
SP. DEFENSE ●●
SPEED ●●●

⊛ EGG GROUPS
Field

● TM & HM MOVES

No.	Name	Type	Kind	Pow.	Acc.	PP	Range	DA
TM06	Toxic	Poison	Status	—	85	10	Normal	—
TM10	Hidden Power	Normal	Special	—	100	15	Normal	—
TM11	Sunny Day	Fire	Status	—	—	5	All	—
TM17	Protect	Normal	Status	—	—	10	Self	—
TM18	Rain Dance	Water	Status	—	—	5	All	—
TM21	Frustration	Normal	Physical	—	100	20	Normal	○
TM23	Iron Tail	Steel	Physical	100	75	15	Normal	○
TM27	Return	Normal	Physical	—	100	20	Normal	○
TM28	Dig	Ground	Physical	80	100	10	Normal	○
TM30	Shadow Ball	Ghost	Special	80	100	15	Normal	—
TM32	Double Team	Normal	Status	—	—	15	Self	—
TM42	Facade	Normal	Physical	70	100	20	Normal	○
TM43	Secret Power	Normal	Physical	70	100	20	Normal	—
TM44	Rest	Psychic	Status	—	—	10	Self	—
TM45	Attract	Normal	Status	—	100	15	Normal	—
TM58	Endure	Normal	Status	—	—	10	Self	—
TM78	Captivate	Normal	Status	—	100	20	2 Foes	—
TM82	Sleep Talk	Normal	Status	—	—	10	Depends	—
TM83	Natural Gift	Normal	Physical	—	100	15	Normal	—
TM87	Swagger	Normal	Status	—	90	15	Normal	—
TM90	Substitute	Normal	Status	—	—	10	Self	—

⊛ PERFORMANCE

SPEED ★★☆☆	STAMINA ★★☆☆
POWER ★★★☆	JUMP ★★☆☆
SKILL ★★☆☆	

● MAIN WAYS TO OBTAIN

Pokémon HeartGold	Receive from Bill in Goldenrod City
Pokémon SoulSilver	Receive from Bill in Goldenrod City
Pokémon Diamond	Trophy Garden at the Pokémon Mansion on Route 212 [after obtaining the National Pokédex, talk to Mr. Backlot]
Pokémon Pearl	Trophy Garden at the Pokémon Mansion on Route 212 [after obtaining the National Pokédex, talk to Mr. Backlot]
Pokémon Platinum	Trophy Garden at the Pokémon Mansion on Route 212 [after obtaining the National Pokédex, talk to Mr. Backlot]

Pokémon HeartGold	Pokémon SoulSilver
It has the ability to alter the composition of its body to suit its surrounding environment.	Its irregularly configured DNA is affected by its surroundings. It evolves if its environment changes.

⊛ EVOLUTION

 Eevee

 Vaporeon — Use Water Stone on Eevee

 Jolteon — Use Thunderstone on Eevee

 Flareon — Use Fire Stone on Eevee

 Espeon — Level up Eevee with high friendship in the morning or afternoon

Umbreon — Level up Eevee with high friendship at night

Leafeon — Level up Eevee in Eterna Forest*

 Glaceon — Level up Eevee on Route 217*

● EGG MOVES

Name	Type	Kind	Pow.	Acc.	PP	Range	DA
Charm	Normal	Status	—	100	20	Normal	—
Flail	Normal	Physical	—	100	15	Normal	○
Endure	Normal	Status	—	—	10	Self	—
Curse	???	Status	—	—	10	Normal/Self	—
Tickle	Normal	Status	—	100	20	Normal	—
Wish	Normal	Status	—	—	10	Self	—
Yawn	Normal	Status	—	—	10	Normal	—
Fake Tears	Dark	Status	—	100	20	Normal	—
Covet	Normal	Physical	40	100	40	Normal	○
Detect	Fighting	Status	—	—	5	Self	—

* Unable to evolve in Pokémon HeartGold or SoulSilver Version. Transfer from Diamond, Pearl, or Platinum Version.

● LEVEL-UP MOVES

Lv.	Name	Type	Kind	Pow.	Acc.	PP	Range	DA
1	Tail Whip	Normal	Status	—	100	30	2 Foes	—
1	Tackle	Normal	Physical	35	95	35	Normal	○
1	Helping Hand	Normal	Status	—	—	20	1 Ally	—
8	Sand-Attack	Ground	Status	—	100	15	Normal	—
15	Water Gun	Water	Special	40	100	25	Normal	—
22	Quick Attack	Normal	Physical	40	100	30	Normal	○
29	Bite	Dark	Physical	60	100	25	Normal	○
36	Aurora Beam	Ice	Special	65	100	20	Normal	—
43	Aqua Ring	Water	Status	—	—	20	Self	—
50	Last Resort	Normal	Physical	130	100	5	Normal	○
57	Haze	Ice	Status	—	—	30	All	—
64	Acid Armor	Poison	Status	—	—	40	Self	—
71	Hydro Pump	Water	Special	120	80	5	Normal	—
78	Muddy Water	Water	Special	95	85	10	2 Foes	—

● MOVE MANIAC

Name	Type	Kind	Pow.	Acc.	PP	Range	DA
Headbutt	Normal	Physical	70	100	15	Normal	○

● BP MOVES

Name	Type	Kind	Pow.	Acc.	PP	Range	DA
Dive	Water	Physical	80	100	10	Normal	○
Icy Wind	Ice	Special	55	95	15	2 Foes	—
Snore	Normal	Special	40	100	15	Normal	—
Helping Hand	Normal	Status	—	—	20	1 Ally	—
Last Resort	Normal	Physical	130	100	5	Normal	○
Swift	Normal	Special	60	—	20	2 Foes	—
Heal Bell	Normal	Status	—	—	5	All Allies	—
Mud-Slap	Ground	Special	20	100	10	Normal	—
Aqua Tail	Water	Physical	90	90	10	Normal	○
Signal Beam	Bug	Special	75	100	15	Normal	—

● TM & HM MOVES

No.	Name	Type	Kind	Pow.	Acc.	PP	Range	DA
TM03	Water Pulse	Water	Special	60	100	20	Normal	—
TM05	Roar	Normal	Status	—	100	20	Normal	—
TM06	Toxic	Poison	Status	—	85	10	Normal	—
TM07	Hail	Ice	Status	—	—	10	All	—
TM10	Hidden Power	Normal	Special	—	100	15	Normal	—
TM11	Sunny Day	Fire	Status	—	—	5	All	—
TM13	Ice Beam	Ice	Special	95	100	10	Normal	—
TM14	Blizzard	Ice	Special	120	70	5	2 Foes	—
TM15	Hyper Beam	Normal	Special	150	90	5	Normal	—
TM17	Protect	Normal	Status	—	—	10	Self	—
TM18	Rain Dance	Water	Status	—	—	5	All	—
TM21	Frustration	Normal	Physical	—	100	20	Normal	○
TM23	Iron Tail	Steel	Physical	100	75	15	Normal	○
TM27	Return	Normal	Physical	—	100	20	Normal	○
TM28	Dig	Ground	Physical	80	100	10	Normal	○
TM30	Shadow Ball	Ghost	Special	80	100	15	Normal	—
TM32	Double Team	Normal	Status	—	—	15	Self	—
TM42	Facade	Normal	Physical	70	100	20	Normal	○
TM43	Secret Power	Normal	Physical	70	100	20	Normal	○
TM44	Rest	Psychic	Status	—	—	10	Self	—
TM45	Attract	Normal	Status	—	100	15	Normal	—
TM55	Brine	Water	Special	65	100	10	Normal	—
TM58	Endure	Normal	Status	—	—	10	Self	—
TM68	Giga Impact	Normal	Physical	150	90	5	Normal	○
TM78	Captivate	Normal	Status	—	100	20	2 Foes	—
TM82	Sleep Talk	Normal	Status	—	—	10	Depends	—
TM83	Natural Gift	Normal	Physical	—	100	15	Normal	—
TM87	Swagger	Normal	Status	—	90	15	Normal	—
TM90	Substitute	Normal	Status	—	—	10	Self	—
HM03	Surf	Water	Special	95	100	15	2 Foes/1 Ally	—
HM04	Strength	Normal	Physical	80	100	15	Normal	○
HM05	Whirlpool	Water	Special	15	70	15	Normal	—
HM06	Rock Smash	Fighting	Physical	40	100	15	Normal	○
HM07	Waterfall	Water	Physical	80	100	15	Normal	○

* Unable to evolve in *Pokémon HeartGold* or *SoulSilver* Version. Transfer from *Diamond, Pearl,* or *Platinum* Version.

No. 134 | Bubble Jet Pokémon
Vaporeon

Water

- **HEIGHT:** 3'03"
- **WEIGHT:** 63.9 lbs.
- **ITEMS:** None

● **SIZE COMPARISON**

● **MALE/FEMALE HAVE SAME FORM**

⊙ ABILITIES
- ● Water Absorb

⊙ EGG GROUPS
Field

⊙ STATS
HP ●●●●●
ATTACK ●●●
DEFENSE ●●
SP. ATTACK ●●●●
SP. DEFENSE ●●●●
SPEED ●●●

⊙ PERFORMANCE

SPEED ★★☆   STAMINA ★★★☆☆
POWER ★☆☆   JUMP ★★★
SKILL ★★★★☆

● MAIN WAYS TO OBTAIN

Pokémon HeartGold   Use Water Stone on Eevee

Pokémon SoulSilver   Use Water Stone on Eevee

Pokémon Diamond   Use Water Stone on Eevee

Pokémon Pearl   Use Water Stone on Eevee

Pokémon Platinum   Use Water Stone on Eevee

Pokémon HeartGold

When VAPOREON's fins begin to vibrate, it is a sign that rain will come within a few hours.

Pokémon SoulSilver

It prefers beautiful shores. With cells similar to water molecules, it could melt in water.

⊙ EVOLUTION

Eevee

Vaporeon
Use Water Stone on Eevee

Jolteon
Use Thunderstone on Eevee

Flareon
Use Fire Stone on Eevee

Espeon
Level up Eevee with high friendship in the morning or afternoon

Umbreon
Level up Eevee with high friendship at night

Leafeon
Level up Eevee in Eterna Forest*

Glaceon
Level up Eevee on Route 217*

No. 135 | Lighting Pokémon
Jolteon

Electric

- **HEIGHT:** 2'02"
- **WEIGHT:** 54.0 lbs.
- **ITEMS:** None

● SIZE COMPARISON

● MALE/FEMALE HAVE SAME FORM

⊙ ABILITIES
● Volt Absorb

⊙ STATS
HP ●●
ATTACK ●●●
DEFENSE ●●●
SP. ATTACK ●●●●●
SP. DEFENSE ●●●●●
SPEED ●●●●●●

⊙ EGG GROUPS
Field

⊙ PERFORMANCE
SPEED ★★★★☆ STAMINA ★★
POWER ★★☆ JUMP ★★★
SKILL ★★★★☆

● MAIN WAYS TO OBTAIN

Pokémon HeartGold	Use Thunderstone on Eevee
Pokémon SoulSilver	Use Thunderstone on Eevee
Pokémon Diamond	Use Thunderstone on Eevee
Pokémon Pearl	Use Thunderstone on Eevee
Pokémon Platinum	Use Thunderstone on Eevee

Pokémon HeartGold
It concentrates the weak electric charges emitted by its cells and launches wicked lightning bolts.

Pokémon SoulSilver
Every hair on its body starts to stand sharply on end if it becomes charged with electricity.

⊙ EVOLUTION
Eevee

Vaporeon
Use Water Stone on Eevee

Jolteon
Use Thunderstone on Eevee

Flareon
Use Fire Stone on Eevee

Espeon
Level up Eevee with high friendship in the morning or afternoon

Umbreon
Level up Eevee with high friendship at night

Leafeon
Level up Eevee in Eterna Forest*

Glaceon
Level up Eevee on Route 217*

● LEVEL-UP MOVES

Lv.	Name	Type	Kind	Pow.	Acc.	PP	Range	DA
1	Tail Whip	Normal	Status	—	100	30	2 Foes	—
1	Tackle	Normal	Physical	35	95	35	Normal	○
1	Helping Hand	Normal	Status	—	—	20	1 Ally	—
8	Sand-Attack	Ground	Status	—	100	15	Normal	—
15	ThunderShock	Electric	Special	40	100	30	Normal	—
22	Quick Attack	Normal	Physical	40	100	30	Normal	○
29	Double Kick	Fighting	Physical	30	100	30	Normal	○
36	Pin Missile	Bug	Physical	14	85	20	Normal	—
43	Thunder Fang	Electric	Physical	65	95	15	Normal	○
50	Last Resort	Normal	Physical	130	100	5	Normal	○
57	Thunder Wave	Electric	Status	—	100	20	Normal	—
64	Agility	Psychic	Status	—	—	30	Self	—
71	Thunder	Electric	Special	120	70	10	Normal	—
78	Discharge	Electric	Special	80	100	15	2 Foes/1 Ally	—

● MOVE MANIAC

Name	Type	Kind	Pow.	Acc.	PP	Range	DA
Headbutt	Normal	Physical	70	100	15	Normal	○

● BP MOVES

Name	Type	Kind	Pow.	Acc.	PP	Range	DA
Snore	Normal	Special	40	100	15	Normal	—
Helping Hand	Normal	Status	—	—	20	1 Ally	—
Magnet Rise	Electric	Status	—	—	10	Self	—
Last Resort	Normal	Physical	130	100	5	Normal	○
Swift	Normal	Special	60	—	20	2 Foes	—
Heal Bell	Normal	Status	—	—	5	All Allies	—
Mud-Slap	Ground	Special	20	100	10	Normal	—
Signal Beam	Bug	Special	75	100	15	Normal	—

● TM & HM MOVES

No.	Name	Type	Kind	Pow.	Acc.	PP	Range	DA
TM05	Roar	Normal	Status	—	100	20	Normal	—
TM06	Toxic	Poison	Status	—	85	10	Normal	—
TM10	Hidden Power	Normal	Special	—	100	15	Normal	—
TM11	Sunny Day	Fire	Status	—	—	5	All	—
TM15	Hyper Beam	Normal	Special	150	90	5	Normal	—
TM16	Light Screen	Psychic	Status	—	—	30	2 Allies	—
TM17	Protect	Normal	Status	—	—	10	Self	—
TM18	Rain Dance	Water	Status	—	—	5	All	—
TM21	Frustration	Normal	Physical	—	100	20	Normal	○
TM23	Iron Tail	Steel	Physical	100	75	15	Normal	○
TM24	Thunderbolt	Electric	Special	95	100	15	Normal	—
TM25	Thunder	Electric	Special	120	70	10	Normal	—
TM27	Return	Normal	Physical	—	100	20	Normal	○
TM28	Dig	Ground	Physical	80	100	10	Normal	○
TM30	Shadow Ball	Ghost	Special	80	100	15	Normal	—
TM32	Double Team	Normal	Status	—	—	15	Self	—
TM34	Shock Wave	Electric	Special	60	—	20	Normal	—
TM42	Facade	Normal	Physical	70	100	20	Normal	—
TM43	Secret Power	Normal	Physical	70	100	20	Normal	○
TM44	Rest	Psychic	Status	—	—	10	Self	—
TM45	Attract	Normal	Status	—	100	15	Normal	—
TM57	Charge Beam	Electric	Special	50	90	10	Normal	—
TM58	Endure	Normal	Status	—	—	10	Self	—
TM68	Giga Impact	Normal	Physical	150	90	5	Normal	○
TM70	Flash	Normal	Status	—	100	20	Normal	—
TM73	Thunder Wave	Electric	Status	—	100	20	Normal	—
TM79	Captivate	Normal	Status	—	100	20	2 Foes	—
TM82	Sleep Talk	Normal	Status	—	—	10	Depends	—
TM83	Natural Gift	Normal	Physical	—	100	15	Normal	—
TM87	Swagger	Normal	Status	—	90	15	Normal	—
TM90	Substitute	Normal	Status	—	—	10	Self	—
HM04	Strength	Normal	Physical	80	100	15	Normal	○
HM06	Rock Smash	Fighting	Physical	40	100	15	Normal	○

* Unable to evolve in Pokémon HeartGold or SoulSilver Version. Transfer from Diamond, Pearl, or Platinum Version.

● LEVEL-UP MOVES

Lv.	Name	Type	Kind	Pow.	Acc.	PP	Range	DA
1	Tail Whip	Normal	Status	—	100	30	2 Foes	—
1	Tackle	Normal	Physical	35	95	35	Normal	○
1	Helping Hand	Normal	Status	—	—	20	1 Ally	—
8	Sand-Attack	Ground	Status	—	100	15	Normal	—
15	Ember	Fire	Special	40	100	25	Normal	—
22	Quick Attack	Normal	Physical	40	100	30	Normal	○
29	Bite	Dark	Physical	60	100	25	Normal	○
36	Fire Spin	Fire	Special	15	70	15	Normal	—
43	Fire Fang	Fire	Physical	65	95	15	Normal	○
50	Last Resort	Normal	Physical	130	100	5	Normal	○
57	Smog	Poison	Special	20	70	20	Normal	—
64	Scary Face	Normal	Status	—	90	10	Normal	—
71	Fire Blast	Fire	Special	120	85	5	Normal	—
78	Lava Plume	Fire	Special	80	100	15	2 Foes/1 Ally	—

● MOVE MANIAC

Name	Type	Kind	Pow.	Acc.	PP	Range	DA
Headbutt	Normal	Physical	70	100	15	Normal	○

● BP MOVES

Name	Type	Kind	Pow.	Acc.	PP	Range	DA
Snore	Normal	Special	40	100	15	Normal	—
Helping Hand	Normal	Status	—	—	20	1 Ally	—
Last Resort	Normal	Physical	130	100	5	Normal	○
Swift	Normal	Special	60	—	20	2 Foes	—
Heal Bell	Normal	Status	—	—	5	All Allies	—
Mud-Slap	Ground	Special	20	100	10	Normal	—
Superpower	Fighting	Physical	120	100	5	Normal	—
Heat Wave	Fire	Special	100	90	10	2 Foes	—

● TM & HM MOVES

No.	Name	Type	Kind	Pow.	Acc.	PP	Range	DA
TM05	Roar	Normal	Status	—	100	20	Normal	—
TM06	Toxic	Poison	Status	—	85	10	Normal	—
TM10	Hidden Power	Normal	Special	—	100	15	Normal	—
TM11	Sunny Day	Fire	Status	—	—	5	All	—
TM15	Hyper Beam	Normal	Special	150	90	5	Normal	—
TM17	Protect	Normal	Status	—	—	10	Self	—
TM18	Rain Dance	Water	Status	—	—	5	All	—
TM21	Frustration	Normal	Physical	—	100	20	Normal	○
TM23	Iron Tail	Steel	Physical	100	75	15	Normal	○
TM27	Return	Normal	Physical	—	100	20	Normal	○
TM28	Dig	Ground	Physical	80	100	10	Normal	○
TM30	Shadow Ball	Ghost	Special	80	100	15	Normal	—
TM32	Double Team	Normal	Status	—	—	15	Self	—
TM35	Flamethrower	Fire	Special	95	100	15	Normal	—
TM38	Fire Blast	Fire	Special	120	85	5	Normal	—
TM42	Facade	Normal	Physical	70	100	20	Normal	○
TM43	Secret Power	Normal	Physical	70	100	20	Normal	○
TM44	Rest	Psychic	Status	—	—	10	Self	—
TM45	Attract	Normal	Status	—	100	15	Normal	—
TM50	Overheat	Fire	Special	140	90	5	Normal	—
TM58	Endure	Normal	Status	—	—	10	Self	—
TM61	Will-O-Wisp	Fire	Status	—	75	15	Normal	—
TM68	Giga Impact	Normal	Physical	150	90	5	Normal	○
TM78	Captivate	Normal	Status	—	100	20	2 Foes	—
TM82	Sleep Talk	Normal	Status	—	—	10	Depends	—
TM83	Natural Gift	Normal	Physical	—	100	15	Normal	—
TM87	Swagger	Normal	Status	—	90	15	Normal	—
TM90	Substitute	Normal	Status	—	—	10	Self	—
HM04	Strength	Normal	Physical	80	100	15	Normal	○
HM06	Rock Smash	Fighting	Physical	40	100	15	Normal	○

No. 136 | Flame Pokémon
Flareon

Fire

- ● HEIGHT: 2'11"
- ● WEIGHT: 55.1 lbs.
- ● ITEMS: None

● SIZE COMPARISON

● MALE/FEMALE HAVE SAME FORM

⊕ ABILITIES
- ● Flash Fire

⊙ STATS
HP	●●
ATTACK	●●●●●
DEFENSE	●●●
SP. ATTACK	●●●●●
SP. DEFENSE	●●●●●
SPEED	●●●

⊕ EGG GROUPS
Field

⊙ PERFORMANCE
SPEED ★★★☆	STAMINA ★★☆
POWER ★★★★☆	JUMP ★★★
SKILL ★★☆	

● MAIN WAYS TO OBTAIN

Pokémon HeartGold	Use Fire Stone on Eevee
Pokémon SoulSilver	Use Fire Stone on Eevee
Pokémon Diamond	Use Fire Stone on Eevee
Pokémon Pearl	Use Fire Stone on Eevee
Pokémon Platinum	Use Fire Stone on Eevee

Pokémon HeartGold	**Pokémon SoulSilver**
It stores some of the air it inhales in its internal flame pouch, which heats it to over 3,000 degrees Fahrenheit.	It fluffs out its fur collar to cool down its body temperature, which can reach 1,650 degrees Fahrenheit.

⊙ EVOLUTION

Eevee

Vaporeon — Use Water Stone on Eevee

Jolteon — Use Thunderstone on Eevee

Flareon — Use Fire Stone on Eevee

Espeon — Level up Eevee with high friendship in the morning or afternoon

Umbreon — Level up Eevee with high friendship at night

Leafeon — Level up Eevee in Eterna Forest*

Glaceon — Level up Eevee on Route 217*

*Unable to evolve in *Pokémon HeartGold* or *SoulSilver Version*. Transfer from *Diamond*, *Pearl*, or *Platinum Version*.

Porygon

Normal

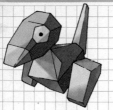

- **HEIGHT:** 2'07"
- **WEIGHT:** 80.5 lbs.
- **ITEMS:** None

● SIZE COMPARISON

● GENDER UNKNOWN

⊙ ABILITIES
- Trace
- Download

⊙ STATS
- HP ●●
- ATTACK ●●●
- DEFENSE ●●●
- SP. ATTACK ●●●●
- SP. DEFENSE ●●●
- SPEED ●●

⊙ EGG GROUPS
Mineral

⊙ PERFORMANCE
SPEED ★★☆	STAMINA ★★★★★
POWER ★★☆	JUMP ★★☆
SKILL ★★☆	

● MAIN WAYS TO OBTAIN

Pokémon HeartGold	Celadon Game Corner prize (9,999 Coins)
Pokémon SoulSilver	Celadon Game Corner prize (9,999 Coins)
Pokémon Diamond	Trophy Garden at the Pokémon Mansion on Route 212 (after obtaining the National Pokédex, talk to Mr. Backlot)
Pokémon Pearl	Trophy Garden at the Pokémon Mansion on Route 212 (after obtaining the National Pokédex, talk to Mr. Backlot)
Pokémon Platinum	Receive from a man in a house in Veilstone City

Pokémon HeartGold	**Pokémon SoulSilver**
It is a manmade Pokémon. Since it doesn't breathe, people are eager to try it in any environment.	A manmade Pokémon that came about as a result of research. It is programmed with only basic motions.

⊙ EVOLUTION

Porygon → (Have it hold Up-Grade and trade it) → Porygon2 → (Have it hold Dubious Disc and trade it) → Porygon-Z

● LEVEL-UP MOVES

Lv.	Name	Type	Kind	Pow.	Acc.	PP	Range	DA
1	Conversion 2	Normal	Status	—	—	30	Self	—
1	Tackle	Normal	Physical	35	95	35	Normal	○
1	Conversion	Normal	Status	—	—	30	Self	—
1	Sharpen	Normal	Status	—	—	30	Self	—
7	Psybeam	Psychic	Special	65	100	20	Normal	—
12	Agility	Psychic	Status	—	—	30	Self	—
18	Recover	Normal	Status	—	—	10	Self	—
23	Magnet Rise	Electric	Status	—	—	10	Self	—
29	Signal Beam	Bug	Special	75	100	15	Normal	—
34	Recycle	Normal	Status	—	—	10	Self	—
40	Discharge	Electric	Special	80	100	15	2 Foes/1 Ally	—
45	Lock-On	Normal	Status	—	—	5	Normal	—
51	Tri Attack	Normal	Special	80	100	10	Normal	—
56	Magic Coat	Psychic	Status	—	—	15	Self	—
62	Zap Cannon	Electric	Special	120	50	5	Normal	—

● MOVE MANIAC

Name	Type	Kind	Pow.	Acc.	PP	Range	DA

● BP MOVES

Name	Type	Kind	Pow.	Acc.	PP	Range	DA
Icy Wind	Ice	Special	55	95	15	2 Foes	—
Zen Headbutt	Psychic	Physical	80	90	15	Normal	○
Trick	Psychic	Status	—	100	10	Normal	—
Snore	Normal	Special	40	100	15	Normal	—
Last Resort	Normal	Physical	130	100	5	Normal	○
Swift	Normal	Special	60	—	20	2 Foes	—
Gravity	Psychic	Status	—	—	5	All	—
Magic Coat	Psychic	Status	—	—	15	Self	—
Signal Beam	Bug	Special	75	100	15	Normal	—
Pain Split	Normal	Status	—	—	20	Normal	—

● TM & HM MOVES

No.	Name	Type	Kind	Pow.	Acc.	PP	Range	DA
TM06	Toxic	Poison	Status	—	85	10	Normal	—
TM10	Hidden Power	Normal	Special	—	100	15	Normal	—
TM11	Sunny Day	Fire	Status	—	—	5	All	—
TM13	Ice Beam	Ice	Special	95	100	10	Normal	—
TM14	Blizzard	Ice	Special	120	70	5	2 Foes	—
TM15	Hyper Beam	Normal	Special	150	90	5	Normal	—
TM17	Protect	Normal	Status	—	—	10	Self	—
TM18	Rain Dance	Water	Status	—	—	5	All	—
TM21	Frustration	Normal	Physical	—	100	20	Normal	○
TM22	SolarBeam	Grass	Special	120	100	10	Normal	—
TM23	Iron Tail	Steel	Physical	100	75	15	Normal	○
TM24	Thunderbolt	Electric	Special	95	100	15	Normal	—
TM25	Thunder	Electric	Special	120	70	10	Normal	—
TM27	Return	Normal	Physical	—	100	20	Normal	○
TM29	Psychic	Psychic	Special	90	100	10	Normal	—
TM30	Shadow Ball	Ghost	Special	80	100	15	Normal	—
TM32	Double Team	Normal	Status	—	—	15	Self	—
TM34	Shock Wave	Electric	Special	60	—	20	Normal	—
TM40	Aerial Ace	Flying	Physical	60	—	20	Normal	—
TM42	Facade	Normal	Physical	70	100	20	Normal	—
TM43	Secret Power	Normal	Physical	70	100	20	Normal	—
TM44	Rest	Psychic	Status	—	—	10	Self	—
TM46	Thief	Dark	Physical	40	100	10	Normal	○
TM57	Charge Beam	Electric	Special	50	90	10	Normal	—
TM58	Endure	Normal	Status	—	—	10	Self	—
TM67	Recycle	Normal	Status	—	—	10	Self	—
TM68	Giga Impact	Normal	Physical	150	90	5	Normal	○
TM70	Flash	Normal	Status	—	100	20	Normal	—
TM73	Thunder Wave	Electric	Status	—	100	20	Normal	—
TM77	Psych Up	Normal	Status	—	—	10	Normal	—
TM82	Sleep Talk	Normal	Status	—	—	10	Depends	—
TM83	Natural Gift	Normal	Physical	—	100	15	Normal	—
TM85	Dream Eater	Psychic	Special	100	100	15	Normal	—
TM87	Swagger	Normal	Status	—	90	15	Normal	—
TM90	Substitute	Normal	Status	—	—	10	Self	—
TM92	Trick Room	Psychic	Status	—	—	5	All	—

● LEVEL-UP MOVES

Lv.	Name	Type	Kind	Pow.	Acc.	PP	Range	DA
1	Constrict	Normal	Physical	10	100	35	Normal	○
1	Withdraw	Water	Status	—	—	40	Self	—
7	Bite	Dark	Physical	60	100	25	Normal	○
10	Water Gun	Water	Special	40	100	25	Normal	—
16	Rollout	Rock	Physical	30	90	20	Normal	○
19	Leer	Normal	Status	—	100	30	2 Foes	—
25	Mud Shot	Ground	Special	55	95	15	Normal	—
28	Brine	Water	Special	65	100	10	Normal	—
34	Protect	Normal	Status	—	—	10	Self	—
37	AncientPower	Rock	Special	60	100	5	Normal	—
43	Tickle	Normal	Status	—	100	20	Normal	—
46	Rock Blast	Rock	Physical	25	80	10	Normal	—
52	Hydro Pump	Water	Special	120	80	5	Normal	—

● MOVE MANIAC

Name	Type	Kind	Pow.	Acc.	PP	Range	DA
Headbutt	Normal	Physical	70	100	15	Normal	—

● BP MOVES

Name	Type	Kind	Pow.	Acc.	PP	Range	DA
Dive	Water	Physical	80	100	10	Normal	○
Icy Wind	Ice	Special	55	95	15	2 Foes	—
Knock Off	Dark	Physical	20	100	20	Normal	○
Snore	Normal	Special	40	100	15	Normal	—
Rollout	Rock	Physical	30	90	20	Normal	○
AncientPower	Rock	Special	60	100	5	Normal	—
Earth Power	Ground	Special	90	100	10	Normal	—
Iron Defense	Steel	Status	—	—	15	Self	—

● TM & HM MOVES

No.	Name	Type	Kind	Pow.	Acc.	PP	Range	DA
TM03	Water Pulse	Water	Special	60	100	20	Normal	—
TM06	Toxic	Poison	Status	—	85	10	Normal	—
TM07	Hail	Ice	Status	—	—	10	All	—
TM10	Hidden Power	Normal	Special	—	100	15	Normal	—
TM13	Ice Beam	Ice	Special	95	100	10	Normal	—
TM14	Blizzard	Ice	Special	120	70	5	2 Foes	—
TM17	Protect	Normal	Status	—	—	10	Self	—
TM18	Rain Dance	Water	Status	—	—	5	All	—
TM21	Frustration	Normal	Physical	—	100	20	Normal	○
TM27	Return	Normal	Physical	—	100	20	Normal	○
TM32	Double Team	Normal	Status	—	—	15	Self	—
TM37	Sandstorm	Rock	Status	—	—	10	All	—
TM39	Rock Tomb	Rock	Physical	50	80	10	Normal	—
TM42	Facade	Normal	Physical	70	100	20	Normal	○
TM43	Secret Power	Normal	Physical	70	100	20	Normal	○
TM44	Rest	Psychic	Status	—	—	10	Self	—
TM45	Attract	Normal	Status	—	100	15	Normal	—
TM46	Thief	Dark	Physical	40	100	10	Normal	○
TM55	Brine	Water	Special	65	100	10	Normal	—
TM58	Endure	Normal	Status	—	—	10	Self	—
TM69	Rock Polish	Rock	Status	—	—	20	Self	—
TM74	Gyro Ball	Steel	Physical	—	100	5	Normal	○
TM76	Stealth Rock	Rock	Status	—	—	20	2 Foes	—
TM78	Captivate	Normal	Status	—	100	20	2 Foes	—
TM80	Rock Slide	Rock	Physical	75	90	10	2 Foes	—
TM82	Sleep Talk	Normal	Status	—	—	10	Depends	—
TM83	Natural Gift	Normal	Physical	—	100	15	Normal	—
TM87	Swagger	Normal	Status	—	90	15	Normal	—
TM90	Substitute	Normal	Status	—	—	10	Self	—
HM03	Surf	Water	Special	95	100	15	2 Foes/1 Ally	—
HM05	Whirlpool	Water	Special	15	70	15	Normal	—
HM06	Rock Smash	Fighting	Physical	40	100	15	Normal	○
HM07	Waterfall	Water	Physical	80	100	15	Normal	○

● EGG MOVES

Name	Type	Kind	Pow.	Acc.	PP	Range	DA
BubbleBeam	Water	Special	65	100	20	Normal	—
Aurora Beam	Ice	Special	65	100	20	Normal	—
Slam	Normal	Physical	80	75	20	Normal	○
Supersonic	Normal	Status	—	55	20	Normal	—
Haze	Ice	Status	—	—	30	All	—
Rock Slide	Rock	Physical	75	90	10	2 Foes	—
Spikes	Ground	Status	—	—	20	2 Foes	—
Knock Off	Dark	Physical	20	100	20	Normal	○
Wring Out	Normal	Special	—	100	5	Normal	—
Toxic Spikes	Poison	Status	—	—	20	2 Foes	—
Muddy Water	Water	Special	95	85	10	2 Foes	—

◉ No. 138 | Spiral Pokémon
Omanyte

`Rock` `Water`

● **HEIGHT:** 1'04"
● **WEIGHT:** 16.5 lbs.
● **ITEMS:** None

● SIZE COMPARISON

● MALE/FEMALE HAVE SAME FORM

◉ ABILITIES
● Swift Swim
● Shell Armor

◉ STATS
- HP ●●
- ATTACK ●●●
- DEFENSE ●●●●
- SP. ATTACK ●●●●
- SP. DEFENSE ●●●
- SPEED ●●

◉ EGG GROUPS
Water 1
Water 3

◉ PERFORMANCE
SPEED ★★☆   STAMINA ★★★☆
POWER ★★☆   JUMP ★★☆
SKILL ★★★☆

● MAIN WAYS TO OBTAIN

Pokémon HeartGold	Have the Helix Fossil restored at the Pewter Museum of Science
Pokémon SoulSilver	—
Pokémon Diamond	After obtaining the National Pokédex, find the Helix Fossil in the Underground and have it restored at the Oreburgh Mining Museum
Pokémon Pearl	After obtaining the National Pokédex, find the Helix Fossil in the Underground and have it restored at the Oreburgh Mining Museum
Pokémon Platinum	After obtaining the National Pokédex, find the Helix Fossil in the Underground and have it restored at the Oreburgh Mining Museum

Pokémon HeartGold	*Pokémon SoulSilver*
Revived from an ancient fossil, this Pokémon uses air stored in its shell to sink and rise in water.	This Pokémon from ancient times is said to have navigated the sea by adeptly twisting its 10 tentacles.

◉ EVOLUTION

 Lv. 40

Omanyte → Omastar

No. 139 | Spiral Pokémon
Omastar

Rock **Water**

- **HEIGHT:** 3'03"
- **WEIGHT:** 77.2 lbs.
- **ITEMS:** None

● SIZE COMPARISON

● MALE/FEMALE HAVE SAME FORM

⊕ ABILITIES
- Swift Swim
- Shell Armor

⊕ STATS
- HP ●●●
- ATTACK ●●●●
- DEFENSE ●●●●●
- SP. ATTACK ●●●●●
- SP. DEFENSE ●●●
- SPEED ●●●

⊕ EGG GROUPS
Water 1

Water 3

⊕ PERFORMANCE
SPEED ★★☆	STAMINA ★★☆
POWER ★★★☆	JUMP ★★
SKILL ★★★★	

● MAIN WAYS TO OBTAIN

Pokémon HeartGold — Level up Omanyte to Lv. 40

Pokémon SoulSilver — —

Pokémon Diamond — Level up Omanyte to Lv. 40

Pokémon Pearl — Level up Omanyte to Lv. 40

Pokémon Platinum — Level up Omanyte to Lv. 40

Pokémon HeartGold
Apparently, it cracked SHELLDER's shell with its sharp fangs and sucked out the insides.

Pokémon SoulSilver
Once wrapped around its prey, it never lets go. It eats the prey by tearing at it with sharp fangs.

⊕ EVOLUTION

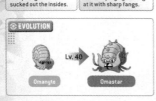

Omanyte — Lv. 40 — Omastar

● LEVEL-UP MOVES
Lv.	Name	Type	Kind	Pow.	Acc.	PP	Range	DA
1	Constrict	Normal	Physical	10	100	35	Normal	○
1	Withdraw	Water	Status	—	—	40	Self	—
1	Bite	Dark	Physical	60	100	25	Normal	○
7	Bite	Dark	Physical	60	100	25	Normal	○
10	Water Gun	Water	Special	40	100	25	Normal	—
16	Rollout	Rock	Physical	30	90	20	Normal	○
19	Leer	Normal	Status	—	100	30	2 Foes	—
25	Mud Shot	Ground	Special	55	95	15	Normal	—
28	Brine	Water	Special	65	100	10	Normal	—
34	Protect	Normal	Status	—	—	10	Self	—
37	AncientPower	Rock	Special	60	100	5	Normal	—
40	Spike Cannon	Normal	Physical	20	100	15	Normal	—
48	Tickle	Normal	Status	—	100	20	Normal	—
56	Rock Blast	Rock	Physical	25	80	10	Normal	—
67	Hydro Pump	Water	Special	120	80	5	Normal	—

● MOVE MANIAC
Name	Type	Kind	Pow.	Acc.	PP	Range	DA
Headbutt	Normal	Physical	70	100	15	Normal	○

● BP MOVES
Name	Type	Kind	Pow.	Acc.	PP	Range	DA
Dive	Water	Physical	80	100	10	Normal	—
Icy Wind	Ice	Special	55	95	15	2 Foes	—
Knock Off	Dark	Physical	20	100	20	Normal	—
Snore	Normal	Special	40	100	15	Normal	—
Rollout	Rock	Physical	30	90	20	Normal	○
AncientPower	Rock	Special	60	100	5	Normal	—
Earth Power	Ground	Special	90	100	10	Normal	—
Iron Defense	Steel	Status	—	—	15	Self	—

● TM & HM MOVES
No.	Name	Type	Kind	Pow.	Acc.	PP	Range	DA
TM03	Water Pulse	Water	Special	60	100	20	Normal	—
TM06	Toxic	Poison	Status	—	85	10	Normal	—
TM07	Hail	Ice	Status	—	—	10	All	—
TM10	Hidden Power	Normal	Special	—	100	15	Normal	—
TM13	Ice Beam	Ice	Special	95	100	10	Normal	—
TM14	Blizzard	Ice	Special	120	70	5	2 Foes	—
TM15	Hyper Beam	Normal	Special	150	90	5	Normal	—
TM17	Protect	Normal	Status	—	—	10	Self	—
TM18	Rain Dance	Water	Status	—	—	5	All	—
TM21	Frustration	Normal	Physical	—	100	20	Normal	○
TM27	Return	Normal	Physical	—	100	20	Normal	○
TM32	Double Team	Normal	Status	—	—	15	Self	—
TM37	Sandstorm	Rock	Status	—	—	10	All	—
TM39	Rock Tomb	Rock	Physical	50	80	10	Normal	—
TM42	Facade	Normal	Physical	70	100	20	Normal	○
TM43	Secret Power	Normal	Physical	70	100	20	Normal	—
TM44	Rest	Psychic	Status	—	—	10	Self	—
TM45	Attract	Normal	Status	—	100	15	Normal	—
TM46	Thief	Dark	Physical	40	100	10	Normal	○
TM55	Brine	Water	Special	65	100	10	Normal	—
TM58	Endure	Normal	Status	—	—	10	Self	—
TM68	Giga Impact	Normal	Physical	150	90	5	Normal	○
TM69	Rock Polish	Rock	Status	—	—	20	Self	—
TM71	Stone Edge	Rock	Physical	100	80	5	Normal	—
TM74	Gyro Ball	Steel	Physical	—	100	5	Normal	○
TM76	Stealth Rock	Rock	Status	—	—	20	2 Foes	—
TM78	Captivate	Normal	Status	—	100	20	2 Foes	—
TM80	Rock Slide	Rock	Physical	75	90	10	2 Foes	—
TM82	Sleep Talk	Normal	Status	—	—	10	Depends	—
TM83	Natural Gift	Normal	Physical	—	100	15	Normal	—
TM87	Swagger	Normal	Status	—	90	15	Normal	—
TM90	Substitute	Normal	Status	—	—	10	Self	—
HM03	Surf	Water	Special	95	100	15	2 Foes/1 Ally	—
HM05	Whirlpool	Water	Special	15	70	15	Normal	—
HM06	Rock Smash	Fighting	Physical	40	100	15	Normal	○
HM07	Waterfall	Water	Physical	80	100	15	Normal	○
HM08	Rock Climb	Normal	Physical	90	85	20	Normal	○

● LEVEL-UP MOVES

Lv.	Name	Type	Kind	Pow.	Acc.	PP	Range	DA
1	Scratch	Normal	Physical	40	100	35	Normal	○
1	Harden	Normal	Status	—	—	30	Self	—
6	Absorb	Grass	Special	20	100	25	Normal	—
11	Leer	Normal	Status	—	100	30	2 Foes	—
16	Mud Shot	Ground	Special	55	95	15	Normal	—
21	Sand-Attack	Ground	Status	—	100	15	Normal	—
26	Endure	Normal	Status	—	—	10	Self	—
31	Aqua Jet	Water	Physical	40	100	20	Normal	○
36	Mega Drain	Grass	Special	40	100	15	Normal	—
41	Metal Sound	Steel	Status	—	85	40	Normal	—
46	AncientPower	Rock	Special	60	100	5	Normal	—
51	Wring Out	Normal	Special	—	100	5	Normal	○

● MOVE MANIAC

Name	Type	Kind	Pow.	Acc.	PP	Range	DA

● BP MOVES

Name	Type	Kind	Pow.	Acc.	PP	Range	DA
Icy Wind	Ice	Special	55	95	15	2 Foes	—
Knock Off	Dark	Physical	20	100	20	Normal	○
Snore	Normal	Special	40	100	15	Normal	—
Mud-Slap	Ground	Special	20	100	10	Normal	—
Rollout	Rock	Physical	30	90	20	Normal	○
AncientPower	Rock	Special	60	100	5	Normal	—
Earth Power	Ground	Special	90	100	10	Normal	—
Iron Defense	Steel	Status	—	—	15	Self	—

● TM & HM MOVES

No.	Name	Type	Kind	Pow.	Acc.	PP	Range	DA
TM03	Water Pulse	Water	Special	60	100	20	Normal	—
TM06	Toxic	Poison	Status	—	85	10	Normal	—
TM07	Hail	Ice	Status	—	—	10	All	—
TM10	Hidden Power	Normal	Special	—	100	15	Normal	—
TM13	Ice Beam	Ice	Special	95	100	10	Normal	—
TM14	Blizzard	Ice	Special	120	70	5	2 Foes	—
TM17	Protect	Normal	Status	—	—	10	Self	—
TM18	Rain Dance	Water	Status	—	—	5	All	—
TM19	Giga Drain	Grass	Special	60	100	10	Normal	—
TM21	Frustration	Normal	Physical	—	100	20	Normal	○
TM27	Return	Normal	Physical	—	100	20	Normal	○
TM28	Dig	Ground	Physical	80	100	10	Normal	○
TM32	Double Team	Normal	Status	—	—	15	Self	—
TM37	Sandstorm	Rock	Status	—	—	10	All	—
TM39	Rock Tomb	Rock	Physical	50	80	10	Normal	—
TM42	Facade	Normal	Physical	70	100	20	Normal	○
TM43	Secret Power	Normal	Physical	70	100	20	Normal	○
TM44	Rest	Psychic	Status	—	—	10	Self	—
TM45	Attract	Normal	Status	—	100	15	Normal	—
TM46	Thief	Dark	Physical	40	100	10	Normal	○
TM55	Brine	Water	Special	65	100	10	Normal	—
TM58	Endure	Normal	Status	—	—	10	Self	—
TM69	Rock Polish	Rock	Status	—	—	20	Self	—
TM76	Stealth Rock	Rock	Status	—	—	20	2 Foes	—
TM78	Captivate	Normal	Status	—	100	20	2 Foes	—
TM80	Rock Slide	Rock	Physical	75	90	10	2 Foes	—
TM82	Sleep Talk	Normal	Status	—	—	10	Self	—
TM83	Natural Gift	Normal	Physical	—	100	15	Normal	○
TM87	Swagger	Normal	Status	—	90	15	Normal	—
TM90	Substitute	Normal	Status	—	—	10	Self	—
HM03	Surf	Water	Special	95	100	15	2 Foes/1 Ally	—
HM05	Whirlpool	Water	Special	15	70	15	Normal	—
HM06	Rock Smash	Fighting	Physical	40	100	15	Normal	○
HM07	Waterfall	Water	Physical	80	100	15	Normal	○

● EGG MOVES

Name	Type	Kind	Pow.	Acc.	PP	Range	DA
BubbleBeam	Water	Special	65	100	20	Normal	—
Aurora Beam	Ice	Special	65	100	20	Normal	—
Rapid Spin	Normal	Physical	20	100	40	Normal	○
Dig	Ground	Physical	80	100	10	Normal	○
Flail	Normal	Physical	—	100	15	Normal	○
Knock Off	Dark	Physical	20	100	20	Normal	○
Confuse Ray	Ghost	Status	—	100	10	Normal	—
Mud Shot	Ground	Special	55	95	15	Normal	—
Icy Wind	Ice	Special	55	95	15	2 Foes	—
Screech	Normal	Status	—	85	40	Normal	—

Kabuto

Rock   Water

- ● HEIGHT: 1'08"
- ● WEIGHT: 25.4 lbs.
- ● ITEMS: None

● SIZE COMPARISON

● MALE/FEMALE HAVE SAME FORM

⊙ ABILITIES
- Swift Swim
- Battle Armor

⊙ STATS

HP	●
ATTACK	●●●
DEFENSE	●●●
SP. ATTACK	●●●●
SP. DEFENSE	●●
SPEED	●●●

⊙ EGG GROUPS

Water 1

Water 3

⊙ PERFORMANCE

SPEED ★★★☆   STAMINA ★★☆
POWER ★★☆☆   JUMP ★★★☆
SKILL ★★☆

● MAIN WAYS TO OBTAIN

Pokémon HeartGold	—
Pokémon SoulSilver	Have the Dome Fossil restored at the Pewter Museum of Science
Pokémon Diamond	After obtaining the National Pokédex, find the Dome Fossil in the Underground and have it restored at Oreburgh Mine Museum
Pokémon Pearl	After obtaining the National Pokédex, find the Dome Fossil in the Underground and have it restored at Oreburgh Mine Museum
Pokémon Platinum	After obtaining the National Pokédex, find the Dome Fossil in the Underground and have it restored at Oreburgh Mine Museum

Pokémon HeartGold	Pokémon SoulSilver
On rare occasions, some have been found as fossils which they became while hiding on the ocean floor.	This Pokémon lived in ancient times. On rare occasions, it has been discovered as a living fossil.

⊙ EVOLUTION

Lv. 40

Kabuto   Kabutops

No. 141 | Shellfish Pokémon
Kabutops

Rock   Water

- **HEIGHT:** 4'03"
- **WEIGHT:** 89.3 lbs.
- **ITEMS:** None

● SIZE COMPARISON

● MALE/FEMALE HAVE SAME FORM

⊙ ABILITIES
- Swift Swim
- Battle Armor

⊙ STATS
HP ●●
ATTACK ●●●●●
DEFENSE ●●●●●
SP. ATTACK ●●●●
SP. DEFENSE ●●●
SPEED ●●●●

⊙ EGG GROUPS
Water 1

Water 3

⊙ PERFORMANCE
SPEED ★★★☆☆   STAMINA ★☆☆
POWER ★★★★☆   JUMP ★★☆
SKILL ★★☆

● MAIN WAYS TO OBTAIN

Pokémon HeartGold —

Pokémon SoulSilver Level up Kabuto to Lv. 40

Pokémon Diamond Level up Kabuto to Lv. 40

Pokémon Pearl Level up Kabuto to Lv. 40

Pokémon Platinum Level up Kabuto to Lv. 40

Pokémon HeartGold
In the water, it tucks in its limbs to become more compact, then it wiggles its shell to swim fast.

Pokémon SoulSilver
With sharp claws, this ferocious, ancient Pokémon rips apart prey and sucks their body fluids.

⊙ EVOLUTION
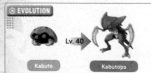

Kabuto — Lv. 40 → Kabutops

● LEVEL-UP MOVES

Lv.	Name	Type	Kind	Pow.	Acc.	PP	Range	DA
1	Feint	Normal	Physical	50	100	10	Normal	—
1	Scratch	Normal	Physical	40	100	35	Normal	○
1	Harden	Normal	Status	—	—	30	Self	—
1	Absorb	Grass	Special	20	100	25	Normal	—
1	Leer	Normal	Status	—	100	30	2 Foes	—
6	Absorb	Grass	Special	20	100	25	Normal	—
11	Leer	Normal	Status	—	100	30	2 Foes	—
16	Mud Shot	Ground	Special	55	95	15	Normal	—
21	Sand-Attack	Ground	Status	—	100	15	Normal	—
26	Endure	Normal	Status	—	—	10	Self	—
31	Aqua Jet	Water	Physical	40	100	20	Normal	○
36	Mega Drain	Grass	Special	40	100	15	Normal	—
40	Slash	Normal	Physical	70	100	20	Normal	○
45	Metal Sound	Steel	Status	—	85	40	Normal	—
54	AncientPower	Rock	Special	60	100	5	Normal	—
63	Wring Out	Normal	Special	—	100	5	Normal	○
72	Night Slash	Dark	Physical	70	100	15	Normal	○

● MOVE MANIAC

Name	Type	Kind	Pow.	Acc.	PP	Range	DA
Headbutt	Normal	Physical	70	100	15	Normal	○

● BP MOVES

Name	Type	Kind	Pow.	Acc.	PP	Range	DA
Dive	Water	Physical	80	100	10	Normal	○
Fury Cutter	Bug	Physical	10	95	20	Normal	○
Icy Wind	Ice	Special	55	95	15	2 Foes	—
Knock Off	Dark	Physical	20	100	20	Normal	○
Snore	Normal	Special	40	100	15	Normal	—
Mud-Slap	Ground	Special	20	100	10	Normal	—
Rollout	Rock	Physical	30	90	20	Normal	○
Superpower	Fighting	Physical	120	100	5	Normal	○
Aqua Tail	Water	Physical	90	90	10	Normal	○
AncientPower	Rock	Special	60	100	5	Normal	—
Earth Power	Ground	Special	90	100	10	Normal	—
Iron Defense	Steel	Status	—	—	15	Self	—
Low Kick	Fighting	Physical	—	100	20	Normal	○

● TM & HM MOVES

No.	Name	Type	Kind	Pow.	Acc.	PP	Range	DA
TM03	Water Pulse	Water	Special	60	100	20	Normal	—
TM06	Toxic	Poison	Status	—	85	10	Normal	—
TM07	Hail	Ice	Status	—	—	10	All	—
TM10	Hidden Power	Normal	Special	—	100	15	Normal	—
TM13	Ice Beam	Ice	Special	95	100	10	Normal	—
TM14	Blizzard	Ice	Special	120	70	5	2 Foes	—
TM15	Hyper Beam	Normal	Special	150	90	5	Normal	—
TM17	Protect	Normal	Status	—	—	10	Self	—
TM18	Rain Dance	Water	Status	—	—	5	All	—
TM19	Giga Drain	Grass	Special	60	100	10	Normal	—
TM21	Frustration	Normal	Physical	—	100	20	Normal	○
TM27	Return	Normal	Physical	—	100	20	Normal	○
TM28	Dig	Ground	Physical	80	100	10	Normal	○
TM31	Brick Break	Fighting	Physical	75	100	15	Normal	○
TM32	Double Team	Normal	Status	—	—	15	Self	—
TM37	Sandstorm	Rock	Status	—	—	10	All	—
TM39	Rock Tomb	Rock	Physical	50	80	10	Normal	—
TM40	Aerial Ace	Flying	Physical	60	—	20	Normal	○
TM42	Facade	Normal	Physical	70	100	20	Normal	○
TM43	Secret Power	Normal	Physical	70	100	20	Normal	○
TM44	Rest	Psychic	Status	—	—	10	Self	—
TM45	Attract	Normal	Status	—	100	15	Normal	—
TM46	Thief	Dark	Physical	40	100	10	Normal	○
TM55	Brine	Water	Special	65	100	10	Normal	—
TM58	Endure	Normal	Status	—	—	10	Self	—
TM68	Giga Impact	Normal	Physical	150	90	5	Normal	○
TM69	Rock Polish	Rock	Status	—	—	20	Self	—
TM71	Stone Edge	Rock	Physical	100	80	5	Normal	—
TM75	Swords Dance	Normal	Status	—	—	30	Self	—
TM76	Stealth Rock	Rock	Status	—	—	20	2 Foes	—
TM78	Captivate	Normal	Status	—	100	20	2 Foes	—
TM80	Rock Slide	Rock	Physical	75	90	10	2 Foes	—
TM81	X-Scissor	Bug	Physical	80	100	15	Normal	○
TM82	Sleep Talk	Normal	Status	—	—	10	Depends	—
TM83	Natural Gift	Normal	Physical	—	100	15	Normal	—
TM87	Swagger	Normal	Status	—	90	15	Normal	—
TM90	Substitute	Normal	Status	—	—	10	Self	—
HM01	Cut	Normal	Physical	50	95	30	Normal	○
HM03	Surf	Water	Special	95	100	15	2 Foes/1 Ally	—
HM05	Whirlpool	Water	Special	15	70	15	Normal	—
HM06	Rock Smash	Fighting	Physical	40	100	15	Normal	○
HM07	Waterfall	Water	Physical	80	100	15	Normal	○
HM08	Rock Climb	Normal	Physical	90	85	20	Normal	○

● LEVEL-UP MOVES

Lv.	Name	Type	Kind	Pow.	Acc.	PP	Range	DA
1	Ice Fang	Ice	Physical	65	95	15	Normal	○
1	Fire Fang	Fire	Physical	65	95	15	Normal	○
1	Thunder Fang	Electric	Physical	65	95	15	Normal	○
1	Wing Attack	Flying	Physical	60	100	35	Normal	○
1	Supersonic	Normal	Status	—	55	20	Normal	—
1	Bite	Dark	Physical	60	100	25	Normal	○
1	Scary Face	Normal	Status	—	90	10	Normal	—
9	Roar	Normal	Status	—	100	20	Normal	—
17	Agility	Psychic	Status	—	—	30	Self	—
25	AncientPower	Rock	Special	60	100	5	Normal	○
33	Crunch	Dark	Physical	80	100	15	Normal	○
41	Take Down	Normal	Physical	90	85	20	Normal	○
49	Iron Head	Steel	Physical	80	100	15	Normal	○
57	Hyper Beam	Normal	Special	150	90	5	Normal	—
65	Rock Slide	Rock	Physical	75	90	10	2 Foes	—
73	Giga Impact	Normal	Physical	150	90	5	Normal	○

● MOVE MANIAC

Name	Type	Kind	Pow.	Acc.	PP	Range	DA
Headbutt	Normal	Physical	70	100	15	Normal	○

● BP MOVES

Name	Type	Kind	Pow.	Acc.	PP	Range	DA
Ominous Wind	Ghost	Special	60	100	5	Normal	—
Air Cutter	Flying	Special	55	95	25	2 Foes	—
Snore	Normal	Special	40	100	15	Normal	—
Swift	Normal	Special	60	—	20	2 Foes	—
Tailwind	Flying	Status	—	—	30	2 Allies	—
Iron Head	Steel	Physical	80	100	15	Normal	○
Aqua Tail	Water	Physical	90	90	10	Normal	○
AncientPower	Rock	Special	60	100	5	Normal	—
Earth Power	Ground	Special	90	100	10	Normal	—
Twister	Dragon	Special	40	100	20	2 Foes	—
Heat Wave	Fire	Special	100	90	10	2 Foes	—
Sky Attack	Flying	Physical	140	90	5	Normal	—

● TM & HM MOVES

No.	Name	Type	Kind	Pow.	Acc.	PP	Range	DA
TM02	Dragon Claw	Dragon	Physical	80	100	15	Normal	○
TM05	Roar	Normal	Status	—	100	20	Normal	—
TM06	Toxic	Poison	Status	—	85	10	Normal	—
TM10	Hidden Power	Normal	Special	—	100	15	Normal	—
TM11	Sunny Day	Fire	Status	—	—	5	All	—
TM12	Taunt	Dark	Status	—	100	20	Normal	—
TM15	Hyper Beam	Normal	Special	150	90	5	Normal	—
TM17	Protect	Normal	Status	—	—	10	Self	—
TM18	Rain Dance	Water	Status	—	—	5	All	—
TM21	Frustration	Normal	Physical	—	100	20	Normal	○
TM23	Iron Tail	Steel	Physical	100	75	15	Normal	○
TM26	Earthquake	Ground	Physical	100	100	10	2 Foes/1 Ally	—
TM27	Return	Normal	Physical	—	100	20	Normal	○
TM32	Double Team	Normal	Status	—	—	15	Self	—
TM35	Flamethrower	Fire	Special	95	100	15	Normal	—
TM37	Sandstorm	Rock	Status	—	—	10	All	—
TM38	Fire Blast	Fire	Special	120	85	5	Normal	—
TM39	Rock Tomb	Rock	Physical	50	80	10	Normal	—
TM40	Aerial Ace	Flying	Physical	60	—	20	Normal	○
TM41	Torment	Dark	Status	—	100	15	Normal	—
TM42	Facade	Normal	Physical	70	100	20	Normal	○
TM43	Secret Power	Normal	Physical	70	100	20	Normal	—
TM44	Rest	Psychic	Status	—	—	10	Self	—
TM45	Attract	Normal	Status	—	100	15	Normal	—
TM46	Thief	Dark	Physical	40	100	10	Normal	○
TM47	Steel Wing	Steel	Physical	70	90	25	Normal	○
TM51	Roost	Flying	Status	—	—	10	Self	—
TM58	Endure	Normal	Status	—	—	10	Self	—
TM59	Dragon Pulse	Dragon	Special	90	100	10	Normal	—
TM66	Payback	Dark	Physical	50	100	10	Normal	○
TM68	Giga Impact	Normal	Physical	150	90	5	Normal	○
TM69	Rock Polish	Rock	Status	—	—	20	Self	—
TM71	Stone Edge	Rock	Physical	100	80	5	Normal	—
TM76	Stealth Rock	Rock	Status	—	—	20	2 Foes	—
TM78	Captivate	Normal	Status	—	100	20	2 Foes	—
TM80	Rock Slide	Rock	Physical	75	90	10	2 Foes	—
TM82	Sleep Talk	Normal	Status	—	—	10	Depends	—
TM83	Natural Gift	Normal	Physical	—	100	15	Normal	—
TM87	Swagger	Normal	Status	—	90	15	Normal	—
TM90	Substitute	Normal	Status	—	—	10	Self	—
HM02	Fly	Flying	Physical	90	95	15	Normal	○
HM04	Strength	Normal	Physical	80	100	15	Normal	○
HM06	Rock Smash	Fighting	Physical	40	100	15	Normal	○

● EGG MOVES

Name	Type	Kind	Pow.	Acc.	PP	Range	DA
Whirlwind	Normal	Status	—	100	20	Normal	—
Pursuit	Dark	Physical	40	100	20	Normal	○
Foresight	Normal	Status	—	—	40	Normal	—
Steel Wing	Steel	Physical	70	90	25	Normal	○
DragonBreath	Dragon	Special	60	100	20	Normal	—
Curse	???	Status	—	—	10	Normal/Self	—
Assurance	Dark	Physical	50	100	10	Normal	○

● No. 142 | Fossil Pokémon
Aerodactyl

Rock Flying

- ● HEIGHT: 5'11"
- ● WEIGHT: 130.1 lbs.
- ● ITEMS: None

● SIZE COMPARISON

● MALE/FEMALE HAVE SAME FORM

⊛ ABILITIES
- ● Rock Head
- ● Pressure

⊛ STATS
HP	●●●
ATTACK	●●●●
DEFENSE	●●●
SP. ATTACK	●●●
SP. DEFENSE	●●●
SPEED	●●●●●●

⊛ EGG GROUPS
Flying

⊛ PERFORMANCE
SPEED ★★★★★	STAMINA ★★☆
POWER ★★☆	JUMP ★★★★★
SKILL ★★	

● MAIN WAYS TO OBTAIN

Pokémon HeartGold	Have the Old Amber restored at the Pewter Museum of Science
Pokémon SoulSilver	Have the Old Amber restored at the Pewter Museum of Science
Pokémon Diamond	After obtaining the National Pokédex, find the Old Amber in the Underground and have it restored at Oreburgh Mine Museum
Pokémon Pearl	After obtaining the National Pokédex, find the Old Amber in the Underground and have it restored at Oreburgh Mine Museum
Pokémon Platinum	After obtaining the National Pokédex, find the Old Amber in the Underground and have it restored at Oreburgh Mine Museum

Pokémon HeartGold	Pokémon SoulSilver
It can transform into anything. When it sleeps, it changes into a stone to avoid being attacked.	Its transformation ability is perfect. However, if made to laugh, it can't maintain its disguise.

⊛ EVOLUTION

Does not evolve

● No. 143 | Sleeping Pokémon
Snorlax

Normal

● HEIGHT: 6'11"
● WEIGHT: 1,014.1 lbs.
● ITEMS: None

● SIZE COMPARISON

● MALE/FEMALE HAVE SAME FORM

◈ ABILITIES
● Immunity
● Thick Fat

◈ STATS
HP ●●●●●●
ATTACK ●●●●●
DEFENSE ●●●●
SP. ATTACK ●●●
SP. DEFENSE ●●●●
SPEED ●

◈ EGG GROUPS
Monster

◈ PERFORMANCE
SPEED ★★☆   STAMINA ★★★☆☆
POWER ★☆☆   JUMP ★★★
SKILL ★★★★☆

● MAIN WAYS TO OBTAIN

Pokémon HeartGold	Wake up the sleeping Snorlax on Route 11 by tuning the radio to the Poké Flute
Pokémon SoulSilver	Wake up the sleeping Snorlax on Route 11 by tuning the radio to the Poké Flute
Pokémon Diamond	Level up Munchlax with high friendship
Pokémon Pearl	Level up Munchlax with high friendship
Pokémon Platinum	Level up Munchlax with high friendship

| Pokémon HeartGold | Pokémon SoulSilver |
| What sounds like its cry may actually be its snores or the rumblings of its hungry belly. | Its stomach's digestive juices can dissolve any kind of poison. It can even eat things off the ground. |

◈ EVOLUTION

  Munchlax — Level it up with high friendship → Snorlax

● LEVEL-UP MOVES

Lv.	Name	Type	Kind	Pow.	Acc.	PP	Range	DA
1	Tackle	Normal	Physical	35	95	35	Normal	○
4	Defense Curl	Normal	Status	—	—	40	Self	—
9	Amnesia	Psychic	Status	—	—	20	Self	—
12	Lick	Ghost	Physical	20	100	30	Normal	○
17	Belly Drum	Normal	Status	—	—	10	Self	—
20	Yawn	Normal	Status	—	—	10	Normal	—
25	Rest	Normal	Status	—	—	10	Self	—
28	Snore	Normal	Special	40	100	15	Normal	—
28	Sleep Talk	Normal	Status	—	—	10	Depends	—
33	Body Slam	Normal	Physical	85	100	15	Normal	—
36	Block	Normal	Status	—	—	5	Normal	—
41	Rollout	Rock	Physical	30	90	20	Normal	○
44	Crunch	Dark	Physical	80	100	15	Normal	—
49	Giga Impact	Normal	Physical	150	90	5	Normal	○

● MOVE MANIAC

Name	Type	Kind	Pow.	Acc.	PP	Range	DA
Headbutt	Normal	Physical	70	100	15	Normal	○

● BP MOVES

Name	Type	Kind	Pow.	Acc.	PP	Range	DA
Icy Wind	Ice	Special	55	95	15	2 Foes	—
ThunderPunch	Electric	Physical	75	100	15	Normal	○
Fire Punch	Fire	Physical	75	100	15	Normal	○
Ice Punch	Ice	Physical	75	100	15	Normal	○
Zen Headbutt	Psychic	Physical	80	90	15	Normal	○
Snore	Normal	Special	40	100	15	Normal	—
Last Resort	Normal	Physical	130	100	5	Normal	○
Block	Normal	Status	—	—	5	Normal	—
Mud-Slap	Ground	Special	20	100	10	Normal	—
Rollout	Rock	Physical	30	90	20	Normal	○
Superpower	Fighting	Physical	120	100	5	Normal	—
Iron Head	Steel	Physical	80	100	15	Normal	—
Outrage	Dragon	Physical	120	100	10	1 Random	—
Gunk Shot	Poison	Physical	120	70	5	Normal	—
Seed Bomb	Grass	Physical	80	100	15	Normal	—

● TM & HM MOVES

No.	Name	Type	Kind	Pow.	Acc.	PP	Range	DA
TM01	Focus Punch	Fighting	Physical	150	100	20	Normal	○
TM03	Water Pulse	Water	Special	60	100	20	Normal	—
TM06	Toxic	Poison	Status	—	85	10	Normal	—
TM10	Hidden Power	Normal	Special	—	100	15	Normal	—
TM11	Sunny Day	Fire	Status	—	—	5	All	—
TM13	Ice Beam	Ice	Special	95	100	10	Normal	—
TM14	Blizzard	Ice	Special	120	70	5	2 Foes	—
TM15	Hyper Beam	Normal	Special	150	90	5	Normal	○
TM17	Protect	Normal	Status	—	—	10	Self	—
TM18	Rain Dance	Water	Status	—	—	5	All	—
TM21	Frustration	Normal	Physical	—	100	20	Normal	○
TM22	SolarBeam	Grass	Special	120	100	10	Normal	—
TM24	Thunderbolt	Electric	Special	95	100	15	Normal	—
TM25	Thunder	Electric	Special	120	70	10	Normal	—
TM26	Earthquake	Ground	Physical	100	100	10	2 Foes/1 Ally	—
TM27	Return	Normal	Physical	—	100	20	Normal	○
TM29	Psychic	Psychic	Special	90	100	10	Normal	—
TM30	Shadow Ball	Ghost	Special	80	100	15	Normal	—
TM31	Brick Break	Fighting	Physical	75	100	15	Normal	○
TM32	Double Team	Normal	Status	—	—	15	Self	—
TM34	Shock Wave	Electric	Special	60	—	20	Normal	—
TM35	Flamethrower	Fire	Special	95	100	15	Normal	—
TM37	Sandstorm	Rock	Status	—	—	10	All	—
TM38	Fire Blast	Fire	Special	120	85	5	Normal	—
TM39	Rock Tomb	Rock	Physical	50	80	10	Normal	—
TM42	Facade	Normal	Physical	70	100	20	Normal	—
TM43	Secret Power	Normal	Physical	70	100	20	Normal	—
TM44	Rest	Psychic	Status	—	—	10	Self	—
TM45	Attract	Normal	Status	—	100	15	Normal	—
TM52	Focus Blast	Fighting	Special	120	70	5	Normal	—
TM56	Fling	Dark	Physical	—	100	10	Normal	—
TM58	Endure	Normal	Status	—	—	10	Self	—
TM67	Recycle	Normal	Status	—	—	10	Self	—
TM68	Giga Impact	Normal	Physical	150	90	5	Normal	○
TM75	Captivate	Normal	Status	—	100	20	2 Foes	—
TM80	Rock Slide	Rock	Physical	75	90	10	2 Foes	—
TM82	Sleep Talk	Normal	Status	—	—	10	Depends	—
TM83	Natural Gift	Normal	Physical	—	100	15	Normal	—
TM87	Swagger	Normal	Status	—	90	15	Normal	—
TM90	Substitute	Normal	Status	—	—	10	Self	—
HM03	Surf	Water	Special	95	100	15	2 Foes/1 Ally	—
HM04	Strength	Normal	Physical	80	100	15	Normal	—
HM05	Whirlpool	Water	Special	15	70	15	Normal	—
HM06	Rock Smash	Fighting	Physical	40	100	15	Normal	—
HM08	Rock Climb	Normal	Physical	90	85	20	Normal	—

● EGG MOVES

Name	Type	Kind	Pow.	Acc.	PP	Range	DA
Lick	Ghost	Physical	20	100	30	Normal	○
Charm	Normal	Status	—	100	20	Normal	—
Double-Edge	Normal	Physical	120	100	15	Normal	—
Curse	???	Status	—	—	10	Normal/Self	—
Fissure	Ground	Physical	—	30	5	Normal	—
Substitute	Normal	Status	—	—	10	Self	—
Whirlwind	Normal	Status	—	100	20	Normal	—
Pursuit	Dark	Physical	40	100	20	Normal	—
Counter	Fighting	Physical	—	100	20	Self	—

● LEVEL-UP MOVES

Lv.	Name	Type	Kind	Pow.	Acc.	PP	Range	DA
1	Gust	Flying	Special	40	100	35	Normal	—
1	Powder Snow	Ice	Special	40	100	25	2 Foes	—
8	Mist	Ice	Status	—	—	30	2 Allies	—
15	Ice Shard	Ice	Physical	40	100	30	Normal	—
22	Mind Reader	Normal	Status	—	—	5	Normal	—
29	AncientPower	Rock	Special	60	100	5	Normal	—
36	Agility	Psychic	Status	—	—	30	Self	—
43	Ice Beam	Ice	Special	95	100	10	Normal	—
50	Reflect	Psychic	Status	—	—	20	2 Allies	—
57	Roost	Flying	Status	—	—	10	Self	—
64	Tailwind	Flying	Status	—	—	30	2 Allies	—
71	Blizzard	Ice	Special	120	70	5	2 Foes	—
78	Sheer Cold	Ice	Special	—	30	5	Normal	—
85	Hail	Ice	Status	—	—	10	All	—

● MOVE MANIAC

Name	Type	Kind	Pow.	Acc.	PP	Range	DA

● BP MOVES

Name	Type	Kind	Pow.	Acc.	PP	Range	DA
Icy Wind	Ice	Special	55	95	15	2 Foes	—
Ominous Wind	Ghost	Special	60	100	5	Normal	—
Air Cutter	Flying	Special	55	95	25	2 Foes	—
Snore	Normal	Special	40	100	15	Normal	—
Swift	Normal	Special	60	—	20	2 Foes	—
Tailwind	Flying	Status	—	—	30	2 Allies	—
Mud-Slap	Ground	Special	20	100	10	Normal	—
AncientPower	Rock	Special	60	100	5	Normal	—
Signal Beam	Bug	Special	75	100	15	Normal	—
Twister	Dragon	Special	40	100	20	2 Foes	—
Sky Attack	Flying	Physical	140	90	5	Normal	—

● TM & HM MOVES

No.	Name	Type	Kind	Pow.	Acc.	PP	Range	DA
TM03	Water Pulse	Water	Special	60	100	20	Normal	—
TM05	Roar	Normal	Status	—	100	20	Normal	—
TM06	Toxic	Poison	Status	—	85	10	Normal	—
TM07	Hail	Ice	Status	—	—	10	All	—
TM10	Hidden Power	Normal	Special	—	100	15	Normal	—
TM11	Sunny Day	Fire	Status	—	—	5	All	—
TM13	Ice Beam	Ice	Special	95	100	10	Normal	—
TM14	Blizzard	Ice	Special	120	70	5	2 Foes	—
TM15	Hyper Beam	Normal	Special	150	90	5	Normal	—
TM17	Protect	Normal	Status	—	—	10	Self	—
TM18	Rain Dance	Water	Status	—	—	5	All	—
TM21	Frustration	Normal	Physical	—	100	20	Normal	○
TM27	Return	Normal	Physical	—	100	20	Normal	○
TM32	Double Team	Normal	Status	—	—	15	Self	—
TM33	Reflect	Psychic	Status	—	—	20	2 Allies	—
TM37	Sandstorm	Rock	Status	—	—	10	All	—
TM40	Aerial Ace	Flying	Physical	60	—	20	Normal	○
TM42	Facade	Normal	Physical	70	100	20	Normal	○
TM43	Secret Power	Normal	Physical	70	100	20	Normal	○
TM44	Rest	Psychic	Status	—	—	10	Self	—
TM47	Steel Wing	Steel	Physical	70	90	25	Normal	○
TM51	Roost	Flying	Status	—	—	10	Self	—
TM58	Endure	Normal	Status	—	—	10	Self	—
TM68	Giga Impact	Normal	Physical	150	90	5	Normal	○
TM72	Avalanche	Ice	Physical	60	100	10	Normal	○
TM82	Sleep Talk	Normal	Status	—	—	10	Depends	—
TM83	Natural Gift	Normal	Physical	—	100	15	Normal	—
TM87	Swagger	Normal	Status	—	90	15	Normal	—
TM88	Pluck	Flying	Physical	60	100	20	Normal	○
TM89	U-turn	Bug	Physical	70	100	20	Normal	○
TM90	Substitute	Normal	Status	—	—	10	Self	—
HM02	Fly	Flying	Physical	90	95	15	Normal	○
HM06	Rock Smash	Fighting	Physical	40	100	15	Normal	○

● No. 144 | Freeze Pokémon
Articuno

Ice   Flying

● HEIGHT: 5'07"
● WEIGHT: 122.1 lbs.
● ITEMS: None

● SIZE COMPARISON

● GENDER UNKNOWN

● ABILITIES
● Pressure

● STATS
HP ●●●○○
ATTACK ●●●●○
DEFENSE ●●●●○
SP. ATTACK ●●●●○
SP. DEFENSE ●●●●●
SPEED ●●●●○

● EGG GROUPS
No Egg has ever been discovered

● PERFORMANCE
SPEED ★★★☆☆   STAMINA ★★★☆☆
POWER ★★★☆☆   JUMP ★★★★★
SKILL ★★★★★

● MAIN WAYS TO OBTAIN

Pokémon HeartGold — Appears in the Seafoam Islands

Pokémon SoulSilver — Appears in the Seafoam Islands

Pokémon Diamond — —

Pokémon Pearl — —

Pokémon Platinum — After you obtain the National Pokédex and talk to Professor Oak in Eterna City, it begins roaming the Sinnoh region

Pokémon HeartGold — The magnificent, seemingly translucent wings of this legendary bird Pokémon are said to be made of ice.

Pokémon SoulSilver — One of the legendary bird Pokémon, it chills moisture in the atmosphere to create snow while flying.

● EVOLUTION
Does not evolve

● No. 145 | Electric Pokémon
Zapdos

Electric | Flying

- ● HEIGHT: 5'03"
- ● WEIGHT: 116.0 lbs.
- ● ITEMS: None

● SIZE COMPARISON

● MALE/FEMALE HAVE SAME FORM

● ABILITIES
- ● Pressure

● STATS
HP ●●●
ATTACK ●●●●
DEFENSE ●●●●
SP. ATTACK ●●●●●
SP. DEFENSE ●●●●●
SPEED ●●●●

● EGG GROUPS
No Egg has ever been discovered

● PERFORMANCE
SPEED ★★★★★	STAMINA ★★☆
POWER ★★★☆☆	JUMP ★★★★★
SKILL ★★★★☆	

● MAIN WAYS TO OBTAIN

Pokémon HeartGold — Appears on Route 10 (after collecting all eight Kanto Gym Badges)

Pokémon SoulSilver — Appears on Route 10 (after collecting all eight Kanto Gym Badges)

Pokémon Diamond — —

Pokémon Pearl — —

Pokémon Platinum — After you obtain the National Pokédex and talk to Professor Oak in Eterna City, it begins roaming the Sinnoh region

Pokémon HeartGold — This legendary bird Pokémon causes savage thunderstorms by flapping its glittering wings.

Pokémon SoulSilver — This legendary bird Pokémon is said to appear only when a thundercloud parts into two halves.

● EVOLUTION
Does not evolve

● LEVEL-UP MOVES
Lv.	Name	Type	Kind	Pow.	Acc.	PP	Range	DA
1	Peck	Flying	Physical	35	100	35	Normal	○
1	ThunderShock	Electric	Special	40	100	30	Normal	—
8	Thunder Wave	Electric	Status	—	100	20	Normal	—
15	Detect	Fighting	Status	—	—	5	Self	—
22	Pluck	Flying	Physical	60	100	20	Normal	○
29	AncientPower	Rock	Special	60	100	5	Normal	—
36	Charge	Electric	Status	—	—	20	Self	—
43	Agility	Psychic	Status	—	—	30	Self	—
50	Discharge	Electric	Special	80	100	15	2 Foes/1 Ally	—
57	Roost	Flying	Status	—	—	10	Self	—
64	Light Screen	Psychic	Status	—	—	30	2 Allies	—
71	Drill Peck	Flying	Physical	80	100	20	Normal	○
78	Thunder	Electric	Special	120	70	10	Normal	—
85	Rain Dance	Water	Status	—	—	5	All	—

● MOVE MANIAC
Name	Type	Kind	Pow.	Acc.	PP	Range	DA

● BP MOVES
Name	Type	Kind	Pow.	Acc.	PP	Range	DA
Ominous Wind	Ghost	Special	60	100	5	Normal	—
Air Cutter	Flying	Special	55	95	25	2 Foes	—
Snore	Normal	Special	40	100	15	Normal	—
Swift	Normal	Special	60	—	20	2 Foes	—
Tailwind	Flying	Status	—	—	30	2 Allies	—
Mud-Slap	Ground	Special	20	100	10	Normal	—
AncientPower	Rock	Special	60	100	5	Normal	—
Signal Beam	Bug	Special	75	100	15	Normal	—
Twister	Dragon	Special	40	100	20	2 Foes	—
Heat Wave	Fire	Special	100	90	10	2 Foes	—
Sky Attack	Flying	Physical	140	90	5	Normal	—

● TM & HM MOVES
No.	Name	Type	Kind	Pow.	Acc.	PP	Range	DA
TM05	Roar	Normal	Status	—	100	20	Normal	—
TM06	Toxic	Poison	Status	—	85	10	Normal	—
TM10	Hidden Power	Normal	Special	—	100	15	Normal	—
TM11	Sunny Day	Fire	Status	—	—	5	All	—
TM15	Hyper Beam	Normal	Special	150	90	5	Normal	—
TM16	Light Screen	Psychic	Status	—	—	30	2 Allies	—
TM17	Protect	Normal	Status	—	—	10	Self	—
TM18	Rain Dance	Water	Status	—	—	5	All	—
TM21	Frustration	Normal	Physical	—	100	20	Normal	○
TM24	Thunderbolt	Electric	Special	95	100	15	Normal	—
TM25	Thunder	Electric	Special	120	70	10	Normal	—
TM27	Return	Normal	Physical	—	100	20	Normal	○
TM32	Double Team	Normal	Status	—	—	15	Self	—
TM34	Shock Wave	Electric	Special	60	—	20	Normal	—
TM37	Sandstorm	Rock	Status	—	—	10	All	—
TM40	Aerial Ace	Flying	Physical	60	—	20	Normal	○
TM42	Facade	Normal	Physical	70	100	20	Normal	○
TM43	Secret Power	Normal	Physical	70	100	20	Normal	—
TM44	Rest	Psychic	Status	—	—	10	Self	—
TM47	Steel Wing	Steel	Physical	70	90	25	Normal	○
TM51	Roost	Flying	Status	—	—	10	Self	—
TM57	Charge Beam	Electric	Special	50	90	10	Normal	—
TM58	Endure	Normal	Status	—	—	10	Self	—
TM68	Giga Impact	Normal	Physical	150	90	5	Normal	○
TM70	Flash	Normal	Status	—	100	20	Normal	—
TM73	Thunder Wave	Electric	Status	—	100	20	Normal	—
TM82	Sleep Talk	Normal	Status	—	—	10	Depends	—
TM83	Natural Gift	Normal	Physical	—	100	15	Normal	—
TM87	Swagger	Normal	Status	—	90	15	Normal	—
TM88	Pluck	Flying	Physical	60	100	20	Normal	○
TM89	U-turn	Bug	Physical	70	100	20	Normal	○
TM90	Substitute	Normal	Status	—	—	10	Self	—
HM02	Fly	Flying	Physical	90	95	15	Normal	○
HM06	Rock Smash	Fighting	Physical	40	100	15	Normal	○

● LEVEL-UP MOVES

Lv.	Name	Type	Kind	Pow.	Acc.	PP	Range	DA
1	Wing Attack	Flying	Physical	60	100	35	Normal	○
1	Ember	Fire	Special	40	100	25	Normal	—
8	Fire Spin	Fire	Special	15	70	15	Normal	—
15	Agility	Psychic	Status	—	—	30	Self	—
22	Endure	Normal	Status	—	—	10	Self	—
29	AncientPower	Rock	Special	60	100	5	Normal	—
36	Flamethrower	Fire	Special	95	100	15	Normal	—
43	Safeguard	Normal	Status	—	—	25	2 Allies	—
50	Air Slash	Flying	Special	75	95	20	Normal	—
57	Roost	Flying	Status	—	—	10	Self	—
64	Heat Wave	Fire	Special	100	90	10	2 Foes	—
71	SolarBeam	Grass	Special	120	100	10	Normal	—
78	Sky Attack	Flying	Physical	140	90	5	Normal	—
85	Sunny Day	Fire	Status	—	—	5	All	—

● MOVE MANIAC

Name	Type	Kind	Pow.	Acc.	PP	Range	DA

● BP MOVES

Name	Type	Kind	Pow.	Acc.	PP	Range	DA
Ominous Wind	Ghost	Special	60	100	5	Normal	—
Air Cutter	Flying	Special	55	95	25	2 Foes	—
Snore	Normal	Special	40	100	15	Normal	—
Swift	Normal	Special	60	—	20	2 Foes	—
Tailwind	Flying	Status	—	—	30	2 Allies	—
Mud-Slap	Ground	Special	20	100	10	Normal	—
AncientPower	Rock	Special	60	100	5	Normal	—
Twister	Dragon	Special	40	100	20	2 Foes	—
Heat Wave	Fire	Special	100	90	10	2 Foes	—
Sky Attack	Flying	Physical	140	90	5	Normal	—

● TM & HM MOVES

No.	Name	Type	Kind	Pow.	Acc.	PP	Range	DA
TM05	Roar	Normal	Status	—	100	20	Normal	—
TM06	Toxic	Poison	Status	—	85	10	Normal	—
TM10	Hidden Power	Normal	Special	—	100	15	Normal	—
TM11	Sunny Day	Fire	Status	—	—	5	All	—
TM15	Hyper Beam	Normal	Special	150	90	5	Normal	—
TM17	Protect	Normal	Status	—	—	10	Self	—
TM18	Rain Dance	Water	Status	—	—	5	All	—
TM20	Safeguard	Normal	Status	—	—	25	2 Allies	—
TM21	Frustration	Normal	Physical	—	100	20	Normal	○
TM22	SolarBeam	Grass	Special	120	100	10	Normal	—
TM27	Return	Normal	Physical	—	100	20	Normal	○
TM32	Double Team	Normal	Status	—	—	15	Self	—
TM35	Flamethrower	Fire	Special	95	100	15	Normal	—
TM37	Sandstorm	Rock	Status	—	—	10	All	—
TM38	Fire Blast	Fire	Special	120	85	5	Normal	—
TM40	Aerial Ace	Flying	Physical	60	—	20	Normal	○
TM42	Facade	Normal	Physical	70	100	20	Normal	○
TM43	Secret Power	Normal	Physical	70	100	20	Normal	○
TM44	Rest	Psychic	Status	—	—	10	Self	—
TM47	Steel Wing	Steel	Physical	70	90	25	Normal	○
TM50	Overheat	Fire	Special	140	90	5	Normal	—
TM51	Roost	Flying	Status	—	—	10	Self	—
TM58	Endure	Normal	Status	—	—	10	Self	—
TM61	Will-O-Wisp	Fire	Status	—	75	15	Normal	—
TM68	Giga Impact	Normal	Physical	150	90	5	Normal	○
TM82	Sleep Talk	Normal	Status	—	—	10	Depends	—
TM83	Natural Gift	Normal	Physical	—	100	15	Normal	○
TM87	Swagger	Normal	Status	—	90	15	Normal	—
TM88	Pluck	Flying	Physical	60	100	20	Normal	○
TM89	U-turn	Bug	Physical	70	100	20	Normal	○
TM90	Substitute	Normal	Status	—	—	10	Self	—
HM02	Fly	Flying	Physical	90	95	15	Normal	○
HM06	Rock Smash	Fighting	Physical	40	100	15	Normal	○

● No. 146 | Flame Pokémon
Moltres

Fire   Flying

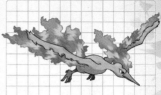

- ● HEIGHT: 6'07"
- ● WEIGHT: 132.3 lbs.
- ● ITEMS: None

● SIZE COMPARISON

● MALE/FEMALE HAVE SAME FORM

● ABILITIES
● Pressure

● STATS
- HP ●●●
- ATTACK ●●●●
- DEFENSE ●●●●
- SP. ATTACK ●●●●●
- SP. DEFENSE ●●●
- SPEED ●●●●

● EGG GROUPS
No Egg has ever been discovered

● PERFORMANCE
SPEED ★★★☆	STAMINA ★★★★☆
POWER ★★★☆☆	JUMP ★★★★★
SKILL ★★★★☆	

● MAIN WAYS TO OBTAIN

Pokémon HeartGold — Appears at Mt. Silver

Pokémon SoulSilver — Appears at Mt. Silver

Pokémon Diamond — —

Pokémon Pearl — —

Pokémon Platinum — After you obtain the National Pokédex and talk to Professor Oak in Eterna City, it begins roaming the Sinnoh region

Pokémon HeartGold
This legendary Pokémon scatters embers with every flap of its wings. It is a thrilling sight to behold.

Pokémon SoulSilver
This legendary bird Pokémon is said to bring early spring to the wintry lands it visits.

● EVOLUTION
Does not evolve

No. 147 | Dragon Pokémon
Dratini

Dragon

- **HEIGHT:** 5'11"
- **WEIGHT:** 7.3 lbs.
- **ITEMS:** Dragon Scale

● SIZE COMPARISON

● MALE/FEMALE HAVE SAME FORM

● ABILITIES
- Shed Skin

● EGG GROUPS
Water 1

Dragon

● PERFORMANCE
SPEED ★★★★☆	STAMINA ★★★☆
POWER ★★☆	JUMP ★★☆
SKILL ★★☆	

● MAIN WAYS TO OBTAIN

Pokémon HeartGold	Dragon's Den (water surface)
Pokémon SoulSilver	Dragon's Den (water surface)
Pokémon Diamond	Mt. Coronet 4F 1(Super Rod)
Pokémon Pearl	Mt. Coronet 4F 1(Super Rod)
Pokémon Platinum	Mt. Coronet 4F 1(Super Rod)

Pokémon HeartGold	**Pokémon SoulSilver**
It is born large to start with. It repeatedly sheds its skin as it steadily grows longer.	This Pokémon is full of life energy. It continually sheds its skin and grows steadily larger.

● EVOLUTION

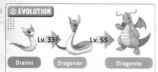

Dratini → Lv. 33 → Dragonair → Lv. 55 → Dragonite

● STATS
- HP ●
- ATTACK ●●●
- DEFENSE ●●●
- SP. ATTACK ●●
- SP. DEFENSE ●●●
- SPEED ●●

● LEVEL-UP MOVES
Lv.	Name	Type	Kind	Pow.	Acc.	PP	Range	DA
1	Wrap	Normal	Physical	15	85	20	Normal	○
1	Leer	Normal	Status	—	100	30	2 Foes	—
5	Thunder Wave	Electric	Status	—	100	20	Normal	—
11	Twister	Dragon	Special	40	100	20	2 Foes	—
15	Dragon Rage	Dragon	Special	—	100	10	Normal	—
21	Slam	Normal	Physical	80	75	20	Normal	○
25	Agility	Psychic	Status	—	—	30	Self	—
31	Aqua Tail	Water	Physical	90	90	10	Normal	○
35	Dragon Rush	Dragon	Physical	100	75	10	Normal	○
41	Safeguard	Normal	Status	—	—	25	2 Allies	—
45	Dragon Dance	Dragon	Status	—	—	20	Self	—
51	Outrage	Dragon	Physical	120	100	15	1 Random	○
55	Hyper Beam	Normal	Special	150	90	5	Normal	—

● MOVE MANIAC
Name	Type	Kind	Pow.	Acc.	PP	Range	DA
Headbutt	Normal	Physical	70	100	15	Normal	○
Draco Meteor	Dragon	Special	140	90	5	Normal	—

● BP MOVES
Name	Type	Kind	Pow.	Acc.	PP	Range	DA
Icy Wind	Ice	Special	55	95	15	2 Foes	—
Snore	Normal	Special	40	100	15	Normal	—
Swift	Normal	Special	60	—	20	2 Foes	—
Aqua Tail	Water	Physical	90	90	10	Normal	○
Outrage	Dragon	Physical	120	100	15	1 Random	○
Twister	Dragon	Special	40	100	20	2 Foes	—

● TM & HM MOVES
No.	Name	Type	Kind	Pow.	Acc.	PP	Range	DA
TM03	Water Pulse	Water	Special	60	100	20	Normal	—
TM06	Toxic	Poison	Status	—	85	10	Normal	—
TM07	Hail	Ice	Status	—	—	10	All	—
TM10	Hidden Power	Normal	Special	—	100	15	Normal	—
TM11	Sunny Day	Fire	Status	—	—	5	All	—
TM13	Ice Beam	Ice	Special	95	100	10	Normal	—
TM14	Blizzard	Ice	Special	120	70	5	2 Foes	—
TM15	Hyper Beam	Normal	Special	150	90	5	Normal	—
TM17	Protect	Normal	Status	—	—	10	Self	—
TM18	Rain Dance	Water	Status	—	—	5	All	—
TM20	Safeguard	Normal	Status	—	—	25	2 Allies	—
TM21	Frustration	Normal	Physical	—	100	20	Normal	○
TM23	Iron Tail	Steel	Physical	100	75	15	Normal	○
TM24	Thunderbolt	Electric	Special	95	100	15	Normal	—
TM25	Thunder	Electric	Special	120	70	10	Normal	—
TM27	Return	Normal	Physical	—	100	20	Normal	○
TM32	Double Team	Normal	Status	—	—	15	Self	—
TM34	Shock Wave	Electric	Special	60	—	20	Normal	—
TM35	Flamethrower	Fire	Special	95	100	15	Normal	—
TM38	Fire Blast	Fire	Special	120	85	5	Normal	—
TM42	Facade	Normal	Physical	70	100	20	Normal	○
TM43	Secret Power	Normal	Physical	70	100	20	Normal	○
TM44	Rest	Psychic	Status	—	—	10	Self	—
TM45	Attract	Normal	Status	—	100	15	Normal	—
TM58	Endure	Normal	Status	—	—	10	Self	—
TM59	Dragon Pulse	Dragon	Special	90	100	10	Normal	—
TM73	Thunder Wave	Electric	Status	—	100	20	Normal	—
TM78	Captivate	Normal	Status	—	100	20	2 Foes	—
TM82	Sleep Talk	Normal	Status	—	—	10	Self	—
TM83	Natural Gift	Normal	Physical	—	100	15	Normal	—
TM87	Swagger	Normal	Status	—	90	15	Normal	—
TM90	Substitute	Normal	Status	—	—	10	Self	—
HM03	Surf	Water	Special	95	100	15	2 Foes/1 Ally	—
HM05	Whirlpool	Water	Special	15	70	15	Normal	—
HM07	Waterfall	Water	Physical	80	100	15	Normal	○

● EGG MOVES
Name	Type	Kind	Pow.	Acc.	PP	Range	DA
Light Screen	Psychic	Status	—	—	30	2 Allies	—
Mist	Ice	Status	—	—	30	2 Allies	—
Haze	Ice	Status	—	—	30	All	—
Supersonic	Normal	Status	—	55	20	Normal	—
DragonBreath	Dragon	Special	60	100	20	Normal	—
Dragon Dance	Dragon	Status	—	—	20	Self	—
Dragon Rush	Dragon	Physical	100	75	10	Normal	○
ExtremeSpeed	Normal	Physical	80	100	5	Normal	○

● LEVEL-UP MOVES

Lv.	Name	Type	Kind	Pow.	Acc.	PP	Range	DA
1	Wrap	Normal	Physical	15	90	20	Normal	○
1	Leer	Normal	Status	–	100	30	2 Foes	–
1	Thunder Wave	Electric	Status	–	100	20	Normal	–
1	Twister	Dragon	Special	40	100	20	2 Foes	–
5	Thunder Wave	Electric	Status	–	100	20	Normal	–
11	Twister	Dragon	Special	40	100	20	2 Foes	–
15	Dragon Rage	Dragon	Special	–	100	10	Normal	–
21	Slam	Normal	Physical	80	75	20	Normal	○
25	Agility	Psychic	Status	–	–	30	Self	–
33	Aqua Tail	Water	Physical	90	90	10	Normal	○
39	Dragon Rush	Dragon	Physical	100	75	10	Normal	○
47	Safeguard	Normal	Status	–	–	25	2 Allies	–
53	Dragon Dance	Dragon	Status	–	–	20	Self	–
61	Outrage	Dragon	Physical	120	100	15	1 Random	○
67	Hyper Beam	Normal	Special	150	90	5	Normal	–

● MOVE MANIAC

Name	Type	Kind	Pow.	Acc.	PP	Range	DA
Headbutt	Normal	Physical	70	100	15	Normal	○
Draco Meteor	Dragon	Special	140	90	5	Normal	–

● BP MOVES

Name	Type	Kind	Pow.	Acc.	PP	Range	DA
Icy Wind	Ice	Special	55	95	15	2 Foes	–
Snore	Normal	Special	40	100	15	Normal	–
Swift	Normal	Special	60	–	20	2 Foes	–
Aqua Tail	Water	Physical	90	90	10	Normal	○
Outrage	Dragon	Physical	120	100	15	1 Random	○
Twister	Dragon	Special	40	100	20	2 Foes	–

● TM & HM MOVES

No.	Name	Type	Kind	Pow.	Acc.	PP	Range	DA
TM03	Water Pulse	Water	Special	60	100	20	Normal	–
TM06	Toxic	Poison	Status	–	85	10	Normal	–
TM07	Hail	Ice	Status	–	–	10	All	–
TM10	Hidden Power	Normal	Special	–	100	15	Normal	–
TM11	Sunny Day	Fire	Status	–	–	5	All	–
TM13	Ice Beam	Ice	Special	95	100	10	Normal	–
TM14	Blizzard	Ice	Special	120	70	5	2 Foes	–
TM15	Hyper Beam	Normal	Special	150	90	5	Normal	–
TM17	Protect	Normal	Status	–	–	10	Self	–
TM18	Rain Dance	Water	Status	–	–	5	All	–
TM20	Safeguard	Normal	Status	–	–	25	2 Allies	–
TM21	Frustration	Normal	Physical	–	100	20	Normal	○
TM23	Iron Tail	Steel	Physical	100	75	15	Normal	○
TM24	Thunderbolt	Electric	Special	95	100	15	Normal	–
TM25	Thunder	Electric	Special	120	70	10	Normal	–
TM27	Return	Normal	Physical	–	100	20	Normal	○
TM32	Double Team	Normal	Status	–	–	15	Self	–
TM34	Shock Wave	Electric	Special	60	–	20	Normal	–
TM35	Flamethrower	Fire	Special	95	100	15	Normal	–
TM38	Fire Blast	Fire	Special	120	85	5	Normal	–
TM42	Facade	Normal	Physical	70	100	20	Normal	○
TM43	Secret Power	Normal	Physical	70	100	20	Normal	○
TM44	Rest	Psychic	Status	–	–	10	Self	–
TM45	Attract	Normal	Status	–	100	15	Normal	–
TM58	Endure	Normal	Status	–	–	10	Self	–
TM59	Dragon Pulse	Dragon	Special	90	100	10	Normal	–
TM73	Thunder Wave	Electric	Status	–	100	20	Normal	–
TM78	Captivate	Normal	Status	–	100	20	2 Foes	–
TM82	Sleep Talk	Normal	Status	–	–	10	Depends	–
TM83	Natural Gift	Normal	Physical	–	100	15	Normal	–
TM87	Swagger	Normal	Status	–	90	15	Normal	–
TM90	Substitute	Normal	Status	–	–	10	Self	–
HM03	Surf	Water	Special	95	100	15	2 Foes/1 Ally	–
HM05	Whirlpool	Water	Special	15	70	15	Normal	–
HM07	Waterfall	Water	Physical	80	100	15	Normal	○

● No. 148 | Dragon Pokémon
Dragonair

Dragon

- ● HEIGHT: 13'01"
- ● WEIGHT: 36.4 lbs.
- ● ITEMS: Dragon Scale

● SIZE COMPARISON

● MALE/FEMALE HAVE SAME FORM

⊚ ABILITIES
● Shed Skin

⊚ STATS
- HP ●●
- ATTACK ●●●●
- DEFENSE ●●●
- SP. ATTACK ●●●●
- SP. DEFENSE ●●●
- SPEED ●●●

⊚ EGG GROUPS
Water 1

Dragon

⊚ PERFORMANCE
SPEED ★★★☆	STAMINA ★★★
POWER ★★☆	JUMP ★★★★☆
SKILL ★★★☆	

● MAIN WAYS TO OBTAIN

Pokémon HeartGold — Dragon's Den (Super Rod)

Pokémon SoulSilver — Dragon's Den (Super Rod)

Pokémon Diamond — Mt. Coronet 4F 1 (Super Rod)

Pokémon Pearl — Mt. Coronet 4F 1 (Super Rod)

Pokémon Platinum — Mt. Coronet 4F 1 (Super Rod)

Pokémon HeartGold
They say that if it emits an aura from its whole body, the weather will begin to change instantly.

Pokémon SoulSilver
Its crystalline orbs appear to give this Pokémon the power to freely control the weather.

⊚ EVOLUTION

Dratini — Lv. 33 — Dragonair — Lv. 55 — Dragonite

No. 149 | Dragon Pokémon
Dragonite

Dragon | **Flying**

● HEIGHT: 7'03"
● WEIGHT: 463.0 lbs.
● ITEMS: None

● SIZE COMPARISON

● MALE/FEMALE HAVE SAME FORM

⊘ ABILITIES
● Inner Focus

⊘ STATS
HP	●●●
ATTACK	●●●●●●●
DEFENSE	●●●●●
SP. ATTACK	●●●●●●
SP. DEFENSE	●●●●●
SPEED	●●●●

⊘ EGG GROUPS
Water 1

Dragon

⊘ PERFORMANCE
SPEED ★★☆☆☆   STAMINA ★★★☆
POWER ★★★★★   JUMP ★★★★★
SKILL ★★☆

● MAIN WAYS TO OBTAIN

Pokémon HeartGold | Level up Dragonair to Lv. 55

Pokémon SoulSilver | Level up Dragonair to Lv. 55

Pokémon Diamond | Level up Dragonair to Lv. 55

Pokémon Pearl | Level up Dragonair to Lv. 55

Pokémon Platinum | Level up Dragonair to Lv. 55

Pokémon HeartGold
It is said that this Pokémon constantly flies over the immense seas and rescues drowning people.

Pokémon SoulSilver
This marine Pokémon has an impressive build that lets it freely fly over raging seas without trouble.

⊘ EVOLUTION

Dratini → Lv. 33 → Dragonair → Lv. 55 → Dragonite

Black and white 2
pokedex

● LEVEL-UP MOVES
Lv.	Name	Type	Kind	Pow.	Acc.	PP	Range	DA
1	Fire Punch	Fire	Physical	75	100	15	Normal	○
1	ThunderPunch	Electric	Physical	75	100	15	Normal	○
1	Roost	Flying	Status	—	—	10	Self	—
1	Wrap	Normal	Physical	15	85	20	Normal	—
1	Leer	Normal	Status	—	100	30	2 Foes	—
1	Thunder Wave	Electric	Status	—	100	20	Normal	—
1	Twister	Dragon	Special	40	100	20	2 Foes	—
5	Thunder Wave	Electric	Status	—	100	20	Normal	—
11	Twister	Dragon	Special	40	100	20	2 Foes	—
15	Dragon Rage	Dragon	Special	—	100	10	Normal	—
21	Slam	Normal	Physical	80	75	20	Normal	○
25	Agility	Psychic	Status	—	—	30	Self	—
33	Aqua Tail	Water	Physical	90	90	10	Normal	○
39	Dragon Rush	Dragon	Physical	100	75	10	Normal	○
47	Safeguard	Normal	Status	—	—	25	2 Allies	—
53	Dragon Dance	Dragon	Status	—	—	20	Self	—
55	Wing Attack	Flying	Physical	60	100	35	Normal	○
64	Outrage	Dragon	Physical	120	100	10	1 Random	○
73	Hyper Beam	Normal	Special	150	90	5	Normal	—

● MOVE MANIAC
Name	Type	Kind	Pow.	Acc.	PP	Range	DA
Headbutt	Normal	Physical	70	100	15	Normal	○
Draco Meteor	Dragon	Special	140	90	5	Normal	—

● BP MOVES
Name	Type	Kind	Pow.	Acc.	PP	Range	DA
Dive	Water	Physical	80	100	10	Normal	○
Fury Cutter	Bug	Physical	10	95	20	Normal	○
Icy Wind	Ice	Special	55	95	15	2 Foes	—
ThunderPunch	Electric	Physical	75	100	15	Normal	○
Fire Punch	Fire	Physical	75	100	15	Normal	○
Ice Punch	Ice	Physical	75	100	15	Normal	○
Ominous Wind	Ghost	Special	60	100	5	Normal	—
Air Cutter	Flying	Special	55	95	25	2 Foes	—
Snore	Normal	Special	40	100	15	Normal	—
Swift	Normal	Special	60	—	20	2 Foes	—
Tailwind	Flying	Status	—	—	30	2 Allies	—
Mud-Slap	Ground	Special	20	100	10	Normal	—
Superpower	Fighting	Physical	120	100	5	Normal	○
Iron Head	Steel	Physical	80	100	15	Normal	○
Aqua Tail	Water	Physical	90	90	10	Normal	○
Outrage	Dragon	Physical	120	100	15	1 Random	○
Twister	Dragon	Special	40	100	20	Normal	—
Heat Wave	Fire	Special	100	90	10	2 Foes	—

● TM & HM MOVES
No.	Name	Type	Kind	Pow.	Acc.	PP	Range	DA
TM01	Focus Punch	Fighting	Physical	150	100	20	Normal	○
TM02	Dragon Claw	Dragon	Physical	80	100	15	Normal	○
TM03	Water Pulse	Water	Special	60	100	20	Normal	—
TM05	Roar	Normal	Status	—	100	20	Normal	—
TM06	Toxic	Poison	Status	—	85	10	Normal	—
TM07	Hail	Ice	Status	—	—	10	All	—
TM10	Hidden Power	Normal	Special	—	100	15	Normal	—
TM11	Sunny Day	Fire	Status	—	—	5	All	—
TM13	Ice Beam	Ice	Special	95	100	10	Normal	—
TM14	Blizzard	Ice	Special	120	70	5	2 Foes	—
TM15	Hyper Beam	Normal	Special	150	90	5	Normal	—
TM17	Protect	Normal	Status	—	—	10	Self	—
TM18	Rain Dance	Water	Status	—	—	5	All	—
TM20	Safeguard	Normal	Status	—	—	25	2 Allies	—
TM21	Frustration	Normal	Physical	—	100	20	Normal	○
TM23	Iron Tail	Steel	Physical	100	75	15	Normal	○
TM24	Thunderbolt	Electric	Special	95	100	15	Normal	—
TM25	Thunder	Electric	Special	120	70	10	Normal	—
TM26	Earthquake	Ground	Physical	100	100	10	2 Foes/1 Ally	—
TM27	Return	Normal	Physical	—	100	20	Normal	○
TM31	Brick Break	Fighting	Physical	75	100	15	Normal	○
TM32	Double Team	Normal	Status	—	—	15	Self	—
TM34	Shock Wave	Electric	Special	60	—	20	Normal	—
TM35	Flamethrower	Fire	Special	95	100	15	Normal	—
TM37	Sandstorm	Rock	Status	—	—	10	All	—
TM38	Fire Blast	Fire	Special	120	85	5	Normal	—
TM39	Rock Tomb	Rock	Physical	50	80	10	Normal	○
TM40	Aerial Ace	Flying	Physical	60	—	20	Normal	○
TM42	Facade	Normal	Physical	70	100	20	Normal	○
TM43	Secret Power	Normal	Physical	70	100	20	Normal	—
TM44	Rest	Psychic	Status	—	—	10	Self	—
TM45	Attract	Normal	Status	—	100	15	Normal	—
TM47	Steel Wing	Steel	Physical	70	90	25	Normal	○
TM51	Roost	Flying	Status	—	—	10	Self	—
TM52	Focus Blast	Fighting	Special	120	70	5	Normal	—
TM56	Fling	Dark	Physical	—	100	10	Normal	○
TM58	Endure	Normal	Status	—	—	10	Self	—
TM59	Dragon Pulse	Dragon	Special	90	100	10	Normal	—
TM68	Giga Impact	Normal	Physical	150	90	5	Normal	○
TM71	Stone Edge	Rock	Physical	100	80	5	Normal	—
TM73	Thunder Wave	Electric	Status	—	100	20	Normal	—
TM78	Captivate	Normal	Status	—	100	20	2 Foes	—
TM80	Rock Slide	Rock	Physical	75	90	10	2 Foes	—
TM82	Sleep Talk	Normal	Status	—	—	10	Depends	—
TM83	Natural Gift	Normal	Physical	—	100	15	Normal	○
TM87	Swagger	Normal	Status	—	90	15	Normal	—
TM90	Substitute	Normal	Status	—	—	10	Self	—
HM01	Cut	Normal	Physical	50	95	30	Normal	○
HM02	Fly	Flying	Physical	90	95	15	Normal	○
HM03	Surf	Water	Special	95	100	15	2 Foes/1 Ally	—
HM04	Strength	Normal	Physical	80	100	15	Normal	○
HM05	Whirlpool	Water	Special	15	70	15	Normal	—
HM06	Rock Smash	Fighting	Physical	40	100	15	Normal	○
HM07	Waterfall	Water	Physical	80	100	15	Normal	○

● LEVEL-UP MOVES

Lv.	Name	Type	Kind	Pow.	Acc.	PP	Range	DA
1	Confusion	Psychic	Special	50	100	25	Normal	—
1	Disable	Normal	Status	—	80	20	Normal	—
8	Barrier	Psychic	Status	—	—	30	Self	—
15	Swift	Normal	Special	60	—	20	2 Foes	—
22	Future Sight	Psychic	Special	80	90	15	Normal	—
29	Psych Up	Normal	Status	—	—	10	Normal	—
36	Miracle Eye	Psychic	Status	—	—	40	Normal	—
43	Mist	Ice	Status	—	—	30	2 Allies	—
50	Psycho Cut	Psychic	Physical	70	100	20	Normal	—
57	Amnesia	Psychic	Status	—	—	20	Self	—
64	Power Swap	Psychic	Status	—	—	10	Normal	—
64	Guard Swap	Psychic	Status	—	—	10	Normal	—
71	Psychic	Psychic	Special	90	100	10	Normal	—
79	Me First	Normal	Status	—	—	20	Depends	—
86	Recover	Normal	Status	—	—	10	Self	—
93	Safeguard	Normal	Status	—	—	25	2 Allies	—
100	Aura Sphere	Fighting	Special	90	—	20	Normal	—

● MOVE MANIAC

Name	Type	Kind	Pow.	Acc.	PP	Range	DA
Headbutt	Normal	Physical	70	100	15	Normal	○

● BP MOVES

Name	Type	Kind	Pow.	Acc.	PP	Range	DA
Icy Wind	Ice	Special	55	95	15	2 Foes	—
ThunderPunch	Electric	Physical	75	100	15	Normal	○
Fire Punch	Fire	Physical	75	100	15	Normal	○
Ice Punch	Ice	Physical	75	100	15	Normal	○
Zen Headbutt	Psychic	Physical	80	90	15	Normal	○
Trick	Psychic	Status	—	100	10	Normal	—
Snore	Normal	Special	40	100	15	Normal	—
Swift	Normal	Special	60	—	20	2 Foes	—
Gravity	Psychic	Status	—	—	5	All	—
Magic Coat	Psychic	Status	—	—	15	Self	—
Role Play	Psychic	Status	—	—	10	Normal	—
Mud-Slap	Ground	Special	20	100	10	Normal	—
Aqua Tail	Water	Physical	90	90	10	Normal	○
Signal Beam	Bug	Special	75	100	15	Normal	—
Low Kick	Fighting	Physical	—	100	20	Normal	○

● TM & HM MOVES

No.	Name	Type	Kind	Pow.	Acc.	PP	Range	DA
TM01	Focus Punch	Fighting	Physical	150	100	20	Normal	○
TM03	Water Pulse	Water	Special	60	100	20	Normal	—
TM04	Calm Mind	Psychic	Status	—	—	20	Self	—
TM06	Toxic	Poison	Status	—	85	10	Normal	—
TM07	Hail	Ice	Status	—	—	10	All	—
TM08	Bulk Up	Fighting	Status	—	—	20	Self	—
TM10	Hidden Power	Normal	Special	—	100	15	Normal	—
TM11	Sunny Day	Fire	Status	—	—	5	All	—
TM12	Taunt	Dark	Status	—	100	20	Normal	—
TM13	Ice Beam	Ice	Special	95	100	10	Normal	—
TM14	Blizzard	Ice	Special	120	70	5	2 Foes	—
TM15	Hyper Beam	Normal	Special	150	90	5	Normal	—
TM16	Light Screen	Psychic	Status	—	—	30	2 Allies	—
TM17	Protect	Normal	Status	—	—	10	Self	—
TM18	Rain Dance	Water	Status	—	—	5	All	—
TM20	Safeguard	Normal	Status	—	—	25	2 Allies	—
TM21	Frustration	Normal	Physical	—	100	20	Normal	○
TM22	SolarBeam	Grass	Special	120	100	10	Normal	—
TM23	Iron Tail	Steel	Physical	100	75	15	Normal	○
TM24	Thunderbolt	Electric	Special	95	100	15	Normal	—
TM25	Thunder	Electric	Special	120	70	10	Normal	—
TM26	Earthquake	Ground	Physical	100	100	10	2 Foes/1 Ally	—
TM27	Return	Normal	Physical	—	100	20	Normal	○
TM29	Psychic	Psychic	Special	90	100	10	Normal	—
TM30	Shadow Ball	Ghost	Special	80	100	15	Normal	—
TM31	Brick Break	Fighting	Physical	75	100	15	Normal	○
TM32	Double Team	Normal	Status	—	—	15	Self	—
TM33	Reflect	Psychic	Status	—	—	20	2 Allies	—
TM34	Shock Wave	Electric	Special	60	—	20	Normal	—
TM35	Flamethrower	Fire	Special	95	100	15	Normal	—
TM37	Sandstorm	Rock	Status	—	—	10	All	—
TM38	Fire Blast	Fire	Special	120	85	5	Normal	—
TM39	Rock Tomb	Rock	Physical	50	80	10	Normal	—
TM40	Aerial Ace	Flying	Physical	60	—	20	Normal	○
TM41	Torment	Dark	Status	—	100	15	Normal	—
TM42	Facade	Normal	Physical	70	100	20	Normal	○
TM43	Secret Power	Normal	Physical	70	100	20	Normal	○
TM44	Rest	Psychic	Status	—	—	10	Self	—
TM48	Skill Swap	Psychic	Status	—	—	10	Normal	—
TM49	Snatch	Dark	Status	—	—	10	Depends	—
TM52	Focus Blast	Fighting	Special	120	70	5	Normal	—
TM53	Energy Ball	Grass	Special	80	100	10	Normal	—
TM56	Fling	Dark	Physical	—	100	10	Normal	—
TM57	Charge Beam	Electric	Special	50	90	10	Normal	—
TM58	Endure	Normal	Status	—	—	10	Self	—
TM60	Drain Punch	Fighting	Physical	60	100	5	Normal	○
TM61	Will-O-Wisp	Fire	Status	—	75	15	Normal	—
TM63	Embargo	Dark	Status	—	100	15	Normal	—
TM67	Recycle	Normal	Status	—	—	10	Self	—
TM68	Giga Impact	Normal	Physical	150	90	5	Normal	○
TM70	Flash	Normal	Status	—	100	20	Normal	—
TM71	Stone Edge	Rock	Physical	100	80	5	Normal	—
TM72	Avalanche	Ice	Physical	60	100	10	Normal	○
TM73	Thunder Wave	Electric	Status	—	100	20	Normal	—
TM77	Psych Up	Normal	Status	—	—	10	Normal	—
TM80	Rock Slide	Rock	Physical	75	90	10	2 Foes	—
TM82	Sleep Talk	Normal	Status	—	—	10	Depends	—
TM83	Natural Gift	Normal	Physical	—	100	15	Normal	—
TM84	Poison Jab	Poison	Physical	80	100	20	Normal	○
TM85	Dream Eater	Psychic	Special	100	100	15	Normal	—
TM86	Grass Knot	Grass	Special	—	100	20	Normal	○
TM87	Swagger	Normal	Status	—	90	15	Normal	—
TM90	Substitute	Normal	Status	—	—	10	Self	—
TM92	Trick Room	Psychic	Status	—	—	5	All	—
HM04	Strength	Normal	Physical	80	100	15	Normal	○
HM06	Rock Smash	Fighting	Physical	40	100	15	Normal	○
HM08	Rock Climb	Normal	Physical	90	85	20	Normal	○

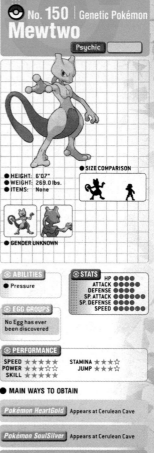

⊙ No. 150 | Genetic Pokémon
Mewtwo

Psychic

- ● HEIGHT: 6'07"
- ● WEIGHT: 269.0 lbs.
- ● ITEMS: None

● SIZE COMPARISON

● GENDER UNKNOWN

⊙ ABILITIES
● Pressure

⊙ STATS
- HP ●●●●○
- ATTACK ●●●●○
- DEFENSE ●●●●○
- SP. ATTACK ●●●●●●
- SP. DEFENSE ●●●●○
- SPEED ●●●●●○

⊙ EGG GROUPS
No Egg has ever been discovered

⊙ PERFORMANCE
SPEED ★★★★★	STAMINA ★★★☆
POWER ★★★☆☆	JUMP ★★★☆
SKILL ★★★★★	

● MAIN WAYS TO OBTAIN

Pokémon HeartGold — Appears at Cerulean Cave

Pokémon SoulSilver — Appears at Cerulean Cave

Pokémon Diamond — —

Pokémon Pearl — —

Pokémon Platinum — —

Pokémon HeartGold	**Pokémon SoulSilver**
Because its battle abilities were raised to the ultimate level, it thinks only of defeating its foes.	It usually remains motionless to conserve energy, so that it may unleash its full power in battle.

⊙ EVOLUTION
Does not evolve

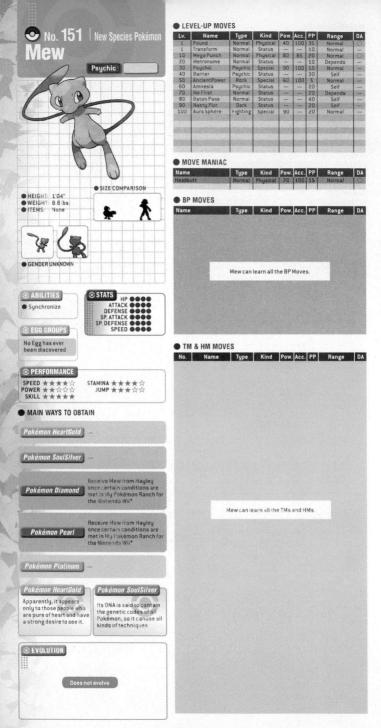

⬤ No. 151 | New Species Pokémon
Mew

Psychic

- ⬤ HEIGHT: 1'04"
- ⬤ WEIGHT: 8.8 lbs
- ⬤ ITEMS: None

⬤ SIZE COMPARISON

⬤ GENDER UNKNOWN

⬤ ABILITIES
- ⬤ Synchronize

⬤ STATS
- HP ●●●●
- ATTACK ●●●●
- DEFENSE ●●●●
- SP. ATTACK ●●●●
- SP. DEFENSE ●●●●
- SPEED ●●●●

⬤ EGG GROUPS
No Egg has ever been discovered

⬤ PERFORMANCE
- SPEED ★★★★☆
- POWER ★★☆☆☆
- SKILL ★★★★★
- STAMINA ★★★★☆
- JUMP ★★★☆☆

⬤ MAIN WAYS TO OBTAIN

Pokémon HeartGold	—
Pokémon SoulSilver	—
Pokémon Diamond	Receive Mew from Hayley once certain conditions are met in My Pokémon Ranch for the Nintendo Wii*
Pokémon Pearl	Receive Mew from Hayley once certain conditions are met in My Pokémon Ranch for the Nintendo Wii*
Pokémon Platinum	—

Pokémon HeartGold
Apparently, it appears only to those people who are pure of heart and have a strong desire to see it.

Pokémon SoulSilver
Its DNA is said to contain the genetic codes of all Pokémon, so it can use all kinds of techniques

⬤ EVOLUTION
Does not evolve

⬤ LEVEL-UP MOVES

Lv.	Name	Type	Kind	Pow.	Acc.	PP	Range	DA
1	Pound	Normal	Physical	40	100	35	Normal	○
1	Transform	Normal	Status	—	—	10	Normal	—
10	Mega Punch	Normal	Physical	80	85	20	Normal	○
20	Metronome	Normal	Status	—	—	10	Depends	—
30	Psychic	Psychic	Special	90	100	10	Normal	—
40	Barrier	Psychic	Status	—	—	30	Self	—
50	AncientPower	Rock	Special	60	100	5	Normal	—
60	Amnesia	Psychic	Status	—	—	20	Self	—
70	Me First	Normal	Status	—	—	20	Depends	—
80	Baton Pass	Normal	Status	—	—	40	Self	—
90	Nasty Plot	Dark	Status	—	—	20	Self	—
100	Aura Sphere	Fighting	Special	90	—	20	Normal	—

⬤ MOVE MANIAC

Name	Type	Kind	Pow.	Acc.	PP	Range	DA
Headbutt	Normal	Physical	70	100	15	Normal	○

⬤ BP MOVES

Name	Type	Kind	Pow.	Acc.	PP	Range	DA

Mew can learn all the BP Moves.

⬤ TM & HM MOVES

No.	Name	Type	Kind	Pow.	Acc.	PP	Range	DA

Mew can learn all the TMs and HMs.

● LEVEL-UP MOVES

Lv.	Name	Type	Kind	Pow.	Acc.	PP	Range	DA
1	Tackle	Normal	Physical	35	95	35	Normal	○
1	Growl	Normal	Status	—	100	40	2 Foes	—
6	Razor Leaf	Grass	Physical	55	95	25	2 Foes	—
9	PoisonPowder	Poison	Status	—	75	35	Normal	—
12	Synthesis	Grass	Status	—	—	5	Self	—
17	Reflect	Psychic	Status	—	—	20	2 Allies	—
20	Magical Leaf	Grass	Special	60	—	20	Normal	—
23	Natural Gift	Normal	Physical	—	100	15	Normal	—
28	Sweet Scent	Normal	Status	—	100	20	2 Foes	—
31	Light Screen	Psychic	Status	—	—	30	2 Allies	—
34	Body Slam	Normal	Physical	85	100	15	Normal	○
39	Safeguard	Normal	Status	—	—	25	2 Allies	—
42	Aromatherapy	Grass	Status	—	—	5	All Allies	—
45	SolarBeam	Grass	Special	120	100	10	Normal	—

● MOVE MANIAC

Name	Type	Kind	Pow.	Acc.	PP	Range	DA
Headbutt	Normal	Physical	70	100	15	Normal	○

● BP MOVES

Name	Type	Kind	Pow.	Acc.	PP	Range	DA
Fury Cutter	Bug	Physical	10	95	20	Normal	○
Snore	Normal	Special	40	100	15	Normal	—
Synthesis	Grass	Status	—	—	5	Self	—
Worry Seed	Grass	Status	—	100	10	Normal	—
Magic Coat	Psychic	Status	—	—	15	Self	—
Mud-Slap	Ground	Special	20	100	10	Normal	—
AncientPower	Rock	Special	60	100	5	Normal	—
Seed Bomb	Grass	Physical	80	100	15	Normal	—

● TM & HM MOVES

No.	Name	Type	Kind	Pow.	Acc.	PP	Range	DA
TM06	Toxic	Poison	Status	—	85	10	Normal	—
TM09	Bullet Seed	Grass	Physical	10	100	30	Normal	—
TM10	Hidden Power	Normal	Special	—	100	15	Normal	—
TM11	Sunny Day	Fire	Status	—	—	5	All	—
TM16	Light Screen	Psychic	Status	—	—	30	2 Allies	—
TM17	Protect	Normal	Status	—	—	10	Self	—
TM19	Giga Drain	Grass	Special	60	100	10	Normal	—
TM20	Safeguard	Normal	Status	—	—	25	2 Allies	—
TM21	Frustration	Normal	Physical	—	100	20	Normal	○
TM22	SolarBeam	Grass	Special	120	100	10	Normal	—
TM23	Iron Tail	Steel	Physical	100	75	15	Normal	○
TM27	Return	Normal	Physical	—	100	20	Normal	○
TM32	Double Team	Normal	Status	—	—	15	Self	—
TM33	Reflect	Psychic	Status	—	—	20	2 Allies	—
TM42	Facade	Normal	Physical	70	100	20	Normal	○
TM43	Secret Power	Normal	Physical	70	100	20	Normal	○
TM44	Rest	Psychic	Status	—	—	10	Self	—
TM45	Attract	Normal	Status	—	100	15	Normal	—
TM53	Energy Ball	Grass	Special	80	100	10	Normal	—
TM58	Endure	Normal	Status	—	—	10	Self	—
TM70	Flash	Normal	Status	—	100	20	Normal	—
TM75	Swords Dance	Normal	Status	—	—	30	Self	—
TM78	Captivate	Normal	Status	—	100	20	2 Foes	—
TM82	Sleep Talk	Normal	Status	—	—	10	Depends	—
TM83	Natural Gift	Normal	Physical	—	100	15	Normal	○
TM86	Grass Knot	Grass	Special	—	100	20	Normal	○
TM87	Swagger	Normal	Status	—	90	15	Normal	—
TM90	Substitute	Normal	Status	—	—	10	Self	—
HM01	Cut	Normal	Physical	50	95	30	Normal	○

● EGG MOVES

Name	Type	Kind	Pow.	Acc.	PP	Range	DA
Vine Whip	Grass	Physical	35	100	15	Normal	○
Leech Seed	Grass	Status	—	90	10	Normal	—
Counter	Fighting	Physical	—	100	20	Self	○
AncientPower	Rock	Special	60	100	5	Normal	—
Flail	Normal	Physical	—	100	15	Normal	○
Nature Power	Normal	Status	—	—	20	Depends	—
Ingrain	Grass	Status	—	—	20	Self	—
GrassWhistle	Grass	Status	—	55	15	Normal	—
Leaf Storm	Grass	Special	140	90	5	Normal	—
Aromatherapy	Grass	Status	—	—	5	All Allies	—
Wring Out	Normal	Special	—	100	5	Normal	—
Body Slam	Normal	Physical	85	100	15	Normal	○

No. 152 | Leaf Pokémon
Chikorita

Grass

- ● HEIGHT: 2'11"
- ● WEIGHT: 14.1 lbs.
- ● ITEMS: None

● SIZE COMPARISON

● MALE/FEMALE HAVE SAME FORM

⊘ ABILITIES
● Overgrow

⊘ STATS
- HP ●●
- ATTACK ●●●
- DEFENSE ●●●
- SP. ATTACK ●●●
- SP. DEFENSE ●●
- SPEED ●●

⊘ EGG GROUPS
Monster

Grass

⊘ PERFORMANCE
- SPEED ★★★☆
- POWER ★★☆
- SKILL ★★☆☆
- STAMINA ★★★★☆
- JUMP ★★★

● MAIN WAYS TO OBTAIN

Pokémon HeartGold	Receive from Professor Elm in New Bark Town at the beginning of the adventure
Pokémon SoulSilver	Receive from Professor Elm in New Bark Town at the beginning of the adventure
Pokémon Diamond	—
Pokémon Pearl	—
Pokémon Platinum	—

| Pokémon HeartGold | A sweet aroma gently wafts from the leaf on its head. It is docile and loves to soak up sunrays. |
| Pokémon SoulSilver | Its pleasantly aromatic leaf has the ability to check humidity and temperature. |

⊘ EVOLUTION

 Lv. 16 Lv.32

Chikorita — Bayleef — Meganium

⦿ No. 153 | Leaf Pokémon
Bayleef

Grass

- **HEIGHT:** 3'11"
- **WEIGHT:** 34.8 lbs.
- **ITEMS:** None

⦿ **SIZE COMPARISON**

⦿ **MALE/FEMALE HAVE SAME FORM**

⦿ ABILITIES
- Overgrow

⦿ STATS
HP	●●
ATTACK	●●●
DEFENSE	●●●
SP. ATTACK	●●●
SP. DEFENSE	●●●
SPEED	●●●

⦿ EGG GROUPS
Monster

Grass

⦿ PERFORMANCE
SPEED ★★☆
POWER ★★☆
SKILL ★★★★☆
STAMINA ★★★★☆
JUMP ★★☆

⦿ MAIN WAYS TO OBTAIN

Pokémon HeartGold Level up Chikorita to Lv. 16

Pokémon SoulSilver Level up Chikorita to Lv. 16

Pokémon Diamond —

Pokémon Pearl —

Pokémon Platinum —

Pokémon HeartGold	Pokémon SoulSilver
The scent of spices comes from around its neck. Somehow, sniffing it makes you want to fight.	A spicy aroma emanates from around its neck. The aroma acts as a stimulant to restore health.

⦿ EVOLUTION

Chikorita — Lv. 16 → Bayleef — Lv.32 → Meganium

⦿ LEVEL-UP MOVES
Lv.	Name	Type	Kind	Pow.	Acc.	PP	Range	DA
1	Tackle	Normal	Physical	35	95	35	Normal	○
1	Growl	Normal	Status	—	100	40	2 Foes	—
1	Razor Leaf	Grass	Physical	55	95	25	2 Foes	—
1	PoisonPowder	Poison	Status	—	75	35	Normal	—
6	Razor Leaf	Grass	Physical	55	95	25	2 Foes	—
6	PoisonPowder	Poison	Status	—	75	35	Normal	—
12	Synthesis	Grass	Status	—	—	5	Self	—
18	Reflect	Psychic	Status	—	—	20	2 Allies	—
22	Magical Leaf	Grass	Special	60	—	20	Normal	—
26	Natural Gift	Normal	Physical	—	100	15	Normal	—
32	Sweet Scent	Normal	Status	—	100	20	2 Foes	—
36	Light Screen	Psychic	Status	—	—	30	2 Allies	—
40	Body Slam	Normal	Physical	85	100	15	Normal	○
46	Safeguard	Normal	Status	—	—	25	2 Allies	—
50	Aromatherapy	Grass	Status	—	—	5	All Allies	—
54	SolarBeam	Grass	Special	120	100	10	Normal	—

⦿ MOVE MANIAC
Name	Type	Kind	Pow.	Acc.	PP	Range	DA
Headbutt	Normal	Physical	70	100	15	Normal	○

⦿ BP MOVES
Name	Type	Kind	Pow.	Acc.	PP	Range	DA
Fury Cutter	Bug	Physical	10	95	20	Normal	○
Snore	Normal	Special	40	100	15	Normal	—
Synthesis	Grass	Status	—	—	5	Self	—
Worry Seed	Grass	Status	—	100	10	Normal	—
Magic Coat	Psychic	Status	—	—	15	Self	—
Mud-Slap	Ground	Special	20	100	10	Normal	—
AncientPower	Rock	Special	60	100	5	Normal	—
Seed Bomb	Grass	Physical	80	100	15	Normal	—

⦿ TM & HM MOVES
No.	Name	Type	Kind	Pow.	Acc.	PP	Range	DA
TM06	Toxic	Poison	Status	—	85	10	Normal	—
TM09	Bullet Seed	Grass	Physical	10	100	30	Normal	—
TM10	Hidden Power	Normal	Special	—	100	15	Normal	—
TM11	Sunny Day	Fire	Status	—	—	5	All	—
TM16	Light Screen	Psychic	Status	—	—	30	2 Allies	—
TM17	Protect	Normal	Status	—	—	10	Self	—
TM19	Giga Drain	Grass	Special	60	100	10	Normal	—
TM20	Safeguard	Normal	Status	—	—	25	2 Allies	—
TM21	Frustration	Normal	Physical	—	100	20	Normal	○
TM22	SolarBeam	Grass	Special	120	100	10	Normal	—
TM23	Iron Tail	Steel	Physical	100	75	15	Normal	○
TM27	Return	Normal	Physical	—	100	20	Normal	○
TM32	Double Team	Normal	Status	—	—	15	Self	—
TM33	Reflect	Psychic	Status	—	—	20	2 Allies	—
TM42	Facade	Normal	Physical	70	100	20	Normal	○
TM43	Secret Power	Normal	Physical	70	100	20	Normal	—
TM44	Rest	Psychic	Status	—	—	10	Self	—
TM45	Attract	Normal	Status	—	100	15	Normal	—
TM53	Energy Ball	Grass	Special	80	100	10	Normal	—
TM58	Endure	Normal	Status	—	—	10	Self	—
TM70	Flash	Normal	Status	—	100	20	Normal	—
TM75	Swords Dance	Normal	Status	—	—	30	Self	—
TM78	Captivate	Normal	Status	—	100	20	2 Foes	—
TM82	Sleep Talk	Normal	Status	—	—	10	Depends	—
TM83	Natural Gift	Normal	Physical	—	100	15	Normal	—
TM86	Grass Knot	Grass	Special	—	100	20	Normal	○
TM87	Swagger	Normal	Status	—	90	15	Normal	—
TM90	Substitute	Normal	Status	—	—	10	Self	—
HM01	Cut	Normal	Physical	50	95	30	Normal	○
HM04	Strength	Normal	Physical	80	100	15	Normal	○
HM06	Rock Smash	Fighting	Physical	40	100	15	Normal	○

● LEVEL-UP MOVES

Lv.	Name	Type	Kind	Pow.	Acc.	PP	Range	DA
1	Tackle	Normal	Physical	35	95	35	Normal	○
1	Growl	Normal	Status	—	100	40	2 Foes	—
1	Razor Leaf	Grass	Physical	55	95	25	2 Foes	—
1	PoisonPowder	Poison	Status	—	75	35	Normal	—
6	Razor Leaf	Grass	Physical	55	95	25	2 Foes	—
9	PoisonPowder	Poison	Status	—	75	35	Normal	—
12	Synthesis	Grass	Status	—	—	5	Self	—
18	Reflect	Psychic	Status	—	—	20	2 Allies	—
22	Magical Leaf	Grass	Special	60	—	20	Normal	—
26	Natural Gift	Normal	Physical	—	100	15	Normal	—
32	Petal Dance	Grass	Special	90	100	20	1 Random	○
34	Sweet Scent	Normal	Status	—	100	20	2 Foes	—
40	Light Screen	Psychic	Status	—	—	30	2 Allies	○
46	Body Slam	Normal	Physical	85	100	15	Normal	—
54	Safeguard	Normal	Status	—	—	25	2 Allies	—
60	Aromatherapy	Grass	Status	—	—	5	All Allies	—
66	SolarBeam	Grass	Special	120	100	10	Normal	—

● MOVE MANIAC

Name	Type	Kind	Pow.	Acc.	PP	Range	DA
Headbutt	Normal	Physical	70	100	15	Normal	○
Frenzy Plant	Grass	Special	150	90	5	Normal	—

● BP MOVES

Name	Type	Kind	Pow.	Acc.	PP	Range	DA
Fury Cutter	Bug	Physical	10	95	20	Normal	○
Snore	Normal	Special	40	100	15	Normal	—
Synthesis	Grass	Status	—	—	5	Self	—
Worry Seed	Grass	Status	—	100	10	Normal	—
Magic Coat	Psychic	Status	—	—	15	Self	—
Mud-Slap	Ground	Special	20	100	10	Normal	—
Outrage	Dragon	Physical	120	100	15	1 Random	○
AncientPower	Rock	Special	60	100	5	Normal	—
Seed Bomb	Grass	Physical	80	100	15	Normal	—

● TM & HM MOVES

No.	Name	Type	Kind	Pow.	Acc.	PP	Range	DA
TM06	Toxic	Poison	Status	—	85	10	Normal	—
TM09	Bullet Seed	Grass	Physical	10	100	30	Normal	—
TM10	Hidden Power	Normal	Special	—	100	15	Normal	—
TM11	Sunny Day	Fire	Status	—	—	5	All	—
TM15	Hyper Beam	Normal	Special	150	90	5	Normal	—
TM16	Light Screen	Psychic	Status	—	—	30	2 Allies	—
TM17	Protect	Normal	Status	—	—	10	Self	—
TM19	Giga Drain	Grass	Special	60	100	10	Normal	—
TM20	Safeguard	Normal	Status	—	—	25	2 Allies	—
TM21	Frustration	Normal	Physical	—	100	20	Normal	○
TM22	SolarBeam	Grass	Special	120	100	10	Normal	—
TM23	Iron Tail	Steel	Physical	100	75	15	Normal	○
TM26	Earthquake	Ground	Physical	100	100	10	2 Foes/1 Ally	○
TM27	Return	Normal	Physical	—	100	20	Normal	○
TM32	Double Team	Normal	Status	—	—	15	Self	—
TM33	Reflect	Psychic	Status	—	—	20	2 Allies	—
TM42	Facade	Normal	Physical	70	100	20	Normal	○
TM43	Secret Power	Normal	Physical	70	100	20	Normal	—
TM44	Rest	Psychic	Status	—	—	10	Self	—
TM45	Attract	Normal	Status	—	100	15	Normal	—
TM53	Energy Ball	Grass	Special	80	100	10	Normal	—
TM58	Endure	Normal	Status	—	—	10	Self	—
TM68	Giga Impact	Normal	Physical	150	90	5	Normal	○
TM70	Flash	Normal	Status	—	100	20	Normal	—
TM75	Swords Dance	Normal	Status	—	—	30	Self	—
TM78	Captivate	Normal	Status	—	100	20	2 Foes	—
TM82	Sleep Talk	Normal	Status	—	—	10	Depends	—
TM83	Natural Gift	Normal	Physical	—	100	15	Normal	—
TM86	Grass Knot	Grass	Special	—	100	20	Normal	○
TM87	Swagger	Normal	Status	—	90	15	Normal	—
TM90	Substitute	Normal	Status	—	—	10	Self	—
HM01	Cut	Normal	Physical	50	95	30	Normal	○
HM04	Strength	Normal	Physical	80	100	15	Normal	○
HM06	Rock Smash	Fighting	Physical	40	100	15	Normal	○
HM08	Rock Climb	Normal	Physical	90	85	20	Normal	○

◉ No. 154 | Herb Pokémon
Meganium

Grass

- **HEIGHT:** 5'11"
- **WEIGHT:** 221.6 lbs.
- **ITEMS:** None

● SIZE COMPARISON

● MALE FORM
Longer stamen

● FEMALE FORM
Shorter stamen

⊙ ABILITIES
- Overgrow

⊙ EGG GROUPS
Monster

Grass

⊙ STATS
- HP ●●●
- ATTACK ●●●●
- DEFENSE ●●●●
- SP. ATTACK ●●●●
- SP. DEFENSE ●●●●
- SPEED ●●●●

⊙ PERFORMANCE
SPEED ★★	STAMINA ★★★★★
POWER ★★★☆☆	JUMP ★★
SKILL ★★★★★	

● MAIN WAYS TO OBTAIN

Pokémon HeartGold — Level up Bayleef to Lv. 32

Pokémon SoulSilver — Level up Bayleef to Lv. 32

Pokémon Diamond — —

Pokémon Pearl — —

Pokémon Platinum — —

Pokémon HeartGold

The aroma that rises from its petals contains a substance that calms aggressive feelings.

Pokémon SoulSilver

MEGANIUM's breath has the power to revive dead grass and plants. It can make them healthy again.

⊙ EVOLUTION

Chikorita — Lv. 16 — Bayleef — Lv.32 — Meganium

No. 155 | Fire Mouse Pokémon
Cyndaquil

Fire

● HEIGHT: 1'08"
● WEIGHT: 17.4 lbs.
● ITEMS: None

● SIZE COMPARISON

● MALE/FEMALE HAVE SAME FORM

⊛ ABILITIES
● Blaze

⊛ STATS
HP ●●
ATTACK ●●
DEFENSE ●●
SP. ATTACK ●●●
SP. DEFENSE ●●●
SPEED ●●●

⊛ EGG GROUPS
Field

⊛ PERFORMANCE
SPEED ★★★★☆　STAMINA ★☆☆
POWER ★☆☆☆　JUMP ★★★
SKILL ★★★

● MAIN WAYS TO OBTAIN

Pokémon HeartGold	Receive from Professor Elm in New Bark Town at the beginning of the adventure
Pokémon SoulSilver	Receive from Professor Elm in New Bark Town at the beginning of the adventure
Pokémon Diamond	—
Pokémon Pearl	—
Pokémon Platinum	—

| Pokémon HeartGold | Pokémon SoulSilver |
| It is timid, and always curls itself up in a ball. If attacked, it flares up its back for protection. | It usually stays hunched over. If it is angry or surprised, it shoots flames out of its back. |

⊛ EVOLUTION

Cyndaquil — Lv. 14 → Quilava — Lv. 36 → Typhlosion

● LEVEL-UP MOVES

Lv.	Name	Type	Kind	Pow.	Acc.	PP	Range	DA
1	Tackle	Normal	Physical	35	95	35	Normal	○
1	Leer	Normal	Status	—	100	30	2 Foes	—
6	SmokeScreen	Normal	Status	—	100	20	Normal	—
10	Ember	Fire	Special	40	100	25	Normal	—
13	Quick Attack	Normal	Physical	40	100	30	Normal	○
19	Flame Wheel	Fire	Physical	60	100	25	Normal	○
22	Defense Curl	Normal	Status	—	—	40	Self	—
28	Swift	Normal	Special	60	—	20	2 Foes	—
31	Lava Plume	Fire	Special	80	100	15	2 Foes/1 Ally	—
37	Flamethrower	Fire	Special	95	100	15	Normal	—
40	Rollout	Rock	Physical	30	90	20	Normal	○
46	Double-Edge	Normal	Physical	120	100	15	Normal	○
49	Eruption	Fire	Special	150	100	5	2 Foes	—

● MOVE MANIAC

Name	Type	Kind	Pow.	Acc.	PP	Range	DA
Headbutt	Normal	Physical	70	100	15	Normal	○

● BP MOVES

Name	Type	Kind	Pow.	Acc.	PP	Range	DA
Snore	Normal	Special	40	100	15	Normal	—
Swift	Normal	Special	60	—	20	2 Foes	—
Mud-Slap	Ground	Special	20	100	10	Normal	—
Rollout	Rock	Physical	30	90	20	Normal	○
Heat Wave	Fire	Special	100	90	10	2 Foes	—

● TM & HM MOVES

No.	Name	Type	Kind	Pow.	Acc.	PP	Range	DA
TM06	Toxic	Poison	Status	—	85	10	Normal	—
TM10	Hidden Power	Normal	Special	—	100	15	Normal	—
TM11	Sunny Day	Fire	Status	—	—	5	All	—
TM17	Protect	Normal	Status	—	—	10	Self	—
TM21	Frustration	Normal	Physical	—	100	20	Normal	○
TM27	Return	Normal	Physical	—	100	20	Normal	○
TM28	Dig	Ground	Physical	80	100	10	Normal	○
TM32	Double Team	Normal	Status	—	—	15	Self	—
TM35	Flamethrower	Fire	Special	95	100	15	Normal	—
TM38	Fire Blast	Fire	Special	120	85	5	Normal	—
TM40	Aerial Ace	Flying	Physical	60	—	20	Normal	○
TM42	Facade	Normal	Physical	70	100	20	Normal	○
TM43	Secret Power	Normal	Physical	70	100	20	Normal	○
TM44	Rest	Psychic	Status	—	—	10	Self	—
TM45	Attract	Normal	Status	—	100	15	Normal	—
TM50	Overheat	Fire	Special	140	90	5	Normal	—
TM58	Endure	Normal	Status	—	—	10	Self	—
TM61	Will-O-Wisp	Fire	Status	—	75	15	Normal	—
TM78	Captivate	Normal	Status	—	100	20	2 Foes	—
TM82	Sleep Talk	Normal	Status	—	—	10	Depends	—
TM83	Natural Gift	Normal	Physical	—	100	15	Normal	○
TM87	Swagger	Normal	Status	—	90	15	Normal	—
TM90	Substitute	Normal	Status	—	—	10	Self	—
HM01	Cut	Normal	Physical	50	95	30	Normal	○

● EGG MOVES

Name	Type	Kind	Pow.	Acc.	PP	Range	DA
Fury Swipes	Normal	Physical	18	80	15	Normal	○
Quick Attack	Normal	Physical	40	100	30	Normal	○
Reversal	Fighting	Physical	—	100	15	Normal	○
Thrash	Normal	Physical	90	100	20	1 Random	○
Foresight	Normal	Status	—	—	40	Normal	—
Covet	Normal	Physical	40	100	40	Normal	○
Howl	Normal	Status	—	—	40	Self	—
Crush Claw	Normal	Physical	75	95	10	Normal	○
Double-Edge	Normal	Physical	120	100	15	Normal	○
Double Kick	Fighting	Physical	30	100	30	Normal	○
Flare Blitz	Fire	Physical	120	100	15	Normal	○
Extrasensory	Psychic	Special	80	100	30	Normal	—

LEVEL-UP MOVES

Lv.	Name	Type	Kind	Pow.	Acc.	PP	Range	DA
1	Tackle	Normal	Physical	35	95	35	Normal	○
1	Leer	Normal	Status	—	100	30	2 Foes	—
1	SmokeScreen	Normal	Status	—	100	20	Normal	—
6	SmokeScreen	Normal	Status	—	100	20	Normal	—
10	Ember	Fire	Special	40	100	25	Normal	—
13	Quick Attack	Normal	Physical	40	100	30	Normal	○
20	Flame Wheel	Fire	Physical	60	100	25	Normal	○
24	Defense Curl	Normal	Status	—	—	40	Self	—
31	Swift	Normal	Special	60	—	20	2 Foes	—
35	Lava Plume	Fire	Special	80	100	15	2 Foes/1 Ally	—
42	Flamethrower	Fire	Special	95	100	15	Normal	—
46	Rollout	Rock	Physical	30	90	20	Normal	○
53	Double-Edge	Normal	Physical	120	100	15	Normal	○
57	Eruption	Fire	Special	150	100	5	2 Foes	—

MOVE MANIAC

Name	Type	Kind	Pow.	Acc.	PP	Range	DA
Headbutt	Normal	Physical	70	100	15	Normal	○

BP MOVES

Name	Type	Kind	Pow.	Acc.	PP	Range	DA
Fury Cutter	Bug	Physical	10	95	20	Normal	○
Snore	Normal	Special	40	100	15	Normal	—
Swift	Normal	Special	60	—	20	2 Foes	—
Mud-Slap	Ground	Special	20	100	10	Normal	—
Rollout	Rock	Physical	30	90	20	Normal	○
Heat Wave	Fire	Special	100	90	10	2 Foes	—

TM & HM MOVES

No.	Name	Type	Kind	Pow.	Acc.	PP	Range	DA
TM01	Focus Punch	Fighting	Physical	150	100	20	Normal	○
TM05	Roar	Normal	Status	—	100	20	Normal	—
TM06	Toxic	Poison	Status	—	85	10	Normal	—
TM10	Hidden Power	Normal	Special	—	100	15	Normal	—
TM11	Sunny Day	Fire	Status	—	—	5	All	—
TM17	Protect	Normal	Status	—	—	10	Self	—
TM21	Frustration	Normal	Physical	—	100	20	Normal	○
TM27	Return	Normal	Physical	—	100	20	Normal	○
TM28	Dig	Ground	Physical	80	100	10	Normal	○
TM31	Brick Break	Fighting	Physical	75	100	15	Normal	○
TM32	Double Team	Normal	Status	—	—	15	Self	—
TM35	Flamethrower	Fire	Special	95	100	15	Normal	—
TM38	Fire Blast	Fire	Special	120	85	5	Normal	—
TM40	Aerial Ace	Flying	Physical	60	—	20	Normal	○
TM42	Facade	Normal	Physical	70	100	20	Normal	○
TM43	Secret Power	Normal	Physical	70	100	20	Normal	—
TM44	Rest	Psychic	Status	—	—	10	Self	—
TM45	Attract	Normal	Status	—	100	15	Normal	—
TM50	Overheat	Fire	Special	140	90	5	Normal	—
TM58	Endure	Normal	Status	—	—	10	Self	—
TM61	Will-O-Wisp	Fire	Status	—	75	15	Normal	—
TM78	Captivate	Normal	Status	—	100	20	2 Foes	—
TM82	Sleep Talk	Normal	Status	—	—	10	Depends	—
TM83	Natural Gift	Normal	Physical	—	100	15	Normal	—
TM87	Swagger	Normal	Status	—	90	15	Normal	—
TM90	Substitute	Normal	Status	—	—	10	Self	—
HM01	Cut	Normal	Physical	50	95	30	Normal	○
HM04	Strength	Normal	Physical	80	100	15	Normal	○
HM06	Rock Smash	Fighting	Physical	40	100	15	Normal	○

No. 156 | Volcano Pokémon
Quilava

Fire

- **HEIGHT:** 2'11"
- **WEIGHT:** 41.9 lbs.
- **ITEMS:** None

● SIZE COMPARISON

● MALE/FEMALE HAVE SAME FORM

ABILITIES
● Blaze

EGG GROUPS
Field

STATS
HP ●●
ATTACK ●●●
DEFENSE ●●
SP. ATTACK ●●●●
SP. DEFENSE ●●
SPEED ●●●●

PERFORMANCE
SPEED ★★★★☆ STAMINA ★★★☆
POWER ★★★☆ JUMP ★★★☆
SKILL ★★☆

MAIN WAYS TO OBTAIN

Pokémon HeartGold	Level up Cyndaquil to Lv. 14
Pokémon SoulSilver	Level up Cyndaquil to Lv. 14
Pokémon Diamond	—
Pokémon Pearl	—
Pokémon Platinum	—

Pokémon HeartGold	Pokémon SoulSilver
Be careful if it turns its back during battle. It means that it will attack with the fire on its back.	Be careful if it turns its back during battle. It means that it will attack with the fire on its back.

EVOLUTION

Cyndaquil — Lv. 14 → Quilava — Lv. 36 → Typhlosion

No. 157 | Volcano Pokémon
Typhlosion

Fire

- **HEIGHT:** 5'07"
- **WEIGHT:** 175.3 lbs.
- **ITEMS:** None

● SIZE COMPARISON

● MALE/FEMALE HAVE SAME FORM

● ABILITIES
- Blaze

● STATS
HP ●●●
ATTACK ●●●●
DEFENSE ●●●
SP. ATTACK ●●●●
SP. DEFENSE ●●●●
SPEED ●●●●

● EGG GROUPS
Field

● PERFORMANCE
SPEED ★★☆☆
POWER ★★★★★
SKILL ★★☆
STAMINA ★★★★☆
JUMP ★★☆

● MAIN WAYS TO OBTAIN

Pokémon HeartGold — Level up Quilava to Lv. 36

Pokémon SoulSilver — Level up Quilava to Lv. 36

Pokémon Diamond — —

Pokémon Pearl — —

Pokémon Platinum — —

Pokémon HeartGold
If its rage peaks, it becomes so hot that anything that touches it will instantly go up in flames.

Pokémon SoulSilver
It has a secret, devastating move. It rubs its blazing fur together to cause huge explosions.

● EVOLUTION

Cyndaquil — Lv. 14 → Quilava — Lv. 36 → Typhlosion

● LEVEL-UP MOVES

Lv.	Name	Type	Kind	Pow.	Acc.	PP	Range	DA
1	Gyro Ball	Steel	Physical	—	100	5	Normal	○
1	Tackle	Normal	Physical	35	95	35	Normal	○
1	Leer	Normal	Status	—	100	30	2 Foes	—
1	SmokeScreen	Normal	Status	—	100	20	Normal	—
1	Ember	Fire	Special	40	100	25	Normal	—
6	SmokeScreen	Normal	Status	—	100	20	Normal	—
10	Ember	Fire	Special	40	100	25	Normal	—
13	Quick Attack	Normal	Physical	40	100	30	Normal	○
20	Flame Wheel	Fire	Physical	60	100	25	Normal	○
24	Defense Curl	Normal	Status	—	—	40	Self	—
31	Swift	Normal	Special	60	—	20	2 Foes	—
35	Lava Plume	Fire	Special	80	100	15	2 Foes/1 Ally	—
42	Flamethrower	Fire	Special	95	100	15	Normal	—
46	Rollout	Rock	Physical	30	90	20	Normal	○
53	Double-Edge	Normal	Physical	120	100	15	Normal	○
57	Eruption	Fire	Special	150	100	5	2 Foes	—

● MOVE MANIAC

Name	Type	Kind	Pow.	Acc.	PP	Range	DA
Headbutt	Normal	Physical	70	100	15	Normal	○
Blast Burn	Fire	Special	150	90	5	Normal	—

● BP MOVES

Name	Type	Kind	Pow.	Acc.	PP	Range	DA
Fury Cutter	Bug	Physical	10	95	20	Normal	○
ThunderPunch	Electric	Physical	75	100	15	Normal	○
Fire Punch	Fire	Physical	75	100	15	Normal	○
Snore	Normal	Special	40	100	15	Normal	—
Swift	Normal	Special	60	—	20	2 Foes	—
Mud-Slap	Ground	Special	20	100	10	Normal	—
Rollout	Rock	Physical	30	90	20	Normal	○
Heat Wave	Fire	Special	100	90	10	2 Foes	—
Low Kick	Fighting	Physical	—	100	20	Normal	○

● TM & HM MOVES

No.	Name	Type	Kind	Pow.	Acc.	PP	Range	DA
TM01	Focus Punch	Fighting	Physical	150	100	20	Normal	○
TM05	Roar	Normal	Status	—	100	20	Normal	—
TM06	Toxic	Poison	Status	—	85	10	Normal	—
TM10	Hidden Power	Normal	Special	—	100	15	Normal	—
TM11	Sunny Day	Fire	Status	—	—	5	All	—
TM15	Hyper Beam	Normal	Special	150	90	5	Normal	—
TM17	Protect	Normal	Status	—	—	10	Self	—
TM21	Frustration	Normal	Physical	—	100	20	Normal	○
TM22	SolarBeam	Grass	Special	120	100	10	2 Foes/1 Ally	—
TM26	Earthquake	Ground	Physical	100	100	10	2 Foes/1 Ally	—
TM27	Return	Normal	Physical	—	100	20	Normal	○
TM28	Dig	Ground	Physical	80	100	10	Normal	○
TM31	Brick Break	Fighting	Physical	75	100	15	Normal	○
TM32	Double Team	Normal	Status	—	—	15	Self	—
TM35	Flamethrower	Fire	Special	95	100	15	Normal	—
TM38	Fire Blast	Fire	Special	120	85	5	Normal	—
TM39	Rock Tomb	Rock	Physical	50	80	10	Normal	○
TM40	Aerial Ace	Flying	Physical	60	—	20	Normal	○
TM42	Facade	Normal	Physical	70	100	20	Normal	○
TM43	Secret Power	Normal	Physical	70	100	20	Normal	○
TM44	Rest	Psychic	Status	—	—	10	Self	—
TM45	Attract	Normal	Status	—	100	15	Normal	—
TM50	Overheat	Fire	Special	140	90	5	Normal	—
TM52	Focus Blast	Fighting	Special	120	70	5	Normal	—
TM56	Fling	Dark	Physical	—	100	10	Normal	○
TM58	Endure	Normal	Status	—	—	10	Self	—
TM61	Will-O-Wisp	Fire	Status	—	75	15	Normal	—
TM65	Shadow Claw	Ghost	Physical	70	100	15	Normal	○
TM68	Giga Impact	Normal	Physical	150	90	5	Normal	○
TM74	Gyro Ball	Steel	Physical	—	100	5	Normal	○
TM78	Captivate	Normal	Status	—	100	20	2 Foes	—
TM80	Rock Slide	Rock	Physical	75	90	10	2 Foes	○
TM82	Sleep Talk	Normal	Status	—	—	10	Depends	—
TM83	Natural Gift	Normal	Physical	—	100	15	Normal	—
TM87	Swagger	Normal	Status	—	90	15	Normal	—
TM90	Substitute	Normal	Status	—	—	10	Self	—
HM01	Cut	Normal	Physical	50	95	30	Normal	○
HM04	Strength	Normal	Physical	80	100	15	Normal	○
HM06	Rock Smash	Fighting	Physical	40	100	15	Normal	○
HM08	Rock Climb	Normal	Physical	90	85	20	Normal	○

● LEVEL-UP MOVES

Lv.	Name	Type	Kind	Pow.	Acc.	PP	Range	DA
1	Scratch	Normal	Physical	40	100	35	Normal	○
1	Leer	Normal	Status	—	100	30	2 Foes	—
6	Water Gun	Water	Special	40	100	25	Normal	—
8	Rage	Normal	Physical	20	100	20	Normal	○
13	Bite	Dark	Physical	60	100	25	Normal	○
15	Scary Face	Normal	Status	—	90	10	Normal	—
20	Ice Fang	Ice	Physical	65	95	15	Normal	○
22	Flail	Normal	Physical	—	100	15	Normal	○
27	Crunch	Dark	Physical	80	100	15	Normal	○
29	Slash	Normal	Physical	70	100	20	Normal	○
34	Screech	Normal	Status	—	85	40	Normal	—
36	Thrash	Normal	Physical	90	100	20	1 Random	○
41	Aqua Tail	Water	Physical	90	90	10	Normal	○
43	Superpower	Fighting	Physical	120	100	5	Normal	○
48	Hydro Pump	Water	Special	120	80	5	Normal	—

● MOVE MANIAC

Name	Type	Kind	Pow.	Acc.	PP	Range	DA
Headbutt	Normal	Physical	70	100	15	Normal	○

● BP MOVES

Name	Type	Kind	Pow.	Acc.	PP	Range	DA
Dive	Water	Physical	80	100	10	Normal	○
Icy Wind	Ice	Special	55	95	15	2 Foes	—
Ice Punch	Ice	Physical	75	100	15	Normal	○
Snore	Normal	Special	40	100	15	Normal	—
Spite	Ghost	Status	—	100	10	Normal	—
Uproar	Normal	Special	50	100	10	1 Random	—
Mud-Slap	Ground	Special	20	100	10	Normal	—
Superpower	Fighting	Physical	120	100	5	Normal	○
Aqua Tail	Water	Physical	90	90	10	Normal	○
AncientPower	Rock	Special	60	100	5	Normal	—
Low Kick	Fighting	Physical	—	100	20	Normal	○

● TM & HM MOVES

No.	Name	Type	Kind	Pow.	Acc.	PP	Range	DA
TM01	Focus Punch	Fighting	Physical	150	100	20	Normal	○
TM03	Water Pulse	Water	Special	60	100	20	Normal	—
TM06	Toxic	Poison	Status	—	85	10	Normal	—
TM07	Hail	Ice	Status	—	—	10	All	—
TM10	Hidden Power	Normal	Special	—	100	15	Normal	—
TM13	Ice Beam	Ice	Special	95	100	10	Normal	—
TM14	Blizzard	Ice	Special	120	70	5	2 Foes	—
TM17	Protect	Normal	Status	—	—	10	Self	—
TM18	Rain Dance	Water	Status	—	—	5	All	—
TM21	Frustration	Normal	Physical	—	100	20	Normal	○
TM23	Iron Tail	Steel	Physical	100	75	15	Normal	○
TM27	Return	Normal	Physical	—	100	20	Normal	○
TM28	Dig	Ground	Physical	80	100	10	Normal	○
TM31	Brick Break	Fighting	Physical	75	100	15	Normal	○
TM32	Double Team	Normal	Status	—	—	15	Self	—
TM39	Rock Tomb	Rock	Physical	50	80	10	Normal	○
TM40	Aerial Ace	Flying	Physical	60	—	20	Normal	○
TM42	Facade	Normal	Physical	70	100	20	Normal	○
TM43	Secret Power	Normal	Physical	70	100	20	Normal	○
TM44	Rest	Psychic	Status	—	—	10	Self	—
TM45	Attract	Normal	Status	—	100	15	Normal	—
TM56	Fling	Dark	Physical	—	100	10	Normal	○
TM58	Endure	Normal	Status	—	—	10	Self	—
TM65	Shadow Claw	Ghost	Physical	70	100	15	Normal	○
TM75	Swords Dance	Normal	Status	—	—	30	Self	—
TM78	Captivate	Normal	Status	—	100	20	2 Foes	—
TM80	Rock Slide	Rock	Physical	75	90	10	2 Foes	○
TM82	Sleep Talk	Normal	Status	—	—	10	Depends	—
TM83	Natural Gift	Normal	Physical	—	100	15	Normal	—
TM87	Swagger	Normal	Status	—	90	15	Normal	—
TM90	Substitute	Normal	Status	—	—	10	Self	—
HM01	Cut	Normal	Physical	50	95	30	Normal	○
HM03	Surf	Water	Special	95	100	15	2 Foes/1 Ally	—
HM05	Whirlpool	Water	Special	15	70	15	Normal	—
HM07	Waterfall	Water	Physical	80	100	15	Normal	○

● EGG MOVES

Name	Type	Kind	Pow.	Acc.	PP	Range	DA
Crunch	Dark	Physical	80	100	15	Normal	○
Thrash	Normal	Physical	90	100	20	1 Random	○
Hydro Pump	Water	Special	120	80	5	Normal	—
AncientPower	Rock	Special	60	100	5	Normal	—
Rock Slide	Rock	Physical	75	90	10	2 Foes	○
Mud Sport	Ground	Status	—	—	15	All	—
Water Sport	Water	Status	—	—	15	All	—
Dragon Claw	Dragon	Physical	80	100	15	Normal	○
Ice Punch	Ice	Physical	75	100	15	Normal	○
Metal Claw	Steel	Physical	50	95	35	Normal	○
Dragon Dance	Dragon	Status	—	—	20	Self	—
Aqua Jet	Water	Physical	40	100	20	Normal	○

No. 158 | Big Jaw Pokémon
Totodile

Water

● HEIGHT: 2'00"
● WEIGHT: 20.9 lbs.
● ITEMS: None

● SIZE COMPARISON

● MALE/FEMALE HAVE SAME FORM

● ABILITIES
● Torrent

● STATS
HP ●●
ATTACK ●●●
DEFENSE ●●●
SP. ATTACK ●●
SP. DEFENSE ●●
SPEED ●●

● EGG GROUPS
Monster
Water 1

● PERFORMANCE
SPEED ★★★☆　　STAMINA ★★☆
POWER ★★★★☆　JUMP ★★★
SKILL ★★☆

● MAIN WAYS TO OBTAIN

Pokémon HeartGold — Receive from Professor Elm in New Bark Town at the beginning of the adventure

Pokémon SoulSilver — Receive from Professor Elm in New Bark Town at the beginning of the adventure

Pokémon Diamond — —

Pokémon Pearl — —

Pokémon Platinum — —

Pokémon HeartGold — Its powerful, well-developed jaws are capable of crushing anything. Even its Trainer must be careful.

Pokémon SoulSilver — It is small but rough and tough. It won't hesitate to take a bite out of anything that moves.

● EVOLUTION

Lv. 18 → Lv. 30

Totodile — Croconew — Feraligatr

No. 159 | Big Jaw Pokémon
Croconaw

Water

● **LEVEL-UP MOVES**

Lv.	Name	Type	Kind	Pow.	Acc.	PP	Range	DA
1	Scratch	Normal	Physical	40	100	35	Normal	—
1	Leer	Normal	Status	—	100	30	2 Foes	—
1	Water Gun	Water	Special	40	100	25	Normal	—
6	Water Gun	Water	Special	40	100	25	Normal	—
8	Rage	Normal	Physical	20	100	20	Normal	—
13	Bite	Dark	Physical	60	100	25	Normal	○
15	Scary Face	Normal	Status	—	90	10	Normal	—
21	Ice Fang	Ice	Physical	65	95	10	Normal	○
24	Flail	Normal	Physical	—	100	15	Normal	—
30	Crunch	Dark	Physical	80	100	15	Normal	○
33	Slash	Normal	Physical	70	100	20	Normal	○
39	Screech	Normal	Status	—	85	40	Normal	—
42	Thrash	Normal	Physical	90	100	10	1 Random	○
48	Aqua Tail	Water	Physical	90	90	10	Normal	○
51	Superpower	Fighting	Physical	120	100	5	Normal	—
57	Hydro Pump	Water	Special	120	80	5	Normal	—

● **MOVE MANIAC**

Name	Type	Kind	Pow.	Acc.	PP	Range	DA
Headbutt	Normal	Physical	70	100	15	Normal	○

● **BP MOVES**

Name	Type	Kind	Pow.	Acc.	PP	Range	DA
Dive	Water	Physical	80	100	10	Normal	—
Fury Cutter	Bug	Physical	10	95	20	Normal	○
Icy Wind	Ice	Special	55	95	15	2 Foes	—
Ice Punch	Ice	Physical	75	100	15	Normal	○
Snore	Normal	Special	40	100	15	Normal	—
Spite	Ghost	Status	—	100	10	Normal	—
Uproar	Normal	Special	50	100	10	1 Random	—
Mud-Slap	Ground	Special	20	100	10	Normal	—
Superpower	Fighting	Physical	120	100	5	Normal	—
AncientPower	Rock	Special	60	100	5	Normal	—
Low Kick	Fighting	Physical	—	100	20	Normal	○

● HEIGHT: 3'02"
● WEIGHT: 55.1 lbs.
● ITEMS: None

● SIZE COMPARISON

● MALE/FEMALE HAVE SAME FORM

⚙ **ABILITIES**
● Torrent

⚙ **STATS**
HP ●●
ATTACK ●●●
DEFENSE ●●●
SP. ATTACK ●●●
SP. DEFENSE ●●●
SPEED ●●●

⚙ **EGG GROUPS**
Monster
Water 1

⚙ **PERFORMANCE**
SPEED ★★☆
POWER ★★★★☆
SKILL ★★☆
STAMINA ★★★★☆
JUMP ★★★

● **MAIN WAYS TO OBTAIN**

Pokémon HeartGold	Level up Totodile to Lv. 18
Pokémon SoulSilver	Level up Totodile to Lv. 18
Pokémon Diamond	—
Pokémon Pearl	—
Pokémon Platinum	—

Pokémon HeartGold	Pokémon SoulSilver
If it loses a fang, a new one grows back in its place. There are always 48 fangs lining its mouth.	It opens its huge jaws wide when attacking. If it loses any fangs while biting, they grow back in.

⚙ **EVOLUTION**

Totodile — Lv. 18 → Croconaw — Lv. 30 → Feraligatr

● **TM & HM MOVES**

No.	Name	Type	Kind	Pow.	Acc.	PP	Range	DA
TM01	Focus Punch	Fighting	Physical	150	100	20	Normal	○
TM03	Water Pulse	Water	Special	60	100	20	Normal	—
TM05	Roar	Normal	Status	—	100	20	Normal	—
TM06	Toxic	Poison	Status	—	85	10	Normal	—
TM07	Hail	Ice	Status	—	—	10	All	—
TM10	Hidden Power	Normal	Special	—	100	15	Normal	—
TM13	Ice Beam	Ice	Special	95	100	10	Normal	—
TM14	Blizzard	Ice	Special	120	70	5	2 Foes	—
TM17	Protect	Normal	Status	—	—	10	Self	—
TM18	Rain Dance	Water	Status	—	—	5	All	—
TM21	Frustration	Normal	Physical	—	100	20	Normal	—
TM23	Iron Tail	Steel	Physical	100	75	15	Normal	○
TM27	Return	Normal	Physical	—	100	20	Normal	—
TM28	Dig	Ground	Physical	80	100	10	Normal	○
TM31	Brick Break	Fighting	Physical	75	100	15	Normal	○
TM32	Double Team	Normal	Status	—	—	15	Self	—
TM39	Rock Tomb	Rock	Physical	50	80	10	Normal	—
TM40	Aerial Ace	Flying	Physical	60	—	20	Normal	○
TM42	Facade	Normal	Physical	70	100	20	Normal	○
TM43	Secret Power	Normal	Physical	70	100	20	Normal	—
TM44	Rest	Psychic	Status	—	—	10	Self	—
TM45	Attract	Normal	Status	—	100	15	Normal	—
TM56	Fling	Dark	Physical	—	100	10	Normal	—
TM58	Endure	Normal	Status	—	—	10	Self	—
TM65	Shadow Claw	Ghost	Physical	70	100	15	Normal	○
TM75	Swords Dance	Normal	Status	—	—	30	Self	—
TM78	Captivate	Normal	Status	—	100	20	2 Foes	—
TM80	Rock Slide	Rock	Physical	75	90	10	2 Foes	—
TM82	Sleep Talk	Normal	Status	—	—	10	Depends	—
TM83	Natural Gift	Normal	Physical	—	100	15	Normal	—
TM87	Swagger	Normal	Status	—	90	15	Normal	—
TM90	Substitute	Normal	Status	—	—	10	Self	—
HM01	Cut	Normal	Physical	50	95	30	Normal	○
HM03	Surf	Water	Special	95	100	15	2 Foes/1 Ally	—
HM04	Strength	Normal	Physical	80	100	15	Normal	○
HM05	Whirlpool	Water	Special	15	70	15	Normal	—
HM06	Rock Smash	Fighting	Physical	40	100	15	Normal	○
HM07	Waterfall	Water	Physical	80	100	15	Normal	○

● LEVEL-UP MOVES

Lv.	Name	Type	Kind	Pow.	Acc.	PP	Range	DA
1	Scratch	Normal	Physical	40	100	35	Normal	○
1	Leer	Normal	Status	—	100	30	2 Foes	—
1	Water Gun	Water	Special	40	100	25	Normal	—
1	Rage	Normal	Physical	20	100	20	Normal	○
6	Water Gun	Water	Special	40	100	25	Normal	—
8	Rage	Normal	Physical	20	100	20	Normal	○
13	Bite	Dark	Physical	60	100	25	Normal	○
15	Scary Face	Normal	Status	—	90	10	Normal	—
21	Ice Fang	Ice	Physical	65	95	15	Normal	○
24	Flail	Normal	Physical	—	100	15	Normal	○
30	Agility	Psychic	Status	—	—	30	Self	—
32	Crunch	Dark	Physical	80	100	15	Normal	○
37	Slash	Normal	Physical	70	100	20	Normal	○
45	Screech	Normal	Status	—	85	40	Normal	—
50	Thrash	Normal	Physical	90	100	10	1 Random	○
58	Aqua Tail	Water	Physical	90	90	10	Normal	○
63	Superpower	Fighting	Physical	120	100	5	Normal	○
71	Hydro Pump	Water	Special	120	80	5	Normal	—

● MOVE MANIAC

Name	Type	Kind	Pow.	Acc.	PP	Range	DA
Headbutt	Normal	Physical	70	100	15	Normal	○
Hydro Cannon	Water	Special	150	90	5	Normal	—

● BP MOVES

Name	Type	Kind	Pow.	Acc.	PP	Range	DA
Dive	Water	Physical	80	100	10	Normal	○
Fury Cutter	Bug	Physical	10	95	20	Normal	○
Icy Wind	Ice	Special	55	95	15	2 Foes	—
Ice Punch	Ice	Physical	75	100	15	Normal	○
Snore	Normal	Special	40	100	15	Normal	—
Spite	Ghost	Status	—	100	10	Normal	—
Uproar	Normal	Special	50	100	10	1 Random	—
Mud-Slap	Ground	Special	20	100	10	Normal	—
Superpower	Fighting	Physical	120	100	5	Normal	○
Aqua Tail	Water	Physical	90	90	10	Normal	○
Outrage	Dragon	Physical	120	100	15	1 Random	○
AncientPower	Rock	Special	60	100	5	Normal	—
Low Kick	Fighting	Physical	—	100	20	Normal	○

● TM & HM MOVES

No.	Name	Type	Kind	Pow.	Acc.	PP	Range	DA
TM01	Focus Punch	Fighting	Physical	150	100	20	Normal	○
TM02	Dragon Claw	Dragon	Physical	80	100	15	Normal	○
TM03	Water Pulse	Water	Special	60	100	20	Normal	—
TM05	Roar	Normal	Status	—	100	20	Normal	—
TM06	Toxic	Poison	Status	—	85	10	Normal	—
TM07	Hail	Ice	Status	—	—	10	All	—
TM10	Hidden Power	Normal	Special	—	100	15	Normal	—
TM13	Ice Beam	Ice	Special	95	100	10	Normal	—
TM14	Blizzard	Ice	Special	120	70	5	2 Foes	—
TM15	Hyper Beam	Normal	Special	150	90	5	Normal	—
TM17	Protect	Normal	Status	—	—	10	Self	—
TM18	Rain Dance	Water	Status	—	—	5	All	—
TM21	Frustration	Normal	Physical	—	100	20	Normal	○
TM23	Iron Tail	Steel	Physical	100	75	15	Normal	○
TM26	Earthquake	Ground	Physical	100	100	10	2 Foes/1 Ally	—
TM27	Return	Normal	Physical	—	100	20	Normal	○
TM28	Dig	Ground	Physical	80	100	10	Normal	○
TM31	Brick Break	Fighting	Physical	75	100	15	Normal	○
TM32	Double Team	Normal	Status	—	—	15	Self	—
TM39	Rock Tomb	Rock	Physical	50	80	10	Normal	○
TM40	Aerial Ace	Flying	Physical	60	—	20	Normal	○
TM42	Facade	Normal	Physical	70	100	20	Normal	○
TM43	Secret Power	Normal	Physical	70	100	20	Normal	○
TM44	Rest	Psychic	Status	—	—	10	Self	—
TM45	Attract	Normal	Status	—	100	15	Normal	—
TM52	Focus Blast	Fighting	Special	120	70	5	Normal	—
TM56	Fling	Dark	Physical	—	100	10	Normal	—
TM58	Endure	Normal	Status	—	—	10	Self	—
TM59	Dragon Pulse	Dragon	Special	90	100	10	Normal	—
TM65	Shadow Claw	Ghost	Physical	70	100	15	Normal	○
TM68	Giga Impact	Normal	Physical	150	90	5	Normal	○
TM72	Avalanche	Ice	Physical	60	100	10	Normal	○
TM75	Swords Dance	Normal	Status	—	—	30	Self	—
TM78	Captivate	Normal	Status	—	100	20	2 Foes	—
TM80	Rock Slide	Rock	Physical	75	90	10	2 Foes	○
TM82	Sleep Talk	Normal	Status	—	—	10	Depends	—
TM83	Natural Gift	Normal	Physical	—	100	15	Normal	—
TM87	Swagger	Normal	Status	—	90	15	Normal	—
TM90	Substitute	Normal	Status	—	—	10	Self	—
HM01	Cut	Normal	Physical	50	95	30	Normal	○
HM03	Surf	Water	Special	95	100	15	2 Foes/1 Ally	—
HM04	Strength	Normal	Physical	80	100	15	Normal	○
HM05	Whirlpool	Water	Special	15	70	15	Normal	—
HM06	Rock Smash	Fighting	Physical	40	100	15	Normal	○
HM07	Waterfall	Water	Physical	80	100	15	Normal	○
HM08	Rock Climb	Normal	Physical	90	85	20	Normal	○

◎ No. 160 | Big Jaw Pokémon
Feraligatr

Water

- ● HEIGHT: 7'07"
- ● WEIGHT: 195.8 lbs.
- ● ITEMS: None

● SIZE COMPARISON

● MALE/FEMALE HAVE SAME FORM

◎ ABILITIES
- ● Torrent

◎ STATS
HP ●●●
ATTACK ●●●●
DEFENSE ●●●●
SP. ATTACK ●●●
SP. DEFENSE ●●●
SPEED ●●●

◎ EGG GROUPS
Monster

Water 1

◎ PERFORMANCE
SPEED ★★★★ STAMINA ★★★☆
POWER ★★★★☆ JUMP ★★
SKILL ★★★☆

● MAIN WAYS TO OBTAIN

Pokémon HeartGold — Level up Croconaw to Lv. 30

Pokémon SoulSilver — Level up Croconaw to Lv. 30

Pokémon Diamond — —

Pokémon Pearl — —

Pokémon Platinum — —

Pokémon HeartGold
When it bites with its massive and powerful jaws, it shakes its head and savagely tears its victim up.

Pokémon SoulSilver
It is hard for it to support its weight out of water, so it sometimes gets down on all fours. But it moves fast.

◎ EVOLUTION

Totodile → Lv. 18 → Croconaw → Lv. 30 → Feraligatr

● No. 161 | Scout Pokémon
Sentret

Normal

● HEIGHT: 2'07"
● WEIGHT: 13.2 lbs.
● ITEMS: Oran Berry

● SIZE COMPARISON

● MALE/FEMALE HAVE SAME FORM

⊛ ABILITIES
- Run Away
- Keen Eye

⊛ STATS
HP ●●
ATTACK ●●
DEFENSE ●●
SP. ATTACK ●●
SP. DEFENSE ●●
SPEED ●

⊛ EGG GROUPS
Field

⊛ PERFORMANCE
SPEED ★★★★☆   STAMINA ★★☆☆
POWER ★★☆   JUMP ★★★☆
SKILL ★★☆☆

● MAIN WAYS TO OBTAIN

Pokémon HeartGold	Route 29 (morning and afternoon only)
Pokémon SoulSilver	Route 29 (morning and afternoon only)
Pokémon Diamond	Route 202 (use Poké Radar)
Pokémon Pearl	Route 202 (use Poké Radar)
Pokémon Platinum	Route 202 (use Poké Radar)

| Pokémon HeartGold | Pokémon SoulSilver |
| A very cautious Pokémon, it raises itself up using its tail to get a better view of its surroundings. | It stands on its tail so it can see a long way. If it spots an enemy, it warns loudly to warn its kind. |

⊛ EVOLUTION

Lv. 15

Sentret → Furret

● LEVEL-UP MOVES

Lv.	Name	Type	Kind	Pow.	Acc.	PP	Range	DA
1	Scratch	Normal	Physical	40	100	35	Normal	○
1	Foresight	Normal	Status	—	—	40	Normal	—
4	Defense Curl	Normal	Status	—	—	40	Self	—
7	Quick Attack	Normal	Physical	40	100	30	Normal	○
13	Fury Swipes	Normal	Physical	18	80	15	Normal	○
16	Helping Hand	Normal	Status	—	—	20	1 Ally	—
19	Follow Me	Normal	Status	—	—	20	Self	—
25	Slam	Normal	Physical	80	75	20	Normal	○
28	Rest	Psychic	Status	—	—	10	Self	—
31	Sucker Punch	Dark	Physical	80	100	5	Normal	○
36	Amnesia	Psychic	Status	—	—	20	Self	—
39	Baton Pass	Normal	Status	—	—	40	Self	—
42	Me First	Normal	Status	—	—	20	Depends	—
47	Hyper Voice	Normal	Special	90	100	10	2 Foes	—

● MOVE MANIAC

Name	Type	Kind	Pow.	Acc.	PP	Range	DA
Headbutt	Normal	Physical	70	100	15	Normal	○

● BP MOVES

Name	Type	Kind	Pow.	Acc.	PP	Range	DA
Fury Cutter	Bug	Physical	10	95	20	Normal	○
ThunderPunch	Electric	Physical	75	100	15	Normal	○
Fire Punch	Fire	Physical	75	100	15	Normal	○
Ice Punch	Ice	Physical	75	100	15	Normal	○
Knock Off	Dark	Physical	20	100	20	Normal	○
Sucker Punch	Dark	Physical	80	100	5	Normal	○
Snore	Normal	Special	40	100	15	Normal	—
Helping Hand	Normal	Status	—	—	20	1 Ally	—
Last Resort	Normal	Physical	130	100	5	Normal	○
Swift	Normal	Special	60	—	20	2 Foes	—
Uproar	Normal	Special	50	100	10	1 Random	—
Mud-Slap	Ground	Special	20	100	10	Normal	—
Rollout	Rock	Physical	30	90	20	Normal	○
Aqua Tail	Water	Physical	90	90	10	Normal	○
Super Fang	Normal	Physical	—	90	10	Normal	○

● TM & HM MOVES

No.	Name	Type	Kind	Pow.	Acc.	PP	Range	DA
TM01	Focus Punch	Fighting	Physical	150	100	20	Normal	○
TM03	Water Pulse	Water	Special	60	100	20	Normal	—
TM06	Toxic	Poison	Status	—	85	10	Normal	—
TM10	Hidden Power	Normal	Special	—	100	15	Normal	—
TM11	Sunny Day	Fire	Status	—	—	5	All	—
TM13	Ice Beam	Ice	Special	95	100	10	Normal	—
TM17	Protect	Normal	Status	—	—	10	Self	—
TM18	Rain Dance	Water	Status	—	—	5	All	—
TM21	Frustration	Normal	Physical	—	100	20	Normal	○
TM22	SolarBeam	Grass	Special	120	100	10	Normal	—
TM23	Iron Tail	Steel	Physical	100	75	15	Normal	○
TM24	Thunderbolt	Electric	Special	95	100	15	Normal	—
TM27	Return	Normal	Physical	—	100	20	Normal	○
TM28	Dig	Ground	Physical	80	100	10	Normal	○
TM30	Shadow Ball	Ghost	Special	80	100	15	Normal	—
TM31	Brick Break	Fighting	Physical	75	100	15	Normal	○
TM32	Double Team	Normal	Status	—	—	15	Self	—
TM34	Shock Wave	Electric	Special	60	—	20	Normal	—
TM35	Flamethrower	Fire	Special	95	100	15	Normal	—
TM42	Facade	Normal	Physical	70	100	20	Normal	○
TM43	Secret Power	Normal	Physical	70	100	20	Normal	○
TM44	Rest	Psychic	Status	—	—	10	Self	—
TM45	Attract	Normal	Status	—	100	15	Normal	—
TM46	Thief	Dark	Physical	40	100	10	Normal	○
TM56	Fling	Dark	Physical	—	100	10	Normal	○
TM57	Charge Beam	Electric	Special	50	90	10	Normal	—
TM58	Endure	Normal	Status	—	—	10	Self	—
TM65	Shadow Claw	Ghost	Physical	70	100	15	Normal	○
TM78	Captivate	Normal	Status	—	100	20	2 Foes	—
TM82	Sleep Talk	Normal	Status	—	—	10	Depends	—
TM83	Natural Gift	Normal	Physical	—	100	15	Normal	—
TM86	Grass Knot	Grass	Special	—	100	20	Normal	—
TM87	Swagger	Normal	Status	—	90	15	Normal	—
TM89	U-turn	Bug	Physical	70	100	20	Normal	○
TM90	Substitute	Normal	Status	—	—	10	Self	—
HM01	Cut	Normal	Physical	50	95	30	Normal	○
HM03	Surf	Water	Special	95	100	15	2 Foes/1 Ally	—
HM05	Whirlpool	Water	Special	15	70	15	Normal	—

● EGG MOVES

Name	Type	Kind	Pow.	Acc.	PP	Range	DA
Double-Edge	Normal	Physical	120	100	15	Normal	○
Pursuit	Dark	Physical	40	100	20	Normal	○
Slash	Normal	Physical	70	100	20	Normal	○
Focus Energy	Normal	Status	—	—	30	Self	—
Reversal	Fighting	Physical	—	100	15	Normal	○
Substitute	Normal	Status	—	—	10	Self	—
Trick	Psychic	Status	—	100	10	Normal	—
Assist	Normal	Status	—	—	20	Depends	—
Last Resort	Normal	Physical	130	100	5	Normal	○
Charm	Normal	Status	—	100	20	Normal	—
Covet	Normal	Physical	40	100	40	Normal	○

● LEVEL-UP MOVES

Lv.	Name	Type	Kind	Pow.	Acc.	PP	Range	DA
1	Scratch	Normal	Physical	40	100	35	Normal	○
1	Foresight	Normal	Status	—	—	40	Normal	—
1	Defense Curl	Normal	Status	—	—	40	Self	—
1	Quick Attack	Normal	Physical	40	100	30	Normal	○
4	Defense Curl	Normal	Status	—	—	40	Self	—
7	Quick Attack	Normal	Physical	40	100	30	Normal	○
13	Fury Swipes	Normal	Physical	18	80	15	Normal	○
17	Helping Hand	Normal	Status	—	—	20	1 Ally	—
21	Follow Me	Normal	Status	—	—	20	Self	—
28	Slam	Normal	Physical	80	75	20	Normal	○
32	Rest	Psychic	Status	—	—	10	Self	—
36	Sucker Punch	Dark	Physical	80	100	5	Normal	○
42	Amnesia	Psychic	Status	—	—	20	Self	—
46	Baton Pass	Normal	Status	—	—	40	Self	—
50	Me First	Normal	Status	—	—	20	Depends	—
56	Hyper Voice	Normal	Special	90	100	10	2 Foes	—

● MOVE MANIAC

Name	Type	Kind	Pow.	Acc.	PP	Range	DA
Headbutt	Normal	Physical	70	100	15	Normal	○

● BP MOVES

Name	Type	Kind	Pow.	Acc.	PP	Range	DA
Fury Cutter	Bug	Physical	10	95	20	Normal	○
ThunderPunch	Electric	Physical	75	100	15	Normal	○
Fire Punch	Fire	Physical	75	100	15	Normal	○
Ice Punch	Ice	Physical	75	100	15	Normal	○
Knock Off	Dark	Physical	20	100	20	Normal	○
Sucker Punch	Dark	Physical	80	100	5	Normal	○
Snore	Normal	Special	40	100	15	Normal	—
Helping Hand	Normal	Status	—	—	20	1 Ally	—
Last Resort	Normal	Physical	130	100	5	Normal	○
Swift	Normal	Special	60	—	20	2 Foes	—
Uproar	Normal	Special	50	100	10	1 Random	—
Mud-Slap	Ground	Special	20	100	10	Normal	—
Rollout	Rock	Physical	30	90	20	Normal	○
Aqua Tail	Water	Physical	90	90	10	Normal	○
Super Fang	Normal	Physical	—	90	10	Normal	○

● TM & HM MOVES

No.	Name	Type	Kind	Pow.	Acc.	PP	Range	DA
TM01	Focus Punch	Fighting	Physical	150	100	20	Normal	○
TM03	Water Pulse	Water	Special	60	100	20	Normal	—
TM06	Toxic	Poison	Status	—	85	10	Normal	—
TM10	Hidden Power	Normal	Special	—	100	15	Normal	—
TM11	Sunny Day	Fire	Status	—	—	5	All	—
TM13	Ice Beam	Ice	Special	95	100	10	Normal	—
TM14	Blizzard	Ice	Special	120	70	5	2 Foes	—
TM15	Hyper Beam	Normal	Special	150	90	5	Normal	—
TM17	Protect	Normal	Status	—	—	10	Self	—
TM18	Rain Dance	Water	Status	—	—	5	All	—
TM21	Frustration	Normal	Physical	—	100	20	Normal	○
TM22	SolarBeam	Grass	Special	120	100	10	Normal	—
TM23	Iron Tail	Steel	Physical	100	75	15	Normal	○
TM24	Thunderbolt	Electric	Special	95	100	15	Normal	—
TM25	Thunder	Electric	Special	120	70	10	Normal	—
TM27	Return	Normal	Physical	—	100	20	Normal	○
TM28	Dig	Ground	Physical	80	100	10	Normal	○
TM30	Shadow Ball	Ghost	Special	80	100	15	Normal	—
TM31	Brick Break	Fighting	Physical	75	100	15	Normal	○
TM32	Double Team	Normal	Status	—	—	15	Self	—
TM34	Shock Wave	Electric	Special	60	—	20	Normal	—
TM35	Flamethrower	Fire	Special	95	100	15	Normal	—
TM42	Facade	Normal	Physical	70	100	20	Normal	○
TM43	Secret Power	Normal	Physical	70	100	20	Normal	○
TM44	Rest	Psychic	Status	—	—	10	Self	—
TM45	Attract	Normal	Status	—	100	15	Normal	—
TM46	Thief	Dark	Physical	40	100	10	Normal	○
TM52	Focus Blast	Fighting	Special	120	70	5	Normal	—
TM56	Fling	Dark	Physical	—	100	10	Normal	○
TM57	Charge Beam	Electric	Special	50	90	10	Normal	—
TM58	Endure	Normal	Status	—	—	10	Self	—
TM65	Shadow Claw	Ghost	Physical	70	100	15	Normal	○
TM68	Giga Impact	Normal	Physical	150	90	5	Normal	○
TM78	Captivate	Normal	Status	—	100	20	2 Foes	—
TM82	Sleep Talk	Normal	Status	—	—	10	Depends	—
TM83	Natural Gift	Normal	Physical	—	100	15	Normal	—
TM86	Grass Knot	Grass	Special	—	100	20	Normal	—
TM87	Swagger	Normal	Status	—	90	15	Normal	—
TM89	U-turn	Bug	Physical	70	100	20	Normal	○
TM90	Substitute	Normal	Status	—	—	10	Self	—
HM01	Cut	Normal	Physical	50	95	30	Normal	○
HM03	Surf	Water	Special	95	100	15	2 Foes/1 Ally	—
HM04	Strength	Normal	Physical	80	100	15	Normal	○
HM05	Whirlpool	Water	Special	15	70	15	Normal	—
HM06	Rock Smash	Fighting	Physical	40	100	15	Normal	○

◎ No. 162 | Long Body Pokémon
Furret

Normal

● HEIGHT: 5'11"
● WEIGHT: 71.6 lbs.
● ITEMS: Oran Berry
  Sitrus Berry

● SIZE COMPARISON

● MALE/FEMALE HAVE SAME FORM

◎ ABILITIES
● Run Away
● Keen Eye

◎ EGG GROUPS
Field

◎ STATS
HP ●●●
ATTACK ●●●
DEFENSE ●●●
SP. ATTACK ●●●
SP. DEFENSE ●●
SPEED ●●●●

◎ PERFORMANCE
SPEED ★★★★★   STAMINA ★★☆
POWER ★★☆   JUMP ★★★
SKILL ★★☆

● MAIN WAYS TO OBTAIN

Pokémon HeartGold — Route 1 [morning and afternoon only] or Safari Zone [Wetland Area: if Grass objects are placed, may appear in tall grass]

Pokémon SoulSilver — Route 1 [morning and afternoon only] or Safari Zone [Wetland Area: if Grass objects are placed, may appear in tall grass]

Pokémon Diamond — Level up Sentret to Lv. 15

Pokémon Pearl — Level up Sentret to Lv. 15

Pokémon Platinum — Level up Sentret to Lv. 15

Pokémon HeartGold — It makes a nest to suit its long and skinny body. The nest is impossible for other Pokémon to enter.

Pokémon SoulSilver — There is no telling where the tail begins. Despite its short legs, it is quick and likes to chase RATTATA.

◎ EVOLUTION

Lv. 15

Sentret → Furret

No. 163 | Owl Pokémon
Hoothoot

Types: **Normal** **Flying**

- **HEIGHT:** 3'03"
- **WEIGHT:** 23.8 lbs.
- **ITEMS:** None

● SIZE COMPARISON

● MALE/FEMALE HAVE SAME FORM

⊙ ABILITIES
- Insomnia
- Keen Eye

⊙ STATS
HP	●●
ATTACK	●●
DEFENSE	●●
SP. ATTACK	●●
SP. DEFENSE	●●
SPEED	●●

⊙ EGG GROUPS
Flying

⊙ PERFORMANCE
SPEED ★★☆	STAMINA ★★☆
POWER ★★☆	JUMP ★★★★
SKILL ★★★☆	

● MAIN WAYS TO OBTAIN

Pokémon HeartGold	Route 29 (night only)
Pokémon SoulSilver	Route 29 (night only)
Pokémon Diamond	Route 210, Celestic Town side (night only)
Pokémon Pearl	Route 210, Celestic Town side (night only)
Pokémon Platinum	Route 210 (night only)

Pokémon HeartGold
It always stands on one foot. It changes feet so fast, the movement can rarely be seen.

Pokémon SoulSilver
It has a perfect sense of time. Whatever happens, it keeps rhythm by precisely tilting its head in time.

⊙ EVOLUTION

Lv. 20

Hoothoot → Noctowl

● LEVEL-UP MOVES

Lv.	Name	Type	Kind	Pow.	Acc.	PP	Range	DA
1	Tackle	Normal	Physical	35	95	35	Normal	○
1	Growl	Normal	Status	—	100	40	2 Foes	—
1	Foresight	Normal	Status	—	—	40	Normal	—
5	Hypnosis	Psychic	Status	—	60	20	Normal	—
9	Peck	Flying	Physical	35	100	35	Normal	○
13	Uproar	Normal	Special	50	100	10	1 Random	—
17	Reflect	Psychic	Status	—	—	20	2 Allies	—
21	Confusion	Psychic	Special	50	100	25	Normal	—
25	Take Down	Normal	Physical	90	85	20	Normal	○
29	Air Slash	Flying	Special	75	95	20	Normal	—
33	Zen Headbutt	Psychic	Physical	80	90	15	Normal	○
37	Extrasensory	Psychic	Special	80	100	30	Normal	—
41	Psycho Shift	Psychic	Status	—	90	10	Normal	—
45	Roost	Flying	Status	—	—	10	Self	—
49	Dream Eater	Psychic	Special	100	100	15	Normal	—

● MOVE MANIAC

Name	Type	Kind	Pow.	Acc.	PP	Range	DA

● BP MOVES

Name	Type	Kind	Pow.	Acc.	PP	Range	DA
Ominous Wind	Ghost	Special	60	100	5	Normal	—
Air Cutter	Flying	Special	55	95	25	2 Foes	—
Zen Headbutt	Psychic	Physical	80	90	15	Normal	○
Swift	Normal	Special	60	—	20	2 Foes	—
Uproar	Normal	Special	50	100	10	1 Random	—
Tailwind	Flying	Status	—	—	30	2 Allies	—
Magic Coat	Psychic	Status	—	—	15	Self	—
Mud-Slap	Ground	Special	20	100	10	Normal	—
Twister	Dragon	Special	40	100	20	2 Foes	—
Heat Wave	Fire	Special	100	90	10	2 Foes	—

● TM & HM MOVES

No.	Name	Type	Kind	Pow.	Acc.	PP	Range	DA
TM06	Toxic	Poison	Status	—	85	10	Normal	—
TM10	Hidden Power	Normal	Special	—	100	15	Normal	—
TM11	Sunny Day	Fire	Status	—	—	5	All	—
TM17	Protect	Normal	Status	—	—	10	Self	—
TM18	Rain Dance	Water	Status	—	—	5	All	—
TM21	Frustration	Normal	Physical	—	100	20	Normal	○
TM27	Return	Normal	Physical	—	100	20	Normal	○
TM29	Psychic	Psychic	Special	90	100	10	Normal	—
TM30	Shadow Ball	Ghost	Special	80	100	15	Normal	—
TM32	Double Team	Normal	Status	—	—	15	Self	—
TM33	Reflect	Psychic	Status	—	—	20	2 Allies	—
TM40	Aerial Ace	Flying	Physical	60	—	20	Normal	○
TM42	Facade	Normal	Physical	70	100	20	Normal	○
TM43	Secret Power	Normal	Physical	70	100	20	Normal	○
TM44	Rest	Psychic	Status	—	—	10	Self	—
TM45	Attract	Normal	Status	—	100	15	Normal	—
TM46	Thief	Dark	Physical	40	100	10	Normal	○
TM47	Steel Wing	Steel	Physical	70	90	25	Normal	○
TM51	Roost	Flying	Status	—	—	10	Self	—
TM58	Endure	Normal	Status	—	—	10	Self	—
TM62	Silver Wind	Bug	Special	60	100	5	Normal	—
TM67	Recycle	Normal	Status	—	—	10	Self	—
TM77	Psych Up	Normal	Status	—	—	10	Normal	—
TM78	Captivate	Normal	Status	—	100	20	2 Foes	—
TM82	Sleep Talk	Normal	Status	—	—	10	Depends	—
TM83	Natural Gift	Normal	Physical	—	100	15	Normal	—
TM85	Dream Eater	Psychic	Special	100	100	15	Normal	—
TM87	Swagger	Normal	Status	—	90	15	Normal	—
TM88	Pluck	Flying	Physical	60	100	20	Normal	○
TM90	Substitute	Normal	Status	—	—	10	Self	—
HM02	Fly	Flying	Physical	90	95	10	Normal	○

● EGG MOVES

Name	Type	Kind	Pow.	Acc.	PP	Range	DA
Mirror Move	Flying	Status	—	—	20	Depends	—
Supersonic	Normal	Status	—	55	20	Normal	—
Faint Attack	Dark	Physical	60	—	20	Normal	○
Wing Attack	Flying	Physical	60	100	35	Normal	○
Whirlwind	Normal	Status	—	100	20	Normal	—
Sky Attack	Flying	Physical	140	90	5	Normal	—
FeatherDance	Flying	Status	—	100	15	Normal	—
Agility	Psychic	Status	—	—	30	Self	—
Night Shade	Ghost	Special	—	100	15	Normal	—

● LEVEL-UP MOVES

Lv.	Name	Type	Kind	Pow.	Acc.	PP	Range	DA
1	Sky Attack	Flying	Physical	140	90	5	Normal	—
1	Tackle	Normal	Physical	35	95	35	Normal	○
1	Growl	Normal	Status	—	100	40	2 Foes	—
1	Foresight	Normal	Status	—	—	40	Normal	—
1	Hypnosis	Psychic	Status	—	60	20	Normal	—
5	Hypnosis	Psychic	Status	—	60	20	Normal	—
9	Peck	Flying	Physical	35	100	35	Normal	○
13	Uproar	Normal	Special	50	100	10	1 Random	—
17	Reflect	Psychic	Status	—	—	20	2 Allies	—
22	Confusion	Psychic	Special	50	100	25	Normal	—
27	Take Down	Normal	Physical	90	85	20	Normal	○
32	Air Slash	Flying	Special	75	95	20	Normal	—
37	Zen Headbutt	Psychic	Physical	80	90	15	Normal	○
42	Extrasensory	Psychic	Special	80	100	30	Normal	—
47	Psycho Shift	Psychic	Status	—	90	10	Normal	—
52	Roost	Flying	Status	—	—	10	Self	—
57	Dream Eater	Psychic	Special	100	100	15	Normal	—

● MOVE MANIAC

Name	Type	Kind	Pow.	Acc.	PP	Range	DA

● BP MOVES

Name	Type	Kind	Pow.	Acc.	PP	Range	DA
Ominous Wind	Ghost	Special	60	100	5	Normal	—
Air Cutter	Flying	Special	55	95	25	2 Foes	—
Zen Headbutt	Psychic	Physical	80	90	15	Normal	○
Swift	Normal	Special	60	—	20	2 Foes	—
Uproar	Normal	Special	50	100	10	1 Random	—
Tailwind	Flying	Status	—	—	30	2 Allies	—
Magic Coat	Psychic	Status	—	—	15	Self	—
Mud-Slap	Ground	Special	20	100	10	Normal	—
Twister	Dragon	Special	40	100	20	2 Foes	—
Heat Wave	Fire	Special	100	90	10	2 Foes	—
Sky Attack	Flying	Physical	140	90	5	Normal	—

● TM & HM MOVES

No.	Name	Type	Kind	Pow.	Acc.	PP	Range	DA
TM06	Toxic	Poison	Status	—	85	10	Normal	—
TM10	Hidden Power	Normal	Special	—	100	15	Normal	—
TM11	Sunny Day	Fire	Status	—	—	5	All	—
TM15	Hyper Beam	Normal	Special	150	90	5	Normal	—
TM17	Protect	Normal	Status	—	—	10	Self	—
TM18	Rain Dance	Water	Status	—	—	5	All	—
TM21	Frustration	Normal	Physical	—	100	20	Normal	○
TM27	Return	Normal	Physical	—	100	20	Normal	○
TM29	Psychic	Psychic	Special	90	100	10	Normal	—
TM30	Shadow Ball	Ghost	Special	80	100	15	Normal	—
TM32	Double Team	Normal	Status	—	—	15	Self	—
TM33	Reflect	Psychic	Status	—	—	20	2 Allies	—
TM40	Aerial Ace	Flying	Physical	60	—	20	Normal	○
TM42	Facade	Normal	Physical	70	100	20	Normal	○
TM43	Secret Power	Normal	Physical	70	100	20	Normal	○
TM44	Rest	Psychic	Status	—	—	10	Self	—
TM45	Attract	Normal	Status	—	100	15	Normal	—
TM46	Thief	Dark	Physical	40	100	10	Normal	○
TM47	Steel Wing	Steel	Physical	70	90	25	Normal	○
TM51	Roost	Flying	Status	—	—	10	Self	—
TM58	Endure	Normal	Status	—	—	10	Self	—
TM62	Silver Wind	Bug	Special	60	100	5	Normal	—
TM67	Recycle	Normal	Status	—	—	10	Self	—
TM68	Giga Impact	Normal	Physical	150	90	5	Normal	○
TM77	Psych Up	Normal	Status	—	—	10	Normal	—
TM78	Captivate	Normal	Status	—	100	20	2 Foes	—
TM82	Sleep Talk	Normal	Status	—	—	10	Depends	—
TM83	Natural Gift	Normal	Physical	—	100	15	Normal	—
TM85	Dream Eater	Psychic	Special	100	100	15	Normal	—
TM87	Swagger	Normal	Status	—	90	15	Normal	—
TM88	Pluck	Flying	Physical	60	100	20	Normal	○
TM90	Substitute	Normal	Status	—	—	10	Self	—
HM02	Fly	Flying	Physical	90	95	15	Normal	○

No. 164 | Owl Pokémon
Noctowl

Normal   Flying

- ● HEIGHT: 5'03"
- ● WEIGHT: 89.9 lbs.
- ● ITEMS: None

● SIZE COMPARISON

● MALE/FEMALE HAVE SAME FORM

⊙ ABILITIES
- ● Insomnia
- ● Keen Eye

⊙ STATS
HP ●●●●
ATTACK ●●
DEFENSE ●●
SP. ATTACK ●●●
SP. DEFENSE ●●●
SPEED ●●●

⊙ EGG GROUPS
Flying

⊙ PERFORMANCE

SPEED ★★★   STAMINA ★★★☆
POWER ★★☆   JUMP ★★★★☆
SKILL ★★☆

● MAIN WAYS TO OBTAIN

Pokémon HeartGold — Route 43 (night only)

Pokémon SoulSilver — Route 43 (night only)

Pokémon Diamond — Route 210, Celestic Town side (night only)

Pokémon Pearl — Route 210, Celestic Town side (night only)

Pokémon Platinum — Route 210 (night only)

Pokémon HeartGold — Its eyes are specially adapted. They concentrate even faint light and enable it to see in the dark.

Pokémon SoulSilver — When it needs to think, it rotates its head 180 degrees to sharpen its intellectual power.

⊙ EVOLUTION

Hoothoot → Lv. 20 → Noctowl

No. 165 | Five Star Pokémon
Ledyba

Bug | Flying

- **HEIGHT:** 3'03"
- **WEIGHT:** 23.8 lbs.
- **ITEMS:** None

● SIZE COMPARISON

● MALE FORM
Longer antennae

● FEMALE FORM
Shorter antennae

⊚ ABILITIES
- Swarm
- Early Bird

⊚ STATS
HP ●
ATTACK ●
DEFENSE ●
SP. ATTACK ●●
SP. DEFENSE ●●●
SPEED ●●●

⊚ EGG GROUPS
Bug

⊚ PERFORMANCE
SPEED ★★★★☆　STAMINA ★☆☆
POWER ★★☆　　JUMP ★★★★☆
SKILL ★★★☆☆

● MAIN WAYS TO OBTAIN

Pokémon HeartGold	—
Pokémon SoulSilver	Route 30 (morning only)
Pokémon Diamond	Find its Egg at the Pokémon Day Care and hatch it
Pokémon Pearl	Find its Egg at the Pokémon Day Care and hatch it
Pokémon Platinum	Find its Egg at the Pokémon Day Care and hatch it

Pokémon HeartGold	Pokémon SoulSilver
It is very timid. It will be afraid to move if it is alone. But it will be active if it is in a group.	When the weather turns cold, lots of LEDYBA gather from everywhere to cluster and keep each other warm.

⊚ EVOLUTION

Ledyba → Lv. 18 → Ledian

● LEVEL-UP MOVES

Lv.	Name	Type	Kind	Pow.	Acc.	PP	Range	DA
1	Tackle	Normal	Physical	35	95	35	Normal	—
6	Supersonic	Normal	Status	—	55	20	Normal	—
9	Comet Punch	Normal	Physical	18	85	15	Normal	○
14	Light Screen	Psychic	Status	—	—	30	2 Allies	—
14	Reflect	Psychic	Status	—	—	20	2 Allies	—
14	Safeguard	Normal	Status	—	—	25	2 Allies	—
17	Mach Punch	Fighting	Physical	40	100	30	Normal	○
22	Baton Pass	Normal	Status	—	—	40	Self	—
25	Silver Wind	Bug	Special	60	100	5	Normal	—
30	Agility	Psychic	Status	—	—	30	Self	—
33	Swift	Normal	Special	60	—	20	2 Foes	—
38	Double-Edge	Normal	Physical	120	100	15	Normal	—
41	Bug Buzz	Bug	Special	90	100	10	Normal	—

● MOVE MANIAC

Name	Type	Kind	Pow.	Acc.	PP	Range	DA
Headbutt	Normal	Physical	70	100	15	Normal	○

● BP MOVES

Name	Type	Kind	Pow.	Acc.	PP	Range	DA
ThunderPunch	Electric	Physical	75	100	15	Normal	○
Ice Punch	Ice	Physical	75	100	15	Normal	○
Ominous Wind	Ghost	Special	60	100	5	Normal	—
Air Cutter	Flying	Special	55	95	25	2 Foes	—
Knock Off	Dark	Physical	20	100	20	Normal	○
Bug Bite	Bug	Physical	60	100	20	Normal	○
Snore	Normal	Special	40	100	15	Normal	—
Swift	Normal	Special	60	—	20	2 Foes	—
Uproar	Normal	Special	50	100	10	1 Random	—
String Shot	Bug	Status	—	95	40	2 Foes	—
Tailwind	Flying	Status	—	—	30	2 Allies	—
Rollout	Rock	Physical	30	90	20	Normal	○

● TM & HM MOVES

No.	Name	Type	Kind	Pow.	Acc.	PP	Range	DA
TM01	Focus Punch	Fighting	Physical	150	100	20	Normal	○
TM06	Toxic	Poison	Status	—	85	10	Normal	—
TM10	Hidden Power	Normal	Special	—	100	15	Normal	—
TM11	Sunny Day	Fire	Status	—	—	5	All	—
TM16	Light Screen	Psychic	Status	—	—	30	2 Allies	—
TM17	Protect	Normal	Status	—	—	10	Self	—
TM19	Giga Drain	Grass	Special	60	100	10	Normal	—
TM20	Safeguard	Normal	Status	—	—	25	2 Allies	—
TM21	Frustration	Normal	Physical	—	100	20	Normal	○
TM22	SolarBeam	Grass	Special	120	100	10	Normal	—
TM27	Return	Normal	Physical	—	100	20	Normal	○
TM28	Dig	Ground	Physical	80	100	10	Normal	○
TM31	Brick Break	Fighting	Physical	75	100	15	Normal	○
TM32	Double Team	Normal	Status	—	—	15	Self	—
TM33	Reflect	Psychic	Status	—	—	20	2 Allies	—
TM40	Aerial Ace	Flying	Physical	60	—	20	Normal	○
TM42	Facade	Normal	Physical	70	100	20	Normal	○
TM43	Secret Power	Normal	Physical	70	100	20	Normal	○
TM44	Rest	Psychic	Status	—	—	10	Self	—
TM45	Attract	Normal	Status	—	100	15	Normal	—
TM46	Thief	Dark	Physical	40	100	10	Normal	○
TM51	Roost	Flying	Status	—	—	10	Self	—
TM56	Fling	Dark	Physical	—	100	10	Normal	○
TM58	Endure	Normal	Status	—	—	10	Self	—
TM60	Drain Punch	Fighting	Physical	60	100	5	Normal	○
TM62	Silver Wind	Bug	Special	60	100	5	Normal	—
TM70	Flash	Normal	Status	—	100	20	Normal	—
TM75	Swords Dance	Normal	Status	—	—	30	Self	—
TM78	Captivate	Normal	Status	—	100	20	2 Foes	—
TM82	Sleep Talk	Normal	Status	—	—	10	Depends	—
TM83	Natural Gift	Normal	Physical	—	100	15	Normal	—
TM87	Swagger	Normal	Status	—	90	15	Normal	—
TM89	U-turn	Bug	Physical	70	100	20	Normal	○
TM90	Substitute	Normal	Status	—	—	10	Self	—

● EGG MOVES

Name	Type	Kind	Pow.	Acc.	PP	Range	DA
Psybeam	Psychic	Special	65	100	20	Normal	—
Bide	Normal	Physical	—	—	10	Self	○
Silver Wind	Bug	Special	60	100	5	Normal	—
Bug Buzz	Bug	Special	90	100	10	Normal	—
Screech	Normal	Status	—	85	40	Normal	—
Encore	Normal	Status	—	100	5	Normal	—
Knock Off	Dark	Physical	20	100	20	Normal	○
Bug Bite	Bug	Physical	60	100	20	Normal	○

● LEVEL-UP MOVES

Lv.	Name	Type	Kind	Pow.	Acc.	PP	Range	DA
1	Tackle	Normal	Physical	35	95	35	Normal	○
1	Growl	Normal	Status	—	100	40	2 Foes	—
1	Razor Leaf	Grass	Physical	55	95	25	2 Foes	—
1	PoisonPowder	Poison	Status	—	75	35	Normal	—
6	Razor Leaf	Grass	Physical	55	95	25	2 Foes	—
9	PoisonPowder	Poison	Status	—	75	35	Normal	—
12	Synthesis	Grass	Status	—	—	5	Self	—
18	Reflect	Psychic	Status	—	—	20	2 Allies	—
22	Magical Leaf	Grass	Special	60	—	20	Normal	—
26	Natural Gift	Normal	Physical	—	100	15	Normal	—
32	Petal Dance	Grass	Special	90	100	20	1 Random	○
34	Sweet Scent	Normal	Status	—	100	20	2 Foes	—
40	Light Screen	Psychic	Status	—	—	30	2 Allies	○
46	Body Slam	Normal	Physical	85	100	15	Normal	—
54	Safeguard	Normal	Status	—	—	25	2 Allies	—
60	Aromatherapy	Grass	Status	—	—	5	All Allies	—
66	SolarBeam	Grass	Special	120	100	10	Normal	—

● MOVE MANIAC

Name	Type	Kind	Pow.	Acc.	PP	Range	DA
Headbutt	Normal	Physical	70	100	15	Normal	○
Frenzy Plant	Grass	Special	150	90	5	Normal	—

● BP MOVES

Name	Type	Kind	Pow.	Acc.	PP	Range	DA
Fury Cutter	Bug	Physical	10	95	20	Normal	○
Snore	Normal	Special	40	100	15	Normal	—
Synthesis	Grass	Status	—	—	5	Self	—
Worry Seed	Grass	Status	—	100	10	Normal	—
Magic Coat	Psychic	Status	—	—	15	Self	—
Mud-Slap	Ground	Special	20	100	10	Normal	—
Outrage	Dragon	Physical	120	100	15	1 Random	○
AncientPower	Rock	Special	60	100	5	Normal	—
Seed Bomb	Grass	Physical	80	100	15	Normal	○

● TM & HM MOVES

No.	Name	Type	Kind	Pow.	Acc.	PP	Range	DA
TM06	Toxic	Poison	Status	—	85	10	Normal	—
TM09	Bullet Seed	Grass	Physical	10	100	30	Normal	—
TM10	Hidden Power	Normal	Special	—	100	15	Normal	—
TM11	Sunny Day	Fire	Status	—	—	5	All	—
TM15	Hyper Beam	Normal	Special	150	90	5	Normal	—
TM16	Light Screen	Psychic	Status	—	—	30	2 Allies	—
TM17	Protect	Normal	Status	—	—	10	Self	—
TM19	Giga Drain	Grass	Special	60	100	10	Normal	—
TM20	Safeguard	Normal	Status	—	—	25	2 Allies	—
TM21	Frustration	Normal	Physical	—	100	20	Normal	○
TM22	SolarBeam	Grass	Special	120	100	10	Normal	—
TM23	Iron Tail	Steel	Physical	100	75	15	Normal	○
TM26	Earthquake	Ground	Physical	100	100	10	2 Foes/1 Ally	—
TM27	Return	Normal	Physical	—	100	20	Normal	○
TM32	Double Team	Normal	Status	—	—	15	Self	—
TM33	Reflect	Psychic	Status	—	—	20	2 Allies	—
TM42	Facade	Normal	Physical	70	100	20	Normal	—
TM43	Secret Power	Normal	Physical	70	100	20	Normal	○
TM44	Rest	Psychic	Status	—	—	10	Self	—
TM45	Attract	Normal	Status	—	100	15	Normal	—
TM53	Energy Ball	Grass	Special	80	100	10	Normal	○
TM58	Endure	Normal	Status	—	—	10	Self	—
TM68	Giga Impact	Normal	Physical	150	90	5	Normal	○
TM70	Flash	Normal	Status	—	100	20	Normal	—
TM75	Swords Dance	Normal	Status	—	—	30	Self	—
TM78	Captivate	Normal	Status	—	100	20	2 Foes	—
TM82	Sleep Talk	Normal	Status	—	—	10	Depends	—
TM83	Natural Gift	Normal	Physical	—	100	15	Normal	—
TM86	Grass Knot	Grass	Special	—	100	20	Normal	○
TM87	Swagger	Normal	Status	—	90	15	Normal	—
TM90	Substitute	Normal	Status	—	—	10	Self	—
HM01	Cut	Normal	Physical	50	95	30	Normal	○
HM04	Strength	Normal	Physical	80	100	15	Normal	○
HM06	Rock Smash	Fighting	Physical	40	100	15	Normal	○
HM08	Rock Climb	Normal	Physical	90	85	20	Normal	○

● HEIGHT: 4'07"
● WEIGHT: 78.5 lbs.
● ITEMS: None

● SIZE COMPARISON

● MALE FORM
Longer antennae

● FEMALE FORM
Shorter antennae

⊙ ABILITIES
● Swarm
● Early Bird

⊙ STATS

HP ●●
ATTACK ●●
DEFENSE ●●
SP. ATTACK ●●
SP. DEFENSE ●●●●
SPEED ●●●●

⊙ EGG GROUPS
Bug

⊙ PERFORMANCE
SPEED ★★★★☆   STAMINA ★★☆
POWER ★☆   JUMP ★★★★★
SKILL ★★★☆☆

● MAIN WAYS TO OBTAIN

Pokémon HeartGold —

Pokémon SoulSilver Route 2 (morning only)

Pokémon Diamond Route 229 (morning only)

Pokémon Pearl Route 229 (morning only)

Pokémon Platinum Route 229 (morning only)

Pokémon HeartGold
When the stars flicker in the night sky, it flutters about, scattering a glowing powder.

Pokémon SoulSilver
The spot patterns on its back grow larger or smaller depending on the number of stars in the night sky.

⊙ EVOLUTION

Ledyba

Lv. 18

Ledian

● No. 167 | String Spit Pokémon
Spinarak

Bug | **Poison**

● HEIGHT: 1'08"
● WEIGHT: 18.7 lbs.
● ITEMS: None

● SIZE COMPARISON

● MALE/FEMALE HAVE SAME FORM

☺ ABILITIES
● Swarm
● Insomnia

☺ STATS
HP ●
ATTACK ●●●
DEFENSE ●●
SP. ATTACK ●●
SP. DEFENSE ●●
SPEED ●

☺ EGG GROUPS
Bug

☺ PERFORMANCE
SPEED ★★★☆☆   STAMINA ★☆☆☆☆
POWER ★★☆☆☆   JUMP ★★☆☆☆
SKILL ★★★★☆

● MAIN WAYS TO OBTAIN

Pokémon HeartGold — Route 30 (night only)

Pokémon SoulSilver — —

Pokémon Diamond — Find its Egg at the Pokémon Day Care and hatch it

Pokémon Pearl — Find its Egg at the Pokémon Day Care and hatch it

Pokémon Platinum — Find its Egg at the Pokémon Day Care and hatch it

Pokémon HeartGold — It lies still in the same pose for days in its web, waiting for its unsuspecting prey to wander close.

Pokémon SoulSilver — It spins a web using fine--but durable--thread. It then waits patiently for prey to be trapped.

● EVOLUTION

Lv. 22 →

Spinarak → Ariados

● LEVEL-UP MOVES

Lv.	Name	Type	Kind	Pow.	Acc.	PP	Range	DA
1	Poison Sting	Poison	Physical	15	100	35	Normal	—
1	String Shot	Bug	Status	—	95	40	2 Foes	—
5	Scary Face	Normal	Status	—	90	10	Normal	—
8	Constrict	Normal	Physical	10	100	35	Normal	—
12	Leech Life	Bug	Physical	20	100	15	Normal	○
15	Night Shade	Ghost	Special	—	100	15	Normal	—
19	Shadow Sneak	Ghost	Physical	40	100	30	Normal	○
22	Fury Swipes	Normal	Physical	18	80	15	Normal	○
26	Sucker Punch	Dark	Physical	80	100	5	Normal	○
29	Spider Web	Bug	Status	—	—	10	Normal	—
33	Agility	Psychic	Status	—	—	30	Self	—
36	Pin Missile	Bug	Physical	14	85	20	Normal	—
40	Psychic	Psychic	Special	90	100	10	Normal	—
43	Poison Jab	Poison	Physical	80	100	20	Normal	○

● MOVE MANIAC

Name	Type	Kind	Pow.	Acc.	PP	Range	DA

● BP MOVES

Name	Type	Kind	Pow.	Acc.	PP	Range	DA
Sucker Punch	Dark	Physical	80	100	5	Normal	○
Bug Bite	Bug	Physical	60	100	20	Normal	○
String Shot	Bug	Status	—	95	40	2 Foes	—
Signal Beam	Bug	Special	75	100	15	Normal	—
Bounce	Flying	Physical	85	85	5	Normal	○

● TM & HM MOVES

No.	Name	Type	Kind	Pow.	Acc.	PP	Range	DA
TM06	Toxic	Poison	Status	—	85	10	Normal	—
TM10	Hidden Power	Normal	Special	—	100	15	Normal	—
TM11	Sunny Day	Fire	Status	—	—	5	All	—
TM17	Protect	Normal	Status	—	—	10	Self	—
TM19	Giga Drain	Grass	Special	60	100	10	Normal	—
TM21	Frustration	Normal	Physical	—	100	20	Normal	○
TM22	SolarBeam	Grass	Special	120	100	10	Normal	—
TM27	Return	Normal	Physical	—	100	20	Normal	○
TM28	Dig	Ground	Physical	80	100	10	Normal	○
TM29	Psychic	Psychic	Special	90	100	10	Normal	—
TM32	Double Team	Normal	Status	—	—	15	Self	—
TM36	Sludge Bomb	Poison	Special	90	100	10	Normal	—
TM42	Facade	Normal	Physical	70	100	20	Normal	○
TM43	Secret Power	Normal	Physical	70	100	20	Normal	—
TM44	Rest	Psychic	Status	—	—	10	Self	—
TM45	Attract	Normal	Status	—	100	15	Normal	—
TM46	Thief	Dark	Physical	40	100	10	Normal	○
TM58	Endure	Normal	Status	—	—	10	Self	—
TM70	Flash	Normal	Status	—	100	20	Normal	—
TM78	Captivate	Normal	Status	—	100	20	2 Foes	—
TM82	Sleep Talk	Normal	Status	—	—	10	Depends	—
TM83	Natural Gift	Normal	Physical	—	100	15	Normal	—
TM84	Poison Jab	Poison	Physical	80	100	20	Normal	○
TM87	Swagger	Normal	Status	—	90	15	Normal	—
TM90	Substitute	Normal	Status	—	—	10	Self	—

● EGG MOVES

Name	Type	Kind	Pow.	Acc.	PP	Range	DA
Psybeam	Psychic	Special	65	100	20	Normal	—
Disable	Normal	Status	—	80	20	Normal	—
SonicBoom	Normal	Special	—	90	20	Normal	—
Baton Pass	Normal	Status	—	—	40	Self	—
Pursuit	Dark	Physical	40	100	20	Normal	○
Signal Beam	Bug	Special	75	100	15	Normal	—
Toxic Spikes	Poison	Status	—	—	20	2 Foes	—
Poison Jab	Poison	Physical	80	100	20	Normal	○

● LEVEL-UP MOVES

Lv.	Name	Type	Kind	Pow.	Acc.	PP	Range	DA
1	Bug Bite	Bug	Physical	60	100	20	Normal	○
1	Poison Sting	Poison	Physical	15	100	35	Normal	○
1	String Shot	Bug	Status	—	95	40	2 Foes	—
1	Scary Face	Normal	Status	—	90	10	Normal	—
1	Constrict	Normal	Physical	10	100	35	Normal	○
5	Scary Face	Normal	Status	—	90	10	Normal	—
8	Constrict	Normal	Physical	10	100	35	Normal	○
12	Leech Life	Bug	Physical	20	100	15	Normal	○
15	Night Shade	Ghost	Special	—	100	15	Normal	—
19	Shadow Sneak	Ghost	Physical	40	100	30	Normal	○
23	Fury Swipes	Normal	Physical	18	80	15	Normal	○
28	Sucker Punch	Dark	Physical	80	100	5	Normal	○
32	Spider Web	Bug	Status	—	—	10	Normal	—
37	Agility	Psychic	Status	—	—	30	Self	—
41	Pin Missile	Bug	Physical	14	85	20	Normal	○
46	Psychic	Psychic	Special	90	100	10	Normal	—
50	Poison Jab	Poison	Physical	80	100	20	Normal	○

● MOVE MANIAC

Name	Type	Kind	Pow.	Acc.	PP	Range	DA

● BP MOVES

Name	Type	Kind	Pow.	Acc.	PP	Range	DA
Sucker Punch	Dark	Physical	80	100	5	Normal	○
Bug Bite	Bug	Physical	60	100	20	Normal	○
String Shot	Bug	Status	—	95	40	2 Foes	—
Signal Beam	Bug	Special	75	100	15	Normal	—
Bounce	Flying	Physical	85	85	5	Normal	○

● TM & HM MOVES

No.	Name	Type	Kind	Pow.	Acc.	PP	Range	DA
TM06	Toxic	Poison	Status	—	85	10	Normal	—
TM10	Hidden Power	Normal	Special	—	100	15	Normal	—
TM11	Sunny Day	Fire	Status	—	—	5	All	—
TM15	Hyper Beam	Normal	Special	150	90	5	Normal	—
TM17	Protect	Normal	Status	—	—	10	Self	—
TM19	Giga Drain	Grass	Special	60	100	10	Normal	—
TM21	Frustration	Normal	Physical	—	100	20	Normal	○
TM22	SolarBeam	Grass	Special	120	100	10	Normal	—
TM27	Return	Normal	Physical	—	100	20	Normal	○
TM28	Dig	Ground	Physical	80	100	10	Normal	○
TM29	Psychic	Psychic	Special	90	100	10	Normal	—
TM32	Double Team	Normal	Status	—	—	15	Self	—
TM36	Sludge Bomb	Poison	Special	90	100	10	Normal	—
TM42	Facade	Normal	Physical	70	100	20	Normal	○
TM43	Secret Power	Normal	Physical	70	100	20	Normal	○
TM44	Rest	Psychic	Status	—	—	10	Self	—
TM45	Attract	Normal	Status	—	100	15	Normal	—
TM46	Thief	Dark	Physical	40	100	10	Normal	○
TM58	Endure	Normal	Status	—	—	10	Self	—
TM68	Giga Impact	Normal	Physical	150	90	5	Normal	○
TM70	Flash	Normal	Status	—	100	20	Normal	—
TM78	Captivate	Normal	Status	—	100	20	2 Foes	—
TM82	Sleep Talk	Normal	Status	—	—	10	Depends	—
TM83	Natural Gift	Normal	Physical	—	100	15	Normal	—
TM84	Poison Jab	Poison	Physical	80	100	20	Normal	○
TM87	Swagger	Normal	Status	—	90	15	Normal	—
TM90	Substitute	Normal	Status	—	—	10	Self	—

● No. 168 | Long Leg Pokémon
Ariados

Bug **Poison**

- **HEIGHT:** 3'07"
- **WEIGHT:** 73.9 lbs.
- **ITEMS:** None

● SIZE COMPARISON

● MALE/FEMALE HAVE SAME FORM

● ABILITIES
- Swarm
- Insomnia

● STATS
HP	●●●
ATTACK	●●●●
DEFENSE	●●●
SP. ATTACK	●●●
SP. DEFENSE	●●
SPEED	●●

● EGG GROUPS
Bug

● PERFORMANCE
SPEED ★★★★	STAMINA ★★☆☆
POWER ★★★	JUMP ★★☆
SKILL ★★★☆	

● MAIN WAYS TO OBTAIN

Pokémon HeartGold	Route 2 (night only)
Pokémon SoulSilver	—
Pokémon Diamond	Route 229 (night only)
Pokémon Pearl	Route 229 (night only)
Pokémon Platinum	Route 229 (night only)

Pokémon HeartGold
It spins string not only from its rear but also from its mouth. It's hard to tell which end is which.

Pokémon SoulSilver
A single strand of a special string is endlessly spun out of its rear. The string leads back to its nest.

● EVOLUTION

Spinarak — Lv. 22 — Ariados

⦿ No. 169 | Bat Pokémon
Crobat

Poison | Flying

● HEIGHT: 5'11"
● WEIGHT: 165.3 lbs.
● ITEMS: None

● SIZE COMPARISON

● MALE/FEMALE HAVE SAME FORM

⦿ ABILITIES
● Inner Focus

⦿ STATS
HP ●●●
ATTACK ●●●●
DEFENSE ●●●
SP. ATTACK ●●●
SP. DEFENSE ●●●
SPEED ●●●●●●

⦿ EGG GROUPS
Flying

⦿ PERFORMANCE
SPEED ★★★★★ STAMINA ★★
POWER ★☆☆ JUMP ★★★★★
SKILL ★★★

● MAIN WAYS TO OBTAIN

Pokémon HeartGold	Level up Golbat with high friendship
Pokémon SoulSilver	Level up Golbat with high friendship
Pokémon Diamond	Level up Golbat with high friendship
Pokémon Pearl	Level up Golbat with high friendship
Pokémon Platinum	Level up Golbat with high friendship

Pokémon HeartGold	Pokémon SoulSilver
It flies so silently through the dark on its four wings that it may not be noticed even when nearby.	The development of wings on its legs enables it to fly fast but also makes it tough to stop and rest.

⦿ EVOLUTION

Zubat → (Lv. 22) Golbat → (Level up with high friendship) Crobat

● LEVEL-UP MOVES

Lv.	Name	Type	Kind	Pow.	Acc.	PP	Range	DA
1	Cross Poison	Poison	Physical	70	100	20	Normal	○
1	Screech	Normal	Status	—	85	40	Normal	—
1	Leech Life	Bug	Physical	20	100	15	Normal	○
1	Supersonic	Normal	Status	—	55	20	Normal	—
1	Astonish	Ghost	Physical	30	100	15	Normal	○
5	Supersonic	Normal	Status	—	55	20	Normal	—
9	Astonish	Ghost	Physical	30	100	15	Normal	○
13	Bite	Dark	Physical	60	100	25	Normal	○
17	Wing Attack	Flying	Physical	60	100	35	Normal	○
21	Confuse Ray	Ghost	Status	—	100	10	Normal	—
27	Air Cutter	Flying	Special	55	95	25	2 Foes	—
33	Mean Look	Normal	Status	—	—	5	Normal	—
39	Poison Fang	Poison	Physical	50	100	15	Normal	○
45	Haze	Ice	Status	—	—	30	Normal	—
51	Air Slash	Flying	Special	75	95	20	Normal	—

● MOVE MANIAC

Name	Type	Kind	Pow.	Acc.	PP	Range	DA

● BP MOVES

Name	Type	Kind	Pow.	Acc.	PP	Range	DA
Ominous Wind	Ghost	Special	60	100	5	Normal	—
Air Cutter	Flying	Special	55	95	25	2 Foes	—
Zen Headbutt	Psychic	Physical	80	90	15	Normal	○
Snore	Normal	Special	40	100	15	Normal	—
Swift	Normal	Special	60	—	20	2 Foes	—
Uproar	Normal	Special	50	100	10	1 Random	—
Tailwind	Flying	Status	—	—	30	2 Allies	—
Twister	Dragon	Special	40	100	20	2 Foes	—
Heat Wave	Fire	Special	100	90	10	2 Foes	—
Super Fang	Normal	Physical	—	90	10	Normal	○
Sky Attack	Flying	Physical	140	90	5	Normal	—

● TM & HM MOVES

No.	Name	Type	Kind	Pow.	Acc.	PP	Range	DA
TM06	Toxic	Poison	Status	—	85	10	Normal	—
TM10	Hidden Power	Normal	Special	—	100	15	Normal	—
TM11	Sunny Day	Fire	Status	—	—	5	All	—
TM12	Taunt	Dark	Status	—	100	20	Normal	—
TM15	Hyper Beam	Normal	Special	150	90	5	Normal	—
TM17	Protect	Normal	Status	—	—	10	Self	—
TM18	Rain Dance	Water	Status	—	—	5	All	—
TM19	Giga Drain	Grass	Special	60	100	10	Normal	—
TM21	Frustration	Normal	Physical	—	100	20	Normal	○
TM27	Return	Normal	Physical	—	100	20	Normal	○
TM30	Shadow Ball	Ghost	Special	80	100	15	Normal	—
TM32	Double Team	Normal	Status	—	—	15	Self	—
TM36	Sludge Bomb	Poison	Special	90	100	10	Normal	—
TM40	Aerial Ace	Flying	Physical	60	—	20	Normal	○
TM41	Torment	Dark	Status	—	100	15	Normal	—
TM42	Facade	Normal	Physical	70	100	20	Normal	○
TM43	Secret Power	Normal	Physical	70	100	20	Normal	—
TM44	Rest	Psychic	Status	—	—	10	Self	—
TM45	Attract	Normal	Status	—	100	15	Normal	—
TM46	Thief	Dark	Physical	40	100	10	Normal	○
TM47	Steel Wing	Steel	Physical	70	90	25	Normal	○
TM49	Snatch	Dark	Status	—	—	10	Depends	—
TM51	Roost	Flying	Status	—	—	10	Self	—
TM58	Endure	Normal	Status	—	—	10	Self	—
TM66	Payback	Dark	Physical	50	100	10	Normal	○
TM68	Giga Impact	Normal	Physical	150	90	5	Normal	○
TM78	Captivate	Normal	Status	—	100	20	2 Foes	—
TM79	Dark Pulse	Dark	Special	80	100	15	Normal	—
TM81	X-Scissor	Bug	Physical	80	100	15	Normal	○
TM82	Sleep Talk	Normal	Status	—	—	10	Depends	—
TM83	Natural Gift	Normal	Physical	—	100	15	Normal	—
TM87	Swagger	Normal	Status	—	90	15	Normal	—
TM88	Pluck	Flying	Physical	60	100	20	Normal	○
TM89	U-turn	Bug	Physical	70	100	20	Normal	○
TM90	Substitute	Normal	Status	—	—	10	Self	—
HM02	Fly	Flying	Physical	90	95	15	Normal	○

● LEVEL-UP MOVES

Lv.	Name	Type	Kind	Pow.	Acc.	PP	Range	DA
1	Scratch	Normal	Physical	40	100	35	Normal	○
1	Leer	Normal	Status	—	100	30	2 Foes	—
6	Water Gun	Water	Special	40	100	25	Normal	—
8	Rage	Normal	Physical	20	100	20	Normal	○
13	Bite	Dark	Physical	60	100	25	Normal	○
15	Scary Face	Normal	Status	—	90	10	Normal	—
20	Ice Fang	Ice	Physical	65	95	15	Normal	○
22	Flail	Normal	Physical	—	100	15	Normal	○
27	Crunch	Dark	Physical	80	100	15	Normal	○
29	Slash	Normal	Physical	70	100	20	Normal	○
34	Screech	Normal	Status	—	85	40	Normal	—
36	Thrash	Normal	Physical	90	100	10	1 Random	○
41	Aqua Tail	Water	Physical	90	90	10	Normal	○
43	Superpower	Fighting	Physical	120	100	5	Normal	○
48	Hydro Pump	Water	Special	120	80	5	Normal	—

● MOVE MANIAC

Name	Type	Kind	Pow.	Acc.	PP	Range	DA
Headbutt	Normal	Physical	70	100	15	Normal	○

● BP MOVES

Name	Type	Kind	Pow.	Acc.	PP	Range	DA
Dive	Water	Physical	80	100	10	Normal	○
Icy Wind	Ice	Special	55	95	15	2 Foes	—
Ice Punch	Ice	Physical	75	100	15	Normal	○
Snore	Normal	Special	40	100	15	Normal	—
Spite	Ghost	Status	—	100	10	Normal	—
Uproar	Normal	Special	50	100	10	1 Random	—
Mud-Slap	Ground	Special	20	100	10	Normal	—
Superpower	Fighting	Physical	120	100	5	Normal	○
Aqua Tail	Water	Physical	90	90	10	Normal	○
AncientPower	Rock	Special	60	100	5	Normal	—
Low Kick	Fighting	Physical	—	100	20	Normal	○

● TM & HM MOVES

No.	Name	Type	Kind	Pow.	Acc.	PP	Range	DA
TM01	Focus Punch	Fighting	Physical	150	100	20	Normal	○
TM03	Water Pulse	Water	Special	60	100	20	Normal	—
TM06	Toxic	Poison	Status	—	85	10	Normal	—
TM07	Hail	Ice	Status	—	—	10	All	—
TM10	Hidden Power	Normal	Special	—	100	15	Normal	—
TM13	Ice Beam	Ice	Special	95	100	10	Normal	—
TM14	Blizzard	Ice	Special	120	70	5	2 Foes	—
TM17	Protect	Normal	Status	—	—	10	Self	—
TM18	Rain Dance	Water	Status	—	—	5	All	—
TM21	Frustration	Normal	Physical	—	100	20	Normal	○
TM23	Iron Tail	Steel	Physical	100	75	15	Normal	○
TM27	Return	Normal	Physical	—	100	20	Normal	○
TM28	Dig	Ground	Physical	80	100	10	Normal	○
TM31	Brick Break	Fighting	Physical	75	100	15	Normal	○
TM32	Double Team	Normal	Status	—	—	15	Self	—
TM39	Rock Tomb	Rock	Physical	50	80	10	Normal	○
TM40	Aerial Ace	Flying	Physical	60	—	20	Normal	○
TM42	Facade	Normal	Physical	70	100	20	Normal	○
TM43	Secret Power	Normal	Physical	70	100	20	Normal	○
TM44	Rest	Psychic	Status	—	—	10	Self	—
TM45	Attract	Normal	Status	—	100	15	Normal	—
TM56	Fling	Dark	Physical	—	100	10	Normal	○
TM58	Endure	Normal	Status	—	—	10	Self	—
TM65	Shadow Claw	Ghost	Physical	70	100	15	Normal	○
TM75	Swords Dance	Normal	Status	—	—	30	Self	—
TM78	Captivate	Normal	Status	—	100	20	2 Foes	—
TM80	Rock Slide	Rock	Physical	75	90	10	2 Foes	—
TM82	Sleep Talk	Normal	Status	—	—	10	Depends	—
TM83	Natural Gift	Normal	Physical	—	100	15	Normal	—
TM87	Swagger	Normal	Status	—	90	15	Normal	—
TM90	Substitute	Normal	Status	—	—	10	Self	—
HM01	Cut	Normal	Physical	50	95	30	Normal	○
HM03	Surf	Water	Special	95	100	15	2 Foes/1 Ally	—
HM05	Whirlpool	Water	Special	15	70	15	Normal	—
HM07	Waterfall	Water	Physical	80	100	15	Normal	○

● EGG MOVES

Name	Type	Kind	Pow.	Acc.	PP	Range	DA
Crunch	Dark	Physical	80	100	15	Normal	○
Thrash	Normal	Physical	90	100	20	1 Random	○
Hydro Pump	Water	Special	120	80	5	Normal	—
AncientPower	Rock	Special	60	100	5	Normal	—
Rock Slide	Rock	Physical	75	90	10	2 Foes	—
Mud Sport	Ground	Status	—	—	15	All	—
Water Sport	Water	Status	—	—	15	All	—
Dragon Claw	Dragon	Physical	80	100	15	Normal	○
Ice Punch	Ice	Physical	75	100	15	Normal	○
Metal Claw	Steel	Physical	50	95	35	Normal	○
Dragon Dance	Dragon	Status	—	—	20	Self	—
Aqua Jet	Water	Physical	40	100	20	Normal	○

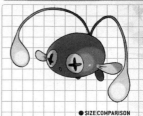

◉ No. 170 | Angler Pokémon
Chinchou
Water Electric

- **HEIGHT:** 1'08"
- **WEIGHT:** 26.5 lbs.
- **ITEMS:** DeepSeaScale

● SIZE COMPARISON

● MALE/FEMALE HAVE SAME FORM

⊛ ABILITIES
- Volt Absorb
- Illuminate

⊛ STATS
- HP ●●●
- ATTACK ●●
- DEFENSE ●●
- SP. ATTACK ●●
- SP. DEFENSE ●●
- SPEED ●●●

⊛ EGG GROUPS
Water 2

⊛ PERFORMANCE
SPEED ★★★☆ STAMINA ★★☆☆
POWER ★★☆ JUMP ★★☆
SKILL ★★★☆☆

● MAIN WAYS TO OBTAIN

Pokémon HeartGold	New Bark Town (Good Rod Super Rod)
Pokémon SoulSilver	New Bark Town (Good Rod Super Rod)
Pokémon Diamond	Route 220 (Super Rod)
Pokémon Pearl	Route 220 (Super Rod)
Pokémon Platinum	Route 220 (Super Rod)

Pokémon HeartGold
It shoots positive and negative electricity between the tips of its two antennae and zaps its enemies.

Pokémon SoulSilver
On the dark ocean floor, its only means of communication is its constantly flashing lights.

⊛ EVOLUTION

Chinchou — Lv. 27 → Lanturn

○ No. 171 | Light Pokémon
Lanturn

Water | Electric

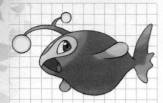

- **HEIGHT:** 3'11"
- **WEIGHT:** 49.6 lbs.
- **ITEMS:** DeepSeaScale

● SIZE COMPARISON

● MALE/FEMALE HAVE SAME FORM

⊛ ABILITIES
- Volt Absorb
- Illuminate

⊛ STATS
HP ●●●●●
ATTACK ●●
DEFENSE ●●
SP. ATTACK ●●●
SP. DEFENSE ●●●
SPEED ●●●

⊛ EGG GROUPS
Water 2

⊛ PERFORMANCE
SPEED ★★★   STAMINA ★★★★
POWER ★★☆   JUMP ★★★☆
SKILL ★★★

● MAIN WAYS TO OBTAIN

Pokémon HeartGold	New Bark Town (Super Rod)
Pokémon SoulSilver	New Bark Town (Super Rod)
Pokémon Diamond	Route 220 (Super Rod)
Pokémon Pearl	Route 220 (Super Rod)
Pokémon Platinum	Level up Chinchou to Lv. 27

Pokémon HeartGold
The light it emits is so bright that it can illuminate the sea's surface from a depth of over three miles.

Pokémon SoulSilver
It blinds prey with an intense burst of light. With the prey incapacitated, the Pokémon swallows it in a single gulp.

⊛ EVOLUTION

Chinchou —Lv. 27→ Lanturn

● LEVEL-UP MOVES

Lv.	Name	Type	Kind	Pow.	Acc.	PP	Range	DA
1	Bubble	Water	Special	20	100	30	2 Foes	—
1	Supersonic	Normal	Status	—	55	20	Normal	—
1	Thunder Wave	Electric	Status	—	100	20	Normal	—
6	Thunder Wave	Electric	Status	—	100	20	Normal	—
9	Flail	Normal	Physical	—	100	15	Normal	○
12	Water Gun	Water	Special	40	100	25	Normal	—
17	Confuse Ray	Ghost	Status	—	100	10	Normal	—
20	Spark	Electric	Physical	65	100	20	Normal	○
23	Take Down	Normal	Physical	90	85	20	Normal	○
27	Stockpile	Normal	Status	—	—	20	Self	—
27	Swallow	Normal	Status	—	—	10	Self	—
27	Spit Up	Normal	Special	—	100	10	Normal	—
30	BubbleBeam	Water	Special	65	100	20	Normal	—
35	Signal Beam	Bug	Special	75	100	15	Normal	—
40	Discharge	Electric	Special	80	100	15	2 Foes/1 Ally	—
47	Aqua Ring	Water	Status	—	—	20	Self	—
52	Hydro Pump	Water	Special	120	80	5	Normal	—
57	Charge	Electric	Status	—	—	20	Self	—

● MOVE MANIAC

Name	Type	Kind	Pow.	Acc.	PP	Range	DA

● BP MOVES

Name	Type	Kind	Pow.	Acc.	PP	Range	DA
Dive	Water	Physical	80	100	10	Normal	○
Icy Wind	Ice	Special	55	95	15	2 Foes	—
Sucker Punch	Dark	Physical	80	100	5	Normal	○
Snore	Normal	Special	40	100	15	Normal	—
Heal Bell	Normal	Status	—	—	5	All Allies	—
Aqua Tail	Water	Physical	90	90	10	Normal	○
Signal Beam	Bug	Special	75	100	15	Normal	—
Bounce	Flying	Physical	85	85	5	Normal	○

● TM & HM MOVES

No.	Name	Type	Kind	Pow.	Acc.	PP	Range	DA
TM03	Water Pulse	Water	Special	60	100	20	Normal	—
TM06	Toxic	Poison	Status	—	85	10	Normal	—
TM07	Hail	Ice	Status	—	—	10	All	—
TM10	Hidden Power	Normal	Special	—	100	15	Normal	—
TM13	Ice Beam	Ice	Special	95	100	10	Normal	—
TM14	Blizzard	Ice	Special	120	70	5	2 Foes	—
TM15	Hyper Beam	Normal	Special	150	90	5	Normal	—
TM17	Protect	Normal	Status	—	—	10	Self	—
TM18	Rain Dance	Water	Status	—	—	5	All	—
TM21	Frustration	Normal	Physical	—	100	20	Normal	○
TM24	Thunderbolt	Electric	Special	95	100	15	Normal	—
TM25	Thunder	Electric	Special	120	70	10	Normal	—
TM27	Return	Normal	Physical	—	100	20	Normal	○
TM32	Double Team	Normal	Status	—	—	15	Self	—
TM34	Shock Wave	Electric	Special	60	—	20	Normal	—
TM42	Facade	Normal	Physical	70	100	20	Normal	○
TM43	Secret Power	Normal	Physical	70	100	20	Normal	—
TM44	Rest	Psychic	Status	—	—	10	Self	—
TM45	Attract	Normal	Status	—	100	15	Normal	—
TM55	Brine	Water	Special	65	100	10	Normal	—
TM57	Charge Beam	Electric	Special	50	90	10	Normal	—
TM58	Endure	Normal	Status	—	—	10	Self	—
TM68	Giga Impact	Normal	Physical	150	90	5	Normal	○
TM70	Flash	Normal	Status	—	100	20	Normal	—
TM73	Thunder Wave	Electric	Status	—	100	20	Normal	—
TM78	Captivate	Normal	Status	—	100	20	2 Foes	—
TM82	Sleep Talk	Normal	Status	—	—	10	Depends	—
TM83	Natural Gift	Normal	Physical	—	100	15	Normal	—
TM87	Swagger	Normal	Status	—	90	15	Normal	—
TM90	Substitute	Normal	Status	—	—	10	Self	—
HM03	Surf	Water	Special	95	100	15	2 Foes/1 Ally	—
HM05	Whirlpool	Water	Special	15	70	15	Normal	—
HM07	Waterfall	Water	Physical	80	100	15	Normal	○

● LEVEL-UP MOVES

Lv.	Name	Type	Kind	Pow.	Acc.	PP	Range	DA
1	ThunderShock	Electric	Special	40	100	30	Normal	—
1	Charm	Normal	Status	—	100	20	Normal	—
5	Tail Whip	Normal	Status	—	100	30	2 Foes	—
10	Thunder Wave	Electric	Status	—	100	20	Normal	—
13	Sweet Kiss	Normal	Status	—	75	10	Normal	—
18	Nasty Plot	Dark	Status	—	—	20	Self	—

● MOVE MANIAC

Name	Type	Kind	Pow.	Acc.	PP	Range	DA
Headbutt	Normal	Physical	70	100	15	Normal	○

● BP MOVES

Name	Type	Kind	Pow.	Acc.	PP	Range	DA
Snore	Normal	Special	40	100	15	Normal	—
Helping Hand	Normal	Status	—	—	20	1 Ally	—
Magnet Rise	Electric	Status	—	—	10	Self	—
Swift	Normal	Special	60	—	20	2 Foes	—
Uproar	Normal	Special	50	100	10	1 Random	—
Mud-Slap	Ground	Special	20	100	10	Normal	—
Rollout	Rock	Physical	30	90	20	Normal	○
Signal Beam	Bug	Special	75	100	15	Normal	—

● TM & HM MOVES

No.	Name	Type	Kind	Pow.	Acc.	PP	Range	DA
TM06	Toxic	Poison	Status	—	85	10	Normal	—
TM10	Hidden Power	Normal	Special	—	100	15	Normal	—
TM16	Light Screen	Psychic	Status	—	—	30	2 Allies	—
TM17	Protect	Normal	Status	—	—	10	Self	—
TM18	Rain Dance	Water	Status	—	—	5	All	—
TM21	Frustration	Normal	Physical	—	100	20	Normal	○
TM23	Iron Tail	Steel	Physical	100	75	15	Normal	○
TM24	Thunderbolt	Electric	Special	95	100	15	Normal	—
TM25	Thunder	Electric	Special	120	70	10	Normal	—
TM27	Return	Normal	Physical	—	100	20	Normal	○
TM32	Double Team	Normal	Status	—	—	15	Self	—
TM34	Shock Wave	Electric	Special	60	—	20	Normal	—
TM42	Facade	Normal	Physical	70	100	20	Normal	○
TM43	Secret Power	Normal	Physical	70	100	20	Normal	—
TM44	Rest	Psychic	Status	—	—	10	Self	—
TM45	Attract	Normal	Status	—	100	15	Normal	—
TM56	Fling	Dark	Physical	—	100	10	Normal	—
TM57	Charge Beam	Electric	Special	50	90	10	Normal	—
TM58	Endure	Normal	Status	—	—	10	Self	—
TM70	Flash	Normal	Status	—	100	20	Normal	—
TM73	Thunder Wave	Electric	Status	—	100	20	Normal	—
TM78	Captivate	Normal	Status	—	100	20	2 Foes	—
TM82	Sleep Talk	Normal	Status	—	—	10	Depends	—
TM83	Natural Gift	Normal	Physical	—	100	15	Normal	—
TM86	Grass Knot	Grass	Special	—	100	20	Normal	○
TM87	Swagger	Normal	Status	—	90	15	Normal	—
TM90	Substitute	Normal	Status	—	—	10	Self	—

● EGG MOVES

Name	Type	Kind	Pow.	Acc.	PP	Range	DA
Reversal	Fighting	Physical	—	100	15	Normal	○
Bide	Normal	Physical	—	—	10	Self	—
Present	Normal	Physical	—	90	15	Normal	—
Encore	Normal	Status	—	100	5	Normal	—
DoubleSlap	Normal	Physical	15	85	10	Normal	○
Wish	Normal	Status	—	—	10	Self	—
Charge	Electric	Status	—	—	20	Self	—
Fake Out	Normal	Physical	40	100	10	Normal	○
ThunderPunch	Electric	Physical	75	100	15	Normal	○
Tickle	Normal	Status	—	100	20	Normal	—
Volt Tackle *	Electric	Physical	120	100	15	Normal	○
Flail	Normal	Physical	—	100	15	Normal	—

○ **No. 172** | Tiny Mouse Pokémon

Pichu

Electric

● HEIGHT: 1'00"
● WEIGHT: 4.4 lbs.
● ITEMS: None

● SIZE COMPARISON

● MALE/FEMALE HAVE SAME FORM

◎ ABILITIES
● Static

◎ STATS
HP ●
ATTACK ●●
DEFENSE ●
SP. ATTACK ●
SP. DEFENSE ●
SPEED ●●●

◎ EGG GROUPS
No Egg has ever been discovered

◎ PERFORMANCE

SPEED ★★★★   STAMINA ★☆☆
POWER ★☆☆   JUMP ★★★
SKILL ★★★★☆

● MAIN WAYS TO OBTAIN

Pokémon HeartGold	Find its Egg at the Pokémon Day Care and hatch it
Pokémon SoulSilver	Find its Egg at the Pokémon Day Care and hatch it
Pokémon Diamond	Trophy Garden at the Pokémon Mansion on Route 212
Pokémon Pearl	Trophy Garden at the Pokémon Mansion on Route 212
Pokémon Platinum	Trophy Garden at the Pokémon Mansion on Route 212

Pokémon HeartGold	**Pokémon SoulSilver**
It is not yet skilled at storing electricity. It may send out a jolt if amused or startled.	Despite its small size, it can zap even adult humans. However, if it does so, it also surprises itself.

◎ EVOLUTION

Level up with high friendship → Use Thunderstone

Pichu → Pikachu → Raichu

No. 173 | Star Shape Pokémon
Cleffa

Normal

- **HEIGHT:** 1'00"
- **WEIGHT:** 6.6 lbs.
- **ITEMS:** None

● SIZE COMPARISON

● MALE/FEMALE HAVE SAME FORM

⊛ ABILITIES
- Cute Charm
- Magic Guard

⊛ STATS
HP	●●
ATTACK	●
DEFENSE	●
SP. ATTACK	●●
SP. DEFENSE	●●
SPEED	●

⊛ EGG GROUPS
No Egg has ever been discovered

⊛ PERFORMANCE
SPEED ★★★★☆	STAMINA ★★★
POWER ★☆	JUMP ★★☆
SKILL ★★★☆	

● MAIN WAYS TO OBTAIN

Pokémon HeartGold — Find its Egg at the Pokémon Day Care and hatch it

Pokémon SoulSilver — Find its Egg at the Pokémon Day Care and hatch it

Pokémon Diamond — Mt. Coronet 1F 1

Pokémon Pearl — Mt. Coronet 1F 1

Pokémon Platinum — Mt. Coronet 1F 1 (morning and night only)

Pokémon HeartGold — Because of its unusual, starlike silhouette, people believe that it came here from on a meteor.

Pokémon SoulSilver — When numerous meteors illuminate the night sky, sightings of CLEFFA strangely increase.

⊛ EVOLUTION

Cleffa — (Level up with high friendship) → Clefairy — (Use Moon Stone) → Clefable

● LEVEL-UP MOVES
Lv.	Name	Type	Kind	Pow.	Acc.	PP	Range	DA
1	Pound	Normal	Physical	40	100	35	Normal	○
1	Charm	Normal	Status	—	100	20	Normal	—
4	Encore	Normal	Status	—	100	5	Normal	—
7	Sing	Normal	Status	—	55	15	Normal	—
10	Sweet Kiss	Normal	Status	—	75	10	Normal	—
13	Copycat	Normal	Status	—	—	20	Depends	—
16	Magical Leaf	Grass	Special	60	—	20	Normal	—

● MOVE MANIAC
Name	Type	Kind	Pow.	Acc.	PP	Range	DA
Headbutt	Normal	Physical	70	100	15	Normal	○

● BP MOVES
Name	Type	Kind	Pow.	Acc.	PP	Range	DA
Icy Wind	Ice	Special	55	95	15	2 Foes	—
Zen Headbutt	Psychic	Physical	80	90	15	Normal	○
Trick	Psychic	Status	—	100	10	Normal	—
Snore	Normal	Special	40	100	15	Normal	—
Helping Hand	Normal	Status	—	—	20	1 Ally	—
Last Resort	Normal	Physical	130	100	5	Normal	○
Uproar	Normal	Special	50	100	10	1 Random	—
Gravity	Psychic	Status	—	—	5	All	—
Magic Coat	Psychic	Status	—	—	15	Self	—
Role Play	Psychic	Status	—	—	10	Normal	—
Mud-Slap	Ground	Special	20	100	10	Normal	—
Rollout	Rock	Physical	30	90	20	Normal	○
Endeavor	Normal	Physical	—	100	5	Normal	○
Signal Beam	Bug	Special	75	100	15	Normal	—

● TM & HM MOVES
No.	Name	Type	Kind	Pow.	Acc.	PP	Range	DA
TM03	Water Pulse	Water	Special	60	100	20	Normal	—
TM06	Toxic	Poison	Status	—	85	10	Normal	—
TM10	Hidden Power	Normal	Special	—	100	15	Normal	—
TM11	Sunny Day	Fire	Status	—	—	5	All	—
TM16	Light Screen	Psychic	Status	—	—	30	2 Allies	—
TM17	Protect	Normal	Status	—	—	10	Self	—
TM18	Rain Dance	Water	Status	—	—	5	All	—
TM20	Safeguard	Normal	Status	—	—	25	2 Allies	—
TM21	Frustration	Normal	Physical	—	100	20	Normal	○
TM22	SolarBeam	Grass	Special	120	100	10	Normal	—
TM23	Iron Tail	Steel	Physical	100	75	15	Normal	○
TM27	Return	Normal	Physical	—	100	20	Normal	○
TM28	Dig	Ground	Physical	80	100	10	Normal	○
TM29	Psychic	Psychic	Special	90	100	10	Normal	—
TM30	Shadow Ball	Ghost	Special	80	100	15	Normal	—
TM32	Double Team	Normal	Status	—	—	15	Self	—
TM33	Reflect	Psychic	Status	—	—	20	2 Allies	—
TM34	Shock Wave	Electric	Special	60	—	20	Normal	—
TM35	Flamethrower	Fire	Special	95	100	15	Normal	—
TM38	Fire Blast	Fire	Special	120	85	5	Normal	—
TM42	Facade	Normal	Physical	70	100	20	Normal	○
TM43	Secret Power	Normal	Physical	70	100	20	Normal	○
TM44	Rest	Psychic	Status	—	—	10	Self	—
TM45	Attract	Normal	Status	—	100	15	Normal	—
TM56	Fling	Dark	Physical	—	100	10	Normal	—
TM58	Endure	Normal	Status	—	—	10	Self	—
TM67	Recycle	Normal	Status	—	—	10	Self	—
TM70	Flash	Normal	Status	—	100	20	Normal	—
TM73	Thunder Wave	Electric	Status	—	100	20	Normal	—
TM77	Psych Up	Normal	Status	—	—	10	Normal	—
TM78	Captivate	Normal	Status	—	100	20	2 Foes	—
TM82	Sleep Talk	Normal	Status	—	—	10	Depends	—
TM83	Natural Gift	Normal	Physical	—	100	15	Normal	—
TM85	Dream Eater	Psychic	Special	100	100	15	Normal	—
TM86	Grass Knot	Grass	Special	—	100	20	Normal	○
TM87	Swagger	Normal	Status	—	90	15	Normal	—
TM90	Substitute	Normal	Status	—	—	10	Self	—

● EGG MOVES
Name	Type	Kind	Pow.	Acc.	PP	Range	DA
Present	Normal	Physical	—	90	15	Normal	—
Metronome	Normal	Status	—	—	10	Depends	—
Amnesia	Psychic	Status	—	—	20	Self	—
Belly Drum	Normal	Status	—	—	10	Self	—
Splash	Normal	Status	—	—	40	Self	—
Mimic	Normal	Status	—	—	10	Normal	—
Wish	Normal	Status	—	—	10	Self	—
Substitute	Normal	Status	—	—	10	Self	—
Fake Tears	Dark	Status	—	100	20	Normal	—
Covet	Normal	Physical	40	100	40	Normal	○
Aromatherapy	Grass	Status	—	—	5	All Allies	—

● LEVEL-UP MOVES

Lv.	Name	Type	Kind	Pow.	Acc.	PP	Range	DA
1	Sing	Normal	Status	—	55	15	Normal	—
1	Charm	Normal	Status	—	100	20	Normal	—
5	Defense Curl	Normal	Status	—	—	40	Self	—
9	Pound	Normal	Physical	40	100	35	Normal	○
13	Sweet Kiss	Normal	Status	—	75	10	Normal	—
17	Copycat	Normal	Status	—	—	20	Depends	—

● MOVE MANIAC

Name	Type	Kind	Pow.	Acc.	PP	Range	DA
Headbutt	Normal	Physical	70	100	15	Normal	○

● BP MOVES

Name	Type	Kind	Pow.	Acc.	PP	Range	DA
Icy Wind	Ice	Special	55	95	15	2 Foes	—
Snore	Normal	Special	40	100	15	Normal	—
Helping Hand	Normal	Status	—	—	20	1 Ally	—
Last Resort	Normal	Physical	130	100	5	Normal	○
Uproar	Normal	Special	50	100	10	1 Random	—
Gravity	Psychic	Status	—	—	5	All	—
Magic Coat	Psychic	Status	—	—	15	Self	—
Role Play	Psychic	Status	—	—	10	Normal	—
Heal Bell	Normal	Status	—	—	5	All Allies	—
Mud-Slap	Ground	Special	20	100	10	Normal	—
Rollout	Rock	Physical	30	90	20	Normal	○
Endeavor	Normal	Physical	—	100	5	Normal	○
Bounce	Flying	Physical	85	85	5	Normal	○
Pain Split	Normal	Status	—	—	20	Normal	—

● TM & HM MOVES

No.	Name	Type	Kind	Pow.	Acc.	PP	Range	DA
TM03	Water Pulse	Water	Special	60	100	20	Normal	—
TM06	Toxic	Poison	Status	—	85	10	Normal	—
TM10	Hidden Power	Normal	Special	—	100	15	Normal	—
TM11	Sunny Day	Fire	Status	—	—	5	All	—
TM16	Light Screen	Psychic	Status	—	—	30	2 Allies	—
TM17	Protect	Normal	Status	—	—	10	Self	—
TM18	Rain Dance	Water	Status	—	—	5	All	—
TM20	Safeguard	Normal	Status	—	—	25	2 Allies	—
TM21	Frustration	Normal	Physical	—	100	20	Normal	○
TM22	SolarBeam	Grass	Special	120	100	10	Normal	—
TM27	Return	Normal	Physical	—	100	20	Normal	○
TM28	Dig	Ground	Physical	80	100	10	Normal	○
TM29	Psychic	Psychic	Special	90	100	10	Normal	—
TM30	Shadow Ball	Ghost	Special	80	100	15	Normal	—
TM32	Double Team	Normal	Status	—	—	15	Self	—
TM33	Reflect	Psychic	Status	—	—	20	2 Allies	—
TM34	Shock Wave	Electric	Special	60	—	20	Normal	—
TM35	Flamethrower	Fire	Special	95	100	15	Normal	—
TM38	Fire Blast	Fire	Special	120	85	5	Normal	—
TM42	Facade	Normal	Physical	70	100	20	Normal	○
TM43	Secret Power	Normal	Physical	70	100	20	Normal	○
TM44	Rest	Psychic	Status	—	—	10	Self	—
TM45	Attract	Normal	Status	—	100	15	Normal	—
TM56	Fling	Dark	Physical	—	100	10	Normal	—
TM58	Endure	Normal	Status	—	—	10	Self	—
TM67	Recycle	Normal	Status	—	—	10	Self	—
TM70	Flash	Normal	Status	—	100	20	Normal	—
TM73	Thunder Wave	Electric	Status	—	100	20	Normal	—
TM77	Psych Up	Normal	Status	—	—	10	Normal	—
TM79	Captivate	Normal	Status	—	100	20	2 Foes	—
TM82	Sleep Talk	Normal	Status	—	—	10	Depends	—
TM83	Natural Gift	Normal	Physical	—	100	15	Normal	—
TM85	Dream Eater	Psychic	Special	100	100	15	Normal	—
TM86	Grass Knot	Grass	Special	—	100	20	Normal	○
TM87	Swagger	Normal	Status	—	90	15	Normal	—
TM90	Substitute	Normal	Status	—	—	10	Self	—

● EGG MOVES

Name	Type	Kind	Pow.	Acc.	PP	Range	DA
Perish Song	Normal	Status	—	—	5	All	—
Present	Normal	Physical	—	90	15	Normal	○
Faint Attack	Dark	Physical	60	—	20	Normal	○
Wish	Normal	Status	—	—	10	Self	—
Fake Tears	Dark	Status	—	100	20	Normal	—
Last Resort	Normal	Physical	130	100	5	Normal	○
Covet	Normal	Physical	40	100	40	Normal	○
Gravity	Psychic	Status	—	—	5	All	—

◉ No. 174 | Balloon Pokémon
Igglybuff

Normal

- ● HEIGHT: 1'00"
- ● WEIGHT: 2.2 lbs.
- ● ITEMS: None

● SIZE COMPARISON

● MALE/FEMALE HAVE SAME FORM

◉ ABILITIES
● Cute Charm

◉ STATS
HP	●●●
ATTACK	●
DEFENSE	●
SP. ATTACK	●
SP. DEFENSE	●●
SPEED	●

◉ EGG GROUPS
No Egg has ever been discovered

◉ PERFORMANCE
SPEED ★★★☆   STAMINA ★★★☆
POWER ★☆☆   JUMP ★★★☆
SKILL ★★☆

● MAIN WAYS TO OBTAIN

Pokémon HeartGold	Find its Egg at the Pokémon Day Care and hatch it
Pokémon SoulSilver	Find its Egg at the Pokémon Day Care and hatch it
Pokémon Diamond	Trophy Garden at the Pokémon Mansion on Route 212 (after obtaining the National Pokédex, talk to Mr. Backlot]
Pokémon Pearl	Trophy Garden at the Pokémon Mansion on Route 212 (after obtaining the National Pokédex, talk to Mr. Backlot]
Pokémon Platinum	Trophy Garden at the Pokémon Mansion on Route 212 (after obtaining the National Pokédex, talk to Mr. Backlot]

Pokémon HeartGold
It has a very soft body. If it starts to roll, it will bounce all over and be impossible to stop.

Pokémon SoulSilver
Its extremely flexible and elastic body makes it bounce continuously--anytime, anywhere.

◉ EVOLUTION

Igglybuff — Level up with high friendship → Jigglypuff — Use Moon Stone → Wigglytuff

Togepi

Normal

- **HEIGHT:** 1'00"
- **WEIGHT:** 3.3 lbs.
- **ITEMS:** None

● SIZE COMPARISON

● MALE/FEMALE HAVE SAME FORM

● ABILITIES
- Hustle
- Serene Grace

● STATS
- HP ●
- ATTACK ●
- DEFENSE ●●●
- SP. ATTACK ●●
- SP. DEFENSE ●●
- SPEED ●

● EGG GROUPS
No Egg has ever been discovered

● PERFORMANCE
SPEED ★★★★☆	STAMINA ★★★★☆
POWER ★☆☆☆	JUMP ★★★☆
SKILL ★★☆☆	

● MAIN WAYS TO OBTAIN

Pokémon HeartGold — Hatch the Mystery Egg received from Mr. Pokémon on Route 30

Pokémon SoulSilver — Hatch the Mystery Egg received from Mr. Pokémon on Route 30

Pokémon Diamond — Route 230 (use Poké Radar)

Pokémon Pearl — Route 230 (use Poké Radar)

Pokémon Platinum — Receive an Egg from Cynthia in Eterna City and hatch it

Pokémon HeartGold — The shell seems to be filled with joy. It is said that it will share good luck when treated kindly.

Pokémon SoulSilver — A proverb claims that happiness will come to anyone who can make a sleeping TOGEPI stand up.

● EVOLUTION

Togepi	Level up with high friendship →	Togetic	Use Shiny Stone →	Togekiss

● LEVEL-UP MOVES

Lv.	Name	Type	Kind	Pow.	Acc.	PP	Range	DA
1	Growl	Normal	Status	—	100	40	2 Foes	—
1	Charm	Normal	Status	—	100	20	Normal	—
6	Metronome	Normal	Status	—	—	10	Depends	—
10	Sweet Kiss	Normal	Status	—	75	10	Normal	—
15	Yawn	Normal	Status	—	—	10	Normal	—
19	Encore	Normal	Status	—	100	5	Normal	—
24	Follow Me	Normal	Status	—	—	20	Self	—
28	Wish	Normal	Status	—	—	10	Self	—
33	AncientPower	Rock	Special	60	100	5	Normal	—
37	Safeguard	Normal	Status	—	—	25	2 Allies	—
42	Baton Pass	Normal	Status	—	—	40	Self	—
46	Double-Edge	Normal	Physical	120	100	15	Normal	○
51	Last Resort	Normal	Physical	130	100	5	Normal	○

● MOVE MANIAC

Name	Type	Kind	Pow.	Acc.	PP	Range	DA
Headbutt	Normal	Physical	70	100	15	Normal	○

● BP MOVES

Name	Type	Kind	Pow.	Acc.	PP	Range	DA
Zen Headbutt	Psychic	Physical	80	90	15	Normal	○
Trick	Psychic	Status	—	100	10	Normal	—
Snore	Normal	Special	40	100	15	Normal	—
Last Resort	Normal	Physical	130	100	5	Normal	○
Swift	Normal	Special	60	—	20	2 Foes	—
Uproar	Normal	Special	50	100	10	1 Random	—
Magic Coat	Psychic	Status	—	—	15	Self	—
Heal Bell	Normal	Status	—	—	5	All Allies	—
Mud-Slap	Ground	Special	20	100	10	Normal	—
Rollout	Rock	Physical	30	90	20	Normal	○
Endeavor	Normal	Physical	—	100	5	Normal	○
AncientPower	Rock	Special	60	100	5	Normal	—
Signal Beam	Bug	Special	75	100	15	Normal	—

● TM & HM MOVES

No.	Name	Type	Kind	Pow.	Acc.	PP	Range	DA
TM03	Water Pulse	Water	Special	60	100	20	Normal	—
TM06	Toxic	Poison	Status	—	85	10	Normal	—
TM10	Hidden Power	Normal	Special	—	100	15	Normal	—
TM11	Sunny Day	Fire	Status	—	—	5	All	—
TM16	Light Screen	Psychic	Status	—	—	30	2 Allies	—
TM17	Protect	Normal	Status	—	—	10	Self	—
TM18	Rain Dance	Water	Status	—	—	5	All	—
TM20	Safeguard	Normal	Status	—	—	25	2 Allies	—
TM21	Frustration	Normal	Physical	—	100	20	Normal	○
TM22	SolarBeam	Grass	Special	120	100	10	Normal	—
TM27	Return	Normal	Physical	—	100	20	Normal	○
TM29	Psychic	Psychic	Special	90	100	10	Normal	—
TM30	Shadow Ball	Ghost	Special	80	100	15	Normal	—
TM32	Double Team	Normal	Status	—	—	15	Self	—
TM33	Reflect	Psychic	Status	—	—	20	2 Allies	—
TM34	Shock Wave	Electric	Special	60	—	20	Normal	—
TM35	Flamethrower	Fire	Special	95	100	15	Normal	—
TM38	Fire Blast	Fire	Special	120	85	5	Normal	—
TM42	Facade	Normal	Physical	70	100	20	Normal	○
TM43	Secret Power	Normal	Physical	70	100	20	Normal	○
TM44	Rest	Psychic	Status	—	—	10	Self	—
TM45	Attract	Normal	Status	—	100	15	Normal	—
TM56	Fling	Dark	Physical	—	100	10	Normal	—
TM58	Endure	Normal	Status	—	—	10	Self	—
TM70	Flash	Normal	Status	—	100	20	Normal	—
TM73	Thunder Wave	Electric	Status	—	100	20	Normal	—
TM77	Psych Up	Normal	Status	—	—	10	Self	—
TM78	Captivate	Normal	Status	—	100	20	2 Foes	—
TM82	Sleep Talk	Normal	Status	—	—	10	Depends	—
TM83	Natural Gift	Normal	Physical	—	100	15	Normal	—
TM85	Dream Eater	Psychic	Special	100	100	15	Normal	—
TM86	Grass Knot	Grass	Special	—	100	20	Normal	○
TM87	Swagger	Normal	Status	—	90	15	Normal	—
TM90	Substitute	Normal	Status	—	—	10	Self	—
HM06	Rock Smash	Fighting	Physical	40	100	15	Normal	○

● EGG MOVES

Name	Type	Kind	Pow.	Acc.	PP	Range	DA
Present	Normal	Physical	—	90	15	Normal	—
Mirror Move	Flying	Status	—	—	20	Depends	—
Peck	Flying	Physical	35	100	35	Normal	○
Foresight	Normal	Status	—	—	40	Normal	—
Future Sight	Psychic	Special	80	90	15	Normal	—
Substitute	Normal	Status	—	—	10	Self	—
Psych Up	Normal	Status	—	—	10	Normal	—
Nasty Plot	Dark	Status	—	—	20	Self	—
Psycho Shift	Psychic	Status	—	90	10	Normal	—
Lucky Chant	Normal	Status	—	—	30	2 Allies	—
Extrasensory	Psychic	Special	80	100	30	Normal	—

● LEVEL-UP MOVES

Lv.	Name	Type	Kind	Pow.	Acc.	PP	Range	DA
1	Magical Leaf	Grass	Special	60	—	20	Normal	—
1	Growl	Normal	Status	—	100	40	2 Foes	—
1	Charm	Normal	Status	—	100	20	Normal	—
1	Metronome	Normal	Status	—	—	10	Depends	—
1	Sweet Kiss	Normal	Status	—	75	10	Normal	—
6	Metronome	Normal	Status	—	—	10	Depends	—
10	Sweet Kiss	Normal	Status	—	75	10	Normal	—
15	Yawn	Normal	Status	—	—	10	Normal	—
19	Encore	Normal	Status	—	100	5	Normal	—
24	Follow Me	Normal	Status	—	—	20	Self	—
28	Wish	Normal	Status	—	—	10	Self	—
33	AncientPower	Rock	Special	60	100	5	Normal	—
37	Safeguard	Normal	Status	—	—	25	2 Allies	—
42	Baton Pass	Normal	Status	—	—	40	Self	—
46	Double-Edge	Normal	Physical	120	100	15	Normal	○
51	Last Resort	Normal	Physical	130	100	5	Normal	○

● MOVE MANIAC

Name	Type	Kind	Pow.	Acc.	PP	Range	DA
Headbutt	Normal	Physical	70	100	15	Normal	○

● BP MOVES

Name	Type	Kind	Pow.	Acc.	PP	Range	DA
Ominous Wind	Ghost	Special	60	100	5	Normal	—
Air Cutter	Flying	Special	55	95	25	2 Foes	—
Zen Headbutt	Psychic	Physical	80	90	15	Normal	○
Trick	Psychic	Status	—	100	10	Normal	—
Snore	Normal	Special	40	100	15	Normal	—
Last Resort	Normal	Physical	130	100	5	Normal	○
Swift	Normal	Special	60	—	20	2 Foes	—
Tailwind	Flying	Status	—	—	30	2 Allies	—
Magic Coat	Psychic	Status	—	—	15	Self	—
Heal Bell	Normal	Status	—	—	5	All Allies	—
Mud-Slap	Ground	Special	20	100	10	Normal	—
Rollout	Rock	Physical	30	90	20	Normal	○
Endeavor	Normal	Physical	—	100	5	Normal	○
AncientPower	Rock	Special	60	100	5	Normal	—
Signal Beam	Bug	Special	75	100	15	Normal	—
Twister	Dragon	Special	40	100	20	2 Foes	—
Heat Wave	Fire	Special	100	90	10	2 Foes	—

● TM & HM MOVES

No.	Name	Type	Kind	Pow.	Acc.	PP	Range	DA
TM01	Focus Punch	Fighting	Physical	150	100	20	Normal	○
TM03	Water Pulse	Water	Special	60	100	20	Normal	—
TM06	Toxic	Poison	Status	—	85	10	Normal	—
TM10	Hidden Power	Normal	Special	—	100	15	Normal	—
TM11	Sunny Day	Fire	Status	—	—	5	All	—
TM15	Hyper Beam	Normal	Special	150	90	5	Normal	—
TM16	Light Screen	Psychic	Status	—	—	30	2 Allies	—
TM17	Protect	Normal	Status	—	—	10	Self	—
TM18	Rain Dance	Water	Status	—	—	5	All	—
TM20	Safeguard	Normal	Status	—	—	25	2 Allies	—
TM21	Frustration	Normal	Physical	—	100	20	Normal	○
TM22	SolarBeam	Grass	Special	120	100	10	Normal	—
TM27	Return	Normal	Physical	—	100	20	Normal	○
TM29	Psychic	Psychic	Special	90	100	10	Normal	—
TM30	Shadow Ball	Ghost	Special	80	100	15	Normal	—
TM31	Brick Break	Fighting	Physical	75	100	15	Normal	○
TM32	Double Team	Normal	Status	—	—	15	Self	—
TM33	Reflect	Psychic	Status	—	—	20	2 Allies	—
TM34	Shock Wave	Electric	Special	60	—	20	Normal	—
TM35	Flamethrower	Fire	Special	95	100	15	Normal	—
TM38	Fire Blast	Fire	Special	120	85	5	Normal	—
TM40	Aerial Ace	Flying	Physical	60	—	20	Normal	○
TM42	Facade	Normal	Physical	70	100	20	Normal	○
TM43	Secret Power	Normal	Physical	70	100	20	Normal	○
TM44	Rest	Psychic	Status	—	—	10	Self	—
TM45	Attract	Normal	Status	—	100	15	Normal	—
TM47	Steel Wing	Steel	Physical	70	90	25	Normal	○
TM51	Roost	Flying	Status	—	—	10	Self	—
TM56	Fling	Dark	Physical	—	100	10	Normal	—
TM58	Endure	Normal	Status	—	—	10	Self	—
TM60	Drain Punch	Fighting	Physical	60	100	5	Normal	○
TM62	Silver Wind	Bug	Special	60	100	5	Normal	—
TM68	Giga Impact	Normal	Physical	150	90	5	Normal	○
TM70	Flash	Normal	Status	—	100	20	Normal	—
TM73	Thunder Wave	Electric	Status	—	100	20	Normal	—
TM77	Psych Up	Normal	Status	—	—	10	Normal	—
TM78	Captivate	Normal	Status	—	100	20	2 Foes	—
TM82	Sleep Talk	Normal	Status	—	—	10	Depends	—
TM83	Natural Gift	Normal	Physical	—	100	15	Normal	—
TM85	Dream Eater	Psychic	Special	100	100	15	Normal	—
TM86	Grass Knot	Grass	Special	—	100	20	Normal	○
TM87	Swagger	Normal	Status	—	90	15	Normal	—
TM90	Substitute	Normal	Status	—	—	10	Self	—
HM02	Fly	Flying	Physical	90	95	15	Normal	○
HM06	Rock Smash	Fighting	Physical	40	100	15	Normal	○

● No. 176 | Happiness Pokémon
Togetic

Normal **Flying**

● HEIGHT: 2'00"
● WEIGHT: 7.1 lbs.
● ITEMS: None

● SIZE COMPARISON

● MALE/FEMALE HAVE SAME FORM

⊙ ABILITIES
● Hustle
● Serene Grace

⊙ STATS
HP ●●
ATTACK ●●
DEFENSE ●●●
SP. ATTACK ●●●
SP. DEFENSE ●●●●
SPEED ●●

⊙ EGG GROUPS
Flying
Fairy

⊙ PERFORMANCE
SPEED ★★★☆ STAMINA ★★★★☆
POWER ★★☆☆☆ JUMP ★★★★☆
SKILL ★★★

● MAIN WAYS TO OBTAIN

Pokémon HeartGold — Level up Togepi with high friendship

Pokémon SoulSilver — Level up Togepi with high friendship

Pokémon Diamond — Level up Togepi with high friendship

Pokémon Pearl — Level up Togepi with high friendship

Pokémon Platinum — Level up Togepi with high friendship

Pokémon HeartGold
They say that it will appear before kindhearted, caring people and shower them with happiness.

Pokémon SoulSilver
It grows dispirited if it is not with kind people. It can float in midair without moving its wings.

⊙ EVOLUTION

Togepi → Level up with high friendship → Togetic → Use Shiny Stone → Togekiss

No. 177 | Tiny Bird Pokémon
Natu

`Psychic` `Flying`

- **HEIGHT:** 0'08"
- **WEIGHT:** 4.4 lbs.
- **ITEMS:** None

● MALE/FEMALE HAVE SAME FORM

● SIZE COMPARISON

⊛ ABILITIES
- Synchronize
- Early Bird

⊛ EGG GROUPS
Flying

⊛ STATS
HP	●
ATTACK	●●
DEFENSE	●●
SP. ATTACK	●●●
SP. DEFENSE	●●●
SPEED	●●●

⊛ PERFORMANCE
SPEED ★★★☆   STAMINA ★★★☆
POWER ★★☆   JUMP ★★★☆
SKILL ★★

● MAIN WAYS TO OBTAIN

Pokémon HeartGold — Ruins of Alph (outside)

Pokémon SoulSilver — Ruins of Alph (outside)

Pokémon Diamond — Route 224 (mass outbreak)

Pokémon Pearl — Route 224 (mass outbreak)

Pokémon Platinum — Route 224 (mass outbreak)

Pokémon HeartGold
Because its wings aren't yet fully grown, it has to hop to get around. It is always staring at something.

Pokémon SoulSilver
It usually forages for food on the ground but may, on rare occasions, hop onto branches to peck at shoots.

⊛ EVOLUTION
  Lv. 25

Natu → Xatu

● LEVEL-UP MOVES
Lv.	Name	Type	Kind	Pow.	Acc.	PP	Range	DA
1	Peck	Flying	Physical	35	100	35	Normal	○
1	Leer	Normal	Status	—	100	30	2 Foes	—
6	Night Shade	Ghost	Special	—	100	15	Normal	—
9	Teleport	Psychic	Status	—	—	20	Self	—
12	Lucky Chant	Normal	Status	—	—	30	2 Allies	—
17	Miracle Eye	Psychic	Status	—	—	40	Normal	—
20	Me First	Normal	Status	—	—	20	Depends	—
23	Confuse Ray	Ghost	Status	—	100	10	Normal	—
28	Wish	Normal	Status	—	—	10	Self	—
33	Psycho Shift	Psychic	Status	—	90	10	Normal	—
36	Future Sight	Psychic	Special	80	90	15	Normal	—
39	Ominous Wind	Ghost	Special	60	100	5	Normal	—
44	Power Swap	Psychic	Status	—	—	10	Normal	—
44	Guard Swap	Psychic	Status	—	—	10	Normal	—
47	Psychic	Psychic	Special	90	100	10	Normal	—

● MOVE MANIAC
Name	Type	Kind	Pow.	Acc.	PP	Range	DA

● BP MOVES
Name	Type	Kind	Pow.	Acc.	PP	Range	DA
Ominous Wind	Ghost	Special	60	100	5	Normal	—
Air Cutter	Flying	Special	55	95	25	2 Foes	—
Zen Headbutt	Psychic	Physical	80	90	15	Normal	○
Trick	Psychic	Status	—	100	10	Normal	—
Sucker Punch	Dark	Physical	80	100	5	Normal	○
Snore	Normal	Special	40	100	15	Normal	—
Swift	Normal	Special	60	—	20	2 Foes	—
Tailwind	Flying	Status	—	—	30	2 Allies	—
Magic Coat	Psychic	Status	—	—	15	Self	—
Signal Beam	Bug	Special	75	100	15	Normal	—
Twister	Dragon	Special	40	100	20	2 Foes	—
Heat Wave	Fire	Special	100	90	10	2 Foes	—
Pain Split	Normal	Status	—	—	20	Normal	—

● TM & HM MOVES
No.	Name	Type	Kind	Pow.	Acc.	PP	Range	DA
TM04	Calm Mind	Psychic	Status	—	—	20	Self	—
TM06	Toxic	Poison	Status	—	85	10	Normal	—
TM10	Hidden Power	Normal	Special	—	100	15	Normal	—
TM11	Sunny Day	Fire	Status	—	—	5	All	—
TM16	Light Screen	Psychic	Status	—	—	30	2 Allies	—
TM17	Protect	Normal	Status	—	—	10	Self	—
TM18	Rain Dance	Water	Status	—	—	5	All	—
TM19	Giga Drain	Grass	Special	60	100	10	Normal	—
TM21	Frustration	Normal	Physical	—	100	20	Normal	○
TM22	SolarBeam	Grass	Special	120	100	10	Normal	—
TM27	Return	Normal	Physical	—	100	20	Normal	○
TM29	Psychic	Psychic	Special	90	100	10	Normal	—
TM30	Shadow Ball	Ghost	Special	80	100	15	Normal	—
TM32	Double Team	Normal	Status	—	—	15	Self	—
TM33	Reflect	Psychic	Status	—	—	20	2 Allies	—
TM40	Aerial Ace	Flying	Physical	60	—	20	Normal	○
TM42	Facade	Normal	Physical	70	100	20	Normal	○
TM43	Secret Power	Normal	Physical	70	100	20	Normal	○
TM44	Rest	Psychic	Status	—	—	10	Self	—
TM45	Attract	Normal	Status	—	100	15	Normal	—
TM46	Thief	Dark	Physical	40	100	10	Normal	○
TM47	Steel Wing	Steel	Physical	70	90	25	Normal	○
TM48	Skill Swap	Psychic	Status	—	—	10	Normal	—
TM51	Roost	Flying	Status	—	—	10	Self	—
TM58	Endure	Normal	Status	—	—	10	Self	—
TM62	Silver Wind	Bug	Special	60	100	5	Normal	—
TM70	Flash	Normal	Status	—	100	20	Normal	—
TM73	Thunder Wave	Electric	Status	—	100	20	Normal	—
TM77	Psych Up	Normal	Status	—	—	10	Normal	—
TM78	Captivate	Normal	Status	—	100	20	2 Foes	—
TM82	Sleep Talk	Normal	Status	—	—	10	Self	—
TM83	Natural Gift	Normal	Physical	—	100	15	Normal	○
TM85	Dream Eater	Psychic	Special	100	100	15	Normal	—
TM86	Grass Knot	Grass	Special	—	100	20	Normal	—
TM87	Swagger	Normal	Status	—	90	15	Normal	—
TM88	Pluck	Flying	Physical	60	100	20	Normal	○
TM89	U-turn	Bug	Physical	70	100	20	Normal	○
TM90	Substitute	Normal	Status	—	—	10	Self	—
TM92	Trick Room	Psychic	Status	—	—	5	All	—

● EGG MOVES
Name	Type	Kind	Pow.	Acc.	PP	Range	DA
Haze	Ice	Status	—	—	30	All	—
Drill Peck	Flying	Physical	80	100	20	Normal	○
Quick Attack	Normal	Physical	40	100	30	Normal	○
Faint Attack	Dark	Physical	60	—	20	Normal	○
Steel Wing	Steel	Physical	70	90	25	Normal	○
Psych Up	Normal	Status	—	—	10	Normal	—
FeatherDance	Flying	Status	—	100	15	Normal	—
Refresh	Normal	Status	—	—	20	Self	—
Zen Headbutt	Psychic	Physical	80	90	15	Normal	○
Sucker Punch	Dark	Physical	80	100	5	Normal	○

● LEVEL-UP MOVES

Lv.	Name	Type	Kind	Pow.	Acc.	PP	Range	DA
1	Peck	Flying	Physical	35	100	35	Normal	○
1	Leer	Normal	Status	—	100	30	2 Foes	—
6	Night Shade	Ghost	Special	—	100	15	Normal	—
9	Teleport	Psychic	Status	—	—	20	Self	—
12	Lucky Chant	Normal	Status	—	—	30	2 Allies	—
17	Miracle Eye	Psychic	Status	—	—	40	Normal	—
20	Me First	Normal	Status	—	—	20	Depends	—
23	Confuse Ray	Ghost	Status	—	100	10	Normal	—
27	Tailwind	Flying	Status	—	—	30	2 Allies	—
30	Wish	Normal	Status	—	—	10	Self	—
37	Psycho Shift	Psychic	Status	—	90	10	Normal	—
42	Future Sight	Psychic	Special	80	90	15	Normal	—
47	Ominous Wind	Ghost	Special	60	100	5	Normal	—
54	Power Swap	Psychic	Status	—	—	10	Normal	—
54	Guard Swap	Psychic	Status	—	—	10	Normal	—
59	Psychic	Psychic	Special	90	100	10	Normal	—

● MOVE MANIAC

Name	Type	Kind	Pow.	Acc.	PP	Range	DA

● BP MOVES

Name	Type	Kind	Pow.	Acc.	PP	Range	DA
Ominous Wind	Ghost	Special	60	100	5	Normal	—
Air Cutter	Flying	Special	55	95	25	2 Foes	—
Zen Headbutt	Psychic	Physical	80	90	15	Normal	○
Trick	Psychic	Status	—	100	10	Normal	—
Sucker Punch	Dark	Physical	80	100	5	Normal	○
Snore	Normal	Special	40	100	15	Normal	—
Swift	Normal	Special	60	—	20	2 Foes	—
Tailwind	Flying	Status	—	—	30	2 Allies	—
Magic Coat	Psychic	Status	—	—	15	Self	—
Signal Beam	Bug	Special	75	100	15	Normal	—
Twister	Dragon	Special	40	100	20	2 Foes	—
Heat Wave	Fire	Special	100	90	10	2 Foes	—
Pain Split	Normal	Status	—	—	20	Normal	—
Sky Attack	Flying	Physical	140	90	5	Normal	—

● TM & HM MOVES

No.	Name	Type	Kind	Pow.	Acc.	PP	Range	DA
TM04	Calm Mind	Psychic	Status	—	—	20	Self	—
TM06	Toxic	Poison	Status	—	85	10	Normal	—
TM10	Hidden Power	Normal	Special	—	100	15	Normal	—
TM11	Sunny Day	Fire	Status	—	—	5	All	—
TM15	Hyper Beam	Normal	Special	150	90	5	Normal	—
TM16	Light Screen	Psychic	Status	—	—	30	2 Allies	—
TM17	Protect	Normal	Status	—	—	10	Self	—
TM18	Rain Dance	Water	Status	—	—	5	All	—
TM19	Giga Drain	Grass	Special	60	100	10	Normal	—
TM21	Frustration	Normal	Physical	—	100	20	Normal	○
TM22	SolarBeam	Grass	Special	120	100	10	Normal	—
TM27	Return	Normal	Physical	—	100	20	Normal	○
TM29	Psychic	Psychic	Special	90	100	10	Normal	—
TM30	Shadow Ball	Ghost	Special	80	100	15	Normal	—
TM32	Double Team	Normal	Status	—	—	15	Self	—
TM33	Reflect	Psychic	Status	—	—	20	2 Allies	—
TM40	Aerial Ace	Flying	Physical	60	—	20	Normal	○
TM42	Facade	Normal	Physical	70	100	20	Normal	○
TM43	Secret Power	Normal	Physical	70	100	20	Normal	○
TM44	Rest	Psychic	Status	—	—	10	Self	—
TM45	Attract	Normal	Status	—	100	15	Normal	—
TM46	Thief	Dark	Physical	40	100	10	Normal	○
TM47	Steel Wing	Steel	Physical	70	90	25	Normal	○
TM48	Skill Swap	Psychic	Status	—	—	10	Normal	—
TM51	Roost	Flying	Status	—	—	10	Self	—
TM58	Endure	Normal	Status	—	—	10	Self	—
TM62	Silver Wind	Bug	Special	60	100	5	Normal	—
TM68	Giga Impact	Normal	Physical	150	90	5	Normal	○
TM70	Flash	Normal	Status	—	100	20	Normal	—
TM73	Thunder Wave	Electric	Status	—	100	20	Normal	—
TM77	Psych Up	Normal	Status	—	—	10	Normal	—
TM78	Captivate	Normal	Status	—	100	20	2 Foes	—
TM82	Sleep Talk	Normal	Status	—	—	10	Depends	—
TM83	Natural Gift	Normal	Physical	—	100	15	Normal	—
TM85	Dream Eater	Psychic	Special	100	100	15	Normal	—
TM86	Grass Knot	Grass	Special	—	100	20	Normal	○
TM87	Swagger	Normal	Status	—	90	15	Normal	—
TM88	Pluck	Flying	Physical	60	100	20	Normal	○
TM89	U-turn	Bug	Physical	70	100	20	Normal	○
TM90	Substitute	Normal	Status	—	—	10	Self	—
TM92	Trick Room	Psychic	Status	—	—	5	All	—
HM02	Fly	Flying	Physical	90	95	15	Normal	○

● No. 178 | Mystic Pokémon
Xatu

Psychic Flying

- ● HEIGHT: 4'07"
- ● WEIGHT: 78.5 lbs.
- ● ITEMS: None

● SIZE COMPARISON

● MALE FORM
Three stripes on body

● FEMALE FORM
Two stripes on body

◉ ABILITIES
- ● Synchronize
- ● Early Bird

◉ STATS
HP	●●
ATTACK	●●●
DEFENSE	●●●
SP. ATTACK	●●●●
SP. DEFENSE	●●●●
SPEED	●●●●

◉ EGG GROUPS
Flying

◉ PERFORMANCE
SPEED ★★☆   STAMINA ★★★★
POWER ★★★   JUMP ★★★☆
SKILL ★★★

● MAIN WAYS TO OBTAIN

Pokémon HeartGold — Trade Haunter to a man at the Pewter City Pokémon Center or level up Natu to Lv. 25

Pokémon SoulSilver — Trade Haunter to a man at the Pewter City Pokémon Center or level up Natu to Lv. 25

Pokémon Diamond — Level up Natu to Lv. 25

Pokémon Pearl — Level up Natu to Lv. 25

Pokémon Platinum — Level up Natu to Lv. 25

Pokémon HeartGold
They say that it stays still and quiet because it is seeing both the past and future at the same time.

Pokémon SoulSilver
In South America, it is said that its right eye sees the future and its left eye views the past.

◉ EVOLUTION

Natu —Lv. 25→ Xatu

No. 179 | Wool Pokémon
Mareep

LEVEL-UP MOVES

Lv.	Name	Type	Kind	Pow.	Acc.	PP	Range	DA
1	Tackle	Normal	Physical	35	95	35	Normal	○
5	Growl	Normal	Status	—	100	40	2 Foes	—
10	ThunderShock	Electric	Special	40	100	30	Normal	—
14	Thunder Wave	Electric	Status	—	100	20	Normal	—
19	Cotton Spore	Grass	Status	—	85	40	Normal	—
23	Charge	Electric	Status	—	—	20	Self	—
28	Discharge	Electric	Special	80	100	15	2 Foes/1 Ally	—
32	Signal Beam	Bug	Special	75	100	15	Normal	—
37	Light Screen	Psychic	Status	—	—	30	2 Allies	—
41	Power Gem	Rock	Special	70	100	20	Normal	—
46	Thunder	Electric	Special	120	70	10	Normal	—

MOVE MANIAC

Name	Type	Kind	Pow.	Acc.	PP	Range	DA
Headbutt	Normal	Physical	70	100	15	Normal	○

BP MOVES

Name	Type	Kind	Pow.	Acc.	PP	Range	DA
Snore	Normal	Special	40	100	15	Normal	—
Magnet Rise	Electric	Status	—	—	10	Self	—
Swift	Normal	Special	60	—	20	2 Foes	—
Heal Bell	Normal	Status	—	—	5	All Allies	—
Signal Beam	Bug	Special	75	100	15	Normal	—

- **HEIGHT:** 2'00"
- **WEIGHT:** 17.2 lbs.
- **ITEMS:** None

- **SIZE COMPARISON**

- **MALE/FEMALE HAVE SAME FORM**

ABILITIES
- Static

STATS
- HP ●●
- ATTACK ●●
- DEFENSE ●●
- SP. ATTACK ●●●
- SP. DEFENSE ●●
- SPEED ●●

EGG GROUPS
Monster

Field

PERFORMANCE
SPEED ★★☆
POWER ★★★
SKILL ★★☆
STAMINA ★★★★
JUMP ★★

MAIN WAYS TO OBTAIN

Pokémon HeartGold — Route 32

Pokémon SoulSilver — Route 32

Pokémon Diamond — Valley Windworks (use Poké Radar)

Pokémon Pearl — Valley Windworks (use Poké Radar)

Pokémon Platinum — Valley Windworks (use Poké Radar)

Pokémon HeartGold

If static electricity builds in its body, its fleece doubles in volume. Touching it will shock you.

Pokémon SoulSilver

Its fleece grows continually. In the summer, the fleece is fully shed, but it grows back in a week.

EVOLUTION

Mareep → Lv. 15 → Flaaffy → Lv. 15 → Ampharos

TM & HM MOVES

No.	Name	Type	Kind	Pow.	Acc.	PP	Range	DA
TM06	Toxic	Poison	Status	—	85	10	Normal	—
TM10	Hidden Power	Normal	Special	—	100	15	Normal	—
TM16	Light Screen	Psychic	Status	—	—	30	2 Allies	—
TM17	Protect	Normal	Status	—	—	10	Self	—
TM18	Rain Dance	Water	Status	—	—	5	All	—
TM21	Frustration	Normal	Physical	—	100	20	Normal	○
TM23	Iron Tail	Steel	Physical	100	75	15	Normal	○
TM24	Thunderbolt	Electric	Special	95	100	15	Normal	—
TM25	Thunder	Electric	Special	120	70	10	Normal	—
TM27	Return	Normal	Physical	—	100	20	Normal	○
TM32	Double Team	Normal	Status	—	—	15	Self	—
TM34	Shock Wave	Electric	Special	60	—	20	Normal	—
TM42	Facade	Normal	Physical	70	100	20	Normal	○
TM43	Secret Power	Normal	Physical	70	100	20	Normal	—
TM44	Rest	Psychic	Status	—	—	10	Self	—
TM45	Attract	Normal	Status	—	100	15	Normal	—
TM57	Charge Beam	Electric	Special	50	90	10	Normal	—
TM58	Endure	Normal	Status	—	—	10	Self	—
TM70	Flash	Normal	Status	—	100	20	Normal	—
TM73	Thunder Wave	Electric	Status	—	100	20	Normal	—
TM78	Captivate	Normal	Status	—	100	20	2 Foes	—
TM82	Sleep Talk	Normal	Status	—	—	10	Self	—
TM83	Natural Gift	Normal	Physical	—	100	15	Normal	—
TM87	Swagger	Normal	Status	—	90	15	Normal	—
TM90	Substitute	Normal	Status	—	—	10	Self	—

EGG MOVES

Name	Type	Kind	Pow.	Acc.	PP	Range	DA
Take Down	Normal	Physical	90	85	20	Normal	○
Body Slam	Normal	Physical	85	100	15	Normal	○
Safeguard	Normal	Status	—	—	25	2 Allies	—
Screech	Normal	Status	—	85	40	Normal	—
Reflect	Psychic	Status	—	—	20	2 Allies	—
Odor Sleuth	Normal	Status	—	—	40	Normal	—
Charge	Electric	Status	—	—	20	Self	—
Flatter	Dark	Status	—	100	15	Normal	—
Sand-Attack	Ground	Status	—	100	15	Normal	—

● LEVEL-UP MOVES

Lv.	Name	Type	Kind	Pow.	Acc.	PP	Range	DA
1	Tackle	Normal	Physical	35	95	35	Normal	○
1	Growl	Normal	Status	—	100	40	2 Foes	—
1	ThunderShock	Electric	Special	40	100	30	Normal	—
5	Growl	Normal	Status	—	100	40	2 Foes	—
10	ThunderShock	Electric	Special	40	100	30	Normal	—
14	Thunder Wave	Electric	Status	—	100	20	Normal	—
20	Cotton Spore	Grass	Status	—	85	40	Normal	—
25	Charge	Electric	Status	—	—	20	Self	—
31	Discharge	Electric	Special	80	100	15	2 Foes/1 Ally	—
36	Signal Beam	Bug	Special	75	100	15	Normal	—
42	Light Screen	Psychic	Status	—	—	30	2 Allies	—
47	Power Gem	Rock	Special	70	100	20	Normal	—
53	Thunder	Electric	Special	120	70	10	Normal	—

● MOVE MANIAC

Name	Type	Kind	Pow.	Acc.	PP	Range	DA
Headbutt	Normal	Physical	70	100	15	Normal	○

● BP MOVES

Name	Type	Kind	Pow.	Acc.	PP	Range	DA
ThunderPunch	Electric	Physical	75	100	15	Normal	○
Fire Punch	Fire	Physical	75	100	15	Normal	○
Snore	Normal	Special	40	100	15	Normal	—
Magnet Rise	Electric	Status	—	—	10	Self	—
Swift	Normal	Special	60	—	20	2 Foes	—
Heal Bell	Normal	Status	—	—	5	All Allies	—
Signal Beam	Bug	Special	75	100	15	Normal	—

● TM & HM MOVES

No.	Name	Type	Kind	Pow.	Acc.	PP	Range	DA
TM01	Focus Punch	Fighting	Physical	150	100	20	Normal	○
TM06	Toxic	Poison	Status	—	85	10	Normal	—
TM10	Hidden Power	Normal	Special	—	100	15	Normal	—
TM16	Light Screen	Psychic	Status	—	—	30	2 Allies	—
TM17	Protect	Normal	Status	—	—	10	Self	—
TM18	Rain Dance	Water	Status	—	—	5	All	—
TM21	Frustration	Normal	Physical	—	100	20	Normal	○
TM23	Iron Tail	Steel	Physical	100	75	15	Normal	○
TM24	Thunderbolt	Electric	Special	95	100	15	Normal	—
TM25	Thunder	Electric	Special	120	70	10	Normal	—
TM27	Return	Normal	Physical	—	100	20	Normal	○
TM31	Brick Break	Fighting	Physical	75	100	15	Normal	○
TM32	Double Team	Normal	Status	—	—	15	Self	—
TM34	Shock Wave	Electric	Special	60	—	20	Normal	—
TM42	Facade	Normal	Physical	70	100	20	Normal	○
TM43	Secret Power	Normal	Physical	70	100	20	Normal	○
TM44	Rest	Psychic	Status	—	—	10	Self	—
TM45	Attract	Normal	Status	—	100	15	Normal	—
TM56	Fling	Dark	Physical	—	100	10	Normal	—
TM57	Charge Beam	Electric	Special	50	90	10	Normal	—
TM58	Endure	Normal	Status	—	—	10	Self	—
TM70	Flash	Normal	Status	—	100	20	Normal	—
TM73	Thunder Wave	Electric	Status	—	100	20	Normal	—
TM78	Captivate	Normal	Status	—	100	20	2 Foes	—
TM82	Sleep Talk	Normal	Status	—	—	10	Depends	—
TM83	Natural Gift	Normal	Physical	—	100	15	Normal	—
TM87	Swagger	Normal	Status	—	90	15	Normal	—
TM90	Substitute	Normal	Status	—	—	10	Self	—
HM04	Strength	Normal	Physical	80	100	15	Normal	○
HM06	Rock Smash	Fighting	Physical	40	100	15	Normal	○

● No. 180 | Wool Pokémon
Flaaffy

Electric

- ● HEIGHT: 2'07"
- ● WEIGHT: 29.3 lbs.
- ● ITEMS: None

● SIZE COMPARISON

● MALE/FEMALE HAVE SAME FORM

● ABILITIES
- ● Static

● STATS
HP ●●●
ATTACK ●●
DEFENSE ●●
SP. ATTACK ●●●●
SP. DEFENSE ●●
SPEED ●●

● EGG GROUPS
Monster

Field

● PERFORMANCE
SPEED ★★☆　　STAMINA ★★★★
POWER ★★★　　JUMP ★★★
SKILL ★★★

● MAIN WAYS TO OBTAIN

Pokémon HeartGold Route 43

Pokémon SoulSilver Route 43

Pokémon Diamond Route 222 (use Poké Radar)

Pokémon Pearl Route 222 (use Poké Radar)

Pokémon Platinum Route 222 (use Poké Radar)

Pokémon HeartGold
As a result of storing too much electricity, it developed patches where even downy wool won't grow.

Pokémon SoulSilver
Its fluffy fleece easily stores electricity. Its rubbery hide keeps it from being electrocuted.

● EVOLUTION

Mareep ── Lv. 15 ── Flaaffy ── Lv. 15 ── Ampharos

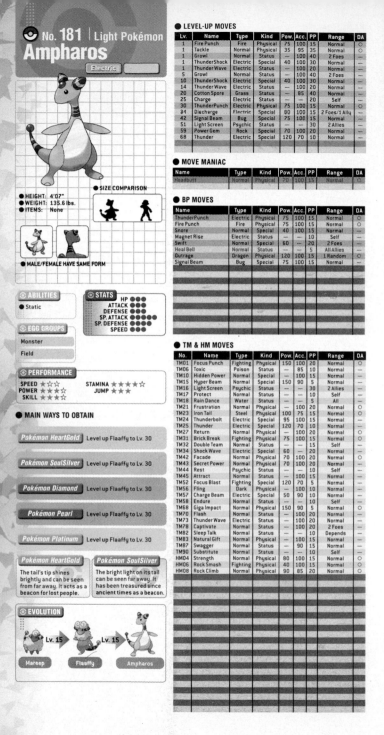

No. 181 | Light Pokémon
Ampharos

Electric

- **HEIGHT:** 4'07"
- **WEIGHT:** 135.6 lbs.
- **ITEMS:** None

● SIZE COMPARISON

● MALE/FEMALE HAVE SAME FORM

⊛ ABILITIES
- Static

⊛ STATS
- HP ●●●
- ATTACK ●●●
- DEFENSE ●●●
- SP. ATTACK ●●●●●
- SP. DEFENSE ●●●●
- SPEED ●●●

⊛ EGG GROUPS
- Monster
- Field

⊛ PERFORMANCE
- SPEED ★☆☆
- POWER ★★☆
- SKILL ★★★☆
- STAMINA ★★★★☆
- JUMP ★★★

● MAIN WAYS TO OBTAIN

Pokémon HeartGold	Level up Flaaffy to Lv. 30
Pokémon SoulSilver	Level up Flaaffy to Lv. 30
Pokémon Diamond	Level up Flaaffy to Lv. 30
Pokémon Pearl	Level up Flaaffy to Lv. 30
Pokémon Platinum	Level up Flaaffy to Lv. 30

Pokémon HeartGold	Pokémon SoulSilver
The tail's tip shines brightly and can be seen from far away. It acts as a beacon for lost people.	The bright light on its tail can be seen far away. It has been treasured since ancient times as a beacon.

⊛ EVOLUTION

Mareep — Lv. 15 → Flaaffy — Lv. 15 → Ampharos

● LEVEL-UP MOVES

Lv.	Name	Type	Kind	Pow.	Acc.	PP	Range	DA
1	Fire Punch	Fire	Physical	75	100	15	Normal	○
1	Tackle	Normal	Physical	35	95	35	Normal	—
1	Growl	Normal	Status	—	100	40	2 Foes	—
1	ThunderShock	Electric	Special	40	100	30	Normal	—
1	Thunder Wave	Electric	Status	—	100	20	Normal	—
5	Growl	Normal	Status	—	100	40	2 Foes	—
10	ThunderShock	Electric	Special	40	100	30	Normal	—
14	Thunder Wave	Electric	Status	—	100	20	Normal	—
20	Cotton Spore	Grass	Status	—	85	40	Normal	—
25	Charge	Electric	Status	—	—	20	Self	—
30	ThunderPunch	Electric	Physical	75	100	15	Normal	○
34	Discharge	Electric	Special	80	100	15	2 Foes; 1 Ally	—
42	Signal Beam	Bug	Special	75	100	15	Normal	—
51	Light Screen	Psychic	Status	—	—	30	2 Allies	—
59	Power Gem	Rock	Special	70	100	20	Normal	—
68	Thunder	Electric	Special	120	70	10	Normal	—

● MOVE MANIAC

Name	Type	Kind	Pow.	Acc.	PP	Range	DA
Headbutt	Normal	Physical	70	100	15	Normal	○

● BP MOVES

Name	Type	Kind	Pow.	Acc.	PP	Range	DA
ThunderPunch	Electric	Physical	75	100	15	Normal	○
Fire Punch	Fire	Physical	75	100	15	Normal	○
Spore	Normal	Special	40	100	15	Normal	—
Magnet Rise	Electric	Status	—	—	10	Self	—
Swift	Normal	Special	60	—	20	2 Foes	—
Heal Bell	Normal	Status	—	—	5	All Allies	—
Outrage	Dragon	Physical	120	100	15	1 Random	○
Signal Beam	Bug	Special	75	100	15	Normal	—

● TM & HM MOVES

No.	Name	Type	Kind	Pow.	Acc.	PP	Range	DA
TM01	Focus Punch	Fighting	Physical	150	100	20	Normal	○
TM06	Toxic	Poison	Status	—	85	10	Normal	—
TM10	Hidden Power	Normal	Special	—	100	15	Normal	—
TM15	Hyper Beam	Normal	Special	150	90	5	Normal	—
TM16	Light Screen	Psychic	Status	—	—	30	2 Allies	—
TM17	Protect	Normal	Status	—	—	10	Self	—
TM18	Rain Dance	Water	Status	—	—	5	All	—
TM21	Frustration	Normal	Physical	—	100	20	Normal	○
TM23	Iron Tail	Steel	Physical	100	75	15	Normal	○
TM24	Thunderbolt	Electric	Special	95	100	15	Normal	—
TM25	Thunder	Electric	Special	120	70	10	Normal	—
TM27	Return	Normal	Physical	—	100	20	Normal	○
TM31	Brick Break	Fighting	Physical	75	100	15	Normal	○
TM32	Double Team	Normal	Status	—	—	15	Self	—
TM34	Shock Wave	Electric	Special	60	—	20	Normal	—
TM42	Facade	Normal	Physical	70	100	20	Normal	○
TM43	Secret Power	Normal	Physical	70	100	20	Normal	—
TM44	Rest	Psychic	Status	—	—	10	Self	—
TM45	Attract	Normal	Status	—	100	15	Normal	—
TM52	Focus Blast	Fighting	Special	120	70	5	Normal	—
TM56	Fling	Dark	Physical	—	100	10	Normal	○
TM57	Charge Beam	Electric	Special	50	90	10	Normal	—
TM58	Endure	Normal	Status	—	—	10	Self	—
TM68	Giga Impact	Normal	Physical	150	90	5	Normal	○
TM70	Flash	Normal	Status	—	100	20	Normal	—
TM73	Thunder Wave	Electric	Status	—	100	20	Normal	—
TM78	Captivate	Normal	Status	—	100	20	2 Foes	—
TM82	Sleep Talk	Normal	Status	—	—	10	Depends	—
TM83	Natural Gift	Normal	Physical	—	100	15	Normal	○
TM87	Swagger	Normal	Status	—	90	15	Normal	—
TM90	Substitute	Normal	Status	—	—	10	Self	—
HM04	Strength	Normal	Physical	80	100	15	Normal	○
HM06	Rock Smash	Fighting	Physical	40	100	15	Normal	○
HM08	Rock Climb	Normal	Physical	90	85	20	Normal	○

● LEVEL-UP MOVES

Lv.	Name	Type	Kind	Pow.	Acc.	PP	Range	DA
1	Leaf Blade	Grass	Physical	90	100	15	Normal	○
1	Mega Drain	Grass	Special	40	100	15	Normal	—
1	Sweet Scent	Normal	Status	—	100	20	2 Foes	—
1	Stun Spore	Grass	Status	—	75	30	Normal	—
1	Sunny Day	Fire	Status	—	—	5	All	—
23	Magical Leaf	Grass	Special	60	—	20	Normal	—
53	Leaf Storm	Grass	Special	140	90	5	Normal	—

● MOVE MANIAC

Name	Type	Kind	Pow.	Acc.	PP	Range	DA

● BP MOVES

Name	Type	Kind	Pow.	Acc.	PP	Range	DA
Snore	Normal	Special	40	100	15	Normal	—
Synthesis	Grass	Status	—	—	5	Self	—
Uproar	Normal	Special	50	100	10	1 Random	—
Worry Seed	Grass	Status	—	100	10	Normal	—
Gastro Acid	Poison	Status	—	100	10	Normal	—
Seed Bomb	Grass	Physical	80	100	15	Normal	—

● TM & HM MOVES

No.	Name	Type	Kind	Pow.	Acc.	PP	Range	DA
TM06	Toxic	Poison	Status	—	85	10	Normal	—
TM09	Bullet Seed	Grass	Physical	10	100	30	Normal	—
TM10	Hidden Power	Normal	Special	—	100	15	Normal	—
TM11	Sunny Day	Fire	Status	—	—	5	All	—
TM15	Hyper Beam	Normal	Special	150	90	5	Normal	—
TM17	Protect	Normal	Status	—	—	10	Self	—
TM19	Giga Drain	Grass	Special	60	100	10	Normal	—
TM20	Safeguard	Normal	Status	—	—	25	2 Allies	—
TM21	Frustration	Normal	Physical	—	100	20	Normal	○
TM22	SolarBeam	Grass	Special	120	100	10	Normal	—
TM27	Return	Normal	Physical	—	100	20	Normal	○
TM32	Double Team	Normal	Status	—	—	15	Self	—
TM36	Sludge Bomb	Poison	Special	90	100	10	Normal	—
TM42	Facade	Normal	Physical	70	100	20	Normal	—
TM43	Secret Power	Normal	Physical	70	100	20	Normal	○
TM44	Rest	Psychic	Status	—	—	10	Self	—
TM45	Attract	Normal	Status	—	100	15	Normal	—
TM53	Energy Ball	Grass	Special	80	100	10	Normal	—
TM56	Fling	Dark	Physical	—	100	10	Normal	—
TM58	Endure	Normal	Status	—	—	10	Self	—
TM60	Drain Punch	Fighting	Physical	60	100	5	Normal	○
TM68	Giga Impact	Normal	Physical	150	90	5	Normal	○
TM70	Flash	Normal	Status	—	100	20	Normal	—
TM75	Swords Dance	Normal	Status	—	—	30	Self	—
TM78	Captivate	Normal	Status	—	100	20	2 Foes	—
TM82	Sleep Talk	Normal	Status	—	—	10	Depends	—
TM83	Natural Gift	Normal	Physical	—	100	15	Normal	—
TM86	Grass Knot	Grass	Special	—	100	20	Normal	○
TM87	Swagger	Normal	Status	—	90	15	Normal	—
TM90	Substitute	Normal	Status	—	—	10	Self	—
HM01	Cut	Normal	Physical	50	95	30	Normal	○

○ **No. 182** | Flower Pokémon

Bellossom

`Grass`

- ● **HEIGHT:** 1'04"
- ● **WEIGHT:** 12.8 lbs.
- ● **ITEMS:** None

● SIZE COMPARISON

● MALE/FEMALE HAVE SAME FORM

◎ ABILITIES
● Chlorophyll

◎ STATS
HP	●●●
ATTACK	●●●
DEFENSE	●●●
SP. ATTACK	●●●●
SP. DEFENSE	●●●●
SPEED	●●

◎ EGG GROUPS
Grass

◎ PERFORMANCE
SPEED ★★★☆	STAMINA ★★★
POWER ★★☆	JUMP ★★★☆
SKILL ★★★★☆	

● MAIN WAYS TO OBTAIN

Pokémon HeartGold	Use Sun Stone on Gloom
Pokémon SoulSilver	Use Sun Stone on Gloom
Pokémon Diamond	Use Sun Stone on Gloom
Pokémon Pearl	Use Sun Stone on Gloom
Pokémon Platinum	Use Sun Stone on Gloom

Pokémon HeartGold
BELLOSSOM gather at times and seem to dance. They say that the dance is a ritual to summon he sun.

Pokémon SoulSilver
Plentiful in the tropics. When it dances, its petals rub together and make a pleasant ringing sound.

◎ EVOLUTION

Oddish — Lv. 21 → Gloom
Gloom — Use Leaf Stone → Vileplume
Gloom — Use Sun Stone → Bellossom

No. 183 | Aqua Mouse Pokémon
Marill

Water

- **HEIGHT:** 1'04"
- **WEIGHT:** 18.7 lbs.
- **ITEMS:** None

● SIZE COMPARISON

● MALE/FEMALE HAVE SAME FORM

⊚ ABILITIES
- Thick Fat
- Huge Power

⊚ STATS
HP	●●●
ATTACK	●
DEFENSE	●●
SP. ATTACK	●●
SP. DEFENSE	●●
SPEED	●●

⊚ EGG GROUPS
Water 1

Fairy

⊚ PERFORMANCE
SPEED ★★★☆	STAMINA ★★☆
POWER ★★★★☆	JUMP ★★★
SKILL ★★☆	

● MAIN WAYS TO OBTAIN

Pokémon HeartGold	Safari Zone (Meadow Area water surface)
Pokémon SoulSilver	Safari Zone (Meadow Area water surface)
Pokémon Diamond	Pastoria Great Marsh
Pokémon Pearl	Pastoria Great Marsh
Pokémon Platinum	Route 215

Pokémon HeartGold
The tip of its tail, which contains oil that is lighter than water, lets it swim without drowning.

Pokémon SoulSilver
The end of its tail serves as a buoy that keeps it from drowning, even in a vicious current.

⊚ EVOLUTION

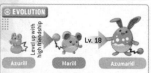

Azurill → Marill (Level up with high friendship) → Azumarill (Lv. 18)

● LEVEL-UP MOVES
Lv.	Name	Type	Kind	Pow.	Acc.	PP	Range	DA
1	Tackle	Normal	Physical	35	95	35	Normal	○
2	Defense Curl	Normal	Status	—	—	40	Self	—
7	Tail Whip	Normal	Status	—	100	30	2 Foes	—
10	Water Gun	Water	Special	40	100	25	Normal	—
15	Rollout	Rock	Physical	30	90	20	Normal	○
18	BubbleBeam	Water	Special	65	100	20	Normal	—
23	Aqua Ring	Water	Status	—	—	20	Self	—
27	Double-Edge	Normal	Physical	120	100	15	Normal	○
32	Rain Dance	Water	Status	—	—	5	All	—
37	Aqua Tail	Water	Physical	90	90	10	Normal	○
42	Hydro Pump	Water	Special	120	80	5	Normal	—

● MOVE MANIAC
Name	Type	Kind	Pow.	Acc.	PP	Range	DA
Headbutt	Normal	Physical	70	100	15	Normal	○

● BP MOVES
Name	Type	Kind	Pow.	Acc.	PP	Range	DA
Dive	Water	Physical	80	100	10	Normal	○
Icy Wind	Ice	Special	55	95	15	2 Foes	—
Ice Punch	Ice	Physical	75	100	20	Normal	○
Knock Off	Dark	Physical	20	100	20	Normal	○
Snore	Normal	Special	40	100	15	Normal	—
Helping Hand	Normal	Status	—	—	20	1 Ally	—
Swift	Normal	Special	60	—	20	2 Foes	—
Mud-Slap	Ground	Special	20	100	10	Normal	—
Rollout	Rock	Physical	30	90	20	Normal	○
Superpower	Fighting	Physical	120	100	5	Normal	○
Aqua Tail	Water	Physical	90	90	10	Normal	○

● TM & HM MOVES
No.	Name	Type	Kind	Pow.	Acc.	PP	Range	DA
TM01	Focus Punch	Fighting	Physical	150	100	20	Normal	○
TM03	Water Pulse	Water	Special	60	100	20	Normal	—
TM06	Toxic	Poison	Status	—	85	10	Normal	—
TM07	Hail	Ice	Status	—	—	10	All	—
TM10	Hidden Power	Normal	Special	—	100	15	Normal	—
TM13	Ice Beam	Ice	Special	95	100	10	Normal	—
TM14	Blizzard	Ice	Special	120	70	5	2 Foes	—
TM17	Protect	Normal	Status	—	—	10	Self	—
TM18	Rain Dance	Water	Status	—	—	5	All	—
TM21	Frustration	Normal	Physical	—	100	20	Normal	○
TM23	Iron Tail	Steel	Physical	100	75	15	Normal	○
TM27	Return	Normal	Physical	—	100	20	Normal	○
TM28	Dig	Ground	Physical	80	100	10	Normal	○
TM31	Brick Break	Fighting	Physical	75	100	15	Normal	○
TM32	Double Team	Normal	Status	—	—	15	Self	—
TM42	Facade	Normal	Physical	70	100	20	Normal	○
TM43	Secret Power	Normal	Physical	70	100	20	Normal	○
TM44	Rest	Psychic	Status	—	—	10	Self	—
TM45	Attract	Normal	Status	—	100	15	Normal	—
TM56	Fling	Dark	Physical	—	100	10	Normal	—
TM58	Endure	Normal	Status	—	—	10	Self	—
TM78	Captivate	Normal	Status	—	100	20	2 Foes	—
TM82	Sleep Talk	Normal	Status	—	—	10	Depends	—
TM83	Natural Gift	Normal	Physical	—	100	15	Normal	—
TM86	Grass Knot	Grass	Special	—	100	20	Normal	○
TM87	Swagger	Normal	Status	—	90	15	Normal	—
TM90	Substitute	Normal	Status	—	—	10	Self	—
HM03	Surf	Water	Special	95	100	15	2 Foes/1 Ally	—
HM04	Strength	Normal	Physical	80	100	15	Normal	○
HM05	Whirlpool	Water	Special	15	70	15	Normal	—
HM06	Rock Smash	Fighting	Physical	40	100	15	Normal	○
HM07	Waterfall	Water	Physical	80	100	15	Normal	○

● EGG MOVES
Name	Type	Kind	Pow.	Acc.	PP	Range	DA
Light Screen	Psychic	Status	—	—	30	2 Allies	—
Present	Normal	Physical	—	90	15	Normal	—
Amnesia	Psychic	Status	—	—	20	Self	—
Future Sight	Psychic	Special	80	90	15	Normal	—
Belly Drum	Normal	Status	—	—	10	Self	—
Perish Song	Normal	Status	—	—	5	All	—
Supersonic	Normal	Status	—	55	20	Normal	—
Substitute	Normal	Status	—	—	10	Self	—
Aqua Jet	Water	Physical	40	100	20	Normal	○
Superpower	Fighting	Physical	120	100	5	Normal	○
Refresh	Normal	Status	—	—	20	Self	—
Body Slam	Normal	Physical	85	100	15	Normal	○

● LEVEL-UP MOVES

Lv.	Name	Type	Kind	Pow.	Acc.	PP	Range	DA
1	Tackle	Normal	Physical	35	95	35	Normal	○
1	Defense Curl	Normal	Status	—	—	40	Self	—
1	Tail Whip	Normal	Status	—	100	30	2 Foes	—
1	Water Gun	Water	Special	40	100	25	Normal	—
2	Defense Curl	Normal	Status	—	—	40	Self	—
7	Tail Whip	Normal	Status	—	100	30	2 Foes	—
10	Water Gun	Water	Special	40	100	25	Normal	—
15	Rollout	Rock	Physical	30	90	20	Normal	○
20	BubbleBeam	Water	Special	65	100	20	Normal	—
27	Aqua Ring	Water	Status	—	—	20	Self	—
33	Double-Edge	Normal	Physical	120	100	15	Normal	○
40	Rain Dance	Water	Status	—	—	5	All	—
47	Aqua Tail	Water	Physical	90	90	10	Normal	○
54	Hydro Pump	Water	Special	120	80	5	Normal	—

● MOVE MANIAC

Name	Type	Kind	Pow.	Acc.	PP	Range	DA
Headbutt	Normal	Physical	70	100	15	Normal	○

● BP MOVES

Name	Type	Kind	Pow.	Acc.	PP	Range	DA
Dive	Water	Physical	80	100	10	Normal	○
Icy Wind	Ice	Special	55	95	15	2 Foes	—
Ice Punch	Ice	Physical	75	100	15	Normal	○
Knock Off	Dark	Physical	20	100	20	Normal	○
Snore	Normal	Special	40	100	15	Normal	—
Helping Hand	Normal	Status	—	—	20	1 Ally	—
Swift	Normal	Special	60	—	20	2 Foes	—
Mud-Slap	Ground	Special	20	100	10	Normal	—
Rollout	Rock	Physical	30	90	20	Normal	○
Superpower	Fighting	Physical	120	100	5	Normal	○
Aqua Tail	Water	Physical	90	90	10	Normal	○

● TM & HM MOVES

No.	Name	Type	Kind	Pow.	Acc.	PP	Range	DA
TM01	Focus Punch	Fighting	Physical	150	100	20	Normal	○
TM03	Water Pulse	Water	Special	60	100	20	Normal	—
TM06	Toxic	Poison	Status	—	85	10	Normal	—
TM07	Hail	Ice	Status	—	—	10	All	—
TM10	Hidden Power	Normal	Special	—	100	15	Normal	—
TM13	Ice Beam	Ice	Special	95	100	10	Normal	—
TM14	Blizzard	Ice	Special	120	70	5	2 Foes	—
TM15	Hyper Beam	Normal	Special	150	90	5	Normal	—
TM17	Protect	Normal	Status	—	—	10	Self	—
TM18	Rain Dance	Water	Status	—	—	5	All	—
TM21	Frustration	Normal	Physical	—	100	20	Normal	○
TM23	Iron Tail	Steel	Physical	100	75	15	Normal	○
TM27	Return	Normal	Physical	—	100	20	Normal	○
TM28	Dig	Ground	Physical	80	100	10	Normal	○
TM31	Brick Break	Fighting	Physical	75	100	15	Normal	○
TM32	Double Team	Normal	Status	—	—	15	Self	—
TM42	Facade	Normal	Physical	70	100	20	Normal	○
TM43	Secret Power	Normal	Physical	70	100	20	Normal	○
TM44	Rest	Psychic	Status	—	—	10	Self	—
TM45	Attract	Normal	Status	—	100	15	Normal	—
TM52	Focus Blast	Fighting	Special	120	70	5	Normal	—
TM56	Fling	Dark	Physical	—	100	10	Normal	—
TM58	Endure	Normal	Status	—	—	10	Self	—
TM68	Giga Impact	Normal	Physical	150	90	5	Normal	○
TM78	Captivate	Normal	Status	—	100	20	2 Foes	—
TM82	Sleep Talk	Normal	Status	—	—	10	Depends	—
TM83	Natural Gift	Normal	Physical	—	100	15	Normal	—
TM86	Grass Knot	Grass	Special	—	100	20	Normal	○
TM87	Swagger	Normal	Status	—	90	15	Normal	—
TM90	Substitute	Normal	Status	—	—	10	Self	—
HM03	Surf	Water	Special	95	100	15	2 Foes/1 Ally	—
HM04	Strength	Normal	Physical	80	100	15	Normal	○
HM05	Whirlpool	Water	Special	15	70	15	Normal	—
HM06	Rock Smash	Fighting	Physical	40	100	15	Normal	○
HM07	Waterfall	Water	Physical	80	100	15	Normal	○

● HEIGHT: 2'02"
● WEIGHT: 62.8 lbs.
● ITEMS: None

● SIZE COMPARISON

● MALE/FEMALE HAVE SAME FORM

◎ ABILITIES
● Thick Fat
● Huge Power

◎ STATS
HP ●●●●
ATTACK ●●
DEFENSE ●●
SP. ATTACK ●●
SP. DEFENSE ●●●
SPEED ●●

◎ EGG GROUPS
Water 1
Fairy

◎ PERFORMANCE

SPEED ★★☆	STAMINA ★★★☆
POWER ★★★★★	JUMP ★★
SKILL ★★★	

● MAIN WAYS TO OBTAIN

Pokémon HeartGold	Level up Marill to Lv. 18
Pokémon SoulSilver	Level up Marill to Lv. 18
Pokémon Diamond	Level up Marill to Lv. 18
Pokémon Pearl	Level up Marill to Lv. 18
Pokémon Platinum	Victory Road 1F Back 2

Pokémon HeartGold	*Pokémon SoulSilver*
By keeping still and listening intently, it can tell what is in even wild, fast-moving rivers.	When it plays in water, it rolls up its elongated ears to prevent their insides from getting wet.

◎ EVOLUTION

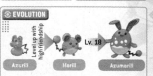

Level up with high friendship → Lv. 18 →

Azurill — Marill — Azumarill

Sudowoodo

`Rock`

- **HEIGHT:** 0'08"
- **WEIGHT:** 4.4 lbs.
- **ITEMS:** None

● **SIZE COMPARISON**

● **MALE FORM**
Larger branches on head

● **FEMALE FORM**
Smaller branches on head

⊙ ABILITIES
- Sturdy
- Rock Head

⊙ STATS
HP	●●●
ATTACK	●●●●
DEFENSE	●●●●●
SP. ATTACK	●●●
SP. DEFENSE	●●
SPEED	●

⊙ EGG GROUPS
Mineral

⊙ PERFORMANCE
SPEED	★★	STAMINA	★★★★☆
POWER	★★★☆	JUMP	★★☆
SKILL	★★★☆		

● MAIN WAYS TO OBTAIN

Pokémon HeartGold	Use the SquirtBottle to water the odd tree on Route 36
Pokémon SoulSilver	Use the SquirtBottle to water the odd tree on Route 36
Pokémon Diamond	Level up Bonsly to Lv. 17 and have it learn Mimic, or level it up once it knows Mimic
Pokémon Pearl	Route 221
Pokémon Platinum	Route 221

Pokémon HeartGold	**Pokémon SoulSilver**
Although it always pretends to be a tree, its composition appears more similar to rock than to vegetation.	It disguises itself as a tree to avoid attack. It hates water, so it will disappear if it starts raining.

⊙ EVOLUTION

Bonsly → Sudowoodo

Level it up to Lv. 17 and teach it Mimic. Or, level it up once it knows Mimic.

● LEVEL-UP MOVES

Lv.	Name	Type	Kind	Pow.	Acc.	PP	Range	DA
1	Wood Hammer	Grass	Physical	120	100	15	Normal	—
1	Copycat	Normal	Status	—	—	20	Depends	—
1	Flail	Normal	Physical	—	100	15	Normal	○
1	Low Kick	Fighting	Physical	—	100	20	Normal	○
1	Rock Throw	Rock	Physical	50	90	15	Normal	—
6	Flail	Normal	Physical	—	100	15	Normal	○
9	Low Kick	Fighting	Physical	—	100	20	Normal	○
14	Rock Throw	Rock	Physical	50	90	15	Normal	—
17	Mimic	Normal	Status	—	—	10	Normal	—
22	Block	Normal	Status	—	—	5	Normal	—
25	Faint Attack	Dark	Physical	60	—	20	Normal	○
30	Rock Tomb	Rock	Physical	50	80	10	Normal	—
33	Rock Slide	Rock	Physical	75	90	10	2 Foes	—
38	Slam	Normal	Physical	80	75	20	Normal	○
41	Sucker Punch	Dark	Physical	80	100	5	Normal	○
46	Double-Edge	Normal	Physical	120	100	15	Normal	○
49	Hammer Arm	Fighting	Physical	100	90	10	Normal	○

● MOVE MANIAC

Name	Type	Kind	Pow.	Acc.	PP	Range	DA
Headbutt	Normal	Physical	70	100	15	Normal	○

● BP MOVES

Name	Type	Kind	Pow.	Acc.	PP	Range	DA
ThunderPunch	Electric	Physical	75	100	15	Normal	○
Fire Punch	Fire	Physical	75	100	15	Normal	○
Ice Punch	Ice	Physical	75	100	15	Normal	○
Sucker Punch	Dark	Physical	80	100	5	Normal	○
Snore	Normal	Special	40	100	15	Normal	—
Helping Hand	Normal	Status	—	—	20	1 Ally	—
Role Play	Psychic	Status	—	—	10	Normal	—
Block	Normal	Status	—	—	5	Normal	—
Mud-Slap	Ground	Special	20	100	10	Normal	—
Rollout	Rock	Physical	30	90	20	Normal	○
Earth Power	Ground	Special	90	100	10	Normal	—
Low Kick	Fighting	Physical	—	100	20	Normal	○

● TM & HM MOVES

No.	Name	Type	Kind	Pow.	Acc.	PP	Range	DA
TM01	Focus Punch	Fighting	Physical	150	100	20	Normal	○
TM04	Calm Mind	Psychic	Status	—	—	20	Self	—
TM06	Toxic	Poison	Status	—	85	10	Normal	—
TM10	Hidden Power	Normal	Special	—	100	15	Normal	—
TM11	Sunny Day	Fire	Status	—	—	5	All	—
TM12	Taunt	Dark	Status	—	100	20	Normal	—
TM17	Protect	Normal	Status	—	—	10	Self	—
TM21	Frustration	Normal	Physical	—	100	20	Normal	○
TM26	Earthquake	Ground	Physical	100	100	10	2 Foes/1 Ally	—
TM27	Return	Normal	Physical	—	100	20	Normal	○
TM28	Dig	Ground	Physical	80	100	10	Normal	—
TM31	Brick Break	Fighting	Physical	75	100	15	Normal	○
TM32	Double Team	Normal	Status	—	—	15	Self	—
TM37	Sandstorm	Rock	Status	—	—	10	All	—
TM39	Rock Tomb	Rock	Physical	50	80	10	Normal	—
TM41	Torment	Dark	Status	—	100	15	Normal	—
TM42	Facade	Normal	Physical	70	100	20	Normal	—
TM43	Secret Power	Normal	Physical	70	100	20	Normal	—
TM44	Rest	Psychic	Status	—	—	10	Self	—
TM45	Attract	Normal	Status	—	100	15	Normal	—
TM46	Thief	Dark	Physical	40	100	10	Normal	—
TM56	Fling	Dark	Physical	—	100	10	Normal	—
TM58	Endure	Normal	Status	—	—	10	Self	—
TM64	Explosion	Normal	Physical	250	100	5	2 Foes/1 Ally	—
TM69	Rock Polish	Rock	Status	—	—	20	Self	—
TM71	Stone Edge	Rock	Physical	100	80	5	Normal	—
TM76	Stealth Rock	Rock	Status	—	—	20	2 Foes	—
TM77	Psych Up	Normal	Status	—	—	10	Normal	—
TM78	Captivate	Normal	Status	—	100	20	2 Foes	—
TM80	Rock Slide	Rock	Physical	75	90	10	2 Foes	—
TM82	Sleep Talk	Normal	Status	—	—	10	Depends	—
TM83	Natural Gift	Normal	Physical	—	100	15	Normal	—
TM87	Swagger	Normal	Status	—	90	15	Normal	—
TM90	Substitute	Normal	Status	—	—	10	Self	—
HM04	Strength	Normal	Physical	80	100	15	Normal	○
HM06	Rock Smash	Fighting	Physical	40	100	15	Normal	○

● EGG MOVES

Name	Type	Kind	Pow.	Acc.	PP	Range	DA
Selfdestruct	Normal	Physical	200	100	5	2 Foes/1 Ally	—
Headbutt	Normal	Physical	70	100	15	Normal	—
Harden	Normal	Status	—	—	30	Self	—
Defense Curl	Normal	Status	—	—	40	Self	—
Rollout	Rock	Physical	30	90	20	Normal	○
Sand Tomb	Ground	Physical	15	70	15	Normal	—

● LEVEL-UP MOVES

Lv.	Name	Type	Kind	Pow.	Acc.	PP	Range	DA
1	BubbleBeam	Water	Special	65	100	20	Normal	—
1	Hypnosis	Psychic	Status	—	60	20	Normal	—
1	DoubleSlap	Normal	Physical	15	85	10	Normal	O
1	Perish Song	Normal	Status	—	—	5	All	—
27	Swagger	Normal	Status	—	90	15	Normal	—
37	Bounce	Flying	Physical	85	85	5	Normal	O
48	Hyper Voice	Normal	Special	90	100	10	2 Foes	—

● MOVE MANIAC

Name	Type	Kind	Pow.	Acc.	PP	Range	DA
Headbutt	Normal	Physical	70	100	15	Normal	O

● BP MOVES

Name	Type	Kind	Pow.	Acc.	PP	Range	DA
Dive	Water	Physical	80	100	10	Normal	O
Icy Wind	Ice	Special	55	95	15	2 Foes	—
Snore	Normal	Special	40	100	15	Normal	—
Helping Hand	Normal	Status	—	—	20	1 Ally	—
Mud-Slap	Ground	Special	20	100	10	Normal	—
Bounce	Flying	Physical	85	85	5	Normal	O

● TM & HM MOVES

No.	Name	Type	Kind	Pow.	Acc.	PP	Range	DA
TM01	Focus Punch	Fighting	Physical	150	100	20	Normal	O
TM03	Water Pulse	Water	Special	60	100	20	Normal	—
TM06	Toxic	Poison	Status	—	85	10	Normal	—
TM07	Hail	Ice	Status	—	—	10	All	—
TM10	Hidden Power	Normal	Special	—	100	15	Normal	—
TM13	Ice Beam	Ice	Special	95	100	10	Normal	—
TM14	Blizzard	Ice	Special	120	70	5	2 Foes	—
TM15	Hyper Beam	Normal	Special	150	90	5	Normal	—
TM17	Protect	Normal	Status	—	—	10	Self	—
TM18	Rain Dance	Water	Status	—	—	5	All	—
TM21	Frustration	Normal	Physical	—	100	20	Normal	O
TM26	Earthquake	Ground	Physical	100	100	10	2 Foes/1 Ally	—
TM27	Return	Normal	Physical	—	100	20	Normal	O
TM28	Dig	Ground	Physical	80	100	10	Normal	O
TM29	Psychic	Psychic	Special	90	100	10	Normal	—
TM31	Brick Break	Fighting	Physical	75	100	15	Normal	O
TM32	Double Team	Normal	Status	—	—	15	Self	—
TM42	Facade	Normal	Physical	70	100	20	Normal	O
TM43	Secret Power	Normal	Physical	70	100	20	Normal	—
TM44	Rest	Psychic	Status	—	—	10	Self	—
TM45	Attract	Normal	Status	—	100	15	Normal	—
TM46	Thief	Dark	Physical	40	100	10	Normal	O
TM52	Focus Blast	Fighting	Special	120	70	5	Normal	—
TM56	Fling	Dark	Physical	—	100	10	Normal	O
TM58	Endure	Normal	Status	—	—	10	Self	—
TM66	Payback	Dark	Physical	50	100	10	Normal	O
TM68	Giga Impact	Normal	Physical	150	90	5	Normal	O
TM78	Captivate	Normal	Status	—	100	20	2 Foes	—
TM82	Sleep Talk	Normal	Status	—	—	10	Depends	—
TM83	Natural Gift	Normal	Physical	—	100	15	Normal	—
TM87	Swagger	Normal	Status	—	90	15	Normal	—
TM90	Substitute	Normal	Status	—	—	10	Self	—
HM03	Surf	Water	Special	95	100	15	2 Foes/1 Ally	—
HM04	Strength	Normal	Physical	80	100	15	Normal	O
HM05	Whirlpool	Water	Special	15	70	15	Normal	—
HM06	Rock Smash	Fighting	Physical	40	100	15	Normal	O
HM07	Waterfall	Water	Physical	80	100	15	Normal	O

◉ No. 186 | Frog Pokémon
Politoed

Water

● HEIGHT: 3'07"
● WEIGHT: 74.7 lbs.
● ITEMS: None

● SIZE COMPARISON

● MALE FORM
Larger cheek spots

● FEMALE FORM
Smaller cheek spots

◎ ABILITIES
● Water Absorb
● Damp

◎ STATS
HP ●●●
ATTACK ●●●
DEFENSE ●●●
SP. ATTACK ●●●
SP. DEFENSE ●●●●
SPEED ●●●

◎ EGG GROUPS
Water 1

◎ PERFORMANCE
SPEED ★★★   STAMINA ★★★☆
POWER ★★★☆ JUMP ★★★★
SKILL ★★★☆

● MAIN WAYS TO OBTAIN

Pokémon HeartGold — Link trade Poliwhirl while it holds the King's Rock

Pokémon SoulSilver — Link trade Poliwhirl while it holds the King's Rock

Pokémon Diamond — Link trade Poliwhirl while it holds the King's Rock

Pokémon Pearl — Link trade Poliwhirl while it holds the King's Rock

Pokémon Platinum — Link trade Poliwhirl while it holds the King's Rock

Pokémon HeartGold
If POLIWAG and POLIWHIRL hear its echoing cry, they respond by gathering from far and wide.

Pokémon SoulSilver
Whenever three or more of these get together, they sing in a loud voice that sounds like bellowing.

◎ EVOLUTION

Use Water Stone → Poliwrath

Poliwag — Lv. 25 → Poliwhirl — Have it hold King's Rock and trade it → Politoed

No. 187 | Cottonweed Pokémon
Hoppip

Grass **Flying**

● HEIGHT: 1'04"
● WEIGHT: 1.1 lbs.
● ITEMS: None

● SIZE COMPARISON

● MALE/FEMALE HAVE SAME FORM

ABILITIES
● Chlorophyll
● Leaf Guard

STATS
HP ●●
ATTACK ●●
DEFENSE ●●
SP. ATTACK ●●
SP. DEFENSE ●●
SPEED ●●

EGG GROUPS
Fairy
Grass

PERFORMANCE
SPEED ★★★☆☆   STAMINA ★
POWER ★☆   JUMP ★★★★★
SKILL ★

MAIN WAYS TO OBTAIN

Pokémon HeartGold	Route 32 (morning and afternoon only)
Pokémon SoulSilver	Route 32 (morning and afternoon only)
Pokémon Diamond	Route 205, Floaroma Town side (use Poké Radar)
Pokémon Pearl	Route 205, Floaroma Town side (use Poké Radar)
Pokémon Platinum	Route 205, Floaroma Town side (use Poké Radar)

Pokémon HeartGold
To keep from being blown away by the wind, they gather in clusters. But they do enjoy gentle breezes.

Pokémon SoulSilver
Its body is so light, it must grip the ground firmly with its feet to keep from being blown away.

EVOLUTION

Lv. 18 Lv. 27

Hoppip — Skiploom — Jumpluff

● LEVEL-UP MOVES

Lv.	Name	Type	Kind	Pow.	Acc.	PP	Range	DA
1	Splash	Normal	Status	—	—	40	Self	—
4	Synthesis	Grass	Status	—	—	5	Self	—
7	Tail Whip	Normal	Status	—	100	30	2 Foes	—
10	Tackle	Normal	Physical	35	95	35	Normal	○
12	PoisonPowder	Poison	Status	—	75	35	Normal	—
14	Stun Spore	Grass	Status	—	75	30	Normal	—
16	Sleep Powder	Grass	Status	—	75	15	Normal	—
19	Bullet Seed	Grass	Physical	10	100	30	Normal	—
22	Leech Seed	Grass	Status	—	90	10	Normal	—
25	Mega Drain	Grass	Special	40	100	15	Normal	—
28	Cotton Spore	Grass	Status	—	85	40	Normal	—
31	U-turn	Bug	Physical	70	100	20	Normal	○
34	Worry Seed	Grass	Status	—	100	10	Normal	—
37	Giga Drain	Grass	Special	60	100	10	Normal	—
40	Bounce	Flying	Physical	85	85	5	Normal	○
43	Memento	Dark	Status	—	100	10	Normal	—

● MOVE MANIAC

Name	Type	Kind	Pow.	Acc.	PP	Range	DA
Headbutt	Normal	Physical	70	100	15	Normal	○

● BP MOVES

Name	Type	Kind	Pow.	Acc.	PP	Range	DA
Snore	Normal	Special	40	100	15	Normal	—
Helping Hand	Normal	Status	—	—	20	1 Ally	—
Synthesis	Grass	Status	—	—	5	Self	—
Worry Seed	Grass	Status	—	100	10	Normal	—
Seed Bomb	Grass	Physical	80	100	15	Normal	—
Bounce	Flying	Physical	85	85	5	Normal	○

● TM & HM MOVES

No.	Name	Type	Kind	Pow.	Acc.	PP	Range	DA
TM06	Toxic	Poison	Status	—	85	10	Normal	—
TM09	Bullet Seed	Grass	Physical	10	100	30	Normal	—
TM10	Hidden Power	Normal	Special	—	100	15	Normal	—
TM11	Sunny Day	Fire	Status	—	—	5	All	—
TM17	Protect	Normal	Status	—	—	10	Self	—
TM19	Giga Drain	Grass	Special	60	100	10	Normal	—
TM21	Frustration	Normal	Physical	—	100	20	Normal	○
TM22	SolarBeam	Grass	Special	120	100	10	Normal	—
TM27	Return	Normal	Physical	—	100	20	Normal	○
TM32	Double Team	Normal	Status	—	—	15	Self	—
TM40	Aerial Ace	Flying	Physical	60	—	20	Normal	○
TM42	Facade	Normal	Physical	70	100	20	Normal	○
TM43	Secret Power	Normal	Physical	70	100	20	Normal	—
TM44	Rest	Psychic	Status	—	—	10	Self	—
TM45	Attract	Normal	Status	—	100	15	Normal	—
TM53	Energy Ball	Grass	Special	80	100	10	Normal	—
TM58	Endure	Normal	Status	—	—	10	Self	—
TM62	Silver Wind	Bug	Special	60	100	5	Normal	—
TM70	Flash	Normal	Status	—	100	20	Normal	—
TM75	Swords Dance	Normal	Status	—	—	30	Self	—
TM78	Captivate	Normal	Status	—	100	20	2 Foes	—
TM82	Sleep Talk	Normal	Status	—	—	10	Self	—
TM83	Natural Gift	Normal	Physical	—	100	15	Normal	—
TM86	Grass Knot	Grass	Special	—	100	20	Normal	○
TM87	Swagger	Normal	Status	—	90	15	Normal	—
TM89	U-turn	Bug	Physical	70	100	20	Normal	○
TM90	Substitute	Normal	Status	—	—	10	Self	—

● EGG MOVES

Name	Type	Kind	Pow.	Acc.	PP	Range	DA
Confusion	Psychic	Special	50	100	25	Normal	—
Encore	Normal	Status	—	100	5	Normal	—
Double-Edge	Normal	Physical	120	100	15	Normal	○
Reflect	Psychic	Status	—	—	20	Self	—
Amnesia	Psychic	Status	—	—	20	Self	—
Helping Hand	Normal	Status	—	—	20	1 Ally	—
Psych Up	Normal	Status	—	—	10	Normal	—
Aromatherapy	Grass	Status	—	—	5	All Allies	—
Worry Seed	Grass	Status	—	100	10	Normal	—

● LEVEL-UP MOVES

Lv.	Name	Type	Kind	Pow.	Acc.	PP	Range	DA
1	Splash	Normal	Status	—	—	40	Self	—
1	Synthesis	Grass	Status	—	—	5	Self	—
1	Tail Whip	Normal	Status	—	100	30	2 Foes	—
1	Tackle	Normal	Physical	35	95	35	Normal	○
4	Synthesis	Grass	Status	—	—	5	Self	—
?	Tail Whip	Normal	Status	—	100	30	2 Foes	—
10	Tackle	Normal	Physical	35	95	35	Normal	○
12	PoisonPowder	Poison	Status	—	75	35	Normal	—
14	Stun Spore	Grass	Status	—	75	30	Normal	—
16	Sleep Powder	Grass	Status	—	75	15	Normal	—
20	Bullet Seed	Grass	Physical	10	100	30	Normal	—
24	Leech Seed	Grass	Status	—	90	10	Normal	—
28	Mega Drain	Grass	Special	40	100	15	Normal	—
32	Cotton Spore	Grass	Status	—	85	40	Normal	—
36	U-turn	Bug	Physical	70	100	20	Normal	○
40	Worry Seed	Grass	Status	—	100	10	Normal	—
44	Giga Drain	Grass	Special	60	100	10	Normal	—
48	Bounce	Flying	Physical	85	85	5	Normal	○
52	Memento	Dark	Status	—	100	10	Normal	—

● MOVE MANIAC

Name	Type	Kind	Pow.	Acc.	PP	Range	DA
Headbutt	Normal	Physical	70	100	15	Normal	○

● BP MOVES

Name	Type	Kind	Pow.	Acc.	PP	Range	DA
Snore	Normal	Special	40	100	15	Normal	—
Helping Hand	Normal	Status	—	—	20	1 Ally	—
Synthesis	Grass	Status	—	—	5	Self	—
Worry Seed	Grass	Status	—	100	10	Normal	—
Seed Bomb	Grass	Physical	80	100	15	Normal	—
Bounce	Flying	Physical	85	85	5	Normal	○

● TM & HM MOVES

No.	Name	Type	Kind	Pow.	Acc.	PP	Range	DA
TM06	Toxic	Poison	Status	—	85	10	Normal	—
TM09	Bullet Seed	Grass	Physical	10	100	30	Normal	—
TM10	Hidden Power	Normal	Special	—	100	15	Normal	—
TM11	Sunny Day	Fire	Status	—	—	5	All	—
TM17	Protect	Normal	Status	—	—	10	Self	—
TM19	Giga Drain	Grass	Special	60	100	10	Normal	—
TM21	Frustration	Normal	Physical	—	100	20	Normal	○
TM22	SolarBeam	Grass	Special	120	100	10	Normal	—
TM27	Return	Normal	Physical	—	100	20	Normal	○
TM32	Double Team	Normal	Status	—	—	15	Self	—
TM40	Aerial Ace	Flying	Physical	60	—	20	Normal	○
TM42	Facade	Normal	Physical	70	100	20	Normal	○
TM43	Secret Power	Normal	Physical	70	100	20	Normal	—
TM44	Rest	Psychic	Status	—	—	10	Self	—
TM45	Attract	Normal	Status	—	100	15	Normal	—
TM53	Energy Ball	Grass	Special	80	100	10	Normal	—
TM58	Endure	Normal	Status	—	—	10	Self	—
TM62	Silver Wind	Bug	Special	60	100	5	Normal	—
TM70	Flash	Normal	Status	—	100	20	Normal	—
TM75	Swords Dance	Normal	Status	—	—	30	Self	—
TM78	Captivate	Normal	Status	—	100	20	2 Foes	—
TM82	Sleep Talk	Normal	Status	—	—	10	Depends	—
TM83	Natural Gift	Normal	Physical	—	100	15	Normal	—
TM86	Grass Knot	Grass	Special	—	100	20	Normal	○
TM87	Swagger	Normal	Status	—	90	15	Normal	—
TM89	U-turn	Bug	Physical	70	100	20	Normal	○
TM90	Substitute	Normal	Status	—	—	10	Self	—

○ No. 188 | Cottonweed Pokémon
Skiploom

Grass　Flying

- ● HEIGHT: 2'00"
- ● WEIGHT: 2.2 lbs.
- ● ITEMS: None

● SIZE COMPARISON

● MALE/FEMALE HAVE SAME FORM

◎ ABILITIES
- ● Chlorophyll
- ● Leaf Guard

◎ STATS
HP ●●
ATTACK ●●
DEFENSE ●●
SP. ATTACK ●●
SP. DEFENSE ●●
SPEED ●●●●

◎ EGG GROUPS
Fairy

Grass

◎ PERFORMANCE

SPEED ★★★★☆　STAMINA ★★
POWER ★★☆　JUMP ★★★★★
SKILL ★

● MAIN WAYS TO OBTAIN

Pokémon HeartGold	Route 14 (morning and afternoon only)
Pokémon SoulSilver	Route 14 (morning and afternoon only)
Pokémon Diamond	Route 205, Eterna City side (occasionally appears when you use Poké Radar)
Pokémon Pearl	Fuego Ironworks (occasionally appears when you use Poké Radar)
Pokémon Platinum	Level up Hoppip to Lv. 18

Pokémon HeartGold	Pokémon SoulSilver
The bloom on top of its head opens and closes as the temperature fluctuates up and down.	It spreads its petals to absorb sunlight. It also floats in the air to get closer to the sun.

◎ EVOLUTION

Lv. 18　　　Lv. 27

Hoppip　　Skiploom　　Jumpluff

No. 189 | Cottonweed Pokémon
Jumpluff

Grass **Flying**

● HEIGHT: 2'07"
● WEIGHT: 6.6 lbs.
● ITEMS: None

● MALE/FEMALE HAVE SAME FORM

● SIZE COMPARISON

⊙ ABILITIES
● Chlorophyll
● Leaf Guard

⊙ STATS
HP ●●●
ATTACK ●●
DEFENSE ●●●
SP. ATTACK ●●
SP. DEFENSE ●●●
SPEED ●●●●●

⊙ EGG GROUPS
Fairy

Grass

⊙ PERFORMANCE
SPEED ★★★★☆
POWER ★☆☆
SKILL ★★
STAMINA ★★
JUMP ★★★★★

● MAIN WAYS TO OBTAIN

Pokémon HeartGold	Level up Skiploom to Lv. 27
Pokémon SoulSilver	Level up Skiploom to Lv. 27
Pokémon Diamond	Level up Skiploom to Lv. 27
Pokémon Pearl	Level up Skiploom to Lv. 27
Pokémon Platinum	Level up Skiploom to Lv. 27

Pokémon HeartGold
Once it catches the wind, it deftly controls its cotton-puff spores-- it can even float around the world.

Pokémon SoulSilver
Drifts on seasonal winds and spreads its cotton-like spores all over the world to make more offspring.

⊙ EVOLUTION

Hoppip — Lv. 18 — Skiploom — Lv. 27 — Jumpluff

● LEVEL-UP MOVES

Lv.	Name	Type	Kind	Pow.	Acc.	PP	Range	DA
1	Splash	Normal	Status	—	—	40	Self	—
1	Synthesis	Grass	Status	—	—	5	Self	—
1	Tail Whip	Normal	Status	—	100	30	2 Foes	—
1	Tackle	Normal	Physical	35	95	35	Normal	○
4	Synthesis	Grass	Status	—	—	5	Self	—
7	Tail Whip	Normal	Status	—	100	30	2 Foes	—
10	Tackle	Normal	Physical	35	95	35	Normal	○
12	PoisonPowder	Poison	Status	—	75	35	Normal	—
14	Stun Spore	Grass	Status	—	75	30	Normal	—
16	Sleep Powder	Grass	Status	—	75	15	Normal	—
20	Bullet Seed	Grass	Physical	10	100	30	Normal	—
24	Leech Seed	Grass	Status	—	90	10	Normal	—
28	Mega Drain	Grass	Special	40	100	15	Normal	—
32	Cotton Spore	Grass	Status	—	85	40	Normal	—
36	U-turn	Bug	Physical	70	100	20	Normal	○
40	Worry Seed	Grass	Status	—	100	10	Normal	—
44	Giga Drain	Grass	Special	60	100	10	Normal	—
48	Bounce	Flying	Physical	85	85	5	Normal	○
52	Memento	Dark	Status	—	100	10	Normal	—

● MOVE MANIAC

Name	Type	Kind	Pow.	Acc.	PP	Range	DA
Headbutt	Normal	Physical	70	100	15	Normal	○

● BP MOVES

Name	Type	Kind	Pow.	Acc.	PP	Range	DA
Snore	Normal	Special	40	100	15	Normal	—
Helping Hand	Normal	Status	—	—	20	1 Ally	—
Synthesis	Grass	Status	—	—	5	Self	—
Worry Seed	Grass	Status	—	100	10	Normal	—
Seed Bomb	Grass	Physical	80	100	15	Normal	—
Bounce	Flying	Physical	85	85	5	Normal	○

● TM & HM MOVES

No.	Name	Type	Kind	Pow.	Acc.	PP	Range	DA
TM06	Toxic	Poison	Status	—	85	10	Normal	—
TM09	Bullet Seed	Grass	Physical	10	100	30	Normal	—
TM10	Hidden Power	Normal	Special	—	100	15	Normal	—
TM11	Sunny Day	Fire	Status	—	—	5	All	—
TM15	Hyper Beam	Normal	Special	150	90	5	Normal	—
TM17	Protect	Normal	Status	—	—	10	Self	—
TM19	Giga Drain	Grass	Special	60	100	10	Normal	—
TM21	Frustration	Normal	Physical	—	100	20	Normal	○
TM22	SolarBeam	Grass	Special	120	100	10	Normal	—
TM27	Return	Normal	Physical	—	100	20	Normal	○
TM32	Double Team	Normal	Status	—	—	15	Self	—
TM40	Aerial Ace	Flying	Physical	60	—	20	Normal	○
TM42	Facade	Normal	Physical	70	100	20	Normal	○
TM43	Secret Power	Normal	Physical	70	100	20	Normal	—
TM44	Rest	Psychic	Status	—	—	10	Self	—
TM45	Attract	Normal	Status	—	100	15	Normal	—
TM53	Energy Ball	Grass	Special	80	100	10	Normal	—
TM58	Endure	Normal	Status	—	—	10	Self	—
TM62	Silver Wind	Bug	Special	60	100	5	Normal	—
TM68	Giga Impact	Normal	Physical	150	90	5	Normal	○
TM70	Flash	Normal	Status	—	100	20	Normal	—
TM75	Swords Dance	Normal	Status	—	—	30	Self	—
TM78	Captivate	Normal	Status	—	100	20	2 Foes	—
TM82	Sleep Talk	Normal	Status	—	—	10	Depends	—
TM83	Natural Gift	Normal	Physical	—	100	15	Normal	—
TM86	Grass Knot	Grass	Special	—	100	20	Normal	○
TM87	Swagger	Normal	Status	—	90	15	Normal	—
TM89	U-turn	Bug	Physical	70	100	20	Normal	○
TM90	Substitute	Normal	Status	—	—	10	Self	—

● LEVEL-UP MOVES

Lv.	Name	Type	Kind	Pow.	Acc.	PP	Range	DA
1	Scratch	Normal	Physical	40	100	35	Normal	○
1	Tail Whip	Normal	Status	—	100	30	2 Foes	—
4	Sand-Attack	Ground	Status	—	100	15	Normal	—
8	Astonish	Ghost	Physical	30	100	15	Normal	○
11	Baton Pass	Normal	Status	—	—	40	Self	—
15	Tickle	Normal	Status	—	100	20	Normal	—
18	Fury Swipes	Normal	Physical	18	80	15	Normal	○
22	Swift	Normal	Special	60	—	20	2 Foes	—
25	Screech	Normal	Status	—	85	40	Normal	—
29	Agility	Psychic	Status	—	—	30	Self	—
32	Double Hit	Normal	Physical	35	90	10	Normal	○
36	Fling	Dark	Physical	—	100	10	Normal	—
39	Nasty Plot	Dark	Status	—	—	20	Self	—
43	Last Resort	Normal	Physical	130	100	5	Normal	○

● MOVE MANIAC

Name	Type	Kind	Pow.	Acc.	PP	Range	DA
Headbutt	Normal	Physical	70	100	15	Normal	○

● BP MOVES

Name	Type	Kind	Pow.	Acc.	PP	Range	DA
Fury Cutter	Bug	Physical	10	95	20	Normal	○
ThunderPunch	Electric	Physical	75	100	15	Normal	○
Fire Punch	Fire	Physical	75	100	15	Normal	○
Ice Punch	Ice	Physical	75	100	15	Normal	○
Knock Off	Dark	Physical	20	100	20	Normal	○
Snore	Normal	Special	40	100	15	Normal	—
Spite	Ghost	Status	—	100	10	Normal	—
Last Resort	Normal	Physical	130	100	5	Normal	○
Swift	Normal	Special	60	—	20	2 Foes	—
Uproar	Normal	Special	50	100	10	1 Random	—
Role Play	Psychic	Status	—	—	10	Normal	—
Mud-Slap	Ground	Special	20	100	10	Normal	—
Gunk Shot	Poison	Physical	120	70	5	Normal	—
Seed Bomb	Grass	Physical	80	100	15	Normal	○
Bounce	Flying	Physical	85	85	5	Normal	○
Low Kick	Fighting	Physical	—	100	20	Normal	○

● TM & HM MOVES

No.	Name	Type	Kind	Pow.	Acc.	PP	Range	DA
TM01	Focus Punch	Fighting	Physical	150	100	20	Normal	○
TM03	Water Pulse	Water	Special	60	100	20	Normal	—
TM06	Toxic	Poison	Status	—	85	10	Normal	—
TM10	Hidden Power	Normal	Special	—	100	15	Normal	—
TM11	Sunny Day	Fire	Status	—	—	5	All	—
TM12	Taunt	Dark	Status	—	100	20	Normal	—
TM17	Protect	Normal	Status	—	—	10	Self	—
TM18	Rain Dance	Water	Status	—	—	5	All	—
TM21	Frustration	Normal	Physical	—	100	20	Normal	○
TM22	SolarBeam	Grass	Special	120	100	10	Normal	—
TM23	Iron Tail	Steel	Physical	100	75	15	Normal	○
TM24	Thunderbolt	Electric	Special	95	100	15	Normal	—
TM25	Thunder	Electric	Special	120	70	10	Normal	—
TM27	Return	Normal	Physical	—	100	20	Normal	○
TM28	Dig	Ground	Physical	80	100	10	Normal	○
TM30	Shadow Ball	Ghost	Special	80	100	15	Normal	—
TM31	Brick Break	Fighting	Physical	75	100	15	Normal	○
TM32	Double Team	Normal	Status	—	—	15	Self	—
TM34	Shock Wave	Electric	Special	60	—	20	Normal	—
TM40	Aerial Ace	Flying	Physical	60	—	20	Normal	○
TM42	Facade	Normal	Physical	70	100	20	Normal	○
TM43	Secret Power	Normal	Physical	70	100	20	Normal	○
TM44	Rest	Psychic	Status	—	—	10	Self	—
TM45	Attract	Normal	Status	—	100	15	Normal	—
TM46	Thief	Dark	Physical	40	100	10	Normal	○
TM49	Snatch	Dark	Status	—	—	10	Depends	—
TM56	Fling	Dark	Physical	—	100	10	Normal	—
TM58	Endure	Normal	Status	—	—	10	Self	—
TM65	Shadow Claw	Ghost	Physical	70	100	15	Normal	○
TM66	Payback	Dark	Physical	50	100	10	Normal	○
TM73	Thunder Wave	Electric	Status	—	100	20	Normal	—
TM78	Captivate	Normal	Status	—	100	20	2 Foes	—
TM82	Sleep Talk	Normal	Status	—	—	10	Depends	—
TM83	Natural Gift	Normal	Physical	—	100	15	Normal	—
TM85	Dream Eater	Psychic	Special	100	100	15	Normal	—
TM86	Grass Knot	Grass	Special	—	100	20	Normal	—
TM87	Swagger	Normal	Status	—	90	15	Normal	—
TM89	U-turn	Bug	Physical	70	100	20	Normal	○
TM90	Substitute	Normal	Status	—	—	10	Self	—
HM01	Cut	Normal	Physical	50	95	30	Normal	○
HM04	Strength	Normal	Physical	80	100	15	Normal	○
HM06	Rock Smash	Fighting	Physical	40	100	15	Normal	○

● EGG MOVES

Name	Type	Kind	Pow.	Acc.	PP	Range	DA
Counter	Fighting	Physical	—	100	20	Self	○
Screech	Normal	Status	—	85	40	Normal	—
Pursuit	Dark	Physical	40	100	20	Normal	○
Agility	Psychic	Status	—	—	30	Self	—
Spite	Ghost	Status	—	100	10	Normal	—
Slam	Normal	Physical	80	75	20	Normal	○
DoubleSlap	Normal	Physical	15	85	10	Normal	○
Beat Up	Dark	Physical	10	100	10	Normal	—
Fake Out	Normal	Physical	40	100	10	Normal	○
Covet	Normal	Physical	40	100	40	Normal	○
Bounce	Flying	Physical	85	85	5	Normal	○

Aipom

Normal

● HEIGHT: 2'07"
● WEIGHT: 25.4 lbs.
● ITEMS: None

● SIZE COMPARISON

● MALE FORM
Shorter fur tuft on head

● FEMALE FORM
Longer fur tuft on head

● ABILITIES
● Chlorophyll
● Leaf Guard

● STATS

HP ●●
ATTACK ●●
DEFENSE ●●
SP. ATTACK ●●
SP. DEFENSE ●●●●
SPEED ●●●●

● EGG GROUPS
Field

● PERFORMANCE
SPEED ★★★★　　STAMINA ★★☆
POWER ★★☆
SKILL ★★★★　　JUMP ★★★☆

● MAIN WAYS TO OBTAIN

Pokémon HeartGold — Azalea Town (use Headbutt)

Pokémon SoulSilver — Azalea Town (use Headbutt)

Pokémon Diamond — Spread Honey on a sweet-smelling tree

Pokémon Pearl — Spread Honey on a sweet-smelling tree

Pokémon Platinum — Spread Honey on a sweet-smelling tree

Pokémon HeartGold
Its tail is so powerful that it can use it to grab a tree branch and hold itself up in the air.

Pokémon SoulSilver
It lives atop tall trees. When leaping from branch to branch, it deftly uses its tail for balance.

● EVOLUTION

Aipom → Ambipom

Level it up to Lv. 32 and teach it Double Hit. Or, level it up once it knows Double Hit.

No. 191 | Seed Pokémon
Sunkern

Grass

- **HEIGHT:** 1'00"
- **WEIGHT:** 4.0 lbs.
- **ITEMS:** Coba Berry

● SIZE COMPARISON

● MALE/FEMALE HAVE SAME FORM

ABILITIES
- Chlorophyll
- Solar Power

STATS
- HP ●
- ATTACK ●
- DEFENSE ●
- SP. ATTACK ●
- SP. DEFENSE ●
- SPEED ●

EGG GROUPS
Grass

PERFORMANCE
SPEED ★★★☆☆	STAMINA ★☆☆☆☆
POWER ★☆☆☆☆	JUMP ★★☆☆☆
SKILL ★☆☆☆☆	

● MAIN WAYS TO OBTAIN

Pokémon HeartGold	National Park (afternoon only)
Pokémon SoulSilver	National Park (afternoon only)
Pokémon Diamond	Route 204, Floaroma Town side (use Poké Radar)
Pokémon Pearl	Route 204, Floaroma Town side (use Poké Radar)
Pokémon Platinum	Route 204 (use Poké Radar)

Pokémon HeartGold	**Pokémon SoulSilver**
It may plummet from the sky. If attacked by a SPEAROW, it will violently shake its leaves.	It lives by drinking only dewdrops from under the leaves of plants. It is said that it eats nothing else.

● EVOLUTION

 Use Sun Stone →

Sunkern → Sunflora

● LEVEL-UP MOVES

Lv.	Name	Type	Kind	Pow.	Acc.	PP	Range	DA
1	Absorb	Grass	Special	20	100	25	Normal	—
1	Growth	Normal	Status	—	—	40	Self	—
5	Mega Drain	Grass	Special	40	100	15	Normal	—
9	Ingrain	Grass	Status	—	—	20	Self	—
13	GrassWhistle	Grass	Status	—	55	15	Normal	—
17	Leech Seed	Grass	Status	—	90	10	Normal	—
21	Endeavor	Normal	Physical	—	100	5	Normal	○
25	Worry Seed	Grass	Status	—	100	10	Normal	—
29	Razor Leaf	Grass	Physical	55	95	25	2 Foes	—
33	Synthesis	Grass	Status	—	—	5	Self	—
37	Sunny Day	Fire	Status	—	—	5	All	—
41	Giga Drain	Grass	Special	60	100	10	Normal	—
45	Seed Bomb	Grass	Physical	80	100	15	Normal	—

● MOVE MANIAC

Name	Type	Kind	Pow.	Acc.	PP	Range	DA

● BP MOVES

Name	Type	Kind	Pow.	Acc.	PP	Range	DA
Snore	Normal	Special	40	100	15	Normal	—
Helping Hand	Normal	Status	—	—	20	1 Ally	—
Synthesis	Grass	Status	—	—	5	Self	—
Uproar	Normal	Special	50	100	10	1 Random	—
Worry Seed	Grass	Status	—	100	10	Normal	—
Endeavor	Normal	Physical	—	100	5	Normal	○
Earth Power	Ground	Special	90	100	10	Normal	—
Seed Bomb	Grass	Physical	80	100	15	Normal	—

● TM & HM MOVES

No.	Name	Type	Kind	Pow.	Acc.	PP	Range	DA
TM06	Toxic	Poison	Status	—	85	10	Normal	—
TM09	Bullet Seed	Grass	Physical	10	100	30	Normal	—
TM10	Hidden Power	Normal	Special	—	100	15	Normal	—
TM11	Sunny Day	Fire	Status	—	—	5	All	—
TM16	Light Screen	Psychic	Status	—	—	30	2 Allies	—
TM17	Protect	Normal	Status	—	—	10	Self	—
TM19	Giga Drain	Grass	Special	60	100	10	Normal	—
TM20	Safeguard	Normal	Status	—	—	25	2 Allies	—
TM21	Frustration	Normal	Physical	—	100	20	Normal	○
TM22	SolarBeam	Grass	Special	120	100	10	Normal	—
TM27	Return	Normal	Physical	—	100	20	Normal	○
TM32	Double Team	Normal	Status	—	—	15	Self	—
TM36	Sludge Bomb	Poison	Special	90	100	10	Normal	—
TM42	Facade	Normal	Physical	70	100	20	Normal	○
TM43	Secret Power	Normal	Physical	70	100	20	Normal	○
TM44	Rest	Psychic	Status	—	—	10	Self	—
TM45	Attract	Normal	Status	—	100	15	Normal	—
TM53	Energy Ball	Grass	Special	80	100	10	Normal	—
TM58	Endure	Normal	Status	—	—	10	Self	—
TM70	Flash	Normal	Status	—	100	20	Normal	—
TM75	Swords Dance	Normal	Status	—	—	30	Self	—
TM78	Captivate	Normal	Status	—	100	20	2 Foes	—
TM82	Sleep Talk	Normal	Status	—	—	10	Depends	—
TM86	Natural Gift	Normal	Physical	—	100	15	Normal	—
TM86	Grass Knot	Grass	Special	—	100	20	Normal	○
TM87	Swagger	Normal	Status	—	90	15	Normal	—
TM90	Substitute	Normal	Status	—	—	10	Self	—
HM01	Cut	Normal	Physical	50	95	30	Normal	○

● EGG MOVES

Name	Type	Kind	Pow.	Acc.	PP	Range	DA
GrassWhistle	Grass	Status	—	55	15	Normal	—
Encore	Normal	Status	—	100	5	Normal	—
Leech Seed	Grass	Status	—	90	10	Normal	—
Nature Power	Normal	Status	—	—	20	Depends	—
Curse	???	Status	—	—	10	Normal/Self	—
Helping Hand	Normal	Status	—	—	20	1 Ally	—
Ingrain	Grass	Status	—	—	20	Self	—
Sweet Scent	Normal	Status	—	100	20	2 Foes	—

● LEVEL-UP MOVES

Lv.	Name	Type	Kind	Pow.	Acc.	PP	Range	DA
1	Absorb	Grass	Special	20	100	25	Normal	—
1	Pound	Normal	Physical	40	100	35	Normal	○
1	Growth	Normal	Status	—	—	40	Self	—
5	Mega Drain	Grass	Special	40	100	15	Normal	—
9	Ingrain	Grass	Status	—	—	20	Self	—
13	GrassWhistle	Grass	Status	—	55	15	Normal	—
17	Leech Seed	Grass	Status	—	90	10	Normal	—
21	Bullet Seed	Grass	Physical	10	100	30	Normal	—
25	Worry Seed	Grass	Status	—	100	10	Normal	—
29	Razor Leaf	Grass	Physical	55	95	25	2 Foes	—
33	Petal Dance	Grass	Special	90	100	20	1 Random	○
37	Sunny Day	Fire	Status	—	—	5	All	—
41	SolarBeam	Grass	Special	120	100	10	Normal	—
43	Leaf Storm	Grass	Special	140	90	5	Normal	—

● MOVE MANIAC

Name	Type	Kind	Pow.	Acc.	PP	Range	DA

● BP MOVES

Name	Type	Kind	Pow.	Acc.	PP	Range	DA
Snore	Normal	Special	40	100	15	Normal	—
Helping Hand	Normal	Status	—	—	20	1 Ally	—
Synthesis	Grass	Status	—	—	5	Self	—
Uproar	Normal	Special	50	100	10	1 Random	—
Worry Seed	Grass	Status	—	100	10	Normal	—
Endeavor	Normal	Physical	—	100	5	Normal	○
Earth Power	Ground	Special	90	100	10	Normal	—
Seed Bomb	Grass	Physical	80	100	15	Normal	—

● TM & HM MOVES

No.	Name	Type	Kind	Pow.	Acc.	PP	Range	DA
TM06	Toxic	Poison	Status	—	85	10	Normal	—
TM09	Bullet Seed	Grass	Physical	10	100	30	Normal	—
TM10	Hidden Power	Normal	Special	—	100	15	Normal	—
TM11	Sunny Day	Fire	Status	—	—	5	All	—
TM15	Hyper Beam	Normal	Special	150	90	5	Normal	—
TM16	Light Screen	Psychic	Status	—	—	30	2 Allies	—
TM17	Protect	Normal	Status	—	—	10	Self	—
TM19	Giga Drain	Grass	Special	60	100	10	Normal	—
TM20	Safeguard	Normal	Status	—	—	25	2 Allies	—
TM21	Frustration	Normal	Physical	—	100	20	Normal	○
TM22	SolarBeam	Grass	Special	120	100	10	Normal	—
TM27	Return	Normal	Physical	—	100	20	Normal	○
TM32	Double Team	Normal	Status	—	—	15	Self	—
TM36	Sludge Bomb	Poison	Special	90	100	10	Normal	—
TM42	Facade	Normal	Physical	70	100	20	Normal	○
TM43	Secret Power	Normal	Physical	70	100	20	Normal	—
TM44	Rest	Psychic	Status	—	—	10	Self	—
TM45	Attract	Normal	Status	—	100	15	Normal	—
TM53	Energy Ball	Grass	Special	80	100	10	Normal	—
TM58	Endure	Normal	Status	—	—	10	Self	—
TM68	Giga Impact	Normal	Physical	150	90	5	Normal	○
TM70	Flash	Normal	Status	—	100	20	Normal	—
TM75	Swords Dance	Normal	Status	—	—	30	Self	—
TM78	Captivate	Normal	Status	—	100	20	2 Foes	—
TM82	Sleep Talk	Normal	Status	—	—	10	Depends	—
TM83	Natural Gift	Normal	Physical	—	100	15	Normal	—
TM86	Grass Knot	Grass	Special	—	100	20	Normal	○
TM87	Swagger	Normal	Status	—	90	15	Normal	—
TM90	Substitute	Normal	Status	—	—	10	Self	—
HM01	Cut	Normal	Physical	50	95	30	Normal	○

⊙ No. 192 | Sun Pokémon
Sunflora

Grass

- **HEIGHT:** 2'07"
- **WEIGHT:** 18.7 lbs.
- **ITEMS:** None

● SIZE COMPARISON

● MALE/FEMALE HAVE SAME FORM

⊙ ABILITIES
- Chlorophyll
- Solar Power

⊙ STATS
- HP ●●●
- ATTACK ●●●
- DEFENSE ●●
- SP. ATTACK ●●●
- SP. DEFENSE ●●●
- SPEED ●

⊙ EGG GROUPS
Grass

⊙ PERFORMANCE
SPEED ★★   STAMINA ★★★★☆
POWER ★★★☆☆   JUMP ★★☆
SKILL ★★★

● MAIN WAYS TO OBTAIN

Pokémon HeartGold	Use Sun Stone on Sunkern

Pokémon SoulSilver	Use Sun Stone on Sunkern

Pokémon Diamond	Use Sun Stone on Sunkern

Pokémon Pearl	Use Sun Stone on Sunkern

Pokémon Platinum	Use Sun Stone on Sunkern

Pokémon HeartGold	**Pokémon SoulSilver**
It converts sunlight into energy. In the darkness after sunset, it closes its petals and becomes still.	In the daytime, it rushes about in a hectic manner, but it comes to a complete stop when the sun sets.

⊙ EVOLUTION

Sunkern → (Use Sun Stone) → Sunflora

● No. 193 | Clear Wing Pokémon
Yanma

Bug　Flying

- **HEIGHT:** 3'11"
- **WEIGHT:** 83,8 lbs.
- **ITEMS:** Wide Lens

● SIZE COMPARISON

● MALE/FEMALE HAVE SAME FORM

⊙ ABILITIES
- Speed Boost
- Compoundeyes

⊙ STATS
HP ●●
ATTACK ●●●
DEFENSE ●●
SP. ATTACK ●●●
SP. DEFENSE ●●
SPEED ●●●●

⊙ EGG GROUPS
Bug

⊙ PERFORMANCE
SPEED ★★★☆☆　STAMINA ★★☆
POWER ★★　JUMP ★★★★★
SKILL ★

● MAIN WAYS TO OBTAIN

Pokémon HeartGold　Route 35

Pokémon SoulSilver　Route 35

Pokémon Diamond　Pastoria Great Marsh (after obtaining the National Poké-dex/changes daily)

Pokémon Pearl　Pastoria Great Marsh (after obtaining the National Poké-dex/changes daily)

Pokémon Platinum　Pastoria Great Marsh

Pokémon HeartGold
If it flaps its wings really fast, it can generate shock waves that will shatter windows in the area.

Pokémon SoulSilver
Its large eyes can scan 360 degrees. It looks in all directions to seek out insects as its prey.

⊙ EVOLUTION

Yanma

Level it up to Lv. 33 and teach it Ancient Power. Or, level it up once it knows AncientPower.

Yanmega

● LEVEL-UP MOVES

Lv.	Name	Type	Kind	Pow.	Acc.	PP	Range	DA
1	Absorb	Grass	Special	20	100	25	Normal	—
1	Pound	Normal	Physical	40	100	35	Normal	○
1	Growth	Normal	Status	—	—	40	Self	—
5	Mega Drain	Grass	Special	40	100	15	Normal	—
9	Ingrain	Grass	Status	—	—	20	Self	—
13	GrassWhistle	Grass	Status	—	55	15	Normal	—
17	Leech Seed	Grass	Status	—	90	10	Normal	—
21	Bullet Seed	Grass	Physical	10	100	30	Normal	—
25	Worry Seed	Grass	Status	—	100	10	Normal	—
29	Razor Leaf	Grass	Special	55	95	25	2 Foes	—
33	Petal Dance	Grass	Special	90	100	20	1 Random	○
37	Sunny Day	Fire	Status	—	—	5	All	—
41	SolarBeam	Grass	Special	120	100	10	Normal	—
43	Leaf Storm	Grass	Special	140	90	5	Normal	—

● MOVE MANIAC

Name	Type	Kind	Pow.	Acc.	PP	Range	DA

● BP MOVES

Name	Type	Kind	Pow.	Acc.	PP	Range	DA
Snore	Normal	Special	40	100	15	Normal	—
Helping Hand	Normal	Status	—	—	20	1 Ally	—
Synthesis	Grass	Status	—	—	5	Self	—
Uproar	Normal	Special	50	100	10	1 Random	—
Worry Seed	Grass	Status	—	100	10	Normal	—
Endeavor	Normal	Physical	—	100	5	Normal	○
Earth Power	Ground	Special	90	100	10	Normal	—
Seed Bomb	Grass	Physical	80	100	15	Normal	—

● TM & HM MOVES

No.	Name	Type	Kind	Pow.	Acc.	PP	Range	DA
TM06	Toxic	Poison	Status	—	85	10	Normal	—
TM09	Bullet Seed	Grass	Physical	10	100	30	Normal	—
TM10	Hidden Power	Normal	Special	—	100	15	Normal	—
TM11	Sunny Day	Fire	Status	—	—	5	All	—
TM15	Hyper Beam	Normal	Special	150	90	5	Normal	—
TM16	Light Screen	Psychic	Status	—	—	30	2 Allies	—
TM17	Protect	Normal	Status	—	—	10	Self	—
TM19	Giga Drain	Grass	Special	60	100	10	Normal	—
TM20	Safeguard	Normal	Status	—	—	25	2 Allies	—
TM21	Frustration	Normal	Physical	—	100	20	Normal	○
TM22	SolarBeam	Grass	Special	120	100	10	Normal	—
TM27	Return	Normal	Physical	—	100	20	Normal	○
TM32	Double Team	Normal	Status	—	—	15	Self	—
TM36	Sludge Bomb	Poison	Special	90	100	10	Normal	—
TM42	Facade	Normal	Physical	70	100	20	Normal	○
TM43	Secret Power	Normal	Physical	70	100	20	Normal	—
TM44	Rest	Psychic	Status	—	—	10	Self	—
TM45	Attract	Normal	Status	—	100	15	Normal	—
TM53	Energy Ball	Grass	Special	80	100	10	Normal	—
TM58	Endure	Normal	Status	—	—	10	Self	—
TM68	Giga Impact	Normal	Physical	150	90	5	Normal	○
TM70	Flash	Normal	Status	—	100	20	Normal	—
TM75	Swords Dance	Normal	Status	—	—	30	Self	—
TM78	Captivate	Normal	Status	—	100	20	2 Foes	—
TM82	Sleep Talk	Normal	Status	—	—	10	Depends	—
TM83	Natural Gift	Normal	Physical	—	100	15	Normal	—
TM86	Grass Knot	Grass	Special	—	100	20	Normal	○
TM87	Swagger	Normal	Status	—	90	15	Normal	—
TM90	Substitute	Normal	Status	—	—	10	Self	—
HM01	Cut	Normal	Physical	50	95	30	Normal	○

● LEVEL-UP MOVES

Lv.	Name	Type	Kind	Pow.	Acc.	PP	Range	DA
1	Water Gun	Water	Special	40	100	25	Normal	—
1	Tail Whip	Normal	Status	—	100	30	2 Foes	—
5	Mud Sport	Ground	Status	—	—	15	All	—
9	Mud Shot	Ground	Special	55	95	15	Normal	—
15	Slam	Normal	Physical	80	75	20	Normal	○
19	Mud Bomb	Ground	Special	65	85	10	Normal	—
23	Amnesia	Psychic	Status	—	—	20	Self	—
29	Yawn	Normal	Status	—	—	10	Normal	—
33	Earthquake	Ground	Physical	100	100	10	2 Foes/1 Ally	—
37	Rain Dance	Water	Status	—	—	5	All	—
43	Mist	Ice	Status	—	—	30	All	—
43	Haze	Ice	Status	—	—	30	All	—
47	Muddy Water	Water	Special	95	85	10	2 Foes	—

● MOVE MANIAC

Name	Type	Kind	Pow.	Acc.	PP	Range	DA
Headbutt	Normal	Physical	70	100	15	Normal	○

● BP MOVES

Name	Type	Kind	Pow.	Acc.	PP	Range	DA
Dive	Water	Physical	80	100	10	Normal	○
Icy Wind	Ice	Special	55	95	15	2 Foes	—
Ice Punch	Ice	Physical	75	100	15	Normal	○
Snore	Normal	Special	40	100	15	Normal	—
Mud-Slap	Ground	Special	20	100	10	Normal	—
Rollout	Rock	Physical	30	90	20	Normal	○
Aqua Tail	Water	Physical	90	90	10	Normal	○
AncientPower	Rock	Special	60	100	5	Normal	—
Earth Power	Ground	Special	90	100	10	Normal	—

● TM & HM MOVES

No.	Name	Type	Kind	Pow.	Acc.	PP	Range	DA
TM03	Water Pulse	Water	Special	60	100	20	Normal	—
TM06	Toxic	Poison	Status	—	85	10	Normal	—
TM07	Hail	Ice	Status	—	—	10	All	—
TM10	Hidden Power	Normal	Special	—	100	15	Normal	—
TM13	Ice Beam	Ice	Special	95	100	10	Normal	—
TM14	Blizzard	Ice	Special	120	70	5	2 Foes	—
TM17	Protect	Normal	Status	—	—	10	Self	—
TM18	Rain Dance	Water	Status	—	—	5	All	—
TM21	Frustration	Normal	Physical	—	100	20	Normal	○
TM23	Iron Tail	Steel	Physical	100	75	15	Normal	○
TM26	Earthquake	Ground	Physical	100	100	10	2 Foes/1 Ally	—
TM27	Return	Normal	Physical	—	100	20	Normal	○
TM28	Dig	Ground	Physical	80	100	10	Normal	○
TM32	Double Team	Normal	Status	—	—	15	Self	—
TM36	Sludge Bomb	Poison	Special	90	100	10	Normal	—
TM37	Sandstorm	Rock	Status	—	—	10	All	—
TM42	Facade	Normal	Physical	70	100	20	Normal	○
TM43	Secret Power	Normal	Physical	70	100	20	Normal	○
TM44	Rest	Psychic	Status	—	—	10	Self	—
TM45	Attract	Normal	Status	—	100	15	Normal	—
TM58	Endure	Normal	Status	—	—	10	Self	—
TM70	Flash	Normal	Status	—	100	20	Normal	—
TM78	Captivate	Normal	Status	—	100	20	2 Foes	—
TM82	Sleep Talk	Normal	Status	—	—	10	Depends	—
TM83	Natural Gift	Normal	Physical	—	100	15	Normal	—
TM87	Swagger	Normal	Status	—	90	15	Normal	—
TM90	Substitute	Normal	Status	—	—	10	Self	—
HM03	Surf	Water	Special	95	100	15	2 Foes/1 Ally	—
HM06	Whirlpool	Water	Special	15	70	15	Normal	—
HM06	Rock Smash	Fighting	Physical	40	100	15	Normal	○
HM07	Waterfall	Water	Physical	80	100	15	Normal	○

● EGG MOVES

Name	Type	Kind	Pow.	Acc.	PP	Range	DA
Body Slam	Normal	Physical	85	100	15	Normal	○
AncientPower	Rock	Special	60	100	5	Normal	—
Safeguard	Normal	Status	—	—	25	2 Allies	—
Curse	???	Status	—	—	10	Normal/Self	—
Mud Sport	Ground	Status	—	—	15	All	—
Stockpile	Normal	Status	—	—	20	Self	—
Swallow	Normal	Status	—	—	10	Self	—
Spit Up	Normal	Special	—	100	10	Normal	—
Counter	Fighting	Physical	—	100	20	Self	○
Encore	Normal	Status	—	100	5	Normal	—
Double Kick	Fighting	Physical	30	100	30	Normal	○
Recover	Normal	Status	—	—	10	Self	—

No. 194 | Water Fish Pokémon
Wooper

Water | Ground

- **HEIGHT:** 1'04"
- **WEIGHT:** 12.8 lbs.
- **ITEMS:** None

● **SIZE COMPARISON**

● **MALE FORM**
Larger gills on head

● **FEMALE FORM**
Smaller gills on head

⊛ ABILITIES
- Damp
- Water Absorb

⊛ STATS
- HP ●●
- ATTACK ●●
- DEFENSE ●●
- SP. ATTACK ●
- SP. DEFENSE ●
- SPEED ●

⊛ EGG GROUPS
Water 1

Field

⊛ PERFORMANCE
- SPEED ★★★
- POWER ★★☆
- SKILL ★★☆
- STAMINA ★★★★
- JUMP ★★☆

● MAIN WAYS TO OBTAIN

Pokémon HeartGold — Route 32 (night only)

Pokémon SoulSilver — Route 32 (night only)

Pokémon Diamond — Pastoria Great Marsh

Pokémon Pearl — Pastoria Great Marsh

Pokémon Platinum — Pastoria Great Marsh

Pokémon HeartGold
This Pokémon lives in cold water. It will leave the water to search for food when it gets cold outside.

Pokémon SoulSilver
When it walks around on the ground, it coats its body with a slimy, poisonous film.

⊛ EVOLUTION

Wooper — Lv. 20 → Quagsire

⚫ No. 195 | Water Fish Pokémon
Quagsire

Water **Ground**

- **HEIGHT:** 4'07"
- **WEIGHT:** 165.3 lbs.
- **ITEMS:** None

● SIZE COMPARISON

● **MALE FORM**
Bigger fin on back

● **FEMALE FORM**
Smaller fin on back

⚙ ABILITIES
- Damp
- Water Absorb

⚙ STATS
HP	●●●●
ATTACK	●●●●
DEFENSE	●●●●
SP. ATTACK	●●●
SP. DEFENSE	●●●
SPEED	●●

⚙ EGG GROUPS
Water 1

Field

⚙ PERFORMANCE
SPEED ★☆   STAMINA ★★★★★
POWER ★★★☆   JUMP ★★
SKILL ★★★☆

● MAIN WAYS TO OBTAIN

Pokémon HeartGold	Route 27 (night only)
Pokémon SoulSilver	Route 27 (night only)
Pokémon Diamond	Pastoria Great Marsh
Pokémon Pearl	Pastoria Great Marsh
Pokémon Platinum	Pastoria Great Marsh

Pokémon HeartGold
This carefree Pokémon has an easy-going nature. While swimming, it always bumps into boat hulls.

Pokémon SoulSilver
Due to its relaxed and carefree attitude, it often bumps its head on boulders and boat hulls as it swims.

⚙ EVOLUTION

Wooper — Lv. 20 → Quagsire

● LEVEL-UP MOVES

Lv.	Name	Type	Kind	Pow.	Acc.	PP	Range	DA
1	Water Gun	Water	Special	40	100	25	Normal	—
1	Tail Whip	Normal	Status	—	100	30	2 Foes	—
1	Mud Sport	Ground	Status	—	—	15	All	—
5	Mud Sport	Ground	Status	—	—	15	All	—
9	Mud Shot	Ground	Special	55	95	15	Normal	—
15	Slam	Normal	Physical	80	75	20	Normal	○
19	Mud Bomb	Ground	Special	65	85	10	Normal	—
24	Amnesia	Psychic	Status	—	—	20	Self	—
31	Yawn	Normal	Status	—	—	10	Normal	—
36	Earthquake	Ground	Physical	100	100	10	2 Foes/1 Ally	—
41	Rain Dance	Water	Status	—	—	5	All	—
48	Mist	Ice	Status	—	—	30	2 Allies	—
48	Haze	Ice	Status	—	—	30	All	—
53	Muddy Water	Water	Special	95	85	10	2 Foes	—

● MOVE MANIAC

Name	Type	Kind	Pow.	Acc.	PP	Range	DA
Headbutt	Normal	Physical	70	100	15	Normal	○

● BP MOVES

Name	Type	Kind	Pow.	Acc.	PP	Range	DA
Dive	Water	Physical	80	100	10	Normal	○
Icy Wind	Ice	Special	55	95	15	2 Foes	—
Ice Punch	Ice	Physical	75	100	15	Normal	○
Snore	Normal	Special	40	100	15	Normal	—
Mud-Slap	Ground	Special	20	100	10	Normal	—
Rollout	Rock	Physical	30	90	20	Normal	○
Aqua Tail	Water	Physical	90	90	10	Normal	○
AncientPower	Rock	Special	60	100	5	Normal	—
Earth Power	Ground	Special	90	100	10	Normal	—

● TM & HM MOVES

No.	Name	Type	Kind	Pow.	Acc.	PP	Range	DA
TM01	Focus Punch	Fighting	Physical	150	100	20	Normal	○
TM03	Water Pulse	Water	Special	60	100	20	Normal	—
TM06	Toxic	Poison	Status	—	85	10	Normal	—
TM07	Hail	Ice	Status	—	—	10	All	—
TM10	Hidden Power	Normal	Special	—	100	15	Normal	—
TM13	Ice Beam	Ice	Special	95	100	10	Normal	—
TM14	Blizzard	Ice	Special	120	70	5	2 Foes	—
TM15	Hyper Beam	Normal	Special	150	90	5	Normal	—
TM17	Protect	Normal	Status	—	—	10	Self	—
TM18	Rain Dance	Water	Status	—	—	5	All	—
TM21	Frustration	Normal	Physical	—	100	20	Normal	○
TM23	Iron Tail	Steel	Physical	100	75	15	Normal	○
TM26	Earthquake	Ground	Physical	100	100	10	2 Foes/1 Ally	○
TM27	Return	Normal	Physical	—	100	20	Normal	○
TM28	Dig	Ground	Physical	80	100	10	Normal	○
TM31	Brick Break	Fighting	Physical	75	100	15	Normal	○
TM32	Double Team	Normal	Status	—	—	15	Self	—
TM36	Sludge Bomb	Poison	Special	90	100	10	Normal	—
TM37	Sandstorm	Rock	Status	—	—	10	All	—
TM39	Rock Tomb	Rock	Physical	50	80	10	Normal	○
TM42	Facade	Normal	Physical	70	100	20	Normal	○
TM43	Secret Power	Normal	Physical	70	100	20	Normal	—
TM44	Rest	Psychic	Status	—	—	10	Self	—
TM45	Attract	Normal	Status	—	100	15	Normal	—
TM52	Focus Blast	Fighting	Special	120	70	5	Normal	—
TM56	Fling	Dark	Physical	—	100	10	Normal	—
TM58	Endure	Normal	Status	—	—	10	Self	—
TM68	Giga Impact	Normal	Physical	150	90	5	Normal	○
TM70	Flash	Normal	Status	—	100	20	Normal	—
TM71	Stone Edge	Rock	Physical	100	80	5	Normal	—
TM78	Captivate	Normal	Status	—	100	20	2 Foes	—
TM80	Rock Slide	Rock	Physical	75	90	10	2 Foes	—
TM82	Sleep Talk	Normal	Status	—	—	10	Depends	—
TM83	Natural Gift	Normal	Physical	—	100	15	Normal	—
TM87	Swagger	Normal	Status	—	90	15	Normal	—
TM90	Substitute	Normal	Status	—	—	10	Self	—
HM03	Surf	Water	Special	95	100	15	2 Foes/1 Ally	—
HM04	Strength	Normal	Physical	80	100	15	Normal	○
HM05	Whirlpool	Water	Special	15	70	15	Normal	—
HM06	Rock Smash	Fighting	Physical	40	100	15	Normal	○
HM07	Waterfall	Water	Physical	80	100	15	Normal	○

● LEVEL-UP MOVES

Lv.	Name	Type	Kind	Pow.	Acc.	PP	Range	DA
1	Tail Whip	Normal	Status	—	100	30	2 Foes	—
1	Tackle	Normal	Physical	35	95	35	Normal	○
1	Helping Hand	Normal	Status	—	—	20	1 Ally	—
8	Sand-Attack	Ground	Status	—	100	15	Normal	—
15	Confusion	Psychic	Special	50	100	25	Normal	—
22	Quick Attack	Normal	Physical	40	100	30	Normal	○
29	Swift	Normal	Special	60	—	20	2 Foes	—
36	Psybeam	Psychic	Special	65	100	10	Normal	—
43	Future Sight	Psychic	Special	80	100	15	Normal	—
50	Last Resort	Normal	Physical	130	100	5	Normal	○
57	Psych Up	Normal	Status	—	—	10	Normal	—
64	Psychic	Psychic	Special	90	100	10	Normal	—
71	Morning Sun	Normal	Status	—	—	5	Self	—
78	Power Swap	Psychic	Status	—	—	10	Normal	—

● MOVE MANIAC

Name	Type	Kind	Pow.	Acc.	PP	Range	DA
Headbutt	Normal	Physical	70	100	15	Normal	○

● BP MOVES

Name	Type	Kind	Pow.	Acc.	PP	Range	DA
Zen Headbutt	Psychic	Physical	80	90	15	Normal	○
Trick	Psychic	Status	—	100	10	Normal	—
Snore	Normal	Special	40	100	15	Normal	—
Helping Hand	Normal	Status	—	—	20	1 Ally	—
Last Resort	Normal	Physical	130	100	5	Normal	○
Swift	Normal	Special	60	—	20	2 Foes	—
Magic Coat	Psychic	Status	—	—	15	Self	—
Heal Bell	Normal	Status	—	—	5	All Allies	—
Mud-Slap	Ground	Special	20	100	10	Normal	—
Signal Beam	Bug	Special	75	100	15	Normal	—

● TM & HM MOVES

No.	Name	Type	Kind	Pow.	Acc.	PP	Range	DA
TM04	Calm Mind	Psychic	Status	—	—	20	Self	—
TM06	Toxic	Poison	Status	—	85	10	Normal	—
TM10	Hidden Power	Normal	Special	—	100	15	Normal	—
TM11	Sunny Day	Fire	Status	—	—	5	All	—
TM15	Hyper Beam	Normal	Special	150	90	5	Normal	—
TM16	Light Screen	Psychic	Status	—	—	30	2 Allies	—
TM17	Protect	Normal	Status	—	—	10	Self	—
TM18	Rain Dance	Water	Status	—	—	5	All	—
TM21	Frustration	Normal	Physical	—	100	20	Normal	○
TM23	Iron Tail	Steel	Physical	100	75	15	Normal	○
TM27	Return	Normal	Physical	—	100	20	Normal	○
TM28	Dig	Ground	Physical	80	100	10	Normal	○
TM29	Psychic	Psychic	Special	90	100	10	Normal	—
TM30	Shadow Ball	Ghost	Special	80	100	15	Normal	—
TM32	Double Team	Normal	Status	—	—	15	Self	—
TM33	Reflect	Psychic	Status	—	—	20	2 Allies	—
TM42	Facade	Normal	Physical	70	100	20	Normal	○
TM43	Secret Power	Normal	Physical	70	100	20	Normal	—
TM44	Rest	Psychic	Status	—	—	10	Self	—
TM45	Attract	Normal	Status	—	100	15	Normal	—
TM48	Skill Swap	Psychic	Status	—	—	10	Normal	—
TM58	Endure	Normal	Status	—	—	10	Self	—
TM68	Giga Impact	Normal	Physical	150	90	5	Normal	○
TM70	Flash	Normal	Status	—	100	20	Normal	—
TM77	Psych Up	Normal	Status	—	—	10	Normal	—
TM78	Captivate	Normal	Status	—	100	20	2 Foes	—
TM82	Sleep Talk	Normal	Status	—	—	10	Depends	—
TM83	Natural Gift	Normal	Physical	—	100	15	Normal	—
TM85	Dream Eater	Psychic	Special	100	100	15	Normal	—
TM86	Grass Knot	Grass	Special	—	100	20	Normal	○
TM87	Swagger	Normal	Status	—	90	15	Normal	—
TM90	Substitute	Normal	Status	—	—	10	Self	—
TM92	Trick Room	Psychic	Status	—	—	5	All	—
HM01	Cut	Normal	Physical	50	95	30	Normal	○

● No. 196 | Sun Pokémon
Espeon
Psychic

● HEIGHT: 2'11"
● WEIGHT: 58.4 lbs.
● ITEMS: None

● SIZE COMPARISON

● MALE/FEMALE HAVE SAME FORM

◎ ABILITIES
● Synchronize

◎ EGG GROUPS
Field

◎ STATS
HP ●●
ATTACK ●●●
DEFENSE ●●
SP. ATTACK ●●●●●●
SP. DEFENSE ●●●●●
SPEED ●●●●●

◎ PERFORMANCE
SPEED ★★★
POWER ★★☆
SKILL ★★★★☆
STAMINA ★★
JUMP ★★★☆

● MAIN WAYS TO OBTAIN

Pokémon HeartGold	Level up Eevee with high friendship between 4:00 A.M. and 8:00 P.M.
Pokémon SoulSilver	Level up Eevee with high friendship between 4:00 A.M. and 8:00 P.M.
Pokémon Diamond	Level up Eevee with high friendship between 4:00 A.M. and 8:00 P.M.
Pokémon Pearl	Level up Eevee with high friendship between 4:00 A.M. and 8:00 P.M.
Pokémon Platinum	Level up Eevee with high friendship between 4:00 A.M. and 8:00 P.M.

Pokémon HeartGold	**Pokémon SoulSilver**
It uses the fine hair that covers its body to sense air currents and predict its enemy's actions.	By reading air currents, it can predict things such as the weather or its foe's next move.

◎ EVOLUTION

Eevee
→ Espeon — Level up Eevee with high friendship in the morning or afternoon

Vaporeon — Use Water Stone on Eevee
Umbreon — Level up Eevee with high friendship at night

Jolteon — Use Thunderstone on Eevee
Leafeon — Level up Eevee in Eterna Forest*

Flareon — Use Fire Stone on Eevee
Glaceon — Level up Eevee on Route 217*

*Unable to evolve in *Pokémon HeartGold* or *SoulSilver Version*. Transfer from *Diamond*, *Pearl*, or *Platinum Version*.

No. 197 | Moonlight Pokémon
Umbreon

Dark

- **HEIGHT:** 3'03"
- **WEIGHT:** 59.5 lbs.
- **ITEMS:** None

● SIZE COMPARISON

● MALE/FEMALE HAVE SAME FORM

● ABILITIES
- Synchronize

● EGG GROUPS
Field

● PERFORMANCE
SPEED ★★☆☆   STAMINA ★★★★☆
POWER ★★★★   JUMP ★★★
SKILL ★★

● STATS
- HP ●●●●
- ATTACK ●●●●
- DEFENSE ●●●●
- SP. ATTACK ●●●●
- SP. DEFENSE ●●●●●
- SPEED ●●●

● MAIN WAYS TO OBTAIN

Pokémon HeartGold	Level up Eevee with high friendship between 8:00 P.M. and 4:00 A.M.
Pokémon SoulSilver	Level up Eevee with high friendship between 8:00 P.M. and 4:00 A.M.
Pokémon Diamond	Level up Eevee with high friendship between 8:00 P.M. and 4:00 A.M.
Pokémon Pearl	Level up Eevee with high friendship between 8:00 P.M. and 4:00 A.M.
Pokémon Platinum	Level up Eevee with high friendship between 8:00 P.M. and 4:00 A.M.

Pokémon HeartGold
When agitated, this Pokémon protects itself by spraying poisonous sweat from its pores.

Pokémon SoulSilver
When darkness falls, the rings on the body begin to glow, striking fear in the hearts of anyone nearby.

● EVOLUTION

- Eevee
- Vaporeon — Use Water Stone on Eevee
- Jolteon — Use Thunderstone on Eevee
- Flareon — Use Fire Stone on Eevee
- Espeon — Level up Eevee with high friendship in the morning or afternoon
- Umbreon — Level up Eevee with high friendship at night
- Leafeon — Level up Eevee in Eterna Forest*
- Glaceon — Level up Eevee on Route 217*

● LEVEL-UP MOVES

Lv.	Name	Type	Kind	Pow.	Acc.	PP	Range	DA
1	Tail Whip	Normal	Status	—	100	30	2 Foes	—
1	Tackle	Normal	Physical	35	95	35	Normal	○
1	Helping Hand	Normal	Status	—	—	20	1 Ally	—
8	Sand-Attack	Ground	Status	—	100	15	Normal	—
15	Pursuit	Dark	Physical	40	100	20	Normal	○
22	Quick Attack	Normal	Physical	40	100	30	Normal	○
29	Confuse Ray	Ghost	Status	—	100	10	Normal	—
36	Faint Attack	Dark	Physical	60	—	20	Normal	○
43	Assurance	Dark	Physical	50	100	10	Normal	○
50	Last Resort	Normal	Physical	130	100	5	Normal	○
57	Mean Look	Normal	Status	—	—	5	Normal	—
64	Screech	Normal	Status	—	85	40	Normal	—
71	Moonlight	Normal	Status	—	—	5	Self	—
78	Guard Swap	Psychic	Status	—	—	10	Normal	—

● MOVE MANIAC

Name	Type	Kind	Pow.	Acc.	PP	Range	DA
Headbutt	Normal	Physical	70	100	15	Normal	○

● BP MOVES

Name	Type	Kind	Pow.	Acc.	PP	Range	DA
Sucker Punch	Dark	Physical	80	100	5	Normal	○
Snore	Normal	Special	40	100	15	Normal	—
Spite	Ghost	Status	—	100	10	Normal	—
Helping Hand	Normal	Status	—	—	20	1 Ally	—
Last Resort	Normal	Physical	130	100	5	Normal	○
Swift	Normal	Special	60	—	20	2 Foes	—
Heal Bell	Normal	Status	—	—	5	All Allies	—
Mud-Slap	Ground	Special	20	100	10	Normal	—

● TM & HM MOVES

No.	Name	Type	Kind	Pow.	Acc.	PP	Range	DA
TM06	Toxic	Poison	Status	—	85	10	Normal	—
TM10	Hidden Power	Normal	Special	—	100	15	Normal	—
TM11	Sunny Day	Fire	Status	—	—	5	All	—
TM12	Taunt	Dark	Status	—	100	20	Normal	—
TM15	Hyper Beam	Normal	Special	150	90	5	Normal	—
TM17	Protect	Normal	Status	—	—	10	Self	—
TM18	Rain Dance	Water	Status	—	—	5	All	—
TM21	Frustration	Normal	Physical	—	100	20	Normal	○
TM23	Iron Tail	Steel	Physical	100	75	15	Normal	○
TM27	Return	Normal	Physical	—	100	20	Normal	○
TM28	Dig	Ground	Physical	80	100	10	Normal	○
TM29	Psychic	Psychic	Special	90	100	10	Normal	—
TM30	Shadow Ball	Ghost	Special	80	100	15	Normal	—
TM32	Double Team	Normal	Status	—	—	15	Self	—
TM41	Torment	Dark	Status	—	100	15	Normal	—
TM42	Facade	Normal	Physical	70	100	20	Normal	○
TM43	Secret Power	Normal	Physical	70	100	20	Normal	○
TM44	Rest	Psychic	Status	—	—	10	Self	—
TM45	Attract	Normal	Status	—	100	15	Normal	—
TM49	Snatch	Dark	Status	—	—	10	Depends	—
TM58	Endure	Normal	Status	—	—	10	Self	—
TM66	Payback	Dark	Physical	50	100	10	Normal	○
TM68	Giga Impact	Normal	Physical	150	90	5	Normal	○
TM70	Flash	Normal	Status	—	100	20	Normal	—
TM77	Psych Up	Normal	Status	—	—	10	Normal	—
TM78	Captivate	Normal	Status	—	100	20	2 Foes	—
TM79	Dark Pulse	Dark	Special	80	100	15	Normal	—
TM82	Sleep Talk	Normal	Status	—	—	10	Depends	—
TM83	Natural Gift	Normal	Physical	—	100	15	Normal	—
TM85	Dream Eater	Psychic	Special	100	100	15	Normal	—
TM87	Swagger	Normal	Status	—	90	15	Normal	—
TM90	Substitute	Normal	Status	—	—	10	Self	—
HM01	Cut	Normal	Physical	50	95	30	Normal	○

*Unable to evolve in Pokémon HeartGold or SoulSilver Version. Transfer from Diamond, Pearl, or Platinum Version.

● LEVEL-UP MOVES

Lv.	Name	Type	Kind	Pow.	Acc.	PP	Range	DA
1	BubbleBeam	Water	Special	65	100	20	Normal	—
1	Hypnosis	Psychic	Status	—	60	20	Normal	—
1	DoubleSlap	Normal	Physical	15	85	10	Normal	○
1	Perish Song	Normal	Status	—	—	5	All	—
27	Swagger	Normal	Status	—	90	15	Normal	—
37	Bounce	Flying	Physical	85	85	5	Normal	○
48	Hyper Voice	Normal	Special	90	100	10	2 Foes	—

● MOVE MANIAC

Name	Type	Kind	Pow.	Acc.	PP	Range	DA
Headbutt	Normal	Physical	70	100	15	Normal	○

● BP MOVES

Name	Type	Kind	Pow.	Acc.	PP	Range	DA
Dive	Water	Physical	80	100	10	Normal	○
Icy Wind	Ice	Special	55	95	15	2 Foes	—
Snore	Normal	Special	40	100	15	Normal	—
Helping Hand	Normal	Status	—	—	20	1 Ally	—
Mud-Slap	Ground	Special	20	100	10	Normal	—
Bounce	Flying	Physical	85	85	5	Normal	○

● TM & HM MOVES

No.	Name	Type	Kind	Pow.	Acc.	PP	Range	DA
TM01	Focus Punch	Fighting	Physical	150	100	20	Normal	○
TM03	Water Pulse	Water	Special	60	100	20	Normal	—
TM06	Toxic	Poison	Status	—	85	10	Normal	—
TM07	Hail	Ice	Status	—	—	10	All	—
TM10	Hidden Power	Normal	Special	—	100	15	Normal	—
TM13	Ice Beam	Ice	Special	95	100	10	Normal	—
TM14	Blizzard	Ice	Special	120	70	5	2 Foes	—
TM15	Hyper Beam	Normal	Special	150	90	5	Normal	—
TM17	Protect	Normal	Status	—	—	10	Self	—
TM18	Rain Dance	Water	Status	—	—	5	All	—
TM21	Frustration	Normal	Physical	—	100	20	Normal	○
TM26	Earthquake	Ground	Physical	100	100	10	2 Foes/1 Ally	—
TM27	Return	Normal	Physical	—	100	20	Normal	○
TM28	Dig	Ground	Physical	80	100	10	Normal	○
TM29	Psychic	Psychic	Special	90	100	10	Normal	—
TM31	Brick Break	Fighting	Physical	75	100	15	Normal	○
TM32	Double Team	Normal	Status	—	—	15	Self	—
TM42	Facade	Normal	Physical	70	100	20	Normal	○
TM43	Secret Power	Normal	Physical	70	100	20	Normal	○
TM44	Rest	Psychic	Status	—	—	10	Self	—
TM45	Attract	Normal	Status	—	100	15	Normal	—
TM46	Thief	Dark	Physical	40	100	10	Normal	○
TM52	Focus Blast	Fighting	Special	120	70	5	Normal	—
TM56	Fling	Dark	Physical	—	100	10	Normal	○
TM58	Endure	Normal	Status	—	—	10	Self	—
TM66	Payback	Dark	Physical	50	100	10	Normal	○
TM68	Giga Impact	Normal	Physical	150	90	5	Normal	○
TM78	Captivate	Normal	Status	—	100	20	2 Foes	—
TM82	Sleep Talk	Normal	Status	—	—	10	Depends	—
TM83	Natural Gift	Normal	Physical	—	100	15	Normal	○
TM87	Swagger	Normal	Status	—	90	15	Normal	—
TM90	Substitute	Normal	Status	—	—	10	Self	—
HM03	Surf	Water	Special	95	100	15	2 Foes/1 Ally	—
HM04	Strength	Normal	Physical	80	100	15	Normal	○
HM05	Whirlpool	Water	Special	15	70	15	Normal	—
HM06	Rock Smash	Fighting	Physical	40	100	15	Normal	○
HM07	Waterfall	Water	Physical	80	100	15	Normal	○

○ No. 198 | Darkness Pokémon
Murkrow

`Dark` `Flying`

- ● **HEIGHT:** 1'08"
- ● **WEIGHT:** 4.6 lbs.
- ● **ITEMS:** None

● **SIZE COMPARISON**

● **MALE FORM**
Larger feather crest

● **FEMALE FORM**
Smaller feather crest

○ ABILITIES
- ● Insomnia
- ● Super Luck

○ STATS
HP	●●
ATTACK	●●●●
DEFENSE	●●
SP. ATTACK	●●●●
SP. DEFENSE	●●
SPEED	●●●●

○ EGG GROUPS
Flying

○ PERFORMANCE
SPEED ★★★☆	STAMINA ★★★☆
POWER ★★☆	JUMP ★★★★
SKILL ★★★☆	

● MAIN WAYS TO OBTAIN

Pokémon HeartGold — Safari Zone (Swamp Area)

Pokémon SoulSilver — Safari Zone (Swamp Area)

Pokémon Diamond — Eterna Forest (night only)

Pokémon Pearl — —

Pokémon Platinum — —

Pokémon HeartGold
Feared and loathed by many, it is believed to bring misfortune to all those who see it at night.

Pokémon SoulSilver
It is said that when chased, it lures its attacker onto dark mountain trails where the foe will get lost.

○ EVOLUTION

Murkrow

Use Dusk Stone →

Honchkrow

No. 199 | Royal Pokémon
Slowking

Water | Psychic

● HEIGHT: 6'07"
● WEIGHT: 175.3 lbs.
● ITEMS: None

● SIZE COMPARISON

● MALE/FEMALE HAVE SAME FORM

● ABILITIES
- Oblivious
- Own Tempo

● STATS
HP	●●●●
ATTACK	●●●
DEFENSE	●●●
SP. ATTACK	●●●
SP. DEFENSE	●●●●
SPEED	●

● EGG GROUPS
Monster
Water 1

● PERFORMANCE
SPEED ★★☆	STAMINA ★★☆
POWER ★★☆	JUMP ★★☆
SKILL ★★★★★	

● MAIN WAYS TO OBTAIN

Pokémon HeartGold	Link trade Slowpoke while it holds the King's Rock
Pokémon SoulSilver	Link trade Slowpoke while it holds the King's Rock
Pokémon Diamond	—
Pokémon Pearl	Link trade Slowpoke while it holds the King's Rock
Pokémon Platinum	Link trade Slowpoke while it holds the King's Rock

Pokémon HeartGold
It has incredible intellect and intuition. Whatever the situation, it remains calm and collected.

Pokémon SoulSilver
When its head was bitten, toxins entered SLOWPOKE's head and unlocked an extraordinary power.

● EVOLUTION

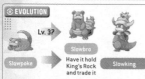

Slowpoke → (Lv. 37) Slowbro
Have it hold King's Rock and trade it → Slowking

● LEVEL-UP MOVES

Lv.	Name	Type	Kind	Pow.	Acc.	PP	Range	DA
1	Power Gem	Rock	Special	70	100	10	Normal	—
1	Hidden Power	Normal	Special	—	100	15	Normal	—
1	Curse	???	Status	—	—	10	Normal/Self	—
1	Yawn	Normal	Status	—	—	10	Normal	—
1	Tackle	Normal	Physical	35	95	35	Normal	○
6	Growl	Normal	Status	—	100	40	2 Foes	—
11	Water Gun	Water	Special	40	100	25	Normal	—
15	Confusion	Psychic	Special	50	100	25	Normal	—
20	Disable	Normal	Status	—	80	20	Normal	—
25	Headbutt	Normal	Physical	70	100	15	Normal	○
29	Water Pulse	Water	Special	60	100	20	Normal	—
34	Zen Headbutt	Psychic	Physical	80	90	15	Normal	○
39	Nasty Plot	Dark	Status	—	—	20	Self	—
43	Swagger	Normal	Status	—	90	15	Normal	—
48	Psychic	Psychic	Special	90	100	10	Normal	—
53	Trump Card	Normal	Special	—	—	5	Normal	○
57	Psych Up	Normal	Status	—	—	10	Normal	—

● MOVE MANIAC

Name	Type	Kind	Pow.	Acc.	PP	Range	DA
Headbutt	Normal	Physical	70	100	15	Normal	○

● BP MOVES

Name	Type	Kind	Pow.	Acc.	PP	Range	DA
Dive	Water	Physical	80	100	10	Normal	○
Fury Cutter	Bug	Physical	10	95	20	Normal	○
Icy Wind	Ice	Special	55	95	15	2 Foes	—
Ice Punch	Ice	Physical	75	100	15	Normal	○
Zen Headbutt	Psychic	Physical	80	90	15	Normal	○
Trick	Psychic	Status	—	100	10	Normal	—
Snore	Normal	Special	40	100	15	Normal	—
Swift	Normal	Special	60	—	20	2 Foes	—
Magic Coat	Psychic	Status	—	—	15	Self	—
Block	Normal	Status	—	—	5	Normal	—
Mud-Slap	Ground	Special	20	100	10	Normal	—
Aqua Tail	Water	Physical	90	90	10	Normal	○
Signal Beam	Bug	Special	75	100	15	Normal	—
Iron Defense	Steel	Status	—	—	15	Self	—

● TM & HM MOVES

No.	Name	Type	Kind	Pow.	Acc.	PP	Range	DA
TM01	Focus Punch	Fighting	Physical	150	100	20	Normal	○
TM03	Water Pulse	Water	Special	60	100	20	Normal	—
TM04	Calm Mind	Psychic	Status	—	—	20	Self	—
TM06	Toxic	Poison	Status	—	85	10	Normal	—
TM07	Hail	Ice	Status	—	—	10	All	—
TM10	Hidden Power	Normal	Special	—	100	15	Normal	—
TM11	Sunny Day	Fire	Status	—	—	5	All	—
TM13	Ice Beam	Ice	Special	95	100	10	Normal	—
TM14	Blizzard	Ice	Special	120	70	5	2 Foes	—
TM15	Hyper Beam	Normal	Special	150	90	5	Normal	—
TM16	Light Screen	Psychic	Status	—	—	30	2 Allies	—
TM17	Protect	Normal	Status	—	—	10	Self	—
TM18	Rain Dance	Water	Status	—	—	5	All	—
TM20	Safeguard	Normal	Status	—	—	25	2 Allies	—
TM21	Frustration	Normal	Physical	—	100	20	Normal	○
TM23	Iron Tail	Steel	Physical	100	75	15	Normal	○
TM26	Earthquake	Ground	Physical	100	100	10	2 Foes/1 Ally	—
TM27	Return	Normal	Physical	—	100	20	Normal	○
TM28	Dig	Ground	Physical	80	100	10	Normal	○
TM29	Psychic	Psychic	Special	90	100	10	Normal	—
TM30	Shadow Ball	Ghost	Special	80	100	15	Normal	—
TM31	Brick Break	Fighting	Physical	75	100	15	Normal	○
TM32	Double Team	Normal	Status	—	—	15	Self	—
TM35	Flamethrower	Fire	Special	95	100	15	Normal	—
TM38	Fire Blast	Fire	Special	120	85	5	Normal	—
TM42	Facade	Normal	Physical	70	100	20	Normal	○
TM43	Secret Power	Normal	Physical	70	100	20	Normal	○
TM44	Rest	Psychic	Status	—	—	10	Self	—
TM45	Attract	Normal	Status	—	100	15	Normal	—
TM48	Skill Swap	Psychic	Status	—	—	10	Normal	—
TM52	Focus Blast	Fighting	Special	120	70	5	Normal	—
TM55	Brine	Water	Special	65	100	10	Normal	—
TM56	Fling	Dark	Physical	—	100	10	Normal	○
TM58	Endure	Normal	Status	—	—	10	Self	—
TM60	Drain Punch	Fighting	Physical	60	100	5	Normal	○
TM67	Recycle	Normal	Status	—	—	10	Self	—
TM68	Giga Impact	Normal	Physical	150	90	5	Normal	○
TM70	Flash	Normal	Status	—	100	20	Normal	—
TM72	Avalanche	Ice	Physical	60	100	10	Normal	○
TM73	Thunder Wave	Electric	Status	—	100	20	Normal	—
TM77	Psych Up	Normal	Status	—	—	10	Normal	—
TM78	Captivate	Normal	Status	—	100	20	2 Foes	—
TM82	Sleep Talk	Normal	Status	—	—	10	Depends	—
TM83	Natural Gift	Normal	Physical	—	100	15	Normal	—
TM85	Dream Eater	Psychic	Special	100	100	15	Normal	—
TM86	Grass Knot	Grass	Special	—	100	20	Normal	○
TM87	Swagger	Normal	Status	—	90	15	Normal	—
TM90	Substitute	Normal	Status	—	—	10	Self	—
TM92	Trick Room	Psychic	Status	—	—	5	All	—
HM03	Surf	Water	Special	95	100	15	2 Foes/1 Ally	—
HM04	Strength	Normal	Physical	80	100	15	Normal	○
HM05	Whirlpool	Water	Special	15	70	15	Normal	—
HM06	Rock Smash	Fighting	Physical	40	100	15	Normal	○

● LEVEL-UP MOVES

Lv.	Name	Type	Kind	Pow.	Acc.	PP	Range	DA
1	Growl	Normal	Status	—	100	40	2 Foes	—
1	Psywave	Psychic	Special	—	80	15	Normal	—
5	Spite	Ghost	Status	—	100	10	Normal	—
10	Astonish	Ghost	Physical	30	100	15	Normal	○
14	Confuse Ray	Ghost	Status	—	100	10	Normal	—
19	Mean Look	Normal	Status	—	—	5	Normal	—
23	Psybeam	Psychic	Special	65	100	20	Normal	—
28	Pain Split	Normal	Status	—	—	20	Normal	—
32	Payback	Dark	Physical	50	100	10	Normal	○
37	Shadow Ball	Ghost	Special	80	100	15	Normal	—
41	Perish Song	Normal	Status	—	—	5	All	—
46	Grudge	Ghost	Status	—	—	5	Self	—
50	Power Gem	Rock	Special	70	100	20	Normal	—

● MOVE MANIAC

Name	Type	Kind	Pow.	Acc.	PP	Range	DA
Headbutt	Normal	Physical	70	100	15	Normal	○

● BP MOVES

Name	Type	Kind	Pow.	Acc.	PP	Range	DA
Icy Wind	Ice	Special	55	95	15	2 Foes	—
Ominous Wind	Ghost	Special	60	100	5	Normal	—
Trick	Psychic	Status	—	100	10	Normal	—
Sucker Punch	Dark	Physical	80	100	5	Normal	○
Snore	Normal	Special	40	100	15	Normal	—
Spite	Ghost	Status	—	100	10	Normal	—
Swift	Normal	Special	60	—	20	2 Foes	—
Uproar	Normal	Special	50	100	10	1 Random	—
Magic Coat	Psychic	Status	—	—	15	Self	—
Heal Bell	Normal	Status	—	—	5	All Allies	—
Pain Split	Normal	Status	—	—	20	Normal	—

● TM & HM MOVES

No.	Name	Type	Kind	Pow.	Acc.	PP	Range	DA
TM04	Calm Mind	Psychic	Status	—	—	20	Self	—
TM06	Toxic	Poison	Status	—	85	10	Normal	—
TM10	Hidden Power	Normal	Special	—	100	15	Normal	—
TM11	Sunny Day	Fire	Status	—	—	5	All	—
TM12	Taunt	Dark	Status	—	100	20	Normal	—
TM17	Protect	Normal	Status	—	—	10	Self	—
TM18	Rain Dance	Water	Status	—	—	5	All	—
TM21	Frustration	Normal	Physical	—	100	20	Normal	○
TM24	Thunderbolt	Electric	Special	95	100	15	Normal	—
TM25	Thunder	Electric	Special	120	70	10	Normal	—
TM27	Return	Normal	Physical	—	100	20	Normal	○
TM29	Psychic	Psychic	Special	90	100	10	Normal	—
TM30	Shadow Ball	Ghost	Special	80	100	15	Normal	—
TM32	Double Team	Normal	Status	—	—	15	Self	—
TM34	Shock Wave	Electric	Special	60	—	20	Normal	—
TM40	Aerial Ace	Flying	Physical	60	—	20	Normal	○
TM41	Torment	Dark	Status	—	100	15	Normal	—
TM42	Facade	Normal	Physical	70	100	20	Normal	○
TM43	Secret Power	Normal	Physical	70	100	20	Normal	○
TM44	Rest	Psychic	Status	—	—	10	Self	—
TM45	Attract	Normal	Status	—	100	15	Normal	—
TM46	Thief	Dark	Physical	40	100	10	Normal	○
TM48	Skill Swap	Psychic	Status	—	—	10	Normal	—
TM49	Snatch	Dark	Status	—	—	10	Depends	—
TM57	Charge Beam	Electric	Special	50	90	10	Normal	—
TM58	Endure	Normal	Status	—	—	10	Self	—
TM61	Will-O-Wisp	Fire	Status	—	75	15	Normal	—
TM63	Embargo	Dark	Status	—	100	15	Normal	—
TM66	Payback	Dark	Physical	50	100	10	Normal	○
TM70	Flash	Normal	Status	—	100	20	Normal	—
TM73	Thunder Wave	Electric	Status	—	100	20	Normal	—
TM77	Psych Up	Normal	Status	—	—	10	Normal	—
TM78	Captivate	Normal	Status	—	100	20	2 Foes	—
TM79	Dark Pulse	Dark	Special	80	100	15	Normal	—
TM82	Sleep Talk	Normal	Status	—	—	10	Depends	—
TM83	Natural Gift	Normal	Physical	—	100	15	Normal	—
TM85	Dream Eater	Psychic	Special	100	100	15	Normal	—
TM87	Swagger	Normal	Status	—	90	15	Normal	—
TM90	Substitute	Normal	Status	—	—	10	Self	—
TM92	Trick Room	Psychic	Status	—	—	5	All	—

● EGG MOVES

Name	Type	Kind	Pow.	Acc.	PP	Range	DA
Screech	Normal	Status	—	85	40	Normal	—
Destiny Bond	Ghost	Status	—	—	5	Self	—
Psych Up	Normal	Status	—	—	10	Normal	—
Imprison	Psychic	Status	—	—	10	Self	—
Memento	Dark	Status	—	100	10	Normal	—
Sucker Punch	Dark	Physical	80	100	5	Normal	○
Shadow Sneak	Ghost	Physical	40	100	30	Normal	○
Curse	???	Status	—	—	10	Normal/Self	—
Spite	Ghost	Status	—	100	10	Normal	—
Ominous Wind	Ghost	Special	60	100	5	Normal	—
Nasty Plot	Dark	Status	—	—	20	Self	—

No. 200 | Screech Pokémon
Misdreavus
Ghost

- ● HEIGHT: 2'04"
- ● WEIGHT: 2.2 lbs.
- ● ITEMS: None

● SIZE COMPARISON

● MALE/FEMALE HAVE SAME FORM

⊘ ABILITIES
- ● Levitate

⊘ STATS
- HP ●●
- ATTACK ●●●
- DEFENSE ●●●
- SP. ATTACK ●●●●
- SP. DEFENSE ●●●●
- SPEED ●●●●

⊘ EGG GROUPS
Amorphous

⊘ PERFORMANCE
SPEED ★★★☆	STAMINA ★★
POWER ★☆	JUMP ★★★★★
SKILL ★★★	

● MAIN WAYS TO OBTAIN

Pokémon HeartGold — Mt. Silver Cave interior (night only)

Pokémon SoulSilver — Mt. Silver Cave interior (night only)

Pokémon Diamond — —

Pokémon Pearl — Eterna Forest (night only)

Pokémon Platinum — —

Pokémon HeartGold
It likes playing mischievous tricks, such as screaming and wailing to startle people at night.

Pokémon SoulSilver
It loves to bite and yank people's hair from behind without warning, just to see their shocked reactions.

⊘ EVOLUTION

Misdreavus → Use Dusk Stone → Mismagius

No. 201 | Symbol Pokémon
Unown

Psychic

- **HEIGHT:** 1'08"
- **WEIGHT:** 11.0 lbs.
- **ITEMS:** None

● SIZE COMPARISON

● GENDER UNKNOWN

⊙ ABILITIES
- Levitate

⊙ STATS
- HP ●●
- ATTACK ●●●
- DEFENSE ●●●
- SP. ATTACK ●●●
- SP. DEFENSE ●●●
- SPEED ●●

⊙ EGG GROUPS
No Egg has ever been discovered

⊙ PERFORMANCE
SPEED ★★★☆☆   STAMINA ★★☆☆☆
POWER ★★☆☆   JUMP ★★☆☆☆
SKILL ★★☆☆☆

● MAIN WAYS TO OBTAIN

Pokémon HeartGold	Ruins of Alph
Pokémon SoulSilver	Ruins of Alph
Pokémon Diamond	Solaceon Ruins
Pokémon Pearl	Solaceon Ruins
Pokémon Platinum	Solaceon Ruins

Pokémon HeartGold	Pokémon SoulSilver
Their shapes look like hieroglyphs on ancient tablets. It is said that the two are somehow related.	Its flat, thin body is always stuck on walls. Its shape appears to have some meaning.

⊙ EVOLUTION
Does not evolve

● LEVEL-UP MOVES

Lv.	Name	Type	Kind	Pow.	Acc.	PP	Range	DA
1	Hidden Power	Normal	Special	—	100	15	Normal	—

● MOVE MANIAC

Name	Type	Kind	Pow.	Acc.	PP	Range	DA

● BP MOVES

Name	Type	Kind	Pow.	Acc.	PP	Range	DA

● UNOWN CHART

A B C D
E F G H
I J K L
M N O P
Q R S T
U V W X
Y Z ! ?

---

*The maximum Skill Performance for Unown ! and ? is 1 star higher

● LEVEL-UP MOVES

Lv.	Name	Type	Kind	Pow.	Acc.	PP	Range	DA
1	Counter	Fighting	Physical	—	100	20	Self	○
1	Mirror Coat	Psychic	Special	—	100	20	Self	—
1	Safeguard	Normal	Status	—	—	25	2 Allies	—
1	Destiny Bond	Ghost	Status	—	—	5	Self	—

● MOVE MANIAC

Name	Type	Kind	Pow.	Acc.	PP	Range	DA

● BP MOVES

Name	Type	Kind	Pow.	Acc.	PP	Range	DA

● TM & HM MOVES

No.	Name	Type	Kind	Pow.	Acc.	PP	Range	DA

◉ No. 202 | Patient Pokémon
Wobbuffet

Psychic

● **HEIGHT:** 4'03"
● **WEIGHT:** 62.8 lbs.
● **ITEMS:** None

● SIZE COMPARISON

● **MALE FORM**
Blue lips

● **FEMALE FORM**
Red lips

◉ ABILITIES
● Shadow Tag

◉ EGG GROUPS
Amorphous

◉ STATS
HP ●●●●●●
ATTACK ●●
DEFENSE ●●
SP. ATTACK ●
SP. DEFENSE ●●
SPEED ●●

◉ PERFORMANCE
SPEED ★☆
POWER ★★★☆
SKILL ★★★☆☆

STAMINA ★★★★★
JUMP ★★☆

● MAIN WAYS TO OBTAIN

Pokémon HeartGold — Dark Cave, Blackthorn City side

Pokémon SoulSilver — Dark Cave, Blackthorn City side

Pokémon Diamond — Lake Valor (use Poké Radar)

Pokémon Pearl — Lake Valor (use Poké Radar)

Pokémon Platinum — Lake Valor (use Poké Radar)

Pokémon HeartGold	Pokémon SoulSilver
It hates light and shock. If attacked, it inflates its body to build up its counterstrike.	To keep its pitch-black tail hidden, it lives quietly in the darkness. It is never first to attack.

◉ EVOLUTION

Wynaut — Lv. 15 — Wobbuffet

⦿ No. 203 | Long Neck Pokémon
Girafarig

`Normal` `Psychic`

- ● **HEIGHT:** 4'11"
- ● **WEIGHT:** 91.5 lbs.
- ● **ITEMS:** Persim Berry

● **SIZE COMPARISON**

- ● **MALE FORM** — Larger dark section
- ● **FEMALE FORM** — Smaller dark section

⊙ ABILITIES
- ● Inner Focus
- ● Early Bird

⊙ STATS
- HP ●●●
- ATTACK ●●●
- DEFENSE ●●●
- SP. ATTACK ●●●●
- SP. DEFENSE ●●●
- SPEED ●●●●

⊙ EGG GROUPS
Field

⊙ PERFORMANCE
SPEED ★★★☆	STAMINA ★★☆
POWER ★★★☆	JUMP ★★☆
SKILL ★★★☆	

● MAIN WAYS TO OBTAIN

Pokémon HeartGold	Route 43
Pokémon SoulSilver	Route 43
Pokémon Diamond	Valor Lakefront
Pokémon Pearl	Valor Lakefront
Pokémon Platinum	Valor Lakefront

Pokémon HeartGold	**Pokémon SoulSilver**
Its tail has a small brain of its own. Beware! If you get close, it may react to your scent by biting.	Its tail, which also contains a small brain, may bite on its own if it notices an alluring smell.

⊙ EVOLUTION
Does not evolve

● LEVEL-UP MOVES
Lv.	Name	Type	Kind	Pow.	Acc.	PP	Range	DA
1	Power Swap	Psychic	Status	—	—	10	Normal	—
1	Guard Swap	Psychic	Status	—	—	10	Normal	—
1	Astonish	Ghost	Physical	30	100	15	Normal	○
1	Tackle	Normal	Physical	35	95	35	Normal	○
1	Growl	Normal	Status	—	100	40	2 Foes	—
1	Confusion	Psychic	Special	50	100	25	Normal	—
5	Odor Sleuth	Normal	Status	—	—	40	Normal	—
10	Stomp	Normal	Physical	65	100	20	Normal	○
14	Agility	Psychic	Status	—	—	30	Self	—
19	Psybeam	Psychic	Special	65	100	20	Normal	—
23	Baton Pass	Normal	Status	—	—	40	Self	—
28	Assurance	Dark	Physical	50	100	10	Normal	○
32	Double Hit	Normal	Physical	35	90	10	Normal	○
37	Psychic	Psychic	Special	90	100	10	Normal	—
41	Zen Headbutt	Psychic	Physical	80	90	15	Normal	○
46	Crunch	Dark	Physical	80	100	15	Normal	○

● MOVE MANIAC
Name	Type	Kind	Pow.	Acc.	PP	Range	DA
Headbutt	Normal	Physical	70	100	15	Normal	○

● BP MOVES
Name	Type	Kind	Pow.	Acc.	PP	Range	DA
Zen Headbutt	Psychic	Physical	80	90	15	Normal	○
Trick	Psychic	Status	—	100	10	Normal	—
Sucker Punch	Dark	Physical	80	100	5	Normal	○
Snore	Normal	Special	40	100	15	Normal	—
Swift	Normal	Special	60	—	20	2 Foes	—
Uproar	Normal	Special	50	100	10	1 Random	—
Gravity	Psychic	Status	—	—	5	All	—
Magic Coat	Psychic	Status	—	—	15	Self	—
Mud-Slap	Ground	Special	20	100	10	Normal	—
Signal Beam	Bug	Special	75	100	15	Normal	—

● TM & HM MOVES
No.	Name	Type	Kind	Pow.	Acc.	PP	Range	DA
TM04	Calm Mind	Psychic	Status	—	—	20	Self	—
TM06	Toxic	Poison	Status	—	85	10	Normal	—
TM10	Hidden Power	Normal	Special	—	100	15	Normal	—
TM11	Sunny Day	Fire	Status	—	—	5	All	—
TM16	Light Screen	Psychic	Status	—	—	30	2 Allies	—
TM17	Protect	Normal	Status	—	—	10	Self	—
TM18	Rain Dance	Water	Status	—	—	5	All	—
TM21	Frustration	Normal	Physical	—	100	20	Normal	○
TM23	Iron Tail	Steel	Physical	100	75	15	Normal	○
TM24	Thunderbolt	Electric	Special	95	100	15	Normal	—
TM25	Thunder	Electric	Special	120	70	10	Normal	—
TM26	Earthquake	Ground	Physical	100	100	10	2 Foes/1 Ally	—
TM27	Return	Normal	Physical	—	100	20	Normal	○
TM29	Psychic	Psychic	Special	90	100	10	Normal	—
TM30	Shadow Ball	Ghost	Special	80	100	15	Normal	—
TM32	Double Team	Normal	Status	—	—	15	Self	—
TM33	Reflect	Psychic	Status	—	—	20	2 Allies	—
TM34	Shock Wave	Electric	Special	60	—	20	Normal	—
TM42	Facade	Normal	Physical	70	100	20	Normal	○
TM43	Secret Power	Normal	Physical	70	100	20	Normal	○
TM44	Rest	Psychic	Status	—	—	10	Self	—
TM45	Attract	Normal	Status	—	100	15	Normal	—
TM46	Thief	Dark	Physical	40	100	10	Normal	○
TM48	Skill Swap	Psychic	Status	—	—	10	Normal	—
TM53	Energy Ball	Grass	Special	80	100	10	Normal	—
TM57	Charge Beam	Electric	Special	50	90	10	Normal	—
TM58	Endure	Normal	Status	—	—	10	Self	—
TM67	Recycle	Normal	Status	—	—	10	Self	—
TM70	Flash	Normal	Status	—	100	20	Normal	—
TM73	Thunder Wave	Electric	Status	—	100	20	Normal	—
TM77	Psych Up	Normal	Status	—	—	10	Normal	—
TM78	Captivate	Normal	Status	—	100	20	2 Foes	—
TM82	Sleep Talk	Normal	Status	—	—	10	Depends	—
TM83	Natural Gift	Normal	Physical	—	100	15	Normal	—
TM85	Dream Eater	Psychic	Special	100	100	15	Normal	—
TM86	Grass Knot	Grass	Special	—	100	20	Normal	○
TM87	Swagger	Normal	Status	—	90	15	Normal	—
TM90	Substitute	Normal	Status	—	—	10	Self	—
TM92	Trick Room	Psychic	Status	—	—	5	All	—
HM04	Strength	Normal	Physical	80	100	15	Normal	○
HM06	Rock Smash	Fighting	Physical	40	100	15	Normal	○

● EGG MOVES
Name	Type	Kind	Pow.	Acc.	PP	Range	DA
Take Down	Normal	Physical	90	85	20	Normal	○
Amnesia	Psychic	Status	—	—	20	Self	—
Foresight	Normal	Status	—	—	40	Normal	—
Future Sight	Psychic	Special	80	90	15	Normal	—
Beat Up	Dark	Physical	10	100	10	Normal	—
Psych Up	Normal	Status	—	—	10	Normal	—
Wish	Normal	Status	—	—	10	Self	—
Magic Coat	Psychic	Status	—	—	15	Self	—
Double Kick	Fighting	Physical	30	100	30	Normal	○
Mirror Coat	Psychic	Special	—	100	20	Self	—
Razor Wind	Normal	Special	80	100	10	2 Foes	—

● LEVEL-UP MOVES

Lv.	Name	Type	Kind	Pow.	Acc.	PP	Range	DA
1	Tackle	Normal	Physical	35	95	35	Normal	○
1	Protect	Normal	Status	—	—	10	Self	—
6	Selfdestruct	Normal	Physical	200	100	5	2 Foes/1 Ally	—
9	Bug Bite	Bug	Physical	60	100	20	Normal	○
12	Take Down	Normal	Physical	90	85	20	Normal	○
17	Rapid Spin	Normal	Physical	20	100	40	Normal	○
20	Bide	Normal	Physical	—	—	10	Self	○
23	Natural Gift	Normal	Physical	—	100	15	Normal	—
28	Spikes	Ground	Status	—	—	20	2 Foes	—
31	Payback	Dark	Physical	50	100	10	Normal	○
34	Explosion	Normal	Physical	250	100	5	2 Foes/1 Ally	—
39	Iron Defense	Steel	Status	—	—	15	Self	—
42	Gyro Ball	Steel	Physical	—	100	5	Normal	○
45	Double-Edge	Normal	Physical	120	100	15	Normal	○

● MOVE MANIAC

Name	Type	Kind	Pow.	Acc.	PP	Range	DA
Headbutt	Normal	Physical	70	100	15	Normal	○

● BP MOVES

Name	Type	Kind	Pow.	Acc.	PP	Range	DA
Bug Bite	Bug	Physical	60	100	20	Normal	○
Snore	Normal	Special	40	100	15	Normal	—
String Shot	Bug	Status	—	95	40	2 Foes	—
Gravity	Psychic	Status	—	—	5	All	—
Rollout	Rock	Physical	30	90	20	Normal	○
Iron Defense	Steel	Status	—	—	15	Self	—
Pain Split	Normal	Status	—	—	20	Normal	—

● TM & HM MOVES

No.	Name	Type	Kind	Pow.	Acc.	PP	Range	DA
TM06	Toxic	Poison	Status	—	85	10	Normal	—
TM10	Hidden Power	Normal	Special	—	100	15	Normal	—
TM11	Sunny Day	Fire	Status	—	—	5	All	—
TM16	Light Screen	Psychic	Status	—	—	30	2 Allies	—
TM17	Protect	Normal	Status	—	—	10	Self	—
TM19	Giga Drain	Grass	Special	60	100	10	Normal	—
TM21	Frustration	Normal	Physical	—	100	20	Normal	○
TM22	SolarBeam	Grass	Special	120	100	10	Normal	—
TM26	Earthquake	Ground	Physical	100	100	10	2 Foes/1 Ally	—
TM27	Return	Normal	Physical	—	100	20	Normal	○
TM28	Dig	Ground	Physical	80	100	10	Normal	○
TM32	Double Team	Normal	Status	—	—	15	Self	—
TM33	Reflect	Psychic	Status	—	—	20	2 Allies	—
TM37	Sandstorm	Rock	Status	—	—	10	All	—
TM39	Rock Tomb	Rock	Physical	50	80	10	Normal	—
TM42	Facade	Normal	Physical	70	100	20	Normal	○
TM43	Secret Power	Normal	Physical	70	100	20	Normal	—
TM44	Rest	Psychic	Status	—	—	10	Self	—
TM45	Attract	Normal	Status	—	100	15	Normal	—
TM58	Endure	Normal	Status	—	—	10	Self	—
TM64	Explosion	Normal	Physical	250	100	5	2 Foes/1 Ally	—
TM66	Payback	Dark	Physical	50	100	10	Normal	○
TM74	Gyro Ball	Steel	Physical	—	100	5	Normal	○
TM76	Stealth Rock	Rock	Status	—	—	20	2 Foes	—
TM78	Captivate	Normal	Status	—	100	20	2 Foes	—
TM80	Rock Slide	Rock	Physical	75	90	10	2 Foes	—
TM82	Sleep Talk	Normal	Status	—	—	10	Depends	—
TM83	Natural Gift	Normal	Physical	—	100	15	Normal	—
TM87	Swagger	Normal	Status	—	90	15	Normal	—
TM90	Substitute	Normal	Status	—	—	10	Self	—
HM04	Strength	Normal	Physical	80	100	15	Normal	○
HM06	Rock Smash	Fighting	Physical	40	100	15	Normal	○

● EGG MOVES

Name	Type	Kind	Pow.	Acc.	PP	Range	DA
Reflect	Psychic	Status	—	—	20	2 Allies	—
Pin Missile	Bug	Physical	14	85	20	Normal	—
Flail	Normal	Physical	—	100	15	Normal	○
Swift	Normal	Special	60	—	20	2 Foes	○
Counter	Fighting	Physical	—	100	20	Self	○
Sand Tomb	Ground	Physical	15	70	15	Normal	—
Revenge	Fighting	Physical	60	100	10	Normal	○
Double-Edge	Normal	Physical	120	100	15	Normal	○
Toxic Spikes	Poison	Status	—	—	20	2 Foes	—
Power Trick	Psychic	Status	—	—	10	Self	—

⊙ No. 204 | Bagwurm Pokémon
Pineco

Bug

- ● HEIGHT: 2'00"
- ● WEIGHT: 15.9 lbs.
- ● ITEMS: None

● SIZE COMPARISON

● MALE/FEMALE HAVE SAME FORM

⊙ ABILITIES
● Sturdy

⊙ STATS
HP ●●
ATTACK ●●●
DEFENSE ●●●●
SP. ATTACK ●
SP. DEFENSE ●
SPEED ●

⊙ EGG GROUPS
Bug

⊙ PERFORMANCE
SPEED ★★☆ STAMINA ★★★☆☆
POWER ★★☆☆☆ JUMP ★★★
SKILL ★★★☆

● MAIN WAYS TO OBTAIN

Pokémon HeartGold	New Bark Town (use Headbutt)
Pokémon SoulSilver	New Bark Town (use Headbutt)
Pokémon Diamond	Route 203 (after obtaining the National Pokédex, insert *Pokémon Emerald* into your Nintendo DS's Game Pak slot)
Pokémon Pearl	Route 203 (after obtaining the National Pokédex, insert *Pokémon Emerald* into your Nintendo DS's Game Pak slot)
Pokémon Platinum	Route 203 (after obtaining the National Pokédex, insert *Pokémon Emerald* into your Nintendo DS's Game Pak slot)

Pokémon HeartGold
It likes to make its shell thicker by adding layers of tree bark. The additional weight doesn't bother it.

Pokémon SoulSilver
It hangs and waits for flying insect prey to come near. It does not move about much on its own.

⊙ EVOLUTION

Lv. 31

Pineco → Forretress

No. 205 | Bagworm Pokémon
Forretress

`Bug` `Steel`

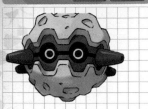

- **HEIGHT:** 3'11"
- **WEIGHT:** 277.3 lbs.
- **ITEMS:** None

● SIZE COMPARISON

● MALE/FEMALE HAVE SAME FORM

ABILITIES
- Sturdy

STATS
HP ●●●
ATTACK ●●●●
DEFENSE ●●●●●
SP. ATTACK ●●●
SP. DEFENSE ●●●
SPEED ●●

EGG GROUPS
Bug

PERFORMANCE
SPEED ★☆☆☆☆   STAMINA ★★★★☆
POWER ★★★★☆   JUMP ★★☆☆☆
SKILL ★★★☆☆

● MAIN WAYS TO OBTAIN

Pokémon HeartGold	Level up Pineco to Lv. 31
Pokémon SoulSilver	Level up Pineco to Lv. 31
Pokémon Diamond	Level up Pineco to Lv. 31
Pokémon Pearl	Level up Pineco to Lv. 31
Pokémon Platinum	Level up Pineco to Lv. 31

Pokémon HeartGold
Its entire body is shielded by a steel-hard shell. What lurks inside this shell is a total mystery.

Pokémon SoulSilver
It remains immovably rooted to its tree. It scatters pieces of its hard shell to drive its enemies away.

EVOLUTION

Pineco → Lv. 31 → Forretress

● LEVEL-UP MOVES

Lv.	Name	Type	Kind	Pow.	Acc.	PP	Range	DA
1	Toxic Spikes	Poison	Status	—	—	20	2 Foes	—
1	Tackle	Normal	Physical	35	95	35	Normal	○
1	Protect	Normal	Status	—	—	10	Self	—
1	Selfdestruct	Normal	Physical	200	100	20	2 Foes/1 Ally	—
1	Bug Bite	Bug	Physical	60	100	20	Normal	○
6	Selfdestruct	Normal	Physical	200	100	5	2 Foes/1 Ally	—
9	Bug Bite	Bug	Physical	60	100	20	Normal	○
12	Take Down	Normal	Physical	90	85	20	Normal	○
17	Rapid Spin	Normal	Physical	20	100	40	Normal	○
20	Bide	Normal	Physical	—	—	10	Self	○
23	Natural Gift	Normal	Physical	—	100	15	Normal	—
28	Spikes	Ground	Status	—	—	20	2 Foes	—
31	Mirror Shot	Steel	Special	65	85	10	Normal	—
33	Payback	Dark	Physical	50	100	10	Normal	○
38	Explosion	Normal	Physical	250	100	5	2 Foes/1 Ally	—
45	Iron Defense	Steel	Status	—	—	15	Self	—
50	Gyro Ball	Steel	Physical	—	100	5	Normal	○
55	Double-Edge	Normal	Physical	120	100	15	Normal	○
62	Magnet Rise	Electric	Status	—	—	10	Self	—
67	Zap Cannon	Electric	Special	120	50	5	Normal	—

● MOVE MANIAC

Name	Type	Kind	Pow.	Acc.	PP	Range	DA
Headbutt	Normal	Physical	70	100	15	Normal	○

● BP MOVES

Name	Type	Kind	Pow.	Acc.	PP	Range	DA
Bug Bite	Bug	Physical	60	100	20	Normal	○
Snore	Normal	Special	40	100	15	Normal	—
Magnet Rise	Electric	Status	—	—	10	Self	—
String Shot	Bug	Status	—	95	40	2 Foes	—
Gravity	Psychic	Status	—	—	5	All	—
Block	Normal	Status	—	—	5	Normal	—
Rollout	Rock	Physical	30	90	20	Normal	○
Signal Beam	Bug	Special	75	100	15	Normal	—
Iron Defense	Steel	Status	—	—	15	Self	—
Pain Split	Normal	Status	—	—	20	Normal	—

● TM & HM MOVES

No.	Name	Type	Kind	Pow.	Acc.	PP	Range	DA
TM06	Toxic	Poison	Status	—	85	10	Normal	—
TM10	Hidden Power	Normal	Special	—	100	15	Normal	—
TM11	Sunny Day	Fire	Status	—	—	5	All	—
TM15	Hyper Beam	Normal	Special	150	90	5	Normal	—
TM16	Light Screen	Psychic	Status	—	—	30	2 Allies	—
TM17	Protect	Normal	Status	—	—	10	Self	—
TM19	Giga Drain	Grass	Special	60	100	10	Normal	—
TM21	Frustration	Normal	Physical	30	90	20	Normal	○
TM22	SolarBeam	Grass	Special	120	100	10	Normal	—
TM26	Earthquake	Ground	Physical	100	100	10	2 Foes/1 Ally	○
TM27	Return	Normal	Physical	—	100	20	Normal	○
TM28	Dig	Ground	Physical	80	100	10	Normal	○
TM32	Double Team	Normal	Status	—	—	15	Self	—
TM33	Reflect	Psychic	Status	—	—	20	2 Allies	—
TM37	Sandstorm	Rock	Status	—	—	10	All	—
TM39	Rock Tomb	Rock	Physical	50	80	10	Normal	—
TM42	Facade	Normal	Physical	70	100	20	Normal	○
TM43	Secret Power	Normal	Physical	70	100	20	Normal	—
TM44	Rest	Psychic	Status	—	—	10	Self	—
TM45	Attract	Normal	Status	—	100	15	Normal	—
TM58	Endure	Normal	Status	—	—	10	Self	—
TM64	Explosion	Normal	Physical	250	100	5	2 Foes/1 Ally	—
TM66	Payback	Dark	Physical	50	100	10	Normal	○
TM68	Giga Impact	Normal	Physical	150	90	5	Normal	○
TM69	Rock Polish	Rock	Status	—	—	20	Self	—
TM74	Gyro Ball	Steel	Physical	—	100	5	Normal	○
TM76	Stealth Rock	Rock	Status	—	—	20	2 Foes	—
TM78	Captivate	Normal	Status	—	100	20	2 Foes	—
TM80	Rock Slide	Rock	Physical	75	90	10	2 Foes	—
TM82	Sleep Talk	Normal	Status	—	—	10	Depends	—
TM83	Natural Gift	Normal	Physical	—	100	15	Normal	—
TM87	Swagger	Normal	Status	—	90	15	Normal	—
TM90	Substitute	Normal	Status	—	—	10	Self	—
TM91	Flash Cannon	Steel	Special	80	100	10	Normal	—
HM04	Strength	Normal	Physical	80	100	15	Normal	○
HM06	Rock Smash	Fighting	Physical	40	100	15	Normal	○

● LEVEL-UP MOVES

Lv.	Name	Type	Kind	Pow.	Acc.	PP	Range	DA
1	Rage	Normal	Physical	20	100	20	Normal	○
5	Defense Curl	Normal	Status	—	—	40	Self	—
9	Yawn	Normal	Status	—	—	10	Normal	—
13	Glare	Normal	Status	—	75	30	Normal	—
17	Rollout	Rock	Physical	30	90	20	Normal	○
21	Spite	Ghost	Status	—	100	10	Normal	—
25	Pursuit	Dark	Physical	40	100	20	Normal	○
29	Screech	Normal	Status	—	85	40	Normal	—
33	Roost	Flying	Status	—	—	10	Self	—
37	Take Down	Normal	Physical	90	85	20	Normal	○
41	AncientPower	Rock	Special	60	100	5	Normal	—
45	Dig	Ground	Physical	80	100	10	Normal	○
49	Endeavor	Normal	Physical	—	100	5	Normal	○
53	Flail	Normal	Physical	—	100	15	Normal	○

● MOVE MANIAC

Name	Type	Kind	Pow.	Acc.	PP	Range	DA
Headbutt	Normal	Physical	70	100	15	Normal	○

● BP MOVES

Name	Type	Kind	Pow.	Acc.	PP	Range	DA
Zen Headbutt	Psychic	Physical	80	90	15	Normal	○
Snore	Normal	Special	40	100	15	Normal	—
Spite	Ghost	Status	—	100	10	Normal	—
Last Resort	Normal	Physical	130	100	5	Normal	○
Magic Coat	Psychic	Status	—	—	15	Self	—
Mud-Slap	Ground	Special	20	100	10	Normal	○
Rollout	Rock	Physical	30	90	20	Normal	○
Aqua Tail	Water	Physical	90	90	10	Normal	○
Endeavor	Normal	Physical	—	100	5	Normal	○
AncientPower	Rock	Special	60	100	5	Normal	—
Pain Split	Normal	Status	—	—	20	Normal	—

● TM & HM MOVES

No.	Name	Type	Kind	Pow.	Acc.	PP	Range	DA
TM03	Water Pulse	Water	Special	60	100	20	Normal	—
TM04	Calm Mind	Psychic	Status	—	—	20	Self	—
TM06	Toxic	Poison	Status	—	85	10	Normal	—
TM10	Hidden Power	Normal	Special	—	100	15	Normal	○
TM11	Sunny Day	Fire	Status	—	—	5	All	—
TM13	Ice Beam	Ice	Special	95	100	10	Normal	—
TM14	Blizzard	Ice	Special	120	70	5	2 Foes	—
TM17	Protect	Normal	Status	—	—	10	Self	—
TM18	Rain Dance	Water	Status	—	—	5	All	—
TM21	Frustration	Normal	Physical	—	100	20	Normal	○
TM22	SolarBeam	Grass	Special	120	100	10	Normal	—
TM23	Iron Tail	Steel	Physical	100	75	15	Normal	○
TM24	Thunderbolt	Electric	Special	95	100	15	Normal	—
TM25	Thunder	Electric	Special	120	70	10	Normal	—
TM26	Earthquake	Ground	Physical	100	100	10	2 Foes / 1 Ally	○
TM27	Return	Normal	Physical	—	100	20	Normal	○
TM28	Dig	Ground	Physical	80	100	10	Normal	○
TM30	Shadow Ball	Ghost	Special	80	100	15	Normal	—
TM32	Double Team	Normal	Status	—	—	15	Self	—
TM34	Shock Wave	Electric	Special	60	—	20	Normal	—
TM35	Flamethrower	Fire	Special	95	100	15	Normal	—
TM38	Fire Blast	Fire	Special	120	85	5	Normal	—
TM39	Rock Tomb	Rock	Physical	50	80	10	Normal	○
TM42	Facade	Normal	Physical	70	100	20	Normal	○
TM43	Secret Power	Normal	Physical	70	100	20	Normal	○
TM44	Rest	Psychic	Status	—	—	10	Self	—
TM45	Attract	Normal	Status	—	100	15	Normal	—
TM46	Thief	Dark	Physical	40	100	10	Normal	○
TM51	Roost	Flying	Status	—	—	10	Self	—
TM57	Charge Beam	Electric	Special	50	90	10	Normal	—
TM58	Endure	Normal	Status	—	—	10	Self	—
TM73	Thunder Wave	Electric	Status	—	100	20	Normal	—
TM74	Gyro Ball	Steel	Physical	—	100	5	Normal	○
TM76	Stealth Rock	Rock	Status	—	—	20	2 Foes	—
TM77	Psych Up	Normal	Status	—	—	10	Normal	—
TM78	Captivate	Normal	Status	—	100	20	2 Foes	—
TM80	Rock Slide	Rock	Physical	75	90	10	2 Foes	—
TM82	Sleep Talk	Normal	Status	—	—	10	Depends	—
TM83	Natural Gift	Normal	Physical	—	100	15	Normal	○
TM84	Poison Jab	Poison	Physical	80	100	20	Normal	○
TM85	Dream Eater	Psychic	Special	100	100	15	Normal	—
TM87	Swagger	Normal	Status	—	90	15	Normal	—
TM90	Substitute	Normal	Status	—	—	10	Self	—
HM04	Strength	Normal	Physical	80	100	15	Normal	○
HM06	Rock Smash	Fighting	Physical	40	100	15	Normal	○

● EGG MOVES

Name	Type	Kind	Pow.	Acc.	PP	Range	DA
Bide	Normal	Physical	—	—	10	Self	○
AncientPower	Rock	Special	60	100	5	Normal	—
Rock Slide	Rock	Physical	75	90	10	2 Foes	—
Bite	Dark	Physical	60	100	25	Normal	—
Headbutt	Normal	Physical	70	100	15	Normal	○
Astonish	Ghost	Physical	30	100	15	Normal	—
Curse	???	Status	—	—	10	Normal/Self	—
Trump Card	Normal	Special	—	—	5	Normal	○
Magic Coat	Psychic	Status	—	—	15	Self	—
Snore	Normal	Special	40	100	15	Normal	—
Agility	Psychic	Status	—	—	30	Self	—

○ No. 206 | Land Snake Pokémon
Dunsparce

Normal

● HEIGHT: 4'11"
● WEIGHT: 30.9 lbs.
● ITEMS: None

● SIZE COMPARISON

● MALE/FEMALE HAVE SAME FORM

● ABILITIES
● Serene Grace
● Run Away

● STATS
HP ●●●●
ATTACK ●●●
DEFENSE ●●●
SP. ATTACK ●●●
SP. DEFENSE ●●●
SPEED ●●

● EGG GROUPS
Field

● PERFORMANCE
SPEED ★★☆
POWER ★★★☆
SKILL ★☆
STAMINA ★★★☆
JUMP ★★★★☆

● MAIN WAYS TO OBTAIN

Pokémon HeartGold — Dark Cave, Violet City side

Pokémon SoulSilver — Dark Cave, Violet City side

Pokémon Diamond — Route 208 (mass outbreak)

Pokémon Pearl — Route 208 (mass outbreak)

Pokémon Platinum — Route 208 (mass outbreak)

Pokémon HeartGold — When spotted, this Pokémon escapes backward by furiously boring into the ground with its tail.

Pokémon SoulSilver — If spotted, it escapes by burrowing with its tail. It can float just slightly using its wings.

● EVOLUTION
Does not evolve

No. 207 | FlyScorpion Pokémon
Gligar

Ground | **Flying**

● **HEIGHT:** 3'07"
● **WEIGHT:** 142.9 lbs.
● **ITEMS:** None

● **SIZE COMPARISON**

● **MALE FORM**
Bigger tail stinger

● **FEMALE FORM**
Smaller tail stinger

● ABILITIES
● Hyper Cutter
● Sand Veil

● STATS
HP ●●
ATTACK ●●●
DEFENSE ●●●●
SP. ATTACK ●
SP. DEFENSE ●●
SPEED ●●●●

● EGG GROUPS
Bug

● PERFORMANCE
SPEED ★★★☆
POWER ★★☆
SKILL ★★★
STAMINA ★★
JUMP ★★★★★

● MAIN WAYS TO OBTAIN

Pokémon HeartGold	Route 45
Pokémon SoulSilver	—
Pokémon Diamond	Route 206 (after obtaining the National Pokédex, insert *Pokémon Emerald* into your Nintendo DS's Game Pak slot)
Pokémon Pearl	Route 206 (after obtaining the National Pokédex, insert *Pokémon Emerald* into your Nintendo DS's Game Pak slot)
Pokémon Platinum	Route 206

Pokémon HeartGold
It flies straight at its target's face, then clamps down on the startled victim to inject poison.

Pokémon SoulSilver
It usually clings to cliffs. When it spots its prey, it spreads its wings and glides down to attack.

● EVOLUTION

Wooper

Have it hold Razor Fang and then level up between 8:00 P.M. and 4:00 A.M.

Quagsire

● LEVEL-UP MOVES

Lv.	Name	Type	Kind	Pow.	Acc.	PP	Range	DA
1	Poison Sting	Poison	Physical	15	100	35	Normal	—
5	Sand-Attack	Ground	Status	—	100	15	Normal	—
9	Harden	Normal	Status	—	—	30	Self	—
12	Knock Off	Dark	Physical	20	100	20	Normal	○
16	Quick Attack	Normal	Physical	40	100	30	Normal	○
20	Fury Cutter	Bug	Physical	10	95	20	Normal	○
23	Faint Attack	Dark	Physical	60	—	20	Normal	○
27	Screech	Normal	Status	—	85	40	Normal	—
31	Slash	Normal	Physical	70	100	20	Normal	○
34	Swords Dance	Normal	Status	—	—	30	Self	—
38	U-turn	Bug	Physical	70	100	20	Normal	○
42	X-Scissor	Bug	Physical	80	100	15	Normal	○
45	Guillotine	Normal	Physical	—	30	5	Normal	—

● MOVE MANIAC

Name	Type	Kind	Pow.	Acc.	PP	Range	DA
Headbutt	Normal	Physical	70	100	15	Normal	○

● BP MOVES

Name	Type	Kind	Pow.	Acc.	PP	Range	DA
Fury Cutter	Bug	Physical	10	95	20	Normal	○
Knock Off	Dark	Physical	20	100	20	Normal	○
Snore	Normal	Special	40	100	15	Normal	—
Swift	Normal	Special	60	—	20	2 Foes	—
Tailwind	Flying	Status	—	—	30	2 Allies	—
Aqua Tail	Water	Physical	90	90	10	Normal	○
Earth Power	Ground	Special	90	100	10	Normal	—

● TM & HM MOVES

No.	Name	Type	Kind	Pow.	Acc.	PP	Range	DA
TM06	Toxic	Poison	Status	—	85	10	Normal	—
TM10	Hidden Power	Normal	Special	—	100	15	Normal	—
TM11	Sunny Day	Fire	Status	—	—	5	All	—
TM12	Taunt	Dark	Status	—	100	20	Normal	—
TM17	Protect	Normal	Status	—	—	10	Self	—
TM18	Rain Dance	Water	Status	—	—	5	All	—
TM21	Frustration	Normal	Physical	—	100	20	Normal	○
TM23	Iron Tail	Steel	Physical	100	75	15	Normal	○
TM26	Earthquake	Ground	Physical	100	100	10	2 Foes/1 Ally	—
TM27	Return	Normal	Physical	—	100	20	Normal	○
TM28	Dig	Ground	Physical	80	100	10	Normal	○
TM31	Brick Break	Fighting	Physical	75	100	15	Normal	○
TM32	Double Team	Normal	Status	—	—	15	Self	—
TM36	Sludge Bomb	Poison	Special	90	100	10	Normal	—
TM37	Sandstorm	Rock	Status	—	—	10	All	—
TM39	Rock Tomb	Rock	Physical	50	80	10	Normal	○
TM40	Aerial Ace	Flying	Physical	60	—	20	Normal	○
TM41	Torment	Dark	Status	—	100	15	Normal	—
TM42	Facade	Normal	Physical	70	100	20	Normal	○
TM43	Secret Power	Normal	Physical	70	100	20	Normal	○
TM44	Rest	Psychic	Status	—	—	10	Self	—
TM45	Attract	Normal	Status	—	100	15	Normal	—
TM46	Thief	Dark	Physical	40	100	10	Normal	○
TM47	Steel Wing	Steel	Physical	70	90	25	Normal	○
TM51	Roost	Flying	Status	—	—	10	Self	—
TM54	False Swipe	Normal	Physical	40	100	40	Normal	○
TM56	Fling	Dark	Physical	—	100	10	Normal	—
TM58	Endure	Normal	Status	—	—	10	Self	—
TM66	Payback	Dark	Physical	50	100	10	Normal	○
TM69	Rock Polish	Rock	Status	—	—	20	Self	—
TM71	Stone Edge	Rock	Physical	100	80	5	Normal	○
TM75	Swords Dance	Normal	Status	—	—	30	Self	—
TM76	Stealth Rock	Rock	Status	—	—	20	2 Foes	—
TM78	Captivate	Normal	Status	—	100	20	2 Foes	—
TM80	Rock Slide	Rock	Physical	75	90	10	2 Foes	—
TM81	X-Scissor	Bug	Physical	80	100	15	Normal	○
TM82	Sleep Talk	Normal	Status	—	—	10	Depends	—
TM83	Natural Gift	Normal	Physical	—	100	15	Normal	○
TM84	Poison Jab	Poison	Physical	80	100	20	Normal	○
TM87	Swagger	Normal	Status	—	90	15	Normal	—
TM89	U-turn	Bug	Physical	70	100	20	Normal	○
TM90	Substitute	Normal	Status	—	—	10	Self	—
HM01	Cut	Normal	Physical	50	95	30	Normal	○
HM04	Strength	Normal	Physical	80	100	15	Normal	○
HM06	Rock Smash	Fighting	Physical	40	100	15	Normal	○

● EGG MOVES

Name	Type	Kind	Pow.	Acc.	PP	Range	DA
Metal Claw	Steel	Physical	50	95	35	Normal	○
Wing Attack	Flying	Physical	60	100	35	Normal	○
Razor Wind	Normal	Special	80	100	10	2 Foes	—
Counter	Fighting	Physical	—	100	20	Self	○
Sand Tomb	Ground	Physical	15	70	15	Normal	—
Agility	Psychic	Status	—	—	30	Self	—
Baton Pass	Normal	Status	—	—	40	Self	—
Double-Edge	Normal	Physical	120	100	15	Normal	○
Feint	Normal	Physical	30	100	10	Normal	—
Night Slash	Dark	Physical	70	100	15	Normal	○
Cross Poison	Poison	Physical	70	100	20	Normal	○
Power Trick	Psychic	Status	—	—	10	Self	—

● LEVEL-UP MOVES

Lv.	Name	Type	Kind	Pow.	Acc.	PP	Range	DA
1	Thunder Fang	Electric	Physical	65	95	15	Normal	○
1	Ice Fang	Ice	Physical	65	95	15	Normal	○
1	Fire Fang	Fire	Physical	65	95	15	Normal	○
1	Mud Sport	Ground	Status	—	—	15	All	—
1	Tackle	Normal	Physical	35	95	35	Normal	○
1	Harden	Normal	Status	—	—	30	Self	—
1	Bind	Normal	Physical	15	85	20	Normal	—
6	Screech	Normal	Status	—	85	40	Normal	—
9	Rock Throw	Rock	Physical	50	90	15	Normal	—
14	Rage	Normal	Physical	20	100	20	Normal	—
17	Rock Tomb	Rock	Physical	50	80	10	Normal	—
22	Sandstorm	Rock	Status	—	—	10	All	—
25	Slam	Normal	Physical	80	75	20	Normal	○
30	Rock Polish	Rock	Status	—	—	20	Self	—
33	DragonBreath	Dragon	Special	60	100	20	Normal	—
38	Curse	???	Status	—	—	10	Normal/Self	—
41	Iron Tail	Steel	Physical	100	75	15	Normal	—
46	Crunch	Dark	Physical	80	100	15	Normal	○
49	Double-Edge	Normal	Physical	120	100	15	Normal	—
54	Stone Edge	Rock	Physical	100	80	5	Normal	—

● MOVE MANIAC

Name	Type	Kind	Pow.	Acc.	PP	Range	DA
Headbutt	Normal	Physical	70	100	15	Normal	○

● BP MOVES

Name	Type	Kind	Pow.	Acc.	PP	Range	DA
Snore	Normal	Special	40	100	15	Normal	—
Magnet Rise	Electric	Status	—	—	10	Self	—
Block	Normal	Status	—	—	5	Normal	—
Mud-Slap	Ground	Special	20	100	10	Normal	—
Rollout	Rock	Physical	30	90	20	Normal	○
Iron Head	Steel	Physical	80	100	15	Normal	○
Aqua Tail	Water	Physical	90	90	10	Normal	—
AncientPower	Rock	Special	60	100	5	Normal	—
Earth Power	Ground	Special	90	100	10	Normal	—
Twister	Dragon	Special	40	100	20	2 Foes	—

● TM & HM MOVES

No.	Name	Type	Kind	Pow.	Acc.	PP	Range	DA
TM05	Roar	Normal	Status	—	100	20	Normal	—
TM06	Toxic	Poison	Status	—	85	10	Normal	—
TM10	Hidden Power	Normal	Special	—	100	15	Normal	—
TM11	Sunny Day	Fire	Status	—	—	5	All	—
TM12	Taunt	Dark	Status	—	100	20	Normal	—
TM15	Hyper Beam	Normal	Special	150	90	5	Normal	—
TM17	Protect	Normal	Status	—	—	10	Self	—
TM21	Frustration	Normal	Physical	—	100	20	Normal	○
TM23	Iron Tail	Steel	Physical	100	75	15	Normal	—
TM26	Earthquake	Ground	Physical	100	100	10	2 Foes/1 Ally	—
TM27	Return	Normal	Physical	—	100	20	Normal	○
TM28	Dig	Ground	Physical	80	100	10	Normal	○
TM32	Double Team	Normal	Status	—	—	15	Self	—
TM37	Sandstorm	Rock	Status	—	—	10	All	—
TM39	Rock Tomb	Rock	Physical	50	80	10	Normal	—
TM41	Torment	Dark	Status	—	100	15	Normal	—
TM42	Facade	Normal	Physical	70	100	20	Normal	○
TM43	Secret Power	Normal	Physical	70	100	20	Normal	—
TM44	Rest	Psychic	Status	—	—	10	Self	—
TM45	Attract	Normal	Status	—	100	15	Normal	—
TM58	Endure	Normal	Status	—	—	10	Self	—
TM59	Dragon Pulse	Dragon	Special	90	100	10	Normal	—
TM64	Explosion	Normal	Physical	250	100	5	2 Foes/1 Ally	—
TM66	Payback	Dark	Physical	50	100	10	Normal	○
TM68	Giga Impact	Normal	Physical	150	90	5	Normal	—
TM69	Rock Polish	Rock	Status	—	—	20	Self	—
TM71	Stone Edge	Rock	Physical	100	80	5	Normal	—
TM74	Gyro Ball	Steel	Physical	—	100	5	Normal	○
TM76	Stealth Rock	Rock	Status	—	—	20	2 Foes	—
TM77	Psych Up	Normal	Status	—	—	10	Normal	—
TM78	Captivate	Normal	Status	—	100	20	2 Foes	—
TM79	Dark Pulse	Dark	Special	80	100	15	Normal	—
TM80	Rock Slide	Rock	Physical	75	90	10	2 Foes	—
TM82	Sleep Talk	Normal	Status	—	—	10	Depends	—
TM83	Natural Gift	Normal	Physical	—	100	15	Normal	—
TM87	Swagger	Normal	Status	—	90	15	Normal	—
TM90	Substitute	Normal	Status	—	—	10	Self	—
TM91	Flash Cannon	Steel	Special	80	100	10	Normal	—
HM01	Cut	Normal	Physical	50	95	30	Normal	○
HM04	Strength	Normal	Physical	80	100	15	Normal	○
HM06	Rock Smash	Fighting	Physical	40	100	15	Normal	○
HM08	Rock Climb	Normal	Physical	90	85	20	Normal	○

● No. 208 | Iron Snake Pokémon
Steelix

Steel Ground

- ● HEIGHT: 30'02"
- ● WEIGHT: 881.8 lbs.
- ● ITEMS: Metal Coat

● SIZE COMPARISON

● MALE FORM
Two fangs

● FEMALE FORM
One fang

⊙ ABILITIES
- ● Rock Head
- ● Sturdy

⊙ STATS
HP ●●●
ATTACK ●●●●
DEFENSE ●●●●●●
SP. ATTACK ●●
SP. DEFENSE ●●
SPEED ●

⊙ EGG GROUPS
Mineral

⊙ PERFORMANCE
SPEED ★☆   STAMINA ★★★★★
POWER ★★★★★   JUMP ★★
SKILL ★★

● MAIN WAYS TO OBTAIN

Pokémon HeartGold — Cliff Cave

Pokémon SoulSilver — Cliff Cave

Pokémon Diamond — Iron Island B3F 1

Pokémon Pearl — Iron Island B3F 1

Pokémon Platinum — Iron Island B3F 1

Pokémon HeartGold

Its body has been compressed deep under the ground. As a result, it is even harder than a diamond.

Pokémon SoulSilver

It's said that if an ONIX lives for 100 years, its composition becomes diamondlike as it evolves into a STEELIX.

⊙ EVOLUTION

Onix — Have it hold Metal Coat and trade it → Steelix

No. 209 | Fairy Pokémon
Snubbull

Normal

- **HEIGHT:** 2'00"
- **WEIGHT:** 17.2 lbs.
- **ITEMS:** None

● SIZE COMPARISON

● MALE/FEMALE HAVE SAME FORM

⊛ ABILITIES
- Intimidate
- Run Away

⊛ STATS
HP ●●●●
ATTACK ●●●●
DEFENSE ●●●●
SP. ATTACK ●●●●
SP. DEFENSE ●●●●●
SPEED ●●●

⊛ EGG GROUPS
Field
Fairy

⊛ PERFORMANCE
SPEED ★★★　　STAMINA ★★★
POWER ★★★☆☆　JUMP ★★☆
SKILL ★★★★

● MAIN WAYS TO OBTAIN

Pokémon HeartGold	Route 38
Pokémon SoulSilver	Route 38
Pokémon Diamond	Route 209 (mass outbreak)
Pokémon Pearl	Route 209 (mass outbreak)
Pokémon Platinum	Route 209 (mass outbreak)

| Pokémon HeartGold | Pokémon SoulSilver |
| Although it looks frightening, it is actually kind and affectionate. It is very popular among women. | It has an active, playful nature. Many women like to frolic with it because of its affectionate ways. |

⊛ EVOLUTION

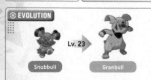

Lv. 23

Snubbull → Granbull

● LEVEL-UP MOVES

Lv.	Name	Type	Kind	Pow.	Acc.	PP	Range	DA
1	Ice Fang	Ice	Physical	65	95	15	Normal	○
1	Fire Fang	Fire	Physical	65	95	15	Normal	○
1	Thunder Fang	Electric	Physical	65	95	15	Normal	○
1	Tackle	Normal	Physical	35	95	35	Normal	○
1	Scary Face	Normal	Status	—	90	10	Normal	—
1	Tail Whip	Normal	Status	—	100	30	2 Foes	—
1	Charm	Normal	Status	—	100	20	Normal	—
7	Bite	Dark	Physical	60	100	25	Normal	○
13	Lick	Ghost	Physical	20	100	30	Normal	○
19	Headbutt	Normal	Physical	70	100	15	Normal	○
25	Roar	Normal	Status	—	100	20	Normal	—
31	Rage	Normal	Physical	20	100	20	Normal	○
37	Take Down	Normal	Physical	90	85	20	Normal	○
43	Payback	Dark	Physical	50	100	10	Normal	○
49	Crunch	Dark	Physical	80	100	15	Normal	○

● MOVE MANIAC

Name	Type	Kind	Pow.	Acc.	PP	Range	DA
Headbutt	Normal	Physical	70	100	15	Normal	○

● BP MOVES

Name	Type	Kind	Pow.	Acc.	PP	Range	DA
ThunderPunch	Electric	Physical	75	100	15	Normal	○
Fire Punch	Fire	Physical	75	100	15	Normal	○
Ice Punch	Ice	Physical	75	100	15	Normal	○
Snore	Normal	Special	40	100	15	Normal	○
Last Resort	Normal	Physical	130	100	5	Normal	○
Heal Bell	Normal	Status	—	—	5	All Allies	—
Mud-Slap	Ground	Special	20	100	10	Normal	○
Superpower	Fighting	Physical	120	100	5	Normal	○
Super Fang	Normal	Physical	—	90	10	Normal	○
Low Kick	Fighting	Physical	—	100	20	Normal	○

● TM & HM MOVES

No.	Name	Type	Kind	Pow.	Acc.	PP	Range	DA
TM01	Focus Punch	Fighting	Physical	150	100	20	Normal	○
TM03	Water Pulse	Water	Special	60	100	20	Normal	—
TM05	Roar	Normal	Status	—	100	20	Normal	—
TM06	Toxic	Poison	Status	—	85	10	Normal	—
TM08	Bulk Up	Fighting	Status	—	—	20	Self	—
TM10	Hidden Power	Normal	Special	—	100	15	Normal	—
TM11	Sunny Day	Fire	Status	—	—	5	All	—
TM12	Taunt	Dark	Status	—	100	20	Normal	—
TM17	Protect	Normal	Status	—	—	10	Self	—
TM18	Rain Dance	Water	Status	—	—	5	All	—
TM21	Frustration	Normal	Physical	—	100	20	Normal	○
TM22	SolarBeam	Grass	Special	120	100	10	Normal	—
TM24	Thunderbolt	Electric	Special	95	100	15	Normal	—
TM25	Thunder	Electric	Special	120	70	10	Normal	—
TM26	Earthquake	Ground	Physical	100	100	10	2 Foes/1 Ally	—
TM27	Return	Normal	Physical	—	100	20	Normal	○
TM28	Dig	Ground	Physical	80	100	10	Normal	○
TM30	Shadow Ball	Ghost	Special	80	100	15	Normal	—
TM31	Brick Break	Fighting	Physical	75	100	15	Normal	○
TM32	Double Team	Normal	Status	—	—	15	Self	—
TM34	Shock Wave	Electric	Special	60	—	20	Normal	—
TM35	Flamethrower	Fire	Special	95	100	15	Normal	—
TM36	Sludge Bomb	Poison	Special	90	100	10	Normal	—
TM38	Fire Blast	Fire	Special	120	85	5	Normal	—
TM41	Torment	Dark	Status	—	100	15	Normal	—
TM42	Facade	Normal	Physical	70	100	20	Normal	○
TM43	Secret Power	Normal	Physical	70	100	20	Normal	—
TM44	Rest	Psychic	Status	—	—	10	Self	—
TM45	Attract	Normal	Status	—	100	15	Normal	—
TM46	Thief	Dark	Physical	40	100	10	Normal	○
TM50	Overheat	Fire	Special	140	90	5	Normal	—
TM56	Fling	Dark	Physical	—	100	10	Normal	○
TM58	Endure	Normal	Status	—	—	10	Self	—
TM66	Payback	Dark	Physical	50	100	10	Normal	○
TM73	Thunder Wave	Electric	Status	—	100	20	Normal	—
TM78	Captivate	Normal	Status	—	100	20	2 Foes	—
TM82	Sleep Talk	Normal	Status	—	—	10	Depends	—
TM83	Natural Gift	Normal	Physical	—	100	15	Normal	—
TM87	Swagger	Normal	Status	—	90	15	Normal	—
TM90	Substitute	Normal	Status	—	—	10	Self	—
HM04	Strength	Normal	Physical	80	100	15	Normal	○
HM06	Rock Smash	Fighting	Physical	40	100	15	Normal	○

● EGG MOVES

Name	Type	Kind	Pow.	Acc.	PP	Range	DA
Metronome	Normal	Status	—	—	10	Depends	—
Faint Attack	Dark	Physical	60	—	20	Normal	○
Reflect	Psychic	Status	—	—	20	2 Allies	—
Present	Normal	Physical	—	90	15	Normal	—
Crunch	Dark	Physical	80	100	15	Normal	○
Heal Bell	Normal	Status	—	—	5	All Allies	—
Snore	Normal	Special	40	100	15	Normal	○
SmellingSalt	Normal	Physical	60	100	10	Normal	○
Close Combat	Fighting	Physical	120	100	5	Normal	○
Ice Fang	Ice	Physical	65	95	15	Normal	○
Fire Fang	Fire	Physical	65	95	15	Normal	○
Thunder Fang	Electric	Physical	65	95	15	Normal	○

● LEVEL-UP MOVES

Lv.	Name	Type	Kind	Pow.	Acc.	PP	Range	DA
1	Ice Fang	Ice	Physical	65	95	15	Normal	○
1	Fire Fang	Fire	Physical	65	95	15	Normal	○
1	Thunder Fang	Electric	Physical	65	95	15	Normal	○
1	Tackle	Normal	Physical	35	95	35	Normal	○
1	Scary Face	Normal	Status	—	90	10	Normal	—
1	Tail Whip	Normal	Status	—	100	30	2 Foes	—
1	Charm	Normal	Status	—	100	20	Normal	—
7	Bite	Dark	Physical	60	100	25	Normal	○
13	Lick	Ghost	Physical	20	100	30	Normal	○
19	Headbutt	Normal	Physical	70	100	15	Normal	○
27	Roar	Normal	Status	—	100	20	Normal	—
35	Rage	Normal	Physical	20	100	20	Normal	○
43	Take Down	Normal	Physical	90	85	20	Normal	○
51	Payback	Dark	Physical	50	100	10	Normal	○
59	Crunch	Dark	Physical	80	100	15	Normal	○

● MOVE MANIAC

Name	Type	Kind	Pow.	Acc.	PP	Range	DA
Headbutt	Normal	Physical	70	100	15	Normal	○

● BP MOVES

Name	Type	Kind	Pow.	Acc.	PP	Range	DA
ThunderPunch	Electric	Physical	75	100	15	Normal	○
Fire Punch	Fire	Physical	75	100	15	Normal	○
Ice Punch	Ice	Physical	75	100	15	Normal	○
Snore	Normal	Special	40	100	15	Normal	—
Last Resort	Normal	Physical	130	100	5	Normal	○
Heal Bell	Normal	Status	—	—	5	All Allies	—
Mud-Slap	Ground	Special	20	100	10	Normal	—
Superpower	Fighting	Physical	120	100	5	Normal	○
Super Fang	Normal	Physical	—	90	10	Normal	○
Low Kick	Fighting	Physical	—	100	20	Normal	○

● TM & HM MOVES

No.	Name	Type	Kind	Pow.	Acc.	PP	Range	DA
TM01	Focus Punch	Fighting	Physical	150	100	20	Normal	○
TM03	Water Pulse	Water	Special	60	100	20	Normal	—
TM05	Roar	Normal	Status	—	100	20	Normal	—
TM06	Toxic	Poison	Status	—	85	10	Normal	—
TM08	Bulk Up	Fighting	Status	—	—	20	Self	—
TM10	Hidden Power	Normal	Special	—	100	15	Normal	—
TM11	Sunny Day	Fire	Status	—	—	5	All	—
TM12	Taunt	Dark	Status	—	100	20	Normal	—
TM15	Hyper Beam	Normal	Special	150	90	5	Normal	—
TM17	Protect	Normal	Status	—	—	10	Self	—
TM18	Rain Dance	Water	Status	—	—	5	All	—
TM21	Frustration	Normal	Physical	—	100	20	Normal	○
TM22	SolarBeam	Grass	Special	120	100	10	Normal	—
TM23	Iron Tail	Steel	Physical	100	75	15	Normal	○
TM24	Thunderbolt	Electric	Special	95	100	15	Normal	—
TM25	Thunder	Electric	Special	120	70	10	Normal	—
TM26	Earthquake	Ground	Physical	100	100	10	2 Foes/1 Ally	—
TM27	Return	Normal	Physical	—	100	20	Normal	○
TM28	Dig	Ground	Physical	80	100	10	Normal	○
TM30	Shadow Ball	Ghost	Special	80	100	15	Normal	—
TM31	Brick Break	Fighting	Physical	75	100	15	Normal	○
TM32	Double Team	Normal	Status	—	—	15	Self	—
TM34	Shock Wave	Electric	Special	60	—	20	Normal	—
TM35	Flamethrower	Fire	Special	95	100	15	Normal	—
TM36	Sludge Bomb	Poison	Special	90	100	10	Normal	—
TM38	Fire Blast	Fire	Special	120	85	5	Normal	—
TM39	Rock Tomb	Rock	Physical	50	80	10	Normal	—
TM41	Torment	Dark	Status	—	100	15	Normal	—
TM42	Facade	Normal	Physical	70	100	20	Normal	○
TM43	Secret Power	Normal	Physical	70	100	20	Normal	—
TM44	Rest	Psychic	Status	—	—	10	Self	—
TM45	Attract	Normal	Status	—	100	15	Normal	—
TM46	Thief	Dark	Physical	40	100	10	Normal	—
TM50	Overheat	Fire	Special	140	90	5	Normal	—
TM52	Focus Blast	Fighting	Special	120	70	5	Normal	—
TM56	Fling	Dark	Physical	—	100	10	Normal	—
TM58	Endure	Normal	Status	—	—	10	Self	—
TM66	Payback	Dark	Physical	50	100	10	Normal	○
TM68	Giga Impact	Normal	Physical	150	90	5	Normal	○
TM71	Stone Edge	Rock	Physical	100	80	5	Normal	—
TM73	Thunder Wave	Electric	Status	—	100	20	Normal	—
TM78	Captivate	Normal	Status	—	100	20	2 Foes	—
TM80	Rock Slide	Rock	Physical	75	90	10	2 Foes	—
TM82	Sleep Talk	Normal	Status	—	—	10	Depends	—
TM83	Natural Gift	Normal	Physical	—	100	15	Normal	—
TM87	Swagger	Normal	Status	—	90	15	Normal	—
TM90	Substitute	Normal	Status	—	—	10	Self	—
HM04	Strength	Normal	Physical	80	100	15	Normal	○
HM06	Rock Smash	Fighting	Physical	40	100	15	Normal	○
HM08	Rock Climb	Normal	Physical	90	85	20	Normal	○

● No. 210 | Fairy Pokémon
Granbull

Normal

- ● HEIGHT: 4'07"
- ● WEIGHT: 107.4 lbs.
- ● ITEMS: None

● SIZE COMPARISON

● MALE/FEMALE HAVE SAME FORM

◎ ABILITIES
- ● Intimidate
- ● Quick Feet

◎ STATS
HP ●●●
ATTACK ●●●●●
DEFENSE ●●●
SP. ATTACK ●●●
SP. DEFENSE ●●●
SPEED ●●

◎ EGG GROUPS
Field
Fairy

◎ PERFORMANCE
SPEED ★★
POWER ★★★★☆
SKILL ★★★★
STAMINA ★★★
JUMP ★★

● MAIN WAYS TO OBTAIN

Pokémon HeartGold — Level up Snubbull to Lv. 23

Pokémon SoulSilver — Level up Snubbull to Lv. 23

Pokémon Diamond — Level up Snubbull to Lv. 23

Pokémon Pearl — Level up Snubbull to Lv. 23

Pokémon Platinum — Level up Snubbull to Lv. 23

Pokémon HeartGold

It is actually timid and easily spooked. If attacked, it flails about to fend off its attacker.

Pokémon SoulSilver

Because its fangs are too heavy, it always keeps its head tilted down. However, its bite is powerful.

◎ EVOLUTION

Snubbull — Lv. 23 → Granbull

No. 211 | Balloon Pokémon
Qwilfish

Water | Poison

- **HEIGHT:** 1'08"
- **WEIGHT:** 8.6 lbs.
- **ITEMS:** Poison Barb

- **SIZE COMPARISON**

- **MALE/FEMALE HAVE SAME FORM**

ABILITIES
- Poison Point
- Swift Swim

STATS
HP ●●
ATTACK ●●●●
DEFENSE ●●●
SP. ATTACK ●●
SP. DEFENSE ●●
SPEED ●●●●

EGG GROUPS
Water 2

PERFORMANCE
SPEED ★★★
POWER ★★★☆
SKILL ★★☆
STAMINA ★★★★☆
JUMP ★★☆

MAIN WAYS TO OBTAIN

Pokémon HeartGold	Route 32 (Good Rod/Super Rod)
Pokémon SoulSilver	Route 32 (Good Rod/Super Rod)
Pokémon Diamond	Iron Island exterior (Super Rod)
Pokémon Pearl	Iron Island exterior (Super Rod)
Pokémon Platinum	Iron Island exterior (Super Rod)

Pokémon HeartGold
To fire its poison spikes, it must inflate its body by drinking over 2.6 gallons of water all at once.

Pokémon SoulSilver
The small spikes covering its body developed from scales. They inject a toxin that causes fainting.

EVOLUTION
Does not evolve

● LEVEL-UP MOVES

Lv.	Name	Type	Kind	Pow.	Acc.	PP	Range	DA
1	Spikes	Ground	Status	—	—	20	2 Foes	—
1	Tackle	Normal	Physical	35	95	35	Normal	○
1	Poison Sting	Poison	Physical	15	100	35	Normal	—
9	Harden	Normal	Status	—	—	30	Self	—
9	Minimize	Normal	Status	—	—	20	Self	—
13	Water Gun	Water	Special	40	100	25	Normal	—
17	Rollout	Rock	Physical	30	90	20	Normal	○
21	Toxic Spikes	Poison	Status	—	—	20	2 Foes	—
25	Stockpile	Normal	Status	—	—	20	Self	—
25	Spit Up	Normal	Special	—	—	10	Normal	—
29	Revenge	Fighting	Physical	60	100	10	Normal	○
33	Brine	Water	Special	55	100	10	Normal	—
37	Pin Missile	Bug	Physical	14	85	20	Normal	—
41	Take Down	Normal	Physical	90	85	20	Normal	○
45	Aqua Tail	Water	Physical	90	90	10	Normal	○
49	Poison Jab	Poison	Physical	80	100	20	Normal	○
53	Destiny Bond	Ghost	Status	—	—	5	Self	—
57	Hydro Pump	Water	Special	120	80	5	Normal	—

● MOVE MANIAC

Name	Type	Kind	Pow.	Acc.	PP	Range	DA
Headbutt	Normal	Physical	70	100	15	Normal	○

● BP MOVES

Name	Type	Kind	Pow.	Acc.	PP	Range	DA
Dive	Water	Physical	80	100	10	Normal	○
Icy Wind	Ice	Special	55	95	15	2 Foes	—
Snore	Normal	Special	40	100	15	Normal	—
Swift	Normal	Special	60	—	20	2 Foes	—
Rollout	Rock	Physical	30	90	20	Normal	○
Aqua Tail	Water	Physical	90	90	10	Normal	○
Signal Beam	Bug	Special	75	100	15	Normal	—
Bounce	Flying	Physical	85	85	5	Normal	○
Pain Split	Normal	Status	—	—	20	Normal	—

● TM & HM MOVES

No.	Name	Type	Kind	Pow.	Acc.	PP	Range	DA
TM03	Water Pulse	Water	Special	60	100	20	Normal	—
TM06	Toxic	Poison	Status	—	85	10	Normal	—
TM07	Hail	Ice	Status	—	—	10	All	—
TM10	Hidden Power	Normal	Special	—	100	15	Normal	—
TM12	Taunt	Dark	Status	—	100	20	Normal	—
TM13	Ice Beam	Ice	Special	95	100	10	Normal	—
TM14	Blizzard	Ice	Special	120	70	5	2 Foes	—
TM17	Protect	Normal	Status	—	—	10	Self	—
TM18	Rain Dance	Water	Status	—	—	5	All	—
TM21	Frustration	Normal	Physical	—	100	20	Normal	○
TM27	Return	Normal	Physical	—	100	20	Normal	○
TM30	Shadow Ball	Ghost	Special	80	100	15	Normal	—
TM32	Double Team	Normal	Status	—	—	15	Self	—
TM34	Shock Wave	Electric	Special	60	—	20	Normal	—
TM36	Sludge Bomb	Poison	Special	90	100	10	Normal	—
TM42	Facade	Normal	Physical	70	100	20	Normal	○
TM43	Secret Power	Normal	Physical	70	100	20	Normal	○
TM44	Rest	Psychic	Status	—	—	10	Self	—
TM45	Attract	Normal	Status	—	100	15	Normal	—
TM55	Brine	Water	Special	65	100	10	Normal	—
TM58	Endure	Normal	Status	—	—	10	Self	—
TM64	Explosion	Normal	Physical	250	100	5	2 Foes/1 Ally	—
TM66	Payback	Dark	Physical	50	100	10	Normal	○
TM73	Thunder Wave	Electric	Status	—	100	20	Normal	—
TM74	Gyro Ball	Steel	Physical	—	100	5	Normal	○
TM78	Captivate	Normal	Status	—	100	20	2 Foes	—
TM82	Sleep Talk	Normal	Status	—	—	10	Self	—
TM83	Natural Gift	Normal	Physical	—	100	15	Normal	—
TM84	Poison Jab	Poison	Physical	80	100	20	Normal	○
TM87	Swagger	Normal	Status	—	90	15	Normal	—
TM90	Substitute	Normal	Status	—	—	10	Self	—
HM03	Surf	Water	Special	95	100	15	2 Foes/1 Ally	—
HM05	Whirlpool	Water	Special	15	70	15	Normal	—
HM07	Waterfall	Water	Physical	80	100	15	Normal	○

● EGG MOVES

Name	Type	Kind	Pow.	Acc.	PP	Range	DA
Flail	Normal	Physical	—	100	15	Normal	○
Haze	Ice	Status	—	—	30	All	—
BubbleBeam	Water	Special	65	100	20	Normal	—
Supersonic	Normal	Status	—	55	20	Normal	—
Astonish	Ghost	Physical	30	100	15	Normal	○
Signal Beam	Bug	Special	75	100	15	Normal	—
Poison Jab	Poison	Physical	80	100	20	Normal	○
Aqua Jet	Water	Physical	40	100	20	Normal	○

● LEVEL-UP MOVES

Lv.	Name	Type	Kind	Pow.	Acc.	PP	Range	DA
1	Bullet Punch	Steel	Physical	40	100	30	Normal	○
1	Quick Attack	Normal	Physical	40	100	30	Normal	○
1	Leer	Normal	Status	—	100	30	2 Foes	—
5	Focus Energy	Normal	Status	—	—	30	Self	—
9	Pursuit	Dark	Physical	40	100	20	Normal	○
13	False Swipe	Normal	Physical	40	100	40	Normal	○
17	Agility	Psychic	Status	—	—	30	Self	—
21	Metal Claw	Steel	Physical	50	95	35	Normal	○
25	Fury Cutter	Bug	Physical	10	95	20	Normal	○
29	Slash	Normal	Physical	70	100	20	Normal	○
33	Razor Wind	Normal	Special	80	100	10	2 Foes	—
37	Iron Defense	Steel	Status	—	—	15	Self	—
41	X-Scissor	Bug	Physical	80	100	15	Normal	○
45	Night Slash	Dark	Physical	70	100	15	Normal	○
49	Double Hit	Normal	Physical	35	90	10	Normal	○
53	Iron Head	Steel	Physical	80	100	15	Normal	○
57	Swords Dance	Normal	Status	—	—	30	Self	—
61	Feint	Normal	Physical	50	100	10	Normal	—

● MOVE MANIAC

Name	Type	Kind	Pow.	Acc.	PP	Range	DA
Headbutt	Normal	Physical	70	100	15	Normal	○

● BP MOVES

Name	Type	Kind	Pow.	Acc.	PP	Range	DA
Fury Cutter	Bug	Physical	10	95	20	Normal	○
Ominous Wind	Ghost	Special	60	100	5	Normal	—
Knock Off	Dark	Physical	20	100	20	Normal	○
Bug Bite	Bug	Physical	60	100	20	Normal	○
Snore	Normal	Special	40	100	15	Normal	—
Swift	Normal	Special	60	—	20	2 Foes	—
Tailwind	Flying	Status	—	—	30	2 Allies	—
Superpower	Fighting	Physical	120	100	5	Normal	○
Iron Head	Steel	Physical	80	100	15	Normal	○
Iron Defense	Steel	Status	—	—	15	Self	—

● TM & HM MOVES

No.	Name	Type	Kind	Pow.	Acc.	PP	Range	DA
TM06	Toxic	Poison	Status	—	85	10	Normal	—
TM10	Hidden Power	Normal	Special	—	100	15	Normal	—
TM11	Sunny Day	Fire	Status	—	—	5	All	—
TM15	Hyper Beam	Normal	Special	150	90	5	Normal	—
TM17	Protect	Normal	Status	—	—	10	Self	—
TM18	Rain Dance	Water	Status	—	—	5	All	—
TM21	Frustration	Normal	Physical	—	100	20	Normal	○
TM27	Return	Normal	Physical	—	100	20	Normal	○
TM31	Brick Break	Fighting	Physical	75	100	15	Normal	○
TM32	Double Team	Normal	Status	—	—	15	Self	—
TM37	Sandstorm	Rock	Status	—	—	10	All	—
TM40	Aerial Ace	Flying	Physical	60	—	20	Normal	○
TM42	Facade	Normal	Physical	70	100	20	Normal	○
TM43	Secret Power	Normal	Physical	70	100	20	Normal	○
TM44	Rest	Psychic	Status	—	—	10	Self	—
TM45	Attract	Normal	Status	—	100	15	Normal	—
TM46	Thief	Dark	Physical	40	100	10	Normal	○
TM47	Steel Wing	Steel	Physical	70	90	25	Normal	○
TM51	Roost	Flying	Status	—	—	10	Self	—
TM54	False Swipe	Normal	Physical	40	100	40	Normal	○
TM56	Fling	Dark	Physical	—	100	10	Normal	○
TM58	Endure	Normal	Status	—	—	10	Self	—
TM62	Silver Wind	Bug	Special	60	100	5	Normal	—
TM68	Giga Impact	Normal	Physical	150	90	5	Normal	○
TM75	Swords Dance	Normal	Status	—	—	30	Self	—
TM78	Captivate	Normal	Status	—	100	20	2 Foes	—
TM81	X-Scissor	Bug	Physical	80	100	15	Normal	○
TM82	Sleep Talk	Normal	Status	—	—	10	Depends	—
TM83	Natural Gift	Normal	Physical	—	100	15	Normal	—
TM87	Swagger	Normal	Status	—	90	15	Normal	—
TM89	U-turn	Bug	Physical	70	100	20	Normal	○
TM90	Substitute	Normal	Status	—	—	10	Self	—
TM91	Flash Cannon	Steel	Special	80	100	10	Normal	—
HM01	Cut	Normal	Physical	50	95	30	Normal	○
HM04	Strength	Normal	Physical	80	100	15	Normal	○
HM06	Rock Smash	Fighting	Physical	40	100	15	Normal	○

◉ No. 212 | Pincer Pokémon
Scizor

Bug   Steel

- **HEIGHT:** 5'11"
- **WEIGHT:** 260.1 lbs.
- **ITEMS:** None

● SIZE COMPARISON

● **MALE FORM**
Shorter abdomen

● **FEMALE FORM**
Longer abdomen

◈ ABILITIES
- Swarm
- Technician

◈ STATS
HP ●●●
ATTACK ●●●●●
DEFENSE ●●●●
SP. ATTACK ●●●
SP. DEFENSE ●●●
SPEED ●●●

◈ EGG GROUPS
Bug

◈ PERFORMANCE
SPEED ★★   STAMINA ★★★★☆
POWER ★★★★☆   JUMP ★★☆
SKILL ★★☆☆☆

● MAIN WAYS TO OBTAIN

Pokémon HeartGold	Link trade Scyther while it holds the Metal Coat
Pokémon SoulSilver	Link trade Scyther while it holds the Metal Coat
Pokémon Diamond	Link trade Scyther while it holds the Metal Coat
Pokémon Pearl	—
Pokémon Platinum	Link trade Scyther while it holds the Metal Coat

Pokémon HeartGold	*Pokémon SoulSilver*
It swings its eye-patterned pincers up to scare its foes. This makes it look like it has three heads.	Its wings are not used for flying. They are flapped at high speed to adjust its body temperature.

◈ EVOLUTION

Scyther

Have it hold Metal Coat and trade it

Scizor

No. 213 | Mold Pokémon
Shuckle

`Bug` `Rock`

- **HEIGHT:** 2'00"
- **WEIGHT:** 45.2 lbs.
- **ITEMS:** Berry Juice

● SIZE COMPARISON

● MALE/FEMALE HAVE SAME FORM

ABILITIES
- Sturdy
- Gluttony

STATS
- HP ●
- ATTACK ●
- DEFENSE ●●●●●
- SP. ATTACK ●
- SP. DEFENSE ●●●●●
- SPEED ●

EGG GROUPS
Bug

PERFORMANCE
SPEED ★☆	STAMINA ★★★★★
POWER ★☆☆☆☆	JUMP ★★
SKILL ★☆	

MAIN WAYS TO OBTAIN

Pokémon HeartGold	Cianwood City (use Rock Smash)
Pokémon SoulSilver	Cianwood City (use Rock Smash)
Pokémon Diamond	Route 224 (after obtaining the National Pokédex, insert *Pokémon Emerald* into your Nintendo DS's Game Pak slot)
Pokémon Pearl	Route 224 (after obtaining the National Pokédex, insert *Pokémon Emerald* into your Nintendo DS's Game Pak slot)
Pokémon Platinum	Route 224 (after obtaining the National Pokédex, insert *Pokémon Emerald* into your Nintendo DS's Game Pak slot)

Pokémon HeartGold	**Pokémon SoulSilver**
The berries it stores in its vase-like shell decompose and become a gooey liquid.	It stores berries inside its shell. To avoid attacks, it hides beneath rocks and remains completely still.

EVOLUTION

Does not evolve

● LEVEL-UP MOVES
Lv.	Name	Type	Kind	Pow.	Acc.	PP	Range	DA
1	Withdraw	Water	Status	—	—	40	Self	—
1	Constrict	Normal	Physical	10	100	35	Normal	○
1	Bide	Normal	Physical	—	—	10	Self	—
9	Encore	Normal	Status	—	100	5	Normal	—
14	Safeguard	Normal	Status	—	—	25	2 Allies	—
22	Wrap	Normal	Physical	15	85	20	Normal	○
27	Rest	Psychic	Status	—	—	10	Self	—
35	Gastro Acid	Poison	Status	—	100	10	Normal	—
40	Bug Bite	Bug	Physical	60	100	20	Normal	○
48	Power Trick	Psychic	Status	—	—	10	Self	—

● MOVE MANIAC
Name	Type	Kind	Pow.	Acc.	PP	Range	DA
Headbutt	Normal	Physical	70	100	15	Normal	○

● BP MOVES
Name	Type	Kind	Pow.	Acc.	PP	Range	DA
Bug Bite	Bug	Physical	60	100	20	Normal	○
Snore	Normal	Special	40	100	15	Normal	—
Helping Hand	Normal	Status	—	—	20	1 Ally	—
String Shot	Bug	Status	—	95	40	2 Foes	—
Mud-Slap	Ground	Special	20	100	10	Normal	—
Rollout	Rock	Physical	30	90	20	Normal	○
Gastro Acid	Poison	Status	—	100	10	Normal	—
AncientPower	Rock	Special	60	100	5	Normal	—
Earth Power	Ground	Special	90	100	10	Normal	—

● TM & HM MOVES
No.	Name	Type	Kind	Pow.	Acc.	PP	Range	DA
TM06	Toxic	Poison	Status	—	85	10	Normal	—
TM10	Hidden Power	Normal	Special	—	100	15	Normal	—
TM11	Sunny Day	Fire	Status	—	—	5	All	—
TM17	Protect	Normal	Status	—	—	10	Self	—
TM20	Safeguard	Normal	Status	—	—	25	2 Allies	—
TM21	Frustration	Normal	Physical	—	100	20	Normal	○
TM26	Earthquake	Ground	Physical	100	100	10	2 Foes/1 Ally	—
TM27	Return	Normal	Physical	—	100	20	Normal	○
TM28	Dig	Ground	Physical	80	100	10	Normal	○
TM32	Double Team	Normal	Status	—	—	15	Self	—
TM36	Sludge Bomb	Poison	Special	90	100	10	Normal	—
TM37	Sandstorm	Rock	Status	—	—	10	All	—
TM39	Rock Tomb	Rock	Physical	50	80	10	Normal	—
TM42	Facade	Normal	Physical	70	100	20	Normal	○
TM43	Secret Power	Normal	Physical	70	100	20	Normal	○
TM44	Rest	Psychic	Status	—	—	10	Self	—
TM45	Attract	Normal	Status	—	100	15	Normal	—
TM58	Endure	Normal	Status	—	—	10	Self	—
TM69	Rock Polish	Rock	Status	—	—	20	Self	—
TM70	Flash	Normal	Status	—	100	20	Normal	—
TM71	Stone Edge	Rock	Physical	100	80	5	Normal	—
TM74	Gyro Ball	Steel	Physical	—	100	5	Normal	○
TM76	Stealth Rock	Rock	Status	—	—	20	2 Foes	—
TM78	Captivate	Normal	Status	—	100	20	2 Foes	—
TM80	Rock Slide	Rock	Physical	75	90	10	2 Foes	—
TM82	Sleep Talk	Normal	Status	—	—	10	Depends	—
TM83	Natural Gift	Normal	Physical	—	100	15	Normal	—
TM87	Swagger	Normal	Status	—	90	15	Normal	—
TM90	Substitute	Normal	Status	—	—	10	Self	—
HM04	Strength	Normal	Physical	80	100	15	Normal	○
HM06	Rock Smash	Fighting	Physical	40	100	15	Normal	○

● EGG MOVES
Name	Type	Kind	Pow.	Acc.	PP	Range	DA
Sweet Scent	Normal	Status	—	100	20	2 Foes	—
Knock Off	Dark	Physical	20	100	20	Normal	○
Helping Hand	Normal	Status	—	—	20	1 Ally	—
Acupressure	Normal	Status	—	—	30	1 Ally	—
Sand Tomb	Ground	Physical	15	70	15	Normal	—
Mud-Slap	Ground	Special	20	100	10	Normal	—

● LEVEL-UP MOVES

Lv.	Name	Type	Kind	Pow.	Acc.	PP	Range	DA
1	Night Slash	Dark	Physical	70	100	15	Normal	○
1	Tackle	Normal	Physical	35	95	35	Normal	○
1	Leer	Normal	Status	—	100	30	2 Foes	—
1	Horn Attack	Normal	Physical	65	100	25	Normal	○
1	Endure	Normal	Status	—	—	10	Self	—
7	Fury Attack	Normal	Physical	15	85	20	Normal	○
13	Aerial Ace	Flying	Physical	60	—	20	Normal	○
19	Brick Break	Fighting	Physical	75	100	15	Normal	○
25	Counter	Fighting	Physical	—	100	20	Self	○
31	Take Down	Normal	Physical	90	85	20	Normal	○
37	Close Combat	Fighting	Physical	120	100	5	Normal	○
43	Reversal	Fighting	Physical	—	100	15	Normal	○
49	Feint	Normal	Physical	50	100	10	Normal	○
55	Megahorn	Bug	Physical	120	85	10	Normal	○

● MOVE MANIAC

Name	Type	Kind	Pow.	Acc.	PP	Range	DA
Headbutt	Normal	Physical	70	100	15	Normal	○

● BP MOVES

Name	Type	Kind	Pow.	Acc.	PP	Range	DA
Fury Cutter	Bug	Physical	10	95	20	Normal	○
Vacuum Wave	Fighting	Special	40	100	30	Normal	○
Knock Off	Dark	Physical	20	100	20	Normal	○
Bug Bite	Bug	Physical	60	100	20	Normal	○
Snore	Normal	Special	40	100	15	Normal	—
Helping Hand	Normal	Status	—	—	20	1 Ally	—
Iron Defense	Steel	Status	—	—	15	Self	—
Low Kick	Fighting	Physical	—	100	20	Normal	○

● TM & HM MOVES

No.	Name	Type	Kind	Pow.	Acc.	PP	Range	DA
TM01	Focus Punch	Fighting	Physical	150	100	20	Normal	○
TM06	Toxic	Poison	Status	—	85	10	Normal	—
TM08	Bulk Up	Fighting	Status	—	—	20	Self	—
TM10	Hidden Power	Normal	Special	—	100	15	Normal	—
TM11	Sunny Day	Fire	Status	—	—	5	All	—
TM15	Hyper Beam	Normal	Special	150	90	5	Normal	—
TM17	Protect	Normal	Status	—	—	10	Self	—
TM18	Rain Dance	Water	Status	—	—	5	All	—
TM21	Frustration	Normal	Physical	—	100	20	Normal	○
TM26	Earthquake	Ground	Physical	100	100	10	2 Foes/1 Ally	—
TM27	Return	Normal	Physical	—	100	20	Normal	○
TM28	Dig	Ground	Physical	80	100	10	Normal	○
TM31	Brick Break	Fighting	Physical	75	100	15	Normal	○
TM32	Double Team	Normal	Status	—	—	15	Self	—
TM39	Rock Tomb	Rock	Physical	50	80	10	Normal	○
TM40	Aerial Ace	Flying	Physical	60	—	20	Normal	○
TM42	Facade	Normal	Physical	70	100	20	Normal	—
TM43	Secret Power	Normal	Physical	70	100	20	Normal	—
TM44	Rest	Psychic	Status	—	—	10	Self	—
TM45	Attract	Normal	Status	—	100	15	Normal	—
TM46	Thief	Dark	Physical	40	100	10	Normal	○
TM52	Focus Blast	Fighting	Special	120	70	5	Normal	—
TM56	Fling	Dark	Physical	—	100	10	Normal	—
TM58	Endure	Normal	Status	—	—	10	Self	—
TM65	Shadow Claw	Ghost	Physical	70	100	15	Normal	○
TM68	Giga Impact	Normal	Physical	150	90	5	Normal	—
TM71	Stone Edge	Rock	Physical	100	80	5	Normal	—
TM75	Swords Dance	Normal	Status	—	—	30	Self	—
TM78	Captivate	Normal	Status	—	100	20	2 Foes	—
TM80	Rock Slide	Rock	Physical	75	90	10	2 Foes	—
TM82	Sleep Talk	Normal	Status	—	—	10	Depends	—
TM83	Natural Gift	Normal	Physical	—	100	15	Normal	—
TM87	Swagger	Normal	Status	—	90	15	Normal	—
TM90	Substitute	Normal	Status	—	—	10	Self	—
HM01	Cut	Normal	Physical	50	95	30	Normal	○
HM04	Strength	Normal	Physical	80	100	15	Normal	○
HM06	Rock Smash	Fighting	Physical	40	100	15	Normal	○

● EGG MOVES

Name	Type	Kind	Pow	Acc	PP	Range	DA
Harden	Normal	Status	—	—	30	Self	—
Bide	Normal	Physical	—	—	10	Self	○
Flail	Normal	Physical	—	100	15	Normal	○
False Swipe	Normal	Physical	40	100	40	Normal	○
Revenge	Fighting	Physical	60	100	10	Normal	○
Pursuit	Dark	Physical	40	100	20	Normal	○
Double-Edge	Normal	Physical	120	100	15	Normal	○

● No. 214 | Single Horn Pokémon

Heracross

Bug Fighting

- ● HEIGHT: 4'11"
- ● WEIGHT: 119.0 lbs.
- ● ITEMS: None

● SIZE COMPARISON

● MALE FORM
Pointed horn

● FEMALE FORM
Rounded horn

⦿ ABILITIES
- Swarm
- Guts

⦿ EGG GROUPS
Bug

⦿ STATS
HP	●●●
ATTACK	●●●●●
DEFENSE	●●●
SP. ATTACK	●●
SP. DEFENSE	●●●●
SPEED	●●●●

⦿ PERFORMANCE
SPEED ★★★
POWER ★★★★☆
SKILL ★★★
STAMINA ★★☆
JUMP ★★☆

● MAIN WAYS TO OBTAIN

Pokémon HeartGold — Azalea Town (use Headbutt)

Pokémon SoulSilver — Azalea Town (use Headbutt)

Pokémon Diamond — Occasionally appears if you spread Honey on a sweet-smelling tree

Pokémon Pearl — Occasionally appears if you spread Honey on a sweet-smelling tree

Pokémon Platinum — Occasionally appears if you spread Honey on a sweet-smelling tree

Pokémon HeartGold — This powerful Pokémon thrusts its prized horn under its enemies' bellies, then lifts and throws them.

Pokémon SoulSilver — It is usually docile, but if it is disturbed while sipping honey, it chases off the intruder with its horn.

⦿ EVOLUTION
Does not evolve

No. 215 | Sharp Claw Pokémon
Sneasel

Dark | **Ice**

● HEIGHT: 2'11"
● WEIGHT: 61.7 lbs.
● ITEMS: Grip Claw
　　　　　Quick Claw

● SIZE COMPARISON

● MALE FORM
Larger ear

● FEMALE FORM
Smaller ear

ABILITIES
● Inner Focus
● Keen Eye

STATS

HP ●●
ATTACK ●●●●
DEFENSE ●●
SP. ATTACK ●
SP. DEFENSE ●●●
SPEED ●●●●●

EGG GROUPS
Field

PERFORMANCE
SPEED ★★★★★　　STAMINA ★
POWER ★★☆　　　 JUMP ★★★☆
SKILL ★★★★☆

● MAIN WAYS TO OBTAIN

Pokémon HeartGold	Mt. Silver Cave interior
Pokémon SoulSilver	Mt. Silver Cave interior
Pokémon Diamond	Route 216
Pokémon Pearl	Route 216
Pokémon Platinum	Route 216

| Pokémon HeartGold | Pokémon SoulSilver |
| Its paws conceal sharp claws. If attacked, it suddenly extends the claws and startles its enemy. | Vicious in nature, it drives PIDGEY from their nests and scavenges any leftovers it can find. |

EVOLUTION

Sneasel → Have it hold Razor Claw and then level up between 8:00 p.m. and 4:00 a.m. → Weavile

● LEVEL-UP MOVES

Lv.	Name	Type	Kind	Pow.	Acc.	PP	Range	DA
1	Scratch	Normal	Physical	40	100	35	Normal	○
1	Leer	Normal	Status	—	100	30	2 Foes	—
1	Taunt	Dark	Status	—	100	20	Normal	—
8	Quick Attack	Normal	Physical	40	100	30	Normal	○
10	Screech	Normal	Status	—	85	40	Normal	—
14	Faint Attack	Dark	Physical	60	—	20	Normal	○
21	Fury Swipes	Normal	Physical	18	80	15	Normal	○
24	Agility	Psychic	Status	—	—	30	Self	—
28	Icy Wind	Ice	Special	55	95	15	2 Foes	—
35	Slash	Normal	Physical	70	100	20	Normal	○
38	Beat Up	Dark	Physical	10	100	10	Normal	—
42	Metal Claw	Steel	Physical	50	95	35	Normal	○
49	Ice Shard	Ice	Physical	40	100	30	Normal	—

● MOVE MANIAC

Name	Type	Kind	Pow.	Acc.	PP	Range	DA
Headbutt	Normal	Physical	70	100	15	Normal	○

● BP MOVES

Name	Type	Kind	Pow.	Acc.	PP	Range	DA
Fury Cutter	Bug	Physical	10	95	20	Normal	○
Icy Wind	Ice	Special	55	95	15	2 Foes	—
Ice Punch	Ice	Physical	75	100	15	Normal	○
Knock Off	Dark	Physical	20	100	20	Normal	○
Snore	Normal	Special	40	100	15	Normal	—
Spite	Ghost	Status	—	100	10	Normal	—
Swift	Normal	Special	60	—	20	2 Foes	—
Mud-Slap	Ground	Special	20	100	10	Normal	—
Low Kick	Fighting	Physical	—	100	20	Normal	—

● TM & HM MOVES

No.	Name	Type	Kind	Pow.	Acc.	PP	Range	DA
TM01	Focus Punch	Fighting	Physical	150	100	20	Normal	○
TM04	Calm Mind	Psychic	Status	—	—	20	Self	—
TM06	Toxic	Poison	Status	—	85	10	Normal	—
TM07	Hail	Ice	Status	—	—	10	All	—
TM10	Hidden Power	Normal	Special	—	100	15	Normal	—
TM11	Sunny Day	Fire	Status	—	—	5	All	—
TM12	Taunt	Dark	Status	—	100	20	Normal	—
TM13	Ice Beam	Ice	Special	95	100	10	Normal	—
TM14	Blizzard	Ice	Special	120	70	5	2 Foes	—
TM17	Protect	Normal	Status	—	—	10	Self	—
TM18	Rain Dance	Water	Status	—	—	5	All	—
TM21	Frustration	Normal	Physical	—	100	20	Normal	○
TM23	Iron Tail	Steel	Physical	100	75	15	Normal	○
TM27	Return	Normal	Physical	—	100	20	Normal	○
TM28	Dig	Ground	Physical	80	100	10	Normal	○
TM30	Shadow Ball	Ghost	Special	80	100	15	Normal	—
TM31	Brick Break	Fighting	Physical	75	100	15	Normal	○
TM32	Double Team	Normal	Status	—	—	15	Self	—
TM40	Aerial Ace	Flying	Physical	60	—	20	Normal	○
TM41	Torment	Dark	Status	—	100	15	Normal	—
TM42	Facade	Normal	Physical	70	100	20	Normal	○
TM43	Secret Power	Normal	Physical	70	100	20	Normal	—
TM44	Rest	Psychic	Status	—	—	10	Self	—
TM45	Attract	Normal	Status	—	100	15	Normal	—
TM46	Thief	Dark	Physical	40	100	10	Normal	○
TM49	Snatch	Dark	Status	—	—	10	Depends	—
TM54	False Swipe	Normal	Physical	40	100	40	Normal	○
TM56	Fling	Dark	Physical	—	100	10	Normal	—
TM58	Endure	Normal	Status	—	—	10	Self	—
TM63	Embargo	Dark	Status	—	100	15	Normal	—
TM65	Shadow Claw	Ghost	Physical	70	100	15	Normal	○
TM66	Payback	Dark	Physical	50	100	10	Normal	○
TM72	Avalanche	Ice	Physical	60	100	10	Normal	○
TM75	Swords Dance	Normal	Status	—	—	30	Self	—
TM77	Psych Up	Normal	Status	—	—	10	Normal	—
TM78	Captivate	Normal	Status	—	100	20	2 Foes	—
TM79	Dark Pulse	Dark	Special	80	100	15	Normal	—
TM81	X-Scissor	Bug	Physical	80	100	15	Normal	○
TM82	Sleep Talk	Normal	Status	—	—	10	Depends	—
TM83	Natural Gift	Normal	Physical	—	100	15	Normal	—
TM84	Poison Jab	Poison	Physical	80	100	20	Normal	○
TM85	Dream Eater	Psychic	Special	100	100	15	Normal	—
TM87	Swagger	Normal	Status	—	90	15	Normal	—
TM90	Substitute	Normal	Status	—	—	10	Self	—
HM01	Cut	Normal	Physical	50	95	30	Normal	○
HM03	Surf	Water	Special	95	100	15	2 Foes/1 Ally	—
HM04	Strength	Normal	Physical	80	100	15	Normal	○
HM05	Whirlpool	Water	Special	15	70	15	Normal	—
HM06	Rock Smash	Fighting	Physical	40	100	15	Normal	○

● EGG MOVES

Name	Type	Kind	Pow.	Acc.	PP	Range	DA
Counter	Fighting	Physical	—	100	20	Self	○
Spite	Ghost	Status	—	100	10	Normal	—
Foresight	Normal	Status	—	—	40	Normal	—
Reflect	Psychic	Status	—	—	20	2 Allies	—
Bite	Dark	Physical	60	100	25	Normal	○
Crush Claw	Normal	Physical	75	95	10	Normal	○
Fake Out	Normal	Physical	40	100	10	Normal	○
Double Hit	Normal	Physical	35	90	10	Normal	○
Punishment	Dark	Physical	—	100	5	Normal	○
Pursuit	Dark	Physical	40	100	20	Normal	○
Ice Shard	Ice	Physical	40	100	30	Normal	—
Ice Punch	Ice	Physical	75	100	15	Normal	○
Assist	Normal	Status	—	—	20	Depends	—

● LEVEL-UP MOVES

Lv.	Name	Type	Kind	Pow.	Acc.	PP	Range	DA
1	Covet	Normal	Physical	40	100	40	Normal	○
1	Scratch	Normal	Physical	40	100	35	Normal	○
1	Leer	Normal	Status	—	100	30	2 Foes	—
1	Lick	Ghost	Physical	20	100	30	Normal	○
1	Fake Tears	Dark	Status	—	100	20	Normal	—
8	Fury Swipes	Normal	Physical	18	80	15	Normal	○
15	Faint Attack	Dark	Physical	60	—	20	Normal	○
22	Sweet Scent	Normal	Status	—	100	20	2 Foes	—
29	Slash	Normal	Physical	70	100	20	Normal	○
36	Charm	Normal	Status	—	100	20	Normal	—
43	Rest	Psychic	Status	—	—	10	Self	—
43	Snore	Normal	Special	40	100	15	Normal	—
50	Thrash	Normal	Physical	90	100	20	1 Random	○
57	Fling	Dark	Physical	—	100	10	Normal	○

● MOVE MANIAC

Name	Type	Kind	Pow.	Acc.	PP	Range	DA
Headbutt	Normal	Physical	70	100	15	Normal	○

● BP MOVES

Name	Type	Kind	Pow.	Acc.	PP	Range	DA
Fury Cutter	Bug	Physical	10	95	20	Normal	○
ThunderPunch	Electric	Physical	75	100	15	Normal	○
Fire Punch	Fire	Physical	75	100	15	Normal	○
Ice Punch	Ice	Physical	75	100	15	Normal	○
Snore	Normal	Special	40	100	15	Normal	—
Last Resort	Normal	Physical	130	100	5	Normal	○
Swift	Normal	Special	60	—	20	2 Foes	—
Mud-Slap	Ground	Special	20	100	10	Normal	—
Rollout	Rock	Physical	30	90	20	Normal	○
Superpower	Fighting	Physical	120	100	5	Normal	○
Gunk Shot	Poison	Physical	120	70	5	Normal	—
Seed Bomb	Grass	Physical	80	100	15	Normal	○

● TM & HM MOVES

No.	Name	Type	Kind	Pow.	Acc.	PP	Range	DA
TM01	Focus Punch	Fighting	Physical	150	100	20	Normal	○
TM05	Roar	Normal	Status	—	100	20	Normal	—
TM06	Toxic	Poison	Status	—	85	10	Normal	—
TM08	Bulk Up	Fighting	Status	—	—	20	Self	—
TM10	Hidden Power	Normal	Special	—	100	15	Normal	—
TM11	Sunny Day	Fire	Status	—	—	5	All	—
TM12	Taunt	Dark	Status	—	100	20	Normal	—
TM17	Protect	Normal	Status	—	—	10	Self	—
TM18	Rain Dance	Water	Status	—	—	5	All	—
TM21	Frustration	Normal	Physical	—	100	20	Normal	○
TM26	Earthquake	Ground	Physical	100	100	10	2 Foes/1 Ally	○
TM27	Return	Normal	Physical	—	100	20	Normal	○
TM28	Dig	Ground	Physical	80	100	10	Normal	○
TM31	Brick Break	Fighting	Physical	75	100	15	Normal	○
TM32	Double Team	Normal	Status	—	—	15	Self	—
TM39	Rock Tomb	Rock	Physical	50	80	10	Normal	○
TM40	Aerial Ace	Flying	Physical	60	—	20	Normal	○
TM41	Torment	Dark	Status	—	100	15	Normal	—
TM42	Facade	Normal	Physical	70	100	20	Normal	○
TM43	Secret Power	Normal	Physical	70	100	20	Normal	○
TM44	Rest	Psychic	Status	—	—	10	Self	—
TM45	Attract	Normal	Status	—	100	15	Normal	—
TM46	Thief	Dark	Physical	40	100	10	Normal	○
TM56	Fling	Dark	Physical	—	100	10	Normal	○
TM58	Endure	Normal	Status	—	—	10	Self	—
TM65	Shadow Claw	Ghost	Physical	70	100	15	Normal	○
TM66	Payback	Dark	Physical	50	100	10	Normal	○
TM75	Swords Dance	Normal	Status	—	—	30	Self	—
TM78	Captivate	Normal	Status	—	100	20	2 Foes	—
TM80	Rock Slide	Rock	Physical	75	90	10	2 Foes	—
TM82	Sleep Talk	Normal	Status	—	—	10	Depends	—
TM83	Natural Gift	Normal	Physical	—	100	15	Normal	—
TM87	Swagger	Normal	Status	—	90	15	Normal	—
TM90	Substitute	Normal	Status	—	—	10	Self	—
HM01	Cut	Normal	Physical	50	95	30	Normal	○
HM04	Strength	Normal	Physical	80	100	15	Normal	○
HM06	Rock Smash	Fighting	Physical	40	100	15	Normal	○

● EGG MOVES

Name	Type	Kind	Pow.	Acc.	PP	Range	DA
Crunch	Dark	Physical	80	100	15	Normal	○
Take Down	Normal	Physical	90	85	20	Normal	○
Seismic Toss	Fighting	Physical	—	100	20	Normal	○
Counter	Fighting	Physical	—	100	20	Self	○
Metal Claw	Steel	Physical	50	95	35	Normal	○
Fake Tears	Dark	Status	—	100	20	Normal	—
Yawn	Normal	Status	—	—	10	Normal	—
Sleep Talk	Normal	Status	—	—	10	Depends	—
Cross Chop	Fighting	Physical	100	80	5	Normal	○
Double-Edge	Normal	Physical	120	100	15	Normal	○
Close Combat	Fighting	Physical	120	100	5	Normal	○
Night Slash	Dark	Physical	70	100	15	Normal	○
Belly Drum	Normal	Status	—	—	10	Self	—

● HEIGHT: 2'00"
● WEIGHT: 19.4 lbs.
● ITEMS: None

● SIZE COMPARISON

● MALE/FEMALE HAVE SAME FORM

● ABILITIES
● Pickup
● Quick Feet

● STATS
HP ●●
ATTACK ●●●
DEFENSE ●●
SP. ATTACK ●●
SP. DEFENSE ●●
SPEED ●●

● EGG GROUPS
Field

● PERFORMANCE
SPEED ★★★
POWER ★★★
SKILL ★★★★

STAMINA ★★★★☆
JUMP ★★☆

● MAIN WAYS TO OBTAIN

Pokémon HeartGold —

Pokémon SoulSilver Route 45

Pokémon Diamond Route 211, Eterna City side (after obtaining the National Pokédex, insert *Pokémon Emerald* into your Nintendo DS's Game Pak slot)

Pokémon Pearl Route 211, Eterna City side (after obtaining the National Pokédex, insert *Pokémon Emerald* into your Nintendo DS's Game Pak slot)

Pokémon Platinum Route 211, Eterna City side (after obtaining the National Pokédex, insert *Pokémon Emerald* into your Nintendo DS's Game Pak slot)

Pokémon HeartGold
If it finds honey, its crescent mark glows. It always licks its paws because they're soaked with honey.

Pokémon SoulSilver
Before food becomes scarce in wintertime, its habit is to hoard food in many hidden locations.

● EVOLUTION

Lv. 30

Teddiursa

Ursaring

● No. 217 | Hibernator Pokémon
Ursaring

Normal

● LEVEL-UP MOVES

Lv.	Name	Type	Kind	Pow.	Acc.	PP	Range	DA
1	Covet	Normal	Physical	40	100	40	Normal	○
1	Scratch	Normal	Physical	40	100	35	Normal	○
1	Leer	Normal	Status	—	100	30	2 Foes	—
1	Lick	Ghost	Physical	20	100	30	Normal	○
1	Fake Tears	Dark	Status	—	100	20	Normal	—
8	Fury Swipes	Normal	Physical	18	80	15	Normal	○
15	Faint Attack	Dark	Physical	60	—	20	Normal	○
22	Sweet Scent	Normal	Status	—	100	20	2 Foes	—
29	Slash	Normal	Physical	70	100	20	Normal	○
38	Scary Face	Normal	Status	—	90	10	Normal	—
47	Rest	Psychic	Status	—	—	10	Self	—
49	Snore	Normal	Special	40	100	15	Normal	—
58	Thrash	Normal	Physical	90	100	20	1 Random	○
67	Hammer Arm	Fighting	Physical	100	90	10	Normal	○

● MOVE MANIAC

Name	Type	Kind	Pow.	Acc.	PP	Range	DA
Headbutt	Normal	Physical	70	100	15	Normal	○

● BP MOVES

Name	Type	Kind	Pow.	Acc.	PP	Range	DA
Fury Cutter	Bug	Physical	10	95	20	Normal	○
ThunderPunch	Electric	Physical	75	100	15	Normal	○
Fire Punch	Fire	Physical	75	100	15	Normal	○
Ice Punch	Ice	Physical	75	100	15	Normal	○
Snore	Normal	Special	40	100	15	Normal	—
Last Resort	Normal	Physical	130	100	5	Normal	○
Swift	Normal	Special	60	—	20	2 Foes	—
Uproar	Normal	Special	50	100	10	1 Random	—
Mud-Slap	Ground	Special	20	100	10	Normal	—
Rollout	Rock	Physical	30	90	20	Normal	○
Superpower	Fighting	Physical	120	100	5	Normal	○
Gunk Shot	Poison	Physical	120	70	5	Normal	—
Seed Bomb	Grass	Physical	80	100	15	Normal	○
Low Kick	Fighting	Physical	—	100	20	Normal	○

● TM & HM MOVES

No.	Name	Type	Kind	Pow.	Acc.	PP	Range	DA
TM01	Focus Punch	Fighting	Physical	150	100	20	Normal	○
TM05	Roar	Normal	Status	—	100	20	Normal	—
TM06	Toxic	Poison	Status	—	85	10	Normal	—
TM08	Bulk Up	Fighting	Status	—	—	20	Self	—
TM10	Hidden Power	Normal	Special	—	100	15	Normal	—
TM11	Sunny Day	Fire	Status	—	—	5	All	—
TM12	Taunt	Dark	Status	—	100	20	Normal	—
TM15	Hyper Beam	Normal	Special	150	90	5	Normal	—
TM17	Protect	Normal	Status	—	—	10	Self	—
TM18	Rain Dance	Water	Status	—	—	5	All	—
TM21	Frustration	Normal	Physical	—	100	20	Normal	○
TM26	Earthquake	Ground	Physical	100	100	10	2 Foes/1 Ally	—
TM27	Return	Normal	Physical	—	100	20	Normal	○
TM28	Dig	Ground	Physical	80	100	10	Normal	○
TM31	Brick Break	Fighting	Physical	75	100	15	Normal	○
TM32	Double Team	Normal	Status	—	—	15	Self	—
TM39	Rock Tomb	Rock	Physical	50	80	10	Normal	—
TM40	Aerial Ace	Flying	Physical	60	—	20	Normal	○
TM41	Torment	Dark	Status	—	100	15	Normal	—
TM42	Facade	Normal	Physical	70	100	20	Normal	○
TM43	Secret Power	Normal	Physical	70	100	20	Normal	○
TM44	Rest	Psychic	Status	—	—	10	Self	—
TM45	Attract	Normal	Status	—	100	15	Normal	—
TM52	Focus Blast	Fighting	Special	120	70	5	Normal	—
TM56	Fling	Dark	Physical	—	100	10	Normal	○
TM58	Endure	Normal	Status	—	—	10	Self	—
TM65	Shadow Claw	Ghost	Physical	70	100	15	Normal	○
TM66	Payback	Dark	Physical	50	100	10	Normal	○
TM68	Giga Impact	Normal	Physical	150	90	5	Normal	○
TM71	Stone Edge	Rock	Physical	100	80	5	Normal	—
TM72	Avalanche	Ice	Physical	60	100	10	Normal	○
TM75	Swords Dance	Normal	Status	—	—	30	Self	—
TM78	Captivate	Normal	Status	—	100	20	2 Foes	—
TM80	Rock Slide	Rock	Physical	75	90	10	2 Foes	—
TM82	Sleep Talk	Normal	Status	—	—	10	Depends	—
TM83	Natural Gift	Normal	Physical	—	100	15	Normal	—
TM87	Swagger	Normal	Status	—	90	15	Normal	—
TM90	Substitute	Normal	Status	—	—	10	Self	—
HM01	Cut	Normal	Physical	50	95	30	Normal	○
HM04	Strength	Normal	Physical	80	100	15	Normal	○
HM06	Rock Smash	Fighting	Physical	40	100	15	Normal	○
HM08	Rock Climb	Normal	Physical	90	85	20	Normal	○

● HEIGHT: 5'11"
● WEIGHT: 277.3 lbs.
● ITEMS: None

● SIZE COMPARISON

● MALE FORM
Shorter fur on shoulders

● FEMALE FORM
Longer fur on shoulders

● ABILITIES
● Guts
● Quick Feet

● STATS
HP ●●●
ATTACK ●●●●●
DEFENSE ●●●●
SP. ATTACK ●●●
SP. DEFENSE ●●●
SPEED ●●●

● EGG GROUPS
Field

● PERFORMANCE
SPEED ★★☆
POWER ★★★★☆
SKILL ★★☆
STAMINA ★★★★★
JUMP ★★

● MAIN WAYS TO OBTAIN

Pokémon HeartGold	—
Pokémon SoulSilver	Victory Road
Pokémon Diamond	Route 216 (after obtaining the National Pokédex, insert *Pokémon Emerald* into your Nintendo DS's Game Pak slot)
Pokémon Pearl	Route 216 (after obtaining the National Pokédex, insert *Pokémon Emerald* into your Nintendo DS's Game Pak slot)
Pokémon Platinum	Route 216 (after obtaining the National Pokédex, insert *Pokémon Emerald* into your Nintendo DS's Game Pak slot)

Pokémon HeartGold
Although it is a good climber, it prefers to snap trees with its forelegs and eat fallen berries.

Pokémon SoulSilver
With its ability to distinguish any aroma, it unfailingly finds all food buried deep underground.

● EVOLUTION

 Teddiursa   Lv. 30   Ursaring

● LEVEL-UP MOVES

Lv.	Name	Type	Kind	Pow.	Acc.	PP	Range	DA
1	Yawn	Normal	Status	—	—	10	Normal	—
1	Smog	Poison	Special	20	70	20	Normal	—
8	Ember	Fire	Special	40	100	25	Normal	—
11	Rock Throw	Rock	Physical	50	90	15	Normal	—
16	Harden	Normal	Status	—	—	30	Self	—
23	Recover	Normal	Status	—	—	10	Self	—
26	AncientPower	Rock	Special	60	100	5	Normal	—
31	Amnesia	Psychic	Status	—	—	20	Self	—
38	Lava Plume	Fire	Special	80	100	15	2 Foes/1 Ally	—
41	Rock Slide	Rock	Physical	75	90	10	2 Foes	—
46	Body Slam	Normal	Physical	85	100	15	Normal	O
53	Flamethrower	Fire	Special	95	100	15	Normal	—
56	Earth Power	Ground	Special	90	100	10	Normal	—

● MOVE MANIAC

Name	Type	Kind	Pow.	Acc.	PP	Range	DA

● BP MOVES

Name	Type	Kind	Pow.	Acc.	PP	Range	DA
Snore	Normal	Special	40	100	15	Normal	—
Mud-Slap	Ground	Special	20	100	10	Normal	—
Rollout	Rock	Physical	30	90	20	Normal	O
AncientPower	Rock	Special	60	100	5	Normal	—
Earth Power	Ground	Special	90	100	10	Normal	—
Iron Defense	Steel	Status	—	—	15	Self	—
Heat Wave	Fire	Special	100	90	10	2 Foes	—
Pain Split	Normal	Status	—	—	20	Normal	—

● TM & HM MOVES

No.	Name	Type	Kind	Pow.	Acc.	PP	Range	DA
TM06	Toxic	Poison	Status	—	85	10	Normal	—
TM10	Hidden Power	Normal	Special	—	100	15	Normal	—
TM11	Sunny Day	Fire	Status	—	—	5	All	—
TM16	Light Screen	Psychic	Status	—	—	30	2 Allies	—
TM17	Protect	Normal	Status	—	—	10	Self	—
TM21	Frustration	Normal	Physical	—	100	20	Normal	O
TM27	Return	Normal	Physical	—	100	20	Normal	O
TM32	Double Team	Normal	Status	—	—	15	Self	—
TM33	Reflect	Psychic	Status	—	—	20	2 Allies	—
TM35	Flamethrower	Fire	Special	95	100	15	Normal	—
TM38	Fire Blast	Fire	Special	120	85	5	Normal	—
TM39	Rock Tomb	Rock	Physical	50	80	10	Normal	—
TM42	Facade	Normal	Physical	70	100	20	Normal	O
TM43	Secret Power	Normal	Physical	70	100	20	Normal	—
TM44	Rest	Psychic	Status	—	—	10	Self	—
TM45	Attract	Normal	Status	—	100	15	Normal	—
TM50	Overheat	Fire	Special	140	90	5	Normal	—
TM58	Endure	Normal	Status	—	—	10	Self	—
TM61	Will-O-Wisp	Fire	Status	—	75	15	Normal	—
TM78	Captivate	Normal	Status	—	100	20	2 Foes	—
TM80	Rock Slide	Rock	Physical	75	90	10	2 Foes	—
TM82	Sleep Talk	Normal	Status	—	—	10	Depends	—
TM83	Natural Gift	Normal	Physical	—	100	15	Normal	—
TM87	Swagger	Normal	Status	—	90	15	Normal	—
TM90	Substitute	Normal	Status	—	—	10	Self	—
HM06	Rock Smash	Fighting	Physical	40	100	15	Normal	O

● EGG MOVES

Name	Type	Kind	Pow.	Acc.	PP	Range	UA
Acid Armor	Poison	Status	—	—	40	Self	—
Heat Wave	Fire	Special	100	90	10	2 Foes	—
Curse	???	Status	—	—	10	Normal/Self	—
SmokeScreen	Normal	Status	—	100	20	Normal	—
Memento	Dark	Status	—	100	10	Normal	—
Stockpile	Normal	Status	—	—	20	Self	—
Spit Up	Normal	Special	—	100	10	Normal	—
Swallow	Normal	Status	—	—	10	Self	—

● No. 218 | Lava Pokémon
Slugma

Fire

- **HEIGHT:** 2'04"
- **WEIGHT:** 77.2 lbs.
- **ITEMS:** None

● SIZE COMPARISON

● MALE/FEMALE HAVE SAME FORM

⊙ ABILITIES
- Magma Armor
- Flame Body

⊙ EGG GROUPS
Amorphous

⊙ STATS
- HP ●●
- ATTACK ●●
- DEFENSE ●●
- SP. ATTACK ●●
- SP. DEFENSE ●●●
- SPEED ●

⊙ PERFORMANCE

SPEED ★★☆	STAMINA ★★★★
POWER ★★☆	JUMP ★★
SKILL ★★☆	

● MAIN WAYS TO OBTAIN

Pokémon HeartGold Route 17

Pokémon SoulSilver Route 17

Pokémon Diamond Stark Mountain interior 1

Pokémon Pearl Stark Mountain interior 1

Pokémon Platinum Stark Mountain interior 1

Pokémon HeartGold
It never sleeps. It has to keep moving because if it stopped, its magma body would cool and harden.

Pokémon SoulSilver
A common sight in volcanic areas, it slowly slithers around in a constant search for warm places.

⊙ EVOLUTION

 Slugma
Lv. 38 ▶
  Magcargo

No. 219 | Lava Pokémon
Magcargo

Fire | Rock

- **HEIGHT:** 2'07"
- **WEIGHT:** 121.3 lbs.
- **ITEMS:** None

● SIZE COMPARISON

● MALE/FEMALE HAVE SAME FORM

● ABILITIES
- Magma Armor
- Flame Body

● STATS

HP	●●
ATTACK	●●
DEFENSE	●●●●●
SP. ATTACK	●●●●
SP. DEFENSE	●●●
SPEED	●

● EGG GROUPS

Amorphous

● PERFORMANCE

SPEED ★		STAMINA ★★★★☆
POWER ★★★★		JUMP ★★
SKILL ★★		

● MAIN WAYS TO OBTAIN

Pokémon HeartGold | Level up Slugma to Lv. 38

Pokémon SoulSilver | Level up Slugma to Lv. 38

Pokémon Diamond | Stark Mountain interior 1

Pokémon Pearl | Stark Mountain interior 1

Pokémon Platinum | Stark Mountain interior 1

Pokémon HeartGold
The shell on its back is just thick skin that has cooled and hardened. It breaks easily with a slight touch.

Pokémon SoulSilver
Its brittle shell occasionally spouts intense flames that circulate throughout its body.

● EVOLUTION

Lv. 38

Slugma | Magcargo

● LEVEL-UP MOVES

Lv.	Name	Type	Kind	Pow.	Acc.	PP	Range	DA
1	Yawn	Normal	Status	—	—	10	Normal	—
1	Smog	Poison	Special	20	70	20	Normal	—
1	Ember	Fire	Special	40	100	25	Normal	—
1	Rock Throw	Rock	Physical	50	90	15	Normal	—
8	Ember	Fire	Special	40	100	25	Normal	—
11	Rock Throw	Rock	Physical	50	90	15	Normal	—
16	Harden	Normal	Status	—	—	30	Self	—
23	Recover	Normal	Status	—	—	10	Self	—
26	AncientPower	Rock	Special	60	100	5	Normal	—
31	Amnesia	Psychic	Status	—	—	20	Self	—
40	Lava Plume	Fire	Special	80	100	15	2 Foes/1 Ally	—
45	Rock Slide	Rock	Physical	75	90	10	2 Foes	—
52	Body Slam	Normal	Physical	85	100	15	Normal	○
61	Flamethrower	Fire	Special	95	100	15	Normal	—
66	Earth Power	Ground	Special	90	100	10	Normal	—

● MOVE MANIAC

Name	Type	Kind	Pow.	Acc.	PP	Range	DA

● BP MOVES

Name	Type	Kind	Pow.	Acc.	PP	Range	DA
Snore	Normal	Special	40	100	15	Normal	—
Mud-Slap	Ground	Special	20	100	10	Normal	—
Rollout	Rock	Physical	30	90	20	Normal	○
AncientPower	Rock	Special	60	100	5	Normal	—
Earth Power	Ground	Special	90	100	10	Normal	—
Iron Defense	Steel	Status	—	—	15	Self	—
Heat Wave	Fire	Special	100	90	10	2 Foes	—
Pain Split	Normal	Status	—	—	20	Normal	—

● TM & HM MOVES

No.	Name	Type	Kind	Pow.	Acc.	PP	Range	DA
TM06	Toxic	Poison	Status	—	85	10	Normal	—
TM10	Hidden Power	Normal	Special	—	100	15	Normal	—
TM11	Sunny Day	Fire	Status	—	—	5	All	—
TM15	Hyper Beam	Normal	Special	150	90	5	Normal	—
TM16	Light Screen	Psychic	Status	—	—	30	2 Allies	—
TM17	Protect	Normal	Status	—	—	10	Self	—
TM21	Frustration	Normal	Physical	—	100	20	Normal	○
TM22	SolarBeam	Grass	Special	120	100	10	Normal	—
TM26	Earthquake	Ground	Physical	100	100	10	2 Foes/1 Ally	—
TM27	Return	Normal	Physical	—	100	20	Normal	○
TM32	Double Team	Normal	Status	—	—	15	Self	—
TM33	Reflect	Psychic	Status	—	—	20	2 Allies	—
TM35	Flamethrower	Fire	Special	95	100	15	Normal	—
TM37	Sandstorm	Rock	Status	—	—	10	All	—
TM38	Fire Blast	Fire	Special	120	85	5	Normal	—
TM39	Rock Tomb	Rock	Physical	50	80	10	Normal	○
TM42	Facade	Normal	Physical	70	100	20	Normal	—
TM43	Secret Power	Normal	Physical	70	100	20	Normal	—
TM44	Rest	Psychic	Status	—	—	10	Self	—
TM45	Attract	Normal	Status	—	100	15	Normal	—
TM50	Overheat	Fire	Special	140	90	5	Normal	—
TM58	Endure	Normal	Status	—	—	10	Self	—
TM61	Will-O-Wisp	Fire	Status	—	75	15	Normal	—
TM64	Explosion	Normal	Physical	250	100	5	2 Foes/1 Ally	—
TM68	Giga Impact	Normal	Physical	150	90	5	Normal	○
TM69	Rock Polish	Rock	Status	—	—	20	Self	—
TM71	Stone Edge	Rock	Physical	100	80	5	Normal	—
TM74	Gyro Ball	Steel	Physical	—	100	5	Normal	○
TM76	Stealth Rock	Rock	Status	—	—	20	2 Foes	—
TM78	Captivate	Normal	Status	—	100	20	2 Foes	—
TM80	Rock Slide	Rock	Physical	75	90	10	2 Foes	—
TM82	Sleep Talk	Normal	Status	—	—	10	Depends	—
TM83	Natural Gift	Normal	Physical	—	100	15	Normal	—
TM87	Swagger	Normal	Status	—	90	15	Normal	—
TM90	Substitute	Normal	Status	—	—	10	Self	—
HM04	Strength	Normal	Physical	80	100	15	Normal	○
HM06	Rock Smash	Fighting	Physical	40	100	15	Normal	○

● LEVEL-UP MOVES

Lv.	Name	Type	Kind	Pow.	Acc.	PP	Range	DA
1	Tackle	Normal	Physical	35	95	35	Normal	○
1	Odor Sleuth	Normal	Status	—	—	40	Normal	—
4	Mud Sport	Ground	Status	—	—	15	All	—
8	Powder Snow	Ice	Special	40	100	25	2 Foes	—
13	Mud-Slap	Ground	Special	20	100	10	Normal	—
16	Endure	Normal	Status	—	—	10	Self	—
20	Mud Bomb	Ground	Special	65	85	10	Normal	—
25	Icy Wind	Ice	Special	55	95	15	2 Foes	—
28	Ice Shard	Ice	Physical	40	100	30	Normal	—
32	Take Down	Normal	Physical	90	85	20	Normal	○
37	Earthquake	Ground	Physical	100	100	10	2 Foes/1 Ally	—
40	Mist	Ice	Status	—	—	30	2 Allies	—
44	Blizzard	Ice	Special	120	70	5	2 Foes	—
49	Amnesia	Psychic	Status	—	—	20	Self	—

● MOVE MANIAC

Name	Type	Kind	Pow.	Acc.	PP	Range	DA
Headbutt	Normal	Physical	70	100	15	Normal	○

● BP MOVES

Name	Type	Kind	Pow.	Acc.	PP	Range	DA
Icy Wind	Ice	Special	55	95	15	2 Foes	—
Snore	Normal	Special	40	100	15	Normal	—
Mud-Slap	Ground	Special	20	100	10	Normal	—
Superpower	Fighting	Physical	120	100	5	Normal	○
Endeavor	Normal	Physical	—	100	5	Normal	○
AncientPower	Rock	Special	60	100	5	Normal	—
Earth Power	Ground	Special	90	100	10	Normal	—

● TM & HM MOVES

No.	Name	Type	Kind	Pow.	Acc.	PP	Range	DA
TM05	Roar	Normal	Status	—	100	20	Normal	—
TM06	Toxic	Poison	Status	—	85	10	Normal	—
TM07	Hail	Ice	Status	—	—	10	All	—
TM10	Hidden Power	Normal	Special	—	100	15	Normal	—
TM13	Ice Beam	Ice	Special	95	100	10	Normal	—
TM14	Blizzard	Ice	Special	120	70	5	2 Foes	—
TM16	Light Screen	Psychic	Status	—	—	30	2 Allies	—
TM17	Protect	Normal	Status	—	—	10	Self	—
TM18	Rain Dance	Water	Status	—	—	5	All	—
TM21	Frustration	Normal	Physical	—	100	20	Normal	○
TM26	Earthquake	Ground	Physical	100	100	10	2 Foes/1 Ally	○
TM27	Return	Normal	Physical	—	100	20	Normal	○
TM28	Dig	Ground	Physical	80	100	10	Normal	○
TM32	Double Team	Normal	Status	—	—	15	Self	—
TM33	Reflect	Psychic	Status	—	—	20	2 Allies	—
TM37	Sandstorm	Rock	Status	—	—	10	All	—
TM39	Rock Tomb	Rock	Physical	50	80	10	Normal	○
TM42	Facade	Normal	Physical	70	100	20	Normal	○
TM43	Secret Power	Normal	Physical	70	100	20	Normal	○
TM44	Rest	Psychic	Status	—	—	10	Self	—
TM45	Attract	Normal	Status	—	100	15	Normal	—
TM58	Endure	Normal	Status	—	—	10	Self	—
TM76	Stealth Rock	Rock	Status	—	—	20	2 Foes	—
TM78	Captivate	Normal	Status	—	100	20	2 Foes	—
TM80	Rock Slide	Rock	Physical	75	90	10	2 Foes	—
TM82	Sleep Talk	Normal	Status	—	—	10	Depends	—
TM83	Natural Gift	Normal	Physical	—	100	15	Normal	—
TM87	Swagger	Normal	Status	—	90	15	Normal	—
TM90	Substitute	Normal	Status	—	—	10	Self	—
HM04	Strength	Normal	Physical	80	100	15	Normal	○
HM06	Rock Smash	Fighting	Physical	40	100	15	Normal	○

● EGG MOVES

Name	Type	Kind	Pow.	Acc.	PP	Range	DA
Take Down	Normal	Physical	90	85	20	Normal	○
Bite	Dark	Physical	60	100	25	Normal	○
Body Slam	Normal	Physical	85	100	15	Normal	○
Rock Slide	Rock	Physical	75	90	10	2 Foes	—
AncientPower	Rock	Special	60	100	5	Normal	—
Mud Shot	Ground	Special	55	95	15	Normal	—
Icicle Spear	Ice	Physical	10	100	30	Normal	—
Double-Edge	Normal	Physical	120	100	15	Normal	○
Fissure	Ground	Physical	—	30	5	Normal	—
Curse	???	Status	—	—	10	Normal/Self	—

○ No. 220 | Pig Pokémon
Swinub

Ice Ground

● HEIGHT: 1'04"
● WEIGHT: 14.3 lbs.
● ITEMS: None

● SIZE COMPARISON

● MALE/FEMALE HAVE SAME FORM

⊙ ABILITIES
● Oblivious
● Snow Cloak

⊙ STATS
HP ●●
ATTACK ●●
DEFENSE ●●
SP. ATTACK ●
SP. DEFENSE ●●
SPEED ●●

⊙ EGG GROUPS
Field

⊙ PERFORMANCE
SPEED ★★★
POWER ★★☆
SKILL ★★
STAMINA ★★★☆
JUMP ★★☆

● MAIN WAYS TO OBTAIN

Pokémon HeartGold	Ice Path
Pokémon SoulSilver	Ice Path
Pokémon Diamond	Route 217 (mass outbreak)
Pokémon Pearl	Route 217 (mass outbreak)
Pokémon Platinum	Route 217

Pokémon HeartGold
It rubs its snout on the ground to find and dig up food. It sometimes discovers hot springs.

Pokémon SoulSilver
If it smells something enticing, it dashes off headlong to find the source of the aroma.

⊙ EVOLUTION

Swinub — Lv. 33 → Piloswine — Teach it AncientPower and level it up* → Mamoswine

*To teach Piloswine AncientPower, give a Heart Scale to the Move Maniac in Blackthorn City or exchange 40 BP at the house in the Battle Frontier.

No. 221 | Swine Pokémon
Piloswine

Ice | Ground

- **HEIGHT:** 3'07"
- **WEIGHT:** 123.0 lbs.
- **ITEMS:** None

● SIZE COMPARISON

● MALE FORM
Longer tusks

● FEMALE FORM
Shorter tusks

ABILITIES
- Oblivious
- Snow Cloak

STATS
- HP ●●●●
- ATTACK ●●●●
- DEFENSE ●●●●
- SP. ATTACK ●●●
- SP. DEFENSE ●●●
- SPEED ●●

EGG GROUPS
Field

PERFORMANCE
SPEED ★★
POWER ★★★☆
SKILL ★☆
STAMINA ★★★★☆
JUMP ★★

● MAIN WAYS TO OBTAIN

Pokémon HeartGold	Level up Swinub to Lv. 33
Pokémon SoulSilver	Level up Swinub to Lv. 33
Pokémon Diamond	Level up Swinub to Lv. 33
Pokémon Pearl	Level up Swinub to Lv. 33
Pokémon Platinum	Route 217 (use Poké Radar)

Pokémon HeartGold
Because the long hair all over its body obscures its sight, it just keeps charging repeatedly.

Pokémon SoulSilver
If it charges at an enemy, the hairs on its back stand up straight. It is very sensitive to sound.

EVOLUTION

Swinub → Lv. 33 → Piloswine → Teach it AncientPower and level it up* → Mamoswine

*To teach Piloswine AncientPower, give a Heart Scale to the Move Maniac in Blackthorn City or exchange 40 BP at the house in the Battle Frontier.

● LEVEL-UP MOVES

Lv.	Name	Type	Kind	Pow.	Acc.	PP	Range	DA
1	AncientPower	Rock	Special	60	100	5	Normal	—
1	Peck	Flying	Physical	35	100	35	Normal	○
1	Odor Sleuth	Normal	Status	—	—	40	Normal	—
1	Mud Sport	Ground	Status	—	—	15	All	—
1	Powder Snow	Ice	Special	40	100	25	2 Foes	—
4	Mud Sport	Ground	Status	—	—	15	All	—
8	Powder Snow	Ice	Special	40	100	25	2 Foes	—
13	Mud-Slap	Ground	Special	20	100	10	Normal	—
16	Endure	Normal	Status	—	—	10	Self	—
20	Mud Bomb	Ground	Special	65	85	10	Normal	—
25	Icy Wind	Ice	Special	55	95	15	2 Foes	—
28	Ice Fang	Ice	Physical	65	95	15	Normal	○
32	Take Down	Normal	Physical	90	85	20	Normal	○
33	Fury Attack	Normal	Physical	15	85	20	Normal	○
40	Earthquake	Ground	Physical	100	100	10	2 Foes/1 Ally	—
48	Mist	Ice	Status	—	—	30	2 Allies	—
56	Blizzard	Ice	Special	120	70	5	2 Foes	—
65	Amnesia	Psychic	Status	—	—	20	Self	—

● MOVE MANIAC

Name	Type	Kind	Pow.	Acc.	PP	Range	DA
Headbutt	Normal	Physical	70	100	15	Normal	○

● BP MOVES

Name	Type	Kind	Pow.	Acc.	PP	Range	DA
Icy Wind	Ice	Special	55	95	15	2 Foes	—
Snore	Normal	Special	40	100	15	Normal	—
Mud-Slap	Ground	Special	20	100	10	Normal	—
Superpower	Fighting	Physical	120	100	5	Normal	○
Endeavor	Normal	Physical	—	100	5	Normal	—
AncientPower	Rock	Special	60	100	5	Normal	—
Earth Power	Ground	Special	90	100	10	Normal	—

● TM & HM MOVES

No.	Name	Type	Kind	Pow.	Acc.	PP	Range	DA
TM05	Roar	Normal	Status	—	100	20	Normal	—
TM06	Toxic	Poison	Status	—	85	10	Normal	—
TM07	Hail	Ice	Status	—	—	10	All	—
TM10	Hidden Power	Normal	Special	—	100	15	Normal	—
TM13	Ice Beam	Ice	Special	95	100	10	Normal	—
TM14	Blizzard	Ice	Special	120	70	5	2 Foes	—
TM15	Hyper Beam	Normal	Special	150	90	5	Normal	—
TM16	Light Screen	Psychic	Status	—	—	30	2 Allies	—
TM17	Protect	Normal	Status	—	—	10	Self	—
TM18	Rain Dance	Water	Status	—	—	5	All	—
TM21	Frustration	Normal	Physical	—	100	20	Normal	○
TM26	Earthquake	Ground	Physical	100	100	10	2 Foes/1 Ally	—
TM27	Return	Normal	Physical	—	100	20	Normal	○
TM28	Dig	Ground	Physical	80	100	10	Normal	○
TM32	Double Team	Normal	Status	—	—	15	Self	—
TM33	Reflect	Psychic	Status	—	—	20	2 Allies	—
TM37	Sandstorm	Rock	Status	—	—	10	All	—
TM39	Rock Tomb	Rock	Physical	50	80	10	Normal	—
TM42	Facade	Normal	Physical	70	100	20	Normal	○
TM43	Secret Power	Normal	Physical	70	100	20	Normal	○
TM44	Rest	Psychic	Status	—	—	10	Self	—
TM45	Attract	Normal	Status	—	100	15	Normal	—
TM58	Endure	Normal	Status	—	—	10	Self	—
TM68	Giga Impact	Normal	Physical	150	90	5	Normal	○
TM71	Stone Edge	Rock	Physical	100	80	5	Normal	—
TM72	Avalanche	Ice	Physical	60	100	10	Normal	○
TM76	Stealth Rock	Rock	Status	—	—	20	2 Foes	—
TM78	Captivate	Normal	Status	—	100	20	2 Foes	—
TM80	Rock Slide	Rock	Physical	75	90	10	2 Foes	—
TM82	Sleep Talk	Normal	Status	—	—	10	Depends	—
TM83	Natural Gift	Normal	Physical	—	100	15	Normal	—
TM87	Swagger	Normal	Status	—	90	15	Normal	—
TM90	Substitute	Normal	Status	—	—	10	Self	—
HM04	Strength	Normal	Physical	80	100	15	Normal	○
HM06	Rock Smash	Fighting	Physical	40	100	15	Normal	○

● LEVEL-UP MOVES

Lv.	Name	Type	Kind	Pow.	Acc.	PP	Range	DA
1	Tackle	Normal	Physical	35	95	35	Normal	○
4	Harden	Normal	Status	—	—	30	Self	—
8	Bubble	Water	Special	20	100	30	2 Foes	—
13	Recover	Normal	Status	—	—	10	Self	—
16	Refresh	Normal	Status	—	—	20	Self	—
20	Rock Blast	Rock	Physical	25	80	10	Normal	—
25	BubbleBeam	Water	Special	65	100	20	Normal	—
28	Lucky Chant	Normal	Status	—	—	30	2 Allies	—
32	AncientPower	Rock	Special	60	100	5	Normal	—
37	Aqua Ring	Water	Status	—	—	20	Self	—
40	Spike Cannon	Normal	Physical	20	100	15	Normal	—
44	Power Gem	Rock	Special	70	100	20	Normal	—
48	Mirror Coat	Psychic	Special	—	100	20	Self	—
53	Earth Power	Ground	Special	90	100	10	Normal	—

● MOVE MANIAC

Name	Type	Kind	Pow.	Acc.	PP	Range	DA
Headbutt	Normal	Physical	70	100	15	Normal	○

● BP MOVES

Name	Type	Kind	Pow.	Acc.	PP	Range	DA
Icy Wind	Ice	Special	55	95	15	2 Foes	—
Sucker Punch	Dark	Physical	80	100	5	Normal	○
Snore	Normal	Special	40	100	15	Normal	—
Magic Coat	Psychic	Status	—	—	15	Self	—
Mud-Slap	Ground	Special	20	100	10	Normal	—
Rollout	Rock	Physical	30	90	20	Normal	○
Endeavor	Normal	Physical	—	100	5	Normal	○
AncientPower	Rock	Special	60	100	5	Normal	—
Earth Power	Ground	Special	90	100	10	Normal	—

● TM & HM MOVES

No.	Name	Type	Kind	Pow.	Acc.	PP	Range	DA
TM03	Water Pulse	Water	Special	60	100	20	Normal	—
TM04	Calm Mind	Psychic	Status	—	—	20	Self	—
TM06	Toxic	Poison	Status	—	85	10	Normal	—
TM07	Hail	Ice	Status	—	—	10	All	—
TM10	Hidden Power	Normal	Special	—	100	15	Normal	—
TM11	Sunny Day	Fire	Status	—	—	5	All	—
TM13	Ice Beam	Ice	Special	95	100	10	Normal	—
TM14	Blizzard	Ice	Special	120	70	5	2 Foes	—
TM16	Light Screen	Psychic	Status	—	—	30	2 Allies	—
TM17	Protect	Normal	Status	—	—	10	Self	—
TM18	Rain Dance	Water	Status	—	—	5	All	—
TM20	Safeguard	Normal	Status	—	—	25	2 Allies	—
TM21	Frustration	Normal	Physical	—	100	20	Normal	○
TM26	Earthquake	Ground	Physical	100	100	10	2 Foes/1 Ally	○
TM27	Return	Normal	Physical	—	100	20	Normal	○
TM28	Dig	Ground	Physical	80	100	10	Normal	○
TM29	Psychic	Psychic	Special	90	100	10	Normal	—
TM30	Shadow Ball	Ghost	Special	80	100	15	Normal	—
TM32	Double Team	Normal	Status	—	—	15	Self	—
TM33	Reflect	Psychic	Status	—	—	20	2 Allies	—
TM37	Sandstorm	Rock	Status	—	—	10	All	—
TM39	Rock Tomb	Rock	Physical	50	80	10	Normal	—
TM42	Facade	Normal	Physical	70	100	20	Normal	○
TM43	Secret Power	Normal	Physical	70	100	20	Normal	—
TM44	Rest	Psychic	Status	—	—	10	Self	—
TM45	Attract	Normal	Status	—	100	15	Normal	—
TM55	Brine	Water	Special	65	100	10	Normal	—
TM58	Endure	Normal	Status	—	—	10	Self	—
TM64	Explosion	Normal	Physical	250	100	5	2 Foes/1 Ally	—
TM69	Rock Polish	Rock	Status	—	—	20	Self	—
TM71	Stone Edge	Rock	Physical	100	80	5	Normal	—
TM76	Stealth Rock	Rock	Status	—	—	20	2 Foes	—
TM78	Captivate	Normal	Status	—	100	20	2 Foes	—
TM80	Rock Slide	Rock	Physical	75	90	10	2 Foes	—
TM82	Sleep Talk	Normal	Status	—	—	10	Depends	—
TM83	Natural Gift	Normal	Physical	—	100	15	Normal	—
TM87	Swagger	Normal	Status	—	90	15	Normal	—
TM90	Substitute	Normal	Status	—	—	10	Self	—
HM03	Surf	Water	Special	95	100	15	2 Foes/1 Ally	—
HM04	Strength	Normal	Physical	80	100	15	Normal	○
HM05	Whirlpool	Water	Special	15	70	15	Normal	—
HM06	Rock Smash	Fighting	Physical	40	100	15	Normal	○

● EGG MOVES

Name	Type	Kind	Pow.	Acc.	PP	Range	DA
Rock Slide	Rock	Physical	75	90	10	2 Foes	—
Screech	Normal	Status	—	85	40	Normal	—
Mist	Ice	Status	—	—	30	2 Allies	—
Amnesia	Psychic	Status	—	—	20	Self	—
Barrier	Psychic	Status	—	—	30	Self	—
Ingrain	Grass	Status	—	—	20	Self	—
Confuse Ray	Ghost	Status	—	100	10	Normal	—
Icicle Spear	Ice	Physical	10	100	30	Normal	—
Nature Power	Normal	Status	—	—	20	Depends	—
Aqua Ring	Water	Status	—	—	20	Self	—
Curse	???	Status	—	—	10	Normal/Self	—

Corsola

Water   Rock

● HEIGHT: 2'00"
● WEIGHT: 11.0 lbs.
● ITEMS: Hard Stone

● SIZE COMPARISON

● MALE/FEMALE HAVE SAME FORM

● ABILITIES
● Hustle
● Natural Cure

● EGG GROUPS
Water 1
Water 3

● STATS
HP ●●
ATTACK ●●
DEFENSE ●●
SP. ATTACK ●●●
SP. DEFENSE ●●●
SPEED ●●

● PERFORMANCE

SPEED ★★★★ STAMINA ★★★
POWER ★★☆ JUMP ★★★
SKILL ★★☆

● MAIN WAYS TO OBTAIN

Pokémon HeartGold — Route 34 (Good Rod/Super Rod, morning and afternoon only)

Pokémon SoulSilver — Route 34 (Good Rod/Super Rod, morning and afternoon only)

Pokémon Diamond — Route 230 (mass outbreak)

Pokémon Pearl — Route 230 (mass outbreak)

Pokémon Platinum — Route 230 (mass outbreak)

Pokémon HeartGold — It continuously sheds and grows. The tip of its head is prized as a treasure because of its beauty.

Pokémon SoulSilver — In a south-sea nation, the people live in communities that are built on groups of these Pokémon.

● EVOLUTION

Does not evolve

No. 223 | Jet Pokémon
Remoraid

Water

- **HEIGHT:** 2'00"
- **WEIGHT:** 26.5 lbs.
- **ITEMS:** None

● SIZE COMPARISON

● MALE/FEMALE HAVE SAME FORM

⊛ ABILITIES
- Hustle
- Sniper

⊛ STATS
HP	●
ATTACK	●●●
DEFENSE	●●
SP. ATTACK	●●●
SP. DEFENSE	●●
SPEED	●●●

⊛ EGG GROUPS
Water 1

Water 2

⊛ PERFORMANCE
SPEED ★★★	STAMINA ★★☆
POWER ★★☆	JUMP ★★★
SKILL ★★★★☆	

● MAIN WAYS TO OBTAIN

Pokémon HeartGold	Route 44 (Good Rod/Super Rod)
Pokémon SoulSilver	Route 44 (Good Rod/Super Rod)
Pokémon Diamond	Route 213 (Good Rod)
Pokémon Pearl	Route 213 (Good Rod)
Pokémon Platinum	Route 213 (Good Rod)

Pokémon HeartGold	Pokémon SoulSilver
It has superb accuracy. The water it shoots out can strike moving prey from more than 300 feet away.	Using its dorsal fin as a suction pad, it clings to a MANTINE's underside to scavenge for leftovers.

⊛ EVOLUTION

Remoraid → Lv. 25 → Octillery

● LEVEL-UP MOVES
Lv.	Name	Type	Kind	Pow.	Acc.	PP	Range	DA
1	Water Gun	Water	Special	40	100	25	Normal	—
6	Lock-On	Normal	Status	—	—	5	Normal	—
10	Psybeam	Psychic	Special	65	100	20	Normal	—
14	Aurora Beam	Ice	Special	65	100	20	Normal	—
19	BubbleBeam	Water	Special	65	100	20	Normal	—
23	Focus Energy	Normal	Status	—	—	30	Self	—
27	Bullet Seed	Grass	Physical	10	100	30	Normal	—
32	Water Pulse	Water	Special	60	100	20	Normal	—
36	Signal Beam	Bug	Special	75	100	15	Normal	—
40	Ice Beam	Ice	Special	95	100	10	Normal	—
45	Hyper Beam	Normal	Special	150	90	5	Normal	—

● MOVE MANIAC
Name	Type	Kind	Pow.	Acc.	PP	Range	DA

● BP MOVES
Name	Type	Kind	Pow.	Acc.	PP	Range	DA
Dive	Water	Physical	80	100	10	Normal	○
Icy Wind	Ice	Special	55	95	15	2 Foes	—
Snore	Normal	Special	40	100	15	Normal	—
Swift	Normal	Special	60	—	20	2 Foes	—
String Shot	Bug	Status	—	95	40	2 Foes	—
Mud-Slap	Ground	Special	20	100	10	Normal	—
Signal Beam	Bug	Special	75	100	15	Normal	—
Gunk Shot	Poison	Physical	120	70	5	Normal	—
Seed Bomb	Grass	Physical	80	100	15	Normal	—
Bounce	Flying	Physical	85	85	5	Normal	○

● TM & HM MOVES
No.	Name	Type	Kind	Pow.	Acc.	PP	Range	DA
TM03	Water Pulse	Water	Special	60	100	20	Normal	—
TM06	Toxic	Poison	Status	—	85	10	Normal	—
TM09	Bullet Seed	Grass	Physical	10	100	30	Normal	—
TM10	Hidden Power	Normal	Special	—	100	15	Normal	—
TM11	Sunny Day	Fire	Status	—	—	5	All	—
TM13	Ice Beam	Ice	Special	95	100	10	Normal	—
TM14	Blizzard	Ice	Special	120	70	5	2 Foes	—
TM15	Hyper Beam	Normal	Special	150	90	5	Normal	—
TM17	Protect	Normal	Status	—	—	10	Self	—
TM18	Rain Dance	Water	Status	—	—	5	All	—
TM21	Frustration	Normal	Physical	—	100	20	Normal	○
TM27	Return	Normal	Physical	—	100	20	Normal	○
TM29	Psychic	Psychic	Special	90	100	10	Normal	—
TM32	Double Team	Normal	Status	—	—	15	Self	—
TM35	Flamethrower	Fire	Special	95	100	15	Normal	—
TM38	Fire Blast	Fire	Special	120	85	5	Normal	—
TM42	Facade	Normal	Physical	70	100	20	Normal	○
TM43	Secret Power	Normal	Physical	70	100	20	Normal	—
TM44	Rest	Psychic	Status	—	—	10	Self	—
TM45	Attract	Normal	Status	—	100	15	Normal	—
TM46	Thief	Dark	Physical	40	100	10	Normal	○
TM55	Brine	Water	Special	65	100	10	Normal	—
TM57	Charge Beam	Electric	Special	50	90	10	Normal	—
TM58	Endure	Normal	Status	—	—	10	Self	—
TM73	Thunder Wave	Electric	Status	—	100	20	Normal	—
TM78	Captivate	Normal	Status	—	100	20	2 Foes	—
TM82	Sleep Talk	Normal	Status	—	—	10	Depends	—
TM83	Natural Gift	Normal	Physical	—	100	15	Normal	—
TM87	Swagger	Normal	Status	—	90	15	Normal	—
TM90	Substitute	Normal	Status	—	—	10	Self	—
HM03	Surf	Water	Special	95	100	15	2 Foes/1 Ally	—
HM05	Whirlpool	Water	Special	15	70	15	Normal	—
HM07	Waterfall	Water	Physical	80	100	15	Normal	○

● EGG MOVES
Name	Type	Kind	Pow.	Acc.	PP	Range	DA
Aurora Beam	Ice	Special	65	100	20	Normal	—
Octazooka	Water	Special	65	85	10	Normal	—
Supersonic	Normal	Status	—	55	20	Normal	—
Haze	Ice	Status	—	—	30	All	—
Screech	Normal	Status	—	85	40	Normal	—
Thunder Wave	Electric	Status	—	100	20	Normal	—
Rock Blast	Rock	Physical	25	80	10	Normal	—
Snore	Normal	Special	40	100	15	Normal	—
Flail	Normal	Physical	—	100	15	Normal	○
Water Spout	Water	Special	150	100	5	2 Foes	—

● LEVEL-UP MOVES

Lv.	Name	Type	Kind	Pow.	Acc.	PP	Range	DA
1	Gunk Shot	Poison	Physical	120	70	5	Normal	—
1	Rock Blast	Rock	Physical	25	80	10	Normal	—
1	Water Gun	Water	Special	40	100	25	Normal	—
1	Constrict	Normal	Physical	10	100	35	Normal	○
1	Psybeam	Psychic	Special	65	100	20	Normal	—
1	Aurora Beam	Ice	Special	65	100	20	Normal	—
6	Constrict	Normal	Physical	10	100	35	Normal	○
10	Psybeam	Psychic	Special	65	100	20	Normal	—
14	Aurora Beam	Ice	Special	65	100	20	Normal	—
19	BubbleBeam	Water	Special	65	100	20	Normal	—
23	Focus Energy	Normal	Status	—	—	30	Self	—
25	Octazooka	Water	Special	65	85	10	Normal	—
29	Bullet Seed	Grass	Physical	10	100	30	Normal	—
36	Wring Out	Normal	Special	—	100	5	Normal	○
42	Signal Beam	Bug	Special	75	100	15	Normal	—
48	Ice Beam	Ice	Special	95	100	10	Normal	—
55	Hyper Beam	Normal	Special	150	90	5	Normal	—

● MOVE MANIAC

Name	Type	Kind	Pow.	Acc.	PP	Range	DA

● BP MOVES

Name	Type	Kind	Pow.	Acc.	PP	Range	DA
Dive	Water	Physical	80	100	10	Normal	○
Icy Wind	Ice	Special	55	95	15	2 Foes	—
Snore	Normal	Special	40	100	15	Normal	—
Swift	Normal	Special	60	—	20	2 Foes	—
String Shot	Bug	Status	—	95	40	2 Foes	—
Mud-Slap	Ground	Special	20	100	10	Normal	—
Signal Beam	Bug	Special	75	100	15	Normal	—
Gunk Shot	Poison	Physical	120	70	5	Normal	—
Seed Bomb	Grass	Physical	80	100	15	Normal	—
Bounce	Flying	Physical	85	85	5	Normal	○

● TM & HM MOVES

No.	Name	Type	Kind	Pow.	Acc.	PP	Range	DA
TM03	Water Pulse	Water	Special	60	100	20	Normal	—
TM06	Toxic	Poison	Status	—	85	10	Normal	—
TM09	Bullet Seed	Grass	Physical	10	100	30	Normal	—
TM10	Hidden Power	Normal	Special	—	100	15	Normal	—
TM11	Sunny Day	Fire	Status	—	—	5	All	—
TM13	Ice Beam	Ice	Special	95	100	10	Normal	—
TM14	Blizzard	Ice	Special	120	70	5	2 Foes	—
TM15	Hyper Beam	Normal	Special	150	90	5	Normal	—
TM17	Protect	Normal	Status	—	—	10	Self	—
TM18	Rain Dance	Water	Status	—	—	5	All	—
TM21	Frustration	Normal	Physical	—	100	20	Normal	○
TM27	Return	Normal	Physical	—	100	20	Normal	○
TM29	Psychic	Psychic	Special	90	100	10	Normal	—
TM32	Double Team	Normal	Status	—	—	15	Self	—
TM35	Flamethrower	Fire	Special	95	100	15	Normal	—
TM36	Sludge Bomb	Poison	Special	90	100	10	Normal	—
TM38	Fire Blast	Fire	Special	120	85	5	Normal	—
TM42	Facade	Normal	Physical	70	100	20	Normal	—
TM43	Secret Power	Normal	Physical	70	100	20	Normal	○
TM44	Rest	Psychic	Status	—	—	10	Self	—
TM45	Attract	Normal	Status	—	100	15	Normal	—
TM46	Thief	Dark	Physical	40	100	10	Normal	○
TM53	Energy Ball	Grass	Special	80	100	10	Normal	—
TM55	Brine	Water	Special	65	100	10	Normal	—
TM57	Charge Beam	Electric	Special	50	90	10	Normal	—
TM58	Endure	Normal	Status	—	—	10	Self	—
TM66	Payback	Dark	Physical	50	100	10	Normal	○
TM68	Giga Impact	Normal	Physical	150	90	5	Normal	○
TM73	Thunder Wave	Electric	Status	—	100	20	Normal	—
TM78	Captivate	Normal	Status	—	100	20	2 Foes	—
TM82	Sleep Talk	Normal	Status	—	—	10	Depends	—
TM83	Natural Gift	Normal	Physical	—	100	15	Normal	—
TM87	Swagger	Normal	Status	—	90	15	Normal	—
TM90	Substitute	Normal	Status	—	—	10	Self	—
TM91	Flash Cannon	Steel	Special	80	100	10	Normal	—
HM03	Surf	Water	Special	95	100	15	2 Foes/1 Ally	—
HM05	Whirlpool	Water	Special	15	70	15	Normal	—
HM07	Waterfall	Water	Physical	80	100	15	Normal	○

◎ No. 224 | Jet Pokémon
Octillery

Water

● SIZE COMPARISON

● HEIGHT: 2'11"
● WEIGHT: 62.8 lbs.
● ITEMS: None

● MALE FORM
Bigger suction cups

● FEMALE FORM
Smaller suction cups

◎ ABILITIES
● Suction Cups
● Sniper

◎ STATS
HP ●●●
ATTACK ●●●●
DEFENSE ●●●
SP. ATTACK ●●●●
SP. DEFENSE ●●●
SPEED ●●

◎ EGG GROUPS
Water 1
Water 2

◎ PERFORMANCE
SPEED ★★
POWER ★★★★
SKILL ★★★☆
STAMINA ★★★★☆
JUMP ★★

● MAIN WAYS TO OBTAIN

Pokémon HeartGold — Level up Remoraid to Lv. 25

Pokémon SoulSilver — Level up Remoraid to Lv. 25

Pokémon Diamond — Route 213 (Super Rod)

Pokémon Pearl — Route 213 (Super Rod)

Pokémon Platinum — Route 213 (Super Rod)

Pokémon HeartGold
It traps foes with the suction cups on its tentacles, then smashes them with its rock-hard head.

Pokémon SoulSilver
It instinctively sneaks into rocky holes. If it gets sleepy, it steals the nest of a fellow OCTILLERY.

◎ EVOLUTION

Lv. 25

Remoraid → Octillery

No. 225 | Delivery Pokémon
Delibird

Ice | Flying

- **HEIGHT:** 2'11"
- **WEIGHT:** 35.3 lbs.
- **ITEMS:** None

● SIZE COMPARISON

● MALE/FEMALE HAVE SAME FORM

ABILITIES
- Vital Spirit
- Hustle

STATS
- HP ●●
- ATTACK ●●
- DEFENSE ●●
- SP. ATTACK ●●●
- SP. DEFENSE ●●●
- SPEED ●●●

EGG GROUPS
Water 1
Field

PERFORMANCE
SPEED ★★★ STAMINA ★★★★☆
POWER ★★★ JUMP ★★★
SKILL ★★★☆

MAIN WAYS TO OBTAIN

Pokémon HeartGold	—
Pokémon SoulSilver	Ice Path
Pokémon Diamond	Route 216 (mass outbreak)
Pokémon Pearl	Route 216 (mass outbreak)
Pokémon Platinum	Route 217 (mass outbreak)

Pokémon HeartGold
It carries food all day long. There are tales about lost people who were saved by its stored food.

Pokémon SoulSilver
It nests at the edge of sharp cliffs. It spends all day carrying food to its awaiting chicks.

EVOLUTION
Does not evolve

● LEVEL-UP MOVES

Lv.	Name	Type	Kind	Pow.	Acc.	PP	Range	DA
1	Present	Normal	Physical	—	90	15	Normal	—

● MOVE MANIAC

Name	Type	Kind	Pow.	Acc.	PP	Range	DA
Headbutt	Normal	Physical	70	100	15	Normal	○

● BP MOVES

Name	Type	Kind	Pow.	Acc.	PP	Range	DA
Icy Wind	Ice	Special	55	95	15	2 Foes	—
Swift	Normal	Special	60	—	20	2 Foes	—
Mud-Slap	Ground	Special	20	100	10	Normal	—
Rollout	Rock	Physical	30	90	20	Normal	○
Signal Beam	Bug	Special	75	100	15	Normal	—
Gunk Shot	Poison	Physical	120	70	5	Normal	—
Seed Bomb	Grass	Physical	80	100	15	Normal	—
Bounce	Flying	Physical	85	85	5	Normal	○
Sky Attack	Flying	Physical	140	90	5	Normal	—

● TM & HM MOVES

No.	Name	Type	Kind	Pow.	Acc.	PP	Range	DA
TM01	Focus Punch	Fighting	Physical	150	100	20	Normal	○
TM03	Water Pulse	Water	Special	60	100	20	Normal	—
TM06	Toxic	Poison	Status	—	85	10	Normal	—
TM07	Hail	Ice	Status	—	—	10	All	—
TM10	Hidden Power	Normal	Special	—	100	15	Normal	—
TM13	Ice Beam	Ice	Special	95	100	10	Normal	—
TM14	Blizzard	Ice	Special	120	70	5	2 Foes	—
TM17	Protect	Normal	Status	—	—	10	Self	—
TM18	Rain Dance	Water	Status	—	—	5	All	—
TM21	Frustration	Normal	Physical	—	100	20	Normal	○
TM27	Return	Normal	Physical	—	100	20	Normal	○
TM31	Brick Break	Fighting	Physical	75	100	15	Normal	○
TM32	Double Team	Normal	Status	—	—	15	Self	—
TM40	Aerial Ace	Flying	Physical	60	—	20	Normal	○
TM42	Facade	Normal	Physical	70	100	20	Normal	○
TM43	Secret Power	Normal	Physical	70	100	20	Normal	—
TM44	Rest	Psychic	Status	—	—	10	Self	—
TM45	Attract	Normal	Status	—	100	15	Normal	—
TM46	Thief	Dark	Physical	40	100	10	Normal	○
TM56	Fling	Dark	Physical	—	100	10	Normal	○
TM58	Endure	Normal	Status	—	—	10	Self	—
TM67	Recycle	Normal	Status	—	—	10	Self	—
TM72	Avalanche	Ice	Physical	60	100	10	Normal	○
TM78	Captivate	Normal	Status	—	100	20	2 Foes	—
TM82	Sleep Talk	Normal	Status	—	—	10	Depends	—
TM83	Natural Gift	Normal	Physical	—	100	15	Normal	—
TM87	Swagger	Normal	Status	—	90	15	Normal	—
TM88	Pluck	Flying	Physical	60	100	20	Normal	○
TM90	Substitute	Normal	Status	—	—	10	Self	—
HM02	Fly	Flying	Physical	90	95	15	Normal	○

● EGG MOVES

Name	Type	Kind	Pow.	Acc.	PP	Range	DA
Aurora Beam	Ice	Special	65	100	20	Normal	—
Quick Attack	Normal	Physical	40	100	30	Normal	○
Future Sight	Psychic	Special	80	90	15	Normal	—
Splash	Normal	Status	—	—	40	Self	—
Rapid Spin	Normal	Physical	20	100	40	Normal	○
Ice Ball	Ice	Physical	30	90	20	Normal	○
Ice Shard	Ice	Physical	40	100	30	Normal	—
Ice Punch	Ice	Physical	75	100	15	Normal	○
Fake Out	Normal	Physical	40	100	10	Normal	○

LEVEL-UP MOVES

Lv.	Name	Type	Kind	Pow.	Acc.	PP	Range	DA
1	Psybeam	Psychic	Special	65	100	20	Normal	—
1	Bullet Seed	Grass	Physical	10	100	30	Normal	—
1	Signal Beam	Bug	Special	75	100	15	Normal	—
1	Tackle	Normal	Physical	35	95	35	Normal	○
1	Bubble	Water	Special	20	100	30	2 Foes	—
1	Supersonic	Normal	Status	—	55	20	Normal	—
1	BubbleBeam	Water	Special	65	100	20	Normal	—
4	Supersonic	Normal	Status	—	55	20	Normal	—
10	BubbleBeam	Water	Special	65	100	20	Normal	—
13	Headbutt	Normal	Physical	70	100	15	Normal	○
19	Agility	Psychic	Status	—	—	30	Self	—
22	Wing Attack	Flying	Physical	60	100	35	Normal	○
28	Water Pulse	Water	Special	60	100	20	Normal	—
31	Take Down	Normal	Physical	90	85	20	Normal	○
37	Confuse Ray	Ghost	Status	—	100	10	Normal	—
40	Bounce	Flying	Physical	85	85	5	Normal	○
46	Aqua Ring	Water	Status	—	—	20	Self	—
49	Hydro Pump	Water	Special	120	80	5	Normal	—

MOVE MANIAC

Name	Type	Kind	Pow.	Acc.	PP	Range	DA
Headbutt	Normal	Physical	70	100	15	Normal	○

BP MOVES

Name	Type	Kind	Pow.	Acc.	PP	Range	DA
Dive	Water	Physical	80	100	10	Normal	○
Icy Wind	Ice	Special	55	95	15	2 Foes	—
Air Cutter	Flying	Special	55	95	25	2 Foes	—
Snore	Normal	Special	40	100	15	Normal	—
Helping Hand	Normal	Status	—	—	20	1 Ally	—
Swift	Normal	Special	60	—	20	2 Foes	—
String Shot	Bug	Status	—	95	40	2 Foes	—
Tailwind	Flying	Status	—	—	30	2 Allies	—
Mud-Slap	Ground	Special	20	100	10	Normal	—
Iron Head	Steel	Physical	80	100	15	Normal	○
Aqua Tail	Water	Physical	90	90	10	Normal	○
Signal Beam	Bug	Special	75	100	15	Normal	—
Gunk Shot	Poison	Physical	120	70	5	Normal	—
Seed Bomb	Grass	Physical	80	100	15	Normal	—
Bounce	Flying	Physical	85	85	5	Normal	—

TM & HM MOVES

No.	Name	Type	Kind	Pow.	Acc.	PP	Range	DA
TM03	Water Pulse	Water	Special	60	100	20	Normal	—
TM06	Toxic	Poison	Status	—	85	10	Normal	—
TM07	Hail	Ice	Status	—	—	10	All	—
TM09	Bullet Seed	Grass	Physical	10	100	30	Normal	—
TM10	Hidden Power	Normal	Special	—	100	15	Normal	—
TM13	Ice Beam	Ice	Special	95	100	10	Normal	—
TM14	Blizzard	Ice	Special	120	70	5	2 Foes	—
TM15	Hyper Beam	Normal	Special	150	90	5	Normal	—
TM17	Protect	Normal	Status	—	—	10	Self	—
TM18	Rain Dance	Water	Status	—	—	5	All	—
TM21	Frustration	Normal	Physical	—	100	20	Normal	○
TM26	Earthquake	Ground	Physical	100	100	10	2 Foes/1 Ally	—
TM27	Return	Normal	Physical	—	100	20	Normal	○
TM32	Double Team	Normal	Status	—	—	15	Self	—
TM39	Rock Tomb	Rock	Physical	50	80	10	Normal	—
TM40	Aerial Ace	Flying	Physical	60	—	20	Normal	○
TM42	Facade	Normal	Physical	70	100	20	Normal	○
TM43	Secret Power	Normal	Physical	70	100	20	Normal	—
TM44	Rest	Psychic	Status	—	—	10	Self	—
TM45	Attract	Normal	Status	—	100	15	Normal	—
TM55	Brine	Water	Special	65	100	10	Normal	—
TM58	Endure	Normal	Status	—	—	10	Self	—
TM68	Giga Impact	Normal	Physical	150	90	5	Normal	○
TM78	Captivate	Normal	Status	—	100	20	2 Foes	—
TM80	Rock Slide	Rock	Physical	75	90	10	2 Foes	—
TM82	Sleep Talk	Normal	Status	—	—	10	Depends	—
TM83	Natural Gift	Normal	Physical	—	100	15	Normal	—
TM87	Swagger	Normal	Status	—	90	15	Normal	—
TM90	Substitute	Normal	Status	—	—	10	Self	—
HM03	Surf	Water	Special	95	100	15	2 Foes/1 Ally	—
HM05	Whirlpool	Water	Special	15	70	15	Normal	—
HM07	Waterfall	Water	Physical	80	100	15	Normal	○

EGG MOVES

Name	Type	Kind	Pow.	Acc.	PP	Range	DA
Twister	Dragon	Special	40	100	20	2 Foes	—
Hydro Pump	Water	Special	120	80	5	Normal	—
Haze	Ice	Status	—	—	30	All	—
Slam	Normal	Physical	80	75	20	Normal	○
Mud Sport	Ground	Status	—	—	15	All	—
Rock Slide	Rock	Physical	75	90	10	2 Foes	—
Mirror Coat	Psychic	Special	—	100	20	Self	—
Water Sport	Water	Status	—	—	15	All	—
Splash	Normal	Status	—	—	40	Self	—

No. 226 | Kite Pokémon
Mantine

Water | Flying

- **HEIGHT:** 6'11"
- **WEIGHT:** 485.0 lbs.
- **ITEMS:** None

● SIZE COMPARISON

● MALE/FEMALE HAVE SAME FORM

⊙ ABILITIES
- Swift Swim
- Water Absorb

⊙ EGG GROUPS
Water 1

⊙ STATS
- HP ●●
- ATTACK ●●●
- DEFENSE ●●●
- SP. ATTACK ●●●●
- SP. DEFENSE ●●●●●●
- SPEED ●●●

⊙ PERFORMANCE
SPEED ★★★☆	STAMINA ★★★★☆
POWER ★★★☆	JUMP ★★☆
SKILL ★★★	

● MAIN WAYS TO OBTAIN

Pokémon HeartGold — Route 41 (water surface)

Pokémon SoulSilver — —

Pokémon Diamond — Put Remoraid in your party and level up Mantyke

Pokémon Pearl — Put Remoraid in your party and level up Mantyke

Pokémon Platinum — Put Remoraid in your party and level up Mantyke

Pokémon HeartGold — As it majestically swims, it doesn't care if REMORAID attach to it for scavenging its leftovers.

Pokémon SoulSilver — Swimming freely in open seas, it may fly out of the water and over the waves if it builds up enough speed.

⊙ EVOLUTION

Mantyke → Level it up while Remoraid is in your party → Mantine

● No. 227 | Armor Bird Pokémon
Skarmory

Steel **Flying**

● **HEIGHT:** 5'07"
● **WEIGHT:** 111.3 lbs.
● **ITEMS:** None

● SIZE COMPARISON

● MALE/FEMALE HAVE SAME FORM

⊙ ABILITIES
● Keen Eye
● Sturdy

⊙ STATS
HP ●●
ATTACK ●●●
DEFENSE ●●●●●
SP. ATTACK ●●
SP. DEFENSE ●●●
SPEED ●●●

⊙ EGG GROUPS
Flying

⊙ PERFORMANCE
SPEED ★★★★☆   STAMINA ★★☆☆
POWER ★★★   JUMP ★★★★★
SKILL ★☆

● MAIN WAYS TO OBTAIN

Pokémon HeartGold	—
Pokémon SoulSilver	Route 45
Pokémon Diamond	Route 227
Pokémon Pearl	Route 227
Pokémon Platinum	Route 227

Pokémon HeartGold
Its sturdy wings look heavy, but they are actually hollow and light, allowing it to fly freely in the sky.

Pokémon SoulSilver
After nesting in bramble bushes, the wings of its chicks grow hard from scratches by thorns.

⊙ EVOLUTION
Does not evolve

● LEVEL-UP MOVES

Lv.	Name	Type	Kind	Pow.	Acc.	PP	Range	DA
1	Leer	Normal	Status	—	100	30	2 Foes	—
1	Peck	Flying	Physical	35	100	35	Normal	○
6	Sand-Attack	Ground	Status	—	100	15	Normal	—
9	Swift	Normal	Special	60	—	20	2 Foes	—
12	Agility	Psychic	Status	—	—	30	Self	—
17	Fury Attack	Normal	Physical	15	85	20	Normal	○
20	Feint	Normal	Physical	50	100	10	Normal	—
23	Air Cutter	Flying	Special	55	95	25	2 Foes	—
28	Spikes	Ground	Status	—	—	20	2 Foes	—
31	Metal Sound	Steel	Status	—	85	40	Normal	—
34	Steel Wing	Steel	Physical	70	90	25	Normal	○
39	Air Slash	Flying	Special	75	95	20	Normal	—
42	Slash	Normal	Physical	70	100	20	Normal	○
45	Night Slash	Dark	Physical	70	100	15	Normal	○

● MOVE MANIAC

Name	Type	Kind	Pow.	Acc.	PP	Range	DA

● BP MOVES

Name	Type	Kind	Pow.	Acc.	PP	Range	DA
Fury Cutter	Bug	Physical	10	95	20	Normal	○
Icy Wind	Ice	Special	55	95	15	2 Foes	—
Ominous Wind	Ghost	Special	60	100	5	Normal	—
Air Cutter	Flying	Special	55	95	25	2 Foes	—
Snore	Normal	Special	40	100	15	Normal	—
Swift	Normal	Special	60	—	20	2 Foes	—
Tailwind	Flying	Status	—	—	30	2 Allies	—
Mud-Slap	Ground	Special	20	100	10	Normal	—
Twister	Dragon	Special	40	100	20	2 Foes	—
Iron Defense	Steel	Status	—	—	15	Self	—
Sky Attack	Flying	Physical	140	90	5	Normal	—

● TM & HM MOVES

No.	Name	Type	Kind	Pow.	Acc.	PP	Range	DA
TM05	Roar	Normal	Status	—	100	20	Normal	—
TM06	Toxic	Poison	Status	—	85	10	Normal	—
TM10	Hidden Power	Normal	Special	—	100	15	Normal	—
TM11	Sunny Day	Fire	Status	—	—	5	All	—
TM12	Taunt	Dark	Status	—	100	20	Normal	—
TM17	Protect	Normal	Status	—	—	10	Self	—
TM21	Frustration	Normal	Physical	—	100	20	Normal	○
TM27	Return	Normal	Physical	—	100	20	Normal	○
TM32	Double Team	Normal	Status	—	—	15	Self	—
TM37	Sandstorm	Rock	Status	—	—	10	All	—
TM39	Rock Tomb	Rock	Physical	50	80	10	Normal	—
TM40	Aerial Ace	Flying	Physical	60	—	20	Normal	○
TM41	Torment	Dark	Status	—	100	15	Normal	—
TM42	Facade	Normal	Physical	70	100	20	Normal	○
TM43	Secret Power	Normal	Physical	70	100	20	Normal	○
TM44	Rest	Psychic	Status	—	—	10	Self	—
TM45	Attract	Normal	Status	—	100	15	Normal	—
TM46	Thief	Dark	Physical	40	100	10	Normal	○
TM47	Steel Wing	Steel	Physical	70	90	25	Normal	○
TM51	Roost	Flying	Status	—	—	10	Self	—
TM58	Endure	Normal	Status	—	—	10	Self	—
TM66	Payback	Dark	Physical	50	100	10	Normal	○
TM70	Flash	Normal	Status	—	100	20	Normal	—
TM75	Swords Dance	Normal	Status	—	—	30	Self	—
TM76	Stealth Rock	Rock	Status	—	—	20	2 Foes	—
TM78	Captivate	Normal	Status	—	100	20	2 Foes	—
TM79	Dark Pulse	Dark	Special	80	100	15	Normal	—
TM80	Rock Slide	Rock	Physical	75	90	10	2 Foes	—
TM81	X-Scissor	Bug	Physical	80	100	15	Normal	○
TM82	Sleep Talk	Normal	Status	—	—	10	Depends	—
TM83	Natural Gift	Normal	Physical	—	100	15	Normal	—
TM87	Swagger	Normal	Status	—	90	15	Normal	—
TM88	Pluck	Flying	Physical	60	100	20	Normal	○
TM90	Substitute	Normal	Status	—	—	10	Self	—
TM91	Flash Cannon	Steel	Special	80	100	10	Normal	—
HM01	Cut	Normal	Physical	50	95	30	Normal	○
HM02	Fly	Flying	Physical	90	95	15	Normal	○
HM06	Rock Smash	Fighting	Physical	40	100	15	Normal	○

● EGG MOVES

Name	Type	Kind	Pow.	Acc.	PP	Range	DA
Drill Peck	Flying	Physical	80	100	20	Normal	○
Pursuit	Dark	Physical	40	100	20	Normal	○
Whirlwind	Normal	Status	—	100	20	Normal	—
Sky Attack	Flying	Physical	140	90	5	Normal	—
Curse	???	Status	—	—	10	Normal/Self	—
Brave Bird	Flying	Physical	120	100	15	Normal	○
Assurance	Dark	Physical	50	100	10	Normal	○
Guard Swap	Psychic	Status	—	—	10	Normal	—

● LEVEL-UP MOVES

Lv.	Name	Type	Kind	Pow.	Acc.	PP	Range	DA
1	Leer	Normal	Status	—	100	30	2 Foes	—
1	Ember	Fire	Special	40	100	25	Normal	—
4	Howl	Normal	Status	—	—	40	Self	—
9	Smog	Poison	Special	20	70	20	Normal	—
14	Roar	Normal	Status	—	100	20	Normal	—
17	Bite	Dark	Physical	60	100	25	Normal	O
22	Odor Sleuth	Normal	Status	—	—	40	Normal	—
27	Beat Up	Dark	Physical	10	100	10	Normal	—
30	Fire Fang	Fire	Physical	65	95	15	Normal	O
35	Faint Attack	Dark	Physical	60	—	20	Normal	O
40	Embargo	Dark	Status	—	100	15	Normal	—
43	Flamethrower	Fire	Special	95	100	15	Normal	—
48	Crunch	Dark	Physical	80	100	15	Normal	O
53	Nasty Plot	Dark	Status	—	—	20	Self	—

● MOVE MANIAC

Name	Type	Kind	Pow.	Acc.	PP	Range	DA
Headbutt	Normal	Physical	70	100	15	Normal	O

● BP MOVES

Name	Type	Kind	Pow.	Acc.	PP	Range	DA
Sucker Punch	Dark	Physical	80	100	5	Normal	O
Snore	Normal	Special	40	100	15	Normal	—
Spite	Ghost	Status	—	100	10	Normal	—
Swift	Normal	Special	60	—	20	2 Foes	—
Uproar	Normal	Special	50	100	10	1 Random	—
Role Play	Psychic	Status	—	—	10	Normal	—
Mud-Slap	Ground	Special	20	100	10	Normal	—
Heat Wave	Fire	Special	100	90	10	2 Foes	—
Super Fang	Normal	Physical	—	90	10	Normal	O

● TM & HM MOVES

No.	Name	Type	Kind	Pow.	Acc.	PP	Range	DA
TM05	Roar	Normal	Status	—	100	20	Normal	—
TM06	Toxic	Poison	Status	—	85	10	Normal	—
TM10	Hidden Power	Normal	Special	—	100	15	Normal	—
TM11	Sunny Day	Fire	Status	—	—	5	All	—
TM12	Taunt	Dark	Status	—	100	20	Normal	—
TM17	Protect	Normal	Status	—	—	10	Self	—
TM21	Frustration	Normal	Physical	—	100	20	Normal	O
TM22	SolarBeam	Grass	Special	120	100	10	Normal	—
TM23	Iron Tail	Steel	Physical	100	75	15	Normal	O
TM27	Return	Normal	Physical	—	100	20	Normal	O
TM30	Shadow Ball	Ghost	Special	80	100	15	Normal	—
TM32	Double Team	Normal	Status	—	—	15	Self	—
TM35	Flamethrower	Fire	Special	95	100	15	Normal	—
TM36	Sludge Bomb	Poison	Special	90	100	10	Normal	—
TM38	Fire Blast	Fire	Special	120	85	5	Normal	—
TM41	Torment	Dark	Status	—	100	15	Normal	—
TM42	Facade	Normal	Physical	70	100	20	Normal	O
TM43	Secret Power	Normal	Physical	70	100	20	Normal	—
TM44	Rest	Psychic	Status	—	—	10	Self	—
TM45	Attract	Normal	Status	—	100	15	Normal	—
TM46	Thief	Dark	Physical	40	100	10	Normal	O
TM49	Snatch	Dark	Status	—	—	10	Depends	—
TM50	Overheat	Fire	Special	140	90	5	Normal	—
TM58	Endure	Normal	Status	—	—	10	Self	—
TM61	Will-O-Wisp	Fire	Status	—	75	15	Normal	—
TM63	Embargo	Dark	Status	—	100	15	Normal	—
TM66	Payback	Dark	Physical	50	100	10	Normal	O
TM78	Captivate	Normal	Status	—	100	20	2 Foes	—
TM79	Dark Pulse	Dark	Special	80	100	15	Normal	—
TM82	Sleep Talk	Normal	Status	—	—	10	Depends	—
TM83	Natural Gift	Normal	Physical	—	100	15	Normal	—
TM85	Dream Eater	Psychic	Special	100	100	15	Normal	—
TM87	Swagger	Normal	Status	—	90	15	Normal	—
TM90	Substitute	Normal	Status	—	—	10	Self	—
HM06	Rock Smash	Fighting	Physical	40	100	15	Normal	O

● EGG MOVES

Name	Type	Kind	Pow.	Acc.	PP	Range	DA
Fire Spin	Fire	Special	15	70	15	Normal	—
Rage	Normal	Physical	20	100	20	Normal	O
Pursuit	Dark	Physical	40	100	20	Normal	O
Counter	Fighting	Physical	—	100	20	Self	O
Spite	Ghost	Status	—	100	10	Normal	—
Reversal	Fighting	Physical	—	100	15	Normal	O
Beat Up	Dark	Physical	10	100	10	Normal	—
Will-O-Wisp	Fire	Status	—	75	15	Normal	—
Fire Fang	Fire	Physical	65	95	15	Normal	O
Thunder Fang	Electric	Physical	65	95	15	Normal	O
Nasty Plot	Dark	Status	—	—	20	Self	—
Punishment	Dark	Physical	—	100	5	Normal	O
Feint	Normal	Physical	50	100	10	Normal	—

🔴 No. 228 | Dark Pokémon
Houndour

`Dark` `Fire`

- **HEIGHT:** 2'00"
- **WEIGHT:** 23.8 lbs.
- **ITEMS:** None

● SIZE COMPARISON

● MALE/FEMALE HAVE SAME FORM

⊙ ABILITIES
- Early Bird
- Flash Fire

⊙ STATS
- HP ●●
- ATTACK ●●●
- DEFENSE ●●●
- SP. ATTACK ●●●●
- SP. DEFENSE ●●●●
- SPEED ●●●

⊙ EGG GROUPS
Field

⊙ PERFORMANCE
SPEED ★★★★ STAMINA ★★★
POWER ★★☆ JUMP ★★★☆
SKILL ★★★★

● MAIN WAYS TO OBTAIN

Pokémon HeartGold Route 7 (night only)

Pokémon SoulSilver Route 7 (night only)

Pokémon Diamond —

Pokémon Pearl Find its Egg at the Pokémon Day Care and hatch it

Pokémon Platinum Route 214

Pokémon HeartGold	*Pokémon SoulSilver*
It uses different kinds of cries for communicating with others of its kind and for pursuing its prey.	To corner prey, they check each other's location using barks that only they can understand.

⊙ EVOLUTION

Houndour — Lv. 24 → Houndoom

No. 229 | Dark Pokémon
Houndoom

`Dark` `Fire`

- **HEIGHT:** 5'11"
- **WEIGHT:** 277.3 lbs.
- **ITEMS:** None

● **SIZE COMPARISON**

● **MALE FORM**
Bigger horns

● **FEMALE FORM**
Smaller horns

⊛ ABILITIES
- Early Bird
- Flash Fire

⊛ STATS
HP	●●●
ATTACK	●●●●
DEFENSE	●●
SP. ATTACK	●●●●●
SP. DEFENSE	●●●●
SPEED	●●●●

⊛ EGG GROUPS
Field

⊛ PERFORMANCE
SPEED ★★★★	STAMINA ★★★☆
POWER ★★★	JUMP ★★★☆
SKILL ★★	

● MAIN WAYS TO OBTAIN

Pokémon HeartGold	Level up Houndour to Lv. 24
Pokémon SoulSilver	Level up Houndour to Lv. 24
Pokémon Diamond	—
Pokémon Pearl	Route 214 (use Poké Radar)
Pokémon Platinum	Level up Houndour to Lv. 24

Pokémon HeartGold	Pokémon SoulSilver
If you are burned by the flames it shoots from its mouth, the pain will never go away.	Upon hearing its eerie howls, other Pokémon get the shivers and head straight back to their nests.

⊛ EVOLUTION

Houndour → Lv. 24 → Houndoom

● LEVEL-UP MOVES
Lv.	Name	Type	Kind	Pow.	Acc.	PP	Range	DA
1	Thunder Fang	Electric	Physical	65	95	15	Normal	○
1	Leer	Normal	Status	—	100	30	2 Foes	—
1	Ember	Fire	Special	40	100	25	Normal	—
1	Howl	Normal	Status	—	—	40	Self	—
1	Smog	Poison	Special	20	70	20	Normal	—
4	Howl	Normal	Status	—	—	40	Self	—
9	Smog	Poison	Special	20	70	20	Normal	—
14	Roar	Normal	Status	—	100	20	Normal	—
17	Bite	Dark	Physical	60	100	25	Normal	○
22	Odor Sleuth	Normal	Status	—	—	40	Normal	—
28	Beat Up	Dark	Physical	10	100	10	Normal	—
32	Fire Fang	Fire	Physical	65	95	15	Normal	○
38	Faint Attack	Dark	Physical	60	—	20	Normal	—
44	Embargo	Dark	Status	—	100	15	Normal	—
48	Flamethrower	Fire	Special	95	100	15	Normal	—
54	Crunch	Dark	Physical	80	100	15	Normal	○
60	Nasty Plot	Dark	Status	—	—	20	Self	—

● MOVE MANIAC
Name	Type	Kind	Pow.	Acc.	PP	Range	DA
Headbutt	Normal	Physical	70	100	15	Normal	○

● BP MOVES
Name	Type	Kind	Pow.	Acc.	PP	Range	DA
Sucker Punch	Dark	Physical	80	100	5	Normal	○
Snore	Normal	Special	40	100	15	Normal	—
Spite	Ghost	Status	—	100	10	Normal	—
Swift	Normal	Special	60	—	20	2 Foes	—
Uproar	Normal	Special	50	100	10	1 Random	—
Role Play	Psychic	Status	—	—	10	Normal	—
Mud-Slap	Ground	Special	20	100	10	Normal	—
Heat Wave	Fire	Special	100	90	10	2 Foes	—
Super Fang	Normal	Physical	—	90	10	Normal	○

● TM & HM MOVES
No.	Name	Type	Kind	Pow.	Acc.	PP	Range	DA
TM05	Roar	Normal	Status	—	100	20	Normal	—
TM06	Toxic	Poison	Status	—	85	10	Normal	—
TM10	Hidden Power	Normal	Special	—	100	15	Normal	—
TM11	Sunny Day	Fire	Status	—	—	5	All	—
TM12	Taunt	Dark	Status	—	100	20	Normal	—
TM15	Hyper Beam	Normal	Special	150	90	5	Normal	—
TM17	Protect	Normal	Status	—	—	10	Self	—
TM21	Frustration	Normal	Physical	—	100	20	Normal	○
TM22	SolarBeam	Grass	Special	120	100	10	Normal	—
TM23	Iron Tail	Steel	Physical	100	75	15	Normal	○
TM27	Return	Normal	Physical	—	100	20	Normal	○
TM30	Shadow Ball	Ghost	Special	80	100	15	Normal	—
TM32	Double Team	Normal	Status	—	—	15	Self	—
TM35	Flamethrower	Fire	Special	95	100	15	Normal	—
TM36	Sludge Bomb	Poison	Special	90	100	10	Normal	—
TM38	Fire Blast	Fire	Special	120	85	5	Normal	—
TM41	Torment	Dark	Status	—	100	15	Normal	—
TM42	Facade	Normal	Physical	70	100	20	Normal	○
TM43	Secret Power	Normal	Physical	70	100	20	Normal	○
TM44	Rest	Psychic	Status	—	—	10	Self	—
TM45	Attract	Normal	Status	—	100	15	Normal	—
TM46	Thief	Dark	Physical	40	100	10	Normal	○
TM49	Snatch	Dark	Status	—	—	10	Depends	—
TM50	Overheat	Fire	Special	140	90	5	Normal	—
TM58	Endure	Normal	Status	—	—	10	Self	—
TM61	Will-O-Wisp	Fire	Status	—	75	15	Normal	—
TM63	Embargo	Dark	Status	—	100	15	Normal	—
TM66	Payback	Dark	Physical	50	100	10	Normal	○
TM68	Giga Impact	Normal	Physical	150	90	5	Normal	○
TM78	Captivate	Normal	Status	—	100	20	2 Foes	—
TM79	Dark Pulse	Dark	Special	80	100	15	Normal	—
TM82	Sleep Talk	Normal	Status	—	—	10	Self	—
TM83	Natural Gift	Normal	Physical	—	100	15	Normal	—
TM85	Dream Eater	Psychic	Special	100	100	15	Normal	—
TM87	Swagger	Normal	Status	—	90	15	Normal	—
TM90	Substitute	Normal	Status	—	—	10	Self	—
HM04	Strength	Normal	Physical	80	100	15	Normal	○
HM06	Rock Smash	Fighting	Physical	40	100	15	Normal	○

● LEVEL-UP MOVES

Lv.	Name	Type	Kind	Pow.	Acc.	PP	Range	DA
1	Yawn	Normal	Status	—	—	10	Normal	—
1	Bubble	Water	Special	20	100	30	2 Foes	—
1	SmokeScreen	Normal	Status	—	100	20	Normal	—
1	Leer	Normal	Status	—	100	30	2 Foes	—
1	Water Gun	Water	Special	40	100	25	Normal	—
4	SmokeScreen	Normal	Status	—	100	20	Normal	—
8	Leer	Normal	Status	—	100	30	2 Foes	—
11	Water Gun	Water	Special	40	100	25	Normal	—
14	Focus Energy	Normal	Status	—	—	30	Self	—
18	BubbleBeam	Water	Special	65	100	20	Normal	—
23	Agility	Psychic	Status	—	—	30	Self	—
26	Twister	Dragon	Special	40	100	20	2 Foes	—
30	Brine	Water	Special	65	100	10	Normal	—
40	Hydro Pump	Water	Special	120	80	5	Normal	—
48	Dragon Dance	Dragon	Status	—	—	20	Self	—
57	Dragon Pulse	Dragon	Special	90	100	10	Normal	—

● MOVE MANIAC

Name	Type	Kind	Pow.	Acc.	PP	Range	DA
Headbutt	Normal	Physical	70	100	15	Normal	○
Draco Meteor	Dragon	Special	140	90	5	Normal	—

● BP MOVES

Name	Type	Kind	Pow.	Acc.	PP	Range	DA
Dive	Water	Physical	80	100	10	Normal	○
Icy Wind	Ice	Special	55	95	15	2 Foes	—
Snore	Normal	Special	40	100	15	Normal	—
Swift	Normal	Special	60	—	20	2 Foes	—
Iron Head	Steel	Physical	80	100	15	Normal	○
Outrage	Dragon	Physical	120	100	15	1 Random	○
Signal Beam	Bug	Special	75	100	15	Normal	—
Twister	Dragon	Special	40	100	20	2 Foes	—
Bounce	Flying	Physical	85	85	5	Normal	○

● TM & HM MOVES

No.	Name	Type	Kind	Pow.	Acc.	PP	Range	DA
TM03	Water Pulse	Water	Special	60	100	20	Normal	—
TM06	Toxic	Poison	Status	—	85	10	Normal	—
TM07	Hail	Ice	Status	—	—	10	All	—
TM10	Hidden Power	Normal	Special	—	100	15	Normal	—
TM13	Ice Beam	Ice	Special	95	100	10	Normal	—
TM14	Blizzard	Ice	Special	120	70	5	2 Foes	—
TM15	Hyper Beam	Normal	Special	150	90	5	Normal	—
TM17	Protect	Normal	Status	—	—	10	Self	—
TM18	Rain Dance	Water	Status	—	—	5	All	—
TM21	Frustration	Normal	Physical	—	100	20	Normal	○
TM27	Return	Normal	Physical	—	100	20	Normal	○
TM32	Double Team	Normal	Status	—	—	15	Self	—
TM42	Facade	Normal	Physical	70	100	20	Normal	○
TM43	Secret Power	Normal	Physical	70	100	20	Normal	—
TM44	Rest	Psychic	Status	—	—	10	Self	—
TM45	Attract	Normal	Status	—	100	15	Normal	—
TM55	Brine	Water	Special	65	100	10	Normal	—
TM58	Endure	Normal	Status	—	—	10	Self	—
TM59	Dragon Pulse	Dragon	Special	90	100	10	Normal	—
TM68	Giga Impact	Normal	Physical	150	90	5	Normal	○
TM78	Captivate	Normal	Status	—	100	20	2 Foes	—
TM82	Sleep Talk	Normal	Status	—	—	10	Depends	—
TM83	Natural Gift	Normal	Physical	—	100	15	Normal	—
TM87	Swagger	Normal	Status	—	90	15	Normal	—
TM90	Substitute	Normal	Status	—	—	10	Self	—
TM91	Flash Cannon	Steel	Special	80	100	10	Normal	—
HM03	Surf	Water	Special	95	100	15	2 Foes/1 Ally	—
HM05	Whirlpool	Water	Special	15	70	15	Normal	—
HM07	Waterfall	Water	Physical	80	100	15	Normal	○

◉ No. 230 | Dragon Pokémon
Kingdra

Water Dragon

● HEIGHT: 5'11"
● WEIGHT: 335.1 lbs.
● ITEMS: None

● SIZE COMPARISON

● MALE/FEMALE HAVE SAME FORM

◈ ABILITIES
● Swift Swim
● Sniper

◈ STATS
HP ●●●
ATTACK ●●●●
DEFENSE ●●●●
SP. ATTACK ●●●●
SP. DEFENSE ●●●●
SPEED ●●●●

◈ EGG GROUPS
Water 1
Dragon

◈ PERFORMANCE
SPEED ★★☆☆☆   STAMINA ★★★★☆
POWER ★★★★   JUMP ★★
SKILL ★★★

● MAIN WAYS TO OBTAIN

Pokémon HeartGold — Link trade Seadra while it holds the Dragon Scale

Pokémon SoulSilver — Link trade Seadra while it holds the Dragon Scale

Pokémon Diamond — Link trade Seadra while it holds the Dragon Scale

Pokémon Pearl — Link trade Seadra while it holds the Dragon Scale

Pokémon Platinum — Link trade Seadra while it holds the Dragon Scale

Pokémon HeartGold
It is said that it usually hides in underwater caves. It can create whirlpools by yawning.

Pokémon SoulSilver
It sleeps deep on the ocean floor to build its energy. It is said to cause tornadoes as it wakes.

◈ EVOLUTION

Horsea → Lv. 32 → Seadra → Have it hold Dragon Scale and trade it → Kingdra

No. 231 | Long Nose Pokémon
Phanpy

Ground

- HEIGHT: 1'08"
- WEIGHT: 73.9 lbs.
- ITEMS: Passho Berry

● SIZE COMPARISON

● MALE/FEMALE HAVE SAME FORM

● ABILITIES
- Pickup

● STATS
HP ●●●
ATTACK ●●●
DEFENSE ●●
SP. ATTACK ●●
SP. DEFENSE ●
SPEED ●●

● EGG GROUPS
Field

● PERFORMANCE
SPEED ★★★   STAMINA ★★★☆
POWER ★★★★☆   JUMP ★★☆
SKILL ★★★

● MAIN WAYS TO OBTAIN

Pokémon HeartGold	Route 45
Pokémon SoulSilver	—
Pokémon Diamond	Route 207 (mass outbreak)
Pokémon Pearl	Route 207 (mass outbreak)
Pokémon Platinum	Route 207 (mass outbreak)

| Pokémon HeartGold | Pokémon SoulSilver |
| It swings its long snout around playfully, but because it is so strong, that can be dangerous. | As a sign of affection, it bumps with its snout. However, it is so strong, it may send you flying. |

● EVOLUTION

Phanpy → Lv. 25 → Donphan

● LEVEL-UP MOVES

Lv.	Name	Type	Kind	Pow.	Acc.	PP	Range	DA
1	Odor Sleuth	Normal	Status	—	—	40	Normal	—
1	Tackle	Normal	Physical	35	95	35	Normal	○
1	Growl	Normal	Status	—	100	40	2 Foes	—
1	Defense Curl	Normal	Status	—	—	40	Self	—
6	Flail	Normal	Physical	—	100	15	Normal	○
10	Take Down	Normal	Physical	90	85	20	Normal	○
15	Rollout	Rock	Physical	30	90	20	Normal	○
19	Natural Gift	Normal	Physical	—	100	15	Normal	—
24	Slam	Normal	Physical	80	75	20	Normal	○
28	Endure	Normal	Status	—	—	10	Self	—
33	Charm	Normal	Status	—	100	20	Normal	—
37	Last Resort	Normal	Physical	130	100	5	Normal	○
42	Double-Edge	Normal	Physical	120	100	15	Normal	○

● MOVE MANIAC

Name	Type	Kind	Pow.	Acc.	PP	Range	DA
Headbutt	Normal	Physical	70	100	15	Normal	○

● BP MOVES

Name	Type	Kind	Pow.	Acc.	PP	Range	DA
Knock Off	Dark	Physical	20	100	20	Normal	○
Snore	Normal	Special	40	100	15	Normal	—
Mud-Slap	Ground	Special	20	100	10	Normal	—
Rollout	Rock	Physical	30	90	20	Normal	○
Superpower	Fighting	Physical	120	100	5	Normal	○
Endeavor	Normal	Physical	—	100	5	Normal	○
AncientPower	Rock	Special	60	100	5	Normal	—
Earth Power	Ground	Special	90	100	10	Normal	—
Gunk Shot	Poison	Physical	120	70	5	Normal	—
Seed Bomb	Grass	Physical	80	100	15	Normal	—

● TM & HM MOVES

No.	Name	Type	Kind	Pow.	Acc.	PP	Range	DA
TM05	Roar	Normal	Status	—	—	30	Normal	—
TM06	Toxic	Poison	Status	—	85	10	Normal	—
TM10	Hidden Power	Normal	Special	—	100	15	Normal	—
TM11	Sunny Day	Fire	Status	—	—	5	All	—
TM17	Protect	Normal	Status	—	—	10	Self	—
TM21	Frustration	Normal	Physical	—	100	20	Normal	○
TM23	Iron Tail	Steel	Physical	100	75	15	Normal	○
TM26	Earthquake	Ground	Physical	100	100	10	2 Foes/1 Ally	—
TM27	Return	Normal	Physical	—	100	20	Normal	○
TM32	Double Team	Normal	Status	—	—	15	Self	—
TM37	Sandstorm	Rock	Status	—	—	10	All	—
TM39	Rock Tomb	Rock	Physical	50	80	10	Normal	—
TM42	Facade	Normal	Physical	70	100	20	Normal	○
TM43	Secret Power	Normal	Physical	70	100	20	Normal	—
TM44	Rest	Psychic	Status	—	—	10	Self	—
TM45	Attract	Normal	Status	—	100	15	Normal	—
TM58	Endure	Normal	Status	—	—	10	Self	—
TM76	Stealth Rock	Rock	Status	—	—	20	2 Foes	—
TM78	Captivate	Normal	Status	—	100	20	2 Foes	—
TM80	Rock Slide	Rock	Physical	75	90	10	2 Foes	—
TM82	Sleep Talk	Normal	Status	—	—	10	Depends	—
TM83	Natural Gift	Normal	Physical	—	100	15	Normal	—
TM87	Swagger	Normal	Status	—	90	15	Normal	—
TM90	Substitute	Normal	Status	—	—	10	Self	—
HM04	Strength	Normal	Physical	80	100	15	Normal	○
HM06	Rock Smash	Fighting	Physical	40	100	15	Normal	○

● EGG MOVES

Name	Type	Kind	Pow.	Acc.	PP	Range	DA
Focus Energy	Normal	Status	—	—	30	Self	—
Body Slam	Normal	Physical	85	100	15	Normal	○
AncientPower	Rock	Special	60	100	5	Normal	—
Snore	Normal	Special	40	100	15	Normal	—
Counter	Fighting	Physical	—	100	20	Self	○
Fissure	Ground	Physical	—	30	5	Normal	—
Endeavor	Normal	Physical	—	100	5	Normal	○
Ice Shard	Ice	Physical	40	100	30	Normal	—
Head Smash	Rock	Physical	150	80	5	Normal	○

● LEVEL-UP MOVES

Lv.	Name	Type	Kind	Pow.	Acc.	PP	Range	DA
1	Fire Fang	Fire	Physical	65	95	15	Normal	○
1	Thunder Fang	Electric	Physical	65	95	15	Normal	○
1	Horn Attack	Normal	Physical	65	100	25	Normal	○
1	Growl	Normal	Status	—	100	40	2 Foes	—
1	Defense Curl	Normal	Status	—	—	40	Self	—
1	Flail	Normal	Physical	—	100	15	Normal	○
6	Rapid Spin	Normal	Physical	20	100	40	Normal	○
10	Knock Off	Dark	Physical	20	100	20	Normal	○
15	Rollout	Rock	Physical	30	90	20	Normal	○
19	Magnitude	Ground	Physical	—	100	30	2 Foes/1 Ally	—
24	Slam	Normal	Physical	80	75	20	Normal	○
25	Fury Attack	Normal	Physical	15	85	20	Normal	○
31	Assurance	Dark	Physical	50	100	10	Normal	○
39	Scary Face	Normal	Status	—	90	10	Normal	—
46	Earthquake	Ground	Physical	100	100	10	2 Foes/1 Ally	—
54	Giga Impact	Normal	Physical	150	90	5	Normal	○

● MOVE MANIAC

Name	Type	Kind	Pow.	Acc.	PP	Range	DA
Headbutt	Normal	Physical	70	100	15	Normal	○

● BP MOVES

Name	Type	Kind	Pow.	Acc.	PP	Range	DA
Knock Off	Dark	Physical	20	100	20	Normal	○
Snore	Normal	Special	40	100	15	Normal	—
Block	Normal	Status	—	—	5	Normal	—
Mud-Slap	Ground	Special	20	100	10	Normal	—
Rollout	Rock	Physical	30	90	20	Normal	○
Superpower	Fighting	Physical	120	100	5	Normal	○
Endeavor	Normal	Physical	—	100	5	Normal	—
AncientPower	Rock	Special	60	100	5	Normal	—
Earth Power	Ground	Special	90	100	10	Normal	—
Gunk Shot	Poison	Physical	120	70	5	Normal	○
Seed Bomb	Grass	Physical	80	100	15	Normal	—
Iron Defense	Steel	Status	—	—	15	Self	—
Bounce	Flying	Physical	85	85	5	Normal	—

● TM & HM MOVES

No.	Name	Type	Kind	Pow.	Acc.	PP	Range	DA
TM05	Roar	Normal	Status	—	100	20	Normal	—
TM06	Toxic	Poison	Status	—	85	10	Normal	—
TM10	Hidden Power	Normal	Special	—	100	15	Normal	—
TM11	Sunny Day	Fire	Status	—	—	5	All	—
TM15	Hyper Beam	Normal	Special	150	90	5	Normal	○
TM17	Protect	Normal	Status	—	—	10	Self	—
TM21	Frustration	Normal	Physical	—	100	20	Normal	○
TM23	Iron Tail	Steel	Physical	100	75	15	Normal	○
TM26	Earthquake	Ground	Physical	100	100	10	2 Foes/1 Ally	—
TM27	Return	Normal	Physical	—	100	20	Normal	○
TM32	Double Team	Normal	Status	—	—	15	Self	—
TM37	Sandstorm	Rock	Status	—	—	10	All	—
TM39	Rock Tomb	Rock	Physical	50	80	10	Normal	—
TM42	Facade	Normal	Physical	70	100	20	Normal	○
TM43	Secret Power	Normal	Physical	70	100	20	Normal	—
TM44	Rest	Psychic	Status	—	—	10	Self	—
TM45	Attract	Normal	Status	—	100	15	Normal	—
TM58	Endure	Normal	Status	—	—	10	Self	—
TM68	Giga Impact	Normal	Physical	150	90	5	Normal	○
TM69	Rock Polish	Rock	Status	—	—	20	Self	—
TM71	Stone Edge	Rock	Physical	100	80	5	Normal	—
TM74	Gyro Ball	Steel	Physical	—	100	5	Normal	○
TM76	Stealth Rock	Rock	Status	—	—	20	2 Foes	—
TM78	Captivate	Normal	Status	—	100	20	2 Foes	—
TM80	Rock Slide	Rock	Physical	75	90	10	2 Foes	—
TM82	Sleep Talk	Normal	Status	—	—	10	Depends	—
TM83	Natural Gift	Normal	Physical	—	100	15	Normal	—
TM84	Poison Jab	Poison	Physical	80	100	20	Normal	○
TM87	Swagger	Normal	Status	—	90	15	Normal	—
TM90	Substitute	Normal	Status	—	—	10	Self	—
HM04	Strength	Normal	Physical	80	100	15	Normal	○
HM06	Rock Smash	Fighting	Physical	40	100	15	Normal	○

● No. 232 | Armor Pokémon

Donphan

Ground

- ● HEIGHT: 3'02"
- ● WEIGHT: 264.6 lbs.
- ● ITEMS: Passho Berry

● SIZE COMPARISON

● MALE FORM
Longer tusks

● FEMALE FORM
Smaller tusks

● ABILITIES
- ● Sturdy

● STATS
- HP ●●●
- ATTACK ●●●●●
- DEFENSE ●●●●●
- SP. ATTACK ●●●
- SP. DEFENSE ●●
- SPEED ●●

● EGG GROUPS
Field

● PERFORMANCE

SPEED ★★☆☆	STAMINA ★★★★
POWER ★★★★★	JUMP ★★
SKILL ★★	

● MAIN WAYS TO OBTAIN

Pokémon HeartGold — Victory Road

Pokémon SoulSilver — —

Pokémon Diamond — Level up Phanpy to Lv. 25

Pokémon Pearl — Level up Phanpy to Lv. 25

Pokémon Platinum — Level up Phanpy to Lv. 25

Pokémon HeartGold
It has sharp, hard tusks and a rugged hide. Its tackle is strong enough to knock down a house.

Pokémon SoulSilver
The longer and bigger its tusks, the higher its rank in its herd. The tusks take long to grow.

● EVOLUTION

Phanpy — Lv. 25 → Donphan

● No. 233 | Virtual Pokémon
Porygon2

Normal

- ● HEIGHT: 2'00"
- ● WEIGHT: 71.6 lbs.
- ● ITEMS: None

● SIZE COMPARISON

● GENDER UNKNOWN

⊙ ABILITIES
- ● Trace
- ● Download

⊙ STATS
HP ●●●
ATTACK ●●●
DEFENSE ●●●
SP. ATTACK ●●●●●
SP. DEFENSE ●●●●
SPEED ●●●

⊙ EGG GROUPS
Mineral

⊙ PERFORMANCE
SPEED ★★★☆
POWER ★★★☆
SKILL ★★★★
STAMINA ★★★☆
JUMP ★★★☆

● MAIN WAYS TO OBTAIN

Pokémon HeartGold — Link trade Porygon while it holds the Up-Grade

Pokémon SoulSilver — Link trade Porygon while it holds the Up-Grade

Pokémon Diamond — Link trade Porygon while it holds the Up-Grade

Pokémon Pearl — Link trade Porygon while it holds the Up-Grade

Pokémon Platinum — Link trade Porygon while it holds the Up-Grade

Pokémon HeartGold
This upgraded version of PORYGON is designed for space exploration. It can't fly, however.

Pokémon SoulSilver
Further research enhanced its abilities. Sometimes, it may exhibit motions that were not programmed.

⊙ EVOLUTION

Porygon — Have it hold Up-Grade and trade it → Porygon2 — Have it hold Dubious Disc and trade it → Porygon-Z

● LEVEL-UP MOVES

Lv.	Name	Type	Kind	Pow.	Acc.	PP	Range	DA
1	Conversion 2	Normal	Status	—	—	30	Self	—
1	Tackle	Normal	Physical	35	95	35	Normal	○
1	Conversion	Normal	Status	—	—	30	Self	—
1	Defense Curl	Normal	Status	—	—	40	Self	—
7	Psybeam	Psychic	Special	65	100	20	Normal	—
12	Agility	Psychic	Status	—	—	30	Self	—
18	Recover	Normal	Status	—	—	10	Self	—
23	Magnet Rise	Electric	Status	—	—	10	Self	—
29	Signal Beam	Bug	Special	75	100	15	Normal	—
34	Recycle	Normal	Status	—	—	10	Self	—
40	Discharge	Electric	Special	80	100	15	2 Foes/1 Ally	—
45	Lock-On	Normal	Status	—	—	5	Normal	—
51	Tri Attack	Normal	Special	80	100	10	Normal	—
56	Magic Coat	Psychic	Status	—	—	15	Self	—
62	Zap Cannon	Electric	Special	120	50	5	Normal	—
67	Hyper Beam	Normal	Special	150	90	5	Normal	—

● MOVE MANIAC

Name	Type	Kind	Pow.	Acc.	PP	Range	DA

● BP MOVES

Name	Type	Kind	Pow.	Acc.	PP	Range	DA
Icy Wind	Ice	Special	55	95	15	2 Foes	—
Zen Headbutt	Psychic	Physical	80	90	15	Normal	○
Trick	Psychic	Status	—	100	10	Normal	—
Snore	Normal	Special	40	100	15	Normal	—
Last Resort	Normal	Physical	130	100	5	Normal	○
Swift	Normal	Special	60	—	20	2 Foes	—
Gravity	Psychic	Status	—	—	5	All	—
Magic Coat	Psychic	Status	—	—	15	Self	—
Signal Beam	Bug	Special	75	100	15	Normal	—
Pain Split	Normal	Status	—	—	20	Normal	—

● TM & HM MOVES

No.	Name	Type	Kind	Pow.	Acc.	PP	Range	DA
TM06	Toxic	Poison	Status	—	85	10	Normal	—
TM10	Hidden Power	Normal	Special	—	100	15	Normal	—
TM11	Sunny Day	Fire	Status	—	—	5	All	—
TM13	Ice Beam	Ice	Special	95	100	10	Normal	—
TM14	Blizzard	Ice	Special	120	70	5	2 Foes	—
TM15	Hyper Beam	Normal	Special	150	90	5	Normal	—
TM17	Protect	Normal	Status	—	—	10	Self	—
TM18	Rain Dance	Water	Status	—	—	5	All	—
TM21	Frustration	Normal	Physical	—	100	20	Normal	○
TM22	SolarBeam	Grass	Special	120	100	10	Normal	—
TM23	Iron Tail	Steel	Physical	100	75	15	Normal	○
TM24	Thunderbolt	Electric	Special	95	100	15	Normal	—
TM25	Thunder	Electric	Special	120	70	10	Normal	—
TM27	Return	Normal	Physical	—	100	20	Normal	○
TM29	Psychic	Psychic	Special	90	100	10	Normal	—
TM30	Shadow Ball	Ghost	Special	80	100	15	Normal	—
TM32	Double Team	Normal	Status	—	—	15	Self	—
TM34	Shock Wave	Electric	Special	60	—	20	Normal	—
TM40	Aerial Ace	Flying	Physical	60	—	20	Normal	○
TM42	Facade	Normal	Physical	70	100	20	Normal	○
TM43	Secret Power	Normal	Physical	70	100	20	Normal	—
TM44	Rest	Psychic	Status	—	—	10	Self	—
TM46	Thief	Dark	Physical	40	100	10	Normal	○
TM57	Charge Beam	Electric	Special	50	90	10	Normal	—
TM58	Endure	Normal	Status	—	—	10	Self	—
TM67	Recycle	Normal	Status	—	—	10	Self	—
TM68	Giga Impact	Normal	Physical	150	90	5	Normal	○
TM70	Flash	Normal	Status	—	100	20	Normal	—
TM73	Thunder Wave	Electric	Status	—	100	20	Normal	—
TM77	Psych Up	Normal	Status	—	—	10	Normal	—
TM82	Sleep Talk	Normal	Status	—	—	10	Depends	—
TM83	Natural Gift	Normal	Physical	—	100	15	Normal	—
TM85	Dream Eater	Psychic	Special	100	100	15	Normal	—
TM87	Swagger	Normal	Status	—	90	15	Normal	—
TM90	Substitute	Normal	Status	—	—	10	Self	—
TM92	Trick Room	Psychic	Status	—	—	5	All	—

● LEVEL-UP MOVES

Lv.	Name	Type	Kind	Pow.	Acc.	PP	Range	DA
1	Tackle	Normal	Physical	35	95	35	Normal	○
3	Leer	Normal	Status	—	100	30	2 Foes	—
7	Astonish	Ghost	Physical	30	100	15	Normal	○
10	Hypnosis	Psychic	Status	—	60	20	Normal	—
13	Stomp	Normal	Physical	65	100	20	Normal	○
16	Sand-Attack	Ground	Status	—	100	15	Normal	—
21	Take Down	Normal	Physical	90	85	20	Normal	○
23	Confuse Ray	Ghost	Status	—	100	10	Normal	—
27	Calm Mind	Psychic	Status	—	—	20	Self	—
33	Role Play	Psychic	Status	—	—	10	Normal	—
38	Zen Headbutt	Psychic	Physical	80	90	15	Normal	○
43	Imprison	Psychic	Status	—	—	10	Self	—
49	Captivate	Normal	Status	—	100	20	2 Foes	—
53	Me First	Normal	Status	—	—	20	Depends	—

● MOVE MANIAC

Name	Type	Kind	Pow.	Acc.	PP	Range	DA
Headbutt	Normal	Physical	70	100	15	Normal	○

● BP MOVES

Name	Type	Kind	Pow.	Acc.	PP	Range	DA
Zen Headbutt	Psychic	Physical	80	90	15	Normal	○
Sucker Punch	Dark	Physical	80	100	5	Normal	○
Snore	Normal	Special	40	100	15	Normal	—
Spite	Ghost	Status	—	100	10	Normal	—
Last Resort	Normal	Physical	130	100	5	Normal	○
Swift	Normal	Special	60	—	20	2 Foes	—
Uproar	Normal	Special	50	100	10	1 Random	—
Gravity	Psychic	Status	—	—	5	All	—
Role Play	Psychic	Status	—	—	10	Normal	—
Mud-Slap	Ground	Special	20	100	10	Normal	—
Signal Beam	Bug	Special	75	100	15	Normal	—
Bounce	Flying	Physical	85	85	5	Normal	○

● TM & HM MOVES

No.	Name	Type	Kind	Pow.	Acc.	PP	Range	DA
TM04	Calm Mind	Psychic	Status	—	—	20	Self	—
TM05	Roar	Normal	Status	—	100	20	Normal	—
TM06	Toxic	Poison	Status	—	85	10	Normal	—
TM10	Hidden Power	Normal	Special	—	100	15	Normal	—
TM11	Sunny Day	Fire	Status	—	—	5	All	—
TM16	Light Screen	Psychic	Status	—	—	30	2 Allies	—
TM17	Protect	Normal	Status	—	—	10	Self	—
TM18	Rain Dance	Water	Status	—	—	5	All	—
TM21	Frustration	Normal	Physical	—	100	20	Normal	○
TM22	SolarBeam	Grass	Special	120	100	10	Normal	—
TM23	Iron Tail	Steel	Physical	100	75	15	Normal	○
TM24	Thunderbolt	Electric	Special	95	100	15	Normal	—
TM25	Thunder	Electric	Special	120	70	10	Normal	—
TM26	Earthquake	Ground	Physical	100	100	10	2 Foes/1 Ally	—
TM27	Return	Normal	Physical	—	100	20	Normal	○
TM29	Psychic	Psychic	Special	90	100	10	Normal	—
TM30	Shadow Ball	Ghost	Special	80	100	15	Normal	—
TM32	Double Team	Normal	Status	—	—	15	Self	—
TM33	Reflect	Psychic	Status	—	—	20	2 Allies	—
TM34	Shock Wave	Electric	Special	60	—	20	Normal	—
TM42	Facade	Normal	Physical	70	100	20	Normal	○
TM43	Secret Power	Normal	Physical	70	100	20	Normal	○
TM44	Rest	Psychic	Status	—	—	10	Self	—
TM45	Attract	Normal	Status	—	100	15	Normal	—
TM46	Thief	Dark	Physical	40	100	10	Normal	○
TM48	Skill Swap	Psychic	Status	—	—	10	Normal	—
TM53	Energy Ball	Grass	Special	80	100	10	Normal	—
TM57	Charge Beam	Electric	Special	50	90	10	Normal	—
TM58	Endure	Normal	Status	—	—	10	Self	—
TM68	Giga Impact	Normal	Physical	150	90	5	Normal	○
TM70	Flash	Normal	Status	—	100	20	Normal	—
TM73	Thunder Wave	Electric	Status	—	100	20	Normal	—
TM77	Psych Up	Normal	Status	—	—	10	Normal	—
TM78	Captivate	Normal	Status	—	100	20	2 Foes	—
TM82	Sleep Talk	Normal	Status	—	—	10	Depends	—
TM83	Natural Gift	Normal	Physical	—	100	15	Normal	—
TM85	Dream Eater	Psychic	Special	100	100	15	Normal	—
TM87	Swagger	Normal	Status	—	90	15	Normal	—
TM90	Substitute	Normal	Status	—	—	10	Self	—
TM92	Trick Room	Psychic	Status	—	—	5	All	—

● EGG MOVES

Name	Type	Kind	Pow.	Acc.	PP	Range	DA
Spite	Ghost	Status	—	100	10	Normal	—
Disable	Normal	Status	—	80	20	Normal	—
Bite	Dark	Physical	60	100	25	Normal	○
Swagger	Normal	Status	—	90	15	Normal	—
Psych Up	Normal	Status	—	—	10	Normal	—
Extrasensory	Psychic	Special	80	100	30	Normal	—
Thrash	Normal	Physical	90	100	10	1 Random	○
Double Kick	Fighting	Physical	30	100	30	Normal	○
Zen Headbutt	Psychic	Physical	80	90	15	Normal	○
Megahorn	Bug	Physical	120	85	10	Normal	○

◉ No. 234 | Big Horn Pokémon
Stantler

Normal

● HEIGHT: 4'07"
● WEIGHT: 157.0 lbs.
● ITEMS: None

● SIZE COMPARISON

● MALE/FEMALE HAVE SAME FORM

◉ ABILITIES
● Intimidate
● Frisk

◉ STATS
HP ●●●
ATTACK ●●●●
DEFENSE ●●●
SP. ATTACK ●●●●
SP. DEFENSE ●●●
SPEED ●●●●

◉ EGG GROUPS
Field

◉ PERFORMANCE
SPEED ★★★
POWER ★★★★
SKILL ★★★
STAMINA ★★★☆
JUMP ★★★

● MAIN WAYS TO OBTAIN

Pokémon HeartGold — Route 36

Pokémon SoulSilver — Route 36

Pokémon Diamond — —

Pokémon Pearl — Route 207 (use Poké Radar)

Pokémon Platinum — Route 207 (use Poké Radar)

Pokémon HeartGold
The curved antlers subtly change the flow of air to create a strange space where reality is distorted.

Pokémon SoulSilver
Those who stare at its antlers will gradually lose control of their senses and be unable to stand.

◉ EVOLUTION

Does not evolve

No. 235 | Painter Pokémon
Smeargle

Normal

- **HEIGHT:** 3'11"
- **WEIGHT:** 127.9 lbs.
- **ITEMS:** None

● SIZE COMPARISON

● MALE/FEMALE HAVE SAME FORM

● ABILITIES
- Own Tempo
- Technician

● STATS
- HP ●●
- ATTACK ●
- DEFENSE ●●
- SP. ATTACK ●
- SP. DEFENSE ●●
- SPEED ●●●

● EGG GROUPS
Field

● PERFORMANCE
SPEED ★★★	STAMINA ★★★
POWER ★★☆	JUMP ★★★
SKILL ★★★★★	

● MAIN WAYS TO OBTAIN

Pokémon HeartGold	Ruins of Alph (outside)
Pokémon SoulSilver	Ruins of Alph (outside)
Pokémon Diamond	Route 212, Hearthome City side (use Poké Radar)
Pokémon Pearl	Route 212, Hearthome City side (use Poké Radar)
Pokémon Platinum	Route 212, Hearthome City side (use Poké Radar)

Pokémon HeartGold
A special fluid oozes from the tip of its tail. It paints the fluid everywhere to mark its territory.

Pokémon SoulSilver
Once it becomes an adult, it has a tendency to let its comrades plant footprints on its back.

● EVOLUTION
Does not evolve

● LEVEL-UP MOVES
Lv.	Name	Type	Kind	Pow.	Acc.	PP	Range	DA
1	Sketch	Normal	Status	—	—	1	Normal	—
11	Sketch	Normal	Status	—	—	1	Normal	—
21	Sketch	Normal	Status	—	—	1	Normal	—
31	Sketch	Normal	Status	—	—	1	Normal	—
41	Sketch	Normal	Status	—	—	1	Normal	—
51	Sketch	Normal	Status	—	—	1	Normal	—
61	Sketch	Normal	Status	—	—	1	Normal	—
71	Sketch	Normal	Status	—	—	1	Normal	—
81	Sketch	Normal	Status	—	—	1	Normal	—
91	Sketch	Normal	Status	—	—	1	Normal	—

● MOVE MANIAC
Name	Type	Kind	Pow.	Acc.	PP	Range	DA

● BP MOVES
Name	Type	Kind	Pow.	Acc.	PP	Range	DA

● TM & HM MOVES
No.	Name	Type	Kind	Pow.	Acc.	PP	Range	DA

● LEVEL-UP MOVES

Lv.	Name	Type	Kind	Pow.	Acc.	PP	Range	DA
1	Tackle	Normal	Physical	35	95	35	Normal	○
1	Helping Hand	Normal	Status	—	—	20	1 Ally	—
1	Fake Out	Normal	Physical	40	100	15	Normal	○
1	Foresight	Normal	Status	—	—	40	Normal	—

● MOVE MANIAC

Name	Type	Kind	Pow.	Acc.	PP	Range	DA
Headbutt	Normal	Physical	70	100	15	Normal	○

● BP MOVES

Name	Type	Kind	Pow.	Acc.	PP	Range	DA
Vacuum Wave	Fighting	Special	40	100	30	Normal	—
Snore	Normal	Special	40	100	15	Normal	—
Helping Hand	Normal	Status	—	—	20	1 Ally	—
Swift	Normal	Special	60	—	20	2 Foes	—
Uproar	Normal	Special	50	100	10	1 Random	—
Role Play	Psychic	Status	—	—	10	Normal	—
Mud-Slap	Ground	Special	20	100	10	Normal	—
Low Kick	Fighting	Physical	—	100	20	Normal	○

● TM & HM MOVES

No.	Name	Type	Kind	Pow.	Acc.	PP	Range	DA
TM06	Toxic	Poison	Status	—	85	10	Normal	—
TM08	Bulk Up	Fighting	Status	—	—	20	Self	—
TM10	Hidden Power	Normal	Special	—	100	15	Normal	—
TM11	Sunny Day	Fire	Status	—	—	5	All	—
TM17	Protect	Normal	Status	—	—	10	Self	—
TM18	Rain Dance	Water	Status	—	—	5	All	—
TM21	Frustration	Normal	Physical	—	100	20	Normal	○
TM26	Earthquake	Ground	Physical	100	100	10	2 Foes/1 Ally	—
TM27	Return	Normal	Physical	—	100	20	Normal	○
TM31	Brick Break	Fighting	Physical	75	100	15	Normal	○
TM32	Double Team	Normal	Status	—	—	15	Self	—
TM42	Facade	Normal	Physical	70	100	20	Normal	○
TM43	Secret Power	Normal	Physical	70	100	20	Normal	○
TM44	Rest	Psychic	Status	—	—	10	Self	—
TM45	Attract	Normal	Status	—	100	15	Normal	—
TM46	Thief	Dark	Physical	40	100	10	Normal	○
TM58	Endure	Normal	Status	—	—	10	Self	—
TM78	Captivate	Normal	Status	—	100	20	2 Foes	—
TM80	Rock Slide	Rock	Physical	75	90	10	2 Foes	—
TM82	Sleep Talk	Normal	Status	—	—	10	Depends	—
TM83	Natural Gift	Normal	Physical	—	100	15	Normal	—
TM87	Swagger	Normal	Status	—	90	15	Normal	—
TM90	Substitute	Normal	Status	—	—	10	Self	—
HM04	Strength	Normal	Physical	80	100	15	Normal	○
HM06	Rock Smash	Fighting	Physical	40	100	15	Normal	○

● EGG MOVES

Name	Type	Kind	Pow.	Acc.	PP	Range	DA
Rapid Spin	Normal	Physical	20	100	40	Normal	○
Hi Jump Kick	Fighting	Physical	100	90	20	Normal	○
Mach Punch	Fighting	Physical	40	100	30	Normal	○
Mind Reader	Normal	Status	—	—	5	Normal	—
Helping Hand	Normal	Status	—	—	20	1 Ally	—
Counter	Fighting	Physical	—	100	20	Self	○
Vacuum Wave	Fighting	Special	40	100	30	Normal	—
Bullet Punch	Steel	Physical	40	100	30	Normal	○

◉ No. 236 | Scuffle Pokémon
Tyrogue

Fighting

- **HEIGHT:** 2'04"
- **WEIGHT:** 46.3 lbs.
- **ITEMS:** None

● SIZE COMPARISON

● MALE FORM

◈ ABILITIES
- Guts
- Steadfast

◈ STATS
- HP ●
- ATTACK ●●
- DEFENSE ●●
- SP. ATTACK ●●
- SP. DEFENSE ●●
- SPEED ●●

◈ EGG GROUPS
No Egg has ever been discovered

◈ PERFORMANCE
- SPEED ★★★★
- POWER ★★☆☆
- SKILL ★★★★
- STAMINA ★★
- JUMP ★★★

● MAIN WAYS TO OBTAIN

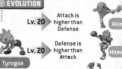

Pokémon HeartGold	Receive from the Karate King at Mt. Mortar B1F
Pokémon SoulSilver	Receive from the Karate King at Mt. Mortar B1F
Pokémon Diamond	Route 211, Eterna City side (use Poké Radar)
Pokémon Pearl	Route 211, Eterna City side (use Poké Radar)
Pokémon Platinum	Route 211, Eterna City side (use Poké Radar)

Pokémon HeartGold
It is always bursting with energy. To make itself stronger, it keeps on fighting even if it loses.

Pokémon SoulSilver
Even though it is small, it can't be ignored because it will slug any handy target without warning.

◈ EVOLUTION

Tyrogue

Lv. 20 — Attack is higher than Defense → Hitmonlee

Lv. 20 — Defense is higher than Attack → Hitmonchan

Lv. 20 — Attack and Defense are the same → Hitmontop

No. 237 | Handstand Pokémon

Hitmontop

Fighting

● **LEVEL-UP MOVES**

Lv.	Name	Type	Kind	Pow.	Acc.	PP	Range	DA
1	Revenge	Fighting	Physical	60	100	10	Normal	○
1	Rolling Kick	Fighting	Physical	60	85	15	Normal	○
6	Focus Energy	Normal	Status	—	—	30	Self	—
10	Pursuit	Dark	Physical	40	100	20	Normal	○
15	Quick Attack	Normal	Physical	40	100	30	Normal	○
19	Triple Kick	Fighting	Physical	10	90	10	Normal	○
24	Rapid Spin	Normal	Physical	20	100	40	Normal	○
28	Counter	Fighting	Physical	—	100	20	Self	—
33	Feint	Normal	Physical	50	100	10	Normal	—
37	Agility	Psychic	Status	—	—	30	Self	—
42	Gyro Ball	Steel	Physical	—	100	5	Normal	○
46	Detect	Fighting	Status	—	—	5	Self	—
51	Close Combat	Fighting	Physical	120	100	5	Normal	○
55	Endeavor	Normal	Physical	—	100	5	Normal	○

● **MOVE MANIAC**

Name	Type	Kind	Pow.	Acc.	PP	Range	DA
Headbutt	Normal	Physical	70	100	15	Normal	○

● **BP MOVES**

Name	Type	Kind	Pow.	Acc.	PP	Range	DA
Vacuum Wave	Fighting	Special	40	100	30	Normal	—
Sucker Punch	Dark	Physical	80	100	5	Normal	○
Snore	Normal	Special	40	100	15	Normal	○
Helping Hand	Normal	Status	—	—	20	1 Ally	—
Swift	Normal	Special	60	—	20	2 Foes	—
Role Play	Psychic	Status	—	—	10	Normal	—
Mud-Slap	Ground	Special	20	100	10	Normal	—
Rollout	Rock	Physical	30	90	20	Normal	○
Endeavor	Normal	Physical	—	100	5	Normal	○
Twister	Dragon	Special	40	100	20	2 Foes	○
Low Kick	Fighting	Physical	—	100	20	Normal	○

● **HEIGHT:** 4'07"
● **WEIGHT:** 105.8 lbs.
● **ITEMS:** None

● **SIZE COMPARISON**

● **MALE FORM**

⊙ **ABILITIES**
● Intimidate
● Technician

⊙ **STATS**
HP ●●
ATTACK ●●●●
DEFENSE ●●●●
SP. ATTACK ●
SP. DEFENSE ●●●●
SPEED ●●●

⊙ **EGG GROUPS**
Human-Like

⊙ **PERFORMANCE**

SPEED ★★★ STAMINA ★★★
POWER ★★★ JUMP ★★★
SKILL ★★★★★

● **MAIN WAYS TO OBTAIN**

Pokémon HeartGold — Make Tyrogue's Attack and Defense equal, then level it up to Lv. 20

Pokémon SoulSilver — Make Tyrogue's Attack and Defense equal, then level it up to Lv. 20

Pokémon Diamond — Make Tyrogue's Attack and Defense equal, then level it up to Lv. 20

Pokémon Pearl — Make Tyrogue's Attack and Defense equal, then level it up to Lv. 20

Pokémon Platinum — Make Tyrogue's Attack and Defense equal, then level it up to Lv. 20

Pokémon HeartGold
If you are enchanted by its smooth, dance-like kicks, you may get a closer experience with one than you'd like.

Pokémon SoulSilver
It launches kicks while spinning. If it spins at high speed, it may bore its way into the ground.

⊙ **EVOLUTION**

Lv. 20 — Attack is higher than Defense → Hitmonlee

Tyrogue

Lv. 20 — Defense is higher than Attack → Hitmonchan

Lv. 20 — Attack and Defense are the same → Hitmontop

● **TM & HM MOVES**

No.	Name	Type	Kind	Pow.	Acc.	PP	Range	DA
TM06	Toxic	Poison	Status	—	85	10	Normal	—
TM08	Bulk Up	Fighting	Status	—	—	20	Self	—
TM10	Hidden Power	Normal	Special	—	100	15	Normal	—
TM11	Sunny Day	Fire	Status	—	—	5	All	—
TM17	Protect	Normal	Status	—	—	10	Self	—
TM18	Rain Dance	Water	Status	—	—	5	All	—
TM21	Frustration	Normal	Physical	—	100	20	Normal	○
TM26	Earthquake	Ground	Physical	100	100	10	2 Foes/1 Ally	—
TM27	Return	Normal	Physical	—	100	20	Normal	○
TM28	Dig	Ground	Physical	80	100	10	Normal	○
TM31	Brick Break	Fighting	Physical	75	100	15	Normal	○
TM32	Double Team	Normal	Status	—	—	15	Self	—
TM37	Sandstorm	Rock	Status	—	—	10	All	—
TM40	Aerial Ace	Flying	Physical	60	—	20	Normal	○
TM42	Facade	Normal	Physical	70	100	20	Normal	○
TM43	Secret Power	Normal	Physical	70	100	20	Normal	○
TM44	Rest	Psychic	Status	—	—	10	Self	—
TM45	Attract	Normal	Status	—	100	15	Normal	—
TM46	Thief	Dark	Physical	40	100	10	Normal	○
TM58	Endure	Normal	Status	—	—	10	Self	—
TM71	Stone Edge	Rock	Physical	100	80	5	Normal	○
TM74	Gyro Ball	Steel	Physical	—	100	5	Normal	○
TM78	Captivate	Normal	Status	—	100	20	2 Foes	—
TM80	Rock Slide	Rock	Physical	75	90	10	2 Foes	—
TM82	Sleep Talk	Normal	Status	—	—	10	Depends	—
TM83	Natural Gift	Normal	Physical	—	100	15	Normal	—
TM87	Swagger	Normal	Status	—	90	15	Normal	—
TM90	Substitute	Normal	Status	—	—	10	Self	—
HM04	Strength	Normal	Physical	80	100	15	Normal	○
HM06	Rock Smash	Fighting	Physical	40	100	15	Normal	○

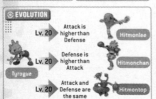

● LEVEL-UP MOVES

Lv.	Name	Type	Kind	Pow.	Acc.	PP	Range	DA
1	Pound	Normal	Physical	40	100	35	Normal	O
5	Lick	Ghost	Physical	20	100	30	Normal	O
8	Sweet Kiss	Normal	Status	—	75	10	Normal	—
11	Powder Snow	Ice	Special	40	100	25	2 Foes	—
15	Confusion	Psychic	Special	50	100	25	Normal	—
18	Sing	Normal	Status	—	55	15	Normal	—
21	Mean Look	Normal	Status	—	—	5	Normal	—
25	Fake Tears	Dark	Status	—	100	20	Normal	—
28	Lucky Chant	Normal	Status	—	—	30	2 Allies	—
31	Avalanche	Ice	Physical	60	100	10	Normal	O
35	Psychic	Psychic	Special	90	100	10	Normal	—
38	Copycat	Normal	Status	—	—	20	Depends	—
41	Perish Song	Normal	Status	—	—	5	All	—
45	Blizzard	Ice	Special	120	70	5	2 Foes	—

● MOVE MANIAC

Name	Type	Kind	Pow.	Acc.	PP	Range	DA

● BP MOVES

Name	Type	Kind	Pow.	Acc.	PP	Range	DA
Icy Wind	Ice	Special	55	95	15	2 Foes	—
Ice Punch	Ice	Physical	75	100	15	Normal	O
Zen Headbutt	Psychic	Physical	80	90	15	Normal	O
Trick	Psychic	Status	—	100	10	Normal	—
Snore	Normal	Special	40	100	15	Normal	—
Helping Hand	Normal	Status	—	—	20	1 Ally	—
Uproar	Normal	Special	50	100	10	1 Random	—
Magic Coat	Psychic	Status	—	—	15	Self	—
Role Play	Psychic	Status	—	—	10	Normal	—
Heal Bell	Normal	Status	—	—	5	All Allies	—
Mud-Slap	Ground	Special	20	100	10	Normal	—
Signal Beam	Bug	Special	75	100	15	Normal	—

● TM & HM MOVES

No.	Name	Type	Kind	Pow.	Acc.	PP	Range	DA
TM03	Water Pulse	Water	Special	60	100	20	Normal	—
TM04	Calm Mind	Psychic	Status	—	—	20	Self	—
TM06	Toxic	Poison	Status	—	85	10	Normal	—
TM07	Hail	Ice	Status	—	—	10	All	—
TM10	Hidden Power	Normal	Special	—	100	15	Normal	—
TM13	Ice Beam	Ice	Special	95	100	10	Normal	—
TM14	Blizzard	Ice	Special	120	70	5	2 Foes	—
TM16	Light Screen	Psychic	Status	—	—	30	2 Allies	—
TM17	Protect	Normal	Status	—	—	10	Self	—
TM18	Rain Dance	Water	Status	—	—	5	All	—
TM21	Frustration	Normal	Physical	—	100	20	Normal	O
TM27	Return	Normal	Physical	—	100	20	Normal	O
TM29	Psychic	Psychic	Special	90	100	10	Normal	—
TM30	Shadow Ball	Ghost	Special	80	100	15	Normal	—
TM32	Double Team	Normal	Status	—	—	15	Self	—
TM33	Reflect	Psychic	Status	—	—	20	2 Allies	—
TM42	Facade	Normal	Physical	70	100	20	Normal	O
TM43	Secret Power	Normal	Physical	70	100	20	Normal	O
TM44	Rest	Psychic	Status	—	—	10	Self	—
TM45	Attract	Normal	Status	—	100	15	Normal	—
TM46	Thief	Dark	Physical	40	100	10	Normal	O
TM48	Skill Swap	Psychic	Status	—	—	10	Normal	—
TM56	Fling	Dark	Physical	—	100	10	Normal	—
TM58	Endure	Normal	Status	—	—	10	Self	—
TM66	Payback	Dark	Physical	50	100	10	Normal	O
TM67	Recycle	Normal	Status	—	—	10	Self	—
TM70	Flash	Normal	Status	—	100	20	Normal	—
TM72	Avalanche	Ice	Physical	60	100	10	Normal	—
TM77	Psych Up	Normal	Status	—	—	10	Normal	—
TM78	Captivate	Normal	Status	—	100	20	2 Foes	—
TM82	Sleep Talk	Normal	Status	—	—	10	Depends	—
TM83	Natural Gift	Normal	Physical	—	100	15	Normal	—
TM85	Dream Eater	Psychic	Special	100	100	15	Normal	—
TM86	Grass Knot	Grass	Special	—	100	20	Normal	O
TM87	Swagger	Normal	Status	—	90	15	Normal	—
TM90	Substitute	Normal	Status	—	—	10	Self	—
TM92	Trick Room	Psychic	Status	—	—	5	All	—

● EGG MOVES

Name	Type	Kind	Pow.	Acc.	PP	Range	DA
Meditate	Psychic	Status	—	—	40	Self	—
Psych Up	Normal	Status	—	—	10	Normal	—
Fake Out	Normal	Physical	40	100	10	Normal	O
Wish	Normal	Status	—	—	10	Self	—
Ice Punch	Ice	Physical	75	100	15	Normal	O
Miracle Eye	Psychic	Status	—	—	40	Normal	—
Nasty Plot	Dark	Status	—	—	20	Self	—

◉ No. 238 | Kiss Pokémon
Smoochum

Ice | Psychic

- ● HEIGHT: 1'04"
- ● WEIGHT: 13.2 lbs.
- ● ITEMS: None

● SIZE COMPARISON

● FEMALE FORM

◉ ABILITIES
- Oblivious
- Forewarn

◉ EGG GROUPS
No Egg has ever been discovered

◉ STATS
- HP ●●
- ATTACK ●
- DEFENSE ●
- SP. ATTACK ●●●●
- SP. DEFENSE ●●●
- SPEED ●●●

◉ PERFORMANCE

SPEED ★★★★ · STAMINA ★☆☆
POWER ★☆ · JUMP ★★★
SKILL ★★★☆

● MAIN WAYS TO OBTAIN

Pokémon HeartGold	Find its Egg at the Pokémon Day Care and hatch it
Pokémon SoulSilver	Find its Egg at the Pokémon Day Care and hatch it
Pokémon Diamond	Lake Acuity [mass outbreak]
Pokémon Pearl	Lake Acuity [mass outbreak]
Pokémon Platinum	Snowpoint Temple1F

Pokémon HeartGold
Its lips are the most sensitive part of its body. It always uses its lips first to examine things.

Pokémon SoulSilver
It always rocks its head slowly backwards and forwards as if it is trying to kiss someone.

◉ EVOLUTION

Lv. 30

Smoochum → Jynx

No. 239 | Electric Pokémon
Elekid

Electric

● HEIGHT: 2'00"
● WEIGHT: 51.8 lbs.
● ITEMS: None

● SIZE COMPARISON

● MALE/FEMALE HAVE SAME FORM

⊛ ABILITIES
● Static

⊛ STATS
HP ●●
ATTACK ●●●
DEFENSE ●●
SP. ATTACK ●●●
SP. DEFENSE ●●●
SPEED ●●●●

⊛ EGG GROUPS
No Egg has ever been discovered

⊛ PERFORMANCE
SPEED ★★★★
POWER ★★☆
SKILL ★★★
STAMINA ★☆
JUMP ★★★

● MAIN WAYS TO OBTAIN

Pokémon HeartGold	Find its Egg at the Pokémon Day Care and hatch it
Pokémon SoulSilver	Find its Egg at the Pokémon Day Care and hatch it
Pokémon Diamond	Valley Windworks (after obtaining the National Pokédex, insert *Pokémon FireRed* into your Nintendo DS's Game Pak slot)
Pokémon Pearl	Valley Windworks (after obtaining the National Pokédex, insert *Pokémon FireRed* into your Nintendo DS's Game Pak slot)
Pokémon Platinum	Find its Egg at the Pokémon Day Care and hatch it

Pokémon HeartGold	*Pokémon SoulSilver*
It rotates its arms to generate electricity, but it tires easily, so it only charges up a little bit.	Even in the most vicious storm, this Pokémon plays happily if thunder rumbles in the sky.

⊛ EVOLUTION

Lv. 30

Have it hold Electirizer and trade it

Elekid → Electabuzz → Electivire

● LEVEL-UP MOVES
Lv.	Name	Type	Kind	Pow.	Acc.	PP	Range	DA
1	Quick Attack	Normal	Physical	40	100	30	Normal	○
1	Leer	Normal	Status	—	100	30	2 Foes	—
7	ThunderShock	Electric	Special	40	100	30	Normal	—
10	Low Kick	Fighting	Physical	—	100	20	Normal	○
16	Swift	Normal	Special	60	—	20	2 Foes	—
19	Shock Wave	Electric	Special	60	—	20	Normal	—
25	Light Screen	Psychic	Status	—	—	30	2 Allies	—
28	ThunderPunch	Electric	Physical	75	100	15	Normal	○
34	Discharge	Electric	Special	80	100	15	2 Foes/1 Ally	—
37	Thunderbolt	Electric	Special	95	100	15	Normal	—
43	Screech	Normal	Status	—	85	40	Normal	—
46	Thunder	Electric	Special	120	70	10	Normal	—

● MOVE MANIAC
Name	Type	Kind	Pow.	Acc.	PP	Range	DA
Headbutt	Normal	Physical	70	100	15	Normal	○

● BP MOVES
Name	Type	Kind	Pow.	Acc.	PP	Range	DA
ThunderPunch	Electric	Physical	75	100	15	Normal	○
Fire Punch	Fire	Physical	75	100	15	Normal	○
Ice Punch	Ice	Physical	75	100	15	Normal	○
Snore	Normal	Special	40	100	15	Normal	—
Helping Hand	Normal	Status	—	—	20	1 Ally	—
Magnet Rise	Electric	Status	—	—	10	Self	—
Swift	Normal	Special	60	—	20	2 Foes	—
Uproar	Normal	Special	50	100	10	1 Random	—
Mud-Slap	Ground	Special	20	100	10	Normal	—
Signal Beam	Bug	Special	75	100	15	Normal	—
Low Kick	Fighting	Physical	—	100	20	Normal	○

● TM & HM MOVES
No.	Name	Type	Kind	Pow.	Acc.	PP	Range	DA
TM01	Focus Punch	Fighting	Physical	150	100	20	Normal	○
TM06	Toxic	Poison	Status	—	85	10	Normal	—
TM10	Hidden Power	Normal	Special	—	100	15	Normal	—
TM16	Light Screen	Psychic	Status	—	—	30	2 Allies	—
TM17	Protect	Normal	Status	—	—	10	Self	—
TM18	Rain Dance	Water	Status	—	—	5	All	—
TM21	Frustration	Normal	Physical	—	100	20	Normal	○
TM24	Thunderbolt	Electric	Special	95	100	15	Normal	—
TM25	Thunder	Electric	Special	120	70	10	Normal	—
TM27	Return	Normal	Physical	—	100	20	Normal	○
TM29	Psychic	Psychic	Special	90	100	10	Normal	—
TM31	Brick Break	Fighting	Physical	75	100	15	Normal	○
TM32	Double Team	Normal	Status	—	—	15	Self	—
TM34	Shock Wave	Electric	Special	60	—	20	Normal	—
TM42	Facade	Normal	Physical	70	100	20	Normal	○
TM43	Secret Power	Normal	Physical	70	100	20	Normal	○
TM44	Rest	Psychic	Status	—	—	10	Self	—
TM45	Attract	Normal	Status	—	100	15	Normal	—
TM46	Thief	Dark	Physical	40	100	10	Normal	○
TM56	Fling	Dark	Physical	—	100	10	Normal	—
TM57	Charge Beam	Electric	Special	50	90	10	Normal	—
TM58	Endure	Normal	Status	—	—	10	Self	—
TM70	Flash	Normal	Status	—	100	20	Normal	—
TM73	Thunder Wave	Electric	Status	—	100	20	Normal	—
TM78	Captivate	Normal	Status	—	100	20	2 Foes	—
TM82	Sleep Talk	Normal	Status	—	—	10	Depends	—
TM83	Natural Gift	Normal	Physical	—	100	15	Normal	○
TM87	Swagger	Normal	Status	—	90	15	Normal	—
TM90	Substitute	Normal	Status	—	—	10	Self	—
HM06	Rock Smash	Fighting	Physical	40	100	15	Normal	○

● EGG MOVES
Name	Type	Kind	Pow.	Acc.	PP	Range	DA
Karate Chop	Fighting	Physical	50	100	25	Normal	○
Barrier	Psychic	Status	—	—	30	Self	—
Rolling Kick	Fighting	Physical	60	85	15	Normal	○
Meditate	Psychic	Status	—	—	40	Self	—
Cross Chop	Fighting	Physical	100	80	5	Normal	○
Fire Punch	Fire	Physical	75	100	15	Normal	○
Ice Punch	Ice	Physical	75	100	15	Normal	○
DynamicPunch	Fighting	Physical	100	50	5	Normal	○
Feint	Normal	Physical	50	100	10	Normal	—

● LEVEL-UP MOVES

Lv.	Name	Type	Kind	Pow.	Acc.	PP	Range	DA
1	Smog	Poison	Special	20	70	20	Normal	—
1	Leer	Normal	Status	—	100	30	2 Foes	—
7	Ember	Fire	Special	40	100	25	Normal	—
10	SmokeScreen	Normal	Status	—	100	20	Normal	—
16	Faint Attack	Dark	Physical	60	—	20	Normal	O
19	Fire Spin	Fire	Special	15	70	15	Normal	—
25	Confuse Ray	Ghost	Status	—	100	10	Normal	—
28	Fire Punch	Fire	Physical	75	100	15	Normal	—
34	Lava Plume	Fire	Special	80	100	15	2 Foes/1 Ally	—
37	Flamethrower	Fire	Special	95	100	15	Normal	—
43	Sunny Day	Fire	Status	—	—	5	All	—
46	Fire Blast	Fire	Special	120	85	5	Normal	—

● MOVE MANIAC

Name	Type	Kind	Pow.	Acc.	PP	Range	DA
Headbutt	Normal	Physical	70	100	15	Normal	O

● BP MOVES

Name	Type	Kind	Pow.	Acc.	PP	Range	DA
ThunderPunch	Electric	Physical	75	100	15	Normal	O
Fire Punch	Fire	Physical	75	100	15	Normal	O
Snore	Normal	Special	40	100	15	Normal	—
Helping Hand	Normal	Status	—	—	20	1 Ally	—
Uproar	Normal	Special	50	100	10	1 Random	—
Mud-Slap	Ground	Special	20	100	10	Normal	—
Heat Wave	Fire	Special	100	90	10	2 Foes	—

● TM & HM MOVES

No.	Name	Type	Kind	Pow.	Acc.	PP	Range	DA
TM01	Focus Punch	Fighting	Physical	150	100	20	Normal	O
TM06	Toxic	Poison	Status	—	85	10	Normal	—
TM10	Hidden Power	Normal	Special	—	100	15	Normal	—
TM11	Sunny Day	Fire	Status	—	—	5	All	—
TM17	Protect	Normal	Status	—	—	10	Self	—
TM21	Frustration	Normal	Physical	—	100	20	Normal	—
TM23	Iron Tail	Steel	Physical	100	75	15	Normal	O
TM27	Return	Normal	Physical	—	100	20	Normal	—
TM29	Psychic	Psychic	Special	90	100	10	Normal	—
TM31	Brick Break	Fighting	Physical	75	100	15	Normal	O
TM32	Double Team	Normal	Status	—	—	15	Self	—
TM35	Flamethrower	Fire	Special	95	100	15	Normal	—
TM38	Fire Blast	Fire	Special	120	85	5	Normal	—
TM42	Facade	Normal	Physical	70	100	20	Normal	O
TM43	Secret Power	Normal	Physical	70	100	20	Normal	—
TM44	Rest	Psychic	Status	—	—	10	Self	—
TM45	Attract	Normal	Status	—	100	15	Normal	—
TM46	Thief	Dark	Physical	40	100	10	Normal	O
TM50	Overheat	Fire	Special	140	90	5	Normal	—
TM56	Fling	Dark	Physical	—	100	10	Normal	—
TM58	Endure	Normal	Status	—	—	10	Self	—
TM61	Will-O-Wisp	Fire	Status	—	75	15	Normal	—
TM78	Captivate	Normal	Status	—	100	20	2 Foes	—
TM82	Sleep Talk	Normal	Status	—	—	10	Depends	—
TM83	Natural Gift	Normal	Physical	—	100	15	Normal	—
TM87	Swagger	Normal	Status	—	90	15	Normal	—
TM90	Substitute	Normal	Status	—	—	10	Self	—
HM06	Rock Smash	Fighting	Physical	40	100	15	Normal	O

● EGG MOVES

Name	Type	Kind	Pow.	Acc.	PP	Range	DA
Karate Chop	Fighting	Physical	50	100	25	Normal	O
Mega Punch	Normal	Physical	80	85	20	Normal	O
Barrier	Psychic	Status	—	—	30	Self	—
Screech	Normal	Status	—	85	40	Normal	—
Cross Chop	Fighting	Physical	100	80	5	Normal	O
ThunderPunch	Electric	Physical	75	100	15	Normal	O
Mach Punch	Fighting	Physical	40	100	30	Normal	O
DynamicPunch	Fighting	Physical	100	50	5	Normal	O
Flare Blitz	Fire	Physical	120	100	15	Normal	O
Belly Drum	Normal	Status	—	—	10	Self	—

○ No. 240 | Live Coal Pokémon
Magby

Fire

● SIZE COMPARISON

- ● HEIGHT: 2'04"
- ● WEIGHT: 47.2 lbs.
- ● ITEMS: None

● MALE/FEMALE HAVE SAME FORM

⊙ ABILITIES
● Flame Body

⊙ STATS
- HP ●●
- ATTACK ●●●
- DEFENSE ●●●
- SP. ATTACK ●●●
- SP. DEFENSE ●●
- SPEED ●●●●

⊙ EGG GROUPS
No Egg has ever been discovered

⊙ PERFORMANCE
- SPEED ★★★
- POWER ★★★
- SKILL ★★★
- STAMINA ★★☆
- JUMP ★★☆

● MAIN WAYS TO OBTAIN

Pokémon HeartGold	Find its Egg at the Pokémon Day Care and hatch it
Pokémon SoulSilver	Find its Egg at the Pokémon Day Care and hatch it
Pokémon Diamond	Route 227 (after obtaining the National Pokédex, insert Pokémon LeafGreen into your Nintendo DS's Game Pak slot)
Pokémon Pearl	Route 227 (after obtaining the National Pokédex, insert Pokémon LeafGreen into your Nintendo DS's Game Pak slot)
Pokémon Platinum	Find its Egg at the Pokémon Day Care and hatch it

Pokémon HeartGold
Each and every time it inhales and exhales, hot embers dribble from its mouth and nostrils.

Pokémon SoulSilver
It is found in volcanic craters. Its body temperature is over 1,100 degrees Fahrenheit, so don't underestimate it.

⊙ EVOLUTION

Lv. 30 → Have it hold Magmarizer and trade it

Magby → Magmar → Magmortar

No. 241 | Milk Cow Pokémon
Miltank

Normal

● LEVEL-UP MOVES

Lv.	Name	Type	Kind	Pow.	Acc.	PP	Range	DA
1	Tackle	Normal	Physical	35	95	35	Normal	O
3	Growl	Normal	Status	—	100	40	2 Foes	—
5	Defense Curl	Normal	Status	—	—	40	Self	—
8	Stomp	Normal	Physical	65	100	20	Normal	O
11	Milk Drink	Normal	Status	—	—	10	Self	—
15	Bide	Normal	Physical	—	—	10	Self	O
19	Rollout	Rock	Physical	30	90	20	Normal	O
24	Body Slam	Normal	Physical	85	100	15	Normal	O
29	Zen Headbutt	Psychic	Physical	80	90	15	Normal	O
35	Captivate	Normal	Status	—	100	20	2 Foes	—
41	Gyro Ball	Steel	Physical	—	100	5	Normal	O
48	Heal Bell	Normal	Status	—	—	5	All Allies	—
55	Wake-Up Slap	Fighting	Physical	60	100	10	Normal	O

● MOVE MANIAC

Name	Type	Kind	Pow.	Acc.	PP	Range	DA
Headbutt	Normal	Physical	70	100	15	Normal	O

● BP MOVES

Name	Type	Kind	Pow.	Acc.	PP	Range	DA
Icy Wind	Ice	Special	55	95	15	2 Foes	—
ThunderPunch	Electric	Physical	75	100	15	Normal	O
Fire Punch	Fire	Physical	75	100	15	Normal	O
Ice Punch	Ice	Physical	75	100	15	Normal	O
Zen Headbutt	Psychic	Physical	80	90	15	Normal	O
Snore	Normal	Special	40	100	15	Normal	—
Helping Hand	Normal	Status	—	—	20	1 Ally	—
Heal Bell	Normal	Status	—	—	5	All Allies	—
Block	Normal	Status	—	—	5	Normal	—
Mud-Slap	Ground	Special	20	100	10	Normal	—
Rollout	Rock	Physical	30	90	20	Normal	O
Iron Head	Steel	Physical	80	100	15	Normal	O

● HEIGHT: 3'11"
● WEIGHT: 166.4 lbs.
● ITEMS: Moomoo Milk

● SIZE COMPARISON

● FEMALE FORM

◎ ABILITIES
● Thick Fat
● Scrappy

◎ STATS
HP ●●●●
ATTACK ●●●●
DEFENSE ●●●●
SP. ATTACK ●●●
SP. DEFENSE ●●●
SPEED ●●●●

◎ EGG GROUPS
Field

◎ PERFORMANCE
SPEED ★★☆
POWER ★★★★
SKILL ★★★☆
STAMINA ★★★★☆
JUMP ★★☆

● MAIN WAYS TO OBTAIN

Pokémon HeartGold	Route 38
Pokémon SoulSilver	Route 38
Pokémon Diamond	Route 210, Solaceon Town side (occasionally appears when you use Poké Radar)
Pokémon Pearl	Route 210, Solaceon Town side (occasionally appears when you use Poké Radar)
Pokémon Platinum	Route 210, Solaceon Town side (occasionally appears when you use Poké Radar)

Pokémon HeartGold	Pokémon SoulSilver
Its milk is packed with nutrition, making it the ultimate beverage for the sick or weary.	If it is around babies, the milk it produces contains much more nutrition than usual.

◎ EVOLUTION

Does not evolve

● TM & HM MOVES

No.	Name	Type	Kind	Pow.	Acc.	PP	Range	DA
TM01	Focus Punch	Fighting	Physical	150	100	20	Normal	O
TM03	Water Pulse	Water	Special	60	100	20	Normal	—
TM06	Toxic	Poison	Status	—	85	10	Normal	—
TM10	Hidden Power	Normal	Special	—	100	15	Normal	—
TM11	Sunny Day	Fire	Status	—	—	5	All	—
TM13	Ice Beam	Ice	Special	95	100	10	Normal	—
TM14	Blizzard	Ice	Special	120	70	5	2 Foes	—
TM15	Hyper Beam	Normal	Special	150	90	5	Normal	—
TM17	Protect	Normal	Status	—	—	10	Self	—
TM18	Rain Dance	Water	Status	—	—	5	All	—
TM21	Frustration	Normal	Physical	—	100	20	Normal	O
TM22	SolarBeam	Grass	Special	120	100	10	Normal	—
TM23	Iron Tail	Steel	Physical	100	75	15	Normal	O
TM24	Thunderbolt	Electric	Special	95	100	15	Normal	—
TM25	Thunder	Electric	Special	120	70	10	Normal	—
TM26	Earthquake	Ground	Physical	100	100	10	2 Foes / 1 Ally	—
TM27	Return	Normal	Physical	—	100	20	Normal	O
TM30	Shadow Ball	Ghost	Special	80	100	15	Normal	—
TM31	Brick Break	Fighting	Physical	75	100	15	Normal	O
TM32	Double Team	Normal	Status	—	—	15	Self	—
TM34	Shock Wave	Electric	Special	60	—	20	Normal	—
TM37	Sandstorm	Rock	Status	—	—	10	All	—
TM39	Rock Tomb	Rock	Physical	50	80	10	Normal	O
TM42	Facade	Normal	Physical	70	100	20	Normal	O
TM43	Secret Power	Normal	Physical	70	100	20	Normal	—
TM44	Rest	Psychic	Status	—	—	10	Self	—
TM45	Attract	Normal	Status	—	100	15	Normal	—
TM52	Focus Blast	Fighting	Special	120	70	5	Normal	—
TM56	Fling	Dark	Physical	—	100	10	Normal	—
TM58	Endure	Normal	Status	—	—	10	Self	—
TM68	Giga Impact	Normal	Physical	150	90	5	Normal	O
TM73	Thunder Wave	Electric	Status	—	100	20	Normal	—
TM74	Gyro Ball	Steel	Physical	—	100	5	Normal	O
TM76	Stealth Rock	Rock	Status	—	—	20	2 Foes	—
TM77	Psych Up	Normal	Status	—	—	10	Self	—
TM78	Captivate	Normal	Status	—	100	20	2 Foes	—
TM80	Rock Slide	Rock	Physical	75	90	10	2 Foes	—
TM82	Sleep Talk	Normal	Status	—	—	10	Depends	—
TM83	Natural Gift	Normal	Physical	—	100	15	Normal	—
TM87	Swagger	Normal	Status	—	90	15	Normal	—
TM90	Substitute	Normal	Status	—	—	10	Self	—
HM03	Surf	Water	Special	95	100	15	2 Foes / 1 Ally	—
HM04	Strength	Normal	Physical	80	100	15	Normal	O
HM05	Whirlpool	Water	Special	15	70	15	Normal	—
HM06	Rock Smash	Fighting	Physical	40	100	15	Normal	O

● EGG MOVES

Name	Type	Kind	Pow.	Acc.	PP	Range	DA
Present	Normal	Physical	—	90	15	Normal	—
Reversal	Fighting	Physical	—	100	15	Normal	O
Seismic Toss	Fighting	Physical	—	100	20	Normal	O
Endure	Normal	Status	—	—	10	Self	—
Psych Up	Normal	Status	—	—	10	Normal	—
Curse	???	Status	—	—	10	Normal/Self	—
Helping Hand	Normal	Status	—	—	20	1 Ally	—
Sleep Talk	Normal	Status	—	—	10	Depends	—
Dizzy Punch	Normal	Physical	70	100	10	Normal	O
Hammer Arm	Fighting	Physical	100	90	10	Normal	O
Double-Edge	Normal	Physical	120	100	15	Normal	O
Punishment	Dark	Physical	—	100	5	Normal	—

● LEVEL-UP MOVES

Lv.	Name	Type	Kind	Pow.	Acc.	PP	Range	DA
1	Pound	Normal	Physical	40	100	35	Normal	○
1	Growl	Normal	Status	—	100	40	2 Foes	—
5	Tail Whip	Normal	Status	—	100	30	2 Foes	—
9	Refresh	Normal	Status	—	—	20	Self	—
12	Softboiled	Normal	Status	—	—	10	Self	—
16	DoubleSlap	Normal	Physical	15	85	10	Normal	○
20	Minimize	Normal	Status	—	—	20	Self	—
23	Sing	Normal	Status	—	55	15	Normal	—
27	Fling	Dark	Physical	—	100	10	Normal	—
31	Defense Curl	Normal	Status	—	—	40	Self	—
34	Light Screen	Psychic	Status	—	—	30	2 Allies	—
38	Egg Bomb	Normal	Physical	100	75	10	Normal	—
42	Healing Wish	Psychic	Status	—	—	10	Self	—
46	Double-Edge	Normal	Physical	120	100	15	Normal	○

● MOVE MANIAC

Name	Type	Kind	Pow.	Acc.	PP	Range	DA
Headbutt	Normal	Physical	70	100	15	Normal	○

● BP MOVES

Name	Type	Kind	Pow.	Acc.	PP	Range	DA
Icy Wind	Ice	Special	55	95	15	2 Foes	—
ThunderPunch	Electric	Physical	75	100	15	Normal	○
Fire Punch	Fire	Physical	75	100	15	Normal	○
Ice Punch	Ice	Physical	75	100	15	Normal	○
Zen Headbutt	Psychic	Physical	80	90	15	Normal	○
Snore	Normal	Special	40	100	15	Normal	—
Helping Hand	Normal	Status	—	—	20	1 Ally	—
Last Resort	Normal	Physical	130	100	5	Normal	○
Gravity	Psychic	Status	—	—	5	All	—
Heal Bell	Normal	Status	—	—	5	All Allies	—
Block	Normal	Status	—	—	5	Normal	—
Mud-Slap	Ground	Special	20	100	10	Normal	—
Rollout	Rock	Physical	30	90	20	Normal	○
Endeavor	Normal	Physical	—	100	5	Normal	—

● TM & HM MOVES

Nu.	Name	Type	Kind	Pow.	Acc.	PP	Range	DA
TM01	Focus Punch	Fighting	Physical	150	100	20	Normal	○
TM03	Water Pulse	Water	Special	60	100	20	Normal	—
TM04	Calm Mind	Psychic	Status	—	—	20	Self	—
TM06	Toxic	Poison	Status	—	85	10	Normal	—
TM07	Hail	Ice	Status	—	—	10	All	—
TM10	Hidden Power	Normal	Special	—	100	15	Normal	—
TM11	Sunny Day	Fire	Status	—	—	5	All	—
TM13	Ice Beam	Ice	Special	95	100	10	Normal	—
TM14	Blizzard	Ice	Special	120	70	5	2 Foes	—
TM15	Hyper Beam	Normal	Special	150	90	5	Normal	—
TM16	Light Screen	Psychic	Status	—	—	30	2 Allies	—
TM17	Protect	Normal	Status	—	—	10	Self	—
TM18	Rain Dance	Water	Status	—	—	5	All	—
TM20	Safeguard	Normal	Status	—	—	25	2 Allies	—
TM21	Frustration	Normal	Physical	—	100	20	Normal	○
TM22	SolarBeam	Grass	Special	120	100	10	Normal	—
TM23	Iron Tail	Steel	Physical	100	75	15	Normal	○
TM24	Thunderbolt	Electric	Special	95	100	15	Normal	—
TM25	Thunder	Electric	Special	120	70	10	Normal	—
TM26	Earthquake	Ground	Physical	100	100	10	2 Foes/1 Ally	—
TM27	Return	Normal	Physical	—	100	20	Normal	○
TM29	Psychic	Psychic	Special	90	100	10	Normal	—
TM30	Shadow Ball	Ghost	Special	80	100	15	Normal	—
TM31	Brick Break	Fighting	Physical	75	100	15	Normal	○
TM32	Double Team	Normal	Status	—	—	15	Self	—
TM34	Shock Wave	Electric	Special	60	—	20	Normal	—
TM35	Flamethrower	Fire	Special	95	100	15	Normal	—
TM37	Sandstorm	Rock	Status	—	—	10	All	—
TM38	Fire Blast	Fire	Special	120	85	5	Normal	—
TM39	Rock Tomb	Rock	Physical	50	80	10	Normal	—
TM42	Facade	Normal	Physical	70	100	20	Normal	○
TM43	Secret Power	Normal	Physical	70	100	20	Normal	○
TM44	Rest	Psychic	Status	—	—	10	Self	—
TM45	Attract	Normal	Status	—	100	15	Normal	—
TM48	Skill Swap	Psychic	Status	—	—	10	Normal	—
TM49	Snatch	Dark	Status	—	—	10	Depends	—
TM52	Focus Blast	Fighting	Special	120	70	5	Normal	—
TM56	Fling	Dark	Physical	—	100	10	Normal	—
TM57	Charge Beam	Electric	Special	50	90	10	Normal	—
TM58	Endure	Normal	Status	—	—	10	Self	—
TM60	Drain Punch	Fighting	Physical	60	100	5	Normal	○
TM67	Recycle	Normal	Status	—	—	10	Self	—
TM68	Giga Impact	Normal	Physical	150	90	5	Normal	○
TM70	Flash	Normal	Status	—	100	20	Normal	—
TM72	Avalanche	Ice	Physical	60	100	10	Normal	○
TM73	Thunder Wave	Electric	Status	—	100	20	Normal	—
TM76	Stealth Rock	Rock	Status	—	—	20	2 Foes	—
TM77	Psych Up	Normal	Status	—	—	10	Normal	—
TM78	Captivate	Normal	Status	—	100	20	2 Foes	—
TM80	Rock Slide	Rock	Physical	75	90	10	2 Foes	—
TM82	Sleep Talk	Normal	Status	—	—	10	Depends	—
TM83	Natural Gift	Normal	Physical	—	100	15	Normal	—
TM85	Dream Eater	Psychic	Special	100	100	15	Normal	—
TM86	Grass Knot	Grass	Special	—	100	20	Normal	—
TM87	Swagger	Normal	Status	—	90	15	Normal	—
TM90	Substitute	Normal	Status	—	—	10	Self	—
HM04	Strength	Normal	Physical	80	100	15	Normal	○
HM06	Rock Smash	Fighting	Physical	40	100	15	Normal	○
HM08	Rock Climb	Normal	Physical	90	85	20	Normal	○

◉ No. 242 | Happiness Pokémon
Blissey

Normal

- ● HEIGHT: 4'11"
- ● WEIGHT: 103.2 lbs.
- ● ITEMS: None

● SIZE COMPARISON

● FEMALE FORM

◉ ABILITIES
- ● Natural Cure
- ● Serene Grace

◉ EGG GROUPS
Fairy

◉ STATS

HP	●●●●●●
ATTACK	●
DEFENSE	●●
SP. ATTACK	●●●
SP. DEFENSE	●●●●●●
SPEED	●●●

◉ PERFORMANCE

SPEED ★★☆ STAMINA ★★★★★
POWER ★★☆ JUMP ★★☆
SKILL ★★★

● MAIN WAYS TO OBTAIN

Pokémon HeartGold — Level up Chansey with high friendship

Pokémon SoulSilver — Level up Chansey with high friendship

Pokémon Diamond — Level up Chansey with high friendship

Pokémon Pearl — Level up Chansey with high friendship

Pokémon Platinum — Level up Chansey with high friendship

Pokémon HeartGold
Anyone who takes even one taste of BLISSEY's egg becomes unfailingly caring and pleasant to everyone.

Pokémon SoulSilver
It has a very compassionate nature. If it sees a sick Pokémon, it will nurse the sufferer back to health.

◉ EVOLUTION

Have it hold Oval Stone and then level up between 4:00 A.M. and 8:00 P.M.

Level up with high friendship

Happiny → Chansey → Blissey

No. 243 | Thunder Pokémon
Raikou

Electric

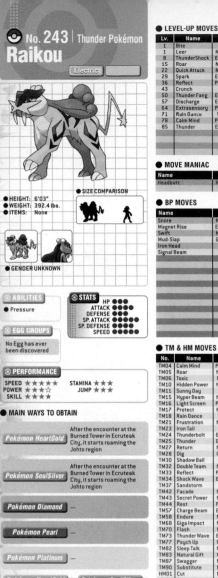

- **HEIGHT:** 6'03"
- **WEIGHT:** 392.4 lbs.
- **ITEMS:** None

● SIZE COMPARISON

● GENDER UNKNOWN

⊙ ABILITIES
- Pressure

⊙ STATS
HP ●●●
ATTACK ●●●●
DEFENSE ●●●●
SP. ATTACK ●●●●●
SP. DEFENSE ●●●●●
SPEED ●●●●●

⊙ EGG GROUPS
No Egg has ever been discovered

⊙ PERFORMANCE
SPEED ★★★★★   STAMINA ★★★
POWER ★★★☆   JUMP ★★★
SKILL ★★★★

● MAIN WAYS TO OBTAIN

Pokémon HeartGold	After the encounter at the Burned Tower in Ecruteak City, it starts roaming the Johto region
Pokémon SoulSilver	After the encounter at the Burned Tower in Ecruteak City, it starts roaming the Johto region
Pokémon Diamond	—
Pokémon Pearl	—
Pokémon Platinum	—

| Pokémon HeartGold | Pokémon SoulSilver |
| The rain clouds it carries let it fire thunderbolts at will. They say that it descended with lightning. | A Pokémon that races across the land while barking a cry that sounds like crashing thunder. |

⊙ EVOLUTION
Does not evolve

● LEVEL-UP MOVES

Lv.	Name	Type	Kind	Pow.	Acc.	PP	Range	DA
1	Bite	Dark	Physical	60	100	25	Normal	○
1	Leer	Normal	Status	—	100	30	2 Foes	—
8	ThunderShock	Electric	Special	40	100	30	Normal	—
15	Roar	Normal	Status	—	100	20	Normal	—
22	Quick Attack	Normal	Physical	40	100	30	Normal	○
29	Spark	Electric	Physical	65	100	20	Normal	○
36	Reflect	Psychic	Status	—	—	20	2 Allies	—
43	Crunch	Dark	Physical	80	100	15	Normal	○
50	Thunder Fang	Electric	Physical	65	95	15	Normal	○
57	Discharge	Electric	Special	80	100	15	2 Foes/1 Ally	—
64	Extrasensory	Psychic	Special	80	100	30	Normal	—
71	Rain Dance	Water	Status	—	—	5	All	—
78	Calm Mind	Psychic	Status	—	—	20	Self	—
85	Thunder	Electric	Special	120	70	10	Normal	—

● MOVE MANIAC

Name	Type	Kind	Pow.	Acc.	PP	Range	DA
Headbutt	Normal	Physical	70	100	15	Normal	○

● BP MOVES

Name	Type	Kind	Pow.	Acc.	PP	Range	DA
Snore	Normal	Special	40	100	15	Normal	—
Magnet Rise	Electric	Status	—	—	10	Self	—
Swift	Normal	Special	60	—	20	2 Foes	—
Mud-Slap	Ground	Special	20	100	10	Normal	—
Iron Head	Steel	Physical	80	100	15	Normal	○
Signal Beam	Bug	Special	75	100	15	Normal	—

● TM & HM MOVES

No.	Name	Type	Kind	Pow.	Acc.	PP	Range	DA
TM04	Calm Mind	Psychic	Status	—	—	20	Self	—
TM05	Roar	Normal	Status	—	100	20	Normal	—
TM06	Toxic	Poison	Status	—	85	10	Normal	—
TM10	Hidden Power	Normal	Special	—	100	15	Normal	—
TM11	Sunny Day	Fire	Status	—	—	5	All	—
TM15	Hyper Beam	Normal	Special	150	90	5	Normal	—
TM16	Light Screen	Psychic	Status	—	—	30	2 Allies	—
TM17	Protect	Normal	Status	—	—	10	Self	—
TM18	Rain Dance	Water	Status	—	—	5	All	—
TM21	Frustration	Normal	Physical	—	100	20	Normal	○
TM23	Iron Tail	Steel	Physical	100	75	15	Normal	○
TM24	Thunderbolt	Electric	Special	95	100	15	Normal	—
TM25	Thunder	Electric	Special	120	70	10	Normal	—
TM27	Return	Normal	Physical	—	100	20	Normal	○
TM28	Dig	Ground	Physical	80	100	10	Normal	○
TM30	Shadow Ball	Ghost	Special	80	100	15	Normal	—
TM32	Double Team	Normal	Status	—	—	15	Self	—
TM33	Reflect	Psychic	Status	—	—	20	2 Allies	—
TM34	Shock Wave	Electric	Special	60	—	20	Normal	—
TM37	Sandstorm	Rock	Status	—	—	10	All	—
TM42	Facade	Normal	Physical	70	100	20	Normal	○
TM44	Secret Power	Normal	Physical	70	100	20	Normal	—
TM44	Rest	Psychic	Status	—	—	10	Self	—
TM57	Charge Beam	Electric	Special	50	90	10	Normal	—
TM58	Endure	Normal	Status	—	—	10	Self	—
TM68	Giga Impact	Normal	Physical	150	90	5	Normal	○
TM70	Flash	Normal	Status	—	100	20	Normal	—
TM73	Thunder Wave	Electric	Status	—	100	20	Normal	—
TM77	Psych Up	Normal	Status	—	—	10	Normal	—
TM82	Sleep Talk	Normal	Status	—	—	10	Depends	—
TM83	Natural Gift	Normal	Physical	—	100	15	Normal	—
TM87	Swagger	Normal	Status	—	90	15	Normal	—
TM90	Substitute	Normal	Status	—	—	10	Self	—
HM01	Cut	Normal	Physical	50	95	30	Normal	○
HM04	Strength	Normal	Physical	80	100	15	Normal	○
HM06	Rock Smash	Fighting	Physical	40	100	15	Normal	○
HM08	Rock Climb	Normal	Physical	90	85	20	Normal	○

● LEVEL-UP MOVES

Lv.	Name	Type	Kind	Pow.	Acc.	PP	Range	DA
1	Bite	Dark	Physical	60	100	25	Normal	○
1	Leer	Normal	Status	—	100	30	2 Foes	—
8	Ember	Fire	Special	40	100	25	Normal	—
15	Roar	Normal	Status	—	100	20	Normal	—
22	Fire Spin	Fire	Special	15	70	15	Normal	—
29	Stomp	Normal	Physical	65	100	20	Normal	○
36	Flamethrower	Fire	Special	95	100	15	Normal	—
43	Swagger	Normal	Status	—	90	15	Normal	—
50	Fire Fang	Fire	Physical	65	95	15	Normal	○
57	Lava Plume	Fire	Special	80	100	15	2 Foes/1 Ally	—
64	Extrasensory	Psychic	Special	80	100	30	Normal	—
71	Fire Blast	Fire	Special	120	85	5	Normal	—
78	Calm Mind	Psychic	Status	—	—	20	Self	—
85	Eruption	Fire	Special	150	100	5	2 Foes	—

● MOVE MANIAC

Name	Type	Kind	Pow.	Acc.	PP	Range	DA
Headbutt	Normal	Physical	70	100	15	Normal	○

● BP MOVES

Name	Type	Kind	Pow.	Acc.	PP	Range	DA
Snore	Normal	Special	40	100	15	Normal	—
Swift	Normal	Special	60	—	20	2 Foes	—
Mud-Slap	Ground	Special	20	100	10	Normal	—
Iron Head	Steel	Physical	80	100	15	Normal	○
Heat Wave	Fire	Special	100	90	10	2 Foes	—

● TM & HM MOVES

No.	Name	Type	Kind	Pow.	Acc.	PP	Range	DA
TM04	Calm Mind	Psychic	Status	—	—	20	Self	—
TM05	Roar	Normal	Status	—	100	20	Normal	—
TM06	Toxic	Poison	Status	—	85	10	Normal	—
TM10	Hidden Power	Normal	Special	—	100	15	Normal	—
TM11	Sunny Day	Fire	Status	—	—	5	All	—
TM15	Hyper Beam	Normal	Special	150	90	5	Normal	—
TM17	Protect	Normal	Status	—	—	10	Self	—
TM18	Rain Dance	Water	Status	—	—	5	All	—
TM21	Frustration	Normal	Physical	—	100	20	Normal	○
TM22	SolarBeam	Grass	Special	120	100	10	Normal	—
TM23	Iron Tail	Steel	Physical	100	75	15	Normal	○
TM27	Return	Normal	Physical	—	100	20	Normal	○
TM28	Dig	Ground	Physical	80	100	10	Normal	○
TM30	Shadow Ball	Ghost	Special	80	100	15	Normal	—
TM32	Double Team	Normal	Status	—	—	15	Self	—
TM33	Reflect	Psychic	Status	—	—	20	2 Allies	—
TM35	Flamethrower	Fire	Special	95	100	15	Normal	—
TM37	Sandstorm	Rock	Status	—	—	10	All	—
TM38	Fire Blast	Fire	Special	120	85	5	Normal	—
TM42	Facade	Normal	Physical	70	100	20	Normal	○
TM43	Secret Power	Normal	Physical	70	100	20	Normal	○
TM44	Rest	Psychic	Status	—	—	10	Self	—
TM50	Overheat	Fire	Special	140	90	5	Normal	—
TM58	Endure	Normal	Status	—	—	10	Self	—
TM61	Will-O-Wisp	Fire	Status	—	75	15	Normal	—
TM68	Giga Impact	Normal	Physical	150	90	5	Normal	○
TM70	Flash	Normal	Status	—	100	20	Normal	—
TM71	Stone Edge	Rock	Physical	100	80	5	Normal	—
TM77	Psych Up	Normal	Status	—	—	10	Normal	—
TM82	Sleep Talk	Normal	Status	—	—	10	Depends	—
TM83	Natural Gift	Normal	Physical	—	100	15	Normal	—
TM87	Swagger	Normal	Status	—	90	15	Normal	—
TM90	Substitute	Normal	Status	—	—	10	Self	—
HM01	Cut	Normal	Physical	50	95	30	Normal	○
HM04	Strength	Normal	Physical	80	100	15	Normal	○
HM06	Rock Smash	Fighting	Physical	40	100	15	Normal	○
HM08	Rock Climb	Normal	Physical	90	85	20	Normal	○

⊙ No. 244 | Volcano Pokémon
Entei

Fire

- ● HEIGHT: 6'11"
- ● WEIGHT: 436.5 lbs.
- ● ITEMS: None

● SIZE COMPARISON

● GENDER UNKNOWN

⊙ ABILITIES
- ● Pressure

⊙ STATS
- HP ●●●●
- ATTACK ●●●●●
- DEFENSE ●●●●
- SP. ATTACK ●●●●
- SP. DEFENSE ●●●●
- SPEED ●●●●

⊙ EGG GROUPS
No Egg has ever been discovered

⊙ PERFORMANCE
SPEED ★★★★	STAMINA ★★★★
POWER ★★★★★	JUMP ★★☆
SKILL ★★★	

● MAIN WAYS TO OBTAIN

Pokémon HeartGold	After the encounter at the Burned Tower in Ecruteak City, it starts roaming the Johto region
Pokémon SoulSilver	After the encounter at the Burned Tower in Ecruteak City, it starts roaming the Johto region
Pokémon Diamond	—
Pokémon Pearl	—
Pokémon Platinum	—

Pokémon HeartGold	Pokémon SoulSilver
Volcanoes erupt when it barks. Unable to contain its sheer power, it races headlong around the land.	A Pokémon that races across the land. It is said that one is born every time a new volcano appears.

⊙ EVOLUTION
Does not evolve

No. 245 | Aurora Pokémon

Suicune

Water

● HEIGHT: 6'07"
● WEIGHT: 412.3 lbs.
● ITEMS: None

● SIZE COMPARISON

● GENDER UNKNOWN

● LEVEL-UP MOVES

Lv.	Name	Type	Kind	Pow.	Acc.	PP	Range	DA
1	Bite	Dark	Physical	60	100	25	Normal	○
1	Leer	Normal	Status	—	100	30	2 Foes	—
8	BubbleBeam	Water	Special	65	100	20	Normal	—
15	Rain Dance	Water	Status	—	—	5	All	—
22	Gust	Flying	Special	40	100	35	Normal	—
29	Aurora Beam	Ice	Special	65	100	20	Normal	—
36	Mist	Ice	Status	—	—	30	2 Allies	—
43	Mirror Coat	Psychic	Special	—	100	20	Self	—
50	Ice Fang	Ice	Physical	65	95	15	Normal	○
57	Tailwind	Flying	Status	—	—	30	2 Allies	—
64	Extrasensory	Psychic	Special	80	100	30	Normal	—
71	Hydro Pump	Water	Special	120	80	5	Normal	—
78	Calm Mind	Psychic	Status	—	—	20	Self	—
85	Blizzard	Ice	Special	120	70	5	2 Foes	—

● MOVE MANIAC

Name	Type	Kind	Pow.	Acc.	PP	Range	DA
Headbutt	Normal	Physical	70	100	15	Normal	○

● BP MOVES

Name	Type	Kind	Pow.	Acc.	PP	Range	DA
Dive	Water	Physical	80	100	10	Normal	○
Icy Wind	Ice	Special	55	95	15	2 Foes	—
Ominous Wind	Ghost	Special	60	100	5	Normal	—
Snore	Normal	Special	40	100	15	Normal	—
Swift	Normal	Special	60	—	20	2 Foes	—
Tailwind	Flying	Status	—	—	30	2 Allies	—
Mud-Slap	Ground	Special	20	100	10	Normal	—
Iron Head	Steel	Physical	80	100	15	Normal	○
Signal Beam	Bug	Special	75	100	15	Normal	—

⊙ ABILITIES

● Pressure

⊙ STATS

HP	●●●●
ATTACK	●●●●
DEFENSE	●●●●●
SP. ATTACK	●●●●●
SP. DEFENSE	●●●●●
SPEED	●●●●

⊙ EGG GROUPS

No Egg has ever been discovered

⊙ PERFORMANCE

SPEED ★★★★☆
POWER ★★★☆
SKILL ★★★★☆

STAMINA ★★★
JUMP ★★★★

● MAIN WAYS TO OBTAIN

Pokémon HeartGold — Hill on east side of Route 25 (after seeing Suicune at Ecruteak City's Burned Tower and all other places it appears)

Pokémon SoulSilver — Hill on east side of Route 25 (after seeing Suicune at Ecruteak City's Burned Tower and all other places it appears)

Pokémon Diamond —

Pokémon Pearl —

Pokémon Platinum —

Pokémon HeartGold — Said to be the embodiment of north winds, it can instantly purify filthy, murky water.

Pokémon SoulSilver — This Pokémon races across the land. It is said that north winds will somehow blow whenever it appears.

⊙ EVOLUTION

Does not evolve

● TM & HM MOVES

No.	Name	Type	Kind	Pow.	Acc.	PP	Range	DA
TM03	Water Pulse	Water	Special	60	100	20	Normal	—
TM04	Calm Mind	Psychic	Status	—	—	20	Self	—
TM05	Roar	Normal	Status	—	100	20	Normal	—
TM06	Toxic	Poison	Status	—	85	10	Normal	—
TM07	Hail	Ice	Status	—	—	10	All	—
TM10	Hidden Power	Normal	Special	—	100	15	Normal	—
TM11	Sunny Day	Fire	Status	—	—	5	All	—
TM13	Ice Beam	Ice	Special	95	100	10	Normal	—
TM14	Blizzard	Ice	Special	120	70	5	2 Foes	—
TM15	Hyper Beam	Normal	Special	150	90	5	Normal	—
TM17	Protect	Normal	Status	—	—	10	Self	—
TM18	Rain Dance	Water	Status	—	—	5	All	—
TM21	Frustration	Normal	Physical	—	100	20	Normal	○
TM23	Iron Tail	Steel	Physical	100	75	15	Normal	○
TM27	Return	Normal	Physical	—	100	20	Normal	○
TM28	Dig	Ground	Physical	80	100	10	Normal	○
TM30	Shadow Ball	Ghost	Special	80	100	15	Normal	—
TM32	Double Team	Normal	Status	—	—	15	Self	—
TM33	Reflect	Psychic	Status	—	—	20	2 Allies	—
TM37	Sandstorm	Rock	Status	—	—	10	All	—
TM42	Facade	Normal	Physical	70	100	20	Normal	○
TM43	Secret Power	Normal	Physical	70	100	20	Normal	—
TM44	Rest	Psychic	Status	—	—	10	Self	—
TM55	Brine	Water	Special	65	100	10	Normal	—
TM58	Endure	Normal	Status	—	—	10	Self	—
TM68	Giga Impact	Normal	Physical	150	90	5	Normal	○
TM72	Avalanche	Ice	Physical	60	100	10	Normal	○
TM77	Psych Up	Normal	Status	—	—	10	Normal	—
TM82	Sleep Talk	Normal	Status	—	—	10	Depends	—
TM83	Natural Gift	Normal	Physical	—	100	15	Normal	—
TM87	Swagger	Normal	Status	—	90	15	Normal	—
TM90	Substitute	Normal	Status	—	—	10	Self	—
HM01	Cut	Normal	Physical	50	95	30	Normal	○
HM03	Surf	Water	Special	95	100	15	2 Foes/1 Ally	—
HM05	Whirlpool	Water	Special	15	70	15	Normal	—
HM06	Rock Smash	Fighting	Physical	40	100	15	Normal	○
HM07	Waterfall	Water	Physical	80	100	15	Normal	○
HM08	Rock Climb	Normal	Physical	90	85	20	Normal	○

● LEVEL-UP MOVES

Lv.	Name	Type	Kind	Pow.	Acc.	PP	Range	DA
1	Bite	Dark	Physical	60	100	25	Normal	○
1	Leer	Normal	Status	—	100	30	2 Foes	—
5	Sandstorm	Rock	Status	—	—	10	All	—
10	Screech	Normal	Status	—	85	40	Normal	—
14	Rock Slide	Rock	Physical	75	90	10	2 Foes	—
19	Scary Face	Normal	Status	—	90	10	Normal	—
23	Thrash	Normal	Physical	90	100	20	1 Random	○
28	Dark Pulse	Dark	Special	80	100	15	Normal	—
32	Payback	Dark	Physical	50	100	10	Normal	○
37	Crunch	Dark	Physical	80	100	15	Normal	—
41	Earthquake	Ground	Physical	100	100	10	2 Foes/1 Ally	—
46	Stone Edge	Rock	Physical	100	80	5	Normal	—
50	Hyper Beam	Normal	Special	150	90	5	Normal	—

● MOVE MANIAC

Name	Type	Kind	Pow.	Acc.	PP	Range	DA
Headbutt	Normal	Physical	70	100	15	Normal	○

● BP MOVES

Name	Type	Kind	Pow.	Acc.	PP	Range	DA
Snore	Normal	Special	40	100	15	Normal	—
Spite	Ghost	Status	—	100	10	Normal	—
Uproar	Normal	Special	50	100	10	1 Random	—
Mud-Slap	Ground	Special	20	100	10	Normal	—
Superpower	Fighting	Physical	120	100	5	Normal	○
Iron Head	Steel	Physical	80	100	15	Normal	○
AncientPower	Rock	Special	60	100	5	Normal	—
Earth Power	Ground	Special	90	100	10	Normal	—

● TM & HM MOVES

No.	Name	Type	Kind	Pow.	Acc.	PP	Range	DA
TM06	Toxic	Poison	Status	—	85	10	Normal	—
TM10	Hidden Power	Normal	Special	—	100	15	Normal	—
TM11	Sunny Day	Fire	Status	—	—	5	All	—
TM12	Taunt	Dark	Status	—	100	20	Normal	—
TM15	Hyper Beam	Normal	Special	150	90	5	Normal	—
TM17	Protect	Normal	Status	—	—	10	Self	—
TM18	Rain Dance	Water	Status	—	—	5	All	—
TM21	Frustration	Normal	Physical	—	100	20	Normal	○
TM26	Earthquake	Ground	Physical	100	100	10	2 Foes/1 Ally	—
TM27	Return	Normal	Physical	—	100	20	Normal	○
TM28	Dig	Ground	Physical	80	100	10	Normal	○
TM31	Brick Break	Fighting	Physical	75	100	15	Normal	○
TM32	Double Team	Normal	Status	—	—	15	Self	—
TM37	Sandstorm	Rock	Status	—	—	10	All	—
TM39	Rock Tomb	Rock	Physical	50	80	10	Normal	—
TM41	Torment	Dark	Status	—	100	15	Normal	—
TM42	Facade	Normal	Physical	70	100	20	Normal	—
TM43	Secret Power	Normal	Physical	70	100	20	Normal	—
TM44	Rest	Psychic	Status	—	—	10	Self	—
TM45	Attract	Normal	Status	—	100	15	Normal	—
TM58	Endure	Normal	Status	—	—	10	Self	—
TM66	Payback	Dark	Physical	50	100	10	Normal	○
TM69	Rock Polish	Rock	Status	—	—	20	Self	—
TM71	Stone Edge	Rock	Physical	100	80	5	Normal	—
TM76	Stealth Rock	Rock	Status	—	—	10	2 Foes	—
TM78	Captivate	Normal	Status	—	100	20	2 Foes	—
TM79	Dark Pulse	Dark	Special	80	100	15	Normal	—
TM80	Rock Slide	Rock	Physical	75	90	10	2 Foes	—
TM82	Sleep Talk	Normal	Status	—	—	10	Depends	—
TM83	Natural Gift	Normal	Physical	—	100	15	Normal	—
TM87	Swagger	Normal	Status	—	90	15	Normal	—
TM90	Substitute	Normal	Status	—	—	10	Self	—
HM06	Rock Smash	Fighting	Physical	40	100	15	Normal	○

● EGG MOVES

Name	Type	Kind	Pow.	Acc.	PP	Range	DA
Pursuit	Dark	Physical	40	100	20	Normal	○
Stomp	Normal	Physical	65	100	20	Normal	○
Outrage	Dragon	Physical	120	100	15	1 Random	○
Focus Energy	Normal	Status	—	—	30	Self	—
AncientPower	Rock	Special	60	100	5	Normal	—
Dragon Dance	Dragon	Status	—	—	20	Self	—
Curse	???	Status	—	—	10	Normal/Self	—
Iron Defense	Steel	Status	—	—	15	Self	—
Assurance	Dark	Physical	50	100	10	Normal	○
Iron Head	Steel	Physical	80	100	15	Normal	○

◉ No. 246 | Rock Skin Pokémon
Larvitar

`Rock` `Ground`

- **● HEIGHT:** 2'00"
- **● WEIGHT:** 158.7 lbs.
- **● ITEMS:** None

● SIZE COMPARISON

● MALE/FEMALE HAVE SAME FORM

◉ ABILITIES
● Guts

◉ STATS
HP ●●
ATTACK ●●●
DEFENSE ●●●
SP. ATTACK ●●
SP. DEFENSE ●●
SPEED ●●

◉ EGG GROUPS
Monster

◉ PERFORMANCE

SPEED ★★★ STAMINA ★★★
POWER ★★☆☆ JUMP ★★★
SKILL ★★★☆

● MAIN WAYS TO OBTAIN

Pokémon HeartGold	Mt. Silver Cave interior
Pokémon SoulSilver	Mt. Silver Cave interior
Pokémon Diamond	Route 207 (use Poké Radar)
Pokémon Pearl	—
Pokémon Platinum	Route 206 (mass outbreak)

Pokémon HeartGold

It feeds on soil. After it has eaten a large mountain, it falls asleep so it can grow.

Pokémon SoulSilver

It is born deep underground. It can't emerge until it has entirely consumed the soil around it.

◉ EVOLUTION

Lv. 30 Lv. 55

Larvitar	Pupitar	Tyranitar

No. 247 | Hard Shell Pokémon
Pupitar

Rock | Ground

- **HEIGHT:** 3'11"
- **WEIGHT:** 335.1 lbs.
- **ITEMS:** None

● SIZE COMPARISON

● MALE/FEMALE HAVE SAME FORM

⊚ ABILITIES
- Shed Skin

⊚ STATS
HP ●●●
ATTACK ●●●●
DEFENSE ●●●
SP. ATTACK ●●●
SP. DEFENSE ●●●
SPEED ●●

⊚ EGG GROUPS
Monster

⊚ PERFORMANCE
SPEED ★★★☆ STAMINA ★★★☆
POWER ★★★★ JUMP ★★☆☆
SKILL ★

● MAIN WAYS TO OBTAIN

Pokémon HeartGold	Small chamber inside Mt. Silver Cave
Pokémon SoulSilver	Small chamber inside Mt. Silver Cave
Pokémon Diamond	Level up Larvitar to Lv. 30
Pokémon Pearl	—
Pokémon Platinum	Level up Larvitar to Lv. 30

Pokémon HeartGold
Its shell is as hard as sheet rock, and it is also very strong. Its thrashing can topple a mountain.

Pokémon SoulSilver
Even sealed in its shell, it can move freely. Hard and fast, it has outstanding destructive power.

⊚ EVOLUTION

Larvitar — Lv. 30 → Pupitar — Lv. 55 → Tyranitar

● LEVEL-UP MOVES

Lv.	Name	Type	Kind	Pow.	Acc.	PP	Range	DA
1	Bite	Dark	Physical	60	100	25	Normal	○
1	Leer	Normal	Status	—	100	30	2 Foes	—
1	Sandstorm	Rock	Status	—	—	10	All	—
1	Screech	Normal	Status	—	85	40	Normal	—
5	Sandstorm	Rock	Status	—	—	10	All	—
10	Screech	Normal	Status	—	85	40	Normal	—
14	Rock Slide	Rock	Physical	75	90	10	2 Foes	—
19	Scary Face	Normal	Status	—	90	10	Normal	—
23	Thrash	Normal	Physical	90	100	20	1 Random	○
28	Dark Pulse	Dark	Special	80	100	15	Normal	—
34	Payback	Dark	Physical	50	100	10	Normal	○
41	Crunch	Dark	Physical	80	100	15	Normal	○
47	Earthquake	Ground	Physical	100	100	10	2 Foes/1 Ally	○
54	Stone Edge	Rock	Physical	100	80	5	Normal	—
60	Hyper Beam	Normal	Special	150	90	5	Normal	—

● MOVE MANIAC

Name	Type	Kind	Pow.	Acc.	PP	Range	DA
Headbutt	Normal	Physical	70	100	15	Normal	○

● BP MOVES

Name	Type	Kind	Pow.	Acc.	PP	Range	DA
Snore	Normal	Special	40	100	15	Normal	—
Spite	Ghost	Status	—	100	10	Normal	—
Uproar	Normal	Special	50	100	10	1 Random	—
Mud-Slap	Ground	Special	20	100	10	Normal	—
Superpower	Fighting	Physical	120	100	5	Normal	○
Iron Head	Steel	Physical	80	100	15	Normal	○
AncientPower	Rock	Special	60	100	5	Normal	—
Earth Power	Ground	Special	90	100	10	Normal	—
Iron Defense	Steel	Status	—	—	15	Self	—

● TM & HM MOVES

No.	Name	Type	Kind	Pow.	Acc.	PP	Range	DA
TM06	Toxic	Poison	Status	—	85	10	Normal	—
TM10	Hidden Power	Normal	Special	—	100	15	Normal	—
TM11	Sunny Day	Fire	Status	—	—	5	All	—
TM12	Taunt	Dark	Status	—	100	20	Normal	—
TM15	Hyper Beam	Normal	Special	150	90	5	Normal	—
TM17	Protect	Normal	Status	—	—	10	Self	—
TM18	Rain Dance	Water	Status	—	—	5	All	—
TM21	Frustration	Normal	Physical	—	100	20	Normal	○
TM26	Earthquake	Ground	Physical	100	100	10	2 Foes/1 Ally	○
TM27	Return	Normal	Physical	—	100	20	Normal	○
TM28	Dig	Ground	Physical	80	100	10	Normal	○
TM31	Brick Break	Fighting	Physical	75	100	15	Normal	○
TM32	Double Team	Normal	Status	—	—	15	Self	—
TM37	Sandstorm	Rock	Status	—	—	10	All	—
TM39	Rock Tomb	Rock	Physical	50	80	10	Normal	—
TM41	Torment	Dark	Status	—	100	15	Normal	—
TM42	Facade	Normal	Physical	70	100	20	Normal	○
TM43	Secret Power	Normal	Physical	70	100	20	Normal	—
TM44	Rest	Psychic	Status	—	—	10	Self	—
TM45	Attract	Normal	Status	—	100	15	Normal	—
TM58	Endure	Normal	Status	—	—	10	Self	—
TM66	Payback	Dark	Physical	50	100	10	Normal	○
TM69	Rock Polish	Rock	Status	—	—	20	Self	—
TM71	Stone Edge	Rock	Physical	100	80	5	Normal	—
TM76	Stealth Rock	Rock	Status	—	—	20	2 Foes	—
TM78	Captivate	Normal	Status	—	100	20	2 Foes	—
TM79	Dark Pulse	Dark	Special	80	100	15	Normal	—
TM80	Rock Slide	Rock	Physical	75	90	10	2 Foes	—
TM82	Sleep Talk	Normal	Status	—	—	10	Depends	—
TM83	Natural Gift	Normal	Physical	—	100	15	Normal	—
TM87	Swagger	Normal	Status	—	90	15	Normal	—
TM90	Substitute	Normal	Status	—	—	10	Self	—
HM06	Rock Smash	Fighting	Physical	40	100	15	Normal	○

● LEVEL-UP MOVES

Lv.	Name	Type	Kind	Pow.	Acc.	PP	Range	DA
1	Thunder Fang	Electric	Physical	65	95	15	Normal	○
1	Ice Fang	Ice	Physical	65	95	15	Normal	○
1	Fire Fang	Fire	Physical	65	95	15	Normal	○
1	Bite	Dark	Physical	60	100	25	Normal	○
1	Leer	Normal	Status	—	100	30	2 Foes	—
1	Sandstorm	Rock	Status	—	—	10	All	—
1	Screech	Normal	Status	—	85	40	Normal	—
5	Sandstorm	Rock	Status	—	—	10	All	—
10	Screech	Normal	Status	—	85	40	Normal	—
14	Rock Slide	Rock	Physical	75	90	10	2 Foes	—
19	Scary Face	Normal	Status	—	90	10	Normal	—
23	Thrash	Normal	Physical	90	100	20	1 Random	○
28	Dark Pulse	Dark	Special	80	100	15	Normal	—
34	Payback	Dark	Physical	50	100	10	Normal	○
41	Crunch	Dark	Physical	80	100	15	Normal	○
47	Earthquake	Ground	Physical	100	100	10	2 Foes/1 Ally	—
54	Stone Edge	Rock	Physical	100	80	5	Normal	—
70	Hyper Beam	Normal	Special	150	90	5	Normal	—

● MOVE MANIAC

Name	Type	Kind	Pow.	Acc.	PP	Range	DA
Headbutt	Normal	Physical	70	100	15	Normal	○

● BP MOVES

Name	Type	Kind	Pow.	Acc.	PP	Range	DA
Fury Cutter	Bug	Physical	10	95	20	Normal	○
ThunderPunch	Electric	Physical	75	100	15	Normal	○
Fire Punch	Fire	Physical	75	100	15	Normal	○
Ice Punch	Ice	Physical	75	100	15	Normal	○
Snore	Normal	Special	40	100	15	Normal	—
Spite	Ghost	Status	—	100	10	Normal	—
Uproar	Normal	Special	50	100	10	1 Random	—
Block	Normal	Status	—	—	5	Normal	—
Mud-Slap	Ground	Special	20	100	10	Normal	—
Superpower	Fighting	Physical	120	100	5	Normal	—
Iron Head	Steel	Physical	80	100	15	Normal	—
Aqua Tail	Water	Physical	90	90	10	Normal	○
Outrage	Dragon	Physical	120	100	15	1 Random	—
AncientPower	Rock	Special	60	100	5	Normal	—
Earth Power	Ground	Special	90	100	10	Normal	—
Low Kick	Fighting	Physical	—	100	20	Normal	—

● TM & HM MOVES

No.	Name	Type	Kind	Pow.	Acc.	PP	Range	DA
TM01	Focus Punch	Fighting	Physical	150	100	20	Normal	○
TM02	Dragon Claw	Dragon	Physical	80	100	15	Normal	○
TM03	Water Pulse	Water	Special	60	100	20	Normal	—
TM05	Roar	Normal	Status	—	100	20	Normal	—
TM06	Toxic	Poison	Status	—	85	10	Normal	—
TM10	Hidden Power	Normal	Special	—	100	15	Normal	—
TM11	Sunny Day	Fire	Status	—	—	5	All	—
TM12	Taunt	Dark	Status	—	100	20	Normal	—
TM13	Ice Beam	Ice	Special	95	100	10	Normal	—
TM14	Blizzard	Ice	Special	120	70	5	2 Foes	—
TM15	Hyper Beam	Normal	Special	150	90	5	Normal	—
TM17	Protect	Normal	Status	—	—	10	Self	—
TM18	Rain Dance	Water	Status	—	—	5	All	—
TM21	Frustration	Normal	Physical	—	100	20	Normal	○
TM23	Iron Tail	Steel	Physical	100	75	15	Normal	○
TM24	Thunderbolt	Electric	Special	95	100	15	Normal	—
TM25	Thunder	Electric	Special	120	70	10	Normal	—
TM26	Earthquake	Ground	Physical	100	100	10	2 Foes/1 Ally	—
TM27	Return	Normal	Physical	—	100	20	Normal	○
TM28	Dig	Ground	Physical	80	100	10	Normal	○
TM31	Brick Break	Fighting	Physical	75	100	15	Normal	○
TM32	Double Team	Normal	Status	—	—	15	Self	—
TM34	Shock Wave	Electric	Special	60	—	20	Normal	—
TM35	Flamethrower	Fire	Special	95	100	15	Normal	—
TM37	Sandstorm	Rock	Status	—	—	10	All	—
TM38	Fire Blast	Fire	Special	120	85	5	Normal	—
TM39	Rock Tomb	Rock	Physical	50	80	10	Normal	—
TM40	Aerial Ace	Flying	Physical	60	—	20	Normal	—
TM41	Torment	Dark	Status	—	100	15	Normal	—
TM42	Facade	Normal	Physical	70	100	20	Normal	○
TM43	Secret Power	Normal	Physical	70	100	20	Normal	—
TM44	Rest	Psychic	Status	—	—	10	Self	—
TM45	Attract	Normal	Status	—	100	15	Normal	—
TM52	Focus Blast	Fighting	Special	120	70	5	Normal	—
TM56	Fling	Dark	Physical	—	100	10	Normal	○
TM58	Endure	Normal	Status	—	—	10	Self	—
TM59	Dragon Pulse	Dragon	Special	90	100	10	Normal	—
TM65	Shadow Claw	Ghost	Physical	70	100	15	Normal	○
TM66	Payback	Dark	Physical	50	100	10	Normal	○
TM68	Giga Impact	Normal	Physical	150	90	5	Normal	○
TM69	Rock Polish	Rock	Status	—	—	20	Self	—
TM71	Stone Edge	Rock	Physical	100	80	5	Normal	—
TM72	Avalanche	Ice	Physical	60	100	10	Normal	○
TM73	Thunder Wave	Electric	Status	—	100	20	Normal	—
TM76	Stealth Rock	Rock	Status	—	—	20	2 Foes	—
TM78	Captivate	Normal	Status	—	100	20	2 Foes	—
TM79	Dark Pulse	Dark	Special	80	100	15	Normal	—
TM80	Rock Slide	Rock	Physical	75	90	10	2 Foes	—
TM82	Sleep Talk	Normal	Status	—	—	10	Depends	—
TM83	Natural Gift	Normal	Physical	—	100	15	Normal	—
TM87	Swagger	Normal	Status	—	90	15	Normal	—
TM90	Substitute	Normal	Status	—	—	10	Self	—
HM01	Cut	Normal	Physical	50	95	30	Normal	○
HM03	Surf	Water	Special	95	100	15	2 Foes/1 Ally	—
HM04	Strength	Normal	Physical	80	100	15	Normal	○
HM05	Whirlpool	Water	Special	15	70	15	Normal	—
HM06	Rock Smash	Fighting	Physical	40	100	15	Normal	○
HM08	Rock Climb	Normal	Physical	90	85	20	Normal	○

◉ No. 248 | Armor Pokémon
Tyranitar

Rock **Dark**

- ● HEIGHT: 6'07"
- ● WEIGHT: 445.3 lbs.
- ● ITEMS: None

● SIZE COMPARISON

● MALE/FEMALE HAVE SAME FORM

◉ ABILITIES
● Sand Stream

◉ STATS
HP ●●●●
ATTACK ●●●●●●
DEFENSE ●●●●●
SP. ATTACK ●●●●
SP. DEFENSE ●●●●
SPEED ●●●

◉ EGG GROUPS
Monster

◉ PERFORMANCE
SPEED ★★
POWER ★★★★★
SKILL ★★★★
STAMINA ★★★★☆
JUMP ★★

● MAIN WAYS TO OBTAIN

Pokémon HeartGold — Level up Pupitar to Lv. 55

Pokémon SoulSilver — Level up Pupitar to Lv. 55

Pokémon Diamond — Level up Pupitar to Lv. 55

Pokémon Pearl — –

Pokémon Platinum — Level up Pupitar to Lv. 55

Pokémon HeartGold
Its body can't be harmed by any sort of attack, so it is very eager to make challenges against enemies.

Pokémon SoulSilver
Extremely strong, it can change the landscape. It has an insolent nature that makes it not care about others.

◉ EVOLUTION

Larvitar — Lv. 30 → Pupitar — Lv. 55 → Tyranitar

No. 249 | Diving Pokémon
Lugia

Psychic | Flying

- **HEIGHT:** 17'01"
- **WEIGHT:** 476.2 lbs.
- **ITEMS:** None

● SIZE COMPARISON

● GENDER UNKNOWN

⊙ ABILITIES
- Pressure

⊙ EGG GROUPS
No Egg has ever been discovered

⊙ STATS
HP	●●●●
ATTACK	●●●●
DEFENSE	●●●●
SP. ATTACK	●●●●
SP. DEFENSE	●●●●●●
SPEED	●●●●●

⊙ PERFORMANCE
SPEED ★★★★	STAMINA ★★★☆
POWER ★★★★☆	JUMP ★★★★★
SKILL ★★★☆	

● MAIN WAYS TO OBTAIN

Pokémon HeartGold	Appears in the Whirl Islands (after entering the Hall of Fame and receiving the Silver Wing in Pewter City)
Pokémon SoulSilver	Appears in the Whirl Islands
Pokémon Diamond	—
Pokémon Pearl	—
Pokémon Platinum	—

Pokémon HeartGold	Pokémon SoulSilver
It is said that it quietly spends its time deep at the bottom of the sea because its powers are too strong.	It is said to be the guardian of the seas. It is rumored to have been seen on the night of a storm.

⊙ EVOLUTION
Does not evolve

● LEVEL-UP MOVES
Lv.	Name	Type	Kind	Pow.	Acc.	PP	Range	DA
1	Whirlwind	Normal	Status	—	100	20	Normal	—
1	Weather Ball	Normal	Special	50	100	10	Normal	—
9	Gust	Flying	Special	40	100	35	Normal	—
15	Dragon Rush	Dragon	Physical	100	75	10	Normal	○
23	Extrasensory	Psychic	Special	80	100	30	Normal	—
29	Rain Dance	Water	Status	—	—	5	All	—
37	Hydro Pump	Water	Special	120	80	5	Normal	—
43	Aeroblast	Flying	Special	100	95	5	Normal	—
50	Punishment	Dark	Physical	—	100	5	Normal	○
57	AncientPower	Rock	Special	60	100	5	Normal	—
65	Safeguard	Normal	Status	—	—	25	2 Allies	—
71	Recover	Normal	Status	—	—	10	Self	—
79	Future Sight	Psychic	Special	80	90	10	Normal	—
85	Natural Gift	Normal	Physical	—	100	15	Normal	—
93	Calm Mind	Psychic	Status	—	—	20	Self	—
99	Sky Attack	Flying	Physical	140	90	5	Normal	—

● MOVE MANIAC
Name	Type	Kind	Pow.	Acc.	PP	Range	DA
Headbutt	Normal	Physical	70	100	15	Normal	○

● BP MOVES
Name	Type	Kind	Pow.	Acc.	PP	Range	DA
Dive	Water	Physical	80	100	10	Normal	○
Icy Wind	Ice	Special	55	95	15	2 Foes	—
Ominous Wind	Ghost	Special	60	100	5	Normal	—
Air Cutter	Flying	Special	55	95	25	2 Foes	—
Zen Headbutt	Psychic	Physical	80	90	15	Normal	○
Trick	Psychic	Status	—	100	10	Normal	—
Snore	Normal	Special	40	100	15	Normal	—
Swift	Normal	Special	60	—	20	2 Foes	—
Tailwind	Flying	Status	—	—	30	2 Allies	—
Mud-Slap	Ground	Special	20	100	10	Normal	—
Iron Head	Steel	Physical	80	100	15	Normal	○
Aqua Tail	Water	Physical	90	90	10	Normal	○
AncientPower	Rock	Special	60	100	5	Normal	—
Signal Beam	Bug	Special	75	100	15	Normal	—
Earth Power	Ground	Special	90	100	10	Normal	—
Twister	Dragon	Special	40	100	20	2 Foes	—
Sky Attack	Flying	Physical	140	90	5	Normal	—

● TM & HM MOVES
No.	Name	Type	Kind	Pow.	Acc.	PP	Range	DA
TM03	Water Pulse	Water	Special	60	100	20	Normal	—
TM04	Calm Mind	Psychic	Status	—	—	20	Self	—
TM05	Roar	Normal	Status	—	100	20	Normal	—
TM06	Toxic	Poison	Status	—	85	10	Normal	—
TM07	Hail	Ice	Status	—	—	10	All	—
TM10	Hidden Power	Normal	Special	—	100	15	Normal	—
TM11	Sunny Day	Fire	Status	—	—	5	All	—
TM13	Ice Beam	Ice	Special	95	100	10	Normal	—
TM14	Blizzard	Ice	Special	120	70	5	2 Foes	—
TM15	Hyper Beam	Normal	Special	150	90	5	Normal	—
TM16	Light Screen	Psychic	Status	—	—	30	2 Allies	—
TM17	Protect	Normal	Status	—	—	10	Self	—
TM18	Rain Dance	Water	Status	—	—	5	All	—
TM19	Giga Drain	Grass	Special	60	100	10	Normal	—
TM20	Safeguard	Normal	Status	—	—	25	2 Allies	—
TM21	Frustration	Normal	Physical	—	100	20	Normal	○
TM23	Iron Tail	Steel	Physical	100	75	15	Normal	○
TM24	Thunderbolt	Electric	Special	95	100	15	Normal	—
TM25	Thunder	Electric	Special	120	70	10	Normal	—
TM26	Earthquake	Ground	Physical	100	100	10	2 Foes/1 Ally	—
TM27	Return	Normal	Physical	—	100	20	Normal	○
TM29	Psychic	Psychic	Special	90	100	10	Normal	—
TM30	Shadow Ball	Ghost	Special	80	100	15	Normal	—
TM32	Double Team	Normal	Status	—	—	15	Self	—
TM33	Reflect	Psychic	Status	—	—	20	2 Allies	—
TM34	Shock Wave	Electric	Special	60	—	20	Normal	—
TM37	Sandstorm	Rock	Status	—	—	10	All	—
TM40	Aerial Ace	Flying	Physical	60	—	20	Normal	○
TM42	Facade	Normal	Physical	70	100	20	Normal	○
TM43	Secret Power	Normal	Physical	70	100	20	Normal	○
TM44	Rest	Psychic	Status	—	—	10	Self	—
TM47	Steel Wing	Steel	Physical	70	90	25	Normal	○
TM48	Skill Swap	Psychic	Status	—	—	10	Normal	—
TM51	Roost	Flying	Status	—	—	10	Self	—
TM55	Brine	Water	Special	65	100	10	Normal	—
TM57	Charge Beam	Electric	Special	50	90	10	Normal	—
TM58	Endure	Normal	Status	—	—	10	Self	—
TM59	Dragon Pulse	Dragon	Special	90	100	10	Normal	—
TM68	Giga Impact	Normal	Physical	150	90	5	Normal	○
TM70	Flash	Normal	Status	—	100	20	Normal	—
TM72	Avalanche	Ice	Physical	60	100	10	Normal	○
TM73	Thunder Wave	Electric	Status	—	100	20	Normal	—
TM77	Psych Up	Normal	Status	—	—	10	Normal	—
TM82	Sleep Talk	Normal	Status	—	—	10	Depends	—
TM83	Natural Gift	Normal	Physical	—	100	15	Normal	—
TM85	Dream Eater	Psychic	Special	100	100	15	Normal	—
TM87	Swagger	Normal	Status	—	90	15	Normal	—
TM90	Substitute	Normal	Status	—	—	10	Self	—
HM02	Fly	Flying	Physical	90	95	15	Normal	○
HM03	Surf	Water	Special	95	100	15	2 Foes/1 Ally	—
HM04	Strength	Normal	Physical	80	100	15	Normal	○
HM05	Whirlpool	Water	Special	15	70	15	Normal	—
HM06	Rock Smash	Fighting	Physical	40	100	15	Normal	○
HM07	Waterfall	Water	Physical	80	100	15	Normal	○

● LEVEL-UP MOVES

Lv.	Name	Type	Kind	Pow.	Acc.	PP	Range	DA
1	Whirlwind	Normal	Status	—	100	20	Normal	—
1	Weather Ball	Normal	Special	50	100	10	Normal	—
9	Gust	Flying	Special	40	100	35	Normal	—
15	Brave Bird	Flying	Physical	120	100	15	Normal	○
23	Extrasensory	Psychic	Special	80	100	30	Normal	—
29	Sunny Day	Fire	Status	—	—	5	All	—
37	Fire Blast	Fire	Special	120	85	5	Normal	—
43	Sacred Fire	Fire	Physical	100	95	5	Normal	—
50	Punishment	Dark	Physical	—	100	5	Normal	○
57	AncientPower	Rock	Special	60	100	5	Normal	—
65	Safeguard	Normal	Status	—	—	25	2 Allies	—
71	Recover	Normal	Status	—	—	10	Self	—
79	Future Sight	Psychic	Special	80	90	5	Normal	—
85	Natural Gift	Normal	Physical	—	100	15	Normal	—
93	Calm Mind	Psychic	Status	—	—	20	Self	—
99	Sky Attack	Flying	Physical	140	90	5	Normal	—

● MOVE MANIAC

Name	Type	Kind	Pow.	Acc.	PP	Range	DA

● BP MOVES

Name	Type	Kind	Pow.	Acc.	PP	Range	DA
Ominous Wind	Ghost	Special	60	100	5	Normal	—
Air Cutter	Flying	Special	55	95	25	2 Foes	—
Zen Headbutt	Psychic	Physical	80	90	15	Normal	○
Snore	Normal	Special	40	100	15	Normal	—
Swift	Normal	Special	60	—	20	2 Foes	—
Tailwind	Flying	Status	—	—	30	2 Allies	—
Mud-Slap	Ground	Special	20	100	10	Normal	—
Iron Head	Steel	Physical	80	100	15	Normal	○
AncientPower	Rock	Special	60	100	5	Normal	—
Signal Beam	Bug	Special	75	100	15	Normal	—
Earth Power	Ground	Special	90	100	10	Normal	—
Twister	Dragon	Special	40	100	20	2 Foes	—
Heat Wave	Fire	Special	100	90	10	2 Foes	—
Sky Attack	Flying	Physical	140	90	5	Normal	—

● TM & HM MOVES

No.	Name	Type	Kind	Pow.	Acc.	PP	Range	DA
TM04	Calm Mind	Psychic	Status	—	—	20	Self	—
TM05	Roar	Normal	Status	—	100	20	Normal	—
TM06	Toxic	Poison	Status	—	85	10	Normal	—
TM10	Hidden Power	Normal	Special	—	100	15	Normal	—
TM11	Sunny Day	Fire	Status	—	—	5	All	—
TM15	Hyper Beam	Normal	Special	150	90	5	Normal	—
TM16	Light Screen	Psychic	Status	—	—	30	2 Allies	—
TM17	Protect	Normal	Status	—	—	10	Self	—
TM18	Rain Dance	Water	Status	—	—	5	All	—
TM19	Giga Drain	Grass	Special	60	100	10	Normal	—
TM20	Safeguard	Normal	Status	—	—	25	2 Allies	—
TM21	Frustration	Normal	Physical	—	100	20	Normal	○
TM22	SolarBeam	Grass	Special	120	100	10	Normal	—
TM24	Thunderbolt	Electric	Special	95	100	15	Normal	—
TM25	Thunder	Electric	Special	120	70	10	Normal	—
TM26	Earthquake	Ground	Physical	100	100	10	2 Foes/1 Ally	—
TM27	Return	Normal	Physical	—	100	20	Normal	○
TM29	Psychic	Psychic	Special	90	100	10	Normal	—
TM30	Shadow Ball	Ghost	Special	80	100	15	Normal	—
TM32	Double Team	Normal	Status	—	—	15	Self	—
TM33	Reflect	Psychic	Status	—	—	20	2 Allies	—
TM34	Shock Wave	Electric	Special	60	—	20	Normal	—
TM35	Flamethrower	Fire	Special	95	100	15	Normal	—
TM37	Sandstorm	Rock	Status	—	—	10	All	—
TM38	Fire Blast	Fire	Special	120	85	5	Normal	—
TM40	Aerial Ace	Flying	Physical	60	—	20	Normal	○
TM42	Facade	Normal	Physical	70	100	20	Normal	○
TM43	Secret Power	Normal	Physical	70	100	20	Normal	—
TM44	Rest	Psychic	Status	—	—	10	Self	—
TM47	Steel Wing	Steel	Physical	70	90	25	Normal	○
TM50	Overheat	Fire	Special	140	90	5	Normal	—
TM51	Roost	Flying	Status	—	—	10	Self	—
TM57	Charge Beam	Electric	Special	50	90	10	Normal	—
TM58	Endure	Normal	Status	—	—	10	Self	—
TM61	Will-O-Wisp	Fire	Status	—	75	15	Normal	—
TM68	Giga Impact	Normal	Physical	150	90	5	Normal	○
TM70	Flash	Normal	Status	—	100	20	Normal	—
TM73	Thunder Wave	Electric	Status	—	100	20	Normal	—
TM77	Psych Up	Normal	Status	—	—	10	Self	—
TM82	Sleep Talk	Normal	Status	—	—	10	Depends	—
TM83	Natural Gift	Normal	Physical	—	100	15	Normal	—
TM85	Dream Eater	Psychic	Special	100	100	15	Normal	—
TM87	Swagger	Normal	Status	—	90	15	Normal	—
TM88	Pluck	Flying	Physical	60	100	20	Normal	○
TM90	Substitute	Normal	Status	—	—	10	Self	—
HM02	Fly	Flying	Physical	90	95	15	Normal	○
HM04	Strength	Normal	Physical	80	100	15	Normal	○
HM06	Rock Smash	Fighting	Physical	40	100	15	Normal	○

◉ No. 250 | Rainbow Pokémon

Ho-Oh

Fire Flying

- **HEIGHT:** 12'06"
- **WEIGHT:** 438.7 lbs.
- **ITEMS:** None

● SIZE COMPARISON

● GENDER UNKNOWN

◉ ABILITIES
- Pressure

◉ STATS
- HP ●●●●○
- ATTACK ●●●●●
- DEFENSE ●●●●○
- SP. ATTACK ●●●●●
- SP. DEFENSE ●●●●●●
- SPEED ●●●●○

◉ EGG GROUPS
No Egg has ever been discovered

◉ PERFORMANCE
- SPEED ★★★★
- POWER ★★★☆
- SKILL ★★★★☆
- STAMINA ★★★☆
- JUMP ★★★★★

● MAIN WAYS TO OBTAIN

Pokémon HeartGold — Appears at Bell Tower

Pokémon SoulSilver — Appears at Bell Tower (after entering the Hall of Fame and receiving the Rainbow Wing in Pewter City)

Pokémon Diamond — —

Pokémon Pearl — —

Pokémon Platinum — —

Pokémon HeartGold
Legends claim this Pokémon flies the world's skies continuously on its magnificent, seven-colored wings.

Pokémon SoulSilver
A legend says that its body glows in seven colors. A rainbow is said to form behind it when it flies.

◉ EVOLUTION
Does not evolve

No. 251 | Time Travel Pokémon
Celebi

Psychic | Grass

● HEIGHT: 2'00"
● WEIGHT: 11.0 lbs.
● ITEMS: None

● SIZE COMPARISON

● GENDER UNKNOWN

● LEVEL-UP MOVES

Lv.	Name	Type	Kind	Pow.	Acc.	PP	Range	DA
1	Leech Seed	Grass	Status	—	90	10	Normal	—
1	Confusion	Psychic	Special	50	100	25	Normal	—
1	Recover	Normal	Status	—	—	10	Self	—
1	Heal Bell	Normal	Status	—	—	5	All Allies	—
10	Safeguard	Normal	Status	—	—	25	2 Allies	—
19	Magical Leaf	Grass	Special	60	—	20	Normal	—
28	AncientPower	Rock	Special	60	100	5	Normal	—
37	Baton Pass	Normal	Status	—	—	40	Self	—
46	Natural Gift	Normal	Physical	—	100	15	Normal	—
55	Heal Block	Psychic	Status	—	100	15	2 Foes	—
64	Future Sight	Psychic	Special	80	90	15	Normal	—
73	Healing Wish	Psychic	Status	—	—	10	Self	—
82	Leaf Storm	Grass	Special	140	90	5	Normal	—
91	Perish Song	Normal	Status	—	—	5	All	—

● MOVE MANIAC

Name	Type	Kind	Pow.	Acc.	PP	Range	DA

● BP MOVES

Name	Type	Kind	Pow.	Acc.	PP	Range	DA
Zen Headbutt	Psychic	Physical	80	90	15	Normal	○
Trick	Psychic	Status	—	100	10	Normal	—
Sucker Punch	Dark	Physical	80	100	5	Normal	○
Snore	Normal	Special	40	100	15	Normal	—
Helping Hand	Normal	Status	—	—	20	1 Ally	—
Synthesis	Grass	Status	—	—	5	Self	—
Last Resort	Normal	Physical	130	100	5	Normal	○
Swift	Normal	Special	60	—	20	2 Foes	—
Uproar	Normal	Special	50	100	10	1 Random	—
Worry Seed	Grass	Status	—	100	10	Normal	—
Magic Coat	Psychic	Status	—	—	15	Self	—
Heal Bell	Normal	Status	—	—	5	All Allies	—
Mud-Slap	Ground	Special	20	100	10	Normal	—
AncientPower	Rock	Special	60	100	5	Normal	—
Signal Beam	Bug	Special	75	100	15	Normal	—
Earth Power	Ground	Special	90	100	10	Normal	—
Seed Bomb	Grass	Physical	80	100	15	Normal	—

● ABILITIES

● Natural Cure

● STATS

HP	●●●●
ATTACK	●●●●
DEFENSE	●●●●
SP. ATTACK	●●●●
SP. DEFENSE	●●●●
SPEED	●●●●

● EGG GROUPS

No Egg has ever been discovered

● PERFORMANCE

SPEED ★★★★★
POWER ★☆☆
SKILL ★★★★★
STAMINA ★★☆
JUMP ★★★★★

● MAIN WAYS TO OBTAIN

Pokémon HeartGold
Migrate it through the Pal Park—cannot be obtained through regular gameplay*

Pokémon SoulSilver
Migrate it through the Pal Park—cannot be obtained through regular gameplay*

Pokémon Diamond
Migrate it through the Pal Park—cannot be obtained through regular gameplay*

Pokémon Pearl
Migrate it through the Pal Park—cannot be obtained through regular gameplay*

Pokémon Platinum
Migrate it through the Pal Park—cannot be obtained through regular gameplay*

Pokémon HeartGold
This Pokémon wanders across time. Grass and trees flourish in the forests in which it has appeared.

Pokémon SoulSilver
When CELEBI disappears deep in a forest, it is said to leave behind an egg brought from the future.

● EVOLUTION

Does not evolve

● TM & HM MOVES

No.	Name	Type	Kind	Pow.	Acc.	PP	Range	DA
TM03	Water Pulse	Water	Special	60	100	20	Normal	—
TM04	Calm Mind	Psychic	Status	—	—	20	Self	—
TM06	Toxic	Poison	Status	—	85	10	Normal	—
TM10	Hidden Power	Normal	Special	—	100	15	Normal	—
TM11	Sunny Day	Fire	Status	—	—	5	All	—
TM15	Hyper Beam	Normal	Special	150	90	5	Normal	—
TM16	Light Screen	Psychic	Status	—	—	30	2 Allies	—
TM17	Protect	Normal	Status	—	—	10	Self	—
TM18	Rain Dance	Water	Status	—	—	5	All	—
TM19	Giga Drain	Grass	Special	60	100	10	Normal	—
TM20	Safeguard	Normal	Status	—	—	25	2 Allies	—
TM21	Frustration	Normal	Physical	—	100	20	Normal	○
TM22	SolarBeam	Grass	Special	120	100	10	Normal	—
TM27	Return	Normal	Physical	—	100	20	Normal	○
TM29	Psychic	Psychic	Special	90	100	10	Normal	—
TM30	Shadow Ball	Ghost	Special	80	100	15	Normal	—
TM32	Double Team	Normal	Status	—	—	15	Self	—
TM33	Reflect	Psychic	Status	—	—	20	2 Allies	—
TM34	Shock Wave	Electric	Special	60	—	20	Normal	—
TM37	Sandstorm	Rock	Status	—	—	10	All	—
TM40	Aerial Ace	Flying	Physical	60	—	20	Normal	○
TM42	Facade	Normal	Physical	70	100	20	Normal	○
TM43	Secret Power	Normal	Physical	70	100	20	Normal	○
TM44	Rest	Psychic	Status	—	—	10	Self	—
TM48	Skill Swap	Psychic	Status	—	—	10	Normal	—
TM53	Energy Ball	Grass	Special	80	100	10	Normal	—
TM56	Fling	Dark	Physical	—	100	10	Normal	—
TM57	Charge Beam	Electric	Special	50	90	10	Normal	—
TM58	Endure	Normal	Status	—	—	10	Self	—
TM62	Silver Wind	Bug	Special	60	100	5	Normal	—
TM68	Giga Impact	Normal	Physical	150	90	5	Normal	○
TM70	Flash	Normal	Status	—	100	20	Normal	—
TM73	Thunder Wave	Electric	Status	—	100	20	Normal	—
TM75	Swords Dance	Normal	Status	—	—	30	Self	—
TM76	Stealth Rock	Rock	Status	—	—	20	2 Foes	—
TM77	Psych Up	Normal	Status	—	—	10	Normal	—
TM82	Sleep Talk	Normal	Status	—	—	10	Depends	—
TM83	Natural Gift	Normal	Physical	—	100	15	Normal	—
TM85	Dream Eater	Psychic	Special	100	100	15	Normal	—
TM86	Grass Knot	Grass	Special	—	100	20	Normal	○
TM87	Swagger	Normal	Status	—	90	15	Normal	—
TM89	U-turn	Bug	Physical	70	100	20	Normal	○
TM90	Substitute	Normal	Status	—	—	10	Self	—
TM92	Trick Room	Psychic	Status	—	—	5	All	—
HM01	Cut	Normal	Physical	50	95	30	Normal	○

*Only available through distribution at special events and not through regular gameplay. Check Pokemon.com for the latest news on how to catch this Pokémon.

● LEVEL-UP MOVES

Lv.	Name	Type	Kind	Pow.	Acc.	PP	Range	DA
1	Ingrain	Grass	Status	—	—	20	Self	—
1	Constrict	Normal	Physical	10	100	35	Normal	○
5	Sleep Powder	Grass	Status	—	75	15	Normal	—
8	Absorb	Grass	Special	20	100	25	Normal	—
12	Growth	Normal	Status	—	—	40	Self	—
15	PoisonPowder	Poison	Status	—	75	35	Normal	—
19	Vine Whip	Grass	Physical	35	100	15	Normal	○
22	Bind	Normal	Physical	15	75	20	Normal	○
26	Mega Drain	Grass	Special	40	100	15	Normal	—
29	Stun Spore	Grass	Status	—	75	30	Normal	—
33	AncientPower	Rock	Special	60	100	5	Normal	—
36	Knock Off	Dark	Physical	20	100	20	Normal	○
40	Natural Gift	Normal	Physical	—	100	15	Normal	○
43	Slam	Normal	Physical	80	75	20	Normal	○
47	Tickle	Normal	Status	—	100	20	Normal	—
50	Wring Out	Normal	Special	—	100	5	Normal	○
54	Power Whip	Grass	Physical	120	85	10	Normal	○

● MOVE MANIAC

Name	Type	Kind	Pow.	Acc.	PP	Range	DA
Headbutt	Normal	Physical	70	100	15	Normal	○

● BP MOVES

Name	Type	Kind	Pow.	Acc.	PP	Range	DA
Knock Off	Dark	Physical	20	100	20	Normal	○
Snore	Normal	Special	40	100	15	Normal	—
Synthesis	Grass	Status	—	—	5	Self	—
Worry Seed	Grass	Status	—	100	10	Normal	—
AncientPower	Rock	Special	60	100	5	Normal	—
Seed Bomb	Grass	Physical	80	100	15	Normal	—
Pain Split	Normal	Status	—	—	20	Normal	—

● TM & HM MOVES

No.	Name	Type	Kind	Pow.	Acc.	PP	Range	DA
TM01	Focus Punch	Fighting	Physical	150	100	20	Normal	○
TM06	Toxic	Poison	Status	—	85	10	Normal	—
TM09	Bullet Seed	Grass	Physical	10	100	30	Normal	—
TM10	Hidden Power	Normal	Special	—	100	15	Normal	—
TM11	Sunny Day	Fire	Status	—	—	5	All	—
TM17	Protect	Normal	Status	—	—	10	Self	—
TM19	Giga Drain	Grass	Special	60	100	10	Normal	—
TM20	Safeguard	Normal	Status	—	—	25	2 Allies	—
TM21	Frustration	Normal	Physical	—	100	20	Normal	○
TM22	SolarBeam	Grass	Special	120	100	10	Normal	—
TM23	Iron Tail	Steel	Physical	100	75	15	Normal	○
TM27	Return	Normal	Physical	—	100	20	Normal	○
TM28	Dig	Ground	Physical	80	100	10	Normal	○
TM31	Brick Break	Fighting	Physical	75	100	15	Normal	○
TM32	Double Team	Normal	Status	—	—	15	Self	—
TM39	Rock Tomb	Rock	Physical	50	80	10	Normal	—
TM40	Aerial Ace	Flying	Physical	60	—	20	Normal	○
TM42	Facade	Normal	Physical	70	100	20	Normal	○
TM43	Secret Power	Normal	Physical	70	100	20	Normal	○
TM44	Rest	Psychic	Status	—	—	10	Self	—
TM45	Attract	Normal	Status	—	100	15	Normal	—
TM53	Energy Ball	Grass	Special	80	100	10	Normal	—
TM56	Fling	Dark	Physical	—	100	10	Normal	○
TM58	Endure	Normal	Status	—	—	10	Self	—
TM60	Drain Punch	Fighting	Physical	60	100	5	Normal	○
TM70	Flash	Normal	Status	—	100	20	Normal	—
TM75	Swords Dance	Normal	Status	—	—	30	Self	—
TM78	Captivate	Normal	Status	—	100	20	2 Foes	—
TM80	Rock Slide	Rock	Physical	75	90	10	2 Foes	—
TM82	Sleep Talk	Normal	Status	—	—	10	Depends	—
TM83	Natural Gift	Normal	Physical	—	100	15	Normal	—
TM86	Grass Knot	Grass	Special	—	100	20	Normal	—
TM87	Swagger	Normal	Status	—	90	15	Normal	—
TM90	Substitute	Normal	Status	—	—	10	Self	—
HM01	Cut	Normal	Physical	50	95	30	Normal	○
HM04	Strength	Normal	Physical	80	100	15	Normal	○
HM06	Rock Smash	Fighting	Physical	40	100	15	Normal	○

● EGG MOVES

Name	Type	Kind	Pow.	Acc.	PP	Range	DA
Crunch	Dark	Physical	80	100	15	Normal	○
Mud Sport	Ground	Status	—	—	15	All	—
Endeavor	Normal	Physical	—	100	5	Normal	○
Leech Seed	Grass	Status	—	90	10	Normal	—
DragonBreath	Dragon	Special	60	100	20	Normal	—
Crush Claw	Normal	Physical	75	95	10	Normal	○
Worry Seed	Grass	Status	—	100	10	Normal	—
Double Kick	Fighting	Physical	30	100	30	Normal	○
GrassWhistle	Grass	Status	—	55	15	Normal	—
Synthesis	Grass	Status	—	—	5	Self	—
Magical Leaf	Grass	Special	60	—	20	Normal	—
Leaf Storm	Grass	Special	140	90	5	Normal	—
Razor Wind	Normal	Special	80	100	10	2 Foes	—

⬤ No. 252 | Wood Gecko Pokémon
Treecko

Grass

- ● HEIGHT: 1'08"
- ● WEIGHT: 11.0 lbs.
- ● ITEMS: None

● SIZE COMPARISON

● MALE/FEMALE HAVE SAME FORM

⊚ ABILITIES
- ● Overgrow

⊚ STATS
- HP ●
- ATTACK ●●
- DEFENSE ●●●
- SP. ATTACK ●●●
- SP. DEFENSE ●●●
- SPEED ●●●

⊚ EGG GROUPS
Monster

Dragon

⊚ PERFORMANCE
- SPEED ★★★★★
- STAMINA ★★
- POWER ★★☆
- JUMP ★★☆
- SKILL ★★★★☆

● MAIN WAYS TO OBTAIN

Pokémon HeartGold — Receive from Steven at Silph Co. in Saffron City [after defeating Red]

Pokémon SoulSilver — Receive from Steven at Silph Co. in Saffron City [after defeating Red]

Pokémon Diamond — —

Pokémon Pearl — —

Pokémon Platinum — —

Pokémon HeartGold — Small hooks on the bottom of its feet catch on walls and ceilings. That is how it can hang from above.

Pokémon SoulSilver — Small hooks on the bottom of its feet catch on walls and ceilings. That is how it can hang from above.

⊚ EVOLUTION

Treecko — Lv. 16 → Grovyle — Lv. 36 → Sceptile

Grovyle

Grass

● HEIGHT: 1'08"
● WEIGHT: 11.0 lbs.
● ITEMS: None

● SIZE COMPARISON

● MALE/FEMALE HAVE SAME FORM

● LEVEL-UP MOVES

Lv.	Name	Type	Kind	Pow.	Acc.	PP	Range	DA
1	Pound	Normal	Physical	40	100	35	Normal	○
1	Leer	Normal	Status	—	100	30	2 Foes	—
1	Absorb	Grass	Special	20	100	25	Normal	—
1	Quick Attack	Normal	Physical	40	100	30	Normal	○
6	Absorb	Grass	Special	20	100	25	Normal	—
11	Quick Attack	Normal	Physical	40	100	30	Normal	○
16	Fury Cutter	Bug	Physical	10	95	20	Normal	○
17	Pursuit	Dark	Physical	40	100	20	Normal	○
23	Screech	Normal	Status	—	85	40	Normal	—
29	Leaf Blade	Grass	Physical	90	100	15	Normal	○
35	Agility	Psychic	Status	—	—	30	Self	—
41	Slam	Normal	Physical	80	75	20	Normal	○
47	Detect	Fighting	Status	—	—	5	Self	—
53	False Swipe	Normal	Physical	40	100	40	Normal	○
59	Leaf Storm	Grass	Special	140	90	5	Normal	—

● MOVE MANIAC

Name	Type	Kind	Pow.	Acc.	PP	Range	DA
Headbutt	Normal	Physical	70	100	15	Normal	○

● BP MOVES

Name	Type	Kind	Pow.	Acc.	PP	Range	DA
Fury Cutter	Bug	Physical	10	95	20	Normal	○
ThunderPunch	Electric	Physical	75	100	15	Normal	○
Snore	Normal	Special	40	100	15	Normal	—
Synthesis	Grass	Status	—	—	5	Self	—
Swift	Normal	Special	60	—	20	2 Foes	—
Worry Seed	Grass	Status	—	100	10	Normal	—
Mud-Slap	Ground	Special	20	100	10	Normal	—
Endeavor	Normal	Physical	—	100	5	Normal	○
Seed Bomb	Grass	Physical	80	100	15	Normal	○
Low Kick	Fighting	Physical	—	100	20	Normal	○

● ABILITIES
● Overgrow

● STATS
HP ●●
ATTACK ●●●
DEFENSE ●●
SP. ATTACK ●●●
SP. DEFENSE ●●●
SPEED ●●●●

● EGG GROUPS
Monster

Dragon

● PERFORMANCE
SPEED ★★★★☆　STAMINA ★★★☆
POWER ★★☆☆　JUMP ★★★★
SKILL ★★★★☆

● MAIN WAYS TO OBTAIN

Pokémon HeartGold — Level up Treecko to Lv. 16

Pokémon SoulSilver — Level up Treecko to Lv. 16

Pokémon Diamond — —

Pokémon Pearl — —

Pokémon Platinum — —

Pokémon HeartGold — It leaps from tree branch to tree branch quite swiftly. It shows astounding agility.

Pokémon SoulSilver — It leaps from tree branch to tree branch quite swiftly. It shows astounding agility.

● EVOLUTION

Treecko　　Lv. 16　Grovyle　　Lv. 36　　Sceptile

● TM & HM MOVES

No.	Name	Type	Kind	Pow.	Acc.	PP	Range	DA
TM01	Focus Punch	Fighting	Physical	150	100	20	Normal	○
TM06	Toxic	Poison	Status	—	85	10	Normal	—
TM09	Bullet Seed	Grass	Physical	10	100	30	Normal	—
TM10	Hidden Power	Normal	Special	—	100	15	Normal	—
TM11	Sunny Day	Fire	Status	—	—	5	All	—
TM17	Protect	Normal	Status	—	—	10	Self	—
TM19	Giga Drain	Grass	Special	60	100	10	Normal	—
TM20	Safeguard	Normal	Status	—	—	25	2 Allies	—
TM21	Frustration	Normal	Physical	—	100	20	Normal	○
TM22	SolarBeam	Grass	Special	120	100	10	Normal	—
TM23	Iron Tail	Steel	Physical	100	75	15	Normal	○
TM27	Return	Normal	Physical	—	100	20	Normal	○
TM28	Dig	Ground	Physical	80	100	10	Normal	○
TM31	Brick Break	Fighting	Physical	75	100	15	Normal	○
TM32	Double Team	Normal	Status	—	—	15	Self	—
TM39	Rock Tomb	Rock	Physical	50	80	10	Normal	○
TM40	Aerial Ace	Flying	Physical	60	—	20	Normal	○
TM42	Facade	Normal	Physical	70	100	20	Normal	○
TM43	Secret Power	Normal	Physical	70	100	20	Normal	○
TM44	Rest	Psychic	Status	—	—	10	Self	—
TM45	Attract	Normal	Status	—	100	20	Normal	—
TM53	Energy Ball	Grass	Special	80	100	10	Normal	—
TM54	False Swipe	Normal	Physical	40	100	40	Normal	○
TM56	Fling	Dark	Physical	—	100	10	Normal	○
TM58	Endure	Normal	Status	—	—	10	Self	—
TM60	Drain Punch	Fighting	Physical	60	100	5	Normal	○
TM70	Flash	Normal	Status	—	100	20	Normal	—
TM75	Swords Dance	Normal	Status	—	—	30	Self	—
TM78	Captivate	Normal	Status	—	100	20	2 Foes	—
TM80	Rock Slide	Rock	Physical	75	90	10	2 Foes	○
TM81	X-Scissor	Bug	Physical	80	100	15	Normal	○
TM82	Sleep Talk	Normal	Status	—	—	10	Depends	—
TM83	Natural Gift	Normal	Physical	—	100	15	Normal	—
TM86	Grass Knot	Grass	Special	—	100	20	Normal	○
TM87	Swagger	Normal	Status	—	90	15	Normal	—
TM90	Substitute	Normal	Status	—	—	10	Self	—
HM01	Cut	Normal	Physical	50	95	30	Normal	○
HM04	Strength	Normal	Physical	80	100	15	Normal	○
HM06	Rock Smash	Fighting	Physical	40	100	15	Normal	○

● LEVEL-UP MOVES

Lv.	Name	Type	Kind	Pow.	Acc.	PP	Range	DA
1	Night Slash	Dark	Physical	70	100	15	Normal	○
1	Pound	Normal	Physical	40	100	35	Normal	○
1	Leer	Normal	Status	—	100	30	2 Foes	○
1	Absorb	Grass	Special	20	100	25	Normal	—
1	Quick Attack	Normal	Physical	40	100	30	Normal	○
6	Absorb	Grass	Special	20	100	25	Normal	—
11	Quick Attack	Normal	Physical	40	100	30	Normal	○
16	X-Scissor	Bug	Physical	80	100	15	Normal	○
17	Pursuit	Dark	Physical	40	100	20	Normal	○
23	Screech	Normal	Status	—	85	40	Normal	—
29	Leaf Blade	Grass	Physical	90	100	15	Normal	○
35	Agility	Psychic	Status	—	—	30	Self	—
43	Slam	Normal	Physical	80	75	20	Normal	○
51	Detect	Fighting	Status	—	—	5	Self	—
59	False Swipe	Normal	Physical	40	100	40	Normal	—
67	Leaf Storm	Grass	Special	140	90	5	Normal	—

● MOVE MANIAC

Name	Type	Kind	Pow.	Acc.	PP	Range	DA
Headbutt	Normal	Physical	70	100	15	Normal	○
Frenzy Plant	Grass	Special	150	90	5	Normal	—

● BP MOVES

Name	Type	Kind	Pow.	Acc.	PP	Range	DA
Fury Cutter	Bug	Physical	10	95	20	Normal	○
ThunderPunch	Electric	Physical	75	100	15	Normal	○
Snore	Normal	Special	40	100	15	Normal	—
Swift	Normal	Special	60	—	20	2 Foes	—
Synthesis	Grass	Status	—	—	5	Self	—
Worry Seed	Grass	Status	—	100	10	Normal	—
Mud-Slap	Ground	Special	20	100	10	Normal	○
Endeavor	Normal	Physical	—	100	5	Normal	○
Outrage	Dragon	Physical	120	100	15	1 Random	○
Seed Bomb	Grass	Physical	80	100	15	Normal	○
Low Kick	Fighting	Physical	—	100	20	Normal	○

● TM & HM MOVES

No.	Name	Type	Kind	Pow.	Acc.	PP	Range	DA
TM01	Focus Punch	Fighting	Physical	150	100	20	Normal	○
TM02	Dragon Claw	Dragon	Physical	80	100	15	Normal	○
TM05	Roar	Normal	Status	—	100	20	Normal	—
TM06	Toxic	Poison	Status	—	85	10	Normal	—
TM09	Bullet Seed	Grass	Physical	10	100	30	Normal	○
TM10	Hidden Power	Normal	Special	—	100	15	Normal	—
TM11	Sunny Day	Fire	Status	—	—	5	All	—
TM15	Hyper Beam	Normal	Special	150	90	5	Normal	—
TM17	Protect	Normal	Status	—	—	10	Self	—
TM19	Giga Drain	Grass	Special	60	100	10	Normal	—
TM20	Safeguard	Normal	Status	—	—	25	2 Allies	—
TM21	Frustration	Normal	Physical	—	100	20	Normal	○
TM22	SolarBeam	Grass	Special	120	100	10	Normal	—
TM23	Iron Tail	Steel	Physical	100	75	15	Normal	○
TM26	Earthquake	Ground	Physical	100	100	10	2 Foes/1 Ally	—
TM27	Return	Normal	Physical	—	100	20	Normal	○
TM28	Dig	Ground	Physical	80	100	10	Normal	○
TM31	Brick Break	Fighting	Physical	75	100	15	Normal	○
TM32	Double Team	Normal	Status	—	—	15	Self	—
TM39	Rock Tomb	Rock	Physical	50	80	10	Normal	○
TM40	Aerial Ace	Flying	Physical	60	—	20	Normal	○
TM42	Facade	Normal	Physical	70	100	20	Normal	○
TM43	Secret Power	Normal	Physical	70	100	20	Normal	○
TM44	Rest	Psychic	Status	—	—	10	Self	—
TM45	Attract	Normal	Status	—	100	15	Normal	—
TM52	Focus Blast	Fighting	Special	120	70	5	Normal	○
TM53	Energy Ball	Grass	Special	80	100	10	Normal	—
TM54	False Swipe	Normal	Physical	40	100	40	Normal	—
TM56	Fling	Dark	Physical	—	100	10	Normal	○
TM58	Endure	Normal	Status	—	—	10	Self	—
TM59	Dragon Pulse	Dragon	Special	90	100	10	Normal	—
TM60	Drain Punch	Fighting	Physical	60	100	5	Normal	○
TM68	Giga Impact	Normal	Physical	150	90	5	Normal	○
TM70	Flash	Normal	Status	—	100	20	Normal	—
TM75	Swords Dance	Normal	Status	—	—	30	Self	—
TM78	Captivate	Normal	Status	—	100	20	2 Foes	—
TM80	Rock Slide	Rock	Physical	75	90	10	2 Foes	—
TM81	X-Scissor	Bug	Physical	80	100	15	Normal	○
TM82	Sleep Talk	Normal	Status	—	—	10	Depends	—
TM83	Natural Gift	Normal	Physical	—	100	15	Normal	—
TM86	Grass Knot	Grass	Special	—	100	20	Normal	○
TM87	Swagger	Normal	Status	—	90	15	Normal	—
TM90	Substitute	Normal	Status	—	—	10	Self	—
HM01	Cut	Normal	Physical	50	95	30	Normal	○
HM04	Strength	Normal	Physical	80	100	15	Normal	○
HM06	Rock Smash	Fighting	Physical	40	100	15	Normal	○
HM08	Rock Climb	Normal	Physical	90	85	20	Normal	○

● No. 254 | Forest Pokémon
Sceptile

Grass

- ● HEIGHT: 5'07"
- ● WEIGHT: 115.1 lbs.
- ● ITEMS: None

● SIZE COMPARISON

● MALE/FEMALE HAVE SAME FORM

● ABILITIES
- ● Overgrow

● STATS
HP	●●●
ATTACK	●●●●
DEFENSE	●●●
SP. ATTACK	●●●●●
SP. DEFENSE	●●●●
SPEED	●●●●●

● EGG GROUPS
Monster

Dragon

● PERFORMANCE
SPEED ★★★★ STAMINA ★★☆☆
POWER ★★★★☆ JUMP ★★★☆
SKILL ★★★★☆

● MAIN WAYS TO OBTAIN

Pokémon HeartGold Level up Grovyle to Lv. 36

Pokémon SoulSilver Level up Grovyle to Lv. 36

Pokémon Diamond —

Pokémon Pearl —

Pokémon Platinum —

Pokémon HeartGold
It agilely leaps about the jungle and uses the sharp leaves on its arms to strike its prey.

Pokémon SoulSilver
It agilely leaps about the jungle and uses the sharp leaves on its arms to strike its prey.

● EVOLUTION

Lv. 16 Lv. 36

Treecko Grovyle Sceptile

No. 255 | Torchic
Chick Pokémon

Fire

- **HEIGHT:** 1'04"
- **WEIGHT:** 5.5 lbs.
- **ITEMS:** None

● SIZE COMPARISON

● MALE FORM
Small speck on rear

● FEMALE FORM
No speck

⊛ ABILITIES
- Blaze

⊛ STATS
- HP ●●
- ATTACK ●●●
- DEFENSE ●●
- SP. ATTACK ●●●
- SP. DEFENSE ●●
- SPEED ●●

⊛ EGG GROUPS
Field

⊛ PERFORMANCE
SPEED ★★★★☆	STAMINA ★★☆☆
POWER ★★☆☆	JUMP ★★☆☆☆
SKILL ★★☆☆☆	

● MAIN WAYS TO OBTAIN

Pokémon HeartGold	Receive from Steven at Silph Co. in Saffron City (after defeating Red)
Pokémon SoulSilver	Receive from Steven at Silph Co. in Saffron City (after defeating Red)
Pokémon Diamond	—
Pokémon Pearl	—
Pokémon Platinum	—

Pokémon HeartGold	Pokémon SoulSilver
Inside its body is a place where it keeps a small flame. Hug it! It will be as warm as a hot-water bottle.	Inside its body is a place where it keeps a small flame. Hug it! It will be as warm as a hot-water bottle.

⊛ EVOLUTION

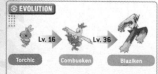

Torchic → Lv. 16 → Combueken → Lv. 36 → Blaziken

● LEVEL-UP MOVES
Lv.	Name	Type	Kind	Pow.	Acc.	PP	Range	DA
1	Scratch	Normal	Physical	40	100	35	Normal	○
1	Growl	Normal	Status	—	100	40	2 Foes	—
7	Focus Energy	Normal	Status	—	—	30	Self	—
10	Ember	Fire	Special	40	100	25	Normal	—
16	Peck	Flying	Physical	35	100	35	Normal	○
19	Sand-Attack	Ground	Status	—	100	15	Normal	—
25	Fire Spin	Fire	Special	15	70	15	Normal	—
28	Quick Attack	Normal	Physical	40	100	30	Normal	○
34	Slash	Normal	Physical	70	100	20	Normal	○
37	Mirror Move	Flying	Status	—	—	20	Depends	—
43	Flamethrower	Fire	Special	95	100	15	Normal	—

● MOVE MANIAC
Name	Type	Kind	Pow.	Acc.	PP	Range	DA
Headbutt	Normal	Physical	70	100	15	Normal	○

● BP MOVES
Name	Type	Kind	Pow.	Acc.	PP	Range	DA
Snore	Normal	Special	40	100	15	Normal	—
Helping Hand	Normal	Status	—	—	20	1 Ally	—
Last Resort	Normal	Physical	130	100	5	Normal	○
Swift	Normal	Special	60	—	20	2 Foes	—
Mud-Slap	Ground	Special	20	100	10	Normal	—
Bounce	Flying	Physical	85	85	5	Normal	○
Heat Wave	Fire	Special	100	90	10	2 Foes	—

● TM & HM MOVES
No.	Name	Type	Kind	Pow.	Acc.	PP	Range	DA
TM06	Toxic	Poison	Status	—	85	10	Normal	—
TM10	Hidden Power	Normal	Special	—	100	15	Normal	—
TM11	Sunny Day	Fire	Status	—	—	5	All	—
TM17	Protect	Normal	Status	—	—	10	Self	—
TM21	Frustration	Normal	Physical	—	100	20	Normal	○
TM27	Return	Normal	Physical	—	100	20	Normal	○
TM28	Dig	Ground	Physical	80	100	10	Normal	○
TM32	Double Team	Normal	Status	—	—	15	Self	—
TM35	Flamethrower	Fire	Special	95	100	15	Normal	—
TM38	Fire Blast	Fire	Special	120	85	5	Normal	—
TM39	Rock Tomb	Rock	Physical	50	80	10	Normal	—
TM40	Aerial Ace	Flying	Physical	60	—	20	Normal	○
TM42	Facade	Normal	Physical	70	100	20	Normal	—
TM43	Secret Power	Normal	Physical	70	100	20	Normal	—
TM44	Rest	Psychic	Status	—	—	10	Self	—
TM45	Attract	Normal	Status	—	100	15	Normal	—
TM50	Overheat	Fire	Special	140	90	5	Normal	—
TM58	Endure	Normal	Status	—	—	10	Self	—
TM61	Will-O-Wisp	Fire	Status	—	75	15	Normal	—
TM65	Shadow Claw	Ghost	Physical	70	100	15	Normal	○
TM75	Swords Dance	Normal	Status	—	—	30	Self	—
TM78	Captivate	Normal	Status	—	100	20	2 Foes	—
TM80	Rock Slide	Rock	Physical	75	90	10	2 Foes	—
TM82	Sleep Talk	Normal	Status	—	—	10	Depends	—
TM83	Natural Gift	Normal	Physical	—	100	15	Normal	—
TM87	Swagger	Normal	Status	—	90	15	Normal	—
TM90	Substitute	Normal	Status	—	—	10	Self	—
HM01	Cut	Normal	Physical	50	95	30	Normal	○
HM04	Strength	Normal	Physical	80	100	15	Normal	○
HM06	Rock Smash	Fighting	Physical	40	100	15	Normal	○

● EGG MOVES
Name	Type	Kind	Pow.	Acc.	PP	Range	DA
Counter	Fighting	Physical	—	100	20	Self	○
Reversal	Fighting	Physical	—	100	15	Normal	○
Endure	Normal	Status	—	—	10	Self	—
Swagger	Normal	Status	—	90	15	Normal	—
Rock Slide	Rock	Physical	75	90	10	2 Foes	—
SmellingSalt	Normal	Physical	60	100	10	Normal	○
Crush Claw	Normal	Physical	75	95	10	Normal	○
Baton Pass	Normal	Status	—	—	40	Self	—
Agility	Psychic	Status	—	—	30	Self	—
Night Slash	Dark	Physical	70	100	15	Normal	○
Last Resort	Normal	Physical	130	100	5	Normal	○
Feint	Normal	Physical	50	100	10	Normal	—
FeatherDance	Flying	Status	—	100	15	Normal	—

● LEVEL-UP MOVES

Lv.	Name	Type	Kind	Pow.	Acc.	PP	Range	DA
1	Scratch	Normal	Physical	40	100	35	Normal	○
1	Growl	Normal	Status	—	100	40	2 Foes	—
1	Focus Energy	Normal	Status	—	—	30	Self	—
1	Ember	Fire	Special	40	100	25	Normal	—
7	Focus Energy	Normal	Status	—	—	30	Self	—
13	Ember	Fire	Special	40	100	25	Normal	—
16	Double Kick	Fighting	Physical	30	100	30	Normal	○
17	Peck	Flying	Physical	35	100	35	Normal	○
21	Sand-Attack	Ground	Status	—	100	15	Normal	—
28	Bulk Up	Fighting	Status	—	—	20	Self	—
32	Quick Attack	Normal	Physical	40	100	30	Normal	○
39	Slash	Normal	Physical	70	100	20	Normal	○
43	Mirror Move	Flying	Status	—	—	20	Depends	—
50	Sky Uppercut	Fighting	Physical	85	90	15	Normal	○
54	Flare Blitz	Fire	Physical	120	100	15	Normal	○

● MOVE MANIAC

Name	Type	Kind	Pow.	Acc.	PP	Range	DA
Headbutt	Normal	Physical	70	100	15	Normal	○

● BP MOVES

Name	Type	Kind	Pow.	Acc.	PP	Range	DA
Fury Cutter	Bug	Physical	10	95	20	Normal	○
ThunderPunch	Electric	Physical	75	100	15	Normal	○
Fire Punch	Fire	Physical	75	100	15	Normal	○
Vacuum Wave	Fighting	Special	40	100	30	Normal	—
Snore	Normal	Special	40	100	15	Normal	—
Helping Hand	Normal	Status	—	—	20	1 Ally	—
Last Resort	Normal	Physical	130	100	5	Normal	○
Swift	Normal	Special	60	—	20	2 Foes	—
Mud-Slap	Ground	Special	20	100	10	Normal	—
Bounce	Flying	Physical	85	85	5	Normal	○
Heat Wave	Fire	Special	100	90	10	2 Foes	—
Low Kick	Fighting	Physical	—	100	20	Normal	○

● TM & HM MOVES

No.	Name	Type	Kind	Pow.	Acc.	PP	Range	DA
TM01	Focus Punch	Fighting	Physical	150	100	20	Normal	○
TM06	Toxic	Poison	Status	—	85	10	Normal	—
TM08	Bulk Up	Fighting	Status	—	—	20	Self	—
TM10	Hidden Power	Normal	Special	—	100	15	Normal	—
TM11	Sunny Day	Fire	Status	—	—	5	All	—
TM17	Protect	Normal	Status	—	—	10	Self	—
TM21	Frustration	Normal	Physical	—	100	20	Normal	○
TM27	Return	Normal	Physical	—	100	20	Normal	○
TM28	Dig	Ground	Physical	80	100	10	Normal	○
TM31	Brick Break	Fighting	Physical	75	100	15	Normal	○
TM32	Double Team	Normal	Status	—	—	15	Self	—
TM35	Flamethrower	Fire	Special	95	100	15	Normal	—
TM38	Fire Blast	Fire	Special	120	85	5	Normal	—
TM39	Rock Tomb	Rock	Physical	50	80	10	Normal	○
TM40	Aerial Ace	Flying	Physical	60	—	20	Normal	○
TM42	Facade	Normal	Physical	70	100	20	Normal	○
TM43	Secret Power	Normal	Physical	70	100	20	Normal	○
TM44	Rest	Psychic	Status	—	—	10	Self	—
TM45	Attract	Normal	Status	—	100	15	Normal	—
TM50	Overheat	Fire	Special	140	90	5	Normal	—
TM52	Focus Blast	Fighting	Special	120	70	5	Normal	—
TM56	Fling	Dark	Physical	—	100	10	Normal	○
TM58	Endure	Normal	Status	—	—	10	Self	—
TM61	Will-O-Wisp	Fire	Status	—	75	15	Normal	—
TM65	Shadow Claw	Ghost	Physical	70	100	15	Normal	○
TM75	Swords Dance	Normal	Status	—	—	30	Self	○
TM78	Captivate	Normal	Status	—	100	20	2 Foes	—
TM80	Rock Slide	Rock	Physical	75	90	10	2 Foes	○
TM82	Sleep Talk	Normal	Status	—	—	10	Depends	—
TM83	Natural Gift	Normal	Physical	—	100	15	Normal	—
TM84	Poison Jab	Poison	Physical	80	100	20	Normal	○
TM87	Swagger	Normal	Status	—	90	15	Normal	—
TM90	Substitute	Normal	Status	—	—	10	Self	—
HM01	Cut	Normal	Physical	50	95	30	Normal	○
HM04	Strength	Normal	Physical	80	100	15	Normal	○
HM06	Rock Smash	Fighting	Physical	40	100	15	Normal	○

● No. 256 | Young Fowl Pokémon
Combusken
Fire Fighting

- **HEIGHT:** 2'11"
- **WEIGHT:** 43.0 lbs.
- **ITEMS:** None

● SIZE COMPARISON

● MALE FORM
Bigger crest

● FEMALE FORM
Smaller crest

⊛ ABILITIES
- Blaze

⊛ STATS
HP ●●
ATTACK ●●●●
DEFENSE ●●●
SP. ATTACK ●●●●
SP. DEFENSE ●●●
SPEED ●●●

⊛ EGG GROUPS
Field

⊛ PERFORMANCE
SPEED ★★★☆
POWER ★★★★☆
SKILL ★★★☆
STAMINA ★★★
JUMP ★★★☆

● MAIN WAYS TO OBTAIN

Pokémon HeartGold — Level up Torchic to Lv. 16

Pokémon SoulSilver — Level up Torchic to Lv. 16

Pokémon Diamond — —

Pokémon Pearl —

Pokémon Platinum — —

Pokémon HeartGold
During a battle, the hot flame in its body increases. Its kicks have outstanding destructive power.

Pokémon SoulSilver
During a battle, the hot flame in its body increases. Its kicks have outstanding destructive power.

⊛ EVOLUTION

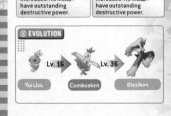

Torchic → Lv. 16 → Combusken → Lv. 36 → Blaziken

● No. 257 | Blaze Pokémon
Blaziken

Fire | Fighting

● LEVEL-UP MOVES

Lv.	Name	Type	Kind	Pow.	Acc.	PP	Range	DA
1	Fire Punch	Fire	Physical	75	100	15	Normal	○
1	Scratch	Normal	Physical	40	100	35	Normal	○
1	Growl	Normal	Status	—	100	40	2 Foes	—
1	Focus Energy	Normal	Status	—	—	30	Self	—
1	Ember	Fire	Special	40	100	25	Normal	—
7	Focus Energy	Normal	Status	—	—	30	Self	—
13	Ember	Fire	Special	40	100	25	Normal	—
16	Double Kick	Fighting	Physical	30	100	30	Normal	○
17	Peck	Flying	Physical	35	100	35	Normal	○
21	Sand-Attack	Ground	Status	—	100	15	Normal	—
28	Bulk Up	Fighting	Status	—	—	20	Self	—
32	Quick Attack	Normal	Physical	40	100	30	Normal	○
36	Blaze Kick	Fire	Physical	85	90	10	Normal	○
42	Slash	Normal	Physical	70	100	20	Normal	○
49	Brave Bird	Flying	Physical	120	100	15	Normal	○
59	Sky Uppercut	Fighting	Physical	85	90	15	Normal	○
66	Flare Blitz	Fire	Physical	120	100	15	Normal	○

● MOVE MANIAC

Name	Type	Kind	Pow.	Acc.	PP	Range	DA
Headbutt	Normal	Physical	70	100	15	Normal	○
Blast Burn	Fire	Special	150	90	5	Normal	—

● BP MOVES

Name	Type	Kind	Pow.	Acc.	PP	Range	DA
Fury Cutter	Bug	Physical	10	95	20	Normal	○
ThunderPunch	Electric	Physical	75	100	15	Normal	○
Fire Punch	Fire	Physical	75	100	15	Normal	○
Vacuum Wave	Fighting	Special	40	100	30	Normal	—
Knock Off	Dark	Physical	20	100	20	Normal	○
Snore	Normal	Special	40	100	15	Normal	—
Helping Hand	Normal	Status	—	—	20	1 Ally	—
Last Resort	Normal	Physical	130	100	5	Normal	○
Swift	Normal	Special	60	—	20	2 Foes	—
Role Play	Psychic	Status	—	—	10	Normal	—
Mud-Slap	Ground	Special	20	100	10	Normal	—
Superpower	Fighting	Physical	120	100	5	Normal	○
Bounce	Flying	Physical	85	85	5	Normal	○
Heat Wave	Fire	Special	100	90	10	2 Foes	—
Low Kick	Fighting	Physical	—	100	20	Normal	○

● TM & HM MOVES

No.	Name	Type	Kind	Pow.	Acc.	PP	Range	DA
TM01	Focus Punch	Fighting	Physical	150	100	20	Normal	○
TM05	Roar	Normal	Status	—	100	20	Normal	—
TM06	Toxic	Poison	Status	—	85	10	Normal	—
TM08	Bulk Up	Fighting	Status	—	—	20	Self	—
TM10	Hidden Power	Normal	Special	—	100	15	Normal	—
TM11	Sunny Day	Fire	Status	—	—	5	All	—
TM15	Hyper Beam	Normal	Special	150	90	5	Normal	—
TM17	Protect	Normal	Status	—	—	10	Self	—
TM21	Frustration	Normal	Physical	—	100	20	Normal	○
TM22	SolarBeam	Grass	Special	120	100	10	Normal	—
TM26	Earthquake	Ground	Physical	100	100	10	2 Foes/1 Ally	—
TM27	Return	Normal	Physical	—	100	20	Normal	○
TM28	Dig	Ground	Physical	80	100	10	Normal	○
TM31	Brick Break	Fighting	Physical	75	100	15	Normal	○
TM32	Double Team	Normal	Status	—	—	15	Self	—
TM35	Flamethrower	Fire	Special	95	100	15	Normal	—
TM38	Fire Blast	Fire	Special	120	85	5	Normal	—
TM39	Rock Tomb	Rock	Physical	50	80	10	Normal	○
TM40	Aerial Ace	Flying	Physical	60	—	20	Normal	○
TM42	Facade	Normal	Physical	70	100	20	Normal	○
TM43	Secret Power	Normal	Physical	70	100	20	Normal	○
TM44	Rest	Psychic	Status	—	—	10	Self	—
TM45	Attract	Normal	Status	—	100	15	Normal	—
TM50	Overheat	Fire	Special	140	90	5	Normal	—
TM52	Focus Blast	Fighting	Special	120	70	5	Normal	—
TM56	Fling	Dark	Physical	—	100	10	Normal	○
TM58	Endure	Normal	Status	—	—	10	Self	—
TM61	Will-O-Wisp	Fire	Status	—	75	15	Normal	—
TM65	Shadow Claw	Ghost	Physical	70	100	15	Normal	○
TM68	Giga Impact	Normal	Physical	150	90	5	Normal	○
TM71	Stone Edge	Rock	Physical	100	80	5	Normal	○
TM75	Swords Dance	Normal	Status	—	—	30	Self	—
TM78	Captivate	Normal	Status	—	100	20	2 Foes	—
TM80	Rock Slide	Rock	Physical	75	90	10	2 Foes	○
TM82	Sleep Talk	Normal	Status	—	—	10	Depends	—
TM83	Natural Gift	Normal	Physical	—	100	15	Normal	—
TM84	Poison Jab	Poison	Physical	80	100	20	Normal	○
TM87	Swagger	Normal	Status	—	90	15	Normal	—
TM90	Substitute	Normal	Status	—	—	10	Self	—
HM01	Cut	Normal	Physical	50	95	30	Normal	○
HM04	Strength	Normal	Physical	80	100	15	Normal	○
HM06	Rock Smash	Fighting	Physical	40	100	15	Normal	○
HM08	Rock Climb	Normal	Physical	90	85	20	Normal	○

- ● HEIGHT: 6'03"
- ● WEIGHT: 114.6 lbs.
- ● ITEMS: None

● SIZE COMPARISON

● MALE FORM
Longer horns and feathers

● FEMALE FORM
Shorter horns and feathers

⊙ ABILITIES
- ● Blaze

⊙ STATS
- HP ●●●
- ATTACK ●●●●●
- DEFENSE ●●●
- SP. ATTACK ●●●●●
- SP. DEFENSE ●●●
- SPEED ●●●●

⊙ EGG GROUPS
Field

⊙ PERFORMANCE
- SPEED ★★☆☆☆
- POWER ★★★★★
- SKILL ★★★☆☆
- STAMINA ★★☆☆
- JUMP ★★★★

● MAIN WAYS TO OBTAIN

Pokémon HeartGold	Level up Combusken to Lv. 36
Pokémon SoulSilver	Level up Combusken to Lv. 36
Pokémon Diamond	—
Pokémon Pearl	—
Pokémon Platinum	—

Pokémon HeartGold	Pokémon SoulSilver
It can clear a 30-story building in a leap. Its fiery punches scorch its foes.	It can clear a 30-story building in a leap. Its fiery punches scorch its foes.

⊙ EVOLUTION

Torchic → Lv. 16 → Combusken → Lv. 36 → Blaziken

● LEVEL-UP MOVES

Lv.	Name	Type	Kind	Pow.	Acc.	PP	Range	DA
1	Tackle	Normal	Physical	35	95	35	Normal	○
1	Growl	Normal	Status	—	100	40	2 Foes	—
6	Mud-Slap	Ground	Special	20	100	10	Normal	—
10	Water Gun	Water	Special	40	100	25	Normal	—
15	Bide	Normal	Physical	—	—	10	Self	○
19	Foresight	Normal	Status	—	—	40	Normal	—
24	Mud Sport	Ground	Status	—	—	15	All	—
28	Take Down	Normal	Physical	90	85	20	Normal	○
33	Whirlpool	Water	Special	15	70	15	Normal	—
37	Protect	Normal	Status	—	—	10	Self	—
42	Hydro Pump	Water	Special	120	80	5	Normal	—
46	Endeavor	Normal	Physical	—	100	5	Normal	○

● MOVE MANIAC

Name	Type	Kind	Pow.	Acc.	PP	Range	DA
Headbutt	Normal	Physical	70	100	15	Normal	○

● BP MOVES

Name	Type	Kind	Pow.	Acc.	PP	Range	DA
Dive	Water	Physical	80	100	10	Normal	○
Icy Wind	Ice	Special	55	95	15	2 Foes	—
Snore	Normal	Special	40	100	15	Normal	—
Mud-Slap	Ground	Special	20	100	10	Normal	—
Rollout	Rock	Physical	30	90	20	Normal	○
Superpower	Fighting	Physical	120	100	5	Normal	○
Aqua Tail	Water	Physical	90	90	10	Normal	○
Endeavor	Normal	Physical	—	100	5	Normal	○
AncientPower	Rock	Special	60	100	5	Normal	—
Earth Power	Ground	Special	90	100	10	Normal	—
Low Kick	Fighting	Physical	—	100	20	Normal	○

● TM & HM MOVES

No.	Name	Type	Kind	Pow.	Acc.	PP	Range	DA
TM03	Water Pulse	Water	Special	60	100	20	Normal	—
TM06	Toxic	Poison	Status	—	85	10	Normal	—
TM07	Hail	Ice	Status	—	—	10	All	—
TM10	Hidden Power	Normal	Special	—	100	15	Normal	—
TM13	Ice Beam	Ice	Special	95	100	10	Normal	—
TM14	Blizzard	Ice	Special	120	70	5	2 Foes	—
TM17	Protect	Normal	Status	—	—	10	Self	—
TM18	Rain Dance	Water	Status	—	—	5	All	—
TM21	Frustration	Normal	Physical	—	100	20	Normal	○
TM23	Iron Tail	Steel	Physical	100	75	15	Normal	○
TM27	Return	Normal	Physical	—	100	20	Normal	○
TM28	Dig	Ground	Physical	80	100	10	Normal	○
TM32	Double Team	Normal	Status	—	—	15	Self	—
TM39	Rock Tomb	Rock	Physical	50	80	10	Normal	○
TM42	Facade	Normal	Physical	70	100	20	Normal	○
TM43	Secret Power	Normal	Physical	70	100	20	Normal	○
TM44	Rest	Psychic	Status	—	—	10	Self	—
TM45	Attract	Normal	Status	—	100	15	Normal	—
TM58	Endure	Normal	Status	—	—	10	Self	—
TM78	Captivate	Normal	Status	—	100	20	2 Foes	—
TM80	Rock Slide	Rock	Physical	75	90	10	2 Foes	○
TM82	Sleep Talk	Normal	Status	—	—	10	Depends	—
TM83	Natural Gift	Normal	Physical	—	100	15	Normal	○
TM87	Swagger	Normal	Status	—	90	15	Normal	—
TM90	Substitute	Normal	Status	—	—	10	Self	—
HM03	Surf	Water	Special	95	100	15	2 Foes/1 Ally	—
HM04	Strength	Normal	Physical	80	100	15	Normal	○
HM05	Whirlpool	Water	Special	15	70	15	Normal	—
HM06	Rock Smash	Fighting	Physical	40	100	15	Normal	○
HM07	Waterfall	Water	Physical	80	100	15	Normal	○

● EGG MOVES

Name	Type	Kind	Pow.	Acc.	PP	Range	DA
Refresh	Normal	Status	—	—	20	Self	—
Uproar	Normal	Special	50	100	10	1 Random	—
Curse	???	Status	—	—	10	Normal/Self	—
Stomp	Normal	Physical	65	100	20	Normal	○
Ice Ball	Ice	Physical	30	90	20	Normal	○
Mirror Coat	Psychic	Special	—	100	20	Self	—
Counter	Fighting	Physical	—	100	20	Self	○
AncientPower	Rock	Special	60	100	5	Normal	—
Whirlpool	Water	Special	15	70	15	Normal	—
Bite	Dark	Physical	60	100	25	Normal	○
Double-Edge	Normal	Physical	120	100	15	Normal	○
Mud Bomb	Ground	Special	65	85	10	Normal	—
Yawn	Normal	Status	—	—	10	Normal	—
Sludge	Poison	Special	65	100	20	Normal	—

◉ No. 258 | Mud Fish Pokémon

Mudkip

Water

● **HEIGHT:** 1'04"
● **WEIGHT:** 16.8 lbs.
● **ITEMS:** None

● SIZE COMPARISON

● MALE/FEMALE HAVE SAME FORM

⊘ ABILITIES
● Torrent

⊘ STATS
HP ●●
ATTACK ●●●
DEFENSE ●●
SP. ATTACK ●●●
SP. DEFENSE ●●
SPEED ●●

⊘ EGG GROUPS
Monster

Water 1

⊘ PERFORMANCE

SPEED ★★☆☆   STAMINA ★★★★☆
POWER ★★★☆   JUMP ★★★
SKILL ★★☆

● MAIN WAYS TO OBTAIN

Pokémon HeartGold	Receive from Steven at Silph Co. in Saffron City (after defeating Red)
Pokémon SoulSilver	Receive from Steven at Silph Co. in Saffron City (after defeating Red)
Pokémon Diamond	—
Pokémon Pearl	—
Pokémon Platinum	—

Pokémon HeartGold	**Pokémon SoulSilver**
Its power can crush boulders. It rests by covering itself with mud at the bottom of a river.	Its power can crush boulders. It rests by covering itself with mud at the bottom of a river.

⊘ EVOLUTION

Mudkip — Lv. 16 → Marshtomp — Lv. 36 → Swampert

No. 259 | Mud Fish Pokémon
Marshtomp

Water　Ground

- **HEIGHT:** 2'04"
- **WEIGHT:** 61.7 lbs.
- **ITEMS:** None

● SIZE COMPARISON

● MALE/FEMALE HAVE SAME FORM

ABILITIES
- Torrent

STATS
HP ●●●
ATTACK ●●●●
DEFENSE ●●●
SP. ATTACK ●●●
SP. DEFENSE ●●●
SPEED ●●

EGG GROUPS
Monster

Water 1

PERFORMANCE
SPEED ★★☆　　STAMINA ★★★★☆
POWER ★★★★　JUMP ★★★
SKILL ★★★☆

MAIN WAYS TO OBTAIN

Pokémon HeartGold | Level up Mudkip to Lv. 16

Pokémon SoulSilver | Level up Mudkip to Lv. 16

Pokémon Diamond | —

Pokémon Pearl | —

Pokémon Platinum | —

Pokémon HeartGold	Pokémon SoulSilver
Living on muddy ground that provides poor footing has made its legs sturdy.	Living on muddy ground that provides poor footing has made its legs sturdy.

EVOLUTION

Lv. 16　　Lv. 36

Mudkip　Marshtomp　Swampert

● LEVEL-UP MOVES

Lv.	Name	Type	Kind	Pow.	Acc.	PP	Range	DA
1	Tackle	Normal	Physical	35	95	35	Normal	○
1	Growl	Normal	Status	—	100	40	2 Foes	—
1	Mud-Slap	Ground	Special	20	100	10	Normal	—
1	Water Gun	Water	Special	40	100	25	Normal	—
6	Mud-Slap	Ground	Special	20	100	10	Normal	—
10	Water Gun	Water	Special	40	100	25	Normal	—
15	Bide	Normal	Physical	—	—	10	Self	○
16	Mud Shot	Ground	Special	55	95	15	Normal	—
20	Foresight	Normal	Status	—	—	40	Normal	—
25	Mud Bomb	Ground	Special	65	85	10	Normal	—
31	Take Down	Normal	Physical	90	85	20	Normal	○
37	Muddy Water	Water	Special	95	85	10	2 Foes	—
42	Protect	Normal	Status	—	—	10	Self	—
46	Earthquake	Ground	Physical	100	100	10	2 Foes/1 Ally	○
53	Endeavor	Normal	Physical	—	100	5	Normal	○

● MOVE MANIAC

Name	Type	Kind	Pow.	Acc.	PP	Range	DA
Headbutt	Normal	Physical	70	100	15	Normal	○

● BP MOVES

Name	Type	Kind	Pow.	Acc.	PP	Range	DA
Dive	Water	Physical	80	100	10	Normal	○
Icy Wind	Ice	Special	55	95	15	2 Foes	—
Ice Punch	Ice	Physical	75	100	15	Normal	○
Snore	Normal	Special	40	100	15	Normal	—
Mud-Slap	Ground	Special	20	100	10	Normal	—
Rollout	Rock	Physical	30	90	20	Normal	○
Superpower	Fighting	Physical	120	100	5	Normal	○
Aqua Tail	Water	Physical	90	90	10	Normal	○
Endeavor	Normal	Physical	—	100	5	Normal	○
AncientPower	Rock	Special	60	100	5	Normal	—
Earth Power	Ground	Special	90	100	10	Normal	—
Low Kick	Fighting	Physical	—	100	20	Normal	○

● TM & HM MOVES

No.	Name	Type	Kind	Pow.	Acc.	PP	Range	DA
TM03	Water Pulse	Water	Special	60	100	20	Normal	—
TM06	Toxic	Poison	Status	—	85	10	Normal	—
TM07	Hail	Ice	Status	—	—	10	All	—
TM10	Hidden Power	Normal	Special	—	100	15	Normal	—
TM13	Ice Beam	Ice	Special	95	100	10	Normal	—
TM14	Blizzard	Ice	Special	120	70	5	2 Foes	—
TM17	Protect	Normal	Status	—	—	10	Self	—
TM18	Rain Dance	Water	Status	—	—	5	All	—
TM21	Frustration	Normal	Physical	—	100	20	Normal	○
TM23	Iron Tail	Steel	Physical	100	75	15	Normal	○
TM26	Earthquake	Ground	Physical	100	100	10	2 Foes/1 Ally	○
TM27	Return	Normal	Physical	—	100	20	Normal	○
TM28	Dig	Ground	Physical	80	100	10	Normal	○
TM31	Brick Break	Fighting	Physical	75	100	15	Normal	○
TM32	Double Team	Normal	Status	—	—	15	Self	—
TM39	Rock Tomb	Rock	Physical	50	80	10	Normal	○
TM42	Facade	Normal	Physical	70	100	20	Normal	○
TM43	Secret Power	Normal	Physical	70	100	20	Normal	—
TM44	Rest	Psychic	Status	—	—	10	Self	—
TM45	Attract	Normal	Status	—	100	15	Normal	—
TM56	Fling	Dark	Physical	—	100	10	Normal	○
TM58	Endure	Normal	Status	—	—	10	Self	—
TM76	Stealth Rock	Rock	Status	—	—	20	2 Foes	—
TM78	Captivate	Normal	Status	—	100	20	2 Foes	—
TM80	Rock Slide	Rock	Physical	75	90	10	2 Foes	—
TM82	Sleep Talk	Normal	Status	—	—	10	Depends	—
TM83	Natural Gift	Normal	Physical	—	100	15	Normal	—
TM87	Swagger	Normal	Status	—	90	15	Normal	—
TM90	Substitute	Normal	Status	—	—	10	Self	—
HM03	Surf	Water	Special	95	100	15	2 Foes/1 Ally	—
HM04	Strength	Normal	Physical	80	100	15	Normal	○
HM05	Whirlpool	Water	Special	15	70	15	Normal	—
HM06	Rock Smash	Fighting	Physical	40	100	15	Normal	○
HM07	Waterfall	Water	Physical	80	100	15	Normal	○

● LEVEL-UP MOVES

Lv.	Name	Type	Kind	Pow.	Acc.	PP	Range	DA
1	Tackle	Normal	Physical	35	95	35	Normal	○
1	Growl	Normal	Status	—	100	40	2 Foes	—
1	Mud-Slap	Ground	Special	20	100	10	Normal	—
1	Water Gun	Water	Special	40	100	25	Normal	—
6	Mud-Slap	Ground	Special	20	100	10	Normal	—
10	Water Gun	Water	Special	40	100	25	Normal	—
15	Bide	Normal	Physical	—	—	10	Self	○
16	Mud Shot	Ground	Special	55	95	15	Normal	—
20	Foresight	Normal	Status	—	—	40	Normal	—
25	Mud Bomb	Ground	Special	65	85	10	Normal	—
31	Take Down	Normal	Physical	90	85	20	Normal	○
39	Muddy Water	Water	Special	95	85	10	2 Foes	—
46	Protect	Normal	Status	—	—	10	Self	—
52	Earthquake	Ground	Physical	100	100	5	2 Foes/1 Ally	—
61	Endeavor	Normal	Physical	—	100	5	Normal	○
69	Hammer Arm	Fighting	Physical	100	90	10	Normal	○

● MOVE MANIAC

Name	Type	Kind	Pow.	Acc.	PP	Range	DA
Headbutt	Normal	Physical	70	100	15	Normal	○
Hydro Cannon	Water	Special	150	90	5	Normal	—

● BP MOVES

Name	Type	Kind	Pow.	Acc.	PP	Range	DA
Dive	Water	Physical	80	100	10	Normal	○
Icy Wind	Ice	Special	55	95	15	2 Foes	—
Ice Punch	Ice	Physical	75	100	15	Normal	○
Snore	Normal	Special	40	100	15	Normal	—
Mud-Slap	Ground	Special	20	100	10	Normal	—
Rollout	Rock	Physical	30	90	20	Normal	○
Superpower	Fighting	Physical	120	100	5	Normal	○
Aqua Tail	Water	Physical	90	90	10	Normal	○
Endeavor	Normal	Physical	—	100	5	Normal	○
Outrage	Dragon	Physical	120	100	15	1 Random	○
AncientPower	Rock	Special	60	100	5	Normal	—
Earth Power	Ground	Special	90	100	10	Normal	—
Low Kick	Fighting	Physical	—	100	20	Self	○

● TM & HM MOVES

No.	Name	Type	Kind	Pow.	Acc.	PP	Range	DA
TM01	Focus Punch	Fighting	Physical	150	100	20	Normal	○
TM03	Water Pulse	Water	Special	60	100	20	Normal	—
TM05	Roar	Normal	Status	—	100	20	Normal	—
TM06	Toxic	Poison	Status	—	85	10	Normal	—
TM07	Hail	Ice	Status	—	—	10	All	—
TM10	Hidden Power	Normal	Special	—	100	15	Normal	—
TM13	Ice Beam	Ice	Special	95	100	10	Normal	—
TM14	Blizzard	Ice	Special	120	70	5	2 Foes	—
TM15	Hyper Beam	Normal	Special	150	90	5	Normal	—
TM17	Protect	Normal	Status	—	—	10	Self	—
TM18	Rain Dance	Water	Status	—	—	5	All	—
TM21	Frustration	Normal	Physical	—	100	20	Normal	○
TM23	Iron Tail	Steel	Physical	100	75	15	Normal	○
TM26	Earthquake	Ground	Physical	100	100	10	2 Foes/1 Ally	—
TM27	Return	Normal	Physical	—	100	20	Normal	○
TM28	Dig	Ground	Physical	80	100	10	Normal	○
TM31	Brick Break	Fighting	Physical	75	100	15	Normal	○
TM32	Double Team	Normal	Status	—	—	15	Self	—
TM39	Rock Tomb	Rock	Physical	50	80	10	Normal	—
TM42	Facade	Normal	Physical	70	100	20	Normal	○
TM43	Secret Power	Normal	Physical	70	100	20	Normal	—
TM44	Rest	Psychic	Status	—	—	10	Self	—
TM45	Attract	Normal	Status	—	100	15	Normal	—
TM52	Focus Blast	Fighting	Special	120	70	5	Normal	—
TM56	Fling	Dark	Physical	—	100	10	Normal	○
TM58	Endure	Normal	Status	—	—	10	Self	—
TM68	Giga Impact	Normal	Physical	150	90	5	Normal	○
TM71	Stone Edge	Rock	Physical	100	80	5	Normal	○
TM72	Avalanche	Ice	Physical	60	100	10	Normal	○
TM76	Stealth Rock	Rock	Status	—	—	20	2 Foes	—
TM78	Captivate	Normal	Status	—	100	20	2 Foes	—
TM80	Rock Slide	Rock	Physical	75	90	10	2 Foes	—
TM82	Sleep Talk	Normal	Status	—	—	10	Depends	—
TM83	Natural Gift	Normal	Physical	—	100	15	Normal	—
TM87	Swagger	Normal	Status	—	90	15	Normal	—
TM90	Substitute	Normal	Status	—	—	10	Self	—
HM03	Surf	Water	Special	95	100	15	2 Foes/1 Ally	—
HM04	Strength	Normal	Physical	80	100	15	Normal	—
HM05	Whirlpool	Water	Special	15	70	15	Normal	—
HM06	Rock Smash	Fighting	Physical	40	100	15	Normal	○
HM07	Waterfall	Water	Physical	80	100	15	Normal	○
HM08	Rock Climb	Normal	Physical	90	85	20	Normal	○

☺ No. 260 | Mud Fish Pokémon
Spampert

`Water` `Ground`

● HEIGHT: 4'11"
● WEIGHT: 180.6 lbs.
● ITEMS: None

● SIZE COMPARISON

● MALE/FEMALE HAVE SAME FORM

☺ ABILITIES
● Torrent

☺ STATS
HP ●●●●○
ATTACK ●●●●●
DEFENSE ●●●●●
SP. ATTACK ●●●●●
SP. DEFENSE ●●●●○
SPEED ●●●○

☺ EGG GROUPS
Monster
Water 1

☺ PERFORMANCE
SPEED ★★☆ STAMINA ★★★★★
POWER ★★★★☆ JUMP ★★
SKILL ★★☆☆☆

● MAIN WAYS TO OBTAIN

Pokémon HeartGold Level up Marshtomp to Lv. 36

Pokémon SoulSilver Level up Marshtomp to Lv. 36

Pokémon Diamond —

Pokémon Pearl —

Pokémon Platinum —

Pokémon HeartGold
Its arms are hard as rock. With one swing, it can break a boulder into pieces.

Pokémon SoulSilver
Its arms are hard as rock. With one swing, it can break a boulder into pieces.

☺ EVOLUTION

Mudkip — Lv. 16 — Marshtomp — Lv. 36 — Swampert

No. 261 | Bite Pokémon
Poochyena
Dark

● HEIGHT: 1'08"
● WEIGHT: 30.0 lbs.
● ITEMS: Pecha Berry

● SIZE COMPARISON

● MALE/FEMALE HAVE SAME FORM

● ABILITIES
● Run Away
● Quick Feet

● STATS
HP ●
ATTACK ●●
DEFENSE ●●
SP. ATTACK ●
SP. DEFENSE ●
SPEED ●●

● EGG GROUPS
Field

● PERFORMANCE
SPEED ★★★☆
POWER ★★★☆
SKILL ★★☆☆
STAMINA ★★★★☆
JUMP ★★☆

● MAIN WAYS TO OBTAIN

Pokémon HeartGold	Route 1 (mass outbreak)
Pokémon SoulSilver	Route 1 (mass outbreak)
Pokémon Diamond	Find its Egg at the Pokémon Day Care and hatch it
Pokémon Pearl	—
Pokémon Platinum	Route 214 (use Poké Radar)

| Pokémon HeartGold | Pokémon SoulSilver |
| It chases its prey until the victim becomes exhausted. However, it turns tail if the prey strikes back. | It chases its prey until the victim becomes exhausted. However, it turns tail if the prey strikes back. |

● EVOLUTION

Poochyena — Lv. 18 → Mightyena

● LEVEL-UP MOVES

Lv.	Name	Type	Kind	Pow.	Acc.	PP	Range	DA
1	Tackle	Normal	Physical	35	95	35	Normal	○
5	Howl	Normal	Status	—	—	40	Self	—
9	Sand-Attack	Ground	Status	—	100	15	Normal	—
13	Bite	Dark	Physical	60	100	25	Normal	○
17	Odor Sleuth	Normal	Status	—	—	40	Normal	—
21	Roar	Normal	Status	—	100	20	Normal	—
25	Swagger	Normal	Status	—	90	15	Normal	—
29	Assurance	Dark	Physical	50	100	10	Normal	○
33	Scary Face	Normal	Status	—	90	10	Normal	—
37	Taunt	Dark	Status	—	100	20	Normal	—
41	Embargo	Dark	Status	—	100	15	Normal	—
45	Take Down	Normal	Physical	90	85	20	Normal	○
49	Sucker Punch	Dark	Physical	80	100	5	Normal	○
53	Crunch	Dark	Physical	80	100	15	Normal	○

● MOVE MANIAC

Name	Type	Kind	Pow.	Acc.	PP	Range	DA
Headbutt	Normal	Physical	70	100	15	Normal	○

● BP MOVES

Name	Type	Kind	Pow.	Acc.	PP	Range	DA
Sucker Punch	Dark	Physical	80	100	5	Normal	○
Snore	Normal	Special	40	100	15	Normal	—
Spite	Ghost	Status	—	100	10	Normal	—
Uproar	Normal	Special	50	100	10	1 Random	—
Mud-Slap	Ground	Special	20	100	10	Normal	—
Super Fang	Normal	Physical	—	90	10	Normal	○

● TM & HM MOVES

No.	Name	Type	Kind	Pow.	Acc.	PP	Range	DA
TM05	Roar	Normal	Status	—	100	20	Normal	—
TM06	Toxic	Poison	Status	—	85	10	Normal	—
TM10	Hidden Power	Normal	Special	—	100	15	Normal	—
TM11	Sunny Day	Fire	Status	—	—	5	All	—
TM12	Taunt	Dark	Status	—	100	20	Normal	—
TM17	Protect	Normal	Status	—	—	10	Self	—
TM18	Rain Dance	Water	Status	—	—	5	All	—
TM21	Frustration	Normal	Physical	—	100	20	Normal	○
TM23	Iron Tail	Steel	Physical	100	75	15	Normal	○
TM27	Return	Normal	Physical	—	100	20	Normal	○
TM28	Dig	Ground	Physical	80	100	10	Normal	○
TM30	Shadow Ball	Ghost	Special	80	100	15	Normal	—
TM32	Double Team	Normal	Status	—	—	15	Self	—
TM41	Torment	Dark	Status	—	100	15	Normal	—
TM42	Facade	Normal	Physical	70	100	20	Normal	○
TM43	Secret Power	Normal	Physical	70	100	20	Normal	—
TM44	Rest	Psychic	Status	—	—	10	Self	—
TM45	Attract	Normal	Status	—	100	15	Normal	—
TM46	Thief	Dark	Physical	40	100	10	Normal	○
TM49	Snatch	Dark	Status	—	—	10	Depends	—
TM58	Endure	Normal	Status	—	—	10	Self	—
TM63	Embargo	Dark	Status	—	100	15	Normal	—
TM66	Payback	Dark	Physical	50	100	10	Normal	○
TM78	Captivate	Normal	Status	—	100	20	2 Foes	—
TM79	Dark Pulse	Dark	Special	80	100	15	Normal	—
TM82	Sleep Talk	Normal	Status	—	—	10	Depends	—
TM83	Natural Gift	Normal	Physical	—	100	15	Normal	○
TM87	Swagger	Normal	Status	—	90	15	Normal	—
TM90	Substitute	Normal	Status	—	—	10	Self	—
HM06	Rock Smash	Fighting	Physical	40	100	15	Normal	○

● EGG MOVES

Name	Type	Kind	Pow.	Acc.	PP	Range	DA
Astonish	Ghost	Physical	30	100	15	Normal	○
Poison Fang	Poison	Physical	50	100	15	Normal	○
Covet	Normal	Physical	40	100	40	Normal	○
Leer	Normal	Status	—	100	30	2 Foes	—
Yawn	Normal	Status	—	—	10	Normal	—
Sucker Punch	Dark	Physical	80	100	5	Normal	○
Ice Fang	Ice	Physical	65	95	15	Normal	○
Fire Fang	Fire	Physical	65	95	15	Normal	○
Thunder Fang	Electric	Physical	65	95	15	Normal	○
Me First	Normal	Status	—	—	20	Depends	—

● LEVEL-UP MOVES

Lv.	Name	Type	Kind	Pow.	Acc.	PP	Range	DA
1	Tackle	Normal	Physical	35	95	35	Normal	○
1	Howl	Normal	Status	—	—	40	Self	—
1	Sand-Attack	Ground	Status	—	100	15	Normal	—
1	Bite	Dark	Physical	60	100	25	Normal	○
5	Howl	Normal	Status	—	—	40	Self	—
9	Sand-Attack	Ground	Status	—	100	15	Normal	—
13	Bite	Dark	Physical	60	100	25	Normal	○
17	Odor Sleuth	Normal	Status	—	—	40	Normal	—
22	Roar	Normal	Status	—	100	20	Normal	—
27	Swagger	Normal	Status	—	90	15	Normal	—
32	Assurance	Dark	Physical	50	100	10	Normal	○
37	Scary Face	Normal	Status	—	90	10	Normal	—
42	Taunt	Dark	Status	—	100	20	Normal	—
47	Embargo	Dark	Status	—	100	15	Normal	—
52	Take Down	Normal	Physical	90	85	20	Normal	○
57	Thief	Dark	Physical	40	100	10	Normal	○
62	Sucker Punch	Dark	Physical	80	100	5	Normal	○

● MOVE MANIAC

Name	Type	Kind	Pow.	Acc.	PP	Range	DA
Headbutt	Normal	Physical	70	100	15	Normal	○

● BP MOVES

Name	Type	Kind	Pow.	Acc.	PP	Range	DA
Sucker Punch	Dark	Physical	80	100	5	Normal	○
Snore	Normal	Special	40	100	15	Normal	—
Spite	Ghost	Status	—	100	10	Normal	—
Uproar	Normal	Special	50	100	10	1 Random	—
Mud-Slap	Ground	Special	20	100	10	Normal	—
Super Fang	Normal	Physical	—	90	10	Normal	○

● TM & HM MOVES

No.	Name	Type	Kind	Pow.	Acc.	PP	Range	DA
TM05	Roar	Normal	Status	—	100	20	Normal	—
TM06	Toxic	Poison	Status	—	85	10	Normal	—
TM10	Hidden Power	Normal	Special	—	100	15	Normal	—
TM11	Sunny Day	Fire	Status	—	—	5	All	—
TM12	Taunt	Dark	Status	—	100	20	Normal	—
TM15	Hyper Beam	Normal	Special	150	90	5	Normal	—
TM17	Protect	Normal	Status	—	—	10	Self	—
TM18	Rain Dance	Water	Status	—	—	5	All	—
TM21	Frustration	Normal	Physical	—	100	20	Normal	○
TM23	Iron Tail	Steel	Physical	100	75	15	Normal	○
TM27	Return	Normal	Physical	—	100	20	Normal	○
TM28	Dig	Ground	Physical	80	100	10	Normal	○
TM30	Shadow Ball	Ghost	Special	80	100	15	Normal	—
TM32	Double Team	Normal	Status	—	—	15	Self	—
TM41	Torment	Dark	Status	—	100	15	Normal	—
TM42	Facade	Normal	Physical	70	100	20	Normal	○
TM43	Secret Power	Normal	Physical	70	100	20	Normal	○
TM44	Rest	Psychic	Status	—	—	10	Self	—
TM45	Attract	Normal	Status	—	100	15	Normal	—
TM46	Thief	Dark	Physical	40	100	10	Normal	○
TM49	Snatch	Dark	Status	—	—	10	Depends	—
TM58	Endure	Normal	Status	—	—	10	Self	—
TM63	Embargo	Dark	Status	—	100	15	Normal	—
TM66	Payback	Dark	Physical	50	100	10	Normal	○
TM68	Giga Impact	Normal	Physical	150	90	5	Normal	○
TM78	Captivate	Normal	Status	—	100	20	2 Foes	—
TM79	Dark Pulse	Dark	Special	80	100	15	Normal	—
TM82	Sleep Talk	Normal	Status	—	—	10	Self	—
TM83	Natural Gift	Normal	Physical	—	100	15	Normal	—
TM87	Swagger	Normal	Status	—	90	15	Normal	—
TM90	Substitute	Normal	Status	—	—	10	Self	—
HM04	Strength	Normal	Physical	80	100	15	Normal	○
HM06	Rock Smash	Fighting	Physical	40	100	15	Normal	○

No. 262 | Bite Pokémon
Mightyena

Dark

- ● HEIGHT: 3'03"
- ● WEIGHT: 81.6 lbs.
- ● ITEMS: None

● SIZE COMPARISON

● MALE/FEMALE HAVE SAME FORM

⊙ ABILITIES
- ● Intimidate
- ● Quick Feet

⊙ STATS
- HP ●●●
- ATTACK ●●●●
- DEFENSE ●●●
- SP. ATTACK ●●●
- SP. DEFENSE ●●●
- SPEED ●●●

⊙ EGG GROUPS
Field

⊙ PERFORMANCE
SPEED ★★☆☆   STAMINA ★★★★★
POWER ★★★★☆   JUMP ★★☆☆
SKILL ★★☆

● MAIN WAYS TO OBTAIN

Pokémon HeartGold   Level up Poochyena to Lv. 18

Pokémon SoulSilver   Level up Poochyena to Lv. 18

Pokémon Diamond   Route 214 (use Poké Radar)

Pokémon Pearl   —

Pokémon Platinum   Level up Poochyena to Lv. 18

Pokémon HeartGold
It chases down prey in a pack of around ten. They defeat foes with perfectly coordinated teamwork.

Pokémon SoulSilver
It chases down prey in a pack of around ten. They defeat foes with perfectly coordinated teamwork.

⊙ EVOLUTION

Poochyena → Lv. 18 → Mightyena

🔵 No. 263 | TinyRaccoon Pokémon
Zigzagoon

`Normal`

- **HEIGHT:** 1'04"
- **WEIGHT:** 38.6 lbs.
- **ITEMS:** Oran Berry

● SIZE COMPARISON

● MALE/FEMALE HAVE SAME FORM

⚙ ABILITIES
- Pick Up
- Gluttony

⚙ STATS
- HP ●
- ATTACK ●
- DEFENSE ●●
- SP. ATTACK ●
- SP. DEFENSE ●●
- SPEED ●●●

⚙ EGG GROUPS
Field

⚙ PERFORMANCE
SPEED ★★★★	STAMINA ★★★★
POWER ★☆☆☆	JUMP ★★☆
SKILL ★★★☆	

● MAIN WAYS TO OBTAIN

Pokémon HeartGold	Burned Tower in Ecruteak City (Hoenn Sound)
Pokémon SoulSilver	Burned Tower in Ecruteak City (Hoenn Sound)
Pokémon Diamond	Route 202 (mass outbreak)
Pokémon Pearl	Route 202 (mass outbreak)
Pokémon Platinum	Route 202 (mass outbreak)

Pokémon HeartGold	Pokémon SoulSilver
It gets interested in everything, which is why it zigs and zags. It is good at finding items.	It gets interested in everything, which is why it zigs and zags. It is good at finding items.

⚙ EVOLUTION

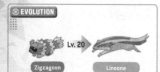

Zigzagoon — Lv. 20 → Linoone

● LEVEL-UP MOVES
Lv.	Name	Type	Kind	Pow.	Acc.	PP	Range	DA
1	Tackle	Normal	Physical	35	95	35	Normal	—
1	Growl	Normal	Status	—	100	40	2 Foes	—
5	Tail Whip	Normal	Status	—	100	30	2 Foes	—
9	Headbutt	Normal	Physical	70	100	15	Normal	○
13	Sand-Attack	Ground	Status	—	100	15	Normal	—
17	Odor Sleuth	Normal	Status	—	—	40	Normal	—
21	Mud Sport	Ground	Status	—	—	15	All	—
25	Pin Missile	Bug	Physical	14	85	20	Normal	—
29	Covet	Normal	Physical	40	100	40	Normal	○
33	Flail	Normal	Physical	—	100	15	Normal	○
37	Rest	Psychic	Status	—	—	10	Self	—
41	Belly Drum	Normal	Status	—	—	10	Self	—
45	Fling	Dark	Physical	—	100	10	Normal	○

● MOVE MANIAC
Name	Type	Kind	Pow.	Acc.	PP	Range	DA
Headbutt	Normal	Physical	70	100	15	Normal	○

● BP MOVES
Name	Type	Kind	Pow.	Acc.	PP	Range	DA
Fury Cutter	Bug	Physical	10	95	20	Normal	○
Icy Wind	Ice	Special	55	95	15	2 Foes	—
Trick	Psychic	Status	—	100	10	Normal	—
Snore	Normal	Special	40	100	15	Normal	—
Helping Hand	Normal	Status	—	—	20	1 Ally	—
Last Resort	Normal	Physical	130	100	5	Normal	○
Swift	Normal	Special	60	—	20	2 Foes	—
Mud-Slap	Ground	Special	20	100	10	Normal	—
Rollout	Rock	Physical	30	90	20	Normal	○
Gunk Shot	Poison	Physical	120	70	5	Normal	—
Seed Bomb	Grass	Physical	80	100	15	Normal	○
Super Fang	Normal	Physical	—	90	10	Normal	○

● TM & HM MOVES
No.	Name	Type	Kind	Pow.	Acc.	PP	Range	DA
TM03	Water Pulse	Water	Special	60	100	20	Normal	—
TM06	Toxic	Poison	Status	—	85	10	Normal	—
TM10	Hidden Power	Normal	Special	—	100	15	Normal	—
TM11	Sunny Day	Fire	Status	—	—	5	All	—
TM13	Ice Beam	Ice	Special	95	100	10	Normal	—
TM14	Blizzard	Ice	Special	120	70	5	2 Foes	—
TM17	Protect	Normal	Status	—	—	10	Self	—
TM18	Rain Dance	Water	Status	—	—	5	All	—
TM21	Frustration	Normal	Physical	—	100	20	Normal	○
TM23	Iron Tail	Steel	Physical	100	75	15	Normal	○
TM24	Thunderbolt	Electric	Special	95	100	15	Normal	—
TM25	Thunder	Electric	Special	120	70	10	Normal	—
TM27	Return	Normal	Physical	—	100	20	Normal	○
TM28	Dig	Ground	Physical	80	100	10	Normal	○
TM30	Shadow Ball	Ghost	Special	80	100	15	Normal	—
TM32	Double Team	Normal	Status	—	—	15	Self	—
TM34	Shock Wave	Electric	Special	60	—	20	Normal	—
TM42	Facade	Normal	Physical	70	100	20	Normal	○
TM43	Secret Power	Normal	Physical	70	100	20	Normal	—
TM44	Rest	Psychic	Status	—	—	10	Self	—
TM45	Attract	Normal	Status	—	100	15	Normal	—
TM46	Thief	Dark	Physical	40	100	10	Normal	—
TM56	Fling	Dark	Physical	—	100	10	Normal	○
TM57	Charge Beam	Electric	Special	50	90	10	Normal	—
TM58	Endure	Normal	Status	—	—	10	Self	—
TM73	Thunder Wave	Electric	Status	—	100	20	Normal	—
TM78	Captivate	Normal	Status	—	100	20	2 Foes	—
TM82	Sleep Talk	Normal	Status	—	—	10	Depends	—
TM83	Natural Gift	Normal	Physical	—	100	15	Normal	○
TM86	Grass Knot	Grass	Special	—	100	20	Normal	○
TM87	Swagger	Normal	Status	—	90	15	Normal	—
TM90	Substitute	Normal	Status	—	—	10	Self	—
HM01	Cut	Normal	Physical	50	95	30	Normal	○
HM03	Surf	Water	Special	95	100	15	2 Foes/1 Ally	—
HM05	Whirlpool	Water	Special	15	70	15	Normal	—
HM06	Rock Smash	Fighting	Physical	40	100	15	Normal	○

● EGG MOVES
Name	Type	Kind	Pow.	Acc.	PP	Range	DA
Charm	Normal	Status	—	100	20	Normal	—
Pursuit	Dark	Physical	40	100	20	Normal	○
Substitute	Normal	Status	—	—	10	Self	—
Tickle	Normal	Status	—	100	20	Normal	—
Trick	Psychic	Status	—	100	10	Normal	—
Helping Hand	Normal	Status	—	—	20	1 Ally	—
Mud-Slap	Ground	Special	20	100	10	Normal	—

● LEVEL-UP MOVES

Lv.	Name	Type	Kind	Pow.	Acc.	PP	Range	DA
1	Switcheroo	Dark	Status	—	100	10	Normal	—
1	Tackle	Normal	Physical	35	95	35	Normal	○
1	Growl	Normal	Status	—	100	40	2 Foes	—
1	Tail Whip	Normal	Status	—	100	30	2 Foes	—
1	Headbutt	Normal	Physical	70	100	15	Normal	○
5	Tail Whip	Normal	Status	—	100	30	2 Foes	—
9	Headbutt	Normal	Physical	70	100	15	Normal	○
13	Sand-Attack	Ground	Status	—	100	15	Normal	—
17	Odor Sleuth	Normal	Status	—	—	40	Normal	—
23	Mud Sport	Ground	Status	—	—	15	All	—
29	Fury Swipes	Normal	Physical	18	80	15	Normal	○
35	Covet	Normal	Physical	40	100	40	Normal	—
41	Slash	Normal	Physical	70	100	20	Normal	○
47	Rest	Psychic	Status	—	—	10	Self	—
53	Belly Drum	Normal	Status	—	—	10	Self	—
59	Fling	Dark	Physical	—	100	10	Normal	—

● MOVE MANIAC

Name	Type	Kind	Pow.	Acc.	PP	Range	DA
Headbutt	Normal	Physical	70	100	15	Normal	○

● BP MOVES

Name	Type	Kind	Pow.	Acc.	PP	Range	DA
Fury Cutter	Bug	Physical	10	95	20	Normal	○
Icy Wind	Ice	Special	55	95	15	2 Foes	—
Trick	Psychic	Status	—	100	10	Normal	—
Snore	Normal	Special	40	100	15	Normal	—
Helping Hand	Normal	Status	—	—	20	1 Ally	—
Last Resort	Normal	Physical	130	100	5	Normal	○
Swift	Normal	Special	60	—	20	2 Foes	—
Mud-Slap	Ground	Special	20	100	10	Normal	—
Rollout	Rock	Physical	30	90	20	Normal	○
Gunk Shot	Poison	Physical	120	70	5	Normal	—
Seed Bomb	Grass	Physical	80	100	15	Normal	○
Super Fang	Normal	Physical	—	90	10	Normal	○

● TM & HM MOVES

No.	Name	Type	Kind	Pow.	Acc.	PP	Range	DA
TM03	Water Pulse	Water	Special	60	100	20	Normal	—
TM05	Roar	Normal	Status	—	100	20	Normal	—
TM06	Toxic	Poison	Status	—	85	10	Normal	—
TM10	Hidden Power	Normal	Special	—	100	15	Normal	—
TM11	Sunny Day	Fire	Status	—	—	5	All	—
TM13	Ice Beam	Ice	Special	95	100	10	Normal	—
TM14	Blizzard	Ice	Special	120	70	5	2 Foes	—
TM15	Hyper Beam	Normal	Special	150	90	5	Normal	—
TM17	Protect	Normal	Status	—	—	10	Self	—
TM18	Rain Dance	Water	Status	—	—	5	All	—
TM21	Frustration	Normal	Physical	—	100	20	Normal	○
TM23	Iron Tail	Steel	Physical	100	75	15	Normal	○
TM24	Thunderbolt	Electric	Special	95	100	15	Normal	—
TM25	Thunder	Electric	Special	120	70	10	Normal	—
TM27	Return	Normal	Physical	—	100	20	Normal	○
TM28	Dig	Ground	Physical	80	100	10	Normal	○
TM30	Shadow Ball	Ghost	Special	80	100	15	Normal	—
TM32	Double Team	Normal	Status	—	—	15	Self	—
TM34	Shock Wave	Electric	Special	60	—	20	Normal	—
TM42	Facade	Normal	Physical	70	100	20	Normal	○
TM43	Secret Power	Normal	Physical	70	100	20	Normal	○
TM44	Rest	Psychic	Status	—	—	10	Self	—
TM45	Attract	Normal	Status	—	100	15	Normal	—
TM46	Thief	Dark	Physical	40	100	10	Normal	—
TM56	Fling	Dark	Physical	—	100	10	Normal	—
TM57	Charge Beam	Electric	Special	50	90	10	Normal	—
TM58	Endure	Normal	Status	—	—	10	Self	—
TM65	Shadow Claw	Ghost	Physical	70	100	15	Normal	○
TM68	Giga Impact	Normal	Physical	150	90	5	Normal	○
TM73	Thunder Wave	Electric	Status	—	100	20	Normal	—
TM78	Captivate	Normal	Status	—	100	20	2 Foes	—
TM82	Sleep Talk	Normal	Status	—	—	10	Self	—
TM83	Natural Gift	Normal	Physical	—	100	15	Normal	—
TM86	Grass Knot	Grass	Special	—	100	20	Normal	○
TM87	Swagger	Normal	Status	—	90	15	Normal	—
TM90	Substitute	Normal	Status	—	—	10	Self	—
HM01	Cut	Normal	Physical	50	95	30	Normal	○
HM03	Surf	Water	Special	95	100	15	2 Foes/1 Ally	—
HM04	Strength	Normal	Physical	80	100	15	Normal	—
HM05	Whirlpool	Water	Special	15	70	15	Normal	—
HM06	Rock Smash	Fighting	Physical	40	100	15	Normal	○

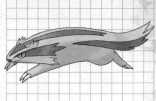

☻ No. 264 | Rushing Pokémon
Linoone

Normal

● HEIGHT: 1'08"
● WEIGHT: 71.6 lbs.
● ITEMS: Oran berry
　　　　　Sitrus Berry

● SIZE COMPARISON

● MALE/FEMALE HAVE SAME FORM

☻ ABILITIES
● Pick Up
● Gluttony

☻ STATS
HP	●●●
ATTACK	●●●
DEFENSE	●●●
SP. ATTACK	●●
SP. DEFENSE	●●
SPEED	●●●●

☻ EGG GROUPS
Field

☻ PERFORMANCE
SPEED ★★★★☆　　STAMINA ★★★★
POWER ★★☆☆☆　　JUMP ★★☆
SKILL ★★☆

● MAIN WAYS TO OBTAIN

Pokémon HeartGold — Route 42 [Hoenn Sound]

Pokémon SoulSilver — Route 42 [Hoenn Sound]

Pokémon Diamond — Level up Zigzagoon to Lv. 20

Pokémon Pearl — Level up Zigzagoon to Lv. 20

Pokémon Platinum — Level up Zigzagoon to Lv. 20

Pokémon HeartGold

When running in a straight line, it can easily top 60 miles an hour. It has a tough time with curved roads.

Pokémon SoulSilver

When running in a straight line, it can easily top 60 miles an hour. It has a tough time with curved roads.

☻ EVOLUTION

Lv. 20

Zigzagoon　　　　　Linoone

No. 265 | Worm Pokémon
Wurmple

Bug

● **LEVEL-UP MOVES**

Lv.	Name	Type	Kind	Pow.	Acc.	PP	Range	DA
1	Tackle	Normal	Physical	35	95	35	Normal	○
1	String Shot	Bug	Status	—	95	40	2 Foes	—
5	Poison Sting	Poison	Physical	15	100	35	Normal	—
15	Bug Bite	Bug	Physical	60	100	20	Normal	○

● **MOVE MANIAC**

Name	Type	Kind	Pow.	Acc.	PP	Range	DA

● **BP MOVES**

Name	Type	Kind	Pow.	Acc.	PP	Range	DA
Bug Bite	Bug	Physical	60	100	20	Normal	○
Snore	Normal	Special	40	100	15	Normal	—
String Shot	Bug	Status	—	95	40	2 Foes	—

● **TM & HM MOVES**

No.	Name	Type	Kind	Pow.	Acc.	PP	Range	DA

● HEIGHT: 1'00"
● WEIGHT: 7.9 lbs.
● ITEMS: None

● SIZE COMPARISON

● MALE/FEMALE HAVE SAME FORM

● **ABILITIES**
● Shield Dust

● **STATS**
HP ●●
ATTACK ●●
DEFENSE ●●
SP. ATTACK ●
SP. DEFENSE ●
SPEED ●

● **EGG GROUPS**
Bug

● **PERFORMANCE**

SPEED ★☆☆	STAMINA ★☆☆☆
POWER ★★☆	JUMP ★★☆
SKILL ★★★★☆	

● **MAIN WAYS TO OBTAIN**

Pokémon HeartGold	Pallet Town (use Headbutt)
Pokémon SoulSilver	Pallet Town (use Headbutt)
Pokémon Diamond	Eterna Forest
Pokémon Pearl	Eterna Forest
Pokémon Platinum	Route 204 (morning and afternoon only)

Pokémon HeartGold
It lives among the tall grass and in forests. It repels attacks by raising up the spikes on its rear.

Pokémon SoulSilver
It lives among the tall grass and in forests. It repels attacks by raising up the spikes on its rear.

● **EVOLUTION**

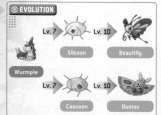

Wurmple
Lv. 7 → Silcoon Lv. 10 → Beautifly
Lv. 7 → Cascoon Lv. 10 → Dustox

LEVEL-UP MOVES

Lv.	Name	Type	Kind	Pow.	Acc.	PP	Range	DA
1	Harden	Normal	Status	—	—	30	Self	—
7	Harden	Normal	Status	—	—	30	Self	—

MOVE MANIAC

Name	Type	Kind	Pow.	Acc.	PP	Range	DA

BP MOVES

Name	Type	Kind	Pow.	Acc.	PP	Range	DA
Bug Bite	Bug	Physical	60	100	20	Normal	○
String Shot	Bug	Status	—	95	40	2 Foes	—
Iron Defense	Steel	Status	—	—	15	Self	—

TM & HM MOVES

No.	Name	Type	Kind	Pow.	Acc.	PP	Range	DA

● HEIGHT: 2'00"
● WEIGHT: 22.0 lbs.
● ITEMS: Wurmple

● SIZE COMPARISON

● MALE/FEMALE HAVE SAME FORM

ABILITIES
● Shed Skin

STATS
HP ●●
ATTACK ●●
DEFENSE ●●
SP. ATTACK ●
SP. DEFENSE ●
SPEED ●

EGG GROUPS
Bug

PERFORMANCE
SPEED ★☆☆
POWER ★☆☆
SKILL ★☆☆
STAMINA ★★★☆☆
JUMP ★★

MAIN WAYS TO OBTAIN

Pokémon HeartGold — Bug-Catching Contest at the National Park [after obtaining the National Pokédex / Thursday]

Pokémon SoulSilver — Bug-Catching Contest at the National Park [after obtaining the National Pokédex / Thursday]

Pokémon Diamond — Eterna Forest

Pokémon Pearl — Level up Wurmple to Lv. 7 [may evolve into Cascoon instead]

Pokémon Platinum — Route 205, Eterna City side

Pokémon HeartGold — Having wrapped silk around the branches of a tree, it quiescently awaits evolution.

Pokémon SoulSilver — Having wrapped silk around the branches of a tree, it quiescently awaits evolution.

EVOLUTION

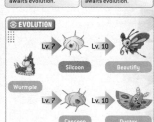

Wurmple — Lv. 7 → Silcoon — Lv. 10 → Beautifly

Wurmple — Lv. 7 → Cascoon — Lv. 10 → Dustox

No. 267 | Butterfly Pokémon
Beautifly

Bug Flying

- **HEIGHT:** 3'03"
- **WEIGHT:** 62.6 lbs.
- **ITEMS:** Shed Shell

● **SIZE COMPARISON**

● **MALE FORM**
Larger red spots on wings

● **FEMALE FORM**
Smaller red spots on wings

⊙ **ABILITIES**
- Swarm

⊙ **STATS**
HP ●●
ATTACK ●●●
DEFENSE ●●
SP. ATTACK ●●●
SP. DEFENSE ●●●
SPEED ●●●

⊙ **EGG GROUPS**
Bug

⊙ **PERFORMANCE**
SPEED ★★★
POWER ★★☆☆
SKILL ★★★
STAMINA ★★★★☆
JUMP ★★★★★

● **MAIN WAYS TO OBTAIN**

Pokémon HeartGold	Bug-Catching Contest at National Park (after obtaining the National Pokédex / Saturday)
Pokémon SoulSilver	Bug-Catching Contest at National Park (after obtaining the National Pokédex / Saturday)
Pokémon Diamond	Route 224
Pokémon Pearl	Route 224
Pokémon Platinum	Route 224

| Pokémon HeartGold | Pokémon SoulSilver |
| Vibrantly patterned wings are its prominent feature. It sucks sweet flower nectar with its long mouth. | Vibrantly patterned wings are its prominent feature. It sucks sweet flower nectar with its long mouth. |

⊙ **EVOLUTION**

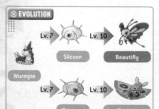

Wurmple — Lv. 7 → Silcoon — Lv. 10 → Beautifly

Wurmple — Lv. 7 → Cascoon — Lv. 10 → Dustox

● **LEVEL-UP MOVES**

Lv.	Name	Type	Kind	Pow.	Acc.	PP	Range	DA
1	Absorb	Grass	Special	20	100	25	Normal	—
10	Absorb	Grass	Special	20	100	25	Normal	—
13	Gust	Flying	Special	40	100	35	Normal	—
17	Stun Spore	Grass	Status	—	75	30	Normal	—
20	Morning Sun	Normal	Status	—	—	5	Self	—
24	Mega Drain	Grass	Special	40	100	15	Normal	—
27	Whirlwind	Normal	Status	—	100	20	Normal	—
31	Attract	Normal	Status	—	100	15	Normal	—
34	Silver Wind	Bug	Special	60	100	5	Normal	—
38	Giga Drain	Grass	Special	60	100	10	Normal	—
41	Bug Buzz	Bug	Special	90	100	10	Normal	—

● **MOVE MANIAC**

Name	Type	Kind	Pow.	Acc.	PP	Range	DA

● **BP MOVES**

Name	Type	Kind	Pow.	Acc.	PP	Range	DA
Ominous Wind	Ghost	Special	60	100	5	Normal	—
Air Cutter	Flying	Special	55	95	25	2 Foes	—
Bug Bite	Bug	Physical	60	100	20	Normal	○
Snore	Normal	Special	40	100	15	Normal	—
Swift	Normal	Special	60	—	20	2 Foes	—
String Shot	Bug	Status	—	95	40	2 Foes	—
Tailwind	Flying	Status	—	—	30	2 Allies	—
Signal Beam	Bug	Special	75	100	15	Normal	—
Twister	Dragon	Special	40	100	20	2 Foes	—

● **TM & HM MOVES**

No.	Name	Type	Kind	Pow.	Acc.	PP	Range	DA
TM06	Toxic	Poison	Status	—	85	10	Normal	—
TM10	Hidden Power	Normal	Special	—	100	15	Normal	—
TM11	Sunny Day	Fire	Status	—	—	5	All	—
TM15	Hyper Beam	Normal	Special	150	90	5	Normal	—
TM17	Protect	Normal	Status	—	—	10	Self	—
TM19	Giga Drain	Grass	Special	60	100	10	Normal	—
TM20	Safeguard	Normal	Status	—	—	25	2 Allies	—
TM21	Frustration	Normal	Physical	—	100	20	Normal	○
TM22	SolarBeam	Grass	Special	120	100	10	Normal	—
TM27	Return	Normal	Physical	—	100	20	Normal	○
TM29	Psychic	Psychic	Special	90	100	10	Normal	—
TM30	Shadow Ball	Ghost	Special	80	100	15	Normal	—
TM32	Double Team	Normal	Status	—	—	15	Self	—
TM40	Aerial Ace	Flying	Physical	60	—	20	Normal	○
TM42	Facade	Normal	Physical	70	100	20	Normal	○
TM43	Secret Power	Normal	Physical	70	100	20	Normal	○
TM44	Rest	Psychic	Status	—	—	10	Self	—
TM45	Attract	Normal	Status	—	100	15	Normal	—
TM46	Thief	Dark	Physical	40	100	10	Normal	○
TM51	Roost	Flying	Status	—	—	10	Self	—
TM53	Energy Ball	Grass	Special	80	100	10	Normal	—
TM58	Endure	Normal	Status	—	—	10	Self	—
TM62	Silver Wind	Bug	Special	60	100	5	Normal	—
TM68	Giga Impact	Normal	Physical	150	90	5	Normal	○
TM70	Flash	Normal	Status	—	100	20	Normal	—
TM78	Captivate	Normal	Status	—	100	20	2 Foes	—
TM82	Sleep Talk	Normal	Status	—	—	10	Depends	—
TM83	Natural Gift	Normal	Physical	—	100	15	Normal	—
TM87	Swagger	Normal	Status	—	90	15	Normal	—
TM89	U-turn	Bug	Physical	70	100	20	Normal	○
TM90	Substitute	Normal	Status	—	—	10	Self	—

● LEVEL-UP MOVES

Lv.	Name	Type	Kind	Pow.	Acc.	PP	Range	DA
1	Harden	Normal	Status	--	--	30	Self	--
?	Harden	Normal	Status	--	--	30	Self	--

● MOVE MANIAC

Name	Type	Kind	Pow.	Acc.	PP	Range	DA
							--

● BP MOVES

Name	Type	Kind	Pow.	Acc.	PP	Range	DA
Bug Bite	Bug	Physical	60	100	20	Normal	○
String Shot	Bug	Status	--	95	40	2 Foes	--
Iron Defense	Steel	Status	--	--	15	Self	--

● TM & HM MOVES

No.	Name	Type	Kind	Pow.	Acc.	PP	Range	DA

⊘ No. 268 | Cocoon Pokémon
Cascoon

Bug

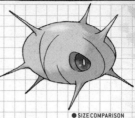

- **HEIGHT:** 2'04"
- **WEIGHT:** 25.4 lbs.
- **ITEMS:** None

● SIZE COMPARISON

● MALE/FEMALE HAVE SAME FORM

⊘ ABILITIES
● Shed Skin

⊘ STATS
HP ●●
ATTACK ●●
DEFENSE ●●
SP. ATTACK ●
SP. DEFENSE ●
SPEED ●

⊘ EGG GROUPS
Bug

⊘ PERFORMANCE
SPEED ★☆☆	STAMINA ★★☆☆
POWER ★★☆	JUMP ★★
SKILL ★☆☆☆	

● MAIN WAYS TO OBTAIN

Pokémon HeartGold	Bug-Catching Contest at the National Park [after obtaining the National Pokédex / Saturday]
Pokémon SoulSilver	Bug-Catching Contest at the National Park [after obtaining the National Pokédex / Saturday]
Pokémon Diamond	Level up Wurmple to Lv. 7 [may evolve into Silcoon instead]
Pokémon Pearl	Eterna Forest
Pokémon Platinum	Route 205, Eterna City side

Pokémon HeartGold	**Pokémon SoulSilver**
It endures attacks with patience, because the more pain before evolution, the sturdier it becomes.	It endures attacks with patience, because the more pain before evolution, the sturdier it becomes.

⊘ EVOLUTION

Wurmple — Lv. 7 → Silcoon — Lv. 10 → Beautifly

Wurmple — Lv. 7 → Cascoon — Lv. 10 → Dustox

No. 269 | Poison Moth Pokémon
Dustox

Bug | Poison

- **HEIGHT:** 3'11"
- **WEIGHT:** 69.7 lbs.
- **ITEMS:** Shed Shell

SIZE COMPARISON

MALE FORM
Longer antennae

FEMALE FORM
Shorter antennae

ABILITIES
- Shield Dust

STATS
- HP ●●
- ATTACK ●●
- DEFENSE ●●●
- SP. ATTACK ●●
- SP. DEFENSE ●●●●
- SPEED ●●●

EGG GROUPS
Bug

PERFORMANCE
- SPEED ★★☆☆
- POWER ★★☆
- SKILL ★★★★☆
- STAMINA ★★☆
- JUMP ★★★★★

MAIN WAYS TO OBTAIN

Pokémon HeartGold
Bug-Catching Contest at the National Park [after obtaining the National Pokédex / Thursday]

Pokémon SoulSilver
Bug-Catching Contest at the National Park [after obtaining the National Pokédex / Thursday]

Pokémon Diamond
Level up Cascoon to Lv. 10

Pokémon Pearl
Route 230

Pokémon Platinum
Route 224

Pokémon HeartGold
It scatters its fine dust all over when it is attacked. It is a nocturnal Pokémon.

Pokémon SoulSilver
It scatters its fine dust all over when it is attacked. It is a nocturnal Pokémon.

EVOLUTION

Wurmple — Lv. 7 → Silcoon — Lv. 10 → Beautifly
Wurmple — Lv. 7 → Cascoon — Lv. 10 → Dustox

● LEVEL-UP MOVES

Lv.	Name	Type	Kind	Pow.	Acc.	PP	Range	DA
1	Confusion	Psychic	Special	50	100	25	Normal	—
10	Confusion	Psychic	Special	50	100	25	Normal	—
13	Gust	Flying	Special	40	100	35	Normal	—
17	Protect	Normal	Status	—	—	10	Self	—
20	Whirlwind	Normal	Status	—	—	5	Self	—
24	Psybeam	Psychic	Special	65	100	20	Normal	—
27	Whirlwind	Normal	Status	—	100	20	Normal	—
31	Light Screen	Psychic	Status	—	—	30	2 Allies	—
34	Silver Wind	Bug	Special	60	100	5	Normal	—
38	Toxic	Poison	Status	—	85	10	Normal	—
41	Bug Buzz	Bug	Special	90	100	10	Normal	—

● MOVE MANIAC

Name	Type	Kind	Pow.	Acc.	PP	Range	DA

● BP MOVES

Name	Type	Kind	Pow.	Acc.	PP	Range	DA
Ominous Wind	Ghost	Special	60	100	5	Normal	—
Air Cutter	Flying	Special	55	95	25	2 Foes	—
Bug Bite	Bug	Physical	60	100	20	Normal	○
Snore	Normal	Special	40	100	15	Normal	—
Swift	Normal	Special	60	—	20	2 Foes	—
String Shot	Bug	Status	—	95	40	2 Foes	—
Tailwind	Flying	Status	—	—	30	2 Allies	—
Signal Beam	Bug	Special	75	100	15	Normal	—
Twister	Dragon	Special	40	100	20	2 Foes	—

● TM & HM MOVES

No.	Name	Type	Kind	Pow.	Acc.	PP	Range	DA
TM06	Toxic	Poison	Status	—	85	10	Normal	—
TM10	Hidden Power	Normal	Special	—	100	15	Normal	—
TM11	Sunny Day	Fire	Status	—	—	5	All	—
TM15	Hyper Beam	Normal	Special	150	90	5	Normal	—
TM16	Light Screen	Psychic	Status	—	—	30	2 Allies	—
TM17	Protect	Normal	Status	—	—	10	Self	—
TM19	Giga Drain	Grass	Special	60	100	10	Normal	—
TM21	Frustration	Normal	Physical	—	100	20	Normal	○
TM22	SolarBeam	Grass	Special	120	100	10	Normal	—
TM27	Return	Normal	Physical	—	100	20	Normal	○
TM29	Psychic	Psychic	Special	90	100	10	Normal	—
TM30	Shadow Ball	Ghost	Special	80	100	15	Normal	—
TM32	Double Team	Normal	Status	—	—	15	Self	—
TM36	Sludge Bomb	Poison	Special	90	100	10	Normal	—
TM40	Aerial Ace	Flying	Physical	60	—	20	Normal	○
TM42	Facade	Normal	Physical	70	100	20	Normal	○
TM43	Secret Power	Normal	Physical	70	100	20	Normal	○
TM44	Rest	Psychic	Status	—	—	10	Self	—
TM45	Attract	Normal	Status	—	100	15	Normal	—
TM46	Thief	Dark	Physical	40	100	10	Normal	○
TM51	Roost	Flying	Status	—	—	10	Self	—
TM53	Energy Ball	Grass	Special	80	100	10	Normal	—
TM58	Endure	Normal	Status	—	—	10	Self	—
TM62	Silver Wind	Bug	Special	60	100	5	Normal	—
TM68	Giga Impact	Normal	Physical	150	90	5	Normal	○
TM70	Flash	Normal	Status	—	100	20	Normal	—
TM78	Captivate	Normal	Status	—	100	20	2 Foes	—
TM82	Sleep Talk	Normal	Status	—	—	10	Depends	—
TM83	Natural Gift	Normal	Physical	—	100	15	Normal	—
TM87	Swagger	Normal	Status	—	90	15	Normal	—
TM89	U-turn	Bug	Physical	70	100	20	Normal	○
TM90	Substitute	Normal	Status	—	—	10	Self	—

● LEVEL-UP MOVES

Lv.	Name	Type	Kind	Pow.	Acc.	PP	Range	DA
1	Astonish	Ghost	Physical	30	100	15	Normal	○
3	Growl	Normal	Status	—	100	40	2 Foes	—
5	Absorb	Grass	Special	20	100	25	Normal	—
7	Nature Power	Normal	Status	—	—	20	Depends	—
11	Mist	Ice	Status	—	—	30	2 Allies	—
15	Natural Gift	Normal	Physical	—	100	15	Normal	—
19	Mega Drain	Grass	Special	40	100	15	Normal	—
25	BubbleBeam	Water	Special	65	100	20	Normal	—
31	Zen Headbutt	Psychic	Physical	80	90	15	Normal	○
37	Rain Dance	Water	Status	—	—	5	All	—
45	Energy Ball	Grass	Special	80	100	10	Normal	—

● MOVE MANIAC

Name	Type	Kind	Pow.	Acc.	PP	Range	DA
Headbutt	Normal	Physical	70	100	15	Normal	—

● BP MOVES

Name	Type	Kind	Pow.	Acc.	PP	Range	DA
Icy Wind	Ice	Special	55	95	15	2 Foes	—
Zen Headbutt	Psychic	Physical	80	90	15	Normal	○
Snore	Normal	Special	40	100	15	Normal	—
Synthesis	Grass	Status	—	—	5	Self	—
Uproar	Normal	Special	50	100	10	1 Random	—
Seed Bomb	Grass	Physical	80	100	15	Normal	—

● TM & HM MOVES

No.	Name	Type	Kind	Pow.	Acc.	PP	Range	DA
TM03	Water Pulse	Water	Special	60	100	20	Normal	—
TM06	Toxic	Poison	Status	—	85	10	Normal	—
TM07	Hail	Ice	Status	—	—	10	All	—
TM09	Bullet Seed	Grass	Physical	10	100	30	Normal	—
TM10	Hidden Power	Normal	Special	—	100	15	Normal	—
TM11	Sunny Day	Fire	Status	—	—	5	All	—
TM13	Ice Beam	Ice	Special	95	100	10	Normal	—
TM14	Blizzard	Ice	Special	120	70	5	2 Foes	—
TM17	Protect	Normal	Status	—	—	10	Self	—
TM18	Rain Dance	Water	Status	—	—	5	All	—
TM19	Giga Drain	Grass	Special	60	100	10	Normal	—
TM21	Frustration	Normal	Physical	—	100	20	Normal	○
TM22	SolarBeam	Grass	Special	120	100	10	Normal	—
TM27	Return	Normal	Physical	—	100	20	Normal	○
TM32	Double Team	Normal	Status	—	—	15	Self	—
TM42	Facade	Normal	Physical	70	100	20	Normal	○
TM43	Secret Power	Normal	Physical	70	100	20	Normal	—
TM44	Rest	Psychic	Status	—	—	10	Self	—
TM45	Attract	Normal	Status	—	100	15	Normal	—
TM46	Thief	Dark	Physical	40	100	10	Normal	○
TM53	Energy Ball	Grass	Special	80	100	10	Normal	—
TM58	Endure	Normal	Status	—	—	10	Self	—
TM70	Flash	Normal	Status	—	100	20	Normal	—
TM75	Swords Dance	Normal	Status	—	—	30	Self	—
TM78	Captivate	Normal	Status	—	100	20	2 Foes	—
TM82	Sleep Talk	Normal	Status	—	—	10	Depends	—
TM83	Natural Gift	Normal	Physical	—	100	15	Normal	—
TM86	Grass Knot	Grass	Special	—	100	20	Normal	—
TM87	Swagger	Normal	Status	—	90	15	Normal	—
TM90	Substitute	Normal	Status	—	—	10	Self	—
HM03	Surf	Water	Special	95	100	15	2 Foes/1 Ally	—
HM05	Whirlpool	Water	Special	15	70	15	Normal	—

● EGG MOVES

Name	Type	Kind	Pow.	Acc.	PP	Range	DA
Synthesis	Grass	Status	—	—	5	Self	—
Razor Leaf	Grass	Physical	55	95	25	2 Foes	—
Sweet Scent	Normal	Status	—	100	20	2 Foes	—
Leech Seed	Grass	Status	—	90	10	Normal	—
Flail	Normal	Physical	—	100	15	Normal	○
Water Gun	Water	Special	40	100	25	Normal	—
Tickle	Normal	Status	—	100	20	Normal	—
Counter	Fighting	Physical	—	100	20	Self	○

Water   Grass

● HEIGHT: 1'08"
● WEIGHT: 5.7 lbs.
● ITEMS: None

● SIZE COMPARISON

● MALE/FEMALE HAVE SAME FORM

◉ ABILITIES
● Swift Swim
● Rain Dish

◉ STATS
HP ●
ATTACK ●
DEFENSE ●
SP. ATTACK ●
SP. DEFENSE ● ●
SPEED ●

◉ EGG GROUPS
Water 1
Grass

◉ PERFORMANCE
SPEED ★★☆
POWER ★★☆☆
SKILL ★★★☆
STAMINA ★★★☆☆
JUMP ★★

● MAIN WAYS TO OBTAIN

Pokémon HeartGold — Safari Zone (Plains Area: if Water objects are placed, may appear in tall grass)

Pokémon SoulSilver — Safari Zone (Plains Area: if Water objects are placed, may appear in tall grass)

Pokémon Diamond — Route 203 (after obtaining the National Pokédex, insert *Pokémon Sapphire* into your Nintendo DS's Game Pak slot)

Pokémon Pearl — Route 203 (after obtaining the National Pokédex, insert *Pokémon Sapphire* into your Nintendo DS's Game Pak slot)

Pokémon Platinum — Route 203 (after obtaining the National Pokédex, insert *Pokémon Sapphire* into your Nintendo DS's Game Pak slot)

Pokémon HeartGold — Its leaf grew too large for it to live on land. That is how it began to live floating in the water.

Pokémon SoulSilver — Its leaf grew too large for it to live on land. That is how it began to live floating in the water.

◉ EVOLUTION

Lotad — Lv. 14 → Lombre — Use Water Stone → Ludicolo

No. 271 | Jolly Pokémon
Lombre

Water | Grass

- **HEIGHT:** 3'11"
- **WEIGHT:** 71.6 lbs.
- **ITEMS:** None

● SIZE COMPARISON

● MALE/FEMALE HAVE SAME FORM

ABILITIES
- Swift Swim
- Rain Dish

STATS
- HP ●●
- ATTACK ●●
- DEFENSE ●●
- SP. ATTACK ●●
- SP. DEFENSE ●●●
- SPEED ●●

EGG GROUPS
- Water 1
- Grass

PERFORMANCE
- SPEED ★★★
- POWER ★★★☆
- SKILL ★★★★☆
- STAMINA ★★☆☆
- JUMP ★★☆

MAIN WAYS TO OBTAIN

Pokémon HeartGold	Safari Zone (Wetland Area): if Grass objects are placed, may appear in tall grass) or level up Lotad to Lv. 14
Pokémon SoulSilver	Safari Zone (Wetland Area): if Grass objects are placed, may appear in tall grass) or level up Lotad to Lv. 14
Pokémon Diamond	Route 212, Pastoria City side (after obtaining the National Pokédex, insert *Pokémon Sapphire* into your Nintendo DS's Game Pak slot)
Pokémon Pearl	Route 212, Pastoria City side (after obtaining the National Pokédex, insert *Pokémon Sapphire* into your Nintendo DS's Game Pak slot)
Pokémon Platinum	Route 212, Pastoria City side (after obtaining the National Pokédex, insert *Pokémon Sapphire* into your Nintendo DS's Game Pak slot)

Pokémon HeartGold	**Pokémon SoulSilver**
It is nocturnal and becomes active at nightfall. It feeds on aquatic mosses that grow in the riverbed.	It is nocturnal and becomes active at nightfall. It feeds on aquatic mosses that grow in the riverbed.

EVOLUTION

Lotad — Lv. 14 → Lombre — Use Water Stone → Ludicolo

● LEVEL-UP MOVES

Lv.	Name	Type	Kind	Pow.	Acc.	PP	Range	DA
1	Astonish	Ghost	Physical	30	100	15	Normal	○
3	Growl	Normal	Status	—	100	40	2 Foes	—
5	Absorb	Grass	Special	20	100	25	Normal	—
7	Nature Power	Normal	Status	—	—	20	Depends	—
11	Fake Out	Normal	Physical	40	100	10	Normal	○
15	Fury Swipes	Normal	Physical	18	80	15	Normal	○
19	Water Sport	Water	Status	—	—	15	All	—
25	BubbleBeam	Water	Special	65	100	10	Normal	○
31	Zen Headbutt	Psychic	Physical	80	90	15	Normal	—
37	Uproar	Normal	Special	50	100	10	1 Random	—
45	Hydro Pump	Water	Special	120	80	5	Normal	—

● MOVE MANIAC

Name	Type	Kind	Pow.	Acc.	PP	Range	DA
Headbutt	Normal	Physical	70	100	15	Normal	○

● BP MOVES

Name	Type	Kind	Pow.	Acc.	PP	Range	DA
Dive	Water	Physical	80	100	10	Normal	○
Icy Wind	Ice	Special	55	95	15	2 Foes	—
ThunderPunch	Electric	Physical	75	100	15	Normal	○
Fire Punch	Fire	Physical	75	100	15	Normal	○
Ice Punch	Ice	Physical	75	100	15	Normal	○
Zen Headbutt	Psychic	Physical	80	90	15	Normal	—
Snore	Normal	Special	40	100	15	Normal	—
Synthesis	Grass	Status	—	—	5	Self	—
Uproar	Normal	Special	50	100	10	1 Random	—
Mud-Slap	Ground	Special	20	100	10	Normal	—
Seed Bomb	Grass	Physical	80	100	15	Normal	—

● TM & HM MOVES

No.	Name	Type	Kind	Pow.	Acc.	PP	Range	DA
TM03	Water Pulse	Water	Special	60	100	20	Normal	—
TM06	Toxic	Poison	Status	—	85	10	Normal	—
TM07	Hail	Ice	Status	—	—	10	All	—
TM09	Bullet Seed	Grass	Physical	10	100	30	Normal	—
TM10	Hidden Power	Normal	Special	—	100	15	Normal	—
TM11	Sunny Day	Fire	Status	—	—	5	All	—
TM13	Ice Beam	Ice	Special	95	100	10	Normal	—
TM14	Blizzard	Ice	Special	120	70	5	2 Foes	—
TM17	Protect	Normal	Status	—	—	10	Self	—
TM18	Rain Dance	Water	Status	—	—	5	All	—
TM19	Giga Drain	Grass	Special	60	100	10	Normal	—
TM21	Frustration	Normal	Physical	—	100	20	Normal	○
TM22	SolarBeam	Grass	Special	120	100	10	Normal	—
TM27	Return	Normal	Physical	—	100	20	Normal	○
TM31	Brick Break	Fighting	Physical	75	100	15	Normal	○
TM32	Double Team	Normal	Status	—	—	15	Self	—
TM42	Facade	Normal	Physical	70	100	20	Normal	○
TM43	Secret Power	Normal	Physical	70	100	20	Normal	—
TM44	Rest	Psychic	Status	—	—	10	Self	—
TM45	Attract	Normal	Status	—	100	15	Normal	—
TM46	Thief	Dark	Physical	40	100	10	Normal	—
TM53	Energy Ball	Grass	Special	80	100	10	Normal	—
TM56	Fling	Dark	Physical	—	100	10	Normal	—
TM58	Endure	Normal	Status	—	—	10	Self	—
TM60	Drain Punch	Fighting	Physical	60	100	5	Normal	○
TM70	Flash	Normal	Status	—	100	20	Normal	—
TM75	Swords Dance	Normal	Status	—	—	30	Self	—
TM78	Captivate	Normal	Status	—	100	20	2 Foes	—
TM82	Sleep Talk	Normal	Status	—	—	10	Self	—
TM83	Natural Gift	Normal	Physical	—	100	15	Normal	—
TM86	Grass Knot	Grass	Special	—	100	20	Normal	○
TM87	Swagger	Normal	Status	—	90	15	Normal	—
TM90	Substitute	Normal	Status	—	—	10	Self	—
HM03	Surf	Water	Special	95	100	15	2 Foes/1 Ally	—
HM04	Strength	Normal	Physical	80	100	15	Normal	○
HM05	Whirlpool	Water	Special	15	70	15	Normal	—
HM06	Rock Smash	Fighting	Physical	40	100	15	Normal	○
HM07	Waterfall	Water	Physical	80	100	15	Normal	○

● LEVEL-UP MOVES

Lv.	Name	Type	Kind	Pow.	Acc.	PP	Range	DA
1	Astonish	Ghost	Physical	30	100	15	Normal	—
1	Growl	Normal	Status	—	100	40	2 Foes	—
1	Mega Drain	Grass	Special	40	100	15	Normal	—
1	Nature Power	Normal	Status	—	—	20	Depends	—

● MOVE MANIAC

Name	Type	Kind	Pow.	Acc.	PP	Range	DA
Headbutt	Normal	Physical	70	100	15	Normal	—

● BP MOVES

Name	Type	Kind	Pow.	Acc.	PP	Range	DA
Dive	Water	Physical	80	100	10	Normal	○
Icy Wind	Ice	Special	55	95	15	2 Foes	—
ThunderPunch	Electric	Physical	75	100	15	Normal	○
Fire Punch	Fire	Physical	75	100	15	Normal	○
Ice Punch	Ice	Physical	75	100	15	Normal	○
Zen Headbutt	Psychic	Physical	80	90	15	Normal	○
Snore	Normal	Special	40	100	15	Normal	—
Synthesis	Grass	Status	—	—	5	Self	—
Uproar	Normal	Special	50	100	10	1 Random	—
Mud-Slap	Ground	Special	20	100	10	Normal	—
Seed Bomb	Grass	Physical	80	100	15	Normal	○

● TM & HM MOVES

No.	Name	Type	Kind	Pow.	Acc.	PP	Range	DA
TM01	Focus Punch	Fighting	Physical	150	100	20	Normal	○
TM03	Water Pulse	Water	Special	60	100	20	Normal	—
TM06	Toxic	Poison	Status	—	85	10	Normal	—
TM07	Hail	Ice	Status	—	—	10	All	—
TM09	Bullet Seed	Grass	Physical	10	100	30	Normal	—
TM10	Hidden Power	Normal	Special	—	100	15	Normal	—
TM11	Sunny Day	Fire	Status	—	—	5	All	—
TM13	Ice Beam	Ice	Special	95	100	10	Normal	—
TM14	Blizzard	Ice	Special	120	70	5	2 Foes	—
TM15	Hyper Beam	Normal	Special	150	90	5	Normal	—
TM17	Protect	Normal	Status	—	—	10	Self	—
TM18	Rain Dance	Water	Status	—	—	5	All	—
TM19	Giga Drain	Grass	Special	60	100	10	Normal	—
TM21	Frustration	Normal	Physical	—	100	20	Normal	○
TM22	SolarBeam	Grass	Special	120	100	10	Normal	—
TM27	Return	Normal	Physical	—	100	20	Normal	○
TM31	Brick Break	Fighting	Physical	75	100	15	Normal	○
TM32	Double Team	Normal	Status	—	—	15	Self	—
TM42	Facade	Normal	Physical	70	100	20	Normal	○
TM43	Secret Power	Normal	Physical	70	100	20	Normal	○
TM44	Rest	Psychic	Status	—	—	10	Self	—
TM45	Attract	Normal	Status	—	100	15	Normal	—
TM46	Thief	Dark	Physical	40	100	10	Normal	○
TM52	Focus Blast	Fighting	Special	120	70	5	Normal	—
TM53	Energy Ball	Grass	Special	80	100	10	Normal	—
TM56	Fling	Dark	Physical	—	100	10	Normal	○
TM58	Endure	Normal	Status	—	—	10	Self	—
TM60	Drain Punch	Fighting	Physical	60	100	5	Normal	○
TM68	Giga Impact	Normal	Physical	150	90	5	Normal	○
TM70	Flash	Normal	Status	—	100	20	Normal	—
TM75	Swords Dance	Normal	Status	—	—	30	Self	—
TM78	Captivate	Normal	Status	—	100	20	2 Foes	—
TM82	Sleep Talk	Normal	Status	—	—	10	Depends	—
TM83	Natural Gift	Normal	Physical	—	100	15	Normal	—
TM86	Grass Knot	Grass	Special	—	100	20	Normal	—
TM87	Swagger	Normal	Status	—	90	15	Normal	—
TM90	Substitute	Normal	Status	—	—	10	Self	—
HM03	Surf	Water	Special	95	100	15	2 Foes/1 Ally	○
HM04	Strength	Normal	Physical	80	100	15	Normal	○
HM05	Whirlpool	Water	Special	15	70	15	Normal	—
HM06	Rock Smash	Fighting	Physical	40	100	15	Normal	○
HM07	Waterfall	Water	Physical	80	100	15	Normal	○
HM08	Rock Climb	Normal	Physical	90	85	20	Normal	○

● **No. 272** | Carefree Pokémon
Ludicolo
Water | Grass

● **HEIGHT:** 4'11"
● **WEIGHT:** 121.3 lbs.
● **ITEMS:** None

● **SIZE COMPARISON**

● **MALE FORM**
Thicker zigzag stripes

● **FEMALE FORM**
Thinner zigzag stripes

◎ ABILITIES
● Swift Swim
● Rain Dish

◎ STATS
HP	●●●
ATTACK	●●●
DEFENSE	●●●
SP. ATTACK	●●●
SP. DEFENSE	●●●●
SPEED	●●●

◎ EGG GROUPS
Water 1
Grass

◎ PERFORMANCE
SPEED ★★☆☆ STAMINA ★★★☆☆
POWER ★★★☆ JUMP ★★☆
SKILL ★★★☆☆

● MAIN WAYS TO OBTAIN

Pokémon HeartGold — Use Water Stone on Lombre

Pokémon SoulSilver — Use Water Stone on Lombre

Pokémon Diamond — Use Water Stone on Lombre

Pokémon Pearl — Use Water Stone on Lombre

Pokémon Platinum — Use Water Stone on Lombre

Pokémon HeartGold — If it hears festive music, it begins moving in rhythm in order to amplify its power.

Pokémon SoulSilver — If it hears festive music, it begins moving in rhythm in order to amplify its power.

◎ EVOLUTION

Lotad → (Lv. 14) Lombre → (Use Water Stone) Ludicolo

No. 273 | Acorn Pokémon
Seedot

Grass

- **HEIGHT:** 1'08"
- **WEIGHT:** 8.8 lbs.
- **ITEMS:** None

● SIZE COMPARISON

● MALE/FEMALE HAVE SAME FORM

ABILITIES
- Chlorophyll
- Early Bird

STATS
HP ●
ATTACK ●●
DEFENSE ●●
SP. ATTACK ●●
SP. DEFENSE ●
SPEED ●

EGG GROUPS
Field

Grass

PERFORMANCE
SPEED ★★★☆   STAMINA ★★☆☆
POWER ★★☆   JUMP ★★☆
SKILL ★★☆☆

● MAIN WAYS TO OBTAIN

Pokémon HeartGold	Viridian Forest (use Headbutt)
Pokémon SoulSilver	Viridian Forest (use Headbutt)
Pokémon Diamond	Route 203 (after obtaining the National Pokédex, insert *Pokémon Ruby* into your Nintendo DS's Game Pak slot)
Pokémon Pearl	Route 203 (after obtaining the National Pokédex, insert *Pokémon Ruby* into your Nintendo DS's Game Pak slot)
Pokémon Platinum	Route 203 (after obtaining the National Pokédex, insert *Pokémon Ruby* into your Nintendo DS's Game Pak slot)

| Pokémon HeartGold | Pokémon SoulSilver |
| It attaches itself to a tree branch using the top of its head. Strong winds can sometimes make it fall. | It attaches itself to a tree branch using the top of its head. Strong winds can sometimes make it fall. |

EVOLUTION

Lv. 14   Use Leaf Stone

Seedot   Nuzleaf   Shiftry

● LEVEL-UP MOVES

Lv.	Name	Type	Kind	Pow.	Acc.	PP	Range	DA
1	Bide	Normal	Physical	—	—	10	Self	○
3	Harden	Normal	Status	—	—	30	Self	—
?	Growth	Normal	Status	—	—	40	Self	—
13	Nature Power	Normal	Status	—	—	20	Depends	—
21	Synthesis	Grass	Status	—	—	5	Self	—
31	Sunny Day	Fire	Status	—	—	5	All	—
43	Explosion	Normal	Physical	250	100	5	2 Foes/1 Ally	—

● MOVE MANIAC

Name	Type	Kind	Pow.	Acc.	PP	Range	DA
Headbutt	Normal	Physical	70	100	15	Normal	○

● BP MOVES

Name	Type	Kind	Pow.	Acc.	PP	Range	DA
Snore	Normal	Special	40	100	15	Normal	—
Spite	Ghost	Status	—	100	10	Normal	—
Synthesis	Grass	Status	—	—	5	Self	—
Worry Seed	Grass	Status	—	100	10	Normal	—
Rollout	Rock	Physical	30	90	20	Normal	○
Seed Bomb	Grass	Physical	80	100	15	Normal	—

● TM & HM MOVES

No.	Name	Type	Kind	Pow.	Acc.	PP	Range	DA
TM06	Toxic	Poison	Status	—	85	10	Normal	—
TM09	Bullet Seed	Grass	Physical	10	100	30	Normal	—
TM10	Hidden Power	Normal	Special	—	100	15	Normal	—
TM11	Sunny Day	Fire	Status	—	—	5	All	—
TM17	Protect	Normal	Status	—	—	10	Self	—
TM19	Giga Drain	Grass	Special	60	100	10	Normal	—
TM21	Frustration	Normal	Physical	—	100	20	Normal	○
TM22	SolarBeam	Grass	Special	120	100	10	Normal	—
TM27	Return	Normal	Physical	—	100	20	Normal	○
TM28	Dig	Ground	Physical	80	100	10	Normal	○
TM30	Shadow Ball	Ghost	Special	80	100	15	Normal	—
TM32	Double Team	Normal	Status	—	—	15	Self	—
TM42	Facade	Normal	Physical	70	100	20	Normal	○
TM43	Secret Power	Normal	Physical	70	100	20	Normal	—
TM44	Rest	Psychic	Status	—	—	10	Self	—
TM45	Attract	Normal	Status	—	100	15	Normal	—
TM53	Energy Ball	Grass	Special	80	100	10	Normal	—
TM58	Endure	Normal	Status	—	—	10	Self	—
TM64	Explosion	Normal	Physical	250	100	5	2 Foes/1 Ally	—
TM70	Flash	Normal	Status	—	100	20	Normal	—
TM75	Swords Dance	Normal	Status	—	—	30	Self	—
TM78	Captivate	Normal	Status	—	100	20	2 Foes	—
TM82	Sleep Talk	Normal	Status	—	—	10	Depends	—
TM83	Natural Gift	Normal	Physical	—	100	15	Normal	—
TM86	Grass Knot	Grass	Special	—	100	20	Normal	○
TM87	Swagger	Normal	Status	—	90	15	Normal	—
TM90	Substitute	Normal	Status	—	—	10	Self	—
HM06	Rock Smash	Fighting	Physical	40	100	15	Normal	○

● EGG MOVES

Name	Type	Kind	Pow.	Acc.	PP	Range	DA
Leech Seed	Grass	Status	—	90	10	Normal	—
Amnesia	Psychic	Status	—	—	20	Self	—
Quick Attack	Normal	Physical	40	100	30	Normal	○
Razor Wind	Normal	Special	80	100	10	2 Foes	—
Take Down	Normal	Physical	90	85	20	Normal	○
False Swipe	Normal	Physical	40	100	40	Normal	○
Worry Seed	Grass	Status	—	100	10	Normal	—
Nasty Plot	Dark	Status	—	—	20	Self	—
Power Swap	Psychic	Status	—	—	10	Normal	—

LEVEL-UP MOVES

Lv.	Name	Type	Kind	Pow.	Acc.	PP	Range	DA
1	Razor Leaf	Grass	Physical	55	95	25	2 Foes	—
1	Pound	Normal	Physical	40	100	35	Normal	○
3	Harden	Normal	Status	—	—	30	Self	—
7	Growth	Normal	Status	—	—	40	Self	—
13	Nature Power	Normal	Status	—	—	20	Depends	—
19	Fake Out	Normal	Physical	40	100	10	Normal	○
25	Torment	Dark	Status	—	100	15	Normal	—
31	Faint Attack	Dark	Physical	60	—	20	Normal	○
37	Razor Wind	Normal	Special	80	100	10	2 Foes	—
43	Swagger	Normal	Status	—	90	15	Normal	—
49	Extrasensory	Psychic	Special	80	100	30	Normal	—

MOVE MANIAC

Name	Type	Kind	Pow.	Acc.	PP	Range	DA
Headbutt	Normal	Physical	70	100	15	Normal	○

BP MOVES

Name	Type	Kind	Pow.	Acc.	PP	Range	DA
Fury Cutter	Bug	Physical	10	95	20	Normal	○
Snore	Normal	Special	40	100	15	Normal	—
Spite	Ghost	Status	—	100	10	Normal	—
Synthesis	Grass	Status	—	—	5	Self	—
Swift	Normal	Special	60	—	20	2 Foes	—
Worry Seed	Grass	Status	—	100	10	Normal	—
Mud-Slap	Ground	Special	20	100	10	Normal	—
Rollout	Rock	Physical	30	90	20	Normal	○
Seed Bomb	Grass	Physical	80	100	15	Normal	○
Low Kick	Fighting	Physical	—	100	20	Normal	○

TM & HM MOVES

Nu.	Name	Type	Kind	Pow.	Acc.	PP	Range	DA
TM06	Toxic	Poison	Status	—	85	10	Normal	—
TM09	Bullet Seed	Grass	Physical	10	100	30	Normal	—
TM10	Hidden Power	Normal	Special	—	100	15	Normal	—
TM11	Sunny Day	Fire	Status	—	—	5	All	—
TM15	Hyper Beam	Normal	Special	150	90	5	Normal	—
TM17	Protect	Normal	Status	—	—	10	Self	—
TM19	Giga Drain	Grass	Special	60	100	10	Normal	—
TM21	Frustration	Normal	Physical	—	100	20	Normal	○
TM22	SolarBeam	Grass	Special	120	100	10	Normal	—
TM27	Return	Normal	Physical	—	100	20	Normal	○
TM28	Dig	Ground	Physical	80	100	10	Normal	○
TM30	Shadow Ball	Ghost	Special	80	100	15	Normal	—
TM31	Brick Break	Fighting	Physical	75	100	15	Normal	—
TM32	Double Team	Normal	Status	—	—	15	Self	—
TM39	Rock Tomb	Rock	Physical	50	80	10	Normal	—
TM41	Torment	Dark	Status	—	100	15	Normal	—
TM42	Facade	Normal	Physical	70	100	20	Normal	—
TM43	Secret Power	Normal	Physical	70	100	20	Normal	—
TM44	Rest	Psychic	Status	—	—	10	Self	—
TM45	Attract	Normal	Status	—	100	15	Normal	—
TM46	Thief	Dark	Physical	40	100	10	Normal	○
TM53	Energy Ball	Grass	Special	80	100	10	Normal	—
TM56	Fling	Dark	Physical	—	100	10	Normal	—
TM58	Endure	Normal	Status	—	—	10	Self	—
TM63	Embargo	Dark	Status	—	100	15	Normal	—
TM64	Explosion	Normal	Physical	250	100	5	2 Foes/1 Ally	—
TM66	Payback	Dark	Physical	50	100	10	Normal	○
TM70	Flash	Normal	Status	—	100	20	Normal	—
TM75	Swords Dance	Normal	Status	—	—	30	Self	—
TM77	Psych Up	Normal	Status	—	—	10	Normal	—
TM78	Captivate	Normal	Status	—	100	20	2 Foes	—
TM79	Dark Pulse	Dark	Special	80	100	15	Normal	—
TM80	Rock Slide	Rock	Physical	75	90	10	2 Foes	—
TM82	Sleep Talk	Normal	Status	—	—	10	Depends	—
TM83	Natural Gift	Normal	Physical	—	100	15	Normal	—
TM86	Grass Knot	Grass	Special	—	100	20	Normal	○
TM87	Swagger	Normal	Status	—	90	15	Normal	—
TM90	Substitute	Normal	Status	—	—	10	Self	—
HM01	Cut	Normal	Physical	50	95	30	Normal	○
HM04	Strength	Normal	Physical	80	100	15	Normal	○
HM06	Rock Smash	Fighting	Physical	40	100	15	Normal	○

No. 274 | Wily Pokémon
Nuzleaf

Grass   Dark

- **HEIGHT:** 3'03"
- **WEIGHT:** 61.7 lbs.
- **ITEMS:** None

SIZE COMPARISON

MALE FORM
Bigger leaf on head

FEMALE FORM
Smaller leaf on head

ABILITIES
- Chlorophyll
- Early Bird

STATS
- HP ●●●
- ATTACK ●●●
- DEFENSE ●●
- SP. ATTACK ●●●
- SP. DEFENSE ●
- SPEED ●●●

EGG GROUPS
Field

Grass

PERFORMANCE

SPEED ★★★☆☆   STAMINA ★★
POWER ★★★☆   JUMP ★★★
SKILL ★★★★

MAIN WAYS TO OBTAIN

Pokémon HeartGold
Safari Zone (Meadow Area: if Forest objects are placed, may appear in tall grass)

Pokémon SoulSilver
Safari Zone (Meadow Area: if Forest objects are placed, may appear in tall grass)

Pokémon Diamond
Route 210, Solaceon Town side (after obtaining the National Pokédex, insert Pokémon Ruby into your Nintendo DS's Game Pak slot)

Pokémon Pearl
Route 210, Solaceon Town side (after obtaining the National Pokédex, insert Pokémon Ruby into your Nintendo DS's Game Pak slot)

Pokémon Platinum
Route 210, Solaceon Town side (after obtaining the National Pokédex, insert Pokémon Ruby into your Nintendo DS's Game Pak slot)

Pokémon HeartGold
It lives deep in forests. With the leaf on its head, it makes a flute whose song makes listeners uneasy.

Pokémon SoulSilver
It lives deep in forests. With the leaf on its head, it makes a flute whose song makes listeners uneasy.

EVOLUTION

Lv. 14 → Use Leaf Stone

Seedot   Nuzleaf   Shiftry

No. 275 | Wicked Pokémon
Shiftry

Grass | Dark

- **HEIGHT:** 4'03"
- **WEIGHT:** 131.4 lbs.
- **ITEMS:** None

● SIZE COMPARISON

- **MALE FORM**
  Bigger leaves
- **FEMALE FORM**
  Smaller leaves

⊚ ABILITIES
- Chlorophyll
- Early Bird

⊚ STATS
- HP ●●●
- ATTACK ●●●●
- DEFENSE ●●
- SP. ATTACK ●●●●
- SP. DEFENSE ●●
- SPEED ●●●●

⊚ EGG GROUPS
- Field
- Grass

⊚ PERFORMANCE
- SPEED ★★★☆
- POWER ★★★☆
- SKILL ★★★☆
- STAMINA ★★★☆
- JUMP ★★★☆

● MAIN WAYS TO OBTAIN

Pokémon HeartGold	Use Leaf Stone on Nuzleaf
Pokémon SoulSilver	Use Leaf Stone on Nuzleaf
Pokémon Diamond	Use Leaf Stone on Nuzleaf
Pokémon Pearl	Use Leaf Stone on Nuzleaf
Pokémon Platinum	Use Leaf Stone on Nuzleaf

Pokémon HeartGold
It lives quietly in the deep forest. It is said to create chilly winter winds with the fans it holds.

Pokémon SoulSilver
It lives quietly in the deep forest. It is said to create chilly winter winds with the fans it holds.

⊚ EVOLUTION

Seedot — Lv. 14 → Nuzleaf — Use Leaf Stone → Shiftry

● LEVEL-UP MOVES

Lv.	Name	Type	Kind	Pow.	Acc.	PP	Range	DA
1	Faint Attack	Dark	Physical	60	—	20	Normal	○
1	Whirlwind	Normal	Status	—	100	20	Normal	—
1	Nasty Plot	Dark	Status	—	—	20	Self	—
1	Razor Leaf	Grass	Physical	55	95	25	2 Foes	—
49	Leaf Storm	Grass	Special	140	90	5	Normal	—

● MOVE MANIAC

Name	Type	Kind	Pow.	Acc.	PP	Range	DA
Headbutt	Normal	Physical	70	100	15	Normal	○

● BP MOVES

Name	Type	Kind	Pow.	Acc.	PP	Range	DA
Fury Cutter	Bug	Physical	10	95	20	Normal	○
Icy Wind	Ice	Special	55	95	15	2 Foes	—
Ominous Wind	Ghost	Special	60	100	5	Normal	—
Air Cutter	Flying	Special	55	95	25	2 Foes	—
Knock Off	Dark	Physical	20	100	20	Normal	○
Sucker Punch	Dark	Physical	80	100	5	Normal	—
Snore	Normal	Special	40	100	15	Normal	—
Spite	Ghost	Status	—	100	10	Normal	—
Synthesis	Grass	Status	—	—	5	Self	—
Swift	Normal	Special	60	—	20	2 Foes	—
Tailwind	Flying	Status	—	—	30	2 Allies	—
Worry Seed	Grass	Status	—	100	10	Normal	—
Mud-Slap	Ground	Special	20	100	10	Normal	—
Rollout	Rock	Physical	30	90	20	Normal	○
Twister	Dragon	Special	40	100	20	2 Foes	—
Seed Bomb	Grass	Physical	80	100	15	Normal	○
Bounce	Flying	Physical	85	85	5	Normal	○
Low Kick	Fighting	Physical	—	100	20	Normal	○

● TM & HM MOVES

No.	Name	Type	Kind	Pow.	Acc.	PP	Range	DA
TM06	Toxic	Poison	Status	—	85	10	Normal	—
TM09	Bullet Seed	Grass	Physical	10	100	30	Normal	—
TM10	Hidden Power	Normal	Special	—	100	15	Normal	—
TM11	Sunny Day	Fire	Status	—	—	5	All	—
TM15	Hyper Beam	Normal	Special	150	90	5	Normal	—
TM17	Protect	Normal	Status	—	—	10	Self	—
TM19	Giga Drain	Grass	Special	60	100	10	Normal	—
TM21	Frustration	Normal	Physical	—	100	20	Normal	○
TM22	SolarBeam	Grass	Special	120	100	10	Normal	—
TM27	Return	Normal	Physical	—	100	20	Normal	○
TM28	Dig	Ground	Physical	80	100	10	Normal	○
TM30	Shadow Ball	Ghost	Special	80	100	15	Normal	—
TM31	Brick Break	Fighting	Physical	75	100	15	Normal	○
TM32	Double Team	Normal	Status	—	—	15	Self	—
TM39	Rock Tomb	Rock	Physical	50	80	10	Normal	○
TM40	Aerial Ace	Flying	Physical	60	—	20	Normal	○
TM41	Torment	Dark	Status	—	100	15	Normal	—
TM42	Facade	Normal	Physical	70	100	20	Normal	○
TM43	Secret Power	Normal	Physical	70	100	20	Normal	○
TM44	Rest	Psychic	Status	—	—	10	Self	—
TM45	Attract	Normal	Status	—	100	15	Normal	—
TM46	Thief	Dark	Physical	40	100	10	Normal	○
TM52	Focus Blast	Fighting	Special	120	70	5	Normal	—
TM53	Energy Ball	Grass	Special	80	100	10	Normal	—
TM56	Fling	Dark	Physical	—	100	10	Normal	—
TM58	Endure	Normal	Status	—	—	10	Self	—
TM62	Silver Wind	Bug	Special	60	100	5	Normal	—
TM63	Embargo	Dark	Status	—	100	15	Normal	—
TM64	Explosion	Normal	Physical	250	100	5	2 Foes/1 Ally	—
TM66	Payback	Dark	Physical	50	100	10	Normal	○
TM68	Giga Impact	Normal	Physical	150	90	5	Normal	○
TM70	Flash	Normal	Status	—	100	20	Normal	—
TM75	Swords Dance	Normal	Status	—	—	30	Self	—
TM77	Psych Up	Normal	Status	—	—	10	Normal	—
TM78	Captivate	Normal	Status	—	100	20	2 Foes	—
TM79	Dark Pulse	Dark	Special	80	100	15	Normal	—
TM80	Rock Slide	Rock	Physical	75	90	10	2 Foes	—
TM81	X-Scissor	Bug	Physical	80	100	15	Normal	○
TM82	Sleep Talk	Normal	Status	—	—	10	Depends	—
TM83	Natural Gift	Normal	Physical	—	100	15	Normal	—
TM86	Grass Knot	Grass	Special	—	100	20	Normal	—
TM87	Swagger	Normal	Status	—	90	15	Normal	—
TM90	Substitute	Normal	Status	—	—	10	Self	—
HM01	Cut	Normal	Physical	50	95	30	Normal	○
HM04	Strength	Normal	Physical	80	100	15	Normal	○
HM06	Rock Smash	Fighting	Physical	40	100	15	Normal	○

● LEVEL-UP MOVES

Lv.	Name	Type	Kind	Pow.	Acc.	PP	Range	DA
1	Peck	Flying	Physical	35	100	35	Normal	○
1	Growl	Normal	Status	—	100	40	2 Foes	—
4	Focus Energy	Normal	Status	—	—	30	Self	—
8	Quick Attack	Normal	Physical	40	100	30	Normal	○
13	Wing Attack	Flying	Physical	60	100	35	Normal	○
19	Double Team	Normal	Status	—	—	15	Self	—
26	Endeavor	Normal	Physical	—	100	5	Normal	○
34	Aerial Ace	Flying	Physical	60	—	20	Normal	○
43	Agility	Psychic	Status	—	—	30	Self	—
53	Air Slash	Flying	Special	75	95	20	Normal	—

● MOVE MANIAC

Name	Type	Kind	Pow.	Acc.	PP	Range	DA

● BP MOVES

Name	Type	Kind	Pow.	Acc.	PP	Range	DA
Ominous Wind	Ghost	Special	60	100	5	Normal	—
Air Cutter	Flying	Special	55	95	25	2 Foes	—
Snore	Normal	Special	40	100	15	Normal	—
Swift	Normal	Special	60	—	20	2 Foes	—
Tailwind	Flying	Status	—	—	30	2 Allies	—
Mud-Slap	Ground	Special	20	100	10	Normal	—
Endeavor	Normal	Physical	—	100	5	Normal	○
Twister	Dragon	Special	40	100	20	2 Foes	—
Heat Wave	Fire	Special	100	90	10	2 Foes	—

● TM & HM MOVES

No.	Name	Type	Kind	Pow.	Acc.	PP	Range	DA
TM06	Toxic	Poison	Status	—	85	10	Normal	—
TM10	Hidden Power	Normal	Special	—	100	15	Normal	—
TM11	Sunny Day	Fire	Status	—	—	5	All	—
TM17	Protect	Normal	Status	—	—	10	Self	—
TM18	Rain Dance	Water	Status	—	—	5	All	—
TM21	Frustration	Normal	Physical	—	100	20	Normal	○
TM27	Return	Normal	Physical	—	100	20	Normal	○
TM32	Double Team	Normal	Status	—	—	15	Self	—
TM40	Aerial Ace	Flying	Physical	60	—	20	Normal	○
TM42	Facade	Normal	Physical	70	100	20	Normal	○
TM43	Secret Power	Normal	Physical	70	100	20	Normal	○
TM44	Rest	Psychic	Status	—	—	10	Self	—
TM45	Attract	Normal	Status	—	100	15	Normal	—
TM46	Thief	Dark	Physical	40	100	10	Normal	○
TM47	Steel Wing	Steel	Physical	70	90	25	Normal	○
TM51	Roost	Flying	Status	—	—	10	Self	—
TM58	Endure	Normal	Status	—	—	10	Self	—
TM78	Captivate	Normal	Status	—	100	20	2 Foes	—
TM82	Sleep Talk	Normal	Status	—	—	10	Depends	—
TM83	Natural Gift	Normal	Physical	—	100	15	Normal	○
TM87	Swagger	Normal	Status	—	90	15	Normal	—
TM88	Pluck	Flying	Physical	60	100	20	Normal	○
TM89	U-turn	Bug	Physical	70	100	20	Normal	○
TM90	Substitute	Normal	Status	—	—	10	Self	—
HM02	Fly	Flying	Physical	90	95	15	Normal	○

● EGG MOVES

Name	Type	Kind	Pow.	Acc.	PP	Range	DA
Pursuit	Dark	Physical	40	100	20	Normal	○
Supersonic	Normal	Status	—	55	20	Normal	—
Refresh	Normal	Status	—	—	20	Self	—
Mirror Move	Flying	Status	—	—	20	Depends	—
Rage	Normal	Physical	20	100	20	Normal	○
Sky Attack	Flying	Physical	140	90	5	Normal	—
Whirlwind	Normal	Status	—	100	20	Normal	—
Brave Bird	Flying	Physical	120	100	15	Normal	○

● No. 276 | TinySwallow Pokémon
Taillow

`Normal` `Flying`

- ● **HEIGHT:** 1'00"
- ● **WEIGHT:** 5.1 lbs.
- ● **ITEMS:** Charti Berry

● **SIZE COMPARISON**

● **MALE/FEMALE HAVE SAME FORM**

⊙ ABILITIES
● Guts

⊙ STATS
- HP ●
- ATTACK ●●
- DEFENSE ●●
- SP. ATTACK ●
- SP. DEFENSE ●●
- SPEED ●●●●

⊙ EGG GROUPS
Flying

⊙ PERFORMANCE
SPEED ★★★☆   STAMINA ★★★★
POWER ★★☆☆   JUMP ★★★★☆
SKILL ★★☆

● MAIN WAYS TO OBTAIN

Pokémon HeartGold	Cherrygrove City (use Rock Climb to reach trees, then use Headbutt)
Pokémon SoulSilver	Cherrygrove City (use Rock Climb to reach trees, then use Headbutt)
Pokémon Diamond	Find its Egg at the Pokémon Day Care and hatch it
Pokémon Pearl	Find its Egg at the Pokémon Day Care and hatch it
Pokémon Platinum	Find its Egg at the Pokémon Day Care and hatch it

Pokémon HeartGold	**Pokémon SoulSilver**
When it gets cold, they migrate, flying over 180 miles a day. It hunts for tasty prey.	When it gets cold, they migrate, flying over 180 miles a day. It hunts for tasty prey.

⊙ EVOLUTION

Lv. 22

`Taillow` → `Swallow`

No. 277 | Swallow Pokémon
Swellow

`Normal` `Flying`

● HEIGHT: 2'04"
● WEIGHT: 43.7 lbs.
● ITEMS: None

● SIZE COMPARISON

● MALE/FEMALE HAVE SAME FORM

⊕ ABILITIES
● Guts

⊕ STATS
HP	●●
ATTACK	●●●●
DEFENSE	●●●
SP. ATTACK	●●
SP. DEFENSE	●●
SPEED	●●●●●●

⊕ EGG GROUPS
Flying

⊕ PERFORMANCE
SPEED ★★★ STAMINA ★★★★
POWER ★★★☆☆ JUMP ★★★★★
SKILL ★☆

● MAIN WAYS TO OBTAIN

Pokémon HeartGold	Level up Taillow to Lv. 22
Pokémon SoulSilver	Level up Taillow to Lv. 22
Pokémon Diamond	Route 213 (use Poké Radar)
Pokémon Pearl	Route 213 (use Poké Radar)
Pokémon Platinum	Route 213 (use Poké Radar)

Pokémon HeartGold	Pokémon SoulSilver
It dives at a steep angle as soon as it spots its prey. It catches its prey with sharp claws.	It dives at a steep angle as soon as it spots its prey. It catches its prey with sharp claws.

⊕ EVOLUTION

Taillow → Lv. 22 → Swellow

● LEVEL-UP MOVES

Lv.	Name	Type	Kind	Pow.	Acc.	PP	Range	DA
1	Pluck	Flying	Physical	60	100	20	Normal	○
1	Peck	Flying	Physical	35	100	35	Normal	—
1	Growl	Normal	Status	—	100	40	2 Foes	—
1	Focus Energy	Normal	Status	—	—	30	Self	—
1	Quick Attack	Normal	Physical	40	100	30	Normal	○
4	Focus Energy	Normal	Status	—	—	30	Self	—
8	Quick Attack	Normal	Physical	40	100	30	Normal	○
13	Wing Attack	Normal	Physical	60	100	35	Normal	○
19	Double Team	Normal	Status	—	—	15	Self	—
28	Endeavor	Normal	Physical	—	100	5	Normal	○
38	Aerial Ace	Flying	Physical	60	—	20	Normal	○
49	Agility	Psychic	Status	—	—	30	Self	—
61	Air Slash	Flying	Special	75	95	20	Normal	—

● MOVE MANIAC

Name	Type	Kind	Pow.	Acc.	PP	Range	DA

● BP MOVES

Name	Type	Kind	Pow.	Acc.	PP	Range	DA
Ominous Wind	Ghost	Special	60	100	5	Normal	—
Air Cutter	Flying	Special	55	95	25	2 Foes	—
Snore	Normal	Special	40	100	15	Normal	—
Swift	Normal	Special	60	—	20	2 Foes	—
Tailwind	Flying	Status	—	—	30	2 Allies	—
Mud-Slap	Ground	Special	20	100	10	Normal	—
Endeavor	Normal	Physical	—	100	5	Normal	○
Twister	Dragon	Special	40	100	20	2 Foes	—
Heat Wave	Fire	Special	100	90	10	2 Foes	—
Sky Attack	Flying	Physical	140	90	5	Normal	—

● TM & HM MOVES

No.	Name	Type	Kind	Pow.	Acc.	PP	Range	DA
TM06	Toxic	Poison	Status	—	85	10	Normal	—
TM10	Hidden Power	Normal	Special	—	100	15	Normal	—
TM11	Sunny Day	Fire	Status	—	—	5	All	—
TM15	Hyper Beam	Normal	Special	150	90	5	Normal	—
TM17	Protect	Normal	Status	—	—	10	Self	—
TM18	Rain Dance	Water	Status	—	—	5	All	—
TM21	Frustration	Normal	Physical	—	100	20	Normal	○
TM27	Return	Normal	Physical	—	100	20	Normal	○
TM32	Double Team	Normal	Status	—	—	15	Self	—
TM40	Aerial Ace	Flying	Physical	60	—	20	Normal	○
TM42	Facade	Normal	Physical	70	100	20	Normal	○
TM43	Secret Power	Normal	Physical	70	100	20	Normal	○
TM44	Rest	Psychic	Status	—	—	10	Self	—
TM45	Attract	Normal	Status	—	100	15	Normal	—
TM46	Thief	Dark	Physical	40	100	10	Normal	○
TM47	Steel Wing	Steel	Physical	70	90	25	Normal	○
TM51	Roost	Flying	Status	—	—	10	Self	—
TM58	Endure	Normal	Status	—	—	10	Self	—
TM68	Giga Impact	Normal	Physical	150	90	5	Normal	○
TM78	Captivate	Normal	Status	—	100	20	2 Foes	—
TM82	Sleep Talk	Normal	Status	—	—	10	Depends	—
TM83	Natural Gift	Normal	Physical	—	100	15	Normal	○
TM87	Swagger	Normal	Status	—	90	15	Normal	—
TM88	Pluck	Flying	Physical	60	100	20	Normal	○
TM89	U-turn	Bug	Physical	70	100	20	Normal	○
TM90	Substitute	Normal	Status	—	—	10	Self	—
HM02	Fly	Flying	Physical	90	95	15	Normal	○

● LEVEL-UP MOVES

Lv.	Name	Type	Kind	Pow.	Acc.	PP	Range	DA
1	Growl	Normal	Status	—	100	40	2 Foes	—
1	Water Gun	Water	Special	40	100	25	Normal	—
6	Supersonic	Normal	Status	—	55	20	Normal	—
11	Wing Attack	Flying	Physical	60	100	35	Normal	○
16	Mist	Ice	Status	—	—	30	2 Allies	—
19	Water Pulse	Water	Special	60	100	20	Normal	—
24	Quick Attack	Normal	Physical	40	100	30	Normal	○
29	Roost	Flying	Status	—	—	10	Self	—
34	Pursuit	Dark	Physical	40	100	20	Normal	○
37	Agility	Psychic	Status	—	—	30	Self	—
42	Aerial Ace	Flying	Physical	60	—	20	Normal	—
47	Air Slash	Flying	Special	75	95	20	Normal	—

● MOVE MANIAC

Name	Type	Kind	Pow.	Acc.	PP	Range	DA

● BP MOVES

Name	Type	Kind	Pow.	Acc.	PP	Range	DA
Icy Wind	Ice	Special	55	95	15	2 Foes	—
Ominous Wind	Ghost	Special	60	100	5	Normal	—
Air Cutter	Flying	Special	55	95	25	2 Foes	—
Knock Off	Dark	Physical	20	100	20	Normal	○
Snore	Normal	Special	40	100	15	Normal	—
Swift	Normal	Special	60	—	20	2 Foes	—
Uproar	Normal	Special	50	100	10	1 Random	—
Tailwind	Flying	Status	—	—	30	2 Allies	—
Mud-Slap	Ground	Special	20	100	10	Normal	—
Twister	Dragon	Special	40	100	20	2 Foes	—

● TM & HM MOVES

No.	Name	Type	Kind	Pow.	Acc.	PP	Range	DA
TM03	Water Pulse	Water	Special	60	100	20	Normal	—
TM06	Toxic	Poison	Status	—	85	10	Normal	—
TM07	Hail	Ice	Status	—	—	10	All	—
TM10	Hidden Power	Normal	Special	—	100	15	Normal	—
TM13	Ice Beam	Ice	Special	95	100	10	Normal	—
TM14	Blizzard	Ice	Special	120	70	5	2 Foes	—
TM17	Protect	Normal	Status	—	—	10	Self	—
TM18	Rain Dance	Water	Status	—	—	5	All	—
TM21	Frustration	Normal	Physical	—	100	20	Normal	○
TM27	Return	Normal	Physical	—	100	20	Normal	○
TM32	Double Team	Normal	Status	—	—	15	Self	—
TM34	Shock Wave	Electric	Special	60	—	20	Normal	—
TM40	Aerial Ace	Flying	Physical	60	—	20	Normal	○
TM42	Facade	Normal	Physical	70	100	20	Normal	○
TM43	Secret Power	Normal	Physical	70	100	20	Normal	○
TM44	Rest	Psychic	Status	—	—	10	Self	—
TM45	Attract	Normal	Status	—	100	15	Normal	—
TM46	Thief	Dark	Physical	40	100	10	Normal	○
TM47	Steel Wing	Steel	Physical	70	90	25	Normal	○
TM51	Roost	Flying	Status	—	—	10	Self	—
TM55	Brine	Water	Special	65	100	10	Normal	—
TM58	Endure	Normal	Status	—	—	10	Self	—
TM78	Captivate	Normal	Status	—	100	20	2 Foes	—
TM82	Sleep Talk	Normal	Status	—	—	10	Depends	—
TM83	Natural Gift	Normal	Physical	—	100	15	Normal	—
TM87	Swagger	Normal	Status	—	90	15	Normal	—
TM88	Pluck	Flying	Physical	60	100	20	Normal	○
TM89	U-turn	Bug	Physical	70	100	20	Normal	○
TM90	Substitute	Normal	Status	—	—	10	Self	—
HM02	Fly	Flying	Physical	90	95	15	Normal	○

● EGG MOVES

Name	Type	Kind	Pow.	Acc.	PP	Range	DA
Mist	Ice	Status	—	—	30	2 Allies	—
Twister	Dragon	Special	40	100	20	2 Foes	—
Agility	Psychic	Status	—	—	30	Self	—
Gust	Flying	Special	40	100	35	Normal	—
Water Sport	Water	Status	—	—	15	All	—
Aqua Ring	Water	Status	—	—	20	Self	—
Knock Off	Dark	Physical	20	100	20	Normal	○

☻ No. 278 | Seagull Pokémon
Wingull

Water | Flying

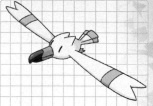

● HEIGHT: 2'00"
● WEIGHT: 20.9 lbs.
● ITEMS: None

● SIZE COMPARISON

● MALE/FEMALE HAVE SAME FORM

✪ ABILITIES
● Keen Eye

✪ STATS
HP ●
ATTACK ●
DEFENSE ●
SP. ATTACK ●●
SP. DEFENSE ●
SPEED ●●●●

✪ EGG GROUPS
Water 1
Flying

✪ PERFORMANCE
SPEED ★★★☆ STAMINA ★★★☆
POWER ★☆☆☆ JUMP ★★★★★
SKILL ★★☆

● MAIN WAYS TO OBTAIN

Pokémon HeartGold — Vermilion City (mass outbreak, water surface)

Pokémon SoulSilver — Vermilion City (mass outbreak, water surface)

Pokémon Diamond — Route 213

Pokémon Pearl — Route 213

Pokémon Platinum — Route 213

Pokémon HeartGold
It soars on updrafts without flapping its wings. It makes a nest on sheer cliffs at the sea's edge.

Pokémon SoulSilver
It soars on updrafts without flapping its wings. It makes a nest on sheer cliffs at the sea's edge.

✪ EVOLUTION

Wingull — Lv. 25 → Pelipper

● No. 279 | Water Bird Pokémon

Pelipper

Water | Flying

● LEVEL-UP MOVES

Lv.	Name	Type	Kind	Pow.	Acc.	PP	Range	DA
1	Growl	Normal	Status	—	100	40	2 Foes	—
1	Water Gun	Water	Special	40	100	25	Normal	—
1	Water Sport	Water	Status	—	—	15	All	—
1	Wing Attack	Flying	Physical	60	100	35	Normal	○
6	Supersonic	Normal	Status	—	55	20	Normal	—
11	Wing Attack	Flying	Physical	60	100	35	Normal	○
16	Mist	Ice	Status	—	—	30	2 Allies	—
19	Water Pulse	Water	Special	60	100	20	Normal	—
24	Payback	Dark	Physical	50	100	10	Normal	○
25	Protect	Normal	Status	—	—	10	Self	—
31	Roost	Flying	Status	—	—	10	Self	—
38	Stockpile	Normal	Status	—	—	20	Self	—
38	Swallow	Normal	Status	—	—	10	Self	—
38	Spit Up	Normal	Special	—	100	10	Normal	—
43	Fling	Dark	Physical	—	100	10	Normal	○
50	Tailwind	Flying	Status	—	—	30	2 Allies	—
57	Hydro Pump	Water	Special	120	80	5	Normal	—

● MOVE MANIAC

Name	Type	Kind	Pow.	Acc.	PP	Range	DA

● BP MOVES

Name	Type	Kind	Pow.	Acc.	PP	Range	DA
Icy Wind	Ice	Special	55	95	15	2 Foes	—
Ominous Wind	Ghost	Special	60	100	5	Normal	—
Air Cutter	Flying	Special	55	95	25	2 Foes	—
Knock Off	Dark	Physical	20	100	20	Normal	○
Snore	Normal	Special	40	100	15	Normal	—
Swift	Normal	Special	60	—	20	2 Foes	—
Uproar	Normal	Special	50	100	10	1 Random	—
Tailwind	Flying	Status	—	—	30	2 Allies	—
Mud-Slap	Ground	Special	20	100	10	Normal	—
Gunk Shot	Poison	Physical	120	70	5	Normal	—
Twister	Dragon	Special	40	100	20	2 Foes	—
Seed Bomb	Grass	Physical	80	100	15	Normal	—
Sky Attack	Flying	Physical	140	90	5	Normal	—

● HEIGHT: 3'11"
● WEIGHT: 61.7 lbs.
● ITEMS: None

● SIZE COMPARISON

● MALE/FEMALE HAVE SAME FORM

⊛ ABILITIES
● Keen Eye

⊛ STATS
HP ●●
ATTACK ●●
DEFENSE ●●●●●
SP. ATTACK ●●●●
SP. DEFENSE ●●●●
SPEED ●●●

⊛ EGG GROUPS
Water
Flying

⊛ PERFORMANCE
SPEED ★★☆
POWER ★★☆☆
SKILL ★★
STAMINA ★★★★☆
JUMP ★★★★★

● MAIN WAYS TO OBTAIN

Pokémon HeartGold	Level up Wingull to Lv. 25
Pokémon SoulSilver	Level up Wingull to Lv. 25
Pokémon Diamond	Route 223 (water surface)
Pokémon Pearl	Route 223 (water surface)
Pokémon Platinum	Route 223 (water surface)

Pokémon HeartGold	Pokémon SoulSilver
It protects its young in its beak. It bobs on waves, resting on them on days when the waters are calm.	It protects its young in its beak. It bobs on waves, resting on them on days when the waters are calm.

⊛ EVOLUTION

Wingull → Lv. 25 → Pelipper

● TM & HM MOVES

No.	Name	Type	Kind	Pow.	Acc.	PP	Range	DA
TM03	Water Pulse	Water	Special	60	100	20	Normal	—
TM06	Toxic	Poison	Status	—	85	10	Normal	—
TM07	Hail	Ice	Status	—	—	10	All	—
TM10	Hidden Power	Normal	Special	—	100	15	Normal	—
TM13	Ice Beam	Ice	Special	95	100	10	Normal	—
TM14	Blizzard	Ice	Special	120	70	5	2 Foes	—
TM15	Hyper Beam	Normal	Special	150	90	5	Normal	—
TM17	Protect	Normal	Status	—	—	10	Self	—
TM18	Rain Dance	Water	Status	—	—	5	All	—
TM21	Frustration	Normal	Physical	—	100	20	Normal	○
TM27	Return	Normal	Physical	—	100	20	Normal	○
TM32	Double Team	Normal	Status	—	—	15	Self	—
TM34	Shock Wave	Electric	Special	60	—	20	Normal	—
TM40	Aerial Ace	Flying	Physical	60	—	20	Normal	○
TM42	Facade	Normal	Physical	70	100	20	Normal	○
TM43	Secret Power	Normal	Physical	70	100	20	Normal	—
TM44	Rest	Psychic	Status	—	—	10	Self	—
TM45	Attract	Normal	Status	—	100	15	Normal	—
TM46	Thief	Dark	Physical	40	100	10	Normal	○
TM47	Steel Wing	Steel	Physical	70	90	25	Normal	○
TM51	Roost	Flying	Status	—	—	10	Self	—
TM55	Brine	Water	Special	65	100	10	Normal	—
TM56	Fling	Dark	Physical	—	100	10	Normal	○
TM58	Endure	Normal	Status	—	—	10	Self	—
TM66	Payback	Dark	Physical	50	100	10	Normal	○
TM68	Giga Impact	Normal	Physical	150	90	5	Normal	○
TM78	Captivate	Normal	Status	—	100	20	2 Foes	—
TM82	Sleep Talk	Normal	Status	—	—	10	Depends	—
TM83	Natural Gift	Normal	Physical	—	100	15	Normal	—
TM87	Swagger	Normal	Status	—	90	15	Normal	—
TM88	Pluck	Flying	Physical	60	100	20	Normal	○
TM89	U-turn	Bug	Physical	70	100	20	Normal	○
TM90	Substitute	Normal	Status	—	—	10	Self	—
HM02	Fly	Flying	Physical	90	95	10	Normal	○
HM03	Surf	Water	Special	95	100	15	2 Foes/1 Ally	—
HM05	Whirlpool	Water	Special	15	70	15	Normal	—

● LEVEL-UP MOVES

Lv.	Name	Type	Kind	Pow.	Acc.	PP	Range	DA
1	Growl	Normal	Status	—	100	40	2 Foes	—
6	Confusion	Psychic	Special	50	100	15	Normal	—
10	Double Team	Normal	Status	—	—	15	Self	—
12	Teleport	Psychic	Status	—	—	20	Self	—
17	Lucky Chant	Normal	Status	—	—	30	2 Allies	—
21	Magical Leaf	Grass	Special	60	—	20	Normal	—
23	Calm Mind	Psychic	Status	—	—	20	Self	—
28	Psychic	Psychic	Special	90	100	10	Normal	—
32	Imprison	Psychic	Status	—	—	10	Self	—
34	Future Sight	Psychic	Special	80	90	15	Normal	—
39	Charm	Normal	Status	—	100	20	Normal	—
43	Hypnosis	Psychic	Status	—	60	20	Normal	—
45	Dream Eater	Psychic	Special	100	100	15	Normal	—

● MOVE MANIAC

Name	Type	Kind	Pow.	Acc.	PP	Range	DA
Headbutt	Normal	Physical	70	100	15	Normal	○

● BP MOVES

Name	Type	Kind	Pow.	Acc.	PP	Range	DA
Icy Wind	Ice	Special	55	95	15	2 Foes	—
ThunderPunch	Electric	Physical	75	100	15	Normal	○
Fire Punch	Fire	Physical	75	100	15	Normal	○
Ice Punch	Ice	Physical	75	100	15	Normal	○
Zen Headbutt	Psychic	Physical	80	90	15	Normal	○
Trick	Psychic	Status	—	100	10	Normal	—
Snore	Normal	Special	40	100	15	Normal	—
Helping Hand	Normal	Status	—	—	20	1 Ally	—
Swift	Normal	Special	60	—	20	2 Foes	—
Magic Coat	Psychic	Status	—	—	15	Self	—
Mud-Slap	Ground	Special	20	100	10	Normal	—
Signal Beam	Bug	Special	75	100	15	Normal	—
Pain Split	Normal	Status	—	—	20	Normal	—

● TM & HM MOVES

No.	Name	Type	Kind	Pow.	Acc.	PP	Range	DA
TM04	Calm Mind	Psychic	Status	—	—	20	Self	—
TM06	Toxic	Poison	Status	—	85	10	Normal	—
TM10	Hidden Power	Normal	Special	—	100	15	Normal	—
TM11	Sunny Day	Fire	Status	—	—	5	All	—
TM12	Taunt	Dark	Status	—	100	20	Normal	—
TM16	Light Screen	Psychic	Status	—	—	30	2 Allies	—
TM17	Protect	Normal	Status	—	—	10	Self	—
TM18	Rain Dance	Water	Status	—	—	5	All	—
TM20	Safeguard	Normal	Status	—	—	25	2 Allies	—
TM21	Frustration	Normal	Physical	—	100	20	Normal	○
TM24	Thunderbolt	Electric	Special	95	100	15	Normal	—
TM27	Return	Normal	Physical	—	100	20	Normal	○
TM29	Psychic	Psychic	Special	90	100	10	Normal	—
TM30	Shadow Ball	Ghost	Special	80	100	15	Normal	—
TM32	Double Team	Normal	Status	—	—	15	Self	—
TM33	Reflect	Psychic	Status	—	—	20	2 Allies	—
TM34	Shock Wave	Electric	Special	60	—	20	Normal	—
TM41	Torment	Dark	Status	—	100	15	Normal	—
TM42	Facade	Normal	Physical	70	100	20	Normal	○
TM43	Secret Power	Normal	Physical	70	100	20	Normal	—
TM44	Rest	Psychic	Status	—	—	10	Self	—
TM45	Attract	Normal	Status	—	100	15	Normal	—
TM46	Thief	Dark	Physical	40	100	10	Normal	○
TM48	Skill Swap	Psychic	Status	—	—	10	Normal	—
TM49	Snatch	Dark	Status	—	—	10	Depends	—
TM56	Fling	Dark	Physical	—	100	10	Normal	—
TM57	Charge Beam	Electric	Special	50	90	10	Normal	—
TM58	Endure	Normal	Status	—	—	10	Self	—
TM67	Recycle	Normal	Status	—	—	10	Self	—
TM70	Flash	Normal	Status	—	100	20	Normal	—
TM73	Thunder Wave	Electric	Status	—	100	20	Normal	—
TM77	Psych Up	Normal	Status	—	—	10	Normal	—
TM78	Captivate	Normal	Status	—	100	20	2 Foes	—
TM82	Sleep Talk	Normal	Status	—	—	10	Depends	—
TM83	Natural Gift	Normal	Physical	—	100	15	Normal	—
TM85	Dream Eater	Psychic	Special	100	100	15	Normal	—
TM86	Grass Knot	Grass	Special	—	100	20	Normal	○
TM87	Swagger	Normal	Status	—	90	15	Normal	—
TM90	Substitute	Normal	Status	—	—	10	Self	—
TM92	Trick Room	Psychic	Status	—	—	5	All	—

● EGG MOVES

Name	Type	Kind	Pow.	Acc.	PP	Range	DA
Disable	Normal	Status	—	80	15	Normal	—
Will-O-Wisp	Fire	Status	—	75	15	Normal	—
Mean Look	Normal	Status	—	—	5	Normal	—
Memento	Dark	Status	—	100	10	Normal	—
Destiny Bond	Ghost	Status	—	—	5	Self	—
Grudge	Ghost	Status	—	—	5	Self	—
Shadow Sneak	Ghost	Physical	40	100	30	Normal	○
Confuse Ray	Ghost	Status	—	100	10	Normal	—
Encore	Normal	Status	—	100	5	Normal	—

☻ No. 280 | Feeling Pokémon
Ralts

Psychic

- **HEIGHT:** 1'04"
- **WEIGHT:** 14.6 lbs.
- **ITEMS:** None

● SIZE COMPARISON

● MALE/FEMALE HAVE SAME FORM

⊕ ABILITIES
- Synchronize
- Trace

⊛ STATS
- HP ●
- ATTACK ●
- DEFENSE ●
- SP. ATTACK ●
- SP. DEFENSE ● ●
- SPEED ● ●

⊕ EGG GROUPS
Amorphous

⊛ PERFORMANCE
SPEED ★★★☆ STAMINA ★☆☆☆
POWER ★ JUMP ★★☆
SKILL ★★★☆☆

● MAIN WAYS TO OBTAIN

Pokémon HeartGold — Route 34 (mass outbreak)

Pokémon SoulSilver — Route 34 (mass outbreak)

Pokémon Diamond — Route 203 (use Poké Radar)

Pokémon Pearl — Route 203 (use Poké Radar)

Pokémon Platinum — Route 208

Pokémon HeartGold
The horns on its head provide a strong power that enables it to sense people's emotions.

Pokémon SoulSilver
The horns on its head provide a strong power that enables it to sense people's emotions.

⊛ EVOLUTION

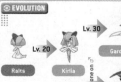

Ralts → Lv. 20 → Kirlia → Lv. 30 → Gardevoir

Use Dawn Stone on ♂ → Gallade

No. 281 | Emotion Pokémon
Kirlia

Psychic

● LEVEL-UP MOVES

Lv.	Name	Type	Kind	Pow.	Acc.	PP	Range	DA
1	Growl	Normal	Status	—	100	40	2 Foes	—
1	Confusion	Psychic	Special	50	100	25	Normal	—
1	Double Team	Normal	Status	—	—	15	Self	—
1	Teleport	Psychic	Status	—	—	20	Self	—
6	Confusion	Psychic	Special	50	100	25	Normal	—
10	Double Team	Normal	Status	—	—	15	Self	—
12	Teleport	Psychic	Status	—	—	20	Self	—
17	Lucky Chant	Normal	Status	—	—	30	2 Allies	—
22	Magical Leaf	Grass	Special	60	—	20	Normal	—
25	Calm Mind	Psychic	Status	—	—	20	Self	—
31	Psychic	Psychic	Special	90	100	10	Normal	—
36	Imprison	Psychic	Status	—	—	10	Self	—
39	Future Sight	Psychic	Special	80	90	15	Normal	—
45	Charm	Normal	Status	—	100	20	Normal	—
50	Hypnosis	Psychic	Status	—	60	20	Normal	—
53	Dream Eater	Psychic	Special	100	100	15	Normal	—

● MOVE MANIAC

Name	Type	Kind	Pow.	Acc.	PP	Range	DA
Headbutt	Normal	Physical	70	100	15	Normal	○

● BP MOVES

Name	Type	Kind	Pow.	Acc.	PP	Range	DA
Icy Wind	Ice	Special	55	95	15	2 Foes	—
ThunderPunch	Electric	Physical	75	100	15	Normal	○
Fire Punch	Fire	Physical	75	100	15	Normal	○
Ice Punch	Ice	Physical	75	100	15	Normal	○
Zen Headbutt	Psychic	Physical	80	90	15	Normal	○
Trick	Psychic	Status	—	100	10	Normal	—
Snore	Normal	Special	40	100	15	Normal	—
Helping Hand	Normal	Status	—	—	20	1 Ally	—
Swift	Normal	Special	60	—	20	2 Foes	—
Magic Coat	Psychic	Status	—	—	15	Self	—
Mud-Slap	Ground	Special	20	100	10	Normal	—
Signal Beam	Bug	Special	75	100	15	Normal	—
Pain Split	Normal	Status	—	—	20	Normal	—

● HEIGHT: 2'07"
● WEIGHT: 44.5 lbs.
● ITEMS: None

● SIZE COMPARISON

● MALE/FEMALE HAVE SAME FORM

⊙ ABILITIES
● Synchronize
● Trace

⊙ STATS
HP ●
ATTACK ●●
DEFENSE ●●
SP. ATTACK ●●●
SP. DEFENSE ●●
SPEED ●●

⊙ EGG GROUPS
Amorphous

⊙ PERFORMANCE
SPEED ★★☆
POWER ★★☆☆
SKILL ★★★★☆
STAMINA ★★☆
JUMP ★★★

● MAIN WAYS TO OBTAIN

Pokémon HeartGold	Level up Ralts to Lv. 20
Pokémon SoulSilver	Level up Ralts to Lv. 20
Pokémon Diamond	Route 203 (occasionally appears when you use Poké Radar)
Pokémon Pearl	Route 203 (occasionally appears when you use Poké Radar)
Pokémon Platinum	Route 212, Hearthome City side

Pokémon HeartGold
It has a psychic power that enables it to distort the space around it and see into the future.

Pokémon SoulSilver
It has a psychic power that enables it to distort the space around it and see into the future.

⊙ EVOLUTION

Ralts → (Lv. 20) → Kirlia → (Lv. 30) → Gardevoir
Kirlia → (Use Dawn Stone on ♂) → Gallade

● TM & HM MOVES

No.	Name	Type	Kind	Pow.	Acc.	PP	Range	DA
TM04	Calm Mind	Psychic	Status	—	—	20	Self	—
TM06	Toxic	Poison	Status	—	85	10	Normal	—
TM10	Hidden Power	Normal	Special	—	100	15	Normal	—
TM11	Sunny Day	Fire	Status	—	—	5	All	—
TM12	Taunt	Dark	Status	—	100	20	Normal	—
TM16	Light Screen	Psychic	Status	—	—	30	2 Allies	—
TM17	Protect	Normal	Status	—	—	10	Self	—
TM18	Rain Dance	Water	Status	—	—	5	All	—
TM20	Safeguard	Normal	Status	—	—	25	2 Allies	—
TM21	Frustration	Normal	Physical	—	100	20	Normal	○
TM24	Thunderbolt	Electric	Special	95	100	15	Normal	—
TM27	Return	Normal	Physical	—	100	20	Normal	○
TM29	Psychic	Psychic	Special	90	100	10	Normal	—
TM30	Shadow Ball	Ghost	Special	80	100	15	Normal	—
TM32	Double Team	Normal	Status	—	—	15	Self	—
TM33	Reflect	Psychic	Status	—	—	20	2 Allies	—
TM34	Shock Wave	Electric	Special	60	—	20	Normal	—
TM41	Torment	Dark	Status	—	100	15	Normal	—
TM42	Facade	Normal	Physical	70	100	20	Normal	○
TM43	Secret Power	Normal	Physical	70	100	20	Normal	○
TM44	Rest	Psychic	Status	—	—	10	Self	—
TM45	Attract	Normal	Status	—	100	15	Normal	—
TM46	Thief	Dark	Physical	40	100	10	Normal	○
TM48	Skill Swap	Psychic	Status	—	—	10	Normal	—
TM49	Snatch	Dark	Status	—	—	10	Depends	—
TM56	Fling	Dark	Physical	—	100	10	Normal	—
TM57	Charge Beam	Electric	Special	50	90	10	Normal	—
TM58	Endure	Normal	Status	—	—	10	Self	—
TM67	Recycle	Normal	Status	—	—	10	Self	—
TM70	Flash	Normal	Status	—	100	20	Normal	—
TM73	Thunder Wave	Electric	Status	—	100	20	Normal	—
TM77	Psych Up	Normal	Status	—	—	10	Normal	—
TM78	Captivate	Normal	Status	—	100	20	2 Foes	—
TM82	Sleep Talk	Normal	Status	—	—	10	Depends	—
TM83	Natural Gift	Normal	Physical	—	100	15	Normal	—
TM85	Dream Eater	Psychic	Special	100	100	15	Normal	—
TM86	Grass Knot	Grass	Special	—	100	20	Normal	○
TM87	Swagger	Normal	Status	—	90	15	Normal	—
TM90	Substitute	Normal	Status	—	—	10	Self	—
TM92	Trick Room	Psychic	Status	—	—	5	All	—

● LEVEL-UP MOVES

Lv.	Name	Type	Kind	Pow.	Acc.	PP	Range	DA
1	Healing Wish	Psychic	Status	—	—	10	Self	—
1	Growl	Normal	Status	—	100	40	2 Foes	—
1	Confusion	Psychic	Special	50	100	25	Normal	—
1	Double Team	Normal	Status	—	—	15	Self	—
1	Teleport	Psychic	Status	—	—	20	Self	—
6	Confusion	Psychic	Special	50	100	25	Normal	—
10	Double Team	Normal	Status	—	—	15	Self	—
12	Teleport	Psychic	Status	—	—	20	Self	—
22	Wish	Normal	Status	—	—	10	Self	—
22	Magical Leaf	Grass	Special	60	—	20	Normal	—
25	Calm Mind	Psychic	Status	—	—	20	Self	—
33	Psychic	Psychic	Special	90	100	10	Normal	—
40	Imprison	Psychic	Status	—	—	10	Self	—
45	Future Sight	Psychic	Special	80	90	15	Normal	—
53	Captivate	Normal	Status	—	100	20	2 Foes	—
60	Hypnosis	Psychic	Status	—	60	20	Normal	—
65	Dream Eater	Psychic	Special	100	100	15	Normal	—

● MOVE MANIAC

Name	Type	Kind	Pow.	Acc.	PP	Range	DA
Headbutt	Normal	Physical	70	100	15	Normal	○

● BP MOVES

Name	Type	Kind	Pow.	Acc.	PP	Range	DA
Icy Wind	Ice	Special	55	95	15	2 Foes	—
ThunderPunch	Electric	Physical	75	100	15	Normal	○
Fire Punch	Fire	Physical	75	100	15	Normal	○
Ice Punch	Ice	Physical	75	100	15	Normal	○
Zen Headbutt	Psychic	Physical	80	90	15	Normal	○
Trick	Psychic	Status	—	100	10	Normal	—
Snore	Normal	Special	40	100	15	Normal	—
Helping Hand	Normal	Status	—	—	20	1 Ally	—
Swift	Normal	Special	60	—	20	2 Foes	—
Magic Coat	Psychic	Status	—	—	15	Self	—
Heal Bell	Normal	Status	—	—	5	All Allies	—
Mud-Slap	Ground	Special	20	100	10	Normal	—
Signal Beam	Bug	Special	75	100	15	Normal	—
Pain Split	Normal	Status	—	—	20	Normal	—

● TM & HM MOVES

No.	Name	Type	Kind	Pow.	Acc.	PP	Range	DA
TM04	Calm Mind	Psychic	Status	—	—	20	Self	—
TM06	Toxic	Poison	Status	—	85	10	Normal	—
TM10	Hidden Power	Normal	Special	—	100	15	Normal	—
TM11	Sunny Day	Fire	Status	—	—	5	All	—
TM12	Taunt	Dark	Status	—	100	20	Normal	—
TM15	Hyper Beam	Normal	Special	150	90	5	Normal	—
TM16	Light Screen	Psychic	Status	—	—	30	2 Allies	—
TM17	Protect	Normal	Status	—	—	10	Self	—
TM18	Rain Dance	Water	Status	—	—	5	All	—
TM20	Safeguard	Normal	Status	—	—	25	2 Allies	—
TM21	Frustration	Normal	Physical	—	100	20	Normal	○
TM24	Thunderbolt	Electric	Special	95	100	15	Normal	—
TM27	Return	Normal	Physical	—	100	20	Normal	○
TM29	Psychic	Psychic	Special	90	100	10	Normal	—
TM30	Shadow Ball	Ghost	Special	80	100	15	Normal	—
TM32	Double Team	Normal	Status	—	—	15	Self	—
TM33	Reflect	Psychic	Status	—	—	20	2 Allies	—
TM34	Shock Wave	Electric	Special	60	—	20	Normal	—
TM41	Torment	Dark	Status	—	100	15	Normal	—
TM42	Facade	Normal	Physical	70	100	20	Normal	○
TM43	Secret Power	Normal	Physical	70	100	20	Normal	○
TM44	Rest	Psychic	Status	—	—	10	Self	—
TM45	Attract	Normal	Status	—	100	15	Normal	—
TM46	Thief	Dark	Physical	40	100	10	Normal	○
TM48	Skill Swap	Psychic	Status	—	—	10	Normal	—
TM49	Snatch	Dark	Status	—	—	10	Depends	—
TM52	Focus Blast	Fighting	Special	120	70	5	Normal	—
TM53	Energy Ball	Grass	Special	80	100	10	Normal	—
TM56	Fling	Dark	Physical	—	100	10	Normal	—
TM57	Charge Beam	Electric	Special	50	90	10	Normal	—
TM58	Endure	Normal	Status	—	—	10	Self	—
TM67	Recycle	Normal	Status	—	—	10	Self	—
TM68	Giga Impact	Normal	Physical	150	90	5	Normal	○
TM70	Flash	Normal	Status	—	100	20	Normal	—
TM73	Thunder Wave	Electric	Status	—	100	20	Normal	—
TM77	Psych Up	Normal	Status	—	—	10	Normal	—
TM78	Captivate	Normal	Status	—	100	20	2 Foes	—
TM82	Sleep Talk	Normal	Status	—	—	10	Self	—
TM83	Natural Gift	Normal	Physical	—	100	15	Normal	—
TM85	Dream Eater	Psychic	Special	100	100	15	Normal	—
TM86	Grass Knot	Grass	Special	—	100	20	Normal	○
TM87	Swagger	Normal	Status	—	90	15	Normal	—
TM90	Substitute	Normal	Status	—	—	10	Self	—
TM92	Trick Room	Psychic	Status	—	—	5	All	—

☺ No. 282 | Embrace Pokémon
Gardevoir

`Psychic`

- ● HEIGHT: 5'03"
- ● WEIGHT: 106.7 lbs.
- ● ITEMS: None

● SIZE COMPARISON

● MALE/FEMALE HAVE SAME FORM

⊛ ABILITIES
- ● Synchronize
- ● Trace

⊛ STATS
- HP ●●●
- ATTACK ●●●
- DEFENSE ●●●
- SP. ATTACK ●●●●●
- SP. DEFENSE ●●●●●
- SPEED ●●●●

⊛ EGG GROUPS
Amorphous

⊛ PERFORMANCE
- SPEED ★★★☆☆
- POWER ★☆☆☆☆
- SKILL ★★★★★
- STAMINA ★★☆☆☆
- JUMP ★★★☆☆

● MAIN WAYS TO OBTAIN

Pokémon HeartGold	Level up Kirlia to Lv. 30
Pokémon SoulSilver	Level up Kirlia to Lv. 30
Pokémon Diamond	Level up Kirlia to Lv. 30
Pokémon Pearl	Level up Kirlia to Lv. 30
Pokémon Platinum	Level up Kirlia to Lv. 30

Pokémon HeartGold
It unleashes psychokinetic energy at full power when protecting a Trainer it has bonded closely with.

Pokémon SoulSilver
It unleashes psychokinetic energy at full power when protecting a Trainer it has bonded closely with.

⊛ EVOLUTION

Ralts — Lv. 20 → Kirlia — Lv. 30 → Gardevoir

Use Dawn Stone on ♂

Gallade

Surskit

Bug | Water

- **HEIGHT:** 1'08"
- **WEIGHT:** 3.7 lbs.
- **ITEMS:** None

● SIZE COMPARISON

● MALE/FEMALE HAVE SAME FORM

⊛ ABILITIES
- Swift Swim

⊛ STATS
- HP ●
- ATTACK ●
- DEFENSE ●
- SP. ATTACK ●●
- SP. DEFENSE ●●
- SPEED ●●●

⊛ EGG GROUPS
Water 1

Bug

⊛ PERFORMANCE
SPEED ★★★☆☆ STAMINA ★★☆
POWER ★☆☆☆ JUMP ★★☆
SKILL ★★☆

● MAIN WAYS TO OBTAIN

Pokémon HeartGold	Safari Zone (Forest Area: if Water objects are placed, may appear in tall grass; Wetland Area: if Grass objects are placed, may appear in tall grass)
Pokémon SoulSilver	Safari Zone (Forest Area: if Water objects are placed, may appear in tall grass; Wetland Area: if Grass objects are placed, may appear in tall grass)
Pokémon Diamond	Lake Verity (mass outbreak)
Pokémon Pearl	Lake Verity (mass outbreak)
Pokémon Platinum	Route 229 (water surface)

Pokémon HeartGold	Pokémon SoulSilver
It secretes a thick, sweet-scented syrup from the tip of its head. It lives on weed-choked ponds.	It secretes a thick, sweet-scented syrup from the tip of its head. It lives on weed-choked ponds.

⊛ EVOLUTION

Surskit — Lv. 22 → Masquerain

● LEVEL-UP MOVES

Lv.	Name	Type	Kind	Pow.	Acc.	PP	Range	DA
1	Confusion	Psychic	Special	50	100	25	Normal	—
10	Confusion	Psychic	Special	50	100	25	Normal	—
13	Gust	Flying	Special	40	100	35	Normal	—
17	Protect	Normal	Status	—	—	10	Self	—
20	Moonlight	Normal	Status	—	—	5	Self	—
24	Psybeam	Psychic	Special	65	100	20	Normal	—
27	Whirlwind	Normal	Status	—	100	20	Normal	—
31	Light Screen	Psychic	Status	—	—	30	2 Allies	—
34	Silver Wind	Bug	Special	60	100	5	Normal	—
38	Toxic	Poison	Status	—	85	10	Normal	—
41	Bug Buzz	Bug	Special	90	100	10	Normal	—

● MOVE MANIAC

Name	Type	Kind	Pow.	Acc.	PP	Range	DA

● BP MOVES

Name	Type	Kind	Pow.	Acc.	PP	Range	DA
Ominous Wind	Ghost	Special	60	100	5	Normal	—
Air Cutter	Flying	Special	55	95	25	2 Foes	—
Bug Bite	Bug	Physical	60	100	20	Normal	○
Snore	Normal	Special	40	100	15	Normal	—
Swift	Normal	Special	60	—	20	2 Foes	—
String Shot	Bug	Status	—	95	40	2 Foes	—
Tailwind	Flying	Status	—	—	30	2 Allies	—
Signal Beam	Bug	Special	75	100	15	Normal	—
Twister	Dragon	Special	40	100	20	2 Foes	—

● TM & HM MOVES

No.	Name	Type	Kind	Pow.	Acc.	PP	Range	DA
TM03	Water Pulse	Water	Special	60	100	20	Normal	—
TM06	Toxic	Poison	Status	—	85	10	Normal	—
TM10	Hidden Power	Normal	Special	—	100	15	Normal	—
TM11	Sunny Day	Fire	Status	—	—	5	All	—
TM13	Ice Beam	Ice	Special	95	100	10	Normal	—
TM14	Blizzard	Ice	Special	120	70	5	2 Foes	—
TM17	Protect	Normal	Status	—	—	10	Self	—
TM18	Rain Dance	Water	Status	—	—	5	All	—
TM19	Giga Drain	Grass	Special	60	100	10	Normal	—
TM21	Frustration	Normal	Physical	—	100	20	Normal	○
TM22	SolarBeam	Grass	Special	120	100	10	Normal	—
TM27	Return	Normal	Physical	—	100	20	Normal	○
TM30	Shadow Ball	Ghost	Special	80	100	15	Normal	—
TM32	Double Team	Normal	Status	—	—	15	Self	—
TM42	Facade	Normal	Physical	70	100	20	Normal	○
TM43	Secret Power	Normal	Physical	70	100	20	Normal	—
TM44	Rest	Psychic	Status	—	—	10	Self	—
TM45	Attract	Normal	Status	—	100	15	Normal	—
TM46	Thief	Dark	Physical	40	100	10	Normal	○
TM58	Endure	Normal	Status	—	—	10	Self	—
TM70	Flash	Normal	Status	—	100	20	Normal	—
TM77	Psych Up	Normal	Status	—	—	10	Normal	—
TM78	Captivate	Normal	Status	—	100	20	2 Foes	—
TM82	Sleep Talk	Normal	Status	—	—	10	Self	—
TM83	Natural Gift	Normal	Physical	—	100	15	Normal	—
TM87	Swagger	Normal	Status	—	90	15	Normal	—
TM90	Substitute	Normal	Status	—	—	10	Self	—

● EGG MOVES

Name	Type	Kind	Pow.	Acc.	PP	Range	DA
Foresight	Normal	Status	—	—	40	Normal	—
Mud Shot	Ground	Special	55	95	15	Normal	—
Psybeam	Psychic	Special	65	100	20	Normal	—
Hydro Pump	Water	Special	120	80	5	Normal	—
Mind Reader	Normal	Status	—	—	5	Normal	—
Signal Beam	Bug	Special	75	100	15	Normal	—
Bug Bite	Bug	Physical	60	100	20	Normal	○

● LEVEL-UP MOVES

Lv.	Name	Type	Kind	Pow.	Acc.	PP	Range	DA
1	Ominous Wind	Ghost	Special	60	100	5	Normal	—
1	Bubble	Water	Special	20	100	30	2 Foes	—
1	Quick Attack	Normal	Physical	40	100	30	Normal	○
1	Sweet Scent	Normal	Status	—	100	20	2 Foes	—
1	Water Sport	Water	Status	—	—	15	All	—
7	Quick Attack	Normal	Physical	40	100	30	Normal	○
13	Sweet Scent	Normal	Status	—	100	20	2 Foes	—
19	Water Sport	Water	Status	—	—	15	All	—
22	Gust	Flying	Special	40	100	35	Normal	—
26	Scary Face	Normal	Status	—	90	10	Normal	—
33	Stun Spore	Grass	Status	—	75	30	Normal	—
40	Silver Wind	Bug	Special	60	100	5	Normal	—
47	Air Slash	Flying	Special	75	95	20	Normal	—
54	Whirlwind	Normal	Status	—	100	20	Normal	—
61	Bug Buzz	Bug	Special	90	100	10	Normal	—

● MOVE MANIAC

Name	Type	Kind	Pow.	Acc.	PP	Range	DA

● BP MOVES

Name	Type	Kind	Pow.	Acc.	PP	Range	DA
Icy Wind	Ice	Special	55	95	15	2 Foes	—
Ominous Wind	Ghost	Special	60	100	5	Normal	—
Air Cutter	Flying	Special	55	95	25	2 Foes	—
Bug Bite	Bug	Physical	60	100	20	Normal	○
Snore	Normal	Special	40	100	15	Normal	—
Swift	Normal	Special	60	—	20	2 Foes	—
String Shot	Bug	Status	—	95	40	2 Foes	—
Tailwind	Flying	Status	—	—	30	2 Allies	—
Mud-Slap	Ground	Special	20	100	10	Normal	—
Signal Beam	Bug	Special	75	100	15	Normal	—
Twister	Dragon	Special	40	100	20	2 Foes	—

● TM & HM MOVES

No.	Name	Type	Kind	Pow.	Acc.	PP	Range	DA
TM03	Water Pulse	Water	Special	60	100	20	Normal	—
TM06	Toxic	Poison	Status	—	85	10	Normal	—
TM10	Hidden Power	Normal	Special	—	100	15	Normal	—
TM11	Sunny Day	Fire	Status	—	—	5	All	—
TM13	Ice Beam	Ice	Special	95	100	10	Normal	—
TM14	Blizzard	Ice	Special	120	70	5	2 Foes	—
TM15	Hyper Beam	Normal	Special	150	90	5	Normal	—
TM17	Protect	Normal	Status	—	—	10	Self	—
TM18	Rain Dance	Water	Status	—	—	5	All	—
TM19	Giga Drain	Grass	Special	60	100	10	Normal	—
TM21	Frustration	Normal	Physical	—	100	20	Normal	○
TM22	SolarBeam	Grass	Special	120	100	10	Normal	—
TM27	Return	Normal	Physical	—	100	20	Normal	○
TM30	Shadow Ball	Ghost	Special	80	100	15	Normal	—
TM32	Double Team	Normal	Status	—	—	15	Self	—
TM40	Aerial Ace	Flying	Physical	60	—	20	Normal	○
TM42	Facade	Normal	Physical	70	100	20	Normal	○
TM43	Secret Power	Normal	Physical	70	100	20	Normal	○
TM44	Rest	Psychic	Status	—	—	10	Self	—
TM45	Attract	Normal	Status	—	100	15	Normal	—
TM46	Thief	Dark	Physical	40	100	10	Normal	○
TM51	Roost	Flying	Status	—	—	10	Self	—
TM53	Energy Ball	Grass	Special	80	100	10	Normal	—
TM58	Endure	Normal	Status	—	—	10	Self	—
TM62	Silver Wind	Bug	Special	60	100	5	Normal	—
TM68	Giga Impact	Normal	Physical	150	90	5	Normal	○
TM70	Flash	Normal	Status	—	100	20	Normal	—
TM77	Psych Up	Normal	Status	—	—	10	Normal	—
TM78	Captivate	Normal	Status	—	100	20	2 Foes	—
TM82	Sleep Talk	Normal	Status	—	—	10	Depends	—
TM83	Natural Gift	Normal	Physical	—	100	15	Normal	—
TM87	Swagger	Normal	Status	—	90	15	Normal	—
TM89	U-turn	Bug	Physical	70	100	20	Normal	○
TM90	Substitute	Normal	Status	—	—	10	Self	—

● No. 284 | Eyeball Pokémon
Masquerain
Bug   Flying

- **● HEIGHT:** 2'07"
- **● WEIGHT:** 7.9 lbs.
- **● ITEMS:** SilverPowder

● SIZE COMPARISON

● MALE/FEMALE HAVE SAME FORM

⊕ ABILITIES
● Intimidate

⊕ STATS
HP ●●●
ATTACK ●●●
DEFENSE ●●●
SP. ATTACK ●●●●
SP. DEFENSE ●●●●
SPEED ●●●

⊕ EGG GROUPS
Water 1

Bug

⊕ PERFORMANCE
SPEED ★★★☆   STAMINA ★★★★
POWER ★★☆   JUMP ★★★★★
SKILL ★★★

● MAIN WAYS TO OBTAIN

Pokémon HeartGold	Safari Zone (Meadow Area: if Water objects are placed, may appear in tall grass)
Pokémon SoulSilver	Safari Zone (Meadow Area: if Water objects are placed, may appear in tall grass)
Pokémon Diamond	Level up Surskit to Lv. 22
Pokémon Pearl	Level up Surskit to Lv. 22
Pokémon Platinum	Route 229 (water surface)

Pokémon HeartGold	**Pokémon SoulSilver**
It flaps its four wings to hover and fly freely in any direction--to and fro and sideways.	It flaps its four wings to hover and fly freely in any direction--to and fro and sideways.

⊕ EVOLUTION

Lv. 22

Surskit   Masquerain

● No. 285 | Mushroom Pokémon
Shroomish

Grass

● **LEVEL-UP MOVES**

Lv.	Name	Type	Kind	Pow.	Acc.	PP	Range	DA
1	Absorb	Grass	Special	20	100	25	Normal	—
5	Tackle	Normal	Physical	35	95	35	Normal	—
9	Stun Spore	Grass	Status	—	75	30	Normal	—
13	Leech Seed	Grass	Status	—	90	10	Normal	—
17	Mega Drain	Grass	Special	40	100	15	Normal	—
21	Headbutt	Normal	Physical	70	100	15	Normal	○
25	PoisonPowder	Poison	Status	—	75	35	Normal	—
29	Worry Seed	Grass	Status	—	100	10	Normal	—
33	Growth	Normal	Status	—	—	40	Self	—
37	Giga Drain	Grass	Special	60	100	10	Normal	—
41	Seed Bomb	Grass	Physical	80	100	15	Normal	—
45	Spore	Grass	Status	—	100	15	Normal	—

● **MOVE MANIAC**

Name	Type	Kind	Pow.	Acc.	PP	Range	DA
Headbutt	Normal	Physical	70	100	15	Normal	○

● **BP MOVES**

Name	Type	Kind	Pow.	Acc.	PP	Range	DA
Snore	Normal	Special	40	100	15	Normal	—
Helping Hand	Normal	Status	—	—	20	1 Ally	—
Synthesis	Grass	Status	—	—	5	Self	—
Worry Seed	Grass	Status	—	100	10	Normal	—
Seed Bomb	Grass	Physical	80	100	15	Normal	—

● **HEIGHT:** 1'04"
● **WEIGHT:** 9.9 lbs.
● **ITEMS:** Kebia Berry

● **SIZE COMPARISON**

● MALE/FEMALE HAVE SAME FORM

● ABILITIES
● Effect Spore
● Poison Heal

● STATS
HP ●●
ATTACK ●●
DEFENSE ●●
SP. ATTACK ●●
SP. DEFENSE ●●
SPEED ●●

● EGG GROUPS
Fairy
Grass

● PERFORMANCE
SPEED ★★☆   STAMINA ★★★★☆
POWER ★★☆   JUMP ★★☆
SKILL ★★

● **TM & HM MOVES**

No.	Name	Type	Kind	Pow.	Acc.	PP	Range	DA
TM06	Toxic	Poison	Status	—	85	10	Normal	—
TM09	Bullet Seed	Grass	Physical	10	100	30	Normal	—
TM10	Hidden Power	Normal	Special	—	100	15	Normal	—
TM11	Sunny Day	Fire	Status	—	—	5	All	—
TM17	Protect	Normal	Status	—	—	10	Self	—
TM19	Giga Drain	Grass	Special	60	100	10	Normal	—
TM20	Safeguard	Normal	Status	—	—	25	2 Allies	—
TM21	Frustration	Normal	Physical	—	100	20	Normal	○
TM22	SolarBeam	Grass	Special	120	100	10	Normal	—
TM27	Return	Normal	Physical	—	100	20	Normal	○
TM32	Double Team	Normal	Status	—	—	15	Self	—
TM36	Sludge Bomb	Poison	Special	90	100	10	Normal	—
TM42	Facade	Normal	Physical	70	100	20	Normal	○
TM43	Secret Power	Normal	Physical	70	100	20	Normal	—
TM44	Rest	Psychic	Status	—	—	10	Self	—
TM45	Attract	Normal	Status	—	100	15	Normal	—
TM49	Snatch	Dark	Status	—	—	10	Depends	—
TM53	Energy Ball	Grass	Special	80	100	10	Normal	—
TM58	Endure	Normal	Status	—	—	10	Self	—
TM70	Flash	Normal	Status	—	100	20	Normal	—
TM75	Swords Dance	Normal	Status	—	—	30	Self	—
TM78	Captivate	Normal	Status	—	100	20	2 Foes	—
TM82	Sleep Talk	Normal	Status	—	—	10	Depends	—
TM83	Natural Gift	Normal	Physical	—	100	15	Normal	—
TM86	Grass Knot	Grass	Special	—	100	20	Normal	○
TM87	Swagger	Normal	Status	—	90	15	Normal	—
TM90	Substitute	Normal	Status	—	—	10	Self	—

● MAIN WAYS TO OBTAIN

Pokémon HeartGold — Viridian Forest (use Headbutt)

Pokémon SoulSilver — Viridian Forest (use Headbutt)

Pokémon Diamond — Pastoria Great Marsh (after obtaining the National Pokédex / changes daily)

Pokémon Pearl — Pastoria Great Marsh (after obtaining the National Pokédex / changes daily)

Pokémon Platinum — Pastoria Great Marsh (after obtaining the National Pokédex / changes daily)

Pokémon HeartGold — If it senses danger, it scatters spores from the top of its head to protect itself.

Pokémon SoulSilver — If it senses danger, it scatters spores from the top of its head to protect itself.

● EVOLUTION

Shroomish — Lv. 23 → Breloom

● **EGG MOVES**

Name	Type	Kind	Pow.	Acc.	PP	Range	DA
Fake Tears	Dark	Status	—	100	20	Normal	—
Swagger	Normal	Status	—	90	15	Normal	—
Charm	Normal	Status	—	100	20	Normal	—
False Swipe	Normal	Physical	40	100	40	Normal	○
Helping Hand	Normal	Status	—	—	20	1 Ally	—
Worry Seed	Grass	Status	—	100	10	Normal	—
Wake-Up Slap	Fighting	Physical	60	100	10	Normal	○
Seed Bomb	Grass	Physical	80	100	15	Normal	—

● LEVEL-UP MOVES

Lv.	Name	Type	Kind	Pow.	Acc.	PP	Range	DA
1	Absorb	Grass	Special	20	100	25	Normal	—
1	Tackle	Normal	Physical	35	95	35	Normal	○
1	Stun Spore	Grass	Status	—	75	30	Normal	—
1	Leech Seed	Grass	Status	—	90	10	Normal	—
5	Tackle	Normal	Physical	35	95	35	Normal	○
9	Stun Spore	Grass	Status	—	75	30	Normal	—
13	Leech Seed	Grass	Status	—	90	10	Normal	—
17	Mega Drain	Grass	Special	40	100	15	Normal	—
21	Headbutt	Normal	Physical	70	100	15	Normal	○
23	Mach Punch	Fighting	Physical	40	100	30	Normal	○
25	Counter	Fighting	Physical	—	100	20	Self	○
29	Force Palm	Fighting	Physical	60	100	10	Normal	○
33	Sky Uppercut	Fighting	Physical	85	90	15	Normal	○
37	Mind Reader	Normal	Status	—	—	5	Normal	—
41	Seed Bomb	Grass	Physical	80	100	15	Normal	○
45	DynamicPunch	Fighting	Physical	100	50	5	Normal	○

● MOVE MANIAC

Name	Type	Kind	Pow.	Acc.	PP	Range	DA
Headbutt	Normal	Physical	70	100	15	Normal	○

● BP MOVES

Name	Type	Kind	Pow.	Acc.	PP	Range	DA
Fury Cutter	Bug	Physical	10	95	20	Normal	○
ThunderPunch	Electric	Physical	75	100	15	Normal	○
Vacuum Wave	Fighting	Special	40	100	30	Normal	—
Snore	Normal	Special	40	100	15	Normal	—
Helping Hand	Normal	Status	—	—	20	1 Ally	—
Synthesis	Grass	Status	—	—	5	Self	—
Worry Seed	Grass	Status	—	100	10	Normal	—
Mud-Slap	Ground	Special	20	100	10	Normal	—
Superpower	Fighting	Physical	120	100	5	Normal	○
Seed Bomb	Grass	Physical	80	100	15	Normal	○

● TM & HM MOVES

No.	Name	Type	Kind	Pow.	Acc.	PP	Range	DA
TM01	Focus Punch	Fighting	Physical	150	100	20	Normal	○
TM06	Toxic	Poison	Status	—	85	10	Normal	—
TM08	Bulk Up	Fighting	Status	—	—	20	Self	—
TM09	Bullet Seed	Grass	Physical	10	100	30	Normal	—
TM10	Hidden Power	Normal	Special	—	100	15	Normal	—
TM11	Sunny Day	Fire	Status	—	—	5	All	—
TM15	Hyper Beam	Normal	Special	150	90	5	Normal	—
TM17	Protect	Normal	Status	—	—	10	Self	—
TM19	Giga Drain	Grass	Special	60	100	10	Normal	—
TM20	Safeguard	Normal	Status	—	—	25	2 Allies	—
TM21	Frustration	Normal	Physical	—	100	20	Normal	○
TM22	SolarBeam	Grass	Special	120	100	10	Normal	—
TM23	Iron Tail	Steel	Physical	100	75	15	Normal	○
TM27	Return	Normal	Physical	—	100	20	Normal	○
TM31	Brick Break	Fighting	Physical	75	100	15	Normal	○
TM32	Double Team	Normal	Status	—	—	15	Self	—
TM36	Sludge Bomb	Poison	Special	90	100	10	Normal	—
TM39	Rock Tomb	Rock	Physical	50	80	10	Normal	○
TM42	Facade	Normal	Physical	70	100	20	Normal	○
TM43	Secret Power	Normal	Physical	70	100	20	Normal	—
TM44	Rest	Psychic	Status	—	—	10	Self	—
TM45	Attract	Normal	Status	—	100	15	Normal	—
TM49	Snatch	Dark	Status	—	—	10	Depends	—
TM52	Focus Blast	Fighting	Special	120	70	5	Normal	—
TM53	Energy Ball	Grass	Special	80	100	10	Normal	—
TM56	Fling	Dark	Physical	—	100	10	Normal	—
TM58	Endure	Normal	Status	—	—	10	Self	—
TM60	Drain Punch	Fighting	Physical	60	100	5	Normal	○
TM68	Giga Impact	Normal	Physical	150	90	5	Normal	○
TM70	Flash	Normal	Status	—	100	20	Normal	—
TM71	Stone Edge	Rock	Physical	100	80	5	Normal	—
TM75	Swords Dance	Normal	Status	—	—	30	Self	—
TM78	Captivate	Normal	Status	—	100	20	2 Foes	—
TM80	Rock Slide	Rock	Physical	75	90	10	2 Foes	—
TM82	Sleep Talk	Normal	Status	—	—	10	Depends	—
TM83	Natural Gift	Normal	Physical	—	100	15	Normal	—
TM86	Grass Knot	Grass	Special	—	100	20	Normal	○
TM87	Swagger	Normal	Status	—	90	15	Normal	—
TM90	Substitute	Normal	Status	—	—	10	Self	—
HM01	Cut	Normal	Physical	50	95	30	Normal	○
HM04	Strength	Normal	Physical	80	100	15	Normal	○
HM06	Rock Smash	Fighting	Physical	40	100	15	Normal	○

Breloom

Grass Fighting

- ●HEIGHT: 3'11"
- ●WEIGHT: 86.4 lbs.
- ●ITEMS: Kebia Berry

● SIZE COMPARISON

● MALE/FEMALE HAVE SAME FORM

● ABILITIES
- Effect Spore
- Poison Heal

● STATS
- HP ●●
- ATTACK ●●●●●
- DEFENSE ●●●
- SP. ATTACK ●●●
- SP. DEFENSE ●●●
- SPEED ●●●

● EGG GROUPS
- Fairy
- Grass

● PERFORMANCE
- SPEED ★★☆☆
- POWER ★★★☆
- SKILL ★★★☆☆
- STAMINA ★★★☆☆
- JUMP ★★☆

● MAIN WAYS TO OBTAIN

Pokémon HeartGold — Safari Zone (Wasteland Area): if Forest objects are placed, may appear in tall grass)

Pokémon SoulSilver — Safari Zone (Wasteland Area): if Forest objects are placed, may appear in tall grass)

Pokémon Diamond — Level up Shroomish to Lv. 23

Pokémon Pearl — Level up Shroomish to Lv. 23

Pokémon Platinum — Level up Shroomish to Lv. 23

Pokémon HeartGold — It scatters poisonous spores and throws powerful punches while its foe is hampered by inhaled spores.

Pokémon SoulSilver — It scatters poisonous spores and throws powerful punches while its foe is hampered by inhaled spores.

● EVOLUTION

Shroomish → Lv. 23 → Breloom

No. 287 | Slacker Pokémon
Slakoth

`Normal`

- **HEIGHT:** 2'07"
- **WEIGHT:** 52.9 lbs.
- **ITEMS:** None

● SIZE COMPARISON

● MALE/FEMALE HAVE SAME FORM

● **ABILITIES**
- Truant

● **STATS**
HP ●●
ATTACK ●●●
DEFENSE ●●●
SP. ATTACK ●
SP. DEFENSE ●
SPEED ●

● **EGG GROUPS**
Field

● **PERFORMANCE**
SPEED ★☆   STAMINA ★★★★☆
POWER ★☆   JUMP ★★
SKILL ★☆

● **MAIN WAYS TO OBTAIN**

Pokémon HeartGold	Route 25 (use Headbutt on four trees in the northwest)
Pokémon SoulSilver	Route 25 (use Headbutt on four trees in the northwest)
Pokémon Diamond	Eterna Forest (mass outbreak)
Pokémon Pearl	Eterna Forest (mass outbreak)
Pokémon Platinum	Eterna Forest (mass outbreak)

| Pokémon HeartGold | Pokémon SoulSilver |
| The way SLAKOTH lolls around makes anyone who watches it feel like doing the same. | The way SLAKOTH lolls around makes anyone who watches it feel like doing the same. |

● **EVOLUTION**

Slakoth — Lv. 18 → Vigoroth — Lv. 36 → Slaking

● LEVEL-UP MOVES

Lv.	Name	Type	Kind	Pow.	Acc.	PP	Range	DA
1	Scratch	Normal	Physical	40	100	35	Normal	—
1	Yawn	Normal	Status	—	—	10	Normal	—
7	Encore	Normal	Status	—	100	5	Normal	—
13	Slack Off	Normal	Status	—	—	10	Self	—
19	Faint Attack	Dark	Physical	60	—	20	Normal	○
25	Amnesia	Psychic	Status	—	—	20	Self	—
31	Covet	Normal	Physical	40	100	40	Normal	○
37	Counter	Fighting	Physical	—	100	20	Self	○
43	Flail	Normal	Physical	—	100	15	Normal	○

● MOVE MANIAC

Name	Type	Kind	Pow.	Acc.	PP	Range	DA
Headbutt	Normal	Physical	70	100	15	Normal	○

● BP MOVES

Name	Type	Kind	Pow.	Acc.	PP	Range	DA
Fury Cutter	Bug	Physical	10	95	20	Normal	○
Icy Wind	Ice	Special	55	95	15	2 Foes	—
ThunderPunch	Electric	Physical	75	100	15	Normal	○
Fire Punch	Fire	Physical	75	100	15	Normal	○
Ice Punch	Ice	Physical	75	100	15	Normal	○
Sucker Punch	Dark	Physical	80	100	5	Normal	○
Snore	Normal	Special	40	100	15	Normal	—
Mud-Slap	Ground	Special	20	100	10	Normal	—
Gunk Shot	Poison	Physical	120	70	5	Normal	—

● TM & HM MOVES

No.	Name	Type	Kind	Pow.	Acc.	PP	Range	DA
TM01	Focus Punch	Fighting	Physical	150	100	20	Normal	○
TM03	Water Pulse	Water	Special	60	100	20	Normal	—
TM06	Toxic	Poison	Status	—	85	10	Normal	—
TM08	Bulk Up	Fighting	Status	—	—	20	Self	—
TM10	Hidden Power	Normal	Special	—	100	15	Normal	—
TM11	Sunny Day	Fire	Status	—	—	5	All	—
TM13	Ice Beam	Ice	Special	95	100	10	Normal	—
TM14	Blizzard	Ice	Special	120	70	5	2 Foes	—
TM17	Protect	Normal	Status	—	—	10	Self	—
TM18	Rain Dance	Water	Status	—	—	5	All	—
TM21	Frustration	Normal	Physical	—	100	20	Normal	○
TM22	SolarBeam	Grass	Special	120	100	10	Normal	—
TM24	Thunderbolt	Electric	Special	95	100	15	Normal	—
TM25	Thunder	Electric	Special	120	70	10	Normal	—
TM27	Return	Normal	Physical	—	100	20	Normal	○
TM30	Shadow Ball	Ghost	Special	80	100	15	Normal	—
TM31	Brick Break	Fighting	Physical	75	100	15	Normal	○
TM32	Double Team	Normal	Status	—	—	15	Self	—
TM34	Shock Wave	Electric	Special	60	—	20	Normal	—
TM35	Flamethrower	Fire	Special	95	100	15	Normal	—
TM38	Fire Blast	Fire	Special	120	85	5	Normal	—
TM39	Rock Tomb	Rock	Physical	50	80	10	Normal	○
TM40	Aerial Ace	Flying	Physical	60	—	20	Normal	○
TM42	Facade	Normal	Physical	70	100	20	Normal	○
TM43	Secret Power	Normal	Physical	70	100	20	Normal	—
TM44	Rest	Psychic	Status	—	—	10	Self	—
TM45	Attract	Normal	Status	—	100	15	Normal	—
TM56	Fling	Dark	Physical	—	100	10	Normal	—
TM58	Endure	Normal	Status	—	—	10	Self	—
TM65	Shadow Claw	Ghost	Physical	70	100	15	Normal	○
TM78	Captivate	Normal	Status	—	100	20	2 Foes	—
TM80	Rock Slide	Rock	Physical	75	90	10	2 Foes	—
TM82	Sleep Talk	Normal	Status	—	—	10	Depends	—
TM83	Natural Gift	Normal	Physical	—	100	15	Normal	—
TM87	Swagger	Normal	Status	—	90	15	Normal	—
TM90	Substitute	Normal	Status	—	—	10	Self	—
HM01	Cut	Normal	Physical	50	95	30	Normal	○
HM04	Strength	Normal	Physical	80	100	15	Normal	○
HM06	Rock Smash	Fighting	Physical	40	100	15	Normal	○

● EGG MOVES

Name	Type	Kind	Pow.	Acc.	PP	Range	DA
Pursuit	Dark	Physical	40	100	20	Normal	○
Slash	Normal	Physical	70	100	20	Normal	○
Body Slam	Normal	Physical	85	100	15	Normal	○
Snore	Normal	Special	40	100	15	Normal	—
Crush Claw	Normal	Physical	75	95	10	Normal	○
Curse	???	Status	—	—	10	Normal/Self	—
Sleep Talk	Normal	Status	—	—	10	Depends	—
Hammer Arm	Fighting	Physical	100	90	10	Normal	○
Night Slash	Dark	Physical	70	100	15	Normal	○

● LEVEL-UP MOVES

Lv.	Name	Type	Kind	Pow.	Acc.	PP	Range	DA
1	Scratch	Normal	Physical	40	100	35	Normal	○
1	Focus Energy	Normal	Status	—	—	30	Self	
1	Encore	Normal	Status	—	100	5	Normal	
1	Uproar	Normal	Special	50	100	10	1 Random	
7	Encore	Normal	Status	—	100	5	Normal	
13	Uproar	Normal	Special	50	100	10	1 Random	
19	Fury Swipes	Normal	Physical	18	80	15	Normal	○
25	Endure	Normal	Status	—	—	10	Self	
31	Slash	Normal	Physical	70	100	20	Normal	○
37	Counter	Fighting	Physical	—	100	20	Self	
43	Focus Punch	Fighting	Physical	150	100	20	Normal	○
49	Reversal	Fighting	Physical	—	100	15	Normal	○

● MOVE MANIAC

Name	Type	Kind	Pow.	Acc.	PP	Range	DA
Headbutt	Normal	Physical	70	100	15	Normal	○

● BP MOVES

Name	Type	Kind	Pow.	Acc.	PP	Range	DA
Fury Cutter	Bug	Physical	10	95	20	Normal	—
Icy Wind	Ice	Special	55	95	15	2 Foes	—
ThunderPunch	Electric	Physical	75	100	15	Normal	○
Fire Punch	Fire	Physical	75	100	15	Normal	○
Ice Punch	Ice	Physical	75	100	15	Normal	○
Sucker Punch	Dark	Physical	80	100	5	Normal	○
Uproar	Normal	Special	50	100	10	1 Random	—
Mud-Slap	Ground	Special	20	100	10	Normal	—
Gunk Shot	Poison	Physical	120	70	5	Normal	—
Low Kick	Fighting	Physical	—	100	20	Normal	○

● TM & HM MOVES

No.	Name	Type	Kind	Pow.	Acc.	PP	Range	DA
TM01	Focus Punch	Fighting	Physical	150	100	20	Normal	○
TM03	Water Pulse	Water	Special	60	100	20	Normal	—
TM05	Roar	Normal	Status	—	100	20	Normal	—
TM06	Toxic	Poison	Status	—	85	10	Normal	—
TM08	Bulk Up	Fighting	Status	—	—	20	Self	—
TM10	Hidden Power	Normal	Special	—	100	15	Normal	—
TM11	Sunny Day	Fire	Status	—	—	5	All	—
TM12	Taunt	Dark	Status	—	100	20	Normal	—
TM13	Ice Beam	Ice	Special	95	100	10	Normal	—
TM14	Blizzard	Ice	Special	120	70	5	2 Foes	—
TM17	Protect	Normal	Status	—	—	10	Self	—
TM18	Rain Dance	Water	Status	—	—	5	All	—
TM21	Frustration	Normal	Physical	—	100	20	Normal	○
TM22	SolarBeam	Grass	Special	120	100	10	Normal	—
TM24	Thunderbolt	Electric	Special	95	100	15	Normal	—
TM25	Thunder	Electric	Special	120	70	10	Normal	—
TM26	Earthquake	Ground	Physical	100	100	10	2 Foes/1 Ally	—
TM27	Return	Normal	Physical	—	100	20	Normal	○
TM30	Shadow Ball	Ghost	Special	80	100	15	Normal	—
TM31	Brick Break	Fighting	Physical	75	100	15	Normal	○
TM32	Double Team	Normal	Status	—	—	15	Self	—
TM34	Shock Wave	Electric	Special	60	—	20	Normal	—
TM35	Flamethrower	Fire	Special	95	100	15	Normal	—
TM38	Fire Blast	Fire	Special	120	85	5	Normal	—
TM39	Rock Tomb	Rock	Physical	50	80	10	Normal	○
TM40	Aerial Ace	Flying	Physical	60	—	20	Normal	○
TM42	Facade	Normal	Physical	70	100	20	Normal	○
TM43	Secret Power	Normal	Physical	70	100	20	Normal	○
TM44	Rest	Psychic	Status	—	—	10	Self	—
TM45	Attract	Normal	Status	—	100	15	Normal	—
TM52	Focus Blast	Fighting	Special	120	70	5	Normal	—
TM56	Fling	Dark	Physical	—	100	10	Normal	—
TM58	Endure	Normal	Status	—	—	10	Self	—
TM65	Shadow Claw	Ghost	Physical	70	100	15	Normal	○
TM78	Captivate	Normal	Status	—	100	20	2 Foes	—
TM80	Rock Slide	Rock	Physical	75	90	10	2 Foes	—
TM82	Sleep Talk	Normal	Status	—	—	10	Depends	—
TM83	Natural Gift	Normal	Physical	—	100	15	Normal	—
TM87	Swagger	Normal	Status	—	90	15	Normal	—
TM90	Substitute	Normal	Status	—	—	10	Self	—
HM01	Cut	Normal	Physical	50	95	30	Normal	○
HM04	Strength	Normal	Physical	80	100	15	Normal	○
HM06	Rock Smash	Fighting	Physical	40	100	15	Normal	○
HM08	Rock Climb	Normal	Physical	90	85	20	Normal	○

No. 288 | Wild Monkey Pokémon

Vigoroth

Normal

- **HEIGHT:** 4'07"
- **WEIGHT:** 102.5 lbs.
- **ITEMS:** None

● SIZE COMPARISON

● MALE/FEMALE HAVE SAME FORM

⚙ ABILITIES
- Vital Spirit

⚙ STATS
- HP ●●●
- ATTACK ●●●
- DEFENSE ●●●
- SP. ATTACK ●●
- SP. DEFENSE ●●
- SPEED ●●●●

⚙ EGG GROUPS
Field

⚙ PERFORMANCE
- SPEED ★★★★☆
- POWER ★★☆
- SKILL ★★☆☆
- STAMINA ★★★☆
- JUMP ★★★☆

● MAIN WAYS TO OBTAIN

Pokémon HeartGold	Safari Zone (Peak Area: if Grass objects are placed, may appear in tall grass)
Pokémon SoulSilver	Safari Zone (Peak Area: if Grass objects are placed, may appear in tall grass)
Pokémon Diamond	Level up Slakoth to Lv. 18
Pokémon Pearl	Level up Slakoth to Lv. 18
Pokémon Platinum	Level up Slakoth to Lv. 18

Pokémon HeartGold	Pokémon SoulSilver
Its stress level rises if it cannot keep moving constantly. Too much stress makes it feel sick.	Its stress level rises if it cannot keep moving constantly. Too much stress makes it feel sick.

⚙ EVOLUTION

Slakoth — Lv. 18 → Vigoroth — Lv. 36 → Slaking

No. 289 | Lazy Pokémon
Slaking

Normal

● HEIGHT: 6'07"
● WEIGHT: 287.7 lbs.
● ITEMS: None

● SIZE COMPARISON

● MALE/FEMALE HAVE SAME FORM

● ABILITIES
● Truant

● STATS
HP ●●●●●
ATTACK ●●●●●
DEFENSE ●●●●
SP. ATTACK ●●●●
SP. DEFENSE ●●●●
SPEED ●●●●

● EGG GROUPS
Field

● PERFORMANCE
SPEED ★
POWER ★★★★★
SKILL ★☆
STAMINA ★★★★☆
JUMP ★★

● MAIN WAYS TO OBTAIN

Pokémon HeartGold | Level up Vigoroth to Lv. 36

Pokémon SoulSilver | Level up Vigoroth to Lv. 36

Pokémon Diamond | Level up Vigoroth to Lv. 36

Pokémon Pearl | Level up Vigoroth to Lv. 36

Pokémon Platinum | Level up Vigoroth to Lv. 36

Pokémon HeartGold	Pokémon SoulSilver
The world's laziest Pokémon. It moves to another spot when there's no food left within its reach.	The world's laziest Pokémon. It moves to another spot when there's no food left within its reach.

● EVOLUTION

Slakoth — Lv. 18 → Vigoroth — Lv. 36 → Slaking

● LEVEL-UP MOVES

Lv.	Name	Type	Kind	Pow.	Acc.	PP	Range	DA
1	Scratch	Normal	Physical	40	100	35	Normal	○
1	Yawn	Normal	Status	—	—	10	Normal	—
1	Encore	Normal	Status	—	100	5	Normal	—
1	Slack Off	Normal	Status	—	—	10	Self	—
?	Encore	Normal	Status	—	100	5	Normal	—
13	Slack Off	Normal	Status	—	—	10	Self	—
19	Faint Attack	Dark	Physical	60	—	20	Normal	○
25	Amnesia	Psychic	Status	—	—	20	Self	—
31	Covet	Normal	Physical	40	100	40	Normal	○
36	Swagger	Normal	Status	—	90	15	Normal	—
37	Counter	Fighting	Physical	—	100	20	Self	—
43	Flail	Normal	Physical	—	100	15	Normal	○
49	Fling	Dark	Physical	—	100	10	Normal	○
55	Punishment	Dark	Physical	—	100	5	Normal	○
61	Hammer Arm	Fighting	Physical	100	90	10	Normal	○

● MOVE MANIAC

Name	Type	Kind	Pow.	Acc.	PP	Range	DA
Headbutt	Normal	Physical	70	100	15	Normal	○

● BP MOVES

Name	Type	Kind	Pow.	Acc.	PP	Range	DA
Fury Cutter	Bug	Physical	10	95	20	Normal	○
Icy Wind	Ice	Special	55	95	15	2 Foes	—
ThunderPunch	Electric	Physical	75	100	15	Normal	○
Fire Punch	Fire	Physical	75	100	15	Normal	○
Ice Punch	Ice	Physical	75	100	15	Normal	○
Sucker Punch	Dark	Physical	80	100	5	Normal	○
Snore	Normal	Special	40	100	15	Normal	—
Block	Normal	Status	—	—	5	Normal	—
Mud-Slap	Ground	Special	20	100	10	Normal	○
Gunk Shot	Poison	Physical	120	70	5	Normal	○
Low Kick	Fighting	Physical	—	100	20	Normal	○

● TM & HM MOVES

No.	Name	Type	Kind	Pow.	Acc.	PP	Range	DA
TM01	Focus Punch	Fighting	Physical	150	100	20	Normal	○
TM03	Water Pulse	Water	Special	60	100	20	Normal	—
TM05	Roar	Normal	Status	—	100	20	Normal	—
TM06	Toxic	Poison	Status	—	85	10	Normal	—
TM08	Bulk Up	Fighting	Status	—	—	20	Self	—
TM10	Hidden Power	Normal	Special	—	100	15	Normal	—
TM11	Sunny Day	Fire	Status	—	—	5	All	—
TM12	Taunt	Dark	Status	—	100	20	Normal	—
TM13	Ice Beam	Ice	Special	95	100	10	Normal	—
TM14	Blizzard	Ice	Special	120	70	5	2 Foes	—
TM15	Hyper Beam	Normal	Special	150	90	5	Normal	—
TM17	Protect	Normal	Status	—	—	10	Self	—
TM18	Rain Dance	Water	Status	—	—	5	All	—
TM21	Frustration	Normal	Physical	—	100	20	Normal	○
TM22	SolarBeam	Grass	Special	120	100	10	Normal	○
TM24	Thunderbolt	Electric	Special	95	100	15	Normal	—
TM25	Thunder	Electric	Special	120	70	10	Normal	—
TM26	Earthquake	Ground	Physical	100	100	10	2 Foes/1 Ally	○
TM27	Return	Normal	Physical	—	100	20	Normal	○
TM30	Shadow Ball	Ghost	Special	80	100	15	Normal	—
TM31	Brick Break	Fighting	Physical	75	100	15	Normal	○
TM32	Double Team	Normal	Status	—	—	15	Self	—
TM34	Shock Wave	Electric	Special	60	—	20	Normal	—
TM35	Flamethrower	Fire	Special	95	100	15	Normal	—
TM38	Fire Blast	Fire	Special	120	85	5	Normal	—
TM39	Rock Tomb	Rock	Physical	50	80	10	Normal	○
TM40	Aerial Ace	Flying	Physical	60	—	20	Normal	○
TM42	Facade	Normal	Physical	70	100	20	Normal	○
TM43	Secret Power	Normal	Physical	70	100	20	Normal	○
TM44	Rest	Psychic	Status	—	—	10	Self	—
TM45	Attract	Normal	Status	—	100	15	Normal	—
TM52	Focus Blast	Fighting	Special	120	70	5	Normal	—
TM56	Fling	Dark	Physical	—	100	10	Normal	○
TM58	Endure	Normal	Status	—	—	10	Self	—
TM65	Shadow Claw	Ghost	Physical	70	100	15	Normal	○
TM68	Giga Impact	Normal	Physical	150	90	5	Normal	○
TM80	Rock Slide	Rock	Physical	75	90	10	2 Foes	—
TM82	Sleep Talk	Normal	Status	—	—	10	Depends	—
TM83	Natural Gift	Normal	Physical	—	100	15	Normal	—
TM87	Swagger	Normal	Status	—	90	15	Normal	—
TM90	Substitute	Normal	Status	—	—	10	Self	—
HM01	Cut	Normal	Physical	50	95	30	Normal	○
HM04	Strength	Normal	Physical	80	100	15	Normal	○
HM06	Rock Smash	Fighting	Physical	40	100	15	Normal	○
HM08	Rock Climb	Normal	Physical	90	85	20	Normal	○

● LEVEL-UP MOVES

Lv.	Name	Type	Kind	Pow.	Acc.	PP	Range	DA
1	Scratch	Normal	Physical	40	100	35	Normal	○
1	Harden	Normal	Status	—	—	30	Self	—
5	Leech Life	Bug	Physical	20	100	15	Normal	○
9	Sand-Attack	Ground	Status	—	100	15	Normal	—
14	Fury Swipes	Normal	Physical	18	80	15	Normal	○
19	Mind Reader	Normal	Status	—	—	5	Normal	—
25	False Swipe	Normal	Physical	40	100	40	Normal	○
31	Mud-Slap	Ground	Special	20	100	10	Normal	—
38	Metal Claw	Steel	Physical	50	95	35	Normal	○
45	Dig	Ground	Physical	80	100	10	Normal	○

● MOVE MANIAC

Name	Type	Kind	Pow.	Acc.	PP	Range	DA

● BP MOVES

Name	Type	Kind	Pow.	Acc.	PP	Range	DA
Fury Cutter	Bug	Physical	10	95	20	Normal	○
Bug Bite	Bug	Physical	60	100	20	Normal	○
Snore	Normal	Special	40	100	15	Normal	—
Spite	Ghost	Status	—	100	10	Normal	—
String Shot	Bug	Status	—	95	40	2 Foes	—
Mud-Slap	Ground	Special	20	100	10	Normal	—

● TM & HM MOVES

No.	Name	Type	Kind	Pow.	Acc.	PP	Range	DA
TM06	Toxic	Poison	Status	—	85	10	Normal	—
TM10	Hidden Power	Normal	Special	—	100	15	Normal	—
TM11	Sunny Day	Fire	Status	—	—	5	All	—
TM17	Protect	Normal	Status	—	—	10	Self	—
TM19	Giga Drain	Grass	Special	60	100	10	Normal	—
TM21	Frustration	Normal	Physical	—	100	20	Normal	○
TM22	SolarBeam	Grass	Special	120	100	10	Normal	—
TM27	Return	Normal	Physical	—	100	20	Normal	○
TM28	Dig	Ground	Physical	80	100	10	Normal	○
TM30	Shadow Ball	Ghost	Special	80	100	15	Normal	—
TM32	Double Team	Normal	Status	—	—	15	Self	—
TM37	Sandstorm	Rock	Status	—	—	10	All	—
TM40	Aerial Ace	Flying	Physical	60	—	20	Normal	○
TM42	Facade	Normal	Physical	70	100	20	Normal	○
TM43	Secret Power	Normal	Physical	70	100	20	Normal	○
TM44	Rest	Psychic	Status	—	—	10	Self	—
TM54	False Swipe	Normal	Physical	40	100	40	Normal	○
TM58	Endure	Normal	Status	—	—	10	Self	—
TM70	Flash	Normal	Status	—	100	20	Normal	—
TM81	X-Scissor	Bug	Physical	80	100	15	Normal	○
TM82	Sleep Talk	Normal	Status	—	—	10	Depends	—
TM83	Natural Gift	Normal	Physical	—	100	15	Normal	—
TM87	Swagger	Normal	Status	—	90	15	Normal	—
TM90	Substitute	Normal	Status	—	—	10	Self	—
HM01	Cut	Normal	Physical	50	95	30	Normal	○

● EGG MOVES

Name	Type	Kind	Pow.	Acc.	PP	Range	UA
Endure	Normal	Status	—	—	10	Self	—
Faint Attack	Dark	Physical	60	—	20	Normal	—
Gust	Flying	Special	40	100	35	Normal	—
Silver Wind	Bug	Special	60	100	5	Normal	—
Bug Buzz	Bug	Special	90	100	10	Normal	—
Night Slash	Dark	Physical	70	100	15	Normal	○
Bug Bite	Bug	Physical	60	100	20	Normal	○

● No. 290 | Trainee Pokémon
Nincada

Bug **Ground**

- **HEIGHT:** 1'08"
- **WEIGHT:** 12.1 lbs.
- **ITEMS:** None

● SIZE COMPARISON

● MALE/FEMALE HAVE SAME FORM

⊕ ABILITIES
● Compoundeyes

⊕ STATS
- HP ●
- ATTACK ●●
- DEFENSE ●●●●
- SP. ATTACK ●
- SP. DEFENSE ●
- SPEED ●●

⊕ EGG GROUPS
Bug

⊕ PERFORMANCE
SPEED ★★☆
POWER ★★☆
SKILL ★★★☆

STAMINA ★★★☆☆
JUMP ★★☆

● MAIN WAYS TO OBTAIN

Pokémon HeartGold	Bug-Catching Contest at the National Park [after obtaining the National Pokédex / Thursday, Saturday]
Pokémon SoulSilver	Bug-Catching Contest at the National Park [after obtaining the National Pokédex / Thursday, Saturday]
Pokémon Diamond	Eterna Forest [use Poké Radar]
Pokémon Pearl	Eterna Forest [use Poké Radar]
Pokémon Platinum	Eterna Forest [use Poké Radar]

Pokémon HeartGold	Pokémon SoulSilver
It can sometimes live underground for more than 10 years. It absorbs nutrients from the roots of trees.	It can sometimes live underground for more than 10 years. It absorbs nutrients from the roots of trees.

⊕ EVOLUTION

Lv. 22 → Ninjask

Have at least one free space in your party and a Poké Ball

 Nincada → Shedinja

No. 291 | Ninja Pokémon
Ninjask

Bug **Flying**

- **HEIGHT:** 2'02"
- **WEIGHT:** 26.5 lbs.
- **ITEMS:** None

● SIZE COMPARISON

● MALE/FEMALE HAVE SAME FORM

● **ABILITIES**
- Speed Boost

● **STATS**
HP	●●
ATTACK	●●●●
DEFENSE	●●
SP. ATTACK	●●
SP. DEFENSE	●●
SPEED	●●●●●●

● **EGG GROUPS**

Bug

● **PERFORMANCE**

SPEED ★★★★★   STAMINA ★★
POWER ★★☆   JUMP ★★★★★
SKILL ★★☆

● MAIN WAYS TO OBTAIN

Pokémon HeartGold	Level up Nincada to Lv. 20
Pokémon SoulSilver	Level up Nincada to Lv. 20
Pokémon Diamond	Level up Nincada to Lv. 20
Pokémon Pearl	Level up Nincada to Lv. 20
Pokémon Platinum	Level up Nincada to Lv. 20

Pokémon HeartGold	Pokémon SoulSilver
Its cry leaves a lasting headache if heard for too long. It moves so quickly that it is almost invisible.	Its cry leaves a lasting headache if heard for too long. It moves so quickly that it is almost invisible.

● **EVOLUTION**

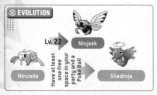

Lv. 22 Ninjask

Nincada → Have at least one free space in your party and a Poké Ball → Shedinja

● **LEVEL-UP MOVES**

Lv.	Name	Type	Kind	Pow.	Acc.	PP	Range	DA
1	Bug Bite	Bug	Physical	60	100	20	Normal	○
1	Scratch	Normal	Physical	40	100	35	Normal	○
1	Harden	Normal	Status	—	—	30	Self	—
1	Leech Life	Bug	Physical	20	100	15	Normal	○
1	Sand-Attack	Ground	Status	—	100	15	Normal	—
5	Leech Life	Bug	Physical	20	100	15	Normal	○
9	Sand-Attack	Ground	Status	—	100	15	Normal	—
14	Fury Swipes	Normal	Physical	18	80	15	Normal	○
19	Mind Reader	Normal	Status	—	—	5	Normal	—
20	Double Team	Normal	Status	—	—	15	Self	—
20	Fury Cutter	Bug	Physical	10	95	20	Normal	○
20	Screech	Normal	Status	—	85	40	Normal	—
25	Swords Dance	Normal	Status	—	—	30	Self	—
31	Slash	Normal	Physical	70	100	20	Normal	○
38	Agility	Psychic	Status	—	—	30	Self	—
45	Baton Pass	Normal	Status	—	—	40	Self	—
52	X-Scissor	Bug	Physical	80	100	15	Normal	○

● **MOVE MANIAC**

Name	Type	Kind	Pow.	Acc.	PP	Range	DA

● **BP MOVES**

Name	Type	Kind	Pow.	Acc.	PP	Range	DA
Fury Cutter	Bug	Physical	10	95	20	Normal	○
Ominous Wind	Ghost	Special	60	100	5	Normal	—
Air Cutter	Flying	Special	55	95	25	2 Foes	—
Bug Bite	Bug	Physical	60	100	20	Normal	○
Snore	Normal	Special	40	100	15	Normal	—
Spite	Ghost	Status	—	100	10	Normal	—
Swift	Normal	Special	60	—	20	2 Foes	—
Uproar	Normal	Special	50	100	10	1 Random	—
String Shot	Bug	Status	—	95	40	2 Foes	—
Mud-Slap	Ground	Special	20	100	10	Normal	—

● **TM & HM MOVES**

No.	Name	Type	Kind	Pow.	Acc.	PP	Range	DA
TM06	Toxic	Poison	Status	—	85	10	Normal	—
TM10	Hidden Power	Normal	Special	—	100	15	Normal	—
TM11	Sunny Day	Fire	Status	—	—	5	All	—
TM15	Hyper Beam	Normal	Special	150	90	5	Normal	—
TM17	Protect	Normal	Status	—	—	10	Self	—
TM19	Giga Drain	Grass	Special	60	100	10	Normal	—
TM21	Frustration	Normal	Physical	—	100	20	Normal	○
TM22	SolarBeam	Grass	Special	120	100	10	Normal	—
TM27	Return	Normal	Physical	—	100	20	Normal	○
TM28	Dig	Ground	Physical	80	100	10	Normal	○
TM30	Shadow Ball	Ghost	Special	80	100	15	Normal	—
TM32	Double Team	Normal	Status	—	—	15	Self	—
TM37	Sandstorm	Rock	Status	—	—	10	All	—
TM40	Aerial Ace	Flying	Physical	60	—	20	Normal	○
TM42	Facade	Normal	Physical	70	100	20	Normal	○
TM43	Secret Power	Normal	Physical	70	100	20	Normal	—
TM44	Rest	Psychic	Status	—	—	10	Self	—
TM45	Attract	Normal	Status	—	100	15	Normal	—
TM46	Thief	Dark	Physical	40	100	10	Normal	○
TM51	Roost	Flying	Status	—	—	10	Self	—
TM54	False Swipe	Normal	Physical	40	100	40	Normal	○
TM58	Endure	Normal	Status	—	—	10	Self	—
TM62	Silver Wind	Bug	Special	60	100	5	Normal	—
TM68	Giga Impact	Normal	Physical	150	90	5	Normal	—
TM70	Flash	Normal	Status	—	100	20	Normal	—
TM75	Swords Dance	Normal	Status	—	—	30	Self	—
TM78	Captivate	Normal	Status	—	100	20	2 Foes	—
TM81	X-Scissor	Bug	Physical	80	100	15	Normal	○
TM82	Sleep Talk	Normal	Status	—	—	10	Self	—
TM83	Natural Gift	Normal	Physical	—	100	15	Normal	○
TM87	Swagger	Normal	Status	—	90	15	Normal	—
TM89	U-turn	Bug	Physical	70	100	20	Normal	○
TM90	Substitute	Normal	Status	—	—	10	Self	—
HM01	Cut	Normal	Physical	50	95	30	Normal	○

● LEVEL-UP MOVES

Lv.	Name	Type	Kind	Pow.	Acc.	PP	Range	DA
1	Scratch	Normal	Physical	40	100	35	Normal	○
1	Harden	Normal	Status	—	—	30	Self	—
5	Leech Life	Bug	Physical	20	100	15	Normal	○
9	Sand-Attack	Ground	Status	—	100	15	Normal	—
14	Fury Swipes	Normal	Physical	18	80	15	Normal	○
19	Mind Reader	Normal	Status	—	—	5	Normal	—
25	Spite	Ghost	Status	—	100	10	Normal	—
31	Confuse Ray	Ghost	Status	—	100	10	Normal	—
38	Shadow Sneak	Ghost	Physical	40	100	30	Normal	○
45	Grudge	Ghost	Status	—	—	5	Self	—
52	Heal Block	Psychic	Status	—	100	15	2 Foes	—
59	Shadow Ball	Ghost	Special	80	100	15	Normal	—

● MOVE MANIAC

Name	Type	Kind	Pow.	Acc.	PP	Range	DA

● BP MOVES

Name	Type	Kind	Pow.	Acc.	PP	Range	DA
Fury Cutter	Bug	Physical	10	95	20	Normal	○
Trick	Psychic	Status	—	100	10	Normal	—
Sucker Punch	Dark	Physical	80	100	5	Normal	—
Bug Bite	Bug	Physical	60	100	20	Normal	○
Snore	Normal	Special	40	100	15	Normal	—
Spite	Ghost	Status	—	100	10	Normal	—
String Shot	Bug	Status	—	95	40	2 Foes	—
Mud-Slap	Ground	Special	20	100	10	Normal	—

● TM & HM MOVES

No.	Name	Type	Kind	Pow.	Acc.	PP	Range	DA
TM06	Toxic	Poison	Status	—	85	10	Normal	—
TM10	Hidden Power	Normal	Special	—	100	15	Normal	—
TM11	Sunny Day	Fire	Status	—	—	5	All	—
TM15	Hyper Beam	Normal	Special	150	90	5	Normal	—
TM17	Protect	Normal	Status	—	—	10	Self	—
TM19	Giga Drain	Grass	Special	60	100	10	Normal	—
TM21	Frustration	Normal	Physical	—	100	20	Normal	○
TM22	SolarBeam	Grass	Special	120	100	10	Normal	—
TM27	Return	Normal	Physical	—	100	20	Normal	○
TM28	Dig	Ground	Physical	80	100	10	Normal	○
TM30	Shadow Ball	Ghost	Special	80	100	15	Normal	—
TM32	Double Team	Normal	Status	—	—	15	Self	—
TM37	Sandstorm	Rock	Status	—	—	10	All	—
TM40	Aerial Ace	Flying	Physical	60	—	20	Normal	○
TM42	Facade	Normal	Physical	70	100	20	Normal	○
TM43	Secret Power	Normal	Physical	70	100	20	Normal	○
TM44	Rest	Psychic	Status	—	—	10	Self	—
TM46	Thief	Dark	Physical	40	100	10	Normal	○
TM54	False Swipe	Normal	Physical	40	100	40	Normal	○
TM58	Endure	Normal	Status	—	—	10	Self	—
TM61	Will-O-Wisp	Fire	Status	—	75	15	Normal	—
TM65	Shadow Claw	Ghost	Physical	70	100	15	Normal	○
TM68	Giga Impact	Normal	Physical	150	90	5	Normal	○
TM70	Flash	Normal	Status	—	100	20	Normal	—
TM81	X-Scissor	Bug	Physical	80	100	15	Normal	○
TM82	Sleep Talk	Normal	Status	—	—	10	Depends	—
TM83	Natural Gift	Normal	Physical	—	100	15	Normal	—
TM85	Dream Eater	Psychic	Special	100	100	15	Normal	—
TM87	Swagger	Normal	Status	—	90	15	Normal	—
TM90	Substitute	Normal	Status	—	—	10	Self	—
HM01	Cut	Normal	Physical	50	95	30	Normal	○

❸ No. 292 | Shed Pokémon
Shedinja

Bug　Ghost

- ● HEIGHT: 2'07"
- ● WEIGHT: 2.6 lbs.
- ● ITEMS: None

● SIZE COMPARISON

● GENDER UNKNOWN

◎ ABILITIES
● Wonder Guard

◎ STATS
- HP ●
- ATTACK ●●●●
- DEFENSE ●●
- SP. ATTACK ●●
- SP. DEFENSE ●●
- SPEED ●●

◎ EGG GROUPS
Mineral

◎ PERFORMANCE
SPEED ★★☆　　STAMINA ★★★★☆
POWER ★☆☆　　JUMP ★★★★★
SKILL ★☆☆

● MAIN WAYS TO OBTAIN

Pokémon HeartGold	Have at least one free space in your party and one Poké Ball, then level up Nincada to Lv. 20
Pokémon SoulSilver	Have at least one free space in your party and one Poké Ball, then level up Nincada to Lv. 20
Pokémon Diamond	Have at least one free space in your party and one Poké Ball, then level up Nincada to Lv. 20
Pokémon Pearl	Have at least one free space in your party and one Poké Ball, then level up Nincada to Lv. 20
Pokémon Platinum	Have at least one free space in your party and one Poké Ball, then level up Nincada to Lv. 20

Pokémon HeartGold	Pokémon SoulSilver
Its cry leaves a lasting headache if heard for too long. It moves so quickly that it is almost invisible.	Its cry leaves a lasting headache if heard for too long. It moves so quickly that it is almost invisible.

◎ EVOLUTION

Lv. 22　Ninjask

Nincada — Have at least one free space in your party and a Poké Ball → Shedinja

● No. 293 | Whisper Pokémon
Whismur

`Normal`

- ● HEIGHT: 2'00"
- ● WEIGHT: 35.9 lbs.
- ● ITEMS: Chesto Berry

● SIZE COMPARISON

● MALE/FEMALE HAVE SAME FORM

⊚ ABILITIES
- ● Soundproof

⊚ STATS
- HP ●●
- ATTACK ●●
- DEFENSE ●
- SP. ATTACK ●●
- SP. DEFENSE ●●
- SPEED ●

⊚ EGG GROUPS
Monster

Field

⊚ PERFORMANCE
SPEED ★★★★☆ STAMINA ★★★
POWER ★★☆   JUMP ★★☆
SKILL ★★☆☆

● MAIN WAYS TO OBTAIN

Pokémon HeartGold	Route 30 [Hoenn Sound]
Pokémon SoulSilver	Route 30 [Hoenn Sound]
Pokémon Diamond	Find its Egg at the Pokémon Day Care and hatch it
Pokémon Pearl	Find its Egg at the Pokémon Day Care and hatch it
Pokémon Platinum	Find its Egg at the Pokémon Day Care and hatch it

| Pokémon HeartGold | Pokémon SoulSilver |
| If it senses danger, it scares the foe by crying out with the volume of a jet-plane engine. | If it senses danger, it scares the foe by crying out with the volume of a jet-plane engine. |

⊚ EVOLUTION

Whismur — Lv. 20 → Loudred — Lv. 40 → Exploud

● LEVEL-UP MOVES

Lv.	Name	Type	Kind	Pow.	Acc.	PP	Range	DA
1	Pound	Normal	Physical	40	100	35	Normal	○
5	Uproar	Normal	Special	50	100	10	1 Random	—
11	Astonish	Ghost	Physical	30	100	15	Normal	○
15	Howl	Normal	Status	—	—	40	Self	—
21	Supersonic	Normal	Status	—	55	20	Normal	—
25	Stomp	Normal	Physical	65	100	20	Normal	○
31	Screech	Normal	Status	—	85	40	Normal	—
35	Roar	Normal	Status	—	100	20	Normal	—
41	Rest	Psychic	Status	—	—	10	Self	—
41	Sleep Talk	Normal	Status	—	—	10	Depends	—
45	Hyper Voice	Normal	Special	90	100	10	2 Foes	—

● MOVE MANIAC

Name	Type	Kind	Pow.	Acc.	PP	Range	DA
Headbutt	Normal	Physical	70	100	15	Normal	○

● BP MOVES

Name	Type	Kind	Pow.	Acc.	PP	Range	DA
Icy Wind	Ice	Special	55	95	15	2 Foes	—
ThunderPunch	Electric	Physical	75	100	15	Normal	○
Fire Punch	Fire	Physical	75	100	15	Normal	○
Ice Punch	Ice	Physical	75	100	15	Normal	○
Zen Headbutt	Psychic	Physical	80	90	15	Normal	○
Snore	Normal	Special	40	100	15	Normal	—
Uproar	Normal	Special	50	100	10	1 Random	—
Mud-Slap	Ground	Special	20	100	10	Normal	—
Rollout	Rock	Physical	30	90	20	Normal	○

● TM & HM MOVES

No.	Name	Type	Kind	Pow.	Acc.	PP	Range	DA
TM03	Water Pulse	Water	Special	60	100	20	Normal	—
TM05	Roar	Normal	Status	—	100	20	Normal	—
TM06	Toxic	Poison	Status	—	85	10	Normal	—
TM10	Hidden Power	Normal	Special	—	100	15	Normal	—
TM11	Sunny Day	Fire	Status	—	—	5	All	—
TM13	Ice Beam	Ice	Special	95	100	10	Normal	—
TM14	Blizzard	Ice	Special	120	70	5	2 Foes	—
TM17	Protect	Normal	Status	—	—	10	Self	—
TM18	Rain Dance	Water	Status	—	—	5	All	—
TM21	Frustration	Normal	Physical	—	100	20	Normal	○
TM22	SolarBeam	Grass	Special	120	100	10	Normal	—
TM27	Return	Normal	Physical	—	100	20	Normal	○
TM30	Shadow Ball	Ghost	Special	80	100	15	Normal	—
TM32	Double Team	Normal	Status	—	—	15	Self	—
TM34	Shock Wave	Electric	Special	60	—	20	Normal	—
TM35	Flamethrower	Fire	Special	95	100	15	Normal	—
TM38	Fire Blast	Fire	Special	120	85	5	Normal	—
TM42	Facade	Normal	Physical	70	100	20	Normal	○
TM43	Secret Power	Normal	Physical	70	100	20	Normal	—
TM44	Rest	Psychic	Status	—	—	10	Self	—
TM45	Attract	Normal	Status	—	100	15	Normal	—
TM56	Fling	Dark	Physical	—	100	10	Normal	—
TM58	Endure	Normal	Status	—	—	10	Self	—
TM78	Captivate	Normal	Status	—	100	20	2 Foes	—
TM82	Sleep Talk	Normal	Status	—	—	10	Depends	—
TM83	Natural Gift	Normal	Physical	—	100	15	Normal	—
TM87	Swagger	Normal	Status	—	90	15	Normal	—
TM90	Substitute	Normal	Status	—	—	10	Self	—

● EGG MOVES

Name	Type	Kind	Pow.	Acc.	PP	Range	DA
Take Down	Normal	Physical	90	85	20	Normal	○
Snore	Normal	Special	40	100	15	Normal	—
Swagger	Normal	Status	—	90	15	Normal	—
Extrasensory	Psychic	Special	80	100	30	Normal	—
SmellingSalt	Normal	Physical	60	100	10	Normal	○
SmokeScreen	Normal	Status	—	100	20	Normal	—
Endeavor	Normal	Physical	—	100	5	Normal	○
Hammer Arm	Fighting	Physical	100	90	10	Normal	○

● LEVEL-UP MOVES

Lv.	Name	Type	Kind	Pow.	Acc.	PP	Range	DA
1	Pound	Normal	Physical	40	100	35	Normal	○
1	Uproar	Normal	Special	50	100	10	1 Random	—
1	Astonish	Ghost	Physical	30	100	15	Normal	○
1	Howl	Normal	Status	—	—	40	Self	—
5	Uproar	Normal	Special	50	100	10	1 Random	—
11	Astonish	Ghost	Physical	30	100	15	Normal	○
15	Howl	Normal	Status	—	—	40	Self	—
20	Bite	Dark	Physical	60	100	25	Normal	○
23	Supersonic	Normal	Status	—	55	20	Normal	—
29	Stomp	Normal	Physical	65	100	20	Normal	○
37	Screech	Normal	Status	—	85	40	Normal	—
43	Roar	Normal	Status	—	100	20	Normal	—
51	Rest	Psychic	Status	—	—	10	Self	—
51	Sleep Talk	Normal	Status	—	—	10	Depends	—
57	Hyper Voice	Normal	Special	90	100	10	2 Foes	—

● MOVE MANIAC

Name	Type	Kind	Pow.	Acc.	PP	Range	DA
Headbutt	Normal	Physical	70	100	15	Normal	○

● BP MOVES

Name	Type	Kind	Pow.	Acc.	PP	Range	DA
Icy Wind	Ice	Special	55	95	15	2 Foes	—
ThunderPunch	Electric	Physical	75	100	15	Normal	○
Fire Punch	Fire	Physical	75	100	15	Normal	○
Ice Punch	Ice	Physical	75	100	15	Normal	○
Zen Headbutt	Psychic	Physical	80	90	15	Normal	○
Snore	Normal	Special	40	100	15	Normal	—
Uproar	Normal	Special	50	100	10	1 Random	—
Mud-Slap	Ground	Special	20	100	10	Normal	—
Rollout	Rock	Physical	30	90	20	Normal	○
Low Kick	Fighting	Physical	—	100	20	Normal	○

● TM & HM MOVES

No.	Name	Type	Kind	Pow.	Acc.	PP	Range	DA
TM03	Water Pulse	Water	Special	60	100	20	Normal	—
TM05	Roar	Normal	Status	—	100	20	Normal	—
TM06	Toxic	Poison	Status	—	85	10	Normal	—
TM10	Hidden Power	Normal	Special	—	100	15	Normal	—
TM11	Sunny Day	Fire	Status	—	—	5	All	—
TM12	Taunt	Dark	Status	—	100	20	Normal	—
TM13	Ice Beam	Ice	Special	95	100	10	Normal	—
TM14	Blizzard	Ice	Special	120	70	5	2 Foes	—
TM17	Protect	Normal	Status	—	—	10	Self	—
TM18	Rain Dance	Water	Status	—	—	5	All	—
TM21	Frustration	Normal	Physical	—	100	20	Normal	○
TM22	SolarBeam	Grass	Special	120	100	10	Normal	—
TM26	Earthquake	Ground	Physical	100	100	10	2 Foes/1 Ally	—
TM27	Return	Normal	Physical	—	100	20	Normal	○
TM30	Shadow Ball	Ghost	Special	80	100	15	Normal	—
TM31	Brick Break	Fighting	Physical	75	100	15	Normal	○
TM32	Double Team	Normal	Status	—	—	15	Self	—
TM34	Shock Wave	Electric	Special	60	—	20	Normal	—
TM35	Flamethrower	Fire	Special	95	100	15	Normal	—
TM38	Fire Blast	Fire	Special	120	85	5	Normal	—
TM39	Rock Tomb	Rock	Physical	50	80	10	Normal	○
TM41	Torment	Dark	Status	—	100	15	Normal	—
TM42	Facade	Normal	Physical	70	100	20	Normal	○
TM43	Secret Power	Normal	Physical	70	100	20	Normal	○
TM44	Rest	Psychic	Status	—	—	10	Self	—
TM45	Attract	Normal	Status	—	100	15	Normal	—
TM50	Overheat	Fire	Special	140	90	5	Normal	—
TM56	Fling	Dark	Physical	—	100	10	Normal	—
TM58	Endure	Normal	Status	—	—	10	Self	—
TM78	Captivate	Normal	Status	—	100	20	2 Foes	—
TM80	Rock Slide	Rock	Physical	75	90	10	2 Foes	—
TM82	Sleep Talk	Normal	Status	—	—	10	Depends	—
TM83	Natural Gift	Normal	Physical	—	100	15	Normal	—
TM87	Swagger	Normal	Status	—	90	15	Normal	—
TM90	Substitute	Normal	Status	—	—	10	Self	—
HM04	Strength	Normal	Physical	80	100	15	Normal	○
HM06	Rock Smash	Fighting	Physical	40	100	15	Normal	○

◉ No. 294 | Big Voice Pokémon
Loudred

Normal

● HEIGHT: 3'03"
● WEIGHT: 89.3 lbs.
● ITEMS: None

● SIZE COMPARISON

● MALE/FEMALE HAVE SAME FORM

◎ ABILITIES
● Soundproof

◎ STATS
HP ●●●
ATTACK ●●●
DEFENSE ●●
SP. ATTACK ●●●
SP. DEFENSE ●●●
SPEED ●●

◎ EGG GROUPS
Monster

Field

◎ PERFORMANCE
SPEED ★★★☆ — STAMINA ★★★☆
POWER ★★★☆ — JUMP ★★☆
SKILL ★★★★

● MAIN WAYS TO OBTAIN

Pokémon HeartGold	Level up Whismur to Lv. 20
Pokémon SoulSilver	Level up Whismur to Lv. 20
Pokémon Diamond	Mt. Coronet exterior (use Poké Radar)
Pokémon Pearl	Mt. Coronet exterior (use Poké Radar)
Pokémon Platinum	Mt. Coronet exterior (use Poké Radar)

Pokémon HeartGold	**Pokémon SoulSilver**
It shouts loudly by inhaling air, and then uses its well-developed stomach muscles to exhale.	It shouts loudly by inhaling air, and then uses its well-developed stomach muscles to exhale.

◎ EVOLUTION

Lv. 20   Lv. 40

Whismur   Loudred   Exploud

Exploud

- **HEIGHT:** 4'11"
- **WEIGHT:** 185.2 lbs.
- **ITEMS:** None

● SIZE COMPARISON

● MALE/FEMALE HAVE SAME FORM

⚙ ABILITIES
- Soundproof

⚙ STATS
HP ●●●●
ATTACK ●●●●
DEFENSE ●●●
SP. ATTACK ●●●●
SP. DEFENSE ●●●
SPEED ●●●

⚙ EGG GROUPS
Monster

Field

⚙ PERFORMANCE
SPEED ★★★
POWER ★★★★
SKILL ★★★★
STAMINA ★★★★☆
JUMP ★★

● MAIN WAYS TO OBTAIN

Pokémon HeartGold Level up Loudred to Lv. 40

Pokémon SoulSilver Level up Loudred to Lv. 40

Pokémon Diamond Level up Loudred to Lv. 40

Pokémon Pearl Level up Loudred to Lv. 40

Pokémon Platinum Level up Loudred to Lv. 40

Pokémon HeartGold
Its roar in battle shakes the ground like a tremor-- or like an earthquake has struck.

Pokémon SoulSilver
Its roar in battle shakes the ground like a tremor-- or like an earthquake has struck.

⚙ EVOLUTION

Lv. 20   Lv. 40

Whismur   Loudred   Exploud

● LEVEL-UP MOVES

Lv.	Name	Type	Kind	Pow.	Acc.	PP	Range	DA
1	Ice Fang	Ice	Physical	65	95	15	Normal	○
1	Fire Fang	Fire	Physical	65	95	15	Normal	○
1	Thunder Fang	Electric	Physical	65	95	15	Normal	○
1	Pound	Normal	Physical	40	100	35	Normal	—
1	Uproar	Normal	Special	50	100	10	1 Random	—
1	Astonish	Ghost	Physical	30	100	15	Normal	—
1	Howl	Normal	Status	—	—	40	Self	—
5	Uproar	Normal	Special	50	100	10	1 Random	—
11	Astonish	Ghost	Physical	30	100	15	Normal	○
15	Howl	Normal	Status	—	—	40	Self	—
20	Bite	Dark	Physical	60	100	25	Normal	—
23	Supersonic	Normal	Status	—	55	20	Normal	—
29	Stomp	Normal	Physical	65	100	20	Normal	○
37	Screech	Normal	Status	—	85	40	Normal	—
40	Crunch	Dark	Physical	80	100	15	Normal	—
45	Roar	Normal	Status	—	100	20	Normal	—
55	Rest	Psychic	Status	—	—	10	Self	—
55	Sleep Talk	Normal	Status	—	—	10	Depends	—
63	Hyper Voice	Normal	Special	90	100	10	2 Foes	—
71	Hyper Beam	Normal	Special	150	90	5	Normal	—

● MOVE MANIAC

Name	Type	Kind	Pow.	Acc.	PP	Range	DA
Headbutt	Normal	Physical	70	100	15	Normal	○

● BP MOVES

Name	Type	Kind	Pow.	Acc.	PP	Range	DA
Icy Wind	Ice	Special	55	95	15	2 Foes	—
ThunderPunch	Electric	Physical	75	100	15	Normal	○
Fire Punch	Fire	Physical	75	100	15	Normal	○
Ice Punch	Ice	Physical	75	100	15	Normal	○
Zen Headbutt	Psychic	Physical	80	90	15	Normal	○
Snore	Normal	Special	40	100	15	Normal	—
Uproar	Normal	Special	50	100	10	1 Random	—
Mud-Slap	Ground	Special	20	100	10	Normal	—
Rollout	Rock	Physical	30	90	20	Normal	○
Outrage	Dragon	Physical	120	100	15	1 Random	○
Low Kick	Fighting	Physical	—	100	20	Normal	○

● TM & HM MOVES

No.	Name	Type	Kind	Pow.	Acc.	PP	Range	DA
TM03	Water Pulse	Water	Special	60	100	20	Normal	—
TM05	Roar	Normal	Status	—	100	20	Normal	—
TM06	Toxic	Poison	Status	—	85	10	Normal	—
TM10	Hidden Power	Normal	Special	—	100	15	Normal	—
TM11	Sunny Day	Fire	Status	—	—	5	All	—
TM12	Taunt	Dark	Status	—	100	20	Normal	—
TM13	Ice Beam	Ice	Special	95	100	10	Normal	—
TM14	Blizzard	Ice	Special	120	70	5	2 Foes	—
TM15	Hyper Beam	Normal	Special	150	90	5	Normal	—
TM17	Protect	Normal	Status	—	—	10	Self	—
TM18	Rain Dance	Water	Status	—	—	5	All	—
TM21	Frustration	Normal	Physical	—	100	20	Normal	○
TM22	SolarBeam	Grass	Special	120	100	10	Normal	—
TM26	Earthquake	Ground	Physical	100	100	10	2 Foes/1 Ally	—
TM27	Return	Normal	Physical	—	100	20	Normal	○
TM30	Shadow Ball	Ghost	Special	80	100	15	Normal	—
TM31	Brick Break	Fighting	Physical	75	100	15	Normal	○
TM32	Double Team	Normal	Status	—	—	15	Self	—
TM34	Shock Wave	Electric	Special	60	—	20	Normal	—
TM35	Flamethrower	Fire	Special	95	100	15	Normal	—
TM38	Fire Blast	Fire	Special	120	85	5	Normal	—
TM39	Rock Tomb	Rock	Physical	50	80	10	Normal	○
TM41	Torment	Dark	Status	—	100	15	Normal	—
TM42	Facade	Normal	Physical	70	100	20	Normal	○
TM43	Secret Power	Normal	Physical	70	100	20	Normal	○
TM44	Rest	Psychic	Status	—	—	10	Self	—
TM45	Attract	Normal	Status	—	100	15	Normal	—
TM50	Overheat	Fire	Special	140	90	5	Normal	—
TM52	Focus Blast	Fighting	Special	120	70	5	Normal	—
TM56	Fling	Dark	Physical	—	100	10	Normal	—
TM58	Endure	Normal	Status	—	—	10	Self	—
TM68	Giga Impact	Normal	Physical	150	90	5	Normal	○
TM72	Avalanche	Ice	Physical	60	100	10	Normal	○
TM78	Captivate	Normal	Status	—	100	20	2 Foes	—
TM80	Rock Slide	Rock	Physical	75	90	10	2 Foes	—
TM82	Sleep Talk	Normal	Status	—	—	10	Depends	—
TM83	Natural Gift	Normal	Physical	—	100	15	Normal	○
TM87	Swagger	Normal	Status	—	90	15	Normal	—
TM90	Substitute	Normal	Status	—	—	10	Self	—
HM03	Surf	Water	Special	95	100	15	2 Foes/1 Ally	—
HM04	Strength	Normal	Physical	80	100	15	Normal	○
HM05	Whirlpool	Water	Special	15	70	15	Normal	—
HM06	Rock Smash	Fighting	Physical	40	100	15	Normal	○
HM08	Rock Climb	Normal	Physical	90	85	20	Normal	○

● LEVEL-UP MOVES

Lv.	Name	Type	Kind	Pow.	Acc.	PP	Range	DA
1	Tackle	Normal	Physical	35	95	35	Normal	○
1	Focus Energy	Normal	Status	—	—	30	Self	—
4	Sand-Attack	Ground	Status	—	100	15	Normal	—
7	Arm Thrust	Fighting	Physical	15	100	20	Normal	○
10	Vital Throw	Fighting	Physical	70	—	10	Normal	○
13	Fake Out	Normal	Physical	40	100	10	Normal	○
16	Whirlwind	Normal	Status	—	100	20	Normal	—
19	Knock Off	Dark	Physical	20	100	20	Normal	○
22	SmellingSalt	Normal	Physical	60	100	10	Normal	○
25	Belly Drum	Normal	Status	—	—	10	Self	—
28	Force Palm	Fighting	Physical	60	100	10	Normal	○
31	Seismic Toss	Fighting	Physical	—	100	20	Normal	—
34	Wake-Up Slap	Fighting	Physical	60	100	10	Normal	○
37	Endure	Normal	Status	—	—	10	Self	—
40	Close Combat	Fighting	Physical	120	100	5	Normal	○
43	Reversal	Fighting	Physical	—	100	15	Normal	○

● MOVE MANIAC

Name	Type	Kind	Pow.	Acc.	PP	Range	DA
Headbutt	Normal	Physical	70	100	15	Normal	○

● BP MOVES

Name	Type	Kind	Pow.	Acc.	PP	Range	DA
ThunderPunch	Electric	Physical	75	100	15	Normal	○
Fire Punch	Fire	Physical	75	100	15	Normal	○
Ice Punch	Ice	Physical	75	100	15	Normal	○
Vacuum Wave	Fighting	Special	40	100	30	Normal	—
Knock Off	Dark	Physical	20	100	20	Normal	—
Snore	Normal	Special	40	100	15	Normal	—
Helping Hand	Normal	Status	—	—	20	1 Ally	—
Role Play	Psychic	Status	—	—	10	Normal	—
Mud-Slap	Ground	Special	20	100	10	Normal	—
Superpower	Fighting	Physical	120	100	5	Normal	○
Low Kick	Fighting	Physical	—	100	20	Normal	○

● TM & HM MOVES

No.	Name	Type	Kind	Pow.	Acc.	PP	Range	DA
TM01	Focus Punch	Fighting	Physical	150	100	20	Normal	○
TM06	Toxic	Poison	Status	—	85	10	Normal	—
TM08	Bulk Up	Fighting	Status	—	—	20	Self	—
TM10	Hidden Power	Normal	Special	—	100	15	Normal	—
TM11	Sunny Day	Fire	Status	—	—	5	All	—
TM17	Protect	Normal	Status	—	—	10	Self	—
TM18	Rain Dance	Water	Status	—	—	5	All	—
TM21	Frustration	Normal	Physical	—	100	20	Normal	○
TM26	Earthquake	Ground	Physical	100	100	10	2 Foes/1 Ally	○
TM27	Return	Normal	Physical	—	100	20	Normal	○
TM28	Dig	Ground	Physical	80	100	10	Normal	○
TM31	Brick Break	Fighting	Physical	75	100	15	Normal	○
TM32	Double Team	Normal	Status	—	—	15	Self	—
TM39	Rock Tomb	Rock	Physical	50	80	10	Normal	—
TM42	Facade	Normal	Physical	70	100	20	Normal	○
TM43	Secret Power	Normal	Physical	70	100	20	Normal	—
TM44	Rest	Psychic	Status	—	—	10	Self	—
TM45	Attract	Normal	Status	—	100	15	Normal	—
TM52	Focus Blast	Fighting	Special	120	70	5	Normal	—
TM56	Fling	Dark	Physical	—	100	10	Normal	—
TM58	Endure	Normal	Status	—	—	10	Self	—
TM78	Captivate	Normal	Status	—	100	20	2 Foes	—
TM80	Rock Slide	Rock	Physical	75	90	10	2 Foes	—
TM82	Sleep Talk	Normal	Status	—	—	10	Depends	—
TM83	Natural Gift	Normal	Physical	—	100	15	Normal	—
TM84	Poison Jab	Poison	Physical	80	100	20	Normal	○
TM87	Swagger	Normal	Status	—	90	15	Normal	—
TM90	Substitute	Normal	Status	—	—	10	Self	—
HM03	Surf	Water	Special	95	100	15	2 Foes/1 Ally	—
HM04	Strength	Normal	Physical	80	100	15	Normal	○
HM05	Whirlpool	Water	Special	15	70	15	Normal	—
HM06	Rock Smash	Fighting	Physical	40	100	15	Normal	○
HM08	Rock Climb	Normal	Physical	90	85	20	Normal	○

● EGG MOVES

Name	Type	Kind	Pow.	Acc.	PP	Range	DA
Faint Attack	Dark	Physical	60	—	20	Normal	○
Detect	Fighting	Status	—	—	5	Self	—
Foresight	Normal	Status	—	—	40	Normal	—
Helping Hand	Normal	Status	—	—	20	1 Ally	—
Cross Chop	Fighting	Physical	100	80	5	Normal	○
Revenge	Fighting	Physical	60	100	10	Normal	○
DynamicPunch	Fighting	Physical	100	50	5	Normal	○
Counter	Fighting	Physical	—	100	20	Self	○
Wake-Up Slap	Fighting	Physical	60	100	10	Normal	○
Bullet Punch	Steel	Physical	40	100	30	Normal	○
Feint	Normal	Physical	50	100	10	Normal	—

○ No. 296 | Guts Pokémon
Makuhita

Fighting

- ● HEIGHT: 3'03"
- ● WEIGHT: 190.5 lbs.
- ● ITEMS: None

● SIZE COMPARISON

● MALE/FEMALE HAVE SAME FORM

⊙ ABILITIES
- ● Thick Fat
- ● Guts

⊙ STATS
HP ●●●
ATTACK ●●●
DEFENSE ●
SP. ATTACK ●
SP. DEFENSE ●
SPEED ●

⊙ EGG GROUPS
Human-Like

⊙ PERFORMANCE
SPEED ★★★		STAMINA ★★★☆
POWER ★★★☆☆		JUMP ★★★☆☆
SKILL ★★★		

● MAIN WAYS TO OBTAIN

Pokémon HeartGold — Union Cave (Hoenn Sound)

Pokémon SoulSilver — Union Cave (Hoenn Sound)

Pokémon Diamond — Route 225 (mass outbreak)

Pokémon Pearl — Route 225 (mass outbreak)

Pokémon Platinum — Route 225 (mass outbreak)

Pokémon HeartGold
It toughens up by slamming into thick trees over and over. It gains a sturdy body and dauntless spirit.

Pokémon SoulSilver
It toughens up by slamming into thick trees over and over. It gains a sturdy body and dauntless spirit.

⊙ EVOLUTION

Makuhita — Lv. 24 — Har0yama

⬤ No. 297 | Arm Thrust Pokémon
Hariyama

Fighting

● LEVEL-UP MOVES

Lv.	Name	Type	Kind	Pow.	Acc.	PP	Range	DA
1	Brine	Water	Special	65	100	10	Normal	—
1	Tackle	Normal	Physical	35	95	35	Normal	○
1	Focus Energy	Normal	Status	—	—	30	Self	—
1	Sand-Attack	Ground	Status	—	100	15	Normal	—
1	Arm Thrust	Fighting	Physical	15	100	20	Normal	○
4	Sand-Attack	Ground	Status	—	100	15	Normal	—
7	Arm Thrust	Fighting	Physical	15	100	20	Normal	○
10	Vital Throw	Fighting	Physical	70	—	10	Normal	○
13	Fake Out	Normal	Physical	40	100	10	Normal	○
16	Whirlwind	Normal	Status	—	100	20	Normal	—
19	Knock Off	Dark	Physical	20	100	20	Normal	○
22	SmellingSalt	Normal	Physical	60	100	10	Normal	○
27	Belly Drum	Normal	Status	—	—	10	Self	—
32	Force Palm	Fighting	Physical	60	100	10	Normal	○
37	Seismic Toss	Fighting	Physical	—	100	20	Normal	○
42	Wake-Up Slap	Fighting	Physical	60	100	10	Normal	○
47	Endure	Normal	Status	—	—	10	Self	—
52	Close Combat	Fighting	Physical	120	100	5	Normal	○
57	Reversal	Fighting	Physical	—	100	15	Normal	○

● MOVE MANIAC

Name	Type	Kind	Pow.	Acc.	PP	Range	DA
Headbutt	Normal	Physical	70	100	15	Normal	

● BP MOVES

Name	Type	Kind	Pow.	Acc.	PP	Range	DA
ThunderPunch	Electric	Physical	75	100	15	Normal	○
Fire Punch	Fire	Physical	75	100	15	Normal	○
Ice Punch	Ice	Physical	75	100	15	Normal	○
Vacuum Wave	Fighting	Special	40	100	30	Normal	—
Knock Off	Dark	Physical	20	100	20	Normal	○
Snore	Normal	Special	40	100	15	Normal	—
Helping Hand	Normal	Status	—	—	20	1 Ally	—
Role Play	Psychic	Status	—	—	10	Normal	—
Mud-Slap	Ground	Special	20	100	10	Normal	○
Superpower	Fighting	Physical	120	100	5	Normal	—
Iron Head	Steel	Physical	80	100	15	Normal	○
Low Kick	Fighting	Physical	—	100	20	Normal	○

● HEIGHT: 7'02"
● WEIGHT: 559.5 lbs.
● ITEMS: None

● SIZE COMPARISON

● MALE/FEMALE HAVE THE SAME FORM

☺ ABILITIES
● Thick Fat
● Guts

☺ STATS
HP ●●●●●
ATTACK ●●●●●
DEFENSE ●●
SP. ATTACK ●●
SP. DEFENSE ●●
SPEED ●●

☺ EGG GROUPS
Human-Like

☺ PERFORMANCE
SPEED ★★☆☆☆ STAMINA ★★★☆
POWER ★★★★★ JUMP ★★☆☆☆
SKILL ★★☆

● MAIN WAYS TO OBTAIN

Pokémon HeartGold	Level up Makuhita to Lv. 24
Pokémon SoulSilver	Level up Makuhita to Lv. 24
Pokémon Diamond	Level up Makuhita to Lv. 24
Pokémon Pearl	Level up Makuhita to Lv. 24
Pokémon Platinum	Level up Makuhita to Lv. 24

Pokémon HeartGold	Pokémon SoulSilver
It loves challenging others to tests of strength. It has the power to stop a train with a slap.	It loves challenging others to tests of strength. It has the power to stop a train with a slap.

☺ EVOLUTION

 Lv. 24 →

Makuhita — Hariyama

● TM & HM MOVES

No.	Name	Type	Kind	Pow.	Acc.	PP	Range	DA
TM01	Focus Punch	Fighting	Physical	150	100	20	Normal	○
TM06	Toxic	Poison	Status	—	85	10	Normal	—
TM08	Bulk Up	Fighting	Status	—	—	20	Self	—
TM10	Hidden Power	Normal	Special	—	100	15	Normal	—
TM11	Sunny Day	Fire	Status	—	—	5	All	—
TM15	Hyper Beam	Normal	Special	150	90	5	Normal	—
TM17	Protect	Normal	Status	—	—	10	Self	—
TM18	Rain Dance	Water	Status	—	—	5	All	—
TM21	Frustration	Normal	Physical	—	100	20	Normal	○
TM26	Earthquake	Ground	Physical	100	100	10	2 Foes/1 Ally	—
TM27	Return	Normal	Physical	—	100	20	Normal	○
TM28	Dig	Ground	Physical	80	100	10	Normal	○
TM31	Brick Break	Fighting	Physical	75	100	15	Normal	○
TM32	Double Team	Normal	Status	—	—	15	Self	—
TM39	Rock Tomb	Rock	Physical	50	80	10	Normal	○
TM42	Facade	Normal	Physical	70	100	20	Normal	○
TM43	Secret Power	Normal	Physical	70	100	20	Normal	○
TM44	Rest	Psychic	Status	—	—	10	Self	—
TM45	Attract	Normal	Status	—	100	15	Normal	—
TM52	Focus Blast	Fighting	Special	120	70	5	Normal	—
TM55	Brine	Water	Special	65	100	10	Normal	—
TM56	Fling	Dark	Physical	—	100	10	Normal	—
TM58	Endure	Normal	Status	—	—	10	Self	—
TM66	Payback	Dark	Physical	50	100	10	Normal	○
TM68	Giga Impact	Normal	Physical	150	90	5	Normal	○
TM71	Stone Edge	Rock	Physical	100	80	5	Normal	—
TM78	Captivate	Normal	Status	—	100	20	2 Foes	—
TM80	Rock Slide	Rock	Physical	75	90	10	2 Foes	—
TM82	Sleep Talk	Normal	Status	—	—	10	Depends	—
TM83	Natural Gift	Normal	Physical	—	100	15	Normal	—
TM84	Poison Jab	Poison	Physical	80	100	20	Normal	○
TM87	Swagger	Normal	Status	—	90	15	Normal	—
TM90	Substitute	Normal	Status	—	—	10	Self	—
HM03	Surf	Water	Special	95	100	15	2 Foes/1 Ally	—
HM04	Strength	Normal	Physical	80	100	15	Normal	○
HM05	Whirlpool	Water	Special	15	70	15	Normal	—
HM06	Rock Smash	Fighting	Physical	40	100	15	Normal	○
HM08	Rock Climb	Normal	Physical	90	85	20	Normal	○

● LEVEL-UP MOVES

Lv.	Name	Type	Kind	Pow.	Acc.	PP	Range	DA
1	Splash	Normal	Status	—	—	40	Self	—
2	Charm	Normal	Status	—	100	20	Normal	—
?	Tail Whip	Normal	Status	—	100	30	2 Foes	—
10	Bubble	Water	Special	20	100	30	2 Foes	—
15	Slam	Normal	Physical	80	75	20	Normal	○
18	Water Gun	Water	Special	40	100	25	Normal	—

● MOVE MANIAC

Name	Type	Kind	Pow.	Acc.	PP	Range	DA
Headbutt	Normal	Physical	70	100	15	Normal	○

● BP MOVES

Name	Type	Kind	Pow.	Acc.	PP	Range	DA
Icy Wind	Ice	Special	55	95	15	2 Foes	—
Knock Off	Dark	Physical	20	100	20	Normal	○
Snore	Normal	Special	40	100	15	Normal	—
Helping Hand	Normal	Status	—	—	20	1 Ally	—
Swift	Normal	Special	60	—	20	2 Foes	—
Uproar	Normal	Special	50	100	10	1 Random	—
Mud-Slap	Ground	Special	20	100	10	Normal	—
Rollout	Rock	Physical	30	90	20	Normal	○

● TM & HM MOVES

No.	Name	Type	Kind	Pow.	Acc.	PP	Range	DA
TM03	Water Pulse	Water	Special	60	100	20	Normal	—
TM06	Toxic	Poison	Status	—	85	10	Normal	—
TM07	Hail	Ice	Status	—	—	10	All	—
TM10	Hidden Power	Normal	Special	—	100	15	Normal	—
TM13	Ice Beam	Ice	Special	95	100	10	Normal	—
TM14	Blizzard	Ice	Special	120	70	5	2 Foes	—
TM17	Protect	Normal	Status	—	—	10	Self	—
TM18	Rain Dance	Water	Status	—	—	5	All	—
TM21	Frustration	Normal	Physical	—	100	20	Normal	○
TM23	Iron Tail	Steel	Physical	100	75	15	Normal	○
TM27	Return	Normal	Physical	—	100	20	Normal	○
TM32	Double Team	Normal	Status	—	—	15	Self	—
TM42	Facade	Normal	Physical	70	100	20	Normal	○
TM43	Secret Power	Normal	Physical	70	100	20	Normal	—
TM44	Rest	Psychic	Status	—	—	10	Self	—
TM45	Attract	Normal	Status	—	100	15	Normal	—
TM58	Endure	Normal	Status	—	—	10	Self	—
TM78	Captivate	Normal	Status	—	100	20	2 Foes	—
TM82	Sleep Talk	Normal	Status	—	—	10	Depends	—
TM83	Natural Gift	Normal	Physical	—	100	15	Normal	—
TM87	Swagger	Normal	Status	—	90	15	Normal	—
TM90	Substitute	Normal	Status	—	—	10	Self	—
HM03	Surf	Water	Special	95	100	15	2 Foes/1 Ally	—
HM05	Whirlpool	Water	Special	15	70	15	Normal	—
HM07	Waterfall	Water	Physical	80	100	15	Normal	○

● EGG MOVES

Name	Type	Kind	Pow.	Acc.	PP	Range	DA
Encore	Normal	Status	—	100	5	Normal	—
Sing	Normal	Status	—	55	15	Normal	—
Refresh	Normal	Status	—	—	20	Self	—
Slam	Normal	Physical	80	75	20	Normal	○
Tickle	Normal	Status	—	100	20	Normal	—
Fake Tears	Dark	Status	—	100	20	Normal	—
Body Slam	Normal	Physical	85	100	15	Normal	○

◎ No. 298 | Polka Dot Pokémon
Azurill

Normal

- ● HEIGHT: 0'08"
- ● WEIGHT: 4.4 lbs.
- ● ITEMS: None

● SIZE COMPARISON

● MALE/FEMALE HAVE SAME FORM

◎ ABILITIES
- ● Thick Fat
- ● Huge Power

◎ STATS
- HP ●●
- ATTACK ●●
- DEFENSE ●●
- SP. ATTACK ●
- SP. DEFENSE ●
- SPEED ●

◎ EGG GROUPS
No Egg has ever been discovered

◎ PERFORMANCE
- SPEED ★★★★☆   STAMINA ★★☆
- POWER ★☆   JUMP ★★★☆
- SKILL ★★☆

● MAIN WAYS TO OBTAIN

Pokémon HeartGold — Safari Zone [Savannah Area: if Water objects are placed, may appear in tall grass]

Pokémon SoulSilver — Safari Zone [Savannah Area: if Water objects are placed, may appear in tall grass]

Pokémon Diamond — Pastoria Great Marsh

Pokémon Pearl — Pastoria Great Marsh

Pokémon Platinum — Have at least one free space in your party and one Poké Ball, then level up Nincada to Lv. 20

Pokémon HeartGold — Its tail is packed full of the nutrients it needs to grow.

Pokémon SoulSilver — Its tail is packed full of the nutrients it needs to grow.

◎ EVOLUTION

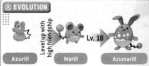

Azurill — Level up with high friendship → Marill — Lv. 18 → Azumarill

No. 299 | Compass Pokémon
Nosepass

`Rock`

● HEIGHT: 3'03"
● WEIGHT: 213.8 lbs.
● ITEMS: Hard Stone

● SIZE COMPARISON

● MALE/FEMALE HAVE SAME FORM

● ABILITIES
- Sturdy
- Magnet Pull

● STATS
HP ●
ATTACK ●●
DEFENSE ●●●●●
SP. ATTACK ●●
SP. DEFENSE ●●●●●
SPEED ●

● EGG GROUPS
Mineral

● PERFORMANCE
SPEED ★☆☆   STAMINA ★★★★☆
POWER ★★★☆   JUMP ★★☆
SKILL ★★☆

● MAIN WAYS TO OBTAIN

Pokémon HeartGold	Safari Zone (Meadow Area: if Rock objects are placed, may appear in tall grass)
Pokémon SoulSilver	Safari Zone (Meadow Area: if Rock objects are placed, may appear in tall grass)
Pokémon Diamond	Route 206 (mass outbreak)
Pokémon Pearl	Route 206 (mass outbreak)
Pokémon Platinum	Mt. Coronet

Pokémon HeartGold	**Pokémon SoulSilver**
If two of these meet, they cannot get too close because their noses repel each other.	If two of these meet, they cannot get too close because their noses repel each other.

● EVOLUTION

Nosepass — Level up at Mt. Coronet* → Probopass

*Unable to evolve in Pokémon HeartGold or SoulSilver Version. Transfer from Pokémon Diamond, Pearl, or Platinum Version.

● LEVEL-UP MOVES

Lv.	Name	Type	Kind	Pow.	Acc.	PP	Range	DA
1	Tackle	Normal	Physical	35	95	35	Normal	○
7	Harden	Normal	Status	—	—	30	Self	—
13	Rock Throw	Rock	Physical	50	90	15	Normal	—
19	Block	Normal	Status	—	—	5	Normal	—
25	Thunder Wave	Electric	Status	—	100	20	Normal	—
31	Rock Slide	Rock	Physical	75	90	10	2 Foes	—
37	Sandstorm	Rock	Status	—	—	10	All	—
43	Rest	Psychic	Status	—	—	10	Self	—
49	Power Gem	Rock	Special	70	100	20	Normal	—
55	Discharge	Electric	Special	80	100	15	2 Foes/1 Ally	—
61	Stone Edge	Rock	Physical	100	80	5	Normal	—
67	Zap Cannon	Electric	Special	120	50	5	Normal	—
73	Lock-On	Normal	Status	—	—	5	Normal	—
79	Earth Power	Ground	Special	90	100	10	Normal	—

● MOVE MANIAC

Name	Type	Kind	Pow.	Acc.	PP	Range	DA
Headbutt	Normal	Physical	70	100	15	Normal	○

● BP MOVES

Name	Type	Kind	Pow.	Acc.	PP	Range	DA
ThunderPunch	Electric	Physical	75	100	15	Normal	○
Fire Punch	Fire	Physical	75	100	15	Normal	○
Ice Punch	Ice	Physical	75	100	15	Normal	○
Snore	Normal	Physical	40	100	15	Normal	—
Magnet Rise	Electric	Status	—	—	10	Self	—
Gravity	Psychic	Status	—	—	5	All	—
Magic Coat	Psychic	Status	—	—	15	Self	—
Block	Normal	Status	—	—	5	Normal	—
Mud-Slap	Ground	Special	20	100	10	Normal	○
Rollout	Rock	Physical	30	90	20	Normal	○
AncientPower	Rock	Special	60	100	5	Normal	—
Earth Power	Ground	Special	90	100	10	Normal	—
Iron Defense	Steel	Status	—	—	15	Self	—
Pain Split	Normal	Status	—	—	20	Normal	—

● TM & HM MOVES

No.	Name	Type	Kind	Pow.	Acc.	PP	Range	DA
TM06	Toxic	Poison	Status	—	85	10	Normal	—
TM10	Hidden Power	Normal	Special	—	100	15	Normal	—
TM11	Sunny Day	Fire	Status	—	—	5	All	—
TM12	Taunt	Dark	Status	—	100	20	Normal	—
TM17	Protect	Normal	Status	—	—	10	Self	—
TM21	Frustration	Normal	Physical	—	100	20	Normal	○
TM24	Thunderbolt	Electric	Special	95	100	15	Normal	—
TM25	Thunder	Electric	Special	120	70	10	Normal	—
TM26	Earthquake	Ground	Physical	100	100	10	2 Foes/1 Ally	—
TM27	Return	Normal	Physical	—	100	20	Normal	○
TM32	Double Team	Normal	Status	—	—	15	Self	—
TM34	Shock Wave	Electric	Special	60	—	20	Normal	—
TM37	Sandstorm	Rock	Status	—	—	10	All	—
TM39	Rock Tomb	Rock	Physical	50	80	10	Normal	—
TM41	Torment	Dark	Status	—	100	15	Normal	—
TM42	Facade	Normal	Physical	70	100	20	Normal	○
TM43	Secret Power	Normal	Physical	70	100	20	Normal	—
TM44	Rest	Psychic	Status	—	—	10	Self	—
TM45	Attract	Normal	Status	—	100	15	Normal	—
TM58	Endure	Normal	Status	—	—	10	Self	—
TM64	Explosion	Normal	Physical	250	100	5	2 Foes/1 Ally	—
TM69	Rock Polish	Rock	Status	—	—	20	Self	—
TM71	Stone Edge	Rock	Physical	100	80	5	Normal	—
TM73	Thunder Wave	Electric	Status	—	100	20	Normal	—
TM76	Stealth Rock	Rock	Status	—	—	20	2 Foes	—
TM78	Captivate	Normal	Status	—	100	20	2 Foes	—
TM80	Rock Slide	Rock	Physical	75	90	10	2 Foes	—
TM82	Sleep Talk	Normal	Status	—	—	10	Depends	—
TM83	Natural Gift	Normal	Physical	—	100	15	Normal	—
TM87	Swagger	Normal	Status	—	90	15	Normal	—
TM90	Substitute	Normal	Status	—	—	10	Self	—
HM04	Strength	Normal	Physical	80	100	15	Normal	○
HM06	Rock Smash	Fighting	Physical	40	100	15	Normal	○

● EGG MOVES

Name	Type	Kind	Pow.	Acc.	PP	Range	DA
Magnitude	Ground	Physical	—	100	30	2 Foes/1 Ally	—
Rollout	Rock	Physical	30	90	20	Normal	○
Explosion	Normal	Physical	250	100	5	2 Foes/1 Ally	○
Double-Edge	Normal	Physical	120	100	15	Normal	○
Block	Normal	Status	—	—	5	Normal	—

● LEVEL-UP MOVES

Lv.	Name	Type	Kind	Pow.	Acc.	PP	Range	DA
1	Fake Out	Normal	Physical	40	100	10	Normal	○
1	Growl	Normal	Status	—	100	40	2 Foes	—
1	Tail Whip	Normal	Status	—	100	30	2 Foes	—
1	Tackle	Normal	Physical	35	95	35	Normal	○
4	Foresight	Normal	Status	—	—	40	Normal	—
8	Attract	Normal	Status	—	100	15	Normal	—
11	Sing	Normal	Status	—	55	15	Normal	—
15	DoubleSlap	Normal	Physical	15	85	10	Normal	○
18	Copycat	Normal	Status	—	—	20	Depends	—
22	Assist	Normal	Status	—	—	20	Depends	—
25	Charm	Normal	Status	—	100	20	Normal	—
29	Faint Attack	Dark	Physical	60	—	20	Normal	○
32	Wake-Up Slap	Fighting	Physical	60	100	10	Normal	○
36	Covet	Normal	Physical	40	100	40	Normal	○
39	Heal Bell	Normal	Status	—	—	5	All Allies	—
42	Double-Edge	Normal	Physical	120	100	15	Normal	○
46	Captivate	Normal	Status	—	100	20	2 Foes	—

● MOVE MANIAC

Name	Type	Kind	Pow.	Acc.	PP	Range	DA
Headbutt	Normal	Physical	70	100	15	Normal	○

● BP MOVES

Name	Type	Kind	Pow.	Acc.	PP	Range	DA
Icy Wind	Ice	Special	55	95	15	2 Foes	—
Zen Headbutt	Psychic	Physical	80	90	15	Normal	○
Sucker Punch	Dark	Physical	80	100	5	Normal	○
Snore	Normal	Special	40	100	15	Normal	—
Helping Hand	Normal	Status	—	—	20	1 Ally	—
Last Resort	Normal	Physical	130	100	5	Normal	○
Swift	Normal	Special	60	—	20	2 Foes	—
Heal Bell	Normal	Status	—	—	5	All Allies	—
Mud-Slap	Ground	Special	20	100	10	Normal	○
Rollout	Rock	Physical	30	90	20	Normal	○

● TM & HM MOVES

No.	Name	Type	Kind	Pow.	Acc.	PP	Range	DA
TM03	Water Pulse	Water	Special	60	100	20	Normal	—
TM04	Calm Mind	Psychic	Status	—	—	20	Self	—
TM06	Toxic	Poison	Status	—	85	10	Normal	—
TM10	Hidden Power	Normal	Special	—	100	15	Normal	—
TM11	Sunny Day	Fire	Status	—	—	5	All	—
TM13	Ice Beam	Ice	Special	95	100	10	Normal	—
TM14	Blizzard	Ice	Special	120	70	5	2 Foes	—
TM17	Protect	Normal	Status	—	—	10	Self	—
TM18	Rain Dance	Water	Status	—	—	5	All	—
TM20	Safeguard	Normal	Status	—	—	25	2 Allies	—
TM21	Frustration	Normal	Physical	—	100	20	Normal	○
TM22	SolarBeam	Grass	Special	120	100	10	Normal	—
TM23	Iron Tail	Steel	Physical	100	75	15	Normal	○
TM24	Thunderbolt	Electric	Special	95	100	15	Normal	—
TM25	Thunder	Electric	Special	120	70	10	Normal	—
TM27	Return	Normal	Physical	—	100	20	Normal	○
TM28	Dig	Ground	Physical	80	100	10	Normal	○
TM30	Shadow Ball	Ghost	Special	80	100	15	Normal	—
TM32	Double Team	Normal	Status	—	—	15	Self	—
TM34	Shock Wave	Electric	Special	60	—	20	Normal	—
TM42	Facade	Normal	Physical	70	100	20	Normal	○
TM43	Secret Power	Normal	Physical	70	100	20	Normal	○
TM44	Rest	Psychic	Status	—	—	10	Self	—
TM45	Attract	Normal	Status	—	100	15	Normal	—
TM57	Charge Beam	Electric	Special	50	90	10	Normal	—
TM58	Endure	Normal	Status	—	—	10	Self	—
TM66	Payback	Dark	Physical	50	100	10	Normal	○
TM70	Flash	Normal	Status	—	100	20	Normal	—
TM73	Thunder Wave	Electric	Status	—	100	20	Normal	—
TM77	Psych Up	Normal	Status	—	—	10	Normal	—
TM78	Captivate	Normal	Status	—	100	20	2 Foes	—
TM82	Sleep Talk	Normal	Status	—	—	10	Depends	—
TM83	Natural Gift	Normal	Physical	—	100	15	Normal	—
TM85	Dream Eater	Psychic	Special	100	100	15	Normal	—
TM86	Grass Knot	Grass	Special	—	100	20	Normal	—
TM87	Swagger	Normal	Status	—	90	15	Normal	—
TM90	Substitute	Normal	Status	—	—	10	Self	—

● EGG MOVES

Name	Type	Kind	Pow.	Acc.	PP	Range	DA
Helping Hand	Normal	Status	—	—	20	1 Ally	—
Psych Up	Normal	Status	—	—	10	Normal	—
Uproar	Normal	Status	50	100	10	1 Random	—
Fake Tears	Dark	Status	—	100	20	Normal	—
Wish	Normal	Status	—	—	10	Self	—
Baton Pass	Normal	Status	—	—	40	Self	—
Substitute	Normal	Status	—	—	10	Self	—
Tickle	Normal	Status	—	—	20	Normal	—
Last Resort	Normal	Physical	130	100	5	Normal	○
Fake Out	Normal	Physical	40	100	10	Normal	○
Zen Headbutt	Psychic	Physical	80	90	15	Normal	○
Sucker Punch	Dark	Physical	80	100	5	Normal	○
Mud Bomb	Ground	Special	65	85	10	Normal	—

◉ No. 300 | Kitten Pokémon
Skitty

Normal

- ● HEIGHT: 2'00"
- ● WEIGHT: 24.3 lbs.
- ● ITEMS: None

● SIZE COMPARISON

● MALE/FEMALE HAVE SAME FORM

⊕ ABILITIES
- ● Cute Charm
- ● Normalize

⊕ STATS
HP	●●
ATTACK	●●
DEFENSE	●●
SP. ATTACK	●●
SP. DEFENSE	●
SPEED	●●

⊕ EGG GROUPS
Field

Fairy

⊕ PERFORMANCE
SPEED ★★★★☆   STAMINA ★★☆
POWER ★★★   JUMP ★★★☆
SKILL ★★★

● MAIN WAYS TO OBTAIN

Pokémon HeartGold — Hoenn Field / Pokéwalker Route

Pokémon SoulSilver — Hoenn Field / Pokéwalker Route

Pokémon Diamond — Route 222 (mass outbreak)

Pokémon Pearl — Route 222 (mass outbreak)

Pokémon Platinum — Route 222 (mass outbreak)

Pokémon HeartGold — It's adorable when it chases its own tail. It's difficult to earn its trust.

Pokémon SoulSilver — It's adorable when it chases its own tail. It's difficult to earn its trust.

⊕ EVOLUTION

Skitty → Use Moon Stone → Delcatty

No. 301 | Prim Pokémon
Delcatty

Normal

- **HEIGHT:** 3'02"
- **WEIGHT:** 71.9 lbs.
- **ITEMS:** None

● SIZE COMPARISON

● MALE/FEMALE HAVE SAME FORM

⊛ ABILITIES
- Cute Charm
- Normalize

⊛ STATS
HP ●●●
ATTACK ●●●
DEFENSE ●●●
SP. ATTACK ●●●
SP. DEFENSE ●●●
SPEED ●●●

⊛ EGG GROUPS
Field

Fairy

⊛ PERFORMANCE
SPEED ★★★★☆   STAMINA ★★★☆
POWER ★★☆☆   JUMP ★★★☆
SKILL ★★★★

● MAIN WAYS TO OBTAIN

Pokémon HeartGold — Use Moon Stone on Skitty

Pokémon SoulSilver — Use Moon Stone on Skitty

Pokémon Diamond — Use Moon Stone on Skitty

Pokémon Pearl — Use Moon Stone on Skitty

Pokémon Platinum — Use Moon Stone on Skitty

Pokémon HeartGold	Pokémon SoulSilver
It dislikes dirty places. It often searches for a comfortable place in which to groom itself.	It dislikes dirty places. It often searches for a comfortable place in which to groom itself.

⊛ EVOLUTION

  Use Moon Stone

Skitty → Delcatty

● LEVEL-UP MOVES

Lv.	Name	Type	Kind	Pow.	Acc.	PP	Range	DA
1	Fake Out	Normal	Physical	40	100	10	Normal	○
1	Attract	Normal	Status	—	100	15	Normal	—
1	Sing	Normal	Status	—	55	15	Normal	—
1	DoubleSlap	Normal	Physical	15	85	10	Normal	○

● MOVE MANIAC

Name	Type	Kind	Pow.	Acc.	PP	Range	DA
Headbutt	Normal	Physical	70	100	15	Normal	○

● BP MOVES

Name	Type	Kind	Pow.	Acc.	PP	Range	DA
Icy Wind	Ice	Special	55	95	15	2 Foes	—
Zen Headbutt	Psychic	Physical	80	90	15	Normal	○
Sucker Punch	Dark	Physical	80	100	5	Normal	○
Snore	Normal	Special	40	100	15	Normal	—
Helping Hand	Normal	Status	—	—	20	1 Ally	—
Last Resort	Normal	Physical	130	100	5	Normal	○
Swift	Normal	Special	60	—	20	2 Foes	—
Heal Bell	Normal	Status	—	—	5	All Allies	—
Mud-Slap	Ground	Special	20	100	10	Normal	—
Rollout	Rock	Physical	30	90	20	Normal	○

● TM & HM MOVES

No.	Name	Type	Kind	Pow.	Acc.	PP	Range	DA
TM03	Water Pulse	Water	Special	60	100	20	Normal	—
TM04	Calm Mind	Psychic	Status	—	—	20	Self	—
TM06	Toxic	Poison	Status	—	85	10	Normal	—
TM10	Hidden Power	Normal	Special	—	100	15	Normal	—
TM11	Sunny Day	Fire	Status	—	—	5	All	—
TM13	Ice Beam	Ice	Special	95	100	10	Normal	—
TM14	Blizzard	Ice	Special	120	70	5	2 Foes	—
TM15	Hyper Beam	Normal	Special	150	90	5	Normal	—
TM17	Protect	Normal	Status	—	—	10	Self	—
TM18	Rain Dance	Water	Status	—	—	5	All	—
TM20	Safeguard	Normal	Status	—	—	25	2 Allies	—
TM21	Frustration	Normal	Physical	—	100	20	Normal	○
TM22	SolarBeam	Grass	Special	120	100	10	Normal	—
TM23	Iron Tail	Steel	Physical	100	75	15	Normal	○
TM24	Thunderbolt	Electric	Special	95	100	15	Normal	—
TM25	Thunder	Electric	Special	120	70	10	Normal	—
TM27	Return	Normal	Physical	—	100	20	Normal	○
TM28	Dig	Ground	Physical	80	100	10	Normal	○
TM30	Shadow Ball	Ghost	Special	80	100	15	Normal	—
TM32	Double Team	Normal	Status	—	—	15	Self	—
TM34	Shock Wave	Electric	Special	60	—	20	Normal	—
TM42	Facade	Normal	Physical	70	100	20	Normal	○
TM43	Secret Power	Normal	Physical	70	100	20	Normal	○
TM44	Rest	Psychic	Status	—	—	10	Self	—
TM45	Attract	Normal	Status	—	100	15	Normal	—
TM57	Charge Beam	Electric	Special	50	90	10	Normal	—
TM58	Endure	Normal	Status	—	—	10	Self	—
TM66	Payback	Dark	Physical	50	100	10	Normal	○
TM68	Giga Impact	Normal	Physical	150	90	5	Normal	○
TM70	Flash	Normal	Status	—	100	20	Normal	—
TM73	Thunder Wave	Electric	Status	—	100	20	Normal	—
TM77	Psych Up	Normal	Status	—	—	10	Normal	—
TM78	Captivate	Normal	Status	—	100	20	2 Foes	—
TM82	Sleep Talk	Normal	Status	—	—	10	Depends	—
TM83	Natural Gift	Normal	Physical	—	100	15	Normal	—
TM85	Dream Eater	Psychic	Special	100	100	15	Normal	—
TM86	Grass Knot	Grass	Special	—	100	20	Normal	○
TM87	Swagger	Normal	Status	—	90	15	Normal	—
TM90	Substitute	Normal	Status	—	—	10	Self	—
HM04	Strength	Normal	Physical	80	100	15	Normal	○
HM06	Rock Smash	Fighting	Physical	40	100	15	Normal	○

● LEVEL-UP MOVES

Lv.	Name	Type	Kind	Pow.	Acc.	PP	Range	DA
1	Leer	Normal	Status	—	100	30	2 Foes	—
1	Scratch	Normal	Physical	40	100	35	Normal	○
4	Foresight	Normal	Status	—	—	40	Normal	—
8	Night Shade	Ghost	Special	—	100	15	Normal	—
11	Astonish	Ghost	Physical	30	100	15	Normal	○
15	Fury Swipes	Normal	Physical	18	80	15	Normal	○
18	Fake Out	Normal	Physical	40	100	10	Normal	○
22	Detect	Fighting	Status	—	—	5	Self	—
25	Shadow Sneak	Ghost	Physical	40	100	30	Normal	○
29	Knock Off	Dark	Physical	20	100	20	Normal	○
32	Faint Attack	Dark	Physical	60	—	20	Normal	○
36	Punishment	Dark	Physical	—	100	5	Normal	○
39	Shadow Claw	Ghost	Physical	70	100	15	Normal	○
43	Power Gem	Rock	Special	70	100	20	Normal	—
46	Confuse Ray	Ghost	Status	—	100	10	Normal	—
50	Zen Headbutt	Psychic	Physical	80	90	15	Normal	○
53	Shadow Ball	Ghost	Special	80	100	15	Normal	—
57	Mean Look	Normal	Status	—	—	5	Normal	—

● MOVE MANIAC

Name	Type	Kind	Pow.	Acc.	PP	Range	DA
Headbutt	Normal	Physical	70	100	15	Normal	○

● BP MOVES

Name	Type	Kind	Pow.	Acc.	PP	Range	DA
Fury Cutter	Bug	Physical	10	95	20	Normal	—
Icy Wind	Ice	Special	55	95	15	2 Foes	—
ThunderPunch	Electric	Physical	75	100	15	Normal	○
Fire Punch	Fire	Physical	75	100	15	Normal	○
Ice Punch	Ice	Physical	75	100	15	Normal	○
Ominous Wind	Ghost	Special	60	100	5	Normal	—
Zen Headbutt	Psychic	Physical	80	90	15	Normal	○
Trick	Psychic	Status	—	100	10	Normal	—
Knock Off	Dark	Physical	20	100	20	Normal	○
Sucker Punch	Dark	Physical	80	100	5	Normal	○
Snore	Normal	Special	40	100	15	Normal	—
Spite	Ghost	Status	—	100	10	Normal	—
Gravity	Psychic	Status	—	—	5	All	—
Magic Coat	Psychic	Status	—	—	15	Self	—
Role Play	Psychic	Status	—	—	10	—	—
Mud-Slap	Ground	Special	20	100	10	Normal	—
Signal Beam	Bug	Special	75	100	15	Normal	—
Pain Split	Normal	Status	—	—	20	Normal	—
Low Kick	Fighting	Physical	—	100	20	Normal	○

● TM & HM MOVES

No.	Name	Type	Kind	Pow.	Acc.	PP	Range	DA
TM01	Focus Punch	Fighting	Physical	150	100	20	Normal	○
TM03	Water Pulse	Water	Special	60	100	20	Normal	—
TM04	Calm Mind	Psychic	Status	—	—	20	Self	—
TM06	Toxic	Poison	Status	—	85	10	Normal	—
TM10	Hidden Power	Normal	Special	—	100	15	Normal	—
TM11	Sunny Day	Fire	Status	—	—	5	All	—
TM12	Taunt	Dark	Status	—	100	20	Normal	—
TM17	Protect	Normal	Status	—	—	10	Self	—
TM18	Rain Dance	Water	Status	—	—	5	All	—
TM21	Frustration	Normal	Physical	—	100	20	Normal	○
TM27	Return	Normal	Physical	—	100	20	Normal	○
TM28	Dig	Ground	Physical	80	100	10	Normal	○
TM29	Psychic	Psychic	Special	90	100	10	Normal	—
TM30	Shadow Ball	Ghost	Special	80	100	15	Normal	—
TM31	Brick Break	Fighting	Physical	75	100	15	Normal	○
TM32	Double Team	Normal	Status	—	—	15	Self	—
TM34	Shock Wave	Electric	Special	60	—	20	Normal	—
TM39	Rock Tomb	Rock	Physical	50	80	10	Normal	○
TM40	Aerial Ace	Flying	Physical	60	—	20	Normal	○
TM41	Torment	Dark	Status	—	100	15	Normal	—
TM42	Facade	Normal	Physical	70	100	20	Normal	○
TM43	Secret Power	Normal	Physical	70	100	20	Normal	—
TM44	Rest	Psychic	Status	—	—	10	Self	—
TM45	Attract	Normal	Status	—	100	15	Normal	—
TM46	Thief	Dark	Physical	40	100	10	Normal	○
TM49	Snatch	Dark	Status	—	—	10	Depends	—
TM56	Fling	Dark	Physical	—	100	10	Normal	—
TM58	Endure	Normal	Status	—	—	10	Self	—
TM61	Will-O-Wisp	Fire	Status	—	75	15	Normal	—
TM63	Embargo	Dark	Status	—	100	15	Normal	—
TM65	Shadow Claw	Ghost	Physical	70	100	15	Normal	○
TM66	Payback	Dark	Physical	50	100	10	Normal	○
TM70	Flash	Normal	Status	—	100	20	Normal	—
TM77	Psych Up	Normal	Status	—	—	10	Normal	—
TM78	Captivate	Normal	Status	—	100	20	2 Foes	—
TM79	Dark Pulse	Dark	Special	80	100	15	Normal	—
TM82	Sleep Talk	Normal	Status	—	—	10	Depends	—
TM83	Natural Gift	Normal	Physical	—	100	15	Normal	—
TM84	Poison Jab	Poison	Physical	80	100	20	Normal	○
TM85	Dream Eater	Psychic	Special	100	100	15	Normal	—
TM87	Swagger	Normal	Status	—	90	15	Normal	—
TM90	Substitute	Normal	Status	—	—	10	Self	—
HM01	Cut	Normal	Physical	50	95	30	Normal	○
HM06	Rock Smash	Fighting	Physical	40	100	15	Normal	○

● EGG MOVES

Name	Type	Kind	Pow.	Acc.	PP	Range	DA
Psych Up	Normal	Status	—	—	10	Normal	—
Recover	Normal	Status	—	—	10	Self	—
Moonlight	Normal	Status	—	—	5	Self	—
Nasty Plot	Dark	Status	—	—	20	Self	—
Flatter	Dark	Status	—	100	15	Normal	—
Feint	Normal	Physical	50	100	10	Normal	—

● HEIGHT: 1'08"
● WEIGHT: 24.3 lbs.
● ITEMS: None

● SIZE COMPARISON

● MALE/FEMALE HAVE SAME FORM

◎ ABILITIES
- Keen Eye
- Stall

◎ EGG GROUPS
Human-Like

◎ STATS
- HP ●●
- ATTACK ●●●
- DEFENSE ●●●
- SP. ATTACK ●●●
- SP. DEFENSE ●●
- SPEED ●●

◎ PERFORMANCE
- SPEED ★★★☆
- POWER ★★★☆
- SKILL ★★★☆
- STAMINA ★★★☆
- JUMP ★★★

● MAIN WAYS TO OBTAIN

Pokémon HeartGold — Route 9 (mass outbreak)

Pokémon SoulSilver — —

Pokémon Diamond — Iron Island (after obtaining the National Pokédex, insert *Pokémon Sapphire* into your Nintendo DS's Game Pak slot)

Pokémon Pearl — Iron Island (after obtaining the National Pokédex, insert *Pokémon Sapphire* into your Nintendo DS's Game Pak slot)

Pokémon Platinum — Iron Island (after obtaining the National Pokédex, insert *Pokémon Sapphire* into your Nintendo DS's Game Pak slot)

Pokémon HeartGold — It dwells in the darkness of caves. It uses its sharp claws to dig up gems to nourish itself.

Pokémon SoulSilver — It dwells in the darkness of caves. It uses its sharp claws to dig up gems to nourish itself.

◎ EVOLUTION
Does not evolve

No. 303 | Deceiver Pokémon
Mawile

Steel

● HEIGHT: 2'00"
● WEIGHT: 25.4 lbs.
● ITEMS: Occa Berry

● SIZE COMPARISON

● MALE/FEMALE HAVE SAME FORM

● ABILITIES
● Hyper Cutter
● Intimidate

● STATS
HP ●●
ATTACK ●●●●
DEFENSE ●●●
SP. ATTACK ●●●
SP. DEFENSE ●●
SPEED ●●

● EGG GROUPS
Field

Fairy

● PERFORMANCE
SPEED ★★★★　　STAMINA ★★★★
POWER ★★★☆　　JUMP ★★☆
SKILL ★★★☆

● MAIN WAYS TO OBTAIN

Pokémon HeartGold	—
Pokémon SoulSilver	Route 9 (mass outbreak)
Pokémon Diamond	Iron Island (after obtaining the National Pokédex, insert Pokémon Ruby into your Nintendo DS's Game Pak slot)
Pokémon Pearl	Iron Island (after obtaining the National Pokédex, insert Pokémon Ruby into your Nintendo DS's Game Pak slot)
Pokémon Platinum	Iron Island (after obtaining the National Pokédex, insert Pokémon Ruby into your Nintendo DS's Game Pak slot)

Pokémon HeartGold
It chomps with its gaping mouth. Its huge jaws are actually steel horns that have been transformed.

Pokémon SoulSilver
It chomps with its gaping mouth. Its huge jaws are actually steel horns that have been transformed.

● EVOLUTION
Does not evolve

● LEVEL-UP MOVES

Lv.	Name	Type	Kind	Pow.	Acc.	PP	Range	DA
1	Astonish	Ghost	Physical	30	100	15	Normal	○
6	Fake Tears	Dark	Status	—	100	20	Normal	—
11	Bite	Dark	Physical	60	100	25	Normal	○
16	Sweet Scent	Normal	Status	—	100	20	2 Foes	—
21	ViceGrip	Normal	Physical	55	100	30	Normal	○
26	Faint Attack	Dark	Physical	60	—	20	Normal	—
31	Baton Pass	Normal	Status	—	—	40	Self	—
36	Crunch	Dark	Physical	80	100	15	Normal	○
41	Iron Defense	Steel	Status	—	—	15	Self	—
46	Sucker Punch	Dark	Physical	80	100	5	Normal	○
51	Stockpile	Normal	Status	—	—	20	Self	—
51	Swallow	Normal	Status	—	—	10	Self	—
51	Spit Up	Normal	Special	—	100	10	Normal	—
56	Iron Head	Steel	Physical	80	100	15	Normal	○

● MOVE MANIAC

Name	Type	Kind	Pow.	Acc.	PP	Range	DA
Headbutt	Normal	Physical	70	100	15	Normal	○

● BP MOVES

Name	Type	Kind	Pow.	Acc.	PP	Range	DA
Icy Wind	Ice	Special	55	95	15	2 Foes	—
ThunderPunch	Electric	Physical	75	100	15	Normal	○
Ice Punch	Ice	Physical	75	100	15	Normal	○
Knock Off	Dark	Physical	20	100	20	Normal	○
Sucker Punch	Dark	Physical	80	100	5	Normal	○
Snore	Normal	Special	40	100	15	Normal	—
Magnet Rise	Electric	Status	—	—	10	Self	—
Mud-Slap	Ground	Special	20	100	10	Normal	—
Iron Head	Steel	Physical	80	100	15	Normal	○
AncientPower	Rock	Special	60	100	5	Normal	—
Iron Defense	Steel	Status	—	—	15	Self	—
Super Fang	Normal	Physical	—	90	10	Normal	○
Pain Split	Normal	Status	—	—	20	Normal	—

● TM & HM MOVES

No.	Name	Type	Kind	Pow.	Acc.	PP	Range	DA
TM01	Focus Punch	Fighting	Physical	150	100	20	Normal	○
TM06	Toxic	Poison	Status	—	85	10	Normal	—
TM10	Hidden Power	Normal	Special	—	100	15	Normal	—
TM11	Sunny Day	Fire	Status	—	—	5	All	—
TM12	Taunt	Dark	Status	—	100	20	Normal	—
TM13	Ice Beam	Ice	Special	95	100	10	Normal	—
TM15	Hyper Beam	Normal	Special	150	90	5	Normal	—
TM17	Protect	Normal	Status	—	—	10	Self	—
TM18	Rain Dance	Water	Status	—	—	5	All	—
TM21	Frustration	Normal	Physical	—	100	20	Normal	○
TM22	SolarBeam	Grass	Special	120	100	10	Normal	—
TM27	Return	Normal	Physical	—	100	20	Normal	○
TM30	Shadow Ball	Ghost	Special	80	100	15	Normal	—
TM31	Brick Break	Fighting	Physical	75	100	15	Normal	○
TM32	Double Team	Normal	Status	—	—	15	Self	—
TM35	Flamethrower	Fire	Special	95	100	15	Normal	—
TM36	Sludge Bomb	Poison	Special	90	100	10	Normal	—
TM37	Sandstorm	Rock	Status	—	—	10	All	—
TM38	Fire Blast	Fire	Special	120	85	5	Normal	—
TM39	Rock Tomb	Rock	Physical	50	80	10	Normal	○
TM41	Torment	Dark	Status	—	100	15	Normal	—
TM42	Facade	Normal	Physical	70	100	20	Normal	○
TM43	Secret Power	Normal	Physical	70	100	20	Normal	○
TM44	Rest	Psychic	Status	—	—	10	Self	—
TM45	Attract	Normal	Status	—	100	15	Normal	—
TM52	Focus Blast	Fighting	Special	120	70	5	Normal	—
TM56	Fling	Dark	Physical	—	100	10	Normal	○
TM57	Charge Beam	Electric	Special	50	90	10	Normal	—
TM58	Endure	Normal	Status	—	—	10	Self	—
TM63	Embargo	Dark	Status	—	100	15	Normal	—
TM66	Payback	Dark	Physical	50	100	10	Normal	○
TM68	Giga Impact	Normal	Physical	150	90	5	Normal	○
TM75	Swords Dance	Normal	Status	—	—	30	Self	—
TM78	Captivate	Normal	Status	—	100	20	2 Foes	—
TM79	Dark Pulse	Dark	Special	80	100	15	Normal	—
TM80	Rock Slide	Rock	Physical	75	90	10	2 Foes	—
TM82	Sleep Talk	Normal	Status	—	—	10	Depends	—
TM83	Natural Gift	Normal	Physical	—	100	15	Normal	○
TM86	Grass Knot	Grass	Special	—	100	20	Normal	○
TM87	Swagger	Normal	Status	—	90	15	Normal	—
TM90	Substitute	Normal	Status	—	—	10	Self	—
TM91	Flash Cannon	Steel	Special	80	100	10	Normal	—
HM04	Strength	Normal	Physical	80	100	15	Normal	○
HM06	Rock Smash	Fighting	Physical	40	100	15	Normal	○

● EGG MOVES

Name	Type	Kind	Pow.	Acc.	PP	Range	DA
Swords Dance	Normal	Status	—	—	30	Self	—
False Swipe	Normal	Physical	40	100	40	Normal	○
Poison Fang	Poison	Physical	50	100	15	Normal	○
Psych Up	Normal	Status	—	—	10	Normal	—
AncientPower	Rock	Special	60	100	5	Normal	—
Tickle	Normal	Status	—	100	20	Normal	—
Sucker Punch	Dark	Physical	80	100	5	Normal	○
Ice Fang	Ice	Physical	65	95	15	Normal	○
Fire Fang	Fire	Physical	65	95	15	Normal	○
Thunder Fang	Electric	Physical	65	95	15	Normal	○
Punishment	Dark	Physical	—	100	5	Normal	—
Guard Swap	Psychic	Status	—	—	10	Normal	—

● LEVEL-UP MOVES

Lv.	Name	Type	Kind	Pow.	Acc.	PP	Range	DA
1	Tackle	Normal	Physical	35	95	35	Normal	○
4	Harden	Normal	Status	—	—	30	Self	—
8	Mud-Slap	Ground	Special	20	100	10	Normal	—
11	Headbutt	Normal	Physical	70	100	15	Normal	○
15	Metal Claw	Steel	Physical	50	95	35	Normal	○
18	Iron Defense	Steel	Status	—	—	15	Self	—
22	Roar	Normal	Status	—	100	20	Normal	—
25	Take Down	Normal	Physical	90	85	20	Normal	○
29	Iron Head	Steel	Physical	80	100	15	Normal	○
32	Protect	Normal	Status	—	—	10	Self	—
36	Metal Sound	Steel	Status	—	85	40	Normal	—
39	Iron Tail	Steel	Physical	100	75	15	Normal	○
43	Double-Edge	Normal	Physical	120	100	15	Normal	○
46	Metal Burst	Steel	Physical	—	100	10	Self	—

● MOVE MANIAC

Name	Type	Kind	Pow.	Acc.	PP	Range	DA
Headbutt	Normal	Physical	70	100	15	Normal	○

● BP MOVES

Name	Type	Kind	Pow.	Acc.	PP	Range	DA
Fury Cutter	Bug	Physical	10	95	20	Normal	○
Snore	Normal	Special	40	100	15	Normal	—
Spite	Ghost	Status	—	100	10	Normal	—
Magnet Rise	Electric	Status	—	—	10	Self	—
Uproar	Normal	Special	50	100	10	1 Random	—
Mud-Slap	Ground	Special	20	100	10	Normal	—
Rollout	Rock	Physical	30	90	20	Normal	○
Superpower	Fighting	Physical	120	100	5	Normal	○
Iron Head	Steel	Physical	80	100	15	Normal	○
Endeavor	Normal	Physical	—	100	5	Normal	○
AncientPower	Rock	Special	60	100	5	Normal	—
Earth Power	Ground	Special	90	100	10	Normal	—
Iron Defense	Steel	Status	—	—	15	Self	—

● TM & HM MOVES

No.	Name	Type	Kind	Pow.	Acc.	PP	Range	DA
TM03	Water Pulse	Water	Special	60	100	20	Normal	—
TM05	Roar	Normal	Status	—	100	20	Normal	—
TM06	Toxic	Poison	Status	—	85	10	Normal	—
TM10	Hidden Power	Normal	Special	—	100	15	Normal	—
TM11	Sunny Day	Fire	Status	—	—	5	All	—
TM17	Protect	Normal	Status	—	—	10	Self	—
TM18	Rain Dance	Water	Status	—	—	5	All	—
TM21	Frustration	Normal	Physical	—	100	20	Normal	○
TM23	Iron Tail	Steel	Physical	100	75	15	Normal	○
TM26	Earthquake	Ground	Physical	100	100	10	2 Foes/1 Ally	—
TM27	Return	Normal	Physical	—	100	20	Normal	○
TM28	Dig	Ground	Physical	80	100	10	Normal	○
TM32	Double Team	Normal	Status	—	—	15	Self	—
TM34	Shock Wave	Electric	Special	60	—	20	Normal	—
TM37	Sandstorm	Rock	Status	—	—	10	All	—
TM39	Rock Tomb	Rock	Physical	50	80	10	Normal	○
TM40	Aerial Ace	Flying	Physical	60	—	20	Normal	○
TM42	Facade	Normal	Physical	70	100	20	Normal	○
TM43	Secret Power	Normal	Physical	70	100	20	Normal	○
TM44	Rest	Psychic	Status	—	—	10	Self	—
TM45	Attract	Normal	Status	—	100	15	Normal	—
TM58	Endure	Normal	Status	—	—	10	Self	—
TM65	Shadow Claw	Ghost	Physical	70	100	15	Normal	○
TM69	Rock Polish	Rock	Status	—	—	20	Self	—
TM76	Stealth Rock	Rock	Status	—	—	20	2 Foes	—
TM78	Captivate	Normal	Status	—	100	20	2 Foes	—
TM80	Rock Slide	Rock	Physical	75	90	10	2 Foes	○
TM82	Sleep Talk	Normal	Status	—	—	10	Depends	—
TM83	Natural Gift	Normal	Physical	—	100	15	Normal	○
TM87	Swagger	Normal	Status	—	90	15	Normal	—
TM90	Substitute	Normal	Status	—	—	10	Self	—
HM01	Cut	Normal	Physical	50	95	30	Normal	○
HM04	Strength	Normal	Physical	80	100	15	Normal	○
HM06	Rock Smash	Fighting	Physical	40	100	15	Normal	○

● EGG MOVES

Name	Type	Kind	Pow.	Acc.	PP	Range	DA
Endeavor	Normal	Physical	—	100	5	Normal	○
Body Slam	Normal	Physical	85	100	15	Normal	○
Stomp	Normal	Physical	65	100	20	Normal	○
SmellingSalt	Normal	Physical	60	100	10	Normal	○
Curse	???	Status	—	—	10	Normal/Self	—
Screech	Normal	Status	—	85	40	Normal	—
Iron Head	Steel	Physical	80	100	15	Normal	○
Dragon Rush	Dragon	Physical	100	75	10	Normal	○
Head Smash	Rock	Physical	150	80	5	Normal	○

◉ No. 304 | Iron Armor Pokémon
Aron

Steel **Rock**

- **HEIGHT:** 1'04"
- **WEIGHT:** 132.3 lbs.
- **ITEMS:** Hard Stone

● SIZE COMPARISON

● MALE/FEMALE HAVE SAME FORM

◎ ABILITIES
- Sturdy
- Rock Head

◎ STATS
HP ●●
ATTACK ●●●
DEFENSE ●●●●
SP. ATTACK ●●
SP. DEFENSE ●
SPEED ●

◎ EGG GROUPS
Monster

◎ PERFORMANCE
SPEED ★★★   STAMINA ★★★
POWER ★★★★   JUMP ★★
SKILL ★★☆

● MAIN WAYS TO OBTAIN

Pokémon HeartGold — Safari Zone (Rocky Beach Area: if Rock objects are placed, may appear in tall grass)

Pokémon SoulSilver — Safari Zone (Rocky Beach Area: if Rock objects are placed, may appear in tall grass)

Pokémon Diamond — Fuego Ironworks (use Poké Radar)

Pokémon Pearl — —

Pokémon Platinum — Fuego Ironworks (use Poké Radar)

Pokémon HeartGold — When it evolves, it sheds the steel carapace that covered its whole body and develops a new one.

Pokémon SoulSilver — When it evolves, it sheds the steel carapace that covered its whole body and develops a new one.

◎ EVOLUTION

Aron — Lv. 32 — Lairon — Lv. 42 — Aggron

No. 305 | Iron Armor Pokémon
Lairon

Steel | Rock

- **HEIGHT:** 2'11"
- **WEIGHT:** 264.6 lbs.
- **ITEMS:** Hard Stone

● **SIZE COMPARISON**

● **MALE/FEMALE HAVE SAME FORM**

⚙ ABILITIES
- Sturdy
- Rock Head

⚙ EGG GROUPS
Monster

⚙ STATS
HP	●●
ATTACK	●●●●
DEFENSE	●●●●●
SP. ATTACK	●●
SP. DEFENSE	●●
SPEED	●●

⚙ PERFORMANCE
- SPEED ★★☆
- POWER ★★★★☆
- SKILL ★★★☆
- STAMINA ★★★☆
- JUMP ★★

● MAIN WAYS TO OBTAIN

Pokémon HeartGold — Safari Zone (Peak Area: if Rock objects are placed, may appear in tall grass)

Pokémon SoulSilver — Safari Zone (Peak Area: if Rock objects are placed, may appear in tall grass)

Pokémon Diamond — Level up Aron to Lv. 32

Pokémon Pearl — —

Pokémon Platinum — Level up Aron to Lv. 32

Pokémon HeartGold — It loves iron ore. Groups of them fight for territory by bashing one another with their steel bodies.

Pokémon SoulSilver — It loves iron ore. Groups of them fight for territory by bashing one another with their steel bodies.

⚙ EVOLUTION
Aron → Lv. 32 → Lairon → Lv. 42 → Aggron

● LEVEL-UP MOVES
Lv.	Name	Type	Kind	Pow.	Acc.	PP	Range	DA
1	Tackle	Normal	Physical	35	95	35	Normal	○
1	Harden	Normal	Status	—	—	30	Self	—
1	Mud-Slap	Ground	Special	20	100	10	Normal	—
1	Headbutt	Normal	Physical	70	100	15	Normal	○
4	Harden	Normal	Status	—	—	30	Self	—
8	Mud-Slap	Ground	Special	20	100	10	Normal	—
11	Headbutt	Normal	Physical	70	100	15	Normal	○
15	Metal Claw	Steel	Physical	50	95	35	Normal	○
18	Iron Defense	Steel	Status	—	—	15	Self	—
22	Roar	Normal	Status	—	100	20	Normal	—
25	Take Down	Normal	Physical	90	85	20	Normal	○
29	Iron Head	Steel	Physical	80	100	15	Normal	○
34	Protect	Normal	Status	—	—	10	Self	—
40	Metal Sound	Steel	Status	—	85	40	Normal	—
45	Iron Tail	Steel	Physical	100	75	15	Normal	○
51	Double-Edge	Normal	Physical	120	100	15	Normal	○
56	Metal Burst	Steel	Physical	—	100	10	Self	○

● MOVE MANIAC
Name	Type	Kind	Pow.	Acc.	PP	Range	DA
Headbutt	Normal	Physical	70	100	15	Normal	○

● BP MOVES
Name	Type	Kind	Pow.	Acc.	PP	Range	DA
Fury Cutter	Bug	Physical	10	95	20	Normal	○
Snore	Normal	Special	40	100	15	Normal	—
Spite	Ghost	Status	—	100	10	Normal	—
Magnet Rise	Electric	Status	—	—	10	Self	—
Uproar	Normal	Special	50	100	10	1 Random	—
Mud-Slap	Ground	Special	20	100	10	Normal	—
Rollout	Rock	Physical	30	90	20	Normal	○
Superpower	Fighting	Physical	120	100	5	Normal	○
Iron Head	Steel	Physical	80	100	15	Normal	○
Endeavor	Normal	Physical	—	100	5	Normal	○
AncientPower	Rock	Special	60	100	5	Normal	—
Earth Power	Ground	Special	90	100	10	Normal	—
Iron Defense	Steel	Status	—	—	15	Self	—

● TM & HM MOVES
No.	Name	Type	Kind	Pow.	Acc.	PP	Range	DA
TM03	Water Pulse	Water	Special	60	100	20	Normal	—
TM05	Roar	Normal	Status	—	100	20	Normal	—
TM06	Toxic	Poison	Status	—	85	10	Normal	—
TM10	Hidden Power	Normal	Special	—	100	15	Normal	—
TM11	Sunny Day	Fire	Status	—	—	5	All	—
TM17	Protect	Normal	Status	—	—	10	Self	—
TM18	Rain Dance	Water	Status	—	—	5	All	—
TM21	Frustration	Normal	Physical	—	100	20	Normal	○
TM23	Iron Tail	Steel	Physical	100	75	15	Normal	○
TM26	Earthquake	Ground	Physical	100	100	10	2 Foes/1 Ally	—
TM27	Return	Normal	Physical	—	100	20	Normal	○
TM28	Dig	Ground	Physical	80	100	10	Normal	○
TM32	Double Team	Normal	Status	—	—	15	Self	—
TM34	Shock Wave	Electric	Special	60	—	20	Normal	—
TM37	Sandstorm	Rock	Status	—	—	10	All	—
TM39	Rock Tomb	Rock	Physical	50	80	10	Normal	○
TM40	Aerial Ace	Flying	Physical	60	—	20	Normal	○
TM42	Facade	Normal	Physical	70	100	20	Normal	○
TM43	Secret Power	Normal	Physical	70	100	20	Normal	○
TM44	Rest	Psychic	Status	—	—	10	Self	—
TM45	Attract	Normal	Status	—	100	15	Normal	—
TM58	Endure	Normal	Status	—	—	10	Self	—
TM65	Shadow Claw	Ghost	Physical	70	100	15	Normal	○
TM69	Rock Polish	Rock	Status	—	—	20	Self	—
TM71	Stone Edge	Rock	Physical	100	80	5	Normal	—
TM76	Stealth Rock	Rock	Status	—	—	20	2 Foes	—
TM78	Captivate	Normal	Status	—	100	20	2 Foes	—
TM80	Rock Slide	Rock	Physical	75	90	10	2 Foes	—
TM82	Sleep Talk	Normal	Status	—	—	10	Depends	—
TM83	Natural Gift	Normal	Physical	—	100	15	Normal	—
TM87	Swagger	Normal	Status	—	90	15	Normal	—
TM90	Substitute	Normal	Status	—	—	10	Self	—
HM01	Cut	Normal	Physical	50	95	30	Normal	○
HM04	Strength	Normal	Physical	80	100	15	Normal	○
HM06	Rock Smash	Fighting	Physical	40	100	15	Normal	○

LEVEL-UP MOVES

Lv.	Name	Type	Kind	Pow.	Acc.	PP	Range	DA
1	Tackle	Normal	Physical	35	95	35	Normal	○
1	Harden	Normal	Status	—	—	30	Self	—
1	Mud-Slap	Ground	Special	20	100	10	Normal	—
1	Headbutt	Normal	Physical	70	100	15	Normal	○
4	Harden	Normal	Status	—	—	30	Self	—
8	Mud-Slap	Ground	Special	20	100	10	Normal	—
11	Headbutt	Normal	Physical	70	100	15	Normal	○
15	Metal Claw	Steel	Physical	50	95	35	Normal	○
18	Iron Defense	Steel	Status	—	—	15	Self	—
22	Roar	Normal	Status	—	100	20	Normal	—
25	Take Down	Normal	Physical	90	85	20	Normal	○
29	Iron Head	Steel	Physical	80	100	15	Normal	○
34	Protect	Normal	Status	—	—	10	Self	—
40	Metal Sound	Steel	Status	—	85	40	Normal	—
48	Iron Tail	Steel	Physical	100	75	15	Normal	○
57	Double-Edge	Normal	Physical	120	100	15	Normal	○
65	Metal Burst	Steel	Physical	—	100	10	Self	—

MOVE MANIAC

Name	Type	Kind	Pow.	Acc.	PP	Range	DA
Headbutt	Normal	Physical	70	100	15	Normal	—

BP MOVES

Name	Type	Kind	Pow.	Acc.	PP	Range	DA
Fury Cutter	Bug	Physical	10	95	20	Normal	○
Icy Wind	Ice	Special	55	95	15	2 Foes	○
ThunderPunch	Electric	Physical	75	100	15	Normal	○
Fire Punch	Fire	Physical	75	100	15	Normal	○
Ice Punch	Ice	Physical	75	100	15	Normal	○
Snore	Normal	Special	40	100	15	Normal	—
Spite	Ghost	Status	—	100	10	Normal	—
Magnet Rise	Electric	Status	—	—	10	Self	—
Uproar	Normal	Special	50	100	10	1 Random	—
Block	Normal	Status	—	—	5	Normal	—
Mud-Slap	Ground	Special	20	100	10	Normal	—
Rollout	Rock	Physical	30	90	20	Normal	○
Superpower	Fighting	Physical	120	100	5	Normal	○
Iron Head	Steel	Physical	80	100	15	Normal	○
Aqua Tail	Water	Physical	90	90	10	Normal	○
Endeavor	Normal	Physical	—	100	5	Normal	—
Outrage	Dragon	Physical	120	100	15	1 Random	○
AncientPower	Rock	Special	60	100	5	Normal	—
Earth Power	Ground	Special	90	100	10	Normal	—
Iron Defense	Steel	Status	—	—	15	Self	—
Low Kick	Fighting	Physical	—	100	20	Normal	○

TM & HM MOVES

No.	Name	Type	Kind	Pow.	Acc.	PP	Range	DA
TM01	Focus Punch	Fighting	Physical	150	100	20	Normal	○
TM02	Dragon Claw	Dragon	Physical	80	100	15	Normal	○
TM03	Water Pulse	Water	Special	60	100	20	Normal	—
TM05	Roar	Normal	Status	—	100	20	Normal	—
TM06	Toxic	Poison	Status	—	85	10	Normal	—
TM10	Hidden Power	Normal	Special	—	100	15	Normal	—
TM11	Sunny Day	Fire	Status	—	—	5	All	—
TM12	Taunt	Dark	Status	—	100	20	Normal	—
TM13	Ice Beam	Ice	Special	95	100	10	Normal	—
TM14	Blizzard	Ice	Special	120	70	5	2 Foes	—
TM15	Hyper Beam	Normal	Special	150	90	5	Normal	—
TM17	Protect	Normal	Status	—	—	10	Self	—
TM18	Rain Dance	Water	Status	—	—	5	All	—
TM21	Frustration	Normal	Physical	—	100	20	Normal	○
TM22	SolarBeam	Grass	Special	120	100	10	Normal	—
TM23	Iron Tail	Steel	Physical	100	75	15	Normal	○
TM24	Thunderbolt	Electric	Special	95	100	15	Normal	—
TM25	Thunder	Electric	Special	120	70	10	Normal	—
TM26	Earthquake	Ground	Physical	100	100	10	2 Foes/1 Ally	○
TM27	Return	Normal	Physical	—	100	20	Normal	○
TM28	Dig	Ground	Physical	80	100	10	Normal	○
TM31	Brick Break	Fighting	Physical	75	100	15	Normal	○
TM32	Double Team	Normal	Status	—	—	15	Self	—
TM34	Shock Wave	Electric	Special	60	—	20	Normal	—
TM35	Flamethrower	Fire	Special	95	100	15	Normal	—
TM37	Sandstorm	Rock	Status	—	—	10	All	—
TM38	Fire Blast	Fire	Special	120	85	5	Normal	—
TM39	Rock Tomb	Rock	Physical	50	80	10	Normal	○
TM40	Aerial Ace	Flying	Physical	60	—	20	Normal	○
TM42	Facade	Normal	Physical	70	100	20	Normal	○
TM43	Secret Power	Normal	Physical	70	100	20	Normal	○
TM44	Rest	Psychic	Status	—	—	10	Self	—
TM45	Attract	Normal	Status	—	100	15	Normal	—
TM52	Focus Blast	Fighting	Special	120	70	5	Normal	—
TM56	Fling	Dark	Physical	—	100	10	Normal	○
TM58	Endure	Normal	Status	—	—	10	Self	—
TM59	Dragon Pulse	Dragon	Special	90	100	10	Normal	—
TM65	Shadow Claw	Ghost	Physical	70	100	15	Normal	○
TM66	Payback	Dark	Physical	50	100	10	Normal	○
TM68	Giga Impact	Normal	Physical	150	90	5	Normal	○
TM69	Rock Polish	Rock	Status	—	—	20	Self	—
TM71	Stone Edge	Rock	Physical	100	80	5	Normal	○
TM72	Avalanche	Ice	Physical	60	100	10	Normal	○
TM73	Thunder Wave	Electric	Status	—	100	20	Normal	—
TM76	Stealth Rock	Rock	Status	—	—	20	2 Foes	—
TM78	Captivate	Normal	Status	—	100	20	2 Foes	—
TM79	Dark Pulse	Dark	Special	80	100	15	Normal	—
TM80	Rock Slide	Rock	Physical	75	90	10	2 Foes	○
TM82	Sleep Talk	Normal	Status	—	—	10	Depends	—
TM83	Natural Gift	Normal	Physical	—	100	15	Normal	○
TM87	Swagger	Normal	Status	—	90	15	Normal	—
TM90	Substitute	Normal	Status	—	—	10	Self	—
TM91	Flash Cannon	Steel	Special	80	100	10	Normal	—
HM01	Cut	Normal	Physical	50	95	30	Normal	○
HM03	Surf	Water	Special	95	100	15	2 Foes/1 Ally	—
HM04	Strength	Normal	Physical	80	100	15	Normal	○
HM05	Whirlpool	Water	Special	15	70	15	Normal	—
HM06	Rock Smash	Fighting	Physical	40	100	15	Normal	○
HM08	Rock Climb	Normal	Physical	90	85	20	Normal	○

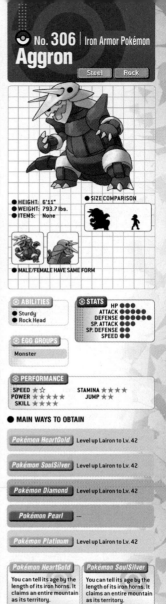

No. 306 | Iron Armor Pokémon
Aggron

Steel **Rock**

- **HEIGHT:** 6'11"
- **WEIGHT:** 793.7 lbs.
- **ITEMS:** None

- **SIZE COMPARISON**

- **MALE/FEMALE HAVE SAME FORM**

ABILITIES
- Sturdy
- Rock Head

STATS
HP ●●●
ATTACK ●●●●●
DEFENSE ●●●●●●
SP. ATTACK ●●●
SP. DEFENSE ●●
SPEED ●●

EGG GROUPS
Monster

PERFORMANCE
SPEED ★☆   STAMINA ★★★★
POWER ★★★★★   JUMP ★★
SKILL ★★★★

MAIN WAYS TO OBTAIN

Pokémon HeartGold — Level up Lairon to Lv. 42

Pokémon SoulSilver — Level up Lairon to Lv. 42

Pokémon Diamond — Level up Lairon to Lv. 42

Pokémon Pearl — —

Pokémon Platinum — Level up Lairon to Lv. 42

Pokémon HeartGold
You can tell its age by the length of its iron horns. It claims an entire mountain as its territory.

Pokémon SoulSilver
You can tell its age by the length of its iron horns. It claims an entire mountain as its territory.

EVOLUTION
Aron — Lv. 32 — Lairon — Lv. 42 — Aggron

◉ No. 307 | Meditate Pokémon
Meditite

Fighting **Psychic**

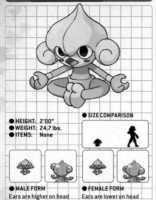

- **HEIGHT:** 2'00"
- **WEIGHT:** 24.7 lbs.
- **ITEMS:** None

● **SIZE COMPARISON**

● **MALE FORM**
Ears are higher on head

● **FEMALE FORM**
Ears are lower on head

◉ ABILITIES
● Pure Power

◉ STATS
- HP ●
- ATTACK ●●
- DEFENSE ●●
- SP. ATTACK ●●
- SP. DEFENSE ●●
- SPEED ●●●

◉ EGG GROUPS
Human-Like

◉ PERFORMANCE
SPEED ★★
POWER ★★
SKILL ★★★★★
STAMINA ★★☆
JUMP ★★☆☆☆

● MAIN WAYS TO OBTAIN

Pokémon HeartGold	Sprout Tower (Sinnoh Sound)
Pokémon SoulSilver	Sprout Tower (Sinnoh Sound)
Pokémon Diamond	Route 211
Pokémon Pearl	Route 211
Pokémon Platinum	Route 211

Pokémon HeartGold	Pokémon SoulSilver
It meditates to heighten its inner energy and to float in the air. It eats one berry a day.	It meditates to heighten its inner energy and to float in the air. It eats one berry a day.

◉ EVOLUTION

Meditite → Lv. 37 → Medicham

● LEVEL-UP MOVES

Lv.	Name	Type	Kind	Pow.	Acc.	PP	Range	DA
1	Bide	Normal	Physical	—	—	10	Self	○
4	Meditate	Psychic	Status	—	—	40	Self	—
8	Confusion	Psychic	Special	50	100	25	Normal	—
11	Detect	Fighting	Status	—	—	5	Self	—
15	Hidden Power	Normal	Special	—	100	15	Normal	—
18	Mind Reader	Normal	Status	—	—	5	Normal	—
22	Feint	Normal	Physical	50	100	10	Normal	—
25	Calm Mind	Psychic	Status	—	—	20	Self	—
29	Force Palm	Fighting	Physical	60	100	10	Normal	○
32	Hi Jump Kick	Fighting	Physical	100	90	20	Normal	○
36	Psych Up	Normal	Status	—	—	10	Self	—
39	Power Trick	Psychic	Status	—	—	10	Self	—
43	Reversal	Fighting	Physical	—	100	15	Normal	○
46	Recover	Normal	Status	—	—	10	Self	—

● MOVE MANIAC

Name	Type	Kind	Pow.	Acc.	PP	Range	DA
Headbutt	Normal	Physical	70	100	15	Normal	○

● BP MOVES

Name	Type	Kind	Pow.	Acc.	PP	Range	DA
ThunderPunch	Electric	Physical	75	100	15	Normal	○
Fire Punch	Fire	Physical	75	100	15	Normal	○
Ice Punch	Ice	Physical	75	100	15	Normal	○
Zen Headbutt	Psychic	Physical	80	90	15	Normal	○
Vacuum Wave	Fighting	Special	40	100	30	Normal	—
Trick	Psychic	Status	—	100	10	Normal	—
Snore	Normal	Special	40	100	15	Normal	—
Helping Hand	Normal	Status	—	—	20	1 Ally	—
Swift	Normal	Special	60	—	20	2 Foes	—
Gravity	Psychic	Status	—	—	5	All	—
Magic Coat	Psychic	Status	—	—	15	Self	—
Role Play	Psychic	Status	—	—	10	Normal	—
Mud-Slap	Ground	Special	20	100	10	Normal	—
Signal Beam	Bug	Special	75	100	15	Normal	—
Pain Split	Normal	Status	—	—	20	Normal	—
Low Kick	Fighting	Physical	—	100	20	Normal	○

● TM & HM MOVES

No.	Name	Type	Kind	Pow.	Acc.	PP	Range	DA
TM01	Focus Punch	Fighting	Physical	150	100	20	Normal	○
TM04	Calm Mind	Psychic	Status	—	—	20	Self	—
TM06	Toxic	Poison	Status	—	85	10	Normal	—
TM08	Bulk Up	Fighting	Status	—	—	20	Self	—
TM10	Hidden Power	Normal	Special	—	100	15	Normal	—
TM11	Sunny Day	Fire	Status	—	—	5	All	—
TM16	Light Screen	Psychic	Status	—	—	30	2 Allies	—
TM17	Protect	Normal	Status	—	—	10	Self	—
TM18	Rain Dance	Water	Status	—	—	5	All	—
TM21	Frustration	Normal	Physical	—	100	20	Normal	○
TM27	Return	Normal	Physical	—	100	20	Normal	○
TM29	Psychic	Psychic	Special	90	100	10	Normal	—
TM30	Shadow Ball	Ghost	Special	80	100	15	Normal	—
TM31	Brick Break	Fighting	Physical	75	100	15	Normal	○
TM32	Double Team	Normal	Status	—	—	15	Self	—
TM33	Reflect	Psychic	Status	—	—	20	2 Allies	—
TM39	Rock Tomb	Rock	Physical	50	80	10	Normal	○
TM42	Facade	Normal	Physical	70	100	20	Normal	○
TM43	Secret Power	Normal	Physical	70	100	20	Normal	○
TM44	Rest	Psychic	Status	—	—	10	Self	—
TM45	Attract	Normal	Status	—	100	15	Normal	—
TM52	Focus Blast	Fighting	Special	120	70	5	Normal	—
TM56	Fling	Dark	Physical	—	100	10	Normal	○
TM58	Endure	Normal	Status	—	—	10	Self	—
TM60	Drain Punch	Fighting	Physical	60	100	5	Normal	○
TM67	Recycle	Normal	Status	—	—	10	Self	—
TM70	Flash	Normal	Status	—	100	20	Normal	—
TM77	Psych Up	Normal	Status	—	—	10	Normal	—
TM78	Captivate	Normal	Status	—	100	20	2 Foes	—
TM80	Rock Slide	Rock	Physical	75	90	10	2 Foes	—
TM82	Sleep Talk	Normal	Status	—	—	10	Depends	—
TM83	Natural Gift	Normal	Physical	—	100	15	Normal	—
TM84	Poison Jab	Poison	Physical	80	100	20	Normal	—
TM85	Dream Eater	Psychic	Special	100	100	15	Normal	—
TM86	Grass Knot	Grass	Special	—	100	20	Normal	—
TM87	Swagger	Normal	Status	—	90	15	Normal	—
TM90	Substitute	Normal	Status	—	—	10	Self	—
HM04	Strength	Normal	Physical	80	100	15	Normal	○
HM06	Rock Smash	Fighting	Physical	40	100	15	Normal	○

● EGG MOVES

Name	Type	Kind	Pow.	Acc.	PP	Range	DA
Fire Punch	Fire	Physical	75	100	15	Normal	○
ThunderPunch	Electric	Physical	75	100	15	Normal	○
Ice Punch	Ice	Physical	75	100	15	Normal	○
Foresight	Normal	Status	—	—	40	Normal	—
Fake Out	Normal	Physical	40	100	10	Normal	○
Baton Pass	Normal	Status	—	—	40	Self	—
DynamicPunch	Fighting	Physical	100	50	5	Normal	○
Power Swap	Psychic	Status	—	—	10	Normal	—
Guard Swap	Psychic	Status	—	—	10	Normal	—
Psycho Cut	Psychic	Physical	70	100	20	Normal	○
Bullet Punch	Steel	Physical	40	100	30	Normal	○

● LEVEL-UP MOVES

Lv.	Name	Type	Kind	Pow.	Acc.	PP	Range	DA
1	Fire Punch	Fire	Physical	75	100	15	Normal	○
1	ThunderPunch	Electric	Physical	75	100	15	Normal	○
1	Ice Punch	Ice	Physical	75	100	15	Normal	○
1	Bide	Normal	Physical	—	—	10	Self	—
1	Meditate	Psychic	Status	—	—	40	Self	—
1	Confusion	Psychic	Special	50	100	25	Normal	—
1	Detect	Fighting	Status	—	—	5	Self	—
4	Meditate	Psychic	Status	—	—	40	Self	—
8	Confusion	Psychic	Special	50	100	25	Normal	—
11	Detect	Fighting	Status	—	—	5	Self	—
15	Hidden Power	Normal	Special	—	100	15	Normal	—
18	Mind Reader	Normal	Status	—	—	5	Normal	—
22	Feint	Normal	Physical	50	100	10	Normal	○
25	Calm Mind	Psychic	Status	—	—	20	Self	—
29	Force Palm	Fighting	Physical	60	100	10	Normal	○
32	Hi Jump Kick	Fighting	Physical	100	90	20	Normal	○
36	Psych Up	Normal	Status	—	—	10	Normal	—
42	Power Trick	Psychic	Status	—	—	10	Self	—
49	Reversal	Fighting	Physical	—	100	15	Normal	○
55	Recover	Normal	Status	—	—	10	Self	—

● MOVE MANIAC

Name	Type	Kind	Pow.	Acc.	PP	Range	DA
Headbutt	Normal	Physical	70	100	15	Normal	○

● BP MOVES

Name	Type	Kind	Pow.	Acc.	PP	Range	DA
ThunderPunch	Electric	Physical	75	100	15	Normal	○
Fire Punch	Fire	Physical	75	100	15	Normal	○
Ice Punch	Ice	Physical	75	100	15	Normal	○
Zen Headbutt	Psychic	Physical	80	90	15	Normal	○
Vacuum Wave	Fighting	Special	40	100	30	Normal	—
Trick	Psychic	Status	—	100	10	Normal	—
Snore	Normal	Special	40	100	15	Normal	—
Helping Hand	Normal	Status	—	—	20	1 Ally	—
Swift	Normal	Special	60	—	20	2 Foes	—
Gravity	Psychic	Status	—	—	5	All	—
Magic Coat	Psychic	Status	—	—	15	Self	—
Role Play	Psychic	Status	—	—	10	Normal	—
Mud-Slap	Ground	Special	20	100	10	Normal	—
Signal Beam	Bug	Special	75	100	15	Normal	—
Pain Split	Normal	Status	—	—	20	Normal	—
Low Kick	Fighting	Physical	—	100	20	Normal	○

● TM & HM MOVES

No.	Name	Type	Kind	Pow.	Acc.	PP	Range	DA
TM01	Focus Punch	Fighting	Physical	150	100	20	Normal	○
TM04	Calm Mind	Psychic	Status	—	—	20	Self	—
TM06	Toxic	Poison	Status	—	85	10	Normal	—
TM08	Bulk Up	Fighting	Status	—	—	20	Self	—
TM10	Hidden Power	Normal	Special	—	100	15	Normal	—
TM11	Sunny Day	Fire	Status	—	—	5	All	—
TM15	Hyper Beam	Normal	Special	150	90	5	Normal	—
TM16	Light Screen	Psychic	Status	—	—	30	2 Allies	—
TM17	Protect	Normal	Status	—	—	10	Self	—
TM18	Rain Dance	Water	Status	—	—	5	All	—
TM21	Frustration	Normal	Physical	—	100	20	Normal	○
TM27	Return	Normal	Physical	—	100	20	Normal	○
TM29	Psychic	Psychic	Special	90	100	10	Normal	—
TM30	Shadow Ball	Ghost	Special	80	100	15	Normal	—
TM31	Brick Break	Fighting	Physical	75	100	15	Normal	○
TM32	Double Team	Normal	Status	—	—	15	Self	—
TM33	Reflect	Psychic	Status	—	—	20	2 Allies	—
TM39	Rock Tomb	Rock	Physical	50	80	10	Normal	○
TM42	Facade	Normal	Physical	70	100	20	Normal	○
TM43	Secret Power	Normal	Physical	70	100	20	Normal	○
TM44	Rest	Psychic	Status	—	—	10	Self	—
TM45	Attract	Normal	Status	—	100	15	Normal	—
TM52	Focus Blast	Fighting	Special	120	70	5	Normal	—
TM53	Energy Ball	Grass	Special	80	100	10	Normal	—
TM56	Fling	Dark	Physical	—	100	10	Normal	○
TM58	Endure	Normal	Status	—	—	10	Self	—
TM60	Drain Punch	Fighting	Physical	60	100	5	Normal	○
TM67	Recycle	Normal	Status	—	—	10	Self	—
TM68	Giga Impact	Normal	Physical	150	90	5	Normal	○
TM70	Flash	Normal	Status	—	100	20	Normal	—
TM77	Psych Up	Normal	Status	—	—	10	Normal	—
TM78	Captivate	Normal	Status	—	100	20	2 Foes	—
TM80	Rock Slide	Rock	Physical	75	90	10	2 Foes	○
TM82	Sleep Talk	Normal	Status	—	—	10	Depends	—
TM83	Natural Gift	Normal	Physical	—	100	15	Normal	○
TM84	Poison Jab	Poison	Physical	80	100	20	Normal	○
TM85	Dream Eater	Psychic	Special	100	100	15	Normal	—
TM86	Grass Knot	Grass	Special	—	100	20	Normal	—
TM87	Swagger	Normal	Status	—	90	15	Normal	—
TM90	Substitute	Normal	Status	—	—	10	Self	—
HM04	Strength	Normal	Physical	80	100	15	Normal	○
HM06	Rock Smash	Fighting	Physical	40	100	15	Normal	○

No. 308 | Meditate Pokémon
Medicham

Fighting | Psychic

- **HEIGHT:** 4'03"
- **WEIGHT:** 69.4 lbs.
- **ITEMS:** None

● **SIZE COMPARISON**

● **MALE FORM**
Bigger extensions on head

● **FEMALE FORM**
Smaller extensions on head

◎ ABILITIES
● Pure Power

◎ STATS
- HP ●●
- ATTACK ●●●
- DEFENSE ●●●
- SP. ATTACK ●●●
- SP. DEFENSE ●●●
- SPEED ●●●●

◎ EGG GROUPS
Human-Like

◎ PERFORMANCE
- SPEED ★★☆
- POWER ★★
- SKILL ★★★★★
- STAMINA ★★☆
- JUMP ★★☆☆☆

● MAIN WAYS TO OBTAIN

Pokémon HeartGold
Safari Zone (Wasteland Area: if Forest objects are placed, may appear in tall grass)

Pokémon SoulSilver
Safari Zone (Wasteland Area: if Forest objects are placed, may appear in tall grass)

Pokémon Diamond — Route 217

Pokémon Pearl — Route 217

Pokémon Platinum — Mt. Coronet

Pokémon HeartGold
It meditates to heighten its inner energy and to float in the air. It eats one berry a day.

Pokémon SoulSilver
It meditates to heighten its inner energy and to float in the air. It eats one berry a day.

◎ EVOLUTION

Meditite

Lv. 37 →

Medicham

No. 309 | Lightning Pokémon
Electrike

Electric

- **HEIGHT:** 2'00"
- **WEIGHT:** 33.5 lbs.
- **ITEMS:** None

● SIZE COMPARISON

● MALE/FEMALE HAVE SAME FORM

ABILITIES
- Static
- Lightningrod

STATS
HP ●
ATTACK ●●
DEFENSE ●●
SP. ATTACK ●●●
SP. DEFENSE ●●
SPEED ●●●

EGG GROUPS
Field

PERFORMANCE
SPEED ★★★★☆   STAMINA ★★☆☆
POWER ★★☆☆   JUMP ★★☆☆
SKILL ★★☆☆

● MAIN WAYS TO OBTAIN

Pokémon HeartGold	Safari Zone (Rocky Beach Area: if Grass objects are placed, may appear in tall grass)
Pokémon SoulSilver	Safari Zone (Rocky Beach Area: if Grass objects are placed, may appear in tall grass)
Pokémon Diamond	Valley Windworks (mass outbreak)
Pokémon Pearl	Valley Windworks (mass outbreak)
Pokémon Platinum	Valley Windworks (mass outbreak)

Pokémon HeartGold	*Pokémon SoulSilver*
It stores electricity in its fur. It gives off sparks from all over its body in seasons when the air is dry.	It stores electricity in its fur. It gives off sparks from all over its body in seasons when the air is dry.

EVOLUTION

 Lv. 26

Electrike   Manectric

● LEVEL-UP MOVES

Lv.	Name	Type	Kind	Pow.	Acc.	PP	Range	DA
1	Tackle	Normal	Physical	35	95	35	Normal	○
4	Thunder Wave	Electric	Status	—	100	20	Normal	—
9	Leer	Normal	Status	—	100	30	2 Foes	—
12	Howl	Normal	Status	—	—	40	Self	—
17	Quick Attack	Normal	Physical	40	100	30	Normal	○
20	Spark	Electric	Physical	65	100	20	Normal	○
25	Odor Sleuth	Normal	Status	—	—	40	Normal	—
28	Bite	Dark	Physical	60	100	25	Normal	○
33	Thunder Fang	Electric	Physical	65	95	15	Normal	○
36	Roar	Normal	Status	—	100	20	Normal	—
41	Discharge	Electric	Special	80	100	15	2 Foes/1 Ally	—
44	Charge	Electric	Status	—	—	20	Self	—
49	Thunder	Electric	Special	120	70	10	Normal	—

● MOVE MANIAC

Name	Type	Kind	Pow.	Acc.	PP	Range	DA
Headbutt	Normal	Physical	70	100	15	Normal	○

● BP MOVES

Name	Type	Kind	Pow.	Acc.	PP	Range	DA
Snore	Normal	Special	40	100	15	Normal	—
Magnet Rise	Electric	Status	—	—	10	Self	—
Swift	Normal	Special	60	—	20	2 Foes	—
Mud-Slap	Ground	Special	20	100	10	Normal	—
Signal Beam	Bug	Special	75	100	15	Normal	—

● TM & HM MOVES

No.	Name	Type	Kind	Pow.	Acc.	PP	Range	DA
TM05	Roar	Normal	Status	—	100	20	Normal	—
TM06	Toxic	Poison	Status	—	85	10	Normal	—
TM10	Hidden Power	Normal	Special	—	100	15	Normal	—
TM16	Light Screen	Psychic	Status	—	—	30	2 Allies	—
TM17	Protect	Normal	Status	—	—	10	Self	—
TM18	Rain Dance	Water	Status	—	—	5	All	—
TM21	Frustration	Normal	Physical	—	100	20	Normal	○
TM23	Iron Tail	Steel	Physical	100	75	15	Normal	○
TM24	Thunderbolt	Electric	Special	95	100	15	Normal	—
TM25	Thunder	Electric	Special	120	70	10	Normal	—
TM27	Return	Normal	Physical	—	100	20	Normal	○
TM32	Double Team	Normal	Status	—	—	15	Self	—
TM34	Shock Wave	Electric	Special	60	—	20	Normal	—
TM35	Flamethrower	Fire	Special	95	100	15	Normal	—
TM42	Facade	Normal	Physical	70	100	20	Normal	○
TM43	Secret Power	Normal	Physical	70	100	20	Normal	○
TM44	Rest	Psychic	Status	—	—	10	Self	—
TM45	Attract	Normal	Status	—	100	15	Normal	—
TM46	Thief	Dark	Physical	40	100	10	Normal	○
TM57	Charge Beam	Electric	Special	50	90	10	Normal	—
TM58	Endure	Normal	Status	—	—	10	Self	—
TM70	Flash	Normal	Status	—	100	20	Normal	—
TM73	Thunder Wave	Electric	Status	—	100	20	Normal	—
TM78	Captivate	Normal	Status	—	100	20	2 Foes	—
TM82	Sleep Talk	Normal	Status	—	—	10	Depends	—
TM83	Natural Gift	Normal	Physical	—	100	15	Normal	—
TM87	Swagger	Normal	Status	—	90	15	Normal	—
TM90	Substitute	Normal	Status	—	—	10	Self	—
HM04	Strength	Normal	Physical	80	100	15	Normal	○

● EGG MOVES

Name	Type	Kind	Pow.	Acc.	PP	Range	DA
Crunch	Dark	Physical	80	100	15	Normal	○
Headbutt	Normal	Physical	70	100	15	Normal	○
Uproar	Normal	Special	50	100	10	1 Random	—
Curse	???	Status	—	—	10	Normal/Self	—
Swift	Normal	Special	60	—	20	2 Foes	—
Discharge	Electric	Special	80	100	15	2 Foes/1 Ally	—
Ice Fang	Ice	Physical	65	95	15	Normal	○
Fire Fang	Fire	Physical	65	95	15	Normal	○
Thunder Fang	Electric	Physical	65	95	15	Normal	○
Switcheroo	Dark	Status	—	100	10	Normal	—

● LEVEL-UP MOVES

Lv.	Name	Type	Kind	Pow.	Acc.	PP	Range	DA
1	Fire Fang	Fire	Physical	65	95	15	Normal	○
1	Tackle	Normal	Physical	35	95	35	Normal	○
1	Thunder Wave	Electric	Status	—	100	20	Normal	—
1	Leer	Normal	Status	—	100	30	2 Foes	—
1	Howl	Normal	Status	—	—	40	Self	—
4	Thunder Wave	Electric	Status	—	100	20	Normal	—
9	Leer	Normal	Status	—	100	30	2 Foes	—
12	Howl	Normal	Status	—	—	40	Self	—
17	Quick Attack	Normal	Physical	40	100	30	Normal	○
20	Spark	Electric	Physical	65	100	20	Normal	○
25	Odor Sleuth	Normal	Status	—	—	40	Normal	—
30	Bite	Dark	Physical	60	100	25	Normal	○
37	Thunder Fang	Electric	Physical	65	95	15	Normal	○
42	Roar	Normal	Status	—	100	20	Normal	—
49	Discharge	Electric	Special	80	100	15	2 Foes/1 Ally	—
54	Charge	Electric	Status	—	—	20	Self	—
61	Thunder	Electric	Special	120	70	10	Normal	—

● MOVE MANIAC

Name	Type	Kind	Pow.	Acc.	PP	Range	DA
Headbutt	Normal	Physical	70	100	15	Normal	○

● BP MOVES

Name	Type	Kind	Pow.	Acc.	PP	Range	DA
Snore	Normal	Special	40	100	15	Normal	—
Magnet Rise	Electric	Status	—	—	10	Self	—
Swift	Normal	Special	60	—	20	2 Foes	—
Mud-Slap	Ground	Special	20	100	10	Normal	—
Signal Beam	Bug	Special	75	100	15	Normal	—

● TM & HM MOVES

No.	Name	Type	Kind	Pow.	Acc.	PP	Range	DA
TM05	Roar	Normal	Status	—	100	20	Normal	—
TM06	Toxic	Poison	Status	—	85	10	Normal	—
TM10	Hidden Power	Normal	Special	—	100	15	Normal	—
TM15	Hyper Beam	Normal	Special	150	90	5	Normal	—
TM16	Light Screen	Psychic	Status	—	—	30	2 Allies	—
TM17	Protect	Normal	Status	—	—	10	Self	—
TM18	Rain Dance	Water	Status	—	—	5	All	—
TM21	Frustration	Normal	Physical	—	100	20	Normal	○
TM23	Iron Tail	Steel	Physical	100	75	15	Normal	○
TM24	Thunderbolt	Electric	Special	95	100	15	Normal	—
TM25	Thunder	Electric	Special	120	70	10	Normal	—
TM27	Return	Normal	Physical	—	100	20	Normal	○
TM32	Double Team	Normal	Status	—	—	15	Self	—
TM34	Shock Wave	Electric	Special	60	—	20	Normal	—
TM35	Flamethrower	Fire	Special	95	100	15	Normal	—
TM42	Facade	Normal	Physical	70	100	20	Normal	○
TM43	Secret Power	Normal	Physical	70	100	20	Normal	○
TM44	Rest	Psychic	Status	—	—	10	Self	—
TM45	Attract	Normal	Status	—	100	15	Normal	—
TM46	Thief	Dark	Physical	40	100	10	Normal	○
TM50	Overheat	Fire	Special	140	90	5	Normal	—
TM57	Charge Beam	Electric	Special	50	90	10	Normal	—
TM58	Endure	Normal	Status	—	—	10	Self	—
TM68	Giga Impact	Normal	Physical	150	90	5	Normal	○
TM70	Flash	Normal	Status	—	100	20	Normal	—
TM73	Thunder Wave	Electric	Status	—	100	20	Normal	—
TM78	Captivate	Normal	Status	—	100	20	2 Foes	—
TM82	Sleep Talk	Normal	Status	—	—	10	Depends	—
TM83	Natural Gift	Normal	Physical	—	100	15	Normal	—
TM87	Swagger	Normal	Status	—	90	15	Normal	—
TM90	Substitute	Normal	Status	—	—	10	Self	—
HM04	Strength	Normal	Physical	80	100	15	Normal	○

● **HEIGHT:** 4'11"
● **WEIGHT:** 88.6 lbs.
● **ITEMS:** None

● SIZE COMPARISON

● MALE/FEMALE HAVE SAME FORM

⊙ ABILITIES

● Static
● Lightningrod

⊙ STATS

HP	●●●
ATTACK	●●●
DEFENSE	●●
SP. ATTACK	●●●●●
SP. DEFENSE	●●●
SPEED	●●●●●

⊙ EGG GROUPS

Field

⊙ PERFORMANCE

SPEED ★★★★☆   STAMINA ★★★
POWER ★★★   JUMP ★★★☆
SKILL ★★★★

● MAIN WAYS TO OBTAIN

Pokémon HeartGold — Safari Zone (Wasteland Area: if Grass objects are placed, may appear in tall grass)

Pokémon SoulSilver — Safari Zone (Wasteland Area: if Grass objects are placed, may appear in tall grass)

Pokémon Diamond — Level up Electrike to Lv. 26

Pokémon Pearl — Level up Electrike to Lv. 26

Pokémon Platinum — Level up Electrike to Lv. 26

Pokémon HeartGold
Its nest can be found where a thunderbolt hits. It is discharging electricity from its mane.

Pokémon SoulSilver
Its nest can be found where a thunderbolt hits. It is discharging electricity from its mane.

⊙ EVOLUTION

Lv. **26**

Electrike → Manectric

◉ No. 311 | Cheering Pokémon
Plusle

Electric

- ●HEIGHT: 1'04"
- ●WEIGHT: 9.3 lbs.
- ●ITEMS: None

● SIZE COMPARISON

●MALE/FEMALE HAVE SAME FORM

◉ ABILITIES
● Plus

◉ STATS
- HP ●●
- ATTACK ●●
- DEFENSE ●●
- SP. ATTACK ●●●●
- SP. DEFENSE ●●●●
- SPEED ●●●●

◉ EGG GROUPS
Fairy

◉ PERFORMANCE
SPEED ★★★★	STAMINA ★★★☆
POWER ★★	JUMP ★★★☆
SKILL ★★	

● MAIN WAYS TO OBTAIN

Pokémon HeartGold	Route 29 (Hoenn Sound)
Pokémon SoulSilver	Route 29 (Hoenn Sound)
Pokémon Diamond	Trophy Garden at the Pokémon Mansion on Route 212 [after obtaining the National Pokédex, talk to Mr. Backlot]
Pokémon Pearl	Trophy Garden at the Pokémon Mansion on Route 212 [after obtaining the National Pokédex, talk to Mr. Backlot]
Pokémon Platinum	Trophy Garden at the Pokémon Mansion on Route 212 [after obtaining the National Pokédex, talk to Mr. Backlot]

Pokémon HeartGold	Pokémon SoulSilver
It absorbs electricity from telephone poles. It shorts out its body to create crackling noises.	It absorbs electricity from telephone poles. It shorts out its body to create crackling noises.

◉ EVOLUTION
Does not evolve

● LEVEL-UP MOVES
Lv.	Name	Type	Kind	Pow.	Acc.	PP	Range	DA
1	Growl	Normal	Status	—	100	40	2 Foes	—
3	Thunder Wave	Electric	Status	—	100	20	Normal	—
7	Quick Attack	Normal	Physical	40	100	30	Normal	○
10	Helping Hand	Normal	Status	—	—	20	1 Ally	—
15	Spark	Electric	Physical	65	100	20	Normal	○
17	Encore	Normal	Status	—	100	5	Normal	—
21	Fake Tears	Dark	Status	—	100	20	Normal	—
24	Copycat	Normal	Status	—	—	20	Depends	—
29	Swift	Normal	Special	60	—	20	2 Foes	—
31	Fake Tears	Dark	Status	—	100	20	Normal	—
35	Charge	Electric	Status	—	—	20	Self	—
38	Thunder	Electric	Special	120	70	10	Normal	—
42	Baton Pass	Normal	Status	—	—	40	Self	—
44	Agility	Psychic	Status	—	—	30	Self	—
48	Last Resort	Normal	Physical	130	100	5	Normal	○
51	Nasty Plot	Dark	Status	—	—	20	Self	—

● MOVE MANIAC
Name	Type	Kind	Pow.	Acc.	PP	Range	DA
Headbutt	Normal	Physical	70	100	15	Normal	○

● BP MOVES
Name	Type	Kind	Pow.	Acc.	PP	Range	DA
ThunderPunch	Electric	Physical	75	100	15	Normal	○
Snore	Normal	Special	40	100	15	Normal	—
Helping Hand	Normal	Status	—	—	20	1 Ally	—
Magnet Rise	Electric	Status	—	—	10	Self	—
Last Resort	Normal	Physical	130	100	5	Normal	○
Swift	Normal	Special	60	—	20	2 Foes	—
Uproar	Normal	Special	50	100	10	1 Random	—
Mud-Slap	Ground	Special	20	100	10	Normal	—
Rollout	Rock	Physical	30	90	20	Normal	○
Signal Beam	Bug	Special	75	100	15	Normal	—

● TM & HM MOVES
No.	Name	Type	Kind	Pow.	Acc.	PP	Range	DA
TM06	Toxic	Poison	Status	—	85	10	Normal	—
TM10	Hidden Power	Normal	Special	—	100	15	Normal	—
TM16	Light Screen	Psychic	Status	—	—	30	2 Allies	—
TM17	Protect	Normal	Status	—	—	10	Self	—
TM18	Rain Dance	Water	Status	—	—	5	All	—
TM21	Frustration	Normal	Physical	100	75	15	Normal	○
TM23	Iron Tail	Steel	Physical	100	75	15	Normal	○
TM24	Thunderbolt	Electric	Special	95	100	15	Normal	—
TM25	Thunder	Electric	Special	120	70	10	Normal	—
TM27	Return	Normal	Physical	—	100	20	Normal	○
TM32	Double Team	Normal	Status	—	—	15	Self	—
TM34	Shock Wave	Electric	Special	60	—	20	Normal	—
TM42	Facade	Normal	Physical	70	100	20	Normal	○
TM43	Secret Power	Normal	Physical	70	100	20	Normal	—
TM44	Rest	Psychic	Status	—	—	10	Self	—
TM45	Attract	Normal	Status	—	100	15	Normal	—
TM56	Fling	Dark	Physical	—	100	10	Normal	—
TM57	Charge Beam	Electric	Special	50	90	10	Normal	—
TM58	Endure	Normal	Status	—	—	10	Self	—
TM70	Flash	Normal	Status	—	100	20	Normal	—
TM73	Thunder Wave	Electric	Status	—	100	20	Normal	—
TM78	Captivate	Normal	Status	—	100	20	2 Foes	—
TM82	Sleep Talk	Normal	Status	—	—	10	Depends	—
TM83	Natural Gift	Normal	Physical	—	100	15	Normal	—
TM86	Grass Knot	Grass	Special	—	100	20	Normal	○
TM87	Swagger	Normal	Status	—	90	15	Normal	—
TM90	Substitute	Normal	Status	—	—	10	Self	—

● EGG MOVES
Name	Type	Kind	Pow.	Acc.	PP	Range	DA
Substitute	Normal	Status	—	—	10	Self	—
Wish	Normal	Status	—	—	10	Self	—
Sing	Normal	Status	—	55	15	Normal	—
Sweet Kiss	Normal	Status	—	75	10	Normal	—
Discharge	Electric	Special	80	100	15	2 Foes/1 Ally	—

● LEVEL-UP MOVES

Lv.	Name	Type	Kind	Pow.	Acc.	PP	Range	DA
1	Growl	Normal	Status	—	100	40	2 Foes	—
3	Thunder Wave	Electric	Status	—	100	20	Normal	—
7	Quick Attack	Normal	Physical	40	100	30	Normal	○
10	Helping Hand	Normal	Status	—	—	20	1 Ally	—
15	Spark	Electric	Physical	65	100	20	Normal	○
17	Encore	Normal	Status	—	100	5	Normal	—
21	Charm	Normal	Status	—	100	20	Normal	—
24	Copycat	Normal	Status	—	—	20	Depends	—
29	Swift	Normal	Special	60	—	20	2 Foes	—
31	Fake Tears	Dark	Status	—	100	20	Normal	—
35	Charge	Electric	Status	—	—	20	Self	—
38	Thunder	Electric	Special	120	70	10	Normal	—
42	Baton Pass	Normal	Status	—	—	40	Self	—
44	Agility	Psychic	Status	—	—	30	Self	—
48	Trump Card	Normal	Special	—	—	5	Normal	○
51	Nasty Plot	Dark	Status	—	—	20	Self	—

● MOVE MANIAC

Name	Type	Kind	Pow.	Acc.	PP	Range	DA
Headbutt	Normal	Physical	70	100	15	Normal	○

● BP MOVES

Name	Type	Kind	Pow.	Acc.	PP	Range	DA
ThunderPunch	Electric	Physical	75	100	15	Normal	○
Snore	Normal	Special	40	100	15	Normal	—
Helping Hand	Normal	Status	—	—	20	1 Ally	—
Magnet Rise	Electric	Status	—	—	10	Self	—
Last Resort	Normal	Physical	130	100	5	Normal	○
Swift	Normal	Special	60	—	20	2 Foes	—
Uproar	Normal	Special	50	100	10	1 Random	—
Mud-Slap	Ground	Special	20	100	10	Normal	—
Rollout	Rock	Physical	30	90	20	Normal	○
Signal Beam	Bug	Special	75	100	15	Normal	—

● TM & HM MOVES

No.	Name	Type	Kind	Pow.	Acc.	PP	Range	DA
TM06	Toxic	Poison	Status	—	85	10	Normal	—
TM10	Hidden Power	Normal	Special	—	100	15	Normal	—
TM16	Light Screen	Psychic	Status	—	—	30	2 Allies	—
TM17	Protect	Normal	Status	—	—	10	Self	—
TM18	Rain Dance	Water	Status	—	—	5	All	—
TM21	Frustration	Normal	Physical	—	100	20	Normal	○
TM23	Iron Tail	Steel	Physical	100	75	15	Normal	○
TM24	Thunderbolt	Electric	Special	95	100	15	Normal	—
TM25	Thunder	Electric	Special	120	70	10	Normal	—
TM27	Return	Normal	Physical	—	100	20	Normal	○
TM32	Double Team	Normal	Status	—	—	15	Self	—
TM34	Shock Wave	Electric	Special	60	—	20	Normal	—
TM42	Facade	Normal	Physical	70	100	20	Normal	○
TM43	Secret Power	Normal	Physical	70	100	20	Normal	—
TM44	Rest	Psychic	Status	—	—	10	Self	—
TM45	Attract	Normal	Status	—	100	15	Normal	—
TM56	Fling	Dark	Physical	—	100	10	Normal	—
TM57	Charge Beam	Electric	Special	50	90	10	Normal	—
TM58	Endure	Normal	Status	—	—	10	Self	—
TM70	Flash	Normal	Status	—	100	20	Normal	—
TM73	Thunder Wave	Electric	Status	—	100	20	Normal	—
TM78	Captivate	Normal	Status	—	100	20	2 Foes	—
TM82	Sleep Talk	Normal	Status	—	—	10	Depends	—
TM83	Natural Gift	Normal	Physical	—	100	15	Normal	—
TM86	Grass Knot	Grass	Special	—	100	20	Normal	○
TM87	Swagger	Normal	Status	—	90	15	Normal	—
TM90	Substitute	Normal	Status	—	—	10	Self	—

● EGG MOVES

Name	Type	Kind	Pow.	Acc.	PP	Range	DA
Substitute	Normal	Status	—	—	10	Self	—
Wish	Normal	Status	—	—	10	Self	—
Sing	Normal	Status	—	55	10	Normal	—
Sweet Kiss	Normal	Status	—	75	10	Normal	—
Discharge	Electric	Special	80	100	15	2 Foes/1 Ally	—

⊙ No. 312 | Cheering Pokémon
Minun

Electric

- **HEIGHT:** 1'04"
- **WEIGHT:** 9.3 lbs.
- **ITEMS:** None

● SIZE COMPARISON

● MALE/FEMALE HAVE SAME FORM

⊙ ABILITIES
● Minus

⊙ STATS
HP ●●
ATTACK ●●
DEFENSE ●●
SP. ATTACK ●●
SP. DEFENSE ●●●
SPEED ●●●●

⊙ EGG GROUPS
Fairy

⊙ PERFORMANCE
SPEED ★★★★　　STAMINA ★★☆
POWER ★★　　　JUMP ★★★☆
SKILL ★★

● MAIN WAYS TO OBTAIN

Pokémon HeartGold — Route 29 (Hoenn Sound)

Pokémon SoulSilver — Route 29 (Hoenn Sound)

Pokémon Diamond — Trophy Garden at the Pokémon Mansion on Route 212 (after obtaining the National Pokédex, talk to Mr. Backlot)

Pokémon Pearl — Trophy Garden at the Pokémon Mansion on Route 212 (after obtaining the National Pokédex, talk to Mr. Backlot)

Pokémon Platinum — Trophy Garden at the Pokémon Mansion on Route 212 (after obtaining the National Pokédex, talk to Mr. Backlot)

Pokémon HeartGold — Exposure to electricity from MINUN and PLUSLE promotes blood circulation and relaxes muscles.

Pokémon SoulSilver — Exposure to electricity from MINUN and PLUSLE promotes blood circulation and relaxes muscles.

⊙ EVOLUTION
Does not evolve

● No. 313 | Firefly Pokémon
Volbeat

Bug

- **HEIGHT:** 2'04"
- **WEIGHT:** 39.0 lbs.
- **ITEMS:** None

● SIZE COMPARISON

● MALE FORM

● ABILITIES
- Illuminate
- Swarm

● STATS
- HP ●●
- ATTACK ●●●
- DEFENSE ●●●
- SP. ATTACK ●●●
- SP. DEFENSE ●●●
- SPEED ●●●●

● EGG GROUPS
Bug

Human-Like

● PERFORMANCE
SPEED ★★★☆	STAMINA ★★☆
POWER ★★★	JUMP ★★★★★
SKILL ★★	

● MAIN WAYS TO OBTAIN

Pokémon HeartGold	Bug-Catching Contest at the National Park (after obtaining the National Pokédex / Thursday)
Pokémon SoulSilver	Bug-Catching Contest at the National Park (after obtaining the National Pokédex / Thursday)
Pokémon Diamond	Route 229
Pokémon Pearl	Route 229
Pokémon Platinum	Route 229

Pokémon HeartGold	Pokémon SoulSilver
It emits light from its tail to communicate. It loves the sweet aroma given off by ILLUMISE.	It emits light from its tail to communicate. It loves the sweet aroma given off by ILLUMISE.

● EVOLUTION
Does not evolve

● LEVEL-UP MOVES
Lv.	Name	Type	Kind	Pow.	Acc.	PP	Range	DA
1	Flash	Normal	Status	—	100	20	Normal	—
1	Tackle	Normal	Physical	35	95	35	Normal	○
5	Double Team	Normal	Status	—	—	15	Self	—
9	Confuse Ray	Ghost	Status	—	100	10	Normal	—
13	Moonlight	Normal	Status	—	⌣	5	Self	—
17	Quick Attack	Normal	Physical	40	100	30	Normal	○
21	Tail Glow	Bug	Status	—	—	20	Self	—
25	Signal Beam	Bug	Special	75	100	15	Normal	—
29	Protect	Normal	Status	—	—	10	Self	—
33	Helping Hand	Normal	Status	—	—	20	1 Ally	—
37	Zen Headbutt	Psychic	Physical	80	90	15	Normal	○
41	Bug Buzz	Bug	Special	90	100	10	Normal	—
45	Double-Edge	Normal	Physical	120	100	15	Normal	○

● MOVE MANIAC
Name	Type	Kind	Pow.	Acc.	PP	Range	DA

● BP MOVES
Name	Type	Kind	Pow.	Acc.	PP	Range	DA
ThunderPunch	Electric	Physical	75	100	15	Normal	○
Ice Punch	Ice	Physical	75	100	15	Normal	○
Ominous Wind	Ghost	Special	60	100	5	Normal	—
Air Cutter	Flying	Special	55	95	25	2 Foes	—
Zen Headbutt	Psychic	Physical	80	90	15	Normal	○
Bug Bite	Bug	Physical	60	100	20	Normal	○
Snore	Normal	Special	40	100	15	Normal	—
Helping Hand	Normal	Status	—	—	20	1 Ally	—
Swift	Normal	Special	60	—	20	2 Foes	—
String Shot	Bug	Status	—	95	40	2 Foes	—
Tailwind	Flying	Status	—	—	30	2 Allies	—
Mud-Slap	Ground	Special	20	100	10	Normal	—
Signal Beam	Bug	Special	75	100	15	Normal	—

● TM & HM MOVES
No.	Name	Type	Kind	Pow.	Acc.	PP	Range	DA
TM01	Focus Punch	Fighting	Physical	150	100	20	Normal	○
TM03	Water Pulse	Water	Special	60	100	20	Normal	—
TM06	Toxic	Poison	Status	—	85	10	Normal	—
TM10	Hidden Power	Normal	Special	—	100	15	Normal	—
TM11	Sunny Day	Fire	Status	—	—	5	All	—
TM16	Light Screen	Psychic	Status	—	—	30	2 Allies	—
TM17	Protect	Normal	Status	—	—	10	Self	—
TM18	Rain Dance	Water	Status	—	—	5	All	—
TM19	Giga Drain	Grass	Special	60	100	10	Normal	—
TM21	Frustration	Normal	Physical	—	100	20	Normal	○
TM22	SolarBeam	Grass	Special	120	100	10	Normal	—
TM24	Thunderbolt	Electric	Special	95	100	15	Normal	—
TM25	Thunder	Electric	Special	120	70	10	Normal	—
TM27	Return	Normal	Physical	—	100	20	Normal	○
TM30	Shadow Ball	Ghost	Special	80	100	15	Normal	—
TM31	Brick Break	Fighting	Physical	75	100	15	Normal	○
TM32	Double Team	Normal	Status	—	—	15	Self	—
TM34	Shock Wave	Electric	Special	60	—	20	Normal	—
TM40	Aerial Ace	Flying	Physical	60	—	20	Normal	○
TM42	Facade	Normal	Physical	70	100	20	Normal	○
TM43	Secret Power	Normal	Physical	70	100	20	Normal	—
TM44	Rest	Psychic	Status	—	—	10	Self	—
TM45	Attract	Normal	Status	—	100	15	Normal	—
TM46	Thief	Dark	Physical	40	100	10	Normal	○
TM51	Roost	Flying	Status	—	—	10	Self	—
TM56	Fling	Dark	Physical	—	100	10	Normal	○
TM57	Charge Beam	Electric	Special	50	90	10	Normal	—
TM58	Endure	Normal	Status	—	—	10	Self	—
TM62	Silver Wind	Bug	Special	60	100	5	Normal	—
TM70	Flash	Normal	Status	—	100	20	Normal	—
TM73	Thunder Wave	Electric	Status	—	100	20	Normal	—
TM77	Psych Up	Normal	Status	—	—	10	Normal	—
TM78	Captivate	Normal	Status	—	100	20	2 Foes	—
TM82	Sleep Talk	Normal	Status	—	—	10	Depends	—
TM83	Natural Gift	Normal	Physical	—	100	15	Normal	—
TM87	Swagger	Normal	Status	—	90	15	Normal	—
TM89	U-turn	Bug	Physical	70	100	20	Normal	○
TM90	Substitute	Normal	Status	—	—	10	Self	—

● EGG MOVES
Name	Type	Kind	Pow.	Acc.	PP	Range	DA
Baton Pass	Normal	Status	—	—	40	Self	—
Silver Wind	Bug	Special	60	100	5	Normal	—
Trick	Psychic	Status	—	100	10	Normal	—
Encore	Normal	Status	—	100	5	Normal	—
Bug Buzz	Bug	Special	90	100	10	Normal	—

● LEVEL-UP MOVES

Lv.	Name	Type	Kind	Pow.	Acc.	PP	Range	DA
1	Tackle	Normal	Physical	35	95	35	Normal	○
5	Sweet Scent	Normal	Status	—	100	20	2 Foes	—
9	Charm	Normal	Status	—	100	20	Normal	—
13	Moonlight	Normal	Status	—	—	5	Self	—
17	Quick Attack	Normal	Physical	40	100	30	Normal	○
21	Wish	Normal	Status	—	—	10	Self	—
25	Encore	Normal	Status	—	100	5	Normal	—
29	Flatter	Dark	Status	—	100	15	Normal	—
33	Helping Hand	Normal	Status	—	—	20	1 Ally	—
37	Zen Headbutt	Psychic	Physical	80	90	15	Normal	○
41	Bug Buzz	Bug	Special	90	100	10	Normal	—
45	Covet	Normal	Physical	40	100	40	Normal	○

● MOVE MANIAC

Name	Type	Kind	Pow.	Acc.	PP	Range	DA

● BP MOVES

Name	Type	Kind	Pow.	Acc.	PP	Range	DA
ThunderPunch	Electric	Physical	75	100	15	Normal	○
Ice Punch	Ice	Physical	75	100	15	Normal	○
Ominous Wind	Ghost	Special	60	100	5	Normal	—
Air Cutter	Flying	Special	55	95	25	2 Foes	—
Zen Headbutt	Psychic	Physical	80	90	15	Normal	○
Bug Bite	Bug	Physical	60	100	20	Normal	○
Snore	Normal	Special	40	100	15	Normal	—
Helping Hand	Normal	Status	—	—	20	1 Ally	—
Swift	Normal	Special	60	—	20	2 Foes	—
String Shot	Bug	Status	—	95	40	2 Foes	—
Tailwind	Flying	Status	—	—	30	2 Allies	—
Mud-Slap	Ground	Special	20	100	10	Normal	—

● TM & HM MOVES

No.	Name	Type	Kind	Pow.	Acc.	PP	Range	DA
TM01	Focus Punch	Fighting	Physical	150	100	20	Normal	○
TM03	Water Pulse	Water	Special	60	100	20	Normal	—
TM06	Toxic	Poison	Status	—	85	10	Normal	—
TM10	Hidden Power	Normal	Special	—	100	15	Normal	—
TM11	Sunny Day	Fire	Status	—	—	5	All	—
TM16	Light Screen	Psychic	Status	—	—	30	2 Allies	—
TM17	Protect	Normal	Status	—	—	10	Self	—
TM18	Rain Dance	Water	Status	—	—	5	All	—
TM19	Giga Drain	Grass	Special	60	100	10	Normal	—
TM21	Frustration	Normal	Physical	—	100	20	Normal	○
TM22	SolarBeam	Grass	Special	120	100	10	Normal	—
TM24	Thunderbolt	Electric	Special	95	100	15	Normal	—
TM25	Thunder	Electric	Special	120	70	10	Normal	—
TM27	Return	Normal	Physical	—	100	20	Normal	○
TM30	Shadow Ball	Ghost	Special	80	100	15	Normal	—
TM31	Brick Break	Fighting	Physical	75	100	15	Normal	○
TM32	Double Team	Normal	Status	—	—	15	Self	—
TM34	Shock Wave	Electric	Special	60	—	20	Normal	—
TM40	Aerial Ace	Flying	Physical	60	—	20	Normal	○
TM42	Facade	Normal	Physical	70	100	20	Normal	○
TM43	Secret Power	Normal	Physical	70	100	20	Normal	○
TM44	Rest	Psychic	Status	—	—	10	Self	—
TM45	Attract	Normal	Status	—	100	15	Normal	—
TM46	Thief	Dark	Physical	40	100	10	Normal	○
TM51	Roost	Flying	Status	—	—	10	Self	—
TM56	Fling	Dark	Physical	—	100	10	Normal	—
TM57	Charge Beam	Electric	Special	50	90	10	Normal	—
TM58	Endure	Normal	Status	—	—	10	Self	—
TM62	Silver Wind	Bug	Special	60	100	5	Normal	—
TM70	Flash	Normal	Status	—	100	20	Normal	—
TM73	Thunder Wave	Electric	Status	—	100	20	Normal	—
TM77	Psych Up	Normal	Status	—	—	10	Normal	—
TM78	Captivate	Normal	Status	—	100	20	2 Foes	—
TM82	Sleep Talk	Normal	Status	—	—	10	Depends	—
TM83	Natural Gift	Normal	Physical	—	100	15	Normal	—
TM87	Swagger	Normal	Status	—	90	15	Normal	—
TM89	U-turn	Bug	Physical	70	100	20	Normal	○
TM90	Substitute	Normal	Status	—	—	10	Self	—

● EGG MOVES

Name	Type	Kind	Pow.	Acc.	PP	Range	DA
Baton Pass	Normal	Status	—	—	40	Self	—
Silver Wind	Bug	Special	60	100	5	Normal	—
Growth	Normal	Status	—	—	40	Self	—
Encore	Normal	Status	—	100	5	Normal	—
Bug Buzz	Bug	Special	90	100	10	Normal	—

◎ No. **314** | Firefly Pokémon
Illumise

Bug

- ● **HEIGHT:** 2'00"
- ● **WEIGHT:** 39.0 lbs.
- ● **ITEMS:** None

● SIZE COMPARISON

● **FEMALE FORM**

◎ **ABILITIES**
- ● Oblivious
- ● Tinted Lens

◎ **STATS**
HP ●●
ATTACK ●●
DEFENSE ●●
SP. ATTACK ●●
SP. DEFENSE ●●●
SPEED ●●●●

◎ **EGG GROUPS**
Bug
Human-Like

◎ **PERFORMANCE**
SPEED ★★★☆ STAMINA ★★★
POWER ★★ JUMP ★★★★★
SKILL ★★★

● **MAIN WAYS TO OBTAIN**

Pokémon HeartGold	Bug-Catching Contest at the National Park [after obtaining the National Pokédex / Saturday]
Pokémon SoulSilver	Bug-Catching Contest at the National Park [after obtaining the National Pokédex / Saturday]
Pokémon Diamond	Route 229
Pokémon Pearl	Route 229
Pokémon Platinum	Route 229

Pokémon HeartGold	Pokémon SoulSilver
Its fragrance attracts a swarm of VOLBEAT, so they draw over 200 patterns in the night sky.	Its fragrance attracts a swarm of VOLBEAT, so they draw over 200 patterns in the night sky.

◎ **EVOLUTION**

Does not evolve

◉ No. 315 | Thorn Pokémon
Roselia

Grass | Poison

● **HEIGHT:** 1'00"
● **WEIGHT:** 4.4 lbs.
● **ITEMS:** Poison Barb

● SIZE COMPARISON

● **MALE FORM**
Smaller leaf on chest

● **FEMALE FORM**
Larger leaf on chest

◉ ABILITIES
● Natural Cure
● Poison Point

◉ STATS
HP	●●
ATTACK	●●●
DEFENSE	●●●
SP. ATTACK	●●●●
SP. DEFENSE	●●●
SPEED	●●●

◉ EGG GROUPS
Fairy

Grass

◉ PERFORMANCE
SPEED ★★★   STAMINA ★★☆
POWER ★★☆   JUMP ★★★
SKILL ★★★★☆

● MAIN WAYS TO OBTAIN

Pokémon HeartGold	Safari Zone (Marshland Area: if Forest objects are placed, may appear in tall grass)
Pokémon SoulSilver	Safari Zone (Marshland Area: if Forest objects are placed, may appear in tall grass)
Pokémon Diamond	Route 212
Pokémon Pearl	Route 212
Pokémon Platinum	Route 208

Pokémon HeartGold	*Pokémon SoulSilver*
ROSELIA that drink nutritionally rich springwater are said to reveal rare coloration when they bloom.	ROSELIA that drink nutritionally rich springwater are said to reveal rare coloration when they bloom.

◉ EVOLUTION

Level it up with high friendship between 4:00 A.M. and 8:00 P.M.

Budew → Roselia → (Use Shiny Stone) → Roserade

● LEVEL-UP MOVES
Lv.	Name	Type	Kind	Pow.	Acc.	PP	Range	DA
1	Absorb	Grass	Special	20	100	25	Normal	—
4	Growth	Normal	Status	—	—	40	Self	—
7	Poison Sting	Poison	Physical	15	100	35	Normal	—
10	Stun Spore	Grass	Status	—	75	30	Normal	—
13	Mega Drain	Grass	Special	40	100	15	Normal	—
16	Leech Seed	Grass	Status	—	90	10	Normal	—
19	Magical Leaf	Grass	Special	60	—	20	Normal	—
22	GrassWhistle	Grass	Status	—	55	15	Normal	—
25	Giga Drain	Grass	Special	60	100	10	Normal	—
28	Toxic Spikes	Poison	Status	—	—	20	2 Foes	—
31	Sweet Scent	Normal	Status	—	100	20	2 Foes	—
34	Ingrain	Grass	Status	—	—	20	Self	—
37	Toxic	Poison	Status	—	85	10	Normal	—
40	Petal Dance	Grass	Special	90	100	20	1 Random	○
43	Aromatherapy	Grass	Status	—	—	5	All Allies	—
46	Synthesis	Grass	Status	—	—	5	Self	—

● MOVE MANIAC
Name	Type	Kind	Pow.	Acc.	PP	Range	DA

● BP MOVES
Name	Type	Kind	Pow.	Acc.	PP	Range	DA
Fury Cutter	Bug	Physical	10	95	20	Normal	○
Snore	Normal	Special	40	100	15	Normal	—
Synthesis	Grass	Status	—	—	5	Self	—
Swift	Normal	Special	60	—	20	2 Foes	—
Worry Seed	Grass	Status	—	100	10	Normal	—
Mud-Slap	Ground	Special	20	100	10	Normal	—
Seed Bomb	Grass	Physical	80	100	15	Normal	—

● TM & HM MOVES
No.	Name	Type	Kind	Pow.	Acc.	PP	Range	DA
TM06	Toxic	Poison	Status	—	85	10	Normal	—
TM09	Bullet Seed	Grass	Physical	10	100	30	Normal	—
TM10	Hidden Power	Normal	Special	—	100	15	Normal	—
TM11	Sunny Day	Fire	Status	—	—	5	All	—
TM17	Protect	Normal	Status	—	—	10	Self	—
TM18	Rain Dance	Water	Status	—	—	5	All	—
TM19	Giga Drain	Grass	Special	60	100	10	Normal	—
TM21	Frustration	Normal	Physical	—	100	20	Normal	○
TM22	SolarBeam	Grass	Special	120	100	10	Normal	—
TM27	Return	Normal	Physical	—	100	20	Normal	○
TM30	Shadow Ball	Ghost	Special	80	100	15	Normal	—
TM32	Double Team	Normal	Status	—	—	15	Self	—
TM36	Sludge Bomb	Poison	Special	90	100	10	Normal	—
TM42	Facade	Normal	Physical	70	100	20	Normal	○
TM43	Secret Power	Normal	Physical	70	100	20	Normal	—
TM44	Rest	Psychic	Status	—	—	10	Self	—
TM45	Attract	Normal	Status	—	100	15	Normal	—
TM53	Energy Ball	Grass	Special	80	100	10	Normal	—
TM58	Endure	Normal	Status	—	—	10	Self	—
TM70	Flash	Normal	Status	—	100	20	Normal	—
TM75	Swords Dance	Normal	Status	—	—	30	Self	—
TM77	Psych Up	Normal	Status	—	—	10	Normal	—
TM78	Captivate	Normal	Status	—	100	20	2 Foes	—
TM82	Sleep Talk	Normal	Status	—	—	10	Depends	—
TM83	Natural Gift	Normal	Physical	—	100	15	Normal	—
TM84	Poison Jab	Poison	Physical	80	100	20	Normal	○
TM86	Grass Knot	Grass	Special	—	100	20	Normal	○
TM87	Swagger	Normal	Status	—	90	15	Normal	—
TM90	Substitute	Normal	Status	—	—	10	Self	—
HM01	Cut	Normal	Physical	50	95	30	Normal	○

● EGG MOVES
Name	Type	Kind	Pow.	Acc.	PP	Range	DA
Spikes	Ground	Status	—	—	20	2 Foes	—
Synthesis	Grass	Status	—	—	5	Self	—
Pin Missile	Bug	Physical	14	85	20	Normal	—
Cotton Spore	Grass	Status	—	85	40	Normal	—
Sleep Powder	Grass	Status	—	75	15	Normal	—
Razor Leaf	Grass	Physical	55	95	25	2 Foes	—
Mind Reader	Normal	Status	—	—	5	Normal	—
Leaf Storm	Grass	Special	140	90	5	Normal	—

● LEVEL-UP MOVES

Lv.	Name	Type	Kind	Pow.	Acc.	PP	Range	DA
1	Pound	Normal	Physical	40	100	35	Normal	○
6	Yawn	Normal	Status	—	—	10	Normal	—
9	Poison Gas	Poison	Status	—	55	40	Normal	—
14	Sludge	Poison	Special	65	100	20	Normal	—
17	Amnesia	Psychic	Status	—	—	20	Self	—
23	Encore	Normal	Status	—	100	5	Normal	—
28	Toxic	Poison	Status	—	85	10	Normal	—
34	Stockpile	Normal	Status	—	—	20	Self	—
34	Spit Up	Normal	Special	—	100	10	Normal	—
34	Swallow	Normal	Status	—	—	10	Self	—
39	Sludge Bomb	Poison	Special	90	100	10	Normal	—
44	Gastro Acid	Poison	Status	—	100	10	Normal	—
49	Wring Out	Normal	Special	—	100	5	Normal	○
54	Gunk Shot	Poison	Physical	120	70	5	Normal	—

● MOVE MANIAC

Name	Type	Kind	Pow.	Acc.	PP	Range	DA
Headbutt	Normal	Physical	70	100	15	Normal	○

● BP MOVES

Name	Type	Kind	Pow.	Acc.	PP	Range	DA
ThunderPunch	Electric	Physical	75	100	15	Normal	○
Fire Punch	Fire	Physical	75	100	15	Normal	○
Ice Punch	Ice	Physical	75	100	15	Normal	○
Snore	Normal	Special	40	100	15	Normal	—
Mud-Slap	Ground	Special	20	100	10	Normal	—
Rollout	Rock	Physical	30	90	20	Normal	○
Gastro Acid	Poison	Status	—	100	10	Normal	—
Gunk Shot	Poison	Physical	120	70	5	Normal	—
Seed Bomb	Grass	Physical	80	100	15	Normal	—
Pain Split	Normal	Status	—	—	20	Normal	—

● TM & HM MOVES

No.	Name	Type	Kind	Pow.	Acc.	PP	Range	DA
TM03	Water Pulse	Water	Special	60	100	20	Normal	—
TM06	Toxic	Poison	Status	—	85	10	Normal	—
TM09	Bullet Seed	Grass	Physical	10	100	30	Normal	—
TM10	Hidden Power	Normal	Special	—	100	15	Normal	—
TM11	Sunny Day	Fire	Status	—	—	5	All	—
TM13	Ice Beam	Ice	Special	95	100	10	Normal	—
TM17	Protect	Normal	Status	—	—	10	Self	—
TM18	Rain Dance	Water	Status	—	—	5	All	—
TM19	Giga Drain	Grass	Special	60	100	10	Normal	—
TM21	Frustration	Normal	Physical	—	100	20	Normal	○
TM22	SolarBeam	Grass	Special	120	100	10	Normal	—
TM27	Return	Normal	Physical	—	100	20	Normal	○
TM30	Shadow Ball	Ghost	Special	80	100	15	Normal	—
TM32	Double Team	Normal	Status	—	—	15	Self	—
TM34	Shock Wave	Electric	Special	60	—	20	Normal	—
TM36	Sludge Bomb	Poison	Special	90	100	10	Normal	—
TM42	Facade	Normal	Physical	70	100	20	Normal	—
TM43	Secret Power	Normal	Physical	70	100	20	Normal	○
TM44	Rest	Psychic	Status	—	—	10	Self	—
TM45	Attract	Normal	Status	—	100	15	Normal	—
TM49	Snatch	Dark	Status	—	—	10	Depends	—
TM58	Endure	Normal	Status	—	—	10	Self	—
TM64	Explosion	Normal	Physical	250	100	5	2 Foes/1 Ally	—
TM78	Captivate	Normal	Status	—	100	20	2 Foes	—
TM82	Sleep Talk	Normal	Status	—	—	10	Depends	—
TM83	Natural Gift	Normal	Physical	—	100	15	Normal	—
TM85	Dream Eater	Psychic	Special	100	100	15	Normal	—
TM87	Swagger	Normal	Status	—	90	15	Normal	—
TM90	Substitute	Normal	Status	—	—	10	Self	—
HM04	Strength	Normal	Physical	80	100	15	Normal	○
HM06	Rock Smash	Fighting	Physical	40	100	15	Normal	○

● EGG MOVES

Name	Type	Kind	Pow.	Acc.	PP	Range	DA
Dream Eater	Psychic	Special	100	100	15	Normal	—
Acid Armor	Poison	Status	—	—	40	Self	—
Smog	Poison	Special	20	70	20	Normal	—
Pain Split	Normal	Status	—	—	20	Normal	—
Curse	???	Status	—	—	10	Normal/Self	—
Destiny Bond	Ghost	Status	—	—	5	Self	—

● No. 316 | Stomach Pokémon
Gulpin

Poison

- ● HEIGHT: 1'04"
- ● WEIGHT: 22.7 lbs.
- ● ITEMS: Big Pearl

● SIZE COMPARISON

● MALE FORM
Longer yellow point

● FEMALE FORM
Shorter yellow point

⊙ ABILITIES
- ● Liquid Ooze
- ● Sticky Hold

⊙ EGG GROUPS
Amorphous

⊙ STATS
- HP ●●●
- ATTACK ●●
- DEFENSE ●●
- SP. ATTACK ●●
- SP. DEFENSE ●●
- SPEED ●●

⊙ PERFORMANCE
SPEED ★★☆	STAMINA ★★★☆
POWER ★☆	JUMP ★★
SKILL ★★	

● MAIN WAYS TO OBTAIN

Pokémon HeartGold —

Pokémon SoulSilver Route 3 (mass outbreak)

Pokémon Diamond Pastoria Great Marsh [after obtaining the National Pokédex / changes daily]

Pokémon Pearl Pastoria Great Marsh [after obtaining the National Pokédex / changes daily]

Pokémon Platinum Pastoria Great Marsh [after obtaining the National Pokédex / changes daily]

Pokémon HeartGold
It has a small heart and brain. Its stomach comprises most of its body, with enzymes to dissolve anything.

Pokémon SoulSilver
It has a small heart and brain. Its stomach comprises most of its body, with enzymes to dissolve anything.

⊙ EVOLUTION

 Lv. 26

Gulpin — Swalot

● No. 317 | Poison Bag Pokémon
Swalot

Poison

● HEIGHT: 5'07"
● WEIGHT: 176.4 lbs.
● ITEMS: None

● SIZE COMPARISON

● MALE FORM
Longer whiskers

● FEMALE FORM
Shorter whiskers

● ABILITIES
● Liquid Ooze
● Sticky Hold

● STATS
HP ●●●●
ATTACK ●●●
DEFENSE ●●●
SP. ATTACK ●●●
SP. DEFENSE ●●●
SPEED ●●●

● EGG GROUPS
Amorphous

● PERFORMANCE
SPEED ★☆
POWER ★★★☆
SKILL ★★★
STAMINA ★★★★☆
JUMP ★★

● MAIN WAYS TO OBTAIN

Pokémon HeartGold	—
Pokémon SoulSilver	Level up Gulpin to Lv. 26
Pokémon Diamond	Level up Gulpin to Lv. 26
Pokémon Pearl	Level up Gulpin to Lv. 26
Pokémon Platinum	Level up Gulpin to Lv. 26

Pokémon HeartGold	Pokémon SoulSilver
It gulps anything that fits in its mouth. Its special enzymes can dissolve anything.	It gulps anything that fits in its mouth. Its special enzymes can dissolve anything.

● EVOLUTION
Gulpin → Lv. 26 → Swalot

● LEVEL-UP MOVES

Lv.	Name	Type	Kind	Pow.	Acc.	PP	Range	DA
1	Pound	Normal	Physical	40	100	35	Normal	○
1	Yawn	Normal	Status	—	—	10	Normal	—
1	Poison Gas	Poison	Status	—	55	40	Normal	—
1	Sludge	Poison	Special	65	100	20	Normal	—
6	Yawn	Normal	Status	—	—	10	Normal	—
9	Poison Gas	Poison	Status	—	55	40	Normal	—
14	Sludge	Poison	Special	65	100	20	Normal	—
17	Amnesia	Psychic	Status	—	—	20	Self	—
23	Encore	Normal	Status	—	100	5	Normal	—
26	Body Slam	Normal	Physical	85	100	15	Normal	○
30	Toxic	Poison	Status	—	85	10	Normal	—
38	Stockpile	Normal	Status	—	—	20	Self	—
38	Spit Up	Normal	Special	—	100	10	Normal	—
38	Swallow	Normal	Status	—	—	10	Self	—
45	Sludge Bomb	Poison	Special	90	100	10	Normal	—
52	Gastro Acid	Poison	Status	—	100	10	Normal	—
59	Wring Out	Normal	Special	—	100	5	Normal	○
66	Gunk Shot	Poison	Physical	120	70	5	Normal	—

● MOVE MANIAC

Name	Type	Kind	Pow.	Acc.	PP	Range	DA
Headbutt	Normal	Physical	70	100	15	Normal	○

● BP MOVES

Name	Type	Kind	Pow.	Acc.	PP	Range	DA
ThunderPunch	Electric	Physical	75	100	15	Normal	○
Fire Punch	Fire	Physical	75	100	15	Normal	○
Ice Punch	Ice	Physical	75	100	15	Normal	○
Snore	Normal	Special	40	100	15	Normal	—
Block	Normal	Status	—	—	5	Normal	—
Mud-Slap	Ground	Special	20	100	10	Normal	—
Rollout	Rock	Physical	30	90	20	Normal	○
Gastro Acid	Poison	Status	—	100	10	Normal	—
Gunk Shot	Poison	Physical	120	70	5	Normal	—
Seed Bomb	Grass	Physical	80	100	15	Normal	—
Pain Split	Normal	Status	—	—	20	Normal	—

● TM & HM MOVES

No.	Name	Type	Kind	Pow.	Acc.	PP	Range	DA
TM03	Water Pulse	Water	Special	60	100	20	Normal	—
TM06	Toxic	Poison	Status	—	85	10	Normal	—
TM09	Bullet Seed	Grass	Physical	10	100	30	Normal	—
TM10	Hidden Power	Normal	Special	—	100	15	Normal	—
TM11	Sunny Day	Fire	Status	—	—	5	All	—
TM13	Ice Beam	Ice	Special	95	100	10	Normal	—
TM15	Hyper Beam	Normal	Special	150	90	5	Normal	—
TM17	Protect	Normal	Status	—	—	10	Self	—
TM18	Rain Dance	Water	Status	—	—	5	All	—
TM19	Giga Drain	Grass	Special	60	100	10	Normal	—
TM21	Frustration	Normal	Physical	—	100	20	Normal	○
TM22	SolarBeam	Grass	Special	120	100	10	Normal	—
TM26	Earthquake	Ground	Physical	100	100	10	2 Foes/1 Ally	—
TM27	Return	Normal	Physical	—	100	20	Normal	○
TM30	Shadow Ball	Ghost	Special	80	100	15	Normal	—
TM32	Double Team	Normal	Status	—	—	15	Self	—
TM34	Shock Wave	Electric	Special	60	—	20	Normal	—
TM36	Sludge Bomb	Poison	Special	90	100	10	Normal	—
TM42	Facade	Normal	Physical	70	100	20	Normal	○
TM43	Secret Power	Normal	Physical	70	100	20	Normal	—
TM44	Rest	Psychic	Status	—	—	10	Self	—
TM45	Attract	Normal	Status	—	100	15	Normal	—
TM49	Snatch	Dark	Status	—	—	10	Depends	—
TM58	Endure	Normal	Status	—	—	10	Self	—
TM64	Explosion	Normal	Physical	250	100	5	2 Foes/1 Ally	—
TM68	Giga Impact	Normal	Physical	150	90	5	Normal	○
TM78	Captivate	Normal	Status	—	100	20	2 Foes	—
TM82	Sleep Talk	Normal	Status	—	—	10	Depends	—
TM83	Natural Gift	Normal	Physical	—	100	15	Normal	—
TM85	Dream Eater	Psychic	Special	100	100	15	Normal	—
TM87	Swagger	Normal	Status	—	90	15	Normal	—
TM90	Substitute	Normal	Status	—	—	10	Self	—
HM04	Strength	Normal	Physical	80	100	15	Normal	○
HM06	Rock Smash	Fighting	Physical	40	100	15	Normal	○

● LEVEL-UP MOVES

Lv.	Name	Type	Kind	Pow.	Acc.	PP	Range	DA
1	Leer	Normal	Status	—	100	30	2 Foes	—
1	Bite	Dark	Physical	60	100	25	Normal	○
6	Rage	Normal	Physical	20	100	20	Normal	○
8	Focus Energy	Normal	Status	—	—	30	Self	—
11	Scary Face	Normal	Status	—	90	10	Normal	—
16	Ice Fang	Ice	Physical	65	95	15	Normal	○
18	Screech	Normal	Status	—	85	40	Normal	—
21	Swagger	Normal	Status	—	90	15	Normal	—
26	Assurance	Dark	Physical	50	100	10	Normal	○
28	Crunch	Dark	Physical	80	100	15	Normal	○
31	Aqua Jet	Water	Physical	40	100	20	Normal	○
36	Agility	Psychic	Status	—	—	30	Self	—
38	Take Down	Normal	Physical	90	85	20	Normal	○

● MOVE MANIAC

Name	Type	Kind	Pow.	Acc.	PP	Range	DA

● BP MOVES

Name	Type	Kind	Pow.	Acc.	PP	Range	DA
Dive	Water	Physical	80	100	10	Normal	○
Fury Cutter	Bug	Physical	10	95	20	Normal	○
Icy Wind	Ice	Special	55	95	15	2 Foes	—
Zen Headbutt	Psychic	Physical	80	90	15	Normal	○
Snore	Normal	Special	40	100	15	Normal	—
Spite	Ghost	Status	—	100	10	Normal	—
Swift	Normal	Special	60	—	20	2 Foes	—
Uproar	Normal	Special	50	100	10	1 Random	—
Mud-Slap	Ground	Special	20	100	10	Normal	—
AncientPower	Rock	Special	60	100	5	Normal	—
Bounce	Flying	Physical	85	85	5	Normal	○
Super Fang	Normal	Physical	—	90	10	Normal	—

● TM & HM MOVES

No.	Name	Type	Kind	Pow.	Acc.	PP	Range	DA
TM03	Water Pulse	Water	Special	60	100	20	Normal	—
TM06	Toxic	Poison	Status	—	85	10	Normal	—
TM07	Hail	Ice	Status	—	—	10	All	—
TM10	Hidden Power	Normal	Special	—	100	15	Normal	—
TM12	Taunt	Dark	Status	—	100	20	Normal	—
TM13	Ice Beam	Ice	Special	95	100	10	Normal	—
TM14	Blizzard	Ice	Special	120	70	5	2 Foes	—
TM17	Protect	Normal	Status	—	—	10	Self	—
TM18	Rain Dance	Water	Status	—	—	5	All	—
TM21	Frustration	Normal	Physical	—	100	20	Normal	○
TM27	Return	Normal	Physical	—	100	20	Normal	○
TM32	Double Team	Normal	Status	—	—	15	Self	—
TM41	Torment	Dark	Status	—	100	15	Normal	—
TM42	Facade	Normal	Physical	70	100	20	Normal	○
TM43	Secret Power	Normal	Physical	70	100	20	Normal	○
TM44	Rest	Psychic	Status	—	—	10	Self	—
TM45	Attract	Normal	Status	—	100	15	Normal	—
TM46	Thief	Dark	Physical	40	100	10	Normal	○
TM55	Brine	Water	Special	65	100	10	Normal	—
TM58	Endure	Normal	Status	—	—	10	Self	—
TM66	Payback	Dark	Physical	50	100	10	Normal	○
TM78	Captivate	Normal	Status	—	100	20	2 Foes	—
TM79	Dark Pulse	Dark	Special	80	100	15	Normal	—
TM82	Sleep Talk	Normal	Status	—	—	10	Depends	—
TM83	Natural Gift	Normal	Physical	—	100	15	Normal	—
TM87	Swagger	Normal	Status	—	90	15	Normal	—
TM90	Substitute	Normal	Status	—	—	10	Self	—
HM03	Surf	Water	Special	95	100	15	2 Foes/1 Ally	—
HM05	Whirlpool	Water	Special	15	70	15	Normal	—
HM07	Waterfall	Water	Physical	80	100	15	Normal	○

● EGG MOVES

Name	Type	Kind	Pow.	Acc.	PP	Range	DA
Hydro Pump	Water	Special	120	80	5	Normal	—
Double-Edge	Normal	Physical	120	100	15	Normal	○
Thrash	Normal	Physical	90	100	20	1 Random	○
AncientPower	Rock	Special	60	100	5	Normal	—

Carvanha

Water | Dark

- ● **HEIGHT:** 2'07"
- ● **WEIGHT:** 45.9 lbs.
- ● **ITEMS:** None

● SIZE COMPARISON

● MALE/FEMALE HAVE SAME FORM

⬡ ABILITIES
● Rough Skin

⬡ STATS
- HP ●●
- ATTACK ●●●●
- DEFENSE ●
- SP. ATTACK ●●●
- SP. DEFENSE ●●
- SPEED ●●●

⬡ EGG GROUPS
Water 2

⬡ PERFORMANCE

SPEED ★★★☆	STAMINA ★★☆
POWER ★★★☆	JUMP ★★☆
SKILL ★★☆☆	

● MAIN WAYS TO OBTAIN

Pokémon HeartGold	Warm Beach Pokéwalker Route
Pokémon SoulSilver	Warm Beach Pokéwalker Route
Pokémon Diamond	Pastoria Great Marsh / Super Rod)
Pokémon Pearl	Pastoria Great Marsh / Super Rod)
Pokémon Platinum	Pastoria Great Marsh / Super Rod)

Pokémon HeartGold	Pokémon SoulSilver
They form packs to attack boats and rip out their hulls to sink them. They live in rivers in the jungle.	They form packs to attack boats and rip out their hulls to sink them. They live in rivers in the jungle.

⬡ EVOLUTION

Carvanha — Lv. 30 → Sharpedo

No. 319 | Brutal Pokémon
Sharpedo

`Water` `Dark`

- **HEIGHT:** 5'11"
- **WEIGHT:** 195.8 lbs.
- **ITEMS:** None

● SIZE COMPARISON

● MALE/FEMALE HAVE SAME FORM

● ABILITIES
● Rough Skin

● STATS
- HP ●●●
- ATTACK ●●●●●
- DEFENSE ●●
- SP. ATTACK ●●●
- SP. DEFENSE ●●●
- SPEED ●●●●

● EGG GROUPS
Water 2

● PERFORMANCE
SPEED ★★★★	STAMINA ★★
POWER ★★★★	JUMP ★★☆
SKILL ★★★★	

● MAIN WAYS TO OBTAIN

Pokémon HeartGold	Level up Carvanha to Lv. 30
Pokémon SoulSilver	Level up Carvanha to Lv. 30
Pokémon Diamond	Route 213 (Super Rod)
Pokémon Pearl	Route 213 (Super Rod)
Pokémon Platinum	Level up Carvanha to Lv. 30

Pokémon HeartGold	Pokémon SoulSilver
It can swim at speeds of 75 mph by jetting sea water through its body. It is the bandit of the sea.	It can swim at speeds of 75 mph by jetting sea water through its body. It is the bandit of the sea.

● EVOLUTION

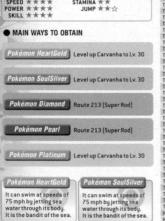

Carvanha → lv. 30 → Sharpedo

● LEVEL-UP MOVES

Lv.	Name	Type	Kind	Pow.	Acc.	PP	Range	DA
1	Feint	Normal	Physical	50	100	10	Normal	—
1	Leer	Normal	Status	—	100	30	2 Foes	—
1	Bite	Dark	Physical	60	100	25	Normal	○
1	Rage	Normal	Physical	20	100	20	Normal	○
1	Focus Energy	Normal	Status	—	—	30	Self	—
6	Rage	Normal	Physical	20	100	20	Normal	○
8	Focus Energy	Normal	Status	—	—	30	Self	—
11	Scary Face	Normal	Status	—	90	10	Normal	—
16	Ice Fang	Ice	Physical	65	95	15	Normal	○
18	Screech	Normal	Status	—	85	40	Normal	—
21	Swagger	Normal	Status	—	90	15	Normal	—
26	Assurance	Dark	Physical	50	100	10	Normal	○
28	Crunch	Dark	Physical	80	100	15	Normal	○
30	Slash	Normal	Physical	70	100	20	Normal	○
34	Aqua Jet	Water	Physical	40	100	20	Normal	○
40	Taunt	Dark	Status	—	100	20	Normal	—
45	Agility	Psychic	Status	—	—	30	Self	—
50	Skull Bash	Normal	Physical	100	100	15	Normal	○
56	Night Slash	Dark	Physical	70	100	15	Normal	○

● MOVE MANIAC

Name	Type	Kind	Pow.	Acc.	PP	Range	DA

● BP MOVES

Name	Type	Kind	Pow.	Acc.	PP	Range	DA
Dive	Water	Physical	80	100	10	Normal	○
Fury Cutter	Bug	Physical	10	95	20	Normal	○
Icy Wind	Ice	Special	55	95	15	2 Foes	—
Zen Headbutt	Psychic	Physical	80	90	15	Normal	○
Snore	Normal	Special	40	100	15	Normal	—
Spite	Ghost	Status	—	100	10	Normal	—
Swift	Normal	Special	60	—	20	2 Foes	—
Uproar	Normal	Special	50	100	10	1 Random	—
Mud-Slap	Ground	Special	20	100	10	Normal	—
AncientPower	Rock	Special	60	100	5	Normal	—
Bounce	Flying	Physical	85	85	5	Normal	○
Super Fang	Normal	Physical	—	90	10	Normal	○

● TM & HM MOVES

No.	Name	Type	Kind	Pow.	Acc.	PP	Range	DA
TM03	Water Pulse	Water	Special	60	100	20	Normal	—
TM05	Roar	Normal	Status	—	100	20	Normal	—
TM06	Toxic	Poison	Status	—	85	10	Normal	—
TM07	Hail	Ice	Status	—	—	10	All	—
TM10	Hidden Power	Normal	Special	—	100	15	Normal	—
TM12	Taunt	Dark	Status	—	100	20	Normal	—
TM13	Ice Beam	Ice	Special	95	100	10	Normal	—
TM14	Blizzard	Ice	Special	120	70	5	2 Foes	—
TM15	Hyper Beam	Normal	Special	150	90	5	Normal	—
TM17	Protect	Normal	Status	—	—	10	Self	—
TM18	Rain Dance	Water	Status	—	—	5	All	—
TM21	Frustration	Normal	Physical	—	100	20	Normal	○
TM26	Earthquake	Ground	Physical	100	100	10	2 Foes/1 Ally	—
TM27	Return	Normal	Physical	—	100	20	Normal	○
TM32	Double Team	Normal	Status	—	—	15	Self	—
TM39	Rock Tomb	Rock	Physical	50	80	10	Normal	—
TM41	Torment	Dark	Status	—	100	15	Normal	—
TM42	Facade	Normal	Physical	70	100	20	Normal	○
TM43	Secret Power	Normal	Physical	70	100	20	Normal	—
TM44	Rest	Psychic	Status	—	—	10	Self	—
TM45	Attract	Normal	Status	—	100	15	Normal	—
TM46	Thief	Dark	Physical	40	100	10	Normal	○
TM55	Brine	Water	Special	65	100	10	Normal	—
TM58	Endure	Normal	Status	—	—	10	Self	—
TM66	Payback	Dark	Physical	50	100	10	Normal	○
TM68	Giga Impact	Normal	Physical	150	90	5	Normal	○
TM72	Avalanche	Ice	Physical	60	100	10	Normal	○
TM78	Captivate	Normal	Status	—	100	20	2 Foes	—
TM79	Dark Pulse	Dark	Special	80	100	15	Normal	—
TM82	Sleep Talk	Normal	Status	—	—	10	Depends	—
TM83	Natural Gift	Normal	Physical	—	100	15	Normal	—
TM84	Poison Jab	Poison	Physical	80	100	20	Normal	○
TM87	Swagger	Normal	Status	—	90	15	Normal	—
TM90	Substitute	Normal	Status	—	—	10	Self	—
HM03	Surf	Water	Special	95	100	15	2 Foes/1 Ally	—
HM04	Strength	Normal	Physical	80	100	15	Normal	○
HM05	Whirlpool	Water	Special	15	70	15	Normal	—
HM06	Rock Smash	Fighting	Physical	40	100	15	Normal	○
HM07	Waterfall	Water	Physical	80	100	15	Normal	○

● LEVEL-UP MOVES

Lv.	Name	Type	Kind	Pow.	Acc.	PP	Range	DA
1	Splash	Normal	Status	—	—	40	Self	—
4	Growl	Normal	Status	—	100	40	2 Foes	—
7	Water Gun	Water	Special	40	100	25	Normal	—
11	Rollout	Rock	Physical	30	90	20	Normal	○
14	Whirlpool	Water	Special	15	70	15	Normal	—
17	Astonish	Ghost	Physical	30	100	15	Normal	○
21	Water Pulse	Water	Special	60	100	20	Normal	—
24	Mist	Ice	Status	—	—	30	2 Allies	—
27	Rest	Psychic	Status	—	—	10	Self	—
31	Brine	Water	Special	65	100	10	Normal	—
34	Water Spout	Water	Special	150	100	5	2 Foes	—
37	Amnesia	Psychic	Status	—	—	20	Self	—
41	Dive	Water	Physical	80	100	10	Normal	○
44	Bounce	Flying	Physical	85	85	5	Normal	○
47	Hydro Pump	Water	Special	120	80	5	Normal	—

● MOVE MANIAC

Name	Type	Kind	Pow.	Acc.	PP	Range	DA
Headbutt	Normal	Physical	70	100	15	Normal	○

● BP MOVES

Name	Type	Kind	Pow.	Acc.	PP	Range	DA
Dive	Water	Physical	80	100	10	Normal	○
Icy Wind	Ice	Special	55	95	15	2 Foes	—
Snore	Normal	Special	40	100	15	Normal	—
Rollout	Rock	Physical	30	90	20	Normal	○
Bounce	Flying	Physical	85	85	5	Normal	○

● TM & HM MOVES

No.	Name	Type	Kind	Pow.	Acc.	PP	Range	DA
TM03	Water Pulse	Water	Special	60	100	20	Normal	—
TM05	Roar	Normal	Status	—	100	20	Normal	—
TM06	Toxic	Poison	Status	—	85	10	Normal	—
TM07	Hail	Ice	Status	—	—	10	All	—
TM10	Hidden Power	Normal	Special	—	100	15	Normal	—
TM13	Ice Beam	Ice	Special	95	100	10	Normal	—
TM14	Blizzard	Ice	Special	120	70	5	2 Foes	—
TM17	Protect	Normal	Status	—	—	10	Self	—
TM18	Rain Dance	Water	Status	—	—	5	All	—
TM21	Frustration	Normal	Physical	—	100	20	Normal	○
TM26	Earthquake	Ground	Physical	100	100	10	2 Foes/1 Ally	○
TM27	Return	Normal	Physical	—	100	20	Normal	○
TM32	Double Team	Normal	Status	—	—	15	Self	—
TM39	Rock Tomb	Rock	Physical	50	80	10	Normal	○
TM42	Facade	Normal	Physical	70	100	20	Normal	○
TM43	Secret Power	Normal	Physical	70	100	20	Normal	○
TM44	Rest	Psychic	Status	—	—	10	Self	—
TM45	Attract	Normal	Status	—	100	15	Normal	—
TM55	Brine	Water	Special	65	100	10	Normal	—
TM58	Endure	Normal	Status	—	—	10	Self	—
TM72	Avalanche	Ice	Physical	60	100	10	Normal	○
TM78	Captivate	Normal	Status	—	100	20	2 Foes	—
TM82	Sleep Talk	Normal	Status	—	—	10	Depends	—
TM83	Natural Gift	Normal	Physical	—	100	15	Normal	○
TM87	Swagger	Normal	Status	—	90	15	Normal	—
TM90	Substitute	Normal	Status	—	—	10	Self	—
HM03	Surf	Water	Special	95	100	15	2 Foes/1 Ally	○
HM04	Strength	Normal	Physical	80	100	15	Normal	○
HM05	Whirlpool	Water	Special	15	70	15	Normal	—
HM06	Rock Smash	Fighting	Physical	40	100	15	Normal	○
HM07	Waterfall	Water	Physical	80	100	15	Normal	○

● EGG MOVES

Name	Type	Kind	Pow.	Acc.	PP	Range	DA
Double-Edge	Normal	Physical	120	100	15	Normal	○
Thrash	Normal	Physical	90	100	20	1 Random	○
Swagger	Normal	Status	—	90	15	Normal	—
Snore	Normal	Special	40	100	15	Normal	—
Sleep Talk	Normal	Status	—	—	10	Depends	—
Curse	???	Status	—	—	10	Normal/Self	—
Fissure	Ground	Physical	—	30	5	Normal	—
Tickle	Normal	Status	—	100	20	Normal	—
Defense Curl	Normal	Status	—	—	40	Self	—
Body Slam	Normal	Physical	85	100	15	Normal	○
Aqua Ring	Water	Status	—	—	20	Self	—

◎ No. 320 | Ball Whale Pokémon
Wailmer

Water

● HEIGHT: 6'07"
● WEIGHT: 286.6 lbs.
● ITEMS: None

● SIZE COMPARISON

● MALE/FEMALE HAVE SAME FORM

◎ ABILITIES
● Water Veil
● Oblivious

◎ STATS
HP ●●●●●
ATTACK ●●●
DEFENSE ●●
SP. ATTACK ●●●
SP. DEFENSE ●
SPEED ●●●

◎ EGG GROUPS
Field
Water 2

◎ PERFORMANCE
SPEED ★★★
POWER ★★★☆
SKILL ★★☆
STAMINA ★★★★☆
JUMP ★★★☆

● MAIN WAYS TO OBTAIN

Pokémon HeartGold — Warm Beach Pokéwalker Route

Pokémon SoulSilver — Warm Beach Pokéwalker Route

Pokémon Diamond — Route 223 (Super Rod)

Pokémon Pearl — Route 223 (Super Rod)

Pokémon Platinum — Route 223 (Super Rod)

Pokémon HeartGold
It bounces playfully like a ball. The more seawater it swallows, the higher it bounces.

Pokémon SoulSilver
It bounces playfully like a ball. The more seawater it swallows, the higher it bounces.

◎ EVOLUTION

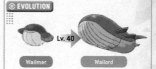

Lv. 40

Wailmer → Wailord

No. 321 | Float Whale Pokémon
Wailord

Water

● LEVEL-UP MOVES

Lv.	Name	Type	Kind	Pow.	Acc.	PP	Range	DA
1	Splash	Normal	Status	—	—	40	Self	—
1	Growl	Normal	Status	—	100	40	2 Foes	—
1	Water Gun	Water	Special	40	100	25	Normal	—
1	Rollout	Rock	Physical	30	90	20	Normal	○
4	Growl	Normal	Status	—	100	40	2 Foes	—
7	Water Gun	Water	Special	40	100	25	Normal	—
11	Rollout	Rock	Physical	30	90	20	Normal	○
14	Whirlpool	Water	Special	15	70	15	Normal	—
17	Astonish	Ghost	Physical	30	100	15	Normal	○
21	Water Pulse	Water	Special	60	100	20	Normal	—
24	Mist	Ice	Status	—	—	30	2 Allies	—
27	Rest	Psychic	Status	—	—	10	Self	—
31	Brine	Water	Special	65	100	10	Normal	—
34	Water Spout	Water	Special	150	100	5	2 Foes	—
37	Amnesia	Psychic	Status	—	—	20	Self	—
46	Dive	Water	Physical	80	100	10	Normal	○
54	Bounce	Flying	Physical	85	85	5	Normal	○
62	Hydro Pump	Water	Special	120	80	5	Normal	—

● MOVE MANIAC

Name	Type	Kind	Pow.	Acc.	PP	Range	DA
Headbutt	Normal	Physical	70	100	15	Normal	○

● BP MOVES

Name	Type	Kind	Pow.	Acc.	PP	Range	DA
Dive	Water	Physical	80	100	10	Normal	○
Icy Wind	Ice	Special	55	95	15	2 Foes	—
Snore	Normal	Special	40	100	15	Normal	—
Block	Normal	Status	—	—	5	Normal	—
Rollout	Rock	Physical	30	90	20	Normal	○
Iron Head	Steel	Physical	80	100	15	Normal	○
Bounce	Flying	Physical	85	85	5	Normal	○

● HEIGHT: 47'07"
● WEIGHT: 877.4 lbs.
● ITEMS: None

● SIZE COMPARISON

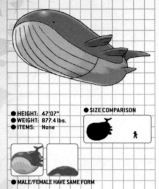

● MALE/FEMALE HAVE SAME FORM

● ABILITIES
● Water Veil
● Oblivious

● STATS
HP ●●●●●●
ATTACK ●●●●
DEFENSE ●●●
SP. ATTACK ●●●●
SP. DEFENSE ●●●
SPEED ●●●

● EGG GROUPS
Field

Water 2

● PERFORMANCE
SPEED ★★☆
POWER ★★★★☆
SKILL ★
STAMINA ★★★★★
JUMP ★★☆☆

● MAIN WAYS TO OBTAIN

| Pokémon HeartGold | Level up Wailmer to Lv. 40 |

| Pokémon SoulSilver | Level up Wailmer to Lv. 40 |

| Pokémon Diamond | Route 223 (Super Rod) |

| Pokémon Pearl | Route 223 (Super Rod) |

| Pokémon Platinum | Route 223 (Super Rod) |

Pokémon HeartGold	Pokémon SoulSilver
It is the largest of all identified Pokémon. They jump as a pack to herd their prey.	It is the largest of all identified Pokémon. They jump as a pack to herd their prey.

● EVOLUTION

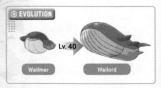

Lv. 40

Wailmer → Wailord

● TM & HM MOVES

No.	Name	Type	Kind	Pow.	Acc.	PP	Range	DA
TM03	Water Pulse	Water	Special	60	100	20	Normal	—
TM05	Roar	Normal	Status	—	100	20	Normal	—
TM06	Toxic	Poison	Status	—	85	10	Normal	—
TM07	Hail	Ice	Status	—	—	10	All	—
TM10	Hidden Power	Normal	Special	—	100	15	Normal	—
TM13	Ice Beam	Ice	Special	95	100	10	Normal	—
TM14	Blizzard	Ice	Special	120	70	5	2 Foes	—
TM15	Hyper Beam	Normal	Special	150	90	5	Normal	—
TM17	Protect	Normal	Status	—	—	10	Self	—
TM18	Rain Dance	Water	Status	—	—	5	All	—
TM21	Frustration	Normal	Physical	—	100	20	Normal	○
TM26	Earthquake	Ground	Physical	100	100	10	2 Foes/1 Ally	—
TM27	Return	Normal	Physical	—	100	20	Normal	○
TM32	Double Team	Normal	Status	—	—	15	Self	—
TM39	Rock Tomb	Rock	Physical	50	80	10	Normal	○
TM42	Facade	Normal	Physical	70	100	20	Normal	○
TM43	Secret Power	Normal	Physical	70	100	20	Normal	—
TM44	Rest	Psychic	Status	—	—	10	Self	—
TM45	Attract	Normal	Status	—	100	15	Normal	—
TM55	Brine	Water	Special	65	100	10	Normal	—
TM58	Endure	Normal	Status	—	—	10	Self	—
TM68	Giga Impact	Normal	Physical	150	90	5	Normal	○
TM72	Avalanche	Ice	Physical	60	100	10	Normal	○
TM78	Captivate	Normal	Status	—	100	20	2 Foes	—
TM82	Sleep Talk	Normal	Status	—	—	10	Depends	—
TM83	Natural Gift	Normal	Physical	—	100	15	Normal	—
TM87	Swagger	Normal	Status	—	90	15	Normal	—
TM90	Substitute	Normal	Status	—	—	10	Self	—
HM03	Surf	Water	Special	95	100	15	2 Foes/1 Ally	—
HM04	Strength	Normal	Physical	80	100	15	Normal	○
HM05	Whirlpool	Water	Special	15	70	15	Normal	—
HM06	Rock Smash	Fighting	Physical	40	100	15	Normal	○
HM07	Waterfall	Water	Physical	80	100	15	Normal	○

● LEVEL-UP MOVES

Lv.	Name	Type	Kind	Pow.	Acc.	PP	Range	DA
1	Growl	Normal	Status	—	100	40	2 Foes	—
1	Tackle	Normal	Physical	35	95	35	Normal	○
5	Ember	Fire	Special	40	100	25	Normal	—
11	Magnitude	Ground	Physical	—	100	30	2 Foes/1 Ally	—
15	Focus Energy	Normal	Status	—	—	30	Self	—
21	Take Down	Normal	Physical	90	85	20	Normal	○
25	Amnesia	Psychic	Status	—	—	20	Self	—
31	Lava Plume	Fire	Special	80	100	15	2 Foes/1 Ally	—
35	Earth Power	Ground	Special	90	100	10	Normal	—
41	Earthquake	Ground	Physical	100	100	10	2 Foes/1 Ally	—
45	Flamethrower	Fire	Special	95	100	15	Normal	—
51	Double-Edge	Normal	Physical	120	100	15	Normal	○

● MOVE MANIAC

Name	Type	Kind	Pow.	Acc.	PP	Range	DA
Headbutt	Normal	Physical	70	100	15	Normal	○

● BP MOVES

Name	Type	Kind	Pow.	Acc.	PP	Range	DA
Snore	Normal	Special	40	100	15	Normal	—
Mud-Slap	Ground	Special	20	100	10	Normal	—
Rollout	Rock	Physical	30	90	20	Normal	○
Earth Power	Ground	Special	90	100	10	Normal	—
Heat Wave	Fire	Special	100	90	10	2 Foes	—

● TM & HM MOVES

No.	Name	Type	Kind	Pow.	Acc.	PP	Range	DA
TM06	Toxic	Poison	Status	—	85	10	Normal	—
TM10	Hidden Power	Normal	Special	—	100	15	Normal	—
TM11	Sunny Day	Fire	Status	—	—	5	All	—
TM17	Protect	Normal	Status	—	—	10	Self	—
TM21	Frustration	Normal	Physical	—	100	20	Normal	○
TM26	Earthquake	Ground	Physical	100	100	10	2 Foes/1 Ally	—
TM27	Return	Normal	Physical	—	100	20	Normal	○
TM28	Dig	Ground	Physical	80	100	10	Normal	○
TM32	Double Team	Normal	Status	—	—	15	Self	—
TM35	Flamethrower	Fire	Special	95	100	15	Normal	—
TM37	Sandstorm	Rock	Status	—	—	10	All	—
TM38	Fire Blast	Fire	Special	120	85	5	Normal	—
TM39	Rock Tomb	Rock	Physical	50	80	10	Normal	—
TM42	Facade	Normal	Physical	70	100	20	Normal	○
TM43	Secret Power	Normal	Physical	70	100	20	Normal	—
TM44	Rest	Psychic	Status	—	—	10	Self	—
TM45	Attract	Normal	Status	—	100	15	Normal	—
TM50	Overheat	Fire	Special	140	90	5	Normal	—
TM58	Endure	Normal	Status	—	—	10	Self	—
TM61	Will-O-Wisp	Fire	Status	—	75	15	Normal	—
TM76	Stealth Rock	Rock	Status	—	—	20	2 Foes	—
TM78	Captivate	Normal	Status	—	100	20	2 Foes	—
TM80	Rock Slide	Rock	Physical	75	90	10	2 Foes	—
TM82	Sleep Talk	Normal	Status	—	—	10	Depends	—
TM83	Natural Gift	Normal	Physical	—	100	15	Normal	—
TM87	Swagger	Normal	Status	—	90	15	Normal	—
TM90	Substitute	Normal	Status	—	—	10	Self	—
HM04	Strength	Normal	Physical	80	100	15	Normal	○
HM06	Rock Smash	Fighting	Physical	40	100	15	Normal	○

● EGG MOVES

Name	Type	Kind	Pow.	Acc.	PP	Range	DA
Howl	Normal	Status	—	—	40	Self	—
Scary Face	Normal	Status	—	90	10	Normal	—
Body Slam	Normal	Physical	85	100	15	Normal	○
Rollout	Rock	Physical	30	90	20	Normal	○
Defense Curl	Normal	Status	—	—	40	Self	—
Stomp	Normal	Physical	65	100	20	Normal	○
Yawn	Normal	Status	—	—	10	Normal	—
AncientPower	Rock	Special	60	100	5	Normal	—
Mud Bomb	Ground	Special	65	85	10	Normal	—
Heat Wave	Fire	Special	100	90	10	2 Foes	—
Stockpile	Normal	Status	—	—	20	Self	—
Swallow	Normal	Status	—	—	10	Self	—
Spit Up	Normal	Special	—	100	10	Normal	—

● **No. 322** | Numb Pokémon

Numel

Fire　Ground

● **HEIGHT:** 2'04"
● **WEIGHT:** 52.9 lbs.
● **ITEMS:** Rawst Berry

● **SIZE COMPARISON**

● **MALE FORM**
Shorter hump

● **FEMALE FORM**
Taller hump

● ABILITIES
● Oblivious
● Simple

● STATS
HP ●●
ATTACK ●●●
DEFENSE ●●●
SP. ATTACK ●●●
SP. DEFENSE ●●
SPEED ●●

● EGG GROUPS
Field

● PERFORMANCE
SPEED ★★☆　　STAMINA ★★★★
POWER ★★★★☆　　JUMP ★★
SKILL ★★

● MAIN WAYS TO OBTAIN

Pokémon HeartGold　Ilex Forest (Hoenn Sound)

Pokémon SoulSilver　Ilex Forest (Hoenn Sound)

Pokémon Diamond　Route 227

Pokémon Pearl　Route 227

Pokémon Platinum　Route 227

Pokémon HeartGold
The flaming magma it stores in the hump on its back is the source of its tremendous power.

Pokémon SoulSilver
The flaming magma it stores in the hump on its back is the source of its tremendous power.

● EVOLUTION

Numel　→ Lv. 33 →　Camerupt

No. 323 | Eruption Pokémon
Camerupt

Fire Ground

- **HEIGHT:** 6'03"
- **WEIGHT:** 485.0 lbs.
- **ITEMS:** None

● **SIZE COMPARISON**

● **MALE FORM**
Shorter humps

● **FEMALE FORM**
Taller humps

● ABILITIES
- Magma Armor
- Solid Rock

● STATS
HP	●●●
ATTACK	●●●●
DEFENSE	●●●●
SP. ATTACK	●●●●●
SP. DEFENSE	●●●
SPEED	●●

● EGG GROUPS
Field

● PERFORMANCE
SPEED ★★★ STAMINA ★★★☆
POWER ★★★★★ JUMP ★★
SKILL ★★

● MAIN WAYS TO OBTAIN

Pokémon HeartGold — Level up Numel to Lv. 33

Pokémon SoulSilver — Level up Numel to Lv. 33

Pokémon Diamond — Route 227

Pokémon Pearl — Route 227

Pokémon Platinum — Route 227

Pokémon HeartGold
It lives in the crater of a volcano. It is well known that the humps on its back erupt every 10 years.

Pokémon SoulSilver
It lives in the crater of a volcano. It is well known that the humps on its back erupt every 10 years.

● EVOLUTION

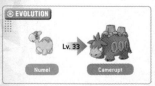

Numel → Lv. 33 → Camerupt

● LEVEL-UP MOVES
Lv.	Name	Type	Kind	Pow.	Acc.	PP	Range	DA
1	Growl	Normal	Status	—	100	40	2 Foes	—
1	Tackle	Normal	Physical	35	95	35	Normal	○
1	Ember	Fire	Special	40	100	25	Normal	—
4	Magnitude	Ground	Physical	—	100	30	2 Foes/1 Ally	—
5	Ember	Fire	Special	40	100	25	Normal	—
11	Magnitude	Ground	Physical	—	100	30	2 Foes/1 Ally	—
15	Focus Energy	Normal	Status	—	—	30	Self	—
21	Take Down	Normal	Physical	90	85	20	Normal	○
25	Amnesia	Psychic	Status	—	—	20	Self	—
31	Lava Plume	Fire	Special	80	100	15	2 Foes/1 Ally	—
33	Rock Slide	Rock	Physical	75	90	10	2 Foes	—
39	Earth Power	Ground	Special	90	100	10	Normal	—
49	Earthquake	Ground	Physical	100	100	10	2 Foes/1 Ally	—
57	Eruption	Fire	Special	150	100	5	2 Foes	—
67	Mist	Ground	Physical	—	30	5	Normal	—

● MOVE MANIAC
Name	Type	Kind	Pow.	Acc.	PP	Range	DA
Headbutt	Normal	Physical	70	100	15	Normal	○

● BP MOVES
Name	Type	Kind	Pow.	Acc.	PP	Range	DA
Snore	Normal	Special	40	100	15	Normal	—
Mud-Slap	Ground	Special	20	100	10	Normal	—
Rollout	Rock	Physical	30	90	20	Normal	○
Iron Head	Steel	Physical	80	100	15	Normal	○
Earth Power	Ground	Special	90	100	10	Normal	—
Heat Wave	Fire	Special	100	90	10	2 Foes	—

● TM & HM MOVES
No.	Name	Type	Kind	Pow.	Acc.	PP	Range	DA
TM05	Roar	Normal	Status	—	100	20	Normal	—
TM06	Toxic	Poison	Status	—	85	10	Normal	—
TM10	Hidden Power	Normal	Special	—	100	15	Normal	—
TM11	Sunny Day	Fire	Status	—	—	5	All	—
TM15	Hyper Beam	Normal	Special	150	90	5	Normal	—
TM17	Protect	Normal	Status	—	—	10	Self	—
TM21	Frustration	Normal	Physical	—	100	20	Normal	○
TM22	SolarBeam	Grass	Special	120	100	10	Normal	—
TM26	Earthquake	Ground	Physical	100	100	10	2 Foes/1 Ally	—
TM27	Return	Normal	Physical	—	100	20	Normal	○
TM28	Dig	Ground	Physical	80	100	10	Normal	○
TM32	Double Team	Normal	Status	—	—	15	Self	—
TM35	Flamethrower	Fire	Special	95	100	15	Normal	—
TM37	Sandstorm	Rock	Status	—	—	10	All	—
TM38	Fire Blast	Fire	Special	120	85	5	Normal	—
TM39	Rock Tomb	Rock	Physical	50	80	10	Normal	—
TM42	Facade	Normal	Physical	70	100	20	Normal	○
TM43	Secret Power	Normal	Physical	70	100	20	Normal	—
TM44	Rest	Psychic	Status	—	—	10	Self	—
TM45	Attract	Normal	Status	—	100	15	Normal	—
TM50	Overheat	Fire	Special	140	90	5	Normal	—
TM58	Endure	Normal	Status	—	—	10	Self	—
TM61	Will-O-Wisp	Fire	Status	—	75	15	Normal	—
TM64	Explosion	Normal	Physical	250	100	5	2 Foes/1 Ally	—
TM68	Giga Impact	Normal	Physical	150	90	5	Normal	○
TM69	Rock Polish	Rock	Status	—	—	20	Self	—
TM71	Stone Edge	Rock	Physical	100	80	5	Normal	—
TM76	Stealth Rock	Rock	Status	—	—	20	2 Foes	—
TM78	Captivate	Normal	Status	—	100	20	2 Foes	—
TM80	Rock Slide	Rock	Physical	75	90	10	2 Foes	—
TM82	Sleep Talk	Normal	Status	—	—	10	Depends	—
TM83	Natural Gift	Normal	Physical	—	100	15	Normal	—
TM87	Swagger	Normal	Status	—	90	15	Normal	—
TM90	Substitute	Normal	Status	—	—	10	Self	—
TM91	Flash Cannon	Steel	Special	80	100	10	Normal	—
HM04	Strength	Normal	Physical	80	100	15	Normal	○
HM06	Rock Smash	Fighting	Physical	40	100	15	Normal	○

● LEVEL-UP MOVES

Lv.	Name	Type	Kind	Pow.	Acc.	PP	Range	DA
1	Ember	Fire	Special	40	100	25	Normal	—
4	Smog	Poison	Special	20	70	20	Normal	—
7	Withdraw	Water	Status	—	—	40	Self	—
12	Curse	???	Status	—	—	10	Normal/Self	—
17	Fire Spin	Fire	Special	15	70	15	Normal	—
20	SmokeScreen	Normal	Status	—	100	20	Normal	—
23	Rapid Spin	Normal	Physical	20	100	40	Normal	○
28	Flamethrower	Fire	Special	95	100	15	Normal	—
33	Body Slam	Normal	Physical	85	100	15	Normal	○
36	Protect	Normal	Status	—	—	10	Self	—
39	Lava Plume	Fire	Special	80	100	15	2 Foes/1 Ally	—
44	Iron Defense	Steel	Status	—	—	15	Self	—
49	Amnesia	Psychic	Status	—	—	20	Self	—
52	Flail	Normal	Physical	—	100	15	Normal	○
55	Heat Wave	Fire	Special	100	90	10	2 Foes	—

● MOVE MANIAC

Name	Type	Kind	Pow.	Acc.	PP	Range	DA
Headbutt	Normal	Physical	70	100	15	Normal	○

● BP MOVES

Name	Type	Kind	Pow.	Acc.	PP	Range	DA
Snore	Normal	Special	40	100	15	Normal	—
Mud-Slap	Ground	Special	20	100	10	Normal	—
Rollout	Rock	Physical	30	90	20	Normal	○
Earth Power	Ground	Special	90	100	10	Normal	—
Iron Defense	Steel	Status	—	—	15	Self	—
Heat Wave	Fire	Special	100	90	10	2 Foes	—

● TM & HM MOVES

No.	Name	Type	Kind	Pow.	Acc.	PP	Range	DA
TM06	Toxic	Poison	Status	—	85	10	Normal	—
TM10	Hidden Power	Normal	Special	—	100	15	Normal	—
TM11	Sunny Day	Fire	Status	—	—	5	All	—
TM15	Hyper Beam	Normal	Special	150	90	5	Normal	—
TM17	Protect	Normal	Status	—	—	10	Self	—
TM21	Frustration	Normal	Physical	—	100	20	Normal	○
TM22	SolarBeam	Grass	Special	120	100	10	Normal	—
TM23	Iron Tail	Steel	Physical	100	75	15	Normal	○
TM26	Earthquake	Ground	Physical	100	100	10	2 Foes/1 Ally	○
TM27	Return	Normal	Physical	—	100	20	Normal	○
TM32	Double Team	Normal	Status	—	—	15	Self	—
TM35	Flamethrower	Fire	Special	95	100	15	Normal	—
TM36	Sludge Bomb	Poison	Special	90	100	10	Normal	—
TM38	Fire Blast	Fire	Special	120	85	5	Normal	—
TM39	Rock Tomb	Rock	Physical	50	80	10	Normal	○
TM42	Facade	Normal	Physical	70	100	20	Normal	○
TM43	Secret Power	Normal	Physical	70	100	20	Normal	○
TM44	Rest	Psychic	Status	—	—	10	Self	—
TM45	Attract	Normal	Status	—	100	15	Normal	—
TM50	Overheat	Fire	Special	140	90	5	Normal	—
TM58	Endure	Normal	Status	—	—	10	Self	—
TM61	Will-O-Wisp	Fire	Status	—	75	15	Normal	—
TM64	Explosion	Normal	Physical	250	100	5	2 Foes/1 Ally	—
TM68	Giga Impact	Normal	Physical	150	90	5	Normal	—
TM71	Stone Edge	Rock	Physical	100	80	5	Normal	—
TM74	Gyro Ball	Steel	Physical	—	100	5	Normal	○
TM76	Stealth Rock	Rock	Status	—	—	20	2 Foes	—
TM78	Captivate	Normal	Status	—	100	20	2 Foes	—
TM80	Rock Slide	Rock	Physical	75	90	10	2 Foes	—
TM82	Sleep Talk	Normal	Status	—	—	10	Depends	—
TM83	Natural Gift	Normal	Physical	—	100	15	Normal	—
TM87	Swagger	Normal	Status	—	90	15	Normal	—
TM90	Substitute	Normal	Status	—	—	10	Self	—
HM04	Strength	Normal	Physical	80	100	15	Normal	○
HM06	Rock Smash	Fighting	Physical	40	100	15	Normal	○

● EGG MOVES

Name	Type	Kind	Pow.	Acc.	PP	Range	DA
Eruption	Fire	Special	150	100	5	2 Foes	—
Endure	Normal	Status	—	—	10	Self	—
Sleep Talk	Normal	Status	—	—	10	Depends	—
Yawn	Normal	Status	—	—	10	Normal	—
Earthquake	Ground	Physical	100	100	10	2 Foes/1 Ally	○
Mist	Ground	Physical	—	30	5	Normal	—
Skull Bash	Normal	Physical	100	100	15	Normal	○

No. 324 | Coal Pokémon

Torkoal

Fire

● **HEIGHT:** 1'08"
● **WEIGHT:** 177.2 lbs.
● **ITEMS:** None

● **SIZE COMPARISON**

● **MALE/FEMALE HAVE SAME FORM**

⊛ ABILITIES
● White Smoke

⊛ STATS
HP ●●●
ATTACK ●●●●
DEFENSE ●●●●●
SP. ATTACK ●●●●
SP. DEFENSE ●●●
SPEED ●

⊛ EGG GROUPS
Field

⊛ PERFORMANCE
SPEED ★☆
POWER ★★★★☆
SKILL ★★☆
STAMINA ★★★★☆
JUMP ★★

● MAIN WAYS TO OBTAIN

Pokémon HeartGold	Safari Zone (Savannah Area: if Rock objects are placed, may appear in tall grass)
Pokémon SoulSilver	Safari Zone (Savannah Area: if Rock objects are placed, may appear in tall grass)
Pokémon Diamond	Route 227 (use Poké Radar)
Pokémon Pearl	Route 227 (use Poké Radar)
Pokémon Platinum	Route 227 (use Poké Radar)

Pokémon HeartGold	**Pokémon SoulSilver**
You find abandoned coal mines full of them. They dig tirelessly in search of coal.	You find abandoned coal mines full of them. They dig tirelessly in search of coal.

⊛ EVOLUTION
Does not evolve

No. 325 | Bounce Pokémon
Spoink

Psychic

● **HEIGHT:** 2'04"
● **WEIGHT:** 67.5 lbs.
● **ITEMS:** Tanga Berry

● SIZE COMPARISON

● MALE/FEMALE HAVE SAME FORM

● ABILITIES
- Thick Fat
- Own Tempo

● STATS
HP ●●
ATTACK ●
DEFENSE ●
SP. ATTACK ●●●
SP. DEFENSE ●●●
SPEED ●●●

● EGG GROUPS
Field

● PERFORMANCE
SPEED ★★☆
POWER ★★☆
SKILL ★★☆
STAMINA ★★★★
JUMP ★★★★☆

● MAIN WAYS TO OBTAIN

Pokémon HeartGold — Ilex Forest (Hoenn Sound)

Pokémon SoulSilver — Ilex Forest (Hoenn Sound)

Pokémon Diamond — Route 214 (mass outbreak)

Pokémon Pearl — Route 214 (mass outbreak)

Pokémon Platinum — Route 214 (mass outbreak)

Pokémon HeartGold
It bounces around on its tail to keep its heart pumping. It carries a pearl from CLAMPERL on its head.

Pokémon SoulSilver
It bounces around on its tail to keep its heart pumping. It carries a pearl from CLAMPERL on its head.

● EVOLUTION

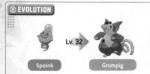

Spoink — Lv. 32 — Grumpig

● LEVEL-UP MOVES

Lv.	Name	Type	Kind	Pow.	Acc.	PP	Range	DA
1	Splash	Normal	Status	—	—	40	Self	—
7	Psywave	Psychic	Special	—	80	15	Normal	—
10	Odor Sleuth	Normal	Status	—	—	40	Normal	—
14	Psybeam	Psychic	Special	65	100	20	Normal	—
15	Psych Up	Normal	Status	—	—	10	Normal	—
18	Confuse Ray	Ghost	Status	—	100	10	Normal	—
21	Magic Coat	Psychic	Status	—	—	15	Self	—
26	Zen Headbutt	Psychic	Physical	80	90	15	Normal	○
29	Rest	Psychic	Status	—	—	10	Self	—
29	Snore	Normal	Special	40	100	15	Normal	—
34	Payback	Dark	Physical	50	100	10	Normal	○
41	Psychic	Psychic	Special	90	100	10	Normal	—
46	Power Gem	Rock	Special	70	100	20	Normal	—
48	Bounce	Flying	Physical	85	85	5	Normal	○

● MOVE MANIAC

Name	Type	Kind	Pow.	Acc.	PP	Range	DA
Headbutt	Normal	Physical	70	100	15	Normal	○

● BP MOVES

Name	Type	Kind	Pow.	Acc.	PP	Range	DA
Icy Wind	Ice	Special	55	95	15	2 Foes	—
Zen Headbutt	Psychic	Physical	80	90	15	Normal	○
Trick	Psychic	Status	—	100	10	Normal	—
Snore	Normal	Special	40	100	15	Normal	—
Swift	Normal	Special	60	—	20	2 Foes	—
Magic Coat	Psychic	Status	—	—	15	Self	—
Role Play	Psychic	Status	—	—	10	Normal	—
Heal Bell	Normal	Status	—	—	5	All Allies	—
Signal Beam	Bug	Special	75	100	15	Normal	—
Bounce	Flying	Physical	85	85	5	Normal	○

● TM & HM MOVES

No.	Name	Type	Kind	Pow.	Acc.	PP	Range	DA
TM04	Calm Mind	Psychic	Status	—	—	20	Self	—
TM06	Toxic	Poison	Status	—	85	10	Normal	—
TM10	Hidden Power	Normal	Special	—	100	15	Normal	—
TM11	Sunny Day	Fire	Status	—	—	5	All	—
TM12	Taunt	Dark	Status	—	100	20	Normal	—
TM16	Light Screen	Psychic	Status	—	—	30	2 Allies	—
TM17	Protect	Normal	Status	—	—	10	Self	—
TM18	Rain Dance	Water	Status	—	—	5	All	—
TM21	Frustration	Normal	Physical	—	100	20	Normal	○
TM23	Iron Tail	Steel	Physical	100	75	15	Normal	○
TM27	Return	Normal	Physical	—	100	20	Normal	○
TM29	Psychic	Psychic	Special	90	100	10	Normal	—
TM30	Shadow Ball	Ghost	Special	80	100	15	Normal	—
TM32	Double Team	Normal	Status	—	—	15	Self	—
TM33	Reflect	Psychic	Status	—	—	20	2 Allies	—
TM34	Shock Wave	Electric	Special	60	—	20	Normal	—
TM41	Torment	Dark	Status	—	100	15	Normal	—
TM42	Facade	Normal	Physical	70	100	20	Normal	○
TM43	Secret Power	Normal	Physical	70	100	20	Normal	—
TM44	Rest	Psychic	Status	—	—	10	Self	—
TM45	Attract	Normal	Status	—	100	15	Normal	—
TM46	Thief	Dark	Physical	40	100	10	Normal	○
TM48	Skill Swap	Psychic	Status	—	—	10	Normal	—
TM49	Snatch	Dark	Status	—	—	10	Depends	—
TM57	Charge Beam	Electric	Special	50	90	10	Normal	—
TM58	Endure	Normal	Status	—	—	10	Self	—
TM66	Payback	Dark	Physical	50	100	10	Normal	○
TM67	Recycle	Normal	Status	—	—	10	Self	—
TM70	Flash	Normal	Status	—	100	20	Normal	—
TM73	Thunder Wave	Electric	Status	—	100	20	Normal	—
TM77	Psych Up	Normal	Status	—	—	10	Normal	—
TM78	Captivate	Normal	Status	—	100	20	2 Foes	—
TM82	Sleep Talk	Normal	Status	—	—	10	Depends	—
TM83	Natural Gift	Normal	Physical	—	100	15	Normal	—
TM85	Dream Eater	Psychic	Special	100	100	15	Normal	—
TM86	Grass Knot	Grass	Special	—	100	20	Normal	○
TM87	Swagger	Normal	Status	—	90	15	Normal	—
TM90	Substitute	Normal	Status	—	—	10	Self	—
TM92	Trick Room	Psychic	Status	—	—	5	All	—

● EGG MOVES

Name	Type	Kind	Pow.	Acc.	PP	Range	DA
Future Sight	Psychic	Special	80	90	15	Normal	—
Extrasensory	Psychic	Special	80	100	30	Normal	—
Substitute	Normal	Status	—	—	10	Self	—
Trick	Psychic	Status	—	100	10	Normal	—
Zen Headbutt	Psychic	Physical	80	90	15	Normal	○
Amnesia	Psychic	Status	—	—	20	Self	—
Mirror Coat	Psychic	Special	—	100	20	Self	—

● LEVEL-UP MOVES

Lv.	Name	Type	Kind	Pow.	Acc.	PP	Range	DA
1	Splash	Normal	Status	—	—	40	Self	—
1	Psywave	Psychic	Special	—	80	15	Normal	—
1	Odor Sleuth	Normal	Status	—	—	40	Normal	—
1	Psybeam	Psychic	Special	65	100	20	Normal	—
7	Psywave	Psychic	Special	—	80	15	Normal	—
10	Odor Sleuth	Normal	Status	—	—	40	Normal	—
14	Psybeam	Psychic	Special	65	100	20	Normal	—
15	Psych Up	Normal	Status	—	—	10	Normal	—
18	Confuse Ray	Ghost	Status	—	100	10	Normal	—
21	Magic Coat	Psychic	Status	—	—	15	Self	—
26	Zen Headbutt	Psychic	Physical	80	90	15	Normal	○
29	Rest	Psychic	Status	—	—	10	Self	—
29	Snore	Normal	Special	40	100	15	Normal	—
37	Payback	Dark	Physical	50	100	10	Normal	○
42	Psychic	Psychic	Special	90	100	10	Normal	—
55	Power Gem	Rock	Special	70	100	20	Normal	—
60	Bounce	Flying	Physical	85	85	5	Normal	○

● MOVE MANIAC

Name	Type	Kind	Pow.	Acc.	PP	Range	DA
Headbutt	Normal	Physical	70	100	15	Normal	○

● BP MOVES

Name	Type	Kind	Pow.	Acc.	PP	Range	DA
Icy Wind	Ice	Special	55	95	15	2 Foes	—
ThunderPunch	Electric	Physical	75	100	15	Normal	○
Fire Punch	Fire	Physical	75	100	15	Normal	○
Ice Punch	Ice	Physical	75	100	15	Normal	○
Zen Headbutt	Psychic	Physical	80	90	15	Normal	○
Trick	Psychic	Status	—	100	10	Normal	—
Snore	Normal	Special	40	100	15	Normal	—
Swift	Normal	Special	60	—	20	2 Foes	—
Magic Coat	Psychic	Status	—	—	15	Self	—
Role Play	Psychic	Status	—	—	10	Normal	—
Heal Bell	Normal	Status	—	—	5	All Allies	—
Mud-Slap	Ground	Special	20	100	10	Normal	—
Signal Beam	Bug	Special	75	100	15	Normal	○
Bounce	Flying	Physical	85	85	5	Normal	○

● TM & HM MOVES

No.	Name	Type	Kind	Pow.	Acc.	PP	Range	DA
TM01	Focus Punch	Fighting	Physical	150	100	20	Normal	○
TM04	Calm Mind	Psychic	Status	—	—	20	Self	—
TM06	Toxic	Poison	Status	—	85	10	Normal	—
TM10	Hidden Power	Normal	Special	—	100	15	Normal	—
TM11	Sunny Day	Fire	Status	—	—	5	All	—
TM12	Taunt	Dark	Status	—	100	20	Normal	—
TM15	Hyper Beam	Normal	Special	150	90	5	Normal	—
TM16	Light Screen	Psychic	Status	—	—	30	2 Allies	—
TM17	Protect	Normal	Status	—	—	10	Self	—
TM18	Rain Dance	Water	Status	—	—	5	All	—
TM21	Frustration	Normal	Physical	—	100	20	Normal	○
TM23	Iron Tail	Steel	Physical	100	75	15	Normal	○
TM27	Return	Normal	Physical	—	100	20	Normal	○
TM29	Psychic	Psychic	Special	90	100	10	Normal	—
TM30	Shadow Ball	Ghost	Special	80	100	15	Normal	—
TM31	Brick Break	Fighting	Physical	75	100	15	Normal	○
TM32	Double Team	Normal	Status	—	—	15	Self	—
TM33	Reflect	Psychic	Status	—	—	20	2 Allies	—
TM34	Shock Wave	Electric	Special	60	—	20	Normal	—
TM41	Torment	Dark	Status	—	100	15	Normal	—
TM42	Facade	Normal	Physical	70	100	20	Normal	○
TM43	Secret Power	Normal	Physical	70	100	20	Normal	○
TM44	Rest	Psychic	Status	—	—	10	Self	—
TM45	Attract	Normal	Status	—	100	15	Normal	—
TM46	Thief	Dark	Physical	40	100	10	Normal	○
TM48	Skill Swap	Psychic	Status	—	—	10	Normal	—
TM49	Snatch	Dark	Status	—	—	10	Depends	—
TM52	Focus Blast	Fighting	Special	120	70	5	Normal	—
TM53	Energy Ball	Grass	Special	80	100	10	Normal	—
TM56	Fling	Dark	Physical	—	100	10	Normal	—
TM57	Charge Beam	Electric	Special	50	90	10	Normal	—
TM58	Endure	Normal	Status	—	—	10	Self	—
TM60	Drain Punch	Fighting	Physical	60	100	5	Normal	○
TM66	Payback	Dark	Physical	50	100	10	Normal	○
TM67	Recycle	Normal	Status	—	—	10	Self	—
TM68	Giga Impact	Normal	Physical	150	90	5	Normal	○
TM70	Flash	Normal	Status	—	100	20	Normal	—
TM73	Thunder Wave	Electric	Status	—	100	20	Normal	—
TM77	Psych Up	Normal	Status	—	—	10	Normal	—
TM78	Captivate	Normal	Status	—	100	20	2 Foes	—
TM82	Sleep Talk	Normal	Status	—	—	10	Depends	—
TM83	Natural Gift	Normal	Physical	—	100	15	Normal	—
TM85	Dream Eater	Psychic	Special	100	100	15	Normal	—
TM86	Grass Knot	Grass	Special	—	100	20	Normal	○
TM87	Swagger	Normal	Status	—	90	15	Normal	—
TM90	Substitute	Normal	Status	—	—	10	Self	—
TM92	Trick Room	Psychic	Status	—	—	5	All	—

No. 326 | Manipulate Pokémon
Grumpig

Psychic

- ● HEIGHT: 2'11"
- ● WEIGHT: 157.6 lbs.
- ● ITEMS: None

● SIZE COMPARISON

● MALE/FEMALE HAVE SAME FORM

⊙ ABILITIES
- ● Thick Fat
- ● Own Tempo

⊙ EGG GROUPS
Field

⊙ STATS
HP ●●●
ATTACK ●●
DEFENSE ●●●
SP. ATTACK ●●●●
SP. DEFENSE ●●●●
SPEED ●●●●

⊙ PERFORMANCE
SPEED ★★
POWER ★★★☆☆
SKILL ★★★☆☆
STAMINA ★★★★☆
JUMP ★★★

● MAIN WAYS TO OBTAIN

Pokémon HeartGold Level up Spoink to Lv. 32

Pokémon SoulSilver Level up Spoink to Lv. 32

Pokémon Diamond Level up Spoink to Lv. 32

Pokémon Pearl Level up Spoink to Lv. 32

Pokémon Platinum Level up Spoink to Lv. 32

Pokémon HeartGold
It can perform odd dance steps to influence foes. Its style of dancing became hugely popular overseas.

Pokémon SoulSilver
It can perform odd dance steps to influence foes. Its style of dancing became hugely popular overseas.

⊙ EVOLUTION

Spoink → Lv. 32 → Grumpig

No. 327 | Spot Panda Pokémon
Spinda

Normal

- **HEIGHT:** 3'02"
- **WEIGHT:** 11.0 lbs.
- **ITEMS:** Chesto Berry

● SIZE COMPARISON

● MALE/FEMALE HAVE SAME FORM

⊙ ABILITIES
- Own Tempo
- Tangled Feet

⊙ STATS
```
         HP ●●
     ATTACK ●●●
    DEFENSE ●●
  SP. ATTACK ●●
 SP. DEFENSE ●●●
      SPEED ●●●
```

⊙ EGG GROUPS
Field

Human-Like

⊙ PERFORMANCE
SPEED ★★☆	STAMINA ★★★	
POWER ★★☆	JUMP ★★☆	
SKILL ★★★☆		

● MAIN WAYS TO OBTAIN

Pokémon HeartGold	Sprout Tower (Hoenn Sound)
Pokémon SoulSilver	Sprout Tower (Hoenn Sound)
Pokémon Diamond	Route 227 (mass outbreak)
Pokémon Pearl	Route 227 (mass outbreak)
Pokémon Platinum	Route 227 (mass outbreak)

Pokémon HeartGold	Pokémon SoulSilver
The chances of two SPINDA having identical spot patterns is less than one in four billion.	The chances of two SPINDA having identical spot patterns is less than one in four billion.

⊙ EVOLUTION
Does not evolve

● LEVEL-UP MOVES
Lv.	Name	Type	Kind	Pow.	Acc.	PP	Range	DA
1	Tackle	Normal	Physical	35	95	35	Normal	○
5	Uproar	Normal	Special	50	100	10	1 Random	—
10	Copycat	Normal	Status	—	—	20	Depends	—
14	Faint Attack	Dark	Physical	60	—	20	Normal	○
19	Psybeam	Psychic	Special	65	100	20	Normal	—
23	Hypnosis	Psychic	Status	—	60	20	Normal	○
28	Dizzy Punch	Normal	Physical	70	100	10	Normal	○
32	Sucker Punch	Dark	Physical	80	100	5	Normal	○
37	Teeter Dance	Normal	Status	—	100	20	2 Foes/1 Ally	—
41	Psych Up	Normal	Status	—	—	10	Normal	—
46	Double-Edge	Normal	Physical	120	100	15	Normal	○
50	Flail	Normal	Physical	—	100	15	Normal	○
55	Thrash	Normal	Physical	90	100	10	1 Random	○

● MOVE MANIAC
Name	Type	Kind	Pow.	Acc.	PP	Range	DA
Headbutt	Normal	Physical	70	100	15	Normal	○

● BP MOVES
Name	Type	Kind	Pow.	Acc.	PP	Range	DA
Icy Wind	Ice	Special	55	95	15	2 Foes	—
ThunderPunch	Electric	Physical	75	100	15	Normal	○
Fire Punch	Fire	Physical	75	100	15	Normal	○
Ice Punch	Ice	Physical	75	100	15	Normal	○
Zen Headbutt	Psychic	Physical	80	90	15	Normal	○
Sucker Punch	Dark	Physical	80	100	5	Normal	○
Snore	Normal	Special	40	100	15	Normal	—
Helping Hand	Normal	Status	—	—	20	1 Ally	—
Last Resort	Normal	Physical	130	100	5	Normal	○
Swift	Normal	Special	60	—	20	2 Foes	—
Uproar	Normal	Special	50	100	10	1 Random	—
Role Play	Psychic	Status	—	—	10	Normal	—
Mud-Slap	Ground	Special	20	100	10	Normal	○
Rollout	Rock	Physical	30	90	20	Normal	○
Low Kick	Fighting	Physical	—	100	20	Normal	○

● TM & HM MOVES
No.	Name	Type	Kind	Pow.	Acc.	PP	Range	DA
TM01	Focus Punch	Fighting	Physical	150	100	20	Normal	○
TM03	Water Pulse	Water	Special	60	100	20	Normal	—
TM04	Calm Mind	Psychic	Status	—	—	20	Self	—
TM06	Toxic	Poison	Status	—	85	10	Normal	—
TM10	Hidden Power	Normal	Special	—	100	15	Normal	—
TM11	Sunny Day	Fire	Status	—	—	5	All	—
TM17	Protect	Normal	Status	—	—	10	Self	—
TM18	Rain Dance	Water	Status	—	—	5	All	—
TM20	Safeguard	Normal	Status	—	—	25	2 Allies	—
TM21	Frustration	Normal	Physical	—	100	20	Normal	○
TM27	Return	Normal	Physical	—	100	20	Normal	○
TM28	Dig	Ground	Physical	80	100	10	Normal	○
TM29	Psychic	Psychic	Special	90	100	10	Normal	—
TM30	Shadow Ball	Ghost	Special	80	100	15	Normal	—
TM31	Brick Break	Fighting	Physical	75	100	15	Normal	○
TM32	Double Team	Normal	Status	—	—	15	Self	—
TM39	Rock Tomb	Rock	Physical	50	80	10	Normal	○
TM42	Facade	Normal	Physical	70	100	20	Normal	○
TM43	Secret Power	Normal	Physical	70	100	20	Normal	○
TM44	Rest	Psychic	Status	—	—	10	Self	—
TM45	Attract	Normal	Status	—	100	15	Normal	—
TM46	Thief	Dark	Physical	40	100	10	Normal	○
TM48	Skill Swap	Psychic	Status	—	—	10	Normal	—
TM49	Snatch	Dark	Status	—	—	10	Depends	—
TM56	Fling	Dark	Physical	—	100	10	Normal	○
TM58	Endure	Normal	Status	—	—	10	Self	—
TM60	Drain Punch	Fighting	Physical	60	100	5	Normal	○
TM67	Recycle	Normal	Status	—	—	10	Self	—
TM70	Flash	Normal	Status	—	100	20	Normal	—
TM77	Psych Up	Normal	Status	—	—	10	Normal	—
TM78	Captivate	Normal	Status	—	100	20	2 Foes	—
TM80	Rock Slide	Rock	Physical	75	90	10	2 Foes	—
TM82	Sleep Talk	Normal	Status	—	—	10	Self	—
TM83	Natural Gift	Normal	Physical	—	100	15	Normal	—
TM85	Dream Eater	Psychic	Special	100	100	15	Normal	—
TM87	Swagger	Normal	Status	—	90	15	Normal	—
TM90	Substitute	Normal	Status	—	—	10	Self	—
TM92	Trick Room	Psychic	Status	—	—	5	All	—
HM04	Strength	Normal	Physical	80	100	15	Normal	○
HM06	Rock Smash	Fighting	Physical	40	100	15	Normal	○

● EGG MOVES
Name	Type	Kind	Pow.	Acc.	PP	Range	DA
Encore	Normal	Status	—	100	5	Normal	—
Rock Slide	Rock	Physical	75	90	10	2 Foes	—
Assist	Normal	Status	—	—	20	Depends	—
Disable	Normal	Status	—	80	20	Normal	—
Flash	Normal	Status	—	100	20	Normal	—
Baton Pass	Normal	Status	—	—	40	Self	—
Wish	Normal	Status	—	—	10	Self	—
Trick	Psychic	Status	—	100	10	Normal	—
SmellingSalt	Normal	Physical	60	100	10	Normal	○
Fake Out	Normal	Physical	40	100	10	Normal	○
Role Play	Psychic	Status	—	—	10	Normal	—
Psycho Cut	Psychic	Physical	70	100	20	Normal	○

● LEVEL-UP MOVES

Lv.	Name	Type	Kind	Pow.	Acc.	PP	Range	DA
1	Bite	Dark	Physical	60	100	25	Normal	○
9	Sand-Attack	Ground	Status	—	100	15	Normal	—
17	Faint Attack	Dark	Physical	60	—	20	Normal	○
25	Sand Tomb	Ground	Physical	15	70	15	Normal	—
33	Crunch	Dark	Physical	80	100	15	Normal	○
41	Dig	Ground	Physical	80	100	10	Normal	○
49	Sandstorm	Rock	Status	—	—	10	All	—
57	Hyper Beam	Normal	Special	150	90	5	Normal	—
65	Earth Power	Ground	Special	90	100	10	Normal	—
73	Earthquake	Ground	Physical	100	100	10	2 Foes/1 Ally	—
81	Feint	Normal	Physical	50	100	10	Normal	—
89	Fissure	Ground	Physical	—	30	5	Normal	—

● MOVE MANIAC

Name	Type	Kind	Pow.	Acc.	PP	Range	DA
Headbutt	Normal	Physical	70	100	15	Normal	○

● BP MOVES

Name	Type	Kind	Pow.	Acc.	PP	Range	DA
Fury Cutter	Bug	Physical	10	95	20	Normal	○
Bug Bite	Bug	Physical	60	100	20	Normal	○
Snore	Normal	Special	40	100	15	Normal	—
Mud-Slap	Ground	Special	20	100	10	Normal	—
Earth Power	Ground	Special	90	100	10	Normal	—

● TM & HM MOVES

No.	Name	Type	Kind	Pow.	Acc.	PP	Range	DA
TM06	Toxic	Poison	Status	—	85	10	Normal	—
TM10	Hidden Power	Normal	Special	—	100	15	Normal	—
TM11	Sunny Day	Fire	Status	—	—	5	All	—
TM15	Hyper Beam	Normal	Special	150	90	5	Normal	—
TM17	Protect	Normal	Status	—	—	10	Self	—
TM19	Giga Drain	Grass	Special	60	100	10	Normal	—
TM21	Frustration	Normal	Physical	—	100	20	Normal	○
TM22	SolarBeam	Grass	Special	120	100	10	Normal	—
TM26	Earthquake	Ground	Physical	100	100	10	2 Foes/1 Ally	—
TM27	Return	Normal	Physical	—	100	20	Normal	○
TM28	Dig	Ground	Physical	80	100	10	Normal	○
TM32	Double Team	Normal	Status	—	—	15	Self	—
TM37	Sandstorm	Rock	Status	—	—	10	All	—
TM39	Rock Tomb	Rock	Physical	50	80	10	Normal	—
TM42	Facade	Normal	Physical	70	100	20	Normal	—
TM43	Secret Power	Normal	Physical	70	100	20	Normal	—
TM44	Rest	Psychic	Status	—	—	10	Self	—
TM45	Attract	Normal	Status	—	100	15	Normal	—
TM58	Endure	Normal	Status	—	—	10	Self	—
TM78	Captivate	Normal	Status	—	100	20	2 Foes	—
TM80	Rock Slide	Rock	Physical	75	90	10	2 Foes	—
TM82	Sleep Talk	Normal	Status	—	—	10	Depends	—
TM83	Natural Gift	Normal	Physical	—	100	15	Normal	—
TM87	Swagger	Normal	Status	—	90	15	Normal	—
TM90	Substitute	Normal	Status	—	—	10	Self	—
HM04	Strength	Normal	Physical	80	100	15	Normal	○
HM06	Rock Smash	Fighting	Physical	40	100	15	Normal	○

● EGG MOVES

Name	Type	Kind	Pow.	Acc.	PP	Range	DA
Focus Energy	Normal	Status	—	—	30	Self	—
Quick Attack	Normal	Physical	40	100	30	Normal	○
Gust	Flying	Special	40	100	35	Normal	○
Flail	Normal	Physical	—	100	15	Normal	○
Fury Cutter	Bug	Physical	10	95	20	Normal	○
Mud Shot	Ground	Special	55	95	15	Normal	—

● No. 328 | Ant Pit Pokémon
Trapinch

Ground

● HEIGHT: 2'04"
● WEIGHT: 33.1 lbs.
● ITEMS: Soft Sand

● SIZE COMPARISON

● MALE/FEMALE HAVE SAME FORM

◎ ABILITIES
● Hyper Cutter
● Arena Trap

◎ STATS
HP ●●
ATTACK ●●●●
DEFENSE ●●●
SP. ATTACK ●●
SP. DEFENSE ●●
SPEED ●

◎ EGG GROUPS
Bug

◎ PERFORMANCE

SPEED ★★☆   STAMINA ★★★☆☆
POWER ★★★☆☆   JUMP ★★
SKILL ★★☆

● MAIN WAYS TO OBTAIN

Pokémon HeartGold	Safari Zone (Desert Area: if Rock objects are placed, may appear in tall grass)
Pokémon SoulSilver	Safari Zone (Desert Area: if Rock objects are placed, may appear in tall grass)
Pokémon Diamond	Route 228 (occasionally appears when you use Poké Radar)
Pokémon Pearl	Route 228 (occasionally appears when you use Poké Radar)
Pokémon Platinum	—

Pokémon HeartGold	**Pokémon SoulSilver**
Its nest is a sloped, bowl-like pit in the desert. Once something has fallen in, there is no escape.	Its nest is a sloped, bowl-like pit in the desert. Once something has fallen in, there is no escape.

◎ EVOLUTION

Lv. 35   Lv. 45

Trapinch   Vibrave   Flygon

No. 329 | Vibration Pokémon
Vibrava

`Ground` `Dragon`

- **HEIGHT:** 3'07"
- **WEIGHT:** 33.7 lbs.
- **ITEMS:** None

● **SIZE COMPARISON**

● MALE/FEMALE HAVE SAME FORM

⊛ ABILITIES
- Levitate

⊛ EGG GROUPS
Bug

⊛ PERFORMANCE
SPEED ★★★☆	STAMINA ★★☆
POWER ★★☆	JUMP ★★★☆
SKILL ★★★★☆	

● MAIN WAYS TO OBTAIN

Pokémon HeartGold — Safari Zone (Desert Area: if Forest objects are placed, may appear in tall grass)

Pokémon SoulSilver — Safari Zone (Desert Area: if Forest objects are placed, may appear in tall grass)

Pokémon Diamond — Route 228 (use Poké Radar)

Pokémon Pearl — Route 228 (use Poké Radar)

Pokémon Platinum — —

Pokémon HeartGold — It vibrates its wings vigorously, creating ultrasonic waves that cause serious headaches.

Pokémon SoulSilver — It vibrates its wings vigorously, creating ultrasonic waves that cause serious headaches.

⊛ EVOLUTION

Trapinch → Lv. 35 → Vibrava → Lv. 45 → Flygon

⊛ STATS
HP	●●
ATTACK	●●
DEFENSE	●●
SP. ATTACK	●●
SP. DEFENSE	●●
SPEED	●●●

● LEVEL-UP MOVES
Lv.	Name	Type	Kind	Pow.	Acc.	PP	Range	DA
1	SonicBoom	Normal	Special	—	90	20	Normal	—
1	Sand-Attack	Ground	Status	—	100	15	Normal	—
1	Faint Attack	Dark	Physical	60	—	20	Normal	○
1	Sand Tomb	Ground	Physical	15	70	15	Normal	—
9	Sand Tomb	Ground	Status	—	100	15	Normal	—
17	Faint Attack	Dark	Physical	60	—	20	Normal	○
25	Sand Tomb	Ground	Physical	15	70	15	Normal	—
33	Supersonic	Normal	Status	—	55	20	Normal	—
35	DragonBreath	Dragon	Special	60	100	20	Normal	—
41	Screech	Normal	Status	—	85	40	Normal	—
49	Sandstorm	Rock	Status	—	—	10	All	—
57	Hyper Beam	Normal	Special	150	90	5	Normal	—

● MOVE MANIAC
Name	Type	Kind	Pow.	Acc.	PP	Range	DA
Headbutt	Normal	Physical	70	100	15	Normal	○
Draco Meteor	Dragon	Special	140	90	5	Normal	—

● BP MOVES
Name	Type	Kind	Pow.	Acc.	PP	Range	DA
Fury Cutter	Bug	Physical	10	95	20	Normal	○
Ominous Wind	Ghost	Special	60	100	5	Normal	—
Air Cutter	Flying	Special	55	95	25	2 Foes	—
Bug Bite	Bug	Physical	60	100	20	Normal	○
Snore	Normal	Special	40	100	15	Normal	—
Swift	Normal	Special	60	—	20	2 Foes	—
Tailwind	Flying	Status	—	—	30	2 Allies	—
Mud-Slap	Ground	Special	20	100	10	Normal	—
Outrage	Dragon	Physical	120	100	15	1 Random	○
Earth Power	Ground	Special	90	100	10	Normal	—
Twister	Dragon	Special	40	100	20	2 Foes	—
Heat Wave	Fire	Special	100	90	10	2 Foes	—

● TM & HM MOVES
No.	Name	Type	Kind	Pow.	Acc.	PP	Range	DA
TM06	Toxic	Poison	Status	—	85	10	Normal	—
TM10	Hidden Power	Normal	Special	—	100	15	Normal	—
TM11	Sunny Day	Fire	Status	—	—	5	All	—
TM15	Hyper Beam	Normal	Special	150	90	5	Normal	—
TM17	Protect	Normal	Status	—	—	10	Self	—
TM19	Giga Drain	Grass	Special	60	100	10	Normal	—
TM21	Frustration	Normal	Physical	—	100	20	Normal	○
TM22	SolarBeam	Grass	Special	120	100	10	Normal	—
TM26	Earthquake	Ground	Physical	100	100	10	2 Foes/1 Ally	—
TM27	Return	Normal	Physical	—	100	20	Normal	○
TM28	Dig	Ground	Physical	80	100	10	Normal	○
TM32	Double Team	Normal	Status	—	—	15	Self	—
TM37	Sandstorm	Rock	Status	—	—	10	All	—
TM39	Rock Tomb	Rock	Physical	50	80	10	Normal	—
TM42	Facade	Normal	Physical	70	100	20	Normal	○
TM43	Secret Power	Normal	Physical	70	100	20	Normal	—
TM44	Rest	Psychic	Status	—	—	10	Self	—
TM45	Attract	Normal	Status	—	100	15	Normal	—
TM47	Steel Wing	Steel	Physical	70	90	25	Normal	○
TM51	Roost	Flying	Status	—	—	10	Self	—
TM58	Endure	Normal	Status	—	—	10	Self	—
TM59	Dragon Pulse	Dragon	Special	90	100	10	Normal	—
TM62	Silver Wind	Bug	Special	60	100	5	Normal	—
TM78	Captivate	Normal	Status	—	100	20	2 Foes	—
TM80	Rock Slide	Rock	Physical	75	90	10	2 Foes	—
TM82	Sleep Talk	Normal	Status	—	—	10	Depends	—
TM83	Natural Gift	Normal	Physical	—	100	15	Normal	—
TM87	Swagger	Normal	Status	—	90	15	Normal	—
TM89	U-turn	Bug	Physical	70	100	20	Normal	○
TM90	Substitute	Normal	Status	—	—	10	Self	—
HM02	Fly	Flying	Physical	90	95	15	Normal	○
HM04	Strength	Normal	Physical	80	100	15	Normal	○
HM06	Rock Smash	Fighting	Physical	40	100	15	Normal	○

● LEVEL-UP MOVES

Lv.	Name	Type	Kind	Pow.	Acc.	PP	Range	DA
1	SonicBoom	Normal	Special	—	90	20	Normal	—
1	Sand-Attack	Ground	Status	—	100	15	Normal	—
1	Faint Attack	Dark	Physical	60	—	20	Normal	○
1	Sand Tomb	Ground	Physical	15	70	15	Normal	—
9	Sand-Attack	Ground	Status	—	100	15	Normal	—
17	Faint Attack	Dark	Physical	60	—	20	Normal	○
25	Sand Tomb	Ground	Physical	15	70	15	Normal	—
33	Supersonic	Normal	Status	—	55	20	Normal	—
35	DragonBreath	Dragon	Special	60	100	20	Normal	—
41	Screech	Normal	Status	—	85	40	Normal	—
45	Dragon Claw	Dragon	Physical	80	100	15	Normal	○
49	Sandstorm	Rock	Status	—	—	10	All	—
57	Hyper Beam	Normal	Special	150	90	5	Normal	—

● MOVE MANIAC

Name	Type	Kind	Pow.	Acc.	PP	Range	DA
Headbutt	Normal	Physical	70	100	15	Normal	○
Draco Meteor	Dragon	Special	140	90	5	Normal	—

● BP MOVES

Name	Type	Kind	Pow.	Acc.	PP	Range	DA
Fury Cutter	Bug	Physical	10	95	20	Normal	○
ThunderPunch	Electric	Physical	75	100	15	Normal	○
Fire Punch	Fire	Physical	75	100	15	Normal	○
Ominous Wind	Ghost	Special	60	100	5	Normal	—
Air Cutter	Flying	Special	55	95	25	2 Foes	—
Bug Bite	Bug	Physical	60	100	20	Normal	○
Snore	Normal	Special	40	100	15	Normal	—
Swift	Normal	Special	60	—	20	2 Foes	—
Tailwind	Flying	Status	—	—	30	2 Allies	—
Mud-Slap	Ground	Special	20	100	10	Normal	—
Outrage	Dragon	Physical	120	100	10	1 Random	○
Earth Power	Ground	Special	90	100	10	Normal	—
Twister	Dragon	Special	40	100	20	2 Foes	—
Heat Wave	Fire	Special	100	90	10	2 Foes	—

● TM & HM MOVES

No.	Name	Type	Kind	Pow.	Acc.	PP	Range	DA
TM02	Dragon Claw	Dragon	Physical	80	100	15	Normal	○
TM06	Toxic	Poison	Status	—	85	10	Normal	—
TM10	Hidden Power	Normal	Special	—	100	15	Normal	—
TM11	Sunny Day	Fire	Status	—	—	5	All	—
TM15	Hyper Beam	Normal	Special	150	90	5	Normal	—
TM17	Protect	Normal	Status	—	—	10	Self	—
TM19	Giga Drain	Grass	Special	60	100	10	Normal	—
TM21	Frustration	Normal	Physical	—	100	20	Normal	○
TM22	SolarBeam	Grass	Special	120	100	10	Normal	—
TM23	Iron Tail	Steel	Physical	100	75	15	Normal	○
TM26	Earthquake	Ground	Physical	100	100	10	2 Foes/1 Ally	○
TM27	Return	Normal	Physical	—	100	20	Normal	○
TM28	Dig	Ground	Physical	80	100	10	Normal	○
TM32	Double Team	Normal	Status	—	—	15	Self	—
TM35	Flamethrower	Fire	Special	95	100	15	Normal	—
TM37	Sandstorm	Rock	Status	—	—	10	All	—
TM38	Fire Blast	Fire	Special	120	85	5	Normal	—
TM39	Rock Tomb	Rock	Physical	50	80	10	Normal	—
TM40	Aerial Ace	Flying	Physical	60	—	20	Normal	○
TM42	Facade	Normal	Physical	70	100	20	Normal	○
TM43	Secret Power	Normal	Physical	70	100	20	Normal	○
TM44	Rest	Psychic	Status	—	—	10	Self	—
TM45	Attract	Normal	Status	—	100	15	Normal	—
TM47	Steel Wing	Steel	Physical	70	90	25	Normal	○
TM51	Roost	Flying	Status	—	—	10	Self	—
TM58	Endure	Normal	Status	—	—	10	Self	—
TM59	Dragon Pulse	Dragon	Special	90	100	10	Normal	—
TM62	Silver Wind	Bug	Special	60	100	5	Normal	—
TM68	Giga Impact	Normal	Physical	150	90	5	Normal	○
TM71	Stone Edge	Rock	Physical	100	80	5	Normal	—
TM78	Captivate	Normal	Status	—	100	20	2 Foes	—
TM80	Rock Slide	Rock	Physical	75	90	10	2 Foes	—
TM82	Sleep Talk	Normal	Status	—	—	10	Depends	—
TM83	Natural Gift	Normal	Physical	—	100	15	Normal	—
TM87	Swagger	Normal	Status	—	90	15	Normal	—
TM89	U-turn	Bug	Physical	70	100	20	Normal	○
TM90	Substitute	Normal	Status	—	—	10	Self	—
HM02	Fly	Flying	Physical	90	95	15	Normal	○
HM04	Strength	Normal	Physical	80	100	15	Normal	○
HM06	Rock Smash	Fighting	Physical	40	100	15	Normal	○

▶ No. 330 | Mystic Pokémon
Flygon

Ground　Dragon

- ● HEIGHT: 6'07"
- ● WEIGHT: 180.8 lbs.
- ● ITEMS: None
- ● SIZE COMPARISON

● MALE/FEMALE HAVE SAME FORM

⚙ ABILITIES
● Levitate

⚙ STATS
HP ●●●○
ATTACK ●●●●
DEFENSE ●●●○
SP. ATTACK ●●●○
SP. DEFENSE ●●●○
SPEED ●●●●

⚙ EGG GROUPS
Bug

⚙ PERFORMANCE
SPEED ★★★☆　　STAMINA ★★
POWER ★★★☆☆　JUMP ★★★★★
SKILL ★★★☆

● MAIN WAYS TO OBTAIN

Pokémon HeartGold　Level up Vibrava to Lv. 45

Pokémon SoulSilver　Level up Vibrava to Lv. 45

Pokémon Diamond　Level up Vibrava to Lv. 45

Pokémon Pearl　Level up Vibrava to Lv. 45

Pokémon Platinum　—

Pokémon HeartGold	Pokémon SoulSilver
It is nicknamed "The Desert Spirit" because the flapping of its wings sounds like a woman singing.	It is nicknamed "The Desert Spirit" because the flapping of its wings sounds like a woman singing.

⚙ EVOLUTION

Trapinch　　Lv. 35　Vibrava　　Lv. 45　Flygon

No. 331 | Cactus Pokémon
Cacnea

Grass

● HEIGHT: 1'04"
● WEIGHT: 113.1 lbs.
● ITEMS: Sticky Barb

● SIZE COMPARISON

● MALE/FEMALE HAVE SAME FORM

● ABILITIES
● Sand Veil

● STATS
HP ●●
ATTACK ●●●●
DEFENSE ●●
SP. ATTACK ●●●●
SP. DEFENSE ●
SPEED ●●

● EGG GROUPS
Grass

Human-Like

● PERFORMANCE
SPEED ★★★
POWER ★★★☆
SKILL ★★★☆

STAMINA ★★★★☆
JUMP ★★☆

● MAIN WAYS TO OBTAIN

Pokémon HeartGold	Safari Zone (Desert Area: if Forest objects are placed, may appear in tall grass)
Pokémon SoulSilver	Safari Zone (Desert Area: if Forest objects are placed, may appear in tall grass)
Pokémon Diamond	Route 228
Pokémon Pearl	Route 228
Pokémon Platinum	Route 228

| Pokémon HeartGold | Pokémon SoulSilver |
| It lives in arid locations. Its yellow flowers bloom once a year. | It lives in arid locations. Its yellow flowers bloom once a year. |

● EVOLUTION

Cacnea → Lv. 32 → Cacturne

● LEVEL-UP MOVES

Lv.	Name	Type	Kind	Pow.	Acc.	PP	Range	DA
1	Poison Sting	Poison	Physical	15	100	35	Normal	—
1	Leer	Normal	Status	—	100	30	2 Foes	—
5	Absorb	Grass	Special	20	100	25	Normal	—
9	Growth	Normal	Status	—	—	40	Self	—
13	Leech Seed	Grass	Status	—	90	10	Normal	—
17	Sand-Attack	Ground	Status	—	100	15	Normal	—
21	Pin Missile	Bug	Physical	14	85	20	Normal	—
25	Ingrain	Grass	Status	—	—	20	Self	—
29	Faint Attack	Dark	Physical	60	—	20	Normal	○
33	Spikes	Ground	Status	—	—	20	2 Foes	—
37	Sucker Punch	Dark	Physical	80	100	5	Normal	○
41	Payback	Dark	Physical	50	100	10	Normal	○
45	Needle Arm	Grass	Physical	60	100	15	Normal	—
49	Cotton Spore	Grass	Status	—	85	40	Normal	—
53	Sandstorm	Rock	Status	—	—	10	All	—
57	Destiny Bond	Ghost	Status	—	—	5	Self	—

● MOVE MANIAC

Name	Type	Kind	Pow.	Acc.	PP	Range	DA
Headbutt	Normal	Physical	70	100	15	Normal	○

● BP MOVES

Name	Type	Kind	Pow.	Acc.	PP	Range	DA
Fury Cutter	Bug	Physical	10	95	20	Normal	○
ThunderPunch	Electric	Physical	75	100	15	Normal	○
Sucker Punch	Dark	Physical	80	100	5	Normal	○
Snore	Normal	Special	40	100	15	Normal	—
Spite	Ghost	Status	—	100	10	Normal	—
Synthesis	Grass	Status	—	—	5	Self	—
Worry Seed	Grass	Status	—	100	10	Normal	—
Role Play	Psychic	Status	—	—	10	Normal	—
Mud-Slap	Ground	Special	20	100	10	Normal	○
Seed Bomb	Grass	Physical	80	100	15	Normal	—
Low Kick	Fighting	Physical	—	100	20	Normal	○

● TM & HM MOVES

No.	Name	Type	Kind	Pow.	Acc.	PP	Range	DA
TM01	Focus Punch	Fighting	Physical	150	100	20	Normal	○
TM06	Toxic	Poison	Status	—	85	10	Normal	—
TM09	Bullet Seed	Grass	Physical	10	100	30	Normal	—
TM10	Hidden Power	Normal	Special	—	100	15	Normal	—
TM11	Sunny Day	Fire	Status	—	—	5	All	—
TM17	Protect	Normal	Status	—	—	10	Self	—
TM19	Giga Drain	Grass	Special	60	100	10	Normal	—
TM21	Frustration	Normal	Physical	—	100	20	Normal	○
TM22	SolarBeam	Grass	Special	120	100	10	Normal	—
TM27	Return	Normal	Physical	—	100	20	Normal	○
TM31	Brick Break	Fighting	Physical	75	100	15	Normal	○
TM32	Double Team	Normal	Status	—	—	15	Self	—
TM37	Sandstorm	Rock	Status	—	—	10	All	—
TM42	Facade	Normal	Physical	70	100	20	Normal	○
TM43	Secret Power	Normal	Physical	70	100	20	Normal	—
TM44	Rest	Psychic	Status	—	—	10	Self	—
TM45	Attract	Normal	Status	—	100	15	Normal	—
TM53	Energy Ball	Grass	Special	80	100	10	Normal	—
TM56	Fling	Dark	Physical	—	100	10	Normal	○
TM58	Endure	Normal	Status	—	—	10	Self	—
TM60	Drain Punch	Fighting	Physical	60	100	5	Normal	○
TM66	Payback	Dark	Physical	50	100	10	Normal	○
TM70	Flash	Normal	Status	—	100	20	Normal	—
TM75	Swords Dance	Normal	Status	—	—	30	Self	—
TM78	Captivate	Normal	Status	—	100	20	2 Foes	—
TM79	Dark Pulse	Dark	Special	80	100	15	Normal	○
TM82	Sleep Talk	Normal	Status	—	—	10	Depends	—
TM83	Natural Gift	Normal	Physical	—	100	15	Normal	—
TM84	Poison Jab	Poison	Physical	80	100	20	Normal	—
TM86	Grass Knot	Grass	Special	—	100	20	Normal	○
TM87	Swagger	Normal	Status	—	90	15	Normal	—
TM90	Substitute	Normal	Status	—	—	10	Self	—
HM01	Cut	Normal	Physical	50	95	30	Normal	○

● EGG MOVES

Name	Type	Kind	Pow.	Acc.	PP	Range	DA
GrassWhistle	Grass	Status	—	55	15	Normal	—
Acid	Poison	Special	40	100	30	2 Foes	—
Teeter Dance	Normal	Status	—	100	20	2 Foes/1 Ally	—
DynamicPunch	Fighting	Physical	100	50	5	Normal	○
Counter	Fighting	Physical	—	100	20	Self	○
Low Kick	Fighting	Physical	—	100	20	Normal	○
SmellingSalt	Normal	Physical	60	100	10	Normal	○
Magical Leaf	Grass	Special	60	—	20	Normal	—
Seed Bomb	Grass	Physical	80	100	15	Normal	—
Nasty Plot	Dark	Status	—	—	20	Self	—

● LEVEL-UP MOVES

Lv.	Name	Type	Kind	Pow.	Acc.	PP	Range	DA
1	Revenge	Fighting	Physical	60	100	10	Normal	○
1	Poison Sting	Poison	Physical	15	100	35	Normal	○
1	Leer	Normal	Status	—	100	30	2 Foes	—
1	Absorb	Grass	Special	20	100	25	Normal	—
1	Growth	Normal	Status	—	—	40	Self	—
5	Absorb	Grass	Special	20	100	25	Normal	—
9	Growth	Normal	Status	—	—	40	Self	—
13	Leech Seed	Grass	Status	—	90	10	Normal	—
17	Sand-Attack	Ground	Status	—	100	15	Normal	—
21	Pin Missile	Bug	Physical	14	85	20	Normal	—
25	Ingrain	Grass	Status	—	—	20	Self	—
29	Faint Attack	Dark	Physical	60	—	20	Normal	○
35	Spikes	Ground	Status	—	—	20	2 Foes	—
41	Sucker Punch	Dark	Physical	80	100	5	Normal	○
47	Payback	Dark	Physical	50	100	10	Normal	○
53	Needle Arm	Grass	Physical	60	100	15	Normal	○
59	Cotton Spore	Grass	Status	—	85	40	Normal	—
65	Sandstorm	Rock	Status	—	—	10	All	—
71	Destiny Bond	Ghost	Status	—	—	5	Self	—

● MOVE MANIAC

Name	Type	Kind	Pow.	Acc.	PP	Range	DA
Headbutt	Normal	Physical	70	100	15	Normal	○

● BP MOVES

Name	Type	Kind	Pow.	Acc.	PP	Range	DA
Fury Cutter	Bug	Physical	10	95	20	Normal	○
ThunderPunch	Electric	Physical	75	100	15	Normal	○
Sucker Punch	Dark	Physical	80	100	5	Normal	○
Snore	Normal	Special	40	100	15	Normal	—
Spite	Ghost	Status	—	100	10	Normal	—
Synthesis	Grass	Status	—	—	5	Self	—
Worry Seed	Grass	Status	—	100	10	Normal	—
Role Play	Psychic	Status	—	—	10	Normal	—
Mud-Slap	Ground	Special	20	100	10	Normal	—
Superpower	Fighting	Physical	120	100	5	Normal	○
Seed Bomb	Grass	Physical	80	100	15	Normal	○
Low Kick	Fighting	Physical	—	100	20	Normal	○

● TM & HM MOVES

No.	Name	Type	Kind	Pow.	Acc.	PP	Range	DA
TM01	Focus Punch	Fighting	Physical	150	100	20	Normal	○
TM06	Toxic	Poison	Status	—	85	10	Normal	—
TM09	Bullet Seed	Grass	Physical	10	100	30	Normal	○
TM10	Hidden Power	Normal	Special	—	100	15	Normal	—
TM11	Sunny Day	Fire	Status	—	—	5	All	—
TM15	Hyper Beam	Normal	Special	150	90	5	Normal	—
TM17	Protect	Normal	Status	—	—	10	Self	—
TM19	Giga Drain	Grass	Special	60	100	10	Normal	○
TM21	Frustration	Normal	Physical	—	100	20	Normal	○
TM22	SolarBeam	Grass	Special	120	100	10	Normal	—
TM27	Return	Normal	Physical	—	100	20	Normal	○
TM31	Brick Break	Fighting	Physical	75	100	15	Normal	○
TM32	Double Team	Normal	Status	—	—	15	Self	—
TM37	Sandstorm	Rock	Status	—	—	10	All	—
TM42	Facade	Normal	Physical	70	100	20	Normal	○
TM43	Secret Power	Normal	Physical	70	100	20	Normal	○
TM44	Rest	Psychic	Status	—	—	10	Self	—
TM45	Attract	Normal	Status	—	100	15	Normal	—
TM52	Focus Blast	Fighting	Special	120	70	5	Normal	—
TM53	Energy Ball	Grass	Special	80	100	10	Normal	○
TM56	Fling	Dark	Physical	—	100	10	Normal	○
TM58	Endure	Normal	Status	—	—	10	Self	—
TM60	Drain Punch	Fighting	Physical	60	100	5	Normal	○
TM63	Embargo	Dark	Status	—	100	15	Normal	—
TM66	Payback	Dark	Physical	50	100	10	Normal	○
TM68	Giga Impact	Normal	Physical	150	90	5	Normal	○
TM70	Flash	Normal	Status	—	100	20	Normal	—
TM75	Swords Dance	Normal	Status	—	—	30	Self	—
TM78	Captivate	Normal	Status	—	100	20	2 Foes	—
TM79	Dark Pulse	Dark	Special	80	100	15	Normal	—
TM82	Sleep Talk	Normal	Status	—	—	10	Depends	—
TM83	Natural Gift	Normal	Physical	—	100	15	Normal	—
TM84	Poison Jab	Poison	Physical	80	100	20	Normal	○
TM86	Grass Knot	Grass	Special	—	100	20	Normal	○
TM87	Swagger	Normal	Status	—	90	15	Normal	—
TM90	Substitute	Normal	Status	—	—	10	Self	—
HM01	Cut	Normal	Physical	50	95	30	Normal	○
HM04	Strength	Normal	Physical	80	100	15	Normal	○

Cacturne

Grass Dark

- ● HEIGHT: 4'03"
- ● WEIGHT: 170.6 lbs.
- ● ITEMS: Sticky Barb

● SIZE COMPARISON

● MALE FORM
Smaller markings on belly

● FEMALE FORM
Larger markings on belly

◎ ABILITIES
● Sand Veil

◎ EGG GROUPS
Grass

Human-Like

◎ STATS
HP ●●●
ATTACK ●●●●●
DEFENSE ●●●
SP. ATTACK ●●●●●
SP. DEFENSE ●●●
SPEED ●●●

◎ PERFORMANCE
SPEED ★★★★
POWER ★★★☆
SKILL ★★★★☆
STAMINA ★★☆
JUMP ★★☆

● MAIN WAYS TO OBTAIN

Pokémon HeartGold	Safari Zone (Savannah Area: if Forest objects are placed, may appear in tall grass)

Pokémon SoulSilver	Safari Zone (Savannah Area: if Forest objects are placed, may appear in tall grass)

Pokémon Diamond	Route 228

Pokémon Pearl	Route 228

Pokémon Platinum	Route 228

Pokémon HeartGold	Pokémon SoulSilver
Packs of them follow travelers through the desert until the travelers can no longer move.	Packs of them follow travelers through the desert until the travelers can no longer move.

◎ EVOLUTION

Lv. 32

Cacnea → Cacturne

No. 333 | Cotton Bird Pokémon
Swablu

`Normal` `Flying`

- **HEIGHT:** 1'04"
- **WEIGHT:** 2.6 lbs.
- **ITEMS:** None

● SIZE COMPARISON

● MALE/FEMALE HAVE SAME FORM

● ABILITIES
- Natural Cure

● EGG GROUPS
Flying

Dragon

● PERFORMANCE
SPEED ★★☆
POWER ★★☆
SKILL ★★★☆
STAMINA ★★★☆
JUMP ★★★★★

● STATS
HP ●●
ATTACK ●●
DEFENSE ●●
SP. ATTACK ●●
SP. DEFENSE ●●●
SPEED ●●

● LEVEL-UP MOVES

Lv.	Name	Type	Kind	Pow.	Acc.	PP	Range	DA
1	Peck	Flying	Physical	35	100	35	Normal	○
1	Growl	Normal	Status	—	100	40	2 Foes	—
5	Astonish	Ghost	Physical	30	100	15	Normal	○
9	Sing	Normal	Status	—	55	15	Normal	—
13	Fury Attack	Normal	Physical	15	85	20	Normal	○
18	Safeguard	Normal	Status	—	—	25	2 Allies	—
23	Mist	Ice	Status	—	—	30	2 Allies	—
28	Take Down	Normal	Physical	90	85	20	Normal	○
32	Natural Gift	Normal	Physical	—	100	15	Normal	—
36	Mirror Move	Flying	Status	—	—	20	Depends	—
40	Refresh	Normal	Status	—	—	20	Self	—
45	Dragon Pulse	Dragon	Special	90	100	10	Normal	—
50	Perish Song	Normal	Status	—	—	5	All	—

● MOVE MANIAC

Name	Type	Kind	Pow.	Acc.	PP	Range	DA
—								
—								

● BP MOVES

Name	Type	Kind	Pow.	Acc.	PP	Range	DA
Ominous Wind	Ghost	Special	60	100	5	Normal	—
Air Cutter	Flying	Special	55	95	25	2 Foes	—
Snore	Normal	Special	40	100	15	Normal	—
Swift	Normal	Special	60	—	20	2 Foes	—
Uproar	Normal	Special	50	100	10	1 Random	—
Tailwind	Flying	Status	—	—	30	2 Allies	—
Heal Bell	Normal	Status	—	—	5	All Allies	—
Mud-Slap	Ground	Special	20	100	10	Normal	—
Outrage	Dragon	Physical	120	100	10	1 Random	○
Twister	Dragon	Special	40	100	20	2 Foes	—
Heat Wave	Fire	Special	100	90	10	2 Foes	—

● MAIN WAYS TO OBTAIN

Pokémon HeartGold — Route 45 (mass outbreak)

Pokémon SoulSilver — Route 45 (mass outbreak)

Pokémon Diamond — Route 210, Celestic Town side (use Poké Radar)

Pokémon Pearl — Route 211, Celestic Town side (use Poké Radar)

Pokémon Platinum — Route 211, Celestic Town side (use Poké Radar)

Pokémon HeartGold	**Pokémon SoulSilver**
Its wings bring cottony clouds to mind. It grooms with springwater and loves to sit on heads.	Its wings bring cottony clouds to mind. It grooms with springwater and loves to sit on heads.

● TM & HM MOVES

No.	Name	Type	Kind	Pow.	Acc.	PP	Range	DA
TM06	Toxic	Poison	Status	—	85	10	Normal	—
TM10	Hidden Power	Normal	Special	—	100	15	Normal	—
TM11	Sunny Day	Fire	Status	—	—	5	All	—
TM13	Ice Beam	Ice	Special	95	100	10	Normal	—
TM17	Protect	Normal	Status	—	—	10	Self	—
TM18	Rain Dance	Water	Status	—	—	5	All	—
TM20	Safeguard	Normal	Status	—	—	25	2 Allies	—
TM21	Frustration	Normal	Physical	—	100	20	Normal	○
TM22	SolarBeam	Grass	Special	120	100	10	Normal	—
TM27	Return	Normal	Physical	—	100	20	Normal	○
TM32	Double Team	Normal	Status	—	—	15	Self	—
TM40	Aerial Ace	Flying	Physical	60	—	20	Normal	○
TM42	Facade	Normal	Physical	70	100	20	Normal	○
TM43	Secret Power	Normal	Physical	70	100	20	Normal	○
TM44	Rest	Psychic	Status	—	—	10	Self	—
TM45	Attract	Normal	Status	—	100	15	Normal	—
TM46	Thief	Dark	Physical	40	100	10	Normal	○
TM47	Steel Wing	Steel	Physical	70	90	25	Normal	○
TM51	Roost	Flying	Status	—	—	10	Self	—
TM58	Endure	Normal	Status	—	—	10	Self	—
TM59	Dragon Pulse	Dragon	Special	90	100	10	Normal	—
TM77	Psych Up	Normal	Status	—	—	10	Normal	—
TM78	Captivate	Normal	Status	—	100	20	2 Foes	—
TM82	Sleep Talk	Normal	Status	—	—	10	Depends	—
TM83	Natural Gift	Normal	Physical	—	100	15	Normal	—
TM85	Dream Eater	Psychic	Special	100	100	15	Normal	—
TM87	Swagger	Normal	Status	—	90	15	Normal	—
TM88	Pluck	Flying	Physical	60	100	20	Normal	○
TM90	Substitute	Normal	Status	—	—	10	Self	—
HM02	Fly	Flying	Physical	90	95	15	Normal	○

● EVOLUTION

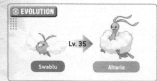

Swablu — Lv. 35 — Altaria

● EGG MOVES

Name	Type	Kind	Pow.	Acc.	PP	Range	DA
Agility	Psychic	Status	—	—	30	Self	—
Haze	Ice	Status	—	—	30	All	—
Pursuit	Dark	Physical	40	100	20	Normal	○
Rage	Normal	Physical	20	100	20	Normal	○
FeatherDance	Flying	Status	—	100	15	Normal	—
Dragon Rush	Dragon	Physical	100	75	10	Normal	○
Power Swap	Psychic	Status	—	—	10	Normal	—

● LEVEL-UP MOVES

Lv.	Name	Type	Kind	Pow.	Acc.	PP	Range	DA
1	Pluck	Flying	Physical	60	100	20	Normal	○
1	Peck	Flying	Physical	35	100	35	Normal	○
1	Growl	Normal	Status	—	100	40	2 Foes	—
1	Astonish	Ghost	Physical	30	100	15	Normal	○
1	Sing	Normal	Status	—	55	15	Normal	—
5	Astonish	Ghost	Physical	30	100	15	Normal	○
9	Sing	Normal	Status	—	55	15	Normal	—
13	Fury Attack	Normal	Physical	15	85	20	Normal	○
18	Safeguard	Normal	Status	—	—	25	2 Allies	—
23	Mist	Ice	Status	—	—	30	2 Allies	—
28	Take Down	Normal	Physical	90	85	20	Normal	○
32	Natural Gift	Normal	Physical	—	100	15	Normal	—
35	DragonBreath	Dragon	Special	60	100	20	Normal	—
39	Dragon Dance	Dragon	Status	—	—	20	Self	—
46	Refresh	Normal	Status	—	—	20	Self	—
54	Dragon Pulse	Dragon	Special	90	100	10	Normal	—
62	Perish Song	Normal	Status	—	—	5	All	—
70	Sky Attack	Flying	Physical	140	90	5	Normal	○

● MOVE MANIAC

Name	Type	Kind	Pow.	Acc.	PP	Range	DA
Draco Meteor	Dragon	Special	140	90	5	Normal	—

● BP MOVES

Name	Type	Kind	Pow.	Acc.	PP	Range	DA
Ominous Wind	Ghost	Special	60	100	5	Normal	—
Air Cutter	Flying	Special	55	95	25	2 Foes	—
Snore	Normal	Special	40	100	15	Normal	—
Swift	Normal	Special	60	—	20	2 Foes	—
Uproar	Normal	Special	50	100	10	1 Random	—
Tailwind	Flying	Status	—	—	30	2 Allies	—
Heal Bell	Normal	Status	—	—	5	All Allies	—
Mud-Slap	Ground	Special	20	100	10	Normal	—
Outrage	Dragon	Physical	120	100	15	1 Random	○
Twister	Dragon	Special	40	100	20	2 Foes	—
Heat Wave	Fire	Special	100	90	10	2 Foes	—
Sky Attack	Flying	Physical	140	90	5	Normal	—

● TM & HM MOVES

No.	Name	Type	Kind	Pow.	Acc.	PP	Range	DA
TM02	Dragon Claw	Dragon	Physical	80	100	15	Normal	○
TM05	Roar	Normal	Status	—	100	20	Normal	—
TM06	Toxic	Poison	Status	—	85	10	Normal	—
TM10	Hidden Power	Normal	Special	—	100	15	Normal	—
TM11	Sunny Day	Fire	Status	—	—	5	All	—
TM13	Ice Beam	Ice	Special	95	100	10	Normal	—
TM15	Hyper Beam	Normal	Special	150	90	5	Normal	—
TM17	Protect	Normal	Status	—	—	10	Self	—
TM18	Rain Dance	Water	Status	—	—	5	All	—
TM20	Safeguard	Normal	Status	—	—	25	2 Allies	—
TM21	Frustration	Normal	Physical	—	100	20	Normal	○
TM22	SolarBeam	Grass	Special	120	100	10	Normal	—
TM23	Iron Tail	Steel	Physical	100	75	15	Normal	○
TM26	Earthquake	Ground	Physical	100	100	10	2 Foes/1 Ally	—
TM27	Return	Normal	Physical	—	100	20	Normal	○
TM32	Double Team	Normal	Status	—	—	15	Self	—
TM35	Flamethrower	Fire	Special	95	100	15	Normal	—
TM38	Fire Blast	Fire	Special	120	85	5	Normal	—
TM40	Aerial Ace	Flying	Physical	60	—	20	Normal	○
TM42	Facade	Normal	Physical	70	100	20	Normal	○
TM43	Secret Power	Normal	Physical	70	100	20	Normal	○
TM44	Rest	Psychic	Status	—	—	10	Self	—
TM45	Attract	Normal	Status	—	100	15	Normal	—
TM46	Thief	Dark	Physical	40	100	10	Normal	○
TM47	Steel Wing	Steel	Physical	70	90	25	Normal	○
TM51	Roost	Flying	Status	—	—	10	Self	—
TM58	Endure	Normal	Status	—	—	10	Self	—
TM59	Dragon Pulse	Dragon	Special	90	100	10	Normal	—
TM68	Giga Impact	Normal	Physical	150	90	5	Normal	○
TM77	Psych Up	Normal	Status	—	—	10	Normal	—
TM78	Captivate	Normal	Status	—	100	20	2 Foes	—
TM82	Sleep Talk	Normal	Status	—	—	10	Depends	—
TM83	Natural Gift	Normal	Physical	—	100	15	Normal	—
TM85	Dream Eater	Psychic	Special	100	100	15	Normal	—
TM87	Swagger	Normal	Status	—	90	15	Normal	—
TM88	Pluck	Flying	Physical	60	100	20	Normal	○
TM90	Substitute	Normal	Status	—	—	10	Self	—
HM02	Fly	Flying	Physical	90	95	15	Normal	○
HM06	Rock Smash	Fighting	Physical	40	100	15	Normal	○

No. 334 | Humming Pokémon
Altaria

`Dragon` `Flying`

- ● HEIGHT: 3'07"
- ● WEIGHT: 45.4 lbs.
- ● ITEMS: None

● SIZE COMPARISON

● MALE/FEMALE HAVE SAME FORM

⊙ ABILITIES
- ● Natural Cure

⊙ STATS
HP ●●●
ATTACK ●●●
DEFENSE ●●●●
SP. ATTACK ●●●
SP. DEFENSE ●●●●
SPEED ●●●●

⊙ EGG GROUPS
Flying

Dragon

⊙ PERFORMANCE
SPEED ★★☆ STAMINA ★★★☆
POWER ★★☆ JUMP ★★★★★
SKILL ★★★★

● MAIN WAYS TO OBTAIN

Pokémon HeartGold	Level up Swablu to Lv. 35
Pokémon SoulSilver	Level up Swablu to Lv. 35
Pokémon Diamond	Level up Swablu to Lv. 35
Pokémon Pearl	Level up Swablu to Lv. 35
Pokémon Platinum	Level up Swablu to Lv. 35

Pokémon HeartGold	**Pokémon SoulSilver**
It flies gracefully through the sky. Its melodic humming makes you feel like you're in a dream.	It flies gracefully through the sky. Its melodic humming makes you feel like you're in a dream.

⊙ EVOLUTION

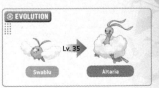

Swablu → Lv. 35 → Altaria

No. 335 | Cat Ferret Pokémon
Zangoose

Normal

● HEIGHT: 4'03"
● WEIGHT: 88.8 lbs.
● ITEMS: Quick Claw

● SIZE COMPARISON

● MALE/FEMALE HAVE SAME FORM

⊕ ABILITIES
● Immunity

⊕ STATS
HP ●●●
ATTACK ●●●●●
DEFENSE ●●●●
SP. ATTACK ●●●
SP. DEFENSE ●●●
SPEED ●●●●

⊕ EGG GROUPS
Field

⊕ PERFORMANCE
SPEED ★★☆ STAMINA ★★★★☆
POWER ★★★☆ JUMP ★★★
SKILL ★★★☆

● MAIN WAYS TO OBTAIN

Pokémon HeartGold
Safari Zone (Rock Area: if Grass objects are placed, may appear in tall grass)

Pokémon SoulSilver
Safari Zone (Rock Area: if Grass objects are placed, may appear in tall grass)

Pokémon Diamond
Route 208 (after obtaining the National Pokédex, insert Pokémon Ruby into your Nintendo DS's Game Pak slot)

Pokémon Pearl
Route 208 (after obtaining the National Pokédex, insert Pokémon Ruby into your Nintendo DS's Game Pak slot)

Pokémon Platinum
Route 208 (after obtaining the National Pokédex, insert Pokémon Ruby into your Nintendo DS's Game Pak slot)

Pokémon HeartGold
Its fur would all stand on end if it smelled a SEVIPER nearby. Its sharp claws tear up its foes.

Pokémon SoulSilver
Its fur would all stand on end if it smelled a SEVIPER nearby. Its sharp claws tear up its foes.

⊕ EVOLUTION
Does not evolve

● LEVEL-UP MOVES

Lv.	Name	Type	Kind	Pow.	Acc.	PP	Range	DA
1	Scratch	Normal	Physical	40	100	35	Normal	—
1	Leer	Normal	Status	—	100	30	2 Foes	—
5	Quick Attack	Normal	Physical	40	100	30	Normal	○
9	Swords Dance	Normal	Status	—	—	30	Self	○
14	Fury Cutter	Bug	Physical	10	95	20	Normal	○
18	Slash	Normal	Physical	70	100	20	Normal	○
22	Pursuit	Dark	Physical	40	100	20	Normal	○
27	Embargo	Dark	Status	—	100	15	Normal	—
31	Crush Claw	Normal	Physical	75	95	10	Normal	○
35	Taunt	Dark	Status	—	100	20	Normal	—
40	Detect	Fighting	Status	—	—	5	Self	—
44	False Swipe	Normal	Physical	40	100	40	Normal	○
48	X-Scissor	Bug	Physical	80	100	15	Normal	○
53	Close Combat	Fighting	Physical	120	100	5	Normal	○

● MOVE MANIAC

Name	Type	Kind	Pow.	Acc.	PP	Range	DA
Headbutt	Normal	Physical	70	100	15	Normal	○

● BP MOVES

Name	Type	Kind	Pow.	Acc.	PP	Range	DA
Fury Cutter	Bug	Physical	10	95	20	Normal	○
Icy Wind	Ice	Special	55	95	15	2 Foes	—
ThunderPunch	Electric	Physical	75	100	15	Normal	○
Fire Punch	Fire	Physical	75	100	15	Normal	○
Ice Punch	Ice	Physical	75	100	15	Normal	○
Knock Off	Dark	Physical	20	100	20	Normal	○
Snore	Normal	Special	40	100	15	Normal	—
Last Resort	Normal	Physical	130	100	5	Normal	○
Swift	Normal	Special	60	—	20	2 Foes	○
Mud-Slap	Ground	Special	20	100	10	Normal	○
Rollout	Rock	Physical	30	90	20	Normal	○
Endeavor	Normal	Physical	—	100	5	Normal	—
Low Kick	Fighting	Physical	—	100	20	Normal	○

● TM & HM MOVES

No.	Name	Type	Kind	Pow.	Acc.	PP	Range	DA
TM01	Focus Punch	Fighting	Physical	150	100	20	Normal	○
TM03	Water Pulse	Water	Special	60	100	20	Normal	—
TM05	Roar	Normal	Status	—	100	20	Normal	—
TM06	Toxic	Poison	Status	—	85	10	Normal	—
TM10	Hidden Power	Normal	Special	—	100	15	Normal	—
TM11	Sunny Day	Fire	Status	—	—	5	All	—
TM12	Taunt	Dark	Status	—	100	20	Normal	—
TM13	Ice Beam	Ice	Special	95	100	10	Normal	—
TM14	Blizzard	Ice	Special	120	70	5	2 Foes	—
TM17	Protect	Normal	Status	—	—	10	Self	—
TM18	Rain Dance	Water	Status	—	—	5	All	—
TM19	Giga Drain	Grass	Special	60	100	10	Normal	—
TM21	Frustration	Normal	Physical	—	100	20	Normal	○
TM22	SolarBeam	Grass	Special	120	100	10	Normal	—
TM23	Iron Tail	Steel	Physical	100	75	15	Normal	○
TM24	Thunderbolt	Electric	Special	95	100	15	Normal	—
TM25	Thunder	Electric	Special	120	70	10	Normal	—
TM27	Return	Normal	Physical	—	100	20	Normal	○
TM28	Dig	Ground	Physical	80	100	10	Normal	○
TM30	Shadow Ball	Ghost	Special	80	100	15	Normal	—
TM31	Brick Break	Fighting	Physical	75	100	15	Normal	○
TM32	Double Team	Normal	Status	—	—	15	Self	—
TM34	Shock Wave	Electric	Special	60	—	20	Normal	—
TM35	Flamethrower	Fire	Special	95	100	15	Normal	—
TM38	Fire Blast	Fire	Special	120	85	5	Normal	—
TM39	Rock Tomb	Rock	Physical	50	80	10	Normal	○
TM40	Aerial Ace	Flying	Physical	60	—	20	Normal	○
TM42	Facade	Normal	Physical	70	100	20	Normal	○
TM43	Secret Power	Normal	Physical	70	100	20	Normal	○
TM44	Rest	Psychic	Status	—	—	10	Self	—
TM45	Attract	Normal	Status	—	100	15	Normal	—
TM46	Thief	Dark	Physical	40	100	10	Normal	○
TM52	Focus Blast	Fighting	Special	120	70	5	Normal	—
TM54	False Swipe	Normal	Physical	40	100	40	Normal	○
TM56	Fling	Dark	Physical	—	100	10	Normal	○
TM58	Endure	Normal	Status	—	—	10	Self	—
TM63	Embargo	Dark	Status	—	100	15	Normal	—
TM65	Shadow Claw	Ghost	Physical	70	100	15	Normal	○
TM66	Payback	Dark	Physical	50	100	10	Normal	○
TM75	Swords Dance	Normal	Status	—	—	30	Self	○
TM78	Captivate	Normal	Status	—	100	20	2 Foes	—
TM80	Rock Slide	Rock	Physical	75	90	10	2 Foes	—
TM81	X-Scissor	Bug	Physical	80	100	15	Normal	○
TM82	Sleep Talk	Normal	Status	—	—	10	Depends	—
TM83	Natural Gift	Normal	Physical	—	100	15	Normal	—
TM84	Poison Jab	Poison	Physical	80	100	20	Normal	○
TM87	Swagger	Normal	Status	—	90	15	Normal	—
TM90	Substitute	Normal	Status	—	—	10	Self	—
HM04	Strength	Normal	Physical	80	100	15	Normal	○
HM06	Rock Smash	Fighting	Physical	40	100	15	Normal	○
HM08	Rock Climb	Normal	Physical	90	85	10	Normal	○

● EGG MOVES

Name	Type	Kind	Pow.	Acc.	PP	Range	DA
Flail	Normal	Physical	—	100	15	Normal	○
Double Kick	Fighting	Physical	30	100	30	Normal	○
Razor Wind	Normal	Special	80	100	10	2 Foes	○
Counter	Fighting	Physical	—	100	20	Self	○
Roar	Normal	Status	—	100	20	Normal	—
Curse	???	Status	—	—	10	Normal/Self	—
Fury Swipes	Normal	Physical	18	80	15	Normal	○
Night Slash	Dark	Physical	70	100	15	Normal	○
Metal Claw	Steel	Physical	50	95	35	Normal	○
Double Hit	Normal	Physical	35	90	10	Normal	○
Disable	Normal	Status	—	80	20	Normal	—

● LEVEL-UP MOVES

Lv.	Name	Type	Kind	Pow.	Acc.	PP	Range	DA
1	Wrap	Normal	Physical	15	85	20	Normal	○
7	Lick	Ghost	Physical	20	100	30	Normal	○
10	Bite	Dark	Physical	60	100	25	Normal	○
16	Poison Tail	Poison	Physical	50	100	25	Normal	○
19	Screech	Normal	Status	—	85	40	Normal	—
25	Glare	Normal	Status	—	75	30	Normal	—
28	Crunch	Dark	Physical	80	100	15	Normal	○
34	Poison Fang	Poison	Physical	50	100	15	Normal	○
37	Swagger	Normal	Status	—	90	15	Normal	—
43	Haze	Ice	Status	—	—	30	All	—
46	Night Slash	Dark	Physical	70	100	15	Normal	○
52	Poison Jab	Poison	Physical	80	100	20	Normal	○
55	Wring Out	Normal	Special	—	100	5	Normal	○

● MOVE MANIAC

Name	Type	Kind	Pow.	Acc.	PP	Range	DA
Headbutt	Normal	Physical	70	100	15	Normal	○

● BP MOVES

Name	Type	Kind	Pow.	Acc.	PP	Range	DA
Fury Cutter	Bug	Physical	10	95	20	Normal	○
Knock Off	Dark	Physical	20	100	20	Normal	○
Sucker Punch	Dark	Physical	80	100	5	Normal	○
Snore	Normal	Special	40	100	15	Normal	—
Swift	Normal	Special	60	—	20	2 Foes	—
Mud-Slap	Ground	Special	20	100	10	Normal	—
Aqua Tail	Water	Physical	90	90	10	Normal	○

● TM & HM MOVES

No.	Name	Type	Kind	Pow.	Acc.	PP	Range	DA
TM06	Toxic	Poison	Status	—	85	10	Normal	—
TM10	Hidden Power	Normal	Special	—	100	15	Normal	—
TM11	Sunny Day	Fire	Status	—	—	5	All	—
TM12	Taunt	Dark	Status	—	100	20	Normal	—
TM17	Protect	Normal	Status	—	—	10	Self	—
TM18	Rain Dance	Water	Status	—	—	5	All	—
TM19	Giga Drain	Grass	Special	60	100	10	Normal	—
TM21	Frustration	Normal	Physical	—	100	20	Normal	○
TM23	Iron Tail	Steel	Physical	100	75	15	Normal	○
TM26	Earthquake	Ground	Physical	100	100	10	2 Foes/1 Ally	—
TM27	Return	Normal	Physical	—	100	20	Normal	○
TM28	Dig	Ground	Physical	80	100	10	Normal	○
TM32	Double Team	Normal	Status	—	—	15	Self	—
TM35	Flamethrower	Fire	Special	95	100	15	Normal	—
TM36	Sludge Bomb	Poison	Special	90	100	10	Normal	—
TM42	Facade	Normal	Physical	70	100	20	Normal	○
TM43	Secret Power	Normal	Physical	70	100	20	Normal	○
TM44	Rest	Psychic	Status	—	—	10	Self	—
TM45	Attract	Normal	Status	—	100	15	Normal	—
TM46	Thief	Dark	Physical	40	100	10	Normal	○
TM49	Snatch	Dark	Status	—	—	10	Depends	—
TM58	Endure	Normal	Status	—	—	10	Self	—
TM66	Payback	Dark	Physical	50	100	10	Normal	○
TM78	Captivate	Normal	Status	—	100	20	2 Foes	—
TM79	Dark Pulse	Dark	Special	80	100	15	Normal	—
TM81	X-Scissor	Bug	Physical	80	100	15	Normal	○
TM82	Sleep Talk	Normal	Status	—	—	10	Depends	—
TM83	Natural Gift	Normal	Physical	—	100	15	Normal	○
TM84	Poison Jab	Poison	Physical	80	100	20	Normal	○
TM87	Swagger	Normal	Status	—	90	15	Normal	—
TM90	Substitute	Normal	Status	—	—	10	Self	—
HM04	Strength	Normal	Physical	80	100	15	Normal	○
HM06	Rock Smash	Fighting	Physical	40	100	15	Normal	○

● EGG MOVES

Name	Type	Kind	Pow.	Acc.	PP	Range	DA
Stockpile	Normal	Status	—	—	20	Self	—
Swallow	Normal	Status	—	—	10	Self	—
Spit Up	Normal	Special	—	100	10	Normal	—
Body Slam	Normal	Physical	85	100	15	Normal	○
Scary Face	Normal	Status	—	90	10	Normal	—
Assurance	Dark	Physical	50	100	10	Normal	○
Night Slash	Dark	Physical	70	100	15	Normal	○
Switcheroo	Dark	Status	—	100	10	Normal	—

No. 336 | Fang Snake Pokémon
Seviper

Poison

- ● HEIGHT: 8'10"
- ● WEIGHT: 115.7 lbs.
- ● ITEMS: None

● SIZE COMPARISON

● MALE/FEMALE HAVE SAME FORM

⊙ ABILITIES
- ● Shed Skin

⊙ STATS
- HP ●●●
- ATTACK ●●●●
- DEFENSE ●●●
- SP. ATTACK ●●●
- SP. DEFENSE ●●●
- SPEED ●●●

⊙ EGG GROUPS
Field

Dragon

⊙ PERFORMANCE

SPEED ★★★☆ STAMINA ★★★★☆
POWER ★★★☆ JUMP ★★
SKILL ★★★★☆

● MAIN WAYS TO OBTAIN

Pokémon HeartGold — Safari Zone [Marshland Area: if Grass objects are placed, may appear in tall grass]

Pokémon SoulSilver — Safari Zone [Marshland Area: if Grass objects are placed, may appear in tall grass]

Pokémon Diamond — Route 208 (after obtaining the National Pokédex, insert Pokémon Sapphire into your Nintendo DS's Game Pak slot)

Pokémon Pearl — Route 208 (after obtaining the National Pokédex, insert Pokémon Sapphire into your Nintendo DS's Game Pak slot)

Pokémon Platinum — Route 208 (after obtaining the National Pokédex, insert Pokémon Sapphire into your Nintendo DS's Game Pak slot)

Pokémon HeartGold — In battle, it uses its bladed tail to counter any ZANGOOSE. It secretes a deadly venom in its tail.

Pokémon SoulSilver — In battle, it uses its bladed tail to counter any ZANGOOSE. It secretes a deadly venom in its tail.

⊙ EVOLUTION

Does not evolve

● No. 337 | Meteorite Pokémon
Lunatone

Rock **Psychic**

● HEIGHT: 3'03"
● WEIGHT: 370.4 lbs.
● ITEMS: Moon Stone

● SIZE COMPARISON

● GENDER UNKNOWN

⊘ ABILITIES
● Levitate

⊘ EGG GROUPS
Mineral

⊘ PERFORMANCE
SPEED ★★☆   STAMINA ★★★★
POWER ★★☆   JUMP ★★★
SKILL ★★★☆

● MAIN WAYS TO OBTAIN

Pokémon HeartGold
Safari Zone [Mountain Area: if Rock objects are placed, may appear in tall grass]

Pokémon SoulSilver
Safari Zone [Mountain Area: if Rock objects are placed, may appear in tall grass]

Pokémon Diamond
Lake Verity [after obtaining the National Pokédex, insert *Pokémon Sapphire* into your Nintendo DS's Game Pak slot]

Pokémon Pearl
Lake Verity [after obtaining the National Pokédex, insert *Pokémon Sapphire* into your Nintendo DS's Game Pak slot]

Pokémon Platinum
Lake Verity [after obtaining the National Pokédex, insert *Pokémon Sapphire* into your Nintendo DS's Game Pak slot]

Pokémon HeartGold
It was discovered at the site of a meteor strike 40 years ago. Its stare can lull its foes to sleep.

Pokémon SoulSilver
It was discovered at the site of a meteor strike 40 years ago. Its stare can lull its foes to sleep.

⊘ EVOLUTION
Does not evolve

● LEVEL-UP MOVES

Lv.	Name	Type	Kind	Pow.	Acc.	PP	Range	DA
1	Tackle	Normal	Physical	35	95	35	Normal	○
1	Harden	Normal	Status	—	—	30	Self	—
1	Confusion	Psychic	Special	50	100	25	Normal	—
9	Rock Throw	Rock	Physical	50	90	15	Normal	—
12	Hypnosis	Psychic	Status	—	60	20	Normal	—
20	Rock Polish	Rock	Status	—	—	20	Self	—
23	Psywave	Psychic	Special	—	80	15	Normal	—
31	Embargo	Dark	Status	—	100	15	Normal	—
34	Cosmic Power	Psychic	Status	—	—	20	Self	—
42	Heal Block	Psychic	Status	—	100	15	2 Foes	—
45	Psychic	Psychic	Special	90	100	10	Normal	—
53	Future Sight	Psychic	Special	80	90	15	Normal	—
56	Explosion	Normal	Physical	250	100	5	2 Foes/1 Ally	—

● MOVE MANIAC

Name	Type	Kind	Pow.	Acc.	PP	Range	DA

● BP MOVES

Name	Type	Kind	Pow.	Acc.	PP	Range	DA
Zen Headbutt	Psychic	Physical	80	90	15	Normal	○
Snore	Normal	Special	40	100	15	Normal	—
Helping Hand	Normal	Status	—	—	20	1 Ally	—
Swift	Normal	Special	60	—	20	2 Foes	—
Gravity	Psychic	Status	—	—	5	All	—
Magic Coat	Psychic	Status	—	—	15	Self	—
Rollout	Rock	Physical	30	90	20	Normal	○
Iron Head	Steel	Physical	80	100	15	Normal	○
AncientPower	Rock	Special	60	100	5	Normal	—
Signal Beam	Bug	Special	75	100	15	Normal	—
Earth Power	Ground	Special	90	100	10	Normal	—
Pain Split	Normal	Status	—	—	20	Normal	—

● TM & HM MOVES

No.	Name	Type	Kind	Pow.	Acc.	PP	Range	DA
TM04	Calm Mind	Psychic	Status	—	—	20	Self	—
TM06	Toxic	Poison	Status	—	85	10	Normal	—
TM10	Hidden Power	Normal	Special	—	100	15	Normal	—
TM13	Ice Beam	Ice	Special	95	100	10	Normal	—
TM14	Blizzard	Ice	Special	120	70	5	2 Foes	—
TM15	Hyper Beam	Normal	Special	150	90	5	Normal	—
TM16	Light Screen	Psychic	Status	—	—	30	2 Allies	—
TM17	Protect	Normal	Status	—	—	10	Self	—
TM18	Rain Dance	Water	Status	—	—	5	All	—
TM20	Safeguard	Normal	Status	—	—	25	2 Allies	—
TM21	Frustration	Normal	Physical	—	100	20	Normal	○
TM26	Earthquake	Ground	Physical	100	100	10	2 Foes/1 Ally	—
TM27	Return	Normal	Physical	—	100	20	Normal	○
TM29	Psychic	Psychic	Special	90	100	10	Normal	—
TM30	Shadow Ball	Ghost	Special	80	100	15	Normal	—
TM32	Double Team	Normal	Status	—	—	15	Self	—
TM33	Reflect	Psychic	Status	—	—	20	2 Allies	—
TM37	Sandstorm	Rock	Status	—	—	10	All	—
TM39	Rock Tomb	Rock	Physical	50	80	10	Normal	—
TM42	Facade	Normal	Physical	70	100	20	Normal	○
TM43	Secret Power	Normal	Physical	70	100	20	Normal	—
TM44	Rest	Psychic	Status	—	—	10	Self	—
TM48	Skill Swap	Psychic	Status	—	—	10	Normal	—
TM57	Charge Beam	Electric	Special	50	90	10	Normal	—
TM58	Endure	Normal	Status	—	—	10	Self	—
TM63	Embargo	Dark	Status	—	100	15	Normal	—
TM64	Explosion	Normal	Physical	250	100	5	2 Foes/1 Ally	—
TM67	Recycle	Normal	Status	—	—	10	Self	—
TM68	Giga Impact	Normal	Physical	150	90	5	Normal	○
TM69	Rock Polish	Rock	Status	—	—	20	Self	—
TM70	Flash	Normal	Status	—	100	20	Normal	—
TM71	Stone Edge	Rock	Physical	100	80	5	Normal	—
TM74	Gyro Ball	Steel	Physical	—	100	5	Normal	—
TM76	Stealth Rock	Rock	Status	—	—	20	2 Foes	—
TM77	Psych Up	Normal	Status	—	—	10	Normal	—
TM80	Rock Slide	Rock	Physical	75	90	10	2 Foes	—
TM82	Sleep Talk	Normal	Status	—	—	10	Depends	—
TM83	Natural Gift	Normal	Physical	—	100	15	Normal	—
TM85	Dream Eater	Psychic	Special	100	100	15	Normal	—
TM86	Grass Knot	Grass	Special	—	100	20	Normal	○
TM87	Swagger	Normal	Status	—	90	15	Normal	—
TM90	Substitute	Normal	Status	—	—	10	Self	—
TM92	Trick Room	Psychic	Status	—	—	5	All	—

⊘ STATS
HP ●●●
ATTACK ●●
DEFENSE ●●●
SP. ATTACK ●●●
SP. DEFENSE ●●●
SPEED ●●●

● LEVEL-UP MOVES

Lv.	Name	Type	Kind	Pow.	Acc.	PP	Range	DA
1	Tackle	Normal	Physical	35	95	35	Normal	○
1	Harden	Normal	Status	—	—	30	Self	—
1	Confusion	Psychic	Special	50	100	25	Normal	—
9	Rock Throw	Rock	Physical	50	90	15	Normal	—
12	Fire Spin	Fire	Special	15	70	15	Normal	—
20	Rock Polish	Rock	Status	—	—	20	Self	—
23	Psywave	Psychic	Special	—	80	15	Normal	—
31	Embargo	Dark	Status	—	100	15	Normal	—
34	Cosmic Power	Psychic	Status	—	—	20	Self	—
42	Heal Block	Psychic	Status	—	100	15	2 Foes	—
45	Rock Slide	Rock	Physical	75	90	10	2 Foes	—
53	SolarBeam	Grass	Special	120	100	10	Normal	—
56	Explosion	Normal	Physical	250	100	5	2 Foes/1 Ally	—

● MOVE MANIAC

Name	Type	Kind	Pow.	Acc.	PP	Range	DA

● BP MOVES

Name	Type	Kind	Pow.	Acc.	PP	Range	DA
Zen Headbutt	Psychic	Physical	80	90	15	Normal	○
Snore	Normal	Special	40	100	15	Normal	—
Helping Hand	Normal	Status	—	—	20	1 Ally	—
Swift	Normal	Special	60	—	20	2 Foes	—
Gravity	Psychic	Status	—	—	5	All	—
Magic Coat	Psychic	Status	—	—	15	Self	—
Rollout	Rock	Physical	30	90	20	Normal	○
Iron Head	Steel	Physical	80	100	15	Normal	○
AncientPower	Rock	Special	60	100	5	Normal	—
Signal Beam	Bug	Special	75	100	15	Normal	—
Earth Power	Ground	Special	90	100	10	Normal	—
Iron Defense	Steel	Status	—	—	15	Self	—
Pain Split	Normal	Status	—	—	20	Normal	—

● TM & HM MOVES

No.	Name	Type	Kind	Pow.	Acc.	PP	Range	DA
TM04	Calm Mind	Psychic	Status	—	—	20	Self	—
TM06	Toxic	Poison	Status	—	85	10	Normal	—
TM10	Hidden Power	Normal	Special	—	100	15	Normal	—
TM11	Sunny Day	Fire	Status	—	—	5	All	—
TM15	Hyper Beam	Normal	Special	150	90	5	Normal	—
TM16	Light Screen	Psychic	Status	—	—	30	2 Allies	—
TM17	Protect	Normal	Status	—	—	10	Self	—
TM20	Safeguard	Normal	Status	—	—	25	2 Allies	—
TM21	Frustration	Normal	Physical	—	100	20	Normal	○
TM22	SolarBeam	Grass	Special	120	100	10	Normal	—
TM26	Earthquake	Ground	Physical	100	100	10	2 Foes/1 Ally	○
TM27	Return	Normal	Physical	—	100	20	Normal	○
TM29	Psychic	Psychic	Special	90	100	10	Normal	—
TM30	Shadow Ball	Ghost	Special	80	100	15	Normal	—
TM32	Double Team	Normal	Status	—	—	15	Self	—
TM33	Reflect	Psychic	Status	—	—	20	2 Allies	—
TM35	Flamethrower	Fire	Special	95	100	15	Normal	—
TM37	Sandstorm	Rock	Status	—	—	10	All	—
TM38	Fire Blast	Fire	Special	120	85	5	Normal	—
TM39	Rock Tomb	Rock	Physical	50	80	10	Normal	—
TM42	Facade	Normal	Physical	70	100	20	Normal	○
TM43	Secret Power	Normal	Physical	70	100	20	Normal	○
TM44	Rest	Psychic	Status	—	—	10	Self	—
TM48	Skill Swap	Psychic	Status	—	—	10	Normal	—
TM50	Overheat	Fire	Special	140	90	5	Normal	—
TM57	Charge Beam	Electric	Special	50	90	10	Normal	—
TM58	Endure	Normal	Status	—	—	10	Self	—
TM61	Will-O-Wisp	Fire	Status	—	75	15	Normal	—
TM63	Embargo	Dark	Status	—	100	15	Normal	—
TM64	Explosion	Normal	Physical	250	100	5	2 Foes/1 Ally	—
TM67	Recycle	Normal	Status	—	—	10	Self	—
TM68	Giga Impact	Normal	Physical	150	90	5	Normal	○
TM69	Rock Polish	Rock	Status	—	—	20	Self	—
TM70	Flash	Normal	Status	—	100	20	Normal	—
TM71	Stone Edge	Rock	Physical	100	80	5	Normal	○
TM74	Gyro Ball	Steel	Physical	—	100	5	Normal	○
TM76	Stealth Rock	Rock	Status	—	—	20	2 Foes	—
TM77	Psych Up	Normal	Status	—	—	10	Normal	—
TM80	Rock Slide	Rock	Physical	75	90	10	2 Foes	—
TM82	Sleep Talk	Normal	Status	—	—	10	Depends	—
TM83	Natural Gift	Normal	Physical	—	100	15	Normal	—
TM85	Dream Eater	Psychic	Special	100	100	15	Normal	—
TM86	Grass Knot	Grass	Special	—	100	20	Normal	—
TM87	Swagger	Normal	Status	—	90	15	Normal	—
TM90	Substitute	Normal	Status	—	—	10	Self	—
TM92	Trick Room	Psychic	Status	—	—	5	All	—

● No. 338 | Meteorite Pokémon
Solrock

Rock | Psychic

● HEIGHT: 3'11"
● WEIGHT: 339.5 lbs.
● ITEMS: Sun Stone

● SIZE COMPARISON

● GENDER UNKNOWN

● ABILITIES
● Levitate

● EGG GROUPS
Mineral

● STATS
HP ●●●
ATTACK ●●●●
DEFENSE ●●●
SP. ATTACK ●●●
SP. DEFENSE ●●
SPEED ●●●

● PERFORMANCE
SPEED ★★☆　　STAMINA ★★★★
POWER ★★★☆☆　JUMP ★★★
SKILL ★★☆☆

● MAIN WAYS TO OBTAIN

Pokémon HeartGold	Safari Zone (Wasteland Area: if Rock objects are placed, may appear in tall grass)
Pokémon SoulSilver	Safari Zone (Wasteland Area: if Rock objects are placed, may appear in tall grass)
Pokémon Diamond	Lake Verity (after obtaining the National Pokédex, insert *Pokémon Ruby* into your Nintendo DS's Game Pak slot)
Pokémon Pearl	Lake Verity (after obtaining the National Pokédex, insert *Pokémon Ruby* into your Nintendo DS's Game Pak slot)
Pokémon Platinum	Lake Verity (after obtaining the National Pokédex, insert *Pokémon Ruby* into your Nintendo DS's Game Pak slot)

Pokémon HeartGold	**Pokémon SoulSilver**
When it rotates itself, it gives off light similar to the sun, thus blinding its foes.	When it rotates itself, it gives off light similar to the sun, thus blinding its foes.

● EVOLUTION
Does not evolve

No. 339 | Whiskers Pokémon

Barboach

Water | Ground

- **HEIGHT:** 1'04"
- **WEIGHT:** 4.2 lbs.
- **ITEMS:** None

- **SIZE COMPARISON**

- **MALE/FEMALE HAVE SAME FORM**

ABILITIES
- Oblivious
- Anticipation

STATS
- HP ●●
- ATTACK ●●
- DEFENSE ●●
- SP. ATTACK ●●
- SP. DEFENSE ●
- SPEED ●●●

EGG GROUPS
Water 2

PERFORMANCE
- SPEED ★★★★
- POWER ★★☆
- SKILL ★★★☆
- STAMINA ★★★☆☆
- JUMP ★★☆

MAIN WAYS TO OBTAIN

Pokémon HeartGold
Safari Zone [Marshland Area: if Water objects are placed, may appear if you fish with the Super Rod]

Pokémon SoulSilver
Safari Zone [Marshland Area: if Water objects are placed, may appear if you fish with the Super Rod]

Pokémon Diamond
Route 205, Eterna City side [Good Rod]

Pokémon Pearl
Route 205, Eterna City side [Good Rod]

Pokémon Platinum
Route 205, Eterna City side [Good Rod]

Pokémon HeartGold
BARBOACH uses its whiskers to taste things just as a person uses his or her tongue to taste things.

Pokémon SoulSilver
BARBOACH uses its whiskers to taste things just as a person uses his or her tongue to taste things.

EVOLUTION

Barboach → [Lv. 30] → Whiscash

LEVEL-UP MOVES

Lv.	Name	Type	Kind	Pow.	Acc.	PP	Range	DA
1	Mud-Slap	Ground	Special	20	100	10	Normal	—
6	Mud Sport	Ground	Status	—	—	15	All	—
6	Water Sport	Water	Status	—	—	15	All	—
10	Water Gun	Water	Special	40	100	25	Normal	—
14	Mud Bomb	Ground	Special	65	85	10	Normal	—
18	Amnesia	Psychic	Status	—	—	20	Self	—
22	Water Pulse	Water	Special	60	100	20	Normal	—
26	Magnitude	Ground	Physical	—	100	30	2 Foes/1 Ally	—
31	Rest	Psychic	Status	—	—	10	Self	—
31	Snore	Normal	Special	40	100	15	Normal	—
35	Aqua Tail	Water	Physical	90	90	10	Normal	○
39	Earthquake	Ground	Physical	100	100	10	2 Foes/1 Ally	—
43	Future Sight	Psychic	Special	80	90	15	Normal	—
47	Fissure	Ground	Physical	—	30	5	Normal	—

MOVE MANIAC

Name	Type	Kind	Pow.	Acc.	PP	Range	DA
Headbutt	Normal	Physical	70	100	15	Normal	○

BP MOVES

Name	Type	Kind	Pow.	Acc.	PP	Range	DA
Dive	Water	Physical	80	100	10	Normal	○
Icy Wind	Ice	Special	55	95	15	2 Foes	—
Snore	Normal	Special	40	100	15	Normal	—
Mud-Slap	Ground	Special	20	100	10	Normal	—
Aqua Tail	Water	Physical	90	90	10	Normal	○
Earth Power	Ground	Special	90	100	10	Normal	—
Bounce	Flying	Physical	85	85	5	Normal	○

TM & HM MOVES

No.	Name	Type	Kind	Pow.	Acc.	PP	Range	DA
TM03	Water Pulse	Water	Special	60	100	20	Normal	—
TM06	Toxic	Poison	Status	—	85	10	Normal	—
TM07	Hail	Ice	Status	—	—	10	All	—
TM10	Hidden Power	Normal	Special	—	100	15	Normal	—
TM13	Ice Beam	Ice	Special	95	100	10	Normal	—
TM14	Blizzard	Ice	Special	120	70	5	2 Foes	—
TM17	Protect	Normal	Status	—	—	10	Self	—
TM18	Rain Dance	Water	Status	—	—	5	All	—
TM21	Frustration	Normal	Physical	—	100	20	Normal	○
TM26	Earthquake	Ground	Physical	100	100	10	2 Foes/1 Ally	—
TM27	Return	Normal	Physical	—	100	20	Normal	○
TM32	Double Team	Normal	Status	—	—	15	Self	—
TM37	Sandstorm	Rock	Status	—	—	10	All	—
TM39	Rock Tomb	Rock	Physical	50	80	10	Normal	—
TM42	Facade	Normal	Physical	70	100	20	Normal	○
TM43	Secret Power	Normal	Physical	70	100	20	Normal	—
TM44	Rest	Psychic	Status	—	—	10	Self	—
TM45	Attract	Normal	Status	—	100	15	Normal	—
TM58	Endure	Normal	Status	—	—	10	Self	—
TM78	Captivate	Normal	Status	—	100	20	2 Foes	—
TM82	Sleep Talk	Normal	Status	—	—	10	Depends	—
TM83	Natural Gift	Normal	Physical	—	100	15	Normal	—
TM87	Swagger	Normal	Status	—	90	15	Normal	—
TM90	Substitute	Normal	Status	—	—	10	Self	—
HM03	Surf	Water	Special	95	100	15	2 Foes/1 Ally	—
HM05	Whirlpool	Water	Special	15	70	15	Normal	—
HM07	Waterfall	Water	Physical	80	100	15	Normal	○

EGG MOVES

Name	Type	Kind	Pow.	Acc.	PP	Range	DA
Thrash	Normal	Physical	90	100	20	1 Random	—
Whirlpool	Water	Special	15	70	15	Normal	—
Spark	Electric	Physical	65	100	20	Normal	—
Hydro Pump	Water	Special	120	80	5	Normal	—
Flail	Normal	Physical	—	100	15	Normal	—
Take Down	Normal	Physical	90	85	20	Normal	—
Dragon Dance	Dragon	Status	—	—	20	Self	—

● LEVEL-UP MOVES

Lv.	Name	Type	Kind	Pow.	Acc.	PP	Range	DA
1	Zen Headbutt	Psychic	Physical	80	90	15	Normal	○
1	Tickle	Normal	Status	—	100	20	Normal	—
1	Mud-Slap	Ground	Special	20	100	10	Normal	—
1	Mud Sport	Ground	Status	—	—	15	All	—
1	Water Sport	Water	Status	—	—	15	All	—
6	Mud Sport	Ground	Status	—	—	15	All	—
6	Water Sport	Water	Status	—	—	15	All	—
10	Water Gun	Water	Special	40	100	25	Normal	—
14	Mud Bomb	Ground	Special	65	85	10	Normal	—
18	Amnesia	Psychic	Status	—	—	20	Self	—
22	Water Pulse	Water	Special	60	100	20	Normal	—
26	Magnitude	Ground	Physical	—	100	30	2 Foes/1 Ally	—
33	Rest	Psychic	Status	—	—	10	Self	—
33	Snore	Normal	Special	40	100	15	Normal	—
39	Aqua Tail	Water	Physical	90	90	10	Normal	○
45	Earthquake	Ground	Physical	100	100	10	2 Foes/1 Ally	—
51	Future Sight	Psychic	Special	80	90	15	Normal	—
57	Fissure	Ground	Physical	—	30	5	Normal	—

● MOVE MANIAC

Name	Type	Kind	Pow.	Acc.	PP	Range	DA
Headbutt	Normal	Physical	70	100	15	Normal	○

● BP MOVES

Name	Type	Kind	Pow.	Acc.	PP	Range	DA
Dive	Water	Physical	80	100	10	Normal	○
Icy Wind	Ice	Special	55	95	15	2 Foes	—
Zen Headbutt	Psychic	Physical	80	90	15	Normal	○
Snore	Normal	Special	40	100	15	Normal	—
Mud-Slap	Ground	Special	20	100	10	Normal	—
Aqua Tail	Water	Physical	90	90	10	Normal	○
Earth Power	Ground	Special	90	100	10	Normal	—
Bounce	Flying	Physical	85	85	5	Normal	○

● TM & HM MOVES

No.	Name	Type	Kind	Pow.	Acc.	PP	Range	DA
TM03	Water Pulse	Water	Special	60	100	20	Normal	—
TM06	Toxic	Poison	Status	—	85	10	Normal	—
TM07	Hail	Ice	Status	—	—	10	All	—
TM10	Hidden Power	Normal	Special	—	100	15	Normal	—
TM13	Ice Beam	Ice	Special	95	100	10	Normal	—
TM14	Blizzard	Ice	Special	120	70	5	2 Foes	—
TM15	Hyper Beam	Normal	Special	150	90	5	Normal	—
TM17	Protect	Normal	Status	—	—	10	Self	—
TM18	Rain Dance	Water	Status	—	—	5	All	—
TM21	Frustration	Normal	Physical	—	100	20	Normal	○
TM26	Earthquake	Ground	Physical	100	100	10	2 Foes/1 Ally	—
TM27	Return	Normal	Physical	—	100	20	Normal	○
TM32	Double Team	Normal	Status	—	—	15	Self	—
TM37	Sandstorm	Rock	Status	—	—	10	All	—
TM39	Rock Tomb	Rock	Physical	50	80	10	Normal	—
TM42	Facade	Normal	Physical	70	100	20	Normal	○
TM43	Secret Power	Normal	Physical	70	100	20	Normal	—
TM44	Rest	Psychic	Status	—	—	10	Self	—
TM45	Attract	Normal	Status	—	100	15	Normal	—
TM58	Endure	Normal	Status	—	—	10	Self	—
TM68	Giga Impact	Normal	Physical	150	90	5	Normal	○
TM71	Stone Edge	Rock	Physical	100	80	5	Normal	—
TM78	Captivate	Normal	Status	—	100	20	2 Foes	—
TM80	Rock Slide	Rock	Physical	75	90	10	2 Foes	—
TM82	Sleep Talk	Normal	Status	—	—	10	Depends	—
TM83	Natural Gift	Normal	Physical	—	100	15	Normal	—
TM87	Swagger	Normal	Status	—	90	15	Normal	—
TM90	Substitute	Normal	Status	—	—	10	Self	—
HM03	Surf	Water	Special	95	100	15	2 Foes/1 Ally	○
HM04	Strength	Normal	Physical	80	100	15	Normal	○
HM05	Whirlpool	Water	Special	15	70	15	Normal	—
HM06	Rock Smash	Fighting	Physical	40	100	15	Normal	○
HM07	Waterfall	Water	Physical	80	100	15	Normal	○

☺ No. 340 | Whiskers Pokémon
Whwatcash

Water Ground

- ● HEIGHT: 2'11"
- ● WEIGHT: 52.0 lbs.
- ● ITEMS: None
- ● SIZE COMPARISON

- ● MALE/FEMALE HAVE SAME FORM

☺ ABILITIES
- ● Oblivious
- ● Anticipation

☺ STATS
- HP ●●●●
- ATTACK ●●●●
- DEFENSE ●●●
- SP. ATTACK ●●●
- SP. DEFENSE ●●●
- SPEED ●●●

☺ EGG GROUPS
Water 2

☺ PERFORMANCE
- SPEED ★★
- POWER ★★★★☆
- SKILL ★★★☆
- STAMINA ★★★★☆
- JUMP ★★

● MAIN WAYS TO OBTAIN

Pokémon HeartGold	Violet City (mass outbreak, fishing)
Pokémon SoulSilver	Violet City (mass outbreak, fishing)
Pokémon Diamond	Route 205, Eterna City side (Super Rod)
Pokémon Pearl	Route 205, Eterna City side (Super Rod)
Pokémon Platinum	Route 205, Eterna City side (Super Rod)

Pokémon HeartGold	Pokémon SoulSilver
It claims a large swamp to itself. If a foe comes near it, it sets off tremors by thrashing around.	It claims a large swamp to itself. If a foe comes near it, it sets off tremors by thrashing around.

☺ EVOLUTION

Lv. 30

Barboach Whiscash

No. 341 | Ruffian Pokémon
Corphish

Water

- **HEIGHT:** 2'00"
- **WEIGHT:** 25.4 lbs.
- **ITEMS:** None

● SIZE COMPARISON

● MALE/FEMALE HAVE SAME FORM

⊙ ABILITIES
- Hyper Cutter
- Shed Armor

⊙ STATS
- HP ●●
- ATTACK ●●●
- DEFENSE ●●●
- SP. ATTACK ●●
- SP. DEFENSE ●
- SPEED ●●

⊙ EGG GROUPS
- Water 1
- Water 3

⊙ PERFORMANCE
- SPEED ★★★☆
- POWER ★★★☆
- SKILL ★★★☆
- STAMINA ★★★☆
- JUMP ★★

● MAIN WAYS TO OBTAIN

Pokémon HeartGold	Safari Zone (Rocky Beach Area: if Water objects are placed, may appear if you fish with the Super Rod)
Pokémon SoulSilver	Safari Zone (Rocky Beach Area: if Water objects are placed, may appear if you fish with the Super Rod)
Pokémon Diamond	Celestic Town (Super Rod)
Pokémon Pearl	Celestic Town (Super Rod)
Pokémon Platinum	Celestic Town (Super Rod)

Pokémon HeartGold	Pokémon SoulSilver
It was originally a Pokémon from afar that escaped to the wild. It can adapt to the dirtiest river.	It was originally a Pokémon from afar that escaped to the wild. It can adapt to the dirtiest river.

⊙ EVOLUTION

Corphish — Lv. 30 → Crawdaunt

● LEVEL-UP MOVES

Lv.	Name	Type	Kind	Pow.	Acc.	PP	Range	DA
1	Bubble	Water	Special	20	100	30	2 Foes	—
7	Harden	Normal	Status	—	—	30	Self	—
10	ViceGrip	Normal	Physical	55	100	30	Normal	○
13	Leer	Normal	Status	—	100	30	2 Foes	—
20	BubbleBeam	Water	Special	65	100	20	Normal	—
23	Protect	Normal	Status	—	—	10	Self	—
26	Knock Off	Dark	Physical	20	100	20	Normal	○
29	Taunt	Dark	Status	—	100	20	Normal	—
35	Night Slash	Dark	Physical	70	100	15	Normal	○
38	Crabhammer	Water	Physical	90	85	10	Normal	○
44	Swords Dance	Normal	Status	—	—	30	Self	—
47	Crunch	Dark	Physical	80	100	15	Normal	○
53	Guillotine	Normal	Physical	—	30	5	Normal	○

● MOVE MANIAC

Name	Type	Kind	Pow.	Acc.	PP	Range	DA

● BP MOVES

Name	Type	Kind	Pow.	Acc.	PP	Range	DA
Fury Cutter	Bug	Physical	10	95	20	Normal	○
Icy Wind	Ice	Special	55	95	15	2 Foes	—
Knock Off	Dark	Physical	20	100	20	Normal	○
Snore	Normal	Special	40	100	15	Normal	—
Spite	Ghost	Status	—	100	10	Normal	—
Mud-Slap	Ground	Special	20	100	10	Normal	—
Superpower	Fighting	Physical	120	100	5	Normal	○
Endeavor	Normal	Physical	—	100	5	Normal	○
AncientPower	Rock	Special	60	100	5	Normal	—
Iron Defense	Steel	Status	—	—	15	Self	—

● TM & HM MOVES

No.	Name	Type	Kind	Pow.	Acc.	PP	Range	DA
TM03	Water Pulse	Water	Special	60	100	20	Normal	—
TM06	Toxic	Poison	Status	—	85	10	Normal	—
TM07	Hail	Ice	Status	—	—	10	All	—
TM10	Hidden Power	Normal	Special	—	100	15	Normal	—
TM12	Taunt	Dark	Status	—	100	20	Normal	—
TM13	Ice Beam	Ice	Special	95	100	10	Normal	—
TM14	Blizzard	Ice	Special	120	70	5	2 Foes	—
TM17	Protect	Normal	Status	—	—	10	Self	—
TM18	Rain Dance	Water	Status	—	—	5	All	—
TM21	Frustration	Normal	Physical	—	100	20	Normal	○
TM27	Return	Normal	Physical	—	100	20	Normal	○
TM28	Dig	Ground	Physical	80	100	10	Normal	○
TM31	Brick Break	Fighting	Physical	75	100	15	Normal	○
TM32	Double Team	Normal	Status	—	—	15	Self	—
TM36	Sludge Bomb	Poison	Special	90	100	10	Normal	—
TM39	Rock Tomb	Rock	Physical	50	80	10	Normal	○
TM40	Aerial Ace	Flying	Physical	60	—	20	Normal	○
TM42	Facade	Normal	Physical	70	100	20	Normal	○
TM43	Secret Power	Normal	Physical	70	100	20	Normal	○
TM44	Rest	Psychic	Status	—	—	10	Self	—
TM45	Attract	Normal	Status	—	100	15	Normal	—
TM54	False Swipe	Normal	Physical	40	100	40	Normal	○
TM56	Fling	Dark	Physical	—	100	10	Normal	○
TM58	Endure	Normal	Status	—	—	10	Self	—
TM66	Payback	Dark	Physical	50	100	10	Normal	○
TM75	Swords Dance	Normal	Status	—	—	30	Self	—
TM78	Captivate	Normal	Status	—	100	20	2 Foes	—
TM80	Rock Slide	Rock	Physical	75	90	10	2 Foes	—
TM81	X-Scissor	Bug	Physical	80	100	15	Normal	○
TM82	Sleep Talk	Normal	Status	—	—	10	Depends	—
TM83	Natural Gift	Normal	Physical	—	100	15	Normal	—
TM87	Swagger	Normal	Status	—	90	15	Normal	—
TM90	Substitute	Normal	Status	—	—	10	Self	—
HM01	Cut	Normal	Physical	50	95	30	Normal	○
HM03	Surf	Water	Special	95	100	15	2 Foes/1 Ally	—
HM04	Strength	Normal	Physical	80	100	15	Normal	○
HM05	Whirlpool	Water	Special	15	70	15	Normal	—
HM06	Rock Smash	Fighting	Physical	40	100	15	Normal	○
HM07	Waterfall	Water	Physical	80	100	15	Normal	○

● EGG MOVES

Name	Type	Kind	Pow.	Acc.	PP	Range	DA
Mud Sport	Ground	Status	—	—	15	All	—
Endeavor	Normal	Physical	—	100	5	Normal	○
Body Slam	Normal	Physical	85	100	15	Normal	○
AncientPower	Rock	Special	60	100	5	Normal	—
Knock Off	Dark	Physical	20	100	20	Normal	○
Superpower	Fighting	Physical	120	100	5	Normal	○
Metal Claw	Steel	Physical	50	95	35	Normal	○
Dragon Dance	Dragon	Status	—	—	20	Self	—

● LEVEL-UP MOVES

Lv.	Name	Type	Kind	Pow.	Acc.	PP	Range	DA
1	Bubble	Water	Special	20	100	30	2 Foes	—
1	Harden	Normal	Status	—	—	30	Self	—
1	ViceGrip	Normal	Physical	55	100	30	Normal	○
1	Leer	Normal	Status	—	100	30	2 Foes	—
7	Harden	Normal	Status	—	—	30	Self	—
10	ViceGrip	Normal	Physical	55	100	30	Normal	○
13	Leer	Normal	Status	—	100	30	2 Foes	—
20	BubbleBeam	Water	Special	65	100	20	Normal	—
23	Protect	Normal	Status	—	—	10	Self	—
26	Knock Off	Dark	Physical	20	100	20	Normal	○
30	Swift	Normal	Special	60	—	20	2 Foes	—
34	Taunt	Dark	Status	—	100	20	Normal	—
39	Night Slash	Dark	Physical	70	100	15	Normal	○
44	Crabhammer	Water	Physical	90	85	10	Normal	○
52	Swords Dance	Normal	Status	—	—	30	Self	—
57	Crunch	Dark	Physical	80	100	15	Normal	○
65	Guillotine	Normal	Physical	—	30	5	Normal	○

● MOVE MANIAC

Name	Type	Kind	Pow.	Acc.	PP	Range	DA

● BP MOVES

Name	Type	Kind	Pow.	Acc.	PP	Range	DA
Dive	Water	Physical	80	100	10	Normal	○
Fury Cutter	Bug	Physical	10	95	20	Normal	○
Icy Wind	Ice	Special	55	95	15	2 Foes	—
Knock Off	Dark	Physical	20	100	20	Normal	○
Snore	Normal	Special	40	100	15	Normal	—
Spite	Ghost	Status	—	100	10	Normal	—
Swift	Normal	Special	60	—	20	2 Foes	—
Mud-Slap	Ground	Special	20	100	10	Normal	—
Superpower	Fighting	Physical	120	100	5	Normal	○
Endeavor	Normal	Physical	—	100	5	Normal	○
AncientPower	Rock	Special	60	100	5	Normal	—
Iron Defense	Steel	Status	—	—	15	Self	—

● TM & HM MOVES

No.	Name	Type	Kind	Pow.	Acc.	PP	Range	DA
TM03	Water Pulse	Water	Special	60	100	20	Normal	—
TM06	Toxic	Poison	Status	—	85	10	Normal	—
TM07	Hail	Ice	Status	—	—	10	All	—
TM10	Hidden Power	Normal	Special	—	100	15	Normal	—
TM12	Taunt	Dark	Status	—	100	20	Normal	—
TM13	Ice Beam	Ice	Special	95	100	10	Normal	—
TM14	Blizzard	Ice	Special	120	70	5	2 Foes	—
TM15	Hyper Beam	Normal	Special	150	90	5	Normal	—
TM17	Protect	Normal	Status	—	—	10	Self	—
TM18	Rain Dance	Water	Status	—	—	5	All	—
TM21	Frustration	Normal	Physical	—	100	20	Normal	○
TM27	Return	Normal	Physical	—	100	20	Normal	○
TM28	Dig	Ground	Physical	80	100	10	Normal	○
TM31	Brick Break	Fighting	Physical	75	100	15	Normal	○
TM32	Double Team	Normal	Status	—	—	15	Self	—
TM36	Sludge Bomb	Poison	Special	90	100	10	Normal	—
TM39	Rock Tomb	Rock	Physical	50	80	10	Normal	○
TM40	Aerial Ace	Flying	Physical	60	—	20	Normal	○
TM42	Facade	Normal	Physical	70	100	20	Normal	○
TM43	Secret Power	Normal	Physical	70	100	20	Normal	○
TM44	Rest	Psychic	Status	—	—	10	Self	—
TM45	Attract	Normal	Status	—	100	15	Normal	—
TM54	False Swipe	Normal	Physical	40	100	40	Normal	○
TM56	Fling	Dark	Physical	—	100	10	Normal	○
TM58	Endure	Normal	Status	—	—	10	Self	—
TM66	Payback	Dark	Physical	50	100	10	Normal	○
TM68	Giga Impact	Normal	Physical	150	90	5	Normal	○
TM72	Avalanche	Ice	Physical	60	100	10	Normal	○
TM75	Swords Dance	Normal	Status	—	—	30	Self	—
TM78	Captivate	Normal	Status	—	100	20	2 Foes	—
TM79	Dark Pulse	Dark	Special	80	100	15	Normal	—
TM80	Rock Slide	Rock	Physical	75	90	10	2 Foes	○
TM81	X-Scissor	Bug	Physical	80	100	15	Normal	○
TM82	Sleep Talk	Normal	Status	—	—	10	Depends	—
TM83	Natural Gift	Normal	Physical	—	100	15	Normal	—
TM87	Swagger	Normal	Status	—	90	15	Normal	—
TM90	Substitute	Normal	Status	—	—	10	Self	—
HM01	Cut	Normal	Physical	50	95	30	Normal	○
HM03	Surf	Water	Special	95	100	15	2 Foes/1 Ally	—
HM04	Strength	Normal	Physical	80	100	15	Normal	○
HM05	Whirlpool	Water	Special	15	70	15	Normal	—
HM06	Rock Smash	Fighting	Physical	40	100	15	Normal	○
HM07	Waterfall	Water	Physical	80	100	15	Normal	○

☺ No. 342 | Rogue Pokémon
Crawdaunt

Water Dark

● **HEIGHT:** 3'07"
● **WEIGHT:** 72.3 lbs.
● **ITEMS:** None

● **SIZE COMPARISON**

● **MALE/FEMALE HAVE SAME FORM**

☺ ABILITIES
● Hyper Cutter
● Shed Armor

☺ EGG GROUPS
Water 1
Water 3

☺ STATS
HP ●●
ATTACK ●●●●●
DEFENSE ●●●
SP. ATTACK ●●
SP. DEFENSE ●●
SPEED ●●●

☺ PERFORMANCE
SPEED ★★☆   STAMINA ★★★☆
POWER ★★★★☆   JUMP ★★☆
SKILL ★★★☆

● MAIN WAYS TO OBTAIN

Pokémon HeartGold — Level up Corphish to Lv. 30

Pokémon SoulSilver — Level up Corphish to Lv. 30

Pokémon Diamond — Level up Corphish to Lv. 30

Pokémon Pearl — Level up Corphish to Lv. 30

Pokémon Platinum — Level up Corphish to Lv. 30

Pokémon HeartGold
A brutish Pokémon that loves to battle. It will crash itself into any foe that approaches its nest.

Pokémon SoulSilver
A brutish Pokémon that loves to battle. It will crash itself into any foe that approaches its nest.

☺ EVOLUTION

Corphish → Lv. 30 → Crawdaunt

☻ No. 343 | Clay Doll Pokémon
Baltoy

`Ground` `Psychic`

- **HEIGHT:** 1'08"
- **WEIGHT:** 47.4 lbs.
- **ITEMS:** None

● SIZE COMPARISON

● GENDER UNKNOWN

☻ ABILITIES
- Levitate

☻ EGG GROUPS
Mineral

☻ PERFORMANCE
SPEED ★★★☆ STAMINA ★★★☆
POWER ★★☆ JUMP ★★☆
SKILL ★★★★☆

● MAIN WAYS TO OBTAIN

Pokémon HeartGold — Route 3 (mass outbreak)

Pokémon SoulSilver — —

Pokémon Diamond — Route 206 (use Poké Radar)

Pokémon Pearl — Route 206 (use Poké Radar)

Pokémon Platinum — Route 206 (use Poké Radar)

Pokémon HeartGold
It moves while spinning around on its single foot. Some BALTOY have been seen spinning on their heads.

Pokémon SoulSilver
It moves while spinning around on its single foot. Some BALTOY have been seen spinning on their heads.

☻ EVOLUTION
Baltoy → Lv. 36 → Claydol

● LEVEL-UP MOVES

Lv.	Name	Type	Kind	Pow.	Acc.	PP	Range	DA
1	Confusion	Psychic	Special	50	100	25	Normal	—
3	Harden	Normal	Status	—	—	30	Self	—
5	Rapid Spin	Normal	Physical	20	100	40	Normal	○
7	Mud-Slap	Ground	Special	20	100	10	Normal	—
11	Psybeam	Psychic	Special	65	100	20	Normal	—
15	Rock Tomb	Rock	Physical	50	80	10	Normal	—
19	Selfdestruct	Normal	Physical	200	100	5	2 Foes/1 Ally	—
25	AncientPower	Rock	Special	60	100	5	Normal	—
31	Power Trick	Psychic	Status	—	—	10	Self	—
37	Sandstorm	Rock	Status	—	—	10	All	—
45	Cosmic Power	Psychic	Status	—	—	20	Self	—
53	Earth Power	Ground	Special	90	100	10	Normal	—
61	Heal Block	Psychic	Status	—	100	15	2 Foes	—
71	Explosion	Normal	Physical	250	100	5	2 Foes/1 Ally	—

● MOVE MANIAC

Name	Type	Kind	Pow.	Acc.	PP	Range	DA
Headbutt	Normal	Physical	70	100	15	Normal	○

● BP MOVES

Name	Type	Kind	Pow.	Acc.	PP	Range	DA
Zen Headbutt	Psychic	Physical	80	90	15	Normal	○
Trick	Psychic	Status	—	—	10	Normal	—
Snore	Normal	Special	40	100	15	Normal	—
Gravity	Psychic	Status	—	—	5	All	—
Magic Coat	Psychic	Status	—	—	15	Self	—
Mud-Slap	Ground	Special	20	100	10	Normal	—
AncientPower	Rock	Special	60	100	5	Normal	—
Signal Beam	Bug	Special	75	100	15	Normal	—
Earth Power	Ground	Special	90	100	10	Normal	—

☻ STATS
- HP ●
- ATTACK ●●
- DEFENSE ●●
- SP. ATTACK ●●
- SP. DEFENSE ●●●
- SPEED ●●●

● TM & HM MOVES

No.	Name	Type	Kind	Pow.	Acc.	PP	Range	DA
TM04	Calm Mind	Psychic	Status	—	—	20	Self	—
TM06	Toxic	Poison	Status	—	85	10	Normal	—
TM10	Hidden Power	Normal	Special	—	100	15	Normal	—
TM11	Sunny Day	Fire	Status	—	—	5	All	—
TM13	Ice Beam	Ice	Special	95	100	10	Normal	—
TM16	Light Screen	Psychic	Status	—	—	30	2 Allies	—
TM17	Protect	Normal	Status	—	—	10	Self	—
TM18	Rain Dance	Water	Status	—	—	5	All	—
TM20	Safeguard	Normal	Status	—	—	25	2 Allies	—
TM21	Frustration	Normal	Physical	—	100	20	Normal	○
TM22	SolarBeam	Grass	Special	120	100	10	Normal	—
TM26	Earthquake	Ground	Physical	100	100	10	2 Foes/1 Ally	—
TM27	Return	Normal	Physical	—	100	20	Normal	○
TM28	Dig	Ground	Physical	80	100	10	Normal	○
TM29	Psychic	Psychic	Special	90	100	10	Normal	—
TM30	Shadow Ball	Ghost	Special	80	100	15	Normal	—
TM32	Double Team	Normal	Status	—	—	15	Self	—
TM33	Reflect	Psychic	Status	—	—	20	2 Allies	—
TM37	Sandstorm	Rock	Status	—	—	10	All	—
TM39	Rock Tomb	Rock	Physical	50	80	10	Normal	—
TM42	Facade	Normal	Physical	70	100	20	Normal	○
TM43	Secret Power	Normal	Physical	70	100	20	Normal	—
TM44	Rest	Psychic	Status	—	—	10	Self	—
TM48	Skill Swap	Psychic	Status	—	—	10	Normal	—
TM57	Charge Beam	Electric	Special	50	90	10	Normal	—
TM58	Endure	Normal	Status	—	—	10	Self	—
TM64	Explosion	Normal	Physical	250	100	5	2 Foes/1 Ally	—
TM67	Recycle	Normal	Status	—	—	10	Self	—
TM69	Rock Polish	Rock	Status	—	—	20	Self	—
TM70	Flash	Normal	Status	—	100	20	Normal	—
TM74	Gyro Ball	Steel	Physical	—	100	5	Normal	○
TM76	Stealth Rock	Rock	Status	—	—	20	2 Foes	—
TM77	Psych Up	Normal	Status	—	—	10	Normal	—
TM80	Rock Slide	Rock	Physical	75	90	10	2 Foes	—
TM82	Sleep Talk	Normal	Status	—	—	10	Depends	—
TM83	Natural Gift	Normal	Physical	—	100	15	Normal	—
TM85	Dream Eater	Psychic	Special	100	100	15	Normal	—
TM86	Grass Knot	Grass	Special	—	100	20	Normal	○
TM87	Swagger	Normal	Status	—	90	15	Normal	—
TM90	Substitute	Normal	Status	—	—	10	Self	—
TM92	Trick Room	Psychic	Status	—	—	5	All	—

● LEVEL-UP MOVES

Lv.	Name	Type	Kind	Pow.	Acc.	PP	Range	DA
1	Teleport	Psychic	Status	—	—	20	Self	—
1	Confusion	Psychic	Special	50	100	25	Normal	—
1	Harden	Normal	Status	—	—	30	Self	—
1	Rapid Spin	Normal	Physical	20	100	40	Normal	○
3	Harden	Normal	Status	—	—	30	Self	—
5	Rapid Spin	Normal	Physical	20	100	40	Normal	○
7	Mud-Slap	Ground	Special	20	100	10	Normal	—
11	Psybeam	Psychic	Special	65	100	20	Normal	—
15	Rock Tomb	Rock	Physical	50	80	10	Normal	—
19	Selfdestruct	Normal	Physical	200	100	5	2 Foes/1 Ally	—
25	AncientPower	Rock	Special	60	100	5	Normal	—
31	Power Trick	Psychic	Status	—	—	10	Self	—
36	Hyper Beam	Normal	Special	150	90	5	Normal	—
40	Sandstorm	Rock	Status	—	—	10	All	—
51	Cosmic Power	Psychic	Status	—	—	20	Self	—
62	Earth Power	Ground	Special	90	100	10	Normal	—
73	Heal Block	Psychic	Status	—	100	15	2 Foes	—
86	Explosion	Normal	Physical	250	100	5	2 Foes/1 Ally	—

● MOVE MANIAC

Name	Type	Kind	Pow.	Acc.	PP	Range	DA
Headbutt	Normal	Physical	70	100	15	Normal	○

● BP MOVES

Name	Type	Kind	Pow.	Acc.	PP	Range	DA
Zen Headbutt	Psychic	Physical	80	90	15	Normal	○
Trick	Psychic	Status	—	100	10	Normal	—
Snore	Normal	Special	40	100	15	Normal	—
Gravity	Psychic	Status	—	—	5	All	—
Magic Coat	Psychic	Status	—	—	15	Self	—
Mud-Slap	Ground	Special	20	100	10	Normal	—
AncientPower	Rock	Special	60	100	5	Normal	—
Signal Beam	Bug	Special	75	100	15	Normal	—
Earth Power	Ground	Special	90	100	10	Normal	—

● TM & HM MOVES

No.	Name	Type	Kind	Pow.	Acc.	PP	Range	DA
TM04	Calm Mind	Psychic	Status	—	—	20	Self	—
TM06	Toxic	Poison	Status	—	85	10	Normal	—
TM10	Hidden Power	Normal	Special	—	100	15	Normal	—
TM11	Sunny Day	Fire	Status	—	—	5	All	—
TM13	Ice Beam	Ice	Special	95	100	10	Normal	—
TM15	Hyper Beam	Normal	Special	150	90	5	Normal	—
TM16	Light Screen	Psychic	Status	—	—	30	2 Allies	—
TM17	Protect	Normal	Status	—	—	10	Self	—
TM18	Rain Dance	Water	Status	—	—	5	All	—
TM20	Safeguard	Normal	Status	—	—	25	2 Allies	—
TM21	Frustration	Normal	Physical	—	100	20	Normal	○
TM22	SolarBeam	Grass	Special	120	100	10	Normal	—
TM26	Earthquake	Ground	Physical	100	100	10	2 Foes/1 Ally	—
TM27	Return	Normal	Physical	—	100	20	Normal	○
TM28	Dig	Ground	Physical	80	100	10	Normal	○
TM29	Psychic	Psychic	Special	90	100	10	Normal	—
TM30	Shadow Ball	Ghost	Special	80	100	15	Normal	—
TM32	Double Team	Normal	Status	—	—	15	Self	—
TM33	Reflect	Psychic	Status	—	—	20	2 Allies	—
TM37	Sandstorm	Rock	Status	—	—	10	All	—
TM39	Rock Tomb	Rock	Physical	50	80	10	Normal	—
TM42	Facade	Normal	Physical	70	100	20	Normal	○
TM43	Secret Power	Normal	Physical	70	100	20	Normal	○
TM44	Rest	Psychic	Status	—	—	10	Self	—
TM48	Skill Swap	Psychic	Status	—	—	10	Normal	—
TM57	Charge Beam	Electric	Special	50	90	10	Normal	—
TM58	Endure	Normal	Status	—	—	10	Self	—
TM64	Explosion	Normal	Physical	250	100	5	2 Foes/1 Ally	—
TM68	Giga Impact	Normal	Physical	150	90	5	Normal	○
TM69	Rock Polish	Rock	Status	—	—	20	Self	—
TM70	Flash	Normal	Status	—	100	20	Normal	—
TM71	Stone Edge	Rock	Physical	100	80	5	Normal	—
TM74	Gyro Ball	Steel	Physical	—	100	5	Normal	○
TM76	Stealth Rock	Rock	Status	—	—	20	2 Foes	—
TM77	Psych Up	Normal	Status	—	—	10	Self	—
TM80	Rock Slide	Rock	Physical	75	90	10	2 Foes	—
TM82	Sleep Talk	Normal	Status	—	—	10	Depends	—
TM83	Natural Gift	Normal	Physical	—	100	15	Normal	—
TM85	Dream Eater	Psychic	Special	100	100	15	Normal	—
TM86	Grass Knot	Grass	Special	—	100	20	Normal	—
TM87	Swagger	Normal	Status	—	90	15	Normal	—
TM90	Substitute	Normal	Status	—	—	10	Self	—
TM92	Trick Room	Psychic	Status	—	—	5	All	—
HM04	Strength	Normal	Physical	80	100	15	Normal	○
HM06	Rock Smash	Fighting	Physical	40	100	15	Normal	○

Claydol

Ground Psychic

- ● HEIGHT: 4'11"
- ● WEIGHT: 238.1 lbs.
- ● ITEMS: None

● SIZE COMPARISON

● GENDER UNKNOWN

● ABILITIES

● Levitate

● STATS

HP ●●
ATTACK ●●●
DEFENSE ●●●●
SP. ATTACK ●●●●
SP. DEFENSE ●●●●●
SPEED ●●●

● EGG GROUPS

Mineral

● PERFORMANCE

SPEED ★★☆ STAMINA ★★★☆
POWER ★★☆ JUMP ★★★★
SKILL ★★★★☆

● MAIN WAYS TO OBTAIN

Pokémon HeartGold — Level up Baltoy to Lv. 36

Pokémon SoulSilver — —

Pokémon Diamond — Level up Baltoy to Lv. 36

Pokémon Pearl — Level up Baltoy to Lv. 36

Pokémon Platinum — Level up Baltoy to Lv. 36

Pokémon HeartGold — It is said that it originates from clay dolls made by an ancient civilization.

Pokémon SoulSilver — It is said that it originates from clay dolls made by an ancient civilization.

● EVOLUTION

Baltoy → Lv. 36 → Claydol

☺ No. 345 | Sea Lily Pokémon
Lileep

`Rock` `Grass`

- **HEIGHT:** 3'03"
- **WEIGHT:** 52.5 lbs.
- **ITEMS:** None

● MALE/FEMALE HAVE SAME FORM

☺ ABILITIES
● Suction Cups

☺ STATS
HP ●●
ATTACK ●●
DEFENSE ●●●
SP. ATTACK ●●●
SP. DEFENSE ●●●
SPEED ●

☺ EGG GROUPS
Water 3

☺ PERFORMANCE
SPEED ★☆☆   STAMINA ★★★★☆
POWER ★★★☆   JUMP ★★
SKILL ★★☆

● MAIN WAYS TO OBTAIN

Pokémon HeartGold	—
Pokémon SoulSilver	Have the Root Fossil restored at the Pewter Museum of Science
Pokémon Diamond	After obtaining the National Pokédex, find the Root Fossil in the Underground and have it restored at the Oreburgh Mining Museum
Pokémon Pearl	After obtaining the National Pokédex, find the Root Fossil in the Underground and have it restored at the Oreburgh Mining Museum
Pokémon Platinum	After obtaining the National Pokédex, find the Root Fossil in the Underground and have it restored at the Oreburgh Mining Museum

Pokémon HeartGold	Pokémon SoulSilver
It disguises its tentacles as flowers to attract and catch prey. It became extinct in ancient times.	It disguises its tentacles as flowers to attract and catch prey. It became extinct in ancient times.

☺ EVOLUTION

Lileep — Lv. 40 ▶ Cradily

● LEVEL-UP MOVES

Lv.	Name	Type	Kind	Pow.	Acc.	PP	Range	DA
1	Astonish	Ghost	Physical	30	100	15	Normal	○
1	Constrict	Normal	Physical	10	100	35	Normal	○
8	Acid	Poison	Special	40	100	30	2 Foes	—
15	Ingrain	Grass	Status	—	—	20	Self	—
22	Confuse Ray	Ghost	Status	—	100	10	Normal	—
29	Amnesia	Psychic	Status	—	—	20	Self	—
36	Gastro Acid	Poison	Status	—	100	10	Normal	—
43	AncientPower	Rock	Special	60	100	5	Normal	—
50	Energy Ball	Grass	Special	80	100	10	Normal	—
57	Stockpile	Normal	Status	—	—	20	Self	—
57	Spit Up	Normal	Special	—	100	10	Normal	—
57	Swallow	Normal	Status	—	—	10	Self	—
64	Wring Out	Normal	Special	—	100	5	Normal	○

● MOVE MANIAC

Name	Type	Kind	Pow.	Acc.	PP	Range	DA

● BP MOVES

Name	Type	Kind	Pow.	Acc.	PP	Range	DA
Snore	Normal	Special	40	100	15	Normal	—
Synthesis	Grass	Status	—	—	5	Self	—
String Shot	Bug	Status	—	95	40	2 Foes	—
Worry Seed	Grass	Status	—	100	10	Normal	—
Mud-Slap	Ground	Special	20	100	10	Normal	—
Gastro Acid	Poison	Status	—	100	10	Normal	—
AncientPower	Rock	Special	60	100	5	Normal	—
Earth Power	Ground	Special	90	100	10	Normal	—
Seed Bomb	Grass	Physical	80	100	15	Normal	—
Pain Split	Normal	Status	—	—	20	Normal	—

● TM & HM MOVES

No.	Name	Type	Kind	Pow.	Acc.	PP	Range	DA
TM06	Toxic	Poison	Status	—	85	10	Normal	—
TM09	Bullet Seed	Grass	Physical	10	100	30	Normal	—
TM10	Hidden Power	Normal	Special	—	100	15	Normal	—
TM11	Sunny Day	Fire	Status	—	—	5	All	—
TM17	Protect	Normal	Status	—	—	10	Self	—
TM19	Giga Drain	Grass	Special	60	100	10	Normal	—
TM21	Frustration	Normal	Physical	—	100	20	Normal	○
TM22	SolarBeam	Grass	Special	120	100	10	Normal	○
TM27	Return	Normal	Physical	—	100	20	Normal	○
TM32	Double Team	Normal	Status	—	—	15	Self	—
TM36	Sludge Bomb	Poison	Special	90	100	10	Normal	—
TM37	Sandstorm	Rock	Status	—	—	10	All	—
TM39	Rock Tomb	Rock	Physical	50	80	10	Normal	—
TM42	Facade	Normal	Physical	70	100	20	Normal	○
TM43	Secret Power	Normal	Physical	70	100	20	Normal	—
TM44	Rest	Psychic	Status	—	—	10	Self	—
TM45	Attract	Normal	Status	—	100	15	Normal	—
TM53	Energy Ball	Grass	Special	80	100	10	Normal	—
TM58	Endure	Normal	Status	—	—	10	Self	—
TM69	Rock Polish	Rock	Status	—	—	20	Self	—
TM70	Flash	Normal	Status	—	100	20	Normal	—
TM75	Swords Dance	Normal	Status	—	—	30	Self	—
TM76	Stealth Rock	Rock	Status	—	—	20	2 Foes	—
TM78	Captivate	Normal	Status	—	100	20	2 Foes	—
TM80	Rock Slide	Rock	Physical	75	90	10	2 Foes	—
TM82	Sleep Talk	Normal	Status	—	—	10	Depends	—
TM83	Natural Gift	Normal	Physical	—	100	15	Normal	—
TM86	Grass Knot	Grass	Special	—	100	20	Normal	○
TM87	Swagger	Normal	Status	—	90	15	Normal	—
TM90	Substitute	Normal	Status	—	—	10	Self	—

● EGG MOVES

Name	Type	Kind	Pow.	Acc.	PP	Range	DA
Barrier	Psychic	Status	—	—	30	Self	—
Recover	Normal	Status	—	—	10	Self	—
Mirror Coat	Psychic	Special	—	—	20	Self	—
Rock Slide	Rock	Physical	75	90	10	2 Foes	—
Wring Out	Normal	Special	—	100	5	Normal	○
Tickle	Normal	Status	—	100	20	Normal	—
Curse	???	Status	—	—	10	Normal/Self	—

● LEVEL-UP MOVES

Lv.	Name	Type	Kind	Pow.	Acc.	PP	Range	DA
1	Astonish	Ghost	Physical	30	100	15	Normal	○
1	Constrict	Normal	Physical	10	100	35	Normal	○
1	Acid	Poison	Special	40	100	30	2 Foes	—
1	Ingrain	Grass	Status	—	—	20	Self	—
8	Acid	Poison	Special	40	100	30	2 Foes	—
15	Ingrain	Grass	Status	—	—	20	Self	—
22	Confuse Ray	Ghost	Status	—	100	10	Normal	—
29	Amnesia	Psychic	Status	—	—	20	Self	—
36	AncientPower	Rock	Special	60	100	5	Normal	—
46	Gastro Acid	Poison	Status	—	100	10	Normal	—
56	Energy Ball	Grass	Special	80	100	10	Normal	—
66	Stockpile	Normal	Status	—	—	20	Self	—
66	Spit Up	Normal	Special	—	100	10	Normal	—
66	Swallow	Normal	Status	—	—	10	Self	—
76	Wring Out	Normal	Special	—	100	5	Normal	○

● MOVE MANIAC

Name	Type	Kind	Pow.	Acc.	PP	Range	DA
Headbutt	Normal	Physical	70	100	15	Normal	○

● BP MOVES

Name	Type	Kind	Pow.	Acc.	PP	Range	DA
Snore	Normal	Special	40	100	15	Normal	—
Synthesis	Grass	Status	—	—	5	Self	—
String Shot	Bug	Status	—	95	40	2 Foes	—
Worry Seed	Grass	Status	—	100	10	Normal	—
Block	Normal	Status	—	—	5	Normal	—
Mud-Slap	Ground	Special	20	100	10	Normal	—
Gastro Acid	Poison	Status	—	100	10	Normal	—
AncientPower	Rock	Special	60	100	5	Normal	—
Earth Power	Ground	Special	90	100	10	Normal	—
Seed Bomb	Grass	Physical	80	100	15	Normal	—
Pain Split	Normal	Status	—	—	20	Normal	—

● TM & HM MOVES

No.	Name	Type	Kind	Pow.	Acc.	PP	Range	DA
TM06	Toxic	Poison	Status	—	85	10	Normal	—
TM09	Bullet Seed	Grass	Physical	10	100	30	Normal	—
TM10	Hidden Power	Normal	Special	—	100	15	Normal	—
TM11	Sunny Day	Fire	Status	—	—	5	All	—
TM15	Hyper Beam	Normal	Special	150	90	5	Normal	—
TM17	Protect	Normal	Status	—	—	10	Self	—
TM19	Giga Drain	Grass	Special	60	100	10	Normal	—
TM21	Frustration	Normal	Physical	—	100	20	Normal	○
TM22	SolarBeam	Grass	Special	120	100	10	Normal	—
TM26	Earthquake	Ground	Physical	100	100	10	2 Foes/1 Ally	—
TM27	Return	Normal	Physical	—	100	20	Normal	○
TM32	Double Team	Normal	Status	—	—	15	Self	—
TM36	Sludge Bomb	Poison	Special	90	100	10	Normal	—
TM37	Sandstorm	Rock	Status	—	—	10	All	—
TM39	Rock Tomb	Rock	Physical	50	80	10	Normal	—
TM42	Facade	Normal	Physical	70	100	20	Normal	—
TM43	Secret Power	Normal	Physical	70	100	20	Normal	—
TM44	Rest	Psychic	Status	—	—	10	Self	—
TM45	Attract	Normal	Status	—	100	15	Normal	—
TM53	Energy Ball	Grass	Special	80	100	10	Normal	—
TM58	Endure	Normal	Status	—	—	10	Self	—
TM68	Giga Impact	Normal	Physical	150	90	5	Normal	○
TM69	Rock Polish	Rock	Status	—	—	20	Self	—
TM70	Flash	Normal	Status	—	100	20	Normal	—
TM71	Stone Edge	Rock	Physical	100	80	5	Normal	—
TM75	Swords Dance	Normal	Status	—	—	30	Self	—
TM76	Stealth Rock	Rock	Status	—	—	20	2 Foes	—
TM78	Captivate	Normal	Status	—	100	20	2 Foes	—
TM80	Rock Slide	Rock	Physical	75	90	10	2 Foes	—
TM82	Sleep Talk	Normal	Status	—	—	10	Depends	—
TM83	Natural Gift	Normal	Physical	—	100	15	Normal	—
TM86	Grass Knot	Grass	Special	—	100	20	Normal	○
TM87	Swagger	Normal	Status	—	90	15	Normal	—
TM90	Substitute	Normal	Status	—	—	10	Self	—
HM04	Strength	Normal	Physical	80	100	15	Normal	○
HM06	Rock Smash	Fighting	Physical	40	100	15	Normal	○

● **HEIGHT:** 4'11"
● **WEIGHT:** 133.2 lbs.
● **ITEMS:** None

● SIZE COMPARISON

● **MALE/FEMALE HAVE SAME FORM**

☉ ABILITIES
● Suction Cups

☉ STATS
HP	●●●
ATTACK	●●●●
DEFENSE	●●●●
SP. ATTACK	●●●●
SP. DEFENSE	●●●●●
SPEED	●●

☉ EGG GROUPS
Water 3

☉ PERFORMANCE
SPEED ★
POWER ★★★★
SKILL ★★☆

STAMINA ★★★★★
JUMP ★★

● **MAIN WAYS TO OBTAIN**

| **Pokémon HeartGold** | — |

Pokémon SoulSilver — Level up Lileep to Lv. 40

Pokémon Diamond — Level up Lileep to Lv. 40

Pokémon Pearl — Level up Lileep to Lv. 40

Pokémon Platinum — Level up Lileep to Lv. 40

Pokémon HeartGold
It lives in warm seas. Its heavy body weighs it down so it won't get washed away in rough weather.

Pokémon SoulSilver
It lives in warm seas. Its heavy body weighs it down so it won't get washed away in rough weather.

☉ EVOLUTION

Lileep → Lv. 40 → Cradily

No. 347 | Old Shrimp Pokémon
Anorith

Rock Bug

- **HEIGHT:** 2'04"
- **WEIGHT:** 27.6 lbs.
- **ITEMS:** None

● SIZE COMPARISON

● MALE/FEMALE HAVE SAME FORM

⊛ ABILITIES
- Battle Armor

⊛ STATS
- HP ●●
- ATTACK ●●●●
- DEFENSE ●●●
- SP. ATTACK ●●
- SP. DEFENSE ●●
- SPEED ●●●

⊛ EGG GROUPS
Water 3

⊛ PERFORMANCE
SPEED ★★★★☆	STAMINA ★★☆
POWER ★★☆	JUMP ★★
SKILL ★★★★☆	

● MAIN WAYS TO OBTAIN

Pokémon HeartGold	Have the Claw Fossil restored at the Pewter Museum of Science
Pokémon SoulSilver	—
Pokémon Diamond	After obtaining the National Pokédex, find the Claw Fossil in the Underground and have it restored at the Oreburgh Mining Museum
Pokémon Pearl	After obtaining the National Pokédex, find the Claw Fossil in the Underground and have it restored at the Oreburgh Mining Museum
Pokémon Platinum	After obtaining the National Pokédex, find the Claw Fossil in the Underground and have it restored at the Oreburgh Mining Museum

Pokémon HeartGold	**Pokémon SoulSilver**
An ancestral Pokémon that lived in the ocean. Over time, its eight feet transformed into wings.	An ancestral Pokémon that lived in the ocean. Over time, its eight feet transformed into wings.

⊛ EVOLUTION

Anorith — Lv. 40 → Armaldo

● LEVEL-UP MOVES
Lv.	Name	Type	Kind	Pow.	Acc.	PP	Range	DA
1	Scratch	Normal	Physical	40	100	35	Normal	○
1	Harden	Normal	Status	—	—	30	Self	—
7	Mud Sport	Ground	Status	—	—	15	All	—
13	Water Gun	Water	Special	40	100	25	Normal	—
19	Metal Claw	Steel	Physical	50	95	35	Normal	○
25	Protect	Normal	Status	—	—	10	Self	—
31	AncientPower	Rock	Special	60	100	5	Normal	—
37	Fury Cutter	Bug	Physical	10	95	20	Normal	○
43	Slash	Normal	Physical	70	100	20	Normal	○
49	Rock Blast	Rock	Physical	25	80	10	Normal	—
55	Crush Claw	Normal	Physical	75	95	10	Normal	○
61	X-Scissor	Bug	Physical	80	100	15	Normal	○

● MOVE MANIAC
Name	Type	Kind	Pow.	Acc.	PP	Range	DA
Headbutt	Normal	Physical	70	100	15	Normal	○

● BP MOVES
Name	Type	Kind	Pow.	Acc.	PP	Range	DA
Fury Cutter	Bug	Physical	10	95	20	Normal	○
Knock Off	Dark	Physical	20	100	20	Normal	○
Snore	Normal	Special	40	100	15	Normal	—
String Shot	Bug	Status	—	95	40	2 Foes	—
Mud-Slap	Ground	Special	20	100	10	Normal	—
AncientPower	Rock	Special	60	100	5	Normal	—
Earth Power	Ground	Special	90	100	10	Normal	—
Iron Defense	Steel	Status	—	—	15	Self	—

● TM & HM MOVES
No.	Name	Type	Kind	Pow.	Acc.	PP	Range	DA
TM03	Water Pulse	Water	Special	60	100	20	Normal	—
TM06	Toxic	Poison	Status	—	85	10	Normal	—
TM10	Hidden Power	Normal	Special	—	100	15	Normal	—
TM11	Sunny Day	Fire	Status	—	—	5	All	—
TM17	Protect	Normal	Status	—	—	10	Self	—
TM21	Frustration	Normal	Physical	—	100	20	Normal	○
TM27	Return	Normal	Physical	—	100	20	Normal	○
TM28	Dig	Ground	Physical	80	100	10	Normal	○
TM31	Brick Break	Fighting	Physical	75	100	15	Normal	○
TM32	Double Team	Normal	Status	—	—	15	Self	—
TM37	Sandstorm	Rock	Status	—	—	10	All	—
TM39	Rock Tomb	Rock	Physical	50	80	10	Normal	○
TM40	Aerial Ace	Flying	Physical	60	—	20	Normal	○
TM42	Facade	Normal	Physical	70	100	20	Normal	○
TM43	Secret Power	Normal	Physical	70	100	20	Normal	○
TM44	Rest	Psychic	Status	—	—	10	Self	—
TM45	Attract	Normal	Status	—	100	15	Normal	—
TM54	False Swipe	Normal	Physical	40	100	40	Normal	○
TM58	Endure	Normal	Status	—	—	10	Self	—
TM69	Rock Polish	Rock	Status	—	—	20	Self	—
TM75	Swords Dance	Normal	Status	—	—	30	Self	—
TM76	Stealth Rock	Rock	Status	—	—	20	2 Foes	—
TM78	Captivate	Normal	Status	—	100	20	2 Foes	—
TM80	Rock Slide	Rock	Physical	75	90	10	2 Foes	—
TM81	X-Scissor	Bug	Physical	80	100	15	Normal	○
TM82	Sleep Talk	Normal	Status	—	—	10	Depends	—
TM83	Natural Gift	Normal	Physical	—	100	15	Normal	○
TM87	Swagger	Normal	Status	—	90	15	Normal	—
TM90	Substitute	Normal	Status	—	—	10	Self	—
HM01	Cut	Normal	Physical	50	95	30	Normal	○
HM06	Rock Smash	Fighting	Physical	40	100	15	Normal	○

● EGG MOVES
Name	Type	Kind	Pow.	Acc.	PP	Range	DA
Rapid Spin	Normal	Physical	20	100	40	Normal	○
Knock Off	Dark	Physical	20	100	20	Normal	○
Swords Dance	Normal	Status	—	—	30	Self	—
Rock Slide	Rock	Physical	75	90	10	2 Foes	—
Screech	Normal	Status	—	85	40	Normal	—
Sand-Attack	Ground	Status	—	100	15	Normal	—
Cross Poison	Poison	Physical	70	100	20	Normal	○
Curse	???	Status	—	—	10	Normal/Self	—

● LEVEL-UP MOVES

Lv.	Name	Type	Kind	Pow.	Acc.	PP	Range	DA
1	Scratch	Normal	Physical	40	100	35	Normal	○
1	Harden	Normal	Status	—	—	30	Self	—
1	Mud Sport	Ground	Status	—	—	15	All	—
1	Water Gun	Water	Special	40	100	25	Normal	—
7	Mud Sport	Ground	Status	—	—	15	All	—
13	Water Gun	Water	Special	40	100	25	Normal	—
19	Metal Claw	Steel	Physical	50	95	35	Normal	○
25	Protect	Normal	Status	—	—	10	Self	—
31	AncientPower	Rock	Special	60	100	5	Normal	—
37	Fury Cutter	Bug	Physical	10	95	20	Normal	○
46	Slash	Normal	Physical	70	100	20	Normal	○
55	Rock Blast	Rock	Physical	25	80	10	Normal	—
67	Crush Claw	Normal	Physical	75	95	10	Normal	○
73	X-Scissor	Bug	Physical	80	100	15	Normal	○

● MOVE MANIAC

Name	Type	Kind	Pow.	Acc.	PP	Range	DA
Headbutt	Normal	Physical	70	100	15	Normal	○

● BP MOVES

Name	Type	Kind	Pow.	Acc.	PP	Range	DA
Fury Cutter	Bug	Physical	10	95	20	Normal	○
Knock Off	Dark	Physical	20	100	20	Normal	○
Snore	Normal	Special	40	100	15	Normal	—
String Shot	Bug	Status	—	95	40	2 Foes	—
Block	Normal	Status	—	—	5	Normal	—
Mud-Slap	Ground	Special	20	100	10	Normal	—
Superpower	Fighting	Physical	120	100	5	Normal	○
Aqua Tail	Water	Physical	90	90	10	Normal	○
AncientPower	Rock	Special	60	100	5	Normal	—
Earth Power	Ground	Special	90	100	10	Normal	—
Iron Defense	Steel	Status	—	—	15	Self	—
Low Kick	Fighting	Physical	—	100	20	Normal	○

● TM & HM MOVES

No.	Name	Type	Kind	Pow.	Acc.	PP	Range	DA
TM03	Water Pulse	Water	Special	60	100	20	Normal	—
TM06	Toxic	Poison	Status	—	85	10	Normal	—
TM10	Hidden Power	Normal	Special	—	100	15	Normal	—
TM11	Sunny Day	Fire	Status	—	—	5	All	—
TM15	Hyper Beam	Normal	Special	150	90	5	Normal	—
TM17	Protect	Normal	Status	—	—	10	Self	—
TM21	Frustration	Normal	Physical	—	100	20	Normal	○
TM23	Iron Tail	Steel	Physical	100	75	15	Normal	○
TM26	Earthquake	Ground	Physical	100	100	10	2 Foes/1 Ally	—
TM27	Return	Normal	Physical	—	100	20	Normal	○
TM28	Dig	Ground	Physical	80	100	10	Normal	○
TM31	Brick Break	Fighting	Physical	75	100	15	Normal	○
TM32	Double Team	Normal	Status	—	—	15	Self	—
TM37	Sandstorm	Rock	Status	—	—	10	All	—
TM39	Rock Tomb	Rock	Physical	50	80	10	Normal	—
TM40	Aerial Ace	Flying	Physical	60	—	20	Normal	○
TM42	Facade	Normal	Physical	70	100	20	Normal	○
TM43	Secret Power	Normal	Physical	70	100	20	Normal	—
TM44	Rest	Psychic	Status	—	—	10	Self	—
TM45	Attract	Normal	Status	—	100	15	Normal	—
TM54	False Swipe	Normal	Physical	40	100	40	Normal	○
TM58	Endure	Normal	Status	—	—	10	Self	—
TM68	Giga Impact	Normal	Physical	150	90	5	Normal	○
TM69	Rock Polish	Rock	Status	—	—	20	Self	—
TM71	Stone Edge	Rock	Physical	100	80	5	Normal	—
TM75	Swords Dance	Normal	Status	—	—	30	Self	—
TM76	Stealth Rock	Rock	Status	—	—	20	2 Foes	—
TM78	Captivate	Normal	Status	—	100	20	2 Foes	—
TM80	Rock Slide	Rock	Physical	75	90	10	2 Foes	—
TM81	X-Scissor	Bug	Physical	80	100	15	Normal	○
TM82	Sleep Talk	Normal	Status	—	—	10	Depends	—
TM83	Natural Gift	Normal	Physical	—	100	15	Normal	—
TM87	Swagger	Normal	Status	—	90	15	Normal	—
TM90	Substitute	Normal	Status	—	—	10	Self	—
TM91	Flash Cannon	Steel	Special	80	100	10	Normal	—
HM01	Cut	Normal	Physical	50	95	30	Normal	○
HM04	Strength	Normal	Physical	80	100	15	Normal	○
HM06	Rock Smash	Fighting	Physical	40	100	15	Normal	○

◎ No. 348 | Plate Pokémon
Armaldo

`Rock` `Bug`

- **HEIGHT:** 4'11"
- **WEIGHT:** 150.4 lbs.
- **ITEMS:** None

● SIZE COMPARISON

● MALE/FEMALE HAVE SAME FORM

◈ ABILITIES
● Battle Armor

◈ STATS
HP	●●●
ATTACK	●●●●●
DEFENSE	●●●●
SP. ATTACK	●●●●
SP. DEFENSE	●●●
SPEED	●●

◈ EGG GROUPS
Water 3

◈ PERFORMANCE
SPEED ★★
POWER ★★★★☆
SKILL ★★★☆

STAMINA ★★★★☆
JUMP ★★

● MAIN WAYS TO OBTAIN

Pokémon HeartGold — Level up Anorith to Lv. 40

Pokémon SoulSilver — —

Pokémon Diamond — Level up Anorith to Lv. 40

Pokémon Pearl — Level up Anorith to Lv. 40

Pokémon Platinum — Level up Anorith to Lv. 40

Pokémon HeartGold
Its enormous, retractable claws can cut through most anything. Its entire body is clad in sturdy plates.

Pokémon SoulSilver
Its enormous, retractable claws can cut through most anything. Its entire body is clad in sturdy plates.

◈ EVOLUTION

Anorith →(Lv. 40)→ Armaldo

No. 349 | Fish Pokémon
Feebas

`Water`

- **HEIGHT:** 2'00"
- **WEIGHT:** 16.3 lbs.
- **ITEMS:** None

● SIZE COMPARISON

● MALE/FEMALE HAVE SAME FORM

⊛ ABILITIES
● Swift Swim

⊛ STATS
HP ●
ATTACK ●
DEFENSE ●
SP. ATTACK ●
SP. DEFENSE ●●
SPEED ●●●●

⊛ EGG GROUPS
Water 1

Dragon

⊛ PERFORMANCE
SPEED ★★☆☆☆   STAMINA ★
POWER ★☆   JUMP ★★
SKILL ★

● MAIN WAYS TO OBTAIN

Pokémon HeartGold	Quiet Cave Pokéwalker Route
Pokémon SoulSilver	Quiet Cave Pokéwalker Route
Pokémon Diamond	Mt. Coronet B1F (Old Rod / location changes daily)
Pokémon Pearl	Mt. Coronet B1F (Old Rod / location changes daily)
Pokémon Platinum	Mt. Coronet B1F (Old Rod / location changes daily)

Pokémon HeartGold
It is the shabbiest Pokémon of all. It forms in schools and lives at the bottom of rivers.

Pokémon SoulSilver
It is the shabbiest Pokémon of all. It forms in schools and lives at the bottom of rivers.

⊛ EVOLUTION

Max out Feebas's beauty and level it up

Feebas → Milotic

● LEVEL-UP MOVES

Lv.	Name	Type	Kind	Pow.	Acc.	PP	Range	DA
1	Splash	Normal	Status	—	—	40	Self	—
15	Tackle	Normal	Physical	35	95	35	Normal	○
30	Flail	Normal	Physical	—	100	15	Normal	○

● MOVE MANIAC

Name	Type	Kind	Pow.	Acc.	PP	Range	DA

● BP MOVES

Name	Type	Kind	Pow.	Acc.	PP	Range	DA
Dive	Water	Physical	80	100	10	Normal	○
Icy Wind	Ice	Special	55	95	15	2 Foes	—
Snore	Normal	Special	40	100	15	Normal	—
Swift	Normal	Special	60	—	20	2 Foes	—

● TM & HM MOVES

No.	Name	Type	Kind	Pow.	Acc.	PP	Range	DA
TM03	Water Pulse	Water	Special	60	100	20	Normal	—
TM06	Toxic	Poison	Status	—	85	10	Normal	—
TM07	Hail	Ice	Status	—	—	10	All	—
TM10	Hidden Power	Normal	Special	—	100	15	Normal	—
TM13	Ice Beam	Ice	Special	95	100	10	Normal	—
TM14	Blizzard	Ice	Special	120	70	5	2 Foes	—
TM17	Protect	Normal	Status	—	—	10	Self	—
TM18	Rain Dance	Water	Status	—	—	5	All	—
TM21	Frustration	Normal	Physical	—	100	20	Normal	—
TM27	Return	Normal	Physical	—	100	20	Normal	—
TM32	Double Team	Normal	Status	—	—	15	Self	—
TM42	Facade	Normal	Physical	70	100	20	Normal	○
TM43	Secret Power	Normal	Physical	70	100	20	Normal	○
TM44	Rest	Psychic	Status	—	—	10	Self	—
TM45	Attract	Normal	Status	—	100	15	Normal	○
TM58	Endure	Normal	Status	—	—	10	Self	—
TM78	Captivate	Normal	Status	—	100	20	2 Foes	—
TM82	Sleep Talk	Normal	Status	—	—	10	Self	—
TM83	Natural Gift	Normal	Physical	—	100	15	Normal	—
TM87	Swagger	Normal	Status	—	90	15	Normal	—
TM90	Substitute	Normal	Status	—	—	10	Self	—
HM03	Surf	Water	Special	95	100	15	2 Foes/1 Ally	—
HM05	Whirlpool	Water	Special	15	70	15	Normal	—
HM07	Waterfall	Water	Physical	80	100	15	Normal	○

● EGG MOVES

Name	Type	Kind	Pow.	Acc.	PP	Range	DA
Mirror Coat	Psychic	Special	—	100	20	Normal	—
DragonBreath	Dragon	Special	60	100	20	Normal	—
Mud Sport	Ground	Status	—	—	15	All	—
Hypnosis	Psychic	Status	—	60	20	Normal	—
Light Screen	Psychic	Status	—	—	30	2 Allies	—
Confuse Ray	Ghost	Status	—	100	10	Normal	—
Mist	Ice	Status	—	—	30	2 Allies	—
Haze	Ice	Status	—	—	30	All	—
Tickle	Normal	Status	—	100	20	Normal	—

● LEVEL-UP MOVES

Lv.	Name	Type	Kind	Pow.	Acc.	PP	Range	DA
1	Water Gun	Water	Special	40	100	25	Normal	—
1	Wrap	Normal	Physical	15	85	20	Normal	○
5	Water Sport	Water	Status	—	—	15	All	—
9	Refresh	Normal	Status	—	—	20	Self	—
13	Water Pulse	Water	Special	60	100	20	Normal	—
17	Twister	Dragon	Special	40	100	20	2 Foes	—
21	Recover	Normal	Status	—	—	10	Self	—
25	Captivate	Normal	Status	—	100	20	2 Foes	—
29	Aqua Tail	Water	Physical	90	90	10	Normal	○
33	Rain Dance	Water	Status	—	—	5	All	—
37	Hydro Pump	Water	Special	120	80	5	Normal	—
41	Attract	Normal	Status	—	100	15	Normal	—
45	Safeguard	Normal	Status	—	—	25	2 Allies	—
49	Aqua Ring	Water	Status	—	—	20	Self	—

● MOVE MANIAC

Name	Type	Kind	Pow.	Acc.	PP	Range	DA

● BP MOVES

Name	Type	Kind	Pow.	Acc.	PP	Range	DA
Dive	Water	Physical	80	100	10	Normal	○
Icy Wind	Ice	Special	55	95	15	2 Foes	—
Snore	Normal	Special	40	100	15	Normal	—
Swift	Normal	Special	60	—	20	2 Foes	—
Magic Coat	Psychic	Status	—	—	15	Self	—
Mud-Slap	Ground	Special	20	100	10	Normal	—
Iron Head	Steel	Physical	80	100	15	Normal	○
Aqua Tail	Water	Physical	90	90	10	Normal	○
Twister	Dragon	Special	40	100	20	2 Foes	—

● TM & HM MOVES

No.	Name	Type	Kind	Pow.	Acc.	PP	Range	DA
TM03	Water Pulse	Water	Special	60	100	20	Normal	—
TM06	Toxic	Poison	Status	—	85	10	Normal	—
TM07	Hail	Ice	Status	—	—	10	All	—
TM10	Hidden Power	Normal	Special	—	100	15	Normal	—
TM13	Ice Beam	Ice	Special	95	100	10	Normal	—
TM14	Blizzard	Ice	Special	120	70	5	2 Foes	—
TM15	Hyper Beam	Normal	Special	150	90	5	Normal	—
TM17	Protect	Normal	Status	—	—	10	Self	—
TM18	Rain Dance	Water	Status	—	—	5	All	—
TM20	Safeguard	Normal	Status	—	—	25	2 Allies	—
TM21	Frustration	Normal	Physical	—	100	20	Normal	○
TM23	Iron Tail	Steel	Physical	100	75	15	Normal	○
TM27	Return	Normal	Physical	—	100	20	Normal	○
TM32	Double Team	Normal	Status	—	—	15	Self	—
TM42	Facade	Normal	Physical	70	100	20	Normal	—
TM43	Secret Power	Normal	Physical	70	100	20	Normal	—
TM44	Rest	Psychic	Status	—	—	10	Self	—
TM45	Attract	Normal	Status	—	100	15	Normal	—
TM58	Endure	Normal	Status	—	—	10	Self	—
TM59	Dragon Pulse	Dragon	Special	90	100	10	Normal	—
TM68	Giga Impact	Normal	Physical	150	90	5	Normal	○
TM72	Avalanche	Ice	Physical	60	100	10	Normal	○
TM77	Psych Up	Normal	Status	—	—	10	Normal	—
TM78	Captivate	Normal	Status	—	100	20	2 Foes	—
TM82	Sleep Talk	Normal	Status	—	—	10	Depends	—
TM83	Natural Gift	Normal	Physical	—	100	15	Normal	—
TM87	Swagger	Normal	Status	—	90	15	Normal	—
TM90	Substitute	Normal	Status	—	—	10	Self	—
HM03	Surf	Water	Special	95	100	15	2 Foes/1 Ally	—
HM05	Whirlpool	Water	Special	15	70	15	Normal	—
HM07	Waterfall	Water	Physical	80	100	15	Normal	○

- ● HEIGHT: 20'04"
- ● WEIGHT: 357.1 lbs.
- ● ITEMS: None

● SIZE COMPARISON

● MALE FORM
Shorter tail fins

● FEMALE FORM
Longer tail fins

☉ ABILITIES
● Marvel Scale

☉ STATS
HP ●●●●
ATTACK ●●●
DEFENSE ●●●
SP. ATTACK ●●●●
SP. DEFENSE ●●●●●
SPEED ●●●●

☉ EGG GROUPS
Water 1

Dragon

☉ PERFORMANCE
SPEED ★★★★	STAMINA ★★★★☆
POWER ★★☆	JUMP ★★★
SKILL ★★★★★	

● MAIN WAYS TO OBTAIN

Pokémon HeartGold	Level up Feebas with high beauty
Pokémon SoulSilver	Level up Feebas with high beauty
Pokémon Diamond	Level up Feebas with high beauty
Pokémon Pearl	Level up Feebas with high beauty
Pokémon Platinum	Level up Feebas with high beauty

Pokémon HeartGold

It's said that a glimpse of a MILOTIC and its beauty will calm any hostile emotions you're feeling.

Pokémon SoulSilver

It's said that a glimpse of a MILOTIC and its beauty will calm any hostile emotions you're feeling.

☉ EVOLUTION

Max out Feebas's beauty and level it up

Feebas → Milotic

No. 351 | Weather Pokémon
Castform

Normal

- **HEIGHT:** 1'00"
- **WEIGHT:** 1.8 lbs.
- **ITEMS:** None

● SIZE COMPARISON

● NORMAL   ● SUNNY FORM   ● RAINY FORM   ● SNOWY FORM

⊙ ABILITIES
● Forecast

⊙ STATS
HP ●●●
ATTACK ●●●
DEFENSE ●●●
SP. ATTACK ●●●
SP. DEFENSE ●●●
SPEED ●●●

⊙ EGG GROUPS
Fairy
Amorphous

⊙ PERFORMANCE
SPEED ★★★★   STAMINA ★★☆☆
POWER ★★☆☆   JUMP ★★★★
SKILL ★★☆☆

● MAIN WAYS TO OBTAIN

| Pokémon HeartGold | Treehouse Pokéwalker Route |

| Pokémon SoulSilver | Treehouse Pokéwalker Route |

| Pokémon Diamond | Trophy Garden at the Pokémon Mansion on Route 212 (after obtaining the National Pokédex, talk to Mr. Backlot) |

| Pokémon Pearl | Trophy Garden at the Pokémon Mansion on Route 212 (after obtaining the National Pokédex, talk to Mr. Backlot) |

| Pokémon Platinum | Trophy Garden at the Pokémon Mansion on Route 212 (after obtaining the National Pokédex, talk to Mr. Backlot) |

| Pokémon HeartGold | Pokémon SoulSilver |
| This Pokémon can change its cells, taking different forms based on the temperature and humidity. | This Pokémon can change its cells, taking different forms based on the temperature and humidity. |

⊙ EVOLUTION
Does not evolve

● LEVEL-UP MOVES

Lv.	Name	Type	Kind	Pow.	Acc.	PP	Range	DA
1	Tackle	Normal	Physical	35	95	35	Normal	○
10	Water Gun	Water	Special	40	100	25	Normal	—
10	Ember	Fire	Special	40	100	25	Normal	—
10	Powder Snow	Ice	Special	40	100	25	2 Foes	—
20	Rain Dance	Water	Status	—	—	5	All	—
20	Sunny Day	Fire	Status	—	—	5	All	—
20	Hail	Ice	Status	—	—	10	All	—
30	Weather Ball	Normal	Special	50	100	10	Normal	—

● MOVE MANIAC

Name	Type	Kind	Pow.	Acc.	PP	Range	DA
							—
							—

● BP MOVES

Name	Type	Kind	Pow.	Acc.	PP	Range	DA
Icy Wind	Ice	Special	55	95	15	2 Foes	—
Ominous Wind	Ghost	Special	60	100	5	Normal	—
Snore	Normal	Special	40	100	15	Normal	—
Last Resort	Normal	Physical	130	100	5	Normal	○
Swift	Normal	Special	60	—	20	2 Foes	—
Tailwind	Flying	Status	—	—	30	2 Allies	—

● TM & HM MOVES

No.	Name	Type	Kind	Pow.	Acc.	PP	Range	DA
TM03	Water Pulse	Water	Special	60	100	20	Normal	—
TM06	Toxic	Poison	Status	—	85	10	Normal	—
TM07	Hail	Ice	Status	—	—	10	All	—
TM10	Hidden Power	Normal	Special	—	100	15	Normal	—
TM11	Sunny Day	Fire	Status	—	—	5	All	—
TM13	Ice Beam	Ice	Special	95	100	10	Normal	—
TM14	Blizzard	Ice	Special	120	70	5	2 Foes	—
TM17	Protect	Normal	Status	—	—	10	Self	—
TM18	Rain Dance	Water	Status	—	—	5	All	—
TM21	Frustration	Normal	Physical	—	100	20	Normal	○
TM22	SolarBeam	Grass	Special	120	100	10	Normal	—
TM24	Thunderbolt	Electric	Special	95	100	15	Normal	—
TM25	Thunder	Electric	Special	120	70	10	Normal	—
TM27	Return	Normal	Physical	—	100	20	Normal	○
TM30	Shadow Ball	Ghost	Special	80	100	15	Normal	—
TM32	Double Team	Normal	Status	—	—	15	Self	—
TM34	Shock Wave	Electric	Special	60	—	20	Normal	—
TM35	Flamethrower	Fire	Special	95	100	15	Normal	—
TM37	Sandstorm	Rock	Status	—	—	10	All	—
TM38	Fire Blast	Fire	Special	120	85	5	Normal	—
TM42	Facade	Normal	Physical	70	100	20	Normal	○
TM43	Secret Power	Normal	Physical	70	100	20	Normal	—
TM44	Rest	Psychic	Status	—	—	10	Self	—
TM45	Attract	Normal	Status	—	100	15	Normal	—
TM46	Thief	Dark	Physical	40	100	10	Normal	○
TM53	Energy Ball	Grass	Special	80	100	10	Normal	—
TM58	Endure	Normal	Status	—	—	10	Self	—
TM70	Flash	Normal	Status	—	100	20	Normal	—
TM72	Avalanche	Ice	Physical	60	100	10	Normal	○
TM73	Thunder Wave	Electric	Status	—	100	20	Normal	—
TM77	Psych Up	Normal	Status	—	—	10	Normal	—
TM78	Captivate	Normal	Status	—	100	20	2 Foes	—
TM82	Sleep Talk	Normal	Status	—	—	10	Depends	—
TM83	Natural Gift	Normal	Physical	—	100	15	Normal	—
TM87	Swagger	Normal	Status	—	90	15	Normal	—
TM90	Substitute	Normal	Status	—	—	10	Self	—

● EGG MOVES

Name	Type	Kind	Pow.	Acc.	PP	Range	DA
Future Sight	Psychic	Special	80	90	15	Normal	—
Psych Up	Normal	Status	—	—	10	Normal	—
Lucky Chant	Normal	Status	—	—	30	2 Allies	—
Disable	Normal	Status	—	80	20	Normal	—
Amnesia	Psychic	Status	—	—	20	Self	—
Ominous Wind	Ghost	Special	60	100	5	Normal	—

● LEVEL-UP MOVES

Lv.	Name	Type	Kind	Pow.	Acc.	PP	Range	DA
1	Thief	Dark	Physical	40	100	10	Normal	○
1	Tail Whip	Normal	Status	—	100	30	2 Foes	—
1	Astonish	Ghost	Physical	30	100	15	Normal	○
1	Lick	Ghost	Physical	20	100	30	Normal	○
1	Scratch	Normal	Physical	40	100	35	Normal	○
4	Bind	Normal	Physical	15	75	20	Normal	—
7	Faint Attack	Dark	Physical	60	—	20	Normal	○
10	Fury Swipes	Normal	Physical	18	80	15	Normal	○
14	Feint	Normal	Physical	50	100	10	Normal	—
18	Psybeam	Psychic	Special	65	100	20	Normal	—
22	Shadow Sneak	Ghost	Physical	40	100	30	Normal	○
27	Slash	Normal	Physical	70	100	20	Normal	○
32	Screech	Normal	Status	—	85	40	Normal	—
37	Substitute	Normal	Status	—	—	10	Self	—
43	Sucker Punch	Dark	Physical	80	100	5	Normal	○
49	Shadow Claw	Ghost	Physical	70	100	15	Normal	○
55	AncientPower	Rock	Special	60	100	5	Normal	—

● MOVE MANIAC

Name	Type	Kind	Pow.	Acc.	PP	Range	DA
Headbutt	Normal	Physical	70	100	15	Normal	○

● BP MOVES

Name	Type	Kind	Pow.	Acc.	PP	Range	DA
Fury Cutter	Bug	Physical	10	95	20	Normal	○
Icy Wind	Ice	Special	55	95	15	2 Foes	—
ThunderPunch	Electric	Physical	75	100	15	Normal	○
Fire Punch	Fire	Physical	75	100	15	Normal	○
Ice Punch	Ice	Physical	75	100	15	Normal	○
Trick	Psychic	Status	—	100	10	Normal	—
Knock Off	Dark	Physical	20	100	20	Normal	○
Sucker Punch	Dark	Physical	80	100	5	Normal	○
Snore	Normal	Special	40	100	15	Normal	—
Last Resort	Normal	Physical	130	100	5	Normal	○
Swift	Normal	Special	60	—	20	2 Foes	—
Magic Coat	Psychic	Status	—	—	15	Self	—
Role Play	Psychic	Status	—	—	10	Normal	—
Mud-Slap	Ground	Special	20	100	10	Normal	—
Rollout	Rock	Physical	30	90	20	Normal	○
Aqua Tail	Water	Physical	90	90	10	Normal	○
AncientPower	Rock	Special	60	100	5	Normal	—
Low Kick	Fighting	Physical	—	100	20	Normal	○

● TM & HM MOVES

No.	Name	Type	Kind	Pow.	Acc.	PP	Range	DA
TM01	Focus Punch	Fighting	Physical	150	100	20	Normal	○
TM03	Water Pulse	Water	Special	60	100	20	Normal	—
TM06	Toxic	Poison	Status	—	85	10	Normal	—
TM10	Hidden Power	Normal	Special	—	100	15	Normal	—
TM11	Sunny Day	Fire	Status	—	—	5	All	—
TM13	Ice Beam	Ice	Special	95	100	10	Normal	—
TM14	Blizzard	Ice	Special	120	70	5	2 Foes	—
TM17	Protect	Normal	Status	—	—	10	Self	—
TM18	Rain Dance	Water	Status	—	—	5	All	—
TM21	Frustration	Normal	Physical	—	100	20	Normal	○
TM22	SolarBeam	Grass	Special	120	100	10	Normal	—
TM23	Iron Tail	Steel	Physical	100	75	15	Normal	○
TM24	Thunderbolt	Electric	Special	95	100	15	Normal	—
TM25	Thunder	Electric	Special	120	70	10	Normal	—
TM27	Return	Normal	Physical	—	100	20	Normal	○
TM28	Dig	Ground	Physical	80	100	10	Normal	○
TM30	Shadow Ball	Ghost	Special	80	100	15	Normal	—
TM31	Brick Break	Fighting	Physical	75	100	15	Normal	○
TM32	Double Team	Normal	Status	—	—	15	Self	—
TM34	Shock Wave	Electric	Special	60	—	20	Normal	—
TM35	Flamethrower	Fire	Special	95	100	15	Normal	—
TM38	Fire Blast	Fire	Special	120	85	5	Normal	—
TM39	Rock Tomb	Rock	Physical	50	80	10	Normal	○
TM40	Aerial Ace	Flying	Physical	60	—	20	Normal	○
TM42	Facade	Normal	Physical	70	100	20	Normal	○
TM43	Secret Power	Normal	Physical	70	100	20	Normal	○
TM44	Rest	Psychic	Status	—	—	10	Self	—
TM45	Attract	Normal	Status	—	100	15	Normal	—
TM46	Thief	Dark	Physical	40	100	10	Normal	○
TM48	Skill Swap	Psychic	Status	—	—	10	Normal	—
TM49	Snatch	Dark	Status	—	—	10	Depends	—
TM56	Fling	Dark	Physical	—	100	10	Normal	○
TM57	Charge Beam	Electric	Special	50	90	10	Normal	—
TM58	Endure	Normal	Status	—	—	10	Self	—
TM60	Drain Punch	Fighting	Physical	60	100	5	Normal	○
TM65	Shadow Claw	Ghost	Physical	70	100	15	Normal	○
TM67	Recycle	Normal	Status	—	—	10	Self	—
TM70	Flash	Normal	Status	—	100	20	Normal	—
TM73	Thunder Wave	Electric	Status	—	100	20	Normal	—
TM76	Stealth Rock	Rock	Status	—	—	20	2 Foes	—
TM77	Psych Up	Normal	Status	—	—	10	Normal	—
TM78	Captivate	Normal	Status	—	100	20	2 Foes	—
TM80	Rock Slide	Rock	Physical	75	90	10	2 Foes	○
TM82	Sleep Talk	Normal	Status	—	—	10	Depends	—
TM83	Natural Gift	Normal	Physical	—	100	15	Normal	○
TM86	Grass Knot	Grass	Special	—	100	20	Normal	—
TM87	Swagger	Normal	Status	—	90	15	Normal	—
TM90	Substitute	Normal	Status	—	—	10	Self	—
TM92	Trick Room	Psychic	Status	—	—	5	All	—
HM01	Cut	Normal	Physical	50	95	30	Normal	○
HM04	Strength	Normal	Physical	80	100	15	Normal	○
HM06	Rock Smash	Fighting	Physical	40	100	15	Normal	○

● EGG MOVES

Name	Type	Kind	Pow.	Acc.	PP	Range	DA
Disable	Normal	Status	—	80	20	Normal	—
Magic Coat	Psychic	Status	—	—	15	Self	—
Trick	Psychic	Status	—	100	10	Normal	—
Fake Out	Normal	Physical	40	100	10	Normal	○
Nasty Plot	Dark	Status	—	—	20	Self	—
Dizzy Punch	Normal	Physical	70	100	10	Normal	○
Recover	Normal	Status	—	—	10	Self	—

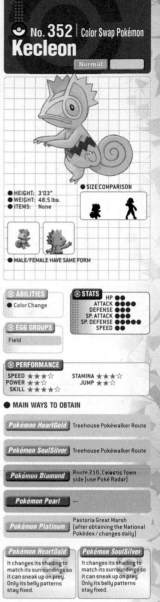

● No. 352 | Color Swap Pokémon

Kecleon

Normal

● HEIGHT: 3'03"
● WEIGHT: 48.5 lbs.
● ITEMS: None

● SIZE COMPARISON

● MALE/FEMALE HAVE SAME FORM

◎ ABILITIES
● Color Change

◎ STATS
- HP ●●
- ATTACK ●●●●
- DEFENSE ●●●
- SP. ATTACK ●●●
- SP. DEFENSE ●●●●●
- SPEED ●●

◎ EGG GROUPS
Field

◎ PERFORMANCE
SPEED ★★★☆   STAMINA ★★★☆
POWER ★★☆   JUMP ★★☆
SKILL ★★★★☆

● MAIN WAYS TO OBTAIN

Pokémon HeartGold	Treehouse Pokéwalker Route
Pokémon SoulSilver	Treehouse Pokéwalker Route
Pokémon Diamond	Route 210, Celestic Town side (use Poké Radar)
Pokémon Pearl	—
Pokémon Platinum	Pastoria Great Marsh (after obtaining the National Pokédex / changes daily)

Pokémon HeartGold
It changes its shading to match its surroundings so it can sneak up on prey. Only its belly patterns stay fixed.

Pokémon SoulSilver
It changes its shading to match its surroundings so it can sneak up on prey. Only its belly patterns stay fixed.

◎ EVOLUTION
Does not evolve

No. 353 | Puppet Pokémon
Shuppet

Ghost

- **HEIGHT:** 2'00"
- **WEIGHT:** 5.1 lbs.
- **ITEMS:** Spell Tag

● SIZE COMPARISON

● MALE/FEMALE HAVE SAME FORM

⊕ ABILITIES
- Insomnia
- Frisk

⊕ STATS
HP	●●
ATTACK	●●●
DEFENSE	●●
SP. ATTACK	●●●
SP. DEFENSE	●
SPEED	●●

⊕ EGG GROUPS
Amorphous

⊕ PERFORMANCE
SPEED ★★★★☆	STAMINA ★☆☆
POWER ★☆	JUMP ★★★★
SKILL ★★☆	

● MAIN WAYS TO OBTAIN

Pokémon HeartGold — Safari Zone (Forest Area: if Forest objects are placed, may appear in tall grass)

Pokémon SoulSilver — Safari Zone (Forest Area: if Forest objects are placed, may appear in tall grass)

Pokémon Diamond — Find its Egg at the Pokémon Day Care and hatch it

Pokémon Pearl — Find its Egg at the Pokémon Day Care and hatch it

Pokémon Platinum — Find its Egg at the Pokémon Day Care and hatch it

Pokémon HeartGold — It uses its horn to feed on envy and malice, or so it's said. It's very active at night.

Pokémon SoulSilver — It uses its horn to feed on envy and malice, or so it's said. It's very active at night.

⊕ EVOLUTION

Lv. 37

Shuppet → Banette

● LEVEL-UP MOVES

Lv.	Name	Type	Kind	Pow.	Acc.	PP	Range	DA
1	Knock Off	Dark	Physical	20	100	20	Normal	○
5	Screech	Normal	Status	—	85	40	Normal	—
8	Night Shade	Ghost	Special	—	100	15	Normal	—
13	Curse	???	Status	—	—	10	Normal/Self	—
16	Spite	Ghost	Status	—	100	10	Normal	—
20	Shadow Sneak	Ghost	Physical	40	100	30	Normal	○
23	Will-O-Wisp	Fire	Status	—	75	15	Normal	—
28	Faint Attack	Dark	Physical	60	—	20	Normal	○
31	Shadow Ball	Ghost	Special	80	100	15	Normal	—
35	Sucker Punch	Dark	Physical	80	100	5	Normal	○
38	Embargo	Dark	Status	—	100	15	Normal	—
43	Snatch	Dark	Status	—	—	10	Depends	—
46	Grudge	Ghost	Status	—	—	5	Self	—
50	Trick	Psychic	Status	—	100	10	Normal	—

● MOVE MANIAC

Name	Type	Kind	Pow.	Acc.	PP	Range	DA
Headbutt	Normal	Physical	70	100	15	Normal	○

● BP MOVES

Name	Type	Kind	Pow.	Acc.	PP	Range	DA
Icy Wind	Ice	Special	55	95	15	2 Foes	—
Ominous Wind	Ghost	Special	60	100	5	Normal	—
Trick	Psychic	Status	—	100	10	Normal	—
Knock Off	Dark	Physical	20	100	20	Normal	○
Sucker Punch	Dark	Physical	80	100	5	Normal	○
Spite	Ghost	Status	—	100	10	Normal	—
Magic Coat	Psychic	Status	—	—	15	Self	—
Role Play	Psychic	Status	—	—	10	Normal	—
Pain Split	Normal	Status	—	—	20	Normal	—

● TM & HM MOVES

No.	Name	Type	Kind	Pow.	Acc.	PP	Range	DA
TM04	Calm Mind	Psychic	Status	—	—	20	Self	—
TM06	Toxic	Poison	Status	—	85	10	Normal	—
TM10	Hidden Power	Normal	Special	—	100	15	Normal	—
TM11	Sunny Day	Fire	Status	—	—	5	All	—
TM12	Taunt	Dark	Status	—	100	20	Normal	—
TM17	Protect	Normal	Status	—	—	10	Self	—
TM18	Rain Dance	Water	Status	—	—	5	All	—
TM21	Frustration	Normal	Physical	—	100	20	Normal	○
TM24	Thunderbolt	Electric	Special	95	100	15	Normal	—
TM25	Thunder	Electric	Special	120	70	10	Normal	—
TM27	Return	Normal	Physical	—	100	20	Normal	○
TM29	Psychic	Psychic	Special	90	100	10	Normal	—
TM30	Shadow Ball	Ghost	Special	80	100	15	Normal	—
TM32	Double Team	Normal	Status	—	—	15	Self	—
TM34	Shock Wave	Electric	Special	60	—	20	Normal	—
TM41	Torment	Dark	Status	—	100	15	Normal	—
TM42	Facade	Normal	Physical	70	100	20	Normal	○
TM43	Secret Power	Normal	Physical	70	100	20	Normal	○
TM44	Rest	Psychic	Status	—	—	10	Self	—
TM45	Attract	Normal	Status	—	100	15	Normal	—
TM46	Thief	Dark	Physical	40	100	10	Normal	○
TM48	Skill Swap	Psychic	Status	—	—	10	Normal	—
TM49	Snatch	Dark	Status	—	—	10	Depends	—
TM57	Charge Beam	Electric	Special	50	90	10	Normal	—
TM58	Endure	Normal	Status	—	—	10	Self	—
TM61	Will-O-Wisp	Fire	Status	—	75	15	Normal	—
TM63	Embargo	Dark	Status	—	100	15	Normal	—
TM66	Payback	Dark	Physical	50	100	10	Normal	○
TM70	Flash	Normal	Status	—	100	20	Normal	—
TM73	Thunder Wave	Electric	Status	—	100	20	Normal	—
TM77	Psych Up	Normal	Status	—	—	10	Normal	—
TM78	Captivate	Normal	Status	—	100	20	2 Foes	—
TM79	Dark Pulse	Dark	Special	80	100	15	Normal	—
TM82	Sleep Talk	Normal	Status	—	—	10	Self	—
TM83	Natural Gift	Normal	Physical	—	100	15	Normal	—
TM85	Dream Eater	Psychic	Special	100	100	15	Normal	—
TM87	Swagger	Normal	Status	—	90	15	Normal	—
TM90	Substitute	Normal	Status	—	—	10	Self	—
TM92	Trick Room	Psychic	Status	—	—	5	All	—

● EGG MOVES

Name	Type	Kind	Pow.	Acc.	PP	Range	DA
Disable	Normal	Status	—	80	20	Normal	—
Destiny Bond	Ghost	Status	—	—	5	Self	—
Foresight	Normal	Status	—	—	40	Normal	—
Astonish	Ghost	Physical	30	100	15	Normal	○
Imprison	Psychic	Status	—	—	10	Self	—
Pursuit	Dark	Physical	40	100	20	Normal	○
Shadow Sneak	Ghost	Physical	40	100	30	Normal	○
Payback	Dark	Physical	50	100	10	Normal	○
Confuse Ray	Ghost	Status	—	100	10	Normal	—

● LEVEL-UP MOVES

Lv.	Name	Type	Kind	Pow.	Acc.	PP	Range	DA
1	Knock Off	Dark	Physical	20	100	20	Normal	○
1	Screech	Normal	Status	—	85	40	Normal	—
1	Night Shade	Ghost	Special	—	100	15	Normal	—
1	Curse	???	Status	—	—	10	Normal/Self	—
5	Night Shade	Ghost	Special	—	100	15	Normal	—
8	Screech	Normal	Status	—	85	40	Normal	—
13	Curse	???	Status	—	—	10	Normal/Self	—
16	Spite	Ghost	Status	—	100	10	Normal	—
20	Shadow Sneak	Ghost	Physical	40	100	30	Normal	○
23	Will-O-Wisp	Fire	Status	—	75	15	Normal	—
28	Faint Attack	Dark	Physical	60	—	20	Normal	○
31	Shadow Ball	Ghost	Special	80	100	15	Normal	—
35	Sucker Punch	Dark	Physical	80	100	5	Normal	○
42	Embargo	Dark	Status	—	100	15	Normal	—
51	Snatch	Dark	Status	—	—	10	Depends	—
58	Grudge	Ghost	Status	—	—	5	Self	—
66	Trick	Psychic	Status	—	100	10	Normal	—

● MOVE MANIAC

Name	Type	Kind	Pow.	Acc.	PP	Range	DA
Headbutt	Normal	Physical	70	100	15	Normal	○

● BP MOVES

Name	Type	Kind	Pow.	Acc.	PP	Range	DA
Icy Wind	Ice	Special	55	95	15	2 Foes	—
Ominous Wind	Ghost	Special	60	100	5	Normal	—
Trick	Psychic	Status	—	100	10	Normal	—
Knock Off	Dark	Physical	20	100	20	Normal	○
Sucker Punch	Dark	Physical	80	100	5	Normal	○
Spite	Ghost	Status	—	100	10	Normal	—
Magic Coat	Psychic	Status	—	—	15	Self	—
Role Play	Psychic	Status	—	—	10	Normal	—
Mud-Slap	Ground	Special	20	100	10	Normal	—
Pain Split	Normal	Status	—	—	20	Normal	—

● TM & HM MOVES

No.	Name	Type	Kind	Pow.	Acc.	PP	Range	DA
TM04	Calm Mind	Psychic	Status	—	—	20	Self	—
TM06	Toxic	Poison	Status	—	85	10	Normal	—
TM10	Hidden Power	Normal	Special	—	100	15	Normal	—
TM11	Sunny Day	Fire	Status	—	—	5	All	—
TM12	Taunt	Dark	Status	—	100	20	Normal	—
TM15	Hyper Beam	Normal	Special	150	90	5	Normal	—
TM17	Protect	Normal	Status	—	—	10	Self	—
TM18	Rain Dance	Water	Status	—	—	5	All	—
TM21	Frustration	Normal	Physical	—	100	20	Normal	○
TM24	Thunderbolt	Electric	Special	95	100	15	Normal	—
TM25	Thunder	Electric	Special	120	70	10	Normal	—
TM27	Return	Normal	Physical	—	100	20	Normal	○
TM29	Psychic	Psychic	Special	90	100	10	Normal	—
TM30	Shadow Ball	Ghost	Special	80	100	15	Normal	—
TM32	Double Team	Normal	Status	—	—	15	Self	—
TM34	Shock Wave	Electric	Special	60	—	20	Normal	—
TM41	Torment	Dark	Status	—	100	15	Normal	—
TM42	Facade	Normal	Physical	70	100	20	Normal	○
TM43	Secret Power	Normal	Physical	70	100	20	Normal	○
TM44	Rest	Psychic	Status	—	—	10	Self	—
TM45	Attract	Normal	Status	—	100	15	Normal	—
TM46	Thief	Dark	Physical	40	100	10	Normal	○
TM48	Skill Swap	Psychic	Status	—	—	10	Normal	—
TM49	Snatch	Dark	Status	—	—	10	Depends	—
TM56	Fling	Dark	Physical	—	100	10	Normal	○
TM57	Charge Beam	Electric	Special	50	90	10	Normal	—
TM58	Endure	Normal	Status	—	—	10	Self	—
TM61	Will-O-Wisp	Fire	Status	—	75	15	Normal	—
TM63	Embargo	Dark	Status	—	100	15	Normal	—
TM65	Shadow Claw	Ghost	Physical	70	100	15	Normal	○
TM66	Payback	Dark	Physical	50	100	10	Normal	○
TM68	Giga Impact	Normal	Physical	150	90	5	Normal	○
TM70	Flash	Normal	Status	—	100	20	Normal	—
TM73	Thunder Wave	Electric	Status	—	100	20	Normal	—
TM77	Psych Up	Normal	Status	—	—	10	Normal	—
TM79	Dark Pulse	Dark	Special	80	100	15	Normal	—
TM82	Sleep Talk	Normal	Status	—	—	10	Self	—
TM83	Natural Gift	Normal	Physical	—	100	15	Normal	○
TM85	Dream Eater	Psychic	Special	100	100	15	Normal	—
TM87	Swagger	Normal	Status	—	90	15	Normal	—
TM90	Substitute	Normal	Status	—	—	10	Self	—
TM92	Trick Room	Psychic	Status	—	—	5	All	—

● No. 354 | Marionette Pokémon
Banette

Ghost

- ● HEIGHT: 3'07"
- ● WEIGHT: 27.6 lbs.
- ● ITEMS: Spell Tag

● SIZE COMPARISON

● MALE/FEMALE HAVE SAME FORM

◈ ABILITIES
- ● Insomnia
- ● Frisk

◈ EGG GROUPS
Amorphous

◈ STATS
HP	●●
ATTACK	●●●●●
DEFENSE	●●●
SP. ATTACK	●●●●
SP. DEFENSE	●●
SPEED	●●●

◈ PERFORMANCE
SPEED ★★★ STAMINA ★★★
POWER ★★★★ JUMP ★★★
SKILL ★★★★

● MAIN WAYS TO OBTAIN

Pokémon HeartGold — Safari Zone (Marshland Area: if Rock objects are placed, may appear in tall grass)

Pokémon SoulSilver — Safari Zone (Marshland Area: if Rock objects are placed, may appear in tall grass)

Pokémon Diamond — Route 225 (night only)

Pokémon Pearl — Route 225 (night only)

Pokémon Platinum — Route 225 (night only)

Pokémon HeartGold — This Pokémon developed from an abandoned doll that amassed a grudge. It is seen in dark alleys.

Pokémon SoulSilver — This Pokémon developed from an abandoned doll that amassed a grudge. It is seen in dark alleys.

◈ EVOLUTION

Shuppet — Lv. 37 → Banette

No. 355 | Requiem Pokémon
Duskull

Ghost

● HEIGHT: 2'07"
● WEIGHT: 33.1 lbs.
● ITEMS: Kasib Berry

● SIZE COMPARISON

● MALE/FEMALE HAVE SAME FORM

⚙ ABILITIES
● Levitate

⚙ STATS
HP ●
ATTACK ●●
DEFENSE ●●●●
SP. ATTACK ●
SP. DEFENSE ●●●●
SPEED ●

⚙ EGG GROUPS
Amorphous

⚙ PERFORMANCE
SPEED ★★★★
POWER ★★☆
SKILL ★☆☆
STAMINA ★★☆
JUMP ★★★★

● MAIN WAYS TO OBTAIN

Pokémon HeartGold	Safari Zone (Swamp Area: if Rock objects are placed, may appear in tall grass)
Pokémon SoulSilver	Safari Zone (Swamp Area: if Rock objects are placed, may appear in tall grass)
Pokémon Diamond	Route 224 (occasionally appears when you use Poké Radar)
Pokémon Pearl	Route 224 (occasionally appears when you use Poké Radar)
Pokémon Platinum	Route 209 (night only)

| Pokémon HeartGold | Pokémon SoulSilver |
| If it finds bad children who won't listen to their parents, it will spirit them away--or so it's said. | If it finds bad children who won't listen to their parents, it will spirit them away--or so it's said. |

⚙ EVOLUTION

Lv. 37

Have it hold Reaper Cloth and trade it

Duskull → Dusclops → Dusknoir

● LEVEL-UP MOVES

Lv.	Name	Type	Kind	Pow.	Acc.	PP	Range	DA
1	Leer	Normal	Status	—	100	30	2 Foes	—
1	Night Shade	Ghost	Special	—	100	15	Normal	—
6	Disable	Normal	Status	—	80	20	Normal	—
9	Foresight	Normal	Status	—	—	40	Normal	—
14	Astonish	Ghost	Physical	30	100	15	Normal	○
17	Confuse Ray	Ghost	Status	—	100	10	Normal	—
22	Shadow Sneak	Ghost	Physical	40	100	30	Normal	○
25	Pursuit	Dark	Physical	40	100	20	Normal	○
30	Curse	???	Status	—	—	10	Normal/Self	—
33	Will-O-Wisp	Fire	Status	—	75	15	Normal	—
38	Mean Look	Normal	Status	—	—	5	Normal	—
41	Payback	Dark	Physical	50	100	10	Normal	○
46	Future Sight	Psychic	Special	80	90	15	Normal	—

● MOVE MANIAC

Name	Type	Kind	Pow.	Acc.	PP	Range	DA
Headbutt	Normal	Physical	70	100	15	Normal	○

● BP MOVES

Name	Type	Kind	Pow.	Acc.	PP	Range	DA
Icy Wind	Ice	Special	55	95	15	2 Foes	—
Ominous Wind	Ghost	Special	60	100	5	Normal	—
Trick	Psychic	Status	—	100	10	Normal	—
Sucker Punch	Dark	Physical	80	100	5	Normal	○
Snore	Normal	Special	40	100	15	Normal	—
Spite	Ghost	Status	—	100	10	Normal	—
Gravity	Psychic	Status	—	—	5	All	—
Pain Split	Normal	Status	—	—	20	Normal	—

● TM & HM MOVES

No.	Name	Type	Kind	Pow.	Acc.	PP	Range	DA
TM04	Calm Mind	Psychic	Status	—	—	20	Self	—
TM06	Toxic	Poison	Status	—	85	10	Normal	—
TM10	Hidden Power	Normal	Special	—	100	15	Normal	—
TM11	Sunny Day	Fire	Status	—	—	5	All	—
TM12	Taunt	Dark	Status	—	100	20	Normal	—
TM13	Ice Beam	Ice	Special	95	100	10	Normal	—
TM14	Blizzard	Ice	Special	120	70	5	2 Foes	—
TM17	Protect	Normal	Status	—	—	10	Self	—
TM18	Rain Dance	Water	Status	—	—	5	All	—
TM21	Frustration	Normal	Physical	—	100	20	Normal	○
TM27	Return	Normal	Physical	—	100	20	Normal	○
TM29	Psychic	Psychic	Special	90	100	10	Normal	—
TM30	Shadow Ball	Ghost	Special	80	100	15	Normal	—
TM32	Double Team	Normal	Status	—	—	15	Self	—
TM41	Torment	Dark	Status	—	100	15	Normal	—
TM42	Facade	Normal	Physical	70	100	20	Normal	○
TM43	Secret Power	Normal	Physical	70	100	20	Normal	—
TM44	Rest	Psychic	Status	—	—	10	Self	—
TM45	Attract	Normal	Status	—	100	15	Normal	—
TM46	Thief	Dark	Physical	40	100	10	Normal	○
TM48	Skill Swap	Psychic	Status	—	—	10	Normal	—
TM49	Snatch	Dark	Status	—	—	10	Depends	—
TM56	Fling	Dark	Physical	—	100	10	Normal	—
TM57	Charge Beam	Electric	Special	50	90	10	Normal	—
TM58	Endure	Normal	Status	—	—	10	Self	—
TM61	Will-O-Wisp	Fire	Status	—	75	15	Normal	—
TM63	Embargo	Dark	Status	—	100	15	Normal	—
TM66	Payback	Dark	Physical	50	100	10	Normal	○
TM70	Flash	Normal	Status	—	100	20	Normal	—
TM77	Psych Up	Normal	Status	—	—	10	Self	—
TM78	Captivate	Normal	Status	—	100	20	2 Foes	—
TM79	Dark Pulse	Dark	Special	80	100	15	Normal	—
TM82	Sleep Talk	Normal	Status	—	—	10	Depends	—
TM83	Natural Gift	Normal	Physical	—	100	15	Normal	—
TM85	Dream Eater	Psychic	Special	100	100	15	Normal	—
TM87	Swagger	Normal	Status	—	90	15	Normal	—
TM90	Substitute	Normal	Status	—	—	10	Self	—
TM92	Trick Room	Psychic	Status	—	—	5	All	—

● EGG MOVES

Name	Type	Kind	Pow.	Acc.	PP	Range	DA
Imprison	Psychic	Status	—	—	10	Self	—
Destiny Bond	Ghost	Status	—	—	5	Self	—
Pain Split	Normal	Status	—	—	20	Normal	—
Grudge	Ghost	Status	—	—	5	Self	—
Memento	Dark	Status	—	100	10	Normal	—
Faint Attack	Dark	Physical	60	—	20	Normal	○
Ominous Wind	Ghost	Special	60	100	5	Normal	—

● LEVEL-UP MOVES

Lv.	Name	Type	Kind	Pow.	Acc.	PP	Range	DA
1	Fire Punch	Fire	Physical	75	100	15	Normal	○
1	Ice Punch	Ice	Physical	75	100	15	Normal	○
1	ThunderPunch	Electric	Physical	75	100	15	Normal	○
1	Gravity	Psychic	Status	—	—	5	All	—
1	Bind	Normal	Physical	15	75	20	Normal	—
1	Leer	Normal	Status	—	100	30	2 Foes	—
1	Night Shade	Ghost	Special	—	100	15	Normal	—
1	Disable	Normal	Status	—	80	20	Normal	—
6	Disable	Normal	Status	—	80	20	Normal	—
9	Foresight	Normal	Status	—	—	40	Normal	—
14	Astonish	Ghost	Physical	30	100	15	Normal	○
17	Confuse Ray	Ghost	Status	—	100	10	Normal	—
22	Shadow Sneak	Ghost	Physical	40	100	30	Normal	○
25	Pursuit	Dark	Physical	40	100	20	Normal	○
30	Curse	???	Status	—	—	10	Normal/Self	—
33	Will-O-Wisp	Fire	Status	—	75	15	Normal	—
37	Shadow Punch	Ghost	Physical	60	—	20	Normal	○
43	Mean Look	Normal	Status	—	—	5	Normal	—
51	Payback	Dark	Physical	50	100	10	Normal	○
61	Future Sight	Psychic	Special	80	90	15	Normal	—

● MOVE MANIAC

Name	Type	Kind	Pow.	Acc.	PP	Range	DA
Headbutt	Normal	Physical	70	100	15	Normal	○

● BP MOVES

Name	Type	Kind	Pow.	Acc.	PP	Range	DA
Icy Wind	Ice	Special	55	95	15	2 Foes	—
ThunderPunch	Electric	Physical	75	100	15	Normal	○
Fire Punch	Fire	Physical	75	100	15	Normal	○
Ice Punch	Ice	Physical	75	100	15	Normal	○
Ominous Wind	Ghost	Special	60	100	5	Normal	—
Trick	Psychic	Status	—	100	10	Normal	—
Sucker Punch	Dark	Physical	80	100	5	Normal	○
Snore	Normal	Special	40	100	15	Normal	—
Spite	Ghost	Status	—	100	10	Normal	—
Gravity	Psychic	Status	—	—	5	All	—
Mud-Slap	Ground	Special	20	100	10	Normal	—
Pain Split	Normal	Status	—	—	20	Normal	—

● TM & HM MOVES

No.	Name	Type	Kind	Pow.	Acc.	PP	Range	DA
TM01	Focus Punch	Fighting	Physical	150	100	20	Normal	○
TM04	Calm Mind	Psychic	Status	—	—	20	Self	—
TM06	Toxic	Poison	Status	—	85	10	Normal	—
TM10	Hidden Power	Normal	Special	—	100	15	Normal	—
TM11	Sunny Day	Fire	Status	—	—	5	All	—
TM12	Taunt	Dark	Status	—	100	20	Normal	—
TM13	Ice Beam	Ice	Special	95	100	10	Normal	—
TM14	Blizzard	Ice	Special	120	70	5	2 Foes	—
TM15	Hyper Beam	Normal	Special	150	90	5	Normal	—
TM17	Protect	Normal	Status	—	—	10	Self	—
TM18	Rain Dance	Water	Status	—	—	5	All	—
TM21	Frustration	Normal	Physical	—	100	20	Normal	○
TM26	Earthquake	Ground	Physical	100	100	10	2 Foes/1 Ally	—
TM27	Return	Normal	Physical	—	100	20	Normal	○
TM29	Psychic	Psychic	Special	90	100	10	Normal	—
TM30	Shadow Ball	Ghost	Special	80	100	15	Normal	—
TM31	Brick Break	Fighting	Physical	75	100	15	Normal	○
TM32	Double Team	Normal	Status	—	—	15	Self	—
TM39	Rock Tomb	Rock	Physical	50	80	10	Normal	○
TM41	Torment	Dark	Status	—	100	15	Normal	—
TM42	Facade	Normal	Physical	70	100	20	Normal	○
TM43	Secret Power	Normal	Physical	70	100	20	Normal	○
TM44	Rest	Psychic	Status	—	—	10	Self	—
TM45	Attract	Normal	Status	—	100	15	Normal	—
TM46	Thief	Dark	Physical	40	100	10	Normal	○
TM48	Skill Swap	Psychic	Status	—	—	10	Normal	—
TM49	Snatch	Dark	Status	—	—	10	Depends	—
TM56	Fling	Dark	Physical	—	100	10	Normal	○
TM57	Charge Beam	Electric	Special	50	90	10	Normal	—
TM58	Endure	Normal	Status	—	—	10	Self	—
TM61	Will-O-Wisp	Fire	Status	—	75	15	Normal	—
TM63	Embargo	Dark	Status	—	100	15	Normal	—
TM66	Payback	Dark	Physical	50	100	10	Normal	○
TM68	Giga Impact	Normal	Physical	150	90	5	Normal	○
TM70	Flash	Normal	Status	—	100	20	Normal	—
TM77	Psych Up	Normal	Status	—	—	10	Normal	—
TM78	Captivate	Normal	Status	—	100	20	2 Foes	—
TM79	Dark Pulse	Dark	Special	80	100	15	Normal	—
TM80	Rock Slide	Rock	Physical	75	90	10	2 Foes	—
TM82	Sleep Talk	Normal	Status	—	—	10	Depends	—
TM83	Natural Gift	Normal	Physical	—	100	15	Normal	○
TM85	Dream Eater	Psychic	Special	100	100	15	Normal	—
TM87	Swagger	Normal	Status	—	90	15	Normal	—
TM90	Substitute	Normal	Status	—	—	10	Self	—
TM92	Trick Room	Psychic	Status	—	—	5	All	—
HM04	Strength	Normal	Physical	80	100	15	Normal	○
HM06	Rock Smash	Fighting	Physical	40	100	15	Normal	○

◉ No. 356 | Beckon Pokémon
Dusclops

Ghost

● HEIGHT: 5'03"
● WEIGHT: 67.5 lbs.
● ITEMS: Kasib Berry

● SIZE COMPARISON

● MALE/FEMALE HAVE SAME FORM

⊘ ABILITIES
● Pressure

⊘ EGG GROUPS
Amorphous

⊘ STATS
HP ●
ATTACK ●●●
DEFENSE ●●●●
SP. ATTACK ●●●
SP. DEFENSE ●●●●
SPEED ●

⊘ PERFORMANCE
SPEED ★★☆ STAMINA ★★★★☆
POWER ★★★☆ JUMP ★★
SKILL ★★★★

● MAIN WAYS TO OBTAIN

Pokémon HeartGold — Safari Zone (Mountain Area: if Forest objects are placed, may appear in tall grass)

Pokémon SoulSilver — Safari Zone (Mountain Area: if Forest objects are placed, may appear in tall grass)

Pokémon Diamond — Route 224 (use Poké Radar)

Pokémon Pearl — Route 224 (use Poké Radar)

Pokémon Platinum — Sendoff Spring

Pokémon HeartGold — Anyone who dares peer into its body to see its spectral ball of fire will have their spirit stolen away.

Pokémon SoulSilver — Anyone who dares peer into its body to see its spectral ball of fire will have their spirit stolen away.

⊘ EVOLUTION

Lv. 37

Have it hold Reaper Cloth and trade it

Duskull → Dusclops → Dusknoir

 No. 357 | Fruit Pokémon
Tropius

Grass Flying

- **HEIGHT:** 6'07"
- **WEIGHT:** 220.5 lbs.
- **ITEMS:** None

● SIZE COMPARISON

● MALE/FEMALE HAVE SAME FORM

⊙ ABILITIES
- Chlorophyll
- Solar Power

⊙ EGG GROUPS
Monster

Grass

⊙ STATS
HP	●●●●
ATTACK	●●●
DEFENSE	●●●
SP. ATTACK	●●●
SP. DEFENSE	●●●
SPEED	●●

⊙ PERFORMANCE
SPEED ★★★☆	STAMINA ★★★☆
POWER ★★★☆☆	JUMP ★★★★★
SKILL ★★	

● MAIN WAYS TO OBTAIN

Pokémon HeartGold	Big Forest Pokéwalker Route
Pokémon SoulSilver	Big Forest Pokéwalker Route
Pokémon Diamond	—
Pokémon Pearl	—
Pokémon Platinum	Pastoria Great Marsh / morning and afternoon only)

Pokémon HeartGold	*Pokémon SoulSilver*
The bunch of fruit around its neck ripens twice a year and is delicious. It's a highly favored tropical snack.	The bunch of fruit around its neck ripens twice a year and is delicious. It's a highly favored tropical snack.

⊙ EVOLUTION
Does not evolve

● LEVEL-UP MOVES
Lv.	Name	Type	Kind	Pow.	Acc.	PP	Range	DA
1	Leer	Normal	Status	—	100	30	2 Foes	—
1	Gust	Flying	Special	40	100	35	Normal	—
7	Growth	Normal	Status	—	—	40	Self	—
11	Razor Leaf	Grass	Physical	55	95	25	2 Foes	—
17	Stomp	Normal	Physical	65	100	20	Normal	○
21	Sweet Scent	Normal	Status	—	100	20	2 Foes	—
27	Whirlwind	Normal	Status	—	100	20	Normal	—
31	Magical Leaf	Grass	Special	60	—	20	Normal	—
37	Body Slam	Normal	Physical	85	100	15	Normal	○
41	Synthesis	Grass	Status	—	—	5	Self	—
47	Air Slash	Flying	Special	75	95	20	Normal	—
51	SolarBeam	Grass	Special	120	100	10	Normal	—
57	Natural Gift	Normal	Physical	—	100	15	Normal	—
61	Leaf Storm	Grass	Special	140	90	5	Normal	—

● MOVE MANIAC
Name	Type	Kind	Pow.	Acc.	PP	Range	DA
Headbutt	Normal	Physical	70	100	15	Normal	○

● BP MOVES
Name	Type	Kind	Pow.	Acc.	PP	Range	DA
Fury Cutter	Bug	Physical	10	95	20	Normal	○
Ominous Wind	Ghost	Special	60	100	5	Normal	—
Air Cutter	Flying	Special	55	95	25	2 Foes	—
Snore	Normal	Special	40	100	15	Normal	—
Synthesis	Grass	Status	—	—	5	Self	—
Tailwind	Flying	Status	—	—	30	2 Allies	—
Worry Seed	Grass	Status	—	100	10	Normal	—
Mud-Slap	Ground	Special	20	100	10	Normal	—
Outrage	Dragon	Physical	120	100	15	1 Random	○
Twister	Dragon	Special	40	100	20	2 Foes	—

● TM & HM MOVES
No.	Name	Type	Kind	Pow.	Acc.	PP	Range	DA
TM05	Roar	Normal	Status	—	100	20	Normal	—
TM06	Toxic	Poison	Status	—	85	10	Normal	—
TM09	Bullet Seed	Grass	Physical	10	100	30	Normal	—
TM10	Hidden Power	Normal	Special	—	100	15	Normal	—
TM11	Sunny Day	Fire	Status	—	—	5	All	—
TM15	Hyper Beam	Normal	Special	150	90	5	Normal	—
TM17	Protect	Normal	Status	—	—	10	Self	—
TM19	Giga Drain	Grass	Special	60	100	10	Normal	—
TM20	Safeguard	Normal	Status	—	—	25	2 Allies	—
TM21	Frustration	Normal	Physical	—	100	20	Normal	○
TM22	SolarBeam	Grass	Special	120	100	10	Normal	—
TM26	Earthquake	Ground	Physical	100	100	10	2 Foes/1 Ally	—
TM27	Return	Normal	Physical	—	100	20	Normal	○
TM32	Double Team	Normal	Status	—	—	15	Self	—
TM40	Aerial Ace	Flying	Physical	60	—	20	Normal	○
TM42	Facade	Normal	Physical	70	100	20	Normal	○
TM43	Secret Power	Normal	Physical	70	100	20	Normal	—
TM44	Rest	Psychic	Status	—	—	10	Self	—
TM45	Attract	Normal	Status	—	100	15	Normal	—
TM47	Steel Wing	Steel	Physical	70	90	25	Normal	○
TM51	Roost	Flying	Status	—	—	10	Self	—
TM53	Energy Ball	Grass	Special	80	100	10	Normal	—
TM58	Endure	Normal	Status	—	—	10	Self	—
TM62	Silver Wind	Bug	Special	60	100	5	Normal	—
TM68	Giga Impact	Normal	Physical	150	90	5	Normal	○
TM70	Flash	Normal	Status	—	100	20	Normal	—
TM75	Swords Dance	Normal	Status	—	—	30	Self	—
TM78	Captivate	Normal	Status	—	100	20	2 Foes	—
TM82	Sleep Talk	Normal	Status	—	—	10	Depends	—
TM83	Natural Gift	Normal	Physical	—	100	15	Normal	—
TM86	Grass Knot	Grass	Special	—	100	20	Normal	—
TM87	Swagger	Normal	Status	—	90	15	Normal	—
TM90	Substitute	Normal	Status	—	—	10	Self	—
HM01	Cut	Normal	Physical	50	95	30	Normal	○
HM02	Fly	Flying	Physical	90	95	15	Normal	○
HM04	Strength	Normal	Physical	80	100	15	Normal	○
HM06	Rock Smash	Fighting	Physical	40	100	15	Normal	○

● EGG MOVES
Name	Type	Kind	Pow.	Acc.	PP	Range	DA
Headbutt	Normal	Physical	70	100	15	Normal	○
Slam	Normal	Physical	80	75	20	Normal	○
Razor Wind	Normal	Special	80	100	10	2 Foes	—
Leech Seed	Grass	Status	—	90	10	Normal	—
Nature Power	Normal	Status	—	—	20	Depends	—
Leaf Storm	Grass	Special	140	90	5	Normal	—
Synthesis	Grass	Status	—	—	5	Self	—
Curse	???	Status	—	—	10	Normal/Self	—
Leaf Blade	Grass	Physical	90	100	15	Normal	○
Dragon Dance	Dragon	Status	—	—	20	Self	—

LEVEL-UP MOVES

Lv.	Name	Type	Kind	Pow.	Acc.	PP	Range	DA
1	Wrap	Normal	Physical	15	85	20	Normal	○
6	Growl	Normal	Status	—	100	40	2 Foes	—
9	Astonish	Ghost	Physical	30	100	15	Normal	○
14	Confusion	Psychic	Special	50	100	25	Normal	—
17	Uproar	Normal	Special	50	100	10	1 Random	—
22	Take Down	Normal	Physical	90	85	20	Normal	○
25	Yawn	Normal	Status	—	—	10	Normal	—
30	Psywave	Psychic	Special	—	80	15	Normal	—
33	Double-Edge	Normal	Physical	120	100	15	Normal	○
38	Heal Bell	Normal	Status	—	—	5	All Allies	—
41	Safeguard	Normal	Status	—	—	25	2 Allies	—
46	Extrasensory	Psychic	Special	80	100	30	Normal	—
49	Healing Wish	Psychic	Status	—	—	10	Self	—

MOVE MANIAC

Name	Type	Kind	Pow.	Acc.	PP	Range	DA

BP MOVES

Name	Type	Kind	Pow.	Acc.	PP	Range	DA
Icy Wind	Ice	Special	55	95	15	2 Foes	—
Zen Headbutt	Psychic	Physical	80	90	15	Normal	○
Trick	Psychic	Status	—	100	10	Normal	—
Knock Off	Dark	Physical	20	100	20	Normal	○
Snore	Normal	Special	40	100	15	Normal	—
Helping Hand	Normal	Status	—	—	20	1 Ally	—
Last Resort	Normal	Physical	130	100	5	Normal	○
Uproar	Normal	Special	50	100	10	1 Random	—
Gravity	Psychic	Status	—	—	5	All	—
Magic Coat	Psychic	Status	—	—	15	Self	—
Heal Bell	Normal	Status	—	—	5	All Allies	—
Rollout	Rock	Physical	30	90	20	Normal	○
Signal Beam	Bug	Special	75	100	15	Normal	—

TM & HM MOVES

No.	Name	Type	Kind	Pow.	Acc.	PP	Range	DA
TM04	Calm Mind	Psychic	Status	—	—	20	Self	—
TM06	Toxic	Poison	Status	—	85	10	Normal	—
TM10	Hidden Power	Normal	Special	—	100	15	Normal	—
TM11	Sunny Day	Fire	Status	—	—	5	All	—
TM12	Taunt	Dark	Status	—	100	20	Normal	—
TM16	Light Screen	Psychic	Status	—	—	30	2 Allies	—
TM17	Protect	Normal	Status	—	—	10	Self	—
TM18	Rain Dance	Water	Status	—	—	5	All	—
TM20	Safeguard	Normal	Status	—	—	25	2 Allies	—
TM21	Frustration	Normal	Physical	—	100	20	Normal	○
TM27	Return	Normal	Physical	—	100	20	Normal	○
TM29	Psychic	Psychic	Special	90	100	10	Normal	—
TM30	Shadow Ball	Ghost	Special	80	100	15	Normal	—
TM32	Double Team	Normal	Status	—	—	15	Self	—
TM33	Reflect	Psychic	Status	—	—	20	2 Allies	—
TM34	Shock Wave	Electric	Special	60	—	20	Normal	—
TM41	Torment	Dark	Status	—	100	15	Normal	—
TM42	Facade	Normal	Physical	70	100	20	Normal	○
TM43	Secret Power	Normal	Physical	70	100	20	Normal	○
TM44	Rest	Psychic	Status	—	—	10	Self	—
TM45	Attract	Normal	Status	—	100	15	Normal	—
TM48	Skill Swap	Psychic	Status	—	—	10	Normal	—
TM49	Snatch	Dark	Status	—	—	10	Depends	—
TM53	Energy Ball	Grass	Special	80	100	10	Normal	—
TM57	Charge Beam	Electric	Special	50	90	10	Normal	—
TM58	Endure	Normal	Status	—	—	10	Self	—
TM67	Recycle	Normal	Status	—	—	10	Self	—
TM70	Flash	Normal	Status	—	100	20	Normal	—
TM73	Thunder Wave	Electric	Status	—	100	20	Normal	—
TM77	Psych Up	Normal	Status	—	—	10	Normal	—
TM78	Captivate	Normal	Status	—	100	20	2 Foes	—
TM82	Sleep Talk	Normal	Status	—	—	10	Depends	—
TM83	Natural Gift	Normal	Physical	—	100	15	Normal	—
TM85	Dream Eater	Psychic	Special	100	100	15	Normal	—
TM86	Grass Knot	Grass	Special	—	100	20	Normal	○
TM87	Swagger	Normal	Status	—	90	15	Normal	—
TM90	Substitute	Normal	Status	—	—	10	Self	—
TM92	Trick Room	Psychic	Status	—	—	5	All	—

EGG MOVES

Name	Type	Kind	Pow.	Acc.	PP	Range	DA
Disable	Normal	Status	—	80	20	Normal	—
Curse	???	Status	—	—	10	Normal/Self	—
Hypnosis	Psychic	Status	—	60	20	Normal	—
Dream Eater	Psychic	Special	100	100	15	Normal	—
Wish	Normal	Status	—	—	10	Self	—
Future Sight	Psychic	Special	80	90	15	Normal	—

No. 358 | Wild Chime Pokémon
Chimecho

Psychic

- **HEIGHT:** 2'00"
- **WEIGHT:** 2.2 lbs.
- **ITEMS:** Colbur Berry

● SIZE COMPARISON

● MALE/FEMALE HAVE SAME FORM

ABILITIES
● Levitate

STATS
HP ●●
ATTACK ●●
DEFENSE ●●●
SP. ATTACK ●●●●
SP. DEFENSE ●●●●
SPEED ●●●

EGG GROUPS
Amorphous

PERFORMANCE
SPEED ★★★☆☆ STAMINA ★★
POWER ★★ JUMP ★★★★☆
SKILL ★☆

MAIN WAYS TO OBTAIN

Pokémon HeartGold	Safari Zone (Swamp Area: if Forest objects are placed, may appear in tall grass)
Pokémon SoulSilver	Safari Zone (Swamp Area: if Forest objects are placed, may appear in tall grass)
Pokémon Diamond	Sendoff Spring
Pokémon Pearl	Sendoff Spring
Pokémon Platinum	Sendoff Spring

| *Pokémon HeartGold* | *Pokémon SoulSilver* |
| It uses the sucker on its head to hang from a tree or from eaves. It an produce seven different tones. | It uses the sucker on its head to hang from a tree or from eaves. It an produce seven different tones. |

EVOLUTION

Chingling → Level up with high friendship between 8:00 P.M. and 4:00 A.M. → Chimecho

No. 359 | Disaster Pokémon
Absol

Dark

● **LEVEL-UP MOVES**

Lv.	Name	Type	Kind	Pow.	Acc.	PP	Range	DA
1	Scratch	Normal	Physical	40	100	35	Normal	—
1	Feint	Normal	Physical	50	100	10	Normal	—
4	Leer	Normal	Status	—	100	30	2 Foes	—
9	Taunt	Dark	Status	—	100	20	Normal	—
12	Quick Attack	Normal	Physical	40	100	30	Normal	○
17	Razor Wind	Normal	Special	80	100	10	2 Foes	○
20	Pursuit	Dark	Physical	40	100	20	Normal	○
25	Swords Dance	Normal	Status	—	—	30	Self	—
28	Bite	Dark	Physical	60	100	25	Normal	○
33	Double Team	Normal	Status	—	—	15	Self	—
36	Slash	Normal	Physical	70	100	20	Normal	○
41	Future Sight	Psychic	Special	80	90	15	Normal	—
44	Sucker Punch	Dark	Physical	80	100	5	Normal	○
49	Detect	Fighting	Status	—	—	5	Self	—
52	Night Slash	Dark	Physical	70	100	15	Normal	○
57	Me First	Normal	Status	—	—	20	Depends	—
60	Psycho Cut	Psychic	Physical	70	100	20	Normal	○
65	Perish Song	Normal	Status	—	—	5	All	—

● **MOVE MANIAC**

Name	Type	Kind	Pow.	Acc.	PP	Range	DA
Headbutt	Normal	Physical	70	100	15	Normal	○

● **BP MOVES**

Name	Type	Kind	Pow.	Acc.	PP	Range	DA
Fury Cutter	Bug	Physical	10	95	20	Normal	○
Icy Wind	Ice	Special	55	95	15	2 Foes	—
Zen Headbutt	Psychic	Physical	80	90	15	Normal	○
Knock Off	Dark	Physical	20	100	20	Normal	○
Sucker Punch	Dark	Physical	80	100	5	Normal	○
Snore	Normal	Special	40	100	15	Normal	—
Spite	Ghost	Status	—	100	10	Normal	—
Swift	Normal	Special	60	—	20	2 Foes	—
Magic Coat	Psychic	Status	—	—	15	Self	—
Role Play	Psychic	Status	—	—	10	Normal	—
Mud-Slap	Ground	Special	20	100	10	Normal	—
Superpower	Fighting	Physical	120	100	5	Normal	○
Bounce	Flying	Physical	85	85	5	Normal	—

● **HEIGHT**: 3'11"
● **WEIGHT**: 103.6 lbs.
● **ITEMS**: None

● **SIZE COMPARISON**

● **MALE/FEMALE HAVE SAME FORM**

● **ABILITIES**
● Pressure
● Super Luck

● **STATS**
HP ●●
ATTACK ●●●●●
DEFENSE ●●●
SP. ATTACK ●●●●
SP. DEFENSE ●●●
SPEED ●●●

● **EGG GROUPS**
Field

● **PERFORMANCE**
SPEED ★★★☆☆   STAMINA ★★★☆
POWER ★★★☆☆   JUMP ★★★
SKILL ★★★

● **MAIN WAYS TO OBTAIN**

Pokémon HeartGold	Union Cave (Hoenn Sound)
Pokémon SoulSilver	Union Cave (Hoenn Sound)
Pokémon Diamond	Route 213 (mass outbreak)
Pokémon Pearl	Route 213 (mass outbreak)
Pokémon Platinum	Mt. Coronet Peak 1

Pokémon HeartGold	**Pokémon SoulSilver**
It has the ability to foretell natural disasters. Its life span is over a hundred years.	It has the ability to foretell natural disasters. Its life span is over a hundred years.

● **EVOLUTION**

Does not evolve

● **TM & HM MOVES**

No.	Name	Type	Kind	Pow.	Acc.	PP	Range	DA
TM03	Water Pulse	Water	Special	60	100	20	Normal	—
TM04	Calm Mind	Psychic	Status	—	—	20	Self	—
TM06	Toxic	Poison	Status	—	85	10	Normal	—
TM07	Hail	Ice	Status	—	—	10	All	—
TM10	Hidden Power	Normal	Special	—	100	15	Normal	—
TM11	Sunny Day	Fire	Status	—	—	5	All	—
TM12	Taunt	Dark	Status	—	100	20	Normal	—
TM13	Ice Beam	Ice	Special	95	100	10	Normal	—
TM14	Blizzard	Ice	Special	120	70	5	2 Foes	—
TM15	Hyper Beam	Normal	Special	150	90	5	Normal	—
TM17	Protect	Normal	Status	—	—	10	Self	—
TM18	Rain Dance	Water	Status	—	—	5	All	—
TM21	Frustration	Normal	Physical	—	100	20	Normal	○
TM23	Iron Tail	Steel	Physical	100	75	15	Normal	○
TM24	Thunderbolt	Electric	Special	95	100	15	Normal	—
TM25	Thunder	Electric	Special	120	70	10	Normal	—
TM27	Return	Normal	Physical	—	100	20	Normal	○
TM30	Shadow Ball	Ghost	Special	80	100	15	Normal	—
TM32	Double Team	Normal	Status	—	—	15	Self	—
TM34	Shock Wave	Electric	Special	60	—	20	Normal	—
TM35	Flamethrower	Fire	Special	95	100	15	Normal	—
TM37	Sandstorm	Rock	Status	—	—	10	All	—
TM38	Fire Blast	Fire	Special	120	85	5	Normal	—
TM39	Rock Tomb	Rock	Physical	50	80	10	Normal	○
TM40	Aerial Ace	Flying	Physical	60	—	20	Normal	○
TM41	Torment	Dark	Status	—	100	15	Normal	—
TM42	Facade	Normal	Physical	70	100	20	Normal	○
TM43	Secret Power	Normal	Physical	70	100	20	Normal	○
TM44	Rest	Psychic	Status	—	—	10	Self	—
TM45	Attract	Normal	Status	—	100	15	Normal	—
TM46	Thief	Dark	Physical	40	100	10	Normal	○
TM49	Snatch	Dark	Status	—	—	10	Depends	—
TM54	False Swipe	Normal	Physical	40	100	40	Normal	○
TM57	Charge Beam	Electric	Special	50	90	10	Normal	—
TM58	Endure	Normal	Status	—	—	10	Self	—
TM61	Will-O-Wisp	Fire	Status	—	75	15	Normal	—
TM65	Shadow Claw	Ghost	Physical	70	100	15	Normal	○
TM66	Payback	Dark	Physical	50	100	10	Normal	○
TM68	Giga Impact	Normal	Physical	150	90	5	Normal	○
TM70	Flash	Normal	Status	—	100	20	Normal	—
TM71	Stone Edge	Rock	Physical	100	80	5	Normal	○
TM73	Thunder Wave	Electric	Status	—	100	20	Normal	—
TM75	Swords Dance	Normal	Status	—	—	30	Self	—
TM77	Psych Up	Normal	Status	—	—	10	Normal	—
TM78	Captivate	Normal	Status	—	100	20	2 Foes	—
TM79	Dark Pulse	Dark	Special	80	100	15	Normal	—
TM80	Rock Slide	Rock	Physical	75	90	10	2 Foes	—
TM81	X-Scissor	Bug	Physical	80	100	15	Normal	○
TM82	Sleep Talk	Normal	Status	—	—	10	Depends	—
TM83	Natural Gift	Normal	Physical	—	100	15	Normal	—
TM85	Dream Eater	Psychic	Special	100	100	15	Normal	—
TM87	Swagger	Normal	Status	—	90	15	Normal	—
TM90	Substitute	Normal	Status	—	—	10	Self	—
HM01	Cut	Normal	Physical	50	95	30	Normal	○
HM04	Strength	Normal	Physical	80	100	15	Normal	○
HM06	Rock Smash	Fighting	Physical	40	100	15	Normal	○

● **EGG MOVES**

Name	Type	Kind	Pow.	Acc.	PP	Range	DA
Baton Pass	Normal	Status	—	—	40	Self	—
Faint Attack	Dark	Physical	60	—	20	Normal	○
Double-Edge	Normal	Physical	120	100	15	Normal	○
Magic Coat	Psychic	Status	—	—	15	Self	—
Curse	???	Status	—	—	10	Normal/Self	—
Substitute	Normal	Status	—	—	10	Self	—
Mean Look	Normal	Status	—	—	5	Normal	—
Zen Headbutt	Psychic	Physical	80	90	15	Normal	○
Punishment	Dark	Physical	—	100	5	Normal	○
Sucker Punch	Dark	Physical	80	100	5	Normal	○
Assurance	Dark	Physical	50	100	10	Normal	○
Me First	Normal	Status	—	—	20	Depends	—
Megahorn	Bug	Physical	120	85	10	Normal	○

LEVEL-UP MOVES

Lv.	Name	Type	Kind	Pow.	Acc.	PP	Range	DA
1	Splash	Normal	Status	—	—	40	Self	—
1	Charm	Normal	Status	—	100	20	Normal	—
1	Encore	Normal	Status	—	100	5	Normal	—
15	Counter	Fighting	Physical	—	100	20	Self	○
15	Mirror Coat	Psychic	Special	—	100	20	Self	—
15	Safeguard	Normal	Status	—	—	25	2 Allies	—
15	Destiny Bond	Ghost	Status	—	—	5	Self	—

MOVE MANIAC

Name	Type	Kind	Pow.	Acc.	PP	Range	DA

BP MOVES

Name	Type	Kind	Pow.	Acc.	PP	Range	DA

TM & HM MOVES

No.	Name	Type	Kind	Pow.	Acc.	PP	Range	DA

No. 360 | Bright Pokémon
Wynaut

Psychic

- **HEIGHT:** 2'00"
- **WEIGHT:** 30.9 lbs.
- **ITEMS:** None

● SIZE COMPARISON

● MALE/FEMALE HAVE SAME FORM

ABILITIES
● Shadow Tag

STATS
HP ●●●●
ATTACK ●●
DEFENSE ●●
SP. ATTACK ●
SP. DEFENSE ●●
SPEED ●

EGG GROUPS
No Egg has ever been discovered

PERFORMANCE
SPEED ★★★☆☆ STAMINA ★★★☆☆
POWER ★☆☆ JUMP ★★☆
SKILL ★☆☆☆

● MAIN WAYS TO OBTAIN

Pokémon HeartGold — Have Wobbuffet ♀ hold the Lax Incense and leave it at the Pokémon Day Care, then find its Egg and hatch it

Pokémon SoulSilver — Have Wobbuffet ♀ hold the Lax Incense and leave it at the Pokémon Day Care, then find its Egg and hatch it

Pokémon Diamond — Have Wobbuffet ♀ hold the Lax Incense and leave it at the Pokémon Day Care, then find its Egg and hatch it

Pokémon Pearl — Have Wobbuffet ♀ hold the Lax Incense and leave it at the Pokémon Day Care, then find its Egg and hatch it

Pokémon Platinum — Have Wobbuffet ♀ hold the Lax Incense and leave it at the Pokémon Day Care, then find its Egg and hatch it

Pokémon HeartGold — It tends to move in a pack. Individuals squash against one another to toughen their spirits.

Pokémon SoulSilver — It tends to move in a pack. Individuals squash against one another to toughen their spirits.

EVOLUTION

Wynaut → Lv. 15 → Wobbuffet

No. 361 | Snow Hat Pokémon
Snorunt

Ice

- **HEIGHT:** 2'04"
- **WEIGHT:** 37.0 lbs.
- **ITEMS:** None

● SIZE COMPARISON

● MALE/FEMALE HAVE SAME FORM

⊙ ABILITIES
- Inner Focus
- Ice Body

⊙ STATS
HP ●●
ATTACK ●●
DEFENSE ●●
SP. ATTACK ●●
SP. DEFENSE ●●
SPEED ●●

⊙ EGG GROUPS
Fairy

Mineral

⊙ PERFORMANCE
SPEED ★★★★☆   STAMINA ★★☆☆
POWER ★★☆☆   JUMP ★★☆☆
SKILL ★★★☆

● MAIN WAYS TO OBTAIN

| Pokémon HeartGold | Icy Mountain Rd. Pokéwalker Route |

| Pokémon SoulSilver | Icy Mountain Rd. Pokéwalker Route |

| Pokémon Diamond | Route 216 [use Poké Radar] |

| Pokémon Pearl | Route 216 [use Poké Radar] |

| Pokémon Platinum | Route 216 [night only] |

| Pokémon HeartGold | Pokémon SoulSilver |
| It's said that if they are seen at midnight, they'll cause heavy snow. They eat snow and ice to survive. | It's said that if they are seen at midnight, they'll cause heavy snow. They eat snow and ice to survive. |

⊙ EVOLUTION

Lv. 42

Glalie

Snorunt   Use Dawn Stone on ♀

Froslass

● LEVEL-UP MOVES

Lv.	Name	Type	Kind	Pow.	Acc.	PP	Range	DA
1	Powder Snow	Ice	Special	40	100	25	2 Foes	—
1	Leer	Normal	Status	—	100	30	2 Foes	—
4	Double Team	Normal	Status	—	—	15	Self	—
10	Bite	Dark	Physical	60	100	25	Normal	○
13	Icy Wind	Ice	Special	55	95	15	2 Foes	—
19	Headbutt	Normal	Physical	70	100	15	Normal	○
22	Protect	Normal	Status	—	—	10	Self	—
28	Ice Fang	Ice	Physical	65	95	15	Normal	○
31	Crunch	Dark	Physical	80	100	15	Normal	○
37	Ice Shard	Ice	Physical	40	100	30	Normal	—
40	Hail	Ice	Status	—	—	10	All	—
46	Blizzard	Ice	Special	120	70	5	2 Foes	—

● MOVE MANIAC

Name	Type	Kind	Pow.	Acc.	PP	Range	DA
Headbutt	Normal	Physical	70	100	15	Normal	○

● BP MOVES

Name	Type	Kind	Pow.	Acc.	PP	Range	DA
Icy Wind	Ice	Special	55	95	15	2 Foes	—
Snore	Normal	Special	40	100	15	Normal	—
Spite	Ghost	Status	—	100	10	Normal	—
Block	Normal	Status	—	—	5	Normal	—
Rollout	Rock	Physical	30	90	20	Normal	○

● TM & HM MOVES

No.	Name	Type	Kind	Pow.	Acc.	PP	Range	DA
TM03	Water Pulse	Water	Special	60	100	20	Normal	—
TM06	Toxic	Poison	Status	—	85	10	Normal	—
TM07	Hail	Ice	Status	—	—	10	All	—
TM10	Hidden Power	Normal	Special	—	100	15	Normal	—
TM13	Ice Beam	Ice	Special	95	100	10	Normal	—
TM14	Blizzard	Ice	Special	120	70	5	2 Foes	—
TM16	Light Screen	Psychic	Status	—	—	30	2 Allies	—
TM17	Protect	Normal	Status	—	—	10	Self	—
TM18	Rain Dance	Water	Status	—	—	5	All	—
TM20	Safeguard	Normal	Status	—	—	25	2 Allies	—
TM21	Frustration	Normal	Physical	—	100	20	Normal	○
TM27	Return	Normal	Physical	—	100	20	Normal	○
TM30	Shadow Ball	Ghost	Special	80	100	15	Normal	—
TM32	Double Team	Normal	Status	—	—	15	Self	—
TM42	Facade	Normal	Physical	70	100	20	Normal	○
TM43	Secret Power	Normal	Physical	70	100	20	Normal	—
TM44	Rest	Psychic	Status	—	—	10	Self	—
TM45	Attract	Normal	Status	—	100	15	Normal	—
TM58	Endure	Normal	Status	—	—	10	Self	—
TM70	Flash	Normal	Status	—	100	20	Normal	—
TM72	Avalanche	Ice	Physical	60	100	10	Normal	○
TM78	Captivate	Normal	Status	—	100	20	2 Foes	—
TM82	Sleep Talk	Normal	Status	—	—	10	Depends	—
TM83	Natural Gift	Normal	Physical	—	100	15	Normal	—
TM87	Swagger	Normal	Status	—	90	15	Normal	—
TM90	Substitute	Normal	Status	—	—	10	Self	—

● EGG MOVES

Name	Type	Kind	Pow.	Acc.	PP	Range	DA
Block	Normal	Status	—	—	5	Normal	—
Spikes	Ground	Status	—	—	20	2 Foes	—
Rollout	Rock	Physical	30	90	20	Normal	○
Disable	Normal	Status	—	80	20	Normal	—
Bide	Normal	Physical	—	—	10	Self	○
Weather Ball	Normal	Special	50	100	10	Normal	—

● LEVEL-UP MOVES

Lv.	Name	Type	Kind	Pow.	Acc.	PP	Range	DA
1	Powder Snow	Ice	Special	40	100	25	2 Foes	—
1	Leer	Normal	Status	—	100	30	2 Foes	—
1	Double Team	Normal	Status	—	—	15	Self	—
1	Bite	Dark	Physical	60	100	25	Normal	○
4	Double Team	Normal	Status	—	—	15	Self	—
10	Bite	Dark	Physical	60	100	25	Normal	○
13	Icy Wind	Ice	Special	55	95	15	2 Foes	—
19	Headbutt	Normal	Physical	70	100	15	Normal	○
22	Protect	Normal	Status	—	—	10	Self	—
28	Ice Fang	Ice	Physical	65	95	15	Normal	○
31	Crunch	Dark	Physical	80	100	15	Normal	○
37	Ice Beam	Ice	Special	95	100	10	Normal	—
40	Hail	Ice	Status	—	—	10	All	—
51	Blizzard	Ice	Special	120	70	5	2 Foes	—
59	Sheer Cold	Ice	Special	—	30	5	Normal	—

● MOVE MANIAC

Name	Type	Kind	Pow.	Acc.	PP	Range	DA
Headbutt	Normal	Physical	70	100	15	Normal	○

● BP MOVES

Name	Type	Kind	Pow.	Acc.	PP	Range	DA
Icy Wind	Ice	Special	55	95	15	2 Foes	—
Snore	Normal	Special	40	100	15	Normal	—
Spite	Ghost	Status	—	100	10	Normal	—
Block	Normal	Status	—	—	5	Normal	—
Rollout	Rock	Physical	30	90	20	Normal	○
Iron Head	Steel	Physical	80	100	15	Normal	○
Signal Beam	Bug	Special	75	100	15	Normal	—
Super Fang	Normal	Physical	—	90	10	Normal	○

● TM & HM MOVES

No.	Name	Type	Kind	Pow.	Acc.	PP	Range	DA
TM03	Water Pulse	Water	Special	60	100	20	Normal	—
TM06	Toxic	Poison	Status	—	85	10	Normal	—
TM07	Hail	Ice	Status	—	—	10	All	—
TM10	Hidden Power	Normal	Special	—	100	15	Normal	—
TM12	Taunt	Dark	Status	—	100	20	Normal	—
TM13	Ice Beam	Ice	Special	95	100	10	Normal	—
TM14	Blizzard	Ice	Special	120	70	5	2 Foes	—
TM15	Hyper Beam	Normal	Special	150	90	5	Normal	—
TM16	Light Screen	Psychic	Status	—	—	30	2 Allies	—
TM17	Protect	Normal	Status	—	—	10	Self	—
TM18	Rain Dance	Water	Status	—	—	5	All	—
TM20	Safeguard	Normal	Status	—	—	25	2 Allies	—
TM21	Frustration	Normal	Physical	—	100	20	Normal	○
TM26	Earthquake	Ground	Physical	100	100	10	2 Foes/1 Ally	—
TM27	Return	Normal	Physical	—	100	20	Normal	○
TM30	Shadow Ball	Ghost	Special	80	100	15	Normal	—
TM32	Double Team	Normal	Status	—	—	15	Self	—
TM41	Torment	Dark	Status	—	100	15	Normal	—
TM42	Facade	Normal	Physical	70	100	20	Normal	○
TM43	Secret Power	Normal	Physical	70	100	20	Normal	—
TM44	Rest	Psychic	Status	—	—	10	Self	—
TM45	Attract	Normal	Status	—	100	15	Normal	—
TM58	Endure	Normal	Status	—	—	10	Self	—
TM64	Explosion	Normal	Physical	250	100	5	2 Foes/1 Ally	—
TM66	Payback	Dark	Physical	50	100	10	Normal	○
TM68	Giga Impact	Normal	Physical	150	90	5	Normal	○
TM70	Flash	Normal	Status	—	100	20	Normal	—
TM72	Avalanche	Ice	Physical	60	100	10	Normal	○
TM74	Gyro Ball	Steel	Physical	—	100	5	Normal	○
TM78	Captivate	Normal	Status	—	100	20	2 Foes	—
TM79	Dark Pulse	Dark	Special	80	100	15	Normal	—
TM82	Sleep Talk	Normal	Status	—	—	10	Depends	—
TM83	Natural Gift	Normal	Physical	—	100	15	Normal	—
TM87	Swagger	Normal	Status	—	90	15	Normal	—
TM90	Substitute	Normal	Status	—	—	10	Self	—

● No. 362 | Face Pokémon
Glalie

Ice

- ● **HEIGHT:** 4'11"
- ● **WEIGHT:** 565.5 lbs.
- ● **ITEMS:** None

● SIZE COMPARISON

● MALE/FEMALE HAVE SAME FORM

⊚ ABILITIES
- ● Inner Focus
- ● Ice Body

⊚ STATS
- HP ●●●
- ATTACK ●●●●
- DEFENSE ●●●
- SP. ATTACK ●●●●
- SP. DEFENSE ●●●●
- SPEED ●●●●

⊚ EGG GROUPS
- Fairy
- Mineral

⊚ PERFORMANCE
- SPEED ★★★☆ — STAMINA ★★★★☆
- POWER ★★★★☆ — JUMP ★★
- SKILL ★★

● MAIN WAYS TO OBTAIN

Pokémon HeartGold — Level up Snorunt to Lv. 42

Pokémon SoulSilver — Level up Snorunt to Lv. 42

Pokémon Diamond — Level up Snorunt to Lv. 42

Pokémon Pearl — Level up Snorunt to Lv. 42

Pokémon Platinum — Level up Snorunt to Lv. 42

Pokémon HeartGold
It can instantly freeze moisture in the atmosphere. It uses this power to freeze its foes.

Pokémon SoulSilver
It can instantly freeze moisture in the atmosphere. It uses this power to freeze its foes.

⊚ EVOLUTION

Snorunt → Lv. 42 → Glalie

Use Dawn Stone on ♀ → Froslass

No. 363 | Clap Pokémon
Spheal

Ice / Water

- **HEIGHT:** 2'02"
- **WEIGHT:** 87.1 lbs.
- **ITEMS:** None

● SIZE COMPARISON

● MALE/FEMALE HAVE SAME FORM

⊙ ABILITIES
- Thick Fat
- Ice Body

⊙ STATS
HP	●●●
ATTACK	●●
DEFENSE	●●
SP. ATTACK	●●
SP. DEFENSE	●●
SPEED	●

⊙ EGG GROUPS
Water 1

Field

⊙ PERFORMANCE
SPEED ★★★☆   STAMINA ★★★☆
POWER ★★★☆   JUMP ★★
SKILL ★☆

● MAIN WAYS TO OBTAIN

Pokémon HeartGold — Safari Zone [Peak Area: if Water objects are placed, may appear in tall grass]

Pokémon SoulSilver — Safari Zone [Peak Area: if Water objects are placed, may appear in tall grass]

Pokémon Diamond — —

Pokémon Pearl — Route 226 [water surface]

Pokémon Platinum — Find its Egg at the Pokémon Day Care and hatch it

Pokémon HeartGold
It crosses the oceans by rolling itself on drifting ice. Fluffy fur keeps it warm when the temperature is below freezing.

Pokémon SoulSilver
It crosses the oceans by rolling itself on drifting ice. Fluffy fur keeps it warm when the temperature is below freezing.

⊙ EVOLUTION

Spheal — Lv. 32 → Sealeo — Lv. 44 → Walrein

● LEVEL-UP MOVES

Lv.	Name	Type	Kind	Pow.	Acc.	PP	Range	DA
1	Defense Curl	Normal	Status	—	—	40	Self	—
1	Powder Snow	Ice	Special	40	100	25	2 Foes	—
1	Growl	Normal	Status	—	100	40	2 Foes	—
1	Water Gun	Water	Special	40	100	25	Normal	—
7	Encore	Normal	Status	—	100	5	Normal	—
13	Ice Ball	Ice	Physical	30	90	20	Normal	○
19	Body Slam	Normal	Physical	85	100	15	Normal	○
25	Aurora Beam	Ice	Special	65	100	20	Normal	—
31	Hail	Ice	Status	—	—	10	All	—
37	Rest	Psychic	Status	—	—	10	Self	—
37	Snore	Normal	Special	40	100	15	Normal	—
43	Blizzard	Ice	Special	120	70	5	2 Foes	—
49	Sheer Cold	Ice	Special	—	30	5	Normal	—

● MOVE MANIAC

Name	Type	Kind	Pow.	Acc.	PP	Range	DA
Headbutt	Normal	Physical	70	100	15	Normal	○

● BP MOVES

Name	Type	Kind	Pow.	Acc.	PP	Range	DA
Dive	Water	Physical	80	100	10	Normal	○
Icy Wind	Ice	Special	55	95	15	2 Foes	—
Snore	Normal	Special	40	100	15	Normal	—
Mud-Slap	Ground	Special	20	100	10	Normal	—
Rollout	Rock	Physical	30	90	20	Normal	○
Aqua Tail	Water	Physical	90	90	10	Normal	○
Signal Beam	Bug	Special	75	100	15	Normal	—
Super Fang	Normal	Physical	—	90	10	Normal	○

● TM & HM MOVES

No.	Name	Type	Kind	Pow.	Acc.	PP	Range	DA
TM03	Water Pulse	Water	Special	60	100	20	Normal	—
TM06	Toxic	Poison	Status	—	85	10	Normal	—
TM07	Hail	Ice	Status	—	—	10	All	—
TM10	Hidden Power	Normal	Special	—	100	15	Normal	—
TM13	Ice Beam	Ice	Special	95	100	10	Normal	—
TM14	Blizzard	Ice	Special	120	70	5	2 Foes	—
TM17	Protect	Normal	Status	—	—	10	Self	—
TM18	Rain Dance	Water	Status	—	—	5	All	—
TM21	Frustration	Normal	Physical	—	100	20	Normal	○
TM23	Iron Tail	Steel	Physical	100	75	15	Normal	○
TM26	Earthquake	Ground	Physical	100	100	10	2 Foes/1 Ally	—
TM27	Return	Normal	Physical	—	100	20	Normal	○
TM32	Double Team	Normal	Status	—	—	15	Self	—
TM39	Rock Tomb	Rock	Physical	50	80	10	Normal	○
TM42	Facade	Normal	Physical	70	100	20	Normal	○
TM43	Secret Power	Normal	Physical	70	100	20	Normal	—
TM44	Rest	Psychic	Status	—	—	10	Self	—
TM45	Attract	Normal	Status	—	100	15	Normal	—
TM55	Brine	Water	Special	65	100	10	Normal	—
TM58	Endure	Normal	Status	—	—	10	Self	—
TM78	Captivate	Normal	Status	—	100	20	2 Foes	—
TM80	Rock Slide	Rock	Physical	75	90	10	2 Foes	—
TM82	Sleep Talk	Normal	Status	—	—	10	Depends	—
TM83	Natural Gift	Normal	Physical	—	100	15	Normal	—
TM87	Swagger	Normal	Status	—	90	15	Normal	—
TM90	Substitute	Normal	Status	—	—	10	Self	—
HM03	Surf	Water	Special	95	100	15	2 Foes/1 Ally	—
HM04	Strength	Normal	Physical	80	100	15	Normal	○
HM05	Whirlpool	Water	Special	15	70	15	Normal	—
HM06	Rock Smash	Fighting	Physical	40	100	15	Normal	○
HM07	Waterfall	Water	Physical	80	100	15	Normal	○

● EGG MOVES

Name	Type	Kind	Pow.	Acc.	PP	Range	DA
Water Sport	Water	Status	—	—	15	All	—
Stockpile	Normal	Status	—	—	20	Self	—
Swallow	Normal	Status	—	—	10	Self	—
Spit Up	Normal	Special	—	100	10	Normal	—
Yawn	Normal	Status	—	—	10	Normal	—
Rock Slide	Rock	Physical	75	90	10	2 Foes	—
Curse	???	Status	—	—	10	Normal/Self	—
Fissure	Ground	Physical	—	30	5	Normal	—
Signal Beam	Bug	Special	75	100	15	Normal	—
Aqua Ring	Water	Status	—	—	20	Self	—

● LEVEL-UP MOVES

Lv.	Name	Type	Kind	Pow.	Acc.	PP	Range	DA
1	Powder Snow	Ice	Special	40	100	25	2 Foes	—
1	Growl	Normal	Status	—	100	40	2 Foes	—
1	Water Gun	Water	Special	40	100	25	Normal	—
1	Encore	Normal	Status	—	100	5	Normal	—
7	Encore	Normal	Status	—	100	5	Normal	—
13	Ice Ball	Ice	Physical	30	90	20	Normal	○
19	Body Slam	Normal	Physical	85	100	15	Normal	○
25	Aurora Beam	Ice	Special	65	100	20	Normal	—
31	Hail	Ice	Status	—	—	10	All	—
32	Swagger	Normal	Status	—	90	15	Normal	—
39	Rest	Psychic	Status	—	—	10	Self	—
39	Snore	Normal	Special	40	100	15	Normal	—
47	Blizzard	Ice	Special	120	70	5	2 Foes	—
55	Sheer Cold	Ice	Special	—	30	5	Normal	—

● MOVE MANIAC

Name	Type	Kind	Pow.	Acc.	PP	Range	DA
Headbutt	Normal	Physical	70	100	15	Normal	○

● BP MOVES

Name	Type	Kind	Pow.	Acc.	PP	Range	DA
Dive	Water	Physical	80	100	10	Normal	○
Icy Wind	Ice	Special	55	95	15	2 Foes	—
Snore	Normal	Special	40	100	15	Normal	—
Mud-Slap	Ground	Special	20	100	10	Normal	—
Rollout	Rock	Physical	30	90	20	Normal	○
Aqua Tail	Water	Physical	90	90	10	Normal	○
Signal Beam	Bug	Special	75	100	15	Normal	—
Super Fang	Normal	Physical	—	90	10	Normal	○

● TM & HM MOVES

No.	Name	Type	Kind	Pow.	Acc.	PP	Range	DA
TM03	Water Pulse	Water	Special	60	100	20	Normal	—
TM05	Roar	Normal	Status	—	100	20	Normal	—
TM06	Toxic	Poison	Status	—	85	10	Normal	—
TM07	Hail	Ice	Status	—	—	10	All	—
TM10	Hidden Power	Normal	Special	—	100	15	Normal	—
TM13	Ice Beam	Ice	Special	95	100	10	Normal	—
TM14	Blizzard	Ice	Special	120	70	5	2 Foes	—
TM17	Protect	Normal	Status	—	—	10	Self	—
TM18	Rain Dance	Water	Status	—	—	5	All	—
TM21	Frustration	Normal	Physical	—	100	20	Normal	○
TM23	Iron Tail	Steel	Physical	100	75	15	Normal	○
TM26	Earthquake	Ground	Physical	100	100	10	2 Foes/1 Ally	○
TM27	Return	Normal	Physical	—	100	20	Normal	○
TM32	Double Team	Normal	Status	—	—	15	Self	—
TM39	Rock Tomb	Rock	Physical	50	80	10	Normal	○
TM42	Facade	Normal	Physical	70	100	20	Normal	○
TM43	Secret Power	Normal	Physical	70	100	20	Normal	○
TM44	Rest	Psychic	Status	—	—	10	Self	—
TM45	Attract	Normal	Status	—	100	15	Normal	—
TM55	Brine	Water	Special	65	100	10	Normal	—
TM58	Endure	Normal	Status	—	—	10	Self	—
TM78	Captivate	Normal	Status	—	100	20	2 Foes	—
TM80	Rock Slide	Rock	Physical	75	90	10	2 Foes	—
TM82	Sleep Talk	Normal	Status	—	—	10	Depends	—
TM83	Natural Gift	Normal	Physical	—	100	15	Normal	—
TM87	Swagger	Normal	Status	—	90	15	Normal	—
TM90	Substitute	Normal	Status	—	—	10	Self	—
HM03	Surf	Water	Special	95	100	15	2 Foes/1 Ally	—
HM04	Strength	Normal	Physical	80	100	15	Normal	○
HM05	Whirlpool	Water	Special	15	70	15	Normal	—
HM06	Rock Smash	Fighting	Physical	40	100	15	Normal	○
HM07	Waterfall	Water	Physical	80	100	15	Normal	○

⊙ No. 364 | Ball Roll Pokémon
Sealeo

Ice Water

● HEIGHT: 3'07"
● WEIGHT: 193.1 lbs.
● ITEMS: None

● SIZE COMPARISON

● MALE/FEMALE HAVE SAME FORM

⊙ ABILITIES
● Thick Fat
● Ice Body

⊙ STATS
HP ●●●
ATTACK ●●●
DEFENSE ●●●
SP. ATTACK ●●●
SP. DEFENSE ●●●
SPEED ●●

⊙ EGG GROUPS
Water 1
Field

⊙ PERFORMANCE
SPEED ★★☆☆　STAMINA ★★★★
POWER ★★★★　JUMP ★★
SKILL ★★

● MAIN WAYS TO OBTAIN

Pokémon HeartGold — Safari Zone (Mountain Area: if Water and Rock objects are placed, may appear in tall grass)

Pokémon SoulSilver — Safari Zone (Mountain Area: if Water and Rock objects are placed, may appear in tall grass)

Pokémon Diamond — —

Pokémon Pearl — Route 226 (water surface)

Pokémon Platinum — Route 230 (water surface)

Pokémon HeartGold — It has a very sensitive nose. It touches new things with its nose to examine them.

Pokémon SoulSilver — It has a very sensitive nose. It touches new things with its nose to examine them.

⊙ EVOLUTION

Spheal　Lv. 32　Sealeo　Lv. 44　Walrein

No. 365 | Ice Break Pokémon
Walrein

`Ice` `Water`

- **HEIGHT:** 4'07"
- **WEIGHT:** 332.0 lbs.
- **ITEMS:** None

● SIZE COMPARISON

● MALE/FEMALE HAVE SAME FORM

⚙ ABILITIES
- Thick Fat
- Ice Body

⚙ STATS
HP	●●●●
ATTACK	●●●●
DEFENSE	●●●●
SP. ATTACK	●●●●
SP. DEFENSE	●●●●
SPEED	●●●

⚙ EGG GROUPS
Water 1

Field

⚙ PERFORMANCE
SPEED ★ ☆

POWER ★ ★ ★ ★ ★

SKILL ★

STAMINA ★ ★ ★ ★ ★

JUMP ★ ★

● MAIN WAYS TO OBTAIN

Pokémon HeartGold	Level up Sealeo to Lv. 44
Pokémon SoulSilver	Level up Sealeo to Lv. 44
Pokémon Diamond	—
Pokémon Pearl	Level up Sealeo to Lv. 44
Pokémon Platinum	Level up Sealeo to Lv. 44

Pokémon HeartGold	**Pokémon SoulSilver**
It shatters drift ice with its strong tusks. Its thick layer of blubber repels enemy attacks.	It shatters drift ice with its strong tusks. Its thick layer of blubber repels enemy attacks.

⚙ EVOLUTION

Spheal → Lv. 32 → Sealeo → Lv. 44 → Walrein

● LEVEL-UP MOVES
Lv.	Name	Type	Kind	Pow.	Acc.	PP	Range	DA
1	Crunch	Dark	Physical	80	100	15	Normal	○
1	Powder Snow	Ice	Special	40	100	25	2 Foes	—
1	Growl	Normal	Status	—	100	40	2 Foes	—
1	Water Gun	Water	Special	40	100	25	Normal	—
1	Encore	Normal	Status	—	100	5	Normal	—
7	Encore	Normal	Status	—	100	5	Normal	—
13	Ice Ball	Ice	Physical	30	90	20	Normal	○
19	Body Slam	Normal	Physical	85	100	15	Normal	○
25	Aurora Beam	Ice	Special	65	100	20	Normal	—
31	Hail	Ice	Status	—	—	10	All	—
32	Swagger	Normal	Status	—	90	15	Normal	—
39	Rest	Psychic	Status	—	—	10	Self	—
39	Snore	Normal	Special	40	100	15	Normal	—
44	Ice Fang	Ice	Physical	65	95	15	Normal	○
52	Blizzard	Ice	Special	120	70	5	2 Foes	—
65	Sheer Cold	Ice	Special	—	30	5	Normal	—

● MOVE MANIAC
Name	Type	Kind	Pow.	Acc.	PP	Range	DA
Headbutt	Normal	Physical	70	100	15	Normal	○

● BP MOVES
Name	Type	Kind	Pow.	Acc.	PP	Range	DA
Dive	Water	Physical	80	100	10	Normal	○
Fury Cutter	Bug	Physical	10	95	20	Normal	○
Icy Wind	Ice	Special	55	95	15	2 Foes	—
Snore	Normal	Special	40	100	15	Normal	—
Block	Normal	Status	—	—	5	Normal	—
Mud-Slap	Ground	Special	20	100	10	Normal	—
Rollout	Rock	Physical	30	90	20	Normal	○
Iron Head	Steel	Physical	80	100	15	Normal	○
Aqua Tail	Water	Physical	90	90	10	Normal	○
Signal Beam	Bug	Special	75	100	15	Normal	—
Super Fang	Normal	Physical	—	90	10	Normal	○

● TM & HM MOVES
No.	Name	Type	Kind	Pow.	Acc.	PP	Range	DA
TM03	Water Pulse	Water	Special	60	100	20	Normal	—
TM05	Roar	Normal	Status	—	100	20	Normal	—
TM06	Toxic	Poison	Status	—	85	10	Normal	—
TM07	Hail	Ice	Status	—	—	10	All	—
TM10	Hidden Power	Normal	Special	—	100	15	Normal	—
TM13	Ice Beam	Ice	Special	95	100	10	Normal	—
TM14	Blizzard	Ice	Special	120	70	5	2 Foes	—
TM15	Hyper Beam	Normal	Special	150	90	5	Normal	—
TM17	Protect	Normal	Status	—	—	10	Self	—
TM18	Rain Dance	Water	Status	—	—	5	All	—
TM21	Frustration	Normal	Physical	—	100	20	Normal	○
TM23	Iron Tail	Steel	Physical	100	75	15	Normal	○
TM26	Earthquake	Ground	Physical	100	100	10	2 Foes/1 Ally	—
TM27	Return	Normal	Physical	—	100	20	Normal	○
TM32	Double Team	Normal	Status	—	—	15	Self	—
TM39	Rock Tomb	Rock	Physical	50	80	10	Normal	○
TM42	Facade	Normal	Physical	70	100	20	Normal	○
TM43	Secret Power	Normal	Physical	70	100	20	Normal	—
TM44	Rest	Psychic	Status	—	—	10	Self	—
TM45	Attract	Normal	Status	—	100	15	Normal	—
TM55	Brine	Water	Special	65	100	10	Normal	—
TM58	Endure	Normal	Status	—	—	10	Self	—
TM68	Giga Impact	Normal	Physical	150	90	5	Normal	○
TM72	Avalanche	Ice	Physical	60	100	10	Normal	○
TM78	Captivate	Normal	Status	—	100	20	2 Foes	—
TM80	Rock Slide	Rock	Physical	75	90	10	2 Foes	○
TM82	Sleep Talk	Normal	Status	—	—	10	Depends	—
TM83	Natural Gift	Normal	Physical	—	100	15	Normal	○
TM87	Swagger	Normal	Status	—	90	15	Normal	—
TM90	Substitute	Normal	Status	—	—	10	Self	—
HM03	Surf	Water	Special	95	100	15	2 Foes/1 Ally	—
HM04	Strength	Normal	Physical	80	100	15	Normal	○
HM05	Whirlpool	Water	Special	15	70	15	Normal	—
HM06	Rock Smash	Fighting	Physical	40	100	15	Normal	○
HM07	Waterfall	Water	Physical	80	100	15	Normal	○

● LEVEL-UP MOVES

Lv.	Name	Type	Kind	Pow.	Acc.	PP	Range	DA
1	Clamp	Water	Physical	35	75	10	Normal	○
1	Water Gun	Water	Special	40	100	25	Normal	—
1	Whirlpool	Water	Special	15	70	15	Normal	—
1	Iron Defense	Steel	Status	—	—	15	Self	—

● MOVE MANIAC

Name	Type	Kind	Pow.	Acc.	PP	Range	DA

● BP MOVES

Name	Type	Kind	Pow.	Acc.	PP	Range	DA
Dive	Water	Physical	80	100	10	Normal	○
Icy Wind	Ice	Special	55	95	15	2 Foes	—
Snore	Normal	Special	40	100	15	Normal	—
Iron Defense	Steel	Status	—	—	15	Self	—

● TM & HM MOVES

No.	Name	Type	Kind	Pow.	Acc.	PP	Range	DA
TM03	Water Pulse	Water	Special	60	100	20	Normal	—
TM06	Toxic	Poison	Status	—	85	10	Normal	—
TM07	Hail	Ice	Status	—	—	10	All	—
TM10	Hidden Power	Normal	Special	—	100	15	Normal	—
TM13	Ice Beam	Ice	Special	95	100	10	Normal	—
TM14	Blizzard	Ice	Special	120	70	5	2 Foes	—
TM17	Protect	Normal	Status	—	—	10	Self	—
TM18	Rain Dance	Water	Status	—	—	5	All	—
TM21	Frustration	Normal	Physical	—	100	20	Normal	○
TM27	Return	Normal	Physical	—	100	20	Normal	○
TM32	Double Team	Normal	Status	—	—	15	Self	—
TM42	Facade	Normal	Physical	70	100	20	Normal	○
TM43	Secret Power	Normal	Physical	70	100	20	Normal	—
TM44	Rest	Psychic	Status	—	—	10	Self	—
TM45	Attract	Normal	Status	—	100	15	Normal	—
TM55	Brine	Water	Special	65	100	10	Normal	—
TM58	Endure	Normal	Status	—	—	10	Self	—
TM78	Captivate	Normal	Status	—	100	20	2 Foes	—
TM82	Sleep Talk	Normal	Status	—	—	10	Depends	—
TM83	Natural Gift	Normal	Physical	—	100	15	Normal	—
TM87	Swagger	Normal	Status	—	90	15	Normal	—
TM90	Substitute	Normal	Status	—	—	10	Self	—
HM03	Surf	Water	Special	95	100	15	2 Foes/1 Ally	—
HM05	Whirlpool	Water	Special	15	70	15	Normal	—
HM07	Waterfall	Water	Physical	80	100	15	Normal	○

● EGG MOVES

Name	Type	Kind	Pow.	Acc.	PP	Range	DA
Refresh	Normal	Status	—	—	20	Self	—
Mud Sport	Ground	Status	—	—	15	All	—
Body Slam	Normal	Physical	85	100	15	Normal	○
Supersonic	Normal	Status	—	55	20	Normal	—
Barrier	Psychic	Status	—	—	30	Self	—
Confuse Ray	Ghost	Status	—	100	10	Normal	—
Aqua Ring	Water	Status	—	—	20	Self	—
Muddy Water	Water	Special	95	85	10	2 Foes	—

● No. 366 | Bivalve Pokémon
Clamperl

Water

● HEIGHT: 1'04"
● WEIGHT: 115.7 lbs.
● ITEMS: Big Pearl

● SIZE COMPARISON

● MALE/FEMALE HAVE SAME FORM

⊙ ABILITIES
● Shell Armor

⊙ STATS
HP ●
ATTACK ★★★
DEFENSE ●●●
SP. ATTACK ●●●
SP. DEFENSE ●●
SPEED ●

⊙ EGG GROUPS
Water 1

⊙ PERFORMANCE

SPEED ★★★
POWER ★★★
SKILL ★★☆

STAMINA ★★★★☆
JUMP ★★☆

● MAIN WAYS TO OBTAIN

Pokémon HeartGold	Route 19 (mass outbreak, water surface)
Pokémon SoulSilver	Route 19 (mass outbreak, water surface)
Pokémon Diamond	Route 219 (Super Rod)
Pokémon Pearl	Route 219 (Super Rod)
Pokémon Platinum	—

Pokémon HeartGold	*Pokémon SoulSilver*
When it evolves, it makes a mysterious pearl that amplifies psychic powers when it's held.	When it evolves, it makes a mysterious pearl that amplifies psychic powers when it's held.

⊙ EVOLUTION

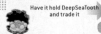

Have it hold DeepSeaTooth and trade it

Huntail

Clamperl

Have it hold DeepSeaScale and trade it

Gorebyss

No. 367 | Deep Sea Pokémon
Huntail

Water

- **HEIGHT:** 5'07"
- **WEIGHT:** 59.5 lbs.
- **ITEMS:** None

● SIZE COMPARISON

● MALE/FEMALE HAVE SAME FORM

● ABILITIES
- Swift Swim

● EGG GROUPS
Water 1

● STATS
HP ●●
ATTACK ●●●●
DEFENSE ●●●●
SP. ATTACK ●●●
SP. DEFENSE ●●●
SPEED ●●

● PERFORMANCE
SPEED ★★★★ STAMINA ★★★
POWER ★★★★ JUMP ★★☆
SKILL ★☆

● MAIN WAYS TO OBTAIN

Pokémon HeartGold — Link trade Clamperl while it holds the DeepSeaTooth

Pokémon SoulSilver — Link trade Clamperl while it holds the DeepSeaTooth

Pokémon Diamond — Link trade Clamperl while it holds the DeepSeaTooth

Pokémon Pearl — Link trade Clamperl while it holds the DeepSeaTooth

Pokémon Platinum — —

Pokémon HeartGold
It lives deep in the pitch-dark sea. It attracts prey by moving its tail in mimicry of a small animal.

Pokémon SoulSilver
It lives deep in the pitch-dark sea. It attracts prey by moving its tail in mimicry of a small animal.

● EVOLUTION

Have it hold DeepSeaTooth and trade it → Huntail

Clamperl

Have it hold DeepSeaScale and trade it → Gorebyss

● LEVEL-UP MOVES

Lv.	Name	Type	Kind	Pow.	Acc.	PP	Range	DA
1	Whirlpool	Water	Special	15	70	15	Normal	—
6	Bite	Dark	Physical	60	100	25	Normal	○
10	Screech	Normal	Status	—	85	40	Normal	—
15	Water Pulse	Water	Special	60	100	20	Normal	—
19	Scary Face	Normal	Status	—	90	10	Normal	—
24	Ice Fang	Ice	Physical	65	95	15	Normal	○
28	Brine	Water	Special	65	100	10	Normal	—
33	Baton Pass	Normal	Status	—	—	40	Self	—
37	Dive	Water	Physical	80	100	10	Normal	○
42	Crunch	Dark	Physical	80	100	15	Normal	○
46	Aqua Tail	Water	Physical	90	90	10	Normal	—
51	Hydro Pump	Water	Special	120	80	5	Normal	—

● MOVE MANIAC

Name	Type	Kind	Pow.	Acc.	PP	Range	DA

● BP MOVES

Name	Type	Kind	Pow.	Acc.	PP	Range	DA
Dive	Water	Physical	80	100	10	Normal	—
Icy Wind	Ice	Special	55	95	15	2 Foes	—
Sucker Punch	Dark	Physical	80	100	5	Normal	○
Snore	Normal	Special	40	100	15	Normal	—
Swift	Normal	Special	60	—	20	2 Foes	—
Mud-Slap	Ground	Special	20	100	10	Normal	—
Aqua Tail	Water	Physical	90	90	10	Normal	○
Bounce	Flying	Physical	85	85	5	Normal	○
Super Fang	Normal	Physical	—	90	10	Normal	—

● TM & HM MOVES

No.	Name	Type	Kind	Pow.	Acc.	PP	Range	DA
TM03	Water Pulse	Water	Special	60	100	20	Normal	—
TM06	Toxic	Poison	Status	—	85	10	Normal	—
TM07	Hail	Ice	Status	—	—	10	All	—
TM10	Hidden Power	Normal	Special	—	100	15	Normal	—
TM13	Ice Beam	Ice	Special	95	100	10	Normal	—
TM14	Blizzard	Ice	Special	120	70	5	2 Foes	—
TM15	Hyper Beam	Normal	Special	150	90	5	Normal	—
TM17	Protect	Normal	Status	—	—	10	Self	—
TM18	Rain Dance	Water	Status	—	—	5	All	—
TM21	Frustration	Normal	Physical	—	100	20	Normal	○
TM27	Return	Normal	Physical	—	100	20	Normal	○
TM32	Double Team	Normal	Status	—	—	15	Self	—
TM39	Rock Tomb	Rock	Physical	50	80	10	Normal	—
TM42	Facade	Normal	Physical	70	100	20	Normal	○
TM43	Secret Power	Normal	Physical	70	100	20	Normal	—
TM44	Rest	Psychic	Status	—	—	10	Self	—
TM45	Attract	Normal	Status	—	100	15	Normal	—
TM49	Snatch	Dark	Status	—	—	10	Depends	—
TM55	Brine	Water	Special	65	100	10	Normal	—
TM58	Endure	Normal	Status	—	—	10	Self	—
TM68	Giga Impact	Normal	Physical	150	90	5	Normal	○
TM78	Captivate	Normal	Status	—	100	20	2 Foes	—
TM82	Sleep Talk	Normal	Status	—	—	10	Depends	—
TM83	Natural Gift	Normal	Physical	—	100	15	Normal	—
TM87	Swagger	Normal	Status	—	90	15	Normal	—
TM90	Substitute	Normal	Status	—	—	10	Self	—
HM03	Surf	Water	Special	95	100	15	2 Foes/1 Ally	—
HM05	Whirlpool	Water	Special	15	70	15	Normal	—
HM07	Waterfall	Water	Physical	80	100	15	Normal	○

● LEVEL-UP MOVES

Lv.	Name	Type	Kind	Pow.	Acc.	PP	Range	DA
1	Whirlpool	Water	Special	15	70	15	Normal	○
6	Confusion	Psychic	Special	50	100	25	Normal	—
10	Agility	Psychic	Status	—	—	30	Self	—
15	Water Pulse	Water	Special	60	100	20	Normal	—
19	Amnesia	Psychic	Status	—	—	20	Self	—
24	Aqua Ring	Water	Status	—	—	20	Self	—
28	Captivate	Normal	Status	—	100	20	2 Foes	—
33	Baton Pass	Normal	Status	—	—	40	Self	—
37	Dive	Water	Physical	80	100	10	Normal	○
42	Psychic	Psychic	Special	90	100	10	Normal	—
46	Aqua Tail	Water	Physical	90	90	10	Normal	○
51	Hydro Pump	Water	Special	120	80	5	Normal	—

● MOVE MANIAC

Name	Type	Kind	Pow.	Acc.	PP	Range	DA

● BP MOVES

Name	Type	Kind	Pow.	Acc.	PP	Range	DA
Dive	Water	Physical	80	100	10	Normal	○
Icy Wind	Ice	Special	55	95	15	2 Foes	—
Snore	Normal	Special	40	100	15	Normal	—
Swift	Normal	Special	60	—	20	2 Foes	—
Mud-Slap	Ground	Special	20	100	10	Normal	—
Aqua Tail	Water	Physical	90	90	10	Normal	○
Signal Beam	Bug	Special	75	100	15	Normal	○
Bounce	Flying	Physical	85	85	5	Normal	○

● TM & HM MOVES

No.	Name	Type	Kind	Pow.	Acc.	PP	Range	DA
TM04	Calm Mind	Psychic	Status	—	—	20	Self	—
TM06	Toxic	Poison	Status	—	85	10	Normal	—
TM10	Hidden Power	Normal	Special	—	100	15	Normal	—
TM11	Sunny Day	Fire	Status	—	—	5	All	—
TM12	Taunt	Dark	Status	—	100	20	Normal	—
TM15	Hyper Beam	Normal	Special	150	90	5	Normal	—
TM17	Protect	Normal	Status	—	—	10	Self	—
TM18	Rain Dance	Water	Status	—	—	5	All	—
TM21	Frustration	Normal	Physical	—	100	20	Normal	○
TM24	Thunderbolt	Electric	Special	95	100	15	Normal	—
TM25	Thunder	Electric	Special	120	70	10	Normal	—
TM27	Return	Normal	Physical	—	100	20	Normal	○
TM29	Psychic	Psychic	Special	90	100	10	Normal	—
TM30	Shadow Ball	Ghost	Special	80	100	15	Normal	—
TM32	Double Team	Normal	Status	—	—	15	Self	—
TM34	Shock Wave	Electric	Special	60	—	20	Normal	—
TM41	Torment	Dark	Status	—	100	15	Normal	—
TM42	Facade	Normal	Physical	70	100	20	Normal	○
TM43	Secret Power	Normal	Physical	70	100	20	Normal	○
TM44	Rest	Psychic	Status	—	—	10	Self	—
TM45	Attract	Normal	Status	—	100	15	Normal	—
TM46	Thief	Dark	Physical	40	100	10	Normal	○
TM48	Skill Swap	Psychic	Status	—	—	10	Normal	—
TM49	Snatch	Dark	Status	—	—	10	Depends	—
TM56	Fling	Dark	Physical	—	100	10	Normal	—
TM57	Charge Beam	Electric	Special	50	90	10	Normal	—
TM58	Endure	Normal	Status	—	—	10	Self	—
TM61	Will-O-Wisp	Fire	Status	—	75	15	Normal	—
TM63	Embargo	Dark	Status	—	100	15	Normal	—
TM65	Shadow Claw	Ghost	Physical	70	100	15	Normal	○
TM66	Payback	Dark	Physical	50	100	10	Normal	○
TM68	Giga Impact	Normal	Physical	150	90	5	Normal	○
TM70	Flash	Normal	Status	—	100	20	Normal	—
TM73	Thunder Wave	Electric	Status	—	100	20	Normal	—
TM77	Psych Up	Normal	Status	—	—	10	Normal	—
TM78	Captivate	Normal	Status	—	100	20	2 Foes	—
TM79	Dark Pulse	Dark	Special	80	100	15	Normal	—
TM82	Sleep Talk	Normal	Status	—	—	10	Depends	—
TM83	Natural Gift	Normal	Physical	—	100	15	Normal	—
TM85	Dream Eater	Psychic	Special	100	100	15	Normal	—
TM87	Swagger	Normal	Status	—	90	15	Normal	—
TM90	Substitute	Normal	Status	—	—	10	Self	—
TM92	Trick Room	Psychic	Status	—	—	5	All	—

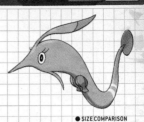

● **HEIGHT:** 5'11"
● **WEIGHT:** 49.8 lbs.
● **ITEMS:** None

● **SIZE COMPARISON**

● MALE/FEMALE HAVE SAME FORM

● ABILITIES

● Swift Swim

● STATS

HP	●●
ATTACK	●●●●
DEFENSE	●●●●
SP. ATTACK	●●●●●
SP. DEFENSE	●●●
SPEED	●●

● EGG GROUPS

Water 1

● PERFORMANCE

SPEED ★★★★   STAMINA ★★★
POWER ★★☆   JUMP ★★☆
SKILL ★★★★

● MAIN WAYS TO OBTAIN

Pokémon HeartGold — Link trade Clamperl while it holds the DeepSeaScale

Pokémon SoulSilver — Link trade Clamperl while it holds the DeepSeaScale

Pokémon Diamond — Link trade Clamperl while it holds the DeepSeaScale

Pokémon Pearl — Link trade Clamperl while it holds the DeepSeaScale

Pokémon Platinum — —

Pokémon HeartGold — Its pink body becomes more vivid with the rise of water temperatures in the springtime.

Pokémon SoulSilver — Its pink body becomes more vivid with the rise of water temperatures in the springtime.

● EVOLUTION

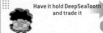

Have it hold DeepSeaTooth and trade it → Huntail

Clamperl

Have it hold DeepSeaScale and trade it → Gorebyss

● No. 369 | Longevity Pokémon
Relicanth

Water | Rock

- **HEIGHT:** 3'03"
- **WEIGHT:** 51.6 lbs.
- **ITEMS:** DeepSeaScale

● SIZE COMPARISON

● MALE FORM
Larger jaw

● FEMALE FORM
Smaller jaw

⊛ ABILITIES
- Swift Swim
- Rock Head

⊛ EGG GROUPS
Water 1
Water 2

⊛ PERFORMANCE
SPEED ★★★★	STAMINA ★★☆
POWER ★★☆	JUMP ★★★★
SKILL ★☆☆	

● MAIN WAYS TO OBTAIN

Pokémon HeartGold — Route 12 [mass outbreak, fishing]

Pokémon SoulSilver — Route 12 [mass outbreak, fishing]

Pokémon Diamond — Route 226 (Super Rod)

Pokémon Pearl — Route 226 (Super Rod)

Pokémon Platinum — Route 226 (Super Rod)

Pokémon HeartGold — Discovered by chance during deep-sea explorations, it has not changed since ancient times.

Pokémon SoulSilver — Discovered by chance during deep-sea explorations, it has not changed since ancient times.

⊛ EVOLUTION
Does not evolve

⊛ STATS
HP ●●●●
ATTACK ●●●●
DEFENSE ●●●●●
SP. ATTACK ●●●
SP. DEFENSE ●●
SPEED ●●●

● LEVEL-UP MOVES
Lv.	Name	Type	Kind	Pow.	Acc.	PP	Range	DA
1	Tackle	Normal	Physical	35	95	35	Normal	○
1	Harden	Normal	Status	—	—	30	Self	—
8	Water Gun	Water	Special	40	100	25	Normal	—
15	Rock Tomb	Rock	Physical	50	80	10	Normal	—
22	Yawn	Normal	Status	—	—	10	Normal	—
29	Take Down	Normal	Physical	90	85	20	Normal	○
36	Mud Sport	Ground	Status	—	—	15	All	—
43	AncientPower	Rock	Special	60	100	5	Normal	—
50	Double-Edge	Normal	Physical	120	100	15	Normal	○
57	Dive	Water	Physical	80	100	10	Normal	○
64	Rest	Psychic	Status	—	—	10	Self	—
71	Hydro Pump	Water	Special	120	80	5	Normal	—
78	Head Smash	Rock	Physical	150	80	5	Normal	○

● MOVE MANIAC
Name	Type	Kind	Pow.	Acc.	PP	Range	DA
Headbutt	Normal	Physical	70	100	15	Normal	○

● BP MOVES
Name	Type	Kind	Pow.	Acc.	PP	Range	DA
Dive	Water	Physical	80	100	10	Normal	○
Icy Wind	Ice	Special	55	95	15	2 Foes	—
Snore	Normal	Special	40	100	15	Normal	—
Mud-Slap	Ground	Special	20	100	10	Normal	—
Aqua Tail	Water	Physical	90	90	10	Normal	○
AncientPower	Rock	Special	60	100	5	Normal	—
Earth Power	Ground	Special	90	100	10	Normal	—
Bounce	Flying	Physical	85	85	5	Normal	○

● TM & HM MOVES
No.	Name	Type	Kind	Pow.	Acc.	PP	Range	DA
TM03	Water Pulse	Water	Special	60	100	20	Normal	—
TM04	Calm Mind	Psychic	Status	—	—	20	Self	—
TM06	Toxic	Poison	Status	—	85	10	Normal	—
TM07	Hail	Ice	Status	—	—	10	All	—
TM10	Hidden Power	Normal	Special	—	100	15	Normal	—
TM13	Ice Beam	Ice	Special	95	100	10	Normal	—
TM14	Blizzard	Ice	Special	120	70	5	2 Foes	—
TM15	Hyper Beam	Normal	Special	150	90	5	Normal	—
TM17	Protect	Normal	Status	—	—	10	Self	—
TM18	Rain Dance	Water	Status	—	—	5	All	—
TM20	Safeguard	Normal	Status	—	—	25	2 Allies	—
TM21	Frustration	Normal	Physical	—	100	20	Normal	○
TM26	Earthquake	Ground	Physical	100	100	10	2 Foes/1 Ally	—
TM27	Return	Normal	Physical	—	100	20	Normal	○
TM32	Double Team	Normal	Status	—	—	15	Self	—
TM37	Sandstorm	Rock	Status	—	—	10	All	—
TM39	Rock Tomb	Rock	Physical	50	80	10	Normal	—
TM42	Facade	Normal	Physical	70	100	20	Normal	○
TM43	Secret Power	Normal	Physical	70	100	20	Normal	—
TM44	Rest	Psychic	Status	—	—	10	Self	—
TM45	Attract	Normal	Status	—	100	15	Normal	—
TM55	Brine	Water	Special	65	100	10	Normal	—
TM58	Endure	Normal	Status	—	—	10	Self	—
TM68	Giga Impact	Normal	Physical	150	90	5	Normal	○
TM69	Rock Polish	Rock	Status	—	—	20	Self	—
TM71	Stone Edge	Rock	Physical	100	80	5	Normal	—
TM76	Stealth Rock	Rock	Status	—	—	20	2 Foes	—
TM77	Psych Up	Normal	Status	—	—	10	Self	—
TM78	Captivate	Normal	Status	—	100	20	2 Foes	—
TM80	Rock Slide	Rock	Physical	75	90	10	2 Foes	—
TM82	Sleep Talk	Normal	Status	—	—	10	Depends	—
TM83	Natural Gift	Normal	Physical	—	100	15	Normal	—
TM87	Swagger	Normal	Status	—	90	15	Normal	—
TM90	Substitute	Normal	Status	—	—	10	Self	—
HM03	Surf	Water	Special	95	100	15	2 Foes/1 Ally	—
HM05	Whirlpool	Water	Special	15	70	15	Normal	—
HM06	Rock Smash	Fighting	Physical	40	100	15	Normal	○
HM07	Waterfall	Water	Physical	80	100	15	Normal	○

● EGG MOVES
Name	Type	Kind	Pow.	Acc.	PP	Range	DA
Magnitude	Ground	Physical	—	100	30	2 Foes/1 Ally	—
Skull Bash	Normal	Physical	100	100	15	Normal	○
Water Sport	Water	Status	—	—	15	All	—
Amnesia	Psychic	Status	—	—	20	Self	—
Sleep Talk	Normal	Status	—	—	10	Depends	—
Rock Slide	Rock	Physical	75	90	10	2 Foes	—
Aqua Tail	Water	Physical	90	90	10	Normal	○
Snore	Normal	Special	40	100	15	Normal	—
Mud-Slap	Ground	Special	20	100	10	Normal	—
Muddy Water	Water	Special	95	85	10	2 Foes	—

● LEVEL-UP MOVES

Lv.	Name	Type	Kind	Pow.	Acc.	PP	Range	DA
1	Tackle	Normal	Physical	35	95	35	Normal	○
4	Charm	Normal	Status	—	100	20	Normal	—
7	Water Gun	Water	Special	40	100	25	Normal	—
9	Agility	Psychic	Status	—	—	30	Self	—
14	Take Down	Normal	Physical	90	85	20	Normal	○
17	Lucky Chant	Normal	Status	—	—	30	2 Allies	—
22	Attract	Normal	Status	—	100	15	Normal	—
27	Sweet Kiss	Normal	Status	—	75	10	Normal	—
31	Water Pulse	Water	Special	60	100	20	Normal	—
37	Aqua Ring	Water	Status	—	—	20	Self	—
40	Captivate	Normal	Status	—	100	20	2 Foes	—
46	Flail	Normal	Physical	—	100	15	Normal	○
51	Safeguard	Normal	Status	—	—	25	2 Allies	—

● MOVE MANIAC

Name	Type	Kind	Pow.	Acc.	PP	Range	DA

● BP MOVES

Name	Type	Kind	Pow.	Acc.	PP	Range	DA
Dive	Water	Physical	80	100	10	Normal	○
Icy Wind	Ice	Special	55	95	15	2 Foes	—
Snore	Normal	Special	40	100	15	Normal	—
Swift	Normal	Special	60	—	20	2 Foes	—
Bounce	Flying	Physical	85	85	5	Normal	○

● TM & HM MOVES

No.	Name	Type	Kind	Pow.	Acc.	PP	Range	DA
TM03	Water Pulse	Water	Special	60	100	20	Normal	—
TM06	Toxic	Poison	Status	—	85	10	Normal	—
TM07	Hail	Ice	Status	—	—	10	All	—
TM10	Hidden Power	Normal	Special	—	100	15	Normal	—
TM13	Ice Beam	Ice	Special	95	100	10	Normal	—
TM14	Blizzard	Ice	Special	120	70	5	2 Foes	—
TM17	Protect	Normal	Status	—	—	10	Self	—
TM18	Rain Dance	Water	Status	—	—	5	All	—
TM20	Safeguard	Normal	Status	—	—	25	2 Allies	—
TM21	Frustration	Normal	Physical	—	100	20	Normal	○
TM27	Return	Normal	Physical	—	100	20	Normal	○
TM32	Double Team	Normal	Status	—	—	15	Self	—
TM42	Facade	Normal	Physical	70	100	20	Normal	○
TM43	Secret Power	Normal	Physical	70	100	20	Normal	—
TM44	Rest	Psychic	Status	—	—	10	Self	—
TM45	Attract	Normal	Status	—	100	15	Normal	—
TM55	Brine	Water	Special	65	100	10	Normal	—
TM58	Endure	Normal	Status	—	—	10	Self	—
TM77	Psych Up	Normal	Status	—	—	10	Normal	—
TM78	Captivate	Normal	Status	—	100	20	2 Foes	—
TM82	Sleep Talk	Normal	Status	—	—	10	Depends	—
TM83	Natural Gift	Normal	Physical	—	100	15	Normal	—
TM87	Swagger	Normal	Status	—	90	15	Normal	—
TM90	Substitute	Normal	Status	—	—	10	Self	—
HM03	Surf	Water	Special	95	100	15	2 Foes/1 Ally	—
HM05	Whirlpool	Water	Special	15	70	15	Normal	—
HM07	Waterfall	Water	Physical	80	100	15	Normal	○

● EGG MOVES

Name	Type	Kind	Pow.	Acc.	PP	Range	DA
Splash	Normal	Status	—	—	40	Self	—
Supersonic	Normal	Status	—	55	20	Normal	—
Water Sport	Water	Status	—	—	15	All	—
Mud Sport	Ground	Status	—	—	15	All	—
Captivate	Normal	Status	—	100	20	2 Foes	—
Aqua Ring	Water	Status	—	—	20	Self	—
Aqua Jet	Water	Physical	40	100	20	Normal	○

☺ No. 370 | Rendezvous Pokémon
Luvdisc

Water

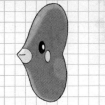

- ● HEIGHT: 2'00"
- ● WEIGHT: 19.2 lbs.
- ● ITEMS: Heart Scale

● SIZE COMPARISON

● MALE/FEMALE HAVE SAME FORM

☺ ABILITIES
● Swift Swim

☺ STATS
- HP ●●
- ATTACK ●
- DEFENSE ●●
- SP. ATTACK ●●
- SP. DEFENSE ●●
- SPEED ●●●●

☺ EGG GROUPS
Water 2

☺ PERFORMANCE
SPEED ★★★☆☆   STAMINA ★★★☆☆
POWER ★   JUMP ★★☆
SKILL ★

● MAIN WAYS TO OBTAIN

Pokémon HeartGold — Route 27 (mass outbreak, water surface)

Pokémon SoulSilver — Route 27 (mass outbreak, water surface)

Pokémon Diamond — Pokémon League (Super Rod)

Pokémon Pearl — Pokémon League (Super Rod)

Pokémon Platinum — Pokémon League (Super Rod)

Pokémon HeartGold
Its heart-shaped body makes it popular. In some places, you would give a LUVDISC to someone you love.

Pokémon SoulSilver
Its heart-shaped body makes it popular. In some places, you would give a LUVDISC to someone you love.

☺ EVOLUTION

Does not evolve

● No. 371 | Rock Head Pokémon
Bagon

Dragon

- ● HEIGHT: 2'00"
- ● WEIGHT: 92.8 lbs.
- ● ITEMS: Dragon Fang

● SIZE COMPARISON

● MALE/FEMALE HAVE SAME FORM

⊙ ABILITIES
- ● Rock Head

⊙ STATS
- HP ●●
- ATTACK ●●●
- DEFENSE ●●
- SP. ATTACK ●●
- SP. DEFENSE ●●
- SPEED ●●

⊙ EGG GROUPS
Dragon

⊙ PERFORMANCE
SPEED ★★★☆	STAMINA ★★★☆
POWER ★★★☆	JUMP ★★★
SKILL ★★★☆	

● MAIN WAYS TO OBTAIN

Pokémon HeartGold
Safari Zone (Swamp Area: if Rock and Forest objects are placed, may appear in tall grass)

Pokémon SoulSilver
Safari Zone (Swamp Area: if Rock and Forest objects are placed, may appear in tall grass)

Pokémon Diamond —

Pokémon Pearl
Route 210, Celestic Town side (use Poké Radar)

Pokémon Platinum
Route 210, Celestic Town side (use Poké Radar)

Pokémon HeartGold
Its well-developed neck muscles and ironlike head can smash boulders into pieces.

Pokémon SoulSilver
Its well-developed neck muscles and ironlike head can smash boulders into pieces.

⊙ EVOLUTION

Lv. 30   Lv. 50

Bagon   Sheigon   Salamence

● LEVEL-UP MOVES
Lv.	Name	Type	Kind	Pow.	Acc.	PP	Range	DA
1	Rage	Normal	Physical	20	100	20	Normal	○
5	Bite	Dark	Physical	60	100	25	Normal	○
10	Leer	Normal	Status	—	100	30	2 Foes	—
16	Headbutt	Normal	Physical	70	100	15	Normal	○
20	Focus Energy	Normal	Status	—	—	30	Self	—
25	Ember	Fire	Special	40	100	25	Normal	—
31	DragonBreath	Dragon	Special	60	100	20	Normal	—
35	Zen Headbutt	Psychic	Physical	80	90	15	Normal	○
40	Scary Face	Normal	Status	—	90	10	Normal	—
46	Crunch	Dark	Physical	80	100	15	Normal	○
50	Dragon Claw	Dragon	Physical	80	100	15	Normal	○
55	Double-Edge	Normal	Physical	120	100	15	Normal	○

● MOVE MANIAC
Name	Type	Kind	Pow.	Acc.	PP	Range	DA
Headbutt	Normal	Physical	70	100	15	Normal	○
Draco Meteor	Dragon	Special	140	90	5	Normal	—

● BP MOVES
Name	Type	Kind	Pow.	Acc.	PP	Range	DA
Fury Cutter	Bug	Physical	10	95	20	Normal	○
Zen Headbutt	Psychic	Physical	80	100	15	Normal	—
Snore	Normal	Special	40	100	15	Normal	—
Mud-Slap	Ground	Special	20	100	10	Normal	—
Outrage	Dragon	Physical	120	100	15	1 Random	○
Twister	Dragon	Special	40	100	20	2 Foes	—

● TM & HM MOVES
No.	Name	Type	Kind	Pow.	Acc.	PP	Range	DA
TM02	Dragon Claw	Dragon	Physical	80	100	15	Normal	○
TM05	Roar	Normal	Status	—	100	20	Normal	—
TM06	Toxic	Poison	Status	—	85	10	Normal	—
TM10	Hidden Power	Normal	Special	—	100	15	Normal	—
TM11	Sunny Day	Fire	Status	—	—	5	All	—
TM17	Protect	Normal	Status	—	—	10	Self	—
TM18	Rain Dance	Water	Status	—	—	5	All	—
TM21	Frustration	Normal	Physical	—	100	20	Normal	○
TM27	Return	Normal	Physical	—	100	20	Normal	○
TM31	Brick Break	Fighting	Physical	75	100	15	Normal	○
TM32	Double Team	Normal	Status	—	—	15	Self	—
TM35	Flamethrower	Fire	Special	95	100	15	Normal	—
TM38	Fire Blast	Fire	Special	120	85	5	Normal	—
TM39	Rock Tomb	Rock	Physical	50	80	10	Normal	—
TM40	Aerial Ace	Flying	Physical	60	—	20	Normal	○
TM42	Facade	Normal	Physical	70	100	20	Normal	○
TM43	Secret Power	Normal	Physical	70	100	20	Normal	—
TM44	Rest	Psychic	Status	—	—	10	Self	—
TM45	Attract	Normal	Status	—	100	15	Normal	—
TM58	Endure	Normal	Status	—	—	10	Self	—
TM59	Dragon Pulse	Dragon	Special	90	100	10	Normal	—
TM65	Shadow Claw	Ghost	Physical	70	100	15	Normal	○
TM78	Captivate	Normal	Status	—	100	20	2 Foes	—
TM80	Rock Slide	Rock	Physical	75	90	10	2 Foes	—
TM82	Sleep Talk	Normal	Status	—	—	10	Depends	—
TM83	Natural Gift	Normal	Physical	—	100	15	Normal	—
TM87	Swagger	Normal	Status	—	90	15	Normal	—
TM90	Substitute	Normal	Status	—	—	10	Self	—
HM01	Cut	Normal	Physical	50	95	30	Normal	○
HM04	Strength	Normal	Physical	80	100	15	Normal	○
HM06	Rock Smash	Fighting	Physical	40	100	15	Normal	○

● EGG MOVES
Name	Type	Kind	Pow.	Acc.	PP	Range	DA
Hydro Pump	Water	Special	120	80	5	Normal	—
Thrash	Normal	Physical	90	100	20	1 Random	○
Dragon Rage	Dragon	Special	—	100	10	Normal	—
Twister	Dragon	Special	40	100	20	2 Foes	—
Dragon Dance	Dragon	Status	—	—	20	Self	—
Fire Fang	Fire	Physical	65	95	15	Normal	○
Shadow Claw	Ghost	Physical	70	100	15	Normal	○
Dragon Rush	Dragon	Physical	100	75	10	Normal	○

● LEVEL-UP MOVES

Lv.	Name	Type	Kind	Pow.	Acc.	PP	Range	DA
1	Rage	Normal	Physical	20	100	20	Normal	○
1	Bite	Dark	Physical	60	100	25	Normal	○
1	Leer	Normal	Status	—	100	30	2 Foes	—
1	Headbutt	Normal	Physical	70	100	15	Normal	○
5	Bite	Dark	Physical	60	100	25	Normal	○
10	Leer	Normal	Status	—	100	30	2 Foes	—
16	Headbutt	Normal	Physical	70	100	15	Normal	○
20	Focus Energy	Normal	Status	—	—	30	Self	—
25	Ember	Fire	Special	40	100	25	Normal	—
30	Protect	Normal	Status	—	—	10	Self	—
32	DragonBreath	Dragon	Special	60	100	20	Normal	—
37	Zen Headbutt	Psychic	Physical	80	90	15	Normal	○
43	Scary Face	Normal	Status	—	90	10	Normal	—
50	Crunch	Dark	Physical	80	100	15	Normal	○
55	Dragon Claw	Dragon	Physical	80	100	15	Normal	○
61	Double-Edge	Normal	Physical	120	100	15	Normal	○

● MOVE MANIAC

Name	Type	Kind	Pow.	Acc.	PP	Range	DA
Headbutt	Normal	Physical	70	100	15	Normal	○
Draco Meteor	Dragon	Special	140	90	5	Normal	—

● BP MOVES

Name	Type	Kind	Pow.	Acc.	PP	Range	DA
Fury Cutter	Bug	Physical	10	95	20	Normal	○
Zen Headbutt	Psychic	Physical	80	90	15	Normal	○
Snore	Normal	Special	40	100	15	Normal	—
Mud-Slap	Ground	Special	20	100	10	Normal	—
Rollout	Rock	Physical	30	90	20	Normal	○
Outrage	Dragon	Physical	120	100	15	1 Random	○
Twister	Dragon	Special	40	100	20	2 Foes	—
Iron Defense	Steel	Status	—	—	15	Self	—

● TM & HM MOVES

No.	Name	Type	Kind	Pow.	Acc.	PP	Range	DA
TM02	Dragon Claw	Dragon	Physical	80	100	15	Normal	○
TM05	Roar	Normal	Status	—	100	20	Normal	—
TM06	Toxic	Poison	Status	—	85	10	Normal	—
TM10	Hidden Power	Normal	Special	—	100	15	Normal	—
TM11	Sunny Day	Fire	Status	—	—	5	All	—
TM17	Protect	Normal	Status	—	—	10	Self	—
TM18	Rain Dance	Water	Status	—	—	5	All	—
TM21	Frustration	Normal	Physical	—	100	20	Normal	○
TM27	Return	Normal	Physical	—	100	20	Normal	○
TM31	Brick Break	Fighting	Physical	75	100	15	Normal	○
TM32	Double Team	Normal	Status	—	—	15	Self	—
TM35	Flamethrower	Fire	Special	95	100	15	Normal	—
TM38	Fire Blast	Fire	Special	120	85	5	Normal	—
TM39	Rock Tomb	Rock	Physical	50	80	10	Normal	○
TM40	Aerial Ace	Flying	Physical	60	—	20	Normal	○
TM42	Facade	Normal	Physical	70	100	20	Normal	○
TM43	Secret Power	Normal	Physical	70	100	20	Normal	○
TM44	Rest	Psychic	Status	—	—	10	Self	—
TM45	Attract	Normal	Status	—	100	15	Normal	—
TM58	Endure	Normal	Status	—	—	10	Self	—
TM59	Dragon Pulse	Dragon	Special	90	100	10	Normal	—
TM65	Shadow Claw	Ghost	Physical	70	100	15	Normal	○
TM78	Captivate	Normal	Status	—	100	20	2 Foes	—
TM80	Rock Slide	Rock	Physical	75	90	10	2 Foes	—
TM82	Sleep Talk	Normal	Status	—	—	10	Depends	—
TM83	Natural Gift	Normal	Physical	—	100	15	Normal	—
TM87	Swagger	Normal	Status	—	90	15	Normal	—
TM90	Substitute	Normal	Status	—	—	10	Self	—
HM01	Cut	Normal	Physical	50	95	30	Normal	○
HM04	Strength	Normal	Physical	80	100	15	Normal	○
HM06	Rock Smash	Fighting	Physical	40	100	15	Normal	○

No. 372 | Endurance Pokémon
Shelgon

Dragon

● HEIGHT: 3'07"
● WEIGHT: 243.6 lbs.
● ITEMS: Dragon Fang

● SIZE COMPARISON

● MALE/FEMALE HAVE SAME FORM

⊚ ABILITIES
● Rock Head

⊛ EGG GROUPS
Dragon

⊛ STATS
HP	●●
ATTACK	●●●●
DEFENSE	●●●●
SP. ATTACK	●●●
SP. DEFENSE	●●
SPEED	●●

⊛ PERFORMANCE
SPEED ★★	STAMINA ★★★★☆
POWER ★★★★☆	JUMP ★★
SKILL ★☆	

● MAIN WAYS TO OBTAIN

Pokémon HeartGold	Safari Zone (Plains Area or Wetland Area: if Rock objects are placed, may appear in tall grass)
Pokémon SoulSilver	Safari Zone (Plains Area or Wetland Area: if Rock objects are placed, may appear in tall grass)
Pokémon Diamond	—
Pokémon Pearl	Level up Bagon to Lv. 30
Pokémon Platinum	Level up Bagon to Lv. 30

Pokémon HeartGold	**Pokémon SoulSilver**
It surrounds its body in an iron-hard shell to accumulate enough power to evolve.	It surrounds its body in an iron-hard shell to accumulate enough power to evolve.

⊛ EVOLUTION

Lv. 30   Lv. 50

Bagon   Shelgon   Salamence

● No. 373 | Dragon Pokémon
Salamence

Dragon Flying

● **HEIGHT:** 4'11"
● **WEIGHT:** 226.2 lbs.
● **ITEMS:** None

● SIZE COMPARISON

● MALE/FEMALE HAVE SAME FORM

● **ABILITIES**
● Intimidate

● **STATS**
HP ●●●●
ATTACK ●●●●●●●
DEFENSE ●●●
SP. ATTACK ●●●●●
SP. DEFENSE ●●●
SPEED ●●●●

● **EGG GROUPS**
Dragon

● **PERFORMANCE**

SPEED ★★★ STAMINA ★★☆
POWER ★★★★★ JUMP ★★★★★
SKILL ★★☆

● **MAIN WAYS TO OBTAIN**

Pokémon HeartGold | Level up Shelgon to Lv. 50

Pokémon SoulSilver | Level up Shelgon to Lv. 50

Pokémon Diamond | —

Pokémon Pearl | Level up Shelgon to Lv. 50

Pokémon Platinum | Level up Shelgon to Lv. 50

Pokémon HeartGold	Pokémon SoulSilver
It's uncontrollable if enraged. It flies around spouting flames and scorching fields and mountains.	It's uncontrollable if enraged. It flies around spouting flames and scorching fields and mountains.

● **EVOLUTION**

Lv. 30 → Lv. 50

Bagon → Shelgon → Salamence

● **LEVEL-UP MOVES**

Lv.	Name	Type	Kind	Pow.	Acc.	PP	Range	DA
1	Fire Fang	Fire	Physical	65	95	15	Normal	○
1	Thunder Fang	Electric	Physical	65	95	15	Normal	○
1	Rage	Normal	Physical	20	100	20	Normal	○
1	Bite	Dark	Physical	60	100	25	Normal	○
1	Leer	Normal	Status	—	100	30	2 Foes	—
1	Headbutt	Normal	Physical	70	100	15	Normal	○
5	Bite	Dark	Physical	60	100	25	Normal	○
10	Leer	Normal	Status	—	100	30	2 Foes	—
16	Headbutt	Normal	Physical	70	100	15	Normal	○
20	Focus Energy	Normal	Status	—	—	30	Self	—
25	Ember	Fire	Special	40	100	25	Normal	—
30	Protect	Normal	Status	—	—	10	Self	—
32	DragonBreath	Dragon	Special	60	100	20	Normal	—
37	Zen Headbutt	Psychic	Physical	80	90	15	Normal	○
43	Scary Face	Normal	Status	—	90	10	Normal	—
50	Fly	Flying	Physical	90	95	15	Normal	○
53	Crunch	Dark	Physical	80	100	15	Normal	○
61	Dragon Claw	Dragon	Physical	80	100	15	Normal	○
70	Double-Edge	Normal	Physical	120	100	15	Normal	○

● **MOVE MANIAC**

Name	Type	Kind	Pow.	Acc.	PP	Range	DA
Headbutt	Normal	Physical	70	100	15	Normal	○
Draco Meteor	Dragon	Special	140	90	5	Normal	—

● **BP MOVES**

Name	Type	Kind	Pow.	Acc.	PP	Range	DA
Fury Cutter	Bug	Physical	10	95	20	Normal	○
Ominous Wind	Ghost	Special	60	100	5	Normal	—
Air Cutter	Flying	Special	55	95	25	2 Foes	—
Zen Headbutt	Psychic	Physical	80	90	15	Normal	○
Snore	Normal	Special	40	100	15	Normal	—
Swift	Normal	Special	60	—	20	2 Foes	—
Tailwind	Flying	Status	—	—	30	2 Allies	—
Mud-Slap	Ground	Special	20	100	10	Normal	—
Rollout	Rock	Physical	30	90	20	Normal	○
Aqua Tail	Water	Physical	90	90	10	Normal	○
Outrage	Dragon	Physical	120	100	15	1 Random	○
Twister	Dragon	Special	40	100	20	2 Foes	—
Heat Wave	Fire	Special	100	90	10	2 Foes	—

● **TM & HM MOVES**

No.	Name	Type	Kind	Pow.	Acc.	PP	Range	DA
TM02	Dragon Claw	Dragon	Physical	80	100	15	Normal	○
TM05	Roar	Normal	Status	—	100	20	Normal	—
TM06	Toxic	Poison	Status	—	85	10	Normal	—
TM10	Hidden Power	Normal	Special	—	100	15	Normal	—
TM11	Sunny Day	Fire	Status	—	—	5	All	—
TM15	Hyper Beam	Normal	Special	150	90	5	Normal	—
TM17	Protect	Normal	Status	—	—	10	Self	—
TM18	Rain Dance	Water	Status	—	—	5	All	—
TM21	Frustration	Normal	Physical	—	100	20	Normal	○
TM23	Iron Tail	Steel	Physical	100	75	15	Normal	○
TM26	Earthquake	Ground	Physical	100	100	10	2 Foes/1 Ally	—
TM27	Return	Normal	Physical	—	100	20	Normal	○
TM31	Brick Break	Fighting	Physical	75	100	15	Normal	○
TM32	Double Team	Normal	Status	—	—	15	Self	—
TM35	Flamethrower	Fire	Special	95	100	15	Normal	—
TM38	Fire Blast	Fire	Special	120	85	5	Normal	—
TM39	Rock Tomb	Rock	Physical	50	80	10	Normal	—
TM40	Aerial Ace	Flying	Physical	60	—	20	Normal	○
TM42	Facade	Normal	Physical	70	100	20	Normal	○
TM43	Secret Power	Normal	Physical	70	100	20	Normal	—
TM44	Rest	Psychic	Status	—	—	10	Self	—
TM45	Attract	Normal	Status	—	100	15	Normal	—
TM47	Steel Wing	Steel	Physical	70	90	25	Normal	○
TM51	Roost	Flying	Status	—	—	10	Self	—
TM58	Endure	Normal	Status	—	—	10	Self	—
TM59	Dragon Pulse	Dragon	Special	90	100	10	Normal	—
TM65	Shadow Claw	Ghost	Physical	70	100	15	Normal	○
TM68	Giga Impact	Normal	Physical	150	90	5	Normal	○
TM71	Stone Edge	Rock	Physical	100	80	5	Normal	—
TM78	Captivate	Normal	Status	—	100	20	2 Foes	—
TM80	Rock Slide	Rock	Physical	75	90	10	2 Foes	—
TM82	Sleep Talk	Normal	Status	—	—	10	Depends	—
TM83	Natural Gift	Normal	Physical	—	100	15	Normal	—
TM87	Swagger	Normal	Status	—	90	15	Normal	—
TM90	Substitute	Normal	Status	—	—	10	Self	—
HM01	Cut	Normal	Physical	50	95	30	Normal	○
HM02	Fly	Flying	Physical	90	95	15	Normal	○
HM04	Strength	Normal	Physical	80	100	15	Normal	○
HM06	Rock Smash	Fighting	Physical	40	100	15	Normal	○

● LEVEL-UP MOVES

Lv.	Name	Type	Kind	Pow.	Acc.	PP	Range	DA
1	Take Down	Normal	Physical	90	85	20	Normal	○

● MOVE MANIAC

Name	Type	Kind	Pow.	Acc.	PP	Range	DA
Headbutt	Normal	Physical	70	100	15	Normal	○

● BP MOVES

Name	Type	Kind	Pow.	Acc.	PP	Range	DA
Zen Headbutt	Psychic	Physical	80	90	15	Normal	○
Iron Head	Steel	Physical	80	100	15	Normal	○
Iron Defense	Steel	Status	—	—	15	Self	—

● TM & HM MOVES

No.	Name	Type	Kind	Pow.	Acc.	PP	Range	DA

● No. 374 | Iron Ball Pokémon
Beldum

Steel **Psychic**

- ● HEIGHT: 2'00"
- ● WEIGHT: 209.9 lbs.
- ● ITEMS: Metal Coat

● SIZE COMPARISON

● GENDER UNKNOWN

⊙ ABILITIES
- ● Clear Body

⊙ EGG GROUPS
Mineral

⊙ STATS
- HP ●
- ATTACK ●●
- DEFENSE ●●●
- SP. ATTACK ●
- SP. DEFENSE ●●
- SPEED ●

⊙ PERFORMANCE
SPEED ★★★☆   STAMINA ★★★
POWER ★★★☆   JUMP ★★★☆
SKILL ★

● MAIN WAYS TO OBTAIN

| **Pokémon HeartGold** | Trade Forretress to Steven at Silph Co. in Saffron City |

| **Pokémon SoulSilver** | Trade Forretress to Steven at Silph Co. in Saffron City |

| **Pokémon Diamond** | Route 228 (mass outbreak) |

| **Pokémon Pearl** | Route 228 (mass outbreak) |

| **Pokémon Platinum** | Route 228 (mass outbreak) |

Pokémon HeartGold
The magnetic force generated by its body repels the ground's natural magnetism, letting it float.

Pokémon SoulSilver
The magnetic force generated by its body repels the ground's natural magnetism, letting it float.

⊙ EVOLUTION

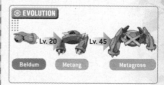

Beldum   Lv. 20   Metang   Lv. 45   Metagross

No. 375 | Iron Claw Pokémon
Metang

Steel **Psychic**

- **HEIGHT:** 3'11"
- **WEIGHT:** 446.4 lbs.
- **ITEMS:** Metal Coat

● SIZE COMPARISON

● GENDER UNKNOWN

⊙ ABILITIES
- Clear Body

⊙ EGG GROUPS
Mineral

⊙ STATS
HP	●●
ATTACK	●●●
DEFENSE	●●●●
SP. ATTACK	●●●
SP. DEFENSE	●●●
SPEED	●●

⊙ PERFORMANCE
SPEED ★★☆ STAMINA ★★★☆
POWER ★★★★ JUMP ★★★☆
SKILL ★★★

● MAIN WAYS TO OBTAIN

Pokémon HeartGold	Safari Zone (Mountain Area: if Rock objects are placed, may appear in tall grass)
Pokémon SoulSilver	Safari Zone (Mountain Area: if Rock objects are placed, may appear in tall grass)
Pokémon Diamond	Level up Beldum to Lv. 20
Pokémon Pearl	Level up Beldum to Lv. 20
Pokémon Platinum	Level up Beldum to Lv. 20

Pokémon HeartGold	**Pokémon SoulSilver**
When two BELDUM fuse together, a magnetic nervous system places their brains in union.	When two BELDUM fuse together, a magnetic nervous system places their brains in union.

⊙ EVOLUTION

Beldum — Lv. 20 — Metang — Lv. 45 — Metagross

● LEVEL-UP MOVES

Lv.	Name	Type	Kind	Pow.	Acc.	PP	Range	DA
1	Magnet Rise	Electric	Status	—	—	10	Self	—
1	Take Down	Normal	Physical	90	85	20	Normal	○
1	Metal Claw	Steel	Physical	50	95	35	Normal	○
1	Confusion	Psychic	Special	50	100	25	Normal	—
20	Metal Claw	Steel	Physical	50	95	35	Normal	○
20	Confusion	Psychic	Special	50	100	25	Normal	—
24	Scary Face	Normal	Status	—	90	10	Normal	—
28	Pursuit	Dark	Physical	40	100	20	Normal	○
32	Bullet Punch	Steel	Physical	40	100	30	Normal	○
36	Psychic	Psychic	Special	90	100	10	Normal	—
40	Iron Defense	Steel	Status	—	—	15	Self	—
44	Agility	Psychic	Status	—	—	30	Self	—
48	Meteor Mash	Steel	Physical	100	85	10	Normal	○
52	Zen Headbutt	Psychic	Physical	80	90	15	Normal	○
56	Hyper Beam	Normal	Special	150	90	5	Normal	—

● MOVE MANIAC

Name	Type	Kind	Pow.	Acc.	PP	Range	DA
Headbutt	Normal	Physical	70	100	15	Normal	○

● BP MOVES

Name	Type	Kind	Pow.	Acc.	PP	Range	DA
Fury Cutter	Bug	Physical	10	95	20	Normal	○
Icy Wind	Ice	Special	55	95	15	2 Foes	—
ThunderPunch	Electric	Physical	75	100	15	Normal	○
Ice Punch	Ice	Physical	75	100	15	Normal	○
Zen Headbutt	Psychic	Physical	80	90	15	Normal	○
Trick	Psychic	Status	—	100	10	Normal	—
Snore	Normal	Special	40	100	15	Normal	—
Magnet Rise	Electric	Status	—	—	10	Self	—
Swift	Normal	Special	60	—	20	2 Foes	—
Gravity	Psychic	Status	—	—	5	All	—
Mud-Slap	Ground	Special	20	100	10	Normal	—
Rollout	Rock	Physical	30	90	20	Normal	○
Iron Head	Steel	Physical	80	100	15	Normal	○
Signal Beam	Bug	Special	75	100	15	Normal	—
Iron Defense	Steel	Status	—	—	15	Self	—

● TM & HM MOVES

No.	Name	Type	Kind	Pow.	Acc.	PP	Range	DA
TM06	Toxic	Poison	Status	—	85	10	Normal	—
TM10	Hidden Power	Normal	Special	—	100	15	Normal	—
TM11	Sunny Day	Fire	Status	—	—	5	All	—
TM15	Hyper Beam	Normal	Special	150	90	5	Normal	—
TM16	Light Screen	Psychic	Status	—	—	30	2 Allies	—
TM17	Protect	Normal	Status	—	—	10	Self	—
TM18	Rain Dance	Water	Status	—	—	5	All	—
TM21	Frustration	Normal	Physical	—	100	20	Normal	○
TM26	Earthquake	Ground	Physical	100	100	10	2 Foes/1 Ally	—
TM27	Return	Normal	Physical	—	100	20	Normal	○
TM29	Psychic	Psychic	Special	90	100	10	Normal	—
TM30	Shadow Ball	Ghost	Special	80	100	15	Normal	—
TM31	Brick Break	Fighting	Physical	75	100	15	Normal	○
TM32	Double Team	Normal	Status	—	—	15	Self	—
TM33	Reflect	Psychic	Status	—	—	20	2 Allies	—
TM36	Sludge Bomb	Poison	Special	90	100	10	Normal	—
TM37	Sandstorm	Rock	Status	—	—	10	All	—
TM39	Rock Tomb	Rock	Physical	50	80	10	Normal	—
TM40	Aerial Ace	Flying	Physical	60	—	20	Normal	○
TM42	Facade	Normal	Physical	70	100	20	Normal	○
TM43	Secret Power	Normal	Physical	70	100	20	Normal	○
TM44	Rest	Psychic	Status	—	—	10	Self	—
TM58	Endure	Normal	Status	—	—	10	Self	—
TM64	Explosion	Normal	Physical	250	100	5	2 Foes/1 Ally	—
TM69	Rock Polish	Rock	Status	—	—	20	Self	—
TM70	Flash	Normal	Status	—	100	20	Normal	—
TM74	Gyro Ball	Steel	Physical	—	100	5	Normal	○
TM76	Stealth Rock	Rock	Status	—	—	20	2 Foes	—
TM77	Psych Up	Normal	Status	—	—	10	Normal	—
TM80	Rock Slide	Rock	Physical	75	90	10	2 Foes	—
TM82	Sleep Talk	Normal	Status	—	—	10	Depends	—
TM83	Natural Gift	Normal	Physical	—	100	15	Normal	—
TM86	Grass Knot	Grass	Special	—	100	20	Normal	○
TM87	Swagger	Normal	Status	—	90	15	Normal	—
TM90	Substitute	Normal	Status	—	—	10	Self	—
TM91	Flash Cannon	Steel	Special	80	100	10	Normal	—
HM01	Cut	Normal	Physical	50	95	30	Normal	○
HM04	Strength	Normal	Physical	80	100	15	Normal	○
HM06	Rock Smash	Fighting	Physical	40	100	15	Normal	○

● LEVEL-UP MOVES

Lv.	Name	Type	Kind	Pow.	Acc.	PP	Range	DA
1	Magnet Rise	Electric	Status	—	—	10	Self	—
1	Take Down	Normal	Physical	90	85	20	Normal	○
1	Metal Claw	Steel	Physical	50	95	35	Normal	○
1	Confusion	Psychic	Special	50	100	25	Normal	—
20	Metal Claw	Steel	Physical	50	95	35	Normal	○
20	Confusion	Psychic	Special	50	100	25	Normal	—
24	Scary Face	Normal	Status	—	90	10	Normal	—
28	Pursuit	Dark	Physical	40	100	20	Normal	○
32	Bullet Punch	Steel	Physical	40	100	30	Normal	○
36	Psychic	Psychic	Special	90	100	10	Normal	—
40	Iron Defense	Steel	Status	—	—	15	Self	—
44	Agility	Psychic	Status	—	—	30	Self	—
45	Hammer Arm	Fighting	Physical	100	90	10	Normal	—
53	Meteor Mash	Steel	Physical	100	85	10	Normal	○
62	Zen Headbutt	Psychic	Physical	80	90	15	Normal	—
71	Hyper Beam	Normal	Special	150	90	5	Normal	—

● MOVE MANIAC

Name	Type	Kind	Pow.	Acc.	PP	Range	DA
Headbutt	Normal	Physical	70	100	15	Normal	○

● BP MOVES

Name	Type	Kind	Pow.	Acc.	PP	Range	DA
Fury Cutter	Bug	Physical	10	95	20	Normal	○
Icy Wind	Ice	Special	55	95	15	2 Foes	—
ThunderPunch	Electric	Physical	75	100	15	Normal	○
Ice Punch	Ice	Physical	75	100	15	Normal	○
Zen Headbutt	Psychic	Physical	80	90	15	Normal	—
Trick	Psychic	Status	—	100	10	Normal	—
Snore	Normal	Special	40	100	15	Normal	—
Magnet Rise	Electric	Status	—	—	10	Self	—
Swift	Normal	Special	60	—	20	2 Foes	—
Gravity	Psychic	Status	—	—	5	All	—
Block	Normal	Status	—	—	5	Normal	—
Mud-Slap	Ground	Special	20	100	10	Normal	—
Rollout	Rock	Physical	30	90	20	Normal	○
Iron Head	Steel	Physical	80	100	15	Normal	○
Signal Beam	Bug	Special	75	100	15	Normal	—
Iron Defense	Steel	Status	—	—	15	Self	—

● TM & HM MOVES

No.	Name	Type	Kind	Pow.	Acc.	PP	Range	DA
TM06	Toxic	Poison	Status	—	85	10	Normal	—
TM10	Hidden Power	Normal	Special	—	100	15	Normal	—
TM11	Sunny Day	Fire	Status	—	—	5	All	—
TM15	Hyper Beam	Normal	Special	150	90	5	Normal	—
TM16	Light Screen	Psychic	Status	—	—	30	2 Allies	—
TM17	Protect	Normal	Status	—	—	10	Self	—
TM18	Rain Dance	Water	Status	—	—	5	All	—
TM21	Frustration	Normal	Physical	—	100	20	Normal	○
TM26	Earthquake	Ground	Physical	100	100	10	2 Foes/1 Ally	○
TM27	Return	Normal	Physical	—	100	20	Normal	○
TM29	Psychic	Psychic	Special	90	100	10	Normal	—
TM30	Shadow Ball	Ghost	Special	80	100	15	Normal	—
TM31	Brick Break	Fighting	Physical	75	100	15	Normal	○
TM32	Double Team	Normal	Status	—	—	15	Self	—
TM33	Reflect	Psychic	Status	—	—	20	2 Allies	—
TM36	Sludge Bomb	Poison	Special	90	100	10	Normal	—
TM37	Sandstorm	Rock	Status	—	—	10	All	—
TM39	Rock Tomb	Rock	Physical	50	80	10	Normal	—
TM40	Aerial Ace	Flying	Physical	60	—	20	Normal	○
TM42	Facade	Normal	Physical	70	100	20	Normal	○
TM43	Secret Power	Normal	Physical	70	100	20	Normal	—
TM44	Rest	Psychic	Status	—	—	10	Self	—
TM58	Endure	Normal	Status	—	—	10	Self	—
TM64	Explosion	Normal	Physical	250	100	5	2 Foes/1 Ally	—
TM68	Giga Impact	Normal	Physical	150	90	5	Normal	○
TM69	Rock Polish	Rock	Status	—	—	20	Self	—
TM70	Flash	Normal	Status	—	100	20	Normal	—
TM74	Gyro Ball	Steel	Physical	—	100	5	Normal	○
TM76	Stealth Rock	Rock	Status	—	—	20	2 Foes	—
TM77	Psych Up	Normal	Status	—	—	10	Normal	—
TM80	Rock Slide	Rock	Physical	75	90	10	2 Foes	—
TM82	Sleep Talk	Normal	Status	—	—	10	Depends	—
TM83	Natural Gift	Normal	Physical	—	100	15	Normal	—
TM86	Grass Knot	Grass	Special	—	100	20	Normal	—
TM87	Swagger	Normal	Status	—	90	15	Normal	—
TM90	Substitute	Normal	Status	—	—	10	Self	—
TM91	Flash Cannon	Steel	Special	80	100	10	Normal	—
HM01	Cut	Normal	Physical	50	95	30	Normal	○
HM04	Strength	Normal	Physical	80	100	15	Normal	○
HM06	Rock Smash	Fighting	Physical	40	100	15	Normal	○

⊙ No. 376 | Iron Leg Pokémon
Metagross

Steel   Psychic

- **HEIGHT:** 5'03"
- **WEIGHT:** 1,212.5 lbs.
- **ITEMS:** None

● SIZE COMPARISON

● GENDER UNKNOWN

⊙ ABILITIES
- Clear Body

⊙ STATS
HP	●●●
ATTACK	●●●●●●
DEFENSE	●●●●●
SP. ATTACK	●●●●●
SP. DEFENSE	●●●●
SPEED	●●●

⊙ EGG GROUPS
Mineral

⊙ PERFORMANCE

SPEED ★☆   STAMINA ★★★★☆
POWER ★★★★☆   JUMP ★★
SKILL ★★★★

● MAIN WAYS TO OBTAIN

Pokémon HeartGold — Level up Metang to Lv. 45

Pokémon SoulSilver — Level up Metang to Lv. 45

Pokémon Diamond — Level up Metang to Lv. 45

Pokémon Pearl — Level up Metang to Lv. 45

Pokémon Platinum — Level up Metang to Lv. 45

Pokémon HeartGold	**Pokémon SoulSilver**
It folds its four legs when flying. Its four brains are said to be superior to a supercomputer.	It folds its four legs when flying. Its four brains are said to be superior to a supercomputer.

⊙ EVOLUTION

Lv. 20   Lv. 45

Beldum   Metang   Metagross

No. 377 | Rock Peak Pokémon
Regirock

Rock

● HEIGHT: 5'07"
● WEIGHT: 507.1 lbs.
● ITEMS: None

● SIZE COMPARISON

● GENDER UNKNOWN

⊛ ABILITIES
● Clear Body

⊛ EGG GROUPS
No Egg has ever been discovered

⊛ STATS
HP ●●●
ATTACK ●●●●
DEFENSE ●●●●●●
SP. ATTACK ●●●●
SP. DEFENSE ●●●●
SPEED ●●

⊛ PERFORMANCE
SPEED ★★
POWER ★★★★★
SKILL ★★★★☆
STAMINA ★★★★★
JUMP ★★

● MAIN WAYS TO OBTAIN

Pokémon HeartGold	—
Pokémon SoulSilver	—
Pokémon Diamond	—
Pokémon Pearl	—
Pokémon Platinum	Put the special Lv. 100 Regigigas in your party and go to the cave on Route 228*

| Pokémon HeartGold | Pokémon SoulSilver |
| The same rocks that form its body have been found in ground layers around the world. | The same rocks that form its body have been found in ground layers around the world. |

⊛ EVOLUTION
Does not evolve

● LEVEL-UP MOVES

Lv.	Name	Type	Kind	Pow.	Acc.	PP	Range	DA
1	Explosion	Normal	Physical	250	100	5	2 Foes/1 Ally	—
1	Stomp	Normal	Physical	65	100	20	Normal	○
9	Rock Throw	Rock	Physical	50	90	15	Normal	—
17	Curse	???	Status	—	—	10	Normal/Self	—
25	Superpower	Fighting	Physical	120	100	5	Normal	○
33	AncientPower	Rock	Special	60	100	5	Normal	—
41	Iron Defense	Steel	Status	—	—	15	Self	—
49	Charge Beam	Electric	Special	50	90	10	Normal	—
57	Lock-On	Normal	Status	—	—	5	Normal	—
65	Zap Cannon	Electric	Special	120	50	5	Normal	—
73	Stone Edge	Rock	Physical	100	80	5	Normal	—
81	Hammer Arm	Fighting	Physical	100	90	10	Normal	○
89	Hyper Beam	Normal	Special	150	90	5	Normal	—

● MOVE MANIAC

Name	Type	Kind	Pow.	Acc.	PP	Range	DA
Headbutt	Normal	Physical	70	100	15	Normal	○

● BP MOVES

Name	Type	Kind	Pow.	Acc.	PP	Range	DA
ThunderPunch	Electric	Physical	75	100	15	Normal	○
Fire Punch	Fire	Physical	75	100	15	Normal	○
Ice Punch	Ice	Physical	75	100	15	Normal	○
Snore	Normal	Special	40	100	15	Normal	—
Gravity	Psychic	Status	—	—	5	All	—
Block	Normal	Status	—	—	5	Normal	—
Mud-Slap	Ground	Special	20	100	10	Normal	○
Rollout	Rock	Physical	30	90	20	Normal	○
Superpower	Fighting	Physical	120	100	5	Normal	○
Iron Head	Steel	Physical	80	100	15	Normal	○
AncientPower	Rock	Special	60	100	5	Normal	—
Earth Power	Ground	Special	90	100	10	Normal	—

● TM & HM MOVES

No.	Name	Type	Kind	Pow.	Acc.	PP	Range	DA
TM01	Focus Punch	Fighting	Physical	150	100	20	Normal	○
TM06	Toxic	Poison	Status	—	85	10	Normal	—
TM10	Hidden Power	Normal	Special	—	100	15	Normal	—
TM11	Sunny Day	Fire	Status	—	—	5	All	—
TM15	Hyper Beam	Normal	Special	150	90	5	Normal	—
TM17	Protect	Normal	Status	—	—	10	Self	—
TM20	Safeguard	Normal	Status	—	—	25	2 Allies	—
TM21	Frustration	Normal	Physical	—	100	20	Normal	○
TM24	Thunderbolt	Electric	Special	95	100	15	Normal	—
TM25	Thunder	Electric	Special	120	70	10	Normal	—
TM26	Earthquake	Ground	Physical	100	100	10	2 Foes/1 Ally	—
TM27	Return	Normal	Physical	—	100	20	Normal	○
TM28	Dig	Ground	Physical	80	100	10	Normal	○
TM31	Brick Break	Fighting	Physical	75	100	15	Normal	○
TM32	Double Team	Normal	Status	—	—	15	Self	—
TM34	Shock Wave	Electric	Special	60	—	20	Normal	—
TM37	Sandstorm	Rock	Status	—	—	10	All	—
TM39	Rock Tomb	Rock	Physical	50	80	10	Normal	—
TM42	Facade	Normal	Physical	70	100	20	Normal	○
TM43	Secret Power	Normal	Physical	70	100	20	Normal	—
TM44	Rest	Psychic	Status	—	—	10	Self	—
TM52	Focus Blast	Fighting	Special	120	70	5	Normal	—
TM56	Fling	Dark	Physical	—	100	10	Normal	—
TM57	Charge Beam	Electric	Special	50	90	10	Normal	—
TM58	Endure	Normal	Status	—	—	10	Self	—
TM60	Drain Punch	Fighting	Physical	60	100	5	Normal	○
TM64	Explosion	Normal	Physical	250	100	5	2 Foes/1 Ally	—
TM68	Giga Impact	Normal	Physical	150	90	5	Normal	○
TM69	Rock Polish	Rock	Status	—	—	20	Self	—
TM71	Stone Edge	Rock	Physical	100	80	5	Normal	—
TM73	Thunder Wave	Electric	Status	—	100	20	Normal	—
TM76	Stealth Rock	Rock	Status	—	—	20	2 Foes	—
TM77	Psych Up	Normal	Status	—	—	10	Normal	—
TM80	Rock Slide	Rock	Physical	75	90	10	2 Foes	—
TM82	Sleep Talk	Normal	Status	—	—	10	Depends	—
TM83	Natural Gift	Normal	Physical	—	100	15	Normal	—
TM87	Swagger	Normal	Status	—	90	15	Normal	—
TM90	Substitute	Normal	Status	—	—	10	Self	—
HM04	Strength	Normal	Physical	80	100	15	Normal	○
HM06	Rock Smash	Fighting	Physical	40	100	15	Normal	○
HM08	Rock Climb	Normal	Physical	90	85	20	Normal	○

*The special Lv. 100 Regigigas is only available through special distribution events. Check Pokemon.com for the latest information on how to catch this Pokémon.

● LEVEL-UP MOVES

Lv.	Name	Type	Kind	Pow.	Acc.	PP	Range	DA
1	Explosion	Normal	Physical	250	100	5	2 Foes/1 Ally	—
1	Stomp	Normal	Physical	65	100	20	Normal	○
9	Icy Wind	Ice	Special	55	95	15	2 Foes	—
17	Curse	???	Status	—	—	10	Normal/Self	—
25	Superpower	Fighting	Physical	120	100	5	Normal	○
33	AncientPower	Rock	Special	60	100	5	Normal	—
41	Amnesia	Psychic	Status	—	—	20	Self	—
49	Charge Beam	Electric	Special	50	90	10	Normal	—
57	Lock-On	Normal	Status	—	—	5	Normal	—
65	Zap Cannon	Electric	Special	120	50	5	Normal	—
73	Ice Beam	Ice	Special	95	100	10	Normal	—
81	Hammer Arm	Fighting	Physical	100	90	10	Normal	○
89	Hyper Beam	Normal	Special	150	90	5	Normal	—

● MOVE MANIAC

Name	Type	Kind	Pow.	Acc.	PP	Range	DA
Headbutt	Normal	Physical	70	100	15	Normal	○

● BP MOVES

Name	Type	Kind	Pow.	Acc.	PP	Range	DA
Icy Wind	Ice	Special	55	95	15	2 Foes	—
ThunderPunch	Electric	Physical	75	100	15	Normal	○
Ice Punch	Ice	Physical	75	100	15	Normal	○
Snore	Normal	Special	40	100	15	Normal	—
Gravity	Psychic	Status	—	—	5	All	—
Block	Normal	Status	—	—	5	Normal	—
Mud-Slap	Ground	Special	20	100	10	Normal	—
Rollout	Rock	Physical	30	90	20	Normal	○
Superpower	Fighting	Physical	120	100	5	Normal	○
Iron Head	Steel	Physical	80	100	15	Normal	○
AncientPower	Rock	Special	60	100	5	Normal	—
Signal Beam	Bug	Special	75	100	15	Normal	—

● TM & HM MOVES

No.	Name	Type	Kind	Pow.	Acc.	PP	Range	DA
TM01	Focus Punch	Fighting	Physical	150	100	20	Normal	○
TM06	Toxic	Poison	Status	—	85	10	Normal	—
TM07	Hail	Ice	Status	—	—	10	All	—
TM10	Hidden Power	Normal	Special	—	100	15	Normal	—
TM13	Ice Beam	Ice	Special	95	100	10	Normal	—
TM14	Blizzard	Ice	Special	120	70	5	2 Foes	—
TM15	Hyper Beam	Normal	Special	150	90	5	Normal	—
TM17	Protect	Normal	Status	—	—	10	Self	—
TM18	Rain Dance	Water	Status	—	—	5	All	—
TM20	Safeguard	Normal	Status	—	—	25	2 Allies	—
TM21	Frustration	Normal	Physical	—	100	20	Normal	○
TM24	Thunderbolt	Electric	Special	95	100	15	Normal	—
TM25	Thunder	Electric	Special	120	70	10	Normal	—
TM26	Earthquake	Ground	Physical	100	100	10	2 Foes/1 Ally	—
TM27	Return	Normal	Physical	—	100	20	Normal	○
TM31	Brick Break	Fighting	Physical	75	100	15	Normal	○
TM32	Double Team	Normal	Status	—	—	15	Self	—
TM34	Shock Wave	Electric	Special	60	—	20	Normal	—
TM39	Rock Tomb	Rock	Physical	50	80	10	Normal	—
TM42	Facade	Normal	Physical	70	100	20	Normal	○
TM43	Secret Power	Normal	Physical	70	100	20	Normal	○
TM44	Rest	Psychic	Status	—	—	10	Self	—
TM52	Focus Blast	Fighting	Special	120	70	5	Normal	—
TM56	Fling	Dark	Physical	—	100	10	Normal	○
TM57	Charge Beam	Electric	Special	50	90	10	Normal	—
TM58	Endure	Normal	Status	—	—	10	Self	—
TM64	Explosion	Normal	Physical	250	100	5	2 Foes/1 Ally	—
TM68	Giga Impact	Normal	Physical	150	90	5	Normal	○
TM69	Rock Polish	Rock	Status	—	—	20	Self	—
TM72	Avalanche	Ice	Physical	60	100	10	Normal	○
TM73	Thunder Wave	Electric	Status	—	100	20	Normal	—
TM77	Psych Up	Normal	Status	—	—	10	Normal	—
TM80	Rock Slide	Rock	Physical	75	90	10	2 Foes	—
TM82	Sleep Talk	Normal	Status	—	—	10	Self	—
TM83	Natural Gift	Normal	Physical	—	100	15	Normal	—
TM87	Swagger	Normal	Status	—	90	15	Normal	—
TM90	Substitute	Normal	Status	—	—	10	Self	—
TM91	Flash Cannon	Steel	Special	80	100	10	Normal	—
HM04	Strength	Normal	Physical	80	100	15	Normal	○
HM06	Rock Smash	Fighting	Physical	40	100	15	Normal	○
HM08	Rock Climb	Normal	Physical	90	85	20	Normal	○

◉ No. 378 | Iceberg Pokémon
Regice

Ice

- ● HEIGHT: 5'11"
- ● WEIGHT: 385.8 lbs.
- ● ITEMS: None

● SIZE COMPARISON

● GENDER UNKNOWN

◈ ABILITIES
- ● Clear Body

◈ STATS
- HP ●●●
- ATTACK ●●●
- DEFENSE ●●●●●
- SP. ATTACK ●●●●
- SP. DEFENSE ●●●●●●
- SPEED ●●

◈ EGG GROUPS
No Egg has ever been discovered

◈ PERFORMANCE

SPEED ★★		STAMINA ★★★★★
POWER ★★★☆		JUMP ★★★
SKILL ★★★★★		

● MAIN WAYS TO OBTAIN

Pokémon HeartGold

Pokémon SoulSilver

Pokémon Diamond

Pokémon Pearl

Pokémon Platinum — Put the special Lv. 100 Regigigas in your party and go to Mt. Coronet 1F*

Pokémon HeartGold — It is said to have slept in a glacier for thousands of years. Its body can't be melted, even by magma.

Pokémon SoulSilver — It is said to have slept in a glacier for thousands of years. Its body can't be melted, even by magma.

◈ EVOLUTION

Does not evolve

---

*The special Lv. 100 Regigigas is only available through special distribution events. Check Pokemon.com for the latest information on how to catch this Pokémon.

● No. 379 | Iron Pokémon

Registeel

Steel

● HEIGHT: 6'03"
● WEIGHT: 451.9 lbs.
● ITEMS: None

● SIZE COMPARISON

● GENDER UNKNOWN

⚙ ABILITIES
● Clear Body

⚙ STATS
HP ●●●
ATTACK ●●●
DEFENSE ●●●●●●
SP. ATTACK ●●●
SP. DEFENSE ●●●●●●
SPEED ●●

⚙ EGG GROUPS
No Egg has ever been discovered

⚙ PERFORMANCE
SPEED ★★
POWER ★★★★☆
SKILL ★★★★★
STAMINA ★★★★★
JUMP ★★

● MAIN WAYS TO OBTAIN

Pokémon HeartGold —

Pokémon SoulSilver —

Pokémon Diamond —

Pokémon Pearl —

Pokémon Platinum
Put the special Lv. 100 Regigigas in your party and go to Iron Island B3F*

Pokémon HeartGold
Its body is said to be harder than any kind of metal. A study has revealed that its body is hollow.

Pokémon SoulSilver
Its body is said to be harder than any kind of metal. A study has revealed that its body is hollow.

⚙ EVOLUTION

Does not evolve

● LEVEL-UP MOVES

Lv.	Name	Type	Kind	Pow.	Acc.	PP	Range	DA
1	Explosion	Normal	Physical	250	100	5	2 Foes/1 Ally	—
1	Stomp	Normal	Physical	65	100	20	Normal	○
9	Metal Claw	Steel	Physical	50	95	35	Normal	○
17	Curse	???	Status	—	—	10	Normal/Self	—
25	Superpower	Fighting	Physical	120	100	5	Normal	○
33	AncientPower	Rock	Special	60	100	5	Normal	—
41	Iron Defense	Steel	Status	—	—	15	Self	—
41	Amnesia	Psychic	Status	—	—	20	Self	—
49	Charge Beam	Electric	Special	50	90	10	Normal	—
57	Lock-On	Normal	Status	—	—	5	Normal	—
65	Zap Cannon	Electric	Special	120	50	5	Normal	—
73	Iron Head	Steel	Physical	80	100	15	Normal	○
73	Flash Cannon	Steel	Special	80	100	10	Normal	—
81	Hammer Arm	Fighting	Physical	100	90	10	Normal	○
89	Hyper Beam	Normal	Special	150	90	5	Normal	—

● MOVE MANIAC

Name	Type	Kind	Pow.	Acc.	PP	Range	DA
Headbutt	Normal	Physical	70	100	15	Normal	○

● BP MOVES

Name	Type	Kind	Pow.	Acc.	PP	Range	DA
ThunderPunch	Electric	Physical	75	100	15	Normal	○
Ice Punch	Ice	Physical	75	100	15	Normal	○
Snore	Normal	Special	40	100	15	Normal	—
Magnet Rise	Electric	Status	—	—	10	Self	—
Gravity	Psychic	Status	—	—	5	All	—
Block	Normal	Status	—	—	5	Normal	—
Mud-Slap	Ground	Special	20	100	10	Normal	—
Rollout	Rock	Physical	30	90	20	Normal	○
Superpower	Fighting	Physical	120	100	5	Normal	○
Iron Head	Steel	Physical	80	100	15	Normal	○
AncientPower	Rock	Special	60	100	5	Normal	—
Iron Defense	Steel	Status	—	—	15	Self	—

● TM & HM MOVES

No.	Name	Type	Kind	Pow.	Acc.	PP	Range	DA
TM01	Focus Punch	Fighting	Physical	150	100	20	Normal	○
TM06	Toxic	Poison	Status	—	85	10	Normal	—
TM10	Hidden Power	Normal	Special	—	100	15	Normal	—
TM11	Sunny Day	Fire	Status	—	—	5	All	—
TM15	Hyper Beam	Normal	Special	150	90	5	Normal	—
TM17	Protect	Normal	Status	—	—	10	Self	—
TM18	Rain Dance	Water	Status	—	—	5	All	—
TM20	Safeguard	Normal	Status	—	—	25	2 Allies	—
TM21	Frustration	Normal	Physical	—	100	20	Normal	○
TM24	Thunderbolt	Electric	Special	95	100	15	Normal	—
TM25	Thunder	Electric	Special	120	70	10	Normal	—
TM26	Earthquake	Ground	Physical	100	100	10	2 Foes/1 Ally	—
TM27	Return	Normal	Physical	—	100	20	Normal	○
TM31	Brick Break	Fighting	Physical	75	100	15	Normal	○
TM32	Double Team	Normal	Status	—	—	15	Self	—
TM34	Shock Wave	Electric	Special	60	—	20	Normal	—
TM37	Sandstorm	Rock	Status	—	—	10	All	—
TM39	Rock Tomb	Rock	Physical	50	80	10	Normal	—
TM40	Aerial Ace	Flying	Physical	60	—	20	Normal	○
TM42	Facade	Normal	Physical	70	100	20	Normal	—
TM43	Secret Power	Normal	Physical	70	100	20	Normal	—
TM44	Rest	Psychic	Status	—	—	10	Self	—
TM52	Focus Blast	Fighting	Special	120	70	5	Normal	—
TM56	Fling	Dark	Physical	—	100	10	Normal	—
TM57	Charge Beam	Electric	Special	50	90	10	Normal	—
TM58	Endure	Normal	Status	—	—	10	Self	—
TM64	Explosion	Normal	Physical	250	100	5	2 Foes/1 Ally	—
TM65	Shadow Claw	Ghost	Physical	70	100	15	Normal	○
TM68	Giga Impact	Normal	Physical	150	90	5	Normal	○
TM69	Rock Polish	Rock	Status	—	—	20	Self	—
TM73	Thunder Wave	Electric	Status	—	100	20	Normal	—
TM76	Stealth Rock	Rock	Status	—	—	20	2 Foes	—
TM77	Psych Up	Normal	Status	—	—	10	Normal	—
TM80	Rock Slide	Rock	Physical	75	90	10	2 Foes	—
TM82	Sleep Talk	Normal	Status	—	—	10	Depends	—
TM83	Natural Gift	Normal	Physical	—	100	15	Normal	—
TM87	Swagger	Normal	Status	—	90	15	Normal	—
TM90	Substitute	Normal	Status	—	—	10	Self	—
TM91	Flash Cannon	Steel	Special	80	100	10	Normal	—
HM04	Strength	Normal	Physical	80	100	15	Normal	○
HM06	Rock Smash	Fighting	Physical	40	100	15	Normal	○
HM08	Rock Climb	Normal	Physical	90	85	20	Normal	○

*The special Lv. 100 Regigigas is only available through special distribution events. Check Pokemon.com for the latest information on how to catch this Pokémon.

● LEVEL-UP MOVES

Lv.	Name	Type	Kind	Pow.	Acc.	PP	Range	DA
1	Psywave	Psychic	Special	—	80	15	Normal	—
5	Wish	Normal	Status	—	—	10	Self	—
10	Helping Hand	Normal	Status	—	—	20	1 Ally	—
15	Safeguard	Normal	Status	—	—	25	2 Allies	—
20	DragonBreath	Dragon	Special	60	100	20	Normal	—
25	Water Sport	Water	Status	—	—	15	All	—
30	Refresh	Normal	Status	—	—	20	Self	—
35	Mist Ball	Psychic	Special	70	100	5	Normal	—
40	Zen Headbutt	Psychic	Physical	80	90	15	Normal	○
45	Recover	Normal	Status	—	—	10	Self	—
50	Psycho Shift	Psychic	Status	—	90	10	Normal	—
55	Charm	Normal	Status	—	100	20	Normal	—
60	Healing Wish	Psychic	Status	—	—	10	Self	—
65	Psychic	Psychic	Special	90	100	10	Normal	—
70	Dragon Pulse	Dragon	Special	90	100	10	Normal	—

● MOVE MANIAC

Name	Type	Kind	Pow.	Acc.	PP	Range	DA
Draco Meteor	Dragon	Special	140	90	5	Normal	—

● BP MOVES

Name	Type	Kind	Pow.	Acc.	PP	Range	DA
Dive	Water	Physical	80	100	10	Normal	○
Fury Cutter	Bug	Physical	10	95	20	Normal	○
Icy Wind	Ice	Special	55	95	15	2 Foes	—
Zen Headbutt	Psychic	Physical	80	90	15	Normal	○
Trick	Psychic	Status	—	100	10	Normal	—
Sucker Punch	Dark	Physical	80	100	5	Normal	○
Snore	Normal	Special	40	100	15	Normal	—
Helping Hand	Normal	Status	—	—	20	1 Ally	—
Last Resort	Normal	Physical	130	100	5	Normal	○
Swift	Normal	Special	60	—	20	2 Foes	—
Tailwind	Flying	Status	—	—	30	2 Allies	—
Magic Coat	Psychic	Status	—	—	15	Self	—
Role Play	Psychic	Status	—	—	10	Normal	—
Mud-Slap	Ground	Special	20	100	10	Normal	—
Outrage	Dragon	Physical	120	100	15	1 Random	○
Twister	Dragon	Special	40	100	20	2 Foes	—

● TM & HM MOVES

No.	Name	Type	Kind	Pow.	Acc.	PP	Range	DA
TM02	Dragon Claw	Dragon	Physical	80	100	15	Normal	○
TM03	Water Pulse	Water	Special	60	100	20	Normal	—
TM04	Calm Mind	Psychic	Status	—	—	20	Self	—
TM05	Roar	Normal	Status	—	100	20	Normal	—
TM06	Toxic	Poison	Status	—	85	10	Normal	—
TM10	Hidden Power	Normal	Special	—	100	15	Normal	—
TM11	Sunny Day	Fire	Status	—	—	5	All	—
TM13	Ice Beam	Ice	Special	95	100	10	Normal	—
TM15	Hyper Beam	Normal	Special	150	90	5	Normal	—
TM16	Light Screen	Psychic	Status	—	—	30	2 Allies	—
TM17	Protect	Normal	Status	—	—	10	Self	—
TM18	Rain Dance	Water	Status	—	—	5	All	—
TM20	Safeguard	Normal	Status	—	—	25	2 Allies	—
TM21	Frustration	Normal	Physical	—	100	20	Normal	○
TM22	SolarBeam	Grass	Special	120	100	10	Normal	—
TM24	Thunderbolt	Electric	Special	95	100	15	Normal	—
TM25	Thunder	Electric	Special	120	70	10	Normal	—
TM26	Earthquake	Ground	Physical	100	100	10	2 Foes/1 Ally	—
TM27	Return	Normal	Physical	—	100	20	Normal	○
TM29	Psychic	Psychic	Special	90	100	10	Normal	—
TM30	Shadow Ball	Ghost	Special	80	100	15	Normal	—
TM32	Double Team	Normal	Status	—	—	15	Self	—
TM33	Reflect	Psychic	Status	—	—	20	2 Allies	—
TM34	Shock Wave	Electric	Special	60	—	20	Normal	—
TM37	Sandstorm	Rock	Status	—	—	10	All	—
TM40	Aerial Ace	Flying	Physical	60	—	20	Normal	○
TM42	Facade	Normal	Physical	70	100	20	Normal	○
TM43	Secret Power	Normal	Physical	70	100	20	Normal	○
TM44	Rest	Psychic	Status	—	—	10	Self	—
TM45	Attract	Normal	Status	—	100	15	Normal	—
TM47	Steel Wing	Steel	Physical	70	90	25	Normal	○
TM51	Roost	Flying	Status	—	—	10	Self	—
TM53	Energy Ball	Grass	Special	80	100	10	Normal	—
TM57	Charge Beam	Electric	Special	50	90	10	Normal	—
TM58	Endure	Normal	Status	—	—	10	Self	—
TM59	Dragon Pulse	Dragon	Special	90	100	10	Normal	—
TM65	Shadow Claw	Ghost	Physical	70	100	15	Normal	○
TM68	Giga Impact	Normal	Physical	150	90	5	Normal	○
TM70	Flash	Normal	Status	—	100	20	Normal	—
TM73	Thunder Wave	Electric	Status	—	100	20	Normal	—
TM77	Psych Up	Normal	Status	—	—	10	Normal	—
TM78	Captivate	Normal	Status	—	100	20	2 Foes	—
TM82	Sleep Talk	Normal	Status	—	—	10	Depends	—
TM83	Natural Gift	Normal	Physical	—	100	15	Normal	—
TM85	Dream Eater	Psychic	Special	100	100	15	Normal	—
TM86	Grass Knot	Grass	Special	—	100	20	Normal	○
TM87	Swagger	Normal	Status	—	90	15	Normal	—
TM90	Substitute	Normal	Status	—	—	10	Self	—
HM01	Cut	Normal	Physical	50	95	30	Normal	○
HM02	Fly	Flying	Physical	90	95	15	Normal	○
HM03	Surf	Water	Special	95	100	15	2 Foes/1 Ally	—
HM05	Whirlpool	Water	Special	15	70	15	Normal	—
HM07	Waterfall	Water	Physical	80	100	15	Normal	○

Latias

Dragon　Psychic

● HEIGHT: 4'07"
● WEIGHT: 88.2 lbs.
● ITEMS: None

● SIZE COMPARISON

● FEMALE FORM

● ABILITIES
● Levitate

● STATS
HP ●●●
ATTACK ●●●
DEFENSE ●●●●
SP. ATTACK ●●●●●
SP. DEFENSE ●●●●●
SPEED ●●●●●

● EGG GROUPS
No Egg has ever been discovered

● PERFORMANCE

SPEED ★★★★★　　STAMINA ★★☆
POWER ★★★☆　　JUMP ★★★★★
SKILL ★★★★☆

● MAIN WAYS TO OBTAIN

Pokémon HeartGold	Starts roaming the Kanto region after you talk to Steven at the Pokémon Fan Club in Vermilion City
Pokémon SoulSilver	—
Pokémon Diamond	
Pokémon Pearl	
Pokémon Platinum	

Pokémon HeartGold	Pokémon SoulSilver
It communicates using telepathy. Its body is covered in down that refracts light to make it invisible.	It communicates using telepathy. Its body is covered in down that refracts light to make it invisible.

● EVOLUTION

Does not evolve

● No. 381 | Eon Pokémon
Latios

Dragon | Psychic

- **HEIGHT:** 6'07"
- **WEIGHT:** 132.3 lbs.
- **ITEMS:** None

● SIZE COMPARISON

● MALE FORM

● ABILITIES
- Levitate

● STATS
HP	●●●
ATTACK	●●●●
DEFENSE	●●●●
SP. ATTACK	●●●●●●
SP. DEFENSE	●●●●●
SPEED	●●●●●

● EGG GROUPS
No Egg has ever been discovered

● PERFORMANCE
SPEED ★★★★☆	STAMINA ★★☆
POWER ★★★☆	JUMP ★★★★★
SKILL ★★★★★	

● MAIN WAYS TO OBTAIN

Pokémon HeartGold — —

Pokémon SoulSilver — Starts roaming the Kanto region after you talk to Steven at the Pokémon Fan Club in Vermilion City

Pokémon Diamond — —

Pokémon Pearl — —

Pokémon Platinum — —

Pokémon HeartGold — It understands human speech and is highly intelligent. It is a tender Pokémon that dislikes fighting.

Pokémon SoulSilver — It understands human speech and is highly intelligent. It is a tender Pokémon that dislikes fighting.

● EVOLUTION
Does not evolve

● LEVEL-UP MOVES
Lv.	Name	Type	Kind	Pow.	Acc.	PP	Range	DA
1	Psywave	Psychic	Special	—	80	15	Normal	—
5	Heal Block	Psychic	Status	—	100	15	2 Foes	—
10	Helping Hand	Normal	Status	—	—	20	1 Ally	—
15	Safeguard	Normal	Status	—	—	25	2 Allies	—
20	DragonBreath	Dragon	Special	60	100	20	Normal	—
25	Protect	Normal	Status	—	—	10	Self	—
30	Refresh	Normal	Status	—	—	20	Self	—
35	Luster Purge	Psychic	Special	70	100	5	Normal	—
40	Zen Headbutt	Psychic	Physical	80	90	15	Normal	○
45	Recover	Normal	Status	—	—	10	Self	—
50	Psycho Shift	Psychic	Status	—	90	10	Normal	—
55	Dragon Dance	Dragon	Status	—	—	20	Self	—
60	Memento	Dark	Status	—	100	10	Normal	—
65	Psychic	Psychic	Special	90	100	10	Normal	—
70	Dragon Pulse	Dragon	Special	90	100	10	Normal	—

● MOVE MANIAC
Name	Type	Kind	Pow.	Acc.	PP	Range	DA
Draco Meteor	Dragon	Special	140	90	5	Normal	—

● BP MOVES
Name	Type	Kind	Pow.	Acc.	PP	Range	DA
Dive	Water	Physical	80	100	10	Normal	○
Fury Cutter	Bug	Physical	10	95	20	Normal	○
Icy Wind	Ice	Special	55	95	15	2 Foes	—
Zen Headbutt	Psychic	Physical	80	90	15	Normal	○
Trick	Psychic	Status	—	100	10	Normal	—
Snore	Normal	Special	40	100	15	Normal	—
Helping Hand	Normal	Status	—	—	20	1 Ally	—
Last Resort	Normal	Physical	130	100	5	Normal	○
Swift	Normal	Special	60	—	20	2 Foes	—
Tailwind	Flying	Status	—	—	30	2 Allies	—
Magic Coat	Psychic	Status	—	—	15	Self	—
Mud-Slap	Ground	Special	20	100	10	Normal	—
Outrage	Dragon	Physical	120	100	15	1 Random	○
Twister	Dragon	Special	40	100	20	2 Foes	—

● TM & HM MOVES
No.	Name	Type	Kind	Pow.	Acc.	PP	Range	DA
TM02	Dragon Claw	Dragon	Physical	80	100	15	Normal	○
TM03	Water Pulse	Water	Special	60	100	20	Normal	—
TM04	Calm Mind	Psychic	Status	—	—	20	Self	—
TM05	Roar	Normal	Status	—	100	20	Normal	—
TM06	Toxic	Poison	Status	—	85	10	Normal	—
TM10	Hidden Power	Normal	Special	—	100	15	Normal	—
TM11	Sunny Day	Fire	Status	—	—	5	All	—
TM13	Ice Beam	Ice	Special	95	100	10	Normal	—
TM15	Hyper Beam	Normal	Special	150	90	5	Normal	—
TM16	Light Screen	Psychic	Status	—	—	30	2 Allies	—
TM17	Protect	Normal	Status	—	—	10	Self	—
TM18	Rain Dance	Water	Status	—	—	5	All	—
TM20	Safeguard	Normal	Status	—	—	25	2 Allies	—
TM21	Frustration	Normal	Physical	—	100	20	Normal	○
TM22	SolarBeam	Grass	Special	120	100	10	Normal	—
TM24	Thunderbolt	Electric	Special	95	100	15	Normal	—
TM25	Thunder	Electric	Special	120	70	10	Normal	—
TM26	Earthquake	Ground	Physical	100	100	10	2 Foes/1 Ally	—
TM27	Return	Normal	Physical	—	100	20	Normal	○
TM29	Psychic	Psychic	Special	90	100	10	Normal	—
TM30	Shadow Ball	Ghost	Special	80	100	15	Normal	—
TM32	Double Team	Normal	Status	—	—	15	Self	—
TM33	Reflect	Psychic	Status	—	—	20	2 Allies	—
TM34	Shock Wave	Electric	Special	60	—	20	Normal	—
TM37	Sandstorm	Rock	Status	—	—	10	All	—
TM40	Aerial Ace	Flying	Physical	60	—	20	Normal	○
TM42	Facade	Normal	Physical	70	100	20	Normal	○
TM43	Secret Power	Normal	Physical	70	100	20	Normal	—
TM44	Rest	Psychic	Status	—	—	10	Self	—
TM45	Attract	Normal	Status	—	100	15	Normal	—
TM47	Steel Wing	Steel	Physical	70	90	25	Normal	○
TM51	Roost	Flying	Status	—	—	10	Self	—
TM53	Energy Ball	Grass	Special	80	100	10	Normal	—
TM57	Charge Beam	Electric	Special	50	90	10	Normal	—
TM58	Endure	Normal	Status	—	—	10	Self	—
TM59	Dragon Pulse	Dragon	Special	90	100	10	Normal	—
TM65	Shadow Claw	Ghost	Physical	70	100	15	Normal	○
TM68	Giga Impact	Normal	Physical	150	90	5	Normal	○
TM70	Flash	Normal	Status	—	100	20	Normal	—
TM73	Thunder Wave	Electric	Status	—	100	20	Normal	—
TM77	Psych Up	Normal	Status	—	—	10	Normal	—
TM78	Captivate	Normal	Status	—	100	20	2 Foes	—
TM82	Sleep Talk	Normal	Status	—	—	10	Depends	—
TM83	Natural Gift	Normal	Physical	—	100	15	Normal	—
TM85	Dream Eater	Psychic	Special	100	100	15	Normal	—
TM86	Grass Knot	Grass	Special	—	100	20	Normal	○
TM87	Swagger	Normal	Status	—	90	15	Normal	—
TM90	Substitute	Normal	Status	—	—	10	Self	—
HM01	Cut	Normal	Physical	50	95	30	Normal	○
HM02	Fly	Flying	Physical	90	95	15	Normal	○
HM03	Surf	Water	Special	95	100	15	2 Foes/1 Ally	—
HM05	Whirlpool	Water	Special	15	70	15	Normal	—
HM07	Waterfall	Water	Physical	80	100	15	Normal	—

● LEVEL-UP MOVES

Lv.	Name	Type	Kind	Pow.	Acc.	PP	Range	DA
1	Water Pulse	Water	Special	60	100	20	Normal	—
5	Scary Face	Normal	Status	—	90	10	Normal	—
15	Body Slam	Normal	Physical	85	100	15	Normal	○
20	Muddy Water	Water	Special	95	85	10	2 Foes	—
30	Aqua Ring	Water	Status	—	—	20	Self	—
35	Ice Beam	Ice	Special	95	100	10	Normal	—
45	AncientPower	Rock	Special	60	100	5	Normal	—
50	Water Spout	Water	Special	150	100	5	2 Foes	—
60	Calm Mind	Psychic	Status	—	—	20	Self	—
65	Aqua Tail	Water	Physical	90	90	10	Normal	○
75	Sheer Cold	Ice	Special	—	30	5	Normal	—
80	Double-Edge	Normal	Physical	120	100	15	Normal	○
90	Hydro Pump	Water	Special	120	80	5	Normal	—

● MOVE MANIAC

Name	Type	Kind	Pow.	Acc.	PP	Range	DA
Headbutt	Normal	Physical	70	100	15	Normal	○

● BP MOVES

Name	Type	Kind	Pow.	Acc.	PP	Range	DA
Dive	Water	Physical	80	100	10	Normal	—
Icy Wind	Ice	Special	55	95	15	2 Foes	—
Snore	Normal	Special	40	100	15	Normal	—
Swift	Normal	Special	60	—	20	2 Foes	—
Uproar	Normal	Special	50	100	10	1 Random	—
Block	Normal	Status	—	—	5	Normal	—
Mud-Slap	Ground	Special	20	100	10	Normal	—
Iron Head	Steel	Physical	80	100	15	Normal	○
Aqua Tail	Water	Physical	90	90	10	Normal	○
AncientPower	Rock	Special	60	100	5	Normal	—
Signal Beam	Bug	Special	75	100	15	Normal	—

● TM & HM MOVES

No.	Name	Type	Kind	Pow.	Acc.	PP	Range	DA
TM03	Water Pulse	Water	Special	60	100	20	Normal	—
TM04	Calm Mind	Psychic	Status	—	—	20	Self	—
TM05	Roar	Normal	Status	—	100	20	Normal	—
TM06	Toxic	Poison	Status	—	85	10	Normal	—
TM07	Hail	Ice	Status	—	—	10	All	—
TM10	Hidden Power	Normal	Special	—	100	15	Normal	—
TM13	Ice Beam	Ice	Special	95	100	10	Normal	—
TM14	Blizzard	Ice	Special	120	70	5	2 Foes	—
TM15	Hyper Beam	Normal	Special	150	90	5	Normal	—
TM17	Protect	Normal	Status	—	—	10	Self	—
TM18	Rain Dance	Water	Status	—	—	5	All	—
TM20	Safeguard	Normal	Status	—	—	25	2 Allies	—
TM21	Frustration	Normal	Physical	—	100	20	Normal	○
TM24	Thunderbolt	Electric	Special	95	100	15	Normal	—
TM25	Thunder	Electric	Special	120	70	10	Normal	—
TM26	Earthquake	Ground	Physical	100	100	10	2 Foes/1 Ally	—
TM27	Return	Normal	Physical	—	100	20	Normal	○
TM31	Brick Break	Fighting	Physical	75	100	15	Normal	○
TM32	Double Team	Normal	Status	—	—	15	Self	—
TM34	Shock Wave	Electric	Special	60	—	20	Normal	—
TM39	Rock Tomb	Rock	Physical	50	80	10	Normal	○
TM42	Facade	Normal	Physical	70	100	20	Normal	○
TM43	Secret Power	Normal	Physical	70	100	20	Normal	○
TM44	Rest	Psychic	Status	—	—	10	Self	—
TM55	Brine	Water	Special	65	100	10	Normal	—
TM58	Endure	Normal	Status	—	—	10	Self	—
TM68	Giga Impact	Normal	Physical	150	90	5	Normal	○
TM72	Avalanche	Ice	Physical	60	100	10	Normal	○
TM73	Thunder Wave	Electric	Status	—	100	20	Normal	—
TM77	Psych Up	Normal	Status	—	—	10	Normal	—
TM80	Rock Slide	Rock	Physical	75	90	10	2 Foes	—
TM82	Sleep Talk	Normal	Status	—	—	10	Depends	—
TM83	Natural Gift	Normal	Physical	—	100	15	Normal	—
TM87	Swagger	Normal	Status	—	90	15	Normal	—
TM90	Substitute	Normal	Status	—	—	10	Self	—
HM03	Surf	Water	Special	95	100	15	2 Foes/1 Ally	—
HM04	Strength	Normal	Physical	80	100	15	Normal	—
HM05	Whirlpool	Water	Special	15	70	15	Normal	—
HM06	Rock Smash	Fighting	Physical	40	100	15	Normal	—
HM07	Waterfall	Water	Physical	80	100	15	Normal	—

No. 382 | Sea Basin Pokémon
Kyogre

Water

- **HEIGHT:** 14'09"
- **WEIGHT:** 776.0 lbs.
- **ITEMS:** None

● SIZE COMPARISON

● GENDER UNKNOWN

● ABILITIES
- Drizzle

● STATS
- HP ●●●●○
- ATTACK ●●●●○
- DEFENSE ●●●●○
- SP. ATTACK ●●●●○
- SP. DEFENSE ●●●●●
- SPEED ●●●●○

● EGG GROUPS
No Egg has ever been discovered

● PERFORMANCE

SPEED ★★★☆ STAMINA ★★★★★
POWER ★★★☆ JUMP ★★★☆
SKILL ★★★★☆

● MAIN WAYS TO OBTAIN

Pokémon HeartGold
Encounter it at the Embedded Tower once you have the Blue Orb

Pokémon SoulSilver

Pokémon Diamond

Pokémon Pearl

Pokémon Platinum

Pokémon HeartGold
A mythical Pokémon said to have swelled the seas with rain and tidal waves. It battled with GROUDON.

Pokémon SoulSilver
A mythical Pokémon said to have swelled the seas with rain and tidal waves. It battled with GROUDON.

● EVOLUTION

Does not evolve

⏺ No. 383 | Continent Pokémon
Groudon

Ground

● HEIGHT: 11'06"
● WEIGHT: 2,094.4 lbs.
● ITEMS: None

● SIZE COMPARISON

● GENDER UNKNOWN

⚙ ABILITIES
● Drought

⚙ EGG GROUPS
No Egg has ever been discovered

⚙ PERFORMANCE

SPEED ★☆
POWER ★★★★★
SKILL ★★★★★
STAMINA ★★★★★
JUMP ★★

⚙ STATS
HP ●●●●
ATTACK ●●●●●●
DEFENSE ●●●●●
SP. ATTACK ●●●●●
SP. DEFENSE ●●●●
SPEED ●●●●

● MAIN WAYS TO OBTAIN

Pokémon HeartGold | —

Pokémon SoulSilver | Encounter it at the Embedded Tower once you have the Red Orb

Pokémon Diamond | —

Pokémon Pearl | —

Pokémon Platinum | —

Pokémon HeartGold | Said to have expanded the lands by evaporating water with raging heat. It battled titanically with KYOGRE.

Pokémon SoulSilver | Said to have expanded the lands by evaporating water with raging heat. It battled titanically with KYOGRE.

⚙ EVOLUTION

Does not evolve

● LEVEL-UP MOVES

Lv.	Name	Type	Kind	Pow.	Acc.	PP	Range	DA
1	Mud Shot	Ground	Special	55	95	15	Normal	—
5	Scary Face	Normal	Status	—	90	10	Normal	—
15	Lava Plume	Fire	Special	80	100	15	2 Foes/1 Ally	—
20	Hammer Arm	Fighting	Physical	100	90	10	Normal	○
30	Rest	Psychic	Status	—	—	10	Self	—
35	Earthquake	Ground	Physical	100	100	10	2 Foes/1 Ally	—
45	AncientPower	Rock	Special	60	100	5	Normal	—
50	Eruption	Fire	Special	150	100	5	2 Foes	—
60	Bulk Up	Fighting	Status	—	—	20	Self	—
65	Earth Power	Ground	Special	90	100	10	Normal	—
75	Fissure	Ground	Physical	—	30	5	Normal	—
80	SolarBeam	Grass	Special	120	100	10	Normal	—
90	Fire Blast	Fire	Special	120	85	5	Normal	—

● MOVE MANIAC

Name	Type	Kind	Pow.	Acc.	PP	Range	DA
Headbutt	Normal	Physical	70	100	15	Normal	○

● BP MOVES

Name	Type	Kind	Pow.	Acc.	PP	Range	DA
Fury Cutter	Bug	Physical	10	95	20	Normal	○
ThunderPunch	Electric	Physical	75	100	15	Normal	○
Fire Punch	Fire	Physical	75	100	15	Normal	○
Snore	Normal	Special	40	100	15	Normal	—
Swift	Normal	Special	60	—	20	2 Foes	—
Uproar	Normal	Special	50	100	10	1 Random	—
Block	Normal	Status	—	—	5	Normal	—
Mud-Slap	Ground	Special	20	100	10	Normal	—
Rollout	Rock	Physical	30	90	20	Normal	○
Iron Head	Steel	Physical	80	100	15	Normal	○
AncientPower	Rock	Special	60	100	5	Normal	—
Earth Power	Ground	Special	90	100	10	Normal	—

● TM & HM MOVES

No.	Name	Type	Kind	Pow.	Acc.	PP	Range	DA
TM02	Dragon Claw	Dragon	Physical	80	100	15	Normal	○
TM05	Roar	Normal	Status	—	100	20	Normal	—
TM06	Toxic	Poison	Status	—	85	10	Normal	—
TM08	Bulk Up	Fighting	Status	—	—	20	Self	—
TM10	Hidden Power	Normal	Special	—	100	15	Normal	—
TM11	Sunny Day	Fire	Status	—	—	5	All	—
TM15	Hyper Beam	Normal	Special	150	90	5	Normal	—
TM17	Protect	Normal	Status	—	—	10	Self	—
TM20	Safeguard	Normal	Status	—	—	25	2 Allies	—
TM21	Frustration	Normal	Physical	—	100	20	Normal	○
TM22	SolarBeam	Grass	Special	120	100	10	Normal	—
TM23	Iron Tail	Steel	Physical	100	75	15	Normal	○
TM24	Thunderbolt	Electric	Special	95	100	15	Normal	—
TM25	Thunder	Electric	Special	120	70	10	Normal	—
TM26	Earthquake	Ground	Physical	100	100	10	2 Foes/1 Ally	—
TM27	Return	Normal	Physical	—	100	20	Normal	○
TM28	Dig	Ground	Physical	80	100	10	Normal	○
TM31	Brick Break	Fighting	Physical	75	100	15	Normal	○
TM32	Double Team	Normal	Status	—	—	15	Self	—
TM34	Shock Wave	Electric	Special	60	—	20	Normal	—
TM35	Flamethrower	Fire	Special	95	100	15	Normal	—
TM37	Sandstorm	Rock	Status	—	—	10	All	—
TM38	Fire Blast	Fire	Special	120	85	5	Normal	—
TM39	Rock Tomb	Rock	Physical	50	80	10	Normal	○
TM40	Aerial Ace	Flying	Physical	60	—	20	Normal	○
TM42	Facade	Normal	Physical	70	100	20	Normal	○
TM43	Secret Power	Normal	Physical	70	100	20	Normal	—
TM44	Rest	Psychic	Status	—	—	10	Self	—
TM50	Overheat	Fire	Special	140	90	5	Normal	—
TM52	Focus Blast	Fighting	Special	120	70	5	Normal	—
TM56	Fling	Dark	Physical	—	100	10	Normal	—
TM58	Endure	Normal	Status	—	—	10	Self	—
TM59	Dragon Pulse	Dragon	Special	90	100	10	Normal	—
TM65	Shadow Claw	Ghost	Physical	70	100	15	Normal	○
TM68	Giga Impact	Normal	Physical	150	90	5	Normal	○
TM69	Rock Polish	Rock	Status	—	—	20	Self	—
TM71	Stone Edge	Rock	Physical	100	80	5	Normal	—
TM73	Thunder Wave	Electric	Status	—	100	20	Normal	—
TM75	Swords Dance	Normal	Status	—	—	30	Self	—
TM76	Stealth Rock	Rock	Status	—	—	20	2 Foes	—
TM77	Psych Up	Normal	Status	—	—	10	Normal	—
TM80	Rock Slide	Rock	Physical	75	90	10	2 Foes	—
TM82	Sleep Talk	Normal	Status	—	—	10	Depends	—
TM83	Natural Gift	Normal	Physical	—	100	15	Normal	—
TM87	Swagger	Normal	Status	—	90	15	Normal	—
TM90	Substitute	Normal	Status	—	—	10	Self	—
HM01	Cut	Normal	Physical	50	95	30	Normal	○
HM04	Strength	Normal	Physical	80	100	15	Normal	○
HM06	Rock Smash	Fighting	Physical	40	100	15	Normal	○
HM08	Rock Climb	Normal	Physical	90	85	20	Normal	○

● LEVEL-UP MOVES

Lv.	Name	Type	Kind	Pow.	Acc.	PP	Range	DA
1	Twister	Dragon	Special	40	100	20	2 Foes	—
5	Scary Face	Normal	Status	—	90	10	Normal	—
15	Crunch	Dark	Physical	80	100	15	Normal	○
20	Hyper Voice	Normal	Special	40	100	10	2 Foes	—
30	Rest	Psychic	Status	—	—	10	Self	—
35	Air Slash	Flying	Special	75	95	20	Normal	—
45	AncientPower	Rock	Special	60	100	5	Normal	—
50	Outrage	Dragon	Physical	120	100	15	1 Random	○
60	Dragon Dance	Dragon	Status	—	—	20	Self	—
65	Fly	Flying	Physical	90	95	15	Normal	—
75	ExtremeSpeed	Normal	Physical	80	100	5	Normal	—
80	Hyper Beam	Normal	Special	150	90	5	Normal	—
90	Dragon Pulse	Dragon	Special	90	100	10	Normal	—

● MOVE MANIAC

Name	Type	Kind	Pow.	Acc.	PP	Range	DA
Headbutt	Normal	Physical	70	100	15	Normal	○
Draco Meteor	Dragon	Special	140	90	5	Normal	—

● BP MOVES

Name	Type	Kind	Pow.	Acc.	PP	Range	DA
Dive	Water	Physical	80	100	10	Normal	○
Fury Cutter	Bug	Physical	10	95	20	Normal	○
Icy Wind	Ice	Special	55	95	15	2 Foes	—
Snore	Normal	Special	40	100	15	Normal	—
Swift	Normal	Special	60	—	20	2 Foes	—
Uproar	Normal	Special	50	100	10	1 Random	—
Tailwind	Flying	Status	—	—	30	2 Allies	—
Mud-Slap	Ground	Special	20	100	10	Normal	—
Iron Head	Steel	Physical	80	100	15	Normal	○
Aqua Tail	Water	Physical	90	90	10	Normal	○
Outrage	Dragon	Physical	120	100	15	1 Random	○
AncientPower	Rock	Special	60	100	5	Normal	—
Earth Power	Ground	Special	90	100	10	Normal	—
Twister	Dragon	Special	40	100	20	2 Foes	—

● TM & HM MOVES

No.	Name	Type	Kind	Pow.	Acc.	PP	Range	DA
TM02	Dragon Claw	Dragon	Physical	80	100	15	Normal	○
TM03	Water Pulse	Water	Special	60	100	20	Normal	—
TM05	Roar	Normal	Status	—	100	20	Normal	—
TM06	Toxic	Poison	Status	—	85	10	Normal	—
TM08	Bulk Up	Fighting	Status	—	—	20	Self	—
TM10	Hidden Power	Normal	Special	—	100	15	Normal	—
TM11	Sunny Day	Fire	Status	—	—	5	All	—
TM13	Ice Beam	Ice	Special	95	100	10	Normal	—
TM14	Blizzard	Ice	Special	120	70	5	2 Foes	—
TM15	Hyper Beam	Normal	Special	150	90	5	Normal	—
TM17	Protect	Normal	Status	—	—	10	Self	—
TM18	Rain Dance	Water	Status	—	—	5	All	—
TM21	Frustration	Normal	Physical	—	100	20	Normal	○
TM22	SolarBeam	Grass	Special	120	100	10	Normal	—
TM23	Iron Tail	Steel	Physical	100	75	15	Normal	○
TM24	Thunderbolt	Electric	Special	95	100	15	Normal	—
TM25	Thunder	Electric	Special	120	70	10	Normal	—
TM26	Earthquake	Ground	Physical	100	100	10	2 Foes/1 Ally	○
TM27	Return	Normal	Physical	—	100	20	Normal	○
TM31	Brick Break	Fighting	Physical	75	100	15	Normal	○
TM32	Double Team	Normal	Status	—	—	15	Self	—
TM34	Shock Wave	Electric	Special	60	—	20	Normal	—
TM35	Flamethrower	Fire	Special	95	100	15	Normal	—
TM37	Sandstorm	Rock	Status	—	—	10	All	—
TM38	Fire Blast	Fire	Special	120	85	5	Normal	—
TM39	Rock Tomb	Rock	Physical	50	80	10	Normal	○
TM40	Aerial Ace	Flying	Physical	60	—	20	Normal	○
TM42	Facade	Normal	Physical	70	100	20	Normal	○
TM43	Secret Power	Normal	Physical	70	100	20	Normal	○
TM44	Rest	Psychic	Status	—	—	10	Self	—
TM50	Overheat	Fire	Special	140	90	5	Normal	—
TM52	Focus Blast	Fighting	Special	120	70	5	Normal	—
TM53	Energy Ball	Grass	Special	80	100	10	Normal	—
TM56	Fling	Dark	Physical	—	100	10	Normal	○
TM58	Endure	Normal	Status	—	—	10	Self	—
TM59	Dragon Pulse	Dragon	Special	90	100	10	Normal	—
TM65	Shadow Claw	Ghost	Physical	70	100	15	Normal	○
TM68	Giga Impact	Normal	Physical	150	90	5	Normal	○
TM71	Stone Edge	Rock	Physical	100	80	5	Normal	○
TM72	Avalanche	Ice	Physical	60	100	10	Normal	○
TM73	Thunder Wave	Electric	Status	—	100	20	Normal	—
TM74	Gyro Ball	Steel	Physical	—	100	5	Normal	○
TM75	Swords Dance	Normal	Status	—	—	30	Self	—
TM77	Psych Up	Normal	Status	—	—	10	Normal	—
TM80	Rock Slide	Rock	Physical	75	90	10	2 Foes	○
TM82	Sleep Talk	Normal	Status	—	—	10	Depends	—
TM83	Natural Gift	Normal	Physical	—	100	15	Normal	○
TM87	Swagger	Normal	Status	—	90	15	Normal	—
TM90	Substitute	Normal	Status	—	—	10	Self	—
HM02	Fly	Flying	Physical	90	95	15	Normal	—
HM03	Surf	Water	Special	95	100	15	2 Foes/1 Ally	—
HM04	Strength	Normal	Physical	80	100	15	Normal	○
HM05	Whirlpool	Water	Special	15	70	15	Normal	—
HM06	Rock Smash	Fighting	Physical	40	100	15	Normal	○
HM07	Waterfall	Water	Physical	80	100	15	Normal	○

Rayquaza

Dragon **Flying**

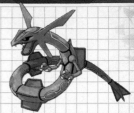

- **HEIGHT:** 23'00"
- **WEIGHT:** 455.2 lbs.
- **ITEMS:** None

● SIZE COMPARISON

● GENDER UNKNOWN

⊛ ABILITIES
- Air Lock

⊛ STATS
- HP ●●●●○○
- ATTACK ●●●●●●
- DEFENSE ●●●●●○
- SP. ATTACK ●●●●●●
- SP. DEFENSE ●●●●●○
- SPEED ●●●●○○

⊛ EGG GROUPS
No Egg has ever been discovered

⊛ PERFORMANCE
- SPEED ★★★★☆   STAMINA ★★★★☆
- POWER ★★★★☆   JUMP ★★★★★
- SKILL ★★★

● MAIN WAYS TO OBTAIN

Pokémon HeartGold	Encounter it at the Embedded Tower once you have the Jade Orb
Pokémon SoulSilver	Encounter it at the Embedded Tower once you have the Jade Orb
Pokémon Diamond	—
Pokémon Pearl	—
Pokémon Platinum	—

Pokémon HeartGold	**Pokémon SoulSilver**
It flies in the ozone layer, way up high in the sky. Until recently, no one had ever seen it.	It flies in the ozone layer, way up high in the sky. Until recently, no one had ever seen it.

⊛ EVOLUTION

Does not evolve

● No. 385 | Wish Pokémon
Jirachi

Steel **Psychic**

- ● **HEIGHT:** 1'00"
- ● **WEIGHT:** 2.4 lbs.
- ● **ITEMS:** None

● **SIZE COMPARISON**

● **GENDER UNKNOWN**

● ABILITIES
- Serene Grace

● STATS
HP	●●●●
ATTACK	●●●●
DEFENSE	●●●●
SP. ATTACK	●●●●
SP. DEFENSE	●●●●
SPEED	●●●●

● EGG GROUPS
No Egg has ever been discovered

● PERFORMANCE
SPEED ★★★☆☆   STAMINA ★★★☆
POWER ★★★   JUMP ★★★★☆
SKILL ★★★★☆

● MAIN WAYS TO OBTAIN

Pokémon HeartGold —

Pokémon SoulSilver —

Pokémon Diamond — Only obtainable through special distribution events—cannot be obtained through regular gameplay*

Pokémon Pearl — Only obtainable through special distribution events—cannot be obtained through regular gameplay*

Pokémon Platinum — Only obtainable through special distribution events—cannot be obtained through regular gameplay*

Pokémon HeartGold — Generations have believed that any wish written on a note on its head will come true when it awakens.

Pokémon SoulSilver — Generations have believed that any wish written on a note on its head will come true when it awakens.

● EVOLUTION
Does not evolve

● LEVEL-UP MOVES
Lv.	Name	Type	Kind	Pow.	Acc.	PP	Range	DA
1	Wish	Normal	Status	—	—	10	Self	—
1	Confusion	Psychic	Special	50	100	25	Normal	—
5	Rest	Psychic	Status	—	—	10	Self	—
10	Swift	Normal	Special	60	—	20	2 Foes	—
15	Helping Hand	Normal	Status	—	—	20	1 Ally	—
20	Psychic	Psychic	Special	90	100	10	Normal	—
25	Refresh	Normal	Status	—	—	20	Self	—
30	Rest	Psychic	Status	—	—	10	Self	—
35	Zen Headbutt	Psychic	Physical	80	90	15	Normal	○
40	Double-Edge	Normal	Physical	120	100	15	Normal	○
45	Gravity	Psychic	Status	—	—	5	All	—
50	Healing Wish	Psychic	Status	—	—	10	Self	—
55	Future Sight	Psychic	Special	80	90	15	Normal	—
60	Cosmic Power	Psychic	Status	—	—	20	Self	—
65	Last Resort	Normal	Physical	130	100	5	Normal	○
70	Doom Desire	Steel	Special	120	85	5	Normal	—

● MOVE MANIAC
Name	Type	Kind	Pow.	Acc.	PP	Range	DA
Headbutt	Normal	Physical	70	100	15	Normal	○

● BP MOVES
Name	Type	Kind	Pow.	Acc.	PP	Range	DA
Icy Wind	Ice	Special	55	95	15	2 Foes	—
ThunderPunch	Electric	Physical	75	100	15	Normal	○
Fire Punch	Fire	Physical	75	100	15	Normal	○
Ice Punch	Ice	Physical	75	100	15	Normal	○
Zen Headbutt	Psychic	Physical	80	90	15	Normal	○
Trick	Psychic	Status	—	100	10	Normal	—
Snore	Normal	Special	40	100	15	Normal	—
Helping Hand	Normal	Status	—	—	20	1 Ally	—
Last Resort	Normal	Physical	130	100	5	Normal	○
Swift	Normal	Special	60	—	20	2 Foes	—
Uproar	Normal	Special	50	100	10	1 Random	—
Gravity	Psychic	Status	—	—	5	All	—
Magic Coat	Psychic	Status	—	—	15	Self	—
Mud-Slap	Ground	Special	20	100	10	Normal	—
Iron Head	Steel	Physical	80	100	15	Normal	○
AncientPower	Rock	Special	60	100	5	Normal	—
Signal Beam	Bug	Special	75	100	15	Normal	—
Iron Defense	Steel	Status	—	—	15	Self	—

● TM & HM MOVES
No.	Name	Type	Kind	Pow.	Acc.	PP	Range	DA
TM03	Water Pulse	Water	Special	60	100	20	Normal	—
TM04	Calm Mind	Psychic	Status	—	—	20	Self	—
TM06	Toxic	Poison	Status	—	85	10	Normal	—
TM10	Hidden Power	Normal	Special	—	100	15	Normal	—
TM11	Sunny Day	Fire	Status	—	—	5	All	—
TM15	Hyper Beam	Normal	Special	150	90	5	Normal	—
TM16	Light Screen	Psychic	Status	—	—	30	2 Allies	—
TM17	Protect	Normal	Status	—	—	10	Self	—
TM18	Rain Dance	Water	Status	—	—	5	All	—
TM20	Safeguard	Normal	Status	—	—	25	2 Allies	—
TM21	Frustration	Normal	Physical	—	100	20	Normal	○
TM24	Thunderbolt	Electric	Special	95	100	15	Normal	—
TM25	Thunder	Electric	Special	120	70	10	Normal	—
TM27	Return	Normal	Physical	—	100	20	Normal	○
TM29	Psychic	Psychic	Special	90	100	10	Normal	—
TM30	Shadow Ball	Ghost	Special	80	100	15	Normal	—
TM32	Double Team	Normal	Status	—	—	15	Self	—
TM33	Reflect	Psychic	Status	—	—	20	2 Allies	—
TM34	Shock Wave	Electric	Special	60	—	20	Normal	—
TM37	Sandstorm	Rock	Status	—	—	10	All	—
TM40	Aerial Ace	Flying	Physical	60	—	20	Normal	○
TM42	Facade	Normal	Physical	70	100	20	Normal	○
TM43	Secret Power	Normal	Physical	70	100	20	Normal	—
TM44	Rest	Psychic	Status	—	—	10	Self	—
TM48	Skill Swap	Psychic	Status	—	—	10	Normal	—
TM53	Energy Ball	Grass	Special	80	100	10	Normal	—
TM56	Fling	Dark	Physical	—	100	10	Normal	—
TM57	Charge Beam	Electric	Special	50	90	10	Normal	—
TM58	Endure	Normal	Status	—	—	10	Self	—
TM60	Drain Punch	Fighting	Physical	60	100	5	Normal	○
TM67	Recycle	Normal	Status	—	—	10	Self	—
TM68	Giga Impact	Normal	Physical	150	90	5	Normal	○
TM70	Flash	Normal	Status	—	100	20	Normal	—
TM73	Thunder Wave	Electric	Status	—	100	20	Normal	—
TM76	Stealth Rock	Rock	Status	—	—	20	2 Foes	—
TM77	Psych Up	Normal	Status	—	—	10	Normal	—
TM82	Sleep Talk	Normal	Status	—	—	10	Depends	—
TM83	Natural Gift	Normal	Physical	—	100	15	Normal	—
TM85	Dream Eater	Psychic	Special	100	100	15	Normal	—
TM86	Grass Knot	Grass	Special	—	100	20	Normal	○
TM87	Swagger	Normal	Status	—	90	15	Normal	—
TM89	U-turn	Bug	Physical	70	100	20	Normal	○
TM90	Substitute	Normal	Status	—	—	10	Self	—
TM91	Flash Cannon	Steel	Special	80	100	10	Normal	—
TM92	Trick Room	Psychic	Status	—	—	5	All	—

● LEVEL-UP MOVES

Lv.	Name	Type	Kind	Pow.	Acc.	PP	Range	DA
1	Leer	Normal	Status	—	100	30	2 Foes	—
1	Wrap	Normal	Physical	15	85	20	Normal	○
9	Night Shade	Ghost	Special	—	100	15	Normal	—
17	Teleport	Psychic	Status	—	—	20	Self	—
25	Knock Off	Dark	Physical	20	100	20	Normal	○
33	Pursuit	Dark	Physical	40	100	20	Normal	○
41	Psychic	Psychic	Special	90	100	10	Normal	—
49	Snatch	Dark	Status	—	—	10	Depends	—
57	Psycho Shift	Psychic	Status	—	90	10	Normal	—
65	Zen Headbutt	Psychic	Physical	80	90	15	Normal	○
73	Cosmic Power	Psychic	Status	—	—	20	Self	—
81	Recover	Normal	Status	—	—	10	Self	—
89	Psycho Boost	Psychic	Special	140	90	5	Normal	—
97	Hyper Beam	Normal	Special	150	90	5	Normal	—

● MOVE MANIAC

Name	Type	Kind	Pow.	Acc.	PP	Range	DA
Headbutt	Normal	Physical	70	100	15	Normal	○

● BP MOVES

Name	Type	Kind	Pow.	Acc.	PP	Range	DA
Icy Wind	Ice	Special	55	95	15	2 Foes	—
ThunderPunch	Electric	Physical	75	100	15	Normal	○
Fire Punch	Fire	Physical	75	100	15	Normal	○
Ice Punch	Ice	Physical	75	100	15	Normal	○
Zen Headbutt	Psychic	Physical	80	90	15	Normal	○
Trick	Psychic	Status	—	100	10	Normal	—
Knock Off	Dark	Physical	20	100	20	Normal	○
Snore	Normal	Special	40	100	15	Normal	—
Swift	Normal	Special	60	—	20	2 Foes	—
Gravity	Psychic	Status	—	—	5	All	—
Magic Coat	Psychic	Status	—	—	15	Self	—
Role Play	Psychic	Status	—	—	10	Normal	—
Mud-Slap	Ground	Special	20	100	10	Normal	—
Signal Beam	Bug	Special	75	100	15	Normal	—
Low Kick	Fighting	Physical	—	100	20	Normal	○

● TM & HM MOVES

No.	Name	Type	Kind	Pow.	Acc.	PP	Range	DA
TM01	Focus Punch	Fighting	Physical	150	100	20	Normal	○
TM03	Water Pulse	Water	Special	60	100	20	Normal	—
TM04	Calm Mind	Psychic	Status	—	—	20	Self	—
TM06	Toxic	Poison	Status	—	85	10	Normal	—
TM10	Hidden Power	Normal	Special	—	100	15	Normal	—
TM11	Sunny Day	Fire	Status	—	—	5	All	—
TM12	Taunt	Dark	Status	—	100	20	Normal	—
TM13	Ice Beam	Ice	Special	95	100	10	Normal	—
TM15	Hyper Beam	Normal	Special	150	90	5	Normal	—
TM16	Light Screen	Psychic	Status	—	—	30	2 Allies	—
TM17	Protect	Normal	Status	—	—	10	Self	—
TM18	Rain Dance	Water	Status	—	—	5	All	—
TM20	Safeguard	Normal	Status	—	—	25	2 Allies	—
TM21	Frustration	Normal	Physical	—	100	20	Normal	○
TM22	SolarBeam	Grass	Special	120	100	10	Normal	—
TM24	Thunderbolt	Electric	Special	95	100	15	Normal	—
TM25	Thunder	Electric	Special	120	70	10	Normal	—
TM27	Return	Normal	Physical	—	100	20	Normal	○
TM29	Psychic	Psychic	Special	90	100	10	Normal	—
TM30	Shadow Ball	Ghost	Special	80	100	15	Normal	—
TM31	Brick Break	Fighting	Physical	75	100	15	Normal	○
TM32	Double Team	Normal	Status	—	—	15	Self	—
TM33	Reflect	Psychic	Status	—	—	20	2 Allies	—
TM34	Shock Wave	Electric	Special	60	—	20	Normal	—
TM39	Rock Tomb	Rock	Physical	50	80	10	Normal	○
TM40	Aerial Ace	Flying	Physical	60	—	20	Normal	○
TM41	Torment	Dark	Status	—	100	15	Normal	—
TM42	Facade	Normal	Physical	70	100	20	Normal	○
TM43	Secret Power	Normal	Physical	70	100	20	Normal	—
TM44	Rest	Psychic	Status	—	—	10	Self	—
TM48	Skill Swap	Psychic	Status	—	—	10	Normal	—
TM49	Snatch	Dark	Status	—	—	10	Depends	—
TM52	Focus Blast	Fighting	Special	120	70	5	Normal	—
TM53	Energy Ball	Grass	Special	80	100	10	Normal	—
TM56	Fling	Dark	Physical	—	100	10	Normal	○
TM57	Charge Beam	Electric	Special	50	90	10	Normal	—
TM58	Endure	Normal	Status	—	—	10	Self	—
TM60	Drain Punch	Fighting	Physical	60	100	5	Normal	○
TM67	Recycle	Normal	Status	—	—	10	Self	—
TM68	Giga Impact	Normal	Physical	150	90	5	Normal	○
TM70	Flash	Normal	Status	—	100	20	Normal	—
TM72	Avalanche	Ice	Physical	60	100	10	Normal	○
TM73	Thunder Wave	Electric	Status	—	100	20	Normal	—
TM76	Stealth Rock	Rock	Status	—	—	20	2 Foes	—
TM77	Psych Up	Normal	Status	—	—	10	Normal	—
TM80	Rock Slide	Rock	Physical	75	90	10	2 Foes	○
TM82	Sleep Talk	Normal	Status	—	—	10	Depends	—
TM83	Natural Gift	Normal	Physical	—	100	15	Normal	—
TM84	Poison Jab	Poison	Physical	80	100	20	Normal	○
TM85	Dream Eater	Psychic	Special	100	100	15	Normal	—
TM86	Grass Knot	Grass	Special	—	100	20	Normal	—
TM87	Swagger	Normal	Status	—	90	15	Normal	—
TM90	Substitute	Normal	Status	—	—	10	Self	—
TM91	Flash Cannon	Steel	Special	80	100	10	Normal	—
TM92	Trick Room	Psychic	Status	—	—	5	All	—
HM01	Cut	Normal	Physical	50	95	30	Normal	○
HM04	Strength	Normal	Physical	80	100	15	Normal	○
HM06	Rock Smash	Fighting	Physical	40	100	15	Normal	○

● No. 386 | DNA Pokémon
Deoxys (Normal Forme)

Psychic

- ● HEIGHT: 5'07"
- ● WEIGHT: 134.0 lbs.
- ● ITEMS: None

- ● SIZE COMPARISON

- ● GENDER UNKNOWN

⊛ ABILITIES
● Pressure

⊛ STATS
HP	●●
ATTACK	●●●●●●●
DEFENSE	●●
SP. ATTACK	●●●●●●●
SP. DEFENSE	●●
SPEED	●●●●●●●

⊛ EGG GROUPS
No Egg has ever been discovered

⊛ PERFORMANCE
SPEED ★★★★   STAMINA ★★★★
POWER ★★★★   JUMP ★★★☆
SKILL ★★★★

● MAIN WAYS TO OBTAIN

Pokémon HeartGold —

Pokémon SoulSilver —

Pokémon Diamond — Only obtainable through special distribution events—cannot be obtained through regular gameplay*

Pokémon Pearl — Only obtainable through special distribution events—cannot be obtained through regular gameplay*

Pokémon Platinum —

Pokémon HeartGold — DNA from a space virus mutated and became a Pokémon. It appears where auroras are seen.

Pokémon SoulSilver — DNA from a space virus mutated and became a Pokémon. It appears where auroras are seen.

⊛ EVOLUTION
Does not evolve

*Deoxys is only available through special distribution events. Check Pokemon.com for the latest information on how to catch this Pokémon.

No. 386 | DNA Pokémon
Deoxys (Attack Forme)
Psychic

- **HEIGHT:** 5'07"
- **WEIGHT:** 134.0 lbs.
- **ITEMS:** None

● SIZE COMPARISON

● GENDER UNKNOWN

⊕ ABILITIES
- Pressure

⊕ STATS
HP	●●
ATTACK	●●●●●●
DEFENSE	●●●
SP. ATTACK	●●●●●●
SP. DEFENSE	●●●
SPEED	●●●●●●

⊕ EGG GROUPS
No Egg has ever been discovered

⊕ PERFORMANCE
SPEED ★★★★★	STAMINA ★★☆
POWER ★★★★★	JUMP ★★★☆
SKILL ★★★★☆	

● MAIN WAYS TO OBTAIN

Pokémon HeartGold — —

Pokémon SoulSilver — —

Pokémon Diamond — Only obtainable through special distribution events—cannot be obtained through regular gameplay*

Pokémon Pearl — Only obtainable through special distribution events—cannot be obtained through regular gameplay*

Pokémon Platinum — —

Pokémon HeartGold — DNA from a space virus mutated and became a Pokémon. It appears where auroras are seen.

Pokémon SoulSilver — DNA from a space virus mutated and became a Pokémon. It appears where auroras are seen.

⊕ EVOLUTION
Does not evolve

● LEVEL-UP MOVES
Lv.	Name	Type	Kind	Pow.	Acc.	PP	Range	DA
1	Leer	Normal	Status	—	100	30	2 Foes	—
1	Wrap	Normal	Physical	15	85	20	Normal	—
9	Night Shade	Ghost	Special	—	100	15	Normal	—
17	Teleport	Psychic	Status	—	100	20	Self	—
25	Taunt	Dark	Status	—	100	20	Normal	—
33	Pursuit	Dark	Physical	40	100	20	Normal	○
41	Psychic	Psychic	Special	90	100	10	Normal	—
49	Superpower	Fighting	Physical	120	100	5	Normal	○
57	Psycho Shift	Psychic	Status	—	90	10	Normal	—
65	Zen Headbutt	Psychic	Physical	80	90	15	Normal	○
73	Cosmic Power	Psychic	Status	—	—	20	Self	—
81	Zap Cannon	Electric	Special	120	50	5	Normal	—
89	Psycho Boost	Psychic	Special	140	90	5	Normal	—
97	Hyper Beam	Normal	Special	150	90	5	Normal	—

● MOVE MANIAC
Name	Type	Kind	Pow.	Acc.	PP	Range	DA
Headbutt	Normal	Physical	70	100	15	Normal	○

● BP MOVES
Name	Type	Kind	Pow.	Acc.	PP	Range	DA
Zen Headbutt	Psychic	Physical	80	90	15	Normal	○
Trick	Psychic	Status	—	100	10	Normal	—
Snore	Normal	Special	40	100	15	Normal	—
Gravity	Psychic	Status	—	—	5	All	—
Magic Coat	Psychic	Status	—	—	15	Self	—
Role Play	Psychic	Status	—	—	10	Normal	—
Mud-Slap	Ground	Special	20	100	10	Normal	—
Superpower	Fighting	Physical	120	100	5	Normal	○
Signal Beam	Bug	Special	75	100	15	Normal	—
Low Kick	Fighting	Physical	—	100	20	Normal	○

● TM & HM MOVES
No.	Name	Type	Kind	Pow.	Acc.	PP	Range	DA
TM01	Focus Punch	Fighting	Physical	150	100	20	Normal	○
TM03	Water Pulse	Water	Special	60	100	20	Normal	—
TM04	Calm Mind	Psychic	Status	—	—	20	Self	—
TM06	Toxic	Poison	Status	—	85	10	Normal	—
TM10	Hidden Power	Normal	Special	—	100	15	Normal	—
TM11	Sunny Day	Fire	Status	—	—	5	All	—
TM12	Taunt	Dark	Status	—	100	20	Normal	—
TM13	Ice Beam	Ice	Special	95	100	10	Normal	—
TM15	Hyper Beam	Normal	Special	150	90	5	Normal	—
TM16	Light Screen	Psychic	Status	—	—	30	2 Allies	—
TM17	Protect	Normal	Status	—	—	10	Self	—
TM18	Rain Dance	Water	Status	—	—	5	All	—
TM20	Safeguard	Normal	Status	—	—	25	2 Allies	—
TM21	Frustration	Normal	Physical	—	100	20	Normal	○
TM22	SolarBeam	Grass	Special	120	100	10	Normal	—
TM24	Thunderbolt	Electric	Special	95	100	15	Normal	—
TM25	Thunder	Electric	Special	120	70	10	Normal	—
TM27	Return	Normal	Physical	—	100	20	Normal	○
TM29	Psychic	Psychic	Special	90	100	10	Normal	—
TM30	Shadow Ball	Ghost	Special	80	100	15	Normal	—
TM31	Brick Break	Fighting	Physical	75	100	15	Normal	○
TM32	Double Team	Normal	Status	—	—	15	Self	—
TM33	Reflect	Psychic	Status	—	—	20	2 Allies	—
TM34	Shock Wave	Electric	Special	60	—	20	Normal	—
TM39	Rock Tomb	Rock	Physical	50	80	10	Normal	○
TM40	Aerial Ace	Flying	Physical	60	—	20	Normal	○
TM41	Torment	Dark	Status	—	100	15	Normal	—
TM42	Facade	Normal	Physical	70	100	20	Normal	○
TM43	Secret Power	Normal	Physical	70	100	20	Normal	○
TM44	Rest	Psychic	Status	—	—	10	Self	—
TM48	Skill Swap	Psychic	Status	—	—	10	Normal	—
TM49	Snatch	Dark	Status	—	—	10	Depends	—
TM52	Focus Blast	Fighting	Special	120	70	5	Normal	—
TM53	Energy Ball	Grass	Special	80	100	10	Normal	—
TM56	Fling	Dark	Physical	—	100	10	Normal	○
TM57	Charge Beam	Electric	Special	50	90	10	Normal	—
TM58	Endure	Normal	Status	—	—	10	Self	—
TM60	Drain Punch	Fighting	Physical	60	100	5	Normal	○
TM67	Recycle	Normal	Status	—	—	10	Self	—
TM68	Giga Impact	Normal	Physical	150	90	5	Normal	○
TM70	Flash	Normal	Status	—	100	20	Normal	—
TM72	Avalanche	Ice	Physical	60	100	10	Normal	○
TM73	Thunder Wave	Electric	Status	—	100	20	Normal	—
TM76	Stealth Rock	Rock	Status	—	—	20	2 Foes	—
TM77	Psych Up	Normal	Status	—	—	10	Normal	—
TM80	Rock Slide	Rock	Physical	75	90	10	2 Foes	○
TM82	Sleep Talk	Normal	Status	—	—	10	Depends	—
TM83	Natural Gift	Normal	Physical	—	100	15	Normal	—
TM84	Poison Jab	Poison	Physical	80	100	20	Normal	○
TM85	Dream Eater	Psychic	Special	100	100	15	Normal	—
TM86	Grass Knot	Grass	Special	—	100	20	Normal	—
TM87	Swagger	Normal	Status	—	90	15	Normal	—
TM90	Substitute	Normal	Status	—	—	10	Self	—
TM91	Flash Cannon	Steel	Special	80	100	10	Normal	—
TM92	Trick Room	Psychic	Status	—	—	5	All	—
HM01	Cut	Normal	Physical	50	95	30	Normal	○
HM04	Strength	Normal	Physical	80	100	15	Normal	○
HM06	Rock Smash	Fighting	Physical	40	100	15	Normal	○

*Deoxys is only available through special distribution events. Check Pokemon.com for the latest information on how to catch this Pokémon.

● LEVEL-UP MOVES

Lv.	Name	Type	Kind	Pow.	Acc.	PP	Range	DA
1	Leer	Normal	Status	—	100	30	2 Foes	—
1	Wrap	Normal	Physical	15	85	20	Normal	○
9	Night Shade	Ghost	Special	—	100	15	Normal	—
17	Teleport	Psychic	Status	—	—	20	Self	—
25	Knock Off	Dark	Physical	20	100	20	Normal	○
33	Spikes	Ground	Status	—	—	20	2 Foes	—
41	Psychic	Psychic	Special	90	100	10	Normal	—
49	Snatch	Dark	Status	—	—	10	Depends	—
57	Psycho Shift	Psychic	Status	—	90	10	Normal	—
65	Zen Headbutt	Psychic	Physical	80	90	15	Normal	○
73	Iron Defense	Steel	Status	—	—	15	Self	—
73	Amnesia	Psychic	Status	—	—	20	Self	—
81	Recover	Normal	Status	—	—	10	Self	—
89	Psycho Boost	Psychic	Special	140	90	5	Normal	—
97	Counter	Fighting	Physical	—	100	20	Self	○
97	Mirror Coat	Psychic	Special	—	100	20	Self	—

● MOVE MANIAC

Name	Type	Kind	Pow.	Acc.	PP	Range	DA
Headbutt	Normal	Physical	70	100	15	Normal	○

● BP MOVES

Name	Type	Kind	Pow.	Acc.	PP	Range	DA
Zen Headbutt	Psychic	Physical	80	90	15	Normal	○
Trick	Psychic	Status	—	100	10	Normal	—
Knock Off	Dark	Physical	20	100	20	Normal	○
Snore	Normal	Special	40	100	15	Normal	—
Gravity	Psychic	Status	—	—	5	All	—
Magic Coat	Psychic	Status	—	—	15	Self	—
Role Play	Psychic	Status	—	—	10	Normal	—
Mud-Slap	Ground	Special	20	100	10	Normal	—
Signal Beam	Bug	Special	75	100	15	Normal	—
Iron Defense	Steel	Status	—	—	15	Self	—
Low Kick	Fighting	Physical	—	100	20	Normal	○

● TM & HM MOVES

No.	Name	Type	Kind	Pow.	Acc.	PP	Range	DA
TM01	Focus Punch	Fighting	Physical	150	100	20	Normal	○
TM03	Water Pulse	Water	Special	60	100	20	Normal	—
TM04	Calm Mind	Psychic	Status	—	—	20	Self	—
TM06	Toxic	Poison	Status	—	85	10	Normal	—
TM10	Hidden Power	Normal	Special	—	100	15	Normal	—
TM11	Sunny Day	Fire	Status	—	—	5	All	—
TM12	Taunt	Dark	Status	—	100	20	Normal	—
TM13	Ice Beam	Ice	Special	95	100	10	Normal	—
TM15	Hyper Beam	Normal	Special	150	90	5	Normal	—
TM16	Light Screen	Psychic	Status	—	—	30	2 Allies	—
TM17	Protect	Normal	Status	—	—	10	Self	—
TM18	Rain Dance	Water	Status	—	—	5	All	—
TM20	Safeguard	Normal	Status	—	—	25	2 Allies	—
TM21	Frustration	Normal	Physical	—	100	20	Normal	○
TM22	SolarBeam	Grass	Special	120	100	10	Normal	—
TM24	Thunderbolt	Electric	Special	95	100	15	Normal	—
TM25	Thunder	Electric	Special	120	70	10	Normal	—
TM27	Return	Normal	Physical	—	100	20	Normal	○
TM29	Psychic	Psychic	Special	90	100	10	Normal	—
TM30	Shadow Ball	Ghost	Special	80	100	15	Normal	—
TM31	Brick Break	Fighting	Physical	75	100	15	Normal	○
TM32	Double Team	Normal	Status	—	—	15	Self	—
TM33	Reflect	Psychic	Status	—	—	20	2 Allies	—
TM34	Shock Wave	Electric	Special	60	—	20	Normal	—
TM39	Rock Tomb	Rock	Physical	50	80	10	Normal	○
TM40	Aerial Ace	Flying	Physical	60	—	20	Normal	○
TM41	Torment	Dark	Status	—	100	15	Normal	—
TM42	Facade	Normal	Physical	70	100	20	Normal	○
TM43	Secret Power	Normal	Physical	70	100	20	Normal	○
TM44	Rest	Psychic	Status	—	—	10	Self	—
TM48	Skill Swap	Psychic	Status	—	—	10	Normal	—
TM49	Snatch	Dark	Status	—	—	10	Depends	—
TM52	Focus Blast	Fighting	Special	120	70	5	Normal	—
TM53	Energy Ball	Grass	Special	80	100	10	Normal	—
TM56	Fling	Dark	Physical	—	100	10	Normal	○
TM57	Charge Beam	Electric	Special	50	90	10	Normal	—
TM58	Endure	Normal	Status	—	—	10	Self	—
TM60	Drain Punch	Fighting	Physical	60	100	5	Normal	○
TM67	Recycle	Normal	Status	—	—	10	Self	—
TM68	Giga Impact	Normal	Physical	150	90	5	Normal	○
TM70	Flash	Normal	Status	—	100	20	Normal	—
TM72	Avalanche	Ice	Physical	60	100	10	Normal	○
TM73	Thunder Wave	Electric	Status	—	100	20	Normal	—
TM76	Stealth Rock	Rock	Status	—	—	20	2 Foes	—
TM77	Psych Up	Normal	Status	—	—	10	Normal	—
TM80	Rock Slide	Rock	Physical	75	90	10	2 Foes	○
TM82	Sleep Talk	Normal	Status	—	—	10	Depends	—
TM83	Natural Gift	Normal	Physical	—	100	15	Normal	—
TM84	Poison Jab	Poison	Physical	80	100	20	Normal	○
TM85	Dream Eater	Psychic	Special	100	100	15	Normal	—
TM86	Grass Knot	Grass	Special	—	100	20	Normal	—
TM87	Swagger	Normal	Status	—	90	15	Normal	—
TM90	Substitute	Normal	Status	—	—	10	Self	—
TM91	Flash Cannon	Steel	Special	80	100	10	Normal	—
TM92	Trick Room	Psychic	Status	—	—	5	All	—
HM01	Cut	Normal	Physical	50	95	30	Normal	—
HM04	Strength	Normal	Physical	80	100	15	Normal	—
HM06	Rock Smash	Fighting	Physical	40	100	15	Normal	—

● No. 386 | DNA Pokémon
Deoxys (Defense Forme)
Psychic

- ● **HEIGHT:** 5'07"
- ● **WEIGHT:** 134.0 lbs.
- ● **ITEMS:** None

● SIZE COMPARISON

● GENDER UNKNOWN

☺ ABILITIES
- ● Pressure

☺ STATS
```
HP           ●●
ATTACK       ●●●
DEFENSE      ●●●●●●
SP. ATTACK   ●●●
SP. DEFENSE  ●●●●●●
SPEED        ●●●●
```

☺ EGG GROUPS
No Egg has ever been discovered

☺ PERFORMANCE
SPEED ★★★ STAMINA ★★★★★
POWER ★★★☆ JUMP ★★☆
SKILL ★★★★☆

● MAIN WAYS TO OBTAIN

Pokémon HeartGold —

Pokémon SoulSilver —

Pokémon Diamond — Only obtainable through special distribution events—cannot be obtained through regular gameplay*

Pokémon Pearl — Only obtainable through special distribution events—cannot be obtained through regular gameplay*

Pokémon Platinum —

Pokémon HeartGold — DNA from a space virus mutated and became a Pokémon. It appears where auroras are seen.

Pokémon SoulSilver — DNA from a space virus mutated and became a Pokémon. It appears where auroras are seen.

☺ EVOLUTION
Does not evolve

*Deoxys is only available through special distribution events. Check Pokemon.com for the latest information on how to catch this Pokémon.

No. 386 | DNA Pokémon
Deoxys (Speed Forme)
Psychic

- HEIGHT: 5'07"
- WEIGHT: 134.0 lbs.
- ITEMS: None

● SIZE COMPARISON

● GENDER UNKNOWN

ABILITIES
- Pressure

STATS
HP	●●
ATTACK	●●●●
DEFENSE	●●●●
SP. ATTACK	●●●●
SP. DEFENSE	●●●●
SPEED	●●●●●●

EGG GROUPS
No Egg has ever been discovered

PERFORMANCE
SPEED ★★★★★ STAMINA ★★★☆
POWER ★★☆ JUMP ★★★★
SKILL ★★★★☆

MAIN WAYS TO OBTAIN

Pokémon HeartGold	—
Pokémon SoulSilver	—
Pokémon Diamond	Only obtainable through special distribution events—cannot be obtained through regular gameplay*
Pokémon Pearl	Only obtainable through special distribution events—cannot be obtained through regular gameplay*
Pokémon Platinum	—
Pokémon HeartGold	DNA from a space virus mutated and became a Pokémon. It appears where auroras are seen.
Pokémon SoulSilver	DNA from a space virus mutated and became a Pokémon. It appears where auroras are seen.

EVOLUTION
Does not evolve

● LEVEL-UP MOVES

Lv.	Name	Type	Kind	Pow.	Acc.	PP	Range	DA
1	Leer	Normal	Status	—	100	30	2 Foes	—
1	Wrap	Normal	Physical	15	85	20	Normal	○
9	Night Shade	Ghost	Special	—	100	15	Normal	—
17	Double Team	Normal	Status	—	—	15	Self	—
25	Knock Off	Dark	Physical	20	100	20	Normal	○
33	Pursuit	Dark	Physical	40	100	20	Normal	○
41	Psychic	Psychic	Special	90	100	10	Normal	—
49	Swift	Normal	Special	60	—	20	2 Foes	—
57	Psycho Shift	Psychic	Status	—	90	10	Normal	—
65	Zen Headbutt	Psychic	Physical	80	90	15	Normal	○
73	Agility	Psychic	Status	—	—	30	Self	—
81	Recover	Normal	Status	—	—	10	Self	—
89	Psycho Boost	Psychic	Special	140	90	5	Normal	—
97	ExtremeSpeed	Normal	Physical	80	100	5	Normal	○

● MOVE MANIAC

Name	Type	Kind	Pow.	Acc.	PP	Range	DA
Headbutt	Normal	Physical	70	100	15	Normal	○

● BP MOVES

Name	Type	Kind	Pow.	Acc.	PP	Range	DA
Zen Headbutt	Psychic	Physical	80	90	15	Normal	—
Trick	Psychic	Status	—	100	10	Normal	—
Knock Off	Dark	Physical	20	100	20	Normal	—
Snore	Normal	Special	40	100	15	Normal	—
Swift	Normal	Special	60	—	20	2 Foes	—
Gravity	Psychic	Status	—	—	5	All	—
Magic Coat	Psychic	Status	—	—	15	Self	—
Role Play	Psychic	Status	—	—	10	Normal	—
Mud-Slap	Ground	Special	20	100	10	Normal	—
Signal Beam	Bug	Special	75	100	15	Normal	—
Low Kick	Fighting	Physical	—	100	20	Normal	○

● TM & HM MOVES

No.	Name	Type	Kind	Pow.	Acc.	PP	Range	DA
TM01	Focus Punch	Fighting	Physical	150	100	20	Normal	○
TM03	Water Pulse	Water	Special	60	100	20	Normal	—
TM04	Calm Mind	Psychic	Status	—	—	20	Self	—
TM06	Toxic	Poison	Status	—	85	10	Normal	—
TM10	Hidden Power	Normal	Special	—	100	15	Normal	—
TM11	Sunny Day	Fire	Status	—	—	5	All	—
TM12	Taunt	Dark	Status	—	100	20	Normal	—
TM13	Ice Beam	Ice	Special	95	100	10	Normal	—
TM15	Hyper Beam	Normal	Special	150	90	5	Normal	—
TM16	Light Screen	Psychic	Status	—	—	30	2 Allies	—
TM17	Protect	Normal	Status	—	—	10	Self	—
TM18	Rain Dance	Water	Status	—	—	5	All	—
TM20	Safeguard	Normal	Status	—	—	25	2 Allies	—
TM21	Frustration	Normal	Physical	—	100	20	Normal	○
TM22	SolarBeam	Grass	Special	120	100	10	Normal	—
TM24	Thunderbolt	Electric	Special	95	100	15	Normal	—
TM25	Thunder	Electric	Special	120	70	10	Normal	—
TM27	Return	Normal	Physical	—	100	20	Normal	○
TM29	Psychic	Psychic	Special	90	100	10	Normal	—
TM30	Shadow Ball	Ghost	Special	80	100	15	Normal	—
TM31	Brick Break	Fighting	Physical	75	100	15	Normal	○
TM32	Double Team	Normal	Status	—	—	15	Self	—
TM33	Reflect	Psychic	Status	—	—	20	2 Allies	—
TM34	Shock Wave	Electric	Special	60	—	20	Normal	—
TM39	Rock Tomb	Rock	Physical	50	80	10	Normal	○
TM40	Aerial Ace	Flying	Physical	60	—	20	Normal	○
TM41	Torment	Dark	Status	—	100	15	Normal	—
TM42	Facade	Normal	Physical	70	100	20	Normal	○
TM43	Secret Power	Normal	Physical	70	100	20	Normal	○
TM44	Rest	Psychic	Status	—	—	10	Self	—
TM48	Skill Swap	Psychic	Status	—	—	10	Normal	—
TM49	Snatch	Dark	Status	—	—	10	Depends	—
TM52	Focus Blast	Fighting	Special	120	70	5	Normal	—
TM53	Energy Ball	Grass	Special	80	100	10	Normal	—
TM56	Fling	Dark	Physical	—	100	10	Normal	○
TM57	Charge Beam	Electric	Special	50	90	10	Normal	—
TM58	Endure	Normal	Status	—	—	10	Self	—
TM60	Drain Punch	Fighting	Physical	60	100	5	Normal	○
TM67	Recycle	Normal	Status	—	—	10	Self	—
TM68	Giga Impact	Normal	Physical	150	90	5	Normal	○
TM70	Flash	Normal	Status	—	100	20	Normal	—
TM72	Avalanche	Ice	Physical	60	100	10	Normal	○
TM73	Thunder Wave	Electric	Status	—	100	20	Normal	—
TM76	Stealth Rock	Rock	Status	—	—	20	2 Foes	—
TM77	Psych Up	Normal	Status	—	—	10	Normal	—
TM80	Rock Slide	Rock	Physical	75	90	10	2 Foes	○
TM82	Sleep Talk	Normal	Status	—	—	10	Depends	—
TM83	Natural Gift	Normal	Physical	—	100	15	Normal	○
TM84	Poison Jab	Poison	Physical	80	100	20	Normal	○
TM85	Dream Eater	Psychic	Special	100	100	15	Normal	—
TM86	Grass Knot	Grass	Special	—	100	20	Normal	○
TM87	Swagger	Normal	Status	—	90	15	Normal	—
TM90	Substitute	Normal	Status	—	—	10	Self	—
TM91	Flash Cannon	Steel	Special	80	100	10	Normal	—
TM92	Trick Room	Psychic	Status	—	—	5	All	—
HM01	Cut	Normal	Physical	50	95	30	Normal	○
HM04	Strength	Normal	Physical	80	100	15	Normal	○
HM06	Rock Smash	Fighting	Physical	40	100	15	Normal	○

*Deoxys is only available through special distribution events. Check Pokemon.com for the latest information on how to catch this Pokémon.

● LEVEL-UP MOVES

Lv.	Name	Type	Kind	Pow.	Acc.	PP	Range	DA
1	Tackle	Normal	Physical	35	95	35	Normal	○
5	Withdraw	Water	Status	—	—	40	Self	—
9	Absorb	Grass	Special	20	100	25	Normal	—
13	Razor Leaf	Grass	Physical	55	95	25	2 Foes	—
17	Curse	???	Status	—	—	10	Normal/Self	—
21	Bite	Dark	Physical	60	100	25	Normal	○
25	Mega Drain	Grass	Special	40	100	15	Normal	—
29	Leech Seed	Grass	Status	—	90	10	Normal	—
33	Synthesis	Grass	Status	—	—	5	Self	—
37	Crunch	Dark	Physical	80	100	15	Normal	○
41	Giga Drain	Grass	Special	60	100	10	Normal	—
45	Leaf Storm	Grass	Special	140	90	5	Normal	—

● MOVE MANIAC

Name	Type	Kind	Pow.	Acc.	PP	Range	DA
Headbutt	Normal	Physical	70	100	15	Normal	○

● BP MOVES

Name	Type	Kind	Pow.	Acc.	PP	Range	DA
Snore	Normal	Special	40	100	15	Normal	—
Synthesis	Grass	Status	—	—	5	Self	—
Worry Seed	Grass	Status	—	100	10	Normal	—
Mud-Slap	Ground	Special	20	100	10	Normal	—
Superpower	Fighting	Physical	120	100	5	Normal	○
Earth Power	Ground	Special	90	100	10	Normal	—
Seed Bomb	Grass	Physical	80	100	15	Normal	—

● TM & HM MOVES

No.	Name	Type	Kind	Pow.	Acc.	PP	Range	DA
TM06	Toxic	Poison	Status	—	85	10	Normal	—
TM09	Bullet Seed	Grass	Physical	10	100	30	Normal	—
TM10	Hidden Power	Normal	Special	—	100	15	Normal	—
TM11	Sunny Day	Fire	Status	—	—	5	All	—
TM16	Light Screen	Psychic	Status	—	—	30	2 Allies	—
TM17	Protect	Normal	Status	—	—	10	Self	—
TM19	Giga Drain	Grass	Special	60	100	10	Normal	—
TM20	Safeguard	Normal	Status	—	—	25	2 Allies	—
TM21	Frustration	Normal	Physical	—	100	20	Normal	○
TM22	SolarBeam	Grass	Special	120	100	10	Normal	—
TM23	Iron Tail	Steel	Physical	100	75	15	Normal	○
TM27	Return	Normal	Physical	—	100	20	Normal	○
TM32	Double Team	Normal	Status	—	—	15	Self	—
TM33	Reflect	Psychic	Status	—	—	20	2 Allies	—
TM42	Facade	Normal	Physical	70	100	20	Normal	○
TM43	Secret Power	Normal	Physical	70	100	20	Normal	○
TM44	Rest	Psychic	Status	—	—	10	Self	—
TM45	Attract	Normal	Status	—	100	15	Normal	—
TM53	Energy Ball	Grass	Special	80	100	10	Normal	—
TM58	Endure	Normal	Status	—	—	10	Self	—
TM70	Flash	Normal	Status	—	100	20	Normal	—
TM75	Swords Dance	Normal	Status	—	—	30	Self	—
TM76	Stealth Rock	Rock	Status	—	—	20	2 Foes	—
TM78	Captivate	Normal	Status	—	100	20	2 Foes	—
TM82	Sleep Talk	Normal	Status	—	—	10	Depends	—
TM83	Natural Gift	Normal	Physical	—	100	15	Normal	○
TM86	Grass Knot	Grass	Special	—	100	20	Normal	○
TM87	Swagger	Normal	Status	—	90	15	Normal	—
TM90	Substitute	Normal	Status	—	—	10	Self	—
HM01	Cut	Normal	Physical	50	95	30	Normal	○
HM04	Strength	Normal	Physical	80	100	15	Normal	○
HM06	Rock Smash	Fighting	Physical	40	100	15	Normal	○
HM08	Rock Climb	Normal	Physical	90	85	20	Normal	○

● EGG MOVES

Name	Type	Kind	Pow.	Acc.	PP	Range	DA
Worry Seed	Grass	Status	—	100	10	Normal	—
Growth	Normal	Status	—	—	40	Self	—
Tickle	Normal	Status	—	100	20	Normal	—
Body Slam	Normal	Physical	85	100	15	Normal	○
Double-Edge	Normal	Physical	120	100	15	Normal	○
Sand Tomb	Ground	Physical	15	70	15	Normal	—
Seed Bomb	Grass	Physical	80	100	15	Normal	—
Thrash	Normal	Physical	90	100	20	1 Random	○
Amnesia	Psychic	Status	—	—	20	Self	—
Superpower	Fighting	Physical	120	100	5	Normal	○
Stockpile	Normal	Status	—	—	20	Self	—
Swallow	Normal	Status	—	—	10	Self	—
Spit Up	Normal	Special	—	100	10	Normal	—

● No. 387 | Tiny Leaf Pokémon
Turtwig

`Grass`

- ● HEIGHT: 1'04"
- ● WEIGHT: 22.5 lbs.
- ● ITEMS: None

● SIZE COMPARISON

● MALE/FEMALE HAVE SAME FORM

⊘ ABILITIES
- ● Overgrow

⊘ STATS
- HP ●●
- ATTACK ●●●
- DEFENSE ●●●
- SP. ATTACK ●●
- SP. DEFENSE ●●
- SPEED ●

⊘ EGG GROUPS
Monster

Grass

⊘ PERFORMANCE
- SPEED ★★★☆
- POWER ★★★☆
- SKILL ★★☆
- STAMINA ★★★☆
- JUMP ★★☆

● MAIN WAYS TO OBTAIN

Pokémon HeartGold	—
Pokémon SoulSilver	—
Pokémon Diamond	Receive from Professor Rowan at the beginning of the adventure
Pokémon Pearl	Receive from Professor Rowan at the beginning of the adventure
Pokémon Platinum	Receive from Professor Rowan at the beginning of the adventure

Pokémon HeartGold
Photosynthesis occurs across its body under the sun. The shell on its back is actually hardened soil.

Pokémon SoulSilver
Photosynthesis occurs across its body under the sun. The shell on its back is actually hardened soil.

⊘ EVOLUTION

Lv. 18 → Lv. 32

Turtwig → Grotle → Torterra

No. 388 | Grove Pokémon
Grotle

Grass

- **HEIGHT:** 3'07"
- **WEIGHT:** 213.8 lbs.
- **ITEMS:** None

● SIZE COMPARISON

● MALE/FEMALE HAVE SAME FORM

⊛ ABILITIES
● Overgrow

⊛ STATS
HP ●●●
ATTACK ●●●●
DEFENSE ●●●
SP. ATTACK ●●●
SP. DEFENSE ●●
SPEED ●●

⊛ EGG GROUPS
Monster

Grass

⊛ PERFORMANCE

SPEED ★★☆　　STAMINA ★★★★☆
POWER ★★★★　JUMP ★★☆
SKILL ★★★

● MAIN WAYS TO OBTAIN

Pokémon HeartGold	—
Pokémon SoulSilver	—
Pokémon Diamond	Level up Turtwig to Lv. 18
Pokémon Pearl	Level up Turtwig to Lv. 18
Pokémon Platinum	Level up Turtwig to Lv. 18

Pokémon HeartGold	Pokémon SoulSilver
A GROTLE that lives in the forest is said to have its own secret springwater.	A GROTLE that lives in the forest is said to have its own secret springwater.

⊛ EVOLUTION

Lv. 18　　Lv. 32

Turtwig　Grotle　Torterra

● LEVEL-UP MOVES

Lv.	Name	Type	Kind	Pow.	Acc.	PP	Range	DA
1	Tackle	Normal	Physical	35	95	35	Normal	○
1	Withdraw	Water	Status	—	—	40	Self	—
5	Withdraw	Water	Status	—	—	40	Self	—
9	Absorb	Grass	Special	20	100	25	Normal	—
13	Razor Leaf	Grass	Physical	55	95	25	2 Foes	—
17	Curse	???	Status	—	—	10	Normal/Self	—
22	Bite	Dark	Physical	60	100	25	Normal	○
27	Mega Drain	Grass	Special	40	100	15	Normal	—
32	Leech Seed	Grass	Status	—	90	10	Normal	—
37	Synthesis	Grass	Status	—	—	5	Self	—
42	Crunch	Dark	Physical	80	100	15	Normal	○
47	Giga Drain	Grass	Special	60	100	10	Normal	—
52	Leaf Storm	Grass	Special	140	90	5	Normal	—

● MOVE MANIAC

Name	Type	Kind	Pow.	Acc.	PP	Range	DA
Headbutt	Normal	Physical	70	100	15	Normal	○

● BP MOVES

Name	Type	Kind	Pow.	Acc.	PP	Range	DA
Snore	Normal	Special	40	100	15	Normal	—
Synthesis	Grass	Status	—	—	5	Self	—
Worry Seed	Grass	Status	—	100	10	Normal	—
Mud-Slap	Ground	Special	20	100	10	Normal	—
Superpower	Fighting	Physical	120	100	5	Normal	○
Earth Power	Ground	Special	90	100	10	Normal	—
Seed Bomb	Grass	Physical	80	100	15	Normal	—

● TM & HM MOVES

No.	Name	Type	Kind	Pow.	Acc.	PP	Range	DA
TM06	Toxic	Poison	Status	—	85	10	Normal	—
TM09	Bullet Seed	Grass	Physical	10	100	30	Normal	—
TM10	Hidden Power	Normal	Special	—	100	15	Normal	—
TM11	Sunny Day	Fire	Status	—	—	5	All	—
TM16	Light Screen	Psychic	Status	—	—	30	2 Allies	—
TM17	Protect	Normal	Status	—	—	10	Self	—
TM19	Giga Drain	Grass	Special	60	100	10	Normal	—
TM20	Safeguard	Normal	Status	—	—	25	2 Allies	—
TM21	Frustration	Normal	Physical	—	100	20	Normal	○
TM22	SolarBeam	Grass	Special	120	100	10	Normal	—
TM23	Iron Tail	Steel	Physical	100	75	15	Normal	○
TM27	Return	Normal	Physical	—	100	20	Normal	○
TM32	Double Team	Normal	Status	—	—	15	Self	—
TM33	Reflect	Psychic	Status	—	—	20	2 Allies	—
TM42	Facade	Normal	Physical	70	100	20	Normal	○
TM43	Secret Power	Normal	Physical	70	100	20	Normal	—
TM44	Rest	Psychic	Status	—	—	10	Self	—
TM45	Attract	Normal	Status	—	100	15	Normal	—
TM53	Energy Ball	Grass	Special	80	100	10	Normal	—
TM58	Endure	Normal	Status	—	—	10	Self	—
TM70	Flash	Normal	Status	—	100	20	Normal	—
TM75	Swords Dance	Normal	Status	—	—	30	Self	—
TM76	Stealth Rock	Rock	Status	—	—	20	2 Foes	—
TM78	Captivate	Normal	Status	—	100	20	2 Foes	—
TM82	Sleep Talk	Normal	Status	—	—	10	Depends	—
TM83	Natural Gift	Normal	Physical	—	100	15	Normal	—
TM86	Grass Knot	Grass	Special	—	100	20	Normal	○
TM87	Swagger	Normal	Status	—	90	15	Normal	—
TM90	Substitute	Normal	Status	—	—	10	Self	—
HM01	Cut	Normal	Physical	50	95	30	Normal	○
HM04	Strength	Normal	Physical	80	100	15	Normal	○
HM06	Rock Smash	Fighting	Physical	40	100	15	Normal	○
HM08	Rock Climb	Normal	Physical	90	85	20	Normal	○

● LEVEL-UP MOVES

Lv.	Name	Type	Kind	Pow.	Acc.	PP	Range	DA
1	Smog	Poison	Special	20	70	20	Normal	—
1	Leer	Normal	Status	—	100	30	2 Foes	—
7	Ember	Fire	Special	40	100	25	Normal	—
10	SmokeScreen	Normal	Status	—	100	20	Normal	—
16	Faint Attack	Dark	Physical	60	—	20	Normal	O
19	Fire Spin	Fire	Special	15	70	15	Normal	—
25	Confuse Ray	Ghost	Status	—	100	10	Normal	—
28	Fire Punch	Fire	Physical	75	100	15	Normal	—
34	Lava Plume	Fire	Special	80	100	15	2 Foes/1 Ally	—
37	Flamethrower	Fire	Special	95	100	15	Normal	—
43	Sunny Day	Fire	Status	—	—	5	All	—
46	Fire Blast	Fire	Special	120	85	5	Normal	—

● MOVE MANIAC

Name	Type	Kind	Pow.	Acc.	PP	Range	DA
Headbutt	Normal	Physical	70	100	15	Normal	O

● BP MOVES

Name	Type	Kind	Pow.	Acc.	PP	Range	DA
ThunderPunch	Electric	Physical	75	100	15	Normal	O
Fire Punch	Fire	Physical	75	100	15	Normal	O
Snore	Normal	Special	40	100	15	Normal	—
Helping Hand	Normal	Status	—	—	20	1 Ally	—
Uproar	Normal	Special	50	100	10	1 Random	—
Mud-Slap	Ground	Special	20	100	10	Normal	—
Heat Wave	Fire	Special	100	90	10	2 Foes	—

● TM & HM MOVES

No.	Name	Type	Kind	Pow.	Acc.	PP	Range	DA
TM01	Focus Punch	Fighting	Physical	150	100	20	Normal	O
TM03	Water Pulse	Water	Special	60	100	20	Normal	—
TM05	Roar	Normal	Status	—	100	20	Normal	—
TM06	Toxic	Poison	Status	—	85	10	Normal	—
TM07	Hail	Ice	Status	—	—	10	All	—
TM10	Hidden Power	Normal	Special	—	100	15	Normal	—
TM13	Ice Beam	Ice	Special	95	100	10	Normal	—
TM14	Blizzard	Ice	Special	120	70	5	2 Foes	—
TM17	Protect	Normal	Status	—	—	10	Self	—
TM18	Rain Dance	Water	Status	—	—	5	All	—
TM21	Frustration	Normal	Physical	—	100	20	Normal	O
TM23	Iron Tail	Steel	Physical	100	75	15	Normal	O
TM27	Return	Normal	Physical	—	100	20	Normal	O
TM28	Dig	Ground	Physical	80	100	10	Normal	O
TM31	Brick Break	Fighting	Physical	75	100	15	Normal	O
TM32	Double Team	Normal	Status	—	—	15	Self	—
TM39	Rock Tomb	Rock	Physical	50	80	10	Normal	—
TM40	Aerial Ace	Flying	Physical	60	—	20	Normal	O
TM42	Facade	Normal	Physical	70	100	20	Normal	O
TM43	Secret Power	Normal	Physical	70	100	20	Normal	—
TM44	Rest	Psychic	Status	—	—	10	Self	—
TM45	Attract	Normal	Status	—	100	15	Normal	—
TM56	Fling	Dark	Physical	—	100	10	Normal	—
TM58	Endure	Normal	Status	—	—	10	Self	—
TM65	Shadow Claw	Ghost	Physical	70	100	15	Normal	O
TM75	Swords Dance	Normal	Status	—	—	30	Self	—
TM78	Captivate	Normal	Status	—	100	20	2 Foes	—
TM80	Rock Slide	Rock	Physical	75	90	10	2 Foes	—
TM82	Sleep Talk	Normal	Status	—	—	10	Self	—
TM83	Natural Gift	Normal	Physical	—	100	15	Normal	—
TM87	Swagger	Normal	Status	—	90	15	Normal	—
TM90	Substitute	Normal	Status	—	—	10	Self	—
HM01	Cut	Normal	Physical	50	95	30	Normal	O
HM03	Surf	Water	Special	95	100	15	2 Foes/1 Ally	—
HM04	Strength	Normal	Physical	80	100	15	Normal	O
HM05	Whirlpool	Water	Special	15	70	15	Normal	—
HM06	Rock Smash	Fighting	Physical	40	100	15	Normal	O
HM07	Waterfall	Water	Physical	80	100	15	Normal	O

● No. 389 | Continent Pokémon
Torterra

 Grass Ground

● **HEIGHT:** 7'03"
● **WEIGHT:** 683.4 lbs.
● **ITEMS:** None

● SIZE COMPARISON

● MALE/FEMALE HAVE SAME FORM

⊙ ABILITIES
● Overgrow

⊙ STATS
HP ●●●●
ATTACK ●●●●●
DEFENSE ●●●●
SP. ATTACK ●●●
SP. DEFENSE ●●●
SPEED ●●●

⊙ EGG GROUPS
Monster

Grass

⊙ PERFORMANCE
SPEED ★☆   STAMINA ★★★★★
POWER ★★★★★   JUMP ★★
SKILL ★★★

● MAIN WAYS TO OBTAIN

Pokémon HeartGold —

Pokémon SoulSilver —

Pokémon Diamond Level up Grotle to Lv. 32

Pokémon Pearl Level up Grotle to Lv. 32

Pokémon Platinum Level up Grotle to Lv. 32

Pokémon HeartGold
Ancient people imagined that beneath the ground, a gigantic TORTERRA dwelled.

Pokémon SoulSilver
Ancient people imagined that beneath the ground, a gigantic TORTERRA dwelled.

⊙ EVOLUTION

Lv. 18   Lv. 32

Turtwig   Grotle   Torterra

No.390 | Chimp Pokémon
Chimchar

Fire

- **HEIGHT:** 1'08"
- **WEIGHT:** 13.7 lbs.
- **ITEMS:** None

● SIZE COMPARISON

● MALE/FEMALE HAVE SAME FORM

● ABILITIES
- Blaze

● STATS
HP ●●
ATTACK ●●
DEFENSE ●●
SP. ATTACK ●●
SP. DEFENSE ●●
SPEED ●●●

● EGG GROUPS
Field

Human-like

● PERFORMANCE
SPEED ★★★★★   STAMINA ★☆
POWER ★★★☆   JUMP ★★★
SKILL ★★★☆

● MAIN WAYS TO OBTAIN

Pokémon HeartGold	—
Pokémon SoulSilver	—
Pokémon Diamond	Receive from Professor Rowan at the beginning of the adventure
Pokémon Pearl	Receive from Professor Rowan at the beginning of the adventure
Pokémon Platinum	Receive from Professor Rowan at the beginning of the adventure

| *Pokémon HeartGold* | *Pokémon SoulSilver* |
| The gas made in its belly burns from its rear end. The fire burns weakly when it feels sick. | The gas made in its belly burns from its rear end. The fire burns weakly when it feels sick. |

● EVOLUTION
Chimchar — Lv. 14 → Monferno — Lv. 36 → Infernape

● LEVEL-UP MOVES

Lv.	Name	Type	Kind	Pow.	Acc.	PP	Range	DA
1	Scratch	Normal	Physical	40	100	35	Normal	○
1	Leer	Normal	Status	—	100	30	2 Foes	—
7	Ember	Fire	Special	40	100	25	Normal	—
9	Taunt	Dark	Status	—	100	20	Normal	—
15	Fury Swipes	Normal	Physical	18	80	15	Normal	○
17	Flame Wheel	Fire	Physical	60	100	25	Normal	○
23	Nasty Plot	Dark	Status	—	—	20	Self	—
25	Torment	Dark	Status	—	100	15	Normal	—
31	Facade	Normal	Physical	70	100	20	Normal	○
33	Fire Spin	Fire	Special	15	70	15	Normal	—
39	Slack Off	Normal	Status	—	—	10	Self	—
41	Flamethrower	Fire	Special	95	100	15	Normal	—

● MOVE MANIAC

Name	Type	Kind	Pow.	Acc.	PP	Range	DA
Headbutt	Normal	Physical	70	100	15	Normal	○

● BP MOVES

Name	Type	Kind	Pow.	Acc.	PP	Range	DA
ThunderPunch	Electric	Physical	75	100	15	Normal	○
Fire Punch	Fire	Physical	75	100	15	Normal	○
Vacuum Wave	Fighting	Special	40	100	30	Normal	—
Snore	Normal	Special	40	100	15	Normal	—
Helping Hand	Normal	Status	—	—	20	1 Ally	—
Swift	Normal	Special	60	—	20	2 Foes	—
Uproar	Normal	Special	50	100	10	1 Random	—
Role Play	Psychic	Status	—	—	10	Normal	—
Mud-Slap	Ground	Special	20	100	10	Normal	—
Rollout	Rock	Physical	30	90	20	Normal	○
Endeavor	Normal	Physical	—	100	5	Normal	—
Gunk Shot	Poison	Physical	120	70	5	Normal	—
Heat Wave	Fire	Special	100	90	10	2 Foes	—
Low Kick	Fighting	Physical	—	100	20	Normal	○

● TM & HM MOVES

No.	Name	Type	Kind	Pow.	Acc.	PP	Range	DA
TM01	Focus Punch	Fighting	Physical	150	100	20	Normal	○
TM06	Toxic	Poison	Status	—	85	10	Normal	—
TM08	Bulk Up	Fighting	Status	—	—	20	Self	—
TM10	Hidden Power	Normal	Special	—	100	15	Normal	—
TM11	Sunny Day	Fire	Status	—	—	5	All	—
TM12	Taunt	Dark	Status	—	100	20	Normal	—
TM17	Protect	Normal	Status	—	—	10	Self	—
TM21	Frustration	Normal	Physical	—	100	20	Normal	○
TM23	Iron Tail	Steel	Physical	100	75	15	Normal	○
TM27	Return	Normal	Physical	—	100	20	Normal	○
TM28	Dig	Ground	Physical	80	100	10	Normal	○
TM31	Brick Break	Fighting	Physical	75	100	15	Normal	○
TM32	Double Team	Normal	Status	—	—	15	Self	—
TM35	Flamethrower	Fire	Special	95	100	15	Normal	—
TM38	Fire Blast	Fire	Special	120	85	5	Normal	—
TM40	Aerial Ace	Flying	Physical	60	—	20	Normal	○
TM41	Torment	Dark	Status	—	100	15	Normal	—
TM42	Facade	Normal	Physical	70	100	20	Normal	○
TM43	Secret Power	Normal	Physical	70	100	20	Normal	○
TM44	Rest	Psychic	Status	—	—	10	Self	—
TM45	Attract	Normal	Status	—	100	15	Normal	—
TM50	Overheat	Fire	Special	140	90	5	Normal	—
TM56	Fling	Dark	Physical	—	100	10	Normal	—
TM58	Endure	Normal	Status	—	—	10	Self	—
TM61	Will-O-Wisp	Fire	Status	—	75	15	Normal	—
TM65	Shadow Claw	Ghost	Physical	70	100	15	Normal	○
TM75	Swords Dance	Normal	Status	—	—	30	Self	—
TM76	Stealth Rock	Rock	Status	—	—	20	2 Foes	—
TM78	Captivate	Normal	Status	—	100	20	2 Foes	—
TM82	Sleep Talk	Normal	Status	—	—	10	Depends	—
TM83	Natural Gift	Normal	Physical	—	100	15	Normal	○
TM86	Grass Knot	Grass	Special	—	100	20	Normal	—
TM87	Swagger	Normal	Status	—	90	15	Normal	—
TM89	U-turn	Bug	Physical	70	100	20	Normal	○
TM90	Substitute	Normal	Status	—	—	10	Self	—
HM01	Cut	Normal	Physical	50	95	30	Normal	○
HM04	Strength	Normal	Physical	80	100	15	Normal	○
HM06	Rock Smash	Fighting	Physical	40	100	15	Normal	○
HM08	Rock Climb	Normal	Physical	90	85	20	Normal	○

● EGG MOVES

Name	Type	Kind	Pow.	Acc.	PP	Range	DA
Fire Punch	Fire	Physical	75	100	15	Normal	○
ThunderPunch	Electric	Physical	75	100	15	Normal	○
Double Kick	Fighting	Physical	30	100	30	Normal	○
Encore	Normal	Status	—	100	5	Normal	—
Heat Wave	Fire	Special	100	90	10	2 Foes	—
Focus Energy	Normal	Status	—	—	30	Self	—
Helping Hand	Normal	Status	—	—	20	1 Ally	—
Fake Out	Normal	Physical	40	100	10	Normal	○
Blaze Kick	Fire	Physical	85	90	10	Normal	○
Counter	Fighting	Physical	—	100	20	Self	○
Assist	Normal	Status	—	—	20	Depends	—

● LEVEL-UP MOVES

Lv.	Name	Type	Kind	Pow.	Acc.	PP	Range	DA
1	Scratch	Normal	Physical	40	100	35	Normal	○
1	Leer	Normal	Status	—	100	30	2 Foes	—
1	Ember	Fire	Special	40	100	25	Normal	—
7	Ember	Fire	Special	40	100	25	Normal	—
9	Taunt	Dark	Status	—	100	20	Normal	—
14	Mach Punch	Fighting	Physical	40	100	30	Normal	○
16	Fury Swipes	Normal	Physical	18	80	15	Normal	○
19	Flame Wheel	Fire	Physical	60	100	25	Normal	○
26	Feint	Normal	Physical	50	100	10	Normal	○
29	Torment	Dark	Status	—	100	15	Normal	—
36	Close Combat	Fighting	Physical	120	100	5	Normal	○
39	Fire Spin	Fire	Special	15	70	15	Normal	—
46	Slack Off	Normal	Status	—	—	10	Self	—
49	Flare Blitz	Fire	Physical	120	100	15	Normal	○

● MOVE MANIAC

Name	Type	Kind	Pow.	Acc.	PP	Range	DA
Headbutt	Normal	Physical	70	100	15	Normal	○

● BP MOVES

Name	Type	Kind	Pow.	Acc.	PP	Range	DA
ThunderPunch	Electric	Physical	75	100	15	Normal	○
Fire Punch	Fire	Physical	75	100	15	Normal	○
Vacuum Wave	Fighting	Special	40	100	30	Normal	—
Snore	Normal	Special	40	100	15	Normal	—
Helping Hand	Normal	Status	—	—	20	1 Ally	—
Swift	Normal	Special	60	—	20	2 Foes	—
Role Play	Psychic	Status	—	—	10	Normal	—
Mud-Slap	Ground	Special	20	100	10	Normal	—
Rollout	Rock	Physical	30	90	20	Normal	○
Endeavor	Normal	Physical	—	100	5	Normal	○
Gunk Shot	Poison	Physical	120	70	5	Normal	○
Heat Wave	Fire	Special	100	90	10	2 Foes	—
Low Kick	Fighting	Physical	—	100	20	Normal	○

● TM & HM MOVES

No.	Name	Type	Kind	Pow.	Acc.	PP	Range	DA
TM01	Focus Punch	Fighting	Physical	150	100	20	Normal	○
TM06	Toxic	Poison	Status	—	85	10	Normal	—
TM08	Bulk Up	Fighting	Status	—	—	20	Self	—
TM10	Hidden Power	Normal	Special	—	100	15	Normal	—
TM11	Sunny Day	Fire	Status	—	—	5	All	—
TM12	Taunt	Dark	Status	—	100	20	Normal	—
TM17	Protect	Normal	Status	—	—	10	Self	—
TM21	Frustration	Normal	Physical	—	100	20	Normal	○
TM23	Iron Tail	Steel	Physical	100	75	15	Normal	○
TM27	Return	Normal	Physical	—	100	20	Normal	○
TM28	Dig	Ground	Physical	80	100	10	Normal	○
TM31	Brick Break	Fighting	Physical	75	100	15	Normal	○
TM32	Double Team	Normal	Status	—	—	15	Self	—
TM35	Flamethrower	Fire	Special	95	100	15	Normal	—
TM38	Fire Blast	Fire	Special	120	85	5	Normal	—
TM39	Rock Tomb	Rock	Physical	50	80	10	Normal	○
TM40	Aerial Ace	Flying	Physical	60	—	20	Normal	○
TM41	Torment	Dark	Status	—	100	15	Normal	—
TM42	Facade	Normal	Physical	70	100	20	Normal	○
TM43	Secret Power	Normal	Physical	70	100	20	Normal	—
TM44	Rest	Psychic	Status	—	—	10	Self	—
TM45	Attract	Normal	Status	—	100	15	Normal	—
TM50	Overheat	Fire	Special	140	90	5	Normal	—
TM52	Focus Blast	Fighting	Special	120	70	5	Normal	—
TM56	Fling	Dark	Physical	—	100	10	Normal	○
TM58	Endure	Normal	Status	—	—	10	Self	—
TM61	Will-O-Wisp	Fire	Status	—	75	15	Normal	—
TM65	Shadow Claw	Ghost	Physical	70	100	15	Normal	○
TM75	Swords Dance	Normal	Status	—	—	30	Self	—
TM76	Stealth Rock	Rock	Status	—	—	20	2 Foes	—
TM78	Captivate	Normal	Status	—	100	20	2 Foes	—
TM80	Rock Slide	Rock	Physical	75	90	10	2 Foes	—
TM82	Sleep Talk	Normal	Status	—	—	10	Depends	—
TM83	Natural Gift	Normal	Physical	—	100	15	Normal	—
TM84	Poison Jab	Poison	Physical	80	100	20	Normal	○
TM86	Grass Knot	Grass	Special	—	100	20	Normal	—
TM87	Swagger	Normal	Status	—	90	15	Normal	—
TM89	U-turn	Bug	Physical	70	100	20	Normal	○
TM90	Substitute	Normal	Status	—	—	10	Self	—
HM01	Cut	Normal	Physical	50	95	30	Normal	○
HM04	Strength	Normal	Physical	80	100	15	Normal	○
HM06	Rock Smash	Fighting	Physical	40	100	15	Normal	○
HM08	Rock Climb	Normal	Physical	90	85	20	Normal	○

No. 391 | Playful Pokémon
Monferno
Fire **Fighting**

- **HEIGHT:** 2'11"
- **WEIGHT:** 48.5 lbs.
- **ITEMS:** None

● SIZE COMPARISON

● MALE/FEMALE HAVE SAME FORM

● ABILITIES
● Blaze

● STATS
HP ●●●
ATTACK ●●●
DEFENSE ●●●
SP. ATTACK ●●●
SP. DEFENSE ●●
SPEED ●●●●

● EGG GROUPS
Field

Human-like

● PERFORMANCE
SPEED ★★★★☆ STAMINA ★★
POWER ★★★☆ JUMP ★★★
SKILL ★★★★☆

● MAIN WAYS TO OBTAIN

Pokémon HeartGold —

Pokémon SoulSilver —

Pokémon Diamond Level up Chimchar to Lv. 14

Pokémon Pearl Level up Chimchar to Lv. 14

Pokémon Platinum Level up Chimchar to Lv. 14

Pokémon HeartGold	**Pokémon SoulSilver**
A bigger fire on its tail and a brighter blue pattern on its face means its rank in its pack is higher.	A bigger fire on its tail and a brighter blue pattern on its face means its rank in its pack is higher.

● EVOLUTION

Lv. 14   Lv. 36

Chimchar   Monferno   Infernape

No. 392 | Flame Pokémon
Infernape

Fire | Fighting

- **HEIGHT:** 3'11"
- **WEIGHT:** 121.3 lbs.
- **ITEMS:** None

● SIZE COMPARISON

● MALE/FEMALE HAVE SAME FORM

⊙ ABILITIES
- Blaze

⊙ STATS
HP	●●●
ATTACK	●●●●
DEFENSE	●●●
SP. ATTACK	●●●●
SP. DEFENSE	●●●
SPEED	●●●●●

⊙ EGG GROUPS
Field

Human-like

⊙ PERFORMANCE
SPEED ★★★★	STAMINA ★☆
POWER ★★★★☆	JUMP ★★★
SKILL ★★★☆	

● MAIN WAYS TO OBTAIN

Pokémon HeartGold	—
Pokémon SoulSilver	—
Pokémon Diamond	Level up Monferno to Lv. 36
Pokémon Pearl	Level up Monferno to Lv. 36
Pokémon Platinum	Level up Monferno to Lv. 36

Pokémon HeartGold	Pokémon SoulSilver
It tosses its enemies around with agility. It uses all its limbs to fight in its own unique style.	It tosses its enemies around with agility. It uses all its limbs to fight in its own unique style.

⊙ EVOLUTION

Chimchar — Lv. 14 → Monferno — Lv. 36 → Infernape

● LEVEL-UP MOVES
Lv.	Name	Type	Kind	Pow.	Acc.	PP	Range	DA
1	Scratch	Normal	Physical	40	100	35	Normal	○
1	Leer	Normal	Status	—	100	30	2 Foes	—
1	Ember	Fire	Special	40	100	25	Normal	—
1	Taunt	Dark	Status	—	100	20	Normal	—
7	Ember	Fire	Special	40	100	25	Normal	—
9	Taunt	Dark	Status	—	100	20	Normal	—
14	Mach Punch	Fighting	Physical	40	100	30	Normal	○
17	Fury Swipes	Normal	Physical	18	80	15	Normal	○
21	Flame Wheel	Fire	Physical	60	100	25	Normal	○
29	Feint	Normal	Physical	50	100	10	Normal	—
33	Punishment	Dark	Physical	—	100	5	Normal	○
41	Close Combat	Fighting	Physical	120	100	5	Normal	○
45	Fire Spin	Fire	Special	15	70	15	Normal	—
53	Calm Mind	Psychic	Status	—	—	20	Self	—
57	Flare Blitz	Fire	Physical	120	100	15	Normal	○

● MOVE MANIAC
Name	Type	Kind	Pow.	Acc.	PP	Range	DA
Headbutt	Normal	Physical	70	100	15	Normal	○
Blast Burn	Fire	Special	150	90	5	Normal	—

● BP MOVES
Name	Type	Kind	Pow.	Acc.	PP	Range	DA
ThunderPunch	Electric	Physical	75	100	15	Normal	○
Fire Punch	Fire	Physical	75	100	15	Normal	○
Vacuum Wave	Fighting	Special	40	100	30	Normal	—
Snore	Normal	Special	40	100	15	Normal	—
Helping Hand	Normal	Status	—	—	20	1 Ally	—
Swift	Normal	Special	60	—	20	2 Foes	—
Role Play	Psychic	Status	—	—	10	Normal	—
Mud-Slap	Ground	Special	20	100	10	Normal	—
Rollout	Rock	Physical	30	90	20	Normal	○
Endeavor	Normal	Physical	—	100	5	Normal	—
Gunk Shot	Poison	Physical	120	70	5	Normal	○
Heat Wave	Fire	Special	100	90	10	2 Foes	—
Low Kick	Fighting	Physical	—	100	20	Normal	○

● TM & HM MOVES
No.	Name	Type	Kind	Pow.	Acc.	PP	Range	DA
TM01	Focus Punch	Fighting	Physical	150	100	20	Normal	○
TM04	Calm Mind	Psychic	Status	—	—	20	Self	—
TM05	Roar	Normal	Status	—	100	20	Normal	—
TM06	Toxic	Poison	Status	—	85	10	Normal	—
TM08	Bulk Up	Fighting	Status	—	—	20	Self	—
TM10	Hidden Power	Normal	Special	—	100	15	Normal	—
TM11	Sunny Day	Fire	Status	—	—	5	All	—
TM12	Taunt	Dark	Status	—	100	20	Normal	—
TM15	Hyper Beam	Normal	Special	150	90	5	Normal	—
TM17	Protect	Normal	Status	—	—	10	Self	—
TM21	Frustration	Normal	Physical	—	100	20	Normal	○
TM22	SolarBeam	Grass	Special	120	100	10	Normal	—
TM23	Iron Tail	Steel	Physical	100	75	15	Normal	○
TM26	Earthquake	Ground	Physical	100	100	10	2 Foes/1 Ally	—
TM27	Return	Normal	Physical	—	100	20	Normal	○
TM28	Dig	Ground	Physical	80	100	10	Normal	○
TM31	Brick Break	Fighting	Physical	75	100	15	Normal	○
TM32	Double Team	Normal	Status	—	—	15	Self	—
TM35	Flamethrower	Fire	Special	95	100	15	Normal	—
TM38	Fire Blast	Fire	Special	120	85	5	Normal	—
TM39	Rock Tomb	Rock	Physical	50	80	10	Normal	○
TM40	Aerial Ace	Flying	Physical	60	—	20	Normal	○
TM41	Torment	Dark	Status	—	100	15	Normal	—
TM42	Facade	Normal	Physical	70	100	20	Normal	○
TM43	Secret Power	Normal	Physical	70	100	20	Normal	○
TM44	Rest	Psychic	Status	—	—	10	Self	—
TM45	Attract	Normal	Status	—	100	15	Normal	—
TM50	Overheat	Fire	Special	140	90	5	Normal	—
TM52	Focus Blast	Fighting	Special	120	70	5	Normal	—
TM56	Fling	Dark	Physical	—	100	10	Normal	—
TM58	Endure	Normal	Status	—	—	10	Self	—
TM61	Will-O-Wisp	Fire	Status	—	75	15	Normal	—
TM65	Shadow Claw	Ghost	Physical	70	100	15	Normal	○
TM68	Giga Impact	Normal	Physical	150	90	5	Normal	○
TM71	Stone Edge	Rock	Physical	100	80	5	Normal	—
TM75	Swords Dance	Normal	Status	—	—	30	Self	—
TM76	Stealth Rock	Rock	Status	—	—	20	2 Foes	—
TM78	Captivate	Normal	Status	—	100	20	2 Foes	—
TM80	Rock Slide	Rock	Physical	75	90	10	2 Foes	○
TM82	Sleep Talk	Normal	Status	—	—	10	Depends	—
TM83	Natural Gift	Normal	Physical	—	100	15	Normal	○
TM84	Poison Jab	Poison	Physical	80	100	20	Normal	○
TM86	Grass Knot	Grass	Special	—	100	20	Normal	○
TM87	Swagger	Normal	Status	—	90	15	Normal	—
TM89	U-turn	Bug	Physical	70	100	20	Normal	○
TM90	Substitute	Normal	Status	—	—	10	Self	—
HM01	Cut	Normal	Physical	50	95	30	Normal	○
HM04	Strength	Normal	Physical	80	100	15	Normal	○
HM06	Rock Smash	Fighting	Physical	40	100	15	Normal	○
HM08	Rock Climb	Normal	Physical	90	85	20	Normal	○

● LEVEL-UP MOVES

Lv.	Name	Type	Kind	Pow.	Acc.	PP	Range	DA
1	Pound	Normal	Physical	40	100	35	Normal	○
4	Growl	Normal	Status	—	100	40	2 Foes	—
8	Bubble	Water	Special	20	100	30	2 Foes	—
11	Water Sport	Water	Status	—	—	15	All	—
15	Peck	Flying	Physical	35	100	35	Normal	○
18	BubbleBeam	Water	Special	65	100	20	Normal	—
22	Bide	Normal	Physical	—	—	10	Self	○
25	Fury Attack	Normal	Physical	15	85	20	Normal	—
29	Brine	Water	Special	55	100	10	Normal	—
32	Whirlpool	Water	Special	15	70	15	Normal	—
36	Mist	Ice	Status	—	—	30	2 Allies	—
39	Drill Peck	Flying	Physical	80	100	20	Normal	○
43	Hydro Pump	Water	Special	120	80	5	Normal	—

● MOVE MANIAC

Name	Type	Kind	Pow.	Acc.	PP	Range	DA
Headbutt	Normal	Physical	70	100	15	Normal	○

● BP MOVES

Name	Type	Kind	Pow.	Acc.	PP	Range	DA
Dive	Water	Physical	80	100	10	Normal	—
Icy Wind	Ice	Special	55	95	15	2 Foes	—
Snore	Normal	Special	40	100	15	Normal	—
Mud-Slap	Ground	Special	20	100	10	Normal	—
Signal Beam	Bug	Special	75	100	15	Normal	—

● TM & HM MOVES

No.	Name	Type	Kind	Pow.	Acc.	PP	Range	DA
TM03	Water Pulse	Water	Special	60	100	20	Normal	—
TM06	Toxic	Poison	Status	—	85	10	Normal	—
TM07	Hail	Ice	Status	—	—	10	All	—
TM10	Hidden Power	Normal	Special	—	100	15	Normal	—
TM13	Ice Beam	Ice	Special	95	100	10	Normal	—
TM14	Blizzard	Ice	Special	120	70	5	2 Foes	—
TM17	Protect	Normal	Status	—	—	10	Self	—
TM18	Rain Dance	Water	Status	—	—	5	All	—
TM21	Frustration	Normal	Physical	—	100	20	Normal	○
TM27	Return	Normal	Physical	—	100	20	Normal	○
TM28	Dig	Ground	Physical	80	100	10	Normal	○
TM31	Brick Break	Fighting	Physical	75	100	15	Normal	○
TM32	Double Team	Normal	Status	—	—	15	Self	—
TM39	Rock Tomb	Rock	Physical	50	80	10	Normal	—
TM40	Aerial Ace	Flying	Physical	60	—	20	Normal	○
TM42	Facade	Normal	Physical	70	100	20	Normal	○
TM43	Secret Power	Normal	Physical	70	100	20	Normal	○
TM44	Rest	Psychic	Status	—	—	10	Self	—
TM45	Attract	Normal	Status	—	100	15	Normal	—
TM55	Brine	Water	Special	65	100	10	Normal	—
TM56	Fling	Dark	Physical	—	100	10	Normal	—
TM58	Endure	Normal	Status	—	—	10	Self	—
TM76	Stealth Rock	Rock	Status	—	—	20	2 Foes	—
TM78	Captivate	Normal	Status	—	100	20	2 Foes	—
TM82	Sleep Talk	Normal	Status	—	—	10	Depends	—
TM83	Natural Gift	Normal	Physical	—	100	15	Normal	—
TM86	Grass Knot	Grass	Special	—	100	20	Normal	○
TM87	Swagger	Normal	Status	—	90	15	Normal	—
TM88	Pluck	Flying	Physical	60	100	20	Normal	○
TM90	Substitute	Normal	Status	—	—	10	Self	—
HM01	Cut	Normal	Physical	50	95	30	Normal	—
HM03	Surf	Water	Special	95	100	15	2 Foes/1 Ally	—
HM05	Whirlpool	Water	Special	15	70	15	Normal	—
HM07	Waterfall	Water	Physical	80	100	15	Normal	○

● EGG MOVES

Name	Type	Kind	Pow	Acc.	PP	Range	DA
Double Hit	Normal	Physical	35	90	10	Normal	○
Supersonic	Normal	Status	—	55	10	Normal	—
Yawn	Normal	Status	—	—	10	Normal	—
Mud Sport	Ground	Status	—	—	15	All	—
Mud-Slap	Ground	Special	20	100	10	Normal	—
Snore	Normal	Special	40	100	15	Normal	—
Flail	Normal	Physical	—	100	15	Normal	○
Agility	Psychic	Status	—	—	30	Self	—
Aqua Ring	Water	Status	—	—	20	Self	—
Hydro Pump	Water	Special	120	80	5	Normal	—
FeatherDance	Flying	Status	—	100	15	Normal	—

Piplup

Water

- ● HEIGHT: 1'04"
- ● WEIGHT: 11.5 lbs.
- ● ITEMS: None

● SIZE COMPARISON

● MALE/FEMALE HAVE SAME FORM

⊛ ABILITIES
● Torrent

⊛ STATS
HP ●●
ATTACK ●●
DEFENSE ●●
SP. ATTACK ●●●
SP. DEFENSE ●●
SPEED ●●

⊛ EGG GROUPS
Water 1
Field

⊛ PERFORMANCE
SPEED ★★★★☆ STAMINA ★★☆
POWER ★★★☆ JUMP ★★★☆☆
SKILL ★★☆

● MAIN WAYS TO OBTAIN

Pokémon HeartGold	—
Pokémon SoulSilver	—
Pokémon Diamond	Receive from Professor Rowan at the beginning of the adventure
Pokémon Pearl	Receive from Professor Rowan at the beginning of the adventure
Pokémon Platinum	Receive from Professor Rowan at the beginning of the adventure

Pokémon HeartGold	Pokémon SoulSilver
It doesn't like to be taken care of. It's difficult to bond with since it won't listen to its Trainer.	It doesn't like to be taken care of. It's difficult to bond with since it won't listen to its Trainer.

⊛ EVOLUTION

Lv. 16 ▶ Lv. 36 ▶

Piplup Prinplup Empoleon

No. 394 | Penguin Pokémon
Prinplup

Water

- **HEIGHT:** 2'02"
- **WEIGHT:** 50.7 lbs.
- **ITEMS:** None

● SIZE COMPARISON

● MALE/FEMALE HAVE SAME FORM

● ABILITIES
- Torrent

● STATS
HP	●●
ATTACK	●●●
DEFENSE	●●●
SP. ATTACK	●●●●
SP. DEFENSE	●●●
SPEED	●●

● EGG GROUPS
Water 1

Field

● PERFORMANCE
SPEED ★★★☆　　STAMINA ★★★☆☆
POWER ★★★☆　　JUMP ★★★☆
SKILL ★★★☆

● MAIN WAYS TO OBTAIN

Pokémon HeartGold	—
Pokémon SoulSilver	—
Pokémon Diamond	Level up Piplup to Lv. 16
Pokémon Pearl	Level up Piplup to Lv. 16
Pokémon Platinum	Level up Piplup to Lv. 16

Pokémon HeartGold	Pokémon SoulSilver
It lives a solitary life. Its wings deliver wicked blows that can snap even the thickest of trees.	It lives a solitary life. Its wings deliver wicked blows that can snap even the thickest of trees.

● EVOLUTION

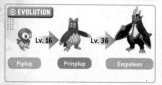

Piplup　→ Lv. 16 →　Prinplup　→ Lv. 36 →　Empoleon

● LEVEL-UP MOVES
Lv.	Name	Type	Kind	Pow.	Acc.	PP	Range	DA
1	Tackle	Normal	Physical	35	95	35	Normal	○
1	Growl	Normal	Status	—	100	40	2 Foes	—
4	Growl	Normal	Status	—	100	40	2 Foes	—
8	Bubble	Water	Special	20	100	30	2 Foes	—
11	Water Sport	Water	Status	—	—	15	All	—
15	Peck	Flying	Physical	35	100	35	Normal	○
16	Metal Claw	Steel	Physical	50	95	35	Normal	○
19	BubbleBeam	Water	Special	65	100	20	Normal	—
24	Bide	Normal	Physical	—	—	10	Self	○
28	Fury Attack	Normal	Physical	15	85	20	Normal	○
33	Brine	Water	Special	65	100	10	Normal	—
37	Whirlpool	Water	Special	15	70	15	Normal	—
42	Mist	Ice	Status	—	—	30	2 Allies	—
46	Drill Peck	Flying	Physical	80	100	20	Normal	○
51	Hydro Pump	Water	Special	120	80	5	Normal	—

● MOVE MANIAC
Name	Type	Kind	Pow.	Acc.	PP	Range	DA
Headbutt	Normal	Physical	70	100	15	Normal	○

● BP MOVES
Name	Type	Kind	Pow.	Acc.	PP	Range	DA
Dive	Water	Physical	80	100	10	Normal	○
Icy Wind	Ice	Special	55	95	15	2 Foes	—
Snore	Normal	Special	40	100	15	Normal	—
Mud-Slap	Ground	Special	20	100	10	Normal	—
Signal Beam	Bug	Special	75	100	15	Normal	—

● TM & HM MOVES
No.	Name	Type	Kind	Pow.	Acc.	PP	Range	DA
TM03	Water Pulse	Water	Special	60	100	20	Normal	—
TM06	Toxic	Poison	Status	—	85	10	Normal	—
TM07	Hail	Ice	Status	—	—	10	All	—
TM10	Hidden Power	Normal	Special	—	100	15	Normal	—
TM13	Ice Beam	Ice	Special	95	100	10	Normal	—
TM14	Blizzard	Ice	Special	120	70	5	2 Foes	—
TM17	Protect	Normal	Status	—	—	10	Self	—
TM18	Rain Dance	Water	Status	—	—	5	All	—
TM21	Frustration	Normal	Physical	—	100	20	Normal	○
TM27	Return	Normal	Physical	—	100	20	Normal	○
TM28	Dig	Ground	Physical	80	100	10	Normal	○
TM31	Brick Break	Fighting	Physical	75	100	15	Normal	○
TM32	Double Team	Normal	Status	—	—	15	Self	—
TM39	Rock Tomb	Rock	Physical	50	80	10	Normal	—
TM40	Aerial Ace	Flying	Physical	60	—	20	Normal	○
TM42	Facade	Normal	Physical	70	100	20	Normal	○
TM43	Secret Power	Normal	Physical	70	100	20	Normal	—
TM44	Rest	Psychic	Status	—	—	10	Self	—
TM45	Attract	Normal	Status	—	100	15	Normal	—
TM55	Brine	Water	Special	65	100	10	Normal	—
TM56	Fling	Dark	Physical	—	100	10	Normal	—
TM58	Endure	Normal	Status	—	—	10	Self	—
TM65	Shadow Claw	Ghost	Physical	70	100	15	Normal	○
TM76	Stealth Rock	Rock	Status	—	—	20	2 Foes	—
TM78	Captivate	Normal	Status	—	100	20	2 Foes	—
TM82	Sleep Talk	Normal	Status	—	—	10	Depends	—
TM83	Natural Gift	Normal	Physical	—	100	15	Normal	—
TM86	Grass Knot	Grass	Special	—	100	20	Normal	—
TM87	Swagger	Normal	Status	—	90	15	Normal	○
TM88	Pluck	Flying	Physical	60	100	20	Normal	○
TM90	Substitute	Normal	Status	—	—	10	Self	—
HM01	Cut	Normal	Physical	50	95	30	Normal	○
HM03	Surf	Water	Special	95	100	15	2 Foes/1 Ally	—
HM04	Strength	Normal	Physical	80	100	15	Normal	○
HM05	Whirlpool	Water	Special	15	70	15	Normal	—
HM06	Rock Smash	Fighting	Physical	40	100	15	Normal	○
HM07	Waterfall	Water	Physical	80	100	15	Normal	○

● LEVEL-UP MOVES

Lv.	Name	Type	Kind	Pow.	Acc.	PP	Range	DA
1	Tackle	Normal	Physical	35	95	35	Normal	○
1	Growl	Normal	Status	—	100	40	2 Foes	—
1	Bubble	Water	Special	20	100	30	2 Foes	—
4	Growl	Normal	Status	—	100	40	2 Foes	—
8	Bubble	Water	Special	20	100	30	2 Foes	—
11	Swords Dance	Normal	Status	—	—	30	Self	—
15	Peck	Flying	Physical	35	100	35	Normal	○
16	Metal Claw	Steel	Physical	50	95	35	Normal	○
19	Swagger	Normal	Status	—	90	15	Normal	—
24	BubbleBeam	Water	Special	65	100	20	Normal	—
28	Fury Attack	Normal	Physical	15	85	20	Normal	○
33	Brine	Water	Special	65	100	10	Normal	—
36	Aqua Jet	Water	Physical	40	100	20	Normal	○
39	Whirlpool	Water	Special	15	70	15	Normal	—
46	Mist	Ice	Status	—	—	30	2 Allies	—
52	Drill Peck	Flying	Physical	80	100	20	Normal	○
59	Hydro Pump	Water	Special	120	80	5	Normal	—

● MOVE MANIAC

Name	Type	Kind	Pow.	Acc.	PP	Range	DA
Headbutt	Normal	Physical	70	100	15	Normal	—
Hydro Cannon	Water	Special	150	90	5	Normal	—

● BP MOVES

Name	Type	Kind	Pow.	Acc.	PP	Range	DA
Dive	Water	Physical	80	100	10	Normal	○
Fury Cutter	Bug	Physical	10	95	20	Normal	○
Icy Wind	Ice	Special	55	95	15	2 Foes	—
Knock Off	Dark	Physical	20	100	20	Normal	○
Snore	Normal	Special	40	100	15	Normal	—
Mud-Slap	Ground	Special	20	100	10	Normal	—
Signal Beam	Bug	Special	75	100	15	Normal	—
Iron Defense	Steel	Status	—	—	15	Self	—

● TM & HM MOVES

No.	Name	Type	Kind	Pow.	Acc.	PP	Range	DA
TM03	Water Pulse	Water	Special	60	100	20	Normal	—
TM05	Roar	Normal	Status	—	100	20	Normal	—
TM06	Toxic	Poison	Status	—	85	10	Normal	—
TM07	Hail	Ice	Status	—	—	10	All	—
TM10	Hidden Power	Normal	Special	—	100	15	Normal	—
TM13	Ice Beam	Ice	Special	95	100	10	Normal	—
TM14	Blizzard	Ice	Special	120	70	5	2 Foes	—
TM15	Hyper Beam	Normal	Special	150	90	5	Normal	—
TM17	Protect	Normal	Status	—	—	10	Self	—
TM18	Rain Dance	Water	Status	—	—	5	All	—
TM21	Frustration	Normal	Physical	—	100	20	Normal	○
TM26	Earthquake	Ground	Physical	100	100	10	2 Foes/1 Ally	○
TM27	Return	Normal	Physical	—	100	20	Normal	○
TM28	Dig	Ground	Physical	80	100	10	Normal	○
TM31	Brick Break	Fighting	Physical	75	100	15	Normal	○
TM32	Double Team	Normal	Status	—	—	15	Self	—
TM39	Rock Tomb	Rock	Physical	50	80	10	Normal	○
TM40	Aerial Ace	Flying	Physical	60	—	20	Normal	○
TM42	Facade	Normal	Physical	70	100	20	Normal	○
TM43	Secret Power	Normal	Physical	70	100	20	Normal	○
TM44	Rest	Psychic	Status	—	—	10	Self	—
TM45	Attract	Normal	Status	—	100	15	Normal	—
TM47	Steel Wing	Steel	Physical	70	90	25	Normal	○
TM55	Brine	Water	Special	65	100	10	Normal	—
TM56	Fling	Dark	Physical	—	100	10	Normal	○
TM58	Endure	Normal	Status	—	—	10	Self	—
TM65	Shadow Claw	Ghost	Physical	70	100	15	Normal	○
TM68	Giga Impact	Normal	Physical	150	90	5	Normal	○
TM72	Avalanche	Ice	Physical	60	100	10	Normal	○
TM75	Swords Dance	Normal	Status	—	—	30	Self	—
TM76	Stealth Rock	Rock	Status	—	—	20	2 Foes	—
TM78	Captivate	Normal	Status	—	100	20	2 Foes	—
TM80	Rock Slide	Rock	Physical	75	90	10	2 Foes	○
TM82	Sleep Talk	Normal	Status	—	—	10	Depends	—
TM83	Natural Gift	Normal	Physical	—	100	15	Normal	○
TM86	Grass Knot	Grass	Special	—	100	20	Normal	—
TM87	Swagger	Normal	Status	—	90	15	Normal	—
TM88	Pluck	Flying	Physical	60	100	20	Normal	○
TM90	Substitute	Normal	Status	—	—	10	Self	—
TM91	Flash Cannon	Steel	Special	80	100	10	Normal	—
HM01	Cut	Normal	Physical	50	95	30	Normal	○
HM03	Surf	Water	Special	95	100	15	2 Foes/1 Ally	○
HM04	Strength	Normal	Physical	80	100	15	Normal	○
HM05	Whirlpool	Water	Special	15	70	15	Normal	—
HM06	Rock Smash	Fighting	Physical	40	100	15	Normal	○
HM07	Waterfall	Water	Physical	80	100	15	Normal	○
HM08	Rock Climb	Normal	Physical	90	85	20	Normal	○

● No. 395 | Emperor Pokémon

Empoleon

Water　Steel

● HEIGHT: 5'07"
● WEIGHT: 186.3 lbs.
● ITEMS: None

● SIZE COMPARISON

● MALE/FEMALE HAVE SAME FORM

⊛ ABILITIES
● Torrent

⊛ STATS
HP ●●●
ATTACK ●●●●
DEFENSE ●●●
SP. ATTACK ●●●●
SP. DEFENSE ●●●●
SPEED ●●●

⊛ EGG GROUPS
Water 1
Field

⊛ PERFORMANCE

SPEED ★★★　　STAMINA ★★★★☆
POWER ★★★☆☆　JUMP ★★★☆
SKILL ★★★

● MAIN WAYS TO OBTAIN

Pokémon HeartGold —

Pokémon SoulSilver —

Pokémon Diamond Level up Prinplup to Lv. 36

Pokémon Pearl Level up Prinplup to Lv. 36

Pokémon Platinum Level up Prinplup to Lv. 36

Pokémon HeartGold
It avoids unnecessary disputes, but it will decimate anything that threatens its pride.

Pokémon SoulSilver
It avoids unnecessary disputes, but it will decimate anything that threatens its pride.

⊛ EVOLUTION

Piplup → Lv. 16 → Prinplup → Lv. 36 → Empoleon

⊙ No. 396 | Starling Pokémon
Starly

`Normal` `Flying`

● **HEIGHT:** 1'00"
● **WEIGHT:** 4.4 lbs.
● **ITEMS:** Yache Berry

● SIZE COMPARISON

● **MALE FORM**
Larger white marking on head

● **FEMALE FORM**
Smaller white marking on head

⊙ ABILITIES
● Keen Eye

⊙ STATS
- HP ●
- ATTACK ●●
- DEFENSE ●●
- SP. ATTACK ●●
- SP. DEFENSE ●●
- SPEED ●●●

⊙ EGG GROUPS
Flying

⊙ PERFORMANCE
SPEED ★★★☆
POWER ★★☆
SKILL ★★
STAMINA ★★☆
JUMP ★★★★☆

● MAIN WAYS TO OBTAIN

Pokémon HeartGold — Pewter City (use Headbutt on two trees at the back of Route 2)

Pokémon SoulSilver — Pewter City (use Headbutt on two trees at the back of Route 2)

Pokémon Diamond — Route 201

Pokémon Pearl — Route 201

Pokémon Platinum — Route 201

Pokémon HeartGold — They flock around mountains and fields, chasing after bug Pokémon. Their singing is noisy and annoying.

Pokémon SoulSilver — They flock around mountains and fields, chasing after bug Pokémon. Their singing is noisy and annoying.

⊙ EVOLUTION

Starly — Lv. 14 → Staravia — Lv. 34 → Staraptor

● LEVEL-UP MOVES

Lv.	Name	Type	Kind	Pow.	Acc.	PP	Range	DA
1	Tackle	Normal	Physical	35	95	35	Normal	○
1	Growl	Normal	Status	—	100	40	2 Foes	—
5	Quick Attack	Normal	Physical	40	100	30	Normal	○
9	Wing Attack	Flying	Physical	60	100	35	Normal	○
13	Double Team	Normal	Status	—	—	15	Self	—
17	Endeavor	Normal	Physical	—	100	5	Normal	○
21	Whirlwind	Normal	Status	—	100	20	Normal	—
25	Aerial Ace	Flying	Physical	60	—	20	Normal	○
29	Take Down	Normal	Physical	90	85	20	Normal	○
33	Agility	Psychic	Status	—	—	30	Self	—
37	Brave Bird	Flying	Physical	120	100	15	Normal	○

● MOVE MANIAC

Name	Type	Kind	Pow.	Acc.	PP	Range	DA

● BP MOVES

Name	Type	Kind	Pow.	Acc.	PP	Range	DA
Ominous Wind	Ghost	Special	60	100	5	Normal	—
Air Cutter	Flying	Special	55	95	25	2 Foes	—
Snore	Normal	Special	40	100	15	Normal	—
Swift	Normal	Special	60	—	20	2 Foes	—
Tailwind	Flying	Status	—	—	30	2 Allies	—
Mud-Slap	Ground	Special	20	100	10	Normal	—
Endeavor	Normal	Physical	—	100	5	Normal	○
Twister	Dragon	Special	40	100	20	2 Foes	—
Heat Wave	Fire	Special	100	90	10	2 Foes	—

● TM & HM MOVES

No.	Name	Type	Kind	Pow.	Acc.	PP	Range	DA
TM06	Toxic	Poison	Status	—	85	10	Normal	—
TM10	Hidden Power	Normal	Special	—	100	15	Normal	—
TM11	Sunny Day	Fire	Status	—	—	5	All	—
TM17	Protect	Normal	Status	—	—	10	Self	—
TM18	Rain Dance	Water	Status	—	—	5	All	—
TM21	Frustration	Normal	Physical	—	100	20	Normal	○
TM27	Return	Normal	Physical	—	100	20	Normal	○
TM32	Double Team	Normal	Status	—	—	15	Self	—
TM40	Aerial Ace	Flying	Physical	60	—	20	Normal	○
TM42	Facade	Normal	Physical	70	100	20	Normal	○
TM43	Secret Power	Normal	Physical	70	100	20	Normal	—
TM44	Rest	Psychic	Status	—	—	10	Self	—
TM45	Attract	Normal	Status	—	100	15	Normal	—
TM46	Thief	Dark	Physical	40	100	10	Normal	○
TM47	Steel Wing	Steel	Physical	70	90	25	Normal	○
TM51	Roost	Flying	Status	—	—	10	Self	—
TM58	Endure	Normal	Status	—	—	10	Self	—
TM78	Captivate	Normal	Status	—	100	20	2 Foes	—
TM82	Sleep Talk	Normal	Status	—	—	10	Depends	—
TM83	Natural Gift	Normal	Physical	—	100	15	Normal	—
TM87	Swagger	Normal	Status	—	90	15	Normal	—
TM88	Pluck	Flying	Physical	60	100	20	Normal	○
TM89	U-turn	Bug	Physical	70	100	20	Normal	○
TM90	Substitute	Normal	Status	—	—	10	Self	—
HM02	Fly	Flying	Physical	90	95	15	Normal	○

● EGG MOVES

Name	Type	Kind	Pow.	Acc.	PP	Range	DA
FeatherDance	Flying	Status	—	100	15	Normal	—
Fury Attack	Normal	Physical	15	85	20	Normal	○
Pursuit	Dark	Physical	40	100	20	Normal	○
Astonish	Ghost	Physical	30	100	15	Normal	○
Sand-Attack	Ground	Status	—	100	15	Normal	—
Foresight	Normal	Status	—	—	40	Normal	—
Double-Edge	Normal	Physical	120	100	15	Normal	○

● LEVEL-UP MOVES

Lv.	Name	Type	Kind	Pow.	Acc.	PP	Range	DA
1	Tackle	Normal	Physical	35	95	35	Normal	○
1	Growl	Normal	Status	—	100	40	2 Foes	—
1	Quick Attack	Normal	Physical	40	100	30	Normal	○
5	Quick Attack	Normal	Physical	40	100	30	Normal	○
9	Wing Attack	Flying	Physical	60	100	35	Normal	○
13	Double Team	Normal	Status	—	—	15	Self	—
18	Endeavor	Normal	Physical	—	100	5	Normal	○
23	Whirlwind	Normal	Status	—	100	20	Normal	—
28	Aerial Ace	Flying	Physical	60	—	20	Normal	○
33	Take Down	Normal	Physical	90	85	20	Normal	○
38	Agility	Psychic	Status	—	—	30	Self	—
43	Brave Bird	Flying	Physical	120	100	15	Normal	○

● MOVE MANIAC

Name	Type	Kind	Pow.	Acc.	PP	Range	DA

● BP MOVES

Name	Type	Kind	Pow.	Acc.	PP	Range	DA
Ominous Wind	Ghost	Special	60	100	5	Normal	—
Air Cutter	Flying	Special	55	95	25	2 Foes	—
Snore	Normal	Special	40	100	15	Normal	—
Swift	Normal	Special	60	—	20	2 Foes	—
Tailwind	Flying	Status	—	—	30	2 Allies	—
Mud-Slap	Ground	Special	20	100	10	Normal	—
Endeavor	Normal	Physical	—	100	5	Normal	○
Twister	Dragon	Special	40	100	20	2 Foes	—
Heat Wave	Fire	Special	100	90	10	2 Foes	—

● TM & HM MOVES

No.	Name	Type	Kind	Pow.	Acc.	PP	Range	DA
TM06	Toxic	Poison	Status	—	85	10	Normal	—
TM10	Hidden Power	Normal	Special	—	100	15	Normal	—
TM11	Sunny Day	Fire	Status	—	—	5	All	—
TM17	Protect	Normal	Status	—	—	10	Self	—
TM18	Rain Dance	Water	Status	—	—	5	All	—
TM21	Frustration	Normal	Physical	—	100	20	Normal	○
TM27	Return	Normal	Physical	—	100	20	Normal	○
TM32	Double Team	Normal	Status	—	—	15	Self	—
TM40	Aerial Ace	Flying	Physical	60	—	20	Normal	○
TM42	Facade	Normal	Physical	70	100	20	Normal	○
TM43	Secret Power	Normal	Physical	70	100	20	Normal	○
TM44	Rest	Psychic	Status	—	—	10	Self	—
TM45	Attract	Normal	Status	—	100	15	Normal	—
TM46	Thief	Dark	Physical	40	100	10	Normal	—
TM47	Steel Wing	Steel	Physical	70	90	25	Normal	○
TM51	Roost	Flying	Status	—	—	10	Self	—
TM58	Endure	Normal	Status	—	—	10	Self	—
TM78	Captivate	Normal	Status	—	100	20	2 Foes	—
TM82	Sleep Talk	Normal	Status	—	—	10	Depends	—
TM83	Natural Gift	Normal	Physical	—	100	15	Normal	—
TM87	Swagger	Normal	Status	—	90	15	Normal	—
TM88	Pluck	Flying	Physical	60	100	20	Normal	○
TM89	U-turn	Bug	Physical	70	100	20	Normal	○
TM90	Substitute	Normal	Status	—	—	10	Self	—
HM02	Fly	Flying	Physical	90	95	15	Normal	○

● No. 397 | Starling Pokémon
Staravia

Normal   Flying

- **HEIGHT:** 2'00"
- **WEIGHT:** 34.2 lbs.
- **ITEMS:** None

● **SIZE COMPARISON**

● **MALE FORM**
Larger gray marking on head

● **FEMALE FORM**
Smaller gray marking on head

● **ABILITIES**
- Intimidate

● **STATS**
- HP ●●
- ATTACK ●●●
- DEFENSE ●●
- SP. ATTACK ●●
- SP. DEFENSE ●
- SPEED ●●●●

● **EGG GROUPS**
Flying

● **PERFORMANCE**

SPEED ★★★☆		STAMINA ★★★☆
POWER ★★★		JUMP ★★★★★
SKILL ★★☆		

● **MAIN WAYS TO OBTAIN**

Pokémon HeartGold	Level up Starly to Lv. 14
Pokémon SoulSilver	Level up Starly to Lv. 14
Pokémon Diamond	Route 209
Pokémon Pearl	Route 209
Pokémon Platinum	Route 209

Pokémon HeartGold	Pokémon SoulSilver
They maintain huge flocks, although fierce scuffles break out between various flocks.	They maintain huge flocks, although fierce scuffles break out between various flocks.

● **EVOLUTION**

 Lv. 14 Lv. 34

Starly   Staravia   Staraptor

Staraptor

Normal **Flying**

- **HEIGHT:** 3'11"
- **WEIGHT:** 54.9 lbs.
- **ITEMS:** None

● SIZE COMPARISON

● MALE FORM
Larger white marking on head

● FEMALE FORM
Smaller white marking on head

⊘ ABILITIES
- Intimidate

⊘ STATS
HP ●●●
ATTACK ●●●●●
DEFENSE ●●●
SP. ATTACK ●●
SP. DEFENSE ●●
SPEED ●●●●

⊘ EGG GROUPS
Flying

⊘ PERFORMANCE

SPEED ★★★
POWER ★★★★☆
SKILL ★☆☆
STAMINA ★★★☆
JUMP ★★★★★

● MAIN WAYS TO OBTAIN

Pokémon HeartGold	Level up Staravia to Lv. 34
Pokémon SoulSilver	Level up Staravia to Lv. 34
Pokémon Diamond	Level up Staravia to Lv. 34
Pokémon Pearl	Level up Staravia to Lv. 34
Pokémon Platinum	Level up Staravia to Lv. 34

Pokémon HeartGold
When STARAVIA evolve into STARAPTOR, they leave the flock to live alone. They have sturdy wings.

Pokémon SoulSilver
When STARAVIA evolve into STARAPTOR, they leave the flock to live alone. They have sturdy wings.

⊘ EVOLUTION

Lv. 14   Lv. 34

Starly   Staravia   Staraptor

● LEVEL-UP MOVES

Lv.	Name	Type	Kind	Pow.	Acc.	PP	Range	DA
1	Tackle	Normal	Physical	35	95	35	Normal	○
1	Growl	Normal	Status	—	100	40	2 Foes	—
1	Quick Attack	Normal	Physical	40	100	30	Normal	○
1	Wing Attack	Flying	Physical	60	100	35	Normal	○
5	Quick Attack	Normal	Physical	40	100	30	Normal	○
9	Wing Attack	Flying	Physical	60	100	35	Normal	○
13	Double Team	Normal	Status	—	—	15	Self	—
18	Endeavor	Normal	Physical	—	100	5	Normal	○
23	Whirlwind	Normal	Status	—	100	20	Normal	—
28	Aerial Ace	Flying	Physical	60	—	20	Normal	○
33	Take Down	Normal	Physical	90	85	20	Normal	○
34	Close Combat	Fighting	Physical	120	100	5	Normal	○
41	Agility	Psychic	Status	—	—	30	Self	—
49	Brave Bird	Flying	Physical	120	100	15	Normal	○

● MOVE MANIAC

Name	Type	Kind	Pow.	Acc.	PP	Range	DA

● BP MOVES

Name	Type	Kind	Pow.	Acc.	PP	Range	DA
Ominous Wind	Ghost	Special	60	100	5	Normal	—
Air Cutter	Flying	Special	55	95	25	2 Foes	—
Snore	Normal	Special	40	100	15	Normal	—
Swift	Normal	Special	60	—	20	2 Foes	—
Tailwind	Flying	Status	—	—	30	2 Allies	—
Mud-Slap	Ground	Special	20	100	10	Normal	—
Endeavor	Normal	Physical	—	100	5	Normal	○
Twister	Dragon	Special	40	100	20	2 Foes	—
Heat Wave	Fire	Special	100	90	10	2 Foes	—
Sky Attack	Flying	Physical	140	90	5	Normal	—

● TM & HM MOVES

No.	Name	Type	Kind	Pow.	Acc.	PP	Range	DA
TM06	Toxic	Poison	Status	—	85	10	Normal	—
TM10	Hidden Power	Normal	Special	—	100	15	Normal	—
TM11	Sunny Day	Fire	Status	—	—	5	All	—
TM15	Hyper Beam	Normal	Special	150	90	5	Normal	—
TM17	Protect	Normal	Status	—	—	10	Self	—
TM18	Rain Dance	Water	Status	—	—	5	All	—
TM21	Frustration	Normal	Physical	—	100	20	Normal	○
TM27	Return	Normal	Physical	—	100	20	Normal	○
TM32	Double Team	Normal	Status	—	—	15	Self	—
TM40	Aerial Ace	Flying	Physical	60	—	20	Normal	○
TM42	Facade	Normal	Physical	70	100	20	Normal	○
TM43	Secret Power	Normal	Physical	70	100	20	Normal	—
TM44	Rest	Psychic	Status	—	—	10	Self	—
TM45	Attract	Normal	Status	—	100	15	Normal	—
TM46	Thief	Dark	Physical	40	100	10	Normal	○
TM47	Steel Wing	Steel	Physical	70	90	25	Normal	○
TM51	Roost	Flying	Status	—	—	10	Self	—
TM58	Endure	Normal	Status	—	—	10	Self	—
TM68	Giga Impact	Normal	Physical	150	90	5	Normal	○
TM78	Captivate	Normal	Status	—	100	20	2 Foes	—
TM82	Sleep Talk	Normal	Status	—	—	10	Depends	—
TM83	Natural Gift	Normal	Physical	—	100	15	Normal	—
TM87	Swagger	Normal	Status	—	90	15	Normal	—
TM88	Pluck	Flying	Physical	60	100	20	Normal	○
TM89	U-turn	Bug	Physical	70	100	20	Normal	○
TM90	Substitute	Normal	Status	—	—	10	Self	—
HM02	Fly	Flying	Physical	90	95	15	Normal	○

● LEVEL-UP MOVES

Lv.	Name	Type	Kind	Pow.	Acc.	PP	Range	DA
1	Tackle	Normal	Physical	35	95	35	Normal	○
5	Growl	Normal	Status	—	100	40	2 Foes	—
9	Defense Curl	Normal	Status	—	—	40	Self	—
13	Rollout	Rock	Physical	30	90	20	Normal	○
17	Headbutt	Normal	Physical	70	100	15	Normal	○
21	Hyper Fang	Normal	Physical	80	90	15	Normal	○
25	Yawn	Normal	Status	—	—	10	Normal	—
29	Amnesia	Psychic	Status	—	—	20	Self	—
33	Take Down	Normal	Physical	90	85	20	Normal	○
37	Super Fang	Normal	Physical	—	90	10	Normal	○
41	Superpower	Fighting	Physical	120	100	5	Normal	○
45	Curse	???	Status	—	—	10	Normal/Self	—

● MOVE MANIAC

Name	Type	Kind	Pow.	Acc.	PP	Range	DA
Headbutt	Normal	Physical	70	100	15	Normal	○

● BP MOVES

Name	Type	Kind	Pow.	Acc.	PP	Range	DA
Fury Cutter	Bug	Physical	10	95	20	Normal	○
Icy Wind	Ice	Special	55	95	15	2 Foes	—
Snore	Normal	Special	40	100	15	Normal	—
Last Resort	Normal	Physical	130	100	5	Normal	○
Swift	Normal	Special	60	—	20	2 Foes	—
Mud-Slap	Ground	Special	20	100	10	Normal	—
Rollout	Rock	Physical	30	90	20	Normal	○
Superpower	Fighting	Physical	120	100	5	Normal	○
Aqua Tail	Water	Physical	90	90	10	Normal	○
Super Fang	Normal	Physical	—	90	10	Normal	○

● TM & HM MOVES

No.	Name	Type	Kind	Pow.	Acc.	PP	Range	DA
TM06	Toxic	Poison	Status	—	85	10	Normal	—
TM10	Hidden Power	Normal	Special	—	100	15	Normal	—
TM11	Sunny Day	Fire	Status	—	—	5	All	—
TM12	Taunt	Dark	Status	—	100	20	Normal	—
TM13	Ice Beam	Ice	Special	95	100	10	Normal	—
TM14	Blizzard	Ice	Special	120	70	5	2 Foes	—
TM17	Protect	Normal	Status	—	—	10	Self	—
TM18	Rain Dance	Water	Status	—	—	5	All	—
TM21	Frustration	Normal	Physical	—	100	20	Normal	○
TM23	Iron Tail	Steel	Physical	100	75	15	Normal	○
TM24	Thunderbolt	Electric	Special	95	100	15	Normal	—
TM25	Thunder	Electric	Special	120	70	10	Normal	—
TM27	Return	Normal	Physical	—	100	20	Normal	○
TM28	Dig	Ground	Physical	80	100	10	Normal	○
TM30	Shadow Ball	Ghost	Special	80	100	15	Normal	—
TM32	Double Team	Normal	Status	—	—	15	Self	—
TM34	Shock Wave	Electric	Special	60	—	20	Normal	—
TM42	Facade	Normal	Physical	70	100	20	Normal	○
TM43	Secret Power	Normal	Physical	70	100	20	Normal	○
TM44	Rest	Psychic	Status	—	—	10	Self	—
TM45	Attract	Normal	Status	—	100	15	Normal	—
TM46	Thief	Dark	Physical	40	100	10	Normal	○
TM57	Charge Beam	Electric	Special	50	90	10	Normal	—
TM58	Endure	Normal	Status	—	—	10	Self	—
TM73	Thunder Wave	Electric	Status	—	100	20	Normal	—
TM76	Stealth Rock	Rock	Status	—	—	20	2 Foes	—
TM78	Captivate	Normal	Status	—	100	20	2 Foes	—
TM82	Sleep Talk	Normal	Status	—	—	10	Depends	—
TM83	Natural Gift	Normal	Physical	—	100	15	Normal	○
TM86	Grass Knot	Grass	Special	—	100	20	Normal	—
TM87	Swagger	Normal	Status	—	90	15	Normal	—
TM88	Pluck	Flying	Physical	60	100	20	Normal	○
TM90	Substitute	Normal	Status	—	—	10	Self	—
HM01	Cut	Normal	Physical	50	95	30	Normal	○
HM06	Rock Smash	Fighting	Physical	40	100	15	Normal	○

● EGG MOVES

Name	Type	Kind	Pow.	Acc.	PP	Range	DA
Quick Attack	Normal	Physical	40	100	30	Normal	○
Water Sport	Water	Status	—	—	15	All	—
Double-Edge	Normal	Physical	120	100	15	Normal	○
Fury Swipes	Normal	Physical	18	80	15	Normal	○
Defense Curl	Normal	Status	—	—	40	Self	—
Rollout	Rock	Physical	30	90	20	Normal	○
Odor Sleuth	Normal	Status	—	—	40	Normal	—
Aqua Tail	Water	Physical	90	90	10	Normal	○

☉ No. 399 | Plump Mouse Pokémon
Bidoof

Normal

● **HEIGHT:** 1'08"
● **WEIGHT:** 44.1 lbs.
● **ITEMS:** None

● **SIZE COMPARISON**

● **MALE FORM**
More tufts of fur on tail

● **FEMALE FORM**
Fewer tufts of fur on tail

⊛ ABILITIES
● Simple
● Unaware

⊛ STATS
HP ●●
ATTACK ●●
DEFENSE ●●
SP. ATTACK ●●
SP. DEFENSE ●
SPEED ●

⊛ EGG GROUPS
Water 1
Field

⊛ PERFORMANCE

SPEED ★★☆☆   STAMINA ★★★☆
POWER ★★☆☆   JUMP ★★
SKILL ☆☆☆☆

● MAIN WAYS TO OBTAIN

Pokémon HeartGold   Route 30 (Sinnoh Sound)

Pokémon SoulSilver   Route 30 (Sinnoh Sound)

Pokémon Diamond   Route 201

Pokémon Pearl   Route 201

Pokémon Platinum   Route 201

Pokémon HeartGold
It lives in groups by the water. It chews up boulders and trees around its nest with its incisors.

Pokémon SoulSilver
It lives in groups by the water. It chews up boulders and trees around its nest with its incisors.

⊛ EVOLUTION

Bidoof   Lv. 15   Bibarel

No. 400 | Beaver Pokémon
Bibarel

Normal | Water

● **HEIGHT:** 3'03"
● **WEIGHT:** 69.4 lbs.
● **ITEMS:** None

● **SIZE COMPARISON**

● **MALE FORM**
Marking on face is wider

● **FEMALE FORM**
Marking on face is more narrow

⊛ **ABILITIES**
● Simple
● Unaware

⊛ **STATS**
HP ●●●
ATTACK ●●●●
DEFENSE ●●
SP. ATTACK ●●
SP. DEFENSE ●●
SPEED ●●●

⊛ **EGG GROUPS**
Water 1
Field

⊛ **PERFORMANCE**
SPEED ★☆☆☆
POWER ★★★☆
SKILL ★★☆☆
STAMINA ★★★★★
JUMP ★★

● **MAIN WAYS TO OBTAIN**

Pokémon HeartGold	Big Forest Pokéwalker Route
Pokémon SoulSilver	Big Forest Pokéwalker Route
Pokémon Diamond	Route 208
Pokémon Pearl	Route 208
Pokémon Platinum	Route 208

| Pokémon HeartGold | Pokémon SoulSilver |
| It busily makes its nest with stacks of branches and roots it has cut up with its sharp incisors. | It busily makes its nest with stacks of branches and roots it has cut up with its sharp incisors. |

⊛ **EVOLUTION**

Bidoof → Lv. 15 → Bibarel

● **LEVEL-UP MOVES**

Lv.	Name	Type	Kind	Pow.	Acc.	PP	Range	DA
1	Tackle	Normal	Physical	35	95	35	Normal	○
1	Growl	Normal	Status	—	100	40	2 Foes	—
5	Growl	Normal	Status	—	100	40	2 Foes	—
9	Defense Curl	Normal	Status	—	—	40	Self	—
13	Rollout	Rock	Physical	30	90	20	Normal	○
15	Water Gun	Water	Special	40	100	25	Normal	—
18	Headbutt	Normal	Physical	70	100	15	Normal	○
23	Hyper Fang	Normal	Physical	80	90	15	Normal	○
28	Yawn	Normal	Status	—	—	10	Normal	—
33	Amnesia	Psychic	Status	—	—	20	Self	—
38	Take Down	Normal	Physical	90	85	20	Normal	○
43	Super Fang	Normal	Physical	—	90	10	Normal	○
48	Superpower	Fighting	Physical	120	100	5	Normal	○
53	Curse	???	Status	—	—	10	Normal/Self	—

● **MOVE MANIAC**

Name	Type	Kind	Pow.	Acc.	PP	Range	DA
Headbutt	Normal	Physical	70	100	15	Normal	○

● **BP MOVES**

Name	Type	Kind	Pow.	Acc.	PP	Range	DA
Dive	Water	Physical	80	100	10	Normal	○
Fury Cutter	Bug	Physical	10	95	20	Normal	○
Icy Wind	Ice	Special	55	95	15	2 Foes	—
Snore	Normal	Special	40	100	15	Normal	—
Last Resort	Normal	Physical	130	100	5	Normal	○
Swift	Normal	Special	60	—	20	2 Foes	—
Mud-Slap	Ground	Special	20	100	10	Normal	—
Rollout	Rock	Physical	30	90	20	Normal	○
Superpower	Fighting	Physical	120	100	5	Normal	○
Aqua Tail	Water	Physical	90	90	10	Normal	○
Super Fang	Normal	Physical	—	90	10	Normal	○

● **TM & HM MOVES**

No.	Name	Type	Kind	Pow.	Acc.	PP	Range	DA
TM01	Focus Punch	Fighting	Physical	150	100	20	Normal	○
TM03	Water Pulse	Water	Special	60	100	20	Normal	—
TM06	Toxic	Poison	Status	—	85	10	Normal	—
TM10	Hidden Power	Normal	Special	—	100	15	Normal	—
TM11	Sunny Day	Fire	Status	—	—	5	All	—
TM12	Taunt	Dark	Status	—	100	20	Normal	—
TM13	Ice Beam	Ice	Special	95	100	10	Normal	—
TM14	Blizzard	Ice	Special	120	70	5	2 Foes	—
TM15	Hyper Beam	Normal	Special	150	90	5	Normal	—
TM17	Protect	Normal	Status	—	—	10	Self	—
TM18	Rain Dance	Water	Status	—	—	5	All	—
TM21	Frustration	Normal	Physical	—	100	20	Normal	○
TM23	Iron Tail	Steel	Physical	100	75	15	Normal	○
TM24	Thunderbolt	Electric	Special	95	100	15	Normal	—
TM25	Thunder	Electric	Special	120	70	10	Normal	—
TM27	Return	Normal	Physical	—	100	20	Normal	○
TM28	Dig	Ground	Physical	80	100	10	Normal	○
TM30	Shadow Ball	Ghost	Special	80	100	15	Normal	—
TM32	Double Team	Normal	Status	—	—	15	Self	—
TM34	Shock Wave	Electric	Special	60	—	20	Normal	—
TM42	Facade	Normal	Physical	70	100	20	Normal	○
TM43	Secret Power	Normal	Physical	70	100	20	Normal	○
TM44	Rest	Psychic	Status	—	—	10	Self	—
TM45	Attract	Normal	Status	—	100	15	Normal	—
TM46	Thief	Dark	Physical	40	100	10	Normal	○
TM56	Fling	Dark	Physical	—	100	10	Normal	○
TM57	Charge Beam	Electric	Special	50	90	10	Normal	—
TM58	Endure	Normal	Status	—	—	10	Self	—
TM68	Giga Impact	Normal	Physical	150	90	5	Normal	○
TM73	Thunder Wave	Electric	Status	—	100	20	Normal	—
TM76	Stealth Rock	Rock	Status	—	—	20	2 Foes	—
TM78	Captivate	Normal	Status	—	100	20	2 Foes	—
TM82	Sleep Talk	Normal	Status	—	—	10	Depends	—
TM83	Natural Gift	Normal	Physical	—	100	15	Normal	—
TM86	Grass Knot	Grass	Special	—	100	20	Normal	—
TM87	Swagger	Normal	Status	—	90	15	Normal	—
TM88	Pluck	Flying	Physical	60	100	20	Normal	○
TM90	Substitute	Normal	Status	—	—	10	Self	—
HM01	Cut	Normal	Physical	50	95	30	Normal	○
HM03	Surf	Water	Special	95	100	15	2 Foes/1 Ally	—
HM04	Strength	Normal	Physical	80	100	15	Normal	○
HM05	Whirlpool	Water	Special	15	70	15	Normal	—
HM06	Rock Smash	Fighting	Physical	40	100	15	Normal	○
HM07	Waterfall	Water	Physical	80	100	15	Normal	○
HM08	Rock Climb	Normal	Physical	90	85	20	Normal	○

● LEVEL-UP MOVES

Lv.	Name	Type	Kind	Pow.	Acc.	PP	Range	DA
1	Growl	Normal	Status	—	100	40	2 Foes	—
1	Bide	Normal	Physical	—	—	10	Self	—
16	Bug Bite	Bug	Physical	60	100	20	Normal	○

● MOVE MANIAC

Name	Type	Kind	Pow.	Acc.	PP	Range	DA

● BP MOVES

Name	Type	Kind	Pow.	Acc.	PP	Range	DA
Bug Bite	Bug	Physical	60	100	20	Normal	○
Snore	Normal	Special	40	100	15	Normal	—
Uproar	Normal	Special	50	100	10	1 Random	—
String Shot	Bug	Status	—	95	40	2 Foes	—
Mud-Slap	Ground	Special	20	100	10	Normal	—
Endeavor	Normal	Physical	—	100	5	Normal	○

● TM & HM MOVES

No.	Name	Type	Kind	Pow.	Acc.	PP	Range	DA

No. 401 | Cricket Pokémon
Kricketot

Bug

- HEIGHT: 1'01"
- WEIGHT: 4.9 lbs.
- ITEMS: Metronome

● SIZE COMPARISON

● MALE FORM
Smaller collar

● FEMALE FORM
Bigger collar

⊙ ABILITIES
- Shed Skin

⊙ STATS
HP	●
ATTACK	●●
DEFENSE	●●
SP. ATTACK	●
SP. DEFENSE	●
SPEED	●

⊙ EGG GROUPS
Bug

⊙ PERFORMANCE

SPEED ★★★★	STAMINA ★★☆
POWER ★★☆	JUMP ★★★
SKILL ★★★☆	

● MAIN WAYS TO OBTAIN

Pokémon HeartGold	Viridian Forest (mass outbreak)
Pokémon SoulSilver	Viridian Forest (mass outbreak)
Pokémon Diamond	Route 202 (morning and night only)
Pokémon Pearl	Route 202 (morning and night only)
Pokémon Platinum	Route 202 (morning and night only)

Pokémon HeartGold	Pokémon SoulSilver
When its antennae hit each other, it sounds like the music of a xylophone.	When its antennae hit each other, it sounds like the music of a xylophone.

⊙ EVOLUTION

Kricketot → Lv. 10 → Kricketune

● No. 402 | Cricket Pokémon
Kricketune

Bug

- **HEIGHT:** 3'03"
- **WEIGHT:** 56.2 lbs.
- **ITEMS:** Metronome

● SIZE COMPARISON

● **MALE FORM**
Longer mustache

● **FEMALE FORM**
Shorter mustache

◎ ABILITIES
- Swarm

◎ STATS
- HP ●●●
- ATTACK ●●●●
- DEFENSE ●●
- SP. ATTACK ●●
- SP. DEFENSE ●●
- SPEED ●●●

◎ EGG GROUPS
Bug

◎ PERFORMANCE
SPEED ★★★☆
POWER ★★☆
SKILL ★★★★☆
STAMINA ★★★
JUMP ★★★

● MAIN WAYS TO OBTAIN

Pokémon HeartGold	Bug-Catching Contest at the National Park (after obtaining the National Pokédex—Thursday, Saturday)
Pokémon SoulSilver	Bug-Catching Contest at the National Park (after obtaining the National Pokédex—Thursday, Saturday)
Pokémon Diamond	Route 206
Pokémon Pearl	Route 206
Pokémon Platinum	Route 206 (morning and night only)

Pokémon HeartGold	**Pokémon SoulSilver**
By allowing its cry to resonate in the hollow of its belly, it produces a captivating sound.	By allowing its cry to resonate in the hollow of its belly, it produces a captivating sound.

◎ EVOLUTION

 Kricketot — Lv. 10 →   Kricketune

● LEVEL-UP MOVES

Lv.	Name	Type	Kind	Pow.	Acc.	PP	Range	DA
1	Growl	Normal	Status	—	100	40	2 Foes	—
1	Bide	Normal	Physical	—	—	10	Self	—
10	Fury Cutter	Bug	Physical	10	95	20	Normal	○
14	Leech Life	Bug	Physical	20	100	15	Normal	○
18	Sing	Normal	Status	—	55	15	Normal	—
22	Focus Energy	Normal	Status	—	—	30	Self	—
26	Slash	Normal	Physical	70	100	20	Normal	○
30	X-Scissor	Bug	Physical	80	100	15	Normal	○
34	Screech	Normal	Status	—	85	40	Normal	—
38	Taunt	Dark	Status	—	100	20	Normal	—
42	Night Slash	Dark	Physical	70	100	15	Normal	○
46	Bug Buzz	Bug	Special	90	100	10	Normal	—
50	Perish Song	Normal	Status	—	—	5	All	—

● MOVE MANIAC

Name	Type	Kind	Pow.	Acc.	PP	Range	DA

● BP MOVES

Name	Type	Kind	Pow.	Acc.	PP	Range	DA
Fury Cutter	Bug	Physical	10	95	20	Normal	○
Knock Off	Dark	Physical	20	100	20	Normal	○
Bug Bite	Bug	Physical	60	100	20	Normal	○
Snore	Normal	Special	40	100	15	Normal	—
Uproar	Normal	Special	50	100	10	1 Random	—
String Shot	Bug	Status	—	95	40	2 Foes	—
Mud-Slap	Ground	Special	20	100	10	Normal	—
Endeavor	Normal	Physical	—	100	5	Normal	○

● TM & HM MOVES

No.	Name	Type	Kind	Pow.	Acc.	PP	Range	DA
TM06	Toxic	Poison	Status	—	85	10	Normal	—
TM10	Hidden Power	Normal	Special	—	100	15	Normal	—
TM11	Sunny Day	Fire	Status	—	—	5	All	—
TM12	Taunt	Dark	Status	—	100	20	Normal	—
TM15	Hyper Beam	Normal	Special	150	90	5	Normal	—
TM17	Protect	Normal	Status	—	—	10	Self	—
TM18	Rain Dance	Water	Status	—	—	5	All	—
TM21	Frustration	Normal	Physical	—	100	20	Normal	○
TM27	Return	Normal	Physical	—	100	20	Normal	○
TM31	Brick Break	Fighting	Physical	75	100	15	Normal	○
TM32	Double Team	Normal	Status	—	—	15	Self	—
TM40	Aerial Ace	Flying	Physical	60	—	20	Normal	○
TM42	Facade	Normal	Physical	70	100	20	Normal	—
TM43	Secret Power	Normal	Physical	70	100	20	Normal	—
TM44	Rest	Psychic	Status	—	—	10	Self	—
TM45	Attract	Normal	Status	—	100	15	Normal	—
TM54	False Swipe	Normal	Physical	40	100	40	Normal	○
TM58	Endure	Normal	Status	—	—	10	Self	—
TM62	Silver Wind	Bug	Special	60	100	5	Normal	—
TM68	Giga Impact	Normal	Physical	150	90	5	Normal	○
TM70	Flash	Normal	Status	—	100	20	Normal	—
TM75	Swords Dance	Normal	Status	—	—	30	Self	—
TM78	Captivate	Normal	Status	—	100	20	2 Foes	—
TM81	X-Scissor	Bug	Physical	80	100	15	Normal	○
TM82	Sleep Talk	Normal	Status	—	—	10	Depends	—
TM83	Natural Gift	Normal	Physical	—	100	15	Normal	—
TM87	Swagger	Normal	Status	—	90	15	Normal	—
TM90	Substitute	Normal	Status	—	—	10	Self	—
HM01	Cut	Normal	Physical	50	95	30	Normal	○
HM04	Strength	Normal	Physical	80	100	15	Normal	○
HM06	Rock Smash	Fighting	Physical	40	100	15	Normal	○

● LEVEL-UP MOVES

Lv.	Name	Type	Kind	Pow.	Acc.	PP	Range	DA
1	Tackle	Normal	Physical	35	95	35	Normal	○
5	Leer	Normal	Status	—	100	30	2 Foes	—
9	Charge	Electric	Status	—	—	20	Self	—
13	Spark	Electric	Physical	65	100	20	Normal	○
17	Bite	Dark	Physical	60	100	25	Normal	○
21	Roar	Normal	Status	—	100	20	Normal	—
25	Swagger	Normal	Status	—	90	15	Normal	—
29	Crunch	Dark	Physical	80	100	15	Normal	○
33	Thunder Fang	Electric	Physical	65	95	15	Normal	○
37	Scary Face	Normal	Status	—	90	10	Normal	—
41	Discharge	Electric	Special	80	100	15	2 Foes/1 Ally	—

● MOVE MANIAC

Name	Type	Kind	Pow.	Acc.	PP	Range	DA
Headbutt	Normal	Physical	70	100	15	Normal	○

● BP MOVES

Name	Type	Kind	Pow.	Acc.	PP	Range	DA
Fury Cutter	Bug	Physical	10	95	20	Normal	○
Snore	Normal	Special	40	100	15	Normal	—
Magnet Rise	Electric	Status	—	—	10	Self	—
Swift	Normal	Special	60	—	20	2 Foes	—
Mud-Slap	Ground	Special	20	100	10	Normal	—
Signal Beam	Bug	Special	75	100	15	Normal	—

● TM & HM MOVES

No.	Name	Type	Kind	Pow.	Acc.	PP	Range	DA
TM05	Roar	Normal	Status	—	100	20	Normal	—
TM06	Toxic	Poison	Status	—	85	10	Normal	—
TM10	Hidden Power	Normal	Special	—	100	15	Normal	—
TM16	Light Screen	Psychic	Status	—	—	30	2 Allies	—
TM17	Protect	Normal	Status	—	—	10	Self	—
TM18	Rain Dance	Water	Status	—	—	5	All	—
TM21	Frustration	Normal	Physical	—	100	20	Normal	○
TM23	Iron Tail	Steel	Physical	100	75	15	Normal	○
TM24	Thunderbolt	Electric	Special	95	100	15	Normal	—
TM25	Thunder	Electric	Special	120	70	10	Normal	—
TM27	Return	Normal	Physical	—	100	20	Normal	○
TM32	Double Team	Normal	Status	—	—	15	Self	—
TM34	Shock Wave	Electric	Special	60	—	20	Normal	—
TM42	Facade	Normal	Physical	70	100	20	Normal	○
TM43	Secret Power	Normal	Physical	70	100	20	Normal	○
TM44	Rest	Psychic	Status	—	—	10	Self	—
TM45	Attract	Normal	Status	—	100	15	Normal	—
TM46	Thief	Dark	Physical	40	100	10	Normal	○
TM57	Charge Beam	Electric	Special	50	90	10	Normal	—
TM58	Endure	Normal	Status	—	—	10	Self	—
TM70	Flash	Normal	Status	—	100	20	Normal	—
TM73	Thunder Wave	Electric	Status	—	100	20	Normal	—
TM78	Captivate	Normal	Status	—	100	20	2 Foes	—
TM82	Sleep Talk	Normal	Status	—	—	10	Depends	—
TM83	Natural Gift	Normal	Physical	—	100	15	Normal	○
TM87	Swagger	Normal	Status	—	90	15	Normal	—
TM90	Substitute	Normal	Status	—	—	10	Self	—
HM04	Strength	Normal	Physical	80	100	15	Normal	○

● EGG MOVES

Name	Type	Kind	Pow.	Acc.	PP	Range	DA
Ice Fang	Ice	Physical	65	95	15	Normal	○
Fire Fang	Fire	Physical	65	95	15	Normal	○
Thunder Fang	Electric	Physical	65	95	15	Normal	○
Quick Attack	Normal	Physical	40	100	30	Normal	○
Howl	Normal	Status	—	—	40	Self	—
Take Down	Normal	Physical	90	85	20	Normal	○
Night Slash	Dark	Physical	70	100	15	Normal	○

● **No. 403** | Flash Pokémon

Shinx

Electric

● **HEIGHT:** 1'08"
● **WEIGHT:** 20.9 lbs.
● **ITEMS:** None

● SIZE COMPARISON

● **MALE FORM**
More fur on head and paws

● **FEMALE FORM**
Less fur on head and paws

● ABILITIES
● Rivalry
● Intimidate

● STATS
HP ●●
ATTACK ●●●
DEFENSE ●●●
SP. ATTACK ●●
SP. DEFENSE ●●
SPEED ●●

● EGG GROUPS
Field

● PERFORMANCE

SPEED ★★★☆	STAMINA ★★★
POWER ★★★☆	JUMP ★★★
SKILL ★★☆☆	

● MAIN WAYS TO OBTAIN

Pokémon HeartGold — Route 29 (Sinnoh Sound)

Pokémon SoulSilver — Route 29 (Sinnoh Sound)

Pokémon Diamond — Route 202

Pokémon Pearl — Route 202

Pokémon Platinum — Route 202

Pokémon HeartGold
The extension and contraction of its muscles generates electricity. Its fur glows when it's in trouble.

Pokémon SoulSilver
The extension and contraction of its muscles generates electricity. Its fur glows when it's in trouble.

● EVOLUTION

Lv. 15 → Lv. 30

Shinx → Luxio → Luxray

No. 404 | Spark Pokémon
Luxio

Electric

- **HEIGHT:** 2'11"
- **WEIGHT:** 67.2 lbs.
- **ITEMS:** None

● SIZE COMPARISON

● MALE FORM
More fur on head and paws

● FEMALE FORM
Less fur on head and paws

⚙ ABILITIES
- Rivalry
- Intimidate

⚙ EGG GROUPS
Field

⚙ STATS
- HP ●●
- ATTACK ●●●●
- DEFENSE ●●●
- SP. ATTACK ●●●
- SP. DEFENSE ●●
- SPEED ●●●

⚙ PERFORMANCE
SPEED ★★★☆
POWER ★★★★
SKILL ★★★
STAMINA ★★★☆
JUMP ★★★

● MAIN WAYS TO OBTAIN

Pokémon HeartGold	Safari Zone (Savannah Area: if Grass objects are placed, may appear in tall grass)
Pokémon SoulSilver	Safari Zone (Savannah Area: if Grass objects are placed, may appear in tall grass)
Pokémon Diamond	Fuego Ironworks
Pokémon Pearl	Fuego Ironworks
Pokémon Platinum	Route 222

Pokémon HeartGold	Pokémon SoulSilver
By gathering their tails together, they collectively generate powerful electricity from their claws.	By gathering their tails together, they collectively generate powerful electricity from their claws.

⚙ EVOLUTION

Lv. 15 → Lv. 30

Shinx — Luxio — Luxray

● LEVEL-UP MOVES
Lv.	Name	Type	Kind	Pow.	Acc.	PP	Range	DA
1	Tackle	Normal	Physical	35	95	35	Normal	○
1	Leer	Normal	Status	—	100	30	2 Foes	—
5	Leer	Normal	Status	—	100	30	2 Foes	—
9	Charge	Electric	Status	—	—	20	Self	—
13	Bite	Dark	Physical	60	100	25	Normal	○
18	Spark	Electric	Physical	65	100	20	Normal	○
23	Roar	Normal	Status	—	100	20	Normal	—
28	Swagger	Normal	Status	—	90	15	Normal	—
33	Crunch	Dark	Physical	80	100	15	Normal	○
38	Thunder Fang	Electric	Physical	65	95	15	Normal	○
43	Scary Face	Normal	Status	—	90	10	Normal	—
48	Discharge	Electric	Special	80	100	15	2 Foes/1 Ally	—

● MOVE MANIAC
Name	Type	Kind	Pow.	Acc.	PP	Range	DA
Headbutt	Normal	Physical	70	100	15	Normal	○

● BP MOVES
Name	Type	Kind	Pow.	Acc.	PP	Range	DA
Fury Cutter	Bug	Physical	10	95	20	Normal	○
Snore	Normal	Special	40	100	15	Normal	—
Magnet Rise	Electric	Status	—	—	10	Self	—
Swift	Normal	Special	60	—	20	2 Foes	—
Mud-Slap	Ground	Special	20	100	10	Normal	—
Signal Beam	Bug	Special	75	100	15	Normal	—

● TM & HM MOVES
No.	Name	Type	Kind	Pow.	Acc.	PP	Range	DA
TM05	Roar	Normal	Status	—	100	20	Normal	—
TM06	Toxic	Poison	Status	—	85	10	Normal	—
TM10	Hidden Power	Normal	Special	—	100	15	Normal	—
TM16	Light Screen	Psychic	Status	—	—	30	2 Allies	—
TM17	Protect	Normal	Status	—	—	10	Self	—
TM18	Rain Dance	Water	Status	—	—	5	All	—
TM21	Frustration	Normal	Physical	—	100	20	Normal	○
TM23	Iron Tail	Steel	Physical	100	75	15	Normal	○
TM24	Thunderbolt	Electric	Special	95	100	15	Normal	—
TM25	Thunder	Electric	Special	120	70	10	Normal	—
TM27	Return	Normal	Physical	—	100	20	Normal	○
TM32	Double Team	Normal	Status	—	—	15	Self	—
TM34	Shock Wave	Electric	Special	60	—	20	Normal	—
TM42	Facade	Normal	Physical	70	100	20	Normal	○
TM43	Secret Power	Normal	Physical	70	100	20	Normal	—
TM44	Rest	Psychic	Status	—	—	10	Self	—
TM45	Attract	Normal	Status	—	100	15	Normal	—
TM46	Thief	Dark	Physical	40	100	10	Normal	○
TM57	Charge Beam	Electric	Special	50	90	10	Normal	—
TM58	Endure	Normal	Status	—	—	10	Self	—
TM70	Flash	Normal	Status	—	100	20	Normal	—
TM73	Thunder Wave	Electric	Status	—	100	20	Normal	—
TM78	Captivate	Normal	Status	—	100	20	2 Foes	—
TM82	Sleep Talk	Normal	Status	—	—	10	Depends	—
TM83	Natural Gift	Normal	Physical	—	100	15	Normal	—
TM87	Swagger	Normal	Status	—	90	15	Normal	—
TM90	Substitute	Normal	Status	—	—	10	Self	—
HM04	Strength	Normal	Physical	80	100	15	Normal	○

● LEVEL-UP MOVES

Lv.	Name	Type	Kind	Pow.	Acc.	PP	Range	DA
1	Tackle	Normal	Physical	35	95	35	Normal	○
1	Leer	Normal	Status	—	100	30	2 Foes	—
1	Charge	Electric	Status	—	—	20	Self	—
5	Leer	Normal	Status	—	100	30	2 Foes	—
9	Charge	Electric	Status	—	—	20	Self	—
13	Bite	Dark	Physical	60	100	25	Normal	○
18	Spark	Electric	Physical	65	100	20	Normal	○
23	Roar	Normal	Status	—	100	20	Normal	—
28	Swagger	Normal	Status	—	90	15	Normal	—
35	Crunch	Dark	Physical	80	100	15	Normal	○
42	Thunder Fang	Electric	Physical	65	95	15	Normal	○
49	Scary Face	Normal	Status	—	90	10	Normal	—
56	Discharge	Electric	Special	80	100	15	2 Foes/1 Ally	—

● MOVE MANIAC

Name	Type	Kind	Pow.	Acc.	PP	Range	DA
Headbutt	Normal	Physical	70	100	15	Normal	○

● BP MOVES

Name	Type	Kind	Pow.	Acc.	PP	Range	DA
Fury Cutter	Bug	Physical	10	95	20	Normal	○
Snore	Normal	Special	40	100	15	Normal	—
Magnet Rise	Electric	Status	—	—	10	Self	—
Swift	Normal	Special	60	—	20	2 Foes	—
Mud-Slap	Ground	Special	20	100	10	Normal	—
Superpower	Fighting	Physical	120	100	5	Normal	○
Signal Beam	Bug	Special	75	100	15	Normal	—

● TM & HM MOVES

No.	Name	Type	Kind	Pow.	Acc.	PP	Range	DA
TM05	Roar	Normal	Status	—	100	20	Normal	—
TM06	Toxic	Poison	Status	—	85	10	Normal	—
TM10	Hidden Power	Normal	Special	—	100	15	Normal	—
TM15	Hyper Beam	Normal	Special	150	90	5	Normal	—
TM16	Light Screen	Psychic	Status	—	—	30	2 Allies	—
TM17	Protect	Normal	Status	—	—	10	Self	—
TM18	Rain Dance	Water	Status	—	—	5	All	—
TM21	Frustration	Normal	Physical	—	100	20	Normal	○
TM23	Iron Tail	Steel	Physical	100	75	15	Normal	○
TM24	Thunderbolt	Electric	Special	95	100	15	Normal	—
TM25	Thunder	Electric	Special	120	70	10	Normal	—
TM27	Return	Normal	Physical	—	100	20	Normal	○
TM32	Double Team	Normal	Status	—	—	15	Self	—
TM34	Shock Wave	Electric	Special	60	—	20	Normal	—
TM42	Facade	Normal	Physical	70	100	20	Normal	—
TM43	Secret Power	Normal	Physical	70	100	20	Normal	—
TM44	Rest	Psychic	Status	—	—	10	Self	—
TM45	Attract	Normal	Status	—	100	15	Normal	—
TM46	Thief	Dark	Physical	40	100	10	Normal	○
TM57	Charge Beam	Electric	Special	50	90	10	Normal	—
TM58	Endure	Normal	Status	—	—	10	Self	—
TM68	Giga Impact	Normal	Physical	150	90	5	Normal	○
TM70	Flash	Normal	Status	—	100	20	Normal	—
TM73	Thunder Wave	Electric	Status	—	100	20	Normal	—
TM78	Captivate	Normal	Status	—	100	20	2 Foes	—
TM82	Sleep Talk	Normal	Status	—	—	10	Depends	—
TM83	Natural Gift	Normal	Physical	—	100	15	Normal	—
TM87	Swagger	Normal	Status	—	90	15	Normal	—
TM90	Substitute	Normal	Status	—	—	10	Self	—
HM04	Strength	Normal	Physical	80	100	15	Normal	○

○ No. 405 | Gleam Eyes Pokémon
Luxray

Electric

- **● HEIGHT:** 4'02"
- **● WEIGHT:** 92.6 lbs.
- **● ITEMS:** None

● SIZE COMPARISON

● MALE FORM
More fur on head

● FEMALE FORM
Less fur on head

⬡ ABILITIES
- Rivalry
- Intimidate

⬡ STATS
HP	●●●
ATTACK	●●●●●
DEFENSE	●●●
SP. ATTACK	●●●●
SP. DEFENSE	●●●
SPEED	●●●

⬡ EGG GROUPS
Field

⬡ PERFORMANCE
SPEED ★★★	STAMINA ★★★★
POWER ★★★★☆	JUMP ★★★
SKILL ★★★★	

● MAIN WAYS TO OBTAIN

Pokémon HeartGold Level up Luxio to Lv. 30

Pokémon SoulSilver Level up Luxio to Lv. 30

Pokémon Diamond Level up Luxio to Lv. 30

Pokémon Pearl Level up Luxio to Lv. 30

Pokémon Platinum Level up Luxio to Lv. 30

Pokémon HeartGold
LUXRAY's ability to see through objects comes in handy when it's scouting for danger.

Pokémon SoulSilver
LUXRAY's ability to see through objects comes in handy when it's scouting for danger.

⬡ EVOLUTION

Shinx → Lv. 15 → Luxio → Lv. 30 → Luxray

● No. 406 | Bud Pokémon
Budew

Grass | **Poison**

- **HEIGHT:** 0'08"
- **WEIGHT:** 2.6 lbs.
- **ITEMS:** Poison Barb

● SIZE COMPARISON

● MALE/FEMALE HAVE SAME FORM

⊙ ABILITIES
- Natural Cure
- Poison Point

⊙ EGG GROUPS
No Egg has ever been discovered

⊙ STATS
HP ●
ATTACK ●
DEFENSE ● ●
SP. ATTACK ● ●
SP. DEFENSE ● ● ●
SPEED ● ● ●

⊙ PERFORMANCE
SPEED ★★★☆☆ STAMINA ★★☆
POWER ★☆☆ JUMP ★★★
SKILL ★★☆

● MAIN WAYS TO OBTAIN

Pokémon HeartGold	Ilex Forest [Sinnoh Sound]
Pokémon SoulSilver	Ilex Forest [Sinnoh Sound]
Pokémon Diamond	Route 204
Pokémon Pearl	Route 204
Pokémon Platinum	Route 204

Pokémon HeartGold
When it feels the sun's warm touch, it opens its bud to release pollen. It lives alongside clear pools.

Pokémon SoulSilver
When it feels the sun's warm touch, it opens its bud to release pollen. It lives alongside clear pools.

⊙ EVOLUTION

Budew — Level up with high friendship between 4:00 A.M. and 8:00 P.M. → Roselia — Use Shiny Stone → Roserade

● LEVEL-UP MOVES

Lv.	Name	Type	Kind	Pow.	Acc.	PP	Range	DA
1	Absorb	Grass	Special	20	100	25	Normal	—
4	Growth	Normal	Status	—	—	40	Self	—
7	Water Sport	Water	Status	—	—	15	All	—
10	Stun Spore	Grass	Status	—	75	30	Normal	—
13	Mega Drain	Grass	Special	40	100	15	Normal	—
16	Worry Seed	Grass	Status	—	100	10	Normal	—

● MOVE MANIAC

Name	Type	Kind	Pow.	Acc.	PP	Range	DA

● BP MOVES

Name	Type	Kind	Pow.	Acc.	PP	Range	DA
Snore	Normal	Special	40	100	15	Normal	—
Synthesis	Grass	Status	—	—	5	Self	—
Swift	Normal	Special	60	—	20	2 Foes	—
Uproar	Normal	Special	50	100	10	1 Random	—
Worry Seed	Grass	Status	—	100	10	Normal	—
Mud-Slap	Ground	Special	20	100	10	Normal	—
Seed Bomb	Grass	Physical	80	100	15	Normal	—

● TM & HM MOVES

No.	Name	Type	Kind	Pow.	Acc.	PP	Range	DA
TM06	Toxic	Poison	Status	—	85	10	Normal	—
TM09	Bullet Seed	Grass	Physical	10	100	30	Normal	—
TM10	Hidden Power	Normal	Special	—	100	15	Normal	—
TM11	Sunny Day	Fire	Status	—	—	5	All	—
TM17	Protect	Normal	Status	—	—	10	Self	—
TM18	Rain Dance	Water	Status	—	—	5	All	—
TM19	Giga Drain	Grass	Special	60	100	10	Normal	—
TM21	Frustration	Normal	Physical	—	100	20	Normal	○
TM22	SolarBeam	Grass	Special	120	100	10	Normal	—
TM27	Return	Normal	Physical	—	100	20	Normal	○
TM30	Shadow Ball	Ghost	Special	80	100	15	Normal	—
TM32	Double Team	Normal	Status	—	—	15	Self	—
TM36	Sludge Bomb	Poison	Special	90	100	10	Normal	—
TM42	Facade	Normal	Physical	70	100	20	Normal	○
TM43	Secret Power	Normal	Physical	70	100	20	Normal	—
TM44	Rest	Psychic	Status	—	—	10	Self	—
TM45	Attract	Normal	Status	—	100	15	Normal	—
TM53	Energy Ball	Grass	Special	80	100	10	Normal	—
TM58	Endure	Normal	Status	—	—	10	Self	—
TM70	Flash	Normal	Status	—	100	20	Normal	—
TM75	Swords Dance	Normal	Status	—	—	30	Self	—
TM77	Psych Up	Normal	Status	—	—	10	Normal	—
TM78	Captivate	Normal	Status	—	100	20	2 Foes	—
TM82	Sleep Talk	Normal	Status	—	—	10	Depends	—
TM83	Natural Gift	Normal	Physical	—	100	15	Normal	—
TM86	Grass Knot	Grass	Special	—	100	20	Normal	○
TM87	Swagger	Normal	Status	—	90	15	Normal	—
TM90	Substitute	Normal	Status	—	—	10	Self	—
HM01	Cut	Normal	Physical	50	95	30	Normal	○

● EGG MOVES

Name	Type	Kind	Pow.	Acc.	PP	Range	DA
Spikes	Ground	Status	—	—	20	2 Foes	—
Synthesis	Grass	Status	—	—	5	Self	—
Pin Missile	Bug	Physical	14	85	20	Normal	—
Cotton Spore	Grass	Status	—	85	40	Normal	—
Sleep Powder	Grass	Status	—	75	15	Normal	—
Razor Leaf	Grass	Physical	55	95	25	2 Foes	—
Mind Reader	Normal	Status	—	—	5	Normal	—
Leaf Storm	Grass	Special	140	90	5	Normal	—
Extrasensory	Psychic	Special	80	100	30	Normal	—

● LEVEL-UP MOVES

Lv.	Name	Type	Kind	Pow.	Acc.	PP	Range	DA
1	Weather Ball	Normal	Special	50	100	10	Normal	—
1	Poison Sting	Poison	Physical	15	100	35	Normal	—
1	Mega Drain	Grass	Special	40	100	15	Normal	—
1	Magical Leaf	Grass	Special	60	—	20	Normal	—
1	Sweet Scent	Normal	Status	—	100	20	2 Foes	—

● MOVE MANIAC

Name	Type	Kind	Pow.	Acc.	PP	Range	DA

● BP MOVES

Name	Type	Kind	Pow.	Acc.	PP	Range	DA
Fury Cutter	Bug	Physical	10	95	20	Normal	○
Snore	Normal	Special	40	100	15	Normal	—
Synthesis	Grass	Status	—	—	5	Self	—
Swift	Normal	Special	60	—	20	2 Foes	—
Worry Seed	Grass	Status	—	100	10	Normal	—
Mud-Slap	Ground	Special	20	100	10	Normal	—
Seed Bomb	Grass	Physical	80	100	15	Normal	—

● TM & HM MOVES

No.	Name	Type	Kind	Pow.	Acc.	PP	Range	DA
TM06	Toxic	Poison	Status	—	85	10	Normal	—
TM09	Bullet Seed	Grass	Physical	10	100	30	Normal	—
TM10	Hidden Power	Normal	Special	—	100	15	Normal	—
TM11	Sunny Day	Fire	Status	—	—	5	All	—
TM15	Hyper Beam	Normal	Special	150	90	5	Normal	—
TM17	Protect	Normal	Status	—	—	10	Self	—
TM18	Rain Dance	Water	Status	—	—	5	All	—
TM19	Giga Drain	Grass	Special	60	100	10	Normal	—
TM21	Frustration	Normal	Physical	—	100	20	Normal	○
TM22	SolarBeam	Grass	Special	120	100	10	Normal	—
TM27	Return	Normal	Physical	—	100	20	Normal	○
TM30	Shadow Ball	Ghost	Special	80	100	15	Normal	—
TM32	Double Team	Normal	Status	—	—	15	Self	—
TM36	Sludge Bomb	Poison	Special	90	100	10	Normal	—
TM42	Facade	Normal	Physical	70	100	20	Normal	○
TM43	Secret Power	Normal	Physical	70	100	20	Normal	—
TM44	Rest	Psychic	Status	—	—	10	Self	—
TM45	Attract	Normal	Status	—	100	15	Normal	—
TM53	Energy Ball	Grass	Special	80	100	10	Normal	—
TM58	Endure	Normal	Status	—	—	10	Self	—
TM68	Giga Impact	Normal	Physical	150	90	5	Normal	○
TM70	Flash	Normal	Status	—	100	20	Normal	—
TM75	Swords Dance	Normal	Status	—	—	30	Self	—
TM77	Psych Up	Normal	Status	—	—	10	Normal	—
TM78	Captivate	Normal	Status	—	100	20	2 Foes	—
TM82	Sleep Talk	Normal	Status	—	—	10	Depends	—
TM83	Natural Gift	Normal	Physical	—	100	15	Normal	—
TM84	Poison Jab	Poison	Physical	80	100	20	Normal	○
TM86	Grass Knot	Grass	Special	—	100	20	Normal	○
TM87	Swagger	Normal	Status	—	90	15	Normal	—
TM90	Substitute	Normal	Status	—	—	10	Self	—
HM01	Cut	Normal	Physical	50	95	30	Normal	○

◉ No. 407 | Bouquet Pokémon
Roserade

Grass   Poison

- ● HEIGHT: 2'11"
- ● WEIGHT: 32.0 lbs.
- ● ITEMS: None

● SIZE COMPARISON

- ● MALE FORM
  Shorter cape
- ● FEMALE FORM
  Longer cape

⊙ ABILITIES
- ● Natural Cure
- ● Poison Point

⊙ STATS
- HP ●●
- ATTACK ●●●
- DEFENSE ●●
- SP. ATTACK ●●●●●
- SP. DEFENSE ●●●●●
- SPEED ●●●●

⊙ EGG GROUPS
Fairy
Grass

⊙ PERFORMANCE
SPEED ★★★☆	STAMINA ★★☆
POWER ★★★☆	JUMP ★★★
SKILL ★★★★★	

● MAIN WAYS TO OBTAIN

Pokémon HeartGold   Use Shiny Stone on Roselia

Pokémon SoulSilver   Use Shiny Stone on Roselia

Pokémon Diamond   Use Shiny Stone on Roselia

Pokémon Pearl   Use Shiny Stone on Roselia

Pokémon Platinum   Use Shiny Stone on Roselia

Pokémon HeartGold

Its sweet aroma attracts prey. Then it spews poison. The more toxic it is, the sweeter its aroma.

Pokémon SoulSilver

Its sweet aroma attracts prey. Then it spews poison. The more toxic it is, the sweeter its aroma.

⊙ EVOLUTION

Budew — Level up with high friendship between 4:00 A.M. and 8:00 P.M. → Roselia — Use Shiny Stone → Roserade

● No. 408 | Head Butt Pokémon
Cranidos

Rock

● HEIGHT: 2'11"
● WEIGHT: 69.4 lbs.
● ITEMS: None

● SIZE COMPARISON

● MALE/FEMALE HAVE SAME FORM

● ABILITIES
● Mold Breaker

● EGG GROUPS
Monster

● STATS
HP ●●
ATTACK ●●●●●
DEFENSE ●●
SP. ATTACK ●
SP. DEFENSE ●
SPEED ●●●

● PERFORMANCE

SPEED ★★★☆
POWER ★★★★☆
SKILL ★★★

STAMINA ★★☆
JUMP ★★☆

● MAIN WAYS TO OBTAIN

Pokémon HeartGold	—
Pokémon SoulSilver	—
Pokémon Diamond	Get the Skull Fossil in the Underground and have it restored at the Oreburgh Mining Museum
Pokémon Pearl	—
Pokémon Platinum	Get the Skull Fossil in the Underground and have it restored at the Oreburgh Mining Museum

| Pokémon HeartGold | Pokémon SoulSilver |
| CRANIDOS toughen up their already rock-hard heads by headbutting one another. | CRANIDOS toughen up their already rock-hard heads by headbutting one another. |

● EVOLUTION

Cranidos → Lv. 30 → Rampardos

● LEVEL-UP MOVES

Lv.	Name	Type	Kind	Pow.	Acc.	PP	Range	DA
1	Headbutt	Normal	Physical	70	100	15	Normal	○
1	Leer	Normal	Status	—	100	30	2 Foes	—
6	Focus Energy	Normal	Status	—	—	30	Self	—
10	Pursuit	Dark	Physical	40	100	20	Normal	○
15	Take Down	Normal	Physical	90	85	20	Normal	○
19	Scary Face	Normal	Status	—	90	10	Normal	—
24	Assurance	Dark	Physical	50	100	10	Normal	○
28	AncientPower	Rock	Special	60	100	5	Normal	—
33	Zen Headbutt	Psychic	Physical	80	90	15	Normal	○
37	Screech	Normal	Status	—	85	40	Normal	—
43	Head Smash	Rock	Physical	150	80	5	Normal	○

● MOVE MANIAC

Name	Type	Kind	Pow.	Acc.	PP	Range	DA
Headbutt	Normal	Physical	70	100	15	Normal	○

● BP MOVES

Name	Type	Kind	Pow.	Acc.	PP	Range	DA
ThunderPunch	Electric	Physical	75	100	15	Normal	○
Fire Punch	Fire	Physical	75	100	15	Normal	○
Zen Headbutt	Psychic	Physical	80	90	15	Normal	○
Snore	Normal	Special	40	100	15	Normal	—
Spite	Ghost	Status	—	100	10	Normal	—
Uproar	Normal	Special	50	100	10	1 Random	—
Mud-Slap	Ground	Special	20	100	10	Normal	—
Superpower	Fighting	Physical	120	100	5	Normal	○
Iron Head	Steel	Physical	80	100	15	Normal	○
Endeavor	Normal	Physical	—	100	5	Normal	○
AncientPower	Rock	Special	60	100	5	Normal	—
Earth Power	Ground	Special	90	100	10	Normal	—

● TM & HM MOVES

No.	Name	Type	Kind	Pow.	Acc.	PP	Range	DA
TM05	Roar	Normal	Status	—	100	20	Normal	—
TM06	Toxic	Poison	Status	—	85	10	Normal	—
TM10	Hidden Power	Normal	Special	—	100	15	Normal	—
TM11	Sunny Day	Fire	Status	—	—	5	All	—
TM13	Ice Beam	Ice	Special	95	100	10	Normal	—
TM14	Blizzard	Ice	Special	120	70	5	2 Foes	—
TM17	Protect	Normal	Status	—	—	10	Self	—
TM18	Rain Dance	Water	Status	—	—	5	All	—
TM21	Frustration	Normal	Physical	—	100	20	Normal	○
TM23	Iron Tail	Steel	Physical	100	75	15	Normal	○
TM24	Thunderbolt	Electric	Special	95	100	15	Normal	—
TM25	Thunder	Electric	Special	120	70	10	Normal	—
TM26	Earthquake	Ground	Physical	100	100	10	2 Foes/1 Ally	—
TM27	Return	Normal	Physical	—	100	20	Normal	○
TM28	Dig	Ground	Physical	80	100	10	Normal	○
TM32	Double Team	Normal	Status	—	—	15	Self	—
TM34	Shock Wave	Electric	Special	60	—	20	Normal	—
TM35	Flamethrower	Fire	Special	95	100	15	Normal	—
TM37	Sandstorm	Rock	Status	—	—	10	All	—
TM38	Fire Blast	Fire	Special	120	85	5	Normal	—
TM39	Rock Tomb	Rock	Physical	50	80	10	Normal	○
TM42	Facade	Normal	Physical	70	100	20	Normal	○
TM43	Secret Power	Normal	Physical	70	100	20	Normal	○
TM44	Rest	Psychic	Status	—	—	10	Self	—
TM45	Attract	Normal	Status	—	100	15	Normal	—
TM46	Thief	Dark	Physical	40	100	10	Normal	○
TM56	Fling	Dark	Physical	—	100	10	Normal	○
TM58	Endure	Normal	Status	—	—	10	Self	—
TM59	Dragon Pulse	Dragon	Special	90	100	10	Normal	—
TM66	Payback	Dark	Physical	50	100	10	Normal	○
TM69	Rock Polish	Rock	Status	—	—	20	Self	—
TM71	Stone Edge	Rock	Physical	100	80	5	Normal	○
TM75	Swords Dance	Normal	Status	—	—	30	Self	—
TM76	Stealth Rock	Rock	Status	—	—	20	2 Foes	—
TM78	Captivate	Normal	Status	—	100	20	2 Foes	—
TM80	Rock Slide	Rock	Physical	75	90	10	2 Foes	—
TM82	Sleep Talk	Normal	Status	—	—	10	Depends	—
TM83	Natural Gift	Normal	Physical	—	100	15	Normal	—
TM87	Swagger	Normal	Status	—	90	15	Normal	—
TM90	Substitute	Normal	Status	—	—	10	Self	—
HM04	Strength	Normal	Physical	80	100	15	Normal	○
HM06	Rock Smash	Fighting	Physical	40	100	15	Normal	○
HM08	Rock Climb	Normal	Physical	90	85	20	Normal	○

● EGG MOVES

Name	Type	Kind	Pow.	Acc.	PP	Range	DA
Crunch	Dark	Physical	80	100	15	Normal	○
Thrash	Normal	Physical	90	100	20	1 Random	○
Double-Edge	Normal	Physical	120	100	15	Normal	○
Leer	Normal	Status	—	100	30	2 Foes	—
Slam	Normal	Physical	80	75	20	Normal	○
Stomp	Normal	Physical	65	100	20	Normal	○
Whirlwind	Normal	Status	—	100	20	Normal	—
Hammer Arm	Fighting	Physical	100	90	10	Normal	○
Curse	???	Status	—	—	10	Normal/Self	—

● LEVEL-UP MOVES

Lv.	Name	Type	Kind	Pow.	Acc.	PP	Range	DA
1	Headbutt	Normal	Physical	70	100	15	Normal	○
1	Leer	Normal	Status	—	100	30	2 Foes	—
6	Focus Energy	Normal	Status	—	—	30	Self	—
10	Pursuit	Dark	Physical	40	100	20	Normal	○
15	Take Down	Normal	Physical	90	85	20	Normal	○
19	Scary Face	Normal	Status	—	90	10	Normal	—
24	Assurance	Dark	Physical	50	100	10	Normal	○
28	AncientPower	Rock	Special	60	100	5	Normal	—
30	Endeavor	Normal	Physical	—	100	5	Normal	○
36	Zen Headbutt	Psychic	Physical	80	90	15	Normal	○
43	Screech	Normal	Status	—	85	40	Normal	—
52	Head Smash	Rock	Physical	150	80	5	Normal	○

● MOVE MANIAC

Name	Type	Kind	Pow.	Acc.	PP	Range	DA
Headbutt	Normal	Physical	70	100	15	Normal	○

● BP MOVES

Name	Type	Kind	Pow.	Acc.	PP	Range	DA
ThunderPunch	Electric	Physical	75	100	15	Normal	—
Fire Punch	Fire	Physical	75	100	15	Normal	○
Zen Headbutt	Psychic	Physical	80	90	15	Normal	○
Snore	Normal	Special	40	100	15	Normal	—
Spite	Ghost	Status	—	100	10	Normal	—
Uproar	Normal	Special	—	100	10	1 Random	—
Mud-Slap	Ground	Special	20	100	10	Normal	—
Superpower	Fighting	Physical	120	100	5	Normal	○
Iron Head	Steel	Physical	80	100	15	Normal	○
Endeavor	Normal	Physical	—	100	5	Normal	○
Outrage	Dragon	Physical	120	100	15	1 Random	○
AncientPower	Rock	Special	60	100	5	Normal	—
Earth Power	Ground	Special	90	100	10	Normal	—
Pain Split	Normal	Status	—	—	20	Normal	—

● TM & HM MOVES

No.	Name	Type	Kind	Pow.	Acc.	PP	Range	DA
TM01	Focus Punch	Fighting	Physical	150	100	20	Normal	○
TM05	Roar	Normal	Status	—	100	20	Normal	—
TM06	Toxic	Poison	Status	—	85	10	Normal	—
TM10	Hidden Power	Normal	Special	—	100	15	Normal	—
TM11	Sunny Day	Fire	Status	—	—	5	All	—
TM13	Ice Beam	Ice	Special	95	100	10	Normal	—
TM14	Blizzard	Ice	Special	120	70	5	2 Foes	—
TM15	Hyper Beam	Normal	Special	150	90	5	Normal	—
TM17	Protect	Normal	Status	—	—	10	Self	—
TM18	Rain Dance	Water	Status	—	—	5	All	—
TM21	Frustration	Normal	Physical	—	100	20	Normal	○
TM23	Iron Tail	Steel	Physical	100	75	15	Normal	○
TM24	Thunderbolt	Electric	Special	95	100	15	Normal	—
TM25	Thunder	Electric	Special	120	70	10	Normal	—
TM26	Earthquake	Ground	Physical	100	100	10	2 Foes/1 Ally	○
TM27	Return	Normal	Physical	—	100	20	Normal	○
TM28	Dig	Ground	Physical	80	100	10	Normal	○
TM31	Brick Break	Fighting	Physical	75	100	15	Normal	○
TM32	Double Team	Normal	Status	—	—	15	Self	—
TM34	Shock Wave	Electric	Special	60	—	20	Normal	—
TM35	Flamethrower	Fire	Special	95	100	15	Normal	—
TM37	Sandstorm	Rock	Status	—	—	10	All	—
TM38	Fire Blast	Fire	Special	120	85	5	Normal	—
TM39	Rock Tomb	Rock	Physical	50	80	10	Normal	○
TM42	Facade	Normal	Physical	70	100	20	Normal	○
TM43	Secret Power	Normal	Physical	70	100	20	Normal	○
TM44	Rest	Psychic	Status	—	—	10	Self	—
TM45	Attract	Normal	Status	—	100	15	Normal	—
TM46	Thief	Dark	Physical	40	100	10	Normal	○
TM52	Focus Blast	Fighting	Special	120	70	5	Normal	—
TM56	Fling	Dark	Physical	—	100	10	Normal	○
TM58	Endure	Normal	Status	—	—	10	Self	—
TM59	Dragon Pulse	Dragon	Special	90	100	10	Normal	—
TM66	Payback	Dark	Physical	50	100	10	Normal	○
TM68	Giga Impact	Normal	Physical	150	90	5	Normal	○
TM69	Rock Polish	Rock	Status	—	—	20	Self	—
TM71	Stone Edge	Rock	Physical	100	80	5	Normal	○
TM72	Avalanche	Ice	Physical	60	100	10	Normal	○
TM75	Swords Dance	Normal	Status	—	—	30	Self	—
TM76	Stealth Rock	Rock	Status	—	—	20	2 Foes	—
TM78	Captivate	Normal	Status	—	100	20	2 Foes	—
TM80	Rock Slide	Rock	Physical	75	90	10	2 Foes	○
TM82	Sleep Talk	Normal	Status	—	—	10	Depends	—
TM83	Natural Gift	Normal	Physical	—	100	15	Normal	—
TM87	Swagger	Normal	Status	—	90	15	Normal	—
TM90	Substitute	Normal	Status	—	—	10	Self	—
HM01	Cut	Normal	Physical	50	95	30	Normal	○
HM03	Surf	Water	Special	95	100	15	2 Foes/1 Ally	—
HM04	Strength	Normal	Physical	80	100	15	Normal	○
HM05	Whirlpool	Water	Special	15	70	15	Normal	—
HM06	Rock Smash	Fighting	Physical	40	100	15	Normal	○
HM08	Rock Climb	Normal	Physical	90	85	20	Normal	○

◎ No. 409 | Head Butt Pokémon
Rampardos
Rock

- **HEIGHT:** 5'03"
- **WEIGHT:** 226.0 lbs.
- **ITEMS:** None

● SIZE COMPARISON

● MALE/FEMALE HAVE SAME FORM

◎ ABILITIES
● Mold Breaker

◎ STATS
- HP ●●●●
- ATTACK ●●●●●●●
- DEFENSE ●●
- SP. ATTACK ●●
- SP. DEFENSE ●●
- SPEED ●●●

◎ EGG GROUPS
Monster

◎ PERFORMANCE
SPEED ★★★   STAMINA ★★★☆
POWER ★★★★★   JUMP ★★☆
SKILL ★★☆

● MAIN WAYS TO OBTAIN

Pokémon HeartGold —

Pokémon SoulSilver —

Pokémon Diamond Level up Cranidos to Lv. 30

Pokémon Pearl —

Pokémon Platinum Level up Cranidos to Lv. 30

Pokémon HeartGold
Its skull withstands impacts of any magnitude. As a result, its brain never gets the chance to grow.

Pokémon SoulSilver
Its skull withstands impacts of any magnitude. As a result, its brain never gets the chance to grow.

◎ EVOLUTION

Cranidos   Lv. 30   Rampardos

● No. 410 | Shield Pokémon
Shieldon

Rock Steel

● LEVEL-UP MOVES

Lv.	Name	Type	Kind	Pow.	Acc.	PP	Range	DA
1	Tackle	Normal	Physical	35	95	35	Normal	○
1	Protect	Normal	Status	—	—	10	Self	—
6	Taunt	Dark	Status	—	100	20	Normal	—
10	Metal Sound	Steel	Status	—	85	40	Normal	—
15	Take Down	Normal	Physical	90	85	20	Normal	○
19	Iron Defense	Steel	Status	—	—	15	Self	—
24	Swagger	Normal	Status	—	90	15	Normal	—
28	AncientPower	Rock	Special	60	100	5	Normal	—
33	Endure	Normal	Status	—	—	10	Self	—
37	Metal Burst	Steel	Physical	—	100	10	Self	—
43	Iron Head	Steel	Physical	80	100	15	Normal	○

● MOVE MANIAC

Name	Type	Kind	Pow.	Acc.	PP	Range	DA
Headbutt	Normal	Physical	70	100	15	Normal	○

● BP MOVES

Name	Type	Kind	Pow.	Acc.	PP	Range	DA
Snore	Normal	Special	40	100	15	Normal	—
Magnet Rise	Electric	Status	—	—	10	Self	—
Mud-Slap	Ground	Special	20	100	10	Normal	—
Iron Head	Steel	Physical	80	100	15	Normal	○
AncientPower	Rock	Special	60	100	5	Normal	—
Earth Power	Ground	Special	90	100	10	Normal	—
Iron Defense	Steel	Status	—	—	15	Self	—

- **HEIGHT:** 1'08"
- **WEIGHT:** 125.7 lbs.
- **ITEMS:** None

● SIZE COMPARISON

● MALE/FEMALE HAVE SAME FORM

⊛ ABILITIES
- Sturdy

⊛ STATS
- HP ●
- ATTACK ●●
- DEFENSE ●●●●●
- SP. ATTACK ●●●
- SP. DEFENSE ●●●
- SPEED ●

⊛ EGG GROUPS
Monster

⊛ PERFORMANCE

SPEED ★★★	STAMINA ★★★★☆
POWER ★★★☆	JUMP ★★
SKILL ★★☆	

● MAIN WAYS TO OBTAIN

Pokémon HeartGold	—
Pokémon SoulSilver	—
Pokémon Diamond	—
Pokémon Pearl	Get the Armor Fossil in the Underground and have it restored at the Oreburgh Mining Museum
Pokémon Platinum	Get the Armor Fossil in the Underground and have it restored at the Oreburgh Mining Museum

Pokémon HeartGold	Pokémon SoulSilver
It was generated from a fossil dug out of a layer of clay that was older than anyone knows. It has a sturdy face.	It was generated from a fossil dug out of a layer of clay that was older than anyone knows. It has a sturdy face.

⊛ EVOLUTION

Shieldon — Lv. 30 → Bastiodon

● TM & HM MOVES

No.	Name	Type	Kind	Pow.	Acc.	PP	Range	DA
TM05	Roar	Normal	Status	—	100	20	Normal	—
TM06	Toxic	Poison	Status	—	85	10	Normal	—
TM10	Hidden Power	Normal	Special	—	100	15	Normal	—
TM11	Sunny Day	Fire	Status	—	—	5	All	—
TM12	Taunt	Dark	Status	—	100	20	Normal	—
TM13	Ice Beam	Ice	Special	95	100	10	Normal	—
TM14	Blizzard	Ice	Special	120	70	5	2 Foes	—
TM17	Protect	Normal	Status	—	—	10	Self	—
TM18	Rain Dance	Water	Status	—	—	5	All	—
TM21	Frustration	Normal	Physical	—	100	20	Normal	○
TM23	Iron Tail	Steel	Physical	100	75	15	Normal	○
TM24	Thunderbolt	Electric	Special	95	100	15	Normal	—
TM25	Thunder	Electric	Special	120	70	10	Normal	—
TM26	Earthquake	Ground	Physical	100	100	10	2 Foes/1 Ally	—
TM27	Return	Normal	Physical	—	100	20	Normal	○
TM28	Dig	Ground	Physical	80	100	10	Normal	○
TM32	Double Team	Normal	Status	—	—	15	Self	—
TM34	Shock Wave	Electric	Special	60	—	20	Normal	—
TM35	Flamethrower	Fire	Special	95	100	15	Normal	—
TM37	Sandstorm	Rock	Status	—	—	10	All	—
TM38	Fire Blast	Fire	Special	120	85	5	Normal	—
TM39	Rock Tomb	Rock	Physical	50	80	10	Normal	—
TM41	Torment	Dark	Status	—	100	15	Normal	—
TM42	Facade	Normal	Physical	70	100	20	Normal	○
TM43	Secret Power	Normal	Physical	70	100	20	Normal	—
TM44	Rest	Psychic	Status	—	—	10	Self	—
TM45	Attract	Normal	Status	—	100	15	Normal	—
TM58	Endure	Normal	Status	—	—	10	Self	—
TM69	Rock Polish	Rock	Status	—	—	20	Self	—
TM71	Stone Edge	Rock	Physical	100	80	5	Normal	—
TM76	Stealth Rock	Rock	Status	—	—	20	2 Foes	—
TM78	Captivate	Normal	Status	—	100	20	2 Foes	—
TM80	Rock Slide	Rock	Physical	75	90	10	2 Foes	—
TM82	Sleep Talk	Normal	Status	—	—	10	Depends	—
TM83	Natural Gift	Normal	Physical	—	100	15	Normal	—
TM87	Swagger	Normal	Status	—	90	15	Normal	—
TM90	Substitute	Normal	Status	—	—	10	Self	—
TM91	Flash Cannon	Steel	Special	80	100	10	Normal	—
HM04	Strength	Normal	Physical	80	100	15	Normal	○
HM06	Rock Smash	Fighting	Physical	40	100	15	Normal	○

● EGG MOVES

Name	Type	Kind	Pow.	Acc.	PP	Range	DA
Headbutt	Normal	Physical	70	100	15	Normal	○
Scary Face	Normal	Status	—	90	10	Normal	—
Focus Energy	Normal	Status	—	—	30	Self	—
Double-Edge	Normal	Physical	120	100	15	Normal	○
Rock Blast	Rock	Physical	25	80	10	Normal	—
Body Slam	Normal	Physical	85	100	15	Normal	○
Screech	Normal	Status	—	85	40	Normal	—
Curse	???	Status	—	—	10	Normal/Self	—
Fissure	Ground	Physical	—	30	5	Normal	—
Counter	Fighting	Physical	—	100	20	Normal	○
							—
							—

● LEVEL-UP MOVES

Lv.	Name	Type	Kind	Pow.	Acc.	PP	Range	DA
1	Tackle	Normal	Physical	35	95	35	Normal	○
1	Protect	Normal	Status	—	—	10	Self	—
1	Taunt	Dark	Status	—	100	20	Normal	—
1	Metal Sound	Steel	Status	—	85	40	Normal	—
6	Taunt	Dark	Status	—	100	20	Normal	—
10	Metal Sound	Steel	Status	—	85	40	Normal	—
15	Take Down	Normal	Physical	90	85	20	Normal	○
19	Iron Defense	Steel	Status	—	—	15	Self	—
24	Swagger	Normal	Status	—	90	15	Normal	—
28	AncientPower	Rock	Special	60	100	5	Normal	—
30	Block	Normal	Status	—	—	5	Normal	—
36	Endure	Normal	Status	—	—	10	Self	—
43	Metal Burst	Steel	Physical	—	100	10	Self	—
52	Iron Head	Steel	Physical	80	100	15	Normal	○

● MOVE MANIAC

Name	Type	Kind	Pow.	Acc.	PP	Range	DA
Headbutt	Normal	Physical	70	100	15	Normal	○

● BP MOVES

Name	Type	Kind	Pow.	Acc.	PP	Range	DA
Snore	Normal	Special	40	100	15	Normal	—
Magnet Rise	Electric	Status	—	—	10	Self	—
Magic Coat	Psychic	Status	—	—	15	Self	—
Block	Normal	Status	—	—	5	Normal	—
Mud-Slap	Ground	Special	20	100	10	Normal	—
Iron Head	Steel	Physical	80	100	15	Normal	○
Outrage	Dragon	Physical	120	100	15	1 Random	○
AncientPower	Rock	Special	60	100	5	Normal	—
Earth Power	Ground	Special	90	100	10	Normal	—
Iron Defense	Steel	Status	—	—	15	Self	—

● TM & HM MOVES

No.	Name	Type	Kind	Pow.	Acc.	PP	Range	DA
TM05	Roar	Normal	Status	—	100	20	Normal	—
TM06	Toxic	Poison	Status	—	85	10	Normal	—
TM10	Hidden Power	Normal	Special	—	100	15	Normal	—
TM11	Sunny Day	Fire	Status	—	—	5	All	—
TM12	Taunt	Dark	Status	—	100	20	Normal	—
TM13	Ice Beam	Ice	Special	95	100	10	Normal	—
TM14	Blizzard	Ice	Special	120	70	5	2 Foes	—
TM15	Hyper Beam	Normal	Special	150	90	5	Normal	—
TM17	Protect	Normal	Status	—	—	10	Self	—
TM18	Rain Dance	Water	Status	—	—	5	All	—
TM21	Frustration	Normal	Physical	—	100	20	Normal	○
TM23	Iron Tail	Steel	Physical	100	75	15	Normal	○
TM24	Thunderbolt	Electric	Special	95	100	15	Normal	—
TM25	Thunder	Electric	Special	120	70	10	Normal	—
TM26	Earthquake	Ground	Physical	100	100	10	2 Foes/1 Ally	○
TM27	Return	Normal	Physical	—	100	20	Normal	○
TM28	Dig	Ground	Physical	80	100	10	Normal	○
TM32	Double Team	Normal	Status	—	—	15	Self	—
TM34	Shock Wave	Electric	Special	60	—	20	Normal	—
TM35	Flamethrower	Fire	Special	95	100	15	Normal	—
TM37	Sandstorm	Rock	Status	—	—	10	All	—
TM38	Fire Blast	Fire	Special	120	85	5	Normal	—
TM39	Rock Tomb	Rock	Physical	50	80	10	Normal	○
TM41	Torment	Dark	Status	—	100	15	Normal	—
TM42	Facade	Normal	Physical	70	100	20	Normal	○
TM43	Secret Power	Normal	Physical	70	100	20	Normal	○
TM44	Rest	Psychic	Status	—	—	10	Self	—
TM45	Attract	Normal	Status	—	100	15	Normal	—
TM58	Endure	Normal	Status	—	—	10	Self	—
TM68	Giga Impact	Normal	Physical	150	90	5	Normal	○
TM69	Rock Polish	Rock	Status	—	—	20	Self	—
TM71	Stone Edge	Rock	Physical	100	80	5	Normal	○
TM72	Avalanche	Ice	Physical	60	100	10	Normal	○
TM76	Stealth Rock	Rock	Status	—	—	20	2 Foes	—
TM78	Captivate	Normal	Status	—	100	20	2 Foes	—
TM80	Rock Slide	Rock	Physical	75	90	10	2 Foes	—
TM82	Sleep Talk	Normal	Status	—	—	10	Depends	—
TM83	Natural Gift	Normal	Physical	—	100	15	Normal	—
TM87	Swagger	Normal	Status	—	90	15	Normal	—
TM90	Substitute	Normal	Status	—	—	10	Self	—
TM91	Flash Cannon	Steel	Special	80	100	10	Normal	○
HM04	Strength	Normal	Physical	80	100	15	Normal	○
HM06	Rock Smash	Fighting	Physical	40	100	15	Normal	○

⊙ No. **411** | Shield Pokémon

Bastiodon

Rock · Steel

- ● HEIGHT: 4'03"
- ● WEIGHT: 329.6 lbs.
- ● ITEMS: None

● SIZE COMPARISON

● MALE/FEMALE HAVE SAME FORM

⊙ ABILITIES
● Sturdy

⊙ STATS
HP ●●
ATTACK ●●●
DEFENSE ●●●●●●
SP. ATTACK ●●
SP. DEFENSE ●●●●●●
SPEED ●

⊙ EGG GROUPS
Monster

⊙ PERFORMANCE
SPEED ★★ STAMINA ★★★★★
POWER ★★★☆☆ JUMP ★★
SKILL ★☆☆

● MAIN WAYS TO OBTAIN

Pokémon HeartGold	—
Pokémon SoulSilver	—
Pokémon Diamond	—
Pokémon Pearl	Level up Shieldon to Lv. 30
Pokémon Platinum	Level up Shieldon to Lv. 30

Pokémon HeartGold
When attacked, they form a wall. Their rock-hard faces serve to protect them from the attacks.

Pokémon SoulSilver
When attacked, they form a wall. Their rock-hard faces serve to protect them from the attacks.

⊙ EVOLUTION

Lv. 30

Shieldon → Bastiodon

● No. 412 | Bagworm Pokémon
Burmy

Bug

Plant Cloak   Sandy Cloak   Trash Cloak

- ● HEIGHT: 0'08"
- ● WEIGHT: 7.5 lbs.
- ● ITEMS: None

● SIZE COMPARISON

● PLANT CLOAK   ● SANDY CLOAK   ● TRASH CLOAK

⊚ ABILITIES
- Shed Skin

⊚ STATS
HP ●
ATTACK ●
DEFENSE ●●
SP. ATTACK ●
SP. DEFENSE ●●
SPEED ●●

⊚ EGG GROUPS
Bug

⊚ PERFORMANCE
SPEED ★☆☆☆☆   STAMINA ★☆☆☆☆
POWER ★☆☆   JUMP ★★☆
SKILL ★☆☆☆☆

* Burmy's Performance depends on its cloak

● MAIN WAYS TO OBTAIN

Pokémon HeartGold	Route 38 (use Rock Climb to reach trees, then use Headbutt)
Pokémon SoulSilver	Route 38 (use Rock Climb to reach trees, then use Headbutt)
Pokémon Diamond	Spread Honey on a the sweet-smelling tree
Pokémon Pearl	Spread Honey on a the sweet-smelling tree
Pokémon Platinum	Spread Honey on a the sweet-smelling tree

| Pokémon HeartGold | Pokémon SoulSilver |
| It covers itself with a cloak to shelter from the cold. When it's hot, its cloak is thinner. | It covers itself with a cloak to shelter from the cold. When it's hot, its cloak is thinner. |

⊚ EVOLUTION

Burmy ♀ [Plant Cloak] — Lv. 20 → Wormadam [Plant Cloak]
Burmy ♀ [Sandy Cloak] — Lv. 20 → Wormadam [Sandy Cloak]
Burmy ♀ [Trash Cloak] — Lv. 20 → Wormadam [Trash Cloak]
Burmy ♂ — Lv. 20 → Mothim

● LEVEL-UP MOVES

Lv.	Name	Type	Kind	Pow.	Acc.	PP	Range	DA
1	Protect	Normal	Status	—	—	10	Self	—
10	Tackle	Normal	Physical	35	95	35	Normal	○
15	Bug Bite	Bug	Physical	60	100	20	Normal	○
20	Hidden Power	Normal	Special	—	100	15	Normal	—

● MOVE MANIAC

Name	Type	Kind	Pow.	Acc.	PP	Range	DA

● BP MOVES

Name	Type	Kind	Pow.	Acc.	PP	Range	DA
Bug Bite	Bug	Physical	60	100	20	Normal	○
Snore	Normal	Special	40	100	15	Normal	—
String Shot	Bug	Status	—	95	40	2 Foes	—

● TM & HM MOVES

No.	Name	Type	Kind	Pow.	Acc.	PP	Range	DA

*Sandy Cloak: Speed ★☆☆☆☆   Power ★☆☆☆☆   Skill ★☆☆   Stamina ★☆☆☆☆   Jump ★★☆
Trash Cloak: Speed ★☆☆☆   Power ★☆☆☆☆   Skill ★☆☆   Stamina ★☆☆☆☆   Jump ★★☆

● LEVEL-UP MOVES

Lv.	Name	Type	Kind	Pow.	Acc.	PP	Range	DA
1	Tackle	Normal	Physical	35	95	35	Normal	○
10	Protect	Normal	Status	—	—	10	Self	—
15	Bug Bite	Bug	Physical	60	100	20	Normal	○
20	Hidden Power	Normal	Special	—	100	15	Normal	—
23	Confusion	Psychic	Special	50	100	25	Normal	—
26	Razor Leaf	Grass	Physical	55	95	25	2 Foes	—
29	Growth	Normal	Status	—	—	40	Self	—
32	Psybeam	Psychic	Special	65	100	20	Normal	—
35	Captivate	Normal	Status	—	100	20	2 Foes	—
38	Flail	Normal	Physical	—	100	15	Normal	○
41	Attract	Normal	Status	—	100	15	Normal	—
44	Psychic	Psychic	Special	90	100	10	Normal	—
47	Leaf Storm	Grass	Special	140	90	5	Normal	—

● MOVE MANIAC

Name	Type	Kind	Pow.	Acc.	PP	Range	DA

● BP MOVES

Name	Type	Kind	Pow.	Acc.	PP	Range	DA
Sucker Punch	Dark	Physical	80	100	5	Normal	○
Bug Bite	Bug	Physical	60	100	20	Normal	○
Snore	Normal	Special	40	100	15	Normal	—
Synthesis	Grass	Status	—	—	5	Self	—
Uproar	Normal	Special	50	100	10	1 Random	—
String Shot	Bug	Status	—	95	40	2 Foes	—
Worry Seed	Grass	Status	—	100	10	Normal	—
Endeavor	Normal	Physical	—	100	5	Normal	○
Signal Beam	Bug	Special	75	100	15	Normal	—
Seed Bomb	Grass	Physical	80	100	15	Normal	—

● TM & HM MOVES

No.	Name	Type	Kind	Pow.	Acc.	PP	Range	DA
TM06	Toxic	Poison	Status	—	85	10	Normal	—
TM09	Bullet Seed	Grass	Physical	10	100	30	Normal	—
TM10	Hidden Power	Normal	Special	—	100	15	Normal	—
TM11	Sunny Day	Fire	Status	—	—	5	All	—
TM15	Hyper Beam	Normal	Special	150	90	5	Normal	—
TM17	Protect	Normal	Status	—	—	10	Self	—
TM18	Rain Dance	Water	Status	—	—	5	All	—
TM19	Giga Drain	Grass	Special	60	100	10	Normal	—
TM20	Safeguard	Normal	Status	—	—	25	2 Allies	—
TM21	Frustration	Normal	Physical	—	100	20	Normal	○
TM22	SolarBeam	Grass	Special	120	100	10	Normal	—
TM27	Return	Normal	Physical	—	100	20	Normal	○
TM29	Psychic	Psychic	Special	90	100	10	Normal	—
TM30	Shadow Ball	Ghost	Special	80	100	15	Normal	—
TM32	Double Team	Normal	Status	—	—	15	Self	—
TM42	Facade	Normal	Physical	70	100	20	Normal	○
TM43	Secret Power	Normal	Physical	70	100	20	Normal	○
TM44	Rest	Psychic	Status	—	—	10	Self	—
TM45	Attract	Normal	Status	—	100	15	Normal	—
TM46	Thief	Dark	Physical	40	100	10	Normal	—
TM48	Skill Swap	Psychic	Status	—	—	10	Normal	—
TM53	Energy Ball	Grass	Special	80	100	10	Normal	—
TM58	Endure	Normal	Status	—	—	10	Self	—
TM68	Giga Impact	Normal	Physical	150	90	5	Normal	○
TM70	Flash	Normal	Status	—	100	20	Normal	—
TM77	Psych Up	Normal	Status	—	—	10	Normal	—
TM78	Captivate	Normal	Status	—	100	20	2 Foes	—
TM82	Sleep Talk	Normal	Status	—	—	10	Depends	—
TM83	Natural Gift	Normal	Physical	—	100	15	Normal	—
TM85	Dream Eater	Psychic	Special	100	100	15	Normal	—
TM86	Grass Knot	Grass	Special	—	100	20	Normal	○
TM87	Swagger	Normal	Status	—	90	15	Normal	—
TM90	Substitute	Normal	Status	—	—	10	Self	—

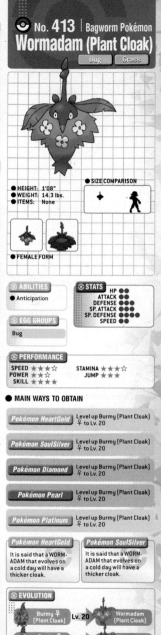

No. 413 | Bagworm Pokémon
Wormadam (Plant Cloak)

Bug　Grass

● HEIGHT: 1'08"
● WEIGHT: 14.3 lbs.
● ITEMS: None

● SIZE COMPARISON

● FEMALE FORM

● ABILITIES
● Anticipation

● STATS
HP ●●
ATTACK ●●
DEFENSE ●●●
SP. ATTACK ●●●
SP. DEFENSE ●●●●
SPEED ●●

● EGG GROUPS
Bug

● PERFORMANCE
SPEED ★★★☆　STAMINA ★★★☆
POWER ★★☆　JUMP ★★★
SKILL ★★★★

● MAIN WAYS TO OBTAIN

Pokémon HeartGold	Level up Burmy (Plant Cloak) ♀ to Lv. 20
Pokémon SoulSilver	Level up Burmy (Plant Cloak) ♀ to Lv. 20
Pokémon Diamond	Level up Burmy (Plant Cloak) ♀ to Lv. 20
Pokémon Pearl	Level up Burmy (Plant Cloak) ♀ to Lv. 20
Pokémon Platinum	Level up Burmy (Plant Cloak) ♀ to Lv. 20

Pokémon HeartGold	Pokémon SoulSilver
It is said that a WORM-ADAM that evolves on a cold day will have a thicker cloak.	It is said that a WORM-ADAM that evolves on a cold day will have a thicker cloak.

● EVOLUTION

Burmy ♀ (Plant Cloak) — Lv. 20 → Wormadam (Plant Cloak)

Burmy ♀ (Sandy Cloak) — Lv. 20 → Wormadam (Sandy Cloak)

Burmy ♀ (Trash Cloak) — Lv. 20 → Wormadam (Trash Cloak)

Burmy ♂ — Lv. 20 → Mothim

No. 413 | Bagworm Pokémon
Wormadam (Sandy Cloak)

Bug | Ground

- **HEIGHT:** 1'08"
- **WEIGHT:** 14.3 lbs.
- **ITEMS:** None

● SIZE COMPARISON

● FEMALE FORM

● ABILITIES
- Anticipation

● STATS
HP ●●
ATTACK ●●●
DEFENSE ●●●●
SP. ATTACK ●●●
SP. DEFENSE ●●●
SPEED ●●

● EGG GROUPS

Bug

● PERFORMANCE

SPEED ★★☆		STAMINA ★★★★☆
POWER ★★★★☆		JUMP ★★☆
SKILL ★★		

● MAIN WAYS TO OBTAIN

Pokémon HeartGold	Level up Burmy (Sandy Cloak) ♀ to Lv. 20
Pokémon SoulSilver	Level up Burmy (Sandy Cloak) ♀ to Lv. 20
Pokémon Diamond	Level up Burmy (Sandy Cloak) ♀ to Lv. 20
Pokémon Pearl	Level up Burmy (Sandy Cloak) ♀ to Lv. 20
Pokémon Platinum	Level up Burmy (Sandy Cloak) ♀ to Lv. 20

Pokémon HeartGold	Pokémon SoulSilver
It is said that a WORMADAM that evolves on a cold day will have a thicker cloak.	It is said that a WORMADAM that evolves on a cold day will have a thicker cloak.

● EVOLUTION

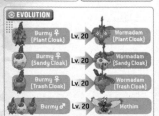

Burmy ♀ (Plant Cloak)	Lv. 20	Wormadam (Plant Cloak)
Burmy ♀ (Sandy Cloak)	Lv. 20	Wormadam (Sandy Cloak)
Burmy ♀ (Trash Cloak)	Lv. 20	Wormadam (Trash Cloak)
Burmy ♂	Lv. 20	Mothim

● LEVEL-UP MOVES

Lv.	Name	Type	Kind	Pow.	Acc.	PP	Range	DA
1	Tackle	Normal	Physical	35	95	35	Normal	○
10	Protect	Normal	Status	—	—	10	Self	—
15	Bug Bite	Bug	Physical	60	100	20	Normal	○
20	Hidden Power	Normal	Special	—	100	15	Normal	—
23	Confusion	Psychic	Special	50	100	25	Normal	—
26	Rock Blast	Rock	Physical	25	80	10	Normal	—
29	Harden	Normal	Status	—	—	30	Self	—
32	Psybeam	Psychic	Special	65	100	20	Normal	—
35	Captivate	Normal	Status	—	100	20	2 Foes	—
38	Flail	Normal	Physical	—	100	15	Normal	○
41	Attract	Normal	Status	—	100	15	Normal	—
44	Psychic	Psychic	Special	90	100	10	Normal	—
47	Fissure	Ground	Physical	—	30	5	Normal	—

● MOVE MANIAC

Name	Type	Kind	Pow.	Acc.	PP	Range	DA

● BP MOVES

Name	Type	Kind	Pow.	Acc.	PP	Range	DA
Sucker Punch	Dark	Physical	80	100	5	Normal	○
Bug Bite	Bug	Physical	60	100	20	Normal	○
Snore	Normal	Special	40	100	15	Normal	—
Uproar	Normal	Special	50	100	10	1 Random	—
String Shot	Bug	Status	—	95	40	2 Foes	—
Mud-Slap	Ground	Special	20	100	10	Normal	—
Rollout	Rock	Physical	30	90	20	Normal	○
Endeavor	Normal	Physical	—	100	5	Normal	○
Signal Beam	Bug	Special	75	100	15	Normal	—
Earth Power	Ground	Special	90	100	10	Normal	—

● TM & HM MOVES

No.	Name	Type	Kind	Pow.	Acc.	PP	Range	DA
TM06	Toxic	Poison	Status	—	85	10	Normal	—
TM10	Hidden Power	Normal	Special	—	100	15	Normal	—
TM11	Sunny Day	Fire	Status	—	—	5	All	—
TM15	Hyper Beam	Normal	Special	150	90	5	Normal	—
TM17	Protect	Normal	Status	—	—	10	Self	—
TM18	Rain Dance	Water	Status	—	—	5	All	—
TM20	Safeguard	Normal	Status	—	—	25	2 Allies	—
TM21	Frustration	Normal	Physical	—	100	20	Normal	○
TM26	Earthquake	Ground	Physical	100	100	10	2 Foes/1 Ally	—
TM27	Return	Normal	Physical	—	100	20	Normal	○
TM28	Dig	Ground	Physical	80	100	10	Normal	○
TM29	Psychic	Psychic	Special	90	100	10	Normal	—
TM30	Shadow Ball	Ghost	Special	80	100	15	Normal	—
TM32	Double Team	Normal	Status	—	—	15	Self	—
TM37	Sandstorm	Rock	Status	—	—	10	All	—
TM39	Rock Tomb	Rock	Physical	50	80	10	Normal	—
TM42	Facade	Normal	Physical	70	100	20	Normal	○
TM43	Secret Power	Normal	Physical	70	100	20	Normal	—
TM44	Rest	Psychic	Status	—	—	10	Self	—
TM45	Attract	Normal	Status	—	100	15	Normal	—
TM46	Thief	Dark	Physical	40	100	10	Normal	○
TM48	Skill Swap	Psychic	Status	—	—	10	Normal	—
TM58	Endure	Normal	Status	—	—	10	Self	—
TM68	Giga Impact	Normal	Physical	150	90	5	Normal	○
TM70	Flash	Normal	Status	—	100	20	Normal	—
TM77	Psych Up	Normal	Status	—	—	10	Normal	—
TM78	Captivate	Normal	Status	—	100	20	2 Foes	—
TM82	Sleep Talk	Normal	Status	—	—	10	Depends	—
TM83	Natural Gift	Normal	Physical	—	100	15	Normal	—
TM85	Dream Eater	Psychic	Special	100	100	15	Normal	—
TM87	Swagger	Normal	Status	—	90	15	Normal	—
TM90	Substitute	Normal	Status	—	—	10	Self	—

● LEVEL-UP MOVES

Lv.	Name	Type	Kind	Pow.	Acc.	PP	Range	DA
1	Tackle	Normal	Physical	35	95	35	Normal	○
10	Protect	Normal	Status	—	—	10	Self	—
15	Bug Bite	Bug	Physical	60	100	20	Normal	○
20	Hidden Power	Normal	Special	—	100	15	Normal	—
23	Confusion	Psychic	Special	50	100	25	Normal	—
26	Mirror Shot	Steel	Special	65	85	10	Normal	—
29	Metal Sound	Steel	Status	—	85	40	Normal	—
32	Psybeam	Psychic	Special	65	100	20	Normal	—
35	Captivate	Normal	Status	—	100	20	2 Foes	—
38	Flail	Normal	Physical	—	100	15	Normal	○
41	Attract	Normal	Status	—	100	15	Normal	—
44	Psychic	Psychic	Special	90	100	10	Normal	—
47	Iron Head	Steel	Physical	80	100	15	Normal	○

● MOVE MANIAC

Name	Type	Kind	Pow.	Acc.	PP	Range	DA

● BP MOVES

Name	Type	Kind	Pow.	Acc.	PP	Range	DA
Sucker Punch	Dark	Physical	80	100	5	Normal	○
Bug Bite	Bug	Physical	60	100	20	Normal	○
Snore	Normal	Special	40	100	15	Normal	—
Magnet Rise	Electric	Status	—	—	10	Self	—
Uproar	Normal	Special	50	100	10	1 Random	—
String Shot	Bug	Status	—	95	40	2 Foes	—
Iron Head	Steel	Physical	80	100	15	Normal	○
Endeavor	Normal	Physical	—	100	5	Normal	○
Signal Beam	Bug	Special	75	100	15	Normal	—
Gunk Shot	Poison	Physical	120	70	5	Normal	—
Iron Defense	Steel	Status	—	—	15	Self	—

● TM & HM MOVES

No.	Name	Type	Kind	Pow.	Acc.	PP	Range	DA
TM06	Toxic	Poison	Status	—	85	10	Normal	—
TM10	Hidden Power	Normal	Special	—	100	15	Normal	—
TM11	Sunny Day	Fire	Status	—	—	5	All	—
TM15	Hyper Beam	Normal	Special	150	90	5	Normal	—
TM17	Protect	Normal	Status	—	—	10	Self	—
TM18	Rain Dance	Water	Status	—	—	5	All	—
TM20	Safeguard	Normal	Status	—	—	25	2 Allies	—
TM21	Frustration	Normal	Physical	—	100	20	Normal	○
TM27	Return	Normal	Physical	—	100	20	Normal	○
TM29	Psychic	Psychic	Special	90	100	10	Normal	—
TM30	Shadow Ball	Ghost	Special	80	100	15	Normal	—
TM32	Double Team	Normal	Status	—	—	15	Self	—
TM42	Facade	Normal	Physical	70	100	20	Normal	—
TM43	Secret Power	Normal	Physical	70	100	20	Normal	—
TM44	Rest	Psychic	Status	—	—	10	Self	—
TM45	Attract	Normal	Status	—	100	15	Normal	—
TM46	Thief	Dark	Physical	40	100	10	Normal	—
TM48	Skill Swap	Psychic	Status	—	—	10	Normal	—
TM58	Endure	Normal	Status	—	—	10	Self	—
TM68	Giga Impact	Normal	Physical	150	90	5	Normal	○
TM70	Flash	Normal	Status	—	100	20	Normal	—
TM74	Gyro Ball	Steel	Physical	—	100	5	Normal	○
TM76	Stealth Rock	Rock	Status	—	—	20	2 Foes	—
TM77	Psych Up	Normal	Status	—	—	10	Normal	—
TM78	Captivate	Normal	Status	—	100	20	2 Foes	—
TM82	Sleep Talk	Normal	Status	—	—	10	Depends	—
TM83	Natural Gift	Normal	Physical	—	100	15	Normal	—
TM85	Dream Eater	Psychic	Special	100	100	15	Normal	—
TM87	Swagger	Normal	Status	—	90	15	Normal	—
TM90	Substitute	Normal	Status	—	—	10	Self	—
TM91	Flash Cannon	Steel	Special	80	100	10	Normal	—

◉ No. 413 | Bagworm Pokémon
Wormadam (Trash Cloak)
Bug   Steel

● HEIGHT: 1'08"
● WEIGHT: 14.3 lbs.
● ITEMS: None

● SIZE COMPARISON

● FEMALE FORM

◉ ABILITIES
● Anticipation

◉ STATS
HP ●●
ATTACK ●●●
DEFENSE ●●●●
SP. ATTACK ●●●
SP. DEFENSE ●●●●
SPEED ●●

◉ EGG GROUPS
Bug

◉ PERFORMANCE
SPEED ★☆☆   STAMINA ★★★★★
POWER ★★★☆☆   JUMP ★★
SKILL ★★☆

● MAIN WAYS TO OBTAIN

Pokémon HeartGold	Level up Burmy (Trash Cloak) ♀ to Lv. 20
Pokémon SoulSilver	Level up Burmy (Trash Cloak) ♀ to Lv. 20
Pokémon Diamond	Level up Burmy (Trash Cloak) ♀ to Lv. 20
Pokémon Pearl	Level up Burmy (Trash Cloak) ♀ to Lv. 20
Pokémon Platinum	Level up Burmy (Trash Cloak) ♀ to Lv. 20

Pokémon HeartGold	**Pokémon SoulSilver**
It is said that a WORM-ADAM that evolves on a cold day will have a thicker cloak.	It is said that a WORM-ADAM that evolves on a cold day will have a thicker cloak.

◉ EVOLUTION

Burmy ♀ (Plant Cloak) — Lv. 20 → Wormadam (Plant Cloak)

Burmy ♀ (Sandy Cloak) — Lv. 20 → Wormadam (Sandy Cloak)

Burmy ♀ (Trash Cloak) — Lv. 20 → Wormadam (Trash Cloak)

Burmy ♂ — Lv. 20 → Mothim

No. 414 | Moth Pokémon
Mothim

`Bug` `Flying`

- **HEIGHT:** 2'11"
- **WEIGHT:** 51.4 lbs.
- **ITEMS:** None

● SIZE COMPARISON

MALE FORM

⊙ ABILITIES
● Swarm

⊙ STATS
HP ●●●
ATTACK ●●●●
DEFENSE ●●●
SP. ATTACK ●●●●
SP. DEFENSE ●●
SPEED ●●●

⊙ EGG GROUPS
Bug

⊙ PERFORMANCE
SPEED ★★★★★ STAMINA ★☆
POWER ★★★☆☆ JUMP ★★★★★
SKILL ★★☆☆☆

● MAIN WAYS TO OBTAIN

Pokémon HeartGold	Level up Burmy ♂ to Lv. 20
Pokémon SoulSilver	Level up Burmy ♂ to Lv. 20
Pokémon Diamond	Level up Burmy ♂ to Lv. 20
Pokémon Pearl	Level up Burmy ♂ to Lv. 20
Pokémon Platinum	Level up Burmy ♂ to Lv. 20

| Pokémon HeartGold | Pokémon SoulSilver |
| It flutters around at night and steals honey from the COMBEE hive. | It flutters around at night and steals honey from the COMBEE hive. |

⊙ EVOLUTION

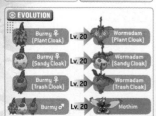

Burmy ♀ (Plant Cloak) — Lv. 20 → Wormadam (Plant Cloak)
Burmy ♀ (Sandy Cloak) — Lv. 20 → Wormadam (Sandy Cloak)
Burmy ♀ (Trash Cloak) — Lv. 20 → Wormadam (Trash Cloak)
Burmy ♂ — Lv. 20 → Mothim

● LEVEL-UP MOVES

Lv.	Name	Type	Kind	Pow.	Acc.	PP	Range	DA
1	Tackle	Normal	Physical	35	95	35	Normal	○
10	Protect	Normal	Status	—	—	10	Self	—
15	Bug Bite	Bug	Physical	60	100	20	Normal	○
20	Hidden Power	Normal	Special	—	100	15	Normal	—
23	Confusion	Psychic	Special	50	100	25	Normal	—
26	Gust	Flying	Special	40	100	35	Normal	—
29	PoisonPowder	Poison	Status	—	75	35	Normal	—
32	Psybeam	Psychic	Special	65	100	20	Normal	—
35	Camouflage	Normal	Status	—	—	20	Self	—
38	Silver Wind	Bug	Special	60	100	5	Normal	—
41	Air Slash	Flying	Special	75	95	20	Normal	—
44	Psychic	Psychic	Special	90	100	10	Normal	—
47	Bug Buzz	Bug	Special	90	100	10	Normal	—

● MOVE MANIAC

Name	Type	Kind	Pow.	Acc.	PP	Range	DA

● BP MOVES

Name	Type	Kind	Pow.	Acc.	PP	Range	DA
Ominous Wind	Ghost	Special	60	100	5	Normal	—
Air Cutter	Flying	Special	55	95	25	2 Foes	—
Bug Bite	Bug	Physical	60	100	20	Normal	○
Snore	Normal	Special	40	100	15	Normal	—
Swift	Normal	Special	60	—	20	2 Foes	—
String Shot	Bug	Status	—	95	40	2 Foes	—
Tailwind	Flying	Status	—	—	30	2 Allies	—
Mud-Slap	Ground	Special	20	100	10	Normal	—
Signal Beam	Bug	Special	75	100	15	Normal	—
Twister	Dragon	Special	40	100	20	2 Foes	—

● TM & HM MOVES

No.	Name	Type	Kind	Pow.	Acc.	PP	Range	DA
TM06	Toxic	Poison	Status	—	85	10	Normal	—
TM10	Hidden Power	Normal	Special	—	100	15	Normal	—
TM11	Sunny Day	Fire	Status	—	—	5	All	—
TM15	Hyper Beam	Normal	Special	150	90	5	Normal	—
TM17	Protect	Normal	Status	—	—	10	Self	—
TM18	Rain Dance	Water	Status	—	—	5	All	—
TM19	Giga Drain	Grass	Special	60	100	10	Normal	—
TM20	Safeguard	Normal	Status	—	—	25	2 Allies	—
TM21	Frustration	Normal	Physical	—	100	20	Normal	○
TM22	SolarBeam	Grass	Special	120	100	10	Normal	—
TM27	Return	Normal	Physical	—	100	20	Normal	○
TM29	Psychic	Psychic	Special	90	100	10	Normal	—
TM30	Shadow Ball	Ghost	Special	80	100	15	Normal	—
TM32	Double Team	Normal	Status	—	—	15	Self	—
TM40	Aerial Ace	Flying	Physical	60	—	20	Normal	○
TM42	Facade	Normal	Physical	70	100	20	Normal	○
TM43	Secret Power	Normal	Physical	70	100	20	Normal	○
TM44	Rest	Psychic	Status	—	—	10	Self	—
TM45	Attract	Normal	Status	—	100	15	Normal	—
TM46	Thief	Dark	Physical	40	100	10	Normal	○
TM48	Skill Swap	Psychic	Status	—	—	10	Normal	—
TM51	Roost	Flying	Status	—	—	10	Self	—
TM53	Energy Ball	Grass	Special	80	100	10	Normal	—
TM58	Endure	Normal	Status	—	—	10	Self	—
TM62	Silver Wind	Bug	Special	60	100	5	Normal	—
TM68	Giga Impact	Normal	Physical	150	90	5	Normal	○
TM70	Flash	Normal	Status	—	100	20	Normal	—
TM77	Psych Up	Normal	Status	—	—	10	Normal	—
TM78	Captivate	Normal	Status	—	100	20	2 Foes	—
TM82	Sleep Talk	Normal	Status	—	—	10	Depends	—
TM83	Natural Gift	Normal	Physical	—	100	15	Normal	—
TM85	Dream Eater	Psychic	Special	100	100	15	Normal	—
TM87	Swagger	Normal	Status	—	90	15	Normal	—
TM89	U-turn	Bug	Physical	70	100	20	Normal	○
TM90	Substitute	Normal	Status	—	—	10	Self	—

● LEVEL-UP MOVES

Lv.	Name	Type	Kind	Pow.	Acc.	PP	Range	DA
1	Sweet Scent	Normal	Status	--	100	20	2 Foes	--
1	Gust	Flying	Special	40	100	35	Normal	--
13	Bug Bite	Bug	Physical	60	100	20	Normal	○

● MOVE MANIAC

Name	Type	Kind	Pow.	Acc.	PP	Range	DA

● BP MOVES

Name	Type	Kind	Pow.	Acc.	PP	Range	DA
Ominous Wind	Ghost	Special	60	100	5	Normal	--
Air Cutter	Flying	Special	55	95	25	2 Foes	--
Bug Bite	Bug	Physical	60	100	20	Normal	○
Snore	Normal	Special	40	100	15	Normal	--
Swift	Normal	Special	60	--	20	2 Foes	--
String Shot	Bug	Status	--	95	40	2 Foes	--
Tailwind	Flying	Status	--	--	30	2 Allies	--
Mud-Slap	Ground	Special	20	100	10	Normal	--
Endeavor	Normal	Physical	--	100	5	Normal	○

● TM & HM MOVES

No.	Name	Type	Kind	Pow.	Acc.	PP	Range	DA

No. 415 | Tiny Bee Pokémon
Combee

Bug Flying

- **HEIGHT:** 1'00"
- **WEIGHT:** 12.1 lbs.
- **ITEMS:** Honey

● SIZE COMPARISON

● MALE FORM
No spot on forehead

● FEMALE FORM
Red spot on forehead

⊙ ABILITIES
● Honey Gather

⊙ EGG GROUPS
Bug

⊙ STATS
HP ●
ATTACK ●
DEFENSE ●●
SP. ATTACK ●
SP. DEFENSE ●●
SPEED ●●●

⊙ PERFORMANCE
SPEED ★★★★★   STAMINA ★☆
POWER ★☆   JUMP ★★★★★
SKILL ★

● MAIN WAYS TO OBTAIN

Pokémon HeartGold	Bug-Catching Contest at the National Park (after obtaining the National Pokédex—Thursday, Saturday)
Pokémon SoulSilver	Bug-Catching Contest at the National Park (after obtaining the National Pokédex—Thursday, Saturday)
Pokémon Diamond	Spread Honey on a the sweet-smelling tree
Pokémon Pearl	Spread Honey on a the sweet-smelling tree
Pokémon Platinum	Spread Honey on a the sweet-smelling tree

Pokémon HeartGold	Pokémon SoulSilver
At night, COMBEE sleep in a group of about a thousand, packed closely together in a lump.	At night, COMBEE sleep in a group of about a thousand, packed closely together in a lump.

⊙ EVOLUTION

Combee ♀ → Lv. 21 → Vespiquen

No. 416 Beehive Pokémon | Vespiquen

Bug **Flying**

- **HEIGHT:** 3'11"
- **WEIGHT:** 84.9 lbs.
- **ITEMS:** None

● SIZE COMPARISON

● FEMALE FORM

⊚ ABILITIES
- Pressure

⊚ STATS
HP ●●●
ATTACK ●●●●
DEFENSE ●●●●
SP. ATTACK ●●●●
SP. DEFENSE ●●●●
SPEED ●●

⊚ EGG GROUPS
Bug

⊚ PERFORMANCE
SPEED ★★★
POWER ★☆☆
SKILL ★★★★☆
STAMINA ★★★☆☆
JUMP ★★★★★

● MAIN WAYS TO OBTAIN

Pokémon HeartGold — Level up Combee ♀ to Lv. 21

Pokémon SoulSilver — Level up Combee ♀ to Lv. 21

Pokémon Diamond — Level up Combee ♀ to Lv. 21

Pokémon Pearl — Level up Combee ♀ to Lv. 21

Pokémon Platinum — Level up Combee ♀ to Lv. 21

Pokémon HeartGold	Pokémon SoulSilver
It raises grubs in the holes in its body. It secretes pheromones to control COMBEE.	It raises grubs in the holes in its body. It secretes pheromones to control COMBEE.

⊚ EVOLUTION

Combee ♀ → Lv. 21 → Vespiquen

● LEVEL-UP MOVES

Lv.	Name	Type	Kind	Pow.	Acc.	PP	Range	DA
1	Sweet Scent	Normal	Status	—	100	20	2 Foes	—
1	Gust	Flying	Special	40	100	35	Normal	—
3	Poison Sting	Poison	Physical	15	100	35	Normal	—
?	Confuse Ray	Ghost	Status	—	100	10	Normal	—
9	Fury Cutter	Bug	Physical	10	95	20	Normal	○
13	Defend Order	Bug	Status	—	—	10	Self	—
15	Pursuit	Dark	Physical	40	100	20	Normal	○
19	Fury Swipes	Normal	Physical	18	80	15	Normal	○
21	Power Gem	Rock	Special	70	100	20	Normal	—
25	Heal Order	Bug	Status	—	—	10	Self	—
27	Toxic	Poison	Status	—	85	10	Normal	—
31	Slash	Normal	Physical	70	100	20	Normal	—
33	Captivate	Normal	Status	—	100	20	2 Foes	○
37	Attack Order	Bug	Physical	90	100	15	Normal	—
39	Swagger	Normal	Status	—	90	15	Normal	—
43	Destiny Bond	Ghost	Status	—	—	5	Self	—

● MOVE MANIAC

Name	Type	Kind	Pow.	Acc.	PP	Range	DA

● BP MOVES

Name	Type	Kind	Pow.	Acc.	PP	Range	DA
Fury Cutter	Bug	Physical	10	95	20	Normal	○
Ominous Wind	Ghost	Special	60	100	5	Normal	—
Air Cutter	Flying	Special	55	95	25	2 Foes	—
Bug Bite	Bug	Physical	60	100	20	Normal	○
Snore	Normal	Special	40	100	15	Normal	—
Swift	Normal	Special	60	—	20	2 Foes	—
String Shot	Bug	Status	—	95	40	2 Foes	—
Tailwind	Flying	Status	—	—	30	2 Allies	—
Mud-Slap	Ground	Special	20	100	10	Normal	—
Endeavor	Normal	Physical	—	100	5	Normal	○
Signal Beam	Bug	Special	75	100	15	Normal	—

● TM & HM MOVES

No.	Name	Type	Kind	Pow.	Acc.	PP	Range	DA
TM06	Toxic	Poison	Status	—	85	10	Normal	—
TM10	Hidden Power	Normal	Special	—	100	15	Normal	—
TM11	Sunny Day	Fire	Status	—	—	5	All	—
TM15	Hyper Beam	Normal	Special	150	90	5	Normal	—
TM17	Protect	Normal	Status	—	—	10	Self	—
TM18	Rain Dance	Water	Status	—	—	5	All	—
TM21	Frustration	Normal	Physical	—	100	20	Normal	○
TM27	Return	Normal	Physical	—	100	20	Normal	○
TM32	Double Team	Normal	Status	—	—	15	Self	—
TM36	Sludge Bomb	Poison	Special	90	100	10	Normal	—
TM40	Aerial Ace	Flying	Physical	60	—	20	Normal	—
TM42	Facade	Normal	Physical	70	100	20	Normal	○
TM43	Secret Power	Normal	Physical	70	100	20	Normal	○
TM44	Rest	Psychic	Status	—	—	10	Self	—
TM45	Attract	Normal	Status	—	100	15	Normal	—
TM46	Thief	Dark	Physical	40	100	10	Normal	○
TM51	Roost	Flying	Status	—	—	10	Self	—
TM56	Fling	Dark	Physical	—	100	10	Normal	—
TM58	Endure	Normal	Status	—	—	10	Self	—
TM62	Silver Wind	Bug	Special	60	100	5	Normal	—
TM68	Giga Impact	Normal	Physical	150	90	5	Normal	○
TM70	Flash	Normal	Status	—	100	20	Normal	—
TM78	Captivate	Normal	Status	—	100	20	2 Foes	—
TM81	X-Scissor	Bug	Physical	80	100	15	Normal	—
TM82	Sleep Talk	Normal	Status	—	—	10	Depends	—
TM83	Natural Gift	Normal	Physical	—	100	15	Normal	—
TM87	Swagger	Normal	Status	—	90	15	Normal	—
TM89	U-turn	Bug	Physical	70	100	20	Normal	○
TM90	Substitute	Normal	Status	—	—	10	Self	—
HM01	Cut	Normal	Physical	50	95	30	Normal	○

● LEVEL-UP MOVES

Lv.	Name	Type	Kind	Pow.	Acc.	PP	Range	DA
1	Growl	Normal	Status	—	100	40	2 Foes	—
1	Bide	Normal	Physical	—	—	10	Self	—
5	Quick Attack	Normal	Physical	40	100	30	Normal	○
9	Charm	Normal	Status	—	100	20	Normal	—
13	Spark	Electric	Physical	65	100	20	Normal	○
17	Endure	Normal	Status	—	—	10	Self	—
21	Swift	Normal	Special	60	—	20	2 Foes	—
25	Sweet Kiss	Normal	Status	—	75	10	Normal	—
29	Discharge	Electric	Special	80	100	15	2 Foes/1 Ally	—
33	Super Fang	Normal	Physical	—	90	10	Normal	○
37	Last Resort	Normal	Physical	130	100	5	Normal	○

● MOVE MANIAC

Name	Type	Kind	Pow.	Acc.	PP	Range	DA
Headbutt	Normal	Physical	70	100	15	Normal	○

● BP MOVES

Name	Type	Kind	Pow.	Acc.	PP	Range	DA
ThunderPunch	Electric	Physical	75	100	15	Normal	○
Snore	Normal	Special	40	100	15	Normal	—
Helping Hand	Normal	Status	—	—	20	1 Ally	—
Magnet Rise	Electric	Status	—	—	10	Self	—
Last Resort	Normal	Physical	130	100	5	Normal	○
Swift	Normal	Special	60	—	20	2 Foes	—
Uproar	Normal	Special	90	100	10	1 Random	—
Mud-Slap	Ground	Special	20	100	10	Normal	—
Rollout	Rock	Physical	30	90	20	Normal	○
Gunk Shot	Poison	Physical	120	70	5	Normal	○
Seed Bomb	Grass	Physical	80	100	15	Normal	○
Super Fang	Normal	Physical	—	90	10	Normal	○

● TM & HM MOVES

No.	Name	Type	Kind	Pow.	Acc.	PP	Range	DA
TM06	Toxic	Poison	Status	—	85	10	Normal	—
TM10	Hidden Power	Normal	Special	—	100	15	Normal	—
TM16	Light Screen	Psychic	Status	—	—	30	2 Allies	—
TM17	Protect	Normal	Status	—	—	10	Self	—
TM18	Rain Dance	Water	Status	—	—	5	All	—
TM21	Frustration	Normal	Physical	—	100	20	Normal	○
TM23	Iron Tail	Steel	Physical	100	75	15	Normal	○
TM24	Thunderbolt	Electric	Special	95	100	15	Normal	—
TM25	Thunder	Electric	Special	120	70	10	Normal	—
TM27	Return	Normal	Physical	—	100	20	Normal	○
TM28	Dig	Ground	Physical	80	100	10	Normal	○
TM32	Double Team	Normal	Status	—	—	15	Self	—
TM34	Shock Wave	Electric	Special	60	—	20	Normal	—
TM42	Facade	Normal	Physical	70	100	20	Normal	○
TM43	Secret Power	Normal	Physical	70	100	20	Normal	○
TM44	Rest	Psychic	Status	—	—	10	Self	—
TM45	Attract	Normal	Status	—	100	15	Normal	—
TM56	Fling	Dark	Physical	—	100	10	Normal	○
TM57	Charge Beam	Electric	Special	50	90	10	Normal	—
TM58	Endure	Normal	Status	—	—	10	Self	—
TM70	Flash	Normal	Status	—	100	20	Normal	—
TM73	Thunder Wave	Electric	Status	—	100	20	Normal	—
TM78	Captivate	Normal	Status	—	100	20	2 Foes	—
TM82	Sleep Talk	Normal	Status	—	—	10	Depends	—
TM83	Natural Gift	Normal	Physical	—	100	15	Normal	—
TM86	Grass Knot	Grass	Special	—	100	20	Normal	○
TM87	Swagger	Normal	Status	—	90	15	Normal	—
TM89	U-turn	Bug	Physical	70	100	20	Normal	○
TM90	Substitute	Normal	Status	—	—	10	Self	—
HM01	Cut	Normal	Physical	50	95	30	Normal	○

● EGG MOVES

Name	Type	Kind	Pow.	Acc.	PP	Range	DA
Covet	Normal	Physical	40	100	40	Normal	○
Bite	Dark	Physical	60	100	25	Normal	○
Fake Tears	Dark	Status	—	100	20	Normal	—
Defense Curl	Normal	Status	—	—	40	Self	—
Rollout	Rock	Physical	30	90	20	Normal	○
Flatter	Dark	Status	—	100	15	Normal	—
Flail	Normal	Physical	—	100	15	Normal	○

No. 417 | Elesquirrel Pokémon
Pachirisu

Electric

● HEIGHT: 1'04"
● WEIGHT: 8.6 lbs.
● ITEMS: None

● SIZE COMPARISON

● MALE FORM
Longer stripe on head

● FEMALE FORM
Shorter stripe on head

⊙ ABILITIES
● Run Away
● Pickup

⊙ STATS
HP ●●
ATTACK ●●
DEFENSE ●●●
SP. ATTACK ●●
SP. DEFENSE ●●●●
SPEED ●●●●

⊙ EGG GROUPS
Field
Fairy

⊙ PERFORMANCE
SPEED ★★★★☆   STAMINA ★★☆
POWER ★★☆   JUMP ★★★
SKILL ★★★☆

● MAIN WAYS TO OBTAIN

Pokémon HeartGold	Safari Zone (Wetlands Area: if Forest objects are placed, may appear in tall grass)
Pokémon SoulSilver	Safari Zone (Wetlands Area: if Forest objects are placed, may appear in tall grass)
Pokémon Diamond	Valley Windworks
Pokémon Pearl	Valley Windworks
Pokémon Platinum	Valley Windworks

Pokémon HeartGold
It's one of the kinds of Pokémon with electric cheek pouches. It shoots charges from its tail.

Pokémon SoulSilver
It's one of the kinds of Pokémon with electric cheek pouches. It shoots charges from its tail.

⊙ EVOLUTION
Does not evolve

No. 418 | Sea Weasel Pokémon
Buizel

Water

- **HEIGHT:** 2'04"
- **WEIGHT:** 65.0 lbs.
- **ITEMS:** Wacan Berry

● SIZE COMPARISON

● MALE FORM
More spots on back

● FEMALE FORM
Less spots on back

⊕ ABILITIES
● Swift Swim

⊕ STATS
HP ●●
ATTACK ●●●
DEFENSE ●●●
SP. ATTACK ●●●
SP. DEFENSE ●
SPEED ●●●●

⊕ EGG GROUPS
Water 1

Field

⊕ PERFORMANCE
SPEED ★★★★★   STAMINA ★★☆☆
POWER ★☆☆☆☆   JUMP ★★★
SKILL ★★☆☆

● MAIN WAYS TO OBTAIN

Pokémon HeartGold	Route 30 (Sinnoh Sound) or Safari Zone (Wetland Area: if Water objects are placed, may appear in tall grass)
Pokémon SoulSilver	Route 30 (Sinnoh Sound) or Safari Zone (Wetland Area: if Water objects are placed, may appear in tall grass)
Pokémon Diamond	Valley Windworks
Pokémon Pearl	Valley Windworks
Pokémon Platinum	Valley Windworks

Pokémon HeartGold	**Pokémon SoulSilver**
It inflates its flotation sac, keeping its face above water in order to watch for prey movement.	It inflates its flotation sac, keeping its face above water in order to watch for prey movement.

⊕ EVOLUTION

Lv. 26

Buizel → Floatzel

● LEVEL-UP MOVES

Lv.	Name	Type	Kind	Pow.	Acc.	PP	Range	DA
1	SonicBoom	Normal	Special	—	90	20	Normal	—
1	Growl	Normal	Status	—	100	40	2 Foes	—
1	Water Sport	Water	Status	—	—	15	All	—
3	Quick Attack	Normal	Physical	40	100	30	Normal	○
6	Water Gun	Water	Special	40	100	25	Normal	—
10	Pursuit	Dark	Physical	40	100	20	Normal	○
15	Swift	Normal	Special	60	—	20	2 Foes	—
21	Aqua Jet	Water	Physical	40	100	20	Normal	○
28	Agility	Psychic	Status	—	—	30	Self	—
36	Whirlpool	Water	Special	15	70	15	Normal	—
45	Razor Wind	Normal	Special	80	100	10	2 Foes	—

● MOVE MANIAC

Name	Type	Kind	Pow.	Acc.	PP	Range	DA
Headbutt	Normal	Physical	70	100	15	Normal	○

● BP MOVES

Name	Type	Kind	Pow.	Acc.	PP	Range	DA
Dive	Water	Physical	80	100	10	Normal	○
Icy Wind	Ice	Special	55	95	15	2 Foes	—
Ice Punch	Ice	Physical	75	100	15	Normal	○
Snore	Normal	Special	40	100	15	Normal	—
Swift	Normal	Special	60	—	20	2 Foes	—
Mud-Slap	Ground	Special	20	100	10	Normal	—

● TM & HM MOVES

No.	Name	Type	Kind	Pow.	Acc.	PP	Range	DA
TM01	Focus Punch	Fighting	Physical	150	100	20	Normal	○
TM03	Water Pulse	Water	Special	60	100	20	Normal	—
TM06	Toxic	Poison	Status	—	85	10	Normal	—
TM07	Hail	Ice	Status	—	—	10	All	—
TM08	Bulk Up	Fighting	Status	—	—	20	Self	—
TM10	Hidden Power	Normal	Special	—	100	15	Normal	—
TM13	Ice Beam	Ice	Special	95	100	10	Normal	—
TM14	Blizzard	Ice	Special	120	70	5	2 Foes	—
TM17	Protect	Normal	Status	—	—	10	Self	—
TM18	Rain Dance	Water	Status	—	—	5	All	—
TM21	Frustration	Normal	Physical	—	100	20	Normal	○
TM23	Iron Tail	Steel	Physical	100	75	15	Normal	○
TM27	Return	Normal	Physical	—	100	20	Normal	○
TM28	Dig	Ground	Physical	80	100	10	Normal	○
TM31	Brick Break	Fighting	Physical	75	100	15	Normal	○
TM32	Double Team	Normal	Status	—	—	15	Self	—
TM39	Rock Tomb	Rock	Physical	50	80	10	Normal	○
TM42	Facade	Normal	Physical	70	100	20	Normal	○
TM43	Secret Power	Normal	Physical	70	100	20	Normal	○
TM44	Rest	Psychic	Status	—	—	10	Self	—
TM45	Attract	Normal	Status	—	100	15	Normal	—
TM55	Brine	Water	Special	65	100	10	Normal	—
TM58	Endure	Normal	Status	—	—	10	Self	—
TM78	Captivate	Normal	Status	—	100	20	2 Foes	—
TM82	Sleep Talk	Normal	Status	—	—	10	Depends	—
TM83	Natural Gift	Normal	Physical	—	100	15	Normal	—
TM87	Swagger	Normal	Status	—	90	15	Normal	—
TM90	Substitute	Normal	Status	—	—	10	Self	—
HM03	Surf	Water	Special	95	100	15	2 Foes/1 Ally	—
HM04	Strength	Normal	Physical	80	100	15	Normal	○
HM05	Whirlpool	Water	Special	15	70	15	Normal	—
HM06	Rock Smash	Fighting	Physical	40	100	15	Normal	○
HM07	Waterfall	Water	Physical	80	100	15	Normal	○

● EGG MOVES

Name	Type	Kind	Pow.	Acc.	PP	Range	DA
Mud-Slap	Ground	Special	20	100	10	Normal	—
Headbutt	Normal	Physical	70	100	15	Normal	○
Fury Swipes	Normal	Physical	18	80	15	Normal	○
Slash	Normal	Physical	70	100	20	Normal	○
Odor Sleuth	Normal	Status	—	—	40	Normal	—
DoubleSlap	Normal	Physical	15	85	10	Normal	○
Fury Cutter	Bug	Physical	10	95	20	Normal	○
Baton Pass	Normal	Status	—	—	40	Self	—

● LEVEL-UP MOVES

Lv.	Name	Type	Kind	Pow.	Acc.	PP	Range	DA
1	Tackle	Normal	Physical	35	95	35	Normal	○
1	Leer	Normal	Status	—	100	30	2 Foes	—
1	Charge	Electric	Status	—	—	20	Self	—
5	Leer	Normal	Status	—	100	30	2 Foes	—
9	Charge	Electric	Status	—	—	20	Self	—
13	Bite	Dark	Physical	60	100	25	Normal	○
18	Spark	Electric	Physical	65	100	20	Normal	○
23	Roar	Normal	Status	—	100	20	Normal	—
28	Swagger	Normal	Status	—	90	15	Normal	—
35	Crunch	Dark	Physical	80	100	15	Normal	○
42	Thunder Fang	Electric	Physical	65	95	15	Normal	○
49	Scary Face	Normal	Status	—	90	10	Normal	—
56	Discharge	Electric	Special	80	100	15	2 Foes/1 Ally	—

● MOVE MANIAC

Name	Type	Kind	Pow.	Acc.	PP	Range	DA
Headbutt	Normal	Physical	70	100	15	Normal	○

● BP MOVES

Name	Type	Kind	Pow.	Acc.	PP	Range	DA
Fury Cutter	Bug	Physical	10	95	20	Normal	○
Snore	Normal	Special	40	100	15	Normal	—
Magnet Rise	Electric	Status	—	—	10	Self	—
Swift	Normal	Special	60	—	20	2 Foes	—
Mud-Slap	Ground	Special	20	100	10	Normal	—
Superpower	Fighting	Physical	120	100	5	Normal	○
Signal Beam	Bug	Special	75	100	15	Normal	—

● TM & HM MOVES

No.	Name	Type	Kind	Pow.	Acc.	PP	Range	DA
TM05	Roar	Normal	Status	—	100	20	Normal	—
TM06	Toxic	Poison	Status	—	85	10	Normal	—
TM10	Hidden Power	Normal	Special	—	100	15	Normal	—
TM15	Hyper Beam	Normal	Special	150	90	5	Normal	—
TM16	Light Screen	Psychic	Status	—	—	30	2 Allies	—
TM17	Protect	Normal	Status	—	—	10	Self	—
TM18	Rain Dance	Water	Status	—	—	5	All	—
TM23	Frustration	Normal	Physical	—	100	20	Normal	○
TM24	Iron Tail	Steel	Physical	100	75	15	Normal	○
TM25	Thunderbolt	Electric	Special	95	100	15	Normal	—
TM25	Thunder	Electric	Special	120	70	10	Normal	—
TM27	Return	Normal	Physical	—	100	20	Normal	○
TM32	Double Team	Normal	Status	—	—	15	Self	—
TM34	Shock Wave	Electric	Special	60	—	20	Normal	—
TM42	Facade	Normal	Physical	70	100	20	Normal	○
TM43	Secret Power	Normal	Physical	70	100	20	Normal	—
TM44	Rest	Psychic	Status	—	—	10	Self	—
TM45	Attract	Normal	Status	—	100	15	Normal	—
TM46	Thief	Dark	Physical	40	100	10	Normal	○
TM57	Charge Beam	Electric	Special	50	90	10	Normal	—
TM58	Endure	Normal	Status	—	—	10	Self	—
TM68	Giga Impact	Normal	Physical	150	90	5	Normal	○
TM70	Flash	Normal	Status	—	100	20	Normal	—
TM73	Thunder Wave	Electric	Status	—	100	20	Normal	—
TM78	Captivate	Normal	Status	—	100	20	2 Foes	—
TM82	Sleep Talk	Normal	Status	—	—	10	Depends	—
TM83	Natural Gift	Normal	Physical	—	100	15	Normal	—
TM87	Swagger	Normal	Status	—	90	15	Normal	—
TM90	Substitute	Normal	Status	—	—	10	Self	—
HM04	Strength	Normal	Physical	80	100	15	Normal	○

Water

● **HEIGHT:** 3'07"
● **WEIGHT:** 73.9 lbs.
● **ITEMS:** Wacan Berry

● **SIZE COMPARISON**

● **MALE FORM**
More spots on back

● **FEMALE FORM**
Fewer spots on back

● ABILITIES
● Swift Swim

● STATS
HP ●●●
ATTACK ●●●●
DEFENSE ●●
SP. ATTACK ●●
SP. DEFENSE ●●●
SPEED ●●●●●

● EGG GROUPS
Water 1
Field

● PERFORMANCE
SPEED ★★★☆   STAMINA ★★★☆☆
POWER ★★★☆   JUMP ★★★
SKILL ★★★☆☆

● MAIN WAYS TO OBTAIN

Pokémon HeartGold	Safari Zone [Swamp Area: if Water objects are placed, may appear in tall grass]
Pokémon SoulSilver	Safari Zone [Swamp Area: if Water objects are placed, may appear in tall grass]
Pokémon Diamond	Route 218
Pokémon Pearl	Route 218
Pokémon Platinum	Route 218

Pokémon HeartGold
With its flotation sac inflated, it can carry people on its back. It deflates the sac before it dives.

Pokémon SoulSilver
With its flotation sac inflated, it can carry people on its back. It deflates the sac before it dives.

● EVOLUTION

 Lv. 26

Buizel → Floatzel

Cherubi

Grass

● HEIGHT: 1'04"
● WEIGHT: 7.3 lbs.
● ITEMS: Miracle Seed

● SIZE COMPARISON

● MALE/FEMALE HAVE SAME FORM

⊕ ABILITIES
● Chlorophyll

⊕ STATS
HP ●●
ATTACK ●●
DEFENSE ●●
SP. ATTACK ●●●
SP. DEFENSE ●●●
SPEED ●●

⊕ EGG GROUPS
Fairy
Grass

⊕ PERFORMANCE
SPEED ★★★☆   STAMINA ★★☆
POWER ★☆☆   JUMP ★★☆
SKILL ★★☆

● MAIN WAYS TO OBTAIN

Pokémon HeartGold	National Park —use Rock Climb to reach trees, then use Headbutt
Pokémon SoulSilver	National Park —use Rock Climb to reach trees, then use Headbutt
Pokémon Diamond	Spread Honey on a sweet-smelling tree
Pokémon Pearl	Spread Honey on a sweet-smelling tree
Pokémon Platinum	Spread Honey on a sweet-smelling tree

Pokémon HeartGold	**Pokémon SoulSilver**
It evolves by sucking the energy out of the small ball where it had been storing nutrients.	It evolves by sucking the energy out of the small ball where it had been storing nutrients.

⊕ EVOLUTION

 Cherubi   Lv. 25   Cherrim

● LEVEL-UP MOVES

Lv.	Name	Type	Kind	Pow.	Acc.	PP	Range	DA
1	Tackle	Normal	Physical	35	95	35	Normal	○
7	Growth	Normal	Status	—	—	40	Self	—
10	Leech Seed	Grass	Status	—	90	10	Normal	—
13	Helping Hand	Normal	Status	—	—	20	1 Ally	—
19	Magical Leaf	Grass	Special	60	—	20	Normal	—
22	Sunny Day	Fire	Status	—	—	5	All	—
28	Worry Seed	Grass	Status	—	100	10	Normal	—
31	Take Down	Normal	Physical	90	85	20	Normal	○
37	SolarBeam	Grass	Special	120	100	10	Normal	—
40	Lucky Chant	Normal	Status	—	—	30	2 Allies	—

● MOVE MANIAC

Name	Type	Kind	Pow.	Acc.	PP	Range	DA

● BP MOVES

Name	Type	Kind	Pow.	Acc.	PP	Range	DA
Snore	Normal	Special	40	100	15	Normal	—
Helping Hand	Normal	Status	—	—	20	1 Ally	—
Synthesis	Grass	Status	—	—	5	Self	—
Worry Seed	Grass	Status	—	100	10	Normal	—
Rollout	Rock	Physical	30	90	20	Normal	○
Seed Bomb	Grass	Physical	80	100	15	Normal	—

● TM & HM MOVES

No.	Name	Type	Kind	Pow.	Acc.	PP	Range	DA
TM06	Toxic	Poison	Status	—	85	10	Normal	—
TM09	Bullet Seed	Grass	Physical	10	100	30	Normal	—
TM10	Hidden Power	Normal	Special	—	100	15	Normal	—
TM11	Sunny Day	Fire	Status	—	—	5	All	—
TM17	Protect	Normal	Status	—	—	10	Self	—
TM19	Giga Drain	Grass	Special	60	100	10	Normal	—
TM20	Safeguard	Normal	Status	—	—	25	2 Allies	—
TM21	Frustration	Normal	Physical	—	100	20	Normal	○
TM22	SolarBeam	Grass	Special	120	100	10	Normal	—
TM27	Return	Normal	Physical	—	100	20	Normal	○
TM32	Double Team	Normal	Status	—	—	15	Self	—
TM42	Facade	Normal	Physical	70	100	20	Normal	○
TM43	Secret Power	Normal	Physical	70	100	20	Normal	—
TM44	Rest	Psychic	Status	—	—	10	Self	—
TM45	Attract	Normal	Status	—	100	15	Normal	—
TM53	Energy Ball	Grass	Special	80	100	10	Normal	—
TM58	Endure	Normal	Status	—	—	10	Self	—
TM70	Flash	Normal	Status	—	100	20	Normal	—
TM75	Swords Dance	Normal	Status	—	—	30	Self	—
TM78	Captivate	Normal	Status	—	100	20	2 Foes	—
TM82	Sleep Talk	Normal	Status	—	—	10	Depends	—
TM83	Natural Gift	Normal	Physical	—	100	15	Normal	—
TM86	Grass Knot	Grass	Special	—	100	20	Normal	○
TM87	Swagger	Normal	Status	—	90	15	Normal	—
TM90	Substitute	Normal	Status	—	—	10	Self	—

● EGG MOVES

Name	Type	Kind	Pow.	Acc.	PP	Range	DA
Razor Leaf	Grass	Physical	55	95	25	2 Foes	—
Sweet Scent	Normal	Status	—	100	20	2 Foes	—
Tickle	Normal	Status	—	100	20	Normal	—
Nature Power	Normal	Status	—	—	20	Depends	—
GrassWhistle	Grass	Status	—	55	15	Normal	—
Aromatherapy	Grass	Status	—	—	5	All Allies	—
Weather Ball	Normal	Special	50	100	10	Normal	—

● LEVEL-UP MOVES

Lv.	Name	Type	Kind	Pow.	Acc.	PP	Range	DA
1	Tackle	Normal	Physical	35	95	35	Normal	○
1	Growth	Normal	Status	—	—	40	Self	—
?	Growth	Normal	Status	—	—	40	Self	—
10	Leech Seed	Grass	Status	—	90	10	Normal	—
13	Helping Hand	Normal	Status	—	—	20	1 Ally	—
19	Magical Leaf	Grass	Special	60	—	20	Normal	—
22	Sunny Day	Fire	Status	—	—	5	All	—
25	Petal Dance	Grass	Special	90	100	20	1 Random	○
30	Worry Seed	Grass	Status	—	100	10	Normal	—
35	Take Down	Normal	Physical	90	85	20	Normal	○
43	SolarBeam	Grass	Special	120	100	10	Normal	—
48	Lucky Chant	Normal	Status	—	—	30	2 Allies	—

● MOVE MANIAC

Name	Type	Kind	Pow.	Acc.	PP	Range	DA

● BP MOVES

Name	Type	Kind	Pow.	Acc.	PP	Range	DA
Snore	Normal	Special	40	100	15	Normal	—
Helping Hand	Normal	Status	—	—	20	1 Ally	—
Synthesis	Grass	Status	—	—	5	Self	—
Worry Seed	Grass	Status	—	100	10	Normal	—
Rollout	Rock	Physical	30	90	20	Normal	○
Seed Bomb	Grass	Physical	80	100	15	Normal	—

● TM & HM MOVES

No.	Name	Type	Kind	Pow.	Acc.	PP	Range	DA
TM06	Toxic	Poison	Status	—	85	10	Normal	—
TM09	Bullet Seed	Grass	Physical	10	100	30	Normal	—
TM10	Hidden Power	Normal	Special	—	100	15	Normal	—
TM11	Sunny Day	Fire	Status	—	—	5	All	—
TM15	Hyper Beam	Normal	Special	150	90	5	Normal	—
TM17	Protect	Normal	Status	—	—	10	Self	—
TM19	Giga Drain	Grass	Special	60	100	10	Normal	—
TM20	Safeguard	Normal	Status	—	—	25	2 Allies	—
TM21	Frustration	Normal	Physical	—	100	20	Normal	○
TM22	SolarBeam	Grass	Special	120	100	10	Normal	—
TM27	Return	Normal	Physical	—	100	20	Normal	○
TM32	Double Team	Normal	Status	—	—	15	Self	—
TM42	Facade	Normal	Physical	70	100	20	Normal	—
TM43	Secret Power	Normal	Physical	70	100	20	Normal	—
TM44	Rest	Psychic	Status	—	—	10	Self	—
TM45	Attract	Normal	Status	—	100	15	Normal	—
TM53	Energy Ball	Grass	Special	80	100	10	Normal	—
TM58	Endure	Normal	Status	—	—	10	Self	—
TM68	Giga Impact	Normal	Physical	150	90	5	Normal	○
TM70	Flash	Normal	Status	—	100	20	Normal	—
TM75	Swords Dance	Normal	Status	—	—	30	Self	—
TM78	Captivate	Normal	Status	—	100	20	2 Foes	—
TM82	Sleep Talk	Normal	Status	—	—	10	Depends	—
TM83	Natural Gift	Normal	Physical	—	100	15	Normal	—
TM86	Grass Knot	Grass	Special	—	100	20	Normal	○
TM87	Swagger	Normal	Status	—	90	15	Normal	—
TM90	Substitute	Normal	Status	—	—	10	Self	—

● No. 421 | Blossom Pokémon
Cherrim

Grass

Overcast Form　　　Sunshine Form

- ● HEIGHT: 1'08"
- ● WEIGHT: 20.5 lbs.
- ● ITEMS: None

● SIZE COMPARISON

● OVERCAST FORM　　● SUNSHINE FORM

⊘ ABILITIES
- ● Flower Gift

⊘ STATS

HP ●●●
ATTACK ●●●●
DEFENSE ●●●●
SP. ATTACK ●●●●
SP. DEFENSE ●●●●
SPEED ●●●●

⊘ EGG GROUPS
Fairy

Grass

⊘ PERFORMANCE
SPEED ★★★☆　　STAMINA ★★☆☆
POWER ★★☆　　JUMP ★★★
SKILL ★★★☆

● MAIN WAYS TO OBTAIN

Pokémon HeartGold	Level up Cherubi to Lv. 25
Pokémon SoulSilver	Level up Cherubi to Lv. 25
Pokémon Diamond	Level up Cherubi to Lv. 25
Pokémon Pearl	Level up Cherubi to Lv. 25
Pokémon Platinum	Level up Cherubi to Lv. 25

Pokémon HeartGold

During times of strong sunlight, its bud blooms, its petals open fully, and it becomes very active.

Pokémon SoulSilver

During times of strong sunlight, its bud blooms, its petals open fully, and it becomes very active.

⊘ EVOLUTION

Cherubi　　Lv. 25　→　Cherrim

No. 422 | Sea Slug Pokémon
Shellos
Water

● LEVEL-UP MOVES

Lv.	Name	Type	Kind	Pow.	Acc.	PP	Range	DA
1	Mud-Slap	Ground	Special	20	100	10	Normal	—
2	Mud Sport	Ground	Status	—	—	15	All	—
4	Harden	Normal	Status	—	—	30	Self	—
7	Water Pulse	Water	Special	60	100	20	Normal	—
11	Mud Bomb	Ground	Special	65	85	10	Normal	—
16	Hidden Power	Normal	Special	—	100	15	Normal	—
22	Rain Dance	Water	Status	—	—	5	All	—
29	Body Slam	Normal	Physical	85	100	15	Normal	—
37	Muddy Water	Water	Special	95	85	10	2 Foes	—
46	Recover	Normal	Status	—	—	10	Self	—

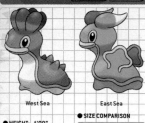

West Sea   East Sea

● HEIGHT: 1'00"
● WEIGHT: 13.9 lbs.
● ITEMS: None

● SIZE COMPARISON

● WEST SEA   ● EAST SEA

● MOVE MANIAC

Name	Type	Kind	Pow.	Acc.	PP	Range	DA
Headbutt	Normal	Physical	70	100	15	Normal	○

● BP MOVES

Name	Type	Kind	Pow.	Acc.	PP	Range	DA
ThunderPunch	Electric	Physical	75	100	15	Normal	○
Fire Punch	Fire	Physical	75	100	15	Normal	○
Zen Headbutt	Psychic	Physical	80	90	15	Normal	○
Snore	Normal	Special	40	100	15	Normal	—
Spite	Ghost	Status	—	100	10	Normal	—
Uproar	Normal	Special	50	100	10	1 Random	—
Mud-Slap	Ground	Special	20	100	10	Normal	—
Superpower	Fighting	Physical	120	100	5	Normal	—
Iron Head	Steel	Physical	80	100	15	Normal	○
Endeavor	Normal	Physical	—	100	5	Normal	—
AncientPower	Rock	Special	60	100	5	Normal	—
Earth Power	Ground	Special	90	100	10	Normal	—

⊙ ABILITIES
● Sticky Hold
● Storm Drain

⊙ STATS
HP ●●●
ATTACK ●●
DEFENSE ●●
SP. ATTACK ●●
SP. DEFENSE ●●
SPEED ●●

⊙ EGG GROUPS
Water 1
Amorphous

⊙ PERFORMANCE
SPEED ★☆☆
POWER ★☆☆
SKILL ★☆☆
STAMINA ★★★☆☆
JUMP ★★

● TM & HM MOVES

No.	Name	Type	Kind	Pow.	Acc.	PP	Range	DA
TM03	Water Pulse	Water	Special	60	100	20	Normal	—
TM06	Toxic	Poison	Status	—	85	10	Normal	—
TM07	Hail	Ice	Status	—	—	10	All	—
TM10	Hidden Power	Normal	Special	—	100	15	Normal	—
TM13	Ice Beam	Ice	Special	95	100	10	Normal	—
TM14	Blizzard	Ice	Special	120	70	5	2 Foes	—
TM17	Protect	Normal	Status	—	—	10	Self	—
TM18	Rain Dance	Water	Status	—	—	5	All	—
TM21	Frustration	Normal	Physical	—	100	20	Normal	○
TM27	Return	Normal	Physical	—	100	20	Normal	○
TM32	Double Team	Normal	Status	—	—	15	Self	—
TM42	Facade	Normal	Physical	70	100	20	Normal	○
TM43	Secret Power	Normal	Physical	70	100	20	Normal	—
TM44	Rest	Psychic	Status	—	—	10	Self	—
TM45	Attract	Normal	Status	—	100	15	Normal	—
TM55	Brine	Water	Special	65	100	10	Normal	—
TM58	Endure	Normal	Status	—	—	10	Self	—
TM78	Captivate	Normal	Status	—	100	20	2 Foes	—
TM82	Sleep Talk	Normal	Status	—	—	10	Depends	—
TM83	Natural Gift	Normal	Physical	—	100	15	Normal	—
TM87	Swagger	Normal	Status	—	90	15	Normal	—
TM90	Substitute	Normal	Status	—	—	10	Self	—
HM03	Surf	Water	Special	95	100	15	2 Foes/1 Ally	—
HM05	Whirlpool	Water	Special	15	70	15	Normal	—

● MAIN WAYS TO OBTAIN

Pokémon HeartGold	Stormy Beach Pokéwalker Route
Pokémon SoulSilver	Stormy Beach Pokéwalker Route
Pokémon Diamond	Valley Windworks [West Sea]—Route 213 [East Sea]
Pokémon Pearl	Valley Windworks [West Sea]—Route 213 [East Sea]
Pokémon Platinum	Valley Windworks [West Sea]—Route 213 [East Sea]

Pokémon HeartGold	Pokémon SoulSilver
Its shape and coloration vary, depending on its habitat.	Its shape and coloration vary, depending on its habitat.

⊙ EVOLUTION

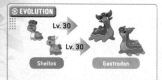

Lv. 30
Lv. 30
Shellos   Gastrodon

● EGG MOVES

Name	Type	Kind	Pow.	Acc.	PP	Range	DA
Counter	Fighting	Physical	—	100	20	Self	○
Mirror Coat	Psychic	Special	—	100	20	Self	—
Stockpile	Normal	Status	—	—	20	Self	—
Swallow	Normal	Status	—	—	10	Self	—
Spit Up	Normal	Special	—	100	10	Normal	—
Yawn	Normal	Status	—	—	10	Normal	—
Memento	Dark	Status	—	100	10	Normal	—
Curse	???	Status	—	—	10	Normal/Self	—
Amnesia	Psychic	Status	—	—	20	Self	—
Fissure	Ground	Physical	—	30	5	Normal	—
Trump Card	Normal	Special	—	—	5	Normal	○
Sludge	Poison	Special	65	100	10	Normal	—

● LEVEL-UP MOVES

Lv.	Name	Type	Kind	Pow.	Acc.	PP	Range	DA
1	Mud-Slap	Ground	Special	20	100	10	Normal	—
1	Mud Sport	Ground	Status	—	—	15	All	—
1	Harden	Normal	Status	—	—	30	Self	—
1	Water Pulse	Water	Special	60	100	20	Normal	—
2	Mud Sport	Ground	Status	—	—	15	All	—
4	Harden	Normal	Status	—	—	30	Self	—
7	Water Pulse	Water	Special	60	100	20	Normal	—
11	Mud Bomb	Ground	Special	65	85	10	Normal	—
16	Hidden Power	Normal	Special	—	100	15	Normal	—
22	Rain Dance	Water	Status	—	—	5	All	—
29	Body Slam	Normal	Physical	85	100	15	Normal	○
41	Muddy Water	Water	Special	95	85	10	2 Foes	—
54	Recover	Normal	Status	—	—	10	Self	—

● MOVE MANIAC

Name	Type	Kind	Pow.	Acc.	PP	Range	DA
Headbutt	Normal	Physical	70	100	15	Normal	○

● BP MOVES

Name	Type	Kind	Pow.	Acc.	PP	Range	DA
Dive	Water	Physical	80	100	10	Normal	○
Icy Wind	Ice	Special	55	95	15	2 Foes	—
Snore	Normal	Special	40	100	15	Normal	—
String Shot	Bug	Status	—	95	40	2 Foes	—
Block	Normal	Status	—	—	5	Normal	—
Mud-Slap	Ground	Special	20	100	10	Normal	—
AncientPower	Rock	Special	60	100	5	Normal	—
Earth Power	Ground	Special	90	100	10	Normal	—
Pain Split	Normal	Status	—	—	20	Normal	—

● TM & HM MOVES

No.	Name	Type	Kind	Pow.	Acc.	PP	Range	DA
TM03	Water Pulse	Water	Special	60	100	20	Normal	—
TM06	Toxic	Poison	Status	—	85	10	Normal	—
TM07	Hail	Ice	Status	—	—	10	All	—
TM10	Hidden Power	Normal	Special	—	100	15	Normal	—
TM13	Ice Beam	Ice	Special	95	100	10	Normal	—
TM14	Blizzard	Ice	Special	120	70	5	2 Foes	—
TM15	Hyper Beam	Normal	Special	150	90	5	Normal	—
TM17	Protect	Normal	Status	—	—	10	Self	—
TM18	Rain Dance	Water	Status	—	—	5	All	—
TM21	Frustration	Normal	Physical	—	100	20	Normal	○
TM26	Earthquake	Ground	Physical	100	100	10	2 Foes/1 Ally	—
TM27	Return	Normal	Physical	—	100	20	Normal	○
TM28	Dig	Ground	Physical	80	100	10	Normal	○
TM32	Double Team	Normal	Status	—	—	15	Self	—
TM36	Sludge Bomb	Poison	Special	90	100	10	Normal	—
TM37	Sandstorm	Rock	Status	—	—	10	All	—
TM39	Rock Tomb	Rock	Physical	50	80	10	Normal	—
TM42	Facade	Normal	Physical	70	100	20	Normal	○
TM43	Secret Power	Normal	Physical	70	100	20	Normal	○
TM44	Rest	Psychic	Status	—	—	10	Self	—
TM45	Attract	Normal	Status	—	100	15	Normal	—
TM55	Brine	Water	Special	65	100	10	Normal	—
TM58	Endure	Normal	Status	—	—	10	Self	—
TM68	Giga Impact	Normal	Physical	150	90	5	Normal	○
TM70	Flash	Normal	Status	—	100	20	Normal	—
TM71	Stone Edge	Rock	Physical	100	80	5	Normal	—
TM78	Captivate	Normal	Status	—	100	20	2 Foes	—
TM80	Rock Slide	Rock	Physical	75	90	10	2 Foes	—
TM82	Sleep Talk	Normal	Status	—	—	10	Depends	—
TM83	Natural Gift	Normal	Physical	—	100	15	Normal	—
TM87	Swagger	Normal	Status	—	90	15	Normal	—
TM90	Substitute	Normal	Status	—	—	10	Self	—
HM03	Surf	Water	Special	95	100	15	2 Foes/1 Ally	—
HM04	Strength	Normal	Physical	80	100	15	Normal	○
HM05	Whirlpool	Water	Special	15	70	15	Normal	—
HM06	Rock Smash	Fighting	Physical	40	100	15	Normal	○
HM07	Waterfall	Water	Physical	80	100	15	Normal	—

No. 423 | Sea Slug Pokémon
Gastrodon

Water　Ground

West Sea　　　East Sea

● SIZE COMPARISON

- **HEIGHT:** 2'11"
- **WEIGHT:** 65.9 lbs.
- **ITEMS:** None

● WEST SEA

⚙ ABILITIES
- Sticky Hold
- Storm Drain

⚙ STATS
- HP ●●●●
- ATTACK ●●●●
- DEFENSE ●●●
- SP. ATTACK ●●●●
- SP. DEFENSE ●●●
- SPEED ●●

⚙ EGG GROUPS
Water 1

Amorphous

⚙ PERFORMANCE
- SPEED ★☆
- POWER ★★★★☆
- SKILL ★★★
- STAMINA ★★★★★
- JUMP ★★

● MAIN WAYS TO OBTAIN

Pokémon HeartGold	Level up Shellos to Lv. 30
Pokémon SoulSilver	Level up Shellos to Lv. 30
Pokémon Diamond	Route 218 (West Sea)— Route 224 (East Sea)
Pokémon Pearl	Route 218 (West Sea)— Route 224 (East Sea)
Pokémon Platinum	Route 218 (West Sea)— Route 224 (East Sea)

Pokémon HeartGold	*Pokémon SoulSilver*
When its natural enemy attacks, it oozes purple fluid and escapes.	When its natural enemy attacks, it oozes purple fluid and escapes.

⚙ EVOLUTION
Lv. 30

Lv. 30

Shellos　　Gastrodon

No. 424 | Long Tail Pokémon
Ambipom

Normal

● HEIGHT: 3'11"
● WEIGHT: 44.8 lbs.
● ITEMS: None

● SIZE COMPARISON

● MALE FORM
Shorter fur tuft on head

● FEMALE FORM
Longer fur tuft on head

● ABILITIES
● Technician
● Pickup

● STATS
HP	●●●
ATTACK	●●●●
DEFENSE	●●●
SP. ATTACK	●●●
SP. DEFENSE	●●
SPEED	●●●●●

● EGG GROUPS
Field

● PERFORMANCE
SPEED ★★★☆
POWER ★★☆☆
SKILL ★★★★★
STAMINA ★★★☆
JUMP ★★★☆

● MAIN WAYS TO OBTAIN

Pokémon HeartGold
Level up Aipom to Lv. 32 and have it learn Double Hit, or level it up once it knows Double Hit

Pokémon SoulSilver
Level up Aipom to Lv. 32 and have it learn Double Hit, or level it up once it knows Double Hit

Pokémon Diamond
Level up Aipom to Lv. 32 and have it learn Double Hit, or level it up once it knows Double Hit

Pokémon Pearl
Level up Aipom to Lv. 32 and have it learn Double Hit, or level it up once it knows Double Hit

Pokémon Platinum
Level up Aipom to Lv. 32 and have it learn Double Hit, or level it up once it knows Double Hit

Pokémon HeartGold
They live on large trees. They are said to communicate by connecting their tails to those of others.

Pokémon SoulSilver
It is very difficult to dodge the consecutive strikes of its two tails.

● EVOLUTION

Aipom

Level it up to Lv. 32 and teach it Double Hit. Or, level it up once it knows Double Hit.

Ambipom

● LEVEL-UP MOVES
Lv.	Name	Type	Kind	Pow.	Acc.	PP	Range	DA
1	Scratch	Normal	Physical	40	100	35	Normal	○
1	Tail Whip	Normal	Status	--	100	30	2 Foes	--
1	Sand-Attack	Ground	Status	--	100	15	Normal	--
1	Astonish	Ghost	Physical	30	100	15	Normal	○
4	Sand-Attack	Ground	Status	--	100	15	Normal	--
8	Astonish	Ghost	Physical	30	100	15	Normal	○
11	Baton Pass	Normal	Status	--	--	40	Self	--
15	Tickle	Normal	Status	--	100	20	Normal	--
18	Fury Swipes	Normal	Physical	18	80	15	Normal	○
22	Swift	Normal	Special	60	--	20	2 Foes	--
25	Screech	Normal	Status	--	85	40	Normal	--
29	Agility	Psychic	Status	--	--	30	Self	--
32	Double Hit	Normal	Physical	35	90	10	Normal	○
36	Fling	Dark	Physical	--	100	10	Normal	--
39	Nasty Plot	Dark	Status	--	--	20	Self	--
43	Last Resort	Normal	Physical	130	100	5	Normal	○

● MOVE MANIAC
Name	Type	Kind	Pow.	Acc.	PP	Range	DA
Headbutt	Normal	Physical	70	100	15	Normal	○

● BP MOVES
Name	Type	Kind	Pow.	Acc.	PP	Range	DA
Fury Cutter	Bug	Physical	10	95	20	Normal	○
ThunderPunch	Electric	Physical	75	100	15	Normal	○
Fire Punch	Fire	Physical	75	100	15	Normal	○
Ice Punch	Ice	Physical	75	100	15	Normal	○
Knock Off	Dark	Physical	20	100	20	Normal	○
Snore	Normal	Special	40	100	15	Normal	--
Spite	Ghost	Status	--	100	10	Normal	--
Last Resort	Normal	Physical	130	100	5	Normal	○
Swift	Normal	Special	60	--	20	2 Foes	--
Uproar	Normal	Special	50	100	10	1 Random	--
Role Play	Psychic	Status	--	--	10	Normal	--
Mud-Slap	Ground	Special	20	100	10	Normal	○
Gunk Shot	Poison	Physical	120	70	5	Normal	○
Seed Bomb	Grass	Physical	80	100	15	Normal	○
Bounce	Flying	Physical	85	85	5	Normal	○
Low Kick	Fighting	Physical	--	100	20	Normal	○

● TM & HM MOVES
No.	Name	Type	Kind	Pow.	Acc.	PP	Range	DA
TM01	Focus Punch	Fighting	Physical	150	100	20	Normal	○
TM03	Water Pulse	Water	Special	60	100	20	Normal	○
TM06	Toxic	Poison	Status	--	85	10	Normal	--
TM10	Hidden Power	Normal	Special	--	100	15	Normal	--
TM11	Sunny Day	Fire	Status	--	--	5	All	--
TM12	Taunt	Dark	Status	--	100	20	Normal	--
TM15	Hyper Beam	Normal	Special	150	90	5	Normal	--
TM17	Protect	Normal	Status	--	--	10	Self	--
TM18	Rain Dance	Water	Status	--	--	5	All	--
TM21	Frustration	Normal	Physical	--	100	20	Normal	○
TM22	SolarBeam	Grass	Special	120	100	10	Normal	○
TM23	Iron Tail	Steel	Physical	100	75	15	Normal	○
TM24	Thunderbolt	Electric	Special	95	100	15	Normal	--
TM25	Thunder	Electric	Special	120	70	10	Normal	--
TM27	Return	Normal	Physical	--	100	20	Normal	○
TM28	Dig	Ground	Physical	80	100	10	Normal	○
TM30	Shadow Ball	Ghost	Special	80	100	15	Normal	--
TM31	Brick Break	Fighting	Physical	75	100	15	Normal	○
TM32	Double Team	Normal	Status	--	--	15	Self	--
TM34	Shock Wave	Electric	Special	60	--	20	Normal	--
TM40	Aerial Ace	Flying	Physical	60	--	20	Normal	○
TM42	Facade	Normal	Physical	70	100	20	Normal	--
TM43	Secret Power	Normal	Physical	70	100	20	Normal	--
TM44	Rest	Psychic	Status	--	--	10	Self	--
TM45	Attract	Normal	Status	--	100	15	Normal	--
TM46	Thief	Dark	Physical	40	100	10	Normal	○
TM49	Snatch	Dark	Status	--	--	10	Depends	--
TM56	Fling	Dark	Physical	--	100	10	Normal	--
TM58	Endure	Normal	Status	--	--	10	Self	--
TM65	Shadow Claw	Ghost	Physical	70	100	15	Normal	○
TM66	Payback	Dark	Physical	50	100	10	Normal	○
TM68	Giga Impact	Normal	Physical	150	90	5	Normal	○
TM73	Thunder Wave	Electric	Status	--	100	20	Normal	--
TM78	Captivate	Normal	Status	--	100	20	2 Foes	--
TM82	Sleep Talk	Normal	Status	--	--	10	Depends	--
TM83	Natural Gift	Normal	Physical	--	100	15	Normal	--
TM85	Dream Eater	Psychic	Special	100	100	15	Normal	--
TM86	Grass Knot	Grass	Special	--	100	20	Normal	○
TM87	Swagger	Normal	Status	--	90	15	Normal	--
TM89	U-turn	Bug	Physical	70	100	20	Normal	○
TM90	Substitute	Normal	Status	--	--	10	Self	--
HM01	Cut	Normal	Physical	50	95	30	Normal	○
HM04	Strength	Normal	Physical	80	100	15	Normal	○
HM06	Rock Smash	Fighting	Physical	40	100	15	Normal	○

● LEVEL-UP MOVES

Lv.	Name	Type	Kind	Pow.	Acc.	PP	Range	DA
1	Constrict	Normal	Physical	10	100	35	Normal	○
1	Minimize	Normal	Status	—	—	20	Self	—
6	Astonish	Ghost	Physical	30	100	15	Normal	○
11	Gust	Flying	Special	40	100	35	Normal	—
14	Focus Energy	Normal	Status	—	—	30	Self	—
17	Payback	Dark	Physical	50	100	10	Normal	○
22	Stockpile	Normal	Status	—	—	20	Self	—
27	Swallow	Normal	Status	—	—	10	Self	—
27	Spit Up	Normal	Special	—	100	10	Normal	—
30	Ominous Wind	Ghost	Special	60	100	5	Normal	—
33	Baton Pass	Normal	Status	—	—	40	Self	—
38	Shadow Ball	Ghost	Special	80	100	15	Normal	—
43	Explosion	Normal	Physical	250	100	5	2 Foes/1 Ally	—

● MOVE MANIAC

Name	Type	Kind	Pow.	Acc.	PP	Range	DA

● BP MOVES

Name	Type	Kind	Pow.	Acc.	PP	Range	DA
Icy Wind	Ice	Special	55	95	15	2 Foes	—
Ominous Wind	Ghost	Special	60	100	5	Normal	—
Air Cutter	Flying	Special	55	95	25	2 Foes	—
Trick	Psychic	Status	—	100	10	Normal	—
Knock Off	Dark	Physical	20	100	20	Normal	○
Sucker Punch	Dark	Physical	80	100	5	Normal	○
Snore	Normal	Special	40	100	15	Normal	—
Spite	Ghost	Status	—	100	10	Normal	—
Swift	Normal	Special	60	—	20	2 Foes	—
Tailwind	Flying	Status	—	—	30	2 Allies	—
Magic Coat	Psychic	Status	—	—	15	Self	—
Mud-Slap	Ground	Special	20	100	10	Normal	—
Rollout	Rock	Physical	30	90	20	Normal	○
Pain Split	Normal	Status	—	—	20	Normal	—

● TM & HM MOVES

No.	Name	Type	Kind	Pow.	Acc.	PP	Range	DA
TM04	Calm Mind	Psychic	Status	—	—	20	Self	—
TM06	Toxic	Poison	Status	—	85	10	Normal	—
TM10	Hidden Power	Normal	Special	—	100	15	Normal	—
TM11	Sunny Day	Fire	Status	—	—	5	All	—
TM17	Protect	Normal	Status	—	—	10	Self	—
TM18	Rain Dance	Water	Status	—	—	5	All	—
TM21	Frustration	Normal	Physical	—	100	20	Normal	○
TM24	Thunderbolt	Electric	Special	95	100	15	Normal	—
TM25	Thunder	Electric	Special	120	70	10	Normal	—
TM27	Return	Normal	Physical	—	100	20	Normal	○
TM29	Psychic	Psychic	Special	90	100	10	Normal	—
TM30	Shadow Ball	Ghost	Special	80	100	15	Normal	—
TM32	Double Team	Normal	Status	—	—	15	Self	—
TM34	Shock Wave	Electric	Special	60	—	20	Normal	—
TM42	Facade	Normal	Physical	70	100	20	Normal	○
TM43	Secret Power	Normal	Physical	70	100	20	Normal	○
TM44	Rest	Psychic	Status	—	—	10	Self	—
TM45	Attract	Normal	Status	—	100	15	Normal	—
TM46	Thief	Dark	Physical	40	100	10	Normal	○
TM48	Skill Swap	Psychic	Status	—	—	10	Normal	—
TM57	Charge Beam	Electric	Special	50	90	10	Normal	—
TM58	Endure	Normal	Status	—	—	10	Self	—
TM61	Will-O-Wisp	Fire	Status	—	75	15	Normal	—
TM62	Silver Wind	Bug	Special	60	100	5	Normal	—
TM63	Embargo	Dark	Status	—	100	15	Normal	—
TM64	Explosion	Normal	Physical	250	100	5	2 Foes/1 Ally	—
TM66	Payback	Dark	Physical	50	100	10	Normal	○
TM67	Recycle	Normal	Status	—	—	10	Self	—
TM70	Flash	Normal	Status	—	100	20	Normal	—
TM73	Thunder Wave	Electric	Status	—	100	20	Normal	—
TM74	Gyro Ball	Steel	Physical	—	100	5	Normal	—
TM77	Psych Up	Normal	Status	—	—	10	Normal	—
TM78	Captivate	Normal	Status	—	100	20	2 Foes	—
TM82	Sleep Talk	Normal	Status	—	—	10	Depends	—
TM83	Natural Gift	Normal	Physical	—	100	15	Normal	—
TM85	Dream Eater	Psychic	Special	100	100	15	Normal	—
TM87	Swagger	Normal	Status	—	90	15	Normal	—
TM90	Substitute	Normal	Status	—	—	10	Self	—
HM01	Cut	Normal	Physical	50	95	30	Normal	○

● EGG MOVES

Name	Type	Kind	Pow.	Acc.	PP	Range	DA
Memento	Dark	Status	—	100	10	Normal	—
Body Slam	Normal	Physical	85	100	15	Normal	○
Destiny Bond	Ghost	Status	—	—	5	Self	—
Disable	Normal	Status	—	80	20	Normal	—
Haze	Ice	Status	—	—	30	All	—
Hypnosis	Psychic	Status	—	60	20	Normal	—
Weather Ball	Normal	Special	50	100	10	Normal	—

No. 425 | Balloon Pokémon
Drifloon

Ghost | Flying

● HEIGHT: 1'04"
● WEIGHT: 2.6 lbs.
● ITEMS: None

● SIZE COMPARISON

● MALE/FEMALE HAVE SAME FORM

● ABILITIES
● Aftermath
● Unburden

● STATS
HP ●●●
ATTACK ●●
DEFENSE ●●
SP. ATTACK ●●●
SP. DEFENSE ●●
SPEED ●●●

● EGG GROUPS
Amorphous

● PERFORMANCE
SPEED ★★★☆☆　　STAMINA ★★★☆
POWER ★　　　　　JUMP ★★★★★
SKILL ★★★★

● MAIN WAYS TO OBTAIN

Pokémon HeartGold	—
Pokémon SoulSilver	—
Pokémon Diamond	Valley Windworks (Friday only)
Pokémon Pearl	Valley Windworks (Friday only)
Pokémon Platinum	Valley Windworks (Friday only)

Pokémon HeartGold
It is whispered that any child who mistakes DRIFLOON for a balloon and holds on to it could wind up missing.

Pokémon SoulSilver
It is whispered that any child who mistakes DRIFLOON for a balloon and holds on to it could wind up missing.

● EVOLUTION

Drifloon — Lv. 28 → Drifblim

No. 426 | Blimp Pokémon
Drifblim

Ghost | Flying

- **HEIGHT:** 3'11"
- **WEIGHT:** 33.1 lbs.
- **ITEMS:** None

● SIZE COMPARISON

● MALE/FEMALE HAVE SAME FORM

⊛ ABILITIES
- Aftermath
- Unburden

⊛ EGG GROUPS
Amorphous

⊛ STATS
HP	●●●●●●
ATTACK	●●●
DEFENSE	●●●
SP. ATTACK	●●●●
SP. DEFENSE	●●
SPEED	●●●●

⊛ PERFORMANCE
SPEED ★★★☆	STAMINA ★★★★☆
POWER ★★★	JUMP ★★★★★
SKILL ★★	

● MAIN WAYS TO OBTAIN

Pokémon HeartGold	—

Pokémon SoulSilver	—

Pokémon Diamond	Level up Drifloon to Lv. 28

Pokémon Pearl	Level up Drifloon to Lv. 28

Pokémon Platinum	Level up Drifloon to Lv. 28

Pokémon HeartGold	Pokémon SoulSilver
It can generate and release gas within its body. That's how it can control the altitude of its drift.	It can generate and release gas within its body. That's how it can control the altitude of its drift.

⊛ EVOLUTION

Drifloon → Lv. 28 → Drifblim

● LEVEL-UP MOVES

Lv.	Name	Type	Kind	Pow.	Acc.	PP	Range	DA
1	Constrict	Normal	Physical	10	100	35	Normal	○
1	Minimize	Normal	Status	—	—	20	Self	—
1	Astonish	Ghost	Physical	30	100	15	Normal	○
1	Gust	Flying	Special	40	100	35	Normal	—
6	Astonish	Ghost	Physical	30	100	15	Normal	○
11	Gust	Flying	Special	40	100	35	Normal	—
14	Focus Energy	Normal	Status	—	—	30	Self	—
17	Payback	Dark	Physical	50	100	10	Normal	○
22	Stockpile	Normal	Status	—	—	20	Self	—
22	Swallow	Normal	Status	—	—	10	Self	—
27	Spit Up	Normal	Special	—	100	10	Normal	—
32	Ominous Wind	Ghost	Special	60	100	5	Normal	—
37	Baton Pass	Normal	Status	—	—	40	Self	—
44	Shadow Ball	Ghost	Special	80	100	15	Normal	—
51	Explosion	Normal	Physical	250	100	5	2 Foes/1 Ally	—

● MOVE MANIAC

Name	Type	Kind	Pow.	Acc.	PP	Range	DA

● BP MOVES

Name	Type	Kind	Pow.	Acc.	PP	Range	DA
Icy Wind	Ice	Special	55	95	15	2 Foes	—
Ominous Wind	Ghost	Special	60	100	5	Normal	—
Air Cutter	Flying	Special	55	95	25	2 Foes	—
Trick	Psychic	Status	—	100	10	Normal	—
Knock Off	Dark	Physical	20	100	20	Normal	○
Sucker Punch	Dark	Physical	80	100	5	Normal	○
Snore	Normal	Special	40	100	15	Normal	—
Spite	Ghost	Status	—	100	10	Normal	—
Swift	Normal	Special	60	—	20	2 Foes	—
Tailwind	Flying	Status	—	—	30	2 Allies	—
Magic Coat	Psychic	Status	—	—	15	Self	—
Mud-Slap	Ground	Special	20	100	10	Normal	—
Rollout	Rock	Physical	30	90	20	Normal	○
Pain Split	Normal	Status	—	—	20	Normal	—

● TM & HM MOVES

No.	Name	Type	Kind	Pow.	Acc.	PP	Range	DA
TM04	Calm Mind	Psychic	Status	—	—	20	Self	—
TM06	Toxic	Poison	Status	—	85	10	Normal	—
TM10	Hidden Power	Normal	Special	—	100	15	Normal	—
TM11	Sunny Day	Fire	Status	—	—	5	All	—
TM15	Hyper Beam	Normal	Special	150	90	5	Normal	—
TM17	Protect	Normal	Status	—	—	10	Self	—
TM18	Rain Dance	Water	Status	—	—	5	All	—
TM21	Frustration	Normal	Physical	—	100	20	Normal	○
TM24	Thunderbolt	Electric	Special	95	100	15	Normal	—
TM25	Thunder	Electric	Special	120	70	10	Normal	—
TM27	Return	Normal	Physical	—	100	20	Normal	○
TM29	Psychic	Psychic	Special	90	100	10	Normal	—
TM30	Shadow Ball	Ghost	Special	80	100	15	Normal	—
TM32	Double Team	Normal	Status	—	—	15	Self	—
TM34	Shock Wave	Electric	Special	60	—	20	Normal	—
TM42	Facade	Normal	Physical	70	100	20	Normal	○
TM43	Secret Power	Normal	Physical	70	100	20	Normal	—
TM44	Rest	Psychic	Status	—	—	10	Self	—
TM45	Attract	Normal	Status	—	100	15	Normal	—
TM46	Thief	Dark	Physical	40	100	10	Normal	○
TM48	Skill Swap	Psychic	Status	—	—	10	Normal	—
TM57	Charge Beam	Electric	Special	50	90	10	Normal	—
TM58	Endure	Normal	Status	—	—	10	Self	—
TM61	Will-O-Wisp	Fire	Status	—	75	15	Normal	—
TM62	Silver Wind	Bug	Special	60	100	5	Normal	—
TM63	Embargo	Dark	Status	—	100	15	Normal	—
TM64	Explosion	Normal	Physical	250	100	5	2 Foes/1 Ally	—
TM66	Payback	Dark	Physical	50	100	10	Normal	○
TM67	Recycle	Normal	Status	—	—	10	Self	—
TM68	Giga Impact	Normal	Physical	150	90	5	Normal	○
TM70	Flash	Normal	Status	—	100	20	Normal	—
TM73	Thunder Wave	Electric	Status	—	100	20	Normal	—
TM74	Gyro Ball	Steel	Physical	—	100	5	Normal	○
TM77	Psych Up	Normal	Status	—	—	10	Normal	—
TM78	Captivate	Normal	Status	—	100	20	2 Foes	—
TM82	Sleep Talk	Normal	Status	—	—	10	Depends	—
TM83	Natural Gift	Normal	Physical	—	100	15	Normal	—
TM85	Dream Eater	Psychic	Special	100	100	15	Normal	—
TM87	Swagger	Normal	Status	—	90	15	Normal	—
TM90	Substitute	Normal	Status	—	—	10	Self	—
HM01	Cut	Normal	Physical	50	95	30	Normal	○
HM02	Fly	Flying	Physical	90	95	15	Normal	○

● LEVEL-UP MOVES

Lv.	Name	Type	Kind	Pow.	Acc.	PP	Range	DA
1	Splash	Normal	Status	—	—	40	Self	—
1	Pound	Normal	Physical	40	100	35	Normal	O
1	Defense Curl	Normal	Status	—	—	40	Self	—
1	Foresight	Normal	Status	—	—	40	Normal	—
6	Endure	Normal	Status	—	—	10	Self	—
13	Frustration	Normal	Physical	—	100	20	Normal	O
16	Quick Attack	Normal	Physical	40	100	30	Normal	O
23	Jump Kick	Fighting	Physical	85	95	25	Normal	O
26	Baton Pass	Normal	Status	—	—	40	Self	—
33	Agility	Psychic	Status	—	—	30	Self	—
36	Dizzy Punch	Normal	Physical	70	100	10	Normal	O
43	Charm	Normal	Status	—	100	20	Normal	—
46	Bounce	Flying	Physical	85	85	5	Normal	O
53	Healing Wish	Psychic	Status	—	—	10	Self	—

● MOVE MANIAC

Name	Type	Kind	Pow.	Acc.	PP	Range	DA
Headbutt	Normal	Physical	70	100	15	Normal	O

● BP MOVES

Name	Type	Kind	Pow.	Acc.	PP	Range	DA
Snore	Normal	Special	40	100	15	Normal	—
Helping Hand	Normal	Status	—	—	20	1 Ally	—
Last Resort	Normal	Physical	130	100	5	Normal	O
Swift	Normal	Special	60	—	20	2 Foes	—
Uproar	Normal	Special	50	100	10	1 Random	—
Magic Coat	Psychic	Status	—	—	15	Self	—
Heal Bell	Normal	Status	—	—	5	All Allies	—
Mud-Slap	Ground	Special	20	100	10	Normal	—
Endeavor	Normal	Physical	—	100	5	Normal	O
Bounce	Flying	Physical	85	85	5	Normal	O
Low Kick	Fighting	Physical	—	100	20	Normal	O

● TM & HM MOVES

No.	Name	Type	Kind	Pow.	Acc.	PP	Range	DA
TM01	Focus Punch	Fighting	Physical	150	100	20	Normal	O
TM03	Water Pulse	Water	Special	60	100	20	Normal	—
TM06	Toxic	Poison	Status	—	85	10	Normal	—
TM10	Hidden Power	Normal	Special	—	100	15	Normal	—
TM11	Sunny Day	Fire	Status	—	—	5	All	—
TM13	Ice Beam	Ice	Special	95	100	10	Normal	—
TM17	Protect	Normal	Status	—	—	10	Self	—
TM18	Rain Dance	Water	Status	—	—	5	All	—
TM21	Frustration	Normal	Physical	—	100	20	Normal	O
TM22	SolarBeam	Grass	Special	120	100	10	Normal	—
TM23	Iron Tail	Steel	Physical	100	75	15	Normal	O
TM24	Thunderbolt	Electric	Special	95	100	15	Normal	—
TM27	Return	Normal	Physical	—	100	20	Normal	O
TM28	Dig	Ground	Physical	80	100	10	Normal	O
TM30	Shadow Ball	Ghost	Special	80	100	15	Normal	—
TM32	Double Team	Normal	Status	—	—	15	Self	—
TM34	Shock Wave	Electric	Special	60	—	20	Normal	—
TM42	Facade	Normal	Physical	70	100	20	Normal	O
TM43	Secret Power	Normal	Physical	70	100	20	Normal	O
TM44	Rest	Psychic	Status	—	—	10	Self	—
TM45	Attract	Normal	Status	—	100	15	Normal	—
TM56	Fling	Dark	Physical	—	100	10	Normal	O
TM57	Charge Beam	Electric	Special	50	90	10	Normal	—
TM58	Endure	Normal	Status	—	—	10	Self	—
TM60	Drain Punch	Fighting	Physical	60	100	5	Normal	O
TM73	Thunder Wave	Electric	Status	—	100	20	Normal	—
TM78	Captivate	Normal	Status	—	100	20	2 Foes	—
TM82	Sleep Talk	Normal	Status	—	—	10	Depends	—
TM83	Natural Gift	Normal	Physical	—	100	15	Normal	O
TM86	Grass Knot	Grass	Special	—	100	20	Normal	O
TM87	Swagger	Normal	Status	—	90	15	Normal	—
TM90	Substitute	Normal	Status	—	—	10	Self	—
HM01	Cut	Normal	Physical	50	95	30	Normal	O
HM06	Rock Smash	Fighting	Physical	40	100	15	Normal	O

● EGG MOVES

Name	Type	Kind	Pow.	Acc.	PP	Range	DA
Fake Tears	Dark	Status	—	100	20	Normal	—
Fake Out	Normal	Physical	40	100	10	Normal	O
Encore	Normal	Status	—	100	5	Normal	—
Sweet Kiss	Normal	Status	—	75	10	Normal	—
Double Hit	Normal	Physical	35	90	10	Normal	O
Attract	Normal	Status	—	100	15	Normal	—
Low Kick	Fighting	Physical	—	100	20	Normal	O
Sky Uppercut	Fighting	Physical	85	90	15	Normal	O
Switcheroo	Dark	Status	—	100	10	Normal	—
ThunderPunch	Electric	Physical	75	100	15	Normal	O
Ice Punch	Ice	Physical	75	100	15	Normal	O
Fire Punch	Fire	Physical	75	100	15	Normal	O
Flail	Normal	Physical	—	100	15	Normal	O

No. 427 | Rabbit Pokémon

Buneary

Normal

- **HEIGHT:** 1'04"
- **WEIGHT:** 12.1 lbs.
- **ITEMS:** Chople Berry

● SIZE COMPARISON

● MALE/FEMALE HAVE SAME FORM

● ABILITIES
- Run Away
- Klutz

● STATS
- HP ●●
- ATTACK ●●●
- DEFENSE ●●
- SP. ATTACK ●●
- SP. DEFENSE ●●
- SPEED ●●●●

● EGG GROUPS
- Field
- Human-Like

● PERFORMANCE
- SPEED ★★★★☆
- POWER ★★★☆☆
- SKILL ★☆
- STAMINA ★★☆☆
- JUMP ★★★★☆

● MAIN WAYS TO OBTAIN

Pokémon HeartGold	Route 25 (mass outbreak)
Pokémon SoulSilver	Route 25 (mass outbreak)
Pokémon Diamond	Eterna Forest
Pokémon Pearl	Eterna Forest
Pokémon Platinum	Eterna Forest

Pokémon HeartGold

You can tell how it feels by the way it rolls its ears. When it's scared, both ears are rolled up.

Pokémon SoulSilver

You can tell how it feels by the way it rolls its ears. When it's scared, both ears are rolled up.

● EVOLUTION

 Buneary → Level up with high friendship → Lopunny

No. 428 | Rabbit Pokémon
Lopunny

`Normal`

- **HEIGHT:** 3'11"
- **WEIGHT:** 73.4 lbs.
- **ITEMS:** None

● SIZE COMPARISON

● MALE/FEMALE HAVE SAME FORM

⊛ ABILITIES
- Cute Charm
- Klutz

⊛ STATS
HP	●●
ATTACK	●●●
DEFENSE	●●●
SP. ATTACK	●●
SP. DEFENSE	●●●
SPEED	●●●●●

⊛ EGG GROUPS
Field

Human-Like

⊛ PERFORMANCE
SPEED	★★★★☆	STAMINA	★★★☆
POWER	★★★☆	JUMP	★★★☆
SKILL	★☆		

● MAIN WAYS TO OBTAIN

Pokémon HeartGold — Level up Buneary with high friendship

Pokémon SoulSilver — Level up Buneary with high friendship

Pokémon Diamond — Level up Buneary with high friendship

Pokémon Pearl — Level up Buneary with high friendship

Pokémon Platinum — Level up Buneary with high friendship

Pokémon HeartGold — It sheds its fur twice a year. Its winter fur is soft and fluffy.

Pokémon SoulSilver — It sheds its fur twice a year. Its winter fur is soft and fluffy.

⊛ EVOLUTION

Buneary → (Level up with high friendship) → Lopunny

● LEVEL-UP MOVES

Lv.	Name	Type	Kind	Pow.	Acc.	PP	Range	DA
1	Mirror Coat	Psychic	Special	—	100	20	Self	—
1	Magic Coat	Psychic	Status	—	—	15	Self	—
1	Splash	Normal	Status	—	—	40	Self	—
1	Pound	Normal	Physical	40	100	35	Normal	○
1	Defense Curl	Normal	Status	—	—	40	Self	—
1	Foresight	Normal	Status	—	—	40	Normal	—
6	Endure	Normal	Status	—	—	10	Self	—
13	Return	Normal	Physical	—	100	20	Normal	○
16	Quick Attack	Normal	Physical	40	100	30	Normal	○
23	Jump Kick	Fighting	Physical	85	95	25	Normal	○
26	Baton Pass	Normal	Status	—	—	40	Self	—
33	Agility	Psychic	Status	—	—	30	Self	—
36	Dizzy Punch	Normal	Physical	70	100	10	Normal	○
43	Charm	Normal	Status	—	100	20	Normal	—
46	Bounce	Flying	Physical	85	85	5	Normal	○
53	Healing Wish	Psychic	Status	—	—	10	Self	—

● MOVE MANIAC

Name	Type	Kind	Pow.	Acc.	PP	Range	DA
Headbutt	Normal	Physical	70	100	15	Normal	○

● BP MOVES

Name	Type	Kind	Pow.	Acc.	PP	Range	DA
Fury Cutter	Bug	Physical	10	95	20	Normal	○
ThunderPunch	Electric	Physical	75	100	15	Normal	○
Fire Punch	Fire	Physical	75	100	15	Normal	○
Ice Punch	Ice	Physical	75	100	15	Normal	○
Snore	Normal	Special	40	100	15	Normal	—
Helping Hand	Normal	Status	—	—	20	1 Ally	—
Last Resort	Normal	Physical	130	100	5	Normal	○
Swift	Normal	Special	60	—	20	2 Foes	—
Uproar	Normal	Special	50	100	10	1 Random	—
Magic Coat	Psychic	Status	—	—	15	Self	—
Heal Bell	Normal	Status	—	—	5	All Allies	—
Mud-Slap	Ground	Special	20	100	10	Normal	—
Endeavor	Normal	Physical	—	100	5	Normal	○
Bounce	Flying	Physical	85	85	5	Normal	○
Low Kick	Fighting	Physical	—	100	20	Normal	○

● TM & HM MOVES

No.	Name	Type	Kind	Pow.	Acc.	PP	Range	DA
TM01	Focus Punch	Fighting	Physical	150	100	20	Normal	○
TM03	Water Pulse	Water	Special	60	100	20	Normal	—
TM06	Toxic	Poison	Status	—	85	10	Normal	—
TM10	Hidden Power	Normal	Special	—	100	15	Normal	—
TM11	Sunny Day	Fire	Status	—	—	5	All	—
TM13	Ice Beam	Ice	Special	95	100	10	Normal	—
TM14	Blizzard	Ice	Special	120	70	5	2 Foes	—
TM15	Hyper Beam	Normal	Special	150	90	5	Normal	—
TM17	Protect	Normal	Status	—	—	10	Self	—
TM18	Rain Dance	Water	Status	—	—	5	All	—
TM21	Frustration	Normal	Physical	—	100	20	Normal	○
TM22	SolarBeam	Grass	Special	120	100	10	Normal	—
TM23	Iron Tail	Steel	Physical	100	75	15	Normal	○
TM24	Thunderbolt	Electric	Special	95	100	15	Normal	—
TM25	Thunder	Electric	Special	120	70	10	Normal	—
TM27	Return	Normal	Physical	—	100	20	Normal	○
TM28	Dig	Ground	Physical	80	100	10	Normal	○
TM30	Shadow Ball	Ghost	Special	80	100	15	Normal	—
TM32	Double Team	Normal	Status	—	—	15	Self	—
TM34	Shock Wave	Electric	Special	60	—	20	Normal	—
TM42	Facade	Normal	Physical	70	100	20	Normal	○
TM43	Secret Power	Normal	Physical	70	100	20	Normal	○
TM44	Rest	Psychic	Status	—	—	10	Self	—
TM45	Attract	Normal	Status	—	100	15	Normal	—
TM52	Focus Blast	Fighting	Special	120	70	5	Normal	—
TM56	Fling	Dark	Physical	—	100	10	Normal	○
TM57	Charge Beam	Electric	Special	50	90	10	Normal	—
TM58	Endure	Normal	Status	—	—	10	Self	—
TM60	Drain Punch	Fighting	Physical	60	100	5	Normal	○
TM68	Giga Impact	Normal	Physical	150	90	5	Normal	○
TM73	Thunder Wave	Electric	Status	—	100	20	Normal	—
TM78	Captivate	Normal	Status	—	100	20	2 Foes	—
TM82	Sleep Talk	Normal	Status	—	—	10	Depends	—
TM83	Natural Gift	Normal	Physical	—	100	15	Normal	○
TM86	Grass Knot	Grass	Special	—	100	20	Normal	—
TM87	Swagger	Normal	Status	—	90	15	Normal	—
TM90	Substitute	Normal	Status	—	—	10	Self	—
HM01	Cut	Normal	Physical	50	95	30	Normal	○
HM04	Strength	Normal	Physical	80	100	15	Normal	○
HM06	Rock Smash	Fighting	Physical	40	100	15	Normal	○

● LEVEL-UP MOVES

Lv.	Name	Type	Kind	Pow.	Acc.	PP	Range	DA
1	Lucky Chant	Normal	Status	—	—	30	2 Allies	—
1	Magical Leaf	Grass	Special	60	—	20	Normal	—
1	Growl	Normal	Status	—	100	40	2 Foes	—
1	Psywave	Psychic	Special	—	80	15	Normal	—
1	Spite	Ghost	Status	—	100	10	Normal	—
1	Astonish	Ghost	Physical	30	100	15	Normal	○

● MOVE MANIAC

Name	Type	Kind	Pow.	Acc.	PP	Range	DA
Headbutt	Normal	Physical	70	100	15	Normal	○

● BP MOVES

Name	Type	Kind	Pow.	Acc.	PP	Range	DA
Icy Wind	Ice	Special	55	95	15	2 Foes	—
Ominous Wind	Ghost	Special	60	100	5	Normal	—
Trick	Psychic	Status	—	100	10	Normal	—
Sucker Punch	Dark	Physical	80	100	5	Normal	○
Snore	Normal	Special	40	100	15	Normal	—
Spite	Ghost	Status	—	100	10	Normal	—
Swift	Normal	Special	60	—	20	2 Foes	—
Uproar	Normal	Special	50	100	10	1 Random	—
Magic Coat	Psychic	Status	—	—	15	Self	—
Heal Bell	Normal	Status	—	—	5	All Allies	—
Pain Split	Normal	Status	—	—	20	Normal	—

● TM & HM MOVES

No.	Name	Type	Kind	Pow.	Acc.	PP	Range	DA
TM04	Calm Mind	Psychic	Status	—	—	20	Self	—
TM06	Toxic	Poison	Status	—	85	10	Normal	—
TM10	Hidden Power	Normal	Special	—	100	15	Normal	—
TM11	Sunny Day	Fire	Status	—	—	5	All	—
TM12	Taunt	Dark	Status	—	100	20	Normal	—
TM15	Hyper Beam	Normal	Special	150	90	5	Normal	—
TM17	Protect	Normal	Status	—	—	10	Self	—
TM18	Rain Dance	Water	Status	—	—	5	All	—
TM21	Frustration	Normal	Physical	—	100	20	Normal	○
TM24	Thunderbolt	Electric	Special	95	100	15	Normal	—
TM25	Thunder	Electric	Special	120	70	10	Normal	—
TM27	Return	Normal	Physical	—	100	20	Normal	○
TM29	Psychic	Psychic	Special	90	100	10	Normal	—
TM30	Shadow Ball	Ghost	Special	80	100	15	Normal	—
TM32	Double Team	Normal	Status	—	—	15	Self	—
TM34	Shock Wave	Electric	Special	60	—	20	Normal	—
TM40	Aerial Ace	Flying	Physical	60	—	20	Normal	○
TM41	Torment	Dark	Status	—	100	15	Normal	—
TM42	Facade	Normal	Physical	70	100	20	Normal	○
TM43	Secret Power	Normal	Physical	70	100	20	Normal	○
TM44	Rest	Psychic	Status	—	—	10	Self	—
TM45	Attract	Normal	Status	—	100	15	Normal	—
TM46	Thief	Dark	Physical	40	100	10	Normal	○
TM48	Skill Swap	Psychic	Status	—	—	10	Normal	—
TM49	Snatch	Dark	Status	—	—	10	Depends	—
TM53	Energy Ball	Grass	Special	80	100	10	Normal	—
TM57	Charge Beam	Electric	Special	50	90	10	Normal	—
TM58	Endure	Normal	Status	—	—	10	Self	—
TM61	Will-O-Wisp	Fire	Status	—	75	15	Normal	—
TM63	Embargo	Dark	Status	—	100	15	Normal	—
TM66	Payback	Dark	Physical	50	100	10	Normal	○
TM68	Giga Impact	Normal	Physical	150	90	5	Normal	—
TM70	Flash	Normal	Status	—	100	20	Normal	—
TM73	Thunder Wave	Electric	Status	—	100	20	Normal	—
TM77	Psych Up	Normal	Status	—	—	10	Normal	—
TM78	Captivate	Normal	Status	—	100	20	2 Foes	—
TM79	Dark Pulse	Dark	Special	80	100	15	Normal	—
TM82	Sleep Talk	Normal	Status	—	—	10	Depends	—
TM83	Natural Gift	Normal	Physical	—	100	15	Normal	—
TM85	Dream Eater	Psychic	Special	100	100	15	Normal	—
TM87	Swagger	Normal	Status	—	90	15	Normal	—
TM90	Substitute	Normal	Status	—	—	10	Self	—
TM92	Trick Room	Psychic	Status	—	—	5	All	—

◉ No. 429 | Magical Pokémon
Mismagius
Ghost

● HEIGHT: 2'11"
● WEIGHT: 9.7 lbs.
● ITEMS: None

● SIZE COMPARISON

● MALE/FEMALE HAVE SAME FORM

⊛ ABILITIES
● Levitate

⊛ STATS
HP ●●
ATTACK ●●●
DEFENSE ●●●
SP. ATTACK ●●●●
SP. DEFENSE ●●●●
SPEED ●●●●●

⊛ EGG GROUPS
Amorphous

⊛ PERFORMANCE
SPEED ★★★★
POWER ★★
SKILL ★★★★☆
STAMINA ★★☆
JUMP ★★★★★

● MAIN WAYS TO OBTAIN

Pokémon HeartGold	Use Dusk Stone on Misdreavus
Pokémon SoulSilver	Use Dusk Stone on Misdreavus
Pokémon Diamond	—
Pokémon Pearl	Use Dusk Stone on Misdreavus
Pokémon Platinum	—

Pokémon HeartGold
Its cries sound like incantations to torment the foe. It appears where you least expect it.

Pokémon SoulSilver
Its cries sound like incantations to torment the foe. It appears where you least expect it.

⊛ EVOLUTION

Use Dusk Stone

Misdreavus → Mismagius

Honchkrow

Dark	Flying

● LEVEL-UP MOVES

Lv.	Name	Type	Kind	Pow.	Acc.	PP	Range	DA
1	Astonish	Ghost	Physical	30	100	15	Normal	○
1	Pursuit	Dark	Physical	40	100	20	Normal	○
1	Haze	Ice	Status	—	—	30	All	—
1	Wing Attack	Flying	Physical	60	100	35	Normal	○
25	Swagger	Normal	Status	—	90	15	Normal	—
35	Nasty Plot	Dark	Status	—	—	20	Self	—
45	Night Slash	Dark	Physical	70	100	15	Normal	○
55	Dark Pulse	Dark	Special	80	100	15	Normal	—

● MOVE MANIAC

Name	Type	Kind	Pow.	Acc.	PP	Range	DA

● BP MOVES

Name	Type	Kind	Pow.	Acc.	PP	Range	DA
Ominous Wind	Ghost	Special	60	100	5	Normal	—
Air Cutter	Flying	Special	55	95	25	2 Foes	—
Sucker Punch	Dark	Physical	80	100	5	Normal	○
Spite	Ghost	Status	—	100	10	Normal	—
Swift	Normal	Special	60	—	20	2 Foes	—
Uproar	Normal	Special	50	100	10	1 Random	—
Tailwind	Flying	Status	—	—	30	2 Allies	—
Mud-Slap	Ground	Special	20	100	10	Normal	—
Superpower	Fighting	Physical	120	100	5	Normal	○
Twister	Dragon	Special	40	100	20	2 Foes	—
Heat Wave	Fire	Special	100	90	10	2 Foes	—
Sky Attack	Flying	Physical	140	90	5	Normal	—

● HEIGHT: 2'11"
● WEIGHT: 60.2 lbs.
● ITEMS: None

● SIZE COMPARISON

● MALE/FEMALE HAVE SAME FORM

⊛ ABILITIES
● Insomnia
● Super Luck

⊛ STATS
HP ●●●●
ATTACK ●●●●●
DEFENSE ●●
SP. ATTACK ●●●
SP. DEFENSE ●●
SPEED ●●●

⊛ EGG GROUPS
Flying

⊛ PERFORMANCE
SPEED ★★☆   STAMINA ★★★★☆
POWER ★★★☆   JUMP ★★★★★
SKILL ★★☆

● MAIN WAYS TO OBTAIN

Pokémon HeartGold	Use Dusk Stone on Murkrow
Pokémon SoulSilver	Use Dusk Stone on Murkrow
Pokémon Diamond	Use Dusk Stone on Murkrow
Pokémon Pearl	—
Pokémon Platinum	—

Pokémon HeartGold	Pokémon SoulSilver
It is merciless by nature. It is said that it never forgives the mistakes of its MURKROW followers.	It is merciless by nature. It is said that it never forgives the mistakes of its MURKROW followers.

⊛ EVOLUTION

  →

Murkrow — Use Dusk Stone → Honchkrow

● TM & HM MOVES

No.	Name	Type	Kind	Pow.	Acc.	PP	Range	DA
TM04	Calm Mind	Psychic	Status	—	—	20	Self	—
TM06	Toxic	Poison	Status	—	85	10	Normal	—
TM10	Hidden Power	Normal	Special	—	100	15	Normal	—
TM11	Sunny Day	Fire	Status	—	—	5	All	—
TM12	Taunt	Dark	Status	—	100	20	Normal	—
TM15	Hyper Beam	Normal	Special	150	90	5	Normal	—
TM17	Protect	Normal	Status	—	—	10	Self	—
TM18	Rain Dance	Water	Status	—	—	5	All	—
TM21	Frustration	Normal	Physical	—	100	20	Normal	○
TM27	Return	Normal	Physical	—	100	20	Normal	○
TM29	Psychic	Psychic	Special	90	100	10	Normal	—
TM30	Shadow Ball	Ghost	Special	80	100	15	Normal	—
TM32	Double Team	Normal	Status	—	—	15	Self	—
TM40	Aerial Ace	Flying	Physical	60	—	20	Normal	○
TM41	Torment	Dark	Status	—	100	15	Normal	—
TM42	Facade	Normal	Physical	70	100	20	Normal	○
TM43	Secret Power	Normal	Physical	70	100	20	Normal	—
TM44	Rest	Psychic	Status	—	—	10	Self	—
TM45	Attract	Normal	Status	—	100	15	Normal	—
TM46	Thief	Dark	Physical	40	100	10	Normal	○
TM47	Steel Wing	Steel	Physical	70	90	25	Normal	○
TM49	Snatch	Dark	Status	—	—	10	Depends	—
TM51	Roost	Flying	Status	—	—	10	Self	—
TM58	Endure	Normal	Status	—	—	10	Self	—
TM63	Embargo	Dark	Status	—	100	15	Normal	—
TM66	Payback	Dark	Physical	50	100	10	Normal	○
TM68	Giga Impact	Normal	Physical	150	90	5	Normal	○
TM73	Thunder Wave	Electric	Status	—	100	20	Normal	—
TM77	Psych Up	Normal	Status	—	—	10	Normal	—
TM78	Captivate	Normal	Status	—	100	20	2 Foes	—
TM79	Dark Pulse	Dark	Special	80	100	15	Normal	—
TM82	Sleep Talk	Normal	Status	—	—	10	Depends	—
TM83	Natural Gift	Normal	Physical	—	100	15	Normal	—
TM85	Dream Eater	Psychic	Special	100	100	15	Normal	—
TM87	Swagger	Normal	Status	—	90	15	Normal	—
TM88	Pluck	Flying	Physical	60	100	20	Normal	○
TM90	Substitute	Normal	Status	—	—	10	Self	—
HM02	Fly	Flying	Physical	90	95	15	Normal	○

● LEVEL-UP MOVES

Lv.	Name	Type	Kind	Pow.	Acc.	PP	Range	DA
1	Fake Out	Normal	Physical	40	100	10	Normal	○
5	Scratch	Normal	Physical	40	100	35	Normal	○
8	Growl	Normal	Status	—	100	40	2 Foes	—
13	Hypnosis	Psychic	Status	—	60	20	Normal	—
17	Faint Attack	Dark	Physical	60	—	20	Normal	○
20	Fury Swipes	Normal	Physical	18	80	15	Normal	○
25	Charm	Normal	Status	—	100	20	Normal	—
29	Assist	Normal	Status	—	—	20	Depends	—
32	Captivate	Normal	Status	—	100	20	2 Foes	—
37	Slash	Normal	Physical	70	100	20	Normal	○
41	Sucker Punch	Dark	Physical	80	100	5	Normal	○
45	Attract	Normal	Status	—	100	15	Normal	—

● MOVE MANIAC

Name	Type	Kind	Pow.	Acc.	PP	Range	DA
Headbutt	Normal	Physical	70	100	15	Normal	○

● BP MOVES

Name	Type	Kind	Pow.	Acc.	PP	Range	DA
Fury Cutter	Bug	Physical	10	95	20	Normal	○
Knock Off	Dark	Physical	20	100	20	Normal	○
Sucker Punch	Dark	Physical	80	100	5	Normal	○
Snore	Normal	Special	40	100	15	Normal	—
Last Resort	Normal	Physical	130	100	5	Normal	○
Swift	Normal	Special	60	—	20	2 Foes	—
Mud-Slap	Ground	Special	20	100	10	Normal	—
Super Fang	Normal	Physical	—	90	10	Normal	○

● TM & HM MOVES

No.	Name	Type	Kind	Pow.	Acc.	PP	Range	DA
TM03	Water Pulse	Water	Special	60	100	20	Normal	—
TM06	Toxic	Poison	Status	—	85	10	Normal	—
TM10	Hidden Power	Normal	Special	—	100	15	Normal	—
TM11	Sunny Day	Fire	Status	—	—	5	All	—
TM12	Taunt	Dark	Status	—	100	20	Normal	—
TM17	Protect	Normal	Status	—	—	10	Self	—
TM18	Rain Dance	Water	Status	—	—	5	All	—
TM21	Frustration	Normal	Physical	—	100	20	Normal	○
TM23	Iron Tail	Steel	Physical	100	75	15	Normal	○
TM24	Thunderbolt	Electric	Special	95	100	15	Normal	—
TM25	Thunder	Electric	Special	120	70	10	Normal	—
TM27	Return	Normal	Physical	—	100	20	Normal	○
TM28	Dig	Ground	Physical	80	100	10	Normal	○
TM30	Shadow Ball	Ghost	Special	80	100	15	Normal	—
TM32	Double Team	Normal	Status	—	—	15	Self	—
TM34	Shock Wave	Electric	Special	60	—	20	Normal	—
TM40	Aerial Ace	Flying	Physical	60	—	20	Normal	○
TM41	Torment	Dark	Status	—	100	15	Normal	—
TM42	Facade	Normal	Physical	70	100	20	Normal	—
TM43	Secret Power	Normal	Physical	70	100	20	Normal	—
TM44	Rest	Psychic	Status	—	—	10	Self	—
TM45	Attract	Normal	Status	—	100	15	Normal	—
TM46	Thief	Dark	Physical	40	100	10	Normal	○
TM49	Snatch	Dark	Status	—	—	10	Depends	—
TM58	Endure	Normal	Status	—	—	10	Self	—
TM65	Shadow Claw	Ghost	Physical	70	100	15	Normal	○
TM66	Payback	Dark	Physical	50	100	10	Normal	○
TM70	Flash	Normal	Status	—	100	20	Normal	—
TM77	Psych Up	Normal	Status	—	—	10	Normal	—
TM78	Captivate	Normal	Status	—	100	20	2 Foes	—
TM82	Sleep Talk	Normal	Status	—	—	10	Depends	—
TM83	Natural Gift	Normal	Physical	—	100	15	Normal	○
TM85	Dream Eater	Psychic	Special	100	100	15	Normal	—
TM87	Swagger	Normal	Status	—	90	15	Normal	—
TM89	U-turn	Bug	Physical	70	100	20	Normal	○
TM90	Substitute	Normal	Status	—	—	10	Self	—
HM01	Cut	Normal	Physical	50	95	30	Normal	○

● EGG MOVES

Name	Type	Kind	Pow.	Acc.	PP	Range	DA
Bite	Dark	Physical	60	100	25	Normal	○
Tail Whip	Normal	Status	—	100	30	2 Foes	—
Quick Attack	Normal	Physical	40	100	30	Normal	○
Sand-Attack	Ground	Status	—	100	15	Normal	—
Fake Tears	Dark	Status	—	100	20	Normal	—
Assurance	Dark	Physical	50	100	10	Normal	○
Flail	Normal	Physical	—	100	15	Normal	○

No. 431 | Catty Pokémon
Glameow

Normal

- HEIGHT: 1'08"
- WEIGHT: 8.6 lbs.
- ITEMS: None

● SIZE COMPARISON

● MALE/FEMALE HAVE SAME FORM

⊙ ABILITIES
- Limber
- Own Tempo

⊙ STATS
HP ●●
ATTACK ●●
DEFENSE ●●
SP. ATTACK ●●
SP. DEFENSE ●
SPEED ●●●●

⊙ EGG GROUPS
Field

⊙ PERFORMANCE
SPEED ★★★★★   STAMINA ★★☆
POWER ★★☆☆☆   JUMP ★★★☆
SKILL ★★☆☆

● MAIN WAYS TO OBTAIN

Pokémon HeartGold	—
Pokémon SoulSilver	—
Pokémon Diamond	—
Pokémon Pearl	Route 218
Pokémon Platinum	—

Pokémon HeartGold
When it's happy, GLAMEOW demonstrates beautiful movements of its tail, like a dancing ribbon.

Pokémon SoulSilver
When it's happy, GLAMEOW demonstrates beautiful movements of its tail, like a dancing ribbon.

⊙ EVOLUTION

Glameow — Lv. 38 → Purugly

No. 432 | Tiger Cat Pokémon
Purugly

Normal

- **HEIGHT:** 3'03"
- **WEIGHT:** 96.6 lbs.
- **ITEMS:** None

● SIZE COMPARISON

● MALE/FEMALE HAVE SAME FORM

⊕ ABILITIES
- Thick Fat
- Own Tempo

⊕ STATS
HP	●●●
ATTACK	●●●
DEFENSE	●●●
SP. ATTACK	●●●
SP. DEFENSE	●●●
SPEED	●●●●●

⊕ EGG GROUPS
Field

⊕ PERFORMANCE
SPEED ★★☆☆	STAMINA ★★★★
POWER ★★★★☆	JUMP ★★☆
SKILL ★☆	

● MAIN WAYS TO OBTAIN

Pokémon HeartGold	—

Pokémon SoulSilver	—

Pokémon Diamond	—

Pokémon Pearl	Route 222

Pokémon Platinum	—

Pokémon HeartGold	Pokémon SoulSilver
It would claim another Pokémon's nest as its own if it finds a nest sufficiently comfortable.	It would claim another Pokémon's nest as its own if it finds a nest sufficiently comfortable.

⊕ EVOLUTION

Glameow	Lv. 38	Purugly

● LEVEL-UP MOVES
Lv.	Name	Type	Kind	Pow.	Acc.	PP	Range	DA
1	Tackle	Normal	Physical	35	95	35	Normal	○
1	Protect	Normal	Status	—	—	10	Self	—
6	Taunt	Dark	Status	—	100	20	Normal	—
10	Metal Sound	Steel	Status	—	85	40	Normal	—
15	Take Down	Normal	Physical	90	85	20	Normal	○
19	Iron Defense	Steel	Status	—	—	15	Self	—
24	Swagger	Normal	Status	—	90	15	Normal	—
28	AncientPower	Rock	Special	60	100	5	Normal	—
33	Endure	Normal	Status	—	—	10	Self	—
37	Metal Burst	Steel	Physical	—	100	10	Self	—
43	Iron Head	Steel	Physical	80	100	15	Normal	○

● MOVE MANIAC
Name	Type	Kind	Pow.	Acc.	PP	Range	DA
Headbutt	Normal	Physical	70	100	15	Normal	○

● BP MOVES
Name	Type	Kind	Pow.	Acc.	PP	Range	DA
Snore	Normal	Special	40	100	15	Normal	—
Magnet Rise	Electric	Status	—	—	10	Self	—
Mud-Slap	Ground	Special	20	100	10	Normal	—
Iron Head	Steel	Physical	80	100	15	Normal	○
AncientPower	Rock	Special	60	100	5	Normal	—
Earth Power	Ground	Special	90	100	10	Normal	—
Iron Defense	Steel	Status	—	—	15	Self	—

● TM & HM MOVES
No.	Name	Type	Kind	Pow.	Acc.	PP	Range	DA
TM05	Roar	Normal	Status	—	—	20	Normal	—
TM06	Toxic	Poison	Status	—	85	10	Normal	—
TM10	Hidden Power	Normal	Special	—	100	15	Normal	—
TM11	Sunny Day	Fire	Status	—	—	5	All	—
TM12	Taunt	Dark	Status	—	100	20	Normal	—
TM13	Ice Beam	Ice	Special	95	100	10	Normal	—
TM14	Blizzard	Ice	Special	120	70	5	2 Foes	—
TM17	Protect	Normal	Status	—	—	10	Self	—
TM18	Rain Dance	Water	Status	—	—	5	All	—
TM21	Frustration	Normal	Physical	—	100	20	Normal	○
TM23	Iron Tail	Steel	Physical	100	75	15	Normal	○
TM24	Thunderbolt	Electric	Special	95	100	15	Normal	—
TM25	Thunder	Electric	Special	120	70	10	Normal	—
TM26	Earthquake	Ground	Physical	100	100	10	2 Foes/1 Ally	—
TM27	Return	Normal	Physical	—	100	20	Normal	○
TM28	Dig	Ground	Physical	80	100	10	Normal	○
TM32	Double Team	Normal	Status	—	—	15	Self	—
TM34	Shock Wave	Electric	Special	60	—	20	Normal	—
TM35	Flamethrower	Fire	Special	95	100	15	Normal	—
TM37	Sandstorm	Rock	Status	—	—	10	All	—
TM38	Fire Blast	Fire	Special	120	85	5	Normal	—
TM39	Rock Tomb	Rock	Physical	50	80	10	Normal	—
TM41	Torment	Dark	Status	—	100	15	Normal	—
TM42	Facade	Normal	Physical	70	100	20	Normal	○
TM43	Secret Power	Normal	Physical	70	100	20	Normal	—
TM44	Rest	Psychic	Status	—	—	10	Self	—
TM45	Attract	Normal	Status	—	100	15	Normal	—
TM58	Endure	Normal	Status	—	—	10	Self	—
TM69	Rock Polish	Rock	Status	—	—	20	Self	—
TM71	Stone Edge	Rock	Physical	100	80	5	Normal	—
TM76	Stealth Rock	Rock	Status	—	—	20	2 Foes	—
TM78	Captivate	Normal	Status	—	100	20	2 Foes	—
TM80	Rock Slide	Rock	Physical	75	90	10	2 Foes	—
TM82	Sleep Talk	Normal	Status	—	—	10	Self	—
TM83	Natural Gift	Normal	Physical	—	100	15	Normal	—
TM87	Swagger	Normal	Status	—	90	15	Normal	—
TM90	Substitute	Normal	Status	—	—	10	Self	—
TM91	Flash Cannon	Steel	Special	80	100	10	Normal	—
HM04	Strength	Normal	Physical	80	100	15	Normal	○
HM06	Rock Smash	Fighting	Physical	40	100	15	Normal	○

● EGG MOVES
Name	Type	Kind	Pow.	Acc.	PP	Range	DA
Headbutt	Normal	Physical	70	100	15	Normal	○
Scary Face	Normal	Status	—	90	10	Normal	—
Focus Energy	Normal	Status	—	—	30	Self	—
Double-Edge	Normal	Physical	120	100	15	Normal	○
Rock Blast	Rock	Physical	25	80	10	Normal	—
Body Slam	Normal	Physical	85	100	15	Normal	○
Screech	Normal	Status	—	85	40	Normal	—
Curse	???	Status	—	—	10	Normal/Self	—
Fissure	Ground	Physical	—	30	5	Normal	○
Counter	Fighting	Physical	—	100	20	Self	—

● LEVEL-UP MOVES

Lv.	Name	Type	Kind	Pow.	Acc.	PP	Range	DA
1	Wrap	Normal	Physical	15	85	20	Normal	○
6	Growl	Normal	Status	—	100	40	2 Foes	—
9	Astonish	Ghost	Physical	30	100	15	Normal	○
14	Confusion	Psychic	Special	50	100	25	Normal	—
17	Uproar	Normal	Special	50	100	10	1 Random	—
22	Last Resort	Normal	Physical	130	100	5	Normal	○

● MOVE MANIAC

Name	Type	Kind	Pow.	Acc.	PP	Range	DA

● BP MOVES

Name	Type	Kind	Pow.	Acc.	PP	Range	DA
Icy Wind	Ice	Special	55	95	15	2 Foes	—
Zen Headbutt	Psychic	Physical	80	90	15	Normal	○
Trick	Psychic	Status	—	100	10	Normal	—
Knock Off	Dark	Physical	20	100	20	Normal	○
Snore	Normal	Special	40	100	15	Normal	—
Helping Hand	Normal	Status	—	—	20	1 Ally	—
Last Resort	Normal	Physical	130	100	5	Normal	○
Swift	Normal	Special	60	—	20	2 Foes	—
Uproar	Normal	Special	50	100	10	1 Random	—
Gravity	Psychic	Status	—	—	5	All	—
Magic Coat	Psychic	Status	—	—	15	Self	—
Heal Bell	Normal	Status	—	—	5	All Allies	—
Rollout	Rock	Physical	30	90	20	Normal	○
Signal Beam	Bug	Special	75	100	15	Normal	—

● TM & HM MOVES

No.	Name	Type	Kind	Pow.	Acc.	PP	Range	DA
TM04	Calm Mind	Psychic	Status	—	—	20	Self	—
TM06	Toxic	Poison	Status	—	85	10	Normal	—
TM10	Hidden Power	Normal	Special	—	100	15	Normal	—
TM11	Sunny Day	Fire	Status	—	—	5	All	—
TM12	Taunt	Dark	Status	—	100	20	Normal	—
TM16	Light Screen	Psychic	Status	—	—	30	2 Allies	—
TM17	Protect	Normal	Status	—	—	10	Self	—
TM18	Rain Dance	Water	Status	—	—	5	All	—
TM20	Safeguard	Normal	Status	—	—	25	2 Allies	—
TM21	Frustration	Normal	Physical	—	100	20	Normal	○
TM27	Return	Normal	Physical	—	100	20	Normal	○
TM29	Psychic	Psychic	Special	90	100	10	Normal	—
TM30	Shadow Ball	Ghost	Special	80	100	15	Normal	—
TM32	Double Team	Normal	Status	—	—	15	Self	—
TM33	Reflect	Psychic	Status	—	—	20	2 Allies	—
TM34	Shock Wave	Electric	Special	60	—	20	Normal	—
TM41	Torment	Dark	Status	—	100	15	Normal	—
TM42	Facade	Normal	Physical	70	100	20	Normal	○
TM43	Secret Power	Normal	Physical	70	100	20	Normal	—
TM44	Rest	Psychic	Status	—	—	10	Self	—
TM45	Attract	Normal	Status	—	100	15	Normal	—
TM48	Skill Swap	Psychic	Status	—	—	10	Normal	—
TM49	Snatch	Dark	Status	—	—	10	Depends	—
TM57	Charge Beam	Electric	Special	50	90	10	Normal	—
TM58	Endure	Normal	Status	—	—	10	Self	—
TM67	Recycle	Normal	Status	—	—	10	Self	—
TM70	Flash	Normal	Status	—	100	20	Normal	—
TM73	Thunder Wave	Electric	Status	—	100	20	Normal	—
TM77	Psych Up	Normal	Status	—	—	10	Normal	—
TM78	Captivate	Normal	Status	—	100	20	2 Foes	—
TM82	Sleep Talk	Normal	Status	—	—	10	Depends	—
TM83	Natural Gift	Normal	Physical	—	100	15	Normal	—
TM85	Dream Eater	Psychic	Special	100	100	15	Normal	—
TM86	Grass Knot	Grass	Special	—	100	20	Normal	○
TM87	Swagger	Normal	Status	—	90	15	Normal	—
TM90	Substitute	Normal	Status	—	—	10	Self	—
TM92	Trick Room	Psychic	Status	—	—	5	All	—

● EGG MOVES

Name	Type	Kind	Pow.	Acc.	PP	Range	DA
Disable	Normal	Status	—	80	20	Normal	—
Curse	???	Status	—	—	10	Normal/Self	—
Hypnosis	Psychic	Status	—	60	20	Normal	—
Dream Eater	Psychic	Special	100	100	15	Normal	—
Wish	Normal	Status	—	—	10	Self	—
Future Sight	Psychic	Special	80	90	15	Normal	—
Recover	Normal	Status	—	—	10	Self	—

● No. 433 | Bell Pokémon
Chingling

Psychic

- ● HEIGHT: 0'08"
- ● WEIGHT: 1.3 lbs.
- ● ITEMS: Colbur Berry

● SIZE COMPARISON

● MALE/FEMALE HAVE SAME FORM

● ABILITIES
● Levitate

● STATS
HP	●●
ATTACK	●
DEFENSE	●●
SP. ATTACK	●●
SP. DEFENSE	●●●
SPEED	●●

● EGG GROUPS
No Egg has ever been discovered

● PERFORMANCE
SPEED ★★☆☆   STAMINA ★★★
POWER ★★☆   JUMP ★★★★☆
SKILL ★★☆

● MAIN WAYS TO OBTAIN

Pokémon HeartGold — Union Cave (Sinnoh Sound)

Pokémon SoulSilver — Union Cave (Sinnoh Sound)

Pokémon Diamond — Route 211

Pokémon Pearl — Route 211

Pokémon Platinum — Route 211

Pokémon HeartGold
It emits high-frequency cries that people can't hear. Once it starts, it can cry for an awfully long time.

Pokémon SoulSilver
It emits high-frequency cries that people can't hear. Once it starts, it can cry for an awfully long time.

● EVOLUTION

Chingling — Level up with high friendship between 8:00 P.M. and 4:00 A.M. — Chimecho

● No. 434 | Skunk Pokémon
Stunky

`Poison` `Dark`

- **HEIGHT:** 1'04"
- **WEIGHT:** 42.3 lbs.
- **ITEMS:** None

● SIZE COMPARISON

● MALE/FEMALE HAVE SAME FORM

● ABILITIES
- Stench
- Aftermath

● STATS
HP	●●
ATTACK	●●●
DEFENSE	●●
SP. ATTACK	●●
SP. DEFENSE	●●
SPEED	●●●

● EGG GROUPS
Field

● PERFORMANCE
SPEED ★★★☆☆ STAMINA ★★☆
POWER ★★☆☆☆ JUMP ★★★
SKILL ★★☆☆

● MAIN WAYS TO OBTAIN

Pokémon HeartGold	—
Pokémon SoulSilver	—
Pokémon Diamond	Route 206
Pokémon Pearl	—
Pokémon Platinum	—

Pokémon HeartGold	Pokémon SoulSilver
The foul fluid from its rear is so revolting that it can make people feel queasy up to a mile and a quarter away.	The foul fluid from its rear is so revolting that it can make people feel queasy up to a mile and a quarter away.

● EVOLUTION

 Lv. 34

Stunky → Skuntank

● LEVEL-UP MOVES

Lv.	Name	Type	Kind	Pow.	Acc.	PP	Range	DA
1	Scratch	Normal	Physical	40	100	35	Normal	○
1	Focus Energy	Normal	Status	—	—	30	Self	—
4	Poison Gas	Poison	Status	—	55	40	Normal	—
7	Screech	Normal	Status	—	85	40	Normal	—
10	Fury Swipes	Normal	Physical	18	80	15	Normal	○
14	SmokeScreen	Normal	Status	—	100	20	Normal	—
18	Feint	Normal	Physical	50	100	10	Normal	—
22	Slash	Normal	Physical	70	100	20	Normal	○
27	Toxic	Poison	Status	—	85	10	Normal	—
32	Night Slash	Dark	Physical	70	100	15	Normal	○
38	Memento	Dark	Status	—	100	10	Normal	—
44	Explosion	Normal	Physical	250	100	5	2 Foes/1 Ally	—

● MOVE MANIAC

Name	Type	Kind	Pow.	Acc.	PP	Range	DA
Headbutt	Normal	Physical	70	100	15	Normal	○

● BP MOVES

Name	Type	Kind	Pow.	Acc.	PP	Range	DA
Fury Cutter	Bug	Physical	10	95	20	Normal	○
Sucker Punch	Dark	Physical	80	100	5	Normal	○
Snore	Normal	Special	40	100	15	Normal	—
Swift	Normal	Special	60	—	20	2 Foes	—
Mud-Slap	Ground	Special	20	100	10	Normal	—

● TM & HM MOVES

No.	Name	Type	Kind	Pow.	Acc.	PP	Range	DA
TM05	Roar	Normal	Status	—	100	20	Normal	—
TM06	Toxic	Poison	Status	—	85	10	Normal	—
TM10	Hidden Power	Normal	Special	—	100	15	Normal	—
TM11	Sunny Day	Fire	Status	—	—	5	All	—
TM12	Taunt	Dark	Status	—	100	20	Normal	—
TM17	Protect	Normal	Status	—	—	10	Self	—
TM18	Rain Dance	Water	Status	—	—	5	All	—
TM21	Frustration	Normal	Physical	—	100	20	Normal	○
TM23	Iron Tail	Steel	Physical	100	75	15	Normal	○
TM27	Return	Normal	Physical	—	100	20	Normal	○
TM28	Dig	Ground	Physical	80	100	10	Normal	○
TM30	Shadow Ball	Ghost	Special	80	100	15	Normal	—
TM32	Double Team	Normal	Status	—	—	15	Self	—
TM35	Flamethrower	Fire	Special	95	100	15	Normal	—
TM36	Sludge Bomb	Poison	Special	90	100	10	Normal	—
TM38	Fire Blast	Fire	Special	120	85	5	Normal	—
TM41	Torment	Dark	Status	—	100	15	Normal	—
TM42	Facade	Normal	Physical	70	100	20	Normal	○
TM43	Secret Power	Normal	Physical	70	100	20	Normal	—
TM44	Rest	Psychic	Status	—	—	10	Self	—
TM45	Attract	Normal	Status	—	100	15	Normal	○
TM46	Thief	Dark	Physical	40	100	10	Normal	—
TM49	Snatch	Dark	Status	—	—	10	Depends	—
TM58	Endure	Normal	Status	—	—	10	Self	—
TM64	Explosion	Normal	Physical	250	100	5	2 Foes/1 Ally	—
TM65	Shadow Claw	Ghost	Physical	70	100	15	Normal	○
TM66	Payback	Dark	Physical	50	100	10	Normal	○
TM78	Captivate	Normal	Status	—	100	20	2 Foes	—
TM79	Dark Pulse	Dark	Special	80	100	15	Normal	—
TM82	Sleep Talk	Normal	Status	—	—	10	Depends	—
TM83	Natural Gift	Normal	Physical	—	100	15	Normal	—
TM87	Swagger	Normal	Status	—	90	15	Normal	—
TM90	Substitute	Normal	Status	—	—	10	Self	—
HM01	Cut	Normal	Physical	50	95	30	Normal	○
HM06	Rock Smash	Fighting	Physical	40	100	15	Normal	○

● EGG MOVES

Name	Type	Kind	Pow.	Acc.	PP	Range	DA
Pursuit	Dark	Physical	40	100	20	Normal	○
Leer	Normal	Status	—	100	30	2 Foes	—
Smog	Poison	Special	20	70	20	Normal	—
Double-Edge	Normal	Physical	120	100	15	Normal	○
Crunch	Dark	Physical	80	100	15	Normal	○
Scary Face	Normal	Status	—	90	10	Normal	—
Astonish	Ghost	Physical	30	100	15	Normal	○
Punishment	Dark	Physical	—	100	5	Normal	○
Haze	Ice	Status	—	—	30	All	—

● LEVEL-UP MOVES

Lv.	Name	Type	Kind	Pow.	Acc.	PP	Range	DA
1	Scratch	Normal	Physical	40	100	35	Normal	○
1	Focus Energy	Normal	Status	—	—	30	Self	—
1	Poison Gas	Poison	Status	—	55	40	Normal	—
4	Poison Gas	Poison	Status	—	55	40	Normal	—
7	Screech	Normal	Status	—	85	40	Normal	—
10	Fury Swipes	Normal	Physical	18	80	15	Normal	○
14	SmokeScreen	Normal	Status	—	100	20	Normal	—
18	Feint	Normal	Physical	50	100	10	Normal	—
22	Slash	Normal	Physical	70	100	20	Normal	○
27	Toxic	Poison	Status	—	85	10	Normal	—
32	Night Slash	Dark	Physical	70	100	15	Normal	○
34	Flamethrower	Fire	Special	95	100	15	Normal	—
42	Memento	Dark	Status	—	100	10	Normal	—
52	Explosion	Normal	Physical	250	100	5	2 Foes/1 Ally	—

● MOVE MANIAC

Name	Type	Kind	Pow.	Acc.	PP	Range	DA
Headbutt	Normal	Physical	70	100	15	Normal	○

● BP MOVES

Name	Type	Kind	Pow.	Acc.	PP	Range	DA
Fury Cutter	Bug	Physical	10	95	20	Normal	○
Sucker Punch	Dark	Physical	80	100	5	Normal	○
Snore	Normal	Special	40	100	15	Normal	—
Swift	Normal	Special	60	—	20	2 Foes	—
Mud-Slap	Ground	Special	20	100	10	Normal	—

● TM & HM MOVES

No.	Name	Type	Kind	Pow.	Acc.	PP	Range	DA
TM05	Roar	Normal	Status	—	100	20	Normal	—
TM06	Toxic	Poison	Status	—	85	10	Normal	—
TM10	Hidden Power	Normal	Special	—	100	15	Normal	—
TM11	Sunny Day	Fire	Status	—	—	5	All	—
TM12	Taunt	Dark	Status	—	100	20	Normal	—
TM15	Hyper Beam	Normal	Special	150	90	5	Normal	—
TM17	Protect	Normal	Status	—	—	10	Self	—
TM18	Rain Dance	Water	Status	—	—	5	All	—
TM21	Frustration	Normal	Physical	—	100	20	Normal	○
TM23	Iron Tail	Steel	Physical	100	75	15	Normal	○
TM27	Return	Normal	Physical	—	100	20	Normal	○
TM28	Dig	Ground	Physical	80	100	10	Normal	○
TM30	Shadow Ball	Ghost	Special	80	100	15	Normal	—
TM32	Double Team	Normal	Status	—	—	15	Self	—
TM35	Flamethrower	Fire	Special	95	100	15	Normal	—
TM36	Sludge Bomb	Poison	Special	90	100	10	Normal	—
TM38	Fire Blast	Fire	Special	120	85	5	Normal	—
TM41	Torment	Dark	Status	—	100	15	Normal	—
TM42	Facade	Normal	Physical	70	100	20	Normal	○
TM43	Secret Power	Normal	Physical	70	100	20	Normal	—
TM44	Rest	Psychic	Status	—	—	10	Self	—
TM45	Attract	Normal	Status	—	100	15	Normal	—
TM46	Thief	Dark	Physical	40	100	10	Normal	○
TM49	Snatch	Dark	Status	—	—	10	Depends	—
TM58	Endure	Normal	Status	—	—	10	Self	—
TM64	Explosion	Normal	Physical	250	100	5	2 Foes/1 Ally	—
TM65	Shadow Claw	Ghost	Physical	70	100	15	Normal	○
TM66	Payback	Dark	Physical	50	100	10	Normal	○
TM68	Giga Impact	Normal	Physical	150	90	5	Normal	○
TM78	Captivate	Normal	Status	—	100	20	2 Foes	—
TM79	Dark Pulse	Dark	Special	80	100	15	Normal	—
TM82	Sleep Talk	Normal	Status	—	—	10	Depends	—
TM83	Natural Gift	Normal	Physical	—	100	15	Normal	—
TM84	Poison Jab	Poison	Physical	80	100	20	Normal	○
TM87	Swagger	Normal	Status	—	90	15	Normal	—
TM90	Substitute	Normal	Status	—	—	10	Self	—
HM01	Cut	Normal	Physical	50	95	30	Normal	○
HM04	Strength	Normal	Physical	80	100	15	Normal	○
HM06	Rock Smash	Fighting	Physical	40	100	15	Normal	○

No. 435 | Skunk Pokémon
Skuntank

`Poison` `Dark`

- ● HEIGHT: 3'03"
- ● WEIGHT: 83.8 lbs.
- ● ITEMS: None

● SIZE COMPARISON

● MALE/FEMALE HAVE SAME FORM

⊘ ABILITIES
- ● Stench
- ● Aftermath

⊘ STATS
HP	●●●●
ATTACK	●●●●
DEFENSE	●●●
SP. ATTACK	●●●
SP. DEFENSE	●●
SPEED	●●●●

⊘ EGG GROUPS
Field

⊘ PERFORMANCE

SPEED ★★☆　　　STAMINA ★★★☆
POWER ★★★★☆　JUMP ★★
SKILL ★★☆☆

● MAIN WAYS TO OBTAIN

Pokémon HeartGold	—
Pokémon SoulSilver	—
Pokémon Diamond	Route 221
Pokémon Pearl	—
Pokémon Platinum	—

Pokémon HeartGold

It attacks by spraying a repugnant fluid from its tail, but the stench dulls after a few squirts.

Pokémon SoulSilver

It attacks by spraying a repugnant fluid from its tail, but the stench dulls after a few squirts.

⊘ EVOLUTION

Stunky　　　Lv. 34　　　Skuntank

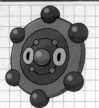

No. 436 | Bronze Pokémon
Bronzor

`Steel` `Psychic`

● **LEVEL-UP MOVES**

Lv.	Name	Type	Kind	Pow.	Acc.	PP	Range	DA
1	Tackle	Normal	Physical	35	95	35	Normal	○
10	Protect	Normal	Status	—	—	10	Self	—
15	Bug Bite	Bug	Physical	60	100	20	Normal	○
20	Hidden Power	Normal	Special	—	100	15	Normal	—
23	Confusion	Psychic	Special	50	100	25	Normal	—
26	Rock Blast	Rock	Physical	25	80	10	Normal	—
29	Harden	Normal	Status	—	—	30	Self	—
32	Psybeam	Psychic	Special	65	100	10	Normal	—
35	Captivate	Normal	Status	—	100	20	2 Foes	—
38	Flail	Normal	Physical	—	100	15	Normal	○
41	Attract	Normal	Status	—	100	15	Normal	—
44	Psychic	Psychic	Special	90	100	10	Normal	—
47	Fissure	Ground	Physical	—	30	5	Normal	—

● **MOVE MANIAC**

Name	Type	Kind	Pow.	Acc.	PP	Range	DA

● **BP MOVES**

Name	Type	Kind	Pow.	Acc.	PP	Range	DA
Sucker Punch	Dark	Physical	80	100	5	Normal	○
Bug Bite	Bug	Physical	60	100	20	Normal	○
Snore	Normal	Special	40	100	15	Normal	—
Uproar	Normal	Special	50	100	10	1 Random	—
String Shot	Bug	Status	—	95	40	2 Foes	—
Mud-Slap	Ground	Special	20	100	10	Normal	—
Rollout	Rock	Physical	30	90	20	Normal	○
Endeavor	Normal	Physical	—	100	5	Normal	○
Signal Beam	Bug	Special	75	100	15	Normal	—
Earth Power	Ground	Special	90	100	10	Normal	—

● HEIGHT: 1'08"
● WEIGHT: 133.4 lbs.
● ITEMS: Metal Coat

● SIZE COMPARISON

● GENDER UNKNOWN

● **ABILITIES**
- Levitate
- Heatproof

● **STATS**
- HP ●●
- ATTACK ●
- DEFENSE ●●●
- SP. ATTACK ●
- SP. DEFENSE ●●●
- SPEED ●

● **EGG GROUPS**

Mineral

● **PERFORMANCE**

SPEED ★★★☆   STAMINA ★★★★☆
POWER ★★☆☆   JUMP ★★★☆
SKILL ★

● **MAIN WAYS TO OBTAIN**

Pokémon HeartGold   Union Cave [Sinnoh Sound]

Pokémon SoulSilver   Union Cave [Sinnoh Sound]

Pokémon Diamond   Wayward Cave

Pokémon Pearl   Wayward Cave

Pokémon Platinum   Wayward Cave

Pokémon HeartGold

Ancient people believed that the pattern on BRONZOR's back contained a mysterious power.

Pokémon SoulSilver

Ancient people believed that the pattern on BRONZOR's back contained a mysterious power.

● **TM & HM MOVES**

No.	Name	Type	Kind	Pow.	Acc.	PP	Range	DA
TM06	Toxic	Poison	Status	—	85	10	Normal	—
TM10	Hidden Power	Normal	Special	—	100	15	Normal	—
TM11	Sunny Day	Fire	Status	—	—	5	All	—
TM15	Hyper Beam	Normal	Special	150	90	5	Normal	—
TM17	Protect	Normal	Status	—	—	10	Self	—
TM18	Rain Dance	Water	Status	—	—	5	All	—
TM20	Safeguard	Normal	Status	—	—	25	2 Allies	—
TM21	Frustration	Normal	Physical	—	100	20	Normal	○
TM26	Earthquake	Ground	Physical	100	100	10	2 Foes/1 Ally	—
TM27	Return	Normal	Physical	—	100	20	Normal	○
TM28	Dig	Ground	Physical	80	100	10	Normal	○
TM29	Psychic	Psychic	Special	90	100	10	Normal	—
TM30	Shadow Ball	Ghost	Special	80	100	15	Normal	—
TM32	Double Team	Normal	Status	—	—	15	Self	—
TM37	Sandstorm	Rock	Status	—	—	10	All	—
TM39	Rock Tomb	Rock	Physical	50	80	10	Normal	—
TM42	Facade	Normal	Physical	70	100	20	Normal	○
TM43	Secret Power	Normal	Physical	70	100	20	Normal	—
TM44	Rest	Psychic	Status	—	—	10	Self	—
TM45	Attract	Normal	Status	—	100	15	Normal	—
TM46	Thief	Dark	Physical	40	100	10	Normal	○
TM48	Skill Swap	Psychic	Status	—	—	10	Normal	—
TM58	Endure	Normal	Status	—	—	10	Self	—
TM68	Giga Impact	Normal	Physical	150	90	5	Normal	○
TM70	Flash	Normal	Status	—	100	20	Normal	—
TM77	Psych Up	Normal	Status	—	—	10	Normal	—
TM78	Captivate	Normal	Status	—	100	20	2 Foes	—
TM82	Sleep Talk	Normal	Status	—	—	10	Depends	—
TM83	Natural Gift	Normal	Physical	—	100	15	Normal	—
TM85	Dream Eater	Psychic	Special	100	100	15	Normal	—
TM87	Swagger	Normal	Status	—	90	15	Normal	—
TM90	Substitute	Normal	Status	—	—	10	Self	—

● **EVOLUTION**

Bronzor   Lv. 33   Bronzong

● LEVEL-UP MOVES

Lv.	Name	Type	Kind	Pow.	Acc.	PP	Range	DA
1	Sunny Day	Fire	Status	—	—	5	All	—
1	Rain Dance	Water	Status	—	—	5	All	—
1	Tackle	Normal	Physical	35	95	35	Normal	○
1	Confusion	Psychic	Special	50	100	25	Normal	—
1	Hypnosis	Psychic	Status	—	60	20	Normal	—
1	Imprison	Psychic	Status	—	—	10	Self	—
7	Hypnosis	Psychic	Status	—	60	20	Normal	—
12	Imprison	Psychic	Status	—	—	10	Self	—
14	Confuse Ray	Ghost	Status	—	100	10	Normal	—
19	Extrasensory	Psychic	Special	80	100	30	Normal	—
26	Iron Defense	Steel	Status	—	—	15	Self	—
30	Safeguard	Normal	Status	—	—	25	2 Allies	—
33	Block	Normal	Status	—	—	5	Normal	—
38	Gyro Ball	Steel	Physical	—	100	5	Normal	○
43	Future Sight	Psychic	Special	80	90	15	Normal	—
50	Faint Attack	Dark	Physical	60	—	20	Normal	○
61	Payback	Dark	Physical	50	100	10	Normal	○
67	Heal Block	Psychic	Status	—	100	15	2 Foes	—

● MOVE MANIAC

Name	Type	Kind	Pow.	Acc.	PP	Range	DA

● BP MOVES

Name	Type	Kind	Pow.	Acc.	PP	Range	DA
Zen Headbutt	Psychic	Physical	80	90	15	Normal	○
Trick	Psychic	Status	—	100	10	Normal	—
Snore	Normal	Special	40	100	15	Normal	—
Gravity	Psychic	Status	—	—	5	All	—
Block	Normal	Status	—	—	5	Normal	—
Rollout	Rock	Physical	30	90	20	Normal	○
Iron Head	Steel	Physical	80	100	15	Normal	—
AncientPower	Rock	Special	60	100	5	Normal	—
Signal Beam	Bug	Special	75	100	15	Normal	—

● TM & HM MOVES

No.	Name	Type	Kind	Pow.	Acc.	PP	Range	DA
TM04	Calm Mind	Psychic	Status	—	—	20	Self	—
TM06	Toxic	Poison	Status	—	85	10	Normal	—
TM10	Hidden Power	Normal	Special	—	100	15	Normal	—
TM11	Sunny Day	Fire	Status	—	—	5	All	—
TM15	Hyper Beam	Normal	Special	150	90	5	Normal	—
TM16	Light Screen	Psychic	Status	—	—	30	2 Allies	—
TM17	Protect	Normal	Status	—	—	10	Self	—
TM18	Rain Dance	Water	Status	—	—	5	All	—
TM20	Safeguard	Normal	Status	—	—	25	2 Allies	—
TM21	Frustration	Normal	Physical	—	100	20	Normal	○
TM22	SolarBeam	Grass	Special	120	100	10	Normal	—
TM26	Earthquake	Ground	Physical	100	100	10	2 Foes/1 Ally	○
TM27	Return	Normal	Physical	—	100	20	Normal	○
TM29	Psychic	Psychic	Special	90	100	10	Normal	—
TM30	Shadow Ball	Ghost	Special	80	100	15	Normal	—
TM32	Double Team	Normal	Status	—	—	15	Self	—
TM33	Reflect	Psychic	Status	—	—	20	2 Allies	—
TM37	Sandstorm	Rock	Status	—	—	10	All	—
TM39	Rock Tomb	Rock	Physical	50	80	10	Normal	—
TM42	Facade	Normal	Physical	70	100	20	Normal	○
TM43	Secret Power	Normal	Physical	70	100	20	Normal	—
TM44	Rest	Psychic	Status	—	—	10	Self	—
TM48	Skill Swap	Psychic	Status	—	—	10	Normal	—
TM57	Charge Beam	Electric	Special	50	90	10	Normal	—
TM58	Endure	Normal	Status	—	—	10	Self	—
TM64	Explosion	Normal	Physical	250	100	5	2 Foes/1 Ally	—
TM66	Payback	Dark	Physical	50	100	10	Normal	○
TM67	Recycle	Normal	Status	—	—	10	Self	—
TM68	Giga Impact	Normal	Physical	150	90	5	Normal	○
TM69	Rock Polish	Rock	Status	—	—	20	Self	—
TM70	Flash	Normal	Status	—	100	20	Normal	—
TM74	Gyro Ball	Steel	Physical	—	100	5	Normal	○
TM76	Stealth Rock	Rock	Status	—	—	20	2 Foes	—
TM77	Psych Up	Normal	Status	—	—	10	Self	—
TM80	Rock Slide	Rock	Physical	75	90	10	2 Foes	—
TM82	Sleep Talk	Normal	Status	—	—	10	Self	—
TM83	Natural Gift	Normal	Physical	—	100	15	Normal	—
TM85	Dream Eater	Psychic	Special	100	100	15	Normal	—
TM86	Grass Knot	Grass	Special	—	100	20	Normal	○
TM87	Swagger	Normal	Status	—	90	15	Normal	—
TM90	Substitute	Normal	Status	—	—	10	Self	—
TM91	Flash Cannon	Steel	Special	80	100	10	Normal	—
TM92	Trick Room	Psychic	Status	—	—	5	All	—
HM04	Strength	Normal	Physical	80	100	15	Normal	○
HM06	Rock Smash	Fighting	Physical	40	100	15	Normal	○

Bronzong

Steel   Psychic

- **HEIGHT:** 4'03"
- **WEIGHT:** 412.3 lbs.
- **ITEMS:** Metal Coat

● SIZE COMPARISON

● GENDER UNKNOWN

● ABILITIES
- Levitate
- Heatproof

● EGG GROUPS
Mineral

● STATS
HP	●●
ATTACK	●●●●
DEFENSE	●●●●●
SP. ATTACK	●●●●
SP. DEFENSE	●●●●●
SPEED	●●

● PERFORMANCE
SPEED ★
POWER ★★★☆☆
SKILL ★★★
STAMINA ★★★★☆
JUMP ★★★☆☆

● MAIN WAYS TO OBTAIN

Pokémon HeartGold	Safari Zone (Forest Area: if Rock and Forest objects are placed, may appear in tall grass)
Pokémon SoulSilver	Safari Zone (Forest Area: if Rock and Forest objects are placed, may appear in tall grass)
Pokémon Diamond	Mt. Coronet 2F
Pokémon Pearl	Mt. Coronet 2F
Pokémon Platinum	Mt. Coronet 2F

Pokémon HeartGold	Pokémon SoulSilver
Ancient people believed that petitioning BRONZONG for rain was the way to make crops grow.	Ancient people believed that petitioning BRONZONG for rain was the way to make crops grow.

● EVOLUTION

Bronzor   →Lv. 33→   Bronzong

No. 438 | Bonsai Pokémon
Bonsly

Rock

● HEIGHT: 1'08"
● WEIGHT: 33,1 lbs.
● ITEMS: None

● SIZE COMPARISON

● MALE/FEMALE HAVE SAME FORM

◎ ABILITIES
● Sturdy
● Rock Head

◎ STATS
HP ●●
ATTACK ●●●
DEFENSE ●●●●
SP. ATTACK ●
SP. DEFENSE ●
SPEED ●

◎ EGG GROUPS
No Egg has ever been discovered

◎ PERFORMANCE
SPEED ★★★☆   STAMINA ★★★★
POWER ★★★   JUMP ★★☆
SKILL ★☆☆

● MAIN WAYS TO OBTAIN

Pokémon HeartGold	Big Forest Pokéwalker Route
Pokémon SoulSilver	Big Forest Pokéwalker Route
Pokémon Diamond	Trophy Garden at the Pokémon Mansion on Route 212 (after obtaining the National Pokédex, talk to Mr. Backlot)
Pokémon Pearl	Route 209
Pokémon Platinum	Trophy Garden at the Pokémon Mansion on Route 212 (after obtaining the National Pokédex, talk to Mr. Backlot)

| Pokémon HeartGold | Pokémon SoulSilver |
| In order to adjust the level of fluids in its body, it exudes water from its eyes. This makes it appear to be crying. | In order to adjust the level of fluids in its body, it exudes water from its eyes. This makes it appear to be crying. |

◎ EVOLUTION

Bonsly — Level it up to Lv. 17 and teach it Mimic. Or, level it up once it knows Mimic. → Sudowoodo

● LEVEL-UP MOVES

Lv.	Name	Type	Kind	Pow.	Acc.	PP	Range	DA
1	Fake Tears	Dark	Status	—	100	20	Normal	—
1	Copycat	Normal	Status	—	—	20	Depends	—
6	Flail	Normal	Physical	—	100	15	Normal	○
9	Low Kick	Fighting	Physical	—	100	20	Normal	○
14	Rock Throw	Rock	Physical	50	90	15	Normal	—
17	Mimic	Normal	Status	—	—	10	Normal	—
22	Block	Normal	Status	—	—	5	Normal	—
25	Faint Attack	Dark	Physical	60	—	20	Normal	○
30	Rock Tomb	Rock	Physical	50	80	10	Normal	—
33	Rock Slide	Rock	Physical	75	90	10	2 Foes	—
38	Slam	Normal	Physical	80	75	20	Normal	○
41	Sucker Punch	Dark	Physical	80	100	5	Normal	○
46	Double-Edge	Normal	Physical	120	100	15	Normal	○

● MOVE MANIAC

Name	Type	Kind	Pow.	Acc.	PP	Range	DA
Headbutt	Normal	Physical	70	100	15	Normal	○

● BP MOVES

Name	Type	Kind	Pow.	Acc.	PP	Range	DA
Sucker Punch	Dark	Physical	80	100	5	Normal	○
Snore	Normal	Special	40	100	15	Normal	—
Helping Hand	Normal	Status	—	—	20	1 Ally	—
Uproar	Normal	Special	50	100	10	1 Random	—
Role Play	Psychic	Status	—	—	10	Normal	—
Block	Normal	Status	—	—	5	Normal	—
Rollout	Rock	Physical	30	90	20	Normal	○
Earth Power	Ground	Special	90	100	10	Normal	—
Low Kick	Fighting	Physical	—	100	20	Normal	○

● TM & HM MOVES

No.	Name	Type	Kind	Pow.	Acc.	PP	Range	DA
TM04	Calm Mind	Psychic	Status	—	—	20	Self	—
TM06	Toxic	Poison	Status	—	85	10	Normal	—
TM10	Hidden Power	Normal	Special	—	100	15	Normal	—
TM11	Sunny Day	Fire	Status	—	—	5	All	—
TM17	Protect	Normal	Status	—	—	10	Self	—
TM21	Frustration	Normal	Physical	—	100	20	Normal	○
TM27	Return	Normal	Physical	—	100	20	Normal	○
TM28	Dig	Ground	Physical	80	100	10	Normal	○
TM31	Brick Break	Fighting	Physical	75	100	15	Normal	○
TM32	Double Team	Normal	Status	—	—	15	Self	—
TM37	Sandstorm	Rock	Status	—	—	10	All	—
TM39	Rock Tomb	Rock	Physical	50	80	10	Normal	—
TM42	Facade	Normal	Physical	70	100	20	Normal	○
TM43	Secret Power	Normal	Physical	70	100	20	Normal	—
TM44	Rest	Psychic	Status	—	—	10	Self	—
TM45	Attract	Normal	Status	—	100	15	Normal	—
TM46	Thief	Dark	Physical	40	100	10	Normal	○
TM58	Endure	Normal	Status	—	—	10	Self	—
TM64	Explosion	Normal	Physical	250	100	5	2 Foes/1 Ally	—
TM69	Rock Polish	Rock	Status	—	—	20	Self	—
TM76	Stealth Rock	Rock	Status	—	—	20	2 Foes	—
TM77	Psych Up	Normal	Status	—	—	10	Normal	—
TM78	Captivate	Normal	Status	—	100	20	2 Foes	—
TM80	Rock Slide	Rock	Physical	75	90	10	2 Foes	—
TM82	Sleep Talk	Normal	Status	—	—	10	Self	—
TM83	Natural Gift	Normal	Physical	—	100	15	Normal	—
TM87	Swagger	Normal	Status	—	90	15	Normal	—
TM90	Substitute	Normal	Status	—	—	10	Self	—

● EGG MOVES

Name	Type	Kind	Pow.	Acc.	PP	Range	DA
Selfdestruct	Normal	Physical	200	100	5	2 Foes/1 Ally	—
Headbutt	Normal	Physical	70	100	15	Normal	○
Harden	Normal	Status	—	—	30	Self	—
Defense Curl	Normal	Status	—	—	40	Self	—
Rollout	Rock	Physical	30	90	20	Normal	○
Sand Tomb	Ground	Physical	15	70	15	Normal	—

● LEVEL-UP MOVES

Lv.	Name	Type	Kind	Pow.	Acc.	PP	Range	DA
1	Tickle	Normal	Status	—	100	20	Normal	—
1	Barrier	Psychic	Status	—	—	30	Self	—
1	Confusion	Psychic	Special	50	100	25	Normal	—
4	Copycat	Normal	Status	—	—	20	Depends	—
8	Meditate	Psychic	Status	—	—	40	Self	—
11	Encore	Normal	Status	—	100	5	Normal	—
15	DoubleSlap	Normal	Physical	15	85	10	Normal	○
18	Mimic	Normal	Status	—	—	10	Normal	—
22	Light Screen	Psychic	Status	—	—	30	2 Allies	—
22	Reflect	Psychic	Status	—	—	20	2 Allies	—
25	Psybeam	Psychic	Special	65	100	20	Normal	—
29	Substitute	Normal	Status	—	—	10	Self	—
32	Recycle	Normal	Status	—	—	10	Self	—
36	Trick	Psychic	Status	—	100	10	Normal	—
39	Psychic	Psychic	Special	90	100	10	Normal	—
43	Role Play	Psychic	Status	—	—	10	Normal	—
46	Baton Pass	Normal	Status	—	—	40	Self	—
50	Safeguard	Normal	Status	—	—	25	2 Allies	—

● MOVE MANIAC

Name	Type	Kind	Pow.	Acc.	PP	Range	DA
Headbutt	Normal	Physical	70	100	15	Normal	○

● BP MOVES

Name	Type	Kind	Pow.	Acc.	PP	Range	DA
Trick	Psychic	Status	—	—	10	Normal	—
Snore	Normal	Special	40	100	15	Normal	—
Helping Hand	Normal	Status	—	—	20	1 Ally	—
Uproar	Normal	Special	50	100	10	1 Random	—
Magic Coat	Psychic	Status	—	—	15	Self	—
Role Play	Psychic	Status	—	—	10	Normal	—
Mud-Slap	Ground	Special	20	100	10	Normal	—
Signal Beam	Bug	Special	75	100	15	Normal	—

● TM & HM MOVES

No.	Name	Type	Kind	Pow.	Acc.	PP	Range	DA
TM01	Focus Punch	Fighting	Physical	150	100	20	Normal	○
TM04	Calm Mind	Psychic	Status	—	—	20	Self	—
TM06	Toxic	Poison	Status	—	85	10	Normal	—
TM10	Hidden Power	Normal	Special	—	100	15	Normal	—
TM11	Sunny Day	Fire	Status	—	—	5	All	—
TM12	Taunt	Dark	Status	—	100	20	Normal	—
TM16	Light Screen	Psychic	Status	—	—	30	2 Allies	—
TM17	Protect	Normal	Status	—	—	10	Self	—
TM18	Rain Dance	Water	Status	—	—	5	All	—
TM20	Safeguard	Normal	Status	—	—	25	2 Allies	—
TM21	Frustration	Normal	Physical	—	100	20	Normal	○
TM22	SolarBeam	Grass	Special	120	100	10	Normal	—
TM24	Thunderbolt	Electric	Special	95	100	15	Normal	—
TM25	Thunder	Electric	Special	120	70	10	Normal	—
TM27	Return	Normal	Physical	—	100	20	Normal	○
TM29	Psychic	Psychic	Special	90	100	10	Normal	—
TM30	Shadow Ball	Ghost	Special	80	100	15	Normal	—
TM31	Brick Break	Fighting	Physical	75	100	15	Normal	○
TM32	Double Team	Normal	Status	—	—	15	Self	—
TM33	Reflect	Psychic	Status	—	—	20	2 Allies	—
TM34	Shock Wave	Electric	Special	60	—	20	Normal	—
TM41	Torment	Dark	Status	—	100	15	Normal	—
TM42	Facade	Normal	Physical	70	100	20	Normal	○
TM43	Secret Power	Normal	Physical	70	100	20	Normal	○
TM44	Rest	Psychic	Status	—	—	10	Self	—
TM45	Attract	Normal	Status	—	100	15	Normal	—
TM46	Thief	Dark	Physical	40	100	10	Normal	○
TM48	Skill Swap	Psychic	Status	—	—	10	Normal	—
TM49	Snatch	Dark	Status	—	—	10	Depends	—
TM56	Fling	Dark	Physical	—	100	10	Normal	—
TM57	Charge Beam	Electric	Special	50	90	10	Normal	—
TM58	Endure	Normal	Status	—	—	10	Self	—
TM60	Drain Punch	Fighting	Physical	60	100	5	Normal	○
TM67	Recycle	Normal	Status	—	—	10	Self	—
TM70	Flash	Normal	Status	—	100	20	Normal	—
TM73	Thunder Wave	Electric	Status	—	100	20	Normal	—
TM77	Psych Up	Normal	Status	—	—	10	Normal	—
TM78	Captivate	Normal	Status	—	100	20	2 Foes	—
TM82	Sleep Talk	Normal	Status	—	—	10	Depends	—
TM83	Natural Gift	Normal	Physical	—	100	15	Normal	—
TM85	Dream Eater	Psychic	Special	100	100	15	Normal	—
TM86	Grass Knot	Grass	Special	—	100	20	Normal	○
TM87	Swagger	Normal	Status	—	90	15	Normal	—
TM90	Substitute	Normal	Status	—	—	10	Self	—
TM92	Trick Room	Psychic	Status	—	—	5	All	—

● EGG MOVES

Name	Type	Kind	Pow.	Acc.	PP	Range	DA
Future Sight	Psychic	Special	80	90	15	Normal	—
Hypnosis	Psychic	Status	—	60	10	Normal	—
Mimic	Normal	Status	—	—	10	Normal	—
Psych Up	Normal	Status	—	—	10	Normal	—
Fake Out	Normal	Physical	40	100	10	Normal	○
Trick	Psychic	Status	—	100	10	Normal	—
Confuse Ray	Ghost	Status	—	100	10	Normal	—
Wake-Up Slap	Fighting	Physical	60	100	10	Normal	○
Teeter Dance	Normal	Status	—	100	20	2 Foes/1 Ally	—
Healing Wish	Psychic	Status	—	—	10	Self	—
Charm	Normal	Status	—	100	20	Normal	—
Nasty Plot	Dark	Status	—	—	20	Self	—

◎ No. 439 | Mime Pokémon
Mime Jr.

Psychic

● HEIGHT: 2'00"
● WEIGHT: 28.7 lbs.
● ITEMS: None

● SIZE COMPARISON

● MALE/FEMALE HAVE SAME FORM

◎ ABILITIES
- Soundproof
- Filter

◎ STATS
HP ●
ATTACK ●
DEFENSE ●●
SP. ATTACK ●●●
SP. DEFENSE ●●●●
SPEED ●●●

◎ EGG GROUPS
No Egg has ever been discovered

◎ PERFORMANCE

SPEED ★★★★☆ STAMINA ★☆☆
POWER ★☆☆ JUMP ★★★
SKILL ★★★☆☆

● MAIN WAYS TO OBTAIN

Pokémon HeartGold	Sinnoh Field Pokéwalker Route
Pokémon SoulSilver	Sinnoh Field Pokéwalker Route
Pokémon Diamond	Route 209
Pokémon Pearl	Trophy Garden at the Pokémon Mansion on Route 212 (after obtaining the National Pokédex, talk to Mr. Backlot)
Pokémon Platinum	Trophy Garden at the Pokémon Mansion on Route 212 (after obtaining the National Pokédex, talk to Mr. Backlot)

Pokémon HeartGold

In an attempt to confuse its enemy, it mimics the enemy's movements. Then it wastes no time in making itself scarce!

Pokémon SoulSilver

In an attempt to confuse its enemy, it mimics the enemy's movements. Then it wastes no time in making itself scarce!

◎ EVOLUTION

Mime Jr.

Mr. Mime

Level it up to Lv. 18 and teach it Mimic. Or, level it up once it knows Mimic.

No. 440 | Playhouse Pokémon
Happiny

`Normal`

- **HEIGHT:** 2'00"
- **WEIGHT:** 53.8 lbs.
- **ITEMS:** None

● **SIZE COMPARISON**

● **FEMALE FORM**

● **ABILITIES**
- Natural Cure
- Serene Grace

● **STATS**
- HP ●●●●
- ATTACK ●
- DEFENSE ●
- SP. ATTACK ●
- SP. DEFENSE ●●
- SPEED ●

● **EGG GROUPS**

No Egg has ever been discovered

● **PERFORMANCE**

SPEED ★★★☆	STAMINA ★★★☆
POWER ★☆☆	JUMP ★★☆
SKILL ★★☆☆	

● **MAIN WAYS TO OBTAIN**

Pokémon HeartGold	Have Chansey or Blissey hold the Luck Incense and leave it at the Pokémon Day Care, then find its Egg and hatch it
Pokémon SoulSilver	Have Chansey or Blissey hold the Luck Incense and leave it at the Pokémon Day Care, then find its Egg and hatch it
Pokémon Diamond	Trophy Garden at the Pokémon Mansion on Route 212 (after obtaining the National Pokédex, talk to Mr. Backlot)
Pokémon Pearl	Trophy Garden at the Pokémon Mansion on Route 212 (after obtaining the National Pokédex, talk to Mr. Backlot)
Pokémon Platinum	Trophy Garden at the Pokémon Mansion on Route 212 (after obtaining the National Pokédex, talk to Mr. Backlot)

Pokémon HeartGold	Pokémon SoulSilver
It carefully carries a round, white rock that it thinks is an egg. It's bothered by how curly its hair looks.	It carefully carries a round, white rock that it thinks is an egg. It's bothered by how curly its hair looks.

● **EVOLUTION**

Happiny — Have it hold Oval Stone and then level up between 4:00 A.M. and 8:00 P.M. → Chansey — Level up with high friendship → Blissey

● **LEVEL-UP MOVES**

Lv.	Name	Type	Kind	Pow.	Acc.	PP	Range	DA
1	Pound	Normal	Physical	40	100	35	Normal	○
1	Charm	Normal	Status	—	100	20	Normal	—
5	Copycat	Normal	Status	—	—	20	Depends	—
9	Refresh	Normal	Status	—	—	20	Self	—
12	Sweet Kiss	Normal	Status	—	75	10	Normal	—

● **MOVE MANIAC**

Name	Type	Kind	Pow.	Acc.	PP	Range	DA
Headbutt	Normal	Physical	70	100	15	Normal	○

● **BP MOVES**

Name	Type	Kind	Pow.	Acc.	PP	Range	DA
Icy Wind	Ice	Special	55	95	15	2 Foes	—
Zen Headbutt	Psychic	Physical	80	90	15	Normal	○
Snore	Normal	Special	40	100	15	Normal	—
Helping Hand	Normal	Status	—	—	20	1 Ally	—
Last Resort	Normal	Physical	130	100	5	Normal	○
Uproar	Normal	Special	50	100	10	1 Random	—
Gravity	Psychic	Status	—	—	5	All	—
Heal Bell	Normal	Status	—	—	5	All Allies	—
Mud-Slap	Ground	Special	20	100	10	Normal	—
Rollout	Rock	Physical	30	90	20	Normal	○
Endeavor	Normal	Physical	—	100	5	Normal	○

● **TM & HM MOVES**

No.	Name	Type	Kind	Pow.	Acc.	PP	Range	DA
TM03	Water Pulse	Water	Special	60	100	20	Normal	—
TM06	Toxic	Poison	Status	—	85	10	Normal	—
TM07	Hail	Ice	Status	—	—	10	All	—
TM10	Hidden Power	Normal	Special	—	100	15	Normal	—
TM11	Sunny Day	Fire	Status	—	—	5	All	—
TM16	Light Screen	Psychic	Status	—	—	30	2 Allies	—
TM17	Protect	Normal	Status	—	—	10	Self	—
TM18	Rain Dance	Water	Status	—	—	5	All	—
TM20	Safeguard	Normal	Status	—	—	25	2 Allies	—
TM21	Frustration	Normal	Physical	—	100	20	Normal	○
TM22	SolarBeam	Grass	Special	120	100	10	Normal	—
TM27	Return	Normal	Physical	—	100	20	Normal	○
TM29	Psychic	Psychic	Special	90	100	10	Normal	—
TM30	Shadow Ball	Ghost	Special	80	100	15	Normal	—
TM32	Double Team	Normal	Status	—	—	15	Self	—
TM34	Shock Wave	Electric	Special	60	—	20	Normal	—
TM35	Flamethrower	Fire	Special	95	100	15	Normal	—
TM38	Fire Blast	Fire	Special	120	85	5	Normal	—
TM42	Facade	Normal	Physical	70	100	20	Normal	○
TM43	Secret Power	Normal	Physical	70	100	20	Normal	○
TM44	Rest	Psychic	Status	—	—	10	Self	—
TM45	Attract	Normal	Status	—	100	15	Normal	—
TM56	Fling	Dark	Physical	—	100	10	Normal	—
TM58	Endure	Normal	Status	—	—	10	Self	—
TM60	Drain Punch	Fighting	Physical	60	100	5	Normal	○
TM67	Recycle	Normal	Status	—	—	10	Self	—
TM70	Flash	Normal	Status	—	100	20	Normal	—
TM73	Thunder Wave	Electric	Status	—	100	20	Normal	—
TM77	Psych Up	Normal	Status	—	—	10	Normal	—
TM78	Captivate	Normal	Status	—	100	20	2 Foes	—
TM82	Sleep Talk	Normal	Status	—	—	10	Self	—
TM83	Natural Gift	Normal	Physical	—	100	15	Normal	—
TM85	Dream Eater	Psychic	Special	100	100	15	Normal	—
TM86	Grass Knot	Grass	Special	—	100	20	Normal	○
TM87	Swagger	Normal	Status	—	90	15	Normal	—
TM90	Substitute	Normal	Status	—	—	10	Self	—

● **EGG MOVES**

Name	Type	Kind	Pow.	Acc.	PP	Range	DA
Present	Normal	Physical	—	90	15	Normal	—
Metronome	Normal	Status	—	—	10	Depends	—
Heal Bell	Normal	Status	—	—	5	All Allies	—
Aromatherapy	Grass	Status	—	—	5	All Allies	—
Substitute	Normal	Status	—	—	10	Self	—
Counter	Fighting	Physical	—	100	20	Self	○
Helping Hand	Normal	Status	—	—	20	1 Ally	—
Gravity	Psychic	Status	—	—	5	All	—
Last Resort	Normal	Physical	130	100	5	Normal	○
Mud Bomb	Ground	Special	65	85	10	Normal	—

● LEVEL-UP MOVES

Lv.	Name	Type	Kind	Pow.	Acc.	PP	Range	DA
1	Peck	Flying	Physical	35	100	35	Normal	○
5	Growl	Normal	Status	—	100	40	2 Foes	—
9	Mirror Move	Flying	Status	—	—	20	Depends	—
13	Sing	Normal	Status	—	55	15	Normal	—
17	Fury Attack	Normal	Physical	15	85	20	Normal	○
21	Chatter	Flying	Special	60	100	20	Normal	—
25	Taunt	Dark	Status	—	100	20	Normal	—
29	Mimic	Normal	Status	—	—	10	Normal	—
33	Roost	Flying	Status	—	—	10	Self	—
37	Uproar	Normal	Special	50	100	10	1 Random	—
41	FeatherDance	Flying	Status	—	100	15	Normal	—
45	Hyper Voice	Normal	Special	90	100	10	2 Foes	—

● MOVE MANIAC

Name	Type	Kind	Pow.	Acc.	PP	Range	DA

● BP MOVES

Name	Type	Kind	Pow.	Acc.	PP	Range	DA
Ominous Wind	Ghost	Special	60	100	5	Normal	—
Air Cutter	Flying	Special	55	95	25	2 Foes	—
Snore	Normal	Special	40	100	15	Normal	—
Swift	Normal	Special	60	—	20	2 Foes	—
Uproar	Normal	Special	50	100	10	1 Random	—
Tailwind	Flying	Status	—	—	30	2 Allies	—
Role Play	Psychic	Status	—	—	10	Normal	—
Mud-Slap	Ground	Special	20	100	10	Normal	—
Twister	Dragon	Special	40	100	20	2 Foes	—
Heat Wave	Fire	Special	100	90	10	2 Foes	—
Sky Attack	Flying	Physical	140	90	5	Normal	—

● TM & HM MOVES

No.	Name	Type	Kind	Pow.	Acc.	PP	Range	DA
TM06	Toxic	Poison	Status	—	85	10	Normal	—
TM10	Hidden Power	Normal	Special	—	100	15	Normal	—
TM11	Sunny Day	Fire	Status	—	—	5	All	—
TM12	Taunt	Dark	Status	—	100	20	Normal	—
TM17	Protect	Normal	Status	—	—	10	Self	—
TM18	Rain Dance	Water	Status	—	—	5	All	—
TM21	Frustration	Normal	Physical	—	100	20	Normal	○
TM27	Return	Normal	Physical	—	100	20	Normal	○
TM32	Double Team	Normal	Status	—	—	15	Self	—
TM40	Aerial Ace	Flying	Physical	60	—	20	Normal	○
TM41	Torment	Dark	Status	—	100	15	Normal	—
TM42	Facade	Normal	Physical	70	100	20	Normal	○
TM43	Secret Power	Normal	Physical	70	100	20	Normal	○
TM44	Rest	Psychic	Status	—	—	10	Self	—
TM45	Attract	Normal	Status	—	100	15	Normal	—
TM46	Thief	Dark	Physical	40	100	10	Normal	○
TM47	Steel Wing	Steel	Physical	70	90	25	Normal	○
TM51	Roost	Flying	Status	—	—	10	Self	—
TM58	Endure	Normal	Status	—	—	10	Self	—
TM78	Captivate	Normal	Status	—	100	20	2 Foes	—
TM82	Sleep Talk	Normal	Status	—	—	10	Self	—
TM83	Natural Gift	Normal	Physical	—	100	15	Normal	—
TM87	Swagger	Normal	Status	—	90	15	Normal	—
TM88	Pluck	Flying	Physical	60	100	20	Normal	○
TM89	U-turn	Bug	Physical	70	100	20	Normal	○
TM90	Substitute	Normal	Status	—	—	10	Self	—
HM02	Fly	Flying	Physical	90	95	15	Normal	○

● EGG MOVES

Name	Type	Kind	Pow.	Acc.	PP	Range	DA
Encore	Normal	Status	—	100	5	Normal	—
Night Shade	Ghost	Special	—	100	15	Normal	—
Agility	Psychic	Status	—	—	30	Self	—
Nasty Plot	Dark	Status	—	—	20	Self	—
Supersonic	Normal	Status	—	55	20	Normal	—

● No. 441 | Music Note Pokémon
Chatot

Normal Flying

● HEIGHT: 1'08"
● WEIGHT: 4.2 lbs.
● ITEMS: Metronome

● SIZE COMPARISON

● MALE/FEMALE HAVE SAME FORM

ABILITIES
● Keen Eye
● Tangled Feet

STATS
HP ●●●
ATTACK ●●●
DEFENSE ●●●
SP. ATTACK ●●●●
SP. DEFENSE ●●●
SPEED ●●●●

EGG GROUPS
Flying

PERFORMANCE
SPEED ★★★☆☆   STAMINA ★★☆
POWER ★★☆   JUMP ★★★★☆
SKILL ★★★☆

● MAIN WAYS TO OBTAIN

Pokémon HeartGold — Sprout Tower (Sinnoh Sound)

Pokémon SoulSilver — Sprout Tower (Sinnoh Sound)

Pokémon Diamond — Route 222 (morning and afternoon only)

Pokémon Pearl — Route 222 (morning and afternoon only)

Pokémon Platinum — Route 213 (morning and afternoon only)

Pokémon HeartGold
It mimics the cries of other Pokémon to trick them into thinking it's one of them. This way they won't attack it.

Pokémon SoulSilver
It mimics the cries of other Pokémon to trick them into thinking it's one of them. This way they won't attack it.

EVOLUTION
Does not evolve

No. 442 | Forbidden Pokémon
Spiritomb

`Ghost` `Dark`

- **HEIGHT:** 3'03"
- **WEIGHT:** 238.1 lbs.
- **ITEMS:** None

● SIZE COMPARISON

● MALE/FEMALE HAVE SAME FORM

⊙ ABILITIES
- Pressure

⊙ STATS
HP	●●
ATTACK	●●●●
DEFENSE	●●●●
SP. ATTACK	●●●●
SP. DEFENSE	●●●●
SPEED	●●

⊙ EGG GROUPS
Amorphous

⊙ PERFORMANCE
SPEED ★☆☆☆☆ STAMINA ★★★★★
POWER ★★★☆☆ JUMP ★★☆☆☆
SKILL ★★☆☆☆

● MAIN WAYS TO OBTAIN

Pokémon HeartGold	Quiet Cave Pokéwalker Route
Pokémon SoulSilver	Quiet Cave Pokéwalker Route
Pokémon Diamond	Broken stone tower on Route 209*
Pokémon Pearl	Broken stone tower on Route 209*
Pokémon Platinum	Broken stone tower on Route 209*

Pokémon HeartGold	Pokémon SoulSilver
It was formed by uniting 108 spirits. It has been bound to the Odd Keystone to keep it from doing any mischief.	It was formed by uniting 108 spirits. It has been bound to the Odd Keystone to keep it from doing any mischief.

⊙ EVOLUTION
Does not evolve

*After you place the Odd Keystone in the broken stone tower, making it into the Hallowed Tower, greet 32 people in the Underground. Afterward, touch the Hallowed Tower and press the A Button to encounter Spiritomb.

● LEVEL-UP MOVES
Lv.	Name	Type	Kind	Pow.	Acc.	PP	Range	DA
1	Curse	???	Status	—	—	10	Normal/Self	—
1	Pursuit	Dark	Physical	40	100	20	Normal	○
1	Confuse Ray	Ghost	Status	—	100	10	Normal	—
1	Spite	Ghost	Status	—	100	10	Normal	—
1	Shadow Sneak	Ghost	Physical	40	100	30	Normal	○
7	Faint Attack	Dark	Physical	60	—	20	Normal	○
13	Hypnosis	Psychic	Status	—	60	20	Normal	—
19	Dream Eater	Psychic	Special	100	100	15	Normal	—
25	Ominous Wind	Ghost	Special	60	100	5	Normal	—
31	Sucker Punch	Dark	Physical	80	100	5	Normal	○
37	Nasty Plot	Dark	Status	—	—	20	Self	—
43	Memento	Dark	Status	—	100	10	Normal	—
49	Dark Pulse	Dark	Special	80	100	15	Normal	—

● MOVE MANIAC
Name	Type	Kind	Pow.	Acc.	PP	Range	DA

● BP MOVES
Name	Type	Kind	Pow.	Acc.	PP	Range	DA
Icy Wind	Ice	Special	55	95	15	2 Foes	—
Ominous Wind	Ghost	Special	60	100	5	Normal	—
Trick	Psychic	Status	—	100	10	Normal	—
Sucker Punch	Dark	Physical	80	100	5	Normal	○
Snore	Normal	Special	40	100	15	Normal	—
Spite	Ghost	Status	—	100	10	Normal	—
Uproar	Normal	Special	50	100	10	1 Random	—
Pain Split	Normal	Status	—	—	20	Normal	—

● TM & HM MOVES
No.	Name	Type	Kind	Pow.	Acc.	PP	Range	DA
TM03	Water Pulse	Water	Special	60	100	20	Normal	—
TM04	Calm Mind	Psychic	Status	—	—	20	Self	—
TM06	Toxic	Poison	Status	—	85	10	Normal	—
TM10	Hidden Power	Normal	Special	—	100	15	Normal	—
TM11	Sunny Day	Fire	Status	—	—	5	All	—
TM12	Taunt	Dark	Status	—	100	20	Normal	—
TM15	Hyper Beam	Normal	Special	150	90	5	Normal	—
TM17	Protect	Normal	Status	—	—	10	Self	—
TM18	Rain Dance	Water	Status	—	—	5	All	—
TM21	Frustration	Normal	Physical	—	100	20	Normal	○
TM27	Return	Normal	Physical	—	100	20	Normal	○
TM29	Psychic	Psychic	Special	90	100	10	Normal	—
TM30	Shadow Ball	Ghost	Special	80	100	15	Normal	—
TM32	Double Team	Normal	Status	—	—	15	Self	—
TM34	Shock Wave	Electric	Special	60	—	20	Normal	—
TM39	Rock Tomb	Rock	Physical	50	80	10	Normal	—
TM41	Torment	Dark	Status	—	100	15	Normal	—
TM42	Facade	Normal	Physical	70	100	20	Normal	○
TM43	Secret Power	Normal	Physical	70	100	20	Normal	—
TM44	Rest	Psychic	Status	—	—	10	Self	—
TM45	Attract	Normal	Status	—	100	15	Normal	—
TM46	Thief	Dark	Physical	40	100	10	Normal	○
TM49	Snatch	Dark	Status	—	—	10	Depends	—
TM58	Endure	Normal	Status	—	—	10	Self	—
TM61	Will-O-Wisp	Fire	Status	—	75	15	Normal	—
TM62	Silver Wind	Bug	Special	60	100	5	Normal	—
TM63	Embargo	Dark	Status	—	100	15	Normal	—
TM68	Giga Impact	Normal	Physical	150	90	5	Normal	○
TM70	Flash	Normal	Status	—	100	20	Normal	—
TM77	Psych Up	Normal	Status	—	—	10	Normal	—
TM78	Captivate	Normal	Status	—	100	20	2 Foes	—
TM79	Dark Pulse	Dark	Special	80	100	15	Normal	—
TM82	Sleep Talk	Normal	Status	—	—	10	Depends	—
TM83	Natural Gift	Normal	Physical	—	100	15	Normal	—
TM85	Dream Eater	Psychic	Special	100	100	15	Normal	—
TM87	Swagger	Normal	Status	—	90	15	Normal	—
TM90	Substitute	Normal	Status	—	—	10	Self	—

● EGG MOVES
Name	Type	Kind	Pow.	Acc.	PP	Range	DA
Destiny Bond	Ghost	Status	—	—	5	Self	—
Pain Split	Normal	Status	—	—	20	Normal	—
SmokeScreen	Normal	Status	—	100	20	Normal	—
Imprison	Psychic	Status	—	—	10	Self	—
Grudge	Ghost	Status	—	—	5	Self	—
Shadow Sneak	Ghost	Physical	40	100	30	Normal	○

● LEVEL-UP MOVES

Lv.	Name	Type	Kind	Pow.	Acc.	PP	Range	DA
1	Tackle	Normal	Physical	35	95	35	Normal	○
3	Sand-Attack	Ground	Status	—	100	15	Normal	—
7	Dragon Rage	Dragon	Special	—	100	10	Normal	—
13	Sandstorm	Rock	Status	—	—	10	All	—
15	Take Down	Normal	Physical	90	85	20	Normal	○
19	Sand Tomb	Ground	Physical	15	70	15	Normal	—
25	Slash	Normal	Physical	70	100	20	Normal	○
27	Dragon Claw	Dragon	Physical	80	100	15	Normal	○
31	Dig	Ground	Physical	80	100	10	Normal	○
37	Dragon Rush	Dragon	Physical	100	75	10	Normal	○

● MOVE MANIAC

Name	Type	Kind	Pow.	Acc.	PP	Range	DA
Headbutt	Normal	Physical	70	100	15	Normal	○
Draco Meteor	Dragon	Special	140	90	5	Normal	—

● BP MOVES

Name	Type	Kind	Pow.	Acc.	PP	Range	DA
Fury Cutter	Bug	Physical	10	95	20	Normal	○
Snore	Normal	Special	40	100	15	Normal	—
Swift	Normal	Special	60	—	20	2 Foes	—
Mud-Slap	Ground	Special	20	100	10	Normal	—
Iron Head	Steel	Physical	80	100	15	Normal	—
Outrage	Dragon	Physical	120	100	15	1 Random	○
Earth Power	Ground	Special	90	100	10	Normal	—
Twister	Dragon	Special	40	100	20	2 Foes	—

● TM & HM MOVES

No.	Name	Type	Kind	Pow.	Acc.	PP	Range	DA
TM02	Dragon Claw	Dragon	Physical	80	100	15	Normal	○
TM05	Roar	Normal	Status	—	100	20	Normal	—
TM06	Toxic	Poison	Status	—	85	10	Normal	—
TM10	Hidden Power	Normal	Special	—	100	15	Normal	—
TM11	Sunny Day	Fire	Status	—	—	5	All	—
TM17	Protect	Normal	Status	—	—	10	Self	—
TM18	Rain Dance	Water	Status	—	—	5	All	—
TM21	Frustration	Normal	Physical	—	100	20	Normal	○
TM26	Earthquake	Ground	Physical	100	100	10	2 Foes/1 Ally	—
TM27	Return	Normal	Physical	—	100	20	Normal	○
TM28	Dig	Ground	Physical	80	100	10	Normal	○
TM32	Double Team	Normal	Status	—	—	15	Self	—
TM35	Flamethrower	Fire	Special	95	100	15	Normal	—
TM37	Sandstorm	Rock	Status	—	—	10	All	—
TM38	Fire Blast	Fire	Special	120	85	5	Normal	—
TM39	Rock Tomb	Rock	Physical	50	80	10	Normal	—
TM40	Aerial Ace	Flying	Physical	60	—	20	Normal	○
TM42	Facade	Normal	Physical	70	100	20	Normal	○
TM43	Secret Power	Normal	Physical	70	100	20	Normal	—
TM44	Rest	Psychic	Status	—	—	10	Self	—
TM45	Attract	Normal	Status	—	100	15	Normal	—
TM58	Endure	Normal	Status	—	—	10	Self	—
TM59	Dragon Pulse	Dragon	Special	90	100	10	Normal	—
TM65	Shadow Claw	Ghost	Physical	70	100	15	Normal	○
TM71	Stone Edge	Rock	Physical	100	80	5	Normal	—
TM76	Stealth Rock	Rock	Status	—	—	20	2 Foes	—
TM78	Captivate	Normal	Status	—	100	20	2 Foes	—
TM80	Rock Slide	Rock	Physical	75	90	10	2 Foes	—
TM82	Sleep Talk	Normal	Status	—	—	10	Depends	—
TM83	Natural Gift	Normal	Physical	—	100	15	Normal	—
TM87	Swagger	Normal	Status	—	90	15	Normal	—
TM90	Substitute	Normal	Status	—	—	10	Self	—
HM01	Cut	Normal	Physical	50	95	30	Normal	○
HM04	Strength	Normal	Physical	80	100	15	Normal	○
HM06	Rock Smash	Fighting	Physical	40	100	15	Normal	○
HM08	Rock Climb	Normal	Physical	90	85	20	Normal	○

● EGG MOVES

Name	Type	Kind	Pow.	Acc.	PP	Range	DA
DragonBreath	Dragon	Special	60	100	20	Normal	—
Outrage	Dragon	Physical	120	100	15	1 Random	○
Twister	Dragon	Special	40	100	20	2 Foes	—
Scary Face	Normal	Status	—	90	10	Normal	—
Double-Edge	Normal	Physical	120	100	15	Normal	○
Thrash	Normal	Physical	120	100	10	1 Random	○
Metal Claw	Steel	Physical	50	95	35	Normal	○
Sand Tomb	Ground	Physical	15	70	15	Normal	—
Body Slam	Normal	Physical	85	100	15	Normal	○
Iron Head	Steel	Physical	80	100	15	Normal	—
Mud Shot	Ground	Special	55	95	15	Normal	—

⊙ No. 443 | Land Shark Pokémon
Gible

Dragon Ground

- ● HEIGHT: 2'04"
- ● WEIGHT: 45.2 lbs.
- ● ITEMS: Haban Berry

● SIZE COMPARISON

● MALE FORM
Notched dorsal fin

● FEMALE FORM
No notch on dorsal fin

⊙ ABILITIES
● Sand Veil

⊙ STATS
- HP ●●
- ATTACK ●●●
- DEFENSE ●●
- SP. ATTACK ●●
- SP. DEFENSE ●●
- SPEED ●●

⊙ EGG GROUPS
Monster

Dragon

⊙ PERFORMANCE
- SPEED ★★★☆
- POWER ★★★☆
- SKILL ★★☆
- STAMINA ★★★
- JUMP ★★

● MAIN WAYS TO OBTAIN

Pokémon HeartGold	Safari Zone (Rocky Beach Area: if Grass and Rock objects are placed, may appear in tall grass)
Pokémon SoulSilver	Safari Zone (Rocky Beach Area: if Grass and Rock objects are placed, may appear in tall grass)
Pokémon Diamond	Wayward Cave B1F (beneath Cycling Road)
Pokémon Pearl	Wayward Cave B1F (beneath Cycling Road)
Pokémon Platinum	Wayward Cave B1F (beneath Cycling Road)

Pokémon HeartGold	**Pokémon SoulSilver**
It nests in horizontal holes warmed by geothermal heat. Foes who get too close can expect to be pounced on and bitten.	It nests in horizontal holes warmed by geothermal heat. Foes who get too close can expect to be pounced on and bitten.

⊙ EVOLUTION

Gible → Lv. 24 → Gabite → Lv. 48 → Garchomp

○ No. 444 | Cave Pokémon
Gabite

Dragon Ground

● HEIGHT: 4'07"
● WEIGHT: 123.5 lbs.
● ITEMS: None

● SIZE COMPARISON

● MALE FORM
Notched dorsal fin

● FEMALE FORM
No notch on dorsal fin

⊙ ABILITIES
● Sand Veil

⊙ STATS
HP ●●●
ATTACK ●●●●
DEFENSE ●●●
SP. ATTACK ●●
SP. DEFENSE ●●
SPEED ●●●●

⊙ EGG GROUPS
Monster
Dragon

⊙ PERFORMANCE
SPEED ★★★
POWER ★★★★
SKILL ★★★☆
STAMINA ★★★☆
JUMP ★★★

● MAIN WAYS TO OBTAIN

Pokémon HeartGold	Level up Gible to Lv. 24
Pokémon SoulSilver	Level up Gible to Lv. 24
Pokémon Diamond	Level up Gible to Lv. 24
Pokémon Pearl	Level up Gible to Lv. 24
Pokémon Platinum	Victory Road 1F

| Pokémon HeartGold | Pokémon SoulSilver |
| As it digs to expand its nest, it habitually digs up gems that it then hoards in its nest. | As it digs to expand its nest, it habitually digs up gems that it then hoards in its nest. |

⊙ EVOLUTION

Lv. 24   Lv. 48

Gible   Gabite   Garchomp

● LEVEL-UP MOVES

Lv.	Name	Type	Kind	Pow.	Acc.	PP	Range	DA
1	Tackle	Normal	Physical	35	95	35	Normal	○
1	Sand-Attack	Ground	Status	—	100	15	Normal	—
3	Sand-Attack	Ground	Status	—	100	15	Normal	—
?	Dragon Rage	Dragon	Special	—	100	10	Normal	—
13	Sandstorm	Rock	Status	—	—	10	All	—
15	Take Down	Normal	Physical	90	85	20	Normal	○
19	Sand Tomb	Ground	Physical	15	70	15	Normal	—
28	Slash	Normal	Physical	70	100	20	Normal	○
33	Dragon Claw	Dragon	Physical	80	100	15	Normal	○
40	Dig	Ground	Physical	80	100	10	Normal	○
49	Dragon Rush	Dragon	Physical	100	75	10	Normal	○

● MOVE MANIAC

Name	Type	Kind	Pow.	Acc.	PP	Range	DA
Headbutt	Normal	Physical	70	100	15	Normal	○
Draco Meteor	Dragon	Special	140	90	5	Normal	—

● BP MOVES

Name	Type	Kind	Pow.	Acc.	PP	Range	DA
Fury Cutter	Bug	Physical	10	95	20	Normal	○
Snore	Normal	Special	40	100	15	Normal	—
Swift	Normal	Special	60	—	20	2 Foes	—
Mud-Slap	Ground	Special	20	100	10	Normal	—
Iron Head	Steel	Physical	80	100	15	Normal	○
Outrage	Dragon	Physical	120	100	15	1 Random	—
Earth Power	Ground	Special	90	100	10	Normal	—
Twister	Dragon	Special	40	100	20	2 Foes	—

● TM & HM MOVES

No.	Name	Type	Kind	Pow.	Acc.	PP	Range	DA
TM02	Dragon Claw	Dragon	Physical	80	100	15	Normal	○
TM05	Roar	Normal	Status	—	100	20	Normal	—
TM06	Toxic	Poison	Status	—	85	10	Normal	—
TM10	Hidden Power	Normal	Special	—	100	15	Normal	—
TM11	Sunny Day	Fire	Status	—	—	5	All	—
TM17	Protect	Normal	Status	—	—	10	Self	—
TM18	Rain Dance	Water	Status	—	—	5	All	—
TM21	Frustration	Normal	Physical	—	100	20	Normal	○
TM23	Iron Tail	Steel	Physical	100	75	15	Normal	○
TM26	Earthquake	Ground	Physical	100	100	10	2 Foes/1 Ally	—
TM27	Return	Normal	Physical	—	100	20	Normal	○
TM28	Dig	Ground	Physical	80	100	10	Normal	○
TM32	Double Team	Normal	Status	—	—	15	Self	—
TM35	Flamethrower	Fire	Special	95	100	15	Normal	—
TM37	Sandstorm	Rock	Status	—	—	10	All	—
TM38	Fire Blast	Fire	Special	120	85	5	Normal	—
TM39	Rock Tomb	Rock	Physical	50	80	10	Normal	—
TM40	Aerial Ace	Flying	Physical	60	—	20	Normal	○
TM42	Facade	Normal	Physical	70	100	20	Normal	○
TM43	Secret Power	Normal	Physical	70	100	20	Normal	—
TM44	Rest	Psychic	Status	—	—	10	Self	—
TM45	Attract	Normal	Status	—	100	15	Normal	—
TM58	Endure	Normal	Status	—	—	10	Self	—
TM59	Dragon Pulse	Dragon	Special	90	100	10	Normal	—
TM65	Shadow Claw	Ghost	Physical	70	100	15	Normal	○
TM71	Stone Edge	Rock	Physical	100	80	5	Normal	—
TM76	Stealth Rock	Rock	Status	—	—	20	2 Foes	—
TM78	Captivate	Normal	Status	—	100	20	2 Foes	—
TM80	Rock Slide	Rock	Physical	75	90	10	2 Foes	—
TM82	Sleep Talk	Normal	Status	—	—	10	Depends	—
TM83	Natural Gift	Normal	Physical	—	100	15	Normal	—
TM87	Swagger	Normal	Status	—	90	15	Normal	—
TM90	Substitute	Normal	Status	—	—	10	Self	—
HM01	Cut	Normal	Physical	50	95	30	Normal	○
HM04	Strength	Normal	Physical	80	100	15	Normal	○
HM06	Rock Smash	Fighting	Physical	40	100	15	Normal	○
HM08	Rock Climb	Normal	Physical	90	85	20	Normal	○

● LEVEL-UP MOVES

Lv.	Name	Type	Kind	Pow.	Acc.	PP	Range	DA
1	Fire Fang	Fire	Physical	65	95	15	Normal	○
1	Tackle	Normal	Physical	35	95	35	Normal	○
1	Sand-Attack	Ground	Status	—	100	15	Normal	—
1	Dragon Rage	Dragon	Special	—	100	10	Normal	—
1	Sandstorm	Rock	Status	—	—	10	All	—
3	Sand-Attack	Ground	Status	—	100	15	Normal	—
7	Dragon Rage	Dragon	Special	—	100	10	Normal	—
13	Sandstorm	Rock	Status	—	—	10	All	—
15	Take Down	Normal	Physical	90	85	20	Normal	○
19	Sand Tomb	Ground	Physical	15	70	15	Normal	—
28	Slash	Normal	Physical	70	100	20	Normal	○
33	Dragon Claw	Dragon	Physical	80	100	15	Normal	○
40	Dig	Ground	Physical	80	100	10	Normal	○
48	Crunch	Dark	Physical	80	100	15	Normal	○
55	Dragon Rush	Dragon	Physical	100	75	10	Normal	○

● MOVE MANIAC

Name	Type	Kind	Pow.	Acc.	PP	Range	DA
Headbutt	Normal	Physical	70	100	15	Normal	○
Draco Meteor	Dragon	Special	140	90	5	Normal	—

● BP MOVES

Name	Type	Kind	Pow.	Acc.	PP	Range	DA
Fury Cutter	Bug	Physical	10	95	20	Normal	○
Snore	Normal	Special	40	100	15	Normal	—
Swift	Normal	Special	60	—	20	2 Foes	—
Mud-Slap	Ground	Special	20	100	10	Normal	—
Iron Head	Steel	Physical	80	100	15	Normal	○
Aqua Tail	Water	Physical	90	90	10	Normal	○
Outrage	Dragon	Physical	120	100	10	1 Random	○
Earth Power	Ground	Special	90	100	10	Normal	—
Twister	Dragon	Special	40	100	20	2 Foes	—

● TM & HM MOVES

No.	Name	Type	Kind	Pow.	Acc.	PP	Range	DA
TM02	Dragon Claw	Dragon	Physical	80	100	15	Normal	○
TM05	Roar	Normal	Status	—	100	20	Normal	—
TM06	Toxic	Poison	Status	—	85	10	Normal	—
TM10	Hidden Power	Normal	Special	—	100	15	Normal	—
TM11	Sunny Day	Fire	Status	—	—	5	All	—
TM15	Hyper Beam	Normal	Special	150	90	5	Normal	—
TM17	Protect	Normal	Status	—	—	10	Self	—
TM18	Rain Dance	Water	Status	—	—	5	All	—
TM21	Frustration	Normal	Physical	—	100	20	Normal	○
TM23	Iron Tail	Steel	Physical	100	75	15	Normal	○
TM26	Earthquake	Ground	Physical	100	100	10	2 Foes/1 Ally	—
TM27	Return	Normal	Physical	—	100	20	Normal	○
TM28	Dig	Ground	Physical	80	100	10	Normal	○
TM31	Brick Break	Fighting	Physical	75	100	15	Normal	○
TM32	Double Team	Normal	Status	—	—	15	Self	—
TM35	Flamethrower	Fire	Special	95	100	15	Normal	—
TM37	Sandstorm	Rock	Status	—	—	10	All	—
TM38	Fire Blast	Fire	Special	120	85	5	Normal	—
TM39	Rock Tomb	Rock	Physical	50	80	10	Normal	—
TM40	Aerial Ace	Flying	Physical	60	—	20	Normal	○
TM42	Facade	Normal	Physical	70	100	20	Normal	○
TM43	Secret Power	Normal	Physical	70	100	20	Normal	○
TM44	Rest	Psychic	Status	—	—	10	Self	—
TM45	Attract	Normal	Status	—	100	15	Normal	—
TM54	False Swipe	Normal	Physical	40	100	40	Normal	○
TM56	Fling	Dark	Physical	—	100	10	Normal	○
TM58	Endure	Normal	Status	—	—	10	Self	—
TM59	Dragon Pulse	Dragon	Special	90	100	10	Normal	—
TM65	Shadow Claw	Ghost	Physical	70	100	15	Normal	○
TM68	Giga Impact	Normal	Physical	150	90	5	Normal	○
TM71	Stone Edge	Rock	Physical	100	80	5	Normal	—
TM75	Swords Dance	Normal	Status	—	—	30	Self	—
TM76	Stealth Rock	Rock	Status	—	—	20	2 Foes	—
TM78	Captivate	Normal	Status	—	100	20	2 Foes	—
TM80	Rock Slide	Rock	Physical	75	90	10	2 Foes	—
TM82	Sleep Talk	Normal	Status	—	—	10	Depends	—
TM83	Natural Gift	Normal	Physical	—	100	15	Normal	—
TM84	Poison Jab	Poison	Physical	80	100	20	Normal	○
TM87	Swagger	Normal	Status	—	90	15	Normal	—
TM90	Substitute	Normal	Status	—	—	10	Self	—
HM01	Cut	Normal	Physical	50	95	30	Normal	○
HM03	Surf	Water	Special	95	100	15	2 Foes/1 Ally	—
HM04	Strength	Normal	Physical	80	100	15	Normal	○
HM05	Whirlpool	Water	Special	15	70	15	Normal	—
HM06	Rock Smash	Fighting	Physical	40	100	15	Normal	○
HM08	Rock Climb	Normal	Physical	90	85	20	Normal	○

● No. 445 | Mach Pokémon
Garchomp

Dragon   Ground

- **HEIGHT:** 6'03"
- **WEIGHT:** 209.4 lbs.
- **ITEMS:** None

● SIZE COMPARISON

● MALE FORM
Notched dorsal fin

● FEMALE FORM
No notch on dorsal fin

⊙ ABILITIES
- Sand Veil

⊙ STATS
HP	●●●●○
ATTACK	●●●●●
DEFENSE	●●●●○
SP. ATTACK	●●●●○
SP. DEFENSE	●●●●○
SPEED	●●●●○

⊙ EGG GROUPS
Monster

Dragon

⊙ PERFORMANCE
SPEED ★★☆   STAMINA ★★★☆
POWER ★★★★☆   JUMP ★★
SKILL ★★★★☆

● MAIN WAYS TO OBTAIN

Pokémon HeartGold Level up Gabite to Lv. 48

Pokémon SoulSilver Level up Gabite to Lv. 48

Pokémon Diamond Level up Gabite to Lv. 48

Pokémon Pearl Level up Gabite to Lv. 48

Pokémon Platinum Level up Gabite to Lv. 48

Pokémon HeartGold	**Pokémon SoulSilver**
Its body is covered in fine scales that reduce drag, enabling it to fly at high speeds.	Its body is covered in fine scales that reduce drag, enabling it to fly at high speeds.

⊙ EVOLUTION

Gible → Lv. 24 → Gabite → Lv. 48 → Garchomp

No. 446 | Big Eater Pokémon
Munchlax
Normal

- **HEIGHT:** 2'00"
- **WEIGHT:** 231.5 lbs.
- **ITEMS:** None

● SIZE COMPARISON

● MALE/FEMALE HAVE SAME FORM

⊘ ABILITIES
- Pickup
- Thick Fat

⊘ EGG GROUPS
No Egg has ever been discovered

⊘ STATS
HP	●●●●●
ATTACK	●●
DEFENSE	●●
SP. ATTACK	●●
SP. DEFENSE	●●●
SPEED	●

⊘ PERFORMANCE
SPEED ★★☆
POWER ★★★☆☆
SKILL ★★☆☆

STAMINA ★★★★☆
JUMP ★★

● MAIN WAYS TO OBTAIN

Pokémon HeartGold	Quiet Cave Pokéwalker Route
Pokémon SoulSilver	Quiet Cave Pokéwalker Route
Pokémon Diamond	Occasionally appears if you spread Honey on a sweet-smelling tree
Pokémon Pearl	Occasionally appears if you spread Honey on a sweet-smelling tree
Pokémon Platinum	Occasionally appears if you spread Honey on a sweet-smelling tree

Pokémon HeartGold	*Pokémon SoulSilver*
It conceals food under the long fur on its body. It carts around this food stash and swallows it without chewing.	It conceals food under the long fur on its body. It carts around this food stash and swallows it without chewing.

⊘ EVOLUTION

 Munchlax — Level up with high friendship → Snorlax

● LEVEL-UP MOVES
Lv.	Name	Type	Kind	Pow.	Acc.	PP	Range	DA
1	Metronome	Normal	Status	—	—	10	Depends	—
1	Odor Sleuth	Normal	Status	—	—	40	Normal	—
1	Tackle	Normal	Physical	35	95	35	Normal	○
4	Defense Curl	Normal	Status	—	—	40	Self	—
9	Amnesia	Psychic	Status	—	—	20	Self	—
12	Lick	Ghost	Physical	20	100	30	Normal	○
17	Recycle	Normal	Status	—	—	10	Self	—
20	Screech	Normal	Status	—	85	40	Normal	—
25	Stockpile	Normal	Status	—	—	20	Self	—
28	Swallow	Normal	Status	—	—	10	Self	—
33	Body Slam	Normal	Physical	85	100	15	Normal	○
36	Fling	Dark	Physical	—	100	10	Normal	—
41	Rollout	Rock	Physical	30	90	20	Normal	○
44	Natural Gift	Normal	Physical	—	100	15	Normal	—
49	Last Resort	Normal	Physical	130	100	5	Normal	○

● MOVE MANIAC
Name	Type	Kind	Pow.	Acc.	PP	Range	DA
Headbutt	Normal	Physical	70	100	15	Normal	○

● BP MOVES
Name	Type	Kind	Pow.	Acc.	PP	Range	DA
Icy Wind	Ice	Special	55	95	15	2 Foes	—
ThunderPunch	Electric	Physical	75	100	15	Normal	○
Fire Punch	Fire	Physical	75	100	15	Normal	○
Ice Punch	Ice	Physical	75	100	15	Normal	○
Zen Headbutt	Psychic	Physical	80	90	15	Normal	○
Snore	Normal	Special	40	100	15	Normal	—
Last Resort	Normal	Physical	130	100	5	Normal	○
Uproar	Normal	Special	50	100	10	1 Random	—
Mud-Slap	Ground	Special	20	100	10	Normal	—
Rollout	Rock	Physical	30	90	20	Normal	○
Superpower	Fighting	Physical	120	100	5	Normal	○
Gunk Shot	Poison	Physical	120	70	5	Normal	—
Seed Bomb	Grass	Physical	80	100	15	Normal	—

● TM & HM MOVES
No.	Name	Type	Kind	Pow.	Acc.	PP	Range	DA
TM01	Focus Punch	Fighting	Physical	150	100	20	Normal	○
TM03	Water Pulse	Water	Special	60	100	20	Normal	—
TM06	Toxic	Poison	Status	—	85	10	Normal	—
TM10	Hidden Power	Normal	Special	—	100	15	Normal	—
TM11	Sunny Day	Fire	Status	—	—	5	All	—
TM13	Ice Beam	Ice	Special	95	100	10	Normal	—
TM14	Blizzard	Ice	Special	120	70	5	2 Foes	—
TM17	Protect	Normal	Status	—	—	10	Self	—
TM18	Rain Dance	Water	Status	—	—	5	All	—
TM21	Frustration	Normal	Physical	—	100	20	Normal	○
TM22	SolarBeam	Grass	Special	120	100	10	Normal	—
TM24	Thunderbolt	Electric	Special	95	100	15	Normal	—
TM25	Thunder	Electric	Special	120	70	10	Normal	—
TM26	Earthquake	Ground	Physical	100	100	10	2 Foes/1 Ally	—
TM27	Return	Normal	Physical	—	100	20	Normal	○
TM29	Psychic	Psychic	Special	90	100	10	Normal	—
TM30	Shadow Ball	Ghost	Special	80	100	15	Normal	—
TM31	Brick Break	Fighting	Physical	75	100	15	Normal	○
TM32	Double Team	Normal	Status	—	—	15	Self	—
TM34	Shock Wave	Electric	Special	60	—	20	Normal	—
TM35	Flamethrower	Fire	Special	95	100	15	Normal	—
TM37	Sandstorm	Rock	Status	—	—	10	All	—
TM38	Fire Blast	Fire	Special	120	85	5	Normal	—
TM39	Rock Tomb	Rock	Physical	50	80	10	Normal	—
TM42	Facade	Normal	Physical	70	100	20	Normal	○
TM43	Secret Power	Normal	Physical	70	100	20	Normal	—
TM44	Rest	Psychic	Status	—	—	10	Self	—
TM45	Attract	Normal	Status	—	100	15	Normal	—
TM56	Fling	Dark	Physical	—	100	10	Normal	—
TM58	Endure	Normal	Status	—	—	10	Self	—
TM67	Recycle	Normal	Status	—	—	10	Self	—
TM78	Captivate	Normal	Status	—	100	20	2 Foes	—
TM80	Rock Slide	Rock	Physical	75	90	10	2 Foes	—
TM82	Sleep Talk	Normal	Status	—	—	10	Depends	—
TM83	Natural Gift	Normal	Physical	—	100	15	Normal	—
TM87	Swagger	Normal	Status	—	90	15	Normal	—
TM90	Substitute	Normal	Status	—	—	10	Self	—
HM03	Surf	Water	Special	95	100	15	2 Foes/1 Ally	—
HM04	Strength	Normal	Physical	80	100	15	Normal	○
HM05	Whirlpool	Water	Special	15	70	15	Normal	—
HM06	Rock Smash	Fighting	Physical	40	100	15	Normal	○
HM08	Rock Climb	Normal	Physical	90	85	20	Normal	—

● EGG MOVES
Name	Type	Kind	Pow.	Acc.	PP	Range	DA
Lick	Ghost	Physical	20	100	30	Normal	○
Charm	Normal	Status	—	100	20	Normal	—
Double-Edge	Normal	Physical	120	100	15	Normal	○
Curse	???	Status	—	—	10	Normal/Self	—
Substitute	Normal	Status	—	—	10	Self	—
Whirlwind	Normal	Status	—	100	20	Normal	—
Pursuit	Dark	Physical	40	100	20	Normal	○
Zen Headbutt	Psychic	Physical	80	90	15	Normal	○
Counter	Fighting	Physical	—	100	20	Self	○

● LEVEL-UP MOVES

Lv.	Name	Type	Kind	Pow.	Acc.	PP	Range	DA
1	Quick Attack	Normal	Physical	40	100	30	Normal	○
1	Foresight	Normal	Status	—	—	40	Normal	—
1	Endure	Normal	Status	—	—	10	Self	—
6	Counter	Fighting	Physical	—	100	20	Self	○
11	Force Palm	Fighting	Physical	60	100	10	Normal	○
15	Feint	Normal	Physical	50	100	10	Normal	—
19	Reversal	Fighting	Physical	—	100	15	Normal	○
24	Screech	Normal	Status	—	85	40	Normal	—
29	Copycat	Normal	Status	—	—	20	Depends	—

● MOVE MANIAC

Name	Type	Kind	Pow.	Acc.	PP	Range	DA
Headbutt	Normal	Physical	70	100	15	Normal	○

● BP MOVES

Name	Type	Kind	Pow.	Acc.	PP	Range	DA
Fury Cutter	Bug	Physical	10	95	20	Normal	○
ThunderPunch	Electric	Physical	75	100	15	Normal	○
Ice Punch	Ice	Physical	75	100	15	Normal	○
Zen Headbutt	Psychic	Physical	80	90	15	Normal	○
Vacuum Wave	Fighting	Special	40	100	30	Normal	—
Snore	Normal	Special	40	100	15	Normal	—
Helping Hand	Normal	Status	—	—	20	1 Ally	—
Magnet Rise	Electric	Status	—	—	10	Self	—
Swift	Normal	Special	60	—	20	2 Foes	—
Role Play	Psychic	Status	—	—	10	Normal	—
Mud-Slap	Ground	Special	20	100	10	Normal	○
Iron Defense	Steel	Status	—	—	15	Self	—
Low Kick	Fighting	Physical	—	100	20	Normal	○

● TM & HM MOVES

No.	Name	Type	Kind	Pow.	Acc.	PP	Range	DA
TM01	Focus Punch	Fighting	Physical	150	100	20	Normal	○
TM05	Roar	Normal	Status	—	100	20	Normal	—
TM06	Toxic	Poison	Status	—	85	10	Normal	—
TM08	Bulk Up	Fighting	Status	—	—	20	Self	—
TM10	Hidden Power	Normal	Special	—	100	15	Normal	—
TM11	Sunny Day	Fire	Status	—	—	5	All	—
TM17	Protect	Normal	Status	—	—	10	Self	—
TM18	Rain Dance	Water	Status	—	—	5	All	—
TM21	Frustration	Normal	Physical	—	100	20	Normal	○
TM23	Iron Tail	Steel	Physical	100	75	15	Normal	○
TM26	Earthquake	Ground	Physical	100	100	10	2 Foes/1 Ally	—
TM27	Return	Normal	Physical	—	100	20	Normal	○
TM28	Dig	Ground	Physical	80	100	10	Normal	○
TM31	Brick Break	Fighting	Physical	75	100	15	Normal	○
TM32	Double Team	Normal	Status	—	—	15	Self	—
TM39	Rock Tomb	Rock	Physical	50	80	10	Normal	—
TM42	Facade	Normal	Physical	70	100	20	Normal	—
TM43	Secret Power	Normal	Physical	70	100	20	Normal	○
TM44	Rest	Psychic	Status	—	—	10	Self	—
TM45	Attract	Normal	Status	—	100	15	Normal	—
TM52	Focus Blast	Fighting	Special	120	70	5	Normal	—
TM56	Fling	Dark	Physical	—	100	10	Normal	○
TM58	Endure	Normal	Status	—	—	10	Self	—
TM60	Drain Punch	Fighting	Physical	60	100	5	Normal	○
TM65	Shadow Claw	Ghost	Physical	70	100	15	Normal	○
TM66	Payback	Dark	Physical	50	100	10	Normal	○
TM75	Swords Dance	Normal	Status	—	—	30	Self	—
TM78	Captivate	Normal	Status	—	100	20	2 Foes	—
TM80	Rock Slide	Rock	Physical	75	90	10	2 Foes	—
TM82	Sleep Talk	Normal	Status	—	—	10	Depends	—
TM83	Natural Gift	Normal	Physical	—	100	15	Normal	○
TM84	Poison Jab	Poison	Physical	80	100	20	Normal	○
TM87	Swagger	Normal	Status	—	90	15	Normal	—
TM90	Substitute	Normal	Status	—	—	10	Self	—
HM04	Strength	Normal	Physical	80	100	15	Normal	○
HM06	Rock Smash	Fighting	Physical	40	100	15	Normal	○

● EGG MOVES

Name	Type	Kind	Pow.	Acc.	PP	Range	DA
Cross Chop	Fighting	Physical	100	80	5	Normal	○
Detect	Fighting	Status	—	—	5	Self	—
Bite	Dark	Physical	60	100	25	Normal	○
Mind Reader	Normal	Status	—	—	5	Normal	—
Sky Uppercut	Fighting	Physical	85	90	15	Normal	○
Hi Jump Kick	Fighting	Physical	100	90	20	Normal	○
Agility	Psychic	Status	—	—	30	Self	—
Vacuum Wave	Fighting	Special	40	100	30	Normal	—
Crunch	Dark	Physical	80	100	15	Normal	○
Low Kick	Fighting	Physical	—	100	20	Normal	○
Iron Defense	Steel	Status	—	—	15	Self	—
Blaze Kick	Fire	Physical	85	90	10	Normal	○
Bullet Punch	Steel	Physical	40	100	30	Normal	○
Follow Me	Normal	Status	—	—	20	Self	—

No. 447 | Emanation Pokémon
Riolu

Fighting

● HEIGHT: 2'04"
● WEIGHT: 44.5 lbs.
● ITEMS: None

● SIZE COMPARISON

● MALE/FEMALE HAVE SAME FORM

● ABILITIES
● Steadfast
● Inner Focus

● STATS
HP ●
ATTACK ●●●
DEFENSE ●●
SP. ATTACK ●●
SP. DEFENSE ●
SPEED ●●●

● EGG GROUPS
No Egg has ever been discovered

● PERFORMANCE
SPEED ★★★★☆ STAMINA ★★☆
POWER ★★☆☆ JUMP ★★★☆
SKILL ★★☆☆☆

● MAIN WAYS TO OBTAIN

Pokémon HeartGold	Safari Zone (Meadow Area) if Rock and Forest objects are placed, may appear in tall grass)
Pokémon SoulSilver	Safari Zone (Meadow Area) if Rock and Forest objects are placed, may appear in tall grass)
Pokémon Diamond	Hatch the Egg you receive from Riley at Iron Island
Pokémon Pearl	Hatch the Egg you receive from Riley at Iron Island
Pokémon Platinum	Hatch the Egg you receive from Riley at Iron Island

Pokémon HeartGold	**Pokémon SoulSilver**
They communicate with one another using their auras. They are able to run all through the night.	They communicate with one another using their auras. They are able to run all through the night.

● EVOLUTION

Level up with high friendship between 4:00 A.M. and 8:00 P.M.

Riolu → Lucario

No. 448 | Aura Pokémon
Lucario

Fighting | **Steel**

● **LEVEL-UP MOVES**

Lv.	Name	Type	Kind	Pow.	Acc.	PP	Range	DA
1	Dark Pulse	Dark	Special	80	100	15	Normal	—
1	Quick Attack	Normal	Physical	40	100	30	Normal	○
1	Foresight	Normal	Status	—	—	40	Normal	—
1	Detect	Fighting	Status	—	—	5	Self	—
1	Metal Claw	Steel	Physical	50	95	35	Normal	○
6	Counter	Fighting	Physical	—	100	20	Self	○
11	Force Palm	Fighting	Physical	60	100	10	Normal	○
15	Feint	Normal	Physical	50	100	10	Normal	—
19	Bone Rush	Ground	Physical	25	80	10	Normal	—
24	Metal Sound	Steel	Status	—	85	40	Normal	—
29	Me First	Normal	Status	—	—	20	Depends	—
33	Swords Dance	Normal	Status	—	—	20	Self	—
37	Aura Sphere	Fighting	Special	90	—	20	Normal	—
42	Close Combat	Fighting	Physical	120	100	5	Normal	○
47	Dragon Pulse	Dragon	Special	90	100	10	Normal	—
51	ExtremeSpeed	Normal	Physical	80	100	5	Normal	○

● **MOVE MANIAC**

Name	Type	Kind	Pow.	Acc.	PP	Range	DA
Headbutt	Normal	Physical	70	100	15	Normal	○

● **BP MOVES**

Name	Type	Kind	Pow.	Acc.	PP	Range	DA
Fury Cutter	Bug	Physical	10	95	20	Normal	○
ThunderPunch	Electric	Physical	75	100	15	Normal	○
Ice Punch	Ice	Physical	75	100	15	Normal	○
Zen Headbutt	Psychic	Physical	80	90	15	Normal	○
Vacuum Wave	Fighting	Special	40	100	30	Normal	—
Snore	Normal	Special	40	100	15	Normal	—
Helping Hand	Normal	Status	—	—	20	1 Ally	—
Magnet Rise	Electric	Status	—	—	10	Self	—
Swift	Normal	Special	60	—	20	2 Foes	—
Role Play	Psychic	Status	—	—	10	Normal	—
Mud-Slap	Ground	Special	20	100	10	Normal	—
Iron Defense	Steel	Status	—	—	15	Self	—
Low Kick	Fighting	Physical	—	100	20	Normal	○

● **HEIGHT:** 3'11"
● **WEIGHT:** 119.0 lbs.
● **ITEMS:** None

● **SIZE COMPARISON**

● **MALE/FEMALE HAVE SAME FORM**

● **ABILITIES**
● Steadfast
● Inner Focus

● **STATS**
- HP ●●●
- ATTACK ●●●●●
- DEFENSE ●●●
- SP. ATTACK ●●●●●
- SP. DEFENSE ●●●
- SPEED ●●●●

● **EGG GROUPS**
Field
Human-Like

● **PERFORMANCE**
SPEED ★★★☆ STAMINA ★★☆
POWER ★★★★☆ JUMP ★★★☆
SKILL ★★★★☆

● **MAIN WAYS TO OBTAIN**

Pokémon HeartGold — Level up Riolu with high friendship between 4:00 A.M. and 8:00 P.M.

Pokémon SoulSilver — Level up Riolu with high friendship between 4:00 A.M. and 8:00 P.M.

Pokémon Diamond — Level up Riolu with high friendship between 4:00 A.M. and 8:00 P.M.

Pokémon Pearl — Level up Riolu with high friendship between 4:00 A.M. and 8:00 P.M.

Pokémon Platinum — Level up Riolu with high friendship between 4:00 A.M. and 8:00 P.M.

Pokémon HeartGold — It's said that no foe can remain invisible to LUCARIO, since it can detect auras. Even foes it could not otherwise see.

Pokémon SoulSilver — It's said that no foe can remain invisible to LUCARIO, since it can detect auras. Even foes it could not otherwise see.

● **EVOLUTION**

 Riolu — Level up with high friendship between 4:00 A.M. and 8:00 P.M. — Lucario

● **TM & HM MOVES**

No.	Name	Type	Kind	Pow.	Acc.	PP	Range	DA
TM01	Focus Punch	Fighting	Physical	150	100	20	Normal	○
TM03	Water Pulse	Water	Special	60	100	20	Normal	—
TM04	Calm Mind	Psychic	Status	—	—	20	Self	—
TM05	Roar	Normal	Status	—	100	20	Normal	—
TM06	Toxic	Poison	Status	—	85	10	Normal	—
TM08	Bulk Up	Fighting	Status	—	—	20	Self	—
TM10	Hidden Power	Normal	Special	—	100	15	Normal	—
TM11	Sunny Day	Fire	Status	—	—	5	All	—
TM15	Hyper Beam	Normal	Special	150	90	5	Normal	—
TM17	Protect	Normal	Status	—	—	10	Self	—
TM18	Rain Dance	Water	Status	—	—	5	All	—
TM21	Frustration	Normal	Physical	—	100	20	Normal	○
TM23	Iron Tail	Steel	Physical	100	75	15	Normal	○
TM26	Earthquake	Ground	Physical	100	100	10	2 Foes/1 Ally	—
TM27	Return	Normal	Physical	—	100	20	Normal	○
TM28	Dig	Ground	Physical	80	100	10	Normal	○
TM29	Psychic	Psychic	Special	90	100	10	Normal	—
TM30	Shadow Ball	Ghost	Special	80	100	15	Normal	—
TM31	Brick Break	Fighting	Physical	75	100	15	Normal	○
TM32	Double Team	Normal	Status	—	—	15	Self	—
TM39	Rock Tomb	Rock	Physical	50	80	10	Normal	—
TM42	Facade	Normal	Physical	70	100	20	Normal	○
TM43	Secret Power	Normal	Physical	70	100	20	Normal	—
TM44	Rest	Psychic	Status	—	—	10	Self	—
TM45	Attract	Normal	Status	—	100	15	Normal	—
TM52	Focus Blast	Fighting	Special	120	70	5	Normal	—
TM56	Fling	Dark	Physical	—	100	10	Normal	—
TM58	Endure	Normal	Status	—	—	10	Self	—
TM59	Dragon Pulse	Dragon	Special	90	100	10	Normal	—
TM60	Drain Punch	Fighting	Physical	60	100	5	Normal	○
TM65	Shadow Claw	Ghost	Physical	70	100	15	Normal	○
TM66	Payback	Dark	Physical	50	100	10	Normal	○
TM68	Giga Impact	Normal	Physical	150	90	5	Normal	○
TM71	Stone Edge	Rock	Physical	100	80	5	Normal	—
TM75	Swords Dance	Normal	Status	—	—	30	Self	—
TM78	Captivate	Normal	Status	—	100	20	2 Foes	—
TM79	Dark Pulse	Dark	Special	80	100	15	Normal	—
TM80	Rock Slide	Rock	Physical	75	90	10	2 Foes	—
TM82	Sleep Talk	Normal	Status	—	—	10	Depends	—
TM83	Natural Gift	Normal	Physical	—	100	15	Normal	—
TM84	Poison Jab	Poison	Physical	80	100	20	Normal	○
TM87	Swagger	Normal	Status	—	90	15	Normal	—
TM90	Substitute	Normal	Status	—	—	10	Self	—
TM91	Flash Cannon	Steel	Special	80	100	10	Normal	—
HM04	Strength	Normal	Physical	80	100	15	Normal	○
HM06	Rock Smash	Fighting	Physical	40	100	15	Normal	○
HM08	Rock Climb	Normal	Physical	90	85	20	Normal	○

● LEVEL-UP MOVES

Lv.	Name	Type	Kind	Pow.	Acc.	PP	Range	DA
1	Tackle	Normal	Physical	35	95	35	Normal	—
1	Sand-Attack	Ground	Status	—	100	15	Normal	—
7	Bite	Dark	Physical	60	100	25	Normal	—
13	Yawn	Normal	Status	—	—	10	Normal	—
19	Take Down	Normal	Physical	90	85	20	Normal	—
19	Dig	Ground	Physical	80	100	10	Normal	—
25	Sand Tomb	Ground	Physical	15	70	15	Normal	—
31	Crunch	Dark	Physical	80	100	15	Normal	—
37	Earthquake	Ground	Physical	100	100	10	2 Foes/1 Ally	—
44	Double-Edge	Normal	Physical	120	100	15	Normal	—
50	Fissure	Ground	Physical	—	30	5	Normal	—

● MOVE MANIAC

Name	Type	Kind	Pow.	Acc.	PP	Range	DA
Headbutt	Normal	Physical	70	100	15	Normal	—

● BP MOVES

Name	Type	Kind	Pow.	Acc.	PP	Range	DA
Snore	Normal	Special	40	100	15	Normal	—
Mud-Slap	Ground	Special	20	100	10	Normal	—
Superpower	Fighting	Physical	120	100	5	Normal	—
Earth Power	Ground	Special	90	100	10	Normal	—

● TM & HM MOVES

No.	Name	Type	Kind	Pow.	Acc.	PP	Range	DA
TM03	Water Pulse	Water	Special	60	100	20	Normal	—
TM05	Roar	Normal	Status	—	100	20	Normal	—
TM06	Toxic	Poison	Status	—	85	10	Normal	—
TM10	Hidden Power	Normal	Special	—	100	15	Normal	—
TM11	Sunny Day	Fire	Status	—	—	5	All	—
TM17	Protect	Normal	Status	—	—	10	Self	—
TM21	Frustration	Normal	Physical	—	100	20	Normal	—
TM23	Iron Tail	Steel	Physical	100	75	15	Normal	—
TM26	Earthquake	Ground	Physical	100	100	10	2 Foes/1 Ally	—
TM27	Return	Normal	Physical	—	100	20	Normal	—
TM28	Dig	Ground	Physical	80	100	10	Normal	—
TM32	Double Team	Normal	Status	—	—	15	Self	—
TM37	Sandstorm	Rock	Status	—	—	10	All	—
TM39	Rock Tomb	Rock	Physical	50	80	10	Normal	—
TM42	Facade	Normal	Physical	70	100	20	Normal	—
TM43	Secret Power	Normal	Physical	70	100	20	Normal	—
TM44	Rest	Psychic	Status	—	—	10	Self	—
TM45	Attract	Normal	Status	—	100	15	Normal	—
TM58	Endure	Normal	Status	—	—	10	Self	—
TM76	Stealth Rock	Rock	Status	—	—	20	2 Foes	—
TM78	Captivate	Normal	Status	—	100	20	2 Foes	—
TM80	Rock Slide	Rock	Physical	75	90	10	2 Foes	—
TM82	Sleep Talk	Normal	Status	—	—	10	Depends	—
TM83	Natural Gift	Normal	Physical	—	100	15	Normal	—
TM87	Swagger	Normal	Status	—	90	15	Normal	—
TM90	Substitute	Normal	Status	—	—	10	Self	—
HM04	Strength	Normal	Physical	80	100	15	Normal	—
HM06	Rock Smash	Fighting	Physical	40	100	15	Normal	—

● EGG MOVES

Name	Type	Kind	Pow.	Acc.	PP	Range	DA
Stockpile	Normal	Status	—	—	20	Self	—
Swallow	Normal	Status	—	—	10	Self	—
Spit Up	Normal	Special	—	100	10	Normal	—
Curse	???	Status	—	—	10	Normal/Self	—
Slack Off	Normal	Status	—	—	10	Self	—
Body Slam	Normal	Physical	85	100	15	Normal	—
Sand Tomb	Ground	Physical	15	70	15	Normal	—
Revenge	Fighting	Physical	60	100	10	Normal	—

● No. 449 | Hippo Pokémon

Hippopotas

Ground

● HEIGHT: 2'07"
● WEIGHT: 109.1 lbs.
● ITEMS: None

● SIZE COMPARISON

● MALE FORM
Beige face

● FEMALE FORM
Brown face

◎ ABILITIES
● Sand Stream

◎ STATS
HP ●●●
ATTACK ●●●
DEFENSE ●●●
SP. ATTACK ●●
SP. DEFENSE ●●
SPEED ●

◎ EGG GROUPS
Field

◎ PERFORMANCE

SPEED ★★☆
POWER ★★★☆☆
SKILL ★★☆
STAMINA ★★★☆☆
JUMP ★★☆

● MAIN WAYS TO OBTAIN

Pokémon HeartGold	Safari Zone (Desert Area: if Rock objects are placed, may appear in tall grass)
Pokémon SoulSilver	Safari Zone (Desert Area: if Rock objects are placed, may appear in tall grass)
Pokémon Diamond	Ruin Maniac Cave/Maniac Tunnel
Pokémon Pearl	Ruin Maniac Cave/Maniac Tunnel
Pokémon Platinum	Ruin Maniac Cave/Maniac Tunnel

Pokémon HeartGold	Pokémon SoulSilver
It shrouds itself in sand to ward off germs. It travels easily through the sands of the desert.	It shrouds itself in sand to ward off germs. It travels easily through the sands of the desert.

◎ EVOLUTION

Lv. 34

Hippopotas → Hippowdon

No. 450 | Heavyweight Pokémon
Hippowdon

Ground

- **HEIGHT:** 6'07"
- **WEIGHT:** 661.4 lbs.
- **ITEMS:** None

● **SIZE COMPARISON**

● **MALE FORM** — Tan body
● **FEMALE FORM** — Gray body

⊕ ABILITIES
● Sand Stream

⊕ STATS
HP ●●●●○
ATTACK ●●●●●
DEFENSE ●●●●●
SP. ATTACK ●●●○○
SP. DEFENSE ●●●○○
SPEED ●●○○○

⊕ EGG GROUPS
Field

⊕ PERFORMANCE
SPEED ★☆
POWER ★★★★☆
SKILL ★★
STAMINA ★★★★☆
JUMP ★★

● **MAIN WAYS TO OBTAIN**

Pokémon HeartGold — Level up Hippopotas to Lv. 34

Pokémon SoulSilver — Level up Hippopotas to Lv. 34

Pokémon Diamond — Route 228

Pokémon Pearl — Route 228

Pokémon Platinum — Route 228

Pokémon HeartGold — It brandishes its gaping mouth in a display of fearsome strength. It raises vast quantities of sand while attacking.

Pokémon SoulSilver — It brandishes its gaping mouth in a display of fearsome strength. It raises vast quantities of sand while attacking.

⊕ EVOLUTION

Hippopotas → Lv. 34 → Hippowdon

● **LEVEL-UP MOVES**

Lv.	Name	Type	Kind	Pow.	Acc.	PP	Range	DA
1	Ice Fang	Ice	Physical	65	95	15	Normal	○
1	Fire Fang	Fire	Physical	65	95	15	Normal	○
1	Thunder Fang	Electric	Physical	65	95	15	Normal	○
1	Tackle	Normal	Physical	35	95	35	Normal	○
1	Sand-Attack	Ground	Status	—	100	15	Normal	—
1	Bite	Dark	Physical	60	100	25	Normal	○
1	Yawn	Normal	Status	—	—	10	Normal	—
7	Bite	Dark	Physical	60	100	25	Normal	○
13	Yawn	Normal	Status	—	—	10	Normal	—
19	Take Down	Normal	Physical	90	85	20	Normal	○
19	Dig	Ground	Physical	80	100	10	Normal	○
25	Sand Tomb	Ground	Physical	15	70	15	Normal	—
31	Crunch	Dark	Physical	80	100	15	Normal	○
40	Earthquake	Ground	Physical	100	100	10	2 Foes/1 Ally	—
50	Double-Edge	Normal	Physical	120	100	15	Normal	○
60	Fissure	Ground	Physical	—	30	5	Normal	—

● **MOVE MANIAC**

Name	Type	Kind	Pow.	Acc.	PP	Range	DA
Headbutt	Normal	Physical	70	100	15	Normal	○

● **BP MOVES**

Name	Type	Kind	Pow.	Acc.	PP	Range	DA
Snore	Normal	Special	40	100	15	Normal	—
Mud-Slap	Ground	Special	20	100	10	Normal	—
Superpower	Fighting	Physical	120	100	5	Normal	○
Iron Head	Steel	Physical	80	100	15	Normal	○
Earth Power	Ground	Special	90	100	10	Normal	—

● **TM & HM MOVES**

No.	Name	Type	Kind	Pow.	Acc.	PP	Range	DA
TM03	Water Pulse	Water	Special	60	100	20	Normal	—
TM05	Roar	Normal	Status	—	100	20	Normal	—
TM06	Toxic	Poison	Status	—	85	10	Normal	—
TM10	Hidden Power	Normal	Special	—	100	15	Normal	—
TM11	Sunny Day	Fire	Status	—	—	5	All	—
TM15	Hyper Beam	Normal	Special	150	90	5	Normal	—
TM17	Protect	Normal	Status	—	—	10	Self	—
TM21	Frustration	Normal	Physical	—	100	20	Normal	○
TM23	Iron Tail	Steel	Physical	100	75	15	Normal	○
TM26	Earthquake	Ground	Physical	100	100	10	2 Foes/1 Ally	—
TM27	Return	Normal	Physical	—	100	20	Normal	○
TM28	Dig	Ground	Physical	80	100	10	Normal	○
TM32	Double Team	Normal	Status	—	—	15	Self	—
TM37	Sandstorm	Rock	Status	—	—	10	All	—
TM39	Rock Tomb	Rock	Physical	50	80	10	Normal	—
TM42	Facade	Normal	Physical	70	100	20	Normal	○
TM43	Secret Power	Normal	Physical	70	100	20	Normal	—
TM44	Rest	Psychic	Status	—	—	10	Self	—
TM45	Attract	Normal	Status	—	100	15	Normal	—
TM58	Endure	Normal	Status	—	—	10	Self	—
TM68	Giga Impact	Normal	Physical	150	90	5	Normal	○
TM71	Stone Edge	Rock	Physical	100	80	5	Normal	—
TM76	Stealth Rock	Rock	Status	—	—	20	2 Foes	—
TM78	Captivate	Normal	Status	—	100	20	2 Foes	—
TM80	Rock Slide	Rock	Physical	75	90	10	2 Foes	—
TM82	Sleep Talk	Normal	Status	—	—	10	Depends	—
TM83	Natural Gift	Normal	Physical	—	100	15	Normal	—
TM87	Swagger	Normal	Status	—	90	15	Normal	—
TM90	Substitute	Normal	Status	—	—	10	Self	—
HM04	Strength	Normal	Physical	80	100	15	Normal	○
HM06	Rock Smash	Fighting	Physical	40	100	15	Normal	○

● LEVEL-UP MOVES

Lv.	Name	Type	Kind	Pow.	Acc.	PP	Range	DA
1	Bite	Dark	Physical	60	100	25	Normal	○
1	Poison Sting	Poison	Physical	15	100	35	Normal	○
1	Leer	Normal	Status	—	100	30	2 Foes	—
6	Knock Off	Dark	Physical	20	100	20	Normal	○
12	Pin Missile	Bug	Physical	14	85	20	Normal	—
17	Acupressure	Normal	Status	—	—	30	1 Ally	—
23	Scary Face	Normal	Status	—	90	10	Normal	—
28	Toxic Spikes	Poison	Status	—	—	20	2 Foes	—
34	Bug Bite	Bug	Physical	60	100	20	Normal	○
39	Poison Fang	Poison	Physical	50	100	15	Normal	○
45	Crunch	Dark	Physical	80	100	15	Normal	○
50	Cross Poison	Poison	Physical	70	100	20	Normal	○

● MOVE MANIAC

Name	Type	Kind	Pow.	Acc.	PP	Range	DA
Headbutt	Normal	Physical	70	100	15	Normal	○

● BP MOVES

Name	Type	Kind	Pow.	Acc.	PP	Range	DA
Fury Cutter	Bug	Physical	10	95	20	Normal	○
Knock Off	Dark	Physical	20	100	20	Normal	○
Bug Bite	Bug	Physical	60	100	20	Normal	○
Snore	Normal	Special	40	100	15	Normal	—
Mud-Slap	Ground	Special	20	100	10	Normal	—
Aqua Tail	Water	Physical	90	90	10	Normal	○

● TM & HM MOVES

No.	Name	Type	Kind	Pow.	Acc.	PP	Range	DA
TM06	Toxic	Poison	Status	—	85	10	Normal	—
TM10	Hidden Power	Normal	Special	—	100	15	Normal	—
TM11	Sunny Day	Fire	Status	—	—	5	All	—
TM12	Taunt	Dark	Status	—	100	20	Normal	—
TM17	Protect	Normal	Status	—	—	10	Self	—
TM18	Rain Dance	Water	Status	—	—	5	All	—
TM21	Frustration	Normal	Physical	—	100	20	Normal	○
TM23	Iron Tail	Steel	Physical	100	75	15	Normal	○
TM27	Return	Normal	Physical	—	100	20	Normal	○
TM28	Dig	Ground	Physical	80	100	10	Normal	○
TM30	Shadow Ball	Ghost	Special	80	100	15	Normal	—
TM31	Brick Break	Fighting	Physical	75	100	15	Normal	○
TM32	Double Team	Normal	Status	—	—	15	Self	—
TM36	Sludge Bomb	Poison	Special	90	100	10	Normal	—
TM39	Rock Tomb	Rock	Physical	50	80	10	Normal	○
TM40	Aerial Ace	Flying	Physical	60	—	20	Normal	○
TM41	Torment	Dark	Status	—	100	15	Normal	—
TM42	Facade	Normal	Physical	70	100	20	Normal	○
TM43	Secret Power	Normal	Physical	70	100	20	Normal	○
TM44	Rest	Psychic	Status	—	—	10	Self	—
TM45	Attract	Normal	Status	—	100	15	Normal	—
TM46	Thief	Dark	Physical	40	100	10	Normal	○
TM54	False Swipe	Normal	Physical	40	100	40	Normal	○
TM56	Fling	Dark	Physical	—	100	10	Normal	○
TM58	Endure	Normal	Status	—	—	10	Self	—
TM66	Payback	Dark	Physical	50	100	10	Normal	○
TM70	Flash	Normal	Status	—	100	20	Normal	—
TM75	Swords Dance	Normal	Status	—	—	30	Self	—
TM78	Captivate	Normal	Status	—	100	20	2 Foes	—
TM79	Dark Pulse	Dark	Special	80	100	15	Normal	—
TM81	X-Scissor	Bug	Physical	80	100	15	Normal	○
TM82	Sleep Talk	Normal	Status	—	—	10	Depends	—
TM83	Natural Gift	Normal	Physical	—	100	15	Normal	○
TM84	Poison Jab	Poison	Physical	80	100	20	Normal	○
TM87	Swagger	Normal	Status	—	90	15	Normal	—
TM90	Substitute	Normal	Status	—	—	10	Self	—
HM01	Cut	Normal	Physical	50	95	30	Normal	○
HM04	Strength	Normal	Physical	80	100	15	Normal	○
HM06	Rock Smash	Fighting	Physical	40	100	15	Normal	○

● EGG MOVES

Name	Type	Kind	Pow.	Acc.	PP	Range	DA
Faint Attack	Dark	Physical	60	—	20	Normal	○
Screech	Normal	Status	—	85	40	Normal	—
Sand-Attack	Ground	Status	—	100	15	Normal	—
Slash	Normal	Physical	70	100	20	Normal	○
Confuse Ray	Ghost	Status	—	100	10	Normal	—
Whirlwind	Normal	Status	—	100	20	Normal	—
Agility	Psychic	Status	—	—	30	Self	—
Pursuit	Dark	Physical	40	100	20	Normal	○
Night Slash	Dark	Physical	70	100	15	Normal	○

● No. 451 | Scorpion Pokémon
Skorupi

Poison | Bug

● HEIGHT: 2'07"
● WEIGHT: 26.5 lbs.
● ITEMS: Poison Barb

● SIZE COMPARISON

● MALE/FEMALE HAVE SAME FORM

⚙ ABILITIES
● Battle Armor
● Sniper

⚙ STATS
HP ●
ATTACK ●●
DEFENSE ●●●●
SP. ATTACK ●
SP. DEFENSE ●●
SPEED ●●●

⚙ EGG GROUPS
Bug

Water 3

⚙ PERFORMANCE

SPEED ★★
POWER ★★★☆
SKILL ★★★★☆
STAMINA ★★★☆
JUMP ★★

● MAIN WAYS TO OBTAIN

Pokémon HeartGold — Safari Zone (Wasteland Area: if Rock objects are placed, may appear in tall grass)

Pokémon SoulSilver — Safari Zone (Wasteland Area: if Rock objects are placed, may appear in tall grass)

Pokémon Diamond — Pastoria Great Marsh (changes daily)

Pokémon Pearl — Pastoria Great Marsh (changes daily)

Pokémon Platinum — Pastoria Great Marsh (changes daily)

Pokémon HeartGold

It burrows under the sand to lie in wait for prey. Its tail claws can inject its prey with a savage poison.

Pokémon SoulSilver

It burrows under the sand to lie in wait for prey. Its tail claws can inject its prey with a savage poison.

⚙ EVOLUTION

Lv. 40

Skorupi → Draplon

No. 452 | Ogre Scorp Pokémon
Drapion

Poison | Dark

- **HEIGHT:** 4'03"
- **WEIGHT:** 135.6 lbs.
- **ITEMS:** None

● MALE/FEMALE HAVE SAME FORM

⊙ ABILITIES
- Battle Armor
- Sniper

⊙ STATS
HP ●●●
ATTACK ●●●●
DEFENSE ●●●●
SP. ATTACK ●●●
SP. DEFENSE ●●●
SPEED ●●●●

⊙ EGG GROUPS
Bug

Water 3

⊙ PERFORMANCE

SPEED ★☆   STAMINA ★★★★
POWER ★★★★☆   JUMP ★★
SKILL ★★★★☆

● MAIN WAYS TO OBTAIN

Pokémon HeartGold	Level up Skorupi to Lv. 40
Pokémon SoulSilver	Level up Skorupi to Lv. 40
Pokémon Diamond	Pastoria Great Marsh (after obtaining the National Pokédex—changes daily)
Pokémon Pearl	Pastoria Great Marsh (after obtaining the National Pokédex—changes daily)
Pokémon Platinum	Pastoria Great Marsh (after obtaining the National Pokédex—changes daily)

| Pokémon HeartGold | Pokémon SoulSilver |
| It attacks people and Pokémon that cross the desert. This has only furthered its bad reputation. | It attacks people and Pokémon that cross the desert. This has only furthered its bad reputation. |

⊙ EVOLUTION

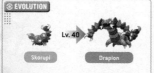

Lv. 40

Skorupi → Drapion

● LEVEL-UP MOVES

Lv.	Name	Type	Kind	Pow.	Acc.	PP	Range	DA
1	Thunder Fang	Electric	Physical	65	95	15	Normal	○
1	Ice Fang	Ice	Physical	65	95	15	Normal	○
1	Fire Fang	Fire	Physical	65	95	15	Normal	○
1	Bite	Dark	Physical	60	100	25	Normal	○
1	Poison Sting	Poison	Physical	15	100	35	Normal	—
1	Leer	Normal	Status	—	100	30	2 Foes	—
1	Knock Off	Dark	Physical	20	100	20	Normal	○
6	Knock Off	Dark	Physical	20	100	20	Normal	○
12	Pin Missile	Bug	Physical	14	85	20	Normal	—
17	Acupressure	Normal	Status	—	—	30	1 Ally	—
23	Scary Face	Normal	Status	—	90	10	Normal	—
28	Toxic Spikes	Poison	Status	—	—	20	2 Foes	—
34	Bug Bite	Bug	Physical	60	100	20	Normal	○
39	Poison Fang	Poison	Physical	50	100	15	Normal	○
49	Crunch	Dark	Physical	80	100	15	Normal	○
58	Cross Poison	Poison	Physical	70	100	20	Normal	○

● MOVE MANIAC

Name	Type	Kind	Pow.	Acc.	PP	Range	DA
Headbutt	Normal	Physical	70	100	15	Normal	○

● BP MOVES

Name	Type	Kind	Pow.	Acc.	PP	Range	DA
Fury Cutter	Bug	Physical	10	95	20	Normal	○
Knock Off	Dark	Physical	20	100	20	Normal	○
Bug Bite	Bug	Physical	60	100	20	Normal	○
Snore	Normal	Special	40	100	15	Normal	—
Mud-Slap	Ground	Special	20	100	10	Normal	—
Aqua Tail	Water	Physical	90	90	10	Normal	○

● TM & HM MOVES

No.	Name	Type	Kind	Pow.	Acc.	PP	Range	DA
TM05	Roar	Normal	Status	—	100	20	Normal	—
TM06	Toxic	Poison	Status	—	85	10	Normal	—
TM10	Hidden Power	Normal	Special	—	100	15	Normal	—
TM11	Sunny Day	Fire	Status	—	—	5	All	—
TM12	Taunt	Dark	Status	—	100	20	Normal	—
TM15	Hyper Beam	Normal	Special	150	90	5	Normal	—
TM17	Protect	Normal	Status	—	—	10	Self	—
TM18	Rain Dance	Water	Status	—	—	5	All	—
TM21	Frustration	Normal	Physical	—	100	20	Normal	○
TM23	Iron Tail	Steel	Physical	100	75	15	Normal	○
TM26	Earthquake	Ground	Physical	100	100	10	2 Foes / 1 Ally	—
TM27	Return	Normal	Physical	—	100	20	Normal	○
TM28	Dig	Ground	Physical	80	100	10	Normal	○
TM30	Shadow Ball	Ghost	Special	80	100	15	Normal	—
TM31	Brick Break	Fighting	Physical	75	100	15	Normal	○
TM32	Double Team	Normal	Status	—	—	15	Self	—
TM36	Sludge Bomb	Poison	Special	90	100	10	Normal	—
TM39	Rock Tomb	Rock	Physical	50	80	10	Normal	○
TM40	Aerial Ace	Flying	Physical	60	—	20	Normal	○
TM41	Torment	Dark	Status	—	100	15	Normal	—
TM42	Facade	Normal	Physical	70	100	20	Normal	○
TM43	Secret Power	Normal	Physical	70	100	20	Normal	○
TM44	Rest	Psychic	Status	—	—	10	Self	—
TM45	Attract	Normal	Status	—	100	15	Normal	—
TM46	Thief	Dark	Physical	40	100	10	Normal	○
TM54	False Swipe	Normal	Physical	40	100	40	Normal	○
TM56	Fling	Dark	Physical	—	100	10	Normal	—
TM58	Endure	Normal	Status	—	—	10	Self	—
TM66	Payback	Dark	Physical	50	100	10	Normal	○
TM68	Giga Impact	Normal	Physical	150	90	5	Normal	○
TM70	Flash	Normal	Status	—	100	20	Normal	—
TM75	Swords Dance	Normal	Status	—	—	30	Self	—
TM78	Captivate	Normal	Status	—	100	20	2 Foes	—
TM79	Dark Pulse	Dark	Special	80	100	15	Normal	—
TM80	Rock Slide	Rock	Physical	75	90	10	2 Foes	—
TM81	X-Scissor	Bug	Physical	80	100	15	Normal	○
TM82	Sleep Talk	Normal	Status	—	—	10	Depends	—
TM83	Natural Gift	Normal	Physical	—	100	15	Normal	—
TM84	Poison Jab	Poison	Physical	80	100	20	Normal	○
TM87	Swagger	Normal	Status	—	90	15	Normal	—
TM90	Substitute	Normal	Status	—	—	10	Self	—
HM01	Cut	Normal	Physical	50	95	30	Normal	○
HM04	Strength	Normal	Physical	80	100	15	Normal	○
HM06	Rock Smash	Fighting	Physical	40	100	15	Normal	○
HM08	Rock Climb	Normal	Physical	90	85	20	Normal	○

● LEVEL-UP MOVES

Lv.	Name	Type	Kind	Pow.	Acc.	PP	Range	DA
1	Astonish	Ghost	Physical	30	100	15	Normal	O
3	Mud-Slap	Ground	Special	20	100	10	Normal	—
8	Poison Sting	Poison	Physical	15	100	35	Normal	—
10	Taunt	Dark	Status	—	100	20	Normal	—
15	Pursuit	Dark	Physical	40	100	20	Normal	O
17	Faint Attack	Dark	Physical	60	—	20	Normal	O
22	Revenge	Fighting	Physical	60	100	10	Normal	O
24	Swagger	Normal	Status	—	90	15	Normal	—
29	Mud Bomb	Ground	Special	65	85	10	Normal	—
31	Sucker Punch	Dark	Physical	80	100	5	Normal	O
36	Nasty Plot	Dark	Status	—	—	20	Self	—
38	Poison Jab	Poison	Physical	80	100	20	Normal	O
43	Sludge Bomb	Poison	Special	90	100	10	Normal	—
45	Flatter	Dark	Status	—	100	15	Normal	—

● MOVE MANIAC

Name	Type	Kind	Pow.	Acc.	PP	Range	DA
Headbutt	Normal	Physical	70	100	15	Normal	O

● BP MOVES

Name	Type	Kind	Pow.	Acc.	PP	Range	DA
Fury Cutter	Bug	Physical	10	95	20	Normal	O
Icy Wind	Ice	Special	55	95	15	2 Foes	O
ThunderPunch	Electric	Physical	75	100	15	Normal	O
Ice Punch	Ice	Physical	75	100	15	Normal	O
Vacuum Wave	Fighting	Special	40	100	30	Normal	—
Knock Off	Dark	Physical	20	100	20	Normal	O
Sucker Punch	Dark	Physical	80	100	5	Normal	O
Snore	Normal	Special	40	100	15	Normal	—
Spite	Ghost	Status	—	100	10	Normal	—
Helping Hand	Normal	Status	—	—	20	1 Ally	—
Role Play	Psychic	Status	—	—	10	Normal	—
Mud-Slap	Ground	Special	20	100	10	Normal	—
Gunk Shot	Poison	Physical	120	70	5	Normal	O
Bounce	Flying	Physical	85	85	5	Normal	O
Super Fang	Normal	Physical	—	90	10	Normal	—
Low Kick	Fighting	Physical	—	100	20	Normal	O

● TM & HM MOVES

No.	Name	Type	Kind	Pow.	Acc.	PP	Range	DA
TM01	Focus Punch	Fighting	Physical	150	100	20	Normal	O
TM06	Toxic	Poison	Status	—	85	10	Normal	—
TM08	Bulk Up	Fighting	Status	—	—	20	Self	—
TM10	Hidden Power	Normal	Special	—	100	15	Normal	—
TM11	Sunny Day	Fire	Status	—	—	5	All	—
TM12	Taunt	Dark	Status	—	100	20	Normal	—
TM17	Protect	Normal	Status	—	—	10	Self	—
TM18	Rain Dance	Water	Status	—	—	5	All	—
TM21	Frustration	Normal	Physical	—	100	20	Normal	O
TM26	Earthquake	Ground	Physical	100	100	10	2 Foes/1 Ally	—
TM27	Return	Normal	Physical	—	100	20	Normal	O
TM28	Dig	Ground	Physical	80	100	10	Normal	O
TM30	Shadow Ball	Ghost	Special	80	100	15	Normal	—
TM31	Brick Break	Fighting	Physical	75	100	15	Normal	O
TM32	Double Team	Normal	Status	—	—	15	Self	—
TM36	Sludge Bomb	Poison	Special	90	100	10	Normal	—
TM39	Rock Tomb	Rock	Physical	50	80	10	Normal	O
TM41	Torment	Dark	Status	—	100	15	Normal	—
TM42	Facade	Normal	Physical	70	100	20	Normal	O
TM43	Secret Power	Normal	Physical	70	100	20	Normal	—
TM44	Rest	Psychic	Status	—	—	10	Self	—
TM45	Attract	Normal	Status	—	100	15	Normal	—
TM46	Thief	Dark	Physical	40	100	10	Normal	O
TM49	Snatch	Dark	Status	—	—	10	Depends	—
TM52	Focus Blast	Fighting	Special	120	70	5	Normal	—
TM56	Fling	Dark	Physical	—	100	10	Normal	—
TM58	Endure	Normal	Status	—	—	10	Self	—
TM63	Embargo	Dark	Status	—	100	15	Normal	—
TM66	Payback	Dark	Physical	50	100	10	Normal	O
TM78	Captivate	Normal	Status	—	100	20	2 Foes	—
TM79	Dark Pulse	Dark	Special	80	100	15	Normal	—
TM80	Rock Slide	Rock	Physical	75	90	10	2 Foes	—
TM81	X-Scissor	Bug	Physical	80	100	15	Normal	O
TM82	Sleep Talk	Normal	Status	—	—	10	Depends	—
TM83	Natural Gift	Normal	Physical	—	100	15	Normal	—
TM84	Poison Jab	Poison	Physical	80	100	20	Normal	O
TM87	Swagger	Normal	Status	—	90	15	Normal	—
TM90	Substitute	Normal	Status	—	—	10	Self	—
HM04	Strength	Normal	Physical	80	100	15	Normal	O
HM06	Rock Smash	Fighting	Physical	40	100	15	Normal	O
HM08	Rock Climb	Normal	Physical	90	85	20	Normal	O

● EGG MOVES

Name	Type	Kind	Pow.	Acc.	PP	Range	DA
Me First	Normal	Status	—	—	20	Depends	—
Feint	Normal	Physical	50	100	10	Normal	—
DynamicPunch	Fighting	Physical	100	50	5	Normal	O
Headbutt	Normal	Physical	70	100	15	Normal	O
Vacuum Wave	Fighting	Special	40	100	30	Normal	—
Meditate	Psychic	Status	—	—	40	Self	—
Fake Out	Normal	Physical	40	100	10	Normal	O
Wake-Up Slap	Fighting	Physical	60	100	10	Normal	O
SmellingSalt	Normal	Physical	60	100	10	Normal	O
Cross Chop	Fighting	Physical	100	80	5	Normal	O
Bullet Punch	Steel	Physical	40	100	30	Normal	O
Counter	Fighting	Physical	—	100	20	Self	O

● No. 453 | Toxic Mouth Pokémon
Croagunk

Poison | **Fighting**

- **HEIGHT:** 2'04"
- **WEIGHT:** 50.7 lbs.
- **ITEMS:** Black Sludge

● SIZE COMPARISON

● **MALE FORM**
Higher stripes on abdomen

● **FEMALE FORM**
Lower stripes on abdomen

● ABILITIES
- Anticipation
- Dry Skin

● STATS
- HP ●●
- ATTACK ●●●
- DEFENSE ●●●
- SP. ATTACK ●●●
- SP. DEFENSE ●
- SPEED ●●

● EGG GROUPS
Human-Like

● PERFORMANCE
- SPEED ★★☆☆☆
- POWER ★★☆☆
- SKILL ★★★☆☆
- STAMINA ★★☆
- JUMP ★★☆☆

● MAIN WAYS TO OBTAIN

Pokémon HeartGold — Safari Zone (Marshland Area: if Forest objects are placed, may appear in tall grass)

Pokémon SoulSilver — Safari Zone (Marshland Area: if Forest objects are placed, may appear in tall grass)

Pokémon Diamond — Pastoria Great Marsh (changes daily)

Pokémon Pearl — Pastoria Great Marsh (changes daily)

Pokémon Platinum — Route 212, Pastoria City side

Pokémon HeartGold — Fluid squeezed from its finger, albeit poisonous, is a significant ingredient in remedies for lower-back pain.

Pokémon SoulSilver — Fluid squeezed from its finger, albeit poisonous, is a significant ingredient in remedies for lower back pain.

● EVOLUTION

Croagunk — Lv. 37 — Toxicroak

No. 454 | Toxic Mouth Pokémon
Toxicroak

Poison | Fighting

● HEIGHT: 4'03"
● WEIGHT: 97.9 lbs.
● ITEMS: None

● SIZE COMPARISON

● MALE FORM
Larger throat sac

● FEMALE FORM
Smaller throat sac

⚙ ABILITIES
● Anticipation
● Dry Skin

⚙ STATS
HP	●●●
ATTACK	●●●●
DEFENSE	●●●
SP. ATTACK	●●●
SP. DEFENSE	●●
SPEED	●●●●

⚙ EGG GROUPS
Human-Like

⚙ PERFORMANCE
SPEED ★★★☆   STAMINA ★★★☆
POWER ★★★☆   JUMP ★★★☆
SKILL ★★★★☆

● MAIN WAYS TO OBTAIN

Pokémon HeartGold	Level up Croagunk to Lv. 37
Pokémon SoulSilver	Level up Croagunk to Lv. 37
Pokémon Diamond	Pastoria Great Marsh (after obtaining the National Pokédex—changes daily)
Pokémon Pearl	Pastoria Great Marsh (after obtaining the National Pokédex—changes daily)
Pokémon Platinum	Pastoria Great Marsh (after obtaining the National Pokédex—changes daily)

Pokémon HeartGold	Pokémon SoulSilver
Swaying and dodging the attacks of its foes, it weaves its flexible body in close, then lunges out with its poisonous claws.	Swaying and dodging the attacks of its foes, it weaves its flexible body in close, then lunges out with its poisonous claws.

⚙ EVOLUTION

Croagunk   Lv. 37   Toxicroak

● LEVEL-UP MOVES

Lv.	Name	Type	Kind	Pow.	Acc.	PP	Range	DA
1	Astonish	Ghost	Physical	30	100	15	Normal	○
1	Mud-Slap	Ground	Special	20	100	10	Normal	—
1	Poison Sting	Poison	Physical	15	100	35	Normal	—
3	Mud-Slap	Ground	Special	20	100	10	Normal	—
8	Poison Sting	Poison	Physical	15	100	35	Normal	—
10	Taunt	Dark	Status	—	100	20	Normal	—
15	Pursuit	Dark	Physical	40	100	20	Normal	○
17	Faint Attack	Dark	Physical	60	—	20	Normal	—
22	Revenge	Fighting	Physical	60	100	10	Normal	○
24	Swagger	Normal	Status	—	90	15	Normal	—
29	Mud Bomb	Ground	Special	65	85	10	Normal	—
31	Sucker Punch	Dark	Physical	80	100	5	Normal	○
36	Nasty Plot	Dark	Status	—	—	20	Self	—
41	Poison Jab	Poison	Physical	80	100	20	Normal	○
49	Sludge Bomb	Poison	Special	90	100	10	Normal	—
54	Flatter	Dark	Status	—	100	15	Normal	—

● MOVE MANIAC

Name	Type	Kind	Pow.	Acc.	PP	Range	DA
Headbutt	Normal	Physical	70	100	15	Normal	○

● BP MOVES

Name	Type	Kind	Pow.	Acc.	PP	Range	DA
Fury Cutter	Bug	Physical	10	95	20	Normal	○
Icy Wind	Ice	Special	55	95	15	2 Foes	—
ThunderPunch	Electric	Physical	75	100	15	Normal	○
Ice Punch	Ice	Physical	75	100	15	Normal	○
Vacuum Wave	Fighting	Special	40	100	30	Normal	—
Knock Off	Dark	Physical	20	100	20	Normal	○
Sucker Punch	Dark	Physical	80	100	5	Normal	○
Snore	Normal	Special	40	100	15	Normal	—
Spite	Ghost	Status	—	100	10	Normal	—
Helping Hand	Normal	Status	—	—	20	1 Ally	—
Role Play	Psychic	Status	—	—	10	—	—
Mud-Slap	Ground	Special	20	100	10	Normal	—
Gunk Shot	Poison	Physical	120	70	5	Normal	○
Bounce	Flying	Physical	85	85	5	Normal	○
Super Fang	Normal	Physical	—	90	10	Normal	○
Low Kick	Fighting	Physical	—	100	20	Normal	○

● TM & HM MOVES

No.	Name	Type	Kind	Pow.	Acc.	PP	Range	DA
TM01	Focus Punch	Fighting	Physical	150	100	20	Normal	○
TM06	Toxic	Poison	Status	—	85	10	Normal	—
TM08	Bulk Up	Fighting	Status	—	—	20	Self	—
TM10	Hidden Power	Normal	Special	—	100	15	Normal	—
TM11	Sunny Day	Fire	Status	—	—	5	All	—
TM12	Taunt	Dark	Status	—	100	20	Normal	—
TM15	Hyper Beam	Normal	Special	150	90	5	Normal	—
TM17	Protect	Normal	Status	—	—	10	Self	—
TM18	Rain Dance	Water	Status	—	—	5	All	—
TM21	Frustration	Normal	Physical	—	100	20	Normal	○
TM26	Earthquake	Ground	Physical	100	100	10	2 Foes/1 Ally	—
TM27	Return	Normal	Physical	—	100	20	Normal	○
TM28	Dig	Ground	Physical	80	100	10	Normal	○
TM30	Shadow Ball	Ghost	Special	80	100	15	Normal	—
TM31	Brick Break	Fighting	Physical	75	100	15	Normal	○
TM32	Double Team	Normal	Status	—	—	15	Self	—
TM36	Sludge Bomb	Poison	Special	90	100	10	Normal	—
TM39	Rock Tomb	Rock	Physical	50	80	10	Normal	○
TM41	Torment	Dark	Status	—	100	15	Normal	—
TM42	Facade	Normal	Physical	70	100	20	Normal	○
TM43	Secret Power	Normal	Physical	70	100	20	Normal	○
TM44	Rest	Psychic	Status	—	—	10	Self	—
TM45	Attract	Normal	Status	—	100	15	Normal	—
TM46	Thief	Dark	Physical	40	100	10	Normal	○
TM49	Snatch	Dark	Status	—	—	10	Depends	—
TM52	Focus Blast	Fighting	Special	120	70	5	Normal	—
TM56	Fling	Dark	Physical	—	100	10	Normal	—
TM58	Endure	Normal	Status	—	—	10	Self	—
TM63	Embargo	Dark	Status	—	100	15	Normal	—
TM66	Payback	Dark	Physical	50	100	10	Normal	○
TM68	Giga Impact	Normal	Physical	150	90	5	Normal	○
TM71	Stone Edge	Rock	Physical	100	80	5	Normal	○
TM75	Swords Dance	Normal	Status	—	—	30	Self	—
TM78	Captivate	Normal	Status	—	100	20	2 Foes	—
TM79	Dark Pulse	Dark	Special	80	100	15	Normal	—
TM80	Rock Slide	Rock	Physical	75	90	10	2 Foes	—
TM81	X-Scissor	Bug	Physical	80	100	15	Normal	○
TM82	Sleep Talk	Normal	Status	—	—	10	Depends	—
TM83	Natural Gift	Normal	Physical	—	100	15	Normal	—
TM84	Poison Jab	Poison	Physical	80	100	20	Normal	○
TM87	Swagger	Normal	Status	—	90	15	Normal	—
TM90	Substitute	Normal	Status	—	—	10	Self	—
HM01	Cut	Normal	Physical	50	95	30	Normal	○
HM04	Strength	Normal	Physical	80	100	15	Normal	○
HM06	Rock Smash	Fighting	Physical	40	100	15	Normal	○
HM08	Rock Climb	Normal	Physical	90	85	20	Normal	—

● LEVEL-UP MOVES

Lv.	Name	Type	Kind	Pow.	Acc.	PP	Range	DA
1	Bind	Normal	Physical	15	75	20	Normal	○
1	Growth	Normal	Status	—	—	40	Self	—
7	Bite	Dark	Physical	60	100	25	Normal	○
11	Vine Whip	Grass	Physical	35	100	15	Normal	—
17	Sweet Scent	Normal	Status	—	100	20	2 Foes	—
21	Ingrain	Grass	Status	—	—	20	Self	—
27	Faint Attack	Dark	Physical	60	—	20	Normal	○
31	Stockpile	Normal	Status	—	—	20	Self	—
31	Spit Up	Normal	Special	—	100	10	Normal	—
31	Swallow	Normal	Status	—	—	10	Self	—
37	Crunch	Dark	Physical	80	100	15	Normal	○
41	Wring Out	Normal	Special	—	100	5	Normal	○
47	Power Whip	Grass	Physical	120	85	10	Normal	○

● MOVE MANIAC

Name	Type	Kind	Pow.	Acc.	PP	Range	DA

● BP MOVES

Name	Type	Kind	Pow.	Acc.	PP	Range	DA
Fury Cutter	Bug	Physical	10	95	20	Normal	○
Knock Off	Dark	Physical	20	100	20	Normal	○
Bug Bite	Bug	Physical	60	100	20	Normal	○
Snore	Normal	Special	40	100	15	Normal	—
Synthesis	Grass	Status	—	—	5	Self	—
Worry Seed	Grass	Status	—	100	10	Normal	—
Mud-Slap	Ground	Special	20	100	10	Normal	—
Gastro Acid	Poison	Status	—	100	10	Normal	—
Seed Bomb	Grass	Physical	80	100	15	Normal	—

● TM & HM MOVES

No.	Name	Type	Kind	Pow.	Acc.	PP	Range	DA
TM06	Toxic	Poison	Status	—	85	10	Normal	—
TM09	Bullet Seed	Grass	Physical	10	100	30	Normal	—
TM10	Hidden Power	Normal	Special	—	100	15	Normal	—
TM11	Sunny Day	Fire	Status	—	—	5	All	—
TM15	Hyper Beam	Normal	Special	150	90	5	Normal	—
TM17	Protect	Normal	Status	—	—	10	Self	—
TM19	Giga Drain	Grass	Special	60	100	10	Normal	—
TM21	Frustration	Normal	Physical	—	100	20	Normal	○
TM22	SolarBeam	Grass	Special	120	100	10	Normal	—
TM27	Return	Normal	Physical	—	100	20	Normal	○
TM32	Double Team	Normal	Status	—	—	15	Self	—
TM42	Facade	Normal	Physical	70	100	20	Normal	○
TM43	Secret Power	Normal	Physical	70	100	20	Normal	—
TM44	Rest	Psychic	Status	—	—	10	Self	—
TM45	Attract	Normal	Status	—	100	15	Normal	—
TM46	Thief	Dark	Physical	40	100	10	Normal	○
TM53	Energy Ball	Grass	Special	80	100	10	Normal	—
TM56	Fling	Dark	Physical	—	100	10	Normal	—
TM58	Endure	Normal	Status	—	—	10	Self	—
TM66	Payback	Dark	Physical	50	100	10	Normal	○
TM68	Giga Impact	Normal	Physical	150	90	5	Normal	○
TM70	Flash	Normal	Status	—	100	20	Normal	—
TM75	Swords Dance	Normal	Status	—	—	30	Self	—
TM78	Captivate	Normal	Status	—	100	20	2 Foes	—
TM82	Sleep Talk	Normal	Status	—	—	10	Depends	—
TM83	Natural Gift	Normal	Physical	—	100	15	Normal	—
TM86	Grass Knot	Grass	Special	—	100	20	Normal	○
TM87	Swagger	Normal	Status	—	90	15	Normal	—
TM90	Substitute	Normal	Status	—	—	10	Self	—
HM01	Cut	Normal	Physical	50	95	30	Normal	○

● EGG MOVES

Name	Type	Kind	Pow.	Acc.	PP	Range	DA
Sleep Powder	Grass	Status	—	75	15	Normal	—
Stun Spore	Grass	Status	—	75	30	Normal	—
Razor Leaf	Grass	Physical	55	95	25	2 Foes	—
Slam	Normal	Physical	80	75	20	Normal	○
Synthesis	Grass	Status	—	—	5	Self	—
Magical Leaf	Grass	Special	60	—	20	Normal	—
Leech Seed	Grass	Status	—	90	10	Normal	—
Worry Seed	Grass	Status	—	100	10	Normal	—

○ No. 455 | Bug Catcher Pokémon
Carnivine

Grass

- **HEIGHT:** 4'07"
- **WEIGHT:** 59.5 lbs.
- **ITEMS:** None

● SIZE COMPARISON

● MALE/FEMALE HAVE SAME FORM

◎ ABILITIES
● Levitate

◎ STATS
HP ●●●
ATTACK ●●●●●
DEFENSE ●●●●
SP. ATTACK ●●●●
SP. DEFENSE ●●●
SPEED ●●

◎ EGG GROUPS
Grass

◎ PERFORMANCE
SPEED ★★☆ STAMINA ★★☆
POWER ★★★☆☆ JUMP ★★★★★
SKILL ★★☆

● MAIN WAYS TO OBTAIN

Pokémon HeartGold — Ilex Forest (Sinnoh Sound)

Pokémon SoulSilver — Ilex Forest (Sinnoh Sound)

Pokémon Diamond — Pastoria Great Marsh (changes daily)

Pokémon Pearl — Pastoria Great Marsh (changes daily)

Pokémon Platinum — Pastoria Great Marsh (changes daily)

Pokémon HeartGold
It walks around on its tentacles in search of a tree branch where it can dangle down and ambush prey.

Pokémon SoulSilver
It walks around on its tentacles in search of a tree branch where it can dangle down and ambush prey.

◎ EVOLUTION
Does not evolve

No. 456 | Wing Fish Pokémon
Finneon

Water

● HEIGHT: 1'04"
● WEIGHT: 15.4 lbs.
● ITEMS: None

● SIZE COMPARISON

● MALE FORM
Bottom lobes of tail fins are smaller

● FEMALE FORM
Bottom lobes of tail fins are larger

⚙ ABILITIES
● Swift Swim
● Storm Drain

⚙ STATS
HP ●●
ATTACK ●●
DEFENSE ●●
SP. ATTACK ●●
SP. DEFENSE ●●
SPEED ●●●

⚙ EGG GROUPS
Water 2

⚙ PERFORMANCE
SPEED ★★★★☆   STAMINA ★★☆☆
POWER ★☆   JUMP ★★★☆
SKILL ★★☆☆

● MAIN WAYS TO OBTAIN

Pokémon HeartGold	Stormy Beach Pokéwalker Route
Pokémon SoulSilver	Stormy Beach Pokéwalker Route
Pokémon Diamond	Route 218 (Good Rod)
Pokémon Pearl	Route 218 (Good Rod)
Pokémon Platinum	Route 218 (Good Rod)

Pokémon HeartGold	Pokémon SoulSilver
Swimming and fluttering its two tail fins, it looks like a BEAUTIFLY. At night, the patterns on its tail fins softly shine.	Swimming and fluttering its two tail fins, it looks like a BEAUTIFLY. At night, the patterns on its tail fins softly shine.

⚙ EVOLUTION

 Lv. 31

Finneon   Lumineon

● LEVEL-UP MOVES

Lv.	Name	Type	Kind	Pow.	Acc.	PP	Range	DA
1	Pound	Normal	Physical	40	100	35	Normal	○
6	Water Gun	Water	Special	40	100	25	Normal	—
10	Attract	Normal	Status	—	100	15	Normal	—
13	Rain Dance	Water	Status	—	—	5	All	—
17	Gust	Flying	Special	40	100	35	Normal	—
22	Water Pulse	Water	Special	60	100	20	Normal	—
26	Captivate	Normal	Status	—	100	20	2 Foes	—
29	Safeguard	Normal	Status	—	—	25	2 Allies	—
33	Aqua Ring	Water	Status	—	—	20	Self	—
38	Whirlpool	Water	Special	15	70	15	Normal	—
42	U-turn	Bug	Physical	70	100	20	Normal	○
45	Bounce	Flying	Physical	85	85	5	Normal	—
49	Silver Wind	Bug	Special	60	100	5	Normal	—

● MOVE MANIAC

Name	Type	Kind	Pow.	Acc.	PP	Range	DA

● BP MOVES

Name	Type	Kind	Pow.	Acc.	PP	Range	DA
Dive	Water	Physical	80	100	10	Normal	○
Icy Wind	Ice	Special	55	95	15	2 Foes	—
Ominous Wind	Ghost	Special	60	100	5	Normal	—
Air Cutter	Flying	Special	55	95	25	2 Foes	—
Snore	Normal	Special	40	100	15	Normal	—
Swift	Normal	Special	60	—	20	2 Foes	—
Tailwind	Flying	Status	—	—	30	2 Allies	—
Aqua Tail	Water	Physical	90	90	10	Normal	○
Twister	Dragon	Special	40	100	20	2 Foes	—
Bounce	Flying	Physical	85	85	5	Normal	○

● TM & HM MOVES

No.	Name	Type	Kind	Pow.	Acc.	PP	Range	DA
TM03	Water Pulse	Water	Special	60	100	20	Normal	—
TM06	Toxic	Poison	Status	—	85	10	Normal	—
TM07	Hail	Ice	Status	—	—	10	All	—
TM10	Hidden Power	Normal	Special	—	100	15	Normal	—
TM13	Ice Beam	Ice	Special	95	100	10	Normal	—
TM14	Blizzard	Ice	Special	120	70	5	2 Foes	—
TM17	Protect	Normal	Status	—	—	10	Self	—
TM18	Rain Dance	Water	Status	—	—	5	All	—
TM20	Safeguard	Normal	Status	—	—	25	2 Allies	—
TM21	Frustration	Normal	Physical	—	100	20	Normal	○
TM27	Return	Normal	Physical	—	100	20	Normal	○
TM32	Double Team	Normal	Status	—	—	15	Self	—
TM42	Facade	Normal	Physical	70	100	20	Normal	○
TM43	Secret Power	Normal	Physical	70	100	20	Normal	○
TM44	Rest	Psychic	Status	—	—	10	Self	—
TM45	Attract	Normal	Status	—	100	15	Normal	—
TM55	Brine	Water	Special	65	100	10	Normal	—
TM58	Endure	Normal	Status	—	—	10	Self	—
TM62	Silver Wind	Bug	Special	60	100	5	Normal	—
TM66	Payback	Dark	Physical	50	100	10	Normal	○
TM70	Flash	Normal	Status	—	100	20	Normal	—
TM77	Psych Up	Normal	Status	—	—	10	Normal	—
TM78	Captivate	Normal	Status	—	100	20	2 Foes	—
TM82	Sleep Talk	Normal	Status	—	—	10	Depends	—
TM83	Natural Gift	Normal	Physical	—	100	15	Normal	—
TM87	Swagger	Normal	Status	—	90	15	Normal	—
TM89	U-turn	Bug	Physical	70	100	20	Normal	○
TM90	Substitute	Normal	Status	—	—	10	Self	—
HM03	Surf	Water	Special	95	100	15	2 Foes/1 Ally	—
HM05	Whirlpool	Water	Special	15	70	15	Normal	—
HM07	Waterfall	Water	Physical	80	100	15	Normal	○

● EGG MOVES

Name	Type	Kind	Pow.	Acc.	PP	Range	DA
Sweet Kiss	Normal	Status	—	75	10	Normal	—
Charm	Normal	Status	—	100	20	Normal	—
Flail	Normal	Physical	—	100	15	Normal	○
Aqua Tail	Water	Physical	90	90	10	Normal	○
Splash	Normal	Status	—	—	40	Self	—
Psybeam	Psychic	Special	65	100	20	Normal	—
Tickle	Normal	Status	—	100	20	Normal	—
Agility	Psychic	Status	—	—	30	Self	—

● LEVEL-UP MOVES

Lv.	Name	Type	Kind	Pow.	Acc.	PP	Range	DA
1	Pound	Normal	Physical	40	100	35	Normal	○
1	Water Gun	Water	Special	40	100	25	Normal	—
1	Attract	Normal	Status	—	100	15	Normal	—
6	Water Gun	Water	Special	40	100	25	Normal	—
10	Attract	Normal	Status	—	100	15	Normal	—
13	Rain Dance	Water	Status	—	—	5	All	—
17	Gust	Flying	Special	40	100	35	Normal	—
22	Water Pulse	Water	Special	60	100	20	Normal	—
26	Captivate	Normal	Status	—	100	20	2 Foes	—
29	Safeguard	Normal	Status	—	—	25	2 Allies	—
35	Aqua Ring	Water	Status	—	—	20	Self	—
42	Whirlpool	Water	Special	15	70	15	Normal	—
48	U-turn	Bug	Physical	70	100	20	Normal	○
53	Bounce	Flying	Physical	85	85	5	Normal	○
59	Silver Wind	Bug	Special	60	100	5	Normal	—

● MOVE MANIAC

Name	Type	Kind	Pow.	Acc.	PP	Range	DA

● BP MOVES

Name	Type	Kind	Pow.	Acc.	PP	Range	DA
Dive	Water	Physical	80	100	10	Normal	○
Icy Wind	Ice	Special	55	95	15	2 Foes	—
Ominous Wind	Ghost	Special	60	100	5	Normal	—
Air Cutter	Flying	Special	55	95	25	2 Foes	—
Snore	Normal	Special	40	100	15	Normal	—
Swift	Normal	Special	60	—	20	2 Foes	—
Tailwind	Flying	Status	—	—	30	2 Allies	—
Aqua Tail	Water	Physical	90	90	10	Normal	○
Twister	Dragon	Special	40	100	20	2 Foes	—
Bounce	Flying	Physical	85	85	5	Normal	○

● TM & HM MOVES

No.	Name	Type	Kind	Pow.	Acc.	PP	Range	DA
TM03	Water Pulse	Water	Special	60	100	20	Normal	—
TM06	Toxic	Poison	Status	—	85	10	Normal	—
TM07	Hail	Ice	Status	—	—	10	All	—
TM10	Hidden Power	Normal	Special	—	100	15	Normal	—
TM13	Ice Beam	Ice	Special	95	100	10	Normal	—
TM14	Blizzard	Ice	Special	120	70	5	2 Foes	—
TM15	Hyper Beam	Normal	Special	150	90	5	Normal	—
TM17	Protect	Normal	Status	—	—	10	Self	—
TM18	Rain Dance	Water	Status	—	—	5	All	—
TM20	Safeguard	Normal	Status	—	—	25	2 Allies	—
TM21	Frustration	Normal	Physical	—	100	20	Normal	○
TM27	Return	Normal	Physical	—	100	20	Normal	○
TM32	Double Team	Normal	Status	—	—	15	Self	—
TM42	Facade	Normal	Physical	70	100	20	Normal	○
TM43	Secret Power	Normal	Physical	70	100	20	Normal	○
TM44	Rest	Psychic	Status	—	—	10	Self	—
TM45	Attract	Normal	Status	—	100	15	Normal	—
TM55	Brine	Water	Special	65	100	10	Normal	—
TM58	Endure	Normal	Status	—	—	10	Self	—
TM62	Silver Wind	Bug	Special	60	100	5	Normal	—
TM66	Payback	Dark	Physical	50	100	10	Normal	○
TM68	Giga Impact	Normal	Physical	150	90	5	Normal	○
TM70	Flash	Normal	Status	—	100	20	Normal	—
TM77	Psych Up	Normal	Status	—	—	10	Normal	—
TM78	Captivate	Normal	Status	—	100	20	2 Foes	—
TM82	Sleep Talk	Normal	Status	—	—	10	Depends	—
TM83	Natural Gift	Normal	Physical	—	100	15	Normal	—
TM87	Swagger	Normal	Status	—	90	15	Normal	—
TM89	U-turn	Bug	Physical	70	100	20	Normal	○
TM90	Substitute	Normal	Status	—	—	10	Self	—
HM03	Surf	Water	Special	95	100	15	2 Foes/1 Ally	—
HM05	Whirlpool	Water	Special	15	70	15	Normal	—
HM07	Waterfall	Water	Physical	80	100	15	Normal	○

◎ No. 457 | Neon Pokémon
Lumineon

Water

● HEIGHT: 3'11"
● WEIGHT: 52.9 lbs.
● ITEMS: None

● SIZE COMPARISON

● MALE FORM
Bottom lobes of tail fins are shorter

● FEMALE FORM
Bottom lobes of tail fins are longer

◎ ABILITIES
● Swift Swim
● Storm Drain

◎ STATS
HP ●●●
ATTACK ●●●
DEFENSE ●●●
SP. ATTACK ●●●
SP. DEFENSE ●●●
SPEED ●●●●

◎ EGG GROUPS
Water 2

◎ PERFORMANCE
SPEED ★★★☆   STAMINA ★★★☆
POWER ★☆☆   JUMP ★★★☆
SKILL ★★★☆

● MAIN WAYS TO OBTAIN

Pokémon HeartGold	Level up Finneon to Lv. 31
Pokémon SoulSilver	Level up Finneon to Lv. 31
Pokémon Diamond	Route 218 (Super Rod)
Pokémon Pearl	Route 218 (Super Rod)
Pokémon Platinum	Route 218 (Super Rod)

Pokémon HeartGold
LUMINEON swimming in the darkness of the deep sea look like stars shining in the night sky.

Pokémon SoulSilver
LUMINEON swimming in the darkness of the deep sea look like stars shining in the night sky.

◎ EVOLUTION

 Lv. 31

Finneon → Lumineon

No. 458 | Kite Pokémon
Mantyke

Water | Flying

- **HEIGHT:** 3'03"
- **WEIGHT:** 143.3 lbs.
- **ITEMS:** None

- **SIZE COMPARISON**

- **MALE/FEMALE HAVE SAME FORM**

⊘ ABILITIES
- Swift Swim
- Water Absorb

⊘ STATS
HP ●●
ATTACK ●●
DEFENSE ●●
SP. ATTACK ●●●
SP. DEFENSE ●●●●●
SPEED ●●

⊘ EGG GROUPS
No Egg has ever been discovered

⊘ PERFORMANCE
SPEED ★★★☆ STAMINA ★★★☆
POWER ★★☆   JUMP ★★★☆
SKILL ★★

● MAIN WAYS TO OBTAIN

Pokémon HeartGold	Have Mantine ♀ hold the Wave Incense and leave it at the Pokémon Day Care, then find its Egg and hatch it
Pokémon SoulSilver	—
Pokémon Diamond	Route 223 (water surface)
Pokémon Pearl	Route 223 (water surface)
Pokémon Platinum	Route 223 (water surface)

Pokémon HeartGold	Pokémon SoulSilver
When it swims close to the surface of the ocean, people aboard ships are able to observe the pattern on its back.	When it swims close to the surface of the ocean, people aboard ships are able to observe the pattern on its back.

⊘ EVOLUTION

Mantyke — Level it up while Remoraid is in your party → Mantine

● LEVEL-UP MOVES

Lv.	Name	Type	Kind	Pow.	Acc.	PP	Range	DA
1	Tackle	Normal	Physical	35	95	35	Normal	○
1	Bubble	Water	Special	20	100	30	2 Foes	—
4	Supersonic	Normal	Status	—	55	20	Normal	—
10	BubbleBeam	Water	Special	65	100	20	Normal	—
13	Headbutt	Normal	Physical	70	100	15	Normal	○
19	Agility	Psychic	Status	—	—	30	Self	—
22	Wing Attack	Flying	Physical	60	100	35	Normal	○
28	Water Pulse	Water	Special	60	100	20	Normal	—
31	Take Down	Normal	Physical	90	85	20	Normal	○
37	Confuse Ray	Ghost	Status	—	100	10	Normal	—
40	Bounce	Flying	Physical	85	85	5	Normal	○
46	Aqua Ring	Water	Status	—	—	20	Self	—
49	Hydro Pump	Water	Special	120	80	5	Normal	—

● MOVE MANIAC

Name	Type	Kind	Pow.	Acc.	PP	Range	DA
Headbutt	Normal	Physical	70	100	15	Normal	○

● BP MOVES

Name	Type	Kind	Pow.	Acc.	PP	Range	DA
Dive	Water	Physical	80	100	10	Normal	○
Icy Wind	Ice	Special	55	95	15	2 Foes	—
Air Cutter	Flying	Special	55	95	25	2 Foes	—
Snore	Normal	Special	40	100	15	Normal	—
Helping Hand	Normal	Status	—	—	20	1 Ally	—
Swift	Normal	Special	60	—	20	2 Foes	—
Mud-Slap	Ground	Special	20	100	10	Normal	—
Bounce	Flying	Physical	85	85	5	Normal	○

● TM & HM MOVES

No.	Name	Type	Kind	Pow.	Acc.	PP	Range	DA
TM03	Water Pulse	Water	Special	60	100	20	Normal	—
TM06	Toxic	Poison	Status	—	100	10	Normal	—
TM07	Hail	Ice	Status	—	—	10	All	—
TM10	Hidden Power	Normal	Special	—	100	15	Normal	—
TM13	Ice Beam	Ice	Special	95	100	10	Normal	—
TM14	Blizzard	Ice	Special	120	70	5	2 Foes	—
TM17	Protect	Normal	Status	—	—	10	Self	—
TM18	Rain Dance	Water	Status	—	—	5	All	—
TM21	Frustration	Normal	Physical	—	100	20	Normal	○
TM26	Earthquake	Ground	Physical	100	100	10	2 Foes/1 Ally	—
TM27	Return	Normal	Physical	—	100	20	Normal	○
TM32	Double Team	Normal	Status	—	—	15	Self	—
TM40	Aerial Ace	Flying	Physical	60	—	20	Normal	○
TM42	Facade	Normal	Physical	70	100	20	Normal	○
TM43	Secret Power	Normal	Physical	70	100	20	Normal	—
TM44	Rest	Psychic	Status	—	—	10	Self	—
TM45	Attract	Normal	Status	—	100	15	Normal	—
TM58	Endure	Normal	Status	—	—	10	Self	—
TM78	Captivate	Normal	Status	—	100	20	2 Foes	—
TM82	Sleep Talk	Normal	Status	—	—	10	Depends	—
TM83	Natural Gift	Normal	Physical	—	100	15	Normal	—
TM87	Swagger	Normal	Status	—	90	15	Normal	—
TM90	Substitute	Normal	Status	—	—	10	Self	—
HM03	Surf	Water	Special	95	100	15	2 Foes/1 Ally	—
HM05	Whirlpool	Water	Special	15	70	15	Normal	—
HM07	Waterfall	Water	Physical	80	100	15	Normal	○

● EGG MOVES

Name	Type	Kind	Pow.	Acc.	PP	Range	DA
Twister	Dragon	Special	40	100	20	2 Foes	—
Hydro Pump	Water	Special	120	80	5	Normal	—
Haze	Ice	Status	—	—	30	All	—
Slam	Normal	Physical	80	75	20	Normal	○
Mud Sport	Ground	Status	—	—	15	All	—
Rock Slide	Rock	Physical	75	90	10	2 Foes	—
Mirror Coat	Psychic	Special	—	100	20	Self	—
Water Sport	Water	Status	—	—	15	All	—
Splash	Normal	Status	—	—	40	Self	—
Signal Beam	Bug	Special	75	100	15	Normal	—

● LEVEL-UP MOVES

Lv.	Name	Type	Kind	Pow.	Acc.	PP	Range	DA
1	Powder Snow	Ice	Special	40	100	25	2 Foes	—
1	Leer	Normal	Status	—	100	30	2 Foes	—
5	Razor Leaf	Grass	Physical	55	95	25	2 Foes	—
9	Icy Wind	Ice	Special	55	95	15	2 Foes	—
13	Grass Whistle	Grass	Status	—	55	15	Normal	—
17	Swagger	Normal	Status	—	90	15	Normal	—
21	Mist	Ice	Status	—	—	30	2 Allies	—
26	Ice Shard	Ice	Physical	40	100	30	Normal	—
31	Ingrain	Grass	Status	—	—	20	Self	—
36	Wood Hammer	Grass	Physical	120	100	15	Normal	○
41	Blizzard	Ice	Special	120	70	5	2 Foes	—
46	Sheer Cold	Ice	Special	—	30	5	Normal	—

● MOVE MANIAC

Name	Type	Kind	Pow.	Acc.	PP	Range	DA
Headbutt	Normal	Physical	70	100	15	Normal	○

● BP MOVES

Name	Type	Kind	Pow.	Acc.	PP	Range	DA
Icy Wind	Ice	Special	55	95	15	2 Foes	—
Ice Punch	Ice	Physical	75	100	15	Normal	○
Snore	Normal	Special	40	100	15	Normal	—
Synthesis	Grass	Status	—	—	5	Self	—
Worry Seed	Grass	Status	—	—	10	Normal	—
Role Play	Psychic	Status	—	—	10	Normal	—
Mud-Slap	Ground	Special	20	100	10	Normal	—
Seed Bomb	Grass	Physical	80	100	15	Normal	—

● TM & HM MOVES

No.	Name	Type	Kind	Pow.	Acc.	PP	Range	DA
TM03	Water Pulse	Water	Special	60	100	20	Normal	—
TM06	Toxic	Poison	Status	—	85	10	Normal	—
TM07	Hail	Ice	Status	—	—	10	All	—
TM09	Bullet Seed	Grass	Physical	10	100	30	Normal	—
TM10	Hidden Power	Normal	Special	—	100	15	Normal	—
TM13	Ice Beam	Ice	Special	95	100	10	Normal	—
TM14	Blizzard	Ice	Special	120	70	5	2 Foes	—
TM16	Light Screen	Psychic	Status	—	—	30	2 Allies	—
TM17	Protect	Normal	Status	—	—	10	Self	—
TM18	Rain Dance	Water	Status	—	—	5	All	—
TM19	Giga Drain	Grass	Special	60	100	10	Normal	—
TM20	Safeguard	Normal	Status	—	—	25	2 Allies	—
TM21	Frustration	Normal	Physical	—	100	20	Normal	○
TM22	SolarBeam	Grass	Special	120	100	10	Normal	—
TM23	Iron Tail	Steel	Physical	100	75	15	Normal	○
TM27	Return	Normal	Physical	—	100	20	Normal	○
TM30	Shadow Ball	Ghost	Special	80	100	15	Normal	—
TM32	Double Team	Normal	Status	—	—	15	Self	—
TM42	Facade	Normal	Physical	70	100	20	Normal	○
TM43	Secret Power	Normal	Physical	70	100	20	Normal	—
TM44	Rest	Psychic	Status	—	—	10	Self	—
TM45	Attract	Normal	Status	—	100	15	Normal	—
TM53	Energy Ball	Grass	Special	80	100	10	Normal	—
TM58	Endure	Normal	Status	—	—	10	Self	—
TM70	Flash	Normal	Status	—	100	20	Normal	—
TM72	Avalanche	Ice	Physical	60	100	10	Normal	○
TM75	Swords Dance	Normal	Status	—	—	30	Self	—
TM78	Captivate	Normal	Status	—	100	20	2 Foes	—
TM82	Sleep Talk	Normal	Status	—	—	10	Depends	—
TM83	Natural Gift	Normal	Physical	—	100	15	Normal	—
TM86	Grass Knot	Grass	Special	—	100	20	Normal	○
TM87	Swagger	Normal	Status	—	90	15	Normal	—
TM90	Substitute	Normal	Status	—	—	10	Self	—

● EGG MOVES

Name	Type	Kind	Pow.	Acc.	PP	Range	DA
Leech Seed	Grass	Status	—	90	10	Normal	—
Magical Leaf	Grass	Special	60	—	20	Normal	—
Seed Bomb	Grass	Physical	80	100	15	Normal	—
Growth	Normal	Status	—	—	40	Self	—
Double-Edge	Normal	Physical	120	100	15	Normal	○
Mist	Ice	Status	—	—	30	2 Allies	—
Stomp	Normal	Physical	65	100	15	Normal	○
Skull Bash	Normal	Physical	100	100	15	Normal	○

 No. 459 | Frost Tree Pokémon

Snover

Grass   Ice

● HEIGHT: 3'03"
● WEIGHT: 111.3 lbs.
● ITEMS: None

● SIZE COMPARISON

● MALE FORM
Shorter white section

● FEMALE FORM
Longer white section

● ABILITIES
● Snow Warning

● STATS
HP ●●
ATTACK ●●●
DEFENSE ●●●
SP. ATTACK ●●●
SP. DEFENSE ●●●
SPEED ●●

● EGG GROUPS
Monster
Grass

● PERFORMANCE
SPEED ★★☆☆   STAMINA ★★★☆
POWER ★★☆☆   JUMP ★★☆
SKILL ★★★☆

● MAIN WAYS TO OBTAIN

Pokémon HeartGold	Icy Mountain Rd. Pokéwalker Route
Pokémon SoulSilver	Icy Mountain Rd. Pokéwalker Route
Pokémon Diamond	Route 216
Pokémon Pearl	Route 216
Pokémon Platinum	Route 216

Pokémon HeartGold

During cold seasons, it migrates to the mountain's lower reaches. It returns to the snow-covered summit in the spring.

Pokémon SoulSilver

During cold seasons, it migrates to the mountain's lower reaches. It returns to the snow-covered summit in the spring.

● EVOLUTION

Snover → Lv. 40 → Abomasnow

● No. 460 | Frost Tree Pokémon
Abomasnow

Grass · Ice

● **HEIGHT:** 7'03"
● **WEIGHT:** 298.7 lbs.
● **ITEMS:** None

● **SIZE COMPARISON**

● **MALE FORM**
Shorter fur on chest

● **FEMALE FORM**
Longer fur on chest

● ABILITIES
● Snow Warning

● STATS
HP	●●●
ATTACK	●●●
DEFENSE	●●●●
SP. ATTACK	●●●
SP. DEFENSE	●●●
SPEED	●●●

● EGG GROUPS
Monster

Grass

● PERFORMANCE
SPEED ★★   STAMINA ★★★★☆
POWER ★★★☆   JUMP ★★
SKILL ★★★★☆

● MAIN WAYS TO OBTAIN

Pokémon HeartGold — Level up Snover to Lv. 40

Pokémon SoulSilver — Level up Snover to Lv. 40

Pokémon Diamond — Mt. Coronet Peak 1

Pokémon Pearl — Mt. Coronet Peak 1

Pokémon Platinum — Mt. Coronet Peak 1

Pokémon HeartGold
It lives a quiet life on mountains that are perpetually covered in snow. It hides itself by whipping up blizzards.

Pokémon SoulSilver
It lives a quiet life on mountains that are perpetually covered in snow. It hides itself by whipping up blizzards.

● EVOLUTION

Snover — Lv. 40 — Abomasnow

● LEVEL-UP MOVES
Lv.	Name	Type	Kind	Pow.	Acc.	PP	Range	DA
1	Ice Punch	Ice	Physical	75	100	15	Normal	○
1	Powder Snow	Ice	Special	40	100	25	2 Foes	—
1	Leer	Normal	Status	—	100	30	2 Foes	—
1	Razor Leaf	Grass	Physical	55	95	25	2 Foes	—
1	Icy Wind	Ice	Special	55	95	15	2 Foes	—
5	Razor Leaf	Grass	Physical	55	95	25	2 Foes	—
9	Icy Wind	Ice	Special	55	95	15	2 Foes	—
13	GrassWhistle	Grass	Status	—	55	15	Normal	—
17	Swagger	Normal	Status	—	90	15	Normal	—
21	Mist	Ice	Status	—	—	30	2 Allies	—
26	Ice Shard	Ice	Physical	40	100	30	Normal	—
31	Ingrain	Grass	Status	—	—	20	Self	—
36	Wood Hammer	Grass	Physical	120	100	15	Normal	○
47	Blizzard	Ice	Special	120	70	5	2 Foes	—
58	Sheer Cold	Ice	Special	—	30	5	Normal	—

● MOVE MANIAC
Name	Type	Kind	Pow.	Acc.	PP	Range	DA
Headbutt	Normal	Physical	70	100	15	Normal	—

● BP MOVES
Name	Type	Kind	Pow.	Acc.	PP	Range	DA
Icy Wind	Ice	Special	55	95	15	2 Foes	—
Ice Punch	Ice	Physical	75	100	15	Normal	○
Snore	Normal	Special	40	100	15	Normal	—
Synthesis	Grass	Status	—	—	5	Self	—
Worry Seed	Grass	Status	—	100	10	Normal	—
Role Play	Psychic	Status	—	—	10	Normal	—
Block	Normal	Status	—	—	5	Normal	—
Mud-Slap	Ground	Special	20	100	10	Normal	—
Outrage	Dragon	Physical	120	100	15	1 Random	—
Seed Bomb	Grass	Physical	80	100	15	Normal	—

● TM & HM MOVES
No.	Name	Type	Kind	Pow.	Acc.	PP	Range	DA
TM01	Focus Punch	Fighting	Physical	150	100	20	Normal	○
TM03	Water Pulse	Water	Special	60	100	20	Normal	—
TM06	Toxic	Poison	Status	—	85	10	Normal	—
TM07	Hail	Ice	Status	—	—	10	All	—
TM09	Bullet Seed	Grass	Physical	10	100	30	Normal	—
TM10	Hidden Power	Normal	Special	—	100	15	Normal	—
TM13	Ice Beam	Ice	Special	95	100	10	Normal	—
TM14	Blizzard	Ice	Special	120	70	5	2 Foes	—
TM15	Hyper Beam	Normal	Special	150	90	5	Normal	—
TM16	Light Screen	Psychic	Status	—	—	30	2 Allies	—
TM17	Protect	Normal	Status	—	—	10	Self	—
TM18	Rain Dance	Water	Status	—	—	5	All	—
TM19	Giga Drain	Grass	Special	60	100	10	Normal	—
TM20	Safeguard	Normal	Status	—	—	25	2 Allies	—
TM21	Frustration	Normal	Physical	—	100	20	Normal	○
TM22	SolarBeam	Grass	Special	120	100	10	Normal	—
TM23	Iron Tail	Steel	Physical	100	75	15	Normal	○
TM26	Earthquake	Ground	Physical	100	100	10	2 Foes/1 Ally	—
TM27	Return	Normal	Physical	—	100	20	Normal	○
TM30	Shadow Ball	Ghost	Special	80	100	15	Normal	—
TM31	Brick Break	Fighting	Physical	75	100	15	Normal	○
TM32	Double Team	Normal	Status	—	—	15	Self	—
TM39	Rock Tomb	Rock	Physical	50	80	10	Normal	—
TM42	Facade	Normal	Physical	70	100	20	Normal	○
TM43	Secret Power	Normal	Physical	70	100	20	Normal	—
TM44	Rest	Psychic	Status	—	—	10	Self	—
TM45	Attract	Normal	Status	—	100	15	Normal	—
TM52	Focus Blast	Fighting	Special	120	70	5	Normal	—
TM53	Energy Ball	Grass	Special	80	100	10	Normal	—
TM56	Fling	Dark	Physical	—	100	10	Normal	—
TM58	Endure	Normal	Status	—	—	10	Self	—
TM68	Giga Impact	Normal	Physical	150	90	5	Normal	○
TM70	Flash	Normal	Status	—	100	20	Normal	—
TM72	Avalanche	Ice	Physical	60	100	10	Normal	○
TM75	Swords Dance	Normal	Status	—	—	30	Self	—
TM78	Captivate	Normal	Status	—	100	20	2 Foes	—
TM80	Rock Slide	Rock	Physical	75	90	10	2 Foes	—
TM82	Sleep Talk	Normal	Status	—	—	10	Depends	—
TM83	Natural Gift	Normal	Physical	—	100	15	Normal	—
TM86	Grass Knot	Grass	Special	—	100	20	Normal	○
TM87	Swagger	Normal	Status	—	90	15	Normal	—
TM90	Substitute	Normal	Status	—	—	10	Self	—
HM04	Strength	Normal	Physical	80	100	15	Normal	○
HM06	Rock Smash	Fighting	Physical	40	100	15	Normal	○
HM08	Rock Climb	Normal	Physical	90	85	20	Normal	○

● LEVEL-UP MOVES

Lv.	Name	Type	Kind	Pow.	Acc.	PP	Range	DA
1	Embargo	Dark	Status	—	100	15	Normal	—
1	Revenge	Fighting	Physical	60	100	10	Normal	○
1	Assurance	Dark	Physical	50	100	10	Normal	○
1	Scratch	Normal	Physical	40	100	35	Normal	○
1	Leer	Normal	Status	—	100	30	2 Foes	—
1	Taunt	Dark	Status	—	100	20	Normal	—
1	Quick Attack	Normal	Physical	40	100	30	Normal	○
8	Quick Attack	Normal	Physical	40	100	30	Normal	○
10	Screech	Normal	Status	—	85	40	Normal	—
14	Faint Attack	Dark	Physical	60	—	20	Normal	○
21	Fury Swipes	Normal	Physical	18	80	15	Normal	○
24	Nasty Plot	Dark	Status	—	—	20	Self	—
28	Icy Wind	Ice	Special	55	95	15	2 Foes	—
35	Night Slash	Dark	Physical	70	100	15	Normal	○
38	Fling	Dark	Physical	—	100	10	Normal	○
42	Metal Claw	Steel	Physical	50	95	35	Normal	○
49	Dark Pulse	Dark	Special	80	100	15	Normal	—

● MOVE MANIAC

Name	Type	Kind	Pow.	Acc.	PP	Range	DA
Headbutt	Normal	Physical	70	100	15	Normal	○

● BP MOVES

Name	Type	Kind	Pow.	Acc.	PP	Range	DA
Fury Cutter	Bug	Physical	10	95	20	Normal	○
Icy Wind	Ice	Special	55	95	15	2 Foes	—
Ice Punch	Ice	Physical	75	100	15	Normal	○
Knock Off	Dark	Physical	20	100	20	Normal	○
Snore	Normal	Special	40	100	15	Normal	—
Spite	Ghost	Status	—	100	10	Normal	—
Swift	Normal	Special	60	—	20	2 Foes	—
Mud-Slap	Ground	Special	20	100	10	Normal	—
Low Kick	Fighting	Physical	—	100	20	Normal	○

● TM & HM MOVES

No.	Name	Type	Kind	Pow.	Acc.	PP	Range	DA
TM01	Focus Punch	Fighting	Physical	150	100	20	Normal	○
TM04	Calm Mind	Psychic	Status	—	—	20	Self	—
TM06	Toxic	Poison	Status	—	85	10	Normal	—
TM07	Hail	Ice	Status	—	—	10	All	—
TM10	Hidden Power	Normal	Special	—	100	15	Normal	—
TM11	Sunny Day	Fire	Status	—	—	5	All	—
TM12	Taunt	Dark	Status	—	100	20	Normal	—
TM13	Ice Beam	Ice	Special	95	100	10	Normal	—
TM14	Blizzard	Ice	Special	120	70	5	2 Foes	—
TM15	Hyper Beam	Normal	Special	150	90	5	Normal	—
TM17	Protect	Normal	Status	—	—	10	Self	—
TM18	Rain Dance	Water	Status	—	—	5	All	—
TM21	Frustration	Normal	Physical	—	100	20	Normal	○
TM23	Iron Tail	Steel	Physical	100	75	15	Normal	○
TM27	Return	Normal	Physical	—	100	20	Normal	○
TM28	Dig	Ground	Physical	80	100	10	Normal	○
TM30	Shadow Ball	Ghost	Special	80	100	15	Normal	—
TM31	Brick Break	Fighting	Physical	75	100	15	Normal	○
TM32	Double Team	Normal	Status	—	—	15	Self	—
TM40	Aerial Ace	Flying	Physical	60	—	20	Normal	○
TM41	Torment	Dark	Status	—	100	15	Normal	—
TM42	Facade	Normal	Physical	70	100	20	Normal	○
TM43	Secret Power	Normal	Physical	70	100	20	Normal	○
TM44	Rest	Psychic	Status	—	—	10	Self	—
TM45	Attract	Normal	Status	—	100	15	Normal	—
TM46	Thief	Dark	Physical	40	100	10	Normal	○
TM49	Snatch	Dark	Status	—	—	10	Depends	—
TM52	Focus Blast	Fighting	Special	120	70	5	Normal	—
TM54	False Swipe	Normal	Physical	40	100	40	Normal	○
TM56	Fling	Dark	Physical	—	100	10	Normal	○
TM58	Endure	Normal	Status	—	—	10	Self	—
TM63	Embargo	Dark	Status	—	100	15	Normal	—
TM65	Shadow Claw	Ghost	Physical	70	100	15	Normal	○
TM66	Payback	Dark	Physical	50	100	10	Normal	○
TM68	Giga Impact	Normal	Physical	150	90	5	Normal	○
TM72	Avalanche	Ice	Physical	60	100	10	Normal	○
TM75	Swords Dance	Normal	Status	—	—	30	Self	—
TM77	Psych Up	Normal	Status	—	—	10	Normal	—
TM78	Captivate	Normal	Status	—	100	20	2 Foes	—
TM79	Dark Pulse	Dark	Special	80	100	15	Normal	—
TM81	X-Scissor	Bug	Physical	80	100	15	Normal	○
TM82	Sleep Talk	Normal	Status	—	—	10	Depends	—
TM83	Natural Gift	Normal	Physical	—	100	15	Normal	—
TM84	Poison Jab	Poison	Physical	80	100	20	Normal	○
TM85	Dream Eater	Psychic	Special	100	100	15	Normal	—
TM87	Swagger	Normal	Status	—	90	15	Normal	—
TM90	Substitute	Normal	Status	—	—	10	Self	—
HM01	Cut	Normal	Physical	50	95	30	Normal	○
HM03	Surf	Water	Special	95	100	15	2 Foes/1 Ally	—
HM04	Strength	Normal	Physical	80	100	15	Normal	○
HM05	Whirlpool	Water	Special	15	70	15	Normal	—
HM06	Rock Smash	Fighting	Physical	40	100	15	Normal	○

● No. 461 | Sharp Claw Pokémon
Weavile

Dark **Ice**

● HEIGHT: 3'07"
● WEIGHT: 75.0 lbs.
● ITEMS: None

● SIZE COMPARISON

● MALE FORM
Longer ears

● FEMALE FORM
Shorter ears

● ABILITIES
● Pressure

● STATS
HP ●●●○
ATTACK ●●●●○
DEFENSE ●●●○
SP. ATTACK ●●●○
SP. DEFENSE ●●●○
SPEED ●●●●●●

● EGG GROUPS
Field

● PERFORMANCE

SPEED ★★★★☆ STAMINA ★★☆
POWER ★★★★☆ JUMP ★★☆
SKILL ★★★☆☆

● MAIN WAYS TO OBTAIN

Pokémon HeartGold	Have Sneasel hold the Razor Claw and level it up between 8:00 P.M. and 4:00 A.M.
Pokémon SoulSilver	Have Sneasel hold the Razor Claw and level it up between 8:00 P.M. and 4:00 A.M.
Pokémon Diamond	Have Sneasel hold the Razor Claw and level it up between 8:00 P.M. and 4:00 A.M.
Pokémon Pearl	Have Sneasel hold the Razor Claw and level it up between 8:00 P.M. and 4:00 A.M.
Pokémon Platinum	Have Sneasel hold the Razor Claw and level it up between 8:00 P.M. and 4:00 A.M.

| Pokémon HeartGold | Pokémon SoulSilver |
| It lives in snowy regions. It carves patterns in trees with its claws as a signal to others. | It lives in snowy regions. It carves patterns in trees with its claws as a signal to others. |

● EVOLUTION

Sneasel → Have it hold Razor Claw and then level it up between 8:00 P.M. and 4:00 A.M. → Weavile

No. 462 | Magnet Area Pokémon
Magnezone

Electric Steel

- **HEIGHT:** 3'11"
- **WEIGHT:** 396.8 lbs.
- **ITEMS:** None

● SIZE COMPARISON

● MALE/FEMALE HAVE SAME FORM

⊙ ABILITIES
- Magnet Pull
- Sturdy

⊙ STATS
HP	●●●
ATTACK	●●●●
DEFENSE	●●●●
SP. ATTACK	●●●●●
SP. DEFENSE	●●●●
SPEED	●●●

⊙ EGG GROUPS
Mineral

⊙ PERFORMANCE
SPEED ★★☆   STAMINA ★★★☆
POWER ★★★   JUMP ★★★★☆
SKILL ★★★★☆

● MAIN WAYS TO OBTAIN

Pokémon HeartGold	—
Pokémon SoulSilver	—
Pokémon Diamond	Make Magneton level up on Mt. Coronet
Pokémon Pearl	Make Magneton level up on Mt. Coronet
Pokémon Platinum	Make Magneton level up on Mt. Coronet

Pokémon HeartGold	Pokémon SoulSilver
Exposure to a special magnetic field changed MAGNETON's molecular structure, turning it into MAGNEZONE.	Exposure to a special magnetic field changed MAGNETON's molecular structure, turning it into MAGNEZONE.

⊙ EVOLUTION

Magnemite — Lv. 30 → Magneton — Level up at Mt. Coronet* → Magnezone

● LEVEL-UP MOVES
Lv.	Name	Type	Kind	Pow.	Acc.	PP	Range	DA
1	Mirror Coat	Psychic	Special	—	100	20	Self	—
1	Barrier	Psychic	Status	—	—	30	Self	—
1	Metal Sound	Steel	Status	—	85	40	Normal	—
1	Tackle	Normal	Physical	35	95	35	Normal	○
1	ThunderShock	Electric	Special	40	100	30	Normal	—
1	Supersonic	Normal	Status	—	55	20	Normal	—
6	ThunderShock	Electric	Special	40	100	30	Normal	—
11	Supersonic	Normal	Status	—	55	20	Normal	—
14	SonicBoom	Normal	Special	—	90	20	Normal	—
17	Thunder Wave	Electric	Status	—	100	20	Normal	—
22	Spark	Electric	Physical	65	100	20	Normal	○
27	Lock-On	Normal	Status	—	—	5	Normal	—
30	Magnet Bomb	Steel	Physical	60	—	20	Normal	—
34	Screech	Normal	Status	—	85	40	Normal	—
40	Discharge	Electric	Special	80	100	15	2 Foes/1 Ally	—
46	Mirror Shot	Steel	Special	65	85	10	Normal	—
50	Magnet Rise	Electric	Status	—	—	10	Self	—
54	Gyro Ball	Steel	Physical	—	100	5	Normal	○
60	Zap Cannon	Electric	Special	120	50	5	Normal	—

● MOVE MANIAC
Name	Type	Kind	Pow.	Acc.	PP	Range	DA

● BP MOVES
Name	Type	Kind	Pow.	Acc.	PP	Range	DA
Snore	Normal	Special	40	100	15	Normal	—
Magnet Rise	Electric	Status	—	—	10	Self	—
Swift	Normal	Special	60	—	20	2 Foes	—
Gravity	Psychic	Status	—	—	5	All	—
Magic Coat	Psychic	Status	—	—	15	Self	—
Rollout	Rock	Physical	30	90	20	Normal	○
Iron Head	Steel	Physical	80	100	15	Normal	○
Signal Beam	Bug	Special	75	100	15	Normal	—
Iron Defense	Steel	Status	—	—	15	Self	—

● TM & HM MOVES
No.	Name	Type	Kind	Pow.	Acc.	PP	Range	DA
TM06	Toxic	Poison	Status	—	85	10	Normal	—
TM10	Hidden Power	Normal	Special	—	100	15	Normal	—
TM11	Sunny Day	Fire	Status	—	—	5	All	—
TM15	Hyper Beam	Normal	Special	150	90	5	Normal	—
TM16	Light Screen	Psychic	Status	—	—	30	2 Allies	—
TM17	Protect	Normal	Status	—	—	10	Self	—
TM18	Rain Dance	Water	Status	—	—	5	All	—
TM21	Frustration	Normal	Physical	—	100	20	Normal	○
TM24	Thunderbolt	Electric	Special	95	100	15	Normal	—
TM25	Thunder	Electric	Special	120	70	10	Normal	—
TM27	Return	Normal	Physical	—	100	20	Normal	○
TM32	Double Team	Normal	Status	—	—	15	Self	—
TM33	Reflect	Psychic	Status	—	—	20	2 Allies	—
TM34	Shock Wave	Electric	Special	60	—	20	Normal	—
TM42	Facade	Normal	Physical	70	100	20	Normal	○
TM43	Secret Power	Normal	Physical	70	100	20	Normal	—
TM44	Rest	Psychic	Status	—	—	10	Self	—
TM57	Charge Beam	Electric	Special	50	90	10	Normal	—
TM58	Endure	Normal	Status	—	—	10	Self	—
TM64	Explosion	Normal	Physical	250	100	5	2 Foes/1 Ally	—
TM67	Recycle	Normal	Status	—	—	10	Self	—
TM68	Giga Impact	Normal	Physical	150	90	5	Normal	○
TM70	Flash	Normal	Status	—	100	20	Normal	—
TM73	Thunder Wave	Electric	Status	—	100	20	Normal	—
TM74	Gyro Ball	Steel	Physical	—	100	5	Normal	○
TM77	Psych Up	Normal	Status	—	—	10	Normal	—
TM82	Sleep Talk	Normal	Status	—	—	10	Depends	—
TM83	Natural Gift	Normal	Physical	—	100	15	Normal	—
TM87	Swagger	Normal	Status	—	90	15	Normal	—
TM90	Substitute	Normal	Status	—	—	10	Self	—
TM91	Flash Cannon	Steel	Special	80	100	10	Normal	—

● LEVEL-UP MOVES

Lv.	Name	Type	Kind	Pow.	Acc.	PP	Range	DA
1	Lick	Ghost	Physical	20	100	30	Normal	○
5	Supersonic	Normal	Status	—	55	20	Normal	—
9	Defense Curl	Normal	Status	—	—	40	Self	—
13	Knock Off	Dark	Physical	20	100	20	Normal	○
17	Wrap	Normal	Physical	15	85	20	Normal	○
21	Stomp	Normal	Physical	65	100	20	Normal	○
25	Disable	Normal	Status	—	80	20	Normal	—
29	Slam	Normal	Physical	80	75	20	Normal	○
33	Rollout	Rock	Physical	30	90	20	Normal	○
37	Me First	Normal	Status	—	—	20	Depends	—
41	Refresh	Normal	Status	—	—	20	Self	—
45	Screech	Normal	Status	—	85	40	Normal	—
49	Power Whip	Grass	Physical	120	85	10	Normal	○
53	Wring Out	Normal	Special	—	100	5	Normal	○
57	Gyro Ball	Steel	Physical	—	100	5	Normal	○

● MOVE MANIAC

Name	Type	Kind	Pow.	Acc.	PP	Range	DA
Headbutt	Normal	Physical	70	100	15	Normal	○

● BP MOVES

Name	Type	Kind	Pow.	Acc.	PP	Range	DA
Icy Wind	Ice	Special	55	95	15	2 Foes	—
ThunderPunch	Electric	Physical	75	100	15	Normal	○
Fire Punch	Fire	Physical	75	100	15	Normal	○
Ice Punch	Ice	Physical	75	100	15	Normal	○
Zen Headbutt	Psychic	Physical	80	90	15	Normal	○
Knock Off	Dark	Physical	20	100	20	Normal	○
Snore	Normal	Special	40	100	15	Normal	—
Block	Normal	Status	—	—	5	Normal	—
Mud-Slap	Ground	Special	20	100	10	Normal	—
Rollout	Rock	Physical	30	90	20	Normal	○
Aqua Tail	Water	Physical	90	90	10	Normal	○

● TM & HM MOVES

No.	Name	Type	Kind	Pow.	Acc.	PP	Range	DA
TM01	Focus Punch	Fighting	Physical	150	100	20	Normal	○
TM03	Water Pulse	Water	Special	60	100	20	Normal	—
TM06	Toxic	Poison	Status	—	85	10	Normal	—
TM10	Hidden Power	Normal	Special	—	100	15	Normal	—
TM11	Sunny Day	Fire	Status	—	—	5	All	—
TM13	Ice Beam	Ice	Special	95	100	10	Normal	—
TM14	Blizzard	Ice	Special	120	100	5	2 Foes	—
TM15	Hyper Beam	Normal	Special	150	90	5	Normal	—
TM17	Protect	Normal	Status	—	—	10	Self	—
TM18	Rain Dance	Water	Status	—	—	5	All	—
TM21	Frustration	Normal	Physical	—	100	20	Normal	○
TM22	SolarBeam	Grass	Special	120	100	10	Normal	—
TM23	Iron Tail	Steel	Physical	100	75	15	Normal	○
TM24	Thunderbolt	Electric	Special	95	100	15	Normal	—
TM25	Thunder	Electric	Special	120	70	10	Normal	—
TM26	Earthquake	Ground	Physical	100	100	10	2 Foes/1 Ally	—
TM27	Return	Normal	Physical	—	100	20	Normal	○
TM28	Dig	Ground	Physical	80	100	10	Normal	○
TM30	Shadow Ball	Ghost	Special	80	100	15	Normal	—
TM31	Brick Break	Fighting	Physical	75	100	15	Normal	○
TM32	Double Team	Normal	Status	—	—	15	Self	—
TM34	Shock Wave	Electric	Special	60	—	20	Normal	—
TM35	Flamethrower	Fire	Special	95	100	15	Normal	—
TM37	Sandstorm	Rock	Status	—	—	10	All	—
TM38	Fire Blast	Fire	Special	120	85	5	Normal	—
TM39	Rock Tomb	Rock	Physical	50	80	10	Normal	○
TM42	Facade	Normal	Physical	70	100	20	Normal	○
TM43	Secret Power	Normal	Physical	70	100	20	Normal	○
TM44	Rest	Psychic	Status	—	—	10	Self	—
TM45	Attract	Normal	Status	—	100	15	Normal	—
TM46	Thief	Dark	Physical	40	100	10	Normal	○
TM52	Focus Blast	Fighting	Special	120	70	5	Normal	—
TM56	Fling	Dark	Physical	—	100	10	Normal	○
TM58	Endure	Normal	Status	—	—	10	Self	—
TM64	Explosion	Normal	Physical	250	100	5	2 Foes/1 Ally	—
TM68	Giga Impact	Normal	Physical	150	90	5	Normal	○
TM74	Gyro Ball	Steel	Physical	—	100	5	Normal	○
TM75	Swords Dance	Normal	Status	—	—	30	Self	—
TM77	Psych Up	Normal	Status	—	—	10	Self	—
TM78	Captivate	Normal	Status	—	100	20	2 Foes	—
TM80	Rock Slide	Rock	Physical	75	90	10	2 Foes	—
TM82	Sleep Talk	Normal	Status	—	—	10	Depends	—
TM83	Natural Gift	Normal	Physical	—	100	15	Normal	○
TM85	Dream Eater	Psychic	Special	100	100	15	Normal	—
TM87	Swagger	Normal	Status	—	90	15	Normal	—
TM90	Substitute	Normal	Status	—	—	10	Self	—
HM01	Cut	Normal	Physical	50	95	30	Normal	○
HM03	Surf	Water	Special	95	100	15	2 Foes/1 Ally	—
HM04	Strength	Normal	Physical	80	100	15	Normal	○
HM05	Whirlpool	Water	Special	15	70	15	Normal	—
HM06	Rock Smash	Fighting	Physical	40	100	15	Normal	○
HM08	Rock Climb	Normal	Physical	90	85	20	Normal	○

◉ No. 463 | Licking Pokémon
Lickilicky

Normal

● **HEIGHT:** 5'02"
● **WEIGHT:** 308.6 lbs.
● **ITEMS:** None

● **SIZE COMPARISON**

● **MALE/FEMALE HAVE SAME FORM**

◉ ABILITIES
● Own Tempo
● Oblivious

◉ STATS
HP ●●●●
ATTACK ●●●●
DEFENSE ●●●●
SP. ATTACK ●●●●
SP. DEFENSE ●●●●
SPEED ●●

◉ EGG GROUPS
Monster

◉ PERFORMANCE
SPEED ★★
POWER ★★★☆
SKILL ★★★★☆
STAMINA ★★★★☆
JUMP ★★

● MAIN WAYS TO OBTAIN

Pokémon HeartGold	Level up Lickitung to Lv. 33 and have it learn Rollout, or level it up once it knows Rollout
Pokémon SoulSilver	Level up Lickitung to Lv. 33 and have it learn Rollout, or level it up once it knows Rollout
Pokémon Diamond	Level up Lickitung to Lv. 33 and have it learn Rollout, or level it up once it knows Rollout
Pokémon Pearl	Level up Lickitung to Lv. 33 and have it learn Rollout, or level it up once it knows Rollout
Pokémon Platinum	Level up Lickitung to Lv. 33 and have it learn Rollout, or level it up once it knows Rollout

Pokémon HeartGold
Its saliva can decompose anything. It wraps its long tongue around things to coat them with its sticky saliva.

Pokémon SoulSilver
It has space in its throat to store saliva. It can also roll up its tongue and store it in the same spot.

◉ EVOLUTION

Lickitung

Lickilicky

Level it up to Lv. 33 and teach it Rollout. Or, level it up once it knows Rollout.

No. 464 | Drill Pokémon
Rhyperior

Ground   Rock

● HEIGHT: 7'10"
● WEIGHT: 623.5 lbs.
● ITEMS: None

● SIZE COMPARISON

MALE FORM
Longer upper horn

● FEMALE FORM
Shorter upper horn

● ABILITIES
● Lightningrod
● Solid Rock

● STATS
HP ●●●●
ATTACK ●●●●●●
DEFENSE ●●●●●●
SP. ATTACK ●●●
SP. DEFENSE ●●●
SPEED ●●

● EGG GROUPS
Monster
Field

● PERFORMANCE
SPEED ★   STAMINA ★★★★★
POWER ★★★★★   JUMP ★★
SKILL ★★☆☆

● MAIN WAYS TO OBTAIN

Pokémon HeartGold	Link trade Rhydon while it holds the Protector
Pokémon SoulSilver	Link trade Rhydon while it holds the Protector
Pokémon Diamond	Link trade Rhydon while it holds the Protector
Pokémon Pearl	Link trade Rhydon while it holds the Protector
Pokémon Platinum	Link trade Rhydon while it holds the Protector

| Pokémon HeartGold | Pokémon SoulSilver |
| From holes in its palms, it fires out GEODUDE. Its carapace can withstand volcanic eruptions. | From holes in its palms, it fires out GEODUDE. Its carapace can withstand volcanic eruptions. |

● EVOLUTION

Rhyhorn   Lv. 42   Rhydon   Have it hold Protector and trade it   Rhyperior

● LEVEL-UP MOVES

Lv.	Name	Type	Kind	Pow.	Acc.	PP	Range	DA
1	Poison Jab	Poison	Physical	80	100	20	Normal	○
1	Horn Attack	Normal	Physical	65	100	25	Normal	○
1	Tail Whip	Normal	Status	—	100	30	2 Foes	—
1	Stomp	Normal	Physical	65	100	20	Normal	○
1	Fury Attack	Normal	Physical	15	85	20	Normal	○
9	Stomp	Normal	Physical	65	100	20	Normal	○
13	Fury Attack	Normal	Physical	15	85	20	Normal	○
21	Scary Face	Normal	Status	—	90	10	Normal	—
25	Rock Blast	Rock	Physical	25	80	10	Normal	—
33	Take Down	Normal	Physical	90	85	20	Normal	○
37	Horn Drill	Normal	Physical	—	30	5	Normal	—
42	Hammer Arm	Fighting	Physical	100	90	10	Normal	○
45	Stone Edge	Rock	Physical	100	80	5	Normal	—
49	Earthquake	Ground	Physical	100	100	10	2 Foes/1 Ally	—
57	Megahorn	Bug	Physical	120	85	10	Normal	—
61	Rock Wrecker	Rock	Physical	150	90	5	Normal	—

● MOVE MANIAC

Name	Type	Kind	Pow.	Acc.	PP	Range	DA
Headbutt	Normal	Physical	70	100	15	Normal	○

● BP MOVES

Name	Type	Kind	Pow.	Acc.	PP	Range	DA
Fury Cutter	Bug	Physical	10	95	20	Normal	○
Icy Wind	Ice	Special	55	95	15	2 Foes	—
ThunderPunch	Electric	Physical	75	100	15	Normal	○
Fire Punch	Fire	Physical	75	100	15	Normal	○
Ice Punch	Ice	Physical	75	100	15	Normal	○
Snore	Normal	Special	40	100	15	Normal	—
Spite	Ghost	Status	—	100	10	Normal	—
Uproar	Normal	Special	50	100	10	1 Random	—
Block	Normal	Status	—	—	5	Normal	—
Mud-Slap	Ground	Physical	20	100	10	Normal	○
Rollout	Rock	Physical	30	90	20	Normal	○
Superpower	Fighting	Physical	120	100	5	Normal	○
Iron Head	Steel	Physical	80	100	15	Normal	○
Endeavor	Normal	Physical	—	100	5	Normal	—
Aqua Tail	Water	Physical	90	90	10	Normal	○
Outrage	Dragon	Physical	120	100	15	1 Random	○
AncientPower	Rock	Special	60	100	5	Normal	—
Earth Power	Ground	Special	90	100	10	Normal	—

● TM & HM MOVES

No.	Name	Type	Kind	Pow.	Acc.	PP	Range	DA
TM01	Focus Punch	Fighting	Physical	150	100	20	Normal	○
TM05	Roar	Normal	Status	—	100	20	Normal	—
TM06	Toxic	Poison	Status	—	85	10	Normal	—
TM10	Hidden Power	Normal	Special	—	100	15	Normal	—
TM11	Sunny Day	Fire	Status	—	—	5	All	—
TM13	Ice Beam	Ice	Special	95	100	10	Normal	—
TM14	Blizzard	Ice	Special	120	70	5	2 Foes	—
TM15	Hyper Beam	Normal	Special	150	90	5	Normal	—
TM17	Protect	Normal	Status	—	—	10	Self	—
TM18	Rain Dance	Water	Status	—	—	5	All	—
TM21	Frustration	Normal	Physical	—	100	20	Normal	○
TM23	Iron Tail	Steel	Physical	100	75	15	Normal	○
TM24	Thunderbolt	Electric	Special	95	100	15	Normal	—
TM25	Thunder	Electric	Special	120	70	10	Normal	—
TM26	Earthquake	Ground	Physical	100	100	10	2 Foes/1 Ally	—
TM27	Return	Normal	Physical	—	100	20	Normal	○
TM28	Dig	Ground	Physical	80	100	10	Normal	○
TM31	Brick Break	Fighting	Physical	75	100	15	Normal	○
TM32	Double Team	Normal	Status	—	—	15	Self	—
TM34	Shock Wave	Electric	Special	60	—	20	Normal	—
TM35	Flamethrower	Fire	Special	95	100	15	Normal	—
TM37	Sandstorm	Rock	Status	—	—	10	All	—
TM38	Fire Blast	Fire	Special	120	85	5	Normal	—
TM39	Rock Tomb	Rock	Physical	50	80	10	Normal	○
TM42	Facade	Normal	Physical	70	100	20	Normal	○
TM43	Secret Power	Normal	Physical	70	100	20	Normal	○
TM44	Rest	Psychic	Status	—	—	10	Self	—
TM45	Attract	Normal	Status	—	100	15	Normal	—
TM46	Thief	Dark	Physical	40	100	10	Normal	○
TM52	Focus Blast	Fighting	Special	120	70	5	Normal	—
TM56	Fling	Dark	Physical	—	100	10	Normal	—
TM58	Endure	Normal	Status	—	—	10	Self	—
TM59	Dragon Pulse	Dragon	Special	90	100	10	Normal	—
TM65	Shadow Claw	Ghost	Physical	70	100	15	Normal	○
TM66	Payback	Dark	Physical	50	100	10	Normal	○
TM68	Giga Impact	Normal	Physical	150	90	5	Normal	○
TM69	Rock Polish	Rock	Status	—	—	20	Self	—
TM71	Stone Edge	Rock	Physical	100	80	5	Normal	—
TM72	Avalanche	Ice	Physical	60	100	10	Normal	○
TM75	Swords Dance	Normal	Status	—	—	30	Self	—
TM76	Stealth Rock	Rock	Status	—	—	20	2 Foes	—
TM78	Captivate	Normal	Status	—	100	20	2 Foes	—
TM80	Rock Slide	Rock	Physical	75	90	10	2 Foes	—
TM82	Sleep Talk	Normal	Status	—	—	10	Depends	—
TM83	Natural Gift	Normal	Physical	—	100	15	Normal	—
TM84	Poison Jab	Poison	Physical	80	100	20	Normal	○
TM87	Swagger	Normal	Status	—	90	15	Normal	—
TM90	Substitute	Normal	Status	—	—	10	Self	—
TM91	Flash Cannon	Steel	Special	80	100	10	Normal	—
HM01	Cut	Normal	Physical	50	95	30	Normal	○
HM03	Surf	Water	Special	95	100	15	2 Foes/1 Ally	—
HM04	Strength	Normal	Physical	80	100	15	Normal	○
HM05	Whirlpool	Water	Special	15	70	15	Normal	○
HM06	Rock Smash	Fighting	Physical	40	100	15	Normal	○
HM08	Rock Climb	Normal	Physical	90	85	20	Normal	○

● LEVEL-UP MOVES

Lv.	Name	Type	Kind	Pow.	Acc.	PP	Range	DA
1	Ingrain	Grass	Status	—	—	20	Self	—
1	Constrict	Normal	Physical	10	100	35	Normal	○
5	Sleep Powder	Grass	Status	—	75	15	Normal	—
8	Absorb	Grass	Special	20	100	25	Normal	—
12	Growth	Normal	Status	—	—	40	Self	—
15	PoisonPowder	Poison	Status	—	75	35	Normal	—
19	Vine Whip	Grass	Physical	35	100	15	Normal	○
22	Bind	Normal	Physical	15	75	20	Normal	○
26	Mega Drain	Grass	Special	40	100	15	Normal	—
29	Stun Spore	Grass	Status	—	75	30	Normal	—
33	AncientPower	Rock	Special	60	100	5	Normal	—
36	Knock Off	Dark	Physical	20	100	20	Normal	○
40	Natural Gift	Normal	Physical	—	100	15	Normal	○
43	Slam	Normal	Physical	80	75	20	Normal	○
47	Tickle	Normal	Status	—	100	20	Normal	—
50	Wring Out	Normal	Special	—	100	5	Normal	—
54	Power Whip	Grass	Physical	120	85	10	Normal	○
57	Block	Normal	Status	—	—	5	Normal	—

● MOVE MANIAC

Name	Type	Kind	Pow.	Acc.	PP	Range	DA
Headbutt	Normal	Physical	70	100	15	Normal	○

● BP MOVES

Name	Type	Kind	Pow.	Acc.	PP	Range	DA
Knock Off	Dark	Physical	20	100	20	Normal	○
Snore	Normal	Special	40	100	15	Normal	—
Synthesis	Grass	Status	—	—	5	Self	—
Worry Seed	Grass	Status	—	100	10	Normal	—
Block	Normal	Status	—	—	5	Normal	—
Mud-Slap	Ground	Special	20	100	10	Normal	—
AncientPower	Rock	Special	60	100	5	Normal	—
Seed Bomb	Grass	Physical	80	100	15	Normal	—
Pain Split	Normal	Status	—	—	20	Normal	—

● TM & HM MOVES

No.	Name	Type	Kind	Pow.	Acc.	PP	Range	DA
TM06	Toxic	Poison	Status	—	85	10	Normal	—
TM09	Bullet Seed	Grass	Physical	10	100	30	Normal	—
TM10	Hidden Power	Normal	Special	—	100	15	Normal	—
TM11	Sunny Day	Fire	Status	—	—	5	All	—
TM15	Hyper Beam	Normal	Special	150	90	5	Normal	—
TM17	Protect	Normal	Status	—	—	10	Self	—
TM19	Giga Drain	Grass	Special	60	100	10	Normal	—
TM21	Frustration	Normal	Physical	—	100	20	Normal	○
TM22	SolarBeam	Grass	Special	120	100	10	Normal	—
TM26	Earthquake	Ground	Physical	100	100	10	2 Foes/1 Ally	—
TM27	Return	Normal	Physical	—	100	20	Normal	○
TM31	Brick Break	Fighting	Physical	75	100	15	Normal	○
TM32	Double Team	Normal	Status	—	—	15	Self	—
TM33	Reflect	Psychic	Status	—	—	20	2 Allies	—
TM34	Shock Wave	Electric	Special	60	—	20	Normal	—
TM36	Sludge Bomb	Poison	Special	90	100	10	Normal	—
TM39	Rock Tomb	Rock	Physical	50	80	10	Normal	—
TM40	Aerial Ace	Flying	Physical	60	—	20	Normal	○
TM42	Facade	Normal	Physical	70	100	20	Normal	○
TM43	Secret Power	Normal	Physical	70	100	20	Normal	○
TM44	Rest	Psychic	Status	—	—	10	Self	—
TM45	Attract	Normal	Status	—	100	15	Normal	—
TM46	Thief	Dark	Physical	40	100	10	Normal	○
TM52	Focus Blast	Fighting	Special	120	70	5	Normal	—
TM53	Energy Ball	Grass	Special	80	100	10	Normal	—
TM56	Fling	Dark	Physical	—	100	10	Normal	○
TM58	Endure	Normal	Status	—	—	10	Self	—
TM66	Payback	Dark	Physical	50	100	10	Normal	○
TM68	Giga Impact	Normal	Physical	150	90	5	Normal	○
TM70	Flash	Normal	Status	—	100	20	Normal	—
TM75	Swords Dance	Normal	Status	—	—	30	Self	—
TM77	Psych Up	Normal	Status	—	—	10	Normal	—
TM78	Captivate	Normal	Status	—	100	20	2 Foes	—
TM80	Rock Slide	Rock	Physical	75	90	10	2 Foes	—
TM82	Sleep Talk	Normal	Status	—	—	10	Depends	—
TM83	Natural Gift	Normal	Physical	—	100	15	Normal	—
TM84	Poison Jab	Poison	Physical	80	100	20	Normal	○
TM86	Grass Knot	Grass	Special	—	100	20	Normal	○
TM87	Swagger	Normal	Status	—	90	15	Normal	—
TM90	Substitute	Normal	Status	—	—	10	Self	—
HM01	Cut	Normal	Physical	50	95	30	Normal	○
HM04	Strength	Normal	Physical	80	100	15	Normal	○
HM06	Rock Smash	Fighting	Physical	40	100	15	Normal	○

Tangrowth

`Grass`

- ● HEIGHT: 6'07"
- ● WEIGHT: 283.5 lbs.
- ● ITEMS: None

● SIZE COMPARISON

● MALE FORM
Hands are partly red

● FEMALE FORM
Hands are completely red

● ABILITIES
- Chlorophyll
- Leaf Guard

● STATS
HP	●●●●
ATTACK	●●●●●
DEFENSE	●●●●●
SP. ATTACK	●●●●●
SP. DEFENSE	●●
SPEED	●●

● EGG GROUPS
Grass

● PERFORMANCE
SPEED ★☆	STAMINA ★★★★★
POWER ★★★☆☆	JUMP ★★
SKILL ★★★★☆	

● MAIN WAYS TO OBTAIN

Pokémon HeartGold — Level up Tangela to Lv. 33 and teach it AncientPower, or level it up once it knows AncientPower

Pokémon SoulSilver — Level up Tangela to Lv. 33 and teach it AncientPower, or level it up once it knows AncientPower

Pokémon Diamond — —

Pokémon Pearl — —

Pokémon Platinum — Level up Tangela to Lv. 33 and teach it AncientPower, or level it up once it knows AncientPower

Pokémon HeartGold

When it remains still, it appears to be a large shrub. Unsuspecting prey that wander near get ensnared by its vines.

Pokémon SoulSilver

Its vines grow so profusely that, in the warm season, you can't even see its eyes.

● EVOLUTION

Level it up to Lv. 33 and teach it AncientPower. Or, level it up once it knows AncientPower.

Tangela → Tangrowth

Level it up to Lv. 33 and teach it AncientPower, level it up once it knows AncientPower.

● No. 466 | Thunderbolt Pokémon
Electivire

Electric

- ● HEIGHT: 5'11"
- ● WEIGHT: 305.6 lbs.
- ● ITEMS: None

● SIZE COMPARISON

● MALE/FEMALE HAVE SAME FORM

● ABILITIES
- ● Motor Drive

● EGG GROUPS
Human-Like

● STATS
HP	●●●
ATTACK	●●●●●
DEFENSE	●●●
SP. ATTACK	●●●●
SP. DEFENSE	●●●
SPEED	●●●●

● PERFORMANCE
SPEED ★★★☆☆	STAMINA ★★★★
POWER ★★★☆	JUMP ★★
SKILL ★★★★☆	

● MAIN WAYS TO OBTAIN

Pokémon HeartGold	Link trade Electabuzz while it holds the Electirizer
Pokémon SoulSilver	Link trade Electabuzz while it holds the Electirizer
Pokémon Diamond	Link trade Electabuzz while it holds the Electirizer
Pokémon Pearl	Link trade Electabuzz while it holds the Electirizer
Pokémon Platinum	Link trade Electabuzz while it holds the Electirizer

Pokémon HeartGold	Pokémon SoulSilver
As its electric charge amplifies, blue sparks begin to crackle between its horns.	As its electric charge amplifies, blue sparks begin to crackle between its horns.

● EVOLUTION

Lv. 30 → Have it hold Electirizer and trade it

Elekid — Electabuzz — Electivire

● LEVEL-UP MOVES
Lv.	Name	Type	Kind	Pow.	Acc.	PP	Range	DA
1	Fire Punch	Fire	Physical	75	100	15	Normal	○
1	Quick Attack	Normal	Physical	40	100	30	Normal	○
1	Leer	Normal	Status	—	100	30	2 Foes	—
1	ThunderShock	Electric	Special	40	100	30	Normal	—
1	Low Kick	Fighting	Physical	—	100	20	Normal	○
7	ThunderShock	Electric	Special	40	100	30	Normal	—
10	Low Kick	Fighting	Physical	—	100	20	Normal	○
16	Swift	Normal	Special	60	—	20	2 Foes	—
19	Shock Wave	Electric	Special	60	—	20	Normal	—
25	Light Screen	Psychic	Status	—	—	30	2 Allies	—
28	ThunderPunch	Electric	Physical	75	100	15	Normal	○
37	Discharge	Electric	Special	80	100	15	2 Foes/1 Ally	—
43	Thunderbolt	Electric	Special	95	100	15	Normal	—
52	Screech	Normal	Status	—	85	40	Normal	—
58	Thunder	Electric	Special	120	70	10	Normal	—
67	Giga Impact	Normal	Physical	150	90	5	Normal	○

● MOVE MANIAC
Name	Type	Kind	Pow.	Acc.	PP	Range	DA
Headbutt	Normal	Physical	70	100	15	Normal	○

● BP MOVES
Name	Type	Kind	Pow.	Acc.	PP	Range	DA
ThunderPunch	Electric	Physical	75	100	15	Normal	○
Fire Punch	Fire	Physical	75	100	15	Normal	○
Ice Punch	Ice	Physical	75	100	15	Normal	○
Snore	Normal	Special	40	100	15	Normal	—
Helping Hand	Normal	Status	—	—	20	1 Ally	—
Magnet Rise	Electric	Status	—	—	10	Self	—
Swift	Normal	Special	60	—	20	2 Foes	—
Mud-Slap	Ground	Special	20	100	10	Normal	—
Signal Beam	Bug	Special	75	100	15	Normal	—
Low Kick	Fighting	Physical	—	100	20	Normal	○

● TM & HM MOVES
No.	Name	Type	Kind	Pow.	Acc.	PP	Range	DA
TM01	Focus Punch	Fighting	Physical	150	100	20	Normal	○
TM06	Toxic	Poison	Status	—	85	10	Normal	—
TM10	Hidden Power	Normal	Special	—	100	15	Normal	—
TM12	Taunt	Dark	Status	—	100	20	Normal	—
TM15	Hyper Beam	Normal	Special	150	90	5	Normal	—
TM16	Light Screen	Psychic	Status	—	—	30	2 Allies	—
TM17	Protect	Normal	Status	—	—	10	Self	—
TM18	Rain Dance	Water	Status	—	—	5	All	—
TM21	Frustration	Normal	Physical	—	100	20	Normal	○
TM23	Iron Tail	Steel	Physical	100	75	15	Normal	○
TM24	Thunderbolt	Electric	Special	95	100	15	Normal	—
TM25	Thunder	Electric	Special	120	70	10	Normal	—
TM26	Earthquake	Ground	Physical	100	100	10	2 Foes/1 Ally	—
TM27	Return	Normal	Physical	—	100	20	Normal	○
TM28	Dig	Ground	Physical	80	100	10	Normal	○
TM29	Psychic	Psychic	Special	90	100	10	Normal	—
TM31	Brick Break	Fighting	Physical	75	100	15	Normal	○
TM32	Double Team	Normal	Status	—	—	15	Self	—
TM34	Shock Wave	Electric	Special	60	—	20	Normal	—
TM35	Flamethrower	Fire	Special	95	100	15	Normal	—
TM39	Rock Tomb	Rock	Physical	50	80	10	Normal	—
TM41	Torment	Dark	Status	—	100	15	Normal	—
TM42	Facade	Normal	Physical	70	100	20	Normal	○
TM43	Secret Power	Normal	Physical	70	100	20	Normal	—
TM44	Rest	Psychic	Status	—	—	10	Self	—
TM45	Attract	Normal	Status	—	100	15	Normal	—
TM46	Thief	Dark	Physical	40	100	10	Normal	○
TM52	Focus Blast	Fighting	Special	120	70	5	Normal	—
TM56	Fling	Dark	Physical	—	100	10	Normal	—
TM57	Charge Beam	Electric	Special	50	90	10	Normal	—
TM58	Endure	Normal	Status	—	—	10	Self	—
TM68	Giga Impact	Normal	Physical	150	90	5	Normal	○
TM70	Flash	Normal	Status	—	100	20	Normal	—
TM73	Thunder Wave	Electric	Status	—	100	20	Normal	—
TM78	Captivate	Normal	Status	—	100	20	2 Foes	—
TM80	Rock Slide	Rock	Physical	75	90	10	2 Foes	—
TM82	Sleep Talk	Normal	Status	—	—	10	Depends	—
TM83	Natural Gift	Normal	Physical	—	100	15	Normal	—
TM87	Swagger	Normal	Status	—	90	15	Normal	—
TM90	Substitute	Normal	Status	—	—	10	Self	—
HM04	Strength	Normal	Physical	80	100	15	Normal	○
HM06	Rock Smash	Fighting	Physical	40	100	15	Normal	○
HM08	Rock Climb	Normal	Physical	90	85	20	Normal	○

● LEVEL-UP MOVES

Lv.	Name	Type	Kind	Pow.	Acc.	PP	Range	DA
1	ThunderPunch	Electric	Physical	75	100	15	Normal	○
1	Smog	Poison	Special	20	70	20	Normal	—
1	Leer	Normal	Status	—	100	30	2 Foes	—
1	Ember	Fire	Special	40	100	25	Normal	—
1	SmokeScreen	Normal	Status	—	100	20	Normal	—
7	Ember	Fire	Special	40	100	25	Normal	—
10	SmokeScreen	Normal	Status	—	100	20	Normal	—
16	Faint Attack	Dark	Physical	60	—	20	Normal	○
19	Fire Spin	Fire	Special	15	70	15	Normal	—
25	Confuse Ray	Ghost	Status	—	100	10	Normal	—
28	Fire Punch	Fire	Physical	75	100	15	Normal	○
37	Lava Plume	Fire	Special	80	100	15	2 Foes/1 Ally	—
43	Flamethrower	Fire	Special	95	100	15	Normal	—
52	Sunny Day	Fire	Status	—	—	5	All	—
58	Fire Blast	Fire	Special	120	85	5	Normal	—
67	Hyper Beam	Normal	Special	150	90	5	Normal	—

● MOVE MANIAC

Name	Type	Kind	Pow.	Acc.	PP	Range	DA
Headbutt	Normal	Physical	70	100	15	Normal	○

● BP MOVES

Name	Type	Kind	Pow.	Acc.	PP	Range	DA
ThunderPunch	Electric	Physical	75	100	15	Normal	○
Fire Punch	Fire	Physical	75	100	15	Normal	○
Snore	Normal	Special	40	100	15	Normal	—
Helping Hand	Normal	Status	—	—	20	1 Ally	—
Mud-Slap	Ground	Special	20	100	10	Normal	—
Heat Wave	Fire	Special	100	90	10	2 Foes	—
Low Kick	Fighting	Physical	—	100	20	Normal	○

● TM & HM MOVES

No.	Name	Type	Kind	Pow.	Acc.	PP	Range	DA
TM01	Focus Punch	Fighting	Physical	150	100	20	Normal	○
TM06	Toxic	Poison	Status	—	85	10	Normal	—
TM10	Hidden Power	Normal	Special	—	100	15	Normal	—
TM11	Sunny Day	Fire	Status	—	—	5	All	—
TM12	Taunt	Dark	Status	—	100	20	Normal	—
TM15	Hyper Beam	Normal	Special	150	90	5	Normal	—
TM17	Protect	Normal	Status	—	—	10	Self	—
TM21	Frustration	Normal	Physical	—	100	20	Normal	○
TM22	SolarBeam	Grass	Special	120	100	10	Normal	—
TM23	Iron Tail	Steel	Physical	100	75	15	Normal	○
TM24	Thunderbolt	Electric	Special	95	100	15	Normal	—
TM26	Earthquake	Ground	Physical	100	100	10	2 Foes/1 Ally	○
TM27	Return	Normal	Physical	—	100	20	Normal	○
TM29	Psychic	Psychic	Special	90	100	10	Normal	—
TM31	Brick Break	Fighting	Physical	75	100	15	Normal	○
TM32	Double Team	Normal	Status	—	—	15	Self	—
TM35	Flamethrower	Fire	Special	95	100	15	Normal	—
TM38	Fire Blast	Fire	Special	120	85	5	Normal	—
TM39	Rock Tomb	Rock	Physical	50	80	10	Normal	○
TM41	Torment	Dark	Status	—	100	15	Normal	—
TM42	Facade	Normal	Physical	70	100	20	Normal	○
TM43	Secret Power	Normal	Physical	70	100	20	Normal	—
TM44	Rest	Psychic	Status	—	—	10	Self	—
TM45	Attract	Normal	Status	—	100	15	Normal	—
TM46	Thief	Dark	Physical	40	100	10	Normal	○
TM50	Overheat	Fire	Special	140	90	5	Normal	—
TM52	Focus Blast	Fighting	Special	120	70	5	Normal	—
TM56	Fling	Dark	Physical	—	100	10	Normal	—
TM58	Endure	Normal	Status	—	—	10	Self	—
TM61	Will-O-Wisp	Fire	Status	—	75	15	Normal	—
TM68	Giga Impact	Normal	Physical	150	90	5	Normal	○
TM78	Captivate	Normal	Status	—	100	20	2 Foes	—
TM80	Rock Slide	Rock	Physical	75	90	10	2 Foes	—
TM82	Sleep Talk	Normal	Status	—	—	10	Depends	—
TM83	Natural Gift	Normal	Physical	—	100	15	Normal	—
TM87	Swagger	Normal	Status	—	90	15	Normal	—
TM90	Substitute	Normal	Status	—	—	10	Self	—
HM04	Strength	Normal	Physical	80	100	15	Normal	○
HM06	Rock Smash	Fighting	Physical	40	100	15	Normal	○
HM08	Rock Climb	Normal	Physical	90	85	20	Normal	○

◎ No. **467** | Blast Pokémon

Magmortar

Fire

● **SIZE COMPARISON**

● HEIGHT: 5'03"
● WEIGHT: 149.9 lbs.
● ITEMS: None

● MALE/FEMALE HAVE SAME FORM

◎ ABILITIES
● Flame Body

◎ STATS
HP	●●●
ATTACK	●●●●
DEFENSE	●●●
SP. ATTACK	●●●●●
SP. DEFENSE	●●●●
SPEED	●●●●

◎ EGG GROUPS
Human-Like

◎ PERFORMANCE
SPEED ★★
POWER ★★★★☆
SKILL ★★★★☆
STAMINA ★★★★☆
JUMP ★★

● MAIN WAYS TO OBTAIN

Pokémon HeartGold	Link trade Magmar while it holds the Magmarizer
Pokémon SoulSilver	Link trade Magmar while it holds the Magmarizer
Pokémon Diamond	Link trade Magmar while it holds the Magmarizer
Pokémon Pearl	Link trade Magmar while it holds the Magmarizer
Pokémon Platinum	Link trade Magmar while it holds the Magmarizer

Pokémon HeartGold

It blasts fireballs of over 3,600 degrees Fahrenheit out of its arms. Its breath also sears and sizzles.

Pokémon SoulSilver

It blasts fireballs of over 3,600 degrees Fahrenheit out of its arms. Its breath also sears and sizzles.

◎ EVOLUTION

Magby → Lv. 30 → Magmar → Have it hold Magmarizer and trade it → Magmortar

○ No. 468 | Jubilee Pokémon
Togekiss

`Normal` `Flying`

- ● **HEIGHT:** 4'11"
- ● **WEIGHT:** 83.8 lbs.
- ● **ITEMS:** None

● **SIZE COMPARISON**

● **MALE/FEMALE HAVE SAME FORM**
Larger white marking on head

⊙ ABILITIES
- Hustle
- Serene Grace

⊙ STATS
HP	●●●
ATTACK	●●
DEFENSE	●●●●
SP. ATTACK	●●●●●
SP. DEFENSE	●●●●●
SPEED	●●●●

⊙ EGG GROUPS
Flying

Fairy

⊙ PERFORMANCE
SPEED ★★★☆　　STAMINA ★★★☆
POWER ★★☆　　JUMP ★★★★★
SKILL ★★★☆

● **MAIN WAYS TO OBTAIN**

Pokémon HeartGold	Use Shiny Stone on Togetic
Pokémon SoulSilver	Use Shiny Stone on Togetic
Pokémon Diamond	Use Shiny Stone on Togetic
Pokémon Pearl	Use Shiny Stone on Togetic
Pokémon Platinum	Use Shiny Stone on Togetic

Pokémon HeartGold	**Pokémon SoulSilver**
As everyone knows, it visits peaceful regions, bringing them gifts of kindness and sweet blessings.	As everyone knows, it visits peaceful regions, bringing them gifts of kindness and sweet blessings.

⊙ EVOLUTION

Togepi → (Level up with high friendship) → Togetic → (Use Shiny Stone) → Togekiss

● LEVEL-UP MOVES
Lv.	Name	Type	Kind	Pow.	Acc.	PP	Range	DA
1	Sky Attack	Flying	Physical	140	90	5	Normal	—
1	ExtremeSpeed	Normal	Physical	80	100	5	Normal	○
1	Aura Sphere	Fighting	Special	90	—	20	Normal	—
1	Air Slash	Flying	Special	75	95	20	Normal	—

● MOVE MANIAC
Name	Type	Kind	Pow.	Acc.	PP	Range	DA
Headbutt	Normal	Physical	70	100	15	Normal	○

● BP MOVES
Name	Type	Kind	Pow.	Acc.	PP	Range	DA
Ominous Wind	Ghost	Special	60	100	5	Normal	—
Air Cutter	Flying	Special	55	95	25	2 Foes	—
Zen Headbutt	Psychic	Physical	80	90	15	Normal	○
Trick	Psychic	Status	—	100	10	Normal	—
Snore	Normal	Special	40	100	15	Normal	—
Last Resort	Normal	Physical	130	100	5	Normal	○
Swift	Normal	Special	60	—	20	2 Foes	—
Tailwind	Flying	Status	—	—	30	2 Allies	—
Magic Coat	Psychic	Status	—	—	15	Self	—
Heal Bell	Normal	Status	—	—	5	All Allies	—
Mud-Slap	Ground	Special	20	100	10	Normal	—
Rollout	Rock	Physical	30	90	20	Normal	○
Endeavor	Normal	Physical	—	100	5	Normal	○
AncientPower	Rock	Special	60	100	5	Normal	—
Signal Beam	Bug	Special	75	100	15	Normal	—
Twister	Dragon	Special	40	100	20	2 Foes	—
Heat Wave	Fire	Special	100	90	10	2 Foes	—
Sky Attack	Flying	Physical	140	90	5	Normal	—

● TM & HM MOVES
No.	Name	Type	Kind	Pow.	Acc.	PP	Range	DA
TM01	Focus Punch	Fighting	Physical	150	100	20	Normal	○
TM03	Water Pulse	Water	Special	60	100	20	Normal	—
TM06	Toxic	Poison	Status	—	85	10	Normal	—
TM10	Hidden Power	Normal	Special	—	100	15	Normal	—
TM11	Sunny Day	Fire	Status	—	—	5	All	—
TM15	Hyper Beam	Normal	Special	150	90	5	Normal	—
TM16	Light Screen	Psychic	Status	—	—	30	2 Allies	—
TM17	Protect	Normal	Status	—	—	10	Self	—
TM18	Rain Dance	Water	Status	—	—	5	All	—
TM20	Safeguard	Normal	Status	—	—	25	2 Allies	—
TM21	Frustration	Normal	Physical	—	100	20	Normal	○
TM22	SolarBeam	Grass	Special	120	100	10	Normal	—
TM27	Return	Normal	Physical	—	100	20	Normal	○
TM29	Psychic	Psychic	Special	90	100	10	Normal	—
TM30	Shadow Ball	Ghost	Special	80	100	15	Normal	—
TM31	Brick Break	Fighting	Physical	75	100	15	Normal	○
TM32	Double Team	Normal	Status	—	—	15	Self	—
TM33	Reflect	Psychic	Status	—	—	20	2 Allies	—
TM34	Shock Wave	Electric	Special	60	—	20	Normal	—
TM35	Flamethrower	Fire	Special	95	100	15	Normal	—
TM38	Fire Blast	Fire	Special	120	85	5	Normal	—
TM40	Aerial Ace	Flying	Physical	60	—	20	Normal	○
TM42	Facade	Normal	Physical	70	100	20	Normal	○
TM43	Secret Power	Normal	Physical	70	100	20	Normal	○
TM44	Rest	Psychic	Status	—	—	10	Self	—
TM45	Attract	Normal	Status	—	100	15	Normal	—
TM47	Steel Wing	Steel	Physical	70	90	25	Normal	○
TM51	Roost	Flying	Status	—	—	10	Self	—
TM56	Fling	Dark	Physical	—	100	10	Normal	○
TM58	Endure	Normal	Status	—	—	10	Self	—
TM60	Drain Punch	Fighting	Physical	60	100	5	Normal	○
TM62	Silver Wind	Bug	Special	60	100	5	Normal	—
TM68	Giga Impact	Normal	Physical	150	90	5	Normal	○
TM70	Flash	Normal	Status	—	100	20	Normal	—
TM73	Thunder Wave	Electric	Status	—	100	20	Normal	—
TM77	Psych Up	Normal	Status	—	—	10	Normal	—
TM78	Captivate	Normal	Status	—	100	20	2 Foes	—
TM82	Sleep Talk	Normal	Status	—	—	10	Depends	—
TM83	Natural Gift	Normal	Physical	—	100	15	Normal	○
TM85	Dream Eater	Psychic	Special	100	100	15	Normal	—
TM86	Grass Knot	Grass	Special	—	100	20	Normal	○
TM87	Swagger	Normal	Status	—	90	15	Normal	—
TM88	Pluck	Flying	Physical	60	100	20	Normal	○
TM90	Substitute	Normal	Status	—	—	10	Self	—
HM02	Fly	Flying	Physical	90	95	15	Normal	○
HM06	Rock Smash	Fighting	Physical	40	100	15	Normal	○

● LEVEL-UP MOVES

Lv.	Name	Type	Kind	Pow.	Acc.	PP	Range	DA
1	Night Slash	Dark	Physical	70	100	15	Normal	○
1	Bug Bite	Bug	Physical	60	100	20	Normal	○
1	Tackle	Normal	Physical	35	95	35	Normal	○
1	Foresight	Normal	Status	—	—	40	Normal	—
1	Quick Attack	Normal	Physical	40	100	30	Normal	○
1	Double Team	Normal	Status	—	—	15	Self	—
6	Quick Attack	Normal	Physical	40	100	30	Normal	○
11	Double Team	Normal	Status	—	—	15	Self	—
14	SonicBoom	Normal	Special	—	90	20	Normal	—
17	Detect	Fighting	Status	—	—	5	Self	—
22	Supersonic	Normal	Status	—	55	20	Normal	—
27	Uproar	Normal	Special	50	100	10	1 Random	—
30	Pursuit	Dark	Physical	40	100	20	Normal	○
33	AncientPower	Rock	Special	60	100	5	Normal	—
38	Feint	Normal	Physical	50	100	10	Normal	—
43	Slash	Normal	Physical	70	100	20	Normal	○
46	Screech	Normal	Status	—	85	40	Normal	—
49	U-turn	Bug	Physical	70	100	20	Normal	○
54	Air Slash	Flying	Special	75	95	20	Normal	—
57	Bug Buzz	Bug	Special	90	100	10	Normal	—

● MOVE MANIAC

Name	Type	Kind	Pow.	Acc.	PP	Range	DA
Headbutt	Normal	Physical	70	100	15	Normal	○

● BP MOVES

Name	Type	Kind	Pow.	Acc.	PP	Range	DA
Ominous Wind	Ghost	Special	60	100	5	Normal	—
Air Cutter	Flying	Special	55	95	25	2 Foes	—
Bug Bite	Bug	Physical	60	100	20	Normal	○
Snore	Normal	Special	40	100	15	Normal	—
Swift	Normal	Special	60	—	20	2 Foes	—
Uproar	Normal	Special	50	100	10	1 Random	—
String Shot	Bug	Status	—	95	40	2 Foes	—
Tailwind	Flying	Status	—	—	30	2 Allies	—
Mud-Slap	Ground	Special	20	100	10	Normal	—
AncientPower	Rock	Special	60	100	5	Normal	—
Signal Beam	Bug	Special	75	100	15	Normal	—

● TM & HM MOVES

No.	Name	Type	Kind	Pow.	Acc.	PP	Range	DA
TM06	Toxic	Poison	Status	—	85	10	Normal	—
TM10	Hidden Power	Normal	Special	—	100	15	Normal	—
TM11	Sunny Day	Fire	Status	—	—	5	All	—
TM15	Hyper Beam	Normal	Special	150	90	5	Normal	—
TM17	Protect	Normal	Status	—	—	10	Self	—
TM19	Giga Drain	Grass	Special	60	100	10	Normal	—
TM21	Frustration	Normal	Physical	—	100	20	Normal	○
TM22	SolarBeam	Grass	Special	120	100	10	Normal	—
TM27	Return	Normal	Physical	—	100	20	Normal	○
TM29	Psychic	Psychic	Special	90	100	10	Normal	—
TM30	Shadow Ball	Ghost	Special	80	100	15	Normal	—
TM32	Double Team	Normal	Status	—	—	15	Self	—
TM40	Aerial Ace	Flying	Physical	60	—	20	Normal	○
TM42	Facade	Normal	Physical	70	100	20	Normal	○
TM43	Secret Power	Normal	Physical	70	100	20	Normal	—
TM44	Rest	Psychic	Status	—	—	10	Self	—
TM45	Attract	Normal	Status	—	100	15	Normal	—
TM46	Thief	Dark	Physical	40	100	10	Normal	○
TM47	Steel Wing	Steel	Physical	70	90	25	Normal	—
TM51	Roost	Flying	Status	—	—	10	Self	—
TM58	Endure	Normal	Status	—	—	10	Self	—
TM62	Silver Wind	Bug	Special	60	100	5	Normal	—
TM68	Giga Impact	Normal	Physical	150	90	5	Normal	○
TM70	Flash	Normal	Status	—	100	20	Normal	—
TM77	Psych Up	Normal	Status	—	—	10	Self	—
TM78	Captivate	Normal	Status	—	100	20	2 Foes	—
TM82	Sleep Talk	Normal	Status	—	—	10	Self	—
TM83	Natural Gift	Normal	Physical	—	100	15	Normal	—
TM85	Dream Eater	Psychic	Special	100	100	15	Normal	—
TM87	Swagger	Normal	Status	—	90	15	Normal	—
TM89	U-turn	Bug	Physical	70	100	20	Normal	○
TM90	Substitute	Normal	Status	—	—	10	Self	—

● No. **469** | Ogre Darner Pokémon
Yanmega

Bug Flying

● HEIGHT: 6'03"
● WEIGHT: 113.5 lbs.
● ITEMS: None

● SIZE COMPARISON

● MALE/FEMALE HAVE SAME FORM

● ABILITIES
● Speed Boost
● Tinted Lens

● STATS
HP ●●●
ATTACK ●●●
DEFENSE ●●●●
SP. ATTACK ●●●●
SP. DEFENSE ●●●
SPEED ●●●●

● EGG GROUPS
Bug

● PERFORMANCE
SPEED ★★★★☆　STAMINA ★★★
POWER ★★☆　JUMP ★★★★★
SKILL ★☆☆

● MAIN WAYS TO OBTAIN

Pokémon HeartGold
Level up Yanma to Lv. 33 and have it learn AncientPower, or level it up once it knows AncientPower

Pokémon SoulSilver
Level up Yanma to Lv. 33 and have it learn AncientPower, or level it up once it knows AncientPower

Pokémon Diamond
Level up Yanma to Lv. 33 and have it learn AncientPower, or level it up once it knows AncientPower

Pokémon Pearl
Level up Yanma to Lv. 33 and have it learn AncientPower, or level it up once it knows AncientPower

Pokémon Platinum
Level up Yanma to Lv. 33 and have it learn AncientPower, or level it up once it knows AncientPower

Pokémon HeartGold
This six-legged Pokémon is easily capable of transporting an adult in flight. The wings on its tail help it stay balanced.

Pokémon SoulSilver
The beat of its wings is so powerful that it accidentally dislodges full-grown trees when it takes off in flight.

● EVOLUTION

Yanma

Level it up to Lv. 33 and teach it AncientPower. Or, level it up once it knows AncientPower.

Yanmega

● No. 470 | Verdant Pokémon
Leafeon

Grass

- ● HEIGHT: 3'03"
- ● WEIGHT: 56.2 lbs.
- ● ITEMS: None

● SIZE COMPARISON

● MALE/FEMALE HAVE SAME FORM

⊙ ABILITIES
- ● Leaf Guard

⊙ STATS
HP	●●
ATTACK	●●●●●
DEFENSE	●●●●●
SP. ATTACK	●●●
SP. DEFENSE	●●
SPEED	●●●●

⊙ EGG GROUPS
Field

⊙ PERFORMANCE
SPEED ★★☆	STAMINA ★★★★☆
POWER ★★★☆	JUMP ★★★☆
SKILL ★★★☆	

● MAIN WAYS TO OBTAIN

Pokémon HeartGold	—
Pokémon SoulSilver	—
Pokémon Diamond	Level up Eevee in Eterna Forest (interior) near the moss-covered rock
Pokémon Pearl	Level up Eevee in Eterna Forest (interior) near the moss-covered rock
Pokémon Platinum	Level up Eevee in Eterna Forest (interior) near the moss-covered rock

Pokémon HeartGold	Pokémon SoulSilver
When you see LEAFEON asleep in a patch of sunshine, you'll know it is using photosynthesis to produce clean air.	When you see LEAFEON asleep in a patch of sunshine, you'll know it is using photosynthesis to produce clean air.

⊙ EVOLUTION

Eevee

Espeon — Level up Eevee with high friendship in the morning or afternoon

Vaporeon — Use Water Stone on Eevee

Umbreon — Level up Eevee with high friendship at night

Jolteon — Use Thunderstone on Eevee

Leafeon — Level up Eevee in Eterna Forest*

Flareon — Use Fire Stone on Eevee

Glaceon — Level up Eevee on Route 217*

● LEVEL-UP MOVES
Lv.	Name	Type	Kind	Pow.	Acc.	PP	Range	DA
1	Tail Whip	Normal	Status	—	100	30	2 Foes	—
1	Tackle	Normal	Physical	35	95	35	Normal	○
1	Helping Hand	Normal	Status	—	—	20	1 Ally	—
8	Sand-Attack	Ground	Status	—	100	15	Normal	—
15	Razor Leaf	Grass	Physical	55	95	25	2 Foes	○
22	Quick Attack	Normal	Physical	40	100	30	Normal	○
29	Synthesis	Grass	Status	—	—	5	Self	—
36	Magical Leaf	Grass	Special	60	—	20	Normal	—
43	Giga Drain	Grass	Special	60	100	10	Normal	—
50	Last Resort	Normal	Physical	130	100	5	Normal	○
57	GrassWhistle	Grass	Status	—	55	15	Normal	—
64	Sunny Day	Fire	Status	—	—	5	All	—
71	Leaf Blade	Grass	Physical	90	100	15	Normal	○
78	Swords Dance	Normal	Status	—	—	30	Self	—

● MOVE MANIAC
Name	Type	Kind	Pow.	Acc.	PP	Range	DA
Headbutt	Normal	Physical	70	100	15	Normal	○

● BP MOVES
Name	Type	Kind	Pow.	Acc.	PP	Range	DA
Fury Cutter	Bug	Physical	10	95	20	Normal	○
Knock Off	Dark	Physical	20	100	20	Normal	○
Snore	Normal	Special	40	100	15	Normal	—
Helping Hand	Normal	Status	—	—	20	1 Ally	—
Synthesis	Grass	Status	—	—	5	Self	—
Last Resort	Normal	Physical	130	100	5	Normal	○
Swift	Normal	Special	60	—	20	2 Foes	—
Worry Seed	Grass	Status	—	100	10	Normal	—
Heal Bell	Normal	Status	—	—	5	All Allies	—
Mud-Slap	Ground	Special	20	100	10	Normal	—
Seed Bomb	Grass	Physical	80	100	15	Normal	—

● TM & HM MOVES
No.	Name	Type	Kind	Pow.	Acc.	PP	Range	DA
TM05	Roar	Normal	Status	—	100	20	Normal	—
TM06	Toxic	Poison	Status	—	85	10	Normal	—
TM09	Bullet Seed	Grass	Physical	10	100	30	Normal	—
TM10	Hidden Power	Normal	Special	—	100	15	Normal	—
TM11	Sunny Day	Fire	Status	—	—	5	All	—
TM15	Hyper Beam	Normal	Special	150	90	5	Normal	—
TM17	Protect	Normal	Status	—	—	10	Self	—
TM18	Rain Dance	Water	Status	—	—	5	All	—
TM19	Giga Drain	Grass	Special	60	100	10	Normal	—
TM21	Frustration	Normal	Physical	—	100	20	Normal	○
TM22	SolarBeam	Grass	Special	120	100	10	Normal	—
TM23	Iron Tail	Steel	Physical	100	75	15	Normal	○
TM27	Return	Normal	Physical	—	100	20	Normal	○
TM28	Dig	Ground	Physical	80	100	10	Normal	○
TM30	Shadow Ball	Ghost	Special	80	100	15	Normal	—
TM32	Double Team	Normal	Status	—	—	15	Self	—
TM40	Aerial Ace	Flying	Physical	60	—	20	Normal	○
TM42	Facade	Normal	Physical	70	100	20	Normal	○
TM43	Secret Power	Normal	Physical	70	100	20	Normal	—
TM44	Rest	Psychic	Status	—	—	10	Self	—
TM45	Attract	Normal	Status	—	100	15	Normal	—
TM53	Energy Ball	Grass	Special	80	100	10	Normal	—
TM58	Endure	Normal	Status	—	—	10	Self	—
TM68	Giga Impact	Normal	Physical	150	90	5	Normal	○
TM70	Flash	Normal	Status	—	100	20	Normal	—
TM75	Swords Dance	Normal	Status	—	—	30	Self	—
TM78	Captivate	Normal	Status	—	100	20	2 Foes	—
TM81	X-Scissor	Bug	Physical	80	100	15	Normal	○
TM82	Sleep Talk	Normal	Status	—	—	10	Depends	—
TM83	Natural Gift	Normal	Physical	—	100	15	Normal	—
TM86	Grass Knot	Grass	Special	—	100	20	Normal	—
TM87	Swagger	Normal	Status	—	90	15	Normal	—
TM90	Substitute	Normal	Status	—	—	10	Self	—
HM04	Strength	Normal	Physical	80	100	15	Normal	○
HM06	Rock Smash	Fighting	Physical	40	100	15	Normal	○

*Unable to evolve in *Pokémon HeartGold* or *SoulSilver Version*. Transfer from *Diamond*, *Pearl*, or *Platinum Version*.

● LEVEL-UP MOVES

Lv.	Name	Type	Kind	Pow.	Acc.	PP	Range	DA
1	Tail Whip	Normal	Status	—	100	30	2 Foes	—
1	Tackle	Normal	Physical	35	95	35	Normal	○
1	Helping Hand	Normal	Status	—	—	20	1 Ally	—
8	Sand-Attack	Ground	Status	—	100	15	Normal	—
15	Icy Wind	Ice	Special	55	95	15	2 Foes	—
22	Quick Attack	Normal	Physical	40	100	30	Normal	○
29	Bite	Dark	Physical	60	100	25	Normal	○
36	Ice Shard	Ice	Physical	40	100	30	Normal	—
43	Ice Fang	Ice	Physical	65	95	15	Normal	○
50	Last Resort	Normal	Physical	130	100	5	Normal	○
5?	Mirror Coat	Psychic	Special	—	100	20	Self	—
64	Hail	Ice	Status	—	—	10	All	—
71	Blizzard	Ice	Special	120	70	5	2 Foes	—
78	Barrier	Psychic	Status	—	—	30	Self	—

● MOVE MANIAC

Name	Type	Kind	Pow.	Acc.	PP	Range	DA
Headbutt	Normal	Physical	70	100	15	Normal	○

● BP MOVES

Name	Type	Kind	Pow.	Acc.	PP	Range	DA
Icy Wind	Ice	Special	55	95	15	2 Foes	—
Snore	Normal	Special	40	100	15	Normal	—
Helping Hand	Normal	Status	—	—	20	1 Ally	—
Last Resort	Normal	Physical	130	100	5	Normal	○
Swift	Normal	Special	60	—	20	2 Foes	—
Heal Bell	Normal	Status	—	—	5	All Allies	—
Mud-Slap	Ground	Special	20	100	10	Normal	—
Aqua Tail	Water	Physical	90	90	10	Normal	○
Signal Beam	Bug	Special	75	100	15	Normal	—

● TM & HM MOVES

No.	Name	Type	Kind	Pow.	Acc.	PP	Range	DA
TM03	Water Pulse	Water	Special	60	100	20	Normal	—
TM05	Roar	Normal	Status	—	100	20	Normal	—
TM06	Toxic	Poison	Status	—	85	10	Normal	—
TM07	Hail	Ice	Status	—	—	10	All	—
TM10	Hidden Power	Normal	Special	—	100	15	Normal	—
TM11	Sunny Day	Fire	Status	—	—	5	All	—
TM13	Ice Beam	Ice	Special	95	100	10	Normal	—
TM14	Blizzard	Ice	Special	120	70	5	2 Foes	—
TM15	Hyper Beam	Normal	Special	150	90	5	Normal	—
TM17	Protect	Normal	Status	—	—	10	Self	—
TM18	Rain Dance	Water	Status	—	—	5	All	—
TM21	Frustration	Normal	Physical	—	100	20	Normal	○
TM23	Iron Tail	Steel	Physical	100	75	15	Normal	○
TM27	Return	Normal	Physical	—	100	20	Normal	○
TM28	Dig	Ground	Physical	80	100	10	Normal	○
TM30	Shadow Ball	Ghost	Special	80	100	15	Normal	—
TM32	Double Team	Normal	Status	—	—	15	Self	—
TM42	Facade	Normal	Physical	70	100	20	Normal	○
TM43	Secret Power	Normal	Physical	70	100	20	Normal	○
TM44	Rest	Psychic	Status	—	—	10	Self	—
TM45	Attract	Normal	Status	—	100	15	Normal	—
TM58	Endure	Normal	Status	—	—	10	Self	—
TM68	Giga Impact	Normal	Physical	150	90	5	Normal	○
TM72	Avalanche	Ice	Physical	60	100	10	Normal	○
TM78	Captivate	Normal	Status	—	100	20	2 Foes	—
TM82	Sleep Talk	Normal	Status	—	—	10	Depends	—
TM83	Natural Gift	Normal	Physical	—	100	15	Normal	—
TM87	Swagger	Normal	Status	—	90	15	Normal	—
TM90	Substitute	Normal	Status	—	—	10	Self	—
HM04	Strength	Normal	Physical	80	100	15	Normal	○
HM06	Rock Smash	Fighting	Physical	40	100	15	Normal	○

○ No. 471 | Fresh Snow Pokémon
Glaceon

Ice

- ● HEIGHT: 2'07"
- ● WEIGHT: 57.1 lbs.
- ● ITEMS: None

● SIZE COMPARISON

● MALE/FEMALE HAVE SAME FORM

○ ABILITIES
- ● Snow Cloak

○ STATS
- HP ●●
- ATTACK ●●●
- DEFENSE ●●●●
- SP. ATTACK ●●●●●
- SP. DEFENSE ●●●●
- SPEED ●●●

○ EGG GROUPS
Field

○ PERFORMANCE
SPEED ★★★☆ STAMINA ★★☆☆
POWER ★★★☆ JUMP ★★★
SKILL ★★★★☆

● MAIN WAYS TO OBTAIN

Pokémon HeartGold	—
Pokémon SoulSilver	—
Pokémon Diamond	Level up Eevee on Route 217 near the ice-covered rock
Pokémon Pearl	Level up Eevee on Route 217 near the ice-covered rock
Pokémon Platinum	Level up Eevee on Route 217 near the ice-covered rock

Pokémon HeartGold
It causes small ice crystals to form by lowering the temperature of the surrounding atmosphere.

Pokémon SoulSilver
It causes small ice crystals to form by lowering the temperature of the surrounding atmosphere.

○ EVOLUTION

Eevee

Espeon — Level up Eevee with high friendship in the morning or afternoon

Vaporeon — Use Water Stone on Eevee

Umbreon — Level up Eevee with high friendship at night

Jolteon — Use Thunderstone on Eevee

Leafeon — Level up Eevee in Eterna Forest*

Flareon — Use Fire Stone on Eevee

Glaceon — Level up Eevee on Route 217*

*Unable to evolve in Pokémon HeartGold or SoulSilver Version. Transfer from Diamond, Pearl, or Platinum Version.

● No. 472 | Fang Scorp Pokémon
Gliscor

`Ground` `Flying`

- **● HEIGHT:** 6'07"
- **● WEIGHT:** 93.7 lbs.
- **● ITEMS:** None

● SIZE COMPARISON

● MALE/FEMALE HAVE SAME FORM

⊛ ABILITIES
- Hyper Cutter
- Sand Veil

⊛ STATS
HP	●●●
ATTACK	●●●●
DEFENSE	●●●●●
SP. ATTACK	●●
SP. DEFENSE	●●●
SPEED	●●●●

⊛ EGG GROUPS
Bug

⊛ PERFORMANCE
SPEED ★★☆☆
POWER ★★★★☆
SKILL ★★★★☆
STAMINA ★★☆☆☆
JUMP ★★★★☆

● MAIN WAYS TO OBTAIN

Pokémon HeartGold — Have Gligar hold the Razor Fang and level up between 8:00 P.M. and 4:00 A.M.

Pokémon SoulSilver — —

Pokémon Diamond — Have Gligar hold the Razor Fang and level up between 8:00 P.M. and 4:00 A.M.

Pokémon Pearl — Have Gligar hold the Razor Fang and level up between 8:00 P.M. and 4:00 A.M.

Pokémon Platinum — Have Gligar hold the Razor Fang and level up between 8:00 P.M. and 4:00 A.M.

Pokémon HeartGold — Its flight is soundless. It uses its lengthy tail to carry off its prey... Then its elongated fangs do the rest.

Pokémon SoulSilver — Its flight is soundless. It uses its lengthy tail to carry off its prey... Then its elongated fangs do the rest.

⊛ EVOLUTION

Gligar — Have it hold Razor Fang and then level up between 8:00 P.M. and 4:00 A.M. — Gliscor

● LEVEL-UP MOVES
Lv.	Name	Type	Kind	Pow.	Acc.	PP	Range	DA
1	Thunder Fang	Electric	Physical	65	95	15	Normal	○
1	Ice Fang	Ice	Physical	65	95	15	Normal	○
1	Fire Fang	Fire	Physical	65	95	15	Normal	○
1	Poison Jab	Poison	Physical	80	100	20	Normal	○
1	Sand-Attack	Ground	Status	—	100	15	Normal	—
1	Harden	Normal	Status	—	—	20	Self	—
1	Knock Off	Dark	Physical	20	100	20	Normal	○
5	Sand-Attack	Ground	Status	—	100	15	Normal	—
9	Harden	Normal	Status	—	—	30	Self	—
12	Knock Off	Dark	Physical	20	100	20	Normal	○
16	Quick Attack	Normal	Physical	40	100	30	Normal	○
20	Fury Cutter	Bug	Physical	10	95	20	Normal	○
23	Faint Attack	Dark	Physical	60	—	20	Normal	○
27	Screech	Normal	Status	—	85	40	Normal	—
31	Night Slash	Dark	Physical	70	100	15	Normal	○
34	Swords Dance	Normal	Status	—	—	30	Self	—
38	U-turn	Bug	Physical	70	100	20	Normal	○
42	X-Scissor	Bug	Physical	80	100	15	Normal	○
45	Guillotine	Normal	Physical	—	30	5	Normal	○

● MOVE MANIAC
Name	Type	Kind	Pow.	Acc.	PP	Range	DA
Headbutt	Normal	Physical	70	100	15	Normal	○

● BP MOVES
Name	Type	Kind	Pow.	Acc.	PP	Range	DA
Fury Cutter	Bug	Physical	10	95	20	Normal	○
Knock Off	Dark	Physical	20	100	20	Normal	○
Snore	Normal	Special	40	100	15	Normal	—
Swift	Normal	Special	60	—	20	Normal	—
Tailwind	Flying	Status	—	—	30	2 Allies	—
Mud-Slap	Ground	Special	20	100	10	Normal	—
Aqua Tail	Water	Physical	90	90	10	Normal	○
Earth Power	Ground	Special	90	100	10	Normal	—
Sky Attack	Flying	Physical	140	90	5	Normal	—

● TM & HM MOVES
No.	Name	Type	Kind	Pow.	Acc.	PP	Range	DA
TM06	Toxic	Poison	Status	—	85	10	Normal	—
TM10	Hidden Power	Normal	Special	—	100	15	Normal	—
TM11	Sunny Day	Fire	Status	—	—	5	All	—
TM12	Taunt	Dark	Status	—	100	20	Normal	—
TM15	Hyper Beam	Normal	Special	150	90	5	Normal	—
TM17	Protect	Normal	Status	—	—	10	Self	—
TM18	Rain Dance	Water	Status	—	—	5	All	—
TM21	Frustration	Normal	Physical	—	100	20	Normal	○
TM23	Iron Tail	Steel	Physical	100	75	15	Normal	○
TM26	Earthquake	Ground	Physical	100	100	10	2 Foes/1 Ally	—
TM27	Return	Normal	Physical	—	100	20	Normal	○
TM28	Dig	Ground	Physical	80	100	10	Normal	○
TM31	Brick Break	Fighting	Physical	75	100	15	Normal	○
TM32	Double Team	Normal	Status	—	—	15	Self	—
TM36	Sludge Bomb	Poison	Special	90	100	10	Normal	—
TM37	Sandstorm	Rock	Status	—	—	10	All	—
TM39	Rock Tomb	Rock	Physical	50	80	10	Normal	○
TM40	Aerial Ace	Flying	Physical	60	—	20	Normal	○
TM41	Torment	Dark	Status	—	100	15	Normal	—
TM42	Facade	Normal	Physical	70	100	20	Normal	○
TM43	Secret Power	Normal	Physical	70	100	20	Normal	○
TM44	Rest	Psychic	Status	—	—	10	Self	—
TM45	Attract	Normal	Status	—	100	15	Normal	—
TM46	Thief	Dark	Physical	40	100	10	Normal	○
TM47	Steel Wing	Steel	Physical	70	90	25	Normal	○
TM51	Roost	Flying	Status	—	—	10	Self	—
TM54	False Swipe	Normal	Physical	40	100	40	Normal	○
TM56	Fling	Dark	Physical	—	100	10	Normal	○
TM58	Endure	Normal	Status	—	—	10	Self	—
TM66	Payback	Dark	Physical	50	100	10	Normal	○
TM68	Giga Impact	Normal	Physical	150	90	5	Normal	○
TM69	Rock Polish	Rock	Status	—	—	20	Self	—
TM71	Stone Edge	Rock	Physical	100	80	5	Normal	○
TM75	Swords Dance	Normal	Status	—	—	30	Self	—
TM76	Stealth Rock	Rock	Status	—	—	20	2 Foes	—
TM78	Captivate	Normal	Status	—	100	20	2 Foes	—
TM79	Dark Pulse	Dark	Special	80	100	15	Normal	—
TM80	Rock Slide	Rock	Physical	75	90	10	2 Foes	○
TM81	X-Scissor	Bug	Physical	80	100	15	Normal	○
TM82	Sleep Talk	Normal	Status	—	—	10	Depends	—
TM83	Natural Gift	Normal	Physical	—	100	15	Normal	—
TM84	Poison Jab	Poison	Physical	80	100	20	Normal	○
TM87	Swagger	Normal	Status	—	90	15	Normal	—
TM89	U-turn	Bug	Physical	70	100	20	Normal	○
TM90	Substitute	Normal	Status	—	—	10	Self	—
HM01	Cut	Normal	Physical	50	95	30	Normal	○
HM04	Strength	Normal	Physical	80	100	15	Normal	○
HM06	Rock Smash	Fighting	Physical	40	100	15	Normal	○

● LEVEL-UP MOVES

Lv.	Name	Type	Kind	Pow.	Acc.	PP	Range	DA
1	AncientPower	Rock	Special	60	100	5	Normal	—
1	Peck	Flying	Physical	35	100	35	Normal	○
1	Odor Sleuth	Normal	Status	—	—	40	Normal	—
1	Mud Sport	Ground	Status	—	—	15	All	—
1	Powder Snow	Ice	Special	40	100	25	2 Foes	—
4	Mud Sport	Ground	Status	—	—	15	All	—
8	Powder Snow	Ice	Special	40	100	25	2 Foes	—
13	Mud-Slap	Ground	Special	20	100	10	Normal	—
16	Endure	Normal	Status	—	—	10	Self	—
20	Mud Bomb	Ground	Special	65	85	10	Normal	—
25	Hail	Ice	Status	—	—	10	All	—
28	Ice Fang	Ice	Physical	65	95	15	Normal	○
32	Take Down	Normal	Physical	90	85	20	Normal	○
33	Double Hit	Normal	Physical	35	90	10	Normal	○
40	Earthquake	Ground	Physical	100	100	10	2 Foes/1 Ally	—
48	Mist	Ice	Status	—	—	30	2 Allies	—
56	Blizzard	Ice	Special	120	70	5	2 Foes	—
65	Scary Face	Normal	Status	—	90	10	Normal	—

● MOVE MANIAC

Name	Type	Kind	Pow.	Acc.	PP	Range	DA
Headbutt	Normal	Physical	70	100	15	Normal	○

● BP MOVES

Name	Type	Kind	Pow.	Acc.	PP	Range	DA
Fury Cutter	Bug	Physical	10	95	20	Normal	○
Icy Wind	Ice	Special	55	95	15	2 Foes	—
Knock Off	Dark	Physical	20	100	20	Normal	○
Snore	Normal	Special	40	100	15	Normal	—
Block	Normal	Status	—	—	5	Normal	—
Mud-Slap	Ground	Special	20	100	10	Normal	—
Superpower	Fighting	Physical	120	100	5	Normal	○
Iron Head	Steel	Physical	80	100	15	Normal	○
Endeavor	Normal	Physical	—	100	5	Normal	○
AncientPower	Rock	Special	60	100	5	Normal	—
Earth Power	Ground	Special	90	100	10	Normal	—

● TM & HM MOVES

No.	Name	Type	Kind	Pow.	Acc.	PP	Range	DA
TM05	Roar	Normal	Status	—	100	20	Normal	—
TM06	Toxic	Poison	Status	—	85	10	Normal	—
TM07	Hail	Ice	Status	—	—	10	All	—
TM10	Hidden Power	Normal	Special	—	100	15	Normal	—
TM13	Ice Beam	Ice	Special	95	100	10	Normal	—
TM14	Blizzard	Ice	Special	120	70	5	2 Foes	—
TM15	Hyper Beam	Normal	Special	150	90	5	Normal	—
TM16	Light Screen	Psychic	Status	—	—	30	2 Allies	—
TM17	Protect	Normal	Status	—	—	10	Self	—
TM18	Rain Dance	Water	Status	—	—	5	All	—
TM21	Frustration	Normal	Physical	—	100	20	Normal	○
TM26	Earthquake	Ground	Physical	100	100	10	2 Foes/1 Ally	—
TM27	Return	Normal	Physical	—	100	20	Normal	○
TM28	Dig	Ground	Physical	80	100	10	Normal	○
TM32	Double Team	Normal	Status	—	—	15	Self	—
TM33	Reflect	Psychic	Status	—	—	20	2 Allies	—
TM37	Sandstorm	Rock	Status	—	—	10	All	—
TM39	Rock Tomb	Rock	Physical	50	80	10	Normal	○
TM42	Facade	Normal	Physical	70	100	20	Normal	○
TM43	Secret Power	Normal	Physical	70	100	20	Normal	○
TM44	Rest	Psychic	Status	—	—	10	Self	—
TM45	Attract	Normal	Status	—	100	15	Normal	—
TM58	Endure	Normal	Status	—	—	10	Self	—
TM68	Giga Impact	Normal	Physical	150	90	5	Normal	○
TM71	Stone Edge	Rock	Physical	100	80	5	Normal	○
TM72	Avalanche	Ice	Physical	60	100	10	Normal	○
TM76	Stealth Rock	Rock	Status	—	—	20	2 Foes	—
TM78	Captivate	Normal	Status	—	100	20	2 Foes	—
TM80	Rock Slide	Rock	Physical	75	90	10	2 Foes	—
TM82	Sleep Talk	Normal	Status	—	—	10	Depends	—
TM83	Natural Gift	Normal	Physical	—	100	15	Normal	○
TM87	Swagger	Normal	Status	—	90	15	Normal	—
TM90	Substitute	Normal	Status	—	—	10	Self	—
HM04	Strength	Normal	Physical	80	100	15	Normal	○
HM06	Rock Smash	Fighting	Physical	40	100	15	Normal	○
HM08	Rock Climb	Normal	Physical	90	85	20	Normal	○

⊙ No. 473 | Twin Tusk Pokémon
Mamoswine

Ice   Ground

● **HEIGHT:** 8'02"
● **WEIGHT:** 641.5 lbs.
● **ITEMS:** None

● **SIZE COMPARISON**

● **MALE FORM**
Longer tusks

● **FEMALE FORM**
Shorter tusks

⊙ ABILITIES
● Oblivious
● Snow Cloak

⊙ STATS
HP ●●●●
ATTACK ●●●●
DEFENSE ●●●●
SP. ATTACK ●●●
SP. DEFENSE ●●●
SPEED ●●●●

⊙ EGG GROUPS
Field

⊙ PERFORMANCE
SPEED ★★★☆   STAMINA ★★★★☆
POWER ★★★★☆   JUMP ★★
SKILL ★★☆

● MAIN WAYS TO OBTAIN

Pokémon HeartGold	Teach Piloswine Ancient-Power and level it up*
Pokémon SoulSilver	Teach Piloswine Ancient-Power and level it up*
Pokémon Diamond	Teach Piloswine Ancient-Power and level it up*
Pokémon Pearl	Teach Piloswine Ancient-Power and level it up*
Pokémon Platinum	Teach Piloswine Ancient-Power and level it up*

Pokémon HeartGold
A frozen MAMOSWINE was dug from ice dating back 10,000 years. This Pokémon has been around a long, long, long time.

Pokémon SoulSilver
It flourished worldwide during the ice age but its population declined when the masses of ice began to dwindle.

⊙ EVOLUTION

Lv. 33 → Teach it AncientPower and level it up*

Swinub → Piloswine → Mamoswine

*To teach Piloswine AncientPower, give a Heart Scale to the Move Maniac in Blackthorn City. Or, exchange 40 BP at a house in the Battle Frontier.

Porygon-Z

Normal

- **HEIGHT:** 2'11"
- **WEIGHT:** 75.0 lbs.
- **ITEMS:** None

● SIZE COMPARISON

● GENDER UNKNOWN

◉ ABILITIES
- Adaptability
- Download

◉ STATS
HP	●●●
ATTACK	●●●
DEFENSE	●●●
SP. ATTACK	●●●●●●
SP. DEFENSE	●●●
SPEED	●●●●

◉ EGG GROUPS
Mineral

◉ PERFORMANCE
SPEED ★★★★
POWER ★★★★☆
SKILL ★★☆☆☆
STAMINA ★
JUMP ★★★★

● MAIN WAYS TO OBTAIN

Pokémon HeartGold — Link trade Porygon2 while it holds the Dubious Disc

Pokémon SoulSilver — Link trade Porygon2 while it holds the Dubious Disc

Pokémon Diamond — Link trade Porygon2 while it holds the Dubious Disc

Pokémon Pearl — Link trade Porygon2 while it holds the Dubious Disc

Pokémon Platinum — Link trade Porygon2 while it holds the Dubious Disc

Pokémon HeartGold — Its programming was modified to enable it to travel through alien dimensions. Seems there might have been an error...

Pokémon SoulSilver — Its programming was modified to enable it to travel through alien dimensions. Seems there might have been an error...

◉ EVOLUTION

Porygon → (Have it hold Up-Grade and trade it) → Porygon2 → (Have it hold Dubious Disc and trade it) → Porygon-Z

● LEVEL-UP MOVES
Lv.	Name	Type	Kind	Pow.	Acc.	PP	Range	DA
1	Trick Room	Psychic	Status	—	—	5	All	—
1	Conversion 2	Normal	Status	—	—	30	Self	—
1	Tackle	Normal	Physical	35	95	35	Normal	○
1	Conversion	Normal	Status	—	—	30	Self	—
1	Nasty Plot	Dark	Status	—	—	20	Self	—
7	Psybeam	Psychic	Special	65	100	20	Normal	—
12	Agility	Psychic	Status	—	—	30	Self	—
18	Recover	Normal	Status	—	—	10	Self	—
23	Magnet Rise	Electric	Status	—	—	10	Self	—
29	Signal Beam	Bug	Special	75	100	15	Normal	—
34	Embargo	Dark	Status	—	100	15	Normal	—
40	Discharge	Electric	Special	80	100	15	2 Foes/1 Ally	—
45	Lock-On	Normal	Status	—	—	5	Normal	—
51	Tri Attack	Normal	Special	80	100	10	Normal	—
56	Magic Coat	Psychic	Status	—	—	15	Self	—
62	Zap Cannon	Electric	Special	120	50	5	Normal	—
67	Hyper Beam	Normal	Special	150	90	5	Normal	—

● MOVE MANIAC
Name	Type	Kind	Pow.	Acc.	PP	Range	DA

● BP MOVES
Name	Type	Kind	Pow.	Acc.	PP	Range	DA
Icy Wind	Ice	Special	55	95	15	2 Foes	—
Zen Headbutt	Psychic	Physical	80	90	15	Normal	○
Trick	Psychic	Status	—	100	10	Normal	—
Snore	Normal	Special	40	100	15	Normal	—
Last Resort	Normal	Physical	130	100	5	Normal	○
Swift	Normal	Special	60	—	20	2 Foes	—
Uproar	Normal	Special	50	100	10	1 Random	—
Gravity	Psychic	Status	—	—	5	All	—
Magic Coat	Psychic	Status	—	—	15	Self	—
Signal Beam	Bug	Special	75	100	15	Normal	—
Pain Split	Normal	Status	—	—	20	Normal	—

● TM & HM MOVES
No.	Name	Type	Kind	Pow.	Acc.	PP	Range	DA
TM06	Toxic	Poison	Status	—	85	10	Normal	—
TM10	Hidden Power	Normal	Special	—	100	15	Normal	—
TM11	Sunny Day	Fire	Status	—	—	5	All	—
TM13	Ice Beam	Ice	Special	95	100	10	Normal	—
TM14	Blizzard	Ice	Special	120	70	5	2 Foes	—
TM15	Hyper Beam	Normal	Special	150	90	5	Normal	—
TM17	Protect	Normal	Status	—	—	10	Self	—
TM18	Rain Dance	Water	Status	—	—	5	All	—
TM21	Frustration	Normal	Physical	—	100	20	Normal	○
TM22	SolarBeam	Grass	Special	120	100	10	Normal	—
TM23	Iron Tail	Steel	Physical	100	75	15	Normal	○
TM24	Thunderbolt	Electric	Special	95	100	15	Normal	—
TM25	Thunder	Electric	Special	120	70	10	Normal	—
TM27	Return	Normal	Physical	—	100	20	Normal	○
TM29	Psychic	Psychic	Special	90	100	10	Normal	—
TM30	Shadow Ball	Ghost	Special	80	100	15	Normal	—
TM32	Double Team	Normal	Status	—	—	15	Self	—
TM34	Shock Wave	Electric	Special	60	—	20	Normal	—
TM40	Aerial Ace	Flying	Physical	60	—	20	Normal	○
TM42	Facade	Normal	Physical	70	100	20	Normal	○
TM43	Secret Power	Normal	Physical	70	100	20	Normal	○
TM44	Rest	Psychic	Status	—	—	10	Self	—
TM46	Thief	Dark	Physical	40	100	10	Normal	○
TM57	Charge Beam	Electric	Special	50	90	10	Normal	—
TM58	Endure	Normal	Status	—	—	10	Self	—
TM63	Embargo	Dark	Status	—	100	15	Normal	—
TM67	Recycle	Normal	Status	—	—	10	Self	—
TM68	Giga Impact	Normal	Physical	150	90	5	Normal	○
TM70	Flash	Normal	Status	—	100	20	Normal	—
TM73	Thunder Wave	Electric	Status	—	100	20	Normal	—
TM77	Psych Up	Normal	Status	—	—	10	Normal	—
TM79	Dark Pulse	Dark	Special	80	100	15	Normal	—
TM82	Sleep Talk	Normal	Status	—	—	10	Depends	—
TM83	Natural Gift	Normal	Physical	—	100	15	Normal	—
TM85	Dream Eater	Psychic	Special	100	100	15	Normal	—
TM87	Swagger	Normal	Status	—	90	15	Normal	—
TM90	Substitute	Normal	Status	—	—	10	Self	—
TM92	Trick Room	Psychic	Status	—	—	5	All	—

● LEVEL-UP MOVES

Lv.	Name	Type	Kind	Pow.	Acc.	PP	Range	DA
1	Leaf Blade	Grass	Physical	90	100	15	Normal	○
1	Night Slash	Dark	Physical	70	100	15	Normal	○
1	Leer	Normal	Status	—	100	30	2 Foes	—
1	Confusion	Psychic	Special	50	100	25	Normal	—
1	Double Team	Normal	Status	—	—	15	Self	—
1	Teleport	Psychic	Status	—	—	20	Self	—
6	Confusion	Psychic	Special	50	100	25	Normal	—
10	Double Team	Normal	Status	—	—	15	Self	—
12	Teleport	Psychic	Status	—	—	20	Self	—
17	Fury Cutter	Bug	Physical	10	95	20	Normal	○
22	Slash	Normal	Physical	70	100	20	Normal	○
25	Swords Dance	Normal	Status	—	—	30	Self	—
31	Psycho Cut	Psychic	Physical	70	100	20	Normal	—
36	Helping Hand	Normal	Status	—	—	20	1 Ally	—
39	Feint	Normal	Physical	50	100	10	Normal	—
45	False Swipe	Normal	Physical	40	100	40	Normal	○
50	Protect	Normal	Status	—	—	10	Self	—
53	Close Combat	Fighting	Physical	120	100	5	Normal	○

● MOVE MANIAC

Name	Type	Kind	Pow.	Acc.	PP	Range	DA
Headbutt	Normal	Physical	70	100	15	Normal	○

● BP MOVES

Name	Type	Kind	Pow.	Acc.	PP	Range	DA
Fury Cutter	Bug	Physical	10	95	20	Normal	○
ThunderPunch	Electric	Physical	75	100	15	Normal	○
Fire Punch	Fire	Physical	75	100	15	Normal	○
Ice Punch	Ice	Physical	75	100	15	Normal	○
Zen Headbutt	Psychic	Physical	80	90	15	Normal	○
Vacuum Wave	Fighting	Special	40	100	30	Normal	—
Trick	Psychic	Status	—	100	10	Normal	—
Knock Off	Dark	Physical	20	100	20	Normal	○
Snore	Normal	Special	40	100	15	Normal	—
Helping Hand	Normal	Status	—	—	20	1 Ally	—
Swift	Normal	Special	60	—	20	2 Foes	—
Magic Coat	Psychic	Status	—	—	15	Self	—
Mud-Slap	Ground	Special	20	100	10	Normal	—
Signal Beam	Bug	Special	75	100	15	Normal	—
Pain Split	Normal	Status	—	—	20	Normal	—
Low Kick	Fighting	Physical	—	100	20	Normal	—

● TM & HM MOVES

No.	Name	Type	Kind	Pow.	Acc.	PP	Range	DA
TM01	Focus Punch	Fighting	Physical	150	100	20	Normal	○
TM04	Calm Mind	Psychic	Status	—	—	20	Self	—
TM06	Toxic	Poison	Status	—	85	10	Normal	—
TM08	Bulk Up	Fighting	Status	—	—	20	Self	—
TM10	Hidden Power	Normal	Special	—	100	15	Normal	—
TM11	Sunny Day	Fire	Status	—	—	5	All	—
TM12	Taunt	Dark	Status	—	100	20	Normal	—
TM15	Hyper Beam	Normal	Special	150	90	5	Normal	—
TM16	Light Screen	Psychic	Status	—	—	30	2 Allies	—
TM17	Protect	Normal	Status	—	—	10	Self	—
TM18	Rain Dance	Water	Status	—	—	5	All	—
TM20	Safeguard	Normal	Status	—	—	25	2 Allies	—
TM21	Frustration	Normal	Physical	—	100	20	Normal	○
TM24	Thunderbolt	Electric	Special	95	100	15	Normal	—
TM26	Earthquake	Ground	Physical	100	100	10	2 Foes/1 Ally	—
TM27	Return	Normal	Physical	—	100	20	Normal	○
TM29	Psychic	Psychic	Special	90	100	10	Normal	—
TM30	Shadow Ball	Ghost	Special	80	100	15	Normal	—
TM31	Brick Break	Fighting	Physical	75	100	15	Normal	○
TM32	Double Team	Normal	Status	—	—	15	Self	—
TM33	Reflect	Psychic	Status	—	—	20	2 Allies	—
TM34	Shock Wave	Electric	Special	60	—	20	Normal	—
TM39	Rock Tomb	Rock	Physical	50	80	10	Normal	—
TM40	Aerial Ace	Flying	Physical	60	—	20	Normal	○
TM41	Torment	Dark	Status	—	100	15	Normal	—
TM42	Facade	Normal	Physical	70	100	20	Normal	○
TM43	Secret Power	Normal	Physical	70	100	20	Normal	—
TM44	Rest	Psychic	Status	—	—	10	Self	—
TM45	Attract	Normal	Status	—	100	15	Normal	—
TM46	Thief	Dark	Physical	40	100	10	Normal	○
TM48	Skill Swap	Psychic	Status	—	—	10	Normal	—
TM49	Snatch	Dark	Status	—	—	10	Depends	—
TM52	Focus Blast	Fighting	Special	120	70	5	Normal	—
TM54	False Swipe	Normal	Physical	40	100	40	Normal	○
TM56	Fling	Dark	Physical	—	100	10	Normal	○
TM57	Charge Beam	Electric	Special	50	90	10	Normal	—
TM58	Endure	Normal	Status	—	—	10	Self	—
TM60	Drain Punch	Fighting	Physical	60	100	5	Normal	○
TM67	Recycle	Normal	Status	—	—	10	Self	—
TM68	Giga Impact	Normal	Physical	150	90	5	Normal	—
TM71	Stone Edge	Rock	Physical	100	80	5	Normal	—
TM73	Thunder Wave	Electric	Status	—	100	20	Normal	—
TM75	Swords Dance	Normal	Status	—	—	30	Self	—
TM77	Psych Up	Normal	Status	—	—	10	Normal	—
TM78	Captivate	Normal	Status	—	100	20	2 Foes	—
TM80	Rock Slide	Rock	Physical	75	90	10	2 Foes	—
TM81	X-Scissor	Bug	Physical	80	100	15	Normal	○
TM82	Sleep Talk	Normal	Status	—	—	10	Depends	—
TM83	Natural Gift	Normal	Physical	—	100	15	Normal	○
TM84	Poison Jab	Poison	Physical	80	100	20	Normal	○
TM85	Dream Eater	Psychic	Special	100	100	15	Normal	—
TM86	Grass Knot	Grass	Special	—	100	20	Normal	—
TM87	Swagger	Normal	Status	—	90	15	Normal	—
TM90	Substitute	Normal	Status	—	—	10	Self	—
TM92	Trick Room	Psychic	Status	—	—	5	All	—
HM01	Cut	Normal	Physical	50	95	30	Normal	○
HM04	Strength	Normal	Physical	80	100	15	Normal	○
HM06	Rock Smash	Fighting	Physical	40	100	15	Normal	○

◎ No. 475 | Blade Pokémon

Gallade

Psychic Fighting

- **HEIGHT:** 5'03"
- **WEIGHT:** 114.6 lbs.
- **ITEMS:** None

● SIZE COMPARISON

● MALE FORM

⊙ ABILITIES
● Steadfast

⊙ STATS
HP	●●●
ATTACK	●●●●●
DEFENSE	●●●●
SP. ATTACK	●●●●
SP. DEFENSE	●●●●●
SPEED	●●●●

⊙ EGG GROUPS
Amorphous

⊙ PERFORMANCE
SPEED ★★★☆ STAMINA ★★
POWER ★★★☆☆ JUMP ★★★☆
SKILL ★★★★★

● MAIN WAYS TO OBTAIN

Pokémon HeartGold	Use Dawn Stone on Kirlia ♂
Pokémon SoulSilver	Use Dawn Stone on Kirlia ♂
Pokémon Diamond	Use Dawn Stone on Kirlia ♂
Pokémon Pearl	Use Dawn Stone on Kirlia ♂
Pokémon Platinum	Use Dawn Stone on Kirlia ♂

Pokémon HeartGold	*Pokémon SoulSilver*
Because it can sense what its foe is thinking, its attacks burst out first, fast, and fierce.	Because it can sense what its foe is thinking, its attacks burst out first, fast, and fierce.

⊙ EVOLUTION

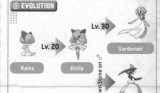

Ralts — Lv. 20 → Kirlia — Lv. 30 → Gardevoir

Kirlia — Use Dawn Stone on ♂ → Gallade

No. 476 | Compass Pokémon
Probopass

Rock Steel

● HEIGHT: 4'07"
● WEIGHT: 749.6 lbs.
● ITEMS: None

● SIZE COMPARISON

● MALE/FEMALE HAVE SAME FORM

⊕ ABILITIES
● Sturdy
● Magnet Pull

⊕ STATS
HP ●●
ATTACK ●●●●
DEFENSE ●●●●●●
SP. ATTACK ●●●●
SP. DEFENSE ●●●●●●
SPEED ●●

⊕ EGG GROUPS
Mineral

⊕ PERFORMANCE
SPEED ★★☆☆☆   STAMINA ★★★★☆
POWER ★★★☆☆   JUMP ★★★☆☆
SKILL ★☆☆☆☆

● MAIN WAYS TO OBTAIN

Pokémon HeartGold	—
Pokémon SoulSilver	—
Pokémon Diamond	Level up Nosepass at Mt. Coronet
Pokémon Pearl	Level up Nosepass at Mt. Coronet
Pokémon Platinum	Level up Nosepass at Mt. Coronet

Pokémon HeartGold
It controls three units called Mini-Noses using magnetic force. With them, it can attack the foe from three directions.

Pokémon SoulSilver
It controls three units called Mini-Noses using magnetic force. With them, it can attack the foe from three directions.

⊕ EVOLUTION

Nosepass — Level up at Mt. Coronet* — Probopass

● LEVEL-UP MOVES

Lv.	Name	Type	Kind	Pow.	Acc.	PP	Range	DA
1	Magnet Rise	Electric	Status	—	—	10	Self	—
1	Gravity	Psychic	Status	—	—	5	All	—
1	Tackle	Normal	Physical	35	95	35	Normal	○
1	Iron Defense	Steel	Status	—	—	15	Self	—
1	Magnet Bomb	Steel	Physical	60	—	20	Normal	—
1	Block	Normal	Status	—	—	5	Normal	—
7	Iron Defense	Steel	Status	—	—	15	Self	—
13	Magnet Bomb	Steel	Physical	60	—	20	Normal	—
19	Block	Normal	Status	—	—	5	Normal	—
25	Thunder Wave	Electric	Status	—	100	20	Normal	—
31	Rock Slide	Rock	Physical	75	90	10	2 Foes	—
37	Sandstorm	Rock	Status	—	—	10	All	—
43	Rest	Psychic	Status	—	—	10	Self	—
49	Power Gem	Rock	Special	70	100	20	Normal	—
55	Discharge	Electric	Special	80	100	15	2 Foes/1 Ally	—
61	Stone Edge	Rock	Physical	100	80	5	Normal	—
67	Zap Cannon	Electric	Special	120	50	5	Normal	—
73	Lock-On	Normal	Status	—	—	5	Normal	—
79	Earth Power	Ground	Special	90	100	10	Normal	—

● MOVE MANIAC

Name	Type	Kind	Pow.	Acc.	PP	Range	DA
Headbutt	Normal	Physical	70	100	15	Normal	○

● BP MOVES

Name	Type	Kind	Pow.	Acc.	PP	Range	DA
ThunderPunch	Electric	Physical	75	100	15	Normal	○
Fire Punch	Fire	Physical	75	100	15	Normal	○
Ice Punch	Ice	Physical	75	100	15	Normal	○
Snore	Normal	Special	40	100	15	Normal	—
Magnet Rise	Electric	Status	—	—	10	Self	—
Gravity	Psychic	Status	—	—	5	All	—
Magic Coat	Psychic	Status	—	—	15	Self	—
Block	Normal	Status	—	—	5	Normal	—
Mud-Slap	Ground	Special	20	100	10	Normal	—
Rollout	Rock	Physical	30	90	20	Normal	○
Iron Head	Steel	Physical	80	100	15	Normal	○
AncientPower	Rock	Special	60	100	5	Normal	—
Earth Power	Ground	Special	90	100	10	Normal	—
Iron Defense	Steel	Status	—	—	15	Self	—
Pain Split	Normal	Status	—	—	20	Normal	—

● TM & HM MOVES

No.	Name	Type	Kind	Pow.	Acc.	PP	Range	DA
TM06	Toxic	Poison	Status	—	85	10	Normal	—
TM10	Hidden Power	Normal	Special	—	100	15	Normal	—
TM11	Sunny Day	Fire	Status	—	—	5	All	—
TM12	Taunt	Dark	Status	—	100	20	Normal	—
TM15	Hyper Beam	Normal	Special	150	90	5	Normal	—
TM17	Protect	Normal	Status	—	—	10	Self	—
TM21	Frustration	Normal	Physical	—	100	20	Normal	○
TM24	Thunderbolt	Electric	Special	95	100	15	Normal	—
TM25	Thunder	Electric	Special	120	70	10	Normal	—
TM26	Earthquake	Ground	Physical	100	100	10	2 Foes/1 Ally	—
TM27	Return	Normal	Physical	—	100	20	Normal	○
TM32	Double Team	Normal	Status	—	—	15	Self	—
TM34	Shock Wave	Electric	Special	60	—	20	Normal	—
TM37	Sandstorm	Rock	Status	—	—	10	All	—
TM39	Rock Tomb	Rock	Physical	50	80	10	Normal	—
TM41	Torment	Dark	Status	—	100	15	Normal	—
TM42	Facade	Normal	Physical	70	100	20	Normal	○
TM43	Secret Power	Normal	Physical	70	100	20	Normal	—
TM44	Rest	Psychic	Status	—	—	10	Self	—
TM45	Attract	Normal	Status	—	100	15	Normal	—
TM58	Endure	Normal	Status	—	—	10	Self	—
TM64	Explosion	Normal	Physical	250	100	5	2 Foes/1 Ally	—
TM68	Giga Impact	Normal	Physical	150	90	5	Normal	○
TM69	Rock Polish	Rock	Status	—	—	20	Self	—
TM71	Stone Edge	Rock	Physical	100	80	5	Normal	—
TM73	Thunder Wave	Electric	Status	—	100	20	Normal	—
TM76	Stealth Rock	Rock	Status	—	—	20	2 Foes	—
TM78	Captivate	Normal	Status	—	100	20	2 Foes	—
TM80	Rock Slide	Rock	Physical	75	90	10	2 Foes	—
TM82	Sleep Talk	Normal	Status	—	—	10	Depends	—
TM83	Natural Gift	Normal	Physical	—	100	15	Normal	—
TM87	Swagger	Normal	Status	—	90	15	Normal	—
TM90	Substitute	Normal	Status	—	—	10	Self	—
TM91	Flash Cannon	Steel	Special	80	100	10	Normal	—
HM04	Strength	Normal	Physical	80	100	15	Normal	○
HM06	Rock Smash	Fighting	Physical	40	100	15	Normal	○

● LEVEL-UP MOVES

Lv.	Name	Type	Kind	Pow.	Acc.	PP	Range	DA
1	Fire Punch	Fire	Physical	75	100	15	Normal	○
1	Ice Punch	Ice	Physical	75	100	15	Normal	○
1	ThunderPunch	Electric	Physical	75	100	15	Normal	○
1	Gravity	Psychic	Status	—	—	5	All	—
1	Bind	Normal	Physical	15	75	20	Normal	○
1	Leer	Normal	Status	—	100	30	2 Foes	—
1	Night Shade	Ghost	Special	—	100	15	Normal	—
1	Disable	Normal	Status	—	80	20	Normal	—
6	Disable	Normal	Status	—	80	20	Normal	—
9	Foresight	Normal	Status	—	—	40	Normal	—
14	Astonish	Ghost	Physical	30	100	15	Normal	○
17	Confuse Ray	Ghost	Status	—	100	10	Normal	—
22	Shadow Sneak	Ghost	Physical	40	100	30	Normal	○
25	Pursuit	Dark	Physical	40	100	20	Normal	○
30	Curse	???	Status	—	—	10	Normal/Self	—
33	Will-O-Wisp	Fire	Status	—	75	15	Normal	—
37	Shadow Punch	Ghost	Physical	60	—	20	Normal	○
43	Mean Look	Normal	Status	—	—	5	Normal	—
51	Payback	Dark	Physical	50	100	10	Normal	○
61	Future Sight	Psychic	Special	80	90	10	Normal	—

● MOVE MANIAC

Name	Type	Kind	Pow.	Acc.	PP	Range	DA
Headbutt	Normal	Physical	70	100	15	Normal	○

● BP MOVES

Name	Type	Kind	Pow.	Acc.	PP	Range	DA
Icy Wind	Ice	Special	55	95	15	2 Foes	—
ThunderPunch	Electric	Physical	75	100	15	Normal	○
Fire Punch	Fire	Physical	75	100	15	Normal	○
Ice Punch	Ice	Physical	75	100	15	Normal	○
Ominous Wind	Ghost	Special	60	100	5	Normal	—
Trick	Psychic	Status	—	100	10	Normal	—
Sucker Punch	Dark	Physical	80	100	5	Normal	○
Snore	Normal	Special	40	100	15	Normal	—
Spite	Ghost	Status	—	100	10	Normal	—
Gravity	Psychic	Status	—	—	5	All	—
Mud-Slap	Ground	Special	20	100	10	Normal	—
Pain Split	Normal	Status	—	—	20	Normal	—

● TM & HM MOVES

No.	Name	Type	Kind	Pow.	Acc.	PP	Range	DA
TM01	Focus Punch	Fighting	Physical	150	100	20	Normal	○
TM04	Calm Mind	Psychic	Status	—	—	20	Self	—
TM06	Toxic	Poison	Status	—	85	10	Normal	—
TM10	Hidden Power	Normal	Special	—	100	15	Normal	—
TM11	Sunny Day	Fire	Status	—	—	5	All	—
TM12	Taunt	Dark	Status	—	100	20	Normal	—
TM13	Ice Beam	Ice	Special	95	100	10	Normal	—
TM14	Blizzard	Ice	Special	120	70	5	2 Foes	—
TM15	Hyper Beam	Normal	Special	150	90	5	Normal	—
TM17	Protect	Normal	Status	—	—	10	Self	—
TM18	Rain Dance	Water	Status	—	—	5	All	—
TM21	Frustration	Normal	Physical	—	100	20	Normal	○
TM26	Earthquake	Ground	Physical	100	100	10	2 Foes/1 Ally	○
TM27	Return	Normal	Physical	—	100	20	Normal	○
TM29	Psychic	Psychic	Special	90	100	10	Normal	—
TM30	Shadow Ball	Ghost	Special	80	100	15	Normal	—
TM31	Brick Break	Fighting	Physical	75	100	15	Normal	○
TM32	Double Team	Normal	Status	—	—	15	Self	—
TM39	Rock Tomb	Rock	Physical	50	80	10	Normal	○
TM41	Torment	Dark	Status	—	100	15	Normal	—
TM42	Facade	Normal	Physical	70	100	20	Normal	○
TM43	Secret Power	Normal	Physical	70	100	20	Normal	○
TM44	Rest	Psychic	Status	—	—	10	Self	—
TM45	Attract	Normal	Status	—	100	15	Normal	—
TM46	Thief	Dark	Physical	40	100	10	Normal	○
TM48	Skill Swap	Psychic	Status	—	—	10	Normal	—
TM49	Snatch	Dark	Status	—	—	10	Depends	—
TM52	Focus Blast	Fighting	Special	120	70	5	Normal	—
TM56	Fling	Dark	Physical	—	100	10	Normal	○
TM57	Charge Beam	Electric	Special	50	90	10	Normal	—
TM58	Endure	Normal	Status	—	—	10	Self	—
TM61	Will-O-Wisp	Fire	Status	—	75	15	Normal	—
TM63	Embargo	Dark	Status	—	100	15	Normal	—
TM66	Payback	Dark	Physical	50	100	10	Normal	○
TM68	Giga Impact	Normal	Physical	150	90	5	Normal	○
TM70	Flash	Normal	Status	—	100	20	Normal	—
TM77	Psych Up	Normal	Status	—	—	10	Normal	—
TM78	Captivate	Normal	Status	—	100	20	2 Foes	—
TM79	Dark Pulse	Dark	Special	80	100	15	Normal	—
TM80	Rock Slide	Rock	Physical	75	90	10	2 Foes	○
TM82	Sleep Talk	Normal	Status	—	—	10	Depends	—
TM83	Natural Gift	Normal	Physical	—	100	15	Normal	—
TM85	Dream Eater	Psychic	Special	100	100	15	Normal	—
TM87	Swagger	Normal	Status	—	90	15	Normal	—
TM90	Substitute	Normal	Status	—	—	10	Self	—
TM92	Trick Room	Psychic	Status	—	—	5	All	—
HM04	Strength	Normal	Physical	80	100	15	Normal	○
HM06	Rock Smash	Fighting	Physical	40	100	15	Normal	○

No. 477 | Gripper Pokémon
Dusknoir

Ghost

- ● HEIGHT: 7'03"
- ● WEIGHT: 235.0 lbs.
- ● ITEMS: None

● SIZE COMPARISON

● MALE/FEMALE HAVE SAME FORM

● ABILITIES
● Pressure

● STATS
HP ●●
ATTACK ●●●●
DEFENSE ●●●●●
SP. ATTACK ●●●●
SP. DEFENSE ●●●●●●
SPEED ●●

● EGG GROUPS
Amorphous

● PERFORMANCE

SPEED ★☆☆☆☆	STAMINA ★★★★
POWER ★★★★	JUMP ★★★★
SKILL ★★★☆	

● MAIN WAYS TO OBTAIN

Pokémon HeartGold	Link trade Dusclops while it holds the Reaper Cloth
Pokémon SoulSilver	Link trade Dusclops while it holds the Reaper Cloth
Pokémon Diamond	Link trade Dusclops while it holds the Reaper Cloth
Pokémon Pearl	Link trade Dusclops while it holds the Reaper Cloth
Pokémon Platinum	Link trade Dusclops while it holds the Reaper Cloth

Pokémon HeartGold
This feared Pokémon is said to travel to worlds unknown. Some even believe that it takes lost spirits along with it.

Pokémon SoulSilver
This feared Pokémon is said to travel to worlds unknown. Some even believe that it takes lost spirits along with it.

● EVOLUTION

Duskull → (Lv. 37) → Dusclops → Dusknoir

Have it hold Reaper Cloth and trade it

⊙ No. 478 | Snow Land Pokémon
Froslass

`Ice` `Ghost`

- **HEIGHT:** 4'03"
- **WEIGHT:** 58.6 lbs.
- **ITEMS:** None

● **SIZE COMPARISON**

● **FEMALE FORM**

⊙ ABILITIES
- Snow Cloak

⊙ STATS
HP	●●●
ATTACK	●●●
DEFENSE	●●●
SP. ATTACK	●●●●
SP. DEFENSE	●●●●
SPEED	●●●●●

⊙ EGG GROUPS
- Fairy
- Mineral

⊙ PERFORMANCE
SPEED ★★★☆	STAMINA ★★☆
POWER ★☆☆	JUMP ★★★☆☆
SKILL ★★★★☆	

● **MAIN WAYS TO OBTAIN**

Pokémon HeartGold	Use Dawn Stone on Snorunt ♀
Pokémon SoulSilver	Use Dawn Stone on Snorunt ♀
Pokémon Diamond	Use Dawn Stone on Snorunt ♀
Pokémon Pearl	Use Dawn Stone on Snorunt ♀
Pokémon Platinum	Use Dawn Stone on Snorunt ♀

Pokémon HeartGold	**Pokémon SoulSilver**
Legends in snowy regions say that a woman who was lost on an icy mountain was reborn as FROSLASS.	Legends in snowy regions say that a woman who was lost on an icy mountain was reborn as FROSLASS.

⊙ EVOLUTION

Snorunt — Lv. 42 → Glalie

Snorunt — Use Dawn Stone on ♀ → Froslass

● **LEVEL-UP MOVES**

Lv.	Name	Type	Kind	Pow.	Acc.	PP	Range	DA
1	Powder Snow	Ice	Special	40	100	25	2 Foes	—
1	Leer	Normal	Status	—	100	30	2 Foes	—
1	Double Team	Normal	Status	—	—	15	Self	—
1	Astonish	Ghost	Physical	30	100	15	Normal	○
4	Double Team	Normal	Status	—	—	15	Self	—
10	Astonish	Ghost	Physical	30	100	15	Normal	○
13	Icy Wind	Ice	Special	55	95	15	2 Foes	—
19	Confuse Ray	Ghost	Status	—	100	10	Normal	—
22	Ominous Wind	Ghost	Special	60	100	5	Normal	—
28	Wake-Up Slap	Fighting	Physical	60	100	10	Normal	○
31	Captivate	Normal	Status	—	100	20	2 Foes	—
37	Ice Shard	Ice	Physical	40	100	30	Normal	—
40	Hail	Ice	Status	—	—	10	All	—
51	Blizzard	Ice	Special	120	70	5	2 Foes	—
59	Destiny Bond	Ghost	Status	—	—	5	Self	—

● **MOVE MANIAC**

Name	Type	Kind	Pow.	Acc.	PP	Range	DA
Headbutt	Normal	Physical	70	100	15	Normal	○

● **BP MOVES**

Name	Type	Kind	Pow.	Acc.	PP	Range	DA
Icy Wind	Ice	Special	55	95	15	2 Foes	—
Ice Punch	Ice	Physical	75	100	15	Normal	○
Ominous Wind	Ghost	Special	60	100	5	Normal	—
Trick	Psychic	Status	—	100	10	Normal	—
Sucker Punch	Dark	Physical	80	100	5	Normal	○
Snore	Normal	Special	40	100	15	Normal	—
Spite	Ghost	Status	—	100	10	Normal	—
Block	Normal	Status	—	—	5	Normal	—
Rollout	Rock	Physical	30	90	20	Normal	○
Mud-Slap	Ground	Special	20	100	10	Normal	○
Signal Beam	Bug	Special	75	100	15	Normal	—
Pain Split	Normal	Status	—	—	20	Normal	—

● **TM & HM MOVES**

No.	Name	Type	Kind	Pow.	Acc.	PP	Range	DA
TM03	Water Pulse	Water	Special	60	100	20	Normal	—
TM06	Toxic	Poison	Status	—	85	10	Normal	—
TM07	Hail	Ice	Status	—	—	10	All	—
TM10	Hidden Power	Normal	Special	—	100	15	Normal	—
TM12	Taunt	Dark	Status	—	100	20	Normal	—
TM13	Ice Beam	Ice	Special	95	100	10	Normal	—
TM14	Blizzard	Ice	Special	120	70	5	2 Foes	—
TM15	Hyper Beam	Normal	Special	150	90	5	Normal	—
TM16	Light Screen	Psychic	Status	—	—	30	2 Allies	—
TM17	Protect	Normal	Status	—	—	10	Self	—
TM18	Rain Dance	Water	Status	—	—	5	All	—
TM20	Safeguard	Normal	Status	—	—	25	2 Allies	—
TM21	Frustration	Normal	Physical	—	100	20	Normal	○
TM24	Thunderbolt	Electric	Special	95	100	15	Normal	—
TM25	Thunder	Electric	Special	120	70	10	Normal	—
TM27	Return	Normal	Physical	—	100	20	Normal	○
TM29	Psychic	Psychic	Special	90	100	10	Normal	—
TM30	Shadow Ball	Ghost	Special	80	100	15	Normal	—
TM32	Double Team	Normal	Status	—	—	15	Self	—
TM34	Shock Wave	Electric	Special	60	—	20	Normal	—
TM41	Torment	Dark	Status	—	100	15	Normal	—
TM42	Facade	Normal	Physical	70	100	20	Normal	○
TM43	Secret Power	Normal	Physical	70	100	20	Normal	○
TM44	Rest	Psychic	Status	—	—	10	Self	—
TM45	Attract	Normal	Status	—	100	15	Normal	—
TM49	Snatch	Dark	Status	—	—	10	Depends	—
TM56	Fling	Dark	Physical	—	100	10	Normal	—
TM58	Endure	Normal	Status	—	—	10	Self	—
TM63	Embargo	Dark	Status	—	100	15	Normal	—
TM66	Payback	Dark	Physical	50	100	10	Normal	○
TM68	Giga Impact	Normal	Physical	150	90	5	Normal	○
TM70	Flash	Normal	Status	—	100	20	Normal	—
TM72	Avalanche	Ice	Physical	60	100	10	Normal	—
TM73	Thunder Wave	Electric	Status	—	100	20	Normal	—
TM77	Psych Up	Normal	Status	—	—	10	Normal	—
TM78	Captivate	Normal	Status	—	100	20	2 Foes	—
TM82	Sleep Talk	Normal	Status	—	—	10	Depends	—
TM83	Natural Gift	Normal	Physical	—	100	15	Normal	—
TM85	Dream Eater	Psychic	Special	100	100	15	Normal	—
TM87	Swagger	Normal	Status	—	90	15	Normal	—
TM90	Substitute	Normal	Status	—	—	10	Self	—

● LEVEL-UP MOVES

Lv.	Name	Type	Kind	Pow.	Acc.	PP	Range	DA
1	Trick	Psychic	Status	—	100	10	Normal	—
1	Astonish	Ghost	Physical	30	100	15	Normal	○
1	Thunder Wave	Electric	Status	—	100	20	Normal	—
1	ThunderShock	Electric	Special	40	100	30	Normal	—
1	Confuse Ray	Ghost	Status	—	100	10	Normal	—
8	Uproar	Normal	Special	50	100	10	1 Random	—
15	Double Team	Normal	Status	—	—	15	Self	—
22	Shock Wave	Electric	Special	60	—	20	Normal	—
29	Ominous Wind	Ghost	Special	60	100	5	Normal	—
36	Substitute	Normal	Status	—	—	10	Self	—
43	Charge	Electric	Status	—	—	20	Self	—
50	Discharge	Electric	Special	80	100	15	2 Foes/1 Ally	—

● MOVE MANIAC

Name	Type	Kind	Pow.	Acc.	PP	Range	DA

● BP MOVES

Name	Type	Kind	Pow.	Acc.	PP	Range	DA
Ominous Wind	Ghost	Special	60	100	5	Normal	—
Trick	Psychic	Status	—	100	10	Normal	—
Sucker Punch	Dark	Physical	80	100	5	Normal	○
Snore	Normal	Special	40	100	15	Normal	—
Spite	Ghost	Status	—	100	10	Normal	—
Swift	Normal	Special	60	—	20	2 Foes	—
Uproar	Normal	Special	50	100	10	1 Random	—
Mud-Slap	Ground	Special	20	100	10	Normal	—
Signal Beam	Bug	Special	75	100	15	Normal	—
Pain Split	Normal	Status	—	—	20	Normal	—

● TM & HM MOVES

No.	Name	Type	Kind	Pow.	Acc.	PP	Range	DA
TM06	Toxic	Poison	Status	—	85	10	Normal	—
TM10	Hidden Power	Normal	Special	—	100	15	Normal	—
TM11	Sunny Day	Fire	Status	—	—	5	All	—
TM16	Light Screen	Psychic	Status	—	—	30	2 Allies	—
TM17	Protect	Normal	Status	—	—	10	Self	—
TM18	Rain Dance	Water	Status	—	—	5	All	—
TM21	Frustration	Normal	Physical	—	100	20	Normal	○
TM24	Thunderbolt	Electric	Special	95	100	15	Normal	—
TM25	Thunder	Electric	Special	120	70	10	Normal	—
TM27	Return	Normal	Physical	—	100	20	Normal	○
TM30	Shadow Ball	Ghost	Special	80	100	15	Normal	—
TM32	Double Team	Normal	Status	—	—	15	Self	—
TM33	Reflect	Psychic	Status	—	—	20	2 Allies	—
TM34	Shock Wave	Electric	Special	60	—	20	Normal	—
TM42	Facade	Normal	Physical	70	100	20	Normal	○
TM43	Secret Power	Normal	Physical	70	100	20	Normal	—
TM44	Rest	Psychic	Status	—	—	10	Self	—
TM46	Thief	Dark	Physical	40	100	10	Normal	○
TM49	Snatch	Dark	Status	—	—	10	Depends	—
TM57	Charge Beam	Electric	Special	50	90	10	Normal	—
TM58	Endure	Normal	Status	—	—	10	Self	—
TM61	Will-O-Wisp	Fire	Status	—	75	15	Normal	—
TM70	Flash	Normal	Status	—	100	20	Normal	—
TM73	Thunder Wave	Electric	Status	—	100	20	Normal	—
TM77	Psych Up	Normal	Status	—	—	10	Normal	—
TM79	Dark Pulse	Dark	Special	80	100	15	Normal	—
TM82	Sleep Talk	Normal	Status	—	—	10	Depends	—
TM83	Natural Gift	Normal	Physical	—	100	15	Normal	—
TM85	Dream Eater	Psychic	Special	100	100	15	Normal	—
TM87	Swagger	Normal	Status	—	90	15	Normal	—
TM90	Substitute	Normal	Status	—	—	10	Self	—

*Rotom's Performance depends on its form:

Heat Rotom .... Speed ★★★★   Power ★★★★   Skill ★★★☆
              Stamina ★★★☆   Jump ★★★★

Wash Rotom .... Speed ★★★★   Power ★★★   Skill ★★★☆
              Stamina ★★★★   Jump ★★☆☆

Frost Rotom .... Speed ★★★☆   Power ★★☆   Skill ★★★★☆
              Stamina ★★★★   Jump ★★★☆

Fan Rotom .... Speed ★★★☆   Power ★★★☆   Skill ★★★
              Stamina ★★☆   Jump ★★★★★

Mow Rotom .... Speed ★★★   Power ★★★   Skill ★★★★★
              Stamina ★★★☆   Jump ★★☆☆

*Put Rotom in your party and take the elevator in Saffron City's Silph Co. It changes by checking out appliances. It learns one move when it transforms but will forget it after it returns to normal.

⬤ No. 479 | Plasma Pokémon
Rotom

Electric   **Ghost**

● SIZE COMPARISON

● HEIGHT: 1'00"
● WEIGHT: 0.7 lbs.
● ITEMS: None

Heat Rotom
Move ● Overheat

Wash Rotom
Move ● Hydro Pump

Frost Rotom
Move ● Blizzard

Fan Rotom
Move ● Air Slash

Mow Rotom
Move ● Leaf Storm

⬤ ABILITIES

● Levitate

⬤ STATS

HP ●●
ATTACK ●●
DEFENSE ●●●
SP. ATTACK ●●●
SP. DEFENSE ●●●
SPEED ●●●●

⬤ EGG GROUPS

Amorphous

⬤ PERFORMANCE

SPEED ★★★☆☆   STAMINA ★★★☆
POWER ★★☆   JUMP ★★★★☆
SKILL ★★★☆☆

● MAIN WAYS TO OBTAIN

Pokémon HeartGold	—
Pokémon SoulSilver	—
Pokémon Diamond	Check the TV in the Old Chateau between 8:00 P.M. and 4:00 A.M. (after obtaining the National Pokédex)
Pokémon Pearl	Check the TV in the Old Chateau between 8:00 P.M. and 4:00 A.M. (after obtaining the National Pokédex)
Pokémon Platinum	Check the TV in the Old Chateau between 8:00 P.M. and 4:00 A.M. (after obtaining the National Pokédex)

Pokémon HeartGold	Pokémon SoulSilver
Research continues on this Pokémon, which could be the power source of a unique motor.	Research continues on this Pokémon, which could be the power source of a unique motor.

⬤ EVOLUTION

Does not evolve

● No. 480 | Knowledge Pokémon
Uxie

Psychic

● HEIGHT: 1'00"
● WEIGHT: 0.7 lbs.
● ITEMS: None

● SIZE COMPARISON

● GENDER UNKNOWN

⊕ ABILITIES
● Levitate

⊕ STATS
HP	●●●
ATTACK	●●●
DEFENSE	●●●●●
SP. ATTACK	●●●
SP. DEFENSE	●●●●●
SPEED	●●●●

⊕ EGG GROUPS
No Egg has ever been discovered

⊕ PERFORMANCE
SPEED ★★★☆   STAMINA ★★★★☆
POWER ★★★☆   JUMP ★★★★☆
SKILL ★★★☆

● MAIN WAYS TO OBTAIN

Pokémon HeartGold —

Pokémon SoulSilver —

Pokémon Diamond | Lake Acuity (inside Acuity Cavern)

Pokémon Pearl | Lake Acuity (inside Acuity Cavern)

Pokémon Platinum | Lake Acuity (inside Acuity Cavern)

Pokémon HeartGold
According to some sources, this Pokémon provided people with the intelligence necessary to solve various problems.

Pokémon SoulSilver
According to some sources, this Pokémon provided people with the intelligence necessary to solve various problems.

⊕ EVOLUTION
Does not evolve

● LEVEL-UP MOVES
Lv.	Name	Type	Kind	Pow.	Acc.	PP	Range	DA
1	Rest	Psychic	Status	—	—	10	Self	—
1	Confusion	Psychic	Special	50	100	25	Normal	—
6	Imprison	Psychic	Status	—	—	10	Self	—
16	Endure	Normal	Status	—	—	10	Self	—
21	Swift	Normal	Special	60	—	20	2 Foes	—
31	Yawn	Normal	Status	—	—	10	Normal	—
36	Future Sight	Psychic	Special	80	100	15	Normal	—
41	Amnesia	Psychic	Status	—	—	20	Self	—
51	Extrasensory	Psychic	Special	80	100	30	Normal	—
61	Flail	Normal	Physical	—	100	15	Normal	○
66	Natural Gift	Normal	Physical	—	100	15	Normal	—
76	Memento	Dark	Status	—	100	10	Normal	—

● MOVE MANIAC
Name	Type	Kind	Pow.	Acc.	PP	Range	DA
Headbutt	Normal	Physical	70	100	15	Normal	—

● BP MOVES
Name	Type	Kind	Pow.	Acc.	PP	Range	DA
ThunderPunch	Electric	Physical	75	100	15	Normal	○
Fire Punch	Fire	Physical	75	100	15	Normal	○
Ice Punch	Ice	Physical	75	100	15	Normal	○
Zen Headbutt	Psychic	Physical	80	90	15	Normal	○
Trick	Psychic	Status	—	100	10	Normal	—
Knock Off	Dark	Physical	20	100	20	Normal	○
Snore	Normal	Special	40	100	15	Normal	—
Helping Hand	Normal	Status	—	—	20	1 Ally	—
Swift	Normal	Special	60	—	20	2 Foes	—
Magic Coat	Psychic	Status	—	—	15	Self	—
Role Play	Psychic	Status	—	—	10	Normal	—
Heal Bell	Normal	Status	—	—	5	All Allies	—
Mud-Slap	Ground	Special	20	100	10	Normal	—
Signal Beam	Bug	Special	75	100	15	Normal	—

● TM & HM MOVES
No.	Name	Type	Kind	Pow.	Acc.	PP	Range	DA
TM03	Water Pulse	Water	Special	60	100	20	Normal	—
TM04	Calm Mind	Psychic	Status	—	—	20	Self	—
TM06	Toxic	Poison	Status	—	85	10	Normal	—
TM10	Hidden Power	Normal	Special	—	100	15	Normal	—
TM11	Sunny Day	Fire	Status	—	—	5	All	—
TM15	Hyper Beam	Normal	Special	150	90	5	Normal	—
TM16	Light Screen	Psychic	Status	—	—	30	2 Allies	—
TM17	Protect	Normal	Status	—	—	10	Self	—
TM18	Rain Dance	Water	Status	—	—	5	All	—
TM19	Giga Drain	Grass	Special	60	100	10	Normal	—
TM20	Safeguard	Normal	Status	—	—	25	2 Allies	—
TM21	Frustration	Normal	Physical	—	100	20	Normal	○
TM22	SolarBeam	Grass	Special	120	100	10	Normal	—
TM23	Iron Tail	Steel	Physical	100	75	15	Normal	○
TM24	Thunderbolt	Electric	Special	95	100	15	Normal	—
TM25	Thunder	Electric	Special	120	70	10	Normal	—
TM27	Return	Normal	Physical	—	100	20	Normal	○
TM29	Psychic	Psychic	Special	90	100	10	Normal	—
TM30	Shadow Ball	Ghost	Special	80	100	15	Normal	—
TM32	Double Team	Normal	Status	—	—	15	Self	—
TM33	Reflect	Psychic	Status	—	—	20	2 Allies	—
TM34	Shock Wave	Electric	Special	60	—	20	Normal	—
TM37	Sandstorm	Rock	Status	—	—	10	All	—
TM42	Facade	Normal	Physical	70	100	20	Normal	○
TM43	Secret Power	Normal	Physical	70	100	20	Normal	○
TM44	Rest	Psychic	Status	—	—	10	Self	—
TM48	Skill Swap	Psychic	Status	—	—	10	Normal	—
TM53	Energy Ball	Grass	Special	80	100	10	Normal	—
TM56	Fling	Dark	Physical	—	100	10	Normal	—
TM57	Charge Beam	Electric	Special	50	90	10	Normal	—
TM58	Endure	Normal	Status	—	—	10	Self	—
TM67	Recycle	Normal	Status	—	—	10	Self	—
TM68	Giga Impact	Normal	Physical	150	90	5	Normal	○
TM70	Flash	Normal	Status	—	100	20	Normal	—
TM73	Thunder Wave	Electric	Status	—	100	20	Normal	—
TM76	Stealth Rock	Rock	Status	—	—	20	2 Foes	—
TM77	Psych Up	Normal	Status	—	—	10	Normal	—
TM82	Sleep Talk	Normal	Status	—	—	10	Depends	—
TM83	Natural Gift	Normal	Physical	—	100	15	Normal	—
TM85	Dream Eater	Psychic	Special	100	100	15	Normal	—
TM86	Grass Knot	Grass	Special	—	100	20	Normal	○
TM87	Swagger	Normal	Status	—	90	15	Normal	—
TM89	U-turn	Bug	Physical	70	100	20	Normal	○
TM90	Substitute	Normal	Status	—	—	10	Self	—
TM92	Trick Room	Psychic	Status	—	—	5	All	—

● LEVEL-UP MOVES

Lv.	Name	Type	Kind	Pow.	Acc.	PP	Range	DA
1	Rest	Psychic	Status	—	—	10	Self	—
1	Confusion	Psychic	Special	50	100	25	Normal	—
6	Imprison	Psychic	Status	—	—	10	Self	—
16	Protect	Normal	Status	—	—	10	Self	—
21	Swift	Normal	Special	60	—	20	2 Foes	—
31	Lucky Chant	Normal	Status	—	—	30	2 Allies	—
36	Future Sight	Psychic	Special	80	90	10	Normal	—
46	Charm	Normal	Status	—	100	20	Normal	—
51	Extrasensory	Psychic	Special	80	100	30	Normal	—
61	Copycat	Normal	Status	—	—	20	Depends	—
66	Natural Gift	Normal	Physical	—	100	15	Normal	—
76	Healing Wish	Psychic	Status	—	—	10	Self	—

● MOVE MANIAC

Name	Type	Kind	Pow.	Acc.	PP	Range	DA
Headbutt	Normal	Physical	70	100	15	Normal	○

● BP MOVES

Name	Type	Kind	Pow.	Acc.	PP	Range	DA
ThunderPunch	Electric	Physical	75	100	15	Normal	○
Fire Punch	Fire	Physical	75	100	15	Normal	○
Ice Punch	Ice	Physical	75	100	15	Normal	○
Zen Headbutt	Psychic	Physical	80	90	15	Normal	○
Trick	Psychic	Status	—	100	10	Normal	—
Knock Off	Dark	Physical	20	100	20	Normal	○
Snore	Normal	Special	40	100	15	Normal	—
Helping Hand	Normal	Status	—	—	20	1 Ally	—
Swift	Normal	Special	60	—	20	2 Foes	—
Magic Coat	Psychic	Status	—	—	15	Self	—
Role Play	Psychic	Status	—	—	10	Normal	—
Mud-Slap	Ground	Special	20	100	10	Normal	—
Signal Beam	Bug	Special	75	100	15	Normal	—

● TM & HM MOVES

No.	Name	Type	Kind	Pow.	Acc.	PP	Range	DA
TM03	Water Pulse	Water	Special	60	100	20	Normal	—
TM04	Calm Mind	Psychic	Status	—	—	20	Self	—
TM06	Toxic	Poison	Status	—	85	10	Normal	—
TM10	Hidden Power	Normal	Special	—	100	15	Normal	—
TM11	Sunny Day	Fire	Status	—	—	5	All	—
TM13	Ice Beam	Ice	Special	95	100	10	Normal	—
TM14	Blizzard	Ice	Special	120	70	5	2 Foes	—
TM15	Hyper Beam	Normal	Special	150	90	5	Normal	—
TM16	Light Screen	Psychic	Status	—	—	30	2 Allies	—
TM17	Protect	Normal	Status	—	—	10	Self	—
TM18	Rain Dance	Water	Status	—	—	5	All	—
TM20	Safeguard	Normal	Status	—	—	25	2 Allies	—
TM21	Frustration	Normal	Physical	—	100	20	Normal	○
TM23	Iron Tail	Steel	Physical	100	75	15	Normal	○
TM24	Thunderbolt	Electric	Special	95	100	15	Normal	—
TM25	Thunder	Electric	Special	120	70	10	Normal	—
TM27	Return	Normal	Physical	—	100	20	Normal	○
TM29	Psychic	Psychic	Special	90	100	10	Normal	—
TM30	Shadow Ball	Ghost	Special	80	100	15	Normal	—
TM32	Double Team	Normal	Status	—	—	15	Self	—
TM33	Reflect	Psychic	Status	—	—	20	2 Allies	—
TM34	Shock Wave	Electric	Special	60	—	20	Normal	—
TM37	Sandstorm	Rock	Status	—	—	10	All	—
TM42	Facade	Normal	Physical	70	100	20	Normal	○
TM43	Secret Power	Normal	Physical	70	100	20	Normal	○
TM44	Rest	Psychic	Status	—	—	10	Self	—
TM48	Skill Swap	Psychic	Status	—	—	10	Normal	—
TM53	Energy Ball	Grass	Special	80	100	10	Normal	—
TM56	Fling	Dark	Physical	—	100	10	Normal	—
TM57	Charge Beam	Electric	Special	50	90	10	Normal	—
TM58	Endure	Normal	Status	—	—	10	Self	—
TM67	Recycle	Normal	Status	—	—	10	Self	—
TM68	Giga Impact	Normal	Physical	150	90	5	Normal	○
TM70	Flash	Normal	Status	—	100	20	Normal	—
TM73	Thunder Wave	Electric	Status	—	100	20	Normal	—
TM76	Stealth Rock	Rock	Status	—	—	20	2 Foes	—
TM77	Psych Up	Normal	Status	—	—	10	Normal	—
TM82	Sleep Talk	Normal	Status	—	—	10	Depends	—
TM83	Natural Gift	Normal	Physical	—	100	15	Normal	—
TM85	Dream Eater	Psychic	Special	100	100	15	Normal	—
TM86	Grass Knot	Grass	Special	—	100	20	Normal	○
TM87	Swagger	Normal	Status	—	90	15	Normal	—
TM89	U-turn	Bug	Physical	70	100	20	Normal	○
TM90	Substitute	Normal	Status	—	—	10	Self	—
TM92	Trick Room	Psychic	Status	—	—	5	All	—

◉ No. 481 | Emotion Pokémon
Mesprit

Psychic

● HEIGHT: 1'00"
● WEIGHT: 0.7 lbs.
● ITEMS: None

● SIZE COMPARISON

● GENDER UNKNOWN

◉ ABILITIES
● Levitate

◉ STATS
HP ●●●
ATTACK ●●●●
DEFENSE ●●●●
SP. ATTACK ●●●●●
SP. DEFENSE ●●●●●
SPEED ●●●●

◉ EGG GROUPS
No Egg has ever been discovered

◉ PERFORMANCE
SPEED ★★☆   STAMINA ★★★☆
POWER ★★★★☆   JUMP ★★★★☆
SKILL ★★★★

● MAIN WAYS TO OBTAIN

Pokémon HeartGold	—
Pokémon SoulSilver	—
Pokémon Diamond	After you meet Mesprit at Lake Verity (inside Verity Cavern), it starts roaming the Sinnoh region
Pokémon Pearl	After you meet Mesprit at Lake Verity (inside Verity Cavern), it starts roaming the Sinnoh region
Pokémon Platinum	After you meet Mesprit at Lake Verity (inside Verity Cavern), it starts roaming the Sinnoh region

Pokémon HeartGold
This Pokémon is said to have endowed the human heart with emotions, such as sorrow and joy.

Pokémon SoulSilver
This Pokémon is said to have endowed the human heart with emotions, such as sorrow and joy.

◉ EVOLUTION
Does not evolve

No. 482 | Willpower Pokémon
Azelf

Psychic

- **HEIGHT:** 1'00"
- **WEIGHT:** 0.7 lbs.
- **ITEMS:** None

● SIZE COMPARISON

● GENDER UNKNOWN

● ABILITIES
- Levitate

● STATS
HP	●●●○○
ATTACK	●●●●○
DEFENSE	●●●○○
SP. ATTACK	●●●●○
SP. DEFENSE	●●●○○
SPEED	●●●●●

● EGG GROUPS
No Egg has ever been discovered

● PERFORMANCE
SPEED ★★★★☆   STAMINA ★★☆☆
POWER ★★☆☆   JUMP ★★★★☆
SKILL ★★★★★

● MAIN WAYS TO OBTAIN

Pokémon HeartGold —

Pokémon SoulSilver —

Pokémon Diamond Lake Valor (inside Valor Cavern)

Pokémon Pearl Lake Valor (inside Valor Cavern)

Pokémon Platinum Lake Valor (inside Valor Cavern)

Pokémon HeartGold
This Pokémon is said to have endowed humans with the determination needed to face any of life's difficulties.

Pokémon SoulSilver
This Pokémon is said to have endowed humans with the determination needed to face any of life's difficulties.

● EVOLUTION
Does not evolve

● LEVEL-UP MOVES
Lv.	Name	Type	Kind	Pow.	Acc.	PP	Range	DA
1	Rest	Psychic	Status	—	—	10	Self	—
1	Confusion	Psychic	Special	50	100	25	Normal	—
6	Imprison	Psychic	Status	—	—	10	Self	—
16	Detect	Fighting	Status	—	—	5	Self	—
21	Swift	Normal	Special	60	—	20	2 Foes	—
31	Uproar	Normal	Special	50	100	10	1 Random	—
36	Future Sight	Psychic	Special	80	90	15	Normal	—
46	Nasty Plot	Dark	Status	—	—	20	Self	—
51	Extrasensory	Psychic	Special	80	100	30	Normal	—
61	Last Resort	Normal	Physical	130	100	5	Normal	○
66	Natural Gift	Normal	Physical	—	100	15	Normal	—
76	Explosion	Normal	Physical	250	100	5	2 Foes/1 Ally	—

● MOVE MANIAC
Name	Type	Kind	Pow.	Acc.	PP	Range	DA
Headbutt	Normal	Physical	70	100	15	Normal	○

● BP MOVES
Name	Type	Kind	Pow.	Acc.	PP	Range	DA
ThunderPunch	Electric	Physical	75	100	15	Normal	○
Fire Punch	Fire	Physical	75	100	15	Normal	○
Ice Punch	Ice	Physical	75	100	15	Normal	○
Zen Headbutt	Psychic	Physical	80	90	15	Normal	○
Trick	Psychic	Status	—	100	10	Normal	—
Knock Off	Dark	Physical	20	100	20	Normal	○
Snore	Normal	Special	40	100	15	Normal	—
Helping Hand	Normal	Status	—	—	20	1 Ally	—
Last Resort	Normal	Physical	130	100	5	Normal	○
Swift	Normal	Special	60	—	20	2 Foes	—
Uproar	Normal	Special	50	100	10	1 Random	—
Magic Coat	Psychic	Status	—	—	15	Self	—
Role Play	Psychic	Status	—	—	10	Normal	—
Mud-Slap	Ground	Special	20	100	10	Normal	—
Signal Beam	Bug	Special	75	100	15	Normal	—

● TM & HM MOVES
No.	Name	Type	Kind	Pow.	Acc.	PP	Range	DA
TM03	Water Pulse	Water	Special	60	100	20	Normal	—
TM04	Calm Mind	Psychic	Status	—	—	20	Self	—
TM06	Toxic	Poison	Status	—	85	10	Normal	—
TM10	Hidden Power	Normal	Special	—	100	15	Normal	—
TM11	Sunny Day	Fire	Status	—	—	5	All	—
TM12	Taunt	Dark	Status	—	100	20	Normal	—
TM15	Hyper Beam	Normal	Special	150	90	5	Normal	—
TM16	Light Screen	Psychic	Status	—	—	30	2 Allies	—
TM17	Protect	Normal	Status	—	—	10	Self	—
TM18	Rain Dance	Water	Status	—	—	5	All	—
TM20	Safeguard	Normal	Status	—	—	25	2 Allies	—
TM21	Frustration	Normal	Physical	—	100	20	Normal	○
TM23	Iron Tail	Steel	Physical	100	75	15	Normal	○
TM24	Thunderbolt	Electric	Special	95	100	15	Normal	—
TM25	Thunder	Electric	Special	120	70	10	Normal	—
TM27	Return	Normal	Physical	—	100	20	Normal	○
TM29	Psychic	Psychic	Special	90	100	10	Normal	—
TM30	Shadow Ball	Ghost	Special	80	100	15	Normal	—
TM32	Double Team	Normal	Status	—	—	15	Self	—
TM33	Reflect	Psychic	Status	—	—	20	2 Allies	—
TM34	Shock Wave	Electric	Special	60	—	20	Normal	—
TM35	Flamethrower	Fire	Special	95	100	15	Normal	—
TM37	Sandstorm	Rock	Status	—	—	10	All	—
TM38	Fire Blast	Fire	Special	120	85	5	Normal	—
TM41	Torment	Dark	Status	—	100	15	Normal	—
TM42	Facade	Normal	Physical	70	100	20	Normal	○
TM43	Secret Power	Normal	Physical	70	100	20	Normal	○
TM44	Rest	Psychic	Status	—	—	10	Self	—
TM48	Skill Swap	Psychic	Status	—	—	10	Normal	—
TM53	Energy Ball	Grass	Special	80	100	10	Normal	—
TM56	Fling	Dark	Physical	—	100	10	Normal	—
TM57	Charge Beam	Electric	Special	50	90	10	Normal	—
TM58	Endure	Normal	Status	—	—	10	Self	—
TM64	Explosion	Normal	Physical	250	100	5	2 Foes/1 Ally	—
TM66	Payback	Dark	Physical	50	100	10	Normal	○
TM67	Recycle	Normal	Status	—	—	10	Self	—
TM68	Giga Impact	Normal	Physical	150	90	5	Normal	○
TM70	Flash	Normal	Status	—	100	20	Normal	—
TM73	Thunder Wave	Electric	Status	—	100	20	Normal	—
TM76	Stealth Rock	Rock	Status	—	—	20	2 Foes	—
TM77	Psych Up	Normal	Status	—	—	10	Normal	—
TM82	Sleep Talk	Normal	Status	—	—	10	Depends	—
TM83	Natural Gift	Normal	Physical	—	100	15	Normal	—
TM85	Dream Eater	Psychic	Special	100	100	15	Normal	—
TM86	Grass Knot	Grass	Special	—	100	20	Normal	—
TM87	Swagger	Normal	Status	—	90	15	Normal	—
TM89	U-turn	Bug	Physical	70	100	20	Normal	○
TM90	Substitute	Normal	Status	—	—	10	Self	—
TM92	Trick Room	Psychic	Status	—	—	5	All	—

● LEVEL-UP MOVES

Lv.	Name	Type	Kind	Pow.	Acc.	PP	Range	DA
1	DragonBreath	Dragon	Special	60	100	20	Normal	—
1	Scary Face	Normal	Status	—	90	10	Normal	—
6	Metal Claw	Steel	Physical	50	95	35	Normal	○
10	AncientPower	Rock	Special	60	100	5	Normal	—
15	Slash	Normal	Physical	70	100	20	Normal	○
19	Power Gem	Rock	Special	70	100	20	Normal	—
24	Metal Burst	Steel	Physical	—	100	10	Self	—
28	Dragon Claw	Dragon	Physical	80	100	15	Normal	○
33	Earth Power	Ground	Special	90	100	10	Normal	—
37	Aura Sphere	Fighting	Special	90	—	20	Normal	—
42	Flash Cannon	Steel	Special	80	100	10	Normal	—
46	Roar of Time	Dragon	Special	150	90	5	Normal	—

● MOVE MANIAC

Name	Type	Kind	Pow.	Acc.	PP	Range	DA
Headbutt	Normal	Physical	70	100	15	Normal	○
Draco Meteor	Dragon	Special	140	90	5	Normal	—

● BP MOVES

Name	Type	Kind	Pow.	Acc.	PP	Range	DA
Fury Cutter	Bug	Physical	10	95	20	Normal	○
Snore	Normal	Special	40	100	15	Normal	—
Magnet Rise	Electric	Status	—	—	10	Self	—
Swift	Normal	Special	60	—	20	2 Foes	—
Gravity	Psychic	Status	—	—	5	All	—
Mud-Slap	Ground	Special	20	100	10	Normal	—
Iron Head	Steel	Physical	80	100	15	Normal	○
Outrage	Dragon	Special	120	100	15	1 Random	○
AncientPower	Rock	Special	60	100	5	Normal	—
Earth Power	Ground	Special	90	100	10	Normal	—
Twister	Dragon	Special	40	100	20	2 Foes	—
Iron Defense	Steel	Status	—	—	15	Self	—

● TM & HM MOVES

No.	Name	Type	Kind	Pow.	Acc.	PP	Range	DA
TM02	Dragon Claw	Dragon	Physical	80	100	15	Normal	○
TM05	Roar	Normal	Status	—	100	20	Normal	—
TM06	Toxic	Poison	Status	—	85	10	Normal	—
TM08	Bulk Up	Fighting	Status	—	—	20	Self	—
TM10	Hidden Power	Normal	Special	—	100	15	Normal	—
TM11	Sunny Day	Fire	Status	—	—	5	All	—
TM13	Ice Beam	Ice	Special	95	100	10	Normal	—
TM14	Blizzard	Ice	Special	120	70	5	2 Foes	—
TM15	Hyper Beam	Normal	Special	150	90	5	Normal	—
TM17	Protect	Normal	Status	—	—	10	Self	—
TM18	Rain Dance	Water	Status	—	—	5	All	—
TM20	Safeguard	Normal	Status	—	—	25	2 Allies	—
TM21	Frustration	Normal	Physical	—	100	20	Normal	○
TM23	Iron Tail	Steel	Physical	100	75	15	Normal	○
TM24	Thunderbolt	Electric	Special	95	100	15	Normal	—
TM25	Thunder	Electric	Special	120	70	10	Normal	—
TM26	Earthquake	Ground	Physical	100	100	10	2 Foes/1 Ally	—
TM27	Return	Normal	Physical	—	100	20	Normal	○
TM31	Brick Break	Fighting	Physical	75	100	15	Normal	○
TM32	Double Team	Normal	Status	—	—	15	Self	—
TM34	Shock Wave	Electric	Special	60	—	20	Normal	—
TM35	Flamethrower	Fire	Special	95	100	15	Normal	—
TM37	Sandstorm	Rock	Status	—	—	10	All	—
TM38	Fire Blast	Fire	Special	120	85	5	Normal	—
TM39	Rock Tomb	Rock	Physical	50	80	10	Normal	—
TM40	Aerial Ace	Flying	Physical	60	—	20	Normal	○
TM42	Facade	Normal	Physical	70	100	20	Normal	○
TM43	Secret Power	Normal	Physical	70	100	20	Normal	○
TM44	Rest	Psychic	Status	—	—	10	Self	—
TM50	Overheat	Fire	Special	140	90	5	Normal	—
TM58	Endure	Normal	Status	—	—	10	Self	—
TM59	Dragon Pulse	Dragon	Special	90	100	10	Normal	—
TM65	Shadow Claw	Ghost	Physical	70	100	15	Normal	○
TM68	Giga Impact	Normal	Physical	150	90	5	Normal	○
TM70	Flash	Normal	Status	—	100	20	Normal	—
TM71	Stone Edge	Rock	Physical	100	80	5	Normal	—
TM73	Thunder Wave	Electric	Status	—	100	20	Normal	—
TM76	Stealth Rock	Rock	Status	—	—	20	2 Foes	—
TM77	Psych Up	Normal	Status	—	—	10	Normal	—
TM80	Rock Slide	Rock	Physical	75	90	10	2 Foes	—
TM82	Sleep Talk	Normal	Status	—	—	10	Depends	—
TM83	Natural Gift	Normal	Physical	—	100	15	Normal	—
TM87	Swagger	Normal	Status	—	90	15	Normal	—
TM90	Substitute	Normal	Status	—	—	10	Self	—
TM91	Flash Cannon	Steel	Special	80	100	10	Normal	—
TM92	Trick Room	Psychic	Status	—	—	5	All	—
HM01	Cut	Normal	Physical	50	95	30	Normal	○
HM04	Strength	Normal	Physical	80	100	15	Normal	○
HM06	Rock Smash	Fighting	Physical	40	100	15	Normal	○

● No. 483 | Temporal Pokémon
Dialga

Steel **Dragon**

- **HEIGHT:** 17'09"
- **WEIGHT:** 1,505.8 lbs.
- **ITEMS:** None

● SIZE COMPARISON

● GENDER UNKNOWN

◈ ABILITIES
● Pressure

◈ STATS
HP ●●●●
ATTACK ●●●●●
DEFENSE ●●●●●
SP. ATTACK ●●●●●
SP. DEFENSE ●●●●
SPEED ●●●●

◈ EGG GROUPS
No Egg has ever been discovered

◈ PERFORMANCE
SPEED ★★☆☆
POWER ★★★★☆
SKILL ★★★★☆
STAMINA ★★★★☆
JUMP ★★★☆☆

● MAIN WAYS TO OBTAIN

Pokémon HeartGold	Bring the Arceus you received in *Pokémon Diamond, Pearl,* or *Platinum* to the Ruins of Alph to receive Dialga*
Pokémon SoulSilver	Bring the Arceus you received in *Pokémon Diamond, Pearl,* or *Platinum* to the Ruins of Alph to receive Dialga*
Pokémon Diamond	Spear Pillar on Mt. Coronet
Pokémon Pearl	—
Pokémon Platinum	Spear Pillar on Mt. Coronet— (after entering the Hall of Fame)

Pokémon HeartGold	Pokémon SoulSilver
This Pokémon completely controls the flow of time. It uses its power to travel at will through the past and future.	This Pokémon completely controls the flow of time. It uses its power to travel at will through the past and future.

◈ EVOLUTION
Does not evolve

---

*Arceus is only available through special distribution events. Check Pokemon.com for the latest information on how to catch this Pokémon. (You can choose only one from Dialga, Palkia, and Giratina.)

No. 484 | Spatial Pokémon
Palkia

`Water` `Dragon`

● SIZE COMPARISON

- **HEIGHT:** 13'09"
- **WEIGHT:** 740.8 lbs.
- **ITEMS:** None

● GENDER UNKNOWN

⊙ ABILITIES
- Pressure

⊙ STATS
HP	●●●
ATTACK	●●●●
DEFENSE	●●●●
SP. ATTACK	●●●●●
SP. DEFENSE	●●●●●
SPEED	●●●●

⊙ EGG GROUPS
No Egg has ever been discovered

⊙ PERFORMANCE
SPEED ★★☆	STAMINA ★★★★☆
POWER ★★★★☆	JUMP ★★★☆☆
SKILL ★★★★★	

● MAIN WAYS TO OBTAIN

Pokémon HeartGold	Bring the Arceus you received in *Pokémon Diamond, Pearl,* or *Platinum* to the Ruins of Alph to receive Palkia*
Pokémon SoulSilver	Bring the Arceus you received in *Pokémon Diamond, Pearl,* or *Platinum* to the Ruins of Alph to receive Palkia*
Pokémon Diamond	—
Pokémon Pearl	Spear Pillar on Mt. Coronet
Pokémon Platinum	Spear Pillar on Mt. Coronet—(after entering the Hall of Fame)

Pokémon HeartGold	**Pokémon SoulSilver**
Its total control over the boundaries of space enable it to transport itself to faraway places or even other dimensions.	Its total control over the boundaries of space enable it to transport itself to faraway places or even other dimensions.

⊙ EVOLUTION

Does not evolve

● LEVEL-UP MOVES

Lv.	Name	Type	Kind	Pow.	Acc.	PP	Range	DA
1	DragonBreath	Dragon	Special	60	100	20	Normal	—
1	Scary Face	Normal	Status	—	90	10	Normal	—
6	Water Pulse	Water	Special	60	100	20	Normal	—
10	AncientPower	Rock	Special	60	100	5	Normal	—
15	Slash	Normal	Physical	70	100	20	Normal	○
19	Power Gem	Rock	Special	70	100	20	Normal	—
24	Aqua Tail	Water	Physical	90	90	10	Normal	○
28	Dragon Claw	Dragon	Physical	80	100	15	Normal	○
33	Earth Power	Ground	Special	90	100	10	Normal	—
37	Aura Sphere	Fighting	Special	90	—	20	Normal	—
42	Hydro Pump	Water	Special	120	80	5	Normal	—
46	Spacial Rend	Dragon	Special	100	95	5	Normal	—

● MOVE MANIAC

Name	Type	Kind	Pow.	Acc.	PP	Range	DA
Headbutt	Normal	Physical	70	100	15	Normal	○
Draco Meteor	Dragon	Special	140	90	5	Normal	—

● BP MOVES

Name	Type	Kind	Pow.	Acc.	PP	Range	DA
Dive	Water	Physical	80	100	10	Normal	○
Fury Cutter	Bug	Physical	10	95	20	Normal	○
Snore	Normal	Special	40	100	15	Normal	—
Swift	Normal	Special	60	—	20	2 Foes	—
Gravity	Psychic	Status	—	—	5	All	—
Mud-Slap	Ground	Special	20	100	10	Normal	—
Aqua Tail	Water	Physical	90	90	10	Normal	○
Outrage	Dragon	Physical	120	100	10	1 Random	○
AncientPower	Rock	Special	60	100	5	Normal	—
Earth Power	Ground	Special	90	100	10	Normal	—
Twister	Dragon	Special	40	100	20	2 Foes	—

● TM & HM MOVES

No.	Name	Type	Kind	Pow.	Acc.	PP	Range	DA
TM01	Focus Punch	Fighting	Physical	150	100	20	Normal	○
TM02	Dragon Claw	Dragon	Physical	80	100	15	Normal	○
TM03	Water Pulse	Water	Special	60	100	20	Normal	—
TM05	Roar	Normal	Status	—	100	20	Normal	—
TM06	Toxic	Poison	Status	—	85	10	Normal	—
TM07	Hail	Ice	Status	—	—	10	All	—
TM08	Bulk Up	Fighting	Status	—	—	20	Self	—
TM10	Hidden Power	Normal	Special	—	100	15	Normal	—
TM11	Sunny Day	Fire	Status	—	—	5	All	—
TM13	Ice Beam	Ice	Special	95	100	10	Normal	—
TM14	Blizzard	Ice	Special	120	70	5	2 Foes	—
TM15	Hyper Beam	Normal	Special	150	90	5	Normal	—
TM17	Protect	Normal	Status	—	—	10	Self	—
TM18	Rain Dance	Water	Status	—	—	5	All	—
TM20	Safeguard	Normal	Status	—	—	25	2 Allies	—
TM21	Frustration	Normal	Physical	—	100	20	Normal	○
TM24	Thunderbolt	Electric	Special	95	100	15	Normal	—
TM25	Thunder	Electric	Special	120	70	10	Normal	—
TM26	Earthquake	Ground	Physical	100	100	10	2 Foes/1 Ally	—
TM27	Return	Normal	Physical	—	100	20	Normal	○
TM31	Brick Break	Fighting	Physical	75	100	15	Normal	○
TM32	Double Team	Normal	Status	—	—	15	Self	—
TM34	Shock Wave	Electric	Special	60	—	20	Normal	—
TM35	Flamethrower	Fire	Special	95	100	15	Normal	—
TM37	Sandstorm	Rock	Status	—	—	10	All	—
TM38	Fire Blast	Fire	Special	120	85	5	Normal	—
TM39	Rock Tomb	Rock	Physical	50	80	10	Normal	—
TM40	Aerial Ace	Flying	Physical	60	—	20	Normal	○
TM42	Facade	Normal	Physical	70	100	20	Normal	○
TM43	Secret Power	Normal	Physical	70	100	20	Normal	○
TM44	Rest	Psychic	Status	—	—	10	Self	—
TM52	Focus Blast	Fighting	Special	120	70	5	Normal	—
TM55	Brine	Water	Special	65	100	10	Normal	—
TM56	Fling	Dark	Physical	—	100	10	Normal	—
TM58	Endure	Normal	Status	—	—	10	Self	—
TM59	Dragon Pulse	Dragon	Special	90	100	10	Normal	—
TM65	Shadow Claw	Ghost	Physical	70	100	15	Normal	○
TM68	Giga Impact	Normal	Physical	150	90	5	Normal	○
TM71	Stone Edge	Rock	Physical	100	80	5	Normal	—
TM72	Avalanche	Ice	Physical	60	100	10	Normal	○
TM73	Thunder Wave	Electric	Status	—	100	20	Normal	—
TM77	Psych Up	Normal	Status	—	—	10	Normal	—
TM80	Rock Slide	Rock	Physical	75	90	10	2 Foes	—
TM82	Sleep Talk	Normal	Status	—	—	10	Depends	—
TM83	Natural Gift	Normal	Physical	—	100	15	Normal	—
TM87	Swagger	Normal	Status	—	90	15	Normal	—
TM90	Substitute	Normal	Status	—	—	10	Self	—
TM92	Trick Room	Psychic	Status	—	—	5	All	—
HM01	Cut	Normal	Physical	50	95	30	Normal	○
HM03	Surf	Water	Special	95	100	15	2 Foes/1 Ally	—
HM04	Strength	Normal	Physical	80	100	15	Normal	○
HM05	Whirlpool	Water	Special	15	70	15	Normal	—
HM06	Rock Smash	Fighting	Physical	40	100	15	Normal	○

---

*Arceus is only available through special distribution events. Check Pokemon.com for the latest information on how to catch this Pokémon. (You can choose only one from Dialga, Palkia, and Giratina.)

● LEVEL-UP MOVES

Lv.	Name	Type	Kind	Pow.	Acc.	PP	Range	DA
1	AncientPower	Rock	Special	60	100	5	Normal	—
9	Leer	Normal	Status	—	100	30	2 Foes	—
17	Fire Fang	Fire	Physical	65	95	15	Normal	○
25	Metal Sound	Steel	Status	—	85	40	Normal	—
33	Crunch	Dark	Physical	80	100	15	Normal	○
41	Scary Face	Normal	Status	—	90	10	Normal	—
49	Lava Plume	Fire	Special	80	100	15	2 Foes/1 Ally	—
57	Fire Spin	Fire	Special	15	70	15	Normal	—
65	Iron Head	Steel	Physical	80	100	15	Normal	○
73	Earth Power	Ground	Special	90	100	10	Normal	—
81	Heat Wave	Fire	Special	100	90	10	2 Foes	—
88	Stone Edge	Rock	Physical	100	80	5	Normal	—
96	Magma Storm	Fire	Special	120	70	5	Normal	—

● MOVE MANIAC

Name	Type	Kind	Pow.	Acc.	PP	Range	DA
Headbutt	Normal	Physical	70	100	15	Normal	○

● BP MOVES

Name	Type	Kind	Pow.	Acc.	PP	Range	DA
Bug Bite	Bug	Physical	60	100	20	Normal	○
Snore	Normal	Special	40	100	15	Normal	—
Uproar	Normal	Special	50	100	10	1 Random	—
Mud-Slap	Ground	Special	20	100	10	Normal	—
Iron Head	Steel	Physical	80	100	15	Normal	○
AncientPower	Rock	Special	60	100	5	Normal	—
Earth Power	Ground	Special	90	100	10	Normal	—
Iron Defense	Steel	Status	—	—	15	Self	—
Heat Wave	Fire	Special	100	90	10	2 Foes	—

● TM & HM MOVES

No.	Name	Type	Kind	Pow.	Acc.	PP	Range	DA
TM05	Roar	Normal	Status	—	100	20	Normal	—
TM06	Toxic	Poison	Status	—	85	10	Normal	—
TM10	Hidden Power	Normal	Special	—	100	15	Normal	—
TM11	Sunny Day	Fire	Status	—	—	5	All	—
TM12	Taunt	Dark	Status	—	100	20	Normal	—
TM15	Hyper Beam	Normal	Special	150	90	5	Normal	—
TM17	Protect	Normal	Status	—	—	10	Self	—
TM21	Frustration	Normal	Physical	—	100	20	Normal	○
TM22	SolarBeam	Grass	Special	120	100	10	Normal	—
TM26	Earthquake	Ground	Physical	100	100	10	2 Foes/1 Ally	—
TM27	Return	Normal	Physical	—	100	20	Normal	○
TM28	Dig	Ground	Physical	80	100	10	Normal	○
TM32	Double Team	Normal	Status	—	—	15	Self	—
TM35	Flamethrower	Fire	Special	95	100	15	Normal	—
TM38	Fire Blast	Fire	Special	120	85	5	Normal	—
TM39	Rock Tomb	Rock	Physical	50	80	10	Normal	—
TM41	Torment	Dark	Status	—	100	15	Normal	—
TM42	Facade	Normal	Physical	70	100	20	Normal	○
TM43	Secret Power	Normal	Physical	70	100	20	Normal	○
TM44	Rest	Psychic	Status	—	—	10	Self	—
TM45	Attract	Normal	Status	—	100	15	Normal	—
TM50	Overheat	Fire	Special	140	90	5	Normal	—
TM58	Endure	Normal	Status	—	—	10	Self	—
TM59	Dragon Pulse	Dragon	Special	90	100	10	Normal	—
TM61	Will-O-Wisp	Fire	Status	—	75	15	Normal	—
TM64	Explosion	Normal	Physical	250	100	5	2 Foes/1 Ally	—
TM66	Payback	Dark	Physical	50	100	10	Normal	○
TM68	Giga Impact	Normal	Physical	150	90	5	Normal	○
TM71	Stone Edge	Rock	Physical	100	80	5	Normal	—
TM76	Stealth Rock	Rock	Status	—	—	20	Normal	—
TM78	Captivate	Normal	Status	—	100	20	2 Foes	—
TM79	Dark Pulse	Dark	Special	80	100	15	Normal	—
TM80	Rock Slide	Rock	Physical	75	90	10	2 Foes	—
TM82	Sleep Talk	Normal	Status	—	—	10	Depends	—
TM83	Natural Gift	Normal	Physical	—	100	15	Normal	—
TM87	Swagger	Normal	Status	—	90	15	Normal	—
TM90	Substitute	Normal	Status	—	—	10	Self	—
TM91	Flash Cannon	Steel	Special	80	100	10	Normal	—
HM04	Strength	Normal	Physical	80	100	15	Normal	○
HM06	Rock Smash	Fighting	Physical	40	100	15	Normal	○
HM08	Rock Climb	Normal	Physical	90	85	20	Normal	○

No. 485 | Lava Dome Pokémon
Heatran

Fire | Steel

- **HEIGHT:** 5'07"
- **WEIGHT:** 948.0 lbs.
- **ITEMS:** None

● SIZE COMPARISON

● MALE/FEMALE HAVE SAME FORM

◉ ABILITIES
- Flash Fire

◉ STATS
- HP ●●●
- ATTACK ●●●●
- DEFENSE ●●●●
- SP. ATTACK ●●●●
- SP. DEFENSE ●●●●
- SPEED ●●●

◉ EGG GROUPS
No Egg has ever been discovered

◉ PERFORMANCE
- SPEED ★★☆
- POWER ★★★★☆
- SKILL ★★★☆☆
- STAMINA ★★★★☆
- JUMP ★★

● MAIN WAYS TO OBTAIN

Pokémon HeartGold	—
Pokémon SoulSilver	—
Pokémon Diamond	Stark Mountain interior (talk to Buck in the Survival Area after exploring Stark Mountain)
Pokémon Pearl	Stark Mountain interior (talk to Buck in the Survival Area after exploring Stark Mountain)
Pokémon Platinum	Stark Mountain interior (talk to Buck in the Survival Area after exploring Stark Mountain)

Pokémon HeartGold	Pokémon SoulSilver
Boiling blood, like magma, circulates through its body. It makes its dwelling place in volcanic caves.	Boiling blood, like magma, circulates through its body. It makes its dwelling place in volcanic caves.

◉ EVOLUTION

Does not evolve

No. 486 | Colossal Pokémon
Regigigas

`Normal`

- **HEIGHT:** 12'02"
- **WEIGHT:** 925.9 lbs.
- **ITEMS:** None

- **SIZE COMPARISON**

- **GENDER UNKNOWN**

ABILITIES
- Slow Start

STATS
HP	●●●●
ATTACK	●●●●●●●
DEFENSE	●●●●●
SP. ATTACK	●●●●●
SP. DEFENSE	●●●●●
SPEED	●●●●

EGG GROUPS
No Egg has ever been discovered

PERFORMANCE
SPEED ★☆☆	STAMINA ★★★★★
POWER ★★★★★	JUMP ★★
SKILL ★★★☆☆	

MAIN WAYS TO OBTAIN

Pokémon HeartGold	—
Pokémon SoulSilver	—
Pokémon Diamond	Snowpoint Temple B5F (put REGIROCK, REGICE, and REGISTEEL in your party)
Pokémon Pearl	Snowpoint Temple B5F (put REGIROCK, REGICE, and REGISTEEL in your party)
Pokémon Platinum	Snowpoint Temple B5F (put REGIROCK, REGICE, and REGISTEEL in your party)

Pokémon HeartGold	**Pokémon SoulSilver**
It is believed to have shaped REGIROCK, REGICE, and REGISTEEL out of clay, ice, and magma.	It is believed to have shaped REGIROCK, REGICE, and REGISTEEL out of clay, ice, and magma.

EVOLUTION
Does not evolve

● LEVEL-UP MOVES
Lv.	Name	Type	Kind	Pow.	Acc.	PP	Range	DA
1	Fire Punch	Fire	Physical	75	100	15	Normal	○
1	Ice Punch	Ice	Physical	75	100	15	Normal	○
1	ThunderPunch	Electric	Physical	75	100	15	Normal	○
1	Mega Punch	Normal	Physical	80	85	20	Normal	○
1	Knock Off	Dark	Physical	20	100	20	Normal	○
1	Confuse Ray	Ghost	Status	—	100	10	Normal	—
1	Stomp	Normal	Physical	65	100	20	Normal	○
25	Superpower	Fighting	Physical	120	100	5	Normal	○
50	Zen Headbutt	Psychic	Physical	80	90	15	Normal	○
75	Crush Grip	Normal	Physical	—	100	5	Normal	○
100	Giga Impact	Normal	Physical	150	90	5	Normal	○

● MOVE MANIAC
Name	Type	Kind	Pow.	Acc.	PP	Range	DA
Headbutt	Normal	Physical	70	100	15	Normal	○

● BP MOVES
Name	Type	Kind	Pow.	Acc.	PP	Range	DA
Icy Wind	Ice	Special	55	95	15	2 Foes	—
ThunderPunch	Electric	Physical	75	100	15	Normal	○
Fire Punch	Fire	Physical	75	100	15	Normal	○
Ice Punch	Ice	Physical	75	100	15	Normal	○
Zen Headbutt	Psychic	Physical	80	90	15	Normal	○
Snore	Normal	Special	40	100	15	Normal	—
Gravity	Psychic	Status	—	—	5	All	—
Block	Normal	Status	—	—	5	Normal	—
Mud-Slap	Ground	Special	20	100	10	Normal	—
Superpower	Fighting	Physical	120	100	5	Normal	○
Iron Head	Steel	Physical	80	100	15	Normal	○
AncientPower	Rock	Special	60	100	5	Normal	—
Earth Power	Ground	Special	90	100	10	Normal	—

● TM & HM MOVES
No.	Name	Type	Kind	Pow.	Acc.	PP	Range	DA
TM01	Focus Punch	Fighting	Physical	150	100	20	Normal	○
TM06	Toxic	Poison	Status	—	85	10	Normal	—
TM10	Hidden Power	Normal	Special	—	100	15	Normal	—
TM11	Sunny Day	Fire	Status	—	—	5	All	—
TM15	Hyper Beam	Normal	Special	150	90	5	Normal	—
TM18	Rain Dance	Water	Status	—	—	5	All	—
TM21	Frustration	Normal	Physical	—	100	20	Normal	○
TM24	Thunderbolt	Electric	Special	95	100	15	Normal	—
TM25	Thunder	Electric	Special	120	70	10	Normal	—
TM26	Earthquake	Ground	Physical	100	100	10	2 Foes/1 Ally	○
TM27	Return	Normal	Physical	—	100	20	Normal	○
TM31	Brick Break	Fighting	Physical	75	100	15	Normal	○
TM32	Double Team	Normal	Status	—	—	15	Self	—
TM34	Shock Wave	Electric	Special	60	—	20	Normal	—
TM39	Rock Tomb	Rock	Physical	50	80	10	Normal	○
TM40	Aerial Ace	Flying	Physical	60	—	20	Normal	○
TM42	Facade	Normal	Physical	70	100	20	Normal	○
TM43	Secret Power	Normal	Physical	70	100	20	Normal	○
TM52	Focus Blast	Fighting	Special	120	70	5	Normal	—
TM56	Fling	Dark	Physical	—	100	10	Normal	○
TM58	Endure	Normal	Status	—	—	10	Self	—
TM60	Drain Punch	Fighting	Physical	60	100	5	Normal	○
TM68	Giga Impact	Normal	Physical	150	90	5	Normal	○
TM69	Rock Polish	Rock	Status	—	—	20	Self	—
TM71	Stone Edge	Rock	Physical	100	80	5	Normal	○
TM72	Avalanche	Ice	Physical	60	100	10	Normal	○
TM73	Thunder Wave	Electric	Status	—	100	20	Normal	—
TM77	Psych Up	Normal	Status	—	—	10	Normal	—
TM80	Rock Slide	Rock	Physical	75	90	10	2 Foes	○
TM82	Sleep Talk	Normal	Status	—	—	10	Depends	—
TM83	Natural Gift	Normal	Physical	—	100	15	Normal	—
TM87	Swagger	Normal	Status	—	90	15	Normal	—
TM90	Substitute	Normal	Status	—	—	10	Self	—
HM04	Strength	Normal	Physical	80	100	15	Normal	○
HM06	Rock Smash	Fighting	Physical	40	100	15	Normal	○
HM08	Rock Climb	Normal	Physical	90	85	20	Normal	○

● LEVEL-UP MOVES

Lv.	Name	Type	Kind	Pow.	Acc.	PP	Range	DA
1	DragonBreath	Dragon	Special	60	100	20	Normal	—
1	Scary Face	Normal	Status	—	90	10	Normal	—
6	Ominous Wind	Ghost	Special	60	100	5	Normal	—
10	AncientPower	Rock	Special	60	100	5	Normal	—
15	Slash	Normal	Physical	70	100	20	Normal	○
19	Shadow Sneak	Ghost	Physical	40	100	30	Normal	○
24	Destiny Bond	Ghost	Status	—	—	5	Self	—
28	Dragon Claw	Dragon	Physical	80	100	15	Normal	○
33	Earth Power	Ground	Special	90	100	10	Normal	—
37	Aura Sphere	Fighting	Special	90	—	20	Normal	—
42	Shadow Claw	Ghost	Physical	70	100	15	Normal	○
46	Shadow Force	Ghost	Physical	120	100	5	Normal	○

● MOVE MANIAC

Name	Type	Kind	Pow.	Acc.	PP	Range	DA
Headbutt	Normal	Physical	70	100	15	Normal	♪
Draco Meteor	Dragon	Special	140	90	5	Normal	—

● BP MOVES

Name	Type	Kind	Pow.	Acc.	PP	Range	DA
Fury Cutter	Bug	Physical	10	95	20	Normal	○
Icy Wind	Ice	Special	55	95	15	2 Foes	—
Ominous Wind	Ghost	Special	60	100	5	Normal	—
Air Cutter	Flying	Special	55	95	25	2 Foes	—
Snore	Normal	Special	40	100	15	Normal	—
Spite	Ghost	Status	—	100	10	Normal	—
Swift	Normal	Special	60	—	20	2 Foes	—
Gravity	Psychic	Status	—	—	5	All	—
Mud-Slap	Ground	Special	20	100	10	Normal	—
Iron Head	Steel	Physical	80	100	15	Normal	○
Aqua Tail	Water	Physical	90	90	10	Normal	○
Outrage	Dragon	Physical	120	100	15	1 Random	○
AncientPower	Rock	Special	60	100	5	Normal	—
Earth Power	Ground	Special	90	100	10	Normal	—
Twister	Dragon	Special	40	100	20	2 Foes	—
Pain Split	Normal	Status	—	—	20	Normal	—

● TM & HM MOVES

No.	Name	Type	Kind	Pow.	Acc.	PP	Range	DA
TM02	Dragon Claw	Dragon	Physical	80	100	15	Normal	○
TM04	Calm Mind	Psychic	Status	—	—	20	Self	—
TM05	Roar	Normal	Status	—	100	20	Normal	—
TM06	Toxic	Poison	Status	—	85	10	Normal	—
TM10	Hidden Power	Normal	Special	—	100	15	Normal	—
TM11	Sunny Day	Fire	Status	—	—	5	All	—
TM15	Hyper Beam	Normal	Special	150	90	5	Normal	—
TM17	Protect	Normal	Status	—	—	10	Self	—
TM18	Rain Dance	Water	Status	—	—	5	All	—
TM20	Safeguard	Normal	Status	—	—	25	2 Allies	—
TM21	Frustration	Normal	Physical	—	100	20	Normal	○
TM23	Iron Tail	Steel	Physical	100	75	15	Normal	○
TM24	Thunderbolt	Electric	Special	95	100	15	Normal	—
TM25	Thunder	Electric	Special	120	70	10	Normal	—
TM26	Earthquake	Ground	Physical	100	100	10	2 Foes/1 Ally	—
TM27	Return	Normal	Physical	—	100	20	Normal	○
TM29	Psychic	Psychic	Special	90	100	10	Normal	—
TM30	Shadow Ball	Ghost	Special	80	100	15	Normal	—
TM32	Double Team	Normal	Status	—	—	15	Self	—
TM34	Shock Wave	Electric	Special	60	—	20	Normal	—
TM40	Aerial Ace	Flying	Physical	60	—	20	Normal	○
TM42	Facade	Normal	Physical	70	100	20	Normal	○
TM43	Secret Power	Normal	Physical	70	100	20	Normal	○
TM44	Rest	Psychic	Status	—	—	10	Self	—
TM47	Steel Wing	Steel	Physical	70	90	25	Normal	○
TM53	Energy Ball	Grass	Special	80	100	10	Normal	—
TM57	Charge Beam	Electric	Special	50	90	10	Normal	—
TM58	Endure	Normal	Status	—	—	10	Self	—
TM59	Dragon Pulse	Dragon	Special	90	100	10	Normal	—
TM61	Will-O-Wisp	Fire	Status	—	75	15	Normal	—
TM62	Silver Wind	Bug	Special	60	100	5	Normal	—
TM65	Shadow Claw	Ghost	Physical	70	100	15	Normal	○
TM66	Payback	Dark	Physical	50	100	10	Normal	○
TM68	Giga Impact	Normal	Physical	150	90	5	Normal	○
TM71	Stone Edge	Rock	Physical	100	80	5	Normal	○
TM73	Thunder Wave	Electric	Status	—	100	20	Normal	—
TM77	Psych Up	Normal	Status	—	—	10	Normal	—
TM79	Dark Pulse	Dark	Special	80	100	15	Normal	—
TM82	Sleep Talk	Normal	Status	—	—	10	Depends	—
TM83	Natural Gift	Normal	Physical	—	100	15	Normal	—
TM85	Dream Eater	Psychic	Special	100	100	15	Normal	—
TM87	Swagger	Normal	Status	—	90	15	Normal	—
TM90	Substitute	Normal	Status	—	—	10	Self	—
HMU1	Cut	Normal	Physical	50	95	30	Normal	○
HM02	Fly	Flying	Physical	90	95	15	Normal	○
HM04	Strength	Normal	Physical	80	100	15	Normal	○
HM06	Rock Smash	Fighting	Physical	40	100	15	Normal	○
HM08	Rock Climb	Normal	Physical	90	85	20	Normal	○

☻ No. 487 | Renegade Pokémon
Giratina (Altered Forme)

`Ghost` `Dragon`

- ● HEIGHT: 14'09"
- ● WEIGHT: 1,653.5 lbs.
- ● ITEMS: None

● SIZE COMPARISON

● GENDER UNKNOWN

◉ ABILITIES
- ● Pressure

◉ STATS
- HP ●●●●●●
- ATTACK ●●●●●
- DEFENSE ●●●●●
- SP. ATTACK ●●●●●
- SP. DEFENSE ●●●●●
- SPEED ●●●●

◉ EGG GROUPS
No Egg has ever been discovered

◉ PERFORMANCE
- SPEED ★★ STAMINA ★★★★★
- POWER ★★★★☆ JUMP ★★☆
- SKILL ★★★☆

● MAIN WAYS TO OBTAIN

Pokémon HeartGold — Bring the Arceus you received in *Pokémon Diamond, Pearl,* or *Platinum* to the Ruins of Alph to receive Giratina*

Pokémon SoulSilver — Bring the Arceus you received in *Pokémon Diamond, Pearl,* or *Platinum* to the Ruins of Alph to receive Giratina*

Pokémon Diamond — Turnback Cave

Pokémon Pearl — Turnback Cave

Pokémon Platinum — Turnback Cave (if you defeat Giratina Origin Forme or flee from the battle in the Distortion World)

Pokémon HeartGold — This Pokémon is said to live in a world on the reverse side of ours, where common knowledge is distorted and strange.

Pokémon SoulSilver — This Pokémon is said to live in a world on the reverse side of ours, where common knowledge is distorted and strange.

◉ EVOLUTION
Does not evolve

*Arceus is only available through special distribution events. Check Pokemon.com for the latest information on how to catch this Pokémon. (You can choose only one from Dialga, Palkia, and Giratina.)

No. 487 | Renegade Pokémon
Giratina (Origin Forme)

Ghost | Dragon

● LEVEL-UP MOVES

Lv.	Name	Type	Kind	Pow.	Acc.	PP	Range	DA
1	DragonBreath	Dragon	Special	60	100	20	Normal	—
1	Scary Face	Normal	Status	—	90	10	Normal	—
6	Ominous Wind	Ghost	Special	60	100	5	Normal	—
10	AncientPower	Rock	Special	60	100	5	Normal	—
15	Slash	Normal	Physical	70	100	20	Normal	○
19	Shadow Sneak	Ghost	Physical	40	100	30	Normal	○
24	Destiny Bond	Ghost	Status	—	—	5	Self	—
28	Dragon Claw	Dragon	Physical	80	100	15	Normal	○
33	Earth Power	Ground	Special	90	100	10	Normal	—
37	Aura Sphere	Fighting	Special	90	—	20	Normal	—
42	Shadow Claw	Ghost	Physical	70	100	15	Normal	○
46	Shadow Force	Ghost	Physical	120	100	5	Normal	—

● MOVE MANIAC

Name	Type	Kind	Pow.	Acc.	PP	Range	DA
Headbutt	Normal	Physical	70	100	15	Normal	○
Draco Meteor	Dragon	Special	140	90	5	Normal	—

● BP MOVES

Name	Type	Kind	Pow.	Acc.	PP	Range	DA
Fury Cutter	Bug	Physical	10	95	20	Normal	○
Icy Wind	Ice	Special	55	95	15	2 Foes	—
Ominous Wind	Ghost	Special	60	100	5	Normal	—
Air Cutter	Flying	Special	55	95	25	2 Foes	—
Snore	Normal	Special	40	100	15	Normal	—
Spite	Ghost	Status	—	100	10	Normal	—
Swift	Normal	Special	60	—	20	2 Foes	—
Tailwind	Flying	Status	—	—	30	2 Allies	—
Gravity	Psychic	Status	—	—	5	All	—
Magic Coat	Psychic	Status	—	—	15	Self	—
Mud-Slap	Ground	Special	20	100	10	Normal	—
Iron Head	Steel	Physical	80	100	15	Normal	○
Aqua Tail	Water	Physical	90	90	10	Normal	○
Outrage	Dragon	Physical	120	100	15	1 Random	○
AncientPower	Rock	Special	60	100	5	Normal	—
Earth Power	Ground	Special	90	100	10	Normal	—
Twister	Dragon	Special	40	100	20	2 Foes	—

● HEIGHT: 22'08"
● WEIGHT: 1,433.0 lbs.
● ITEMS: None

● SIZE COMPARISON

● GENDER UNKNOWN

◉ ABILITIES
● Levitate

◉ STATS
HP	●●●●●●
ATTACK	●●●●●
DEFENSE	●●●●
SP. ATTACK	●●●●●
SP. DEFENSE	●●●●
SPEED	●●●●

◉ EGG GROUPS
No Egg has ever been discovered

◉ PERFORMANCE
SPEED ★★★☆☆   STAMINA ★★★☆☆
POWER ★★★☆☆   JUMP ★★★☆☆
SKILL ★★★☆☆

● MAIN WAYS TO OBTAIN

Pokémon HeartGold
Bring the Arceus you received in *Pokémon Diamond, Pearl,* or *Platinum* to the Ruins of Alph to receive Giratina*

Pokémon SoulSilver
Bring the Arceus you received in *Pokémon Diamond, Pearl,* or *Platinum* to the Ruins of Alph to receive Giratina*

Pokémon Diamond —

Pokémon Pearl —

Pokémon Platinum Distortion World

Pokémon HeartGold
This Pokémon is said to live in a world on the reverse side of ours, where common knowledge is distorted and strange.

Pokémon SoulSilver
This Pokémon is said to live in a world on the reverse side of ours, where common knowledge is distorted and strange.

◉ EVOLUTION

Does not evolve

● TM & HM MOVES

No.	Name	Type	Kind	Pow.	Acc.	PP	Range	DA
TM02	Dragon Claw	Dragon	Physical	80	100	15	Normal	○
TM04	Calm Mind	Psychic	Status	—	—	20	Self	—
TM05	Roar	Normal	Status	—	100	20	Normal	—
TM06	Toxic	Poison	Status	—	85	10	Normal	—
TM10	Hidden Power	Normal	Special	—	100	15	Normal	—
TM11	Sunny Day	Fire	Status	—	—	5	All	—
TM15	Hyper Beam	Normal	Special	150	90	5	Normal	—
TM17	Protect	Normal	Status	—	—	10	Self	—
TM18	Rain Dance	Water	Status	—	—	5	All	—
TM20	Safeguard	Normal	Status	—	—	25	2 Allies	—
TM21	Frustration	Normal	Physical	—	100	20	Normal	○
TM23	Iron Tail	Steel	Physical	100	75	15	Normal	○
TM24	Thunderbolt	Electric	Special	95	100	15	Normal	—
TM25	Thunder	Electric	Special	120	70	10	Normal	—
TM26	Earthquake	Ground	Physical	100	100	10	2 Foes/1 Ally	—
TM27	Return	Normal	Physical	—	100	20	Normal	○
TM29	Psychic	Psychic	Special	90	100	10	Normal	—
TM30	Shadow Ball	Ghost	Special	80	100	15	Normal	—
TM32	Double Team	Normal	Status	—	—	15	Self	—
TM34	Shock Wave	Electric	Special	60	—	20	Normal	—
TM40	Aerial Ace	Flying	Physical	60	—	20	Normal	○
TM42	Facade	Normal	Physical	70	100	20	Normal	○
TM43	Secret Power	Normal	Physical	70	100	20	Normal	○
TM44	Rest	Psychic	Status	—	—	10	Self	—
TM47	Steel Wing	Steel	Physical	70	90	25	Normal	○
TM53	Energy Ball	Grass	Special	80	100	10	Normal	—
TM57	Charge Beam	Electric	Special	50	90	10	Normal	—
TM58	Endure	Normal	Status	—	—	10	Self	—
TM59	Dragon Pulse	Dragon	Special	90	100	10	Normal	—
TM61	Will-O-Wisp	Fire	Status	—	75	15	Normal	—
TM62	Silver Wind	Bug	Special	60	100	5	Normal	—
TM65	Shadow Claw	Ghost	Physical	70	100	15	Normal	○
TM66	Payback	Dark	Physical	50	100	10	Normal	○
TM68	Giga Impact	Normal	Physical	150	90	5	Normal	○
TM71	Stone Edge	Rock	Physical	100	80	5	Normal	○
TM73	Thunder Wave	Electric	Status	—	100	20	Normal	—
TM77	Psych Up	Normal	Status	—	—	10	Self	—
TM79	Dark Pulse	Dark	Special	80	100	15	Normal	—
TM82	Sleep Talk	Normal	Status	—	—	10	Depends	—
TM83	Natural Gift	Normal	Physical	—	100	15	Normal	○
TM85	Dream Eater	Psychic	Special	100	100	15	Normal	—
TM87	Swagger	Normal	Status	—	90	15	Normal	—
TM90	Substitute	Normal	Status	—	—	10	Self	—
HM01	Cut	Normal	Physical	50	95	30	Normal	○
HM02	Fly	Flying	Physical	90	95	15	Normal	○
HM04	Strength	Normal	Physical	80	100	15	Normal	○
HM06	Rock Smash	Fighting	Physical	40	100	15	Normal	○
HM08	Rock Climb	Normal	Physical	90	85	20	Normal	○

*Arceus is only available through special distribution events. Check Pokemon.com for the latest information on how to catch this Pokémon. (You can choose only one from Dialga, Palkia, and Giratina.)

● LEVEL-UP MOVES

Lv.	Name	Type	Kind	Pow.	Acc.	PP	Range	DA
1	Confusion	Psychic	Special	50	100	25	Normal	—
1	Double Team	Normal	Status	—	—	15	Self	—
11	Safeguard	Normal	Status	—	—	25	2 Allies	—
20	Mist	Ice	Status	—	—	30	2 Allies	—
29	Aurora Beam	Ice	Special	65	100	20	Normal	—
38	Future Sight	Psychic	Special	80	90	15	Normal	—
47	Slash	Normal	Physical	70	100	20	Normal	○
57	Moonlight	Normal	Status	—	—	5	Self	—
66	Psycho Cut	Psychic	Physical	70	100	20	Normal	—
75	Psycho Shift	Psychic	Status	—	90	10	Normal	—
84	Lunar Dance	Psychic	Status	—	—	10	Self	—
93	Psychic	Psychic	Special	90	100	10	Normal	—

● MOVE MANIAC

Name	Type	Kind	Pow.	Acc.	PP	Range	DA

● BP MOVES

Name	Type	Kind	Pow.	Acc.	PP	Range	DA
Fury Cutter	Bug	Physical	10	95	20	Normal	○
Icy Wind	Ice	Special	55	95	15	2 Foes	—
Zen Headbutt	Psychic	Physical	80	90	15	Normal	○
Trick	Psychic	Status	—	100	10	Normal	—
Snore	Normal	Special	40	100	15	Normal	—
Helping Hand	Normal	Status	—	—	20	1 Ally	—
Swift	Normal	Special	60	—	20	2 Foes	—
Gravity	Psychic	Status	—	—	5	All	—
Magic Coat	Psychic	Status	—	—	15	Self	—
Mud-Slap	Ground	Special	20	100	10	Normal	—
Signal Beam	Bug	Special	75	100	15	Normal	—

● TM & HM MOVES

No.	Name	Type	Kind	Pow.	Acc.	PP	Range	DA
TM04	Calm Mind	Psychic	Status	—	—	20	Self	—
TM06	Toxic	Poison	Status	—	85	10	Normal	—
TM10	Hidden Power	Normal	Special	—	100	15	Normal	—
TM11	Sunny Day	Fire	Status	—	—	5	All	—
TM13	Ice Beam	Ice	Special	95	100	10	Normal	—
TM15	Hyper Beam	Normal	Special	150	90	5	Normal	—
TM16	Light Screen	Psychic	Status	—	—	30	2 Allies	—
TM17	Protect	Normal	Status	—	—	10	Self	—
TM18	Rain Dance	Water	Status	—	—	5	All	—
TM20	Safeguard	Normal	Status	—	—	25	2 Allies	—
TM21	Frustration	Normal	Physical	—	100	20	Normal	○
TM22	SolarBeam	Grass	Special	120	100	10	Normal	—
TM27	Return	Normal	Physical	—	100	20	Normal	○
TM29	Psychic	Psychic	Special	90	100	10	Normal	—
TM30	Shadow Ball	Ghost	Special	80	100	15	Normal	—
TM33	Reflect	Psychic	Status	—	—	20	2 Allies	—
TM42	Facade	Normal	Physical	70	100	20	Normal	○
TM43	Secret Power	Normal	Physical	70	100	20	Normal	○
TM44	Rest	Psychic	Status	—	—	10	Self	—
TM45	Attract	Normal	Status	—	100	15	Normal	—
TM48	Skill Swap	Psychic	Status	—	—	10	Normal	—
TM53	Energy Ball	Grass	Special	80	100	10	Normal	—
TM57	Charge Beam	Electric	Special	50	90	10	Normal	—
TM58	Endure	Normal	Status	—	—	10	Self	—
TM67	Recycle	Normal	Status	—	—	10	Self	—
TM68	Giga Impact	Normal	Physical	150	90	5	Normal	○
TM70	Flash	Normal	Status	—	100	20	Normal	—
TM73	Thunder Wave	Electric	Status	—	100	20	Normal	—
TM77	Psych Up	Normal	Status	—	—	10	Normal	—
TM78	Captivate	Normal	Status	—	100	20	2 Foes	—
TM82	Sleep Talk	Normal	Status	—	—	10	Depends	—
TM83	Natural Gift	Normal	Physical	—	100	15	Normal	—
TM85	Dream Eater	Psychic	Special	100	100	15	Normal	—
TM86	Grass Knot	Grass	Special	—	100	20	Normal	○
TM87	Swagger	Normal	Status	—	90	15	Normal	—
TM90	Substitute	Normal	Status	—	—	10	Self	—
TM92	Trick Room	Psychic	Status	—	—	5	All	—

No. 488 | Lunar Pokémon
Cresselia

 Psychic

- **HEIGHT:** 4'11"
- **WEIGHT:** 188.7 lbs.
- **ITEMS:** None

● SIZE COMPARISON

● FEMALE FORM

⊘ ABILITIES
● Levitate

⊘ STATS
HP	●●●●●
ATTACK	●●●●
DEFENSE	●●●●●
SP. ATTACK	●●●●
SP. DEFENSE	●●●●●
SPEED	●●●●

⊘ EGG GROUPS
No Egg has ever been discovered

⊘ PERFORMANCE
SPEED ★★★☆ STAMINA ★★★☆
POWER ★★★★☆ JUMP ★★★★☆
SKILL ★★★★

● MAIN WAYS TO OBTAIN

Pokémon HeartGold —

Pokémon SoulSilver —

Pokémon Diamond After you meet it at Fullmoon Island, it starts roaming the Sinnoh region

Pokémon Pearl After you meet it at Fullmoon Island, it starts roaming the Sinnoh region

Pokémon Platinum After you meet it at Fullmoon Island, it starts roaming the Sinnoh region

Pokémon HeartGold Those who sleep holding CRESSELIA's feather are assured of joyful dreams. It is said to represent the crescent moon.

Pokémon SoulSilver Those who sleep holding CRESSELIA's feather are assured of joyful dreams. It is said to represent the crescent moon.

⊘ EVOLUTION
Does not evolve

No. 489 | Sea Drifter Pokémon
Phione

Water

- **HEIGHT:** 1'04"
- **WEIGHT:** 6.8 lbs.
- **ITEMS:** None

● SIZE COMPARISON

● GENDER UNKNOWN

⊕ ABILITIES
● Hydration

⊕ STATS
HP	●●●
ATTACK	●●●
DEFENSE	●●●
SP. ATTACK	●●●
SP. DEFENSE	●●●●
SPEED	●●●●

⊕ EGG GROUPS
Water 1

Fairy

⊕ PERFORMANCE
SPEED ★★★★☆   STAMINA ★☆☆
POWER ★★☆   JUMP ★★☆
SKILL ★★★☆☆

● MAIN WAYS TO OBTAIN

Pokémon HeartGold — Leave Manaphy and Ditto together at the Pokémon Day Care, then find its Egg and hatch it*

Pokémon SoulSilver — Leave Manaphy and Ditto together at the Pokémon Day Care, then find its Egg and hatch it*

Pokémon Diamond — Leave Manaphy and Ditto together at the Pokémon Day Care, then find its Egg and hatch it*

Pokémon Pearl — Leave Manaphy and Ditto together at the Pokémon Day Care, then find its Egg and hatch it*

Pokémon Platinum — Leave Manaphy and Ditto together at the Pokémon Day Care, then find its Egg and hatch it*

Pokémon HeartGold — When the water warms, they inflate the flotation sac on their heads and drift languidly on the sea in packs.

Pokémon SoulSilver — When the water warms, they inflate the flotation sac on their heads and drift languidly on the sea in packs.

⊕ EVOLUTION

Does not evolve

● LEVEL-UP MOVES
Lv.	Name	Type	Kind	Pow.	Acc.	PP	Range	DA
1	Bubble	Water	Special	20	100	30	2 Foes	—
1	Water Sport	Water	Status	—	—	15	All	—
9	Charm	Normal	Status	—	100	20	Normal	—
16	Supersonic	Normal	Status	—	55	20	Normal	—
24	BubbleBeam	Water	Special	65	100	20	Normal	—
31	Acid Armor	Poison	Status	—	—	40	Self	—
39	Whirlpool	Water	Special	15	70	15	Normal	—
46	Water Pulse	Water	Special	60	100	20	Normal	—
54	Aqua Ring	Water	Status	—	—	20	Self	—
61	Dive	Water	Physical	80	100	10	Normal	○
69	Rain Dance	Water	Status	—	—	5	All	—

● MOVE MANIAC
Name	Type	Kind	Pow.	Acc.	PP	Range	DA

● BP MOVES
Name	Type	Kind	Pow.	Acc.	PP	Range	DA
Dive	Water	Physical	80	100	10	Normal	○
Icy Wind	Ice	Special	55	95	15	2 Foes	—
Knock Off	Dark	Physical	20	100	20	Normal	○
Snore	Normal	Special	40	100	15	Normal	—
Helping Hand	Normal	Status	—	—	20	1 Ally	—
Last Resort	Normal	Physical	130	100	5	Normal	○
Swift	Normal	Special	60	—	20	2 Foes	—
Uproar	Normal	Special	50	100	10	1 Random	—
Heal Bell	Normal	Status	—	—	5	All Allies	—
Mud-Slap	Ground	Special	20	100	10	Normal	—
AncientPower	Rock	Special	60	100	5	Normal	—
Signal Beam	Bug	Special	75	100	15	Normal	—
Bounce	Flying	Physical	85	85	5	Normal	○

● TM & HM MOVES
No.	Name	Type	Kind	Pow.	Acc.	PP	Range	DA
TM03	Water Pulse	Water	Special	60	100	20	Normal	—
TM06	Toxic	Poison	Status	—	85	10	Normal	—
TM07	Hail	Ice	Status	—	—	10	All	—
TM10	Hidden Power	Normal	Special	—	100	15	Normal	—
TM13	Ice Beam	Ice	Special	95	100	10	Normal	—
TM14	Blizzard	Ice	Special	120	70	5	2 Foes	—
TM17	Protect	Normal	Status	—	—	10	Self	—
TM18	Rain Dance	Water	Status	—	—	5	All	—
TM20	Safeguard	Normal	Status	—	—	25	2 Allies	—
TM21	Frustration	Normal	Physical	—	100	20	Normal	○
TM27	Return	Normal	Physical	—	100	20	Normal	○
TM32	Double Team	Normal	Status	—	—	15	Self	—
TM42	Facade	Normal	Physical	70	100	20	Normal	○
TM43	Secret Power	Normal	Physical	70	100	20	Normal	—
TM44	Rest	Psychic	Status	—	—	10	Self	—
TM55	Brine	Water	Special	65	100	10	Normal	—
TM56	Fling	Dark	Physical	—	100	10	Normal	—
TM58	Endure	Normal	Status	—	—	10	Self	—
TM77	Psych Up	Normal	Status	—	—	10	Self	—
TM82	Sleep Talk	Normal	Status	—	—	10	Depends	—
TM83	Natural Gift	Normal	Physical	—	100	15	Normal	—
TM86	Grass Knot	Grass	Special	—	100	20	Normal	○
TM87	Swagger	Normal	Status	—	90	15	Normal	—
TM89	U-turn	Bug	Physical	70	100	20	Normal	○
TM90	Substitute	Normal	Status	—	—	10	Self	—
HM03	Surf	Water	Special	95	100	15	2 Foes/1 Ally	—
HM05	Whirlpool	Water	Special	15	70	15	Normal	—
HM07	Waterfall	Water	Physical	80	100	15	Normal	○

*Manaphy is only available through special distribution events. Check Pokemon.com for the latest information on how to catch this Pokémon.

● LEVEL-UP MOVES

Lv.	Name	Type	Kind	Pow.	Acc.	PP	Range	DA
1	Tail Glow	Bug	Status	—	—	20	Self	—
1	Bubble	Water	Special	20	100	30	2 Foes	—
1	Water Sport	Water	Status	—	—	15	All	—
9	Charm	Normal	Status	—	100	20	Normal	—
16	Supersonic	Normal	Status	—	55	20	Normal	—
24	BubbleBeam	Water	Special	65	100	20	Normal	—
31	Acid Armor	Poison	Status	—	—	40	Self	—
39	Whirlpool	Water	Special	15	70	15	Normal	—
46	Water Pulse	Water	Special	60	100	20	Normal	—
54	Aqua Ring	Water	Status	—	—	20	Self	—
61	Dive	Water	Physical	80	100	10	Normal	○
69	Rain Dance	Water	Status	—	—	5	All	—
76	Heart Swap	Psychic	Status	—	—	10	Normal	—

● MOVE MANIAC

Name	Type	Kind	Pow.	Acc.	PP	Range	DA

● BP MOVES

Name	Type	Kind	Pow.	Acc.	PP	Range	DA
Dive	Water	Physical	80	100	10	Normal	○
Icy Wind	Ice	Special	55	95	15	2 Foes	—
Knock Off	Dark	Physical	20	100	20	Normal	○
Snore	Normal	Special	40	100	15	Normal	—
Helping Hand	Normal	Status	—	—	20	1 Ally	—
Last Resort	Normal	Physical	130	100	5	Normal	○
Swift	Normal	Special	60	—	20	2 Foes	—
Uproar	Normal	Special	50	100	10	1 Random	—
Heal Bell	Normal	Status	—	—	5	All Allies	—
Mud-Slap	Ground	Special	20	100	10	Normal	—
AncientPower	Rock	Special	60	100	5	Normal	—
Signal Beam	Bug	Special	75	100	15	Normal	—
Bounce	Flying	Physical	85	85	5	Normal	○

● TM & HM MOVES

No.	Name	Type	Kind	Pow.	Acc.	PP	Range	DA
TM03	Water Pulse	Water	Special	60	100	20	Normal	—
TM04	Calm Mind	Psychic	Status	—	—	20	Self	—
TM06	Toxic	Poison	Status	—	85	10	Normal	—
TM07	Hail	Ice	Status	—	—	10	All	—
TM10	Hidden Power	Normal	Special	—	100	15	Normal	—
TM13	Ice Beam	Ice	Special	95	100	10	Normal	—
TM14	Blizzard	Ice	Special	120	70	5	2 Foes	—
TM15	Hyper Beam	Normal	Special	150	90	5	Normal	—
TM16	Light Screen	Psychic	Status	—	—	30	2 Allies	—
TM17	Protect	Normal	Status	—	—	10	Self	—
TM18	Rain Dance	Water	Status	—	—	5	All	—
TM20	Safeguard	Normal	Status	—	—	25	2 Allies	—
TM21	Frustration	Normal	Physical	—	100	20	Normal	○
TM27	Return	Normal	Physical	—	100	20	Normal	○
TM29	Psychic	Psychic	Special	90	100	10	Normal	—
TM30	Shadow Ball	Ghost	Special	80	100	15	Normal	—
TM32	Double Team	Normal	Status	—	—	15	Self	—
TM33	Reflect	Psychic	Status	—	—	20	2 Allies	—
TM42	Facade	Normal	Physical	70	100	20	Normal	○
TM43	Secret Power	Normal	Physical	70	100	20	Normal	○
TM44	Rest	Psychic	Status	—	—	10	Self	—
TM48	Skill Swap	Psychic	Status	—	—	10	Normal	—
TM53	Energy Ball	Grass	Special	80	100	10	Normal	—
TM55	Brine	Water	Special	65	100	10	Normal	—
TM56	Fling	Dark	Physical	—	100	10	Normal	—
TM58	Endure	Normal	Status	—	—	10	Self	—
TM68	Giga Impact	Normal	Physical	150	90	5	Normal	○
TM70	Flash	Normal	Status	—	100	20	Normal	—
TM77	Psych Up	Normal	Status	—	—	10	Normal	—
TM82	Sleep Talk	Normal	Status	—	—	10	Depends	—
TM83	Natural Gift	Normal	Physical	—	100	15	Normal	—
TM86	Grass Knot	Grass	Special	—	100	20	Normal	○
TM87	Swagger	Normal	Status	—	90	15	Normal	—
TM89	U-turn	Bug	Physical	70	100	20	Normal	○
TM90	Substitute	Normal	Status	—	—	10	Self	—
HM03	Surf	Water	Special	95	100	15	2 Foes/1 Ally	—
HM05	Whirlpool	Water	Special	15	70	15	Normal	—
HM07	Waterfall	Water	Physical	80	100	15	Normal	○

Manaphy

Water

- **HEIGHT:** 1'00"
- **WEIGHT:** 3.1 lbs.
- **ITEMS:** None

● SIZE COMPARISON

● GENDER UNKNOWN

● ABILITIES
- Hydration

● STATS
HP ●●●●
ATTACK ●●●●
DEFENSE ●●●●
SP. ATTACK ●●●●
SP. DEFENSE ●●●●
SPEED ●●●●

● EGG GROUPS
Water 1
Fairy

● PERFORMANCE

SPEED ★★★☆ STAMINA ★★★☆
POWER ★★☆ JUMP ★★★
SKILL ★★★★☆

● MAIN WAYS TO OBTAIN

Pokémon HeartGold
Only obtainable through special distribution events: check Pokemon.com for the latest updates on how to catch this Pokémon

Pokémon SoulSilver
Only obtainable through special distribution events: check Pokemon.com for the latest updates on how to catch this Pokémon

Pokémon Diamond
Only obtainable through special distribution events: check Pokemon.com for the latest updates on how to catch this Pokémon

Pokémon Pearl
Only obtainable through special distribution events: check Pokemon.com for the latest updates on how to catch this Pokémon

Pokémon Platinum
Only obtainable through special distribution events: check Pokemon.com for the latest updates on how to catch this Pokémon

Pokémon HeartGold
It starts its life with a wondrous power that permits it to bond with any kind of Pokémon.

Pokémon SoulSilver
It starts its life with a wondrous power that permits it to bond with any kind of Pokémon.

● EVOLUTION

Does not evolve

No. 491 | Pitch-Black Pokémon
Darkrai

`Dark`

- **HEIGHT:** 4'11"
- **WEIGHT:** 111.3 lbs.
- **ITEMS:** None

● **SIZE COMPARISON**

● **GENDER UNKNOWN**

⊙ ABILITIES
- Bad Dreams

⊙ EGG GROUPS
No Egg has ever been discovered

⊙ STATS
HP	●●●
ATTACK	●●●●
DEFENSE	●●●●
SP. ATTACK	●●●●●●
SP. DEFENSE	●●●●●
SPEED	●●●●●●

⊙ PERFORMANCE
SPEED ★★★☆	STAMINA ★★★
POWER ★★☆☆	JUMP ★★★☆☆
SKILL ★★★★☆	

● MAIN WAYS TO OBTAIN

Pokémon HeartGold	—
Pokémon SoulSilver	—
Pokémon Diamond	—
Pokémon Pearl	—
Pokémon Platinum	Only obtainable through special distribution events: check Pokemon.com for the latest updates on how to catch this Pokémon

Pokémon HeartGold	Pokémon SoulSilver
It chases people and Pokémon from its territory by causing them to experience deep, nightmarish slumbers.	It chases people and Pokémon from its territory by causing them to experience deep, nightmarish slumbers.

⊙ EVOLUTION
Does not evolve

● LEVEL-UP MOVES
Lv.	Name	Type	Kind	Pow.	Acc.	PP	Range	DA
1	Ominous Wind	Ghost	Special	60	100	5	Normal	—
1	Disable	Normal	Status	—	80	20	Normal	—
11	Quick Attack	Normal	Physical	40	100	30	Normal	○
20	Hypnosis	Psychic	Status	—	60	20	Normal	—
29	Faint Attack	Dark	Physical	60	—	20	Normal	○
38	Nightmare	Ghost	Status	—	100	15	Normal	—
47	Double Team	Normal	Status	—	—	15	Self	—
57	Haze	Ice	Status	—	—	30	All	—
66	Dark Void	Dark	Status	—	80	10	2 Foes	—
75	Nasty Plot	Dark	Status	—	—	10	Self	—
84	Dream Eater	Psychic	Special	100	100	15	Normal	—
93	Dark Pulse	Dark	Special	80	100	15	Normal	—

● MOVE MANIAC
Name	Type	Kind	Pow.	Acc.	PP	Range	DA
Headbutt	Normal	Physical	70	100	15	Normal	○

● BP MOVES
Name	Type	Kind	Pow.	Acc.	PP	Range	DA
Icy Wind	Ice	Special	55	95	15	2 Foes	—
Ominous Wind	Ghost	Special	60	100	5	Normal	—
Trick	Psychic	Status	—	100	10	Normal	—
Knock Off	Dark	Physical	20	100	20	Normal	○
Sucker Punch	Dark	Physical	80	100	5	Normal	○
Snore	Normal	Special	40	100	15	Normal	—
Spite	Ghost	Status	—	100	10	Normal	—
Last Resort	Normal	Physical	130	100	5	Normal	○
Swift	Normal	Special	60	—	20	2 Foes	—
Mud-Slap	Ground	Special	20	100	10	Normal	—

● TM & HM MOVES
No.	Name	Type	Kind	Pow.	Acc.	PP	Range	DA
TM01	Focus Punch	Fighting	Physical	150	100	20	Normal	○
TM04	Calm Mind	Psychic	Status	—	—	20	Self	—
TM06	Toxic	Poison	Status	—	85	10	Normal	—
TM10	Hidden Power	Normal	Special	—	100	15	Normal	—
TM11	Sunny Day	Fire	Status	—	—	5	All	—
TM12	Taunt	Dark	Status	—	100	20	Normal	—
TM13	Ice Beam	Ice	Special	95	100	10	Normal	—
TM14	Blizzard	Ice	Special	120	70	5	2 Foes	—
TM15	Hyper Beam	Normal	Special	150	90	5	Normal	—
TM17	Protect	Normal	Status	—	—	10	Self	—
TM18	Rain Dance	Water	Status	—	—	5	All	—
TM21	Frustration	Normal	Physical	—	100	20	Normal	○
TM24	Thunderbolt	Electric	Special	95	100	15	Normal	—
TM25	Thunder	Electric	Special	120	70	10	Normal	—
TM27	Return	Normal	Physical	—	100	20	Normal	○
TM29	Psychic	Psychic	Special	90	100	10	Normal	—
TM30	Shadow Ball	Ghost	Special	80	100	15	Normal	—
TM31	Brick Break	Fighting	Physical	75	100	15	Normal	○
TM32	Double Team	Normal	Status	—	—	15	Self	—
TM34	Shock Wave	Electric	Special	60	—	20	Normal	—
TM36	Sludge Bomb	Poison	Special	90	100	10	Normal	—
TM39	Rock Tomb	Rock	Physical	50	80	10	Normal	—
TM40	Aerial Ace	Flying	Physical	60	—	20	Normal	○
TM41	Torment	Dark	Status	—	100	15	Normal	—
TM42	Facade	Normal	Physical	70	100	20	Normal	○
TM43	Secret Power	Normal	Physical	70	100	20	Normal	—
TM44	Rest	Psychic	Status	—	—	10	Self	—
TM46	Thief	Dark	Physical	40	100	10	Normal	○
TM49	Snatch	Dark	Status	—	—	10	Depends	—
TM52	Focus Blast	Fighting	Special	120	70	5	Normal	—
TM56	Fling	Dark	Physical	—	100	10	Normal	○
TM57	Charge Beam	Electric	Special	50	90	10	Normal	—
TM58	Endure	Normal	Status	—	—	10	Self	—
TM60	Drain Punch	Fighting	Physical	60	100	5	Normal	○
TM61	Will-O-Wisp	Fire	Status	—	75	15	Normal	—
TM63	Embargo	Dark	Status	—	100	15	Normal	—
TM65	Shadow Claw	Ghost	Physical	70	100	15	Normal	○
TM66	Payback	Dark	Physical	50	100	10	Normal	○
TM68	Giga Impact	Normal	Physical	150	90	5	Normal	○
TM70	Flash	Normal	Status	—	100	20	Normal	—
TM73	Thunder Wave	Electric	Status	—	100	20	Normal	—
TM75	Swords Dance	Normal	Status	—	—	30	Self	—
TM77	Psych Up	Normal	Status	—	—	10	Normal	—
TM79	Dark Pulse	Dark	Special	80	100	15	Normal	—
TM80	Rock Slide	Rock	Physical	75	90	10	2 Foes	—
TM81	X-Scissor	Bug	Physical	80	100	15	Normal	○
TM82	Sleep Talk	Normal	Status	—	—	10	Depends	—
TM83	Natural Gift	Normal	Physical	—	100	15	Normal	—
TM84	Poison Jab	Poison	Physical	80	100	20	Normal	○
TM85	Dream Eater	Psychic	Special	100	100	15	Normal	—
TM87	Swagger	Normal	Status	—	90	15	Normal	—
TM90	Substitute	Normal	Status	—	—	10	Self	—
HM01	Cut	Normal	Physical	50	95	30	Normal	○
HM04	Strength	Normal	Physical	80	100	15	Normal	○
HM06	Rock Smash	Fighting	Physical	40	100	15	Normal	○
HM08	Rock Climb	Normal	Physical	90	85	20	Normal	○

● LEVEL-UP MOVES

Lv.	Name	Type	Kind	Pow.	Acc.	PP	Range	DA
1	Growth	Normal	Status	—	—	40	Self	—
10	Magical Leaf	Grass	Special	60	—	20	Normal	—
19	Leech Seed	Grass	Status	—	90	10	Normal	—
28	Synthesis	Grass	Status	—	—	5	Self	—
37	Sweet Scent	Normal	Status	—	100	20	2 Foes	—
46	Natural Gift	Normal	Physical	—	100	15	Normal	—
55	Worry Seed	Grass	Status	—	100	10	Normal	—
64	Aromatherapy	Grass	Status	—	—	5	All Allies	—
73	Energy Ball	Grass	Special	80	100	10	Normal	—
82	Sweet Kiss	Normal	Status	—	75	10	Normal	—
91	Healing Wish	Psychic	Status	—	—	10	Self	—
100	Seed Flare	Grass	Special	120	85	5	Normal	—

● MOVE MANIAC

Name	Type	Kind	Pow.	Acc.	PP	Range	DA
Headbutt	Normal	Physical	70	100	15	Normal	○

● BP MOVES

Name	Type	Kind	Pow.	Acc.	PP	Range	DA
Zen Headbutt	Psychic	Physical	80	90	15	Normal	○
Snore	Normal	Special	40	100	15	Normal	—
Synthesis	Grass	Status	—	—	5	Self	—
Last Resort	Normal	Physical	130	100	5	Normal	○
Swift	Normal	Special	60	—	20	2 Foes	—
Worry Seed	Grass	Status	—	100	10	Normal	—
Mud-Slap	Ground	Special	20	100	10	Normal	—
Endeavor	Normal	Physical	—	100	5	Normal	○
Earth Power	Ground	Special	90	100	10	Normal	—
Seed Bomb	Grass	Physical	80	100	15	Normal	—

● TM & HM MOVES

No.	Name	Type	Kind	Pow.	Acc.	PP	Range	DA
TM06	Toxic	Poison	Status	—	85	10	Normal	—
TM09	Bullet Seed	Grass	Physical	10	100	30	Normal	—
TM10	Hidden Power	Normal	Special	—	100	15	Normal	—
TM11	Sunny Day	Fire	Status	—	—	5	All	—
TM15	Hyper Beam	Normal	Special	150	90	5	Normal	—
TM17	Protect	Normal	Status	—	—	10	Self	—
TM19	Giga Drain	Grass	Special	60	100	10	Normal	—
TM20	Safeguard	Normal	Status	—	—	25	2 Allies	—
TM21	Frustration	Normal	Physical	—	100	20	Normal	○
TM22	SolarBeam	Grass	Special	120	100	10	Normal	—
TM27	Return	Normal	Physical	—	100	20	Normal	○
TM29	Psychic	Psychic	Special	90	100	10	Normal	—
TM32	Double Team	Normal	Status	—	—	15	Self	—
TM42	Facade	Normal	Physical	70	100	20	Normal	○
TM43	Secret Power	Normal	Physical	70	100	20	Normal	—
TM44	Rest	Psychic	Status	—	—	10	Self	—
TM53	Energy Ball	Grass	Special	80	100	10	Normal	—
TM58	Endure	Normal	Status	—	—	10	Self	—
TM68	Giga Impact	Normal	Physical	150	90	5	Normal	○
TM70	Flash	Normal	Status	—	100	20	Normal	—
TM75	Swords Dance	Normal	Status	—	—	30	Self	—
TM77	Psych Up	Normal	Status	—	—	10	Normal	—
TM82	Sleep Talk	Normal	Status	—	—	10	Depends	—
TM83	Natural Gift	Normal	Physical	—	100	15	Normal	—
TM86	Grass Knot	Grass	Special	—	100	20	Normal	○
TM87	Swagger	Normal	Status	—	90	15	Normal	—
TM90	Substitute	Normal	Status	—	—	10	Self	—

● No. 492 | Gratitude Pokémon

Shaymin (Land Forme)

Grass

- **HEIGHT:** 0'08"
- **WEIGHT:** 4.6 lbs.
- **ITEMS:** None

● SIZE COMPARISON

● GENDER UNKNOWN

⊙ ABILITIES
● Natural Cure

⊙ STATS
- HP ●●●●
- ATTACK ●●●●
- DEFENSE ●●●●
- SP. ATTACK ●●●●
- SP. DEFENSE ●●●●
- SPEED ●●●●

⊙ EGG GROUPS
No Egg has ever been discovered

⊙ PERFORMANCE
SPEED ★★★☆	STAMINA ★★★
POWER ★★☆☆	JUMP ★★★☆☆
SKILL ★★★★☆	

● MAIN WAYS TO OBTAIN

Pokémon HeartGold —

Pokémon SoulSilver —

Pokémon Diamond —

Pokémon Pearl —

Pokémon Platinum — Only obtainable through special distribution events: check Pokemon.com for the latest updates on how to catch this Pokémon

Pokémon HeartGold
The blooming of Gracidea flowers confers the power of flight upon it. Feelings of gratitude are the message it delivers.

Pokémon SoulSilver
The blooming of Gracidea flowers confers the power of flight upon it. Feelings of gratitude are the message it delivers.

⊙ EVOLUTION
Does not evolve

No. 492 | Gratitude Pokémon
Shaymin (Sky Forme)

Grass　Flying

- **HEIGHT:** 1'04"
- **WEIGHT:** 11.5 lbs.
- **ITEMS:** None

● GENDER UNKNOWN

ABILITIES
- Serene Grace

STATS
HP ●●●●
ATTACK ●●●●
DEFENSE ●●●
SP. ATTACK ●●●●
SP. DEFENSE ●●●
SPEED ●●●●●●

EGG GROUPS
No Egg has ever been discovered

PERFORMANCE
SPEED ★★★☆☆　STAMINA ★★★
POWER ★★★★　JUMP ★★★★★
SKILL ★★★☆

MAIN WAYS TO OBTAIN

Pokémon HeartGold	Use Gracidea flower on Shaymin (Land Forme)*
Pokémon SoulSilver	Use Gracidea flower on Shaymin (Land Forme)*
Pokémon Diamond	Use Gracidea flower on Shaymin (Land Forme)*
Pokémon Pearl	Use Gracidea flower on Shaymin (Land Forme)*
Pokémon Platinum	Use Gracidea flower on Shaymin (Land Forme)*

| Pokémon HeartGold | Pokémon SoulSilver |
| The blooming of Gracidea flowers confers the power of flight upon it. Feelings of gratitude are the message it delivers. | The blooming of Gracidea flowers confers the power of flight upon it. Feelings of gratitude are the message it delivers. |

EVOLUTION
Does not evolve

● LEVEL-UP MOVES

Lv.	Name	Type	Kind	Pow.	Acc.	PP	Range	DA
1	Growth	Normal	Status	—	—	40	Self	—
10	Magical Leaf	Grass	Special	60	—	20	Normal	—
19	Leech Seed	Grass	Status	—	90	10	Normal	—
28	Quick Attack	Normal	Physical	40	100	30	Normal	○
37	Sweet Scent	Normal	Status	—	100	20	2 Foes	—
46	Natural Gift	Normal	Physical	—	100	15	Normal	—
55	Worry Seed	Grass	Status	—	100	10	Normal	—
64	Air Slash	Flying	Special	75	95	20	Normal	—
73	Energy Ball	Grass	Special	80	100	10	Normal	—
82	Sweet Kiss	Normal	Status	—	75	10	Normal	—
91	Leaf Storm	Grass	Special	140	90	5	Normal	—
100	Seed Flare	Grass	Special	120	85	5	Normal	—

● MOVE MANIAC

Name	Type	Kind	Pow.	Acc.	PP	Range	DA
Headbutt	Normal	Physical	70	100	15	Normal	○

● BP MOVES

Name	Type	Kind	Pow.	Acc.	PP	Range	DA
Ominous Wind	Ghost	Special	60	100	5	Normal	—
Air Cutter	Flying	Special	55	95	25	2 Foes	—
Zen Headbutt	Psychic	Physical	80	90	15	Normal	○
Snore	Normal	Special	40	100	15	Normal	—
Synthesis	Grass	Status	—	—	5	Self	—
Last Resort	Normal	Physical	130	100	5	Normal	○
Swift	Normal	Special	60	—	20	2 Foes	—
Tailwind	Flying	Status	—	—	30	2 Allies	—
Worry Seed	Grass	Status	—	100	10	Normal	—
Mud-Slap	Ground	Special	20	100	10	Normal	—
Seed Bomb	Grass	Physical	80	100	15	Normal	—

● TM & HM MOVES

No.	Name	Type	Kind	Pow.	Acc.	PP	Range	DA
TM06	Toxic	Poison	Status	—	85	10	Normal	—
TM09	Bullet Seed	Grass	Physical	10	100	30	Normal	—
TM10	Hidden Power	Normal	Special	—	100	15	Normal	—
TM11	Sunny Day	Fire	Status	—	—	5	All	—
TM15	Hyper Beam	Normal	Special	150	90	5	Normal	—
TM17	Protect	Normal	Status	—	—	10	Self	—
TM19	Giga Drain	Grass	Special	60	100	10	Normal	—
TM20	Safeguard	Normal	Status	—	—	25	2 Allies	—
TM21	Frustration	Normal	Physical	—	100	20	Normal	○
TM22	SolarBeam	Grass	Special	120	100	10	Normal	—
TM27	Return	Normal	Physical	—	100	20	Normal	○
TM29	Psychic	Psychic	Special	90	100	10	Normal	—
TM32	Double Team	Normal	Status	—	—	15	Self	—
TM42	Facade	Normal	Physical	70	100	20	Normal	○
TM43	Secret Power	Normal	Physical	70	100	20	Normal	—
TM44	Rest	Psychic	Status	—	—	10	Self	—
TM53	Energy Ball	Grass	Special	80	100	10	Normal	—
TM58	Endure	Normal	Status	—	—	10	Self	—
TM68	Giga Impact	Normal	Physical	150	90	5	Normal	○
TM70	Flash	Normal	Status	—	100	20	Normal	—
TM75	Swords Dance	Normal	Status	—	—	30	Self	—
TM77	Psych Up	Normal	Status	—	—	10	Normal	—
TM82	Sleep Talk	Normal	Status	—	—	10	Depends	—
TM83	Natural Gift	Normal	Physical	—	100	15	Normal	—
TM86	Grass Knot	Grass	Special	—	100	20	Normal	○
TM87	Swagger	Normal	Status	—	90	15	Normal	—
TM90	Substitute	Normal	Status	—	—	10	Self	—

*Shaymin is only available through special distribution events. Check Pokemon.com for the latest information on how to catch this Pokémon.

MULTITYPE

The type of Arceus changes depending on the type of Plate it holds. There are 16 Plates altogether, and you can get one a day when you talk to the Captain of the Fast Ship S.S. Aqua. (You won't get a Plate on your first visit to the ship.)

 ● NORMAL

 ● FIRE

 ● WATER

 ● GRASS

 ● ELECTRIC

 ● ICE

 ● FIGHTING

 ● POISON

 ● GROUND

 ● FLYING

 ● PSYCHIC

 ● BUG

 ● ROCK

 ● GHOST

 ● DRAGON

 ● DARK

 ● STEEL

● Arceus

No. 493 | Alpha Pokémon
Normal

- HEIGHT: 10'06"
- WEIGHT: 705.5 lbs.
- ITEMS: None

● SIZE COMPARISON

● GENDER UNKNOWN

ABILITIES
● Multitype

STATS
HP ●●●●●
ATTACK ●●●●●
DEFENSE ●●●●●
SP. ATTACK ●●●●●
SP. DEFENSE ●●●●●
SPEED ●●●●●

EGG GROUPS
No Egg has ever been discovered

PERFORMANCE

■ **Normal, Fire, Ground, Rock**
SPEED ★★★★☆   STAMINA ★★★★
POWER ★★★★★   JUMP ★★★★☆
SKILL ★★★★☆

■ **Water, Electric, Psychic**
SPEED ★★★★★   STAMINA ★★★★☆
POWER ★★★★☆   JUMP ★★★★☆
SKILL ★★★★★

■ **Grass**
SPEED ★★★★☆   STAMINA ★★★★
POWER ★★★★☆   JUMP ★★★★★
SKILL ★★★★☆

■ **Ice**
SPEED ★★★★★   STAMINA ★★★★☆
POWER ★★★★★   JUMP ★★★★☆
SKILL ★★★★☆

■ **Fighting, Dark**
SPEED ★★★★☆   STAMINA ★★★★☆
POWER ★★★★★   JUMP ★★★★☆
SKILL ★★★★★

■ **Poison, Steel**
SPEED ★★★★☆   STAMINA ★★★★★
POWER ★★★★☆   JUMP ★★★★☆
SKILL ★★★★★

■ **Flying, Bug**
SPEED ★★★★☆   STAMINA ★★★★☆
POWER ★★★★☆   JUMP ★★★★★
SKILL ★★★★☆

■ **Ghost**
SPEED ★★★★☆   STAMINA ★★★★☆
POWER ★★★★☆   JUMP ★★★★★
SKILL ★★★★★

■ **Dragon**
SPEED ★★★☆☆   STAMINA ★★★★★
POWER ★★★★☆   JUMP ★★★★★
SKILL ★★★★★

● LEVEL-UP MOVES

Lv.	Name	Type	Kind	Pow.	Acc.	PP	Range	DA
1	Seismic Toss	Fighting	Physical	—	100	20	Normal	○
1	Cosmic Power	Psychic	Status	—	—	20	Self	—
1	Natural Gift	Normal	Physical	—	100	15	Normal	—
1	Punishment	Dark	Physical	—	100	5	Normal	○
10	Gravity	Psychic	Status	—	—	5	All	—
20	Earth Power	Ground	Special	90	100	10	Normal	—
30	Hyper Voice	Normal	Special	90	100	10	2 Foes	—
40	ExtremeSpeed	Normal	Physical	80	100	5	Normal	○
50	Refresh	Normal	Status	—	—	20	Self	—
60	Future Sight	Psychic	Special	80	90	15	Normal	—
70	Recover	Normal	Status	—	—	10	Self	—
80	Hyper Beam	Normal	Special	150	90	5	Normal	—
90	Perish Song	Normal	Status	—	—	5	All	—
100	Judgment	Normal	Special	100	100	10	Normal	—

● MOVE MANIAC

Name	Type	Kind	Pow.	Acc.	PP	Range	DA
Headbutt	Normal	Physical	70	100	15	Normal	○
Draco Meteor*	Dragon	Special	140	90	5	Normal	—

*Can be taught if Arceus holds the Draco Plate and has high enough friendship

See next page for the TM & HM MOVES and MAIN WAYS TO OBTAIN ▶▶▶

● MAIN WAYS TO OBTAIN

Pokémon HeartGold —

Pokémon SoulSilver —

Pokémon Diamond — Arceus is only available through special distribution events. Check Pokemon.com for the latest information on how to catch this Pokémon.

Pokémon Pearl — Arceus is only available through special distribution events. Check Pokemon.com for the latest information on how to catch this Pokémon.

Pokémon Platinum — Arceus is only available through special distribution events. Check Pokemon.com for the latest information on how to catch this Pokémon.

Pokémon HeartGold	Pokémon SoulSilver
According to the legends of Sinnoh, this Pokémon emerged from an egg and shaped all there is in this world.	According to the legends of Sinnoh, this Pokémon emerged from an egg and shaped all there is in this world.

⊕ EVOLUTION

Does not evolve

● BP MOVES

Name	Type	Kind	Pow.	Acc.	PP	Range	DA
Dive	Water	Physical	80	100	10	Normal	○
Fury Cutter	Bug	Physical	10	95	20	Normal	○
Icy Wind	Ice	Special	55	95	15	2 Foes	—
Ominous Wind	Ghost	Special	60	100	5	Normal	—
Zen Headbutt	Psychic	Physical	80	90	15	Normal	—
Trick	Psychic	Status	—	100	10	Normal	—
Snore	Normal	Special	40	100	15	Normal	—
Last Resort	Normal	Physical	130	100	5	Normal	—
Swift	Normal	Special	60	—	20	2 Foes	—
Tailwind	Flying	Status	—	—	30	2 Allies	—
Gravity	Psychic	Status	—	—	5	All	—
Magic Coat	Psychic	Status	—	—	15	Self	—
Mud-Slap	Ground	Special	20	100	10	Normal	—
Iron Head	Steel	Physical	80	100	15	Normal	○
Aqua Tail	Water	Physical	90	90	10	Normal	○
Outrage	Dragon	Physical	120	100	15	1 Random	○
AncientPower	Rock	Special	60	100	5	Normal	—
Signal Beam	Bug	Special	75	100	15	Normal	—
Earth Power	Ground	Special	90	100	10	Normal	—
Twister	Dragon	Special	40	100	20	2 Foes	—
Iron Defense	Steel	Status	—	—	15	Self	—
Heat Wave	Fire	Special	100	90	10	2 Foes	—

● TM & HM MOVES

No.	Name	Type	Kind	Pow.	Acc.	PP	Range	DA
TM02	Dragon Claw	Dragon	Physical	80	100	15	Normal	—
TM03	Water Pulse	Water	Special	60	100	20	Normal	—
TM04	Calm Mind	Psychic	Status	—	—	20	Self	—
TM05	Roar	Normal	Status	—	100	20	Normal	—
TM06	Toxic	Poison	Status	—	85	10	Normal	—
TM07	Hail	Ice	Status	—	—	10	All	—
TM09	Bullet Seed	Grass	Physical	10	100	30	Normal	—
TM10	Hidden Power	Normal	Special	—	100	15	Normal	—
TM11	Sunny Day	Fire	Status	—	—	5	All	—
TM13	Ice Beam	Ice	Special	95	100	10	Normal	—
TM14	Blizzard	Ice	Special	120	70	5	2 Foes	—
TM15	Hyper Beam	Normal	Special	150	90	5	Normal	—
TM16	Light Screen	Psychic	Status	—	—	30	2 Allies	—
TM17	Protect	Normal	Status	—	—	10	Self	—
TM18	Rain Dance	Water	Status	—	—	5	All	—
TM19	Giga Drain	Grass	Special	60	100	10	Normal	—
TM20	Safeguard	Normal	Status	—	—	25	2 Allies	—
TM21	Frustration	Normal	Physical	—	100	20	Normal	○
TM22	SolarBeam	Grass	Special	120	100	10	Normal	—
TM23	Iron Tail	Steel	Physical	100	75	15	Normal	○
TM24	Thunderbolt	Electric	Special	95	100	15	Normal	—
TM25	Thunder	Electric	Special	120	70	10	Normal	—
TM26	Earthquake	Ground	Physical	100	100	10	2 Foes/1 Ally	—
TM27	Return	Normal	Physical	—	100	20	Normal	○
TM29	Psychic	Psychic	Special	90	100	10	Normal	—
TM30	Shadow Ball	Ghost	Special	80	100	15	Normal	—
TM31	Brick Break	Fighting	Physical	75	100	15	Normal	○
TM32	Double Team	Normal	Status	—	—	15	Self	—
TM33	Reflect	Psychic	Status	—	—	20	2 Allies	—
TM34	Shock Wave	Electric	Special	60	—	20	Normal	—
TM35	Flamethrower	Fire	Special	95	100	15	Normal	—
TM36	Sludge Bomb	Poison	Special	90	100	10	Normal	—
TM37	Sandstorm	Rock	Status	—	—	10	All	—
TM38	Fire Blast	Fire	Special	120	85	5	Normal	—
TM39	Rock Tomb	Rock	Physical	50	80	10	Normal	—
TM40	Aerial Ace	Flying	Physical	60	—	20	Normal	○
TM42	Facade	Normal	Physical	70	100	20	Normal	○
TM43	Secret Power	Normal	Physical	70	100	20	Normal	—
TM44	Rest	Psychic	Status	—	—	10	Self	—
TM50	Overheat	Fire	Special	140	90	5	Normal	—
TM52	Focus Blast	Fighting	Special	120	70	5	Normal	—
TM53	Energy Ball	Grass	Special	80	100	10	Normal	—
TM55	Brine	Water	Special	65	100	10	Normal	—
TM57	Charge Beam	Electric	Special	50	90	10	Normal	—
TM58	Endure	Normal	Status	—	—	10	Self	—
TM59	Dragon Pulse	Dragon	Special	90	100	10	Normal	—
TM61	Will-O-Wisp	Fire	Status	—	75	15	Normal	—
TM62	Silver Wind	Bug	Special	60	100	5	Normal	—
TM65	Shadow Claw	Ghost	Physical	70	100	15	Normal	○
TM66	Payback	Dark	Physical	50	100	10	Normal	○
TM67	Recycle	Normal	Status	—	—	10	Self	—
TM68	Giga Impact	Normal	Physical	150	90	5	Normal	○
TM70	Flash	Normal	Status	—	100	20	Normal	—
TM71	Stone Edge	Rock	Physical	100	80	5	Normal	—
TM72	Avalanche	Ice	Physical	60	100	10	Normal	—
TM73	Thunder Wave	Electric	Status	—	100	20	Normal	—
TM75	Swords Dance	Normal	Status	—	—	30	Self	—
TM76	Stealth Rock	Rock	Status	—	—	20	2 Foes	—
TM77	Psych Up	Normal	Status	—	—	10	Normal	—
TM79	Dark Pulse	Dark	Special	80	100	15	Normal	—
TM80	Rock Slide	Rock	Physical	75	90	10	2 Foes	—
TM81	X-Scissor	Bug	Physical	80	100	15	Normal	○
TM82	Sleep Talk	Normal	Status	—	—	10	Depends	○
TM83	Natural Gift	Normal	Physical	—	100	15	Normal	—
TM84	Poison Jab	Poison	Physical	80	100	20	Normal	○
TM85	Dream Eater	Psychic	Special	100	100	15	Normal	—
TM86	Grass Knot	Grass	Special	—	100	20	Normal	○
TM87	Swagger	Normal	Status	—	90	15	Normal	—
TM90	Substitute	Normal	Status	—	—	10	Self	—
TM91	Flash Cannon	Steel	Special	80	100	10	Normal	—
TM92	Trick Room	Psychic	Status	—	—	5	All	—
HM01	Cut	Normal	Physical	50	95	30	Normal	○
HM02	Fly	Flying	Physical	90	95	15	Normal	○
HM03	Surf	Water	Special	95	1	15	2 Foes/1 Ally	—
HM04	Strength	Normal	Physical	80	100	15	Normal	○
HM05	Whirlpool	Water	Special	15	70	15	Normal	—
HM06	Rock Smash	Fighting	Physical	40	100	15	Normal	○
HM07	Waterfall	Water	Physical	80	100	15	Normal	○
HM08	Rock Climb	Normal	Physical	90	85	20	Normal	○

Pokémon Moves

Move	Effect
Absorb	Restores HP equal to half of damage inflicted on the target.
Acid	There is a 10% chance of lowering the target's Sp. Defense by 1. The attack power decreases in Double Battles.
Acid Armor	Raises user's Defense by 2.
Acupressure	Raises a random stat by 2.
Aerial Ace	Always strikes the target.
Aeroblast	High critical-hit rate.
Agility	Raises user's Speed by 2.
Air Cutter	High critical-hit rate. The attack is weaker in Double Battles.
Air Slash	This move has a 30% chance of making the target flinch (target cannot use moves for that turn).
Amnesia	Raises user's Sp. Defense by 2.
AncientPower	Has a 10% chance of raising Attack, Defense, Sp. Attack, Sp. Defense, and Speed by 1.
Aqua Jet	Move always attacks first (if both opponents use this move, the one with the higher Speed goes first).
Aqua Ring	Gradually restores HP with every turn.
Aqua Tail	Regular attack.
Arm Thrust	Attacks 2–5 times in a row in a single turn.
Aromatherapy	Heals status ailments of all ally Pokémon in your party.
Assist	Uses a random move from one of the non-participating Pokémon in your party.
Assurance	Does twice the damage if the target has already taken damage that turn.
Astonish	This move has a 30% chance of making the target flinch (target cannot use moves for that turn).
Attack Order	High critical hit rate.
Attract	This move has a 50% chance of making the target unable to attack. Only works if the user and target are different genders.
Aura Sphere	Always strikes the target.
Aurora Beam	This move has a 10% chance of lowering the target's Attack by 1.
Avalanche	This move deals double the damage if the user has already received damage from the target that turn.
Barrage	Attacks 2–5 times in a row in a single turn.
Barrier	Raises user's Defense by 2.
Baton Pass	Swaps out with an ally Pokémon, passing along any stat changes.
Beat Up	Attacks according to the number of Pokémon in your party, including the user, but not Pokémon that have fainted.
Belly Drum	Halves the user's HP, but raises its Attack to the maximum.
Bide	Counter-inflicts twice the damage received in the next 2 turns.
Bind	Inflicts damage over 2–5 turns. Target cannot escape during that time.
Bite	This move has a 30% chance of making the target flinch (target cannot use moves for that turn).
Blast Burn	Cannot move on the next turn. If the target is afflicted with the Frozen condition, this move melts the ice.
Blaze Kick	This move has a 10% chance of inflicting the Burned condition on the target. If the target is afflicted with the Frozen condition, this move melts the ice.
Blizzard	This move has a 10% chance of inflicting the Frozen condition on the target. The attack power decreases in Double Battles.
Block	This move prevents the target from escaping. If used in a Trainer battle, the Trainer cannot switch Pokémon.
Body Slam	This move has a 30% chance of inflicting the Paralysis condition on the target.

Bone Club	This move has a 10% chance of making the target flinch (target cannot use moves for that turn).
Bone Rush	Attacks 2–5 times in a row in a single turn.
Bonemerang	Attacks twice in a row in a single turn.
Bounce	Flies into the air on first turn, then attacks on the second. This move has a 30% chance of inflicting the Paralysis condition on the target.
Brave Bird	User takes 1/3 of the damage inflicted on the target.
Brick Break	This move breaks through Reflect and Light Screen.
Brine	This move delivers twice the damage if the target has less than half its maximum HP.
Bubble	This move has a 10% chance of lowering the target's Speed. The attack is weaker in Double Battles.
BubbleBeam	This move has a 10% chance of lowering the target's Speed by 1.
Bug Bite	Eats and uses the effects of opponent's Berry in battle.
Bug Buzz	This move has a 10% chance of lowering the target's Sp. Defense by 1.
Bulk Up	Raises the user's Attack and Defense by 1.
Bullet Punch	This move always attacks first. (If both opponents use this move, the one with the higher Speed goes first.)
Bullet Seed	Attacks 2–5 times in a single turn.
Calm Mind	Raises the user's Sp. Attack and Sp. Defense by 1.
Camouflage	Changes user's type in accordance with the terrain. Tall grass/water puddle: Grass type. Sandy ground/marsh: Ground type. Rocky ground/cave: Rock type. Water surface: Water type. Snowy/icy ground: Ice type. Floor: Normal Type.
Captivate	Lowers Sp. Attack by 2. Only works if the user and target are opposite genders.
Charge	Doubles attack power of an Electric-type move used on following turn. Raises user's Sp. Defense by 1.
Charge Beam	This move has a 70% chance of raising the user's Sp. Attack by 1.
Charm	Lowers the target's Attack by 2.
Chatter	May Confuse the target—likelihood depends on the volume of the sound you recorded (Chatot only).
Clamp	Inflicts damage for 2–5 turns. Target cannot escape during that time.
Close Combat	Lowers user's Defense and Sp. Defense by 1.
Comet Punch	Attacks 2–5 times in a single turn.
Confuse Ray	Inflicts the Confused condition on the target.
Confusion	This move has a 10% chance of inflicting the Confused condition on the target.
Constrict	This move has a 10% chance of lowering the target's Speed by 1.
Conversion	Changes user's type to that of one of its moves.
Conversion 2	Changes user's type to type that is strong against foe's last-used move.
Copycat	Uses the last move executed.
Cosmic Power	Raises user's Defense and Sp. Defense by 1.
Cotton Spore	Lowers the target's Speed by 2.
Counter	If user is attacked physically, this move counter-inflicts twice the damage. Always strikes last.
Covet	If the target has an item and user has none, the user steals the target's item.
Crabhammer	High critical-hit rate.
Cross Chop	High critical-hit rate.
Cross Poison	High critical-hit rate. This move has a 10% chance of inflicting the Poison condition on the target.
Crunch	This move has a 20% chance of lowering the target's Defense by 1.
Crush Claw	This move has a 50% chance of lowering the target's Defense by 1.
Crush Grip	If the target has high HP remaining, the damage of the move is increased (max attack power: 120).

Curse	Lowers user's Speed by 1 and raises its Attack and Defense by 1. If used by a Ghost-type Pokémon, it halves user's HP, but lowers the target's HP by 1/4 of maximum every turn.
Cut	Regular attack.
Dark Pulse	There is a 20% chance of making the target flinch (target cannot use moves for that turn).
Dark Void	Inflicts the Sleep condition on the target.
Defend Order	Raises the user's Defense and Sp. Defense by 1.
Defense Curl	Raises the user's Defense by 1.
Defog	Lowers the target's evasion by 1. Nullifies the effects of the target's Light Screen, Reflect, Safeguard, Mist, Spikes, or Toxic Spikes, and nullifies the Fog weather condition.
Destiny Bond	When executed, if the user faints due to damage from the target, the target faints as well.
Detect	Protects against a move used by the target on that turn. Chance of failure increases with each successive use.
Dig	User burrows underground on the first turn, and then attacks on the second.
Disable	Prevents the target from using the last move it used for several turns.
Discharge	This move has a 30% chance of inflicting the Paralysis condition on the target. The attack power decreases in Double Battles.
Dive	Dives underwater on the first turn, then attacks on the second.
Dizzy Punch	This move has a 20% chance of inflicting the Confused condition on the target.
Doom Desire	Attacks the target after 2 turns. Inflicts damage regardless of the target's type.
Double Hit	Attacks twice in a row in a single turn.
Double Kick	Attacks twice in a row in a single turn.
Double Team	Raises user's evasion by 1.
Double-Edge	User takes damage equal to 1/3 of damage inflicted on the target.
DoubleSlap	Attacks consecutively 2–5 times.
Draco Meteor	Lowers the user's Sp. Attack by 2.
Dragon Claw	Regular attack.
Dragon Dance	Raises the user's Attack and Speed by 1.
Dragon Pulse	Regular attack.
Dragon Rage	Deals a fixed 40 points of damage.
Dragon Rush	This move has a 20% chance of making the target flinch (target cannot use moves for that turn).
DragonBreath	This move has a 30% chance of inflicting the Paralyzed condition on the target.
Drain Punch	Restores HP equal to 1/2 the damage dealt to the target.
Dream Eater	Restores HP equal to 1/2 the damage inflicted on the target. Only works when the target is asleep.
Drill Peck	Regular attack.
DynamicPunch	This move has a 100% chance of inflicting the Confused condition on the target.
Earth Power	Has a 10% chance of lowering the target's Sp. Defense by 1.
Earthquake	Regular attack. Does double damage to foes using Dig. Attack power is lower in Double Battles.
Egg Bomb	Regular attack.
Embargo	The target is unable to use items for 5 turns. Trainer cannot use items on that Pokémon either.
Ember	This move has a 10% chance of inflicting the Burned condition on the target. If the target is Frozen, this move melts the ice.
Encore	Forces the target to use its last move again. Works for 2–6 turns.
Endeavor	Inflicts damage equal to the target's HP minus user's HP.
Endure	Leaves the user with 1 HP even after moves that deliver a KO hit. The chance of failure rises with each successive use.
Energy Ball	This move has a 10% chance of lowering the target's Sp. Defense by 1.

Eruption	If the user's HP is low, this attack's power is decreased. If the target is afflicted with the Frozen condition, this move melts the ice. The attack power decreases in Double Battles.
Explosion	User faints after using. This move deals damage as if the target's Defense were halved and has lower attack power in Double Battles.
Extrasensory	This move has a 10% chance of making the target flinch (cannot use a move for this turn).
ExtremeSpeed	Move always attacks first (if both opponents use this move, the one with the higher Speed goes first).
Facade	This move inflicts twice the damage if user has the Poison, Paralyzed, or Burned condition.
Faint Attack	Always strikes the target.
Fake Out	Always strikes first, with 100% chance of making the target flinch. Only works on the turn where user is sent out.
Fake Tears	Lowers the target's Sp. Defense by 2.
False Swipe	Leaves the target with 1 HP remaining, even when hit with KO moves.
FeatherDance	Lowers the target's Attack by 2.
Feint	Only hits targets using Protect or Detect, and eliminates the effects from those moves.
Fire Blast	This move has a 10% chance of inflicting the Burned condition on the target. If the target is Frozen, this move melts the ice.
Fire Fang	This move has a 10% chance of inflicting the Burned condition or making the target flinch. If the target is afflicted with the Frozen condition, this move melts the ice.
Fire Punch	This move has a 10% chance of inflicting the Burned condition on the target. If the target is afflicted with the Frozen condition, this move melts the ice.
Fire Spin	Inflicts damage and prevents the target from fleeing for 2–5 turns. If the target is afflicted with the Frozen condition, this move melts the ice.
Fissure	It KOs the foe in one move. This move doesn't work if the target's level is higher than the user's, and is more accurate the higher the user's level compared to the target's.
Flail	If the user's HP is low, this move does greater damage to the target.
Flame Wheel	This move has a 10% chance of inflicting the Burned condition on the target. If the target is afflicted with the Frozen condition, this move melts the ice. If the user is Frozen, this also melts its ice.
Flamethrower	This move has a 10% chance of inflicting the Burned condition. If foe is Frozen, this move melts its ice.
Flare Blitz	User takes 1/3 of the damage inflicted. There is a 10% chance of inflicting the Burn condition on the target. If the target is afflicted with the Frozen condition, this move melts its ice. This move can also be used if the user is Frozen and will melt its ice.
Flash	Lowers the target's accuracy by 1.
Flash Cannon	This move has a 10% chance of lowering the target's Sp. Attack by 1.
Flatter	Confuses the target but raises its Sp. Attack by 1.
Fling	Attacks by throwing user's held item at the target. Power and effect depend on item thrown.
Fly	User flies into the air on the first turn, then attacks on the second.
Focus Blast	This move has a 10% chance of lowering the target's Sp. Defense by 1.
Focus Energy	Raises critical-hit rate for next move.
Focus Punch	Strikes last. If the target lands a hit before this move lands, then this move misses.
Follow Me	Draws all the target's attacks to the user.
Force Palm	This move has a 30% chance of inflicting the Paralysis condition on the target.
Foresight	Hits the target regardless of the target's evasion stat. Makes Ghost-type Pokémon vulnerable to Normal- and Fighting-type moves.
Frenzy Plant	User cannot use a move on the next turn.
Frustration	If the user's friendship level is low, this move's attack power increases.
Fury Attack	Attacks 2–5 times in a row in a single turn.
Fury Cutter	This move doubles in power every time it strikes (up to 5 times). Power returns to normal once it misses.
Fury Swipes	Attacks 2–5 times in a row in a single turn.
Future Sight	Attacks the target after 2 turns. Inflicts damage regardless of the target's type.

Gastro Acid	Nullifies the target's Ability.
Giga Drain	Restores HP equal to half the damage inflicted on the target.
Giga Impact	The user cannot move on the next turn.
Glare	Inflicts the Paralysis condition on the target.
Grass Knot	Has higher attack power against heavier targets.
GrassWhistle	Inflicts the Sleep condition on the target.
Gravity	Raises the accuracy of all Pokémon in battle for 5 turns. Makes Flying-type Pokémon and Pokémon with the Ability Levitate vulnerable to Ground-type moves. Prevents use of Fly, Splash, Bounce, and Magnet Rise. Pulls any airborne Pokémon to the ground.
Growl	Lowers the target's Attack by 1.
Growth	Raises user's Sp. Attack by 1.
Grudge	If the user faints because of an enemy's move, that move's PP drops to 0.
Guard Swap	Swaps Defense and Sp. Defense differences between user and the target.
Guillotine	It KOs the foe in one move. This move doesn't work if the target's level is higher than the user's, and is more accurate the higher the user's level compared to the target's.
Gunk Shot	This move has a 30% chance of inflicting the Poison condition on the target.
Gust	Regular attack. This does twice the damage if the target is using Fly or Bounce when it hits.
Gyro Ball	If the target has a higher Speed stat than the user, the damage of the move is increased (max attack power 150).
Hail	Changes the weather condition to Hail for 5 turns, damaging all Pokémon except Ice types every turn.
Hammer Arm	Lowers user's Speed by 1.
Harden	Raises user's Defense by 1.
Haze	Restores user's and target's stats to their original state.
Head Smash	User takes 1/2 the damage inflicted on the target.
Headbutt	This move has a 30% chance of making the target flinch (cannot use a move for that turn).
Heal Bell	Heals status ailments for all ally Pokémon in your party.
Heal Block	Target cannot use moves to recover HP for 5 turns.
Heal Order	Restores half of maximum HP.
Healing Wish	Makes user faint, but completely heals the HP and status of the next Pokémon you send out.
Heart Swap	Swaps all stat changes between user and the target.
Heat Wave	This move has a 10% chance of inflicting the Burned condition on the target. If the target is Frozen, it melts the ice. The attack power decreases in Double Battles.
Helping Hand	Strengthens ally's attack power by 1.5 times.
Hi Jump Kick	If this attack misses, user takes 1/2 of the damage that would have been inflicted.
Hidden Power	Type and power will change depending on the user.
Horn Attack	Regular attack.
Horn Drill	It KOs the foe in one move. This move doesn't work if the target's level is higher than the user's, and is more accurate as the difference between the target's level and user's level increases.
Howl	Raises user's Attack by 1.
Hydro Cannon	User cannot use a move on the next turn.
Hydro Pump	Regular attack.
Hyper Beam	Cannot use a move on the next turn.
Hyper Fang	This move has a 10% chance of making the target flinch (target cannot use moves for that turn).
Hyper Voice	Regular attack. The attack power decreases in Double Battles.
Hypnosis	Inflicts the Sleep condition on the target.
Ice Ball	Attacks consecutively for 5 turns or until it misses. Damage rises with each strike. Use Defense Curl first to double the damage.
Ice Beam	This move has a 10% chance of inflicting the Frozen condition on the target.

Ice Fang	This move has a 10% chance of inflicting the Frozen condition on the target or making it flinch.
Ice Punch	This move has a 10% chance of inflicting the Frozen condition on the target.
Ice Shard	Move always attacks first (if both opponents use this move, the one with higher Speed goes first).
Icicle Spear	Attacks 2–5 times in a row in a single turn.
Icy Wind	Has a 100% chance of lowering target's Speed by 1. The attack power decreases in Double Battles.
Imprison	Makes target unable to use a move if the user knows it as well.
Ingrain	Restores a little HP each turn. User cannot be switched out after using this move. Flying-type Pokémon and Pokémon with the Levitate Ability become vulnerable to Ground-type moves.
Iron Defense	Raises user's Defense by 2.
Iron Head	This move has a 30% chance of making the target flinch (target cannot use moves for that turn).
Iron Tail	This move has a 30% chance of lowering the target's Defense by 1.
Judgment	Regular attack. Type changes according to the Plate Arceus is holding.
Jump Kick	If this attack misses, user takes 1/2 of the damage that would have been inflicted.
Karate Chop	High critical-hit rate.
Kinesis	Lowers the target's accuracy by 1.
Knock Off	Foe loses its held item for the duration of the battle.
Last Resort	Damage is inflicted only if user has executed each of its other moves at least once.
Lava Plume	There is a 30% chance of inflicting the Burned condition on the target. If the target is afflicted with the Frozen condition, this move melts the ice. The attack power decreases in Double Battles.
Leaf Blade	High critical-hit rate.
Leaf Storm	Lowers the user's Sp. Attack by 2.
Leech Life	Restores HP equal to half the damage inflicted on the target.
Leech Seed	Steals HP from the target every turn. Effect lasts even if the user switches out.
Leer	Lowers the target's Defense by 1.
Lick	This move has a 30% chance of inflicting the Paralysis condition on the target.
Light Screen	Halves damage from the target's special moves for 5 turns. Effect lasts for 5 turns even if user is switched out. Effect is weaker in Double Battles.
Lock-On	Attack on the subsequent turn is a guaranteed hit.
Lovely Kiss	Inflicts the Sleep condition on the target.
Low Kick	Has higher attack power against heavier targets.
Lucky Chant	Target cannot land critical hits for 5 turns.
Lunar Dance	Knocks out the user, but completely restores the PP and status of the next Pokémon you send out.
Luster Purge	This move has a 50% chance of lowering the target's Sp. Defense by 1.
Mach Punch	Move always attacks first (if both opponents use this move, the one with higher Speed goes first).
Magic Coat	Reflects moves with effects like Leech Seed or those that inflict the Sleep, Poison, Paralysis, or Confused conditions.
Magical Leaf	Always strikes the target.
Magma Storm	Inflicts damage and prevents the target from fleeing for 2–5 turns. If the target is afflicted with the Frozen condition, this move melts the ice.
Magnet Bomb	Always strikes the target.
Magnet Rise	Nullifies Ground-type moves for 5 turns.
Magnitude	Attack power shifts between 10, 30, 50, 70, 90, 110, and 150. This move deals double damage against targets using Dig and has lower power in Double Battles.
Me First	Copies the foe's chosen move and uses it with increased power. Fails if it does not strike first.
Mean Look	This move prevents the target from escaping. If used in a Trainer battle, the Trainer cannot switch Pokémon.
Meditate	Raises the user's Attack by 1.
Mega Drain	Recovers HP equal to 1/2 the damage inflicted on the target.

Mega Kick	Regular attack.
Mega Punch	Regular attack.
Megahorn	Regular attack.
Memento	User faints, but the target's Attack and Sp. Attack are lowered by 2.
Metal Burst	Inflicts damage on the target equal to 1.5 times the damage last received from the target in that same turn.
Metal Claw	This move has a 10% chance of raising the user's Attack stat by 1.
Metal Sound	Lowers the target's Sp. Defense by 2.
Meteor Mash	This move has a 20% chance of raising user's Attack by 1.
Metronome	Uses one move randomly chosen from all possible moves.
Milk Drink	Restores half of user's maximum HP.
Mimic	Allows opponent's last-used move to be copied by user (copied move has a PP of 5).
Mind Reader	The user's next attack will have perfect accuracy.
Minimize	Raises user's evasion by 1.
Miracle Eye	Hits the target regardless of the target's evasion stat. Makes Dark-type Pokémon vulnerable to Psychic-type attacks.
Mirror Coat	Returns double the damage received from a special move delivered by the target.
Mirror Move	Uses the last move that the target just used.
Mirror Shot	This move has a 30% chance of lowering the target's accuracy by 1.
Mist	For 5 turns, this move protects against stat-lowering moves and side effects.
Mist Ball	There is a 50% chance of lowering the target's Sp. Attack by 1.
Moonlight	Restores HP, the amount of which is based on the weather. Sunny weather condition: recovers 2/3 of HP (normally recovers 1/2). Rain/Sandstorm/Hail/Fog weather condition: recovers 1/4 of HP.
Morning Sun	Restores HP by an amount determined by the weather. Sunny weather condition: recovers 2/3 of HP (normally recovers 1/2). Rainy/Sandstorm/Hail/Fog weather condition: recovers 1/4 of HP.
Mud Bomb	This move has a 30% chance of lowering the target's accuracy by 1.
Mud Shot	This move has a 100% chance of lowering the target's Speed by 1.
Mud Sport	Halves the power of Electric-type moves as long as user is in play.
Muddy Water	This move has a 30% chance of lowering the target's accuracy by 1. The attack power decreases in Double Battles.
Mud-Slap	This move has a 100% chance of lowering the target's accuracy by 1.
Nasty Plot	Raises the user's Sp. Attack by 2.
Natural Gift	Type and attack power change according to the Berry held by user.
Nature Power	Move varies depending on terrain. Tall grass/puddle: Seed Bomb. Sand: Earthquake. Rocks/cave: Rockslide. Swamp: Mud Bomb. Water: Hydro Pump. Snow: Blizzard. Ice: Ice Beam. Floor: Tri Attack.
Needle Arm	This move has a 30% chance of making the target flinch (target cannot use moves for that turn).
Night Shade	Deals fixed damage equal to user's level.
Night Slash	High critical-hit rate.
Nightmare	Lowers the target's HP by 1/4 of maximum every turn. Fails if the target is not asleep.
Octazooka	This move has a 50% chance of lowering the target's accuracy by 1.
Odor Sleuth	Always hits, regardless of the target's evasion stat. Makes Ghost-type Pokémon vulnerable to Normal- and Fighting-type moves.
Ominous Wind	This move has a 10% chance of raising all of the user's stats by 1. Weaker in Double Battles.
Outrage	Attacks consecutively for 2–3 turns. If attack is interrupted, the user becomes Confused.
Overheat	Lowers user's Sp. Attack by 2. If foe is Frozen, this move also melts the ice.
Pain Split	Averages user's HP and the target's HP.
Payback	This move delivers twice the damage if the user strikes after the target strikes.

Payday	Increases the amount of prize money received after battle (level multiplied by number of attacks, multiplied by five).
Peck	Regular attack.
Perish Song	All Pokémon in battle will faint after 3 turns, unless switched out.
Petal Dance	Attacks 2–3 turns in succession. If attack is interrupted, the user becomes Confused.
Pin Missile	Attacks 2–5 times in a row in a single turn.
Pluck	Eats and uses the effects of opponent's Berry in battle.
Poison Fang	This move has a 30% chance of inflicting the Badly Poisoned condition on the target. Damage from being Badly Poisoned increases with every turn.
Poison Gas	Inflicts the Poison condition on the target.
Poison Jab	This move has a 30% chance of inflicting the Poison condition on the target.
Poison Sting	This move has a 30% chance of inflicting the Poison condition on the target.
Poison Tail	This move has a 10% chance of inflicting the Poison condition on the target. High critical-hit rate.
PoisonPowder	Inflicts the Poison condition on the target.
Pound	Regular attack.
Powder Snow	This move has a 10% chance of inflicting the Frozen condition on the target. The attack power decreases in Double Battles.
Power Gem	Regular attack.
Power Swap	Swaps any changes to Attack and Sp. Attack between the user and the target.
Power Trick	Swaps original Attack and Defense stats (does not swap changes made to the stats).
Power Whip	Regular attack.
Present	Attack power varies: 40 (40% chance), 80 (30%), 120 (10%). Has 20% of healing foe by 1/4 max HP.
Protect	Protects against moves used by the target on that turn. Chance of failure increases with each successive use.
Psybeam	This move has a 10% chance of inflicting the Confused condition.
Psych Up	Gives the target's stat changes to user.
Psychic	This move has a 10% chance of lowering foe's Sp. Defense by 1.
Psycho Boost	Lowers user's Sp. Attack by 2.
Psycho Cut	High critical-hit rate.
Psycho Shift	Transfers user's Poison, Badly Poisoned, Sleep, Paralysis, or Burned status to foe, healing the user.
Psywave	Inflicts damage equal to user's level multiplied by a random number between 0.5 and 1.5.
Punishment	Has higher attack power if the target has elevated stats.
Pursuit	Does twice the damage against a target Pokémon that's switching out.
Quick Attack	Move always attacks first (if both opponents use this move, the one with higher Speed goes first).
Rage	Attack power rises as user takes hits from the target.
Rain Dance	Changes the weather condition to Rain for 5 turns, thus strengthening Water-type moves.
Rapid Spin	Releases user from Bind, Wrap, Leech Seed, or Spikes.
Razor Leaf	High critical-hit rate. The attack power decreases in Double Battles.
Razor Wind	Builds power on the first turn and attacks on the second turn. High critical-hit rate. The attack power decreases in Double Battles.
Recover	Restores half of maximum HP.
Recycle	Makes a used held item useable again.
Reflect	Halves damage from the target's physical moves for 5 turns. Effect lasts for 5 turns even if user is switched out. Effect is weaker in Double Battles.
Refresh	Heals the Poison, Paralysis, and Burned conditions.
Rest	Completely restores HP, but user is asleep for 2 turns.
Return	If the user's friendship level is high, this move's attack power increases.

Revenge	This move deals double the damage if the user has already received damage from the target that turn.
Reversal	If user's HP is low, this move does more damage to the target.
Roar	Ends wild Pokémon battles. In Trainer battles, this move forces the opponent to swap Pokémon.
Roar of Time	User cannot move on the next turn.
Rock Blast	Attacks 2–5 times in a single turn.
Rock Climb	This move has a 20% chance of inflicting the Confused condition on the target.
Rock Polish	Raises the user's Speed by 2.
Rock Slide	This move has a 30% chance of making the target flinch (target cannot use moves for that turn). The attack is weaker in Double Battles.
Rock Smash	This move has a 50% chance of lowering the target's Defense by 1.
Rock Throw	Regular attack.
Rock Tomb	This move has a 100% chance of lowering the target's Speed by 1.
Rock Wrecker	The user cannot use a move on the next turn.
Role Play	Copies the target's Ability (cannot copy Wonder Guard).
Rolling Kick	There is a 30% chance of making the target flinch (target cannot use moves for that turn).
Rollout	Attacks consecutively over 5 turns or until it misses. Inflicts greater damage with every successful hit, and inflicts twice the damage if used after Defense Curl.
Roost	Restores half of maximum HP, but pulls the Flying-type Pokémon to the ground.
Sacred Fire	This move has a 50% chance of inflicting the Burned condition on the target. If the target is inflicted with the Frozen condition, this move melts the ice. If the user is Frozen, this also melts the ice.
Safeguard	Protects against status conditions for 5 turns. Effects last even if the user switches Pokémon.
Sand Tomb	Inflicts damage over 2–5 turns. Target cannot escape during that time.
Sand-Attack	Lowers the target's accuracy by 1.
Sandstorm	Changes the weather condition to Sandstorm for 5 turns. All Pokémon but Rock, Steel, and Ground types take damage every turn.
Scary Face	Lowers the target's Speed by 2.
Scratch	Regular attack.
Screech	Lowers the target's Defense by 2.
Secret Power	Regular attack with a 30% chance of one of the following side effects, depending on the terrain: Tall grass/water puddle: Sleep condition. Sandy ground: lowers accuracy by 1. Rocky ground/cave: target flinches. Marsh: lowers Speed by 1. Water surface: lowers Attack by 1. Snowy/icy ground: Frozen condition. Floor: Paralysis condition.
Seed Bomb	Regular attack.
Seed Flare	This move has a 40% chance of lowering the target's Sp. Defense by 2.
Seismic Toss	Deals fixed damage equal to user's level.
Selfdestruct	User faints after using. This move deals damage as if the target's Defense were halved and has lower attack power in Double Battles.
Shadow Ball	This move has a 20% chance of lowering the target's Sp. Defense by 1.
Shadow Claw	High critical hit rate.
Shadow Force	Makes user invisible on the first turn, then attacks on the second. Strikes the target even if it's using Protect or Detect.
Shadow Punch	Always strikes the target.
Shadow Sneak	This move always attacks first. (If both opponents use this move, the one with the higher Speed goes first.)
Sharpen	Raises user's Attack by 1.
Sheer Cold	It KOs the foe in one move. This move doesn't work if the target's level is higher than the user's, and is more accurate the higher the user's level compared to the target's.
Shock Wave	Always strikes the target.
Signal Beam	This move has a 10% chance of inflicting the Confused condition on the target.
Silver Wind	This move has a 10% chance of raising Attack, Defense, Speed, Sp. Attack, and Sp. Defense by 1.

Sing	Inflicts the Sleep condition on the target.
Sketch	Copies the last move used by the target. User then forgets the Sketch and learns the new move.
Skill Swap	Swaps Abilities between the user and target (except for Wonder Guard).
Skull Bash	Powers up on the first turn and attacks on the second turn. On the first turn, this move raises user's Defense by 1.
Sky Attack	Builds power on the first turn and attacks on the second turn and has a high critical-hit rate. This move has a 30% chance of making the target flinch (target cannot use moves for that turn).
Sky Uppercut	Deals damage even to targets using Fly or Bounce.
Slack Off	Restores 1/2 of maximum HP.
Slam	Regular attack.
Slash	High critical-hit rate.
Sleep Powder	Inflicts the Sleep condition on the target.
Sleep Talk	Randomly executes one of user's moves. Only works when user is asleep.
Sludge	There is a 30% chance of inflicting the Poison condition on the target.
Sludge Bomb	There is a 30% chance of inflicting the Poison condition on the target.
Shadow Ball	This move has a 20% chance of lowering the target's Sp. Defense by 1.
Shadow Claw	High critical hit rate.
Shadow Force	Makes user invisible on the first turn, then attacks on the second. Strikes the target even if it's using Protect or Detect.
Shadow Punch	Always strikes the target.
Shadow Sneak	This move always attacks first. (If both opponents use this move, the one with the higher Speed goes first.)
Sharpen	Raises user's Attack by 1.
Sheer Cold	It KOs the foe in one move. This move doesn't work if the target's level is higher than the user's, and is more accurate the higher the user's level compared to the target's.
Shock Wave	Always strikes the target.
Signal Beam	This move has a 10% chance of inflicting the Confused condition on the target.
Silver Wind	This move has a 10% chance of raising Attack, Defense, Speed, Sp. Attack, and Sp. Defense by 1.
Sing	Inflicts the Sleep condition on the target.
Sketch	Copies the last move used by the target. User then forgets the Sketch and learns the new move.
Skill Swap	Swaps Abilities between the user and target (except for Wonder Guard).
Skull Bash	Powers up on the first turn and attacks on the second turn. On the first turn, this move raises user's Defense by 1.
Sky Attack	Builds power on the first turn and attacks on the second turn and has a high critical-hit rate. This move has a 30% chance of making the target flinch (target cannot use moves for that turn).
Sky Uppercut	Deals damage even to targets using Fly or Bounce.
Slack Off	Restores 1/2 of maximum HP.
Slam	Regular attack.
Slash	High critical-hit rate.
Sleep Powder	Inflicts the Sleep condition on the target.
Sleep Talk	Randomly executes one of user's moves. Only works when user is asleep.
Sludge	There is a 30% chance of inflicting the Poison condition on the target.
Sludge Bomb	There is a 30% chance of inflicting the Poison condition on the target.
SmellingSalt	This move does twice the damage against targets with Paralysis, but heals this condition.
Smog	This move has a 40% chance of inflicting the Poison condition on the target.
SmokeScreen	Lowers the target's accuracy by 1.
Snatch	Steals the effects of recovery or stat-altering moves used by the target on that turn.

Snore	Only works when user is asleep. Has a 30% chance of making the target flinch.
Softboiled	Restores half of maximum HP.
SolarBeam	Powers up on the first move, then attacks on the second. Can attack without charging in a Sunny weather condition. Attack power is halved in Rain, Sandstorm, Hail, and Fog weather conditions.
SonicBoom	This move deals a fixed 20 points of damage.
Spacial Rend	High critical-hit rate.
Spark	This move has a 30% chance of inflicting the Paralysis condition on the target.
Spider Web	This move prevents the target from escaping. If used in a Trainer battle, the Trainer cannot switch Pokémon.
Spike Cannon	Attacks 2–5 times in a row in a single turn.
Spikes	Damages the target as it switches out. Power rises with each use, up to 3 times. Ineffective against Flying-type Pokémon and Pokémon with the Levitate Ability.
Spit Up	Deals damage, the amount of which is determined by how many times the user performed Stockpile (does not work if user has not used Stockpile first). Nullifies Defense and Sp. Defense stat increases caused by Stockpile.
Spite	Takes 4 points from the PP of the target's last move used.
Splash	No effect.
Spore	Inflicts the Sleep condition on the target.
Stealth Rock	Target takes damage when sending out Pokémon. Damage is subject to type matchups.
Steel Wing	This move has a 10% chance of raising the user's Defense by 1.
Stockpile	Raises user's Defense and Sp. Defense by 1. Can be used up to 3 times.
Stomp	This move has a 30% chance of making the target flinch (target cannot use moves for that turn). It deals twice the damage if the target is using Minimize.
Stone Edge	High critical-hit rate.
Strength	Regular attack.
String Shot	Lowers the target's Speed by 1.
Struggle	This move becomes available when all other moves are out of Power Points. User takes 1/4 of its maximum HP as damage. Inflicts damage regardless of type compatibility.
Stun Spore	Inflicts the Paralysis condition on the target.
Submission	User takes 1/4 of the damage inflicted on foe.
Substitute	Uses 1/4 of maximum HP to create a copy of the user.
Sucker Punch	This move attacks first and deals damage if the target's chosen move is an attack move.
Sunny Day	Changes the weather condition to Sunny for 5 turns, strengthening Fire-type moves.
Super Fang	Halves the target's HP.
Super Power	Lowers user's Attack and Defense by 1.
Supersonic	Inflicts the Confused condition on the target.
Surf	Regular attack. Does double the damage to foes using Dive. The attack power decreases in Double Battles.
Swagger	Confuses target but raises its Attack by 2.
Swallow	Restores HP, the amount of which is determined by how many times the user performed Stockpile (does not work if user has not used Stockpile first). Nullifies Defense and Sp. Defense stat increases caused by Stockpile.
Sweet Kiss	Inflicts the Confused condition on the target.
Sweet Scent	Lowers the target's evasion by 1.
Swift	Always strikes the target. Has lower attack power in Double Battles.
Switcheroo	Swaps items between the user and the target.
Swords Dance	Raises user's Attack by 2.
Synthesis	Restores HP by an amount determined by the weather. Sunny weather condition: recovers 2/3 of HP (normally recovers 1/2). Rain/Sandstorm/Hail/Fog weather condition: recovers 1/4 of HP.
Tackle	Regular attack.
Tail Glow	Raises the user's Sp. Attack by 2.

Tail Whip	Lowers the target's Defense by 1.
Tailwind	Doubles user's and ally's Speed for 3 turns.
Take Down	User takes damage equal to 1/4 of the damage inflicted on the target.
Taunt	Prevents the target from using anything other than attack moves for 2–4 turns.
Teeter Dance	Inflicts the Confused condition on the target.
Teleport	Ends wild Pokémon battles.
Thief	If the target has an item and the user has none, the user steals the target's item.
Thrash	Attacks 2–3 times consecutively, then the user becomes Confused.
Thunder	This move has a 30% chance of inflicting the Paralyzed condition on a target. It is 100% accurate in the Rain weather condition and 50% accurate in the Sunny weather condition. It can also hit foes using Fly or Bounce.
Thunder Fang	This move has a 10% chance of paralyzing a target or making it flinch (target cannot use moves for that turn).
Thunder Wave	Inflicts the Paralyzed condition on the target.
Thunderbolt	This move has a 10% chance of inflicting the Paralysis condition on the target.
ThunderPunch	This move has a 10% chance of inflicting the Paralysis condition on the target.
ThunderShock	This move has a 10% chance of inflicting the Paralysis condition on the target.
Tickle	Lowers the target's Attack and Defense by 1.
Torment	Target cannot use same move twice in a row.
Toxic	Badly poisons the target. Damage from being Badly Poisoned increases with every turn.
Toxic Spikes	Lays a trap of poison spikes that inflict the Poison condition on foes that switch into battle. Using Toxic Spikes twice will inflict the Badly Poisoned condition. Ineffective against Poison-type Pokémon. Ineffective against Flying-type Pokémon and Pokémon with the Levitate Ability.
Transform	User transforms into the target. User has the same moves and Ability as the target (all moves have 5 PP).
Tri Attack	This move has a 20% chance of inflicting the Paralysis, Burned, or Frozen condition on the target.
Trick	Swaps items between user and the target.
Trick Room	For 5 turns, the Pokémon with lower Speed strikes first. First-strike moves still go first. If performed again by user while still in play, it cancels the effect.
Triple Kick	Attacks 3 times in a row in a single turn. Power rises from 10 to 20 to 30 as long as it continues to hit.
Trump Card	If this move has low PP, its attack power is increased.
Twineedle	Attacks twice in a row in a single turn. There is also a 20% chance of inflicting the Poison condition on the target.
Twister	This move has a 20% chance of making the target flinch (the target cannot use moves for that turn). Deals double the damage to targets using Fly or Bounce. The attack power decreases in Double Battles.
Uproar	User is in an uproar for 2-5 turns. During that time, neither Pokémon can fall asleep.
U-turn	After attacking, user switches out with the next Pokémon in the party.
Vacuum Wave	Move always attacks first (if both opponents use this move, the one with higher Speed goes first).
ViceGrip	Regular attack.
Vine Whip	Regular attack.
Vital Throw	Strikes last, but always hits.
Volt Tackle	User takes 1/3 of the damage inflicted on the target. There is a 10% chance of inflicting the Paralysis condtion on the target.
Wake-Up Slap	Deals twice the damage against sleeping targets, but awakes them from the Sleep condition.
Water Gun	Regular attack.
Water Pulse	There is a 20% chance of inflicting the Confused condition on the target.
Water Sport	Halves the power of Fire-type moves for as long as the user is in play.
Water Spout	If the user's HP is low, this move has lower attack power. Attack power is also lower in Double Battles.
Waterfall	This move has a 20% chance of making the target flinch (target cannot use moves for that turn).

Weather Ball	Move type changes in special weather conditions. Sunny weather condition: Fire type. Rain weather condition: Water type. Hail weather condition: Ice type. Sandstorm weather condition: Rock type. Has double attack power in the above weather conditions.
Whirlpool	Inflicts damage over 2–5 turns. Target cannot flee during that time. Does double damage if the target is using Dive when attacked.
Whirlwind	Ends wild Pokémon battles. In Trainer battles, this move forces the opponent to swap Pokémon.
Will-O-Wisp	Burns the target.
Wing Attack	Regular attack.
Wish	Restores 1/2 of maximum HP at the end of the next turn. Works even if the user has switched out.
Withdraw	Raises user's Defense by 1.
Wood Hammer	User takes 1/3 of the damage inflicted on the target.
Worry Seed	Changes the target's Ability to Insomnia. Does not work against Pokémon with the Truant Ability.
Wrap	Inflicts damage and prevents the target from fleeing for 2-5 turns.
Wring Out	If the target has high HP remaining, the damage of the move is increased (max attack power: 120).
X-Scissor	Regular attack.
Yawn	Inflicts the Sleep condition on the target on the next turn. No effect if the target switches out before then.
Zap Cannon	This move has a 100% chance of inflicting the Paralysis condition on the target.
Zen Headbutt	This move has a 20% chance of making the target flinch (target cannot use moves for that turn).

Moves that can be used in the field

Move	Field effect
Cut	Cuts down small trees so your party may pass.
Defog	Dispels fog so you can see.
Dig	Pulls you out of spaces like caves, returning you to the last entrance you went through.
Flash	Illuminates dark caves.
Fly	Whisks you instantly to a town or city you've visited before.
Milk Drink	Distributes part of user's own HP among teammates.
Rock Climb	Lets you climb up and down craggy rock faces.
Rock Smash	Smashes cracked rocks so your party may pass.
Softboiled	Distributes part of user's own HP among teammates.
Strength	Moves large rocks so your party may pass.
Surf	Lets you move across water.
Sweet Scent	Attracts wild Pokémon and makes them appear.
Teleport	Transports you to the last Pokémon Center you used (cannot be used in caves or similar places).
Waterfall	Lets you climb up waterfalls.
Whirlpool	Lets you pass over whirlpools in the water.

Moves taught by people

Move	Field effect
Blast Burn	Pokémon move house in Blackthorn City (Ultimate Move Tutor)
Draco Meteor	Pokémon move house in Blackthorn City (Grandma Wilma)
Frenzy Plant	Pokémon move house in Blackthorn City (Ultimate Move Tutor)
Headbutt	Large boy in Ilex Forest
Hydro Cannon	Pokémon move house in Blackthorn City (Ultimate Move Tutor)

Moves taught in exchange for BP

Technical Moves			
Move	BP	Move	BP
Air Cutter	48	Knock Off	40
Bug Bite	32	Ominous Wind	48
Dive	40	Sucker Punch	40
Fire Punch	64	Thunderpunch	64
Fury Cutter	32	Trick	48
Ice Punch	64	Vacuum Wave	48
Icy Wind	48	Zen Headbutt	64
Influential Moves			
Block	32	Spite	40
Gravity	32	String Shot	32
Heal Bell	48	Swift	40
Helping Hand	40	Synthesis	40
Last Resort	48	Tailwind	48
Magic Coat	32	Uproar	48
Magnet Rise	40	Worry Seed	32
Snore	32		
Powerful Moves			
Ancient Power	40	Mud-Slap	32
Aqua Tail	40	Outrage	48
Bounce	32	Pain Split	64
Earth Power	40	Rollout	32
Endeavor	64	Seed Bomb	40
Gastro Acid	32	Signal Beam	40
Gunk Shot	32	Sky Attack	64
Heat Wave	48	Super Fang	40
Iron Defense	40	Super Power	48
Iron Head	40	Twister	40
Low Kick	32		

TMs

No.	Move	Ways to obtain	Price
1	Focus Punch	Win at Cianwood Gym.	—
2	Dragon Claw	Route 27 or Goldenrod City Department Store drawing 1st prize (Sunday)	—
3	Water Pulse	Win at Cerulean Gym	—
4	Calm Mind	Receive for 48 BP at the Battle Frontier	—
5	Roar	Receive from young man on Route 32 (HM Cut required)	—
6	Toxic	Receive for 32 BP at the Battle Frontier.	—
7	Hail	Win at Mahogany Gym/Obtain on the Poké Walker	—
8	Bulk Up	Receive for 48 BP at the Battle Frontier	—
9	Bullet Seed	Route 32	—
10	Hidden Power	Receive from a man at the house northwest of the Lake of Rage, obtain on the Pokéwalker, or Celadon Game Corner prize (6,000 Coins)	—
11	Sunny Day	Receive from a girl at Goldenrod Radio Tower 3F (after freeing the tower) or obtain on the Pokéwalker.	—
12	Taunt	Burned Tower B1F (HM Strength required) or Celadon Department Store 3F	1,500
13	Ice Beam	Goldenrod Game Corner prize (10,000 Coins) or Seafoam Islands B4F	—
14	Blizzard	Goldenrod City Department Store 5F	5,500
15	Hyper Beam	Goldenrod City Department Store 5F or obtain on the Pokéwalker	7,500
16	Light Screen	Goldenrod City Department Store 5F	2,000
17	Protect	Goldenrod City Department Store 5F	2,000
18	Rain Dance	SLOWPOKE Well B2F (HM Strength required) or obtain on the Pokéwalker	—

19	Giga Drain	Win at Celadon Gym	—
20	Safeguard	Celadon Department Store 3F	2,000
21	Frustration	Receive from a lady on Goldenrod City Department Store 5F (if your lead Pokémon has a low friendship level) on Sunday or Celadon Department Store 3F	1,000
22	SolarBeam	Goldenrod City Department Store 5F	3,000
23	Iron Tail	Win at Olivine Gym	—
24	Thunderbolt	Goldenrod Game Corner prize (10,000 Coins) or Cerulean Cave 2F	—
25	Thunder	Goldenrod City Department Store 5F	5,500
26	Earthquake	Victory Road 2F, Pickup Ability, or receive for 80 BP at the Battle Frontier	—
27	Return	Receive from a lady on Goldenrod Department Store 5F (if your lead Pokémon has a high friendship level) on Sunday or Celadon Department Store 3F	1,000
28	Dig	National Park or Celadon Department Store 3F	2,000
29	Psychic	Celadon Game Corner prize (10,000 Coins) or receive from Mr. Psychic in Saffron City	—
30	Shadow Ball	Win at Ecruteak Gym or receive for 64 BP at the Battle Frontier	—
31	Brick Break	Receive for 40 BP at the Battle Frontier	—
32	Double Team	Celadon Game Corner prize (4,000 Coins)	—
33	Reflect	Goldenrod City Department Store 5F	2,000
34	Shock Wave	Win at the Vermilion Gym	—
35	Flamethrower	Goldenrod Game Corner prize (10,000 Coins) or Route 28	—
36	Sludge Bomb	Receive from Route 43 gate attendant (after defeating Team Rocket) or receive for 80 BP at the Battle Frontier	—
37	Sandstorm	Receive from old lady in house on Route 27 (if lead Pokémon has high friendship) or obtain on the Pokéwalker	—
38	Fire Blast	Goldenrod City Department Store 5F	5,500
39	Rock Tomb	Union Cave B1F	—
40	Aerial Ace	Receive for 40 BP at the Battle Frontier	—
41	Torment	Route 8 or Celadon Department Store 3F	1,500
42	Facade	Goldenrod Department Store drawing 1st prize (Friday)	—
43	Secret Power	Lake of Rage	—
44	Rest	Deliver Spearow to the large boy on Route 31 or Goldenrod Game Corner prize (6,000 Coins)	—
45	Attract	Win at the Goldenrod Gym or receive for 32 BP at the Battle Frontier	—
46	Thief	Team Rocket HQ B2F	—
47	Steel Wing	Receive from a retired Idol hiding at the house on Route 28	—
48	Skill Swap	Win at Saffron Gym	—
49	Snatch	Team Rocket HQ B3F	—
50	Overheat	Win at Cinnabar Island Gym (in the Seafoam Islands)	—
51	Roost	Win at Violet Gym	—
52	Focus Blast	Goldenrod City Department Store 5F	5,500
53	Energy Ball	Receive for 64 BP at the Battle Frontier	—
54	False Swipe	Goldenrod City Department Store 5F or Dark Cave (Blackthorn side)	7,000
55	Brine	Route 19 or Celadon Department Store 3F	3,000
56	Fling	Rock Tunnel 1F or Pickup Ability	—
57	Charge Beam	Olivine City or Goldenrod Department Store drawing 1st prize (Wednesday) or receive from the Power Plant's manager (after delivering the Machine Part)	—
58	Endure	Celadon Game Corner prize (2,000 Coins)	—
59	Dragon Pulse	Receive from Clair at Dragon's Den (after winning at the Blackthorn Gym) or receive for 80 BP at the Battle Frontier	—

60	Drain Punch	Route 39 or Goldenrod City Department Store drawing 1st prize (Thursday)	—
61	Will-O-Wisp	Receive for 32 BP at the Battle Frontier	—
62	Silver Wind	Goldenrod Department Store drawing 1st prize (Saturday) or Route 6	—
63	Embargo	Route 34	—
64	Explosion	Receive for a RageCandyBar from a man in the Underground Path connecting Routes 5 and 6	—
65	Shadow Claw	Route 42 or Goldenrod City Department Store drawing 1st prize (Monday)	—
66	Payback	Route 35	—
67	Recycle	Celadon City	—
68	Giga Impact	Obtain on the Pokéwalker or Celadon Game Corner prize (15,000 Coins)	—
69	Rock Polish	Route 10	—
70	Flash	Defeat the Elder on Sprout Tower 3F or Goldenrod City Department Store 5F	1,000
71	Stone Edge	Receive for 80 BP at the Battle Frontier	—
72	Avalanche	Ice Path B2F or Celadon Department Store 3F	3,000
73	Thunder Wave	Receive for 32 BP at the Battle Frontier	—
74	Gyro Ball	Celadon Game Corner prize (10,000 Coins)	—
75	Swords Dance	Goldenrod Game Corner prize (4,000 Coins)	—
76	Stealth Rock	Mt. Silver Cave or Celadon Department Store 3F	2,000
77	Psych Up	Viridian Forest	—
78	Captivate	Goldenrod Game Corner or Celadon Department Store 3F	2,500
79	Dark Pulse	Victory Road 3F or Celadon Department Store 3F	3,000
80	Rock Slide	Win at the Pewter Gym	—
81	X-Scissor	Receive for 64 BP at the Battle Frontier	—
82	Sleep Talk	Goldenrod Tunnel B2F	—
83	Natural Gift	Goldenrod City Department Store 5F or receive from the farmer lady at Moomoo Farm on Route 39 (after helping Miltank)	2,000
84	Poison Jab	Win at Fuchsia Gym	—
85	Dream Eater	Receive from a man in Viridian City	—
86	Grass Knot	Route 11 or Pickup Ability	—
87	Swagger	Lighthouse in Olivine City or Celadon Department Store 3F	1,500
88	Pluck	Route 40	—
89	U-turn	Win at Azalea Gym or receive for 40 BP at the Battle Frontier	—
90	Substitute	Goldenrod Game Corner prize (2,000 Coins)	—
91	Flash Cannon	Route 9 or Goldenrod Department Store drawing 1st prize (Tuesday)	—
92	Trick Room	Win at Viridian Gym	—

HMs

No.	Move	Ways to obtain	Price
1	Cut	Receive from the Charcoal Man in Ilex Forest (after catching both Farfetch'd)	—
2	Fly	Receive from Chuck's wife in Cianwood City (after winning in Cianwood Gym)	—
3	Surf	Receive from the Gentleman in Ecruteak Dance Theater (after saving the Kimono Girl from Team Rocket)	—
4	Strength	Receive from the Hiker who comes out of Mt. Mortar on Route 42	—
5	Whirlpool	Receive from Lance at Team Rocket HQ (after the Double Battle)	—
6	Rock Smash	Receive from the large boy on Route 36	—
7	Waterfall	Obtain on Ice Path 1F	—
8	Rock Climb	Receive from Professor Oak in Pallet Town (after obtaining eight Kanto Badges)	—